European Edition

Marketing Research

An Applied Approach

Naresh Malhotra
David Birks

An imprint of Pearson Education

Harlow, England • London • New York • Reading, Massachusetts • San Francisco • Toronto • Don Mills, Ontario • Sydney
Tokyo • Singapore • Hong Kong • Seoul • Taipei • Cape Town • Madrid • Mexico City • Amsterdam • Munich • Paris • Milan

Pearson Education Ltd
Edinburgh Gate
Harlow
Essex CM20 2JE
England

and Associated Companies throughout the world

Visit us on the World Wide Web at:
www.pearsoneduc.com

Original 3rd edition entitled *Marketing Research: An Applied Orientation* published by Prentice Hall, Inc.
A Pearson Education company

This edition published by Pearson Education Limited 2000

ISBN 0139-22964-7

British Library Cataloguing-in-Publication Data
A catalogue record for this book can be obtained from the British Library.

10 9 8 7 6 5 4
06 05 04 03 02

Typeset by 30 in Stone Serif 9.5pt
Printed and bound by Grafos S.A., Arte sobre papel, Barcelona, Spain

Marketing Research

An Applied Approach

Contents

Preface

The three USA editions, the international edition and the Australia and New Zealand edition are testaments to the success of Malhotra's *Marketing Research* text. It is widely recognised as a comprehensive, applied and authoritative book on the nature and scope of marketing research. Lecturers and students in Europe have long appreciated the qualities of the text, using it in preference to locally produced texts that do not possess either the depth and breadth of its topics or its pedagogical features.

This European edition sacrifices none of the qualities that lie in the original format. It does, however, clarify the differences between Europe and the USA in marketing research practice. It includes an array of European examples, practices and illustrations throughout the text. There are also two additional chapters reflecting the growth of geodemographics and databases in marketing research and the wide use of qualitative research in Europe. This edition attempts to build on the success of the USA editions, making the book more current, contemporary, illustrative and sensitive to the needs of European lecturers and students.

AUDIENCE

This book is suitable for use at both the undergraduate and the graduate levels. This positioning is confirmed by the response to the first three editions of *Marketing Research*. The coverage is comprehensive and the depth and breadth of topics encompass both levels. The material is presented in a manner that is easy to read and understand. There are numerous diagrams, tables, pictures, illustrations and examples that help to explain the basic concepts. The accompanying CD-ROM presents demonstrations of two major software packages that enhance the coverage in the chapters. The Internet links to major Web sites on the CD-ROM facilitate an extensive means to explore contemporary material. The *Instructor's Manual* offers specific suggestions for teaching each chapter at the undergraduate and graduate levels. Not only is the book suitable for use in courses on marketing research, it can also be used effectively in courses on marketing data analysis. All the commonly used univariate and multivariate data analysis techniques are discussed extensively yet simply.

ORGANISATION

The book is organised into four parts, based on a six-step framework for conducting marketing research. Part I provides an introduction and discusses problem definition, the first and most important stage of the marketing research process. The nature and scope of research undertaken to develop an approach to the problem, the second step in the marketing research process, is also described. Part II covers research design, the third step, and describes the techniques that allow exploratory, descriptive and causal research designs. We describe the types of information commonly obtained in marketing research and the appropriate scales for obtaining such information. We present guidelines for designing questionnaires and explain the procedures, techniques and statistical considerations involved in sampling. Part III presents a pratical and managerially orientated discussion of field work, the fourth stage of the marketing research process. We discuss in detail the basic and advanced statistical techniques, with the emphasis on explaining the procedures, interpreting the results, and understanding managerial implications rather than on statistical elegance. Communicating the research by preparing and presenting a formal report constitutes the sixth step in the marketing research process and forms the subject of Part IV. This last part is also devoted to the complex process of international marketing research. Throughout the book, the orientation is applied and managerial.

NEW FOR THE EUROPEAN EDITION

While retaining the desirable features of the first three editions of the USA text, the European edition contains major revisions. Several significant changes have been made. Major changes include:

1 *The impact of geodemographics and databases on the marketing research industry*. Many major marketing research companies in Europe are now involved in the development of databases to support

marketing decision makers. The distinction between 'traditional' marketing research and database marketing is increasingly blurred with many companies using database and survey data in a 'fused' manner, utilising geodemographic systems as the focus of their decision support systems. To reflect this trend, a new chapter is presented that highlights these issues. The chapter is supported with a software demonstration disk describing the nature and use of geodemographics.

2 *The different perspectives of qualitative research in Europe compared to the USA*. The balance of quantitative to qualitative topics in previous editions did not reflect the widespread and varied use of qualitative research in Europe. A new chapter on qualitative research allows focus groups, in-depth interviews, projective techniques and the analysis of qualitative data to be tackled in more detail. Qualitative research applications are illustrated in a range of new examples and practitioners' perspectives. Underlying the widespread applications of qualitative research are a number of fundamental ways that qualitative research in Europe differs from the USA. These differences are highlighted with reference to their impact in conducting international qualitative research.

3 *An accompanying CD-ROM containing demonstration disks on the survey design and analysis, and geodemographics programs*. The first demo disk, SNAP5, is a package widely used in industry and academic institutions for survey design and data analysis. This demo enhances the chapters in this text dealing with survey and observation methods, scaling techniques, questionnaire design, data preparation, frequency distribution, cross tabulation and hypothesis testing. The second demo disk, MOSAIC by Experian, is again a package used widely in industry that many academic institutions are eager to acquire and use. The disk helps to explain the principles behind geodemographics, different ways that consumers may be classified, the display of statistics using maps and the marketing research and marketing applications of the system. The CD-ROM also includes many Internet links to organisations, adding an additional depth to the text, allowing exploration and discovery of contemporary research issues.

4 *Addition of a pan-European case throughout the book*. GlobalCash is a research project that was conducted in 1994, 1996 and 1998 (with plans for the 2000 project in place) in 20 European countries, using a major survey translated into 10 languages and requiring the support of 19 leading European business schools. The project uses both qualitative and quantitative techniques to great effect, supporting decision-making in major pan-European and American banks. The European author was the marketing research director on this project and he uses this position to provide an insight to the problems faced, the integration of techniques and the value of research findings to decision-makers.

5 *New professional perspectives*. The text has 12 new practitioners' perspectives covering an array of techniques, issues and applications of marketing research in Europe. IT developments are fundamentally changing the way that marketing research is planned, implemented and presented. These changes are reflected in individual chapters but are illustrated well in a number of the perspectives. New and fascinating techniques using the Internet, mystery shopping, geodemographics and research amongst children are also presented. Interesting applications of research findings are also presented, reflecting the realities of marketing decision making and the nature of research support demanded.

6 *Modifications to chapters*. Where appropriate, to reflect practice in Europe, new examples, figures and text have been added to clarify practice, update technology and present new ideas. These modifications occur throughout the text.

7 *New and updated examples*. The majority of USA examples have been replaced with European or other international examples. These examples have been chosen to reflect the diversity of marketing research problems faced in the current marketing and marketing research environment.

KEY FEATURES OF THE TEXT

This book has several salient and unique features, both in terms of content and pedagogy.

Content features

1 A separate chapter has been devoted to problem definition and developing an approach. These important steps in the marketing research process are discussed thoroughly and extensively (Chapter 2).

2 A separate chapter covers secondary data collection and analysis. In addition to traditional sources, computerised databases and syndicated sources are also covered extensively. Use of the Internet for secondary data collection and analysis is discussed in detail (Chapter 4).
3 The use of geodemographics and databases as a distinct form of secondary data collection and analysis is covered in detail. This chapter illustrates how leading marketing research organisations and marketers combine the use of database and survey data (Chapter 5).
4 Qualitative research is covered in two chapters. Focus groups, in-depth interviews, projective techniques and qualitative observation are covered in detail, with an emphasis on the type of problem for which a qualitative approach is the only solution. The use of the Internet for qualitative research is discussed as is the use of qualitative data analysis packages (Chapters 6 and 7).
5 A separate chapter presents survey and observation methods (Chapter 8), while another discusses experimentation (Chapter 9). Thus, description and causal designs are covered in detail.
6 Two chapters have been devoted to scaling techniques. One chapter is devoted to the fundamentals and comparative scaling techniques (Chapter 10). The other covers non-comparative techniques, including multi-item scales, and procedures for assessing their reliability, validity and generalisability (Chapter 11).
7 A separate chapter discusses questionnaire design. A step-by-step procedure and several guidelines are provided for constructing questionnaires (Chapter 12).
8 Two chapters cover sampling techniques. One chapter discusses the qualitative issues involved in sampling and the various non-probability and probability sampling techniques (Chapter 13). The other chapter explains statistical issues as well as final and initial sample size determination (Chapter 14).
9 A separate chapter presents fieldwork. We give several guidelines on interviewer training, interviewing and supervision of fieldworkers (Chapter 15).
10 This book is unique in the treatment of marketing research data analysis. Separate chapters have been devoted to:
   a Data preparation (Chapter 16)
   b Frequency distribution, cross-tabulation, and hypothesis testing (Chapter 17)
   c Analysis of variance and covariance (Chapter 18)
   d Regression analysis (Chapter 19)
   e Discriminant analysis (Chapter 20)
   f Factor analysis (Chapter 21)
   g Cluster analysis (Chapter 22)
   h Multidimensional scaling and conjoint analysis (Chapter 23)

   Data analysis is illustrated for five statistical packages: SPSS, SAS, BMDP, Minitab and Excel.
11 A separate chapter discusses report writing and presentation. Several guidelines are presented to create reports that utilise but do not totally rely upon IT developments (Chapters 24).
12 To supplement the discussions throughout the text, an additional chapter explains international marketing research. The environment in which international marketing research is conducted is described, followed by a discussion of some advanced concepts (Chapter 25).

Pedagogical features

1 Scholarship is appropriately blended with a highly applied and managerial orientation. Throughout, we illustrate the application of concepts and techniques by marketing researchers and implementation of findings by managers to improve marketing practice.
2 Numerous real-life examples are given. These examples describe in some detail the kind of marketing research used to address a specific managerial problem and decision that was based on those findings. Additional examples have been integrated throughout the text to further explain and illustrate the concepts in each chapter.
3 In addition, a real-life project is used as a running example to illustrate the various concepts throughout the text. These illustrations have been entitled 'GlobalCash Project'. As the project involves sensitive data collected at the time of the launch of the European Monetary Union, several aspects

have been disguised. The GlobalCash project spans the whole book and is easy to pick up in any chapter.

4 Another way in which a contemporary focus is achieved is by integrating the coverage of international marketing research and ethics in marketing research throughout the text. We show how the concepts discussed in each chapter can be applied in an international setting and discuss the ethical issues that may arise when implementing those concepts domestically and internationally.
5 The use of the Internet and computers has also been integrated throughout the text. Each chapter has a section entitled 'Internet and Computer Application'. We show how the Internet and computers can be integrated in each step of the marketing research process and how they can be used to implement the concepts discussed in each chapter. The attached CD-ROM demo disks further illustrate the use of computers in the marketing research process.
6 Data analysis procedures are illustrated with respect to SPSS, SAS, BMDP, Minitab and Excel, along with other popular programs. This book can be used as a text, regardless of the statistical package being used by the instructor.
7 Each part contains 'Professional Perspectives', which feature articles by leading marketing research practitioners. These articles complement the material in the chapters and further strengthen the applied orientation of the book.
8 Extensive 'Exercise' sections in the text cover questions and problems. In the *Instructor's Manual*, questions and problems are enhanced with Internet and computer exercises, role playing, fieldwork and group discussion. This provides ample opportunities for learning and testing the concepts covered in the chapter.
9 A complete set of learning aids including a functional and useful Web site, an *Instructor's Manual*, PowerPoint slides, Exercises in Marketing Research and Test Bank have been provided.

INSTRUCTIONAL SUPPORT

The *Instructor's Manual*, written by the authors, is very closely tied to the text. The manual shows how to tailor the material in each chapter to the undergraduate and graduate levels. Each chapter contains chapter objectives, authors' notes, chapter outline, teaching suggestions, and answers to all end-of-chapter exercises and activities (questions, problems, Internet and computer exercises). In addition, cases from Malhotra's 3rd edition are presented along with solutions, including those that involve data analysis. The *Instructor's Manual* also contains four comprehensive cases with data: DuPont carpets (consumer products), Gucci catalogue (direct marketing), Kosair Children's Hospital (services), and Astec (industrial marketing).

ACKNOWLEDGEMENTS

Several people have been extremely helpful in writing this European edition. Most fundamental was the foundation provided in Naresh Malhotra's excellent original text.

I would also like to acknowledge the Consumer Behaviour teaching of John Southan; his efforts were fundamental in developing my interest and direction in marketing research. My friend and former work colleague, Kevin Fogarty, deserves mentioning for his humour and creativity and for teaching me the value of teamwork.

My colleagues at the University of Bath have been very supportive. I particularly want to mention my Research Assistant at Bath, Jackie Guinness, who worked so hard and creatively in gathering and critically reviewing new material. The students in my Management Research, Consumer Research, Market Analysis and PhD research training courses provided useful feedback as the material was class tested.

The GlobalCash Project running throughout this text could not have been completed without the inspiration and drive of David Middleton and Tony de Caux of the Bank Relationship Consultancy; they have been very supportive and helpful. The support of Peter Wills, Managing Director of Mercator, and Richard Webber, Group Director of Experian, is gratefully acknowledged. I am very thankful for their willingness to provide SNAP and MOSAIC demonstration disks and for their contributions to the Professional Perspectives. In putting together the new Professional Perspectives, I would like to thank Gavin Emsden (Nestlé,), Mike Pepp and Ian Becattelli (Context Research International), Trevor Fenwick (Euromonitor), Virginia Monk (Network Research and Marketing), Tim Macer (Tim Macer Services), David Backinsell (NOP Mystery Shopping), Marsha Hemmingway (Good Sense Research) and Nathalie Watkins of the Market Research Society.

The reviewers of this European edition have provided many constructive and valuable suggestions, and their help is gratefully acknowledged.

Reviewers for this European edition:
Howard Jackson, University of Huddersfield
Paul Baines, Middlesex University
Dr Martin Wetzels, University of Maastricht
Dr David Longbottom, University of Derby
John Beaumont-Kerridge, University of Luton
Marc De Laet, Hogeschool, Antwerp
Kare Sandvik, Buskerud College, Norway

Reviewers for the third US edition:
Tom Anastasti, Boston University
John Weiss, Colorado State University
Subash Lonial, University of Louisville
Joel Herche, University of the Pacific
Paul L. Sauer, Canisius College

Reviewers for the second US edition:
Rick Andrews, University of Delaware
Holland Blades Jr., Missouri Southern State College
Sharmila Chatterjee, Santa Clara University
Rajshekhar Javalgi, Cleveland State University
Mustaq Luqmani, Western Michigan University
Jeanne Munger, University of Southern Maine
Audesh Paswan, University of South Dakota
Venkatram Ramaswamy, University of Michigan
Gillian Rice, Thunderbird University
Paul L. Sauer, Canisius College
Hans Srinivasan, University of Conneticut

Reviewers for the first edition:
David M. Andrus, Kansas State University
Joe Ballenger, Stephen F. Austin State University
Joseph D. Brown, Ball State University
Thomas E. Buzas, Eastern Michigan University
Rajendar K. Garg, Northeastern Illinois University
Lawrence D. Gibson, Consultant
Ronald E. Goldsmith, Florida State University
Rajshekhar G. Javalgi, Cleveland State University
Charlotte H. Mason, University of North Carolina
Kent Nakamoto, University of Colorado
Thomas J. Page Jr, Michigan State University
William S. Perkins, Pennsylvania State University
Sudhi Seshadri, University of Maryland at College Park
David Shani, Baruch College

I would like to thank the team at Pearson Education for their support. To Liz Sproat, Acquisitions Editor, Jacqueline Senior, Development Editor and Julie Knight, Editor: many thanks for your patience, good humour and excellent all-round help.

I am eternally grateful for the love and support of my mother Maria Birks and my nephew James Birks. And for putting up with me, helping me in many stages of writing, being extremely patient and tolerant, with much love I thank my partner Jane Clothier.

David F. Birks

About the Authors

Dr. Naresh K. Malhotra is Regents' Professor, DuPree College of Management, Georgia Institute of Technology. He is listed in *Marquis Who's Who in America*, 51st Edition (1997), 52nd Edition (1998), 53rd Edition (1999), and in the *National Registry of Who's Who* (1999).

In an article by Wheatley and Wilson (1987 AMA Educators' Proceedings), Professor Malhotra was ranked number one in the country based on articles published in the *Journal of Marketing Research* from 1980 to 1985. He also holds the all time record for the most publications in the *Journal of Health Care Marketing*. He is ranked number one based on publications in the *Journal of the Academy of Marketing Science* (JAMS) from its inception through volume 23, 1995. He is also number one based on publications in JAMS from 1986 to 1995. He is listed as one of the best researchers in marketing in John Fraedrich, "The Best Researchers in Marketing," *Marketing Educator* (Summer 1997), p. 5.

He has published more than 75 papers in major refereed journals including the *Journal of Marketing Research, Journal of Consumer Research, Marketing Science, Journal of Marketing, Journal of Academy of Marketing Science, Journal of Retailing, Journal of Health Care Marketing*, and leading journals in statistics, management science, and psychology. In addition, he has also published numerous refereed articles in the proceedings of major national and international conferences. Several articles have received research awards.

He was Chairman, Academy of Marketing Science Foundation, 1996–1998, and was President, Academy of Marketing Science, 1994–1996, and Chairman of the Board of Governors from 1990 to 1992. He is a Distinguished Fellow of the Academy and Fellow of the Decision Sciences Institute. He serves as an Associate Editor of *Decision Sciences Journal* and has served as Section Editor, Health Care Marketing Abstracts, *Journal of Health Care Marketing*. Also, he serves on the Editorial Boards of eight journals.

His book entitled *Marketing Research: An Applied Orientation*, Third Edition, was published by Prentice Hall, Inc. An International Edition and an Australian Edition of his book have also been published, along with a Spanish translation. The book has received widespread adoption at both the graduate and undergraduate levels with more than 100 schools using it in the United States.

Dr. Malhotra has consulted for business, non-profit, and government organizations in the United States and abroad and has served as an expert witness in legal and regulatory proceedings. He is the winner of numerous awards and honours for research, teaching, and service to the profession.

Dr. Malhotra is a member and Deacon, First Baptist Church of Atlanta. He lives in the Atlanta area with his wife, Veena, and children, Ruth and Paul.

Dr. David Frederick Birks is a Lecturer in Marketing in the School of Management at the University of Bath, England. He teaches marketing research and management research on Undergraduate, taught Postgraduate and Research degree programmes. David's industrial experience was gained in the construction and housing industry in England and Germany. Before university lecturing he worked in purchasing, planning, marketing and research. He has Masters degrees in Marketing Management and in Social Statistics and a PhD in Marketing Information Systems.

David has continued to practise marketing research throughout his University career, managing projects in financial institutions, retailers, industrial organisations, local authorities and charities. He has managed projects as part of the undergraduate, M.Sc. M.B.A. and Ph.D. degree programmes at the University of Bath. He was the Head of Marketing Research on the GlobalCash Project detailed throughout this text. He helped to develop the methodology, research instruments and analyses of this project. This involved coordinating the demands of major pan-European and American banks, and the research requirements of 19 Business Schools throughout Europe. He edited and made a major contribution to the text *Global Cash Management in Europe* that resulted from the combined research efforts of colleagues in Britain, Denmark, Germany, Ireland, Italy, Norway and Sweden. He has published further research from GlobalCash with colleagues from Aarhus, Denmark. In addition to his Cash Management work, David's publications have covered the fields of Housing, Statistics and Marketing.

David lives in the beautiful rural village of Vobster in the Mendip Hills of Somerset. From this very English setting, he brings a cosmopolitan background to this European edition having an English father, German mother, French grandfather and Belgian great-grandparents.

Part I

INTRODUCTION AND EARLY PHASES OF MARKETING RESEARCH

In this part, we discuss the nature and scope of marketing research and its role in supporting marketing decision-making. We describe characteristics of the marketing research industry and illustrate the benefits as well as the limitations of marketing research support. We set out a basic six-step marketing research process and discuss problem definition, the first and most important step in detail. In establishing the nature of a research problem we describe the steps required to develop a research brief and a research proposal. Finally, we describe the development of an approach to the problem, the second step in the marketing research process, and discuss in detail the various components of the approach. The perspective given in these chapters should be useful to both the decision-maker and the marketing researcher.

Chapter 1

Introduction to marketing research

The task of marketing researchers is to support management with the information needed to identify and solve marketing problems

OBJECTIVES

After reading this chapter, the student should be able to:

1 understand the nature and scope of marketing research and its role in designing and implementing successful marketing programmes;
2 explain the role of marketing research in decision support systems in providing data, marketing models and specialised software;
3 discuss the types and roles of research suppliers including internal and external, full-service and limited-service suppliers;
4 describe a conceptual framework for conducting marketing research as well as the steps of the marketing research process;
5 acquire an appreciation of the complexity involved in international marketing research;
6 gain an understanding of the ethical aspects of marketing research and the responsibilities that marketing research stakeholders have to themselves, each other, and to the research project.

OVERVIEW

Marketing research comprises one of the most important and fascinating facets of marketing. In this chapter, we describe the nature and scope of marketing research, emphasising its role of supporting marketing decision-making and provide several real-life examples to illustrate the basic concepts of marketing research. We give a formal definition of marketing research and subdivide marketing research into two areas: problem identification and problem-solving research. We show that marketing research may be conducted on an ad hoc basis but is also an integral part of marketing information systems or decision support systems. Next, we provide an overview of marketing research suppliers and services. We go through a simple six-stage linear description of the marketing research process. This description is extended to illustrate many of the interconnected activities in the marketing research process. There are many successful marketing decisions that have used marketing research support; however, marketing research does not replace decision-making. The limitations of marketing research are established. To illustrate the marketing research process, we examine the GlobalCash study, a live marketing research project that is run every two years throughout Europe. GlobalCash will be used as a running example throughout this book. The topic of international marketing research is introduced and discussed systematically in the subsequent chapters. The ethical aspects of marketing research and the responsibilities that marketing research stakeholders have to themselves, each other, and to the research project are presented and developed in more detail throughout the text.

WHAT DOES MARKETING RESEARCH ENCOMPASS?

The term 'marketing research' is broad in meaning; it is related to all aspects of marketing decision-making. The following examples provide a flavour of the varied nature of marketing research.

EXAMPLE

For Eurostar's star regulars, there truly is a free dinner[1]

European Passenger Services (EPS), the UK operator which, with the French and Belgian national railways, now runs Eurostar, faced decisions in refining the service to compete profitably in the business travel market. With the whole project taking many years to complete, EPS took advantage of the lead-time to undertake a project which provided feedback from a panel of frequent business travellers. The panel collected both qualitative and quantitative data and consisted of 560 frequent business travellers. Once recruited, each business traveller was sent three sets of travel diaries: one each for travel by air, ferry and rail. The diaries provided quantitative data about modes of travel and performance of carriers on specific service elements on out- and inbound trips. Just as important as the quantitative data was the qualitative feedback obtained from travellers during group discussions. The discussions took place in a private room in Central London (although in one case they were preceded by an exploration of the then newly finished International Terminal at Waterloo). Each evening's discussion was followed by dinner. So, while panellists had to work fairly hard for a couple of hours, they had the opportunity to network over good food and wine. EPS and its European partners used the groups and the analysis of the diaries to answer individual questions about many aspects of the needs, expectations, perceptions and habits of business travellers. Many of the questions were ones that might have proved difficult to answer using classic ad hoc survey methods. ■

EXAMPLE

Make us laugh, make us cry ...[2]

Many factors are driving companies towards developing manufacturing, distribution and marketing programmes to exploit fully the 340 million Western European consumers. The realisation of EMU in 1999 and the launch of the 'Euro' in 2002 will give a further boost towards these developments. Retailers are preparing: *Continent*, the French-owned hypermarket chain, now operates stores in Belgium, France, Germany, Spain and Italy. Research companies are also adapting; for example, GfK maintains offices in 26 European countries and has developed techniques for use across the whole of Europe. GfK publishes a purchasing power guide that examines relative purchasing power by region. It shows that the Swiss have the highest disposable income levels, the Portuguese the lowest, while the German score is still depressed as a result of unification. Their Consumer Confidence survey for the European Union shows that confidence about the future is always high in some countries – Finland, for example, and Denmark. Other countries – Spain, Portugal – seem to be permanently depressed, while Ireland has the wildest swings in confidence of all the countries surveyed. Fortunately the young in all countries are always confident and hence are the drivers of the various economies; older citizens express more concerns about the future. ■

EXAMPLE

Football fever – caught by the nation or just those most at risk?[3]

The BARB TV audience research panel is one of the largest in the world with 4500 metered homes producing a continuous sample of some 11,500 individuals. TV viewing is reported for 25 channels and data from the system is widely used for buying and selling airtime and planning TV schedules. In June 1996, between Saturday 8 June and Sunday 30 June, the TV schedules of ITV and BBC1 took on a different look. For these three weeks, the early evening and peak-time schedules were packed with 27 live football games – Euro 96. The BARB database can tell us much more about football fever and who caught it than simply how many men, women or children sat down to watch the games at home. Not so long ago, detailed analysis of the BARB database was possible only with large mainframe computers. In recent years the accessibility of BARB data has greatly changed, with the availability of Windows-based PC systems to allow easy analysis and the ability to address specific questions regarding who is viewing.

So what of Euro 96? Did everyone in the UK catch football fever? The level of addiction is illustrated by the reach levels, based on viewers who watched at least 45 minutes (non-consecutively) of the matches. This amount of viewing was chosen to include viewers who were committed to watching a large part of the game. Based on these viewing criteria, 82 per cent of men saw at least one game, with 15 per cent watching around half the games to this extent. The English matches achieved a high reach of all men, with 73 per cent watching at least one of the five England games and 9 per cent watching a full 45 minutes or more of all five. Women viewers were gripped to a lesser extent but 3 per cent of all women still 'loyally' followed England from their sofa throughout the tournament, by viewing at least 45 minutes of every England game. ■

EXAMPLE

From Armani to AIDS: the hopes, the fears, of Europe's youth[4]

Today's youth live in a fast-changing world, and their attitudes, behaviour and exposure to the media and to brands differs from their predecessors of just a few years ago. A major qualitative research study, interviewing more than 500 young people across 16 countries, has been conducted. Four workshops of 7–9 participants were held in each capital city, each lasting up to 5 hours. The countries covered were: Austria, the Czech Republic, Denmark, Finland, France, Germany, Hungary, Italy, the Netherlands, Norway, Poland, Russia, Spain, Sweden, Switzerland and the UK. The target of the research was 'trend-setters', that is young opinion leaders and leading edge youth aged 15–19 years, those who decide what is 'in', the early adopters and disseminators of opinions and tastes. Participants were given disposable cameras to take photographs ahead of the groups; these were used, with other materials, to create collages illustrating what makes them 'happy' or 'sad', and what it means to be young living in their country. A self-completion questionnaire provided data on favourite pastimes, music and media stars, sports, teams and so on, and 'awareness', 'usage' and 'preferences' of brands.

On clothing, for example, valuable insight was gained on the rationale behind both aspirational desires and actual behaviour. Male participants aspired to the most obviously status-giving brands, the opulent and clearly expensive (Versace,

Armani) reflecting their desire to buy into a world of success, money, power that everyone (they feel) would appreciate. Female participants however, were far more interested in standing out from the crowd. They were attracted to the non-mainstream brands which also came with their own strong set of values (e.g. Mambo, Stussy), as well as the more expensive (e.g. Prada and Gucci). What was especially interesting to the researchers was the way that these girls wore brands, mixing and matching, personalising their outfits. As both the boys and girls matured and their repertoire of brands and their financial status grew, they were more inclined to temper their 'ideals'. They moved toward the more High Street designer brands of Diesel, Calvin Klein, Ralph Lauren and DKNY and 'older' stores such as Next and The Gap. ■

EXAMPLE

What's in store?[5]

Geographical information systems (GIS) have always been important for retailers in determining the best location for stores, and in planning routes for distribution. Using detailed maps and associated geographical data, planners would look at the demographics, analyse the transport infrastructure and check to see if there were any competitors nearby. Today these systems are being used for a much wider variety of applications: to select targets for database marketing; to support merchandisers by matching product mix to demographics; and to define sales territories for marketing campaigns. They are also being used for store performance analysis. Tesco started its Site Research Unit in 1980, developing a reputation for combining technology with 'gut feeling', something retailers pride themselves on. The unit employs a number of qualified forecasters, statisticians and researchers and uses the Smallworld GIS to integrate its existing, largely homegrown applications and yet accommodate future data sources. Tesco analyses traditional map data as well as geographical and non-geographical information from external sources such as customer demand files. It makes recommendations on potential sites for development but also provides marketing support to stores and corporate departments. ■

The previous examples illustrate only a few of the methods used to conduct marketing research: one-on-one participatory surveys, questionnaires to a limited sample, large surveys, geodemographic information systems, published sources of information and database analyses, consumer panels and focus groups. This book will introduce you to the full complement of marketing research techniques. These examples also illustrate the crucial role played by marketing research in designing and implementing successful marketing plans.[6] Perhaps the role of marketing research can be better understood in light of the basic marketing paradigm depicted in Figure 1.1.

The emphasis in marketing is on the identification and satisfaction of customer needs. To determine customer needs and to implement marketing strategies and plans aimed at satisfying those needs, marketing managers need information about customers, competitors and other forces in the marketplace. In recent years, many factors have increased the need for more and better information. As firms have become national and international in scope, the need for information on larger, and more distant, markets has increased. As consumers have become more affluent, discerning and sophisticated, marketing managers need better information on how they will respond to products and other marketing offerings. As competition has become more intense, managers need information on the effectiveness of their marketing tools. As the environment is changing more rapidly, marketing managers need more timely information.[7]

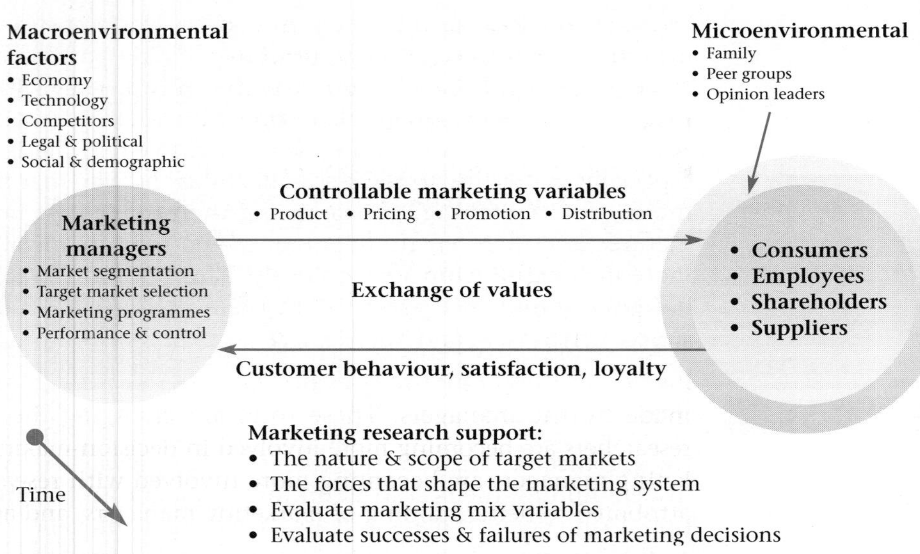

Figure 1.1
The role of marketing research within the marketing system

The task of marketing research is to assess the information needs and provide management with relevant, accurate, reliable, valid and current information. Today's competitive marketing environment and the ever-increasing costs attributed to poor decision-making require that marketing research provide sound information. Sound decisions are not based on gut feeling, intuition, or even pure judgement. In the absence of sound information, an incorrect management decision may result, as illustrated by the case of Johnson & Johnson baby aspirin.

EXAMPLE

Johnson & Johnson's gentleness could not handle pain[8]

Johnson & Johnson's attempt to use its company name on baby aspirin proved to be unsuccessful. Johnson & Johnson products are perceived as gentle, but gentleness is not what people want in a baby aspirin. Although baby aspirin should be safe, gentleness *per se* is not a desirable feature. Rather, some people perceived that a gentle aspirin might not be effective enough. So here is an example of what seemed, intuitively, to be a natural move but turned out to be an incorrect decision. ■

As illustrated by the Johnson & Johnson example, marketing managers make numerous strategic and tactical decisions in the process of identifying and satisfying customer needs. As shown in Figure 1.1, marketers make decisions about potential opportunities and problems and the most effective means to capitalise upon their opportunities and overcome their problems. They do this by creating a 'vision' of their markets and customer groups through market segmentation and target market selection. From this 'vision' they develop, implement and control marketing programmes. The marketing managers' 'vision' of markets and subsequent marketing plans decisions are complicated by the interactive effects of macroenvironmental forces that shape the nature and scope of target markets and their ability to satisfy those target markets. Further complications arise in understanding the interactive effects of microenvironmental forces that strongly influence the attitudes and behaviour of consumers. Marketing research helps the marketing manager link the marketing variables with the environment and the customer groups. It helps remove some of the uncertainty by providing relevant information about the marketing variables, environment, and consumers. In the absence of relevant information, consumers' responses to marketing plans cannot be predicted reliably or accurately.

The role of the marketing researcher in supporting the marketing decision-maker can be summarised as helping to:

- describe the nature and scope of customer groups
- understand the nature of forces that shape the needs of customer groups and the marketer's ability to satisfy those groups
- test individual and interactive controllable marketing variables
- monitor and reflect upon past successes and failures in marketing decisions.

Traditionally, marketing researchers were responsible for assessing information needs and providing the relevant information while marketing decisions were made by the managers. These roles are changing, however, and marketing researchers are becoming more involved in decision-making and conversely, marketing managers are becoming more involved with research. This trend can be attributed to better training of marketing managers, and advances in technology. There has also been a shift in the marketing research paradigm where increasingly marketing research is being undertaken on an ongoing basis rather than in response to specific marketing problems or opportunities on an ad hoc basis.[9]

This crucial role of marketing research is recognised in its definition, which is given in the next section.

DEFINITION OF MARKETING RESEARCH

The European Society for Opinion and Marketing Research (ESOMAR) definition of marketing research is given below. For the purpose of this book, which emphasises the need for information in the support of decision-making, marketing research is defined as follows:

> **Marketing research** is the systematic and objective identification, collection, analysis, and dissemination of information for improving decision-making related to the identification and solution of problems and opportunities in marketing.

Marketing research
The systematic and objective identification, collection, analysis and dissemination of information for improving decision-making related to the identification and solution of problems and opportunities in marketing.

Marketing research process
A set of six steps which defines the taks to be accomplished in conducting a marketing research study. These include problem definition, developing an approach to the problem, research design formulation, fieldwork, data preparation and analysis, and report generation and presentation.

Several aspects of this definition are noteworthy. First, marketing research is systematic. Thus, systematic planning is required at all stages of the **marketing research process**. The procedures followed at each stage are methodologically sound, well documented and, as much as possible, planned.

Marketing research involves the identification, collection, analysis and dissemination of information. Each phase of this process is important. We identify or define the marketing research problem or opportunity and then determine what information is needed to investigate it. Because every marketing opportunity translates into a research problem to be investigated, the terms 'problem' and 'opportunity' are used interchangeably here. Next, the relevant information sources are identified and a range of data collection methods varying in sophistication and complexity are evaluated for their usefulness. The data are collected using the most appropriate method; they are analysed and interpreted, and inferences are drawn. Finally, the findings, implications and recommendations are provided in a format that allows the information to be used for marketing decision-making and to be acted upon directly. The next section elaborates this definition by classifying different types of marketing research.

Marketing research should be objective. It attempts to provide accurate information that reflects a true state of affairs. It should be conducted impartially. Although research is always influenced by the researcher's research philosophy, it should be free from the personal or political biases of the researcher or the management. Research motivated by personal or political gain involves a breach of professional standards. Such research is deliberately biased to result in predetermined findings. The motto of every researcher should be, 'Find it and tell it like it is'.

ESOMAR definition of marketing research

Marketing research is a key element within the total field of marketing information. It links the consumer, customer and public to the marketer through information which is used to identify and define marketing opportunities and problems; generate, refine and evaluate marketing actions; improve understanding of marketing as a process and of the ways in which specific marketing activities can be made more effective.

ESOMAR further distinguishes marketing research from other forms of data gathering, through the issue of the anonymity of respondents. It stresses that in marketing research the identity of the provider of information is not disclosed. It makes a clear distinction between marketing research and database marketing where the names and addresses of the people contacted are to be used for individual selling, promotional, fund-raising or other non-research purposes. These issues will be explored more fully in the section 'Ethics in Marketing Research' in this chapter. The distinction between marketing research and the database as a research tool is not so clear. There is a growing amount of support given to marketing decision-makers from database analyses that is not 'respondent specific'. Database analyses can be performed with the same purpose as outlined in the definition of marketing research and with the same level of professional standards, especially when related to database analyses of existing customers.

There are many instances where database analyses can add clarity and focus to marketing research activities. For example, since the start of 1995 the highly respected marketing research agency, Taylor Nelson AGB, has been building the European Toiletries & Cosmetics Database (ETCD). Some 14,000-usage diaries of personal care products are collected each year, across Britain, France, Germany, Italy and Spain. Given the huge impact that database analyses are having upon marketing decision-making, these issues will be developed more fully in Chapter 5. In the meantime, the maxim stated by ESOMAR of preserving the anonymity of respondents is vital for the continuing support of respondents and ultimate health of the marketing research industry.

A CLASSIFICATION OF MARKETING RESEARCH

Our definition states that organisations use marketing research for two reasons: (1) to identify and (2) to solve marketing problems. This distinction serves as a basis for classifying marketing research into problem identification research and problem-solving research, as shown in Figure 1.2.

Problem identification research
Research undertaken to help identify problems that are not necessarily apparent on the surface, yet exist or are likely to arise in the future.

Problem identification research is undertaken to help identify problems that are, perhaps, not apparent on the surface and yet exist or are likely to arise in the future. Examples of problem identification research include market potential, market share, brand or company image, market characteristics, sales analysis, short-range forecasting, long-range forecasting and business trends research.

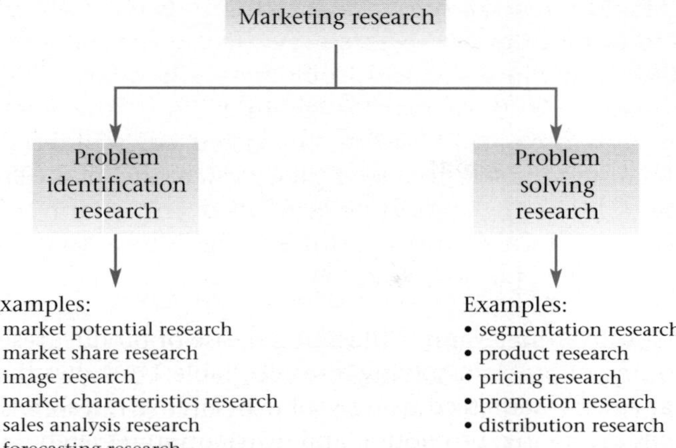

Examples:
- market potential research
- market share research
- image research
- market characteristics research
- sales analysis research
- forecasting research
- business trends research

Examples:
- segmentation research
- product research
- pricing research
- promotion research
- distribution research

Figure 1.2 A classification of marketing research

Research of this type provides information about the marketing environment and helps diagnose a problem. For example, a declining market potential indicates that the firm is likely to have a problem achieving its growth targets. Similarly, a problem exists if the market potential is increasing but the firm is losing market share. The recognition of economic, social or cultural trends, such as changes in consumer behaviour, may point to underlying problems or opportunities.

EXAMPLE

Beer research shows overspill[10]

The proliferation of new brands in Europe's booming beer market could result in shorter product lifecycles and, ultimately, destroy brand loyalty. The report 'Western European Beer' reveals that the industry is in danger of an overspill of brands, with the number of brands available exceeding demand. As a result, consumers are likely to fall back on 'tried and tested brands', normally owned by large manufacturers, at the expense of lesser known brands, which are likely to fall by the wayside. In Western Europe, there is an average per head consumption of 84 litres per year, the highest level in the world. ■

The above research presents either a problem or an opportunity for beer manufacturers, depending largely upon whether your brand is 'tried and tested' or not. The research could be classified as 'business trends research' or even 'market potential research'. It could be followed by individual beer manufacturers conducting their own 'image research' to reveal the extent to which their brand(s) are perceived as being 'tried and tested'.

Problem-solving research
Research undertaken to help solve specific marketing problems.

Once a problem or opportunity has been identified, **problem-solving research** may be undertaken to help develop a solution. The findings of problem-solving research are used to support decisions that tackle specific marketing problems. An example of problem-solving research is provided by the repositioning of Ovaltine.

EXAMPLE

Ovaltine wakes up the chocolate drink mix market[11]

Originally popular during the 1940s as a bedtime drink, Ovaltine hot chocolate mix began losing market share in the 1960s. The first response of management was to bring back the popular characters used in the 1940s advertisements. These outdated characters, however, did not fit in well with the period and only served to reinforce the image of Ovaltine as a drink before bedtime.

Management employed marketing research to help develop their product. Brand repositioning research revealed several opportunities. As Ovaltine had only natural ingredients, it could be positioned as a health food drink, targeted at mothers 20 to 35 years of age. In addition, the demand for instant beverages was increasing and a low-calorie version was well received in concept testing in which respondents provided their evaluations of different hot chocolate mixes and drinks. The company developed an instant hot chocolate mix and a reduced-calorie Ovaltine drink to meet these needs. This helped Ovaltine to regain some of its lost share. ■

The Ovaltine example illustrates a case of product research that falls under the heading of problem-solving research. Table 1.1 shows the different types of issues that can be addressed using problem-solving research, including segmentation, product, pricing, promotion and distribution research.

Table 1.1 Examples of problem-solving research

Segmentation research	Determine basis of segmentation Establish market potential and responsiveness for various segments Select target markets and create lifestyle profiles: demography, media, and product image characteristics
Product research	Test concept Determine optimal product design Package tests Product modification Brand positioning and repositioning Test marketing
Pricing research	Importance of price in brand selection Pricing policies Product line pricing Price elasticity of demand Initiating and responding to price changes
Promotions research	Optimal promotional budget Optimal promotion mix Copy decisions Creative advertising testing Evaluation of advertising effectiveness
Distribution research	Attitudes of channel members Intensity of wholesale and retail coverage Channel margins Retail and wholesale locations

Classifying marketing research into two main types is useful from a conceptual as well as a practical viewpoint. The Ovaltine example is clearly one of problem-solving research. A problem-solving perspective enabled management to focus on the product development of Ovaltine. Problem identification research and problem-solving research go hand-in-hand, however, and a given marketing research project may combine both types of research. A marketing research project for a European beer manufacturer that sees its market share diminish may determine through Image Research that its brand is perceived in a most positive manner. This may indicate that the brand be extended into other types of beer or even clothes and fashion accessories! Appropriate target markets may be selected, with detailed profiles of potential customers and an associated media and product image. These decisions can clearly be supported with problem-solving research.

THE ROLE OF MARKETING RESEARCH IN MkIS AND DSS

Earlier we defined marketing research as the systematic and objective identification, collection, analysis, and dissemination of information for use in marketing decision-making.[12] The information obtained through marketing research and sources such as internal records and marketing intelligence becomes an integral part of a firm's marketing information systems (MkIS). A **marketing information system (MkIS)** is a formalised set of procedures for generating, analysing, storing and distributing pertinent information to marketing decision-makers on an ongoing basis. Note that the definition of a MkIS is similar to that of marketing research. The difference lies in the MkIS providing information on a continuous basis, guided by a marketing plan. Marketing research forms a component of the MkIS, providing primarily ad hoc studies. The design of the MkIS focuses upon each marketing decision-maker's responsibilities, information needs and decision style. The MkIS is designed around information gathered from a variety of sources, such as customer analyses from invoices and marketing intelligence reported by sales personnel. The continuously gathered information is combined and presented in a format that can be readily used in decision-making. More information can be obtained from a MkIS than from ad hoc marketing research projects. However, a MkIS may be limited in the nature of information it provides and the manner in which the information is structured and cannot easily be manipulated.

Marketing information systems (MkIS)
A formalised set of procedures for generating, analysing, sorting and distributing pertinent information to marketing decision-makers on an ongoing basis.

Developed to overcome the limitations of the MkIS, decision support systems (DSS) enable marketing decision-makers to interact directly with databases and analysis models.[13] A **decision support system (DSS)** is an integrated information system including hardware, communications network, database, model base, software base and the marketing decision-maker, that collects and interprets information for decision-making. Marketing research contributes research data to the database, marketing models and analytical techniques to the model base, and specialised programs for analysing marketing data to the software base. DSSs differ from MkISs in various ways (see Figure 1.3).[14] A DSS can combine the use of models or analytical techniques with the traditional access and retrieval functions of an MkIS. They are easier to use in an interactive mode and can be adapted as changes in the marketing system occur, as well as to the decision-making approach of the user. In addition to improving efficiency, a DSS can also enhance decision-making effectiveness by using 'what if' analyses, allowing the creativity of the marketing decision-maker to be reflected in the search and connection between different internal and external data sources. An example of a DSS is the use of geodemographic information systems, which will be covered in more detail in Chapter 5 but is illustrated in the following example.

Decision support systems (DSS)
An information system that enables decision-makers to interact directly with both databases and analysis models. The important components of a DSS include hardware and a communication network, database, model base, software base and the DSS user (decision-maker).

MkIS	DSS
• structured problems • reports 'fed' to decision makers • rigid structure • information display restricted • combines quantitative and qualitative data	• unstructured problems • use of models • user-friendly interaction • adaptability • uses 'what if' analyses

Figure 1.3
Marketing information systems versus decision support systems

EXAMPLE

Geographic marketing at Banco Central Hispanoamericano[15]

There are two important geographic features of the Spanish banking market: the concentration of the population in cities and the large number of bank branches. Forty-two per cent of the population is concentrated in cities with more than 100,000 inhabitants. In these cities, the potential of a geodemographic information system (GIS) which combines customer data with the geographic data on a map of a city is very useful to define customer distribution areas based on their financial behaviour.

Banco Central Hispanoamericano have designed a model within their GIS which allows them to assign customers to branches, maximising the number of customers assigned to each branch while minimising the distance they have to travel. To do this, the system considers the maximum distance (by street) which a customer is capable of travelling to go to a branch, the maximum number of branches along which to distribute the customers, the total number of branches to analyse, and the maximum distance over which to carry out the analysis.

The system also allows the bank to select new locations for automated teller machines (ATMs) in an 'intelligent' way. When opening a new ATM, it is possible to select customers of the Bank who use the machines of competitor banks close by and who also live in its area of influence. This facilitates promotions activities, targeted at customers with the greatest likelihood of using the new service. ■

As shown by the experience of Banco Central Hispanoamericano, a DSS can greatly enhance the support given to marketing decision-makers. To make a MkIS or a DSS work properly, the data used in the systems has to be accurate and totally dependable. To generate data to support specific marketing decisions, management relies on marketing research suppliers and services.

MARKETING RESEARCH SUPPLIERS AND SERVICES

Internal suppliers
Marketing research departments located within a firm.

Marketing research suppliers provide most of the information needed for making marketing decisions. Figure 1.4 classifies marketing research suppliers and services. Broadly speaking, research suppliers can be classified as internal or external. An **internal supplier** is a marketing research department or function located within a firm. Many firms, particularly large ones maintain in-house marketing research departments. A marketing research department's place in an organisation structure may vary quite considerably. At one extreme, the research function may be centralised and located at the corporate headquarters, allowing the development of a range of skills and expertise to be built up in a team. At the other extreme is a decentralised structure in which the marketing research function is organised along divisional lines, allowing specific and focused expertise to be developed but without the breadth of experience that may lie in a centralised team. In a decentralised scheme, the company may be organised into divisions by products, customers or geographical regions, with marketing research personnel assigned to the various divisions. These personnel generally report to a division manager rather than to a corporate-level executive. In addition, between these two extremes is a variety of types of organisation. Even if a firm has its own marketing research specialists, they may still turn to external suppliers to perform specific marketing research tasks.

External suppliers
Outside marketing research companies hired to supply marketing research services.

External suppliers are outside firms hired to supply marketing research data. These external suppliers collectively comprise the marketing research industry. These suppliers range from small (one or a few persons) operations to very large global corporations. Table 1.2 lists the top ten marketing research suppliers in the world, while Table 1.3 lists where marketing research monies are spent world-wide through external suppliers. External suppliers can be classified as full-service or limited-service suppliers. **Full-service suppliers** offer the entire range of marketing research services, for example, defining a problem, developing an research design, conducting focus group interviews, designing questionnaires, sampling, collecting, analysing and interpreting data, and presenting reports. They may also address the marketing implications of the information they present. The services provided by these suppliers can be further broken down into syndicated services, standardised services and customised services (see Figure 1.4).

Full-service suppliers
Companies that offer the full range of marketing research activities.

Syndicated services collect information that they provide to subscribers. Surveys, diary panels, scanners and audits are the main means by which these data are collected.

Standardised services
Companies that use standardised procedures to provide marketing research to various clients.

Standardised services are research studies conducted for different clients but in a standard way. For example, procedures for measuring advertising effectiveness have been standardised so that the results can be compared across studies and evaluative norms can be established.

Customised services
Companies that tailor research procedures to best meet the needs of each client.

Customised services offer a variety of marketing research services specifically designed to suit a client's particular needs. Each marketing research project is treated uniquely.

Limited-service suppliers
Companies that specialise in one or a few phases of a marketing research project.

Limited-service suppliers specialise in one or a few phases of a marketing research project. Services offered by such suppliers are classified as field services, coding and data entry, data analysis, analytical services, and branded products.

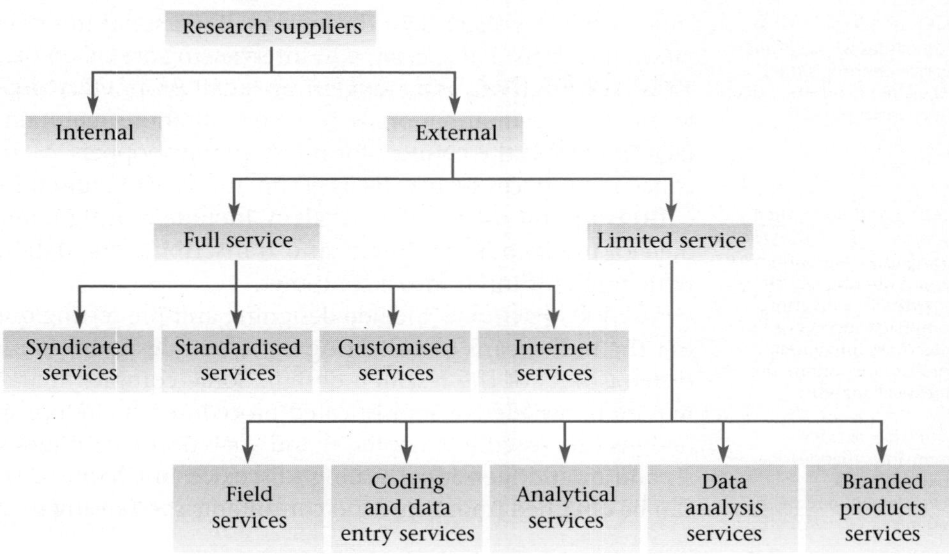

Figure 1.4 Marketing research suppliers

Table 1.2 World Top 10 market research companies 1996[16]

Company	Turnover ($US m)	Countries with office	Head office	Ownership
1 A.C. Nielsen Corp	1363	73	USA	D&B Marketing Information Services, USA. Became a separate public company in Nov. 1996.
2 IMS International Inc.	907	79	USA/UK	D&B Marketing Information Services, USA. Became part of a public co. in Nov. 1996: Cognizant Corp. (also incorporating Nielsen Media Research Inc. & Gartner Group)
3 Information Resources Inc	406	21	USA	Public Company, USA
4 GfK	317	33	Germany	Public Company, Germany
5 Sofres Group	277	23	France	Fimalac-led Group, France
6 Research International	248	55	UK	The Kantar Group, UK
7 Infratest/Burke	168	15	Germany	Public Company, Germany
8 IPSOS Group	162	16	France	Public Company, France
9 Millward Brown Int.	156	26	UK	The Kantar Group, UK
10 The Arbitron Co.	154	1	USA	Ceridian Corp., USA

Table 1.3 Europe still has the largest research market in the world![17]

Region	Turnover ($US m)*	Percentage of world turnover	Index 1995/1994
EU 15	4656	42	110
Other Europe	411	4	127
Total Europe	5067	46	110
USA	3940	36	109
Japan	947	9	94
Other	1143	10	106
Total World	11097	100	109

* *Excludes in-house research by marketing departments, advertising agencies, governmental and academic institutions, etc.; using average calendar year 1996 exchange rates at 1 ECU = US$ 1.27 = Yen 138.03*

Field services
Companies whose primary service offering is their expertise in collecting data for research projects.

Field services collect data through mail, personal interviews or telephone interviews and firms that specialise in interviewing are called field service organisations. These organisations may range from small proprietary organisations that operate locally to large multinationals. Some organisations maintain extensive interviewing facilities across the country for interviewing shoppers. Many offer qualitative data collection services such as focus group interviewing (discussed in Chapter 6).

Coding and data entry services
Companies whose primary service offering is their expertise in converting completed surveys or interviews into a usable database for conducting statistical analysis.

Coding and data entry services include editing completed questionnaires, developing a coding scheme, and transcribing the data onto diskettes or magnetic tapes for input into a computer.

Analytical services
Companies that provide guidance in the development of research design.

Analytical services include designing and pre-testing questionnaires, determining the best means of collecting data, and designing sampling plans, as well as other aspects of the research design. Some complex marketing research projects require knowledge of sophisticated procedures, including specialised experimental designs (discussed in Chapter 9) and analytical techniques such as conjoint analysis and multidimensional scaling (discussed in Chapter 23). This kind of expertise can be obtained from firms and consultants specialising in analytical services.

Data analysis services
Firms whose primay service is to conduct statistical analysis of quantitative data.

Data analysis services are offered by firms, also known as tab houses, that specialise in computer analysis of quantitative data such as those obtained in large surveys. Initially, most data analysis firms supplied only tabulations (frequency counts) and cross-tabulations (frequency counts that describe two or more variables simultaneously). Now, many firms offer sophisticated data analysis using advanced statistical techniques. With the proliferation of microcomputers and software, many firms now have the capability to analyse their own data, but data analysis firms are still in demand.

Branded marketing research products
Specialised data collection and analysis procedures developed to address specific types of marketing research problems.

Branded marketing research products and services are specialised data collection and analysis procedures developed to address specific types of marketing research problems. These procedures may be patented, given brand names, and marketed like any other branded product. *Microscope* by Retail Marketing (In-Store) Services is an example of a branded product. *Microscope* is a test marketing package for new product development that supplies cost-effective measurements of new product performance.

Every year ESOMAR (European Society for Opinion and Marketing Research) conducts a study to estimate the total size of the market for market research. The 1996 report shows that the world-wide value of the research market was estimated to be worth just over US$ 11 billion which was 9 per cent more than in 1995.

The market in Europe grew by 10 per cent over the year and accounted for 46 per cent of the world-wide total in 1996 compared to 45 per cent in 1995. The US market grew by 9 per cent taking 36 per cent of the world-wide total; Japan's market shrank and its share decreased from 10 per cent to 9 per cent and the market for the rest of the world fell from 11 per cent to 10 per cent.

The estimated size of the research market in 1996 was as shown in Table 1.3. Germany continues to have the largest market (US$ 1171 m) followed by the UK (US$ 1045 m) and France (US$ 883 m). Together the three major markets account for nearly two thirds of all European research turnover.

THE MARKETING RESEARCH PROCESS

The marketing research process consists of six broad stages. Each of these stages is discussed in detail in subsequent chapters; thus, the discussion here is brief. The process illustrated in Figure 1.5 is of a simple linear nature, Figure 1.6 takes the process a stage further to show the many iterations and connections between stages. This section will explain the stages and illustrate the connections between the stages.

Step 1: Problem definition. The logical starting point in wishing to support the decision-maker is trying to understand what marketing problem is being tackled. Marketing problems are not simple 'givens', as will be discussed in Chapter 2, and the symptoms and causes of a problem are not as neatly presented as they may be in a case-study. In Figure 1.6, the first three stages show the iterations between *evaluating the nature of the marketing problem, identifying gaps in the information that decision-makers need*, to an *initial evaluation of readily available information*. These steps combine to define the nature of the marketing problem and the research problem. In defining these problems, the researcher should take into account the purpose of the study, relevant background information, what information is needed, and how it will be used in

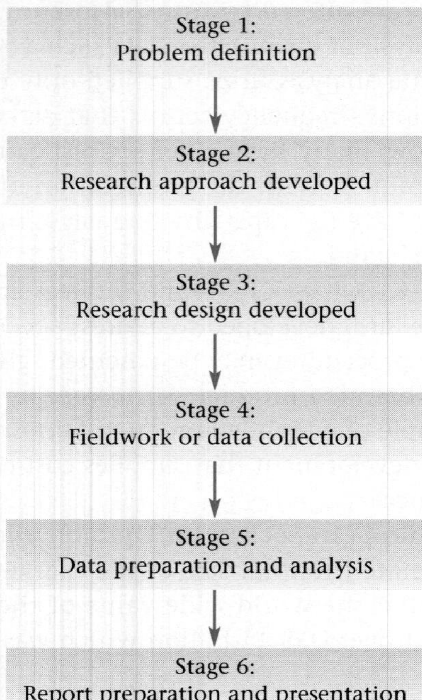

Figure 1.5 Simple linear description of the marketing research process

decision-making. Problem definition involves discussion with the decision-makers, in-depth interviews with industry experts, and the collection and analysis of readily available published information (from both inside and outside the firm). Once the problem has been precisely defined, the research can be designed and conducted properly (see Chapter 2).

Step 2: Development of an approach to the problem development. Development of an approach to the problem involves identifying characteristics or factors that can influence the research design and may include formulating an objective or theoretical framework; preparing analytical models, research questions, and hypotheses. From a clear understanding of the nature of a research problem should emerge the nature and scope of what should be either measured or encapsulated (see Chapter 2).

Step 3: Research design developed. A research design is a framework or blueprint for conducting a marketing research project. It details the procedures necessary for obtaining the required information. Its purpose is to establish a study design that will either: test the hypotheses of interest, and/or determine possible answers to set research questions, and ultimately provide the information needed for decision-making. Conducting exploratory research, precisely defining the variables, and designing appropriate scales to measure them are also a part of the research design. The issue of how the data should be obtained from the respondents (for example, by conducting a survey or an experiment) must be addressed. It may also be necessary to design a questionnaire which would entail outlining the details of measurements to be taken. These steps are discussed in detail in Chapters 3 through to 12.

Step 4: Fieldwork or data collection. In Figure 1.5, this stage is simplified to 'collecting the required data'. In Figure 1.6, the relationship between

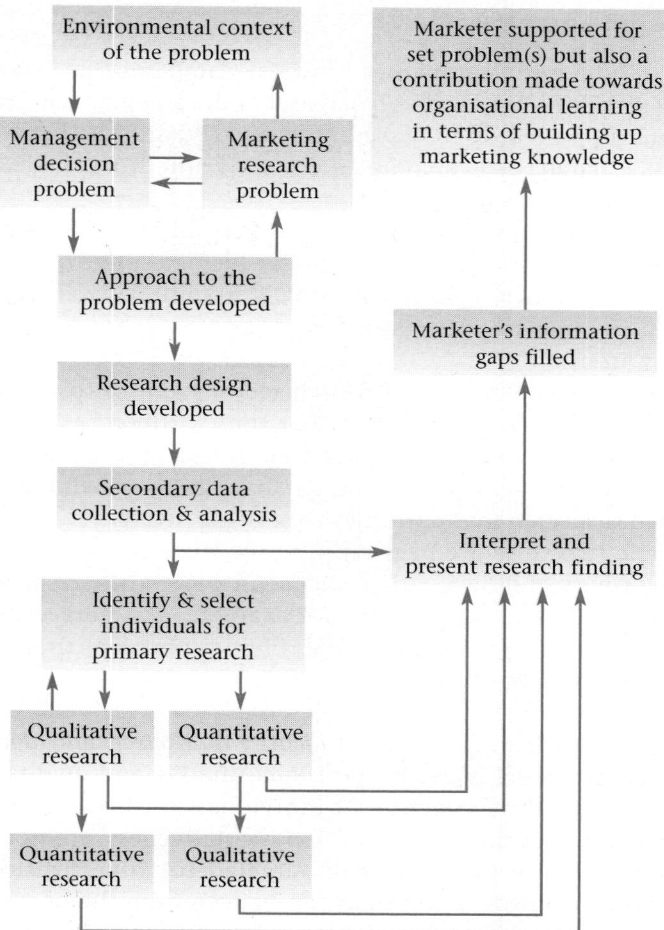

Figure 1.6
The marketing research process detailing iterations between stages

stages of data collection is shown. This starts with a more thorough collection and analysis of secondary data sources. Secondary data are data collected for some other purpose than the problem at hand. Secondary data may be held within the organisation such as databases that detail the nature and frequency of customer purchases, through to surveys that may have been completed some time ago that may be accessed through libraries, CD-ROMs or even the Internet. Going through this stage avoids replication of work and gives guidance in sampling plans and in deciding what to measure or encapsulate using quantitative or qualitative techniques. Secondary data collection and analysis may complete the research process, i.e. sufficient information may exist to interpret and report findings to a point whereby the information gaps that the decision-maker has are filled. The case may be that the secondary data forms a vital foundation and a clear focus to primary data collection. A good illustration of the connection between secondary data and primary data is seen in the connections between analysed characteristics of customers on company databases and the use of surveys or in-depth interviews to elaborate or focus upon particular questions; this is shown in the following example.

EXAMPLE

Complementary forces[18]

A trend among companies to utilise databases that provide facts and accurate predictions of consumer behaviour is developing. Databases utilise quantitative data supported by in-depth interviews. Traditional marketing research and customer databases can complement each other to provide a more comprehensive analysis of consumer behaviour.

In a market where the goalposts keep moving, research consultants are confused. According to Tony Cowling, Chief Executive of the UK's largest marketing research agency, Taylor Nelson AGB, 'traditionally, in-depth interviewing comes first to understand an issue, and then it is quantified. Now it's done the other way around'.

The key could be the research sector's ability to see the growth of database activity as an opportunity rather than a threat. As David Sneesby, Marketing Director of Taylor Nelson AGB's marketing services division, points out: 'In the past, the market research and database industries did not work closely together. Each suspected that territories were being invaded'.

The two sides are beginning to see the advantage of mutuality rather than exclusivity and have either bought into each other's area of business or formed useful alliances. Taylor AGB, for example, has merged its consumer-purchasing panel with Calyx, which handles lifestyle and demographic databases to produce SMARTbase. ■

In Figure 1.6, the stage of *identify and select individuals for primary research* covers sampling issues for both quantitative and qualitative studies. This stage may include the selection of individuals for in-depth qualitative research. In qualitative research, issues of 'representativeness' are not so important as much as the quality of individuals targeted for investigation and the quality of response elicited. However, as can be seen from the line leading up from *qualitative research* to *identify and select individuals for primary research*, the qualitative research process may help in the identification and classification of individuals, that may be targeted using more formal sampling methods. These sampling methods are covered in detail in Chapters 13 and 14.

Beyond issues of identifying and selecting individuals, the options available for primary data collection vary considerably. A stage of *qualitative research* alone may be sufficient to support the decision-maker, as indeed could a stage of *quantitative research*. The following example illustrates the use of qualitative observation, a method that can be used without quantitative confirmation of the findings.

EXAMPLE

Supermarket sweep[19]

Video camera analysis can be used to gain vital information about the way in which supermarket consumers spend their money. People behave in certain ways within the supermarket environment, according to store design specialist company ID Magasin. Patterns of consumer behaviour can be used to maximise profits. Store managers who work on store design without video footage are sometimes wrong about their conclusions. Consumers, for example, often ignore the products placed on shelves at eye-level, despite popular belief to the contrary. ■

The research problem may require a stage of qualitative and quantitative research to run concurrently, perhaps measuring and encapsulating different characteristics of the problem under investigation.

A stage of qualitative research could be used to precede a stage of quantitative research. For example, a series of focus groups may elicit a series of statements or expectations as illustrated in the following example of choosing and using contraceptives.

EXAMPLE

Choosing and using contraceptives[20]

A survey to determine ways to improve the delivery of family planning services in the UK was carried out in the Wessex Health Region. The work started with 19 focus groups of contraceptive users and potential users. These groups included single-sex groups of teenage men and women, those in their twenties and those aged over 30. The results of these focus groups were then used to develop a series of questionnaires that were sent to random samples of family doctors, and specialised family planning doctors and nurses. A feature of these questionnaires was the development of a battery of attitudinal questions based on statements made by members of the focus groups. ■

Conversely, a survey may be conducted and, upon analysis, there may be clear statistically significant differences between two distinct target markets. A series of qualitative in-depth interviews may follow to allow a more full exploration and understanding of the reasons for the differences between the two groups.

Step 5: Data preparation and analysis. Data preparation includes the editing, coding, transcription and verification of data. This process is the same for both quantitative and qualitative data analysis. Considerations of data analysis do not occur after data has been collected; such considerations are an integral part of the development of a research design and the implementation of individual quantitative or qualitative methods. As an example of this process, each questionnaire or observation form is inspected or edited and, if necessary, corrected. Number or letter codes are assigned to represent each response to each question in the questionnaire. The data from the questionnaires are transcribed or keypunched onto magnetic tape or disks or are inputted directly into a computer. Verification ensures that the data from the original questionnaires have been accurately transcribed, whereas data analysis gives meaning to the data that have been collected. Univariate techniques are used for analysing data when there is a single measurement of each element or unit in the sample, or if there are several measurements of each element, each variable is analysed in isolation. On the other hand, multivariate techniques are used for analysing data when there are two or more measurements on each element and the variables are analysed simultaneously (see Chapters 16 through 23).

Step 6: Report preparation and presentation. The entire project should be documented in a written report that addresses the specific research questions identified; describes the approach, research design, data collection and data analysis procedures adopted; and presents the results and major findings. The findings should be presented in a comprehensible format so that they can be readily used in the decision-making process. In addition, an oral presentation to management should be made using tables, figures, and graphs to enhance clarity and impact. This stage should see information gaps of the decision-maker filled, allowing the marketing problem to be tackled with confidence. As indicated in Figure 1.6 there is an added bonus in receiving the research findings. As well as tackling the set problem, there is also a contribution made towards organisational learning in terms of building up marketing knowledge (see Chapter 24).

Our description of the marketing research process is typical of the research being done by major corporations. The following case of Land Rover illustrates some of the activities involved in the marketing research process. Most importantly it shows the vital link between marketing decision-makers and marketing researchers in generating information that can give a clear competitive edge.

EXAMPLE

Land Rover brand values across Europe[21]

For Land Rover, it is vitally important for them to regularly measure consumers' knowledge, image and desirability of the Land Rover brand. To this end, Land Rover monitors its brand values across Europe via its image tracking study, CATS, which provides a measure of the health of the brand and its composite values in each country surveyed. Since Europe is the most important region for Rover in terms of product sales, this defined the focus of their research. The countries covered on a continuous basis were Britain, France, Germany, Italy, Portugal and Spain.

The need for research to address the issue of brand values within Rover Group Marketing Research stemmed from the fact that they were embarking on a global strategy of brand value focus. The challenge was how to convert the strategy into something that was measurable. In other words, how to make the marketing information requirements operational from a research standpoint. Translating this challenge into the development of a research design, set the challenge of how to quantify the overtly emotional brand values and the values that are based on the more concrete products. This had to be achieved, keeping the study as simple and elegant as possible.

The data collection methodology adopted used Computer Assisted Personal Interviewing (CAPI). New car buyers were interviewed covering the sectors that Land Rover competes:

- 4x4 sector – with Range Rover, Discovery and Defender
- Luxury sector – with Range Rover
- 4x2 sector – with Discovery and Range Rover

With a clear research design, the most important element to address their set objectives was to design a workable international questionnaire. The most important needs in developing the questionnaire were as follows:

- Common measures needed to be developed and adopted across all markets
- To distinguish between the emotional and rational elements of brand image
- To measure the Land Rover brand in a meaningful context

These requirements resulted in a questionnaire development process of four stages:

1. Contents determination e.g. image dimensions
2. Questionnaire piloting – using a qualitative studio facility
3. Questionnaire translation
4. Agency face-to-face briefing (in individual countries where the fieldwork was to be conducted)

A great deal of time was allocated to the structure of the reports to ensure that they focused on the most salient findings of Land Rover's progress in its competitive context. The information was carefully marshalled to provide brand management with input into the brand planning cycle without swamping them with masses of data.

The philosophy of taking data to wisdom is at the heart of Rover Group Marketing Research. The objective was to transform data along the continuum to information, then knowledge and ultimately wisdom. Land Rover clearly sees the wisdom of being focused and driven by the consumer. Such a focus requires regular, timely and actionable consumer-based research. By being passionate about the brand and the customer, Land Rover survives and indeed thrives in today's fiercely competitive environment. ■

THE LIMITATIONS OF MARKETING RESEARCH

If decision-makers have a gap in their knowledge, if they perceive risk and uncertainty in their decision-making and cannot find support at hand within their organisation, they can gain support from marketing research. However, there are cases where the use of marketing research has resulted in failure and so it is worth examining the limitations of marketing research.

There are two areas of misconception of the role of marketing research:[22]

1 *Marketing research does not make decisions.* The role of marketing research is not to make decisions. Rather, research replaces hunches, impressions or a total lack of knowledge with pertinent information.
2 *Marketing research does not guarantee success.* Research, at best, can improve the odds of making a correct decision. Anyone who expects to eliminate the possibility of failure by doing research is both unrealistic and likely to be disappointed. The real value of research can be seen over a long period where increasing the percentage of good decisions should be manifested in improved bottom-line performance and in the occasional revelation that arises from research.

The last point shows the long-term benefits of conducting marketing research, i.e. that the results of a study may help decision-makers with an immediate problem, but by building their knowledge they can also have long-term benefits.

A great proportion of marketing research money has been spent on developing and testing new products. 'If marketing research is as useful as marketing researchers believe it to be, there should have been more successes and fewer failures'.[23] Questions have been posed that examine the role marketing research plays in poor success rates of new products across a wide range of industries. Clearly, marketing research cannot be blamed for every failure, and the following two reasons may explain why decision-makers can make poor decisions when sound research has been conducted:[24]

1 *Blind optimism/disbelief in research.* Many patently bad products have been launched because marketing management did not believe research findings.
2 *Political pressures.* Given how many personal reputations may be at stake in the lengthy and costly process of new product development, there may be political pressures to launch a 'borderline' case.

The following example illustrates where research was used in new product development but the designer and entrepreneur chose to ignore the findings, and ultimately achieved immense levels of success.

EXAMPLE

Doing a Dyson[25]

Just 23 months after launch in the UK, the Dyson bagless vacuum cleaner became Britain's best seller, overtaking sales of Hoover, Electrolux, Panasonic, Miele and all other vacuum cleaners.

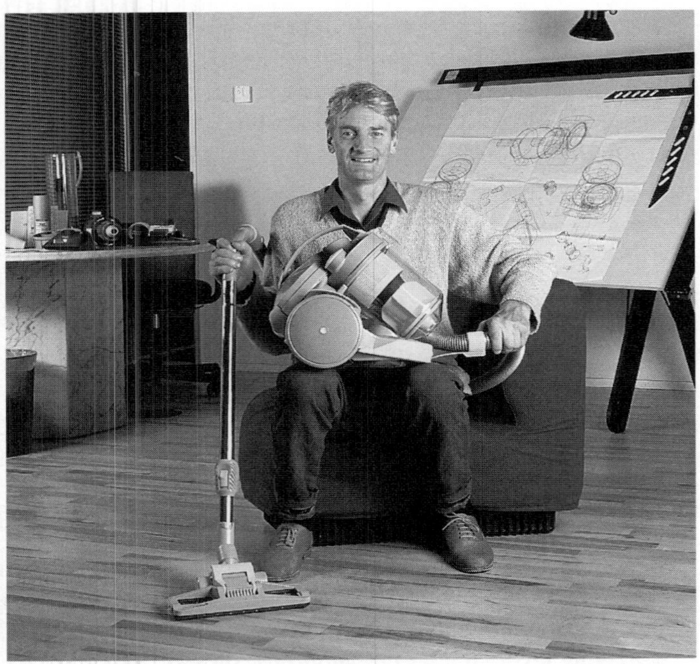

James Dyson has retained the clear bin in his design for the latest model, the Dyson DC05

Paul Lange

The Dyson clear bin was given a resounding thumbs-down in marketing research. People said they did not like the dirt being visible in the bin in case their neighbours saw how much dirt had been picked up in their homes. Some retailers said they would not want to have dust on display in demonstration machines. Yet, the dust was there because they began using Dyson display machines to clean their shops. Dyson felt compelled to launch their vacuum cleaner with a clear bin, believing that it is important to see when it is full. Moreover, what better way was there to show stockists, sales staff and customers proof of its increased efficiency than to see the dirt being collected?

How would consumers react to a new vacuum cleaner with totally radical styling, revolutionary internal engineering and a price tag almost twice that of the current brand leader? The public's response proved immediately that innovative products do sell, even at a premium price.

However, marketing research did not point to this product having the potential to be a success. Dyson argued that 'marketing research will only tell you what has happened. No research can tell you what is going to happen'. ■

Other researchers offer reasons why decision-makers may reject research findings. These go beyond the confines of developing and testing new products; examples of these reasons include:[26]

1 *Invalidity of research methods*. If the decision-maker suspects the accuracy or appropriateness of the methods for the problem faced, lack of confidence would lead to a rejection of findings.
2 *Faulty communication*. This would lead to the findings being difficult to comprehend or utilise, or being unconvincing.
3 *Irrelevance*. The decision-maker may see the findings to be irrelevant to the perceived marketing problem.

If decision-makers reject research findings, and have been taken to task as a consequence, they can easily support their stance. They could question the time taken to conduct research (and the possible consequences of delays in decision-making), and the cost required (not only in paying for marketing research projects but also in managerial effort). They could point to the few reliable methods of evaluating the return on investment. They may also question the amount of support that can be given from a researcher who may have little understanding of the context and environment in which the decisions are made.

The following example concludes the limitations of marketing research. It shows other industries where decision-makers may be sceptical of using research findings. The essence of this example is a criticism of researchers who may focus upon techniques of data collection and analysis at the expense of understanding of the problems faced by marketing decision-makers.

EXAMPLE

Buy the numbers?

Negative marketing research caused Hollywood studios to pass on the modestly budgeted *The English Patient* for some multimillion-dollar action flick – probably about a tornado in a blocked tunnel full of invading aliens. As another example, Proctor & Gamble has realised that 12 flavours of Listerine or 22 variations of toothpaste is not a good thing. Now they are telling us that while the Clove-Cinnamon-Herbal-Chablis Listerine tested well, it helped give customers too many choices, and this resulted in profit-dropping confusion. For Proctor and Gamble, positive marketing research caused myriad desired but confusing mutant strains of household and personal care products. Of course, the cheap shot would be to rain derision on marketing research. However, research is vital, I think we can all agree on that. No, the real problem is when we begin to be 'blinded by science'. Or, rather, faux science. The grim and savage lesson to be learned from these events is that marketing from the numbers is not the same as marketing by the numbers. Not by a long shot.

It seems, to me at least, that marketing, with its past reputation as a 'soft' profession, has sought to reinvent itself in NASA-like hard-science terms. The numbers and the statistics have sometimes become ends in themselves, instead of points of departure for marketing strategies. In the aggressive desire for minimised risk, ideas, products and services that don't test well are simply not pursued, while ones that do are – even in the face of common sense.

Think back 15 years ago – you're Sony and you've surveyed the market. The chances that your sample would have articulated the need for a small, battery-powered stereo tape player would have been nil. And, from another angle, asking a focus group of professional men and women in 1981 whether they had any desire to be ensconced in headphones while walking down the street would not have tested well either. Quite simply, in marketing by the numbers situation, the Sony Walkman would have been killed on the drawing board. ■

Like the Dyson example, the Sony Walkman is a classic example of decision-makers ignoring what they see as misleading research findings and going on to great success by following a hunch. Many cases of less significance like the Hollywood and Proctor & Gamble examples above serve to illustrate that marketing research does not replace marketing decision-making or guarantee success. Collectively, these examples illustrate that out of the array of research and information support approaches, there is no guaranteed approach to supporting marketing decision-makers. Given the vast array of marketing decisions and styles of marketing decision-maker, the hallmark of marketing decision-making is creativity. Creativity in decision-making can be supported well by accurate and relevant information. Generating accurate and relevant information is also a creative act. The diagnosis of problems, the measurement of consumers and the interpretation of those measurements are all creative acts, not a set system.

If decision-makers complain that research is misleading or is only telling them what they already know, the marketing researcher may argue that the fault lies with managers who pose the wrong questions or problem in the first place. If one takes the narrow view that the decision-maker poses the questions and the researcher finds the answers, there may be some validity in such an argument. It does not hold if one considers that the decision-maker and the researcher have a joint commitment to solve problems. That they have quite distinct but complementary creative skills that they can bring together to understand what problem they should be researching, how they conduct the research, and how they interpret their findings.

GLOBALCASH PROJECT

Supporting pan-European banking decisions

A research project designed to understand the cash management and electronic banking practices of Europe's largest companies is used as a running example throughout this text to illustrate concepts and data analysis procedures. The project was directed by the English co-author, coordinating 19 business schools throughout Europe. GlobalCash is a study conducted every two years utilising a mixture of quantitative and qualitative methods. The targets to be researched are the largest companies in 19 European countries including the Eastern European countries of the Czech Republic, Hungary and Poland. The whole project is funded by major banks from Britain, France, Germany, Ireland, Spain and the USA, with additional sponsorship from Treasury Management Associations in individual countries. The subjects tackled in the study focus upon cash management practices, electronic banking and the impact of European Monetary Union. Of particular importance to banks are questions that indicate changes in market share in individual countries', evaluations of their service delivery and companies' plans for the future.

The headquarters of Commerzbank in Frankfurt – one of the major pan-European banks that supported the GlobalCash project

The main methods used were:

- a postal survey of companies
- in-depth interviews in each country
- a feedback workshop in Brussels, whereby the survey findings were presented to questionnaire respondents followed by qualitative workshops.

The findings of the GlobalCash studies were used to develop the marketing, operational and IT strategies of the major banks operating in Europe. As the study is conducted every two years, measurement of the effect or outcome of past strategies can be conducted. ■

INTERNATIONAL MARKETING RESEARCH

Conducting international marketing research is much more complex than domestic marketing research. All research of this kind will be discussed and illustrated in individual chapters as individual techniques are developed and in greater detail in Chapter 25. The marketing, government, legal, economic, structural, socio-cultural and informational environments, prevailing in target international markets, and characteristics of target consumers that are being studied, influence the manner in which the six steps of the marketing research process should be performed. Examples of these environmental factors and their impact on the marketing research process are illustrated in detail in subsequent chapters. Despite the complexity, international marketing research is expected to grow at a faster rate than domestic research as illustrated in the following example.

EXAMPLE

The world shrinks, maybe, but there's still the need to travel[28]

Twenty-five years ago the world seemed much larger than it does today and international researchers were only a small community of competitive but like-minded mavericks, all with their travellers' tales. In those days, the problems of working overseas, especially in the developing world, justified the belief that international research was a category apart and those international practitioners were living a very different kind of life. Not many people had the resources for international travel in the early 1970s and certainly not as part of an all-paid working mission. Twenty-five years on, international research has changed, in both obvious and subtle ways. The most obvious is in terms of growth; international research has remained one of the most consistently buoyant sectors, maintaining growth through two major recessions. Consumer marketing has reached most cities in most countries in the world and, along with marketing, advertising and market research are commonplace.

> A month ago I sat in a small house in a black township in Cape Town with a group of young men whose prospects seemed limited to casual labour and, possibly, crime. Then one of them chided me for showing them a dull advertisement: 'Surely you must remember AIDA,' he said. 'Attention Interest Desire Action – well I don't see much Interest and Desire in that advert.' ■

With the spread of marketing and research skills has come a noticeable decline in the 'national research culture'. There was a time, when each country had a stubbornly distinctive approach to research, making it extremely difficult to get a consistent research design across markets. Most people are aware now that there are different, equally legitimate, ways to approach research problems and that no one school of thought has absolute authority for all types of problem. This greater flexibility has made multi-country coordinated projects much more feasible – not easier, as they represent intellectually, logistically and diplomatically the most demanding of problems.

ETHICS IN MARKETING RESEARCH

Ethical issues arise in marketing research for several reasons. Marketing research often involves contact with the respondents and the general public, usually by way of data collection, dissemination of the research findings, and marketing activities such as advertising campaigns based on these findings. Thus, there is the potential to abuse or misuse marketing research by taking advantage of these people, for example by misrepresenting the research findings in advertising. As explained earlier, marketing research is generally conducted by commercial (i.e. for-profit) firms which are either independent research organisations (external suppliers) or departments within corporations (internal suppliers). Most marketing research is conducted for clients representing commercial firms. The following example summarises the basic principles of the Code of Conduct for the Market Research Society in the UK. These principles will be developed and illustrated at the end of each chapter.

EXAMPLE

Code of Conduct: basic principles

Research is founded upon the willing cooperation of the public and of business organisations. It depends upon public and business confidence that it is conducted honestly, objectively, without unwelcome intrusion and without harm to informants. Its purpose is to collect and analyse information, and not directly to create sales nor to influence the opinions of anyone participating in it. It is in this spirit that the Code of Conduct has been devised.

The general public and other interested parties shall be entitled to complete assurance that every research project is carried out strictly in accordance with this Code, and that their rights of privacy are respected.

In particular, they must be assured that no information which could be used to identify them will be made available without their agreement to anyone outside the agency responsible for conducting the research. They must also be assured that the information they supply will not be used for any purposes other than research and that they will in no way be adversely affected or embarrassed as a direct result of their participation in a research project.

Finally, the research findings themselves must always be reported accurately and never used to mislead anyone, in any way. ■

Sugging
The use of marketing research to deliberately disguise a sales effort.

Frugging
The use of marketing research to deliberately disguise fundraising activities.

Classic examples of breaches of these principles come in the guise of **sugging** and **frugging**. Sugging occurs when surveys are used to gain access to respondents to deliver a sales pitch or to generate sales by other means. Frugging occurs when surveys are used to raise funds for a charity or other cause under the guise of conducting research.

INTERNET AND COMPUTER APPLICATIONS

The Internet is possibly the greatest communication medium since the telephone. The World Wide Web (www or Web) is the dominant component of the Internet and many use the terms Web and Internet synonymously. Each document on the Web has a specific electronic address called a Uniform Resource Locator (URL). In this text we list on p.403 the URLs of many sites of use to marketing researchers. These sites are not guaranteed to be available or to be at the same URL when you read this text, as the Internet changes rapidly. However, you will develop the skills to track down URLs that have changed for particular organisations and track down other URLs of specific use to your own research work.

There are many ways in which the Internet can be useful to marketing researchers. It can be used as a source of marketing research providers: a source of secondary data; a source for marketing research software; and as a source for data gathering such as focus groups and surveys. It is another source of information that can feed into a firm's marketing information system. One of the big advantages of conducting focus groups and surveys on the Internet is that the data is ready for processing as soon as it comes in. Internet data does not require the step of data input because data is electronically sent from respondents – wherever they are in the world. The Internet is also very useful for project management. Email combined with the ability to attach files is used extensively for communication between researchers and clients through every stage of the marketing research process.

Throughout this book we show how the stages of the marketing research process are facilitated by Internet research.[29] Computers, mainframes followed by microcomputers, have had a profound effect upon marketing and marketing research. In this text we show how computing technology can be integrated in each step of the marketing research process. The demonstration disks enclosed with this text illustrate the use of computing technology in the process of questionnaire design, data entry, data analysis and reporting; and the application of geodemographic information systems. Later in the text we illustrate the use of popular quantitative and qualitative data analysis packages.

SUMMARY

Marketing research provides support to marketing decision-makers by helping to: describe the nature and scope of customer groups, understand the nature of forces that shape the needs of customer groups and the marketer's ability to satisfy those groups, test individual and interactive controllable marketing variables, monitor and reflect upon past successes and failures in marketing decisions. The overall purpose of marketing research is to assess information needs and provide the relevant information in a systematic and objective manner to improve marketing decision-making. Marketing research may be classified into problem identification research and problem-solving research. Information obtained using marketing research can become an integral part of a Marketing Information System (MkIS) and a Decision Support System (DSS). The contribution of marketing research to such systems illustrates that research has a role in developing marketing learning within organisations.

Marketing research may be conducted internally (by internal suppliers) or may be purchased from external suppliers. Full-service suppliers provide the entire range of marketing research services, from problem definition to report preparation and presentation. The services provided by these suppliers can be classified as syndicated services, standardised services or customised services. Limited-service suppliers specialise in one or a few phases of the marketing research project. Services offered by these suppliers can be classified as field services, coding and data entry, data analysis, analytical services or branded products.

The marketing research process consists of six broad steps that must be followed systematically. The process involves: problem definition, research approach developed, research design formulated, fieldwork or data collection, data preparation and analysis, and report preparation and presentation. Within these six broad steps are many iterations and routes that can be taken, reflecting the reality of practising marketing research.

Marketing research is not a panacea for all marketing problems. There are examples where marketing research has not adequately supported decision-makers. Many of the problems that arise from poor marketing research derive from poor communications between decision-makers and researchers. International marketing research is much more complex than domestic research because the researcher must consider the environments prevailing in the international markets being researched. Research is founded upon the willing cooperation of the public and of business organisations. Ethical marketing research practices nurture that cooperation allowing a more professional approach and more accurate research information.

QUESTIONS AND PROBLEMS

1 Describe the task of marketing research.

2 What decisions are made by marketing managers? How does marketing research help in supporting these decisions?

3 Define marketing research.

4 What problems are associated with using consumer databases in marketing research?

5 Describe one classification of marketing research.

6 What is a marketing information system?

7 How does a DSS differ from a MkIS?

8 Explain one way to classify marketing research suppliers and services.

9 What are syndicated services?

10 Describe the steps in the simple linear marketing research process.

11 Explain why there may be the need for iterations between stages of the marketing research process.

12 What arguments would be used by sceptics of marketing research?

13 What arguments would you use to defend investment in marketing research?

14 What factors fuel the growth of international marketing research?

15 Discuss the ethical issues in marketing research that relate to (a) the client, (b) the supplier, and (c) the respondent.

NOTES

1 Hall, J. 'For Eurostar's star regulars, there truly is a free dinner', *ResearchPlus* (June 1995), 12.

2 Jagger, S. 'Make us laugh, make us cry', *ResearchPlus* (November 1996), 12.

3 Davies, B. 'Football fever – caught by the nation or just those most at risk?', *ResearchPlus* (September 1996), 10.

4 Bradford, S. 'From Armani to AIDS: the hopes, the fears, of Europe's youth', *ResearchPlus* (November 1997), 4.

5 Field, C. 'What's in store?',*Computer Weekly* (7 November 1996), 52.

6 For the strategic role of marketing research, see Noel B. Zabriskie and Alan B. Huellmantel, 'Marketing Research as a Strategic Tool', *Long-Range Planning* 27 (February 1994), 107–18.

7 For relationships between information processing, marketing decisions and performance, see Rashi Glazer and Allen M. Weiss, 'Marketing in Turbulent Environments: Decision Process and the Time-Sensitivity of Information', *Journal of Marketing Research* 30 (November 1993), 509–21.

8 Rebecca Fannin, 'More Marketers Are Using Creative Brand Extensions to Expand Their Franchises. The Question Is: Can the Practice Be too Much of a Stretch?', *Marketing and Media Decisions* (January 1987), 22–28.

9 Malhotra, N.K. 'Shifting Perspective on the Shifting Paradigm in Marketing Research', *Journal of the Academy of Marketing Science* 20 (Fall 1992): 379i37; and William Perreault, 'The Shifting Paradigm in Marketing Research', *Journal of the Academy of Marketing Science* 20 (Fall 1992), 367–75.

10 *Marketing*, 'Beer research shows overspill', (9 October 1997), 6.

11 'Say Goodnight Ovaltineys', *Marketing* (27 November 1986), 25–27.

12 Cowan, D., 'Good Information – Generals Can't Do Without It. Why Do CEOs Think They Can?', *Journal of the Market Research Society*, 36 (April 1994), 105–14.

13 Turban, E. *Decision Support and Expert Systems* (New York: Macmillan, 1990); McCann, J., Tadlaoui, A. and Gallagher, J. 'Knowledge Systems in Merchandising: Advertising Designs', *Journal of Retailing* (Fall 1990), 257–77.

14 Gupta, S., and Kohli, R., 'A Knowledge-Based System for Advertising Design', *Marketing Science* (Summer 1990), 212–29.

15 Calmet, A.V. 'Geographic Marketing in Financial Institutions: The Experience of Banco Central Hispanoamericano', *Marketing and Research Today* (August 1996), 182–89.

16 ESOMAR Press Release, Amsterdam, 7 September 1997.

17 ESOMAR Press Release, Amsterdam, 7 September 1997.

18 Bond, C. 'Complementary forces', *Marketing* (16 January 1997), 29.

19 'Supermarket sweep', *The Grocer* (13 July 1996), 28.

20 Cooper, P. Diamond, I. and High, S. 'Choosing and Using Contraceptives: Integrating Qualitative and Quantitative Methods in Family Planning', *Journal of the Market Research Society* 35(4) (October 1993), 325.

21 Bull, N. and Oxley, M. The Search for Focus – Brand Values across Europe', *Marketing and Research Today* (November 1996), 239.

22 Lehmann, D.R., *Market Research and Analysis*, 3rd edn (Homewood, IL: Irwin, 1994), 14.

23 Sampson, P. and Standen, P. 'Predicting Sales Volume and Market Shares', in *New Product Development Research Contributions to Strategy Formulation, Idea Generation and Screening Product, Product Testing and Final Marketing*, ESOMAR (November 1983).

24 Ibid.

25 Muranka, T. and Rootes, N. *Doing a Dyson*, (Dyson Appliances, 1996), 22.

26 Luck, D.J., Wales, H.C., Taylor, D.A. and Rubin, R.S. *Marketing Research*, 5th edn (Englewood Cliffs, NJ: Prentice Hall, 1978).

27 Sheridan, K. 'Buy the numbers?' *Bank Marketing* 29(3) (March 1997), 5.

28 Goodyear, M. 'The world shrinks, maybe, but there's still the need to travel', *ResearchPlus* (May 1996), 12.

29 De Ville, B., 'Internet for marketing research', *Marketing Research* 7(3), (Summer 1995), 36–38.

Chapter 2

Defining the marketing research problem and developing a research approach

Problem definition is the most important step in a marketing research project. Failure to diagnose a problem correctly will, at best, lead to wasted resources at worst, totally misguided decisions

OBJECTIVES

After reading this chapter, the student should be able to:

1 understand the importance of, and process used in defining marketing research problems;
2 describe the tasks involved in problem definition;
3 discuss in detail the nature and various components of a research brief and a research proposal;
4 discuss the environmental factors affecting the definition of the research problem;
5 clarify the distinction between the management decision problem and the marketing research problem;
6 explain the structure of a well-defined marketing research problem, including the broad statement and the specific components;
7 acquire an appreciation of the complexity involved in defining the problem and developing a research approach in international marketing research;
8 understand the ethical issues and conflicts that arise in defining the problem and developing a research approach.

OVERVIEW

This chapter covers the first two of the six steps of the marketing research process described in Chapter 1: defining the marketing research problem and developing a research approach to tackle the problem. Defining the problem is the most important step, since only when a problem has been clearly and accurately identified can a research project be conducted properly. Defining the marketing research problem sets the course of the entire project. Regardless of how well a research plan is designed and subsequent stages carried out, if the problem is not correctly diagnosed, research findings could be misleading or even dangerous! In this chapter, we allow the reader to appreciate the complexities involved in defining a problem, by identifying the factors to be considered and the tasks involved.

In practical terms, the means to communicate and facilitate the diagnosis of research problems is achieved through the preparation of a research brief and research proposal. The rationale and components of the research brief and research proposal are presented. We provide guidelines for appropriately defining the marketing research problem and avoiding common types of errors. We also discuss in detail the characteristics or factors influencing the research design and components of an approach to the problem: objective/theoretical framework, analytical models, research questions and hypotheses. The special considerations involved in defining the problem and developing a research approach in international marketing research are discussed. Finally, several ethical issues that arise at this stage of the marketing research process are considered.

We introduce our discussion with two examples. The first example is based upon the tourism industry. This example illustrates the difficulties that a marketing researcher may face in diagnosing marketing problems and their related research problems. The macroenvironmental context of the tourism industry presents difficulties for the marketing researcher in developing an appropriate research design. However, the biggest problem for the marketing researcher lies in organisational cultures that do not see any value in using marketing research. The diagnosis of research problems with a corresponding research design is difficult to achieve in cooperation with decision-makers whose perspective is mainly short-term and tactical.

The second example, the ABC Global Kids study, illustrates that from broad research questions a clear set of research questions can be developed. There are many difficulties in designing a research approach that will allow comparable findings from six countries in three continents and in questioning children. Without a precise diagnosis of management and research problems, such a complicated research approach would be doomed to failure.

EXAMPLE

Travelling so fast, they can't stop for research[1]

Although travel and tourism probably account for 12 per cent of the world's economy, less than 5 per cent of total marketing research turnover is in the sector. The tourism industry's management culture is very entrepreneurial and introspective, being dominated by 'operations men' and by those whose career has been mainly within the industry itself. Since travel expertise can be seen as more important than broader management experience gained elsewhere, newcomers reliant on modern marketing sciences rather than on years in travel can sometimes be regarded suspiciously.

The highly competitive nature of travel and tourism and its narrow profit margins means that short-term tactical needs can be more important than a long-term strategic overview. There is a constant need to react rapidly because international political and economic changes have a greater, more immediate effect on travel and tourism than on other industries. Often managers feel they do not have time for detailed research before reacting, if they hesitate, a once off opportunity can be lost. The intangible nature of the travel product itself can make research difficult, especially when it comes to new product development. It is often easier for travel marketers to check out the viability of new products in the real world rather than via traditional research-based test marketing techniques.

Travel marketers have a tendency to query the usefulness and value of research. Will it actually shift products or will it provide data that experienced travel insiders knew anyway? Is the diversion of expenditure to research from advertising or below-the-line activities justifiable when the latter will hopefully yield sales tomorrow? ■

EXAMPLE

Is there one global village for our future generation?[2]

The ABC Global Kids Study was conducted in the Spring of 1996 among 2400 children aged 7 to 12 years and their mothers, in China, Japan, France, Britain, Germany and the United States. The study was sponsored by multinational corporations such as Mars, Kodak and MacDonalds. The key topic areas were as follows:

- Child wealth and spending patterns
- Influence on household purchases
- Media habits
- Technology ownership and usage
- Social issues and concerns
- Daily activities
- Food and beverages
- Toys and games
- Cartoon and movie awareness and attitudes
- Recreation

The study was designed to quantify the size of business opportunities in given product categories and to provide fact-based direction on how to create an exciting child product portfolio and marketing programme.

While uniformity of survey, method and instrument were maintained for cross-country comparison, adaptations were sought locally to capture unique retail and cultural characteristics. A pictorial response scale was used when interviewing children on emotions and preferences. Product usage frequency was asked of mothers, instead of children.

The survey revealed considerable spending power for children aged 7–12, as well as active participation from children in making family purchase decision in a number of product categories. It was apparent that world-wide, children basically have many common dreams and aspirations. ■

IMPORTANCE OF DEFINING THE PROBLEM

Although each step in a marketing research project is important, problem definition is the most important step. As mentioned in Chapter 1, for the purpose of marketing research, problems and opportunities are treated interchangeably. **Problem definition** involves stating the general problem and identifying the specific components of the marketing research problem. Only when the marketing research problem has been clearly defined can research be designed and conducted properly. 'Of all the tasks in a marketing research project, none is more vital to the ultimate fulfilment of a client's needs than an accurate and adequate definition of the research problem. All the effort, time, and money spent from this point on will be wasted if the problem is misunderstood and ill-defined.'[3] Without a thorough and accurate evaluation of the marketing problem to be solved and its translation into a research approach, research techniques, however well designed and executed, may be of little use or even harmful. An analogy to this is the medical doctor prescribing treatment after a cursory examination of a patient – the medicine may be even more dangerous than the condition it is supposed to cure!

Problem definition
A broad statement of the general problem and identification of the specific components of the marketing research problem.

The importance of clearly identifying and defining the research problem cannot be overstated. The foundation of defining a research problem is the communication that develops between marketing decision-makers and marketing researchers. In some form or another the marketing decision-makers must communicate what they see as being the problems they face and what research support they need. This communication usually comes in the form of a research brief. The marketing researcher responds to the research brief with a research proposal, which is their outline of a practical solution to the set research problem. The following example illustrates that a research brief may not always be particularly well thought-out. The marketing researcher is expected to develop the brief into a research proposal and in doing so has a vital role to play in the diagnosis of research problems.

EXAMPLE

How to bait the interview hook for those Top 1000 big fish[4]

The groans from researchers when another brief arrives asking for 100 or 200 interviews with Chief Executive Officers (CEOs) or equivalents within the *Times* Top 1000 companies typify the attitude generated by business-to-business marketers' constant demand to reach this audience. When the research brief arrives, it is certainly worth examining whether, practically, what is requested can actually be done. The research proposal developed must reflect the practicalities of questioning managers who are constantly bombarded with requests to respond to research questions. The number of interviews, the time scale, the nature of questions and the structure of the sample all need to be taken into account. For example, is it really worth undertaking 200 interviews within any single European country? If we were limited to one per organisation, we would be interviewing to strike rates of between 1 in 2.5 to 1 in 5. If the research targets companies throughout Europe, individual countries such as Britain and France may have few large companies if compared to the USA, while Italy has a limited number of very large companies and a great many smaller ones. In actually reaching the target audience, a number of issues need to be taken into account. International business-to-business research with senior business audiences brings with it not only the particular difficulties of reaching them but also the need to understand both country and cultural issues that impact on the research. Telephone interviews (even if possible) are considered inappropriate for these audiences in many Far East and Middle East markets, especially South Korea and Japan, while in Singapore and Hong Kong, provided the interviews are not too long (over 15 minutes), telephone is fine. ■

THE MARKETING RESEARCH BRIEF

Research brief
A document produced by the users of research findings or the buyers of a piece of marketing research. The brief is used to communicate the perceived requirements of a marketing research project.

The marketing **research brief** is a document produced by the users of research findings or the buyers of a piece of marketing research. The brief may be used to communicate the perceived requirements of a marketing research project to external agencies or internally within an organisation to marketing research professionals. *The marketing research brief should not be carved in tablets of stone!* It should act as the first stage in expressing the nature of a research problem and agreeing an appropriate research approach.

It has been contended that the greatest form of potential error in marketing research lies in the initial relationship between marketing decision makers and marketing researchers.[5] In developing a sound initial relationship, the research brief plays a vital role. Without some formal method of communicating the nature of a management problem, there is great potential for ambiguities, illogical actions (by both parties), misunderstandings and even forgetfulness. The purpose of a written marketing research brief may be summarised as:

- It makes the initiator of the brief more certain of how the information to be collected will support decision-making.
- It ensures an amount of agreement or cohesion among all parties who may benefit from the research findings.
- It helps both the marketer and the researcher to plan and administer the research programme.
- It helps to reduce disputes that can occur when the gaps in marketers' knowledge are not 'filled' as intended.
- It can form the basis for negotiation with a variety of research organisations.

In all, the research brief saves resources in time and money by helping to ensure that the nature of the problem or opportunity under investigation has been thought through.

Components of the marketing research brief

The rationale for a marketing research brief may be logical, but actually generating a brief from marketing decision-makers can be extremely difficult. These difficulties will be tackled later in this chapter. The following format for a research brief has two great advantages. First, it does not demand a great deal of knowledge about research techniques from decision-makers. Second, it allows the researchers the opportunity to demonstrate their creativity. They have the possibility to examine the marketing problem from different perspectives, and to develop an approach to the research problem that supports the marketing decision-maker within clear time and cost parameters.

1 *Background information.* The background serves to put research objectives into context, helping the researcher to understand *why* certain research objectives are being pursued. The marketer would detail what they see as being the main events that have caused or contributed to the problem under study. Such a background gives a framework for the researcher to investigate other potential events, contributory factors or causes.

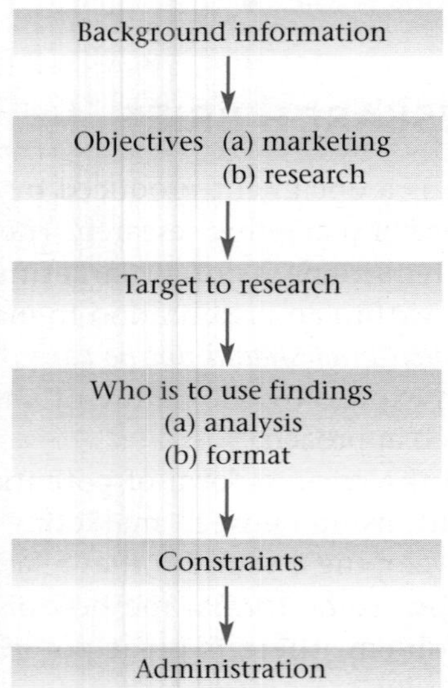

Figure 2.1
Components of the marketing research brief

2 *Objectives*. This would detail what marketing decisions are to be completed once the research has been undertaken. Decisions are made to accomplish objectives. The formulation of the management decision problem must be based on a clear understanding of two types of objectives: the organisational objectives (the goals of the organisation) and the personal objectives of the decision-maker. For the project to be successful, it must serve the objectives of the organisation and of the decision-maker. This, however, is not an easy task. The decision-maker rarely formulates personal or organisational objectives accurately. Rather, it is likely that these objectives will be stated in terms that have no operational significance, such as 'to improve corporate image'. Direct questioning of the decision-maker is unlikely to reveal all the relevant objectives. Researchers rely heavily upon their interviewing and probing skills to extract these objectives. Generating decision-makers' perspectives of objectives, even if they have no operational significance, helps the process of extracting and developing an understanding of what the decision-maker is trying to achieve.

3 *Target to research*. Any marketing research project will measure or observe a target group of individuals. These may be distinct groups of consumers or channel members such as retailers or competitors. Here, details of the characteristics of the target group help in the decisions of identification, gaining access and measurement or observation.

4 *Who is to use the findings*. This section would outline brief details of the decision-makers who will use the research findings. As with the example of the tourist industry at the start of this chapter, certain decision-makers may be entrepreneurial and introspective, looking for short-term tactical advantages. Presenting research findings that make tactical advantages apparent would be the best way to communicate to such managers. This has an impact upon the extent of analysis conducted upon the data collected and the style and format in which research findings will be presented.

5 *Constraints*. The main limitation to marketing researchers carrying out what they may perceive as being the correct way to research a problem, is the time and money that a marketer can afford. Proposing a large-scale project that would cost €200,000 when only €50,000 has been budgeted obviously will not meet management approval. In many instances, the scope of the marketing research problem may have to be reduced to accommodate budget constraints. With knowledge of time and cost constraints, the researcher can develop a research design to suit these needs. The researcher may also demonstrate other courses of action that could demand greater amounts of money or time, but could have clear benefits that the marketer may be unaware of. Other constraints, such as those imposed by the client firm's personnel, organisational structure and culture, or decision-making styles, should be identified to determine the scope of the research project. Yet, constraints should not be allowed to diminish the value of the research to the decision-maker or to compromise the integrity of the research process. In instances where the resources are too limited to allow a project of sufficient quality, the firm should be advised not to undertake formal marketing research. Thus, it becomes necessary to identify resources and constraints, a task that can be better understood when examined in the light of the objectives of the organisation and the decision-maker.

6 *Administrative considerations*. This would lay out administration details in completing the research project. Examples of this could be the expected delivery of interim reports, contacts in an organisation that may be able to help supply further information, or reference to sources of materials that are needed to successfully complete the research.

With a formal marketing research brief and perhaps preliminary discussions with the organisation that is to commission the research, the marketing researcher has the necessary material to develop a research proposal.

The above outline of a marketing research brief is an example that allows the researcher to offer their wide range of expertise. Research briefs may also be far more explicit in terms of specifying methods of measurement and analysis. Such research briefs act as tender documents. In many instances however, the marketing researcher does not enjoy the luxury of a written research brief. The marketing decision-maker may outline their ideas in an oral manner, perhaps on an informal basis. If the marketing researcher is faced with an oral brief, they can use the proposed brief outline above as a guideline to the issues they should elicit in order to develop a proposal.

THE MARKETING RESEARCH PROPOSAL

Research proposal
The official layout of the planned marketing research activity.

In response to a research brief, the marketing researcher will develop a research plan (covered in detail in Chapter 3) and will develop a **research proposal** to communicate this plan. The marketing research proposal contains the essence of the project and, in its final format, serves as a contract between the researcher and management. The research proposal covers all phases of the marketing research process. It allows the researcher to present their interpretation of the problems faced by management and to be creative in developing a research solution that will effectively support decision-makers. Although the format of a research proposal may vary considerably, most proposals address all the steps of the marketing research process and contain the elements as shown in Figure 2.2.

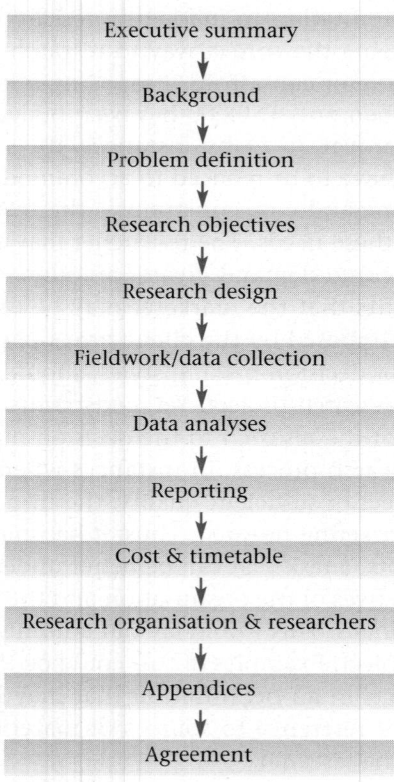

Figure 2.2
Components of the marketing research proposal

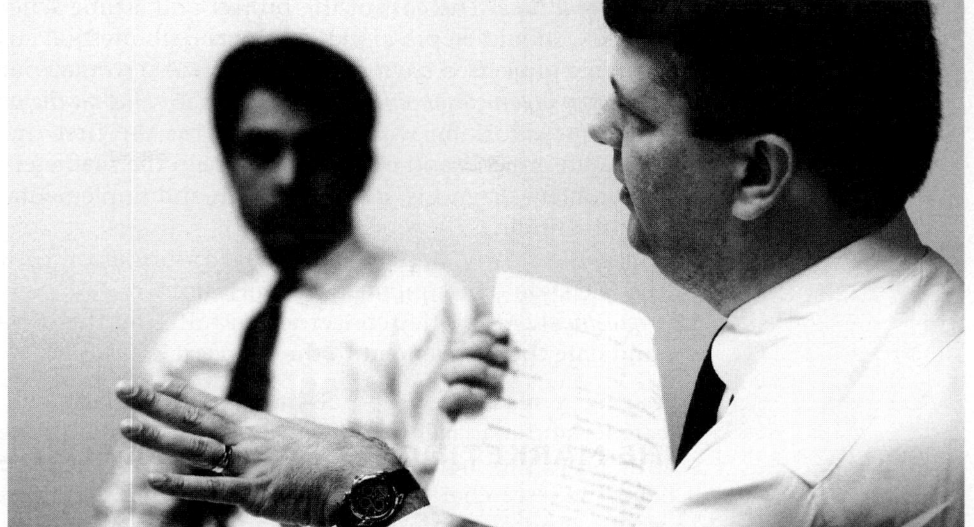

There should be a written statement of the marketing research problem that has been agreed to or by the client. Burke consultant discussing the marketing research problem definition with the client

1 *Executive summary*. The proposal should begin with a summary of the major points from each of the other sections, presenting an overview of the entire proposal.
2 *Background*. The researcher would be expected to go beyond the background presented in the brief. Other potential causes of the problems faced or alternative interpretations of the factors that shape the background in an environmental context should be presented.
3 *Problem definition*. Again, if necessary, the researcher may go beyond the problem definition presented in the brief. If the researcher sees potential to add value for the marketer through alternative diagnoses of the problem presented in the brief, then these should be shown. If the researcher sees a problem in the brief that is ambiguous or unattainable, again alternative diagnoses should be presented. From this section, the marketer's gaps in knowledge should be apparent.
4 *Research objectives*. This may be presented in the form of clear hypotheses that may be tested. It may also cover broader areas that are to be explored that may not be measured or tested at this stage.
5 *Research design*. The research design to be adopted – whether exploratory, descriptive or causal – should be specified. Information should be provided on the following components: methods of collecting the desired data; nature of the instrument to collect data, e.g. details of questionnaire or focus group interview; sampling plan and sample size.
6 *Field work/data collection*. The proposal should discuss how the data will be collected and who will collect it. If the fieldwork is to be subcontracted to another supplier, this should be stated. Control mechanisms to ensure the quality of data collected should be described.
7 *Data analysis*. The kind of data analysis that will be conducted (simple cross-tabulations, univariate analysis, multivariate analysis) and the extent to which the results will be interpreted should be described.
8 *Reporting*. The proposal should specify the nature of any intermediate reports to be presented; what will be the form of the final report; and whether an oral presentation of the results will be made.

9 *Cost and time*. The cost of the project and a time schedule, broken down by phases, should be presented. A critical path method chart might be included. In large projects, a payment schedule is also worked out in advance.
10 *Research organisation and key researchers working on the project*. When an organisation is working with researchers for the first time, some idea of past research projects and clients should help the marketer to trust the researcher in problem diagnosis, research design and implementation, and in interpreting the findings.
11 *Appendices*. Any statistical or other information of interest to only a few people should be contained in appendices.
12 *Agreement*. All parties concerned in fulfilling the research plan should sign and date their agreement to the proposal.

Preparing a research proposal has several advantages. It ensures that the researcher and management agree about the nature of the project, and it helps sell the project to management. As preparation of the proposal entails planning, it helps the researcher conceptualise and execute the marketing research project. The following example illustrates the language problems in writing a pan-European research proposal. In this example, a problem lies with English speakers wanting to negotiate and work with other English speakers and having little experience of the countries in which they will undertake research.

EXAMPLE

Some dos and don'ts of pan-European research[6]

Many European studies are commissioned by English speakers who want to work with English speakers. They want to agree questionnaires in English, and they want reports and tables in English. And so they come to Britain.

In addition, it is simpler for someone commissioning international research to accept an English proposal written by a first-language English speaker. Even the best European – used here in its not-British sense – English speaker finds it hard to write a creative proposal in good idiomatic English. *But it is creativity that sells proposals*.

A problem in writing proposals for research in Europe is often lack of familiarity with European habits and behaviour. Most British researchers' experience of Europe is derived from holidays backed up (in all too few cases) by limited work experience in one or more countries. Faced by a proposal on TV viewing, on grocery purchasing, on holiday habits or on headache remedies, few British researchers have any notion of how Italians, Spaniards or Germans treat these subjects. Hence the first step in writing an international proposal on an unfamiliar subject is secondary research. This may also involve calling a dozen homes in the relevant country, and chatting on the phone for an hour or two with locals. Soon you start to identify how Italians, Spaniards and Germans differ from the UK and what these main differences are. Designing a piece of European research in an unfamiliar area without taking this first simple step is like taking up power boating without learning to swim. It is a route to disaster, not maybe with the proposal, but with the research when commissioned. ■

THE PROCESS OF DEFINING THE PROBLEM AND DEVELOPING A RESEARCH APPROACH

By formally developing and exchanging a marketing research brief and research proposal, the marketing decision-maker and the marketing researcher utilise their distinctive skills. They ensure that the marketing problem and research

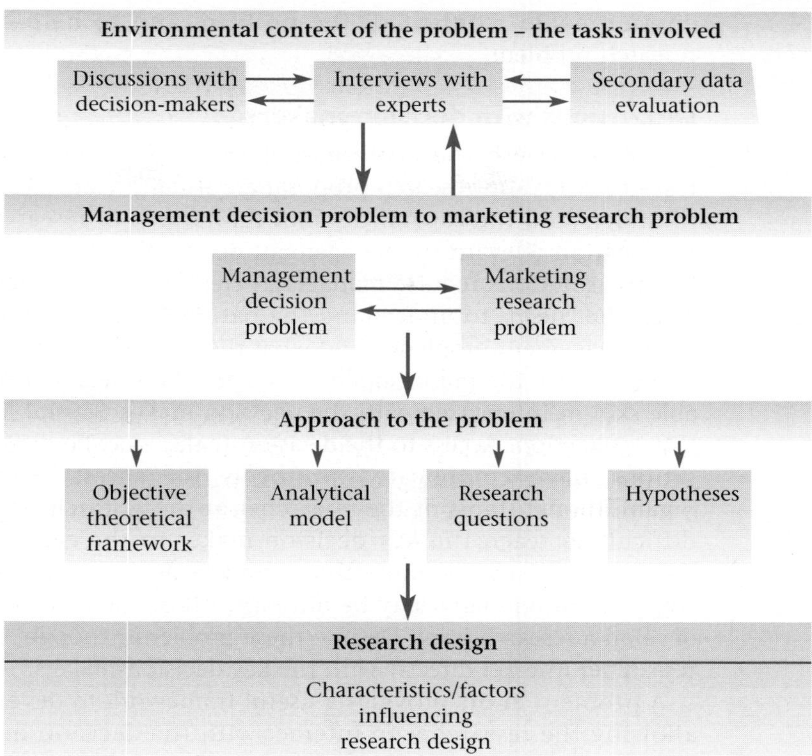

Figure 2.3
The process of defining the problem and developing an approach

problems have been correctly defined and an appropriate research approach is developed. The research brief and the research proposal are the formal documents that ensure each party is clear about the nature and scope of a research task. These are not the only means of communications and activities, conducted by the parties involved in the process of defining research problems and an appropriate research approach. The detail of defining the nature of problems and developing an appropriate research approach is shown in Figure 2.3.

The tasks involved in problem definition consist of discussions with decision-makers, qualitative interviews with industry experts and other knowledgeable individuals, and analysis of readily available secondary data. These tasks help the researcher to understand the background of the problem by analysing the environmental context. Certain essential environmental factors bearing on the problem should be evaluated. An understanding of the environmental context facilitates the identification of the management decision problem. Then, the management decision problem is translated into a marketing research problem. Based on the definition of the marketing research problem, an approach to the problem is established and an appropriate research design is developed. The components of the approach may consist of an objective/theoretical framework, analytical models, research questions and hypotheses. Further explanation of the problem definition process begins with a discussion of the tasks involved.

TASKS INVOLVED

The tasks involved in problem definition can include discussions with the decision-makers, qualitative interviews with industry experts, and secondary data analysis. The purposes of these tasks are to obtain information on the environmental context of the problem and to help define the marketing research problem.

Discussions with decision-makers

Discussions with the decision-makers beyond the formal presentation of a research brief and research proposal are usually vital. The decision-maker needs to understand the capabilities and limitations of research.[7] Research provides information relevant to management decisions, but it cannot provide solutions, because solutions require managerial creativity and judgement. Conversely, the researcher needs to understand the nature of the decision the managers face – the management problem – and what they hope to learn from the research.

To identify the management problem, the researcher must possess considerable skill in interacting with the decision-maker. Several factors may complicate this interaction. Access to the decision-maker may be difficult, and some organisations have complicated protocols for access to top executives. The organisational status of the researcher or the research department may make it difficult to reach the key decision-maker in the early stages of the project. Finally, there may be more than one key decision-maker and meeting collectively or individually may be difficult. All of the problems make it difficult to develop a research brief. Despite these problems, though, it is necessary that the researcher interact directly with the key decision-makers.[8]

Problem audit
A comprehensive examination of a marketing problem to understand its origin and nature.

A **problem audit** provides a useful framework to develop ideas from a brief, allowing the researcher to interact with the decision-maker and identify the underlying causes of the problem. A problem audit, like any other type of audit, is a comprehensive examination of a marketing problem with the purpose of understanding its origin and nature.[9] A problem audit involves discussions with the decision-maker on the following issues:

1. The events that led to the decision that action is needed, or the history of the problem.
2. The corporate culture as it relates to decision-making.
3. The alternative courses of action available to the decision-maker. The set of alternatives may be incomplete at this stage, and qualitative research may be needed to identify the more innovative courses of action.
4. The criteria that will be used to evaluate the alternative courses of action. For example, new product offerings might be evaluated based on sales, market share, profitability, or return on investment.
5. What the decision-maker perceives to be as gaps in their knowledge.
6. The manner in which the decision-maker will use each item of information in making the decision.

In some firms, the decision-making process is dominant, in others, the personality of the decision-maker is more important. Awareness of corporate culture may be one of the most important factors that distinguishes researchers who affect strategic marketing decisions from those who do not.[10]

It may be necessary to perform a problem audit because the decision-maker may have only a vague idea of what the problem is. For example, the decision-maker may know that the firm is losing market share but may not know why; decision-makers may tend to focus on symptoms rather than on causes. Inability to meet sales forecasts, loss of market share and decline in profits are all symptoms. The researcher should treat the underlying causes, not merely address the symptoms. For example, loss of market share may be caused by a superior promotion by the competition, inadequate distribution of the company's products, or any number of other factors. Only when the underlying causes are identified can the problem be successfully addressed.

A problem audit, which involves extensive interaction between the decision-maker and the researcher, can greatly facilitate problem definition by determining the underlying causes. The interaction between the researcher and the decision-maker is facilitated when one or more people in the client organisation serve to liaise and form a team with the marketing researcher. To be fruitful, the interaction between the decision-maker and the researcher can be characterised by the following:

1 *Communication*. A free exchange of ideas between the decision-maker and the researcher is essential.
2 *Cooperation*. Marketing research is a team project in which both parties (decision-maker and researcher) must cooperate, from problem diagnosis through to the interpretation and presentation of findings.
3 *Confidence*. Mutual trust of each other's distinct skills and contribution should underlie the interaction between the decision-maker and the researcher.
4 *Candour*. There should not be any hidden agendas, and an attitude of openness should prevail.
5 *Closeness*. An understanding of each other's problems should result in a closeness that should characterise the relationship between the decision-maker and the researcher.
6 *Continuity*. The decision-maker and the researcher must interact continually rather than sporadically.
7 *Creativity*. The interaction between the decision-maker and the researcher should be creative rather than formulaic. Though the research process may be laid out in a systematic manner, in reality great amounts of creativity are needed at every stage.

Interviews with industry experts

In addition to discussions with the decision-maker, qualitative interviews with industry experts, individuals knowledgeable about the firm and the industry can help in diagnosing the nature of the marketing research problem.[11] These experts may be found both inside and outside the firm. Typically, expert information is obtained by unstructured personal interviews, without a formal questionnaire. It is helpful, however, to prepare a list of topics to be covered during the interview. The order in which these topics are covered and the questions to ask should not be predetermined. Instead, they should be decided as the interview progresses, which allows greater flexibility in capturing the insights of the experts. The list of topics to cover and the type of expert sought should evolve as the researcher becomes more attuned to the nature of the management problem. The purpose of interviewing experts is to explore ideas, make new connections between ideas and create new perspectives in defining the marketing research problem. Unfortunately, two potential difficulties may arise when seeking advice from experts:

1 Some individuals who claim to be knowledgeable and are eager to participate may not really possess expertise.
2 It may be difficult to locate and obtain the help from experts who are outside the client organisation.

For these reasons, interviews with experts are more useful in conducting marketing research for industrial firms and for products of a technical nature, where it is relatively easy to identify and approach the experts. This method is also helpful in situations where little information is available from other sources, as in the case of radically new products. Experts can provide valuable insights in modifying or repositioning existing products, as illustrated by the development of brand values at Visa.

EXAMPLE

Visa to travel[12]

Visa ran a major brand-building campaign spanning Europe, excluding the UK where the brand already has 100 per cent awareness. The aim of the campaign was to create the same brand values in different countries. Although the benefits of a uniform branding are obvious, many companies have found that targeting a number of countries with the same campaign is fraught with danger. However, with research that revealed perceptions of Visa and cash to be consistent across Europe that 'plastic is better than cash', the message was simple to translate – simple if one is aware of cultural sensibilities and the relationship between countries, the company and the target audience. With industry expertise emphasising the appeal of locally produced campaigns, Visa have succeeded. As an example, they have been running a separate campaign for the Electron debit card in Spain, Portugal and Italy for some time. It has won many awards in Spain where they think it is a Spanish campaign, but then they think the ad is locally produced in Italy and Portugal as well. ■

Initial secondary data analyses

Secondary data
Data collected for some purpose other than the problem at hand.

Primary data
Data originated by the researcher specifically to address the research problem.

Secondary data collection and analysis will be addressed in detail in Chapters 4 and 5. A brief introduction here will demonstrate the worth of secondary data at the stage of problem diagnosis. **Secondary data** are data collected for some purpose other than the problem at hand. **Primary data**, on the other hand, are originated by the researcher for the specific purpose of addressing the research problem. Secondary data include data generated within an organisation, information made available by business and government sources, commercial marketing research firms, and computerised databases. Secondary data are an economical and quick source of background information. Analysis of available secondary data is an essential step in the problem definition process: primary data should not be collected until the available secondary data have been fully analysed. Past information and forecasts of trends with respect to sales, market share, profitability, technology, population, demographics and lifestyle can help the researcher to understand the underlying marketing research problem. Where appropriate, this kind of analysis should be carried out at the industry and firm levels. For example, if a firm's sales have decreased but industry sales have increased, the problems will be very different than if the industry sales have also decreased. In the former case, the problems are likely to be specific to the firm. Past information and forecasts can be valuable in uncovering potential opportunities and problems.

MANAGEMENT DECISION PROBLEM AND MARKETING RESEARCH PROBLEM

Management decision problem
The problem confronting the decision-maker, which asks what the decision-maker needs to do.

Marketing research problem
A problem that entails determining what information is needed and how it can be obtained in the most feasible way.

The **management decision problem** asks what the decision-maker needs to do, whereas the **marketing research problem** asks what information is needed and how it can best be obtained.[13] Research can provide the necessary information to make a sound decision.[14] The management decision problem is action oriented. It is concerned with the possible actions the decision-maker can take. How should the loss of market share be arrested? Should the market be segmented differently? Should a new product be introduced? Should the promotional budget be increased?

In contrast, the marketing research problem is information oriented. It involves determining what information is needed and how that information can be obtained effectively and efficiently. Consider, for example, the loss of market share for a particular product line. The decision-maker's problem is how to recover this loss. Alternative courses of action include modifying existing products, introducing new products, changing other elements in the marketing mix, and segmenting the market. Suppose that the decision-maker and the researcher believe that the problem is caused by inappropriate segmentation of the market and wanted research to provide information on this issue. The research problem would then become the identification and evaluation of an alternative basis for segmenting the market. Note that this process is interactive. The GlobalCash Project illustrates further the distinction between the management decision problem and the marketing research problem as well as the interactive nature of the problem definition process.

GLOBALCASH PROJECT

Defining the problem

Bank X: We are experiencing a loss of market share in Ireland in corporate banking.

Researcher: Is it just Ireland?

Bank X: No, but as we conduct the majority of our business there, the loss is causing us the greatest amount of concern.

Researcher: Why do you think you are losing market share?

Bank X: We wish we knew!

Researcher: How are your competitors coping?

Bank X: We suspect that other Irish banks are also suffering, but that the multinational banks are capturing market share.

Researcher: How do your customers feel about the quality of services you deliver?

Bank X: We recently attained our ISO 9000 for service quality, which we are proud of!

Researcher: But how does your service delivery compare to your competitors?

After a series of discussions with key decision-makers, analysis of secondary data within the bank and from other sources, the problem was identified as follows:

- *Management decision problem*
  What should be done to arrest the decline in market share of Bank X?

- *Marketing research problem*
  Determine the relative strengths and weaknesses of Bank X, *vis-à-vis* other major competitors in Ireland. This would be done with respect to factors that influence a company in its choice of a bank to handle its treasury transactions. ■

The GlobalCash Project shows the interactive nature of the process to identify the management decision problem and the marketing problem. The following examples further distinguish between the management decision problem and the marketing research problem.

Management decision problem	Marketing research problem
Should a new product be introduced?	To determine consumer preferences and purchase intentions for the proposed new product.
Should the advertising campaign be changed?	To determine the effectiveness of the current advertising campaign.
Should the price of the brand be increased?	To determine the price elasticity of demand and the impact on sales and profits of various levels of price changes.

DEFINING THE MARKETING RESEARCH PROBLEM

The general rule to be followed in defining the research problem is that the definition should:

1 allow the researcher to obtain all the information needed to address the management decision problem;
2 guide the researcher in proceeding with the project.

Researchers make two common errors in problem definition. The first arises when the research problem is defined too broadly. A broad definition does not provide clear guidelines for the subsequent steps involved in the project. Some examples of overly broad marketing research problem definitions are: developing a marketing strategy for a brand, improving the competitive position of the firm, or improving the company's image. These are not specific enough to suggest an approach to the problem or a research design.

The second type of error is just the opposite: the marketing research problem is defined too narrowly. A narrow focus may preclude consideration of some courses of action, particularly those that are innovative and not obvious. It may also prevent the researcher from addressing important components of the management decision problem. For example, in a project conducted for a consumer products firm, the management problem was how to respond to a price cut initiated by a competitor. The alternative courses of action initially identified by the firm's research staff were to:

1 Decrease the price of the firm's brand to match the competitor's price cut.
2 Maintain price but increase advertising heavily.
3 Decrease the price somewhat, without matching the competitor's price, and moderately increase advertising.

None of these alternatives seemed promising. When outside marketing research experts were brought in, the problem was redefined as improving the market share and profitability of the product line. Qualitative research indicated that in blind tests, consumers could not differentiate products offered under different brand names. Furthermore, consumers relied on price as an

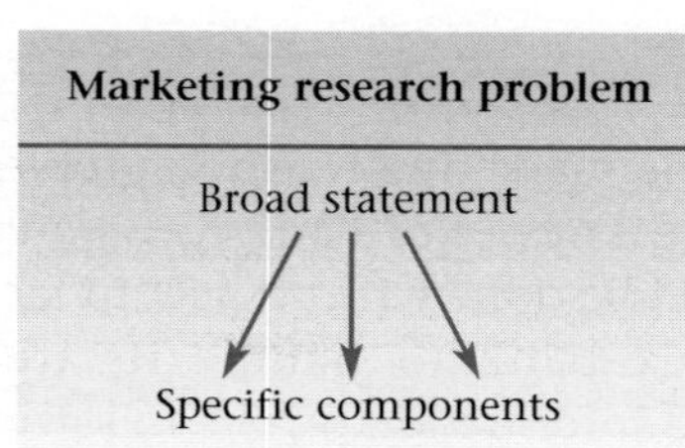

Figure 2.4 Proper definition of the marketing research problem

Broad statement of the problem
The initial statement of the marketing research problem that provides an appropriate perspective on the problem.

Specific components of the problem
The second part of the marketing research problem definition that focuses on the key aspects of the problem and provides clear guidelines on how to proceed further.

indicator of product quality. These findings led to a creative alternative: increase the price of the existing brand and introduce two new brands: one priced to match the competitor and the other priced to undercut it.

The likelihood of committing either error of problem definition can be reduced by stating the marketing research problem in broad, general terms and identifying its specific components (see Figure 2.4). The **broad statement of the problem** provides perspective and acts as a safeguard against committing the second type of error. The **specific components of the problem** focus on the key aspects and provide clear guidelines on how to proceed further. Examples of appropriate marketing research problem definitions are provided in the two following examples.

EXAMPLE

Net has yet to prove its value[15]

As the stampede to set up Web sites continues, those companies without a clear long-term strategy are looking increasingly rudderless as they search for ways to capitalise on their investment. A recent survey by Gallup and the Wall Street Journal of 603 board-level executives in Britain, France and Germany has revealed that Europe's businesses continue to embrace the Internet on the somewhat vague grounds that it is in the interests of their 'competitiveness'. Yet, they remain unsure about how, specifically, to use the medium for generating profits in the longer term.

The notable exception has been the financial services sector. Exploratory secondary data gathering and analyses revealed the opportunities that have been grasped by this sector. It also revealed the strategies adopted by financial companies. To develop these ideas into relevant actions, case histories of exemplary financial companies were built, key decision-makers targeted and questions focused upon technology, design and financial returns were developed.

Specifically the following issues could be addressed (as examples of many) for a company embarking on developing a Web site:

1 To what extent is the Net used by competitors?
2 What specific information types and services do they offer?
3 How can the Net generate knowledge of customers?
4 How can the Net add to marketing communication strategies?
5 How can the Net help to generate actual sales?
6 What types of existing or potential customers could use our site? ■

Problem definition in the GlobalCash project followed the following pattern.

Problem definition

In the GlobalCash project, the marketing research problem was to determine the relative strengths and weaknesses of Bank X, *vis-à-vis* other major competitors in Ireland. This would be done with respect to factors that influence a company in its choice of a bank to handle its treasury transactions. Specifically, research provided information on the following questions:

1 What criteria do companies use when choosing a bank for the first time?
2 What criteria do companies use to allocate business between existing banks?
3 Which banks are used for domestic business and pan-European business?
4 How do those banks fare on a range of service quality delivery criteria?
5 What is the market share of Bank X and its competitors in Ireland?
6 What is the profile of companies that use Bank X? Does it differ from the profile of customers from competing banks?

Once the marketing research problem has been broadly stated and its specific components identified, the researcher is in a position to develop a suitable approach. ■

COMPONENTS OF THE APPROACH

In the process of developing an approach, we must not lose sight of the goal: the outputs. The outputs of the approach development process should include the following components: objective/theoretical framework, analytical models, research questions, and hypotheses. Each of these components is discussed in the following sections.

Objective/theoretical framework

Theory
A conceptual scheme based on foundational statements, or axioms, that are assumed to be true.

Objective evidence
Unbiased evidence that is supported by empirical findings.

In general, research should be based on objective evidence and supported by **theory**. A theory is a conceptual scheme based on foundational statements called axioms that are assumed true. **Objective evidence** (evidence that is unbiased and supported by empirical findings) is gathered by compiling relevant findings from secondary sources. Likewise, an appropriate theory to guide the research might be identified by reviewing academic literature contained in books, journals and monographs. The researcher should rely on theory to determine which variables should be investigated. Past research on theory development and testing can provide important guidelines on determining dependent variables (variables that depend on the values of other variables) and independent variables (those values affect the values of other variables). Furthermore, theoretical considerations provide information on how the variables should be operationalised and measured, as well as how the research design and sample should be selected. A theory also serves as a foundation on which the researcher can organise and interpret the findings: 'nothing is so practical as a good theory.'[16] Conversely, by neglecting theory, the researcher increases the likelihood that he or she will fail to understand the data obtained or be unable to interpret and integrate the findings of the project with findings obtained by others. The role of theory in the various phases of an applied marketing research project is summarised in Table 2.1.

Theory also plays a vital role in influencing the research procedures adopted in basic research. Applying a theory to an applied marketing research problem

Table 2.1 The role of theory in applied marketing research

Research task	*Role of theory*
Conceptualising and identifying key variables	Provides a conceptual foundation and understanding of the basic processes underlying the problem situation. These processes will suggest key dependent and independent variables.
Operationalising key variables	Provides guidance for the practical means to measure or encapsulate the concepts or key variables identified.
Selecting a research design	Causal or associative relationships suggested by the theory may indicate whether a causal, descriptive or exploratory research design should be adopted (see Chapter 3).
Selecting a sample	Helps in defining the nature of a population, characteristics that may be used to stratify populations or to validate samples (see Chapter 13).
Analysing and interpreting data	The theoretical framework and the models, research questions and hypotheses based on it guide the selection of a data analysis strategy and the interpretation of results (see Chapter 16).
Integrating findings	The findings obtained in the research project can be interpreted in the light of previous research and integrated with the existing body of knowledge.

requires creativity on the part of the researcher, however. A theory may not specify adequately how its abstract constructs (variables) can be embodied in a real-world phenomenon. Moreover, theories are incomplete; they deal with only a subset of variables that exist in the real world. Hence, the researcher must also identify and examine other variables that have yet to be published as theories.[17]

Analytical model

Analytical model
An explicit specification of a set of variables and their interrelationships designed to represent some real system or process in whole or in part.

Verbal models
Analytical models that provide a written representation of the relationships between variables.

Graphical models
Analytical models that provide a visual picture of the relationships between variables.

Mathematical models
Analytical models that explicitly describe the relationships between variables, usually in equation form.

An **analytical model** is a set of variables and their interrelationships designed to represent, in whole or in part, some real system or process. Models can have many different forms. The most common are verbal, graphical and mathematical structures. In **verbal models**, the variables and their relationships are stated in prose form. Such models may be mere restatements of the main tenets of a theory. **Graphical models** are visual. They are used to isolate variables and to suggest directions of relationships but are not designed to provide numerical results. They are logical, preliminary steps to developing mathematical models.[18] **Mathematical models** explicitly specify the relationships among variables, usually in equation form.[19] These models can be used as guides for formulating the research design and have the advantage of being amenable to manipulation.[20] The different models are illustrated in the context of the GlobalCash project.

As can be seen from this example, the verbal, graphical and mathematical models depict the same phenomenon or theoretical framework in different ways. The phenomenon of 'threshold effect', stated verbally, is represented for clarity through a figure (graphical model) and is put in equation form (mathematical model) for ease of statistical estimation and testing. Graphical models are particularly helpful in clarifying the concept or approach to the problem.

The verbal, graphical and mathematical models complement each other and help the researcher identify relevant research questions and hypotheses.

Model building

Verbal model

A treasury manager first becomes aware of a bank's ability to perform a particular cash management service. That manager then gains a greater understanding of the service by evaluating the bank in terms of the factors comprising the choice criteria. Based on the evaluation, the manager forms a degree of preference for the bank. If preference exceeds a certain threshold level, the manager will switch business to the bank.

Graphical model

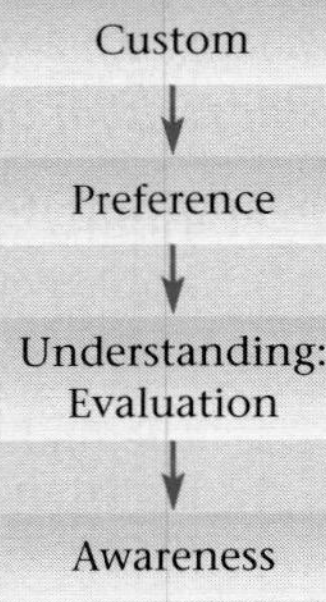

Mathematical model

$$y = a_0 + \sum_{i=1}^{n} a_i x_i$$

where

y = degree of preference

a_0, a_i = model parameters to be estimated statisically

x_i = bank custom factors that constitute the choice criteria

Research questions

Research questions Research questions are refined statements of the specific components of the problem.

Research questions are refined statements of the specific components of the problem. Although the components of the problem define the problem in specific terms, further detail may be needed to develop an approach. Each component of the problem may have to be broken down into subcomponents or research questions. Research questions ask what specific information is required with respect to the problem components. If the research questions are answered by the research, then the information obtained should aid the decision-maker. The formulation of the research questions should be guided not only by the problem definition, but also by the theoretical framework and the analytical model adopted. For a given problem component, there are likely to be several research questions, as in the GlobalCash project.

GLOBALCASH PROJECT

Research questions

One of the major events occurring during the GlobalCash project was the introduction of systems to cope with Economic and Monetary Union (EMU). This is of major importance to cash management banks, whose business is based upon the problems of conducting business across borders and paying for goods and services in a variety of currencies. Companies pay banks to cope with these transactions in an environment of complicated legislation. The marketplace will change dramatically when there is one currency for all the countries, with no currency exchange to conduct.

Key research questions for the banks that may lose business relate to relationships. Examples of these are shown in the following two questions:

Question: How will Economic and Monetary Union (EMU) affect your cash management banking relationships within the expected 'Euro zone'?

Answers: (please circle appropriate numbers)
1 Existing country relationships to be maintained within the Euro zone
2 Fewer banks to be used in each country
3 Fewer banks to be used across the Euro zone
4 One major bank to coordinate all Euro accounts where possible

Question: What process will you go through in selecting your cash management banks?

Answers: (please circle appropriate numbers)
1 Formal tender in each country
2 Formal tender for a regional bank
3 Informal evaluation
4 Other (*please state*)......................................

Hypotheses

Hypothesis
An unproven statement or proposition about a factor or phenomenon that is of interest to the researcher.

A **hypothesis** is an unproven statement or proposition about a factor or phenomenon that is of interest to the researcher. For example, it may be a tentative statement about relationships between two or more variables as stipulated by the theoretical framework or the analytical model. Often, a hypothesis is a possible answer to the research question.[21] Hypotheses go beyond research questions because they are statements of relationships or propositions rather than merely questions to which answers are sought. Research questions are interrogative, hypotheses are declarative and can be tested empirically (see Chapter 17). An important role of a hypothesis is to suggest variables to be included in the research design.[22] The relationship between the marketing research problem, research questions and hypotheses, along with the influence of the objective/theoretical framework and analytical models, is described in Figure 2.5 and illustrated by the following example from GlobalCash.

Hypotheses are an important part of the approach to a research problem. When stated in operational terms, as *H*1 and *H*2 in the GlobalCash example, they provide guidelines on what, and how, data are to be collected and analysed. When operational hypotheses are stated using symbolic notation, they are commonly referred to as statistical hypotheses.

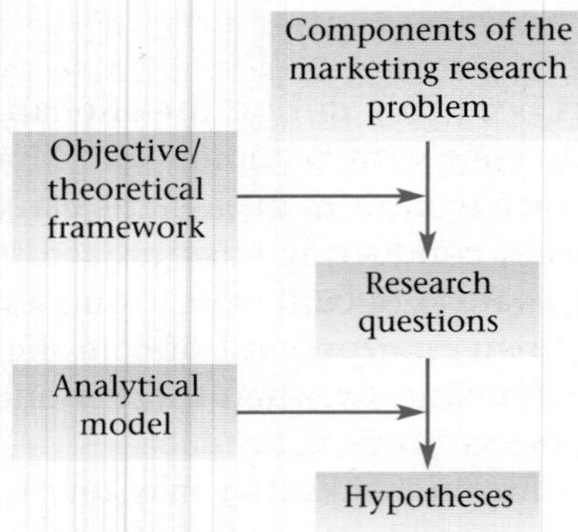

Figure 2.5 Development of research questions and hypotheses

Hypotheses

The following hypotheses were formulated in relation to the research question on bank–company relationships.

H_1: Companies within the Euro-zone plan to use fewer banks after the introduction of EMU compared to companies outside the Euro-zone.
H_2: Companies that will select cash management banks on an informal basis have fewer bank relationships than those that will select through formal tenders.

The additional research question that will allow *H*1 to be tested relates to the country that an ultimate parent country operates. The European Union has assigned countries as being 'within' or 'outside' for the first wave of EMU. The additional question that will allow *H*2 to be tested asks how many banks are used for domestic cash management. In countries like Switzerland and Norway, the mean can be around three, in Italy the mean is around 10, with one respondent having 70 banks! ■

These hypotheses guided the research by ensuring that variables which affect relationships were included in the research design. The connection between questions that form hypotheses, and the appropriate analyses needed, were thought out clearly before the research approach and questionnaire were designed.

Another example in a consumer goods environment is shown in the following example of Chanel.

EXAMPLE

Chanel perfumes[23]

A research question may have more than one hypothesis associated with it, as in the case of Chanel. Chanel was considering advertising its perfumes in magazines it formerly considered too 'down-market' for its prestigious brand. The Chanel brand had a 3 per cent share of department store sales (the leader was Estee Lauder with a 21 per cent share). By expanding its advertising beyond high-fashion magazines, Chanel hoped to improve its share of department store sales. The following research question and hypotheses may be posed:

Research question: Does Chanel have an 'upmarket' image?

H_1: Chanel is perceived to be an expensive brand.
H_2: Users of Chanel have higher-than-average incomes.
H_3: Users of Chanel associate this perfume with status. ■

Note that to test H_1, the researcher would have to operationalise and measure the perceived price associated with Chanel. Empirical testing of H_2 would require that respondents be classified as users or non-users of Chanel and provide information on their incomes. Finally, H_3 tells us that we need to operationalise another variable or a set of variables that measure the status associated with Chanel. The results of this research provided support for Hypotheses 1 and 3 but not for Hypothesis 2. Although Chanel did have an 'up-market' image, its appeal was not limited to 'up-market' buyers or users of the product. Broadening the target market by advertising in magazines formerly considered 'down-market' led to improved department store sales of Chanel.

Relevant characteristics

Relevant characteristics Characteristics, factors, product attributes, or variables that may affect a research design.

As mentioned earlier, a useful way of conceptualising the development of an approach is to view it as a bridge between step 1 (problem definition) and step 3 (research design) of the marketing research process. Specifically, we focus here on one important aspect of research design: developing a questionnaire. The key question to ask – given the problem definition, research questions and hypotheses – is what additional characteristics, factors, product attributes or variables should be identified so that a questionnaire can be constructed? The answer to this question will result in the identification of the relevant characteristics. Let us consider the GlobalCash Project and focus on the components of the problem identified earlier in this chapter.

GLOBALCASH PROJECT

Relevant characteristics

Component 1 involves the criteria companies use to choose a bank. Unless the specific factors comprising these criteria are identified, we cannot formulate a question asking respondents which of these are important to them.

Based on the process outlined earlier, examples of characteristics were identified as follows: domestic branch network, electronic banking security, ability to send payment instructions to other banks, timeliness of information provision, ability to replicate structure across Europe.

Component 2 involves the criteria companies use to allocate business between banks. Again, unless these specific criteria are identified, we cannot formulate a question asking respondents which of these are important to them.

Examples would be: level of commitment to your business, bank's credit rating, good relationship with bank.

Component 3 is concerned with competition. Unless the competing banks are identified, it would be impossible to obtain information related to this component. Five indigenous banks and three pan-European banks were identified as competitors to Bank X.

Component 4 is concerned with how identified competing banks fare on a range of service quality delivery criteria. Where companies have experience of named banks, criteria are set to evaluate their service delivery.

Examples would be: high speed of error correction, level of electronic banking support, local support, low numbers of payment/statement errors.

Component 5 involves the market share of Bank X and its competitors in Ireland. This will be determined through a valid representation of the total market through a sound sampling plan.

▶

Component 6 concerns the profile of companies that use Bank X. Does it differ from the profile of customers from competing banks? Classification questions were used to identify the size of companies, their industry, sphere of operations, and the nationality of parent company. As well as validating the sample compared to the population, these questions allow detailed profiles of Bank X customers compared to competing banks. ■

The process of identifying the relevant characteristics and the other components of the approach to the problem, lead to a specification of the information needed. By focusing on each component of the problem and the related theory, models, research questions, hypotheses and characteristics that have been identified in developing an approach, the researcher can determine what information should be obtained. This facilitates the formulation of an appropriate research design.

INTERNATIONAL MARKETING RESEARCH

The precise definition of the marketing research problem is more difficult in international marketing research than in domestic marketing research. Unfamiliarity with the environmental factors of the country where the research is being conducted can greatly increase the difficulty of understanding the problem's environmental context and uncovering its causes.

EXAMPLE

Heinz Ketchup couldn't catch up in Brazil[24]

Despite good records of accomplishment inland and overseas, the H.J. Heinz Company failed in Brazil, a market that seemed to be South America's biggest and most promising market. Heinz entered a joint venture with Citrosuco Paulista, a giant orange juice exporter, because of the future possibility of buying the profitable company. Yet, the sales of its products, including ketchup, did not take off. Where was the problem? A problem audit revealed that the company lacked a strong local distribution system. Heinz lost control of the distribution because it worked on consignment. Distribution could not reach 25 per cent penetration. The other related problem was that Heinz concentrated on neighbourhood shops because this strategy was successful in Mexico. The problem audit, however, revealed that 75 per cent of the grocery shopping in Sao Paulo is done in supermarkets and not the smaller shops. Although Mexico and Brazil may appear to have similar cultural and demographic characteristics, consumer behaviour can vary greatly. A closer and intensive look at the Brazilian food distribution system and the behaviour of consumers could have averted this failure.

As the Heinz example illustrates, many international marketing efforts fail not because research was not conducted but because the relevant environmental factors were not taken into account. Generally, this leads to a definition of the problem that is too narrow. A major problem for researchers is that their perception of problems may be reflected through their own social and cultural development. Before defining the problem, researchers should reflect upon their unconscious reference to cultural values. The following steps help researchers to reflect upon their own cultural values.[25]

1 Define the marketing research problem in terms of domestic environmental and cultural factors. This involves an identification of relevant European traits, economics, values, needs or habits.
2 Define the marketing research problem in terms of foreign environmental and cultural factors. Make no judgements. This involves an identification of the related traits, economics, values, needs or habits in the proposed market culture. This task requires input from researchers familiar with the foreign environment.
3 Examine the differences between steps 1 and 2. The unconscious reference to cultural values can be seen to account for these differences.
4 Redefine the problem without the social/cultural influence and address it for the foreign market situation. If the differences in steps 3 are significant, the impact of the social/cultural influences should be carefully considered.

While developing theoretical frameworks, models, research questions and hypotheses, remember that differences in the environmental factors, especially the socio-cultural environment, may lead to differences in the formation of perceptions, attitudes, preferences and choice behaviour. For example, orientation toward time varies considerably across cultures. In Asia, Latin America and the Middle East, people are not as time-conscious as Westerners. This influences their perceptions of and preferences for convenience foods such as frozen foods and prepared dinners. In developing an approach to the problem, the researcher should consider the equivalence of consumption and purchase behaviour and the underlying factors that influence them. This is critical to the identification of the correct research questions, hypotheses and characteristics/factors that influence the research design.

The following example reveals how the use of focus groups could have helped to reveal social/cultural characteristics of the Japanese. Focus groups would have allowed the correct identification of research questions, leading to more successful product launch.

Investigation on appropriate research questions and hypotheses lead to a broadening of the market for Chanel perfume

EXAMPLE

Surf Superconcentrate faces a super washout in Japan[26]

Unilever attempted to break into the Japanese detergent market with Surf Superconcentrate. It initially achieved 14.5 per cent of the market share during test marketing but fell down to a shocking 2.8 per cent when the product was introduced nationally. Where did they go wrong? Surf was designed to have a distinctive pre-measured packet as in teabag-like sachets, joined in pairs because convenience was an important attribute to Japanese consumers. It also had a 'fresh smell' appeal. Japanese consumers, however, noticed that the detergents did not dissolve in the wash, partly because of weather conditions and because of the popularity of low-agitation washing machines. Surf was not designed to work in the new washing machines. Unilever also found that the 'fresh smell' positioning of new Surf had little relevance since most consumers hang their wash out in the fresh air. The research approach was certainly not without flaw as Unilever failed to identify critical attributes that are relevant in the Japanese detergent market. Furthermore, it identified factors such as 'smell fresh' that had no relevance in the Japanese context. Appropriate qualitative research such as focus groups across samples from the target market could have revealed the correct characteristics or factors leading to a suitable research design. ■

ETHICS IN MARKETING RESEARCH

Ethical situations arising from the process of problem definition and developing an approach are likely to occur between the market researcher and the client. As explained earlier, identifying the correct marketing research problem is crucial to the success of the project. This process can however, be compromised by the personal agendas of the researcher or the decision-maker. For example, the researcher, after performing the tasks involved in problem definition and analysing the environmental context of the problem, realises that the correct marketing research problem may be defined in a way that makes primary research unnecessary. This would reduce the cost of the project and the research firm's profit margin substantially. Does the researcher define the problem correctly, fabricate a research problem that involves primary data collection, or does the researcher refuse to proceed with this project in lieu of those more profitable? The researcher is faced with an ethical dilemma, as in the following example.

EXAMPLE

Taste (profits) or image (ethics)?[27]

A marketing research firm is hired by a soft drink company to conduct taste tests to determine why its newly introduced soft drink brand has not captured the expected market share. The researcher, after following the process outlined in this chapter, determines that the problem is not one of taste but of the image and its positioning. The client, however, has already defined the problem as a taste problem and not as the broader, market-share problem. The researcher must also weigh the relatively high profit margin of taste test research to the less lucrative survey research needed to answer questions pertaining to soft drink image. What should researchers do? Should they simply conduct the research the client wants rather than the research they feel the client needs? The guidelines indicate that 'the researcher has a professional obligation to indicate to the client that, in his or her judgement, the research expenditure is not warranted. If, after this judgement has been clearly stated, the client still desires the research, the researcher should feel free to conduct the study. The reason for this is that the researcher can never know for certain the risk preferences and strategies that are guiding the client's behaviour.' ■

Such ethical situations would be satisfactorily resolved if the client/researcher relationship developed with both the client and the researcher adhering to the seven Cs discussed earlier: communication, cooperation, confidence, candour, closeness, continuity and creativity. This would provide a relationship of mutual trust that would check any unethical tendencies.

Ethical situations affecting the researcher and the client may also arise in developing an approach to the problem. When researchers conduct studies for different clients in related industries (i.e. banking and financial services) or in similar research areas (i.e. customer satisfaction) they may be tempted to cut corners in theoretical framework and model development. Take an example where a grocery chain client has on its board of directors the chairman of a bank. The bank had recently conducted customer satisfaction research using a client-specific model and the bank-affiliated board member has access to this research. The researcher feels that a customer satisfaction model for the bank could be easily adapted to work for the grocery chain. The client feels that it would not be a good business decision to have access to this information and not use it. Is it ethical for the client and researcher to obtain and use this model developed for another company by another research firm? There is an underlying trust between the researcher and the client that the research firm is honour-bound not to reuse client specific models or findings for other projects.

The client also has an ethical responsibility not to solicit proposals merely to gain the expertise of the research firms without pay. It is unethical for a client to solicit proposals from a few research firms, then adopt one or a combination of the approaches suggested in them, and conduct the project in-house. The client must respect the rights of a realising firm by releasing that an unpaid proposal belongs to the research firm that generated it. However, if the client firm pays for the development of the proposal, it has a right to use the information contained in it.

INTERNET AND COMPUTER APPLICATIONS

There are several ways in which the Internet can help in defining the problem and developing an approach to a research problem. The following summarises where the Internet can support the process of problem diagnosis and research design.

Discussions with the decision-maker

The Internet can help the researcher gain access to a wide variety of marketing decision-makers who may use and benefit from proposed research. Thanks to email, it is possible to reach decision-makers anywhere, at any time. The Internet can also provide chat rooms so that decision-makers and researchers can exchange and test ideas. The availability of the responses to be seen by whomever enters the chat room has the effect of getting all the relevant decision-makers together at the same time without requiring that they be physically present at the same time.

Interviews with industry experts

The Internet can be used to enhance the researcher's ability to obtain advice from experts. The Internet can be searched to find industry experts outside of the organisation that commissions a research project.

Secondary data location and analysis

Search engines can be used to locate secondary data quickly and economically. This can be vital in helping to understand the issues to be examined and the approach to examining those issues. We will discuss the availability and acquisition of secondary data on the Internet in more detail in Chapter 4.

In setting the environmental context of the research problem, client-specific information can be gained from the company home page. Generally, the companies provide information about their products and services in their home page, making it the ideal starting point for information about the company. Further, the user can also search for competitor and industry information on the Internet. While these searches may not provide complete answers for the marketing researcher, they may raises issues and identify contacts where further exploration may prove beneficial.

SUMMARY

Defining the marketing research problem is the most important step in a research project. Problem definition is a difficult step, because frequently management has not determined the actual problem or has only a vague notion about it. The marketing researcher's role is to help management identify and isolate the problem.

The formal ways in which decision-makers and researchers communicate their perspectives of a research problem and how to solve it are through the development of a research brief and a research proposal. To fully develop these documents, researchers should develop active discussions with key decision-makers, including a problem audit. They should also conduct where necessary, interviews with relevant experts, and secondary data analyses. These tasks should lead to an understanding of the environmental context of the problem.

Analysis of the environmental context should assist in the identification of the management decision problem, which should then be translated into a marketing research problem. The management decision asks what the decision-maker needs to do, whereas the marketing research problem asks what information is needed and how it can be obtained effectively and efficiently. The researcher should avoid defining the marketing research problem either too broadly or too narrowly. An appropriate way of defining the marketing research problem is to make a broad statement of the problem and then identify its specific components.

Developing an approach to the problem is the second step in the marketing research process. The components of an approach may consist of an objective/theoretical framework, analytical models, research questions and hypotheses. It is necessary that the approach developed be based upon objective evidence or empirical evidence and be grounded in theory as far as it is developed. The relevant variables and their interrelationships may be neatly summarised via an analytical model. The most common kinds of model structures are verbal, graphical and mathematical. The research questions are refined statements of the specific components of the problem that ask what specific information is required with respect to the problem components. Research questions may be further refined into hypotheses. Finally, given the problem definition, research questions and hypotheses should be used to develop a method to either measure or elicit an understanding of target respondents.

When defining the problem in international marketing research, the researcher must be aware of the impact of their own cultural values when evaluating the environmental impact upon the nature of a problem. Likewise, when developing an approach, the differences in the environment prevailing in the domestic market and the foreign markets should be carefully considered. Several ethical issues that have an impact on the client and the researcher can arise at this stage but can be resolved by adhering to the seven Cs: communication, cooperation, confidence, candour, closeness, continuity and creativity.

QUESTIONS AND PROBLEMS

1 What is the nature of the first step in conducting a marketing research project?

2 Why is it vital to define the marketing research problem correctly?

3 What is the role of the researcher in the problem definition process?

4 What are the components of a marketing research brief?

5 What are the components of a marketing research proposal?

6 How may a marketing researcher be creative in interpreting a research brief and developing a research proposal?

7 What is the significance of the 'background' section of a research brief and research proposal?

8 Describe some of the reasons why management is often not clear about the real problem.

9 What interrelated events occur in the environmental context of a research problem?

10 What are some differences between a management decision problem and a marketing research problem?

11 Describe the factors that may affect the approach to a research problem.

12 What is the role of theory in the development of a research approach?

13 What are the most common forms of analytical models?

14 What are the differences between research questions and hypotheses?

15 Is it necessary for every research project to have a set of hypotheses? Why or why not?

NOTES

1 Hodgson, P., 'Travelling so fast, they can't stop for research', *ResearchPlus* (June 1995), 5.

2 Carey, G., Zhao, X., Chiaramonte, J. and Eden, D. 'Is There a Global Village for our Future Generation? Talking to 7–12-year-olds around the World', *Marketing and Research Today* (February 1997), 12.

3 Joselyn, R.W. *Designing the Marketing Research Project* (New York: Mason/Charter, 1977), 46.

4 Ingledew, S. How to bait the interview hood for those Top 1000 big fish, *ResearchPlus* (October 1996), 4

5 Greenhalgh, C., 'How should we initiate effective research?' The Market Research Society Conference, 1983.

6 Clemens, J., 'Some dos and don'ts of pan-European research', *ResearchPlus* (November 1996), 4

7 Curren, M.T., Folkes, V.S. and Joel H. Steckel, 'Explanations for Successful and Unsuccessful Marketing

Decisions: The Decision Maker's Perspective', *Journal of Marketing* 56 (April 1992), 18–31.

8 Jones, S., 'Problem-Definition in Marketing Research: Facilitating between Clients and Researchers', *Psychology and Marketing* (Summer 1985), 83–93.

9 Berry, L.L., Conant, J.S. and Parasuraman, A., 'A Framework for Conducting a Services Marketing Audit', *Journal of the Academy of Marketing Science* 19 (Summer 1991), 255–68; Russell L. Ackoff, *Scientific Method* (New York: Wiley, 1961), 71; Russell L. Ackoff, *The Art of Problem Solving* (New York: Wiley, 1978).

10 Levine, J., 'Six Factors Mark Researchers Who Sway Strategic Decisions', *Marketing News* (4 February 1983), 1.

11 Armstrong, J.S., 'Prediction of Consumer Behaviour by Experts and Novices', *Journal of Consumer Research* 18 (September 1991), 251–56; Phillip Kotler, 'A Guide to Gathering Expert Estimates', *Business Horizons* 13 (October 1970), 79–87.

12 Barrett, P., 'Abroad minded', *Marketing* (24 April 1997), 20.

13 Conner, P.W., 'Research Request Step Can Enhance Use of Results', *Marketing News* 19 (4 January 1985), 41.

14 Boughton, P.D., 'Marketing Research and Small Business: Pitfalls and Potential', *Journal of Small Business Management* 21 (July 1983), 36–42, for a list of questions small business managers (and decision makers) can ask to make sure they get the most from their research.

15 Shannon, J., 'Net has yet to prove its value', *Marketing Week* (26 June 1997), 25.

16 Jacoby, J., 'Consumer Research: A State of the Art Review', *Journal of Marketing* 42 (April 1978), 87–96. See also Hunt, S.D., 'Truth in Marketing Theory and Research', *Journal of Marketing* 54 (July 1990), 1–15; Hunt, S.D., 'For Reason and Realism in Marketing', *Journal of Marketing* 56 (April 1992), 89–102.

17 Calder, B.J., Phillips, L.W. and Tybout, A.M., 'Designing Research for Applications', *Journal of Consumer Research* 8 (September 1981), 197–207. A positivist perspective on research is used here. Positivism encompasses logical positivism, logical empiricism, and all forms of falsificationism. This is the perspective adopted in a great amount of quantitative commercial marketing research.

18 For an illustration of a graphical model of software piracy, see Figure 1 of Givon, M., Mahajan, V. and Muller, E., 'Software Piracy: Estimation of Lost Sales and the Impact on Software Diffusion', *Journal of Marketing* 59 (January 1995), 29–37.

19 For an example of developing a theoretical framework and a mathematical model based on it, see Miller, C.M., McIntyre, S.H. and Mantrala, M.K. 'Toward Formalizing Fashion Theory', *Journal of Marketing Research* 30 (May 1993), 142–57.

20 Lilien, G.L., Kotler, P. and Moorthy, K.S., *Marketing Models* (Englewood Cliffs, NJ: Prentice Hall, 1992).

21 For an example of hypotheses formulation, see Gundlach, G.T., Ravi, S., Achrol, R.S. and Mentzer, J.T., 'The Structure of Commitment in Exchange', *Journal of Marketing* 59 (January 1995), 78–92.

22 Kerlinger, F.N., *Foundations of Behavioural Research*, 3rd edn (New York: Holt, Rinehart, and Winston, 1986). See pp. 17–20 for a detailed discussion of the characteristics and role of hypotheses in research. For an alternative view, see Lawrence, R.J., 'To Hypothesize or Not to Hypothesize? The Correct "Approach" to Survey Research', *Journal of the Market Research Society* 24 (October 1982), 335–43. For an example of model development and hypotheses formulation see Bitner, M.J., 'Servicescapes: The Impact of Physical Surroundings on Customers and Employees', *Journal of Marketing* 56 (April 1992), 57–71.

23 'Chanel Plans to Run Ads in Magazines with Less Cachet', *Wall Street Journal* (27 January 1988), 30.

24 Judann, D., 'Why Heinz Went Sour in Brazil', *Advertising Age* (5 December 1988).

25 J.A., 'Cultural Analysis of Overseas Operations', *Harvard Business Review* 44 (March–April 1966), 106–14; and Douglas, S.P. and Craig, C.S., *International Marketing Research* (Englewood Cliffs, NJ: Prentice Hall, 1983).

26 Kilbum, D., 'Unilever Struggles with Surf in Japan', *Advertising Age* (6 May 1991).

27 Laczniak, G.R. and Murphy, P.E., *Ethical Marketing Decisions, the Higher Road* (Boston: Allyn and Bacon, 1993), p. 64.

PROFESSIONAL PERSPECTIVES for Part I

Decision-making at Heineken

A review of the keynote speech presented by the Chairman of Heineken to the ESOMAR congress[1]

The ESOMAR congress is a forum where marketing researchers, primarily from European countries, meet to discuss and debate the latest developments in the industry. The congress attracts practitioners involved in the design and collection of marketing research and those who buy and use marketing research findings. The congress offers an environment that is lively and provocative, and offers the chance for participants to develop insights by meeting other researchers and managers who may not be accessible on a day-to-day basis. Mr Karel Vuursteen, the Chairman of Heineken, presented a keynote speech to the 1995 ESOMAR Congress. Though this is a number of years ago and practices at Heineken may have moved on, his message provoked much thought, retaining a clarity and freshness that is relevant today.

In Chapter 1, we discussed the limitations of marketing research, contending that not all successful decision making is founded upon marketing research. The success story of Heineken in the USA was build upon a very limited contribution from marketing research. Exporting had been a priority for Heineken for many years, expecially to the USA, it was the first beer imported into the States. However, decisions on new product launches, pricing, and advertising were made without product tests, price meters, pre-tests or other sophisticated research methodologies. These decisions were taken on personal insight, on intuition, on a 'feel' for the market. These qualifications were shared by the USA importer and Mr Alfred Heineken. Heineken today is a global brand, a large international organisation with high ambitions for further expansion. Past successes built largely upon intuition do not mean there is no role for marketing research at Heineken today. Marketing research within Heineken focuses upon:

- understanding consumers in different cultures;
- describing the many different markets they operate in;
- measuring the performance of brands;
- developing new products or brands.

[1] The full transcript of this speech was published in *Marketing and Research Today* (February 1996), 42–45.

Over the past 10 to 15 years research has come to play an increasingly important role in the company. Mose marketing decisions are based or supported on research information. They have, as do most companies of a similar size – tracking surveys, retail audits, advertising tests, sponsorship monitors and more. They introduced 'brand health checks', to be executed by all operating companies. The results of these brand health checks are used in long-term planning discussions. This research supports operating companies in allocating the financial means and efforts in the most effective way. Also, in many strategic company decisions, marketing research becomes involved. Mr Vuursteen presented examples of the decisions the Heineken Executive Board had to make and where research findings play a role.

Brand sourcing

Where the Heineken brand actually is produced is an issue for decision making for many markets. Several factors play a role in such a decision, such as production capacity issues, financial, political and marketing considerations. Many pros and cons have to be balanced. In guiding and supporting decisions in this area, marketing research support was sought. It led to the decision not to change the imported status of the Heineken brand in the USA, because of the value consumers attached to this aspect.

Kameleon

An idea was launched to harmonise the identity of local brands from European operating companies. Several studies helped to convince the management layers involved here about the feasibility of this strategy. It furthermore provided guidance as to how this process could best be implemented in order to be successful.

Referring back to Chapter 1 where the contention was made that marketing research does not make decisions, we see this theme developed and illustrated.

At Heineken, research is primarily viewed as a decision support tool. The emphasis is on support which should not be confused with decision making. Decision making is seen to be about making choices, taking risks, looking ahead, and anticipating changes. In contrast, marketing research is seen as describing, about facts, and analysing. Marketing research is seen to add to the knowledge already held by managers.

Mr Vuursteen voiced his hear that the outcomes of reasearch may be too easily accepted and followed. That managers run away with research findings as the 'truth'. And that they don't take enough room for personal interpretation, for a personal vision. Not using their 'gut-feel' which basically is created by research. He noted that many young managers have difficulty with making decisions. To the question "What would you do.....?" too often comes the answer "The research findings say that we should....."

A key contention presented by Mr Vuursteen, was whether the answer to a continuously changing and increasingly more competitive environment, lay in more data, more facts and more research projects. He argued that there should be more interpretation of already known facts, instead of generating more data. An argument was made for a more responsible use of research. A less absolute and more relative approach towards its findings, one that leaves room for the more undefined factor in decision making. That of personal insight, judgement and intuition.

He described how at Heineken, they try to develop a culture in such a way that the *feel* for the company and for its values, its main asset, the Heineken brand, is stimulated. A culture where creativity and innovation are stimilated and that personal style is appreciated. Managers are stimulated to use more of their intuition, their feel and judgement. To develop these qualities it is seen to be essential to have a very good understanding of markets and consumers – beer drinkers. To develop knowledge about their motivations, their interests, their habits and their environment.

The role of traditional marketing research was seen as necessary, but an argument was made for decision makers to supplement this data by trying to view the product through the eyes of the consumer. Managers should experience the environments where consumers are, where they use Heineken products. Alongside figures, there are great lessons to be learnt from being in the market place, observing consumers, participating in their activities, being close to them, understanding them better.

This attitude of curiousity towards consumers was seen as essential for managers in their role of decision makers. Mr Vuursteen recognised that he was fortun the sense that Heineken's business is beer and not vinegar, and that most managers do not have any problem in visiting bars, pubs and restaurants to observe customers in their natural environment. He admitted that he does not know whether this form of 'particpating observation' fits within ESOMAR definitions of market research. It certainly falls into the descriptions of qualitative observation techniques and ethnographic approaches as discussed in Chapter 7.

Mr Vuursteen concluded by supporting the role of marketing research in its contribution to Heineken's insight and understanding of consumer needs. He contended that this may not only be achieved through traditional marketing research methods. He argued that researchers may need new research 'tools', but more distinctly he argued that researchers have to choose where they want to be, what role they want to play. Is the role an expert on consumer behaviour or a marketing innovator? Should that role be to provide necessary and reliable information or be a strategic thinker? A decision support tool or a decision maker? He confessed that he did not know, he could only advise that this choice should not be postponed or even researched! Like good decision making at Heineken, the answer does not lie in more data collection – researchers should follow their intuition!

The acid test

GAVIN EMSDEN

At Nestlé, product testing among consumers is taken very seriously. Understanding how consumers react to products is considered critical to the continued success of both existing and new products – after all, it is the consumer, not techincal or marketing experts, who determines the success or otherwise of products.

Product testing can be looked at broadly in two areas:

- product benchmarking and reformulation – to ensure the continued success of existing products;
- new product development – to ensure the business has a stream of rising stars to retain interest in the category and take advantage of changing consumer needs.

Gavin Emsden

Gavin began his career specialising in research in fast moving consumer goods and new product development, working on brands such as Golden Wonder, Elisabeth Shaw and Martini. His career developed to broaden his research experience into retail and service industries working with clients such as KFC, Thomas Cook and London Transport. The last 3 years have been spent at Nestlé as Consumer Research Manager for beverages. His main focus of research is on the Nescafé range of coffees as well as the Coffee Mate and Nesquik brands.

Product benchmarking and changing consumer needs

Benchmarking, as the name implies, is about taking a snapshot in time to assess how your products are performing against the competitors. Understanding your product's strengths and weaknesses versus the competition is critical if you are serious about maintaining a product advantage. Of course, product quality is only one part of the equation – other elements of the marketing mix, such as price and positioning, also play a key part in product performance.

Choosing the most appropriate approach: In-home versus in-hall

When it comes to coffee products, Nestlé tends to opt for in-home testing. This allows for coffee to be tested in the most natural environment. It does mean an element of control is lost: each consumer 'adjusting' the test product to suit their individual preferences – the amount of coffee, milk and sugar used. (It is therefore important to ensure that the sample is balanced not only in terms of demographics but also in the way they drink their coffee.)

However, it is precisely for these reasons that we prefer in-home, as it allows consumers to experiment and adjust dosages, rather than presenting them with *our* idea of the 'right' dosage. In-home also means consumers are drinking products on the occasions they would normally use them (as opposed to dragging them into a hall to try a product just once, that they may neither want nor is made up to their preferred taste). It also ensures a full cup is drunk, and on more than one occasion. While you have no control over this, this is a realistic scenario and some products that at first taste are liked, can become 'too much' by the end of the portion. Where a product is not normally consumed at home, then a hall is probably a better option. It is also less of an issue where products are usually consumed exactly 'as bought', e.g. chocolates or chilled desserts which are normally consumed without any 'tampering'.

Test design

Having chosen an in-home test, there are still many more decisions to be made. One of these is whether to opt for a monadic, paired comparison, or sequential monadic approach. As with in-home v. in-hall, there is no right or wrong approach – it should reflect the objectives and the action that is likely to be taken based on the results. There are often time and cost considerations too. How often have we heard marketing say, 'I need top line by the end of the week. Oh, and I've only got a budget of £10,000!'

From a purist's perspective, as consumers tend to buy and drink coffee one jar at a time, a monadic approach is the best way to test them. This is a very 'hard' measure and will often lead to no clear preference between products branded on monadic scores. It is therefore worth considering a sequential monadic design, as this allows for a direct preference result (rather than inferred) – although you need to consider how preference is established, the strength of that preference and the role the products play in the consumers' repertoire. In most product areas, it is rare to find a consumer 100 per cent loyal to one brand. It is also worth probing reasons for no preference. The consumer may simply not be able to tell the products apart, or alternatively, may notice a difference between products but not have a preference.

Paired preference is more likely to force a preference but you have less control over order of testing, and cannot prevent consumers trying products side by side. This is likely to be the preferred approach for products bought as part of a 'bundle' of meal solutions, e.g. most people tend to have a range of chilled desserts sitting in their fridge at any one time.

Blind v. branded

Another decision is whether to test blind or branded. Again, this should relate back to the project objectives. Branding has a significant impact on the way consumers perceive and use products, and this needs to be taken into consideration, yet there is a role for testing products both blind and branded:

- blind to understand how the product performs, away from the influence of branding and packaging;
- branded to understand the impact of branding on the way consumers perceive the product.

Testing products blind is often not an easy task. Many products are very distinctive, either by virtue of their shape or texture, or because they have the product name embossed on them – my colleagues in confectionery are often faced with these problems, and it is not unknown to ask consumers to test products blindfolded. This is not an issue for coffee testing, but where a product is tested in-home, it does mean the coffee needs to be repackaged into generic jars.

The questionnaire and sample

A good deal of thought needs to be given to sample size (ensuring samples are robust enough for sensible confidence limits yet not cost-prohibitive), target audience (do you make assumptions about the target audience, or do you use a nationally representative group to help understand the most suitable target?), and then there's the questionnaire. It is true that overall opinion, inclination to buy, and preference (where relevant) will tend to be the key questions, but getting 'under the skin' of these results is all-important, and a carefully designed questionnaire will help with analysis and interpretation. Because consumers often have difficulty in expressing themselves meaningfully, it is all the more important to have an understanding of product attributes and consumer language, which may necessitate some qualitative work prior to product testing. It is also important to have a sensory profile to understand how the product compares to key competitors.

New product development

The thought processes and considerations given to testing new products tend to be similar to those for benchmarking and reformulation. How the new product ideas are generated and developed is a very different matter. Assuming the basic idea has already been researched and agreed, the role of research now becomes to test the suitability of products against the new concept.

Ideally, products should be developed against the concept – although there can also be a temptation to take what already exists or can easily be produced and build a concept around it.

Hopefully, a product profile will have been developed by the marketing, technical and sensory departments, against which a product will be sought and tested. This is based on our current understanding of the market and any research around the product concept. For example, with the launch of Black Gold, we had a concept that delivered a highly motivating consumer promise and it was important to fit a product that not only was of high quality but met the concept of a 'rich and smooth taste with a mouth-feel of velvet'.

Depending on the product or products the business comes up with, research may be carried out blind initially to understand how each product performs against the brief, or research may go straight to a concept product test.

So how do sensory and product optimisation fit in?

At Nestlé, we have our own in-house sensory department, and it is important it is involved from day one, as it will assist with profiling products and developing a brief for the new product. In developing new products, it is critical to understand technically how they compare against competitors. The sensory department will also ensure products are close to brief and of sufficient quality before testing among consumers – to avoid wasting time and effort with a substandard product. Furthermore, it is important that sensory work establishes there is a detectable difference between products – if it cannot tell the difference, the consumer certainly will not!

Consumers tend to be good at telling us what they like/dislike, but not so good at telling us why. Even when they are able to verbalise what they like/dislike, the words used will often mean different things to each consumer, and almost certainly to us. For example, consumers will often talk about coffee being 'too bitter' when in fact they mean 'too acidic', which is at the opposite end of the 'bitter scale'. Product optimisation can help to overcome this by combining consumer liking scores with sensory panel language and profiling. In this way, it is possible to infer which attributes are driving consumer preference.

A final thought

It is also worth checking that the product being tested can be reproduced in a factory environment. It is not unknown for products to test extremely well among consumers, only to find the factory is not able to produce product to the same spec!

Originally published in *Research* (February 1999), 44–45.

Ronald L. Tatham, *chairman, Burke, Inc. Ronald L. Tatham is actively involved in both the general management of the corporation and the design and analysis of research. Burke operates with the concept of the "producing manager." Every senior manager is involved in client-related activities and the delivery of Burke's research efforts.*

The Marketing Research Problem: From the DM's Desk to Study Execution

RONALD L. TATHAM

As a practising researcher, I find that much of the satisfaction of this profession comes from the sense of discovery and achievement in the unique and interesting problems waiting to be solved. It is this uniqueness that prevents the development of a simple cookbook approach to problem solving and allows creativity in our professional lives. Still, we must have foundations for how we define or examine marketing research problems.

The decision maker (DM) tends to focus on the symptoms and usually defines problems in terms of a desired outcome, such as why are my sales down (desired outcome = high levels of sales), or how do I choose the best of the two test products (desired outcome = product that produces the largest share and/or revenue). To a researcher, on the other hand, a problem is appropriately defined when it states the needed information such that a level of measurement is specified. For example:

DM: Our sales are going down – what can we do?

Researcher: Declining sales are symptoms of problems in the marketplace in general (all products in our category are declining in popularity) or problems with our product. The resolution is sequential:

1 What are the causes of the decline? (A research issue)
2 What actions are we capable of taking against these causes once identified? (A management issue)
3 Which of these actions produces the optimal result for us? (A research issue)
4 How do we monitor the impact of these actions once they are taken? (A research issue)
5 How do we implement ongoing modifications to continue to improve sales? (Another sequence of management and research issues)

Thus from the researcher's point of view, the problem definition has to result in a specific set of components.

In the simplest case, a DM asks, "Which of these two proposed new products is better?" The researcher must now define "better" in such a way that specific components of the marketing research problem can be identified and appropriate measurements made. The definition stage could result in defining "better" as some combination of:

1 Has an image most consistent with that sought by our company in terms of specific measurable image characteristics.
2 Has the greatest appeal when measured in a concept test prior to product creation (appeal defined in terms of a purchase interest scale).
3 Has the highest sales forecast in a simulated test market that includes a home use period.
4 Results in the highest net sales in a minitest market.

Each of these four definitions of "better" implies a specific measurement to be taken by the researcher. However, the researcher must address the more specific issues of:

1 There are many components of image. Which are appropriate to this occasion and how do we assess them?
2 Which purchase interest scale do we use, and how do we evaluate the results?
3 There are several approaches to simulated test markets. Which do we select?

These do not exhaust the components of the problem that must be addressed, but they show that the researcher must eventually define the problem in terms of specific components and measurements. At the exploratory stage of problem development the measures may be 'expert opinion.' However, at later stages the measures will likely be obtained from the eventual purchasers or purchase deciders for the product or service.

A general statement of proper problem definition is as follows: "When the problem is properly defined the researcher knows all of the possible answers, but the researcher has not counted the answers yet." In other words, the best problem definition, from the researcher's point of view, leads to such a precise definition of measurement that the nature of the answers are known, only their frequencies are unknown. For example, problem definition meetings may have led the researcher to measure the following characteristics of a sample of current users of a product:

1 Age
2 Number of times the product was purchased in the past seven days
3 Number of items purchased at each purchase occasion (past seven days)
4 Number of times competitive products were purchased in past seven days
5 Number of competitive items purchased at each purchase occasion (past seven days)
6 Ratings of client's product and competitive products on five 10-point image questions

For each of the six information areas listed above, the researcher knows the form of the answer and the limits within which acceptable answers can be given. That is, we know the population distribution of ages and we know the specific units (years of age) we will get for answers; we know that only answers of the numbers 1 through 10 are permitted on information item #6, and so forth. We do not know the actual values of the answers among our target population. This may sound naively simple, but it illustrates the point that you must know what you are measuring before you attempt to gather information.

If the problem is defined rigorously, the usefulness of the information can be tested with the DM. The basic question to be asked of the DM is, "If the data the respondents give us take the following forms, what would you or could you do?" The researcher can show the DM hypothetical results based on the researcher's conjecture. If the DM says, "I'm not sure what I would do with that information," the researcher must stop and ask, "What additional information would you need to make this information more useful or what about this information limits its usefulness to you?" Because you know the form of all of the possible answers, you must test the likely results for usefulness with the DM even if you do not know the outcome of the study. A proper definition of the problem will provide the DM with the relevant information needed for decision making and guide the researcher in proceeding with the research project.

Mike Pepp and Ian Becattelli

Mike and Ian work for Context Research International which is a medium-sized specialist qualitative research agency operating at an international level across a variety of sectors. Mike is an Associate Director who works extensively on international branding and advertising research, primarily in the pharmaceutical industry. Ian is a Senior Research Executive who is fluent in English, German and Italian, he also works extensively on international projects.

Researching the way into adland Europe

MIKE PEPP AND IAN BECATTELLI

Pan-European advertising is a double-edged sword. On one hand it offers strategic brand advantages and cost savings; on the other, it can present internal political difficulties and require creative ideas that cross cultural boundaries. I would like to explore the creative difficulties presented by pan-European advertising and suggest how research can assist the advertising development process and allow brands to achieve the advantages of a pan-European campaign.

Foreign travel, Europe-wide satellite TV and the Internet have accelerated the convergence of assumptions and expectations in European markets. This offers the opportunity for advertising campaigns to be shown in more than one country. Such pan-European campaigns can strengthen brand image, as recent Levi's advertising has shown.

Advertising – and research – agencies too often develop pan-European advertising that is palatable in each of the different markets, but which may not be actively motivating in any one of them. We term this the 'black hole' approach, since it exerts an enormous attraction, but is frequently destructive to creative ideas. We believe advertising development research can assist the creation of motivating panEuropean campaigns.

Culture, codes and advertising

Besides language, there are a variety of other mutually dependent signs, rules and conventions which contribute meaning to advertising. Successful communication requires that we share an interpretation of these elements: the closer our interpretation, the closer our two meanings will be. Advertising, like other elements of popular culture, has developed its own particular systems of meanings, or codes. These are culturally defined and frequently vary between countries, meaning that advertising is composed and read differently across European markets.

There are also different cultural references (including myths, history and humour) across Europe. German advertising, for example, has frequent references to ecology and individuality, while reflecting interest in hedonistic consumption and technology. Historically, French advertising has been notable for its representation of personal style and patriotism. This is not surprising: an advert which does not tap successfully into local references is less likely to motivate in that locality than one that does.

A key difference in advertising cultures between markets relates to the use of metaphors and metonyms. Although used in similar situations, the two have fundamentally different mechanisms:

- Metaphors transpose qualities/ values from one plane of reality onto another (e.g. 'the train snaked up the mountain'). Imagination is required, to seek similarities between two different planes. Metaphors can be used to suggest that a product is in some way 'like' something else.
- Metonyms make part of an object represent the whole (e.g. 'the crowned heads of Europe'). A less imaginative reading is required. In advertising, metonyms usually show the consumer, and often the moment of brand consumption.

An example of metaphorical advertising is a BMW advert in which we are asked to transfer the values of power and speed normally associated with lightning to a new gear box. Six prongs of lightning are shown, as visual symbols of the six gear-speeds.

By contrast, metonymical advertising is laden with lifestyle clues. It depicts an aspirational customer to make others want to be associated with the brand. A well-known metonymical advert is the Ferrero Rocher 'Ambassador's Reception'.

Certain cultures favour metonymical, others metaphorical advertising styles. For example, the metonymical style is favoured in Germany, where ads tend to feature a central character who represents the wider target audience. Metaphorical advertising tends to work better in the UK. Thus, the Orange Tango ads are metaphorical of the product experience. In consequence, there are different expectations of advertising between cultures.

Since a metaphor requires a transfer of values from one object to another, metaphorical advertising is dependent upon the symbol being understood. As interpretation of symbols is culturally dependent, there is a strong possibility of mis-communication with a pan-European campaign.

We have recently tested the metaphor of a clockwork mechanism, to suggest speed and accuracy, with respondents from sixteen European countries. Respondents from Western Europe identified the mechanism as belonging to an accurate, efficient and prestigious Swiss watch and drew appropriate messages. Respondents from the former Easter bloc identified the mechanism as inefficient, old-fashioned and less accurate than a digital mechanism. All respondents agreed accuracy and speed to be highly motivating communications, but they demand different visual interpretations of this.

The pan-European code

Pan-European advertising therefore tends to avoid metaphorical images and concentrate on the metonymical style. In short, pan-European advertising tends to show consumers and consumption, because it is easier than applying metaphors across cultures.

However, metonymical advertising is less effective at communicating intangible brand attributes. At best, it can encourage the audience to identify with the characters shown and share vicariously in the satisfaction they get from brand usage. However, this style of advertising can seem bland and lack the ability to motivate, as illustrated by the Ferrero Rocher ads which centre on communicating only 'aspiration'.

The way forward: a research programme

Advertisers planning a pan-European campaign must understand the prevailing advertising codes in the target countries. They should also be aware that cross-cultural differences may mean that a campaign communicates common values and has a single underlying creative idea, but with its executional context tailored to maximise its motivational impact in each market. The pan-European advertiser should, therefore, anticipate a centrally coordinated campaign incorporating local variations to maximise its appeal in each target market.

A research programme to support advertising development should not be designed to find common ground between cultures. Instead, it should look for a theme that is motivating across markets, and then examine how this theme can best be expressed in each one. When faced with this research problem, we recommend a three-stage research programme, thus:

1. *Brand evaluations and choice of advertising theme.* This stage of research identifies the current brand position in each market and chooses core themes which promote the desired brand values in each market. It is concerned largely with the form of the advertising: the mechanisms and codes that can be employed. It is also likely to identify the broad advertising content, such as whether humour is an appropriate device.
2. *Creative development theme.* Here, research identifies how the advertising theme can be expressed in each culture. It is concerned with fine-tuning the chosen core advertising message, to maximise its appeal and relevance in each culture. This may involve tactical changes, such as varying the type of humour used, or using alternative symbols/ references, to tie brand communication to local needs.

   This will allow subtle variations between markets to communicate common brand values with maximum effectiveness. The financial cost of executing these variations is likely to be relatively small, probably involving the inclusion of slightly different symbols and references in some markets, but with the core communication remaining constant.
3. *Creative evaluation and assessment.* Evaluating these creative ideas requires testing, in each market, of the local variation of the potential campaign. By evaluating the results, it is possible to create advertising which offers the greatest brand fit and ability to motivate across markets. This is the optimal pan-European campaign for the brand, providing a common brand identity across markets, with maximised communication strength, relevance and appeal.

While not as cheap as a single advert used in all markets, this tailored pan-European campaign will achieve economy of scale, since most of the advertising material is shared between markets and development costs can be controlled centrally. It will also provide much greater cost-effectiveness, since brand communication and motivation will be maximised in each targeted market.

We conclude that a core campaign tailored to individual markets produces a better value campaign and is in the long-term interests of the brand. It allows for the strongest possible communication of the chosen brand values, and maximises the ability of the advertising to motivate in each market.

Originally published in *ResearchPlus* (Autumn 1999), 18–195.

Part II

RESEARCH DESIGN FORMULATION

After a research problem has been defined and an approach developed, a research design is formulated. This part of the text describes in detail the techniques that help to form exploratory, descriptive and causal research designs. We describe the primary scales of measurement and the comparative and non-comparative scaling techniques commonly used. We present several guidelines for designing questionnaires and explain the procedures, techniques and statistical considerations involved in sampling. Managers and researchers should find this material helpful.

Chapter 3

Research design

There is never a single, perfect research design that is the best for all marketing research projects, or even for a specific type of marketing research task

OBJECTIVES

After reading this chapter, the student should be able to:

1 define research design, classify various research designs, and explain the differences between exploratory and conclusive research designs;
2 compare and contrast the basic research designs: exploratory, descriptive, and causal;
3 understand how respondents or the subjects of research design affect research design choices;
4 describe the major sources of errors in a research design including random sampling error and the various sources of non-sampling error;
5 explain research design formulation in international marketing research;
6 understand the ethical issues and conflicts that arise in formulating a research design.

OVERVIEW

Chapter 2 discussed how to define a marketing research problem and develop a suitable approach. These first two steps are critical to the success of the whole marketing research project. Once they have been completed, attention should be devoted to designing the formal research project by formulating a detailed research design (see Figure 2.1).

This chapter defines and classifies research designs. We describe the two major types of research design: exploratory and conclusive. We further classify conclusive research designs as descriptive or causal and discuss both types in detail. We then consider the differences between the two types of descriptive designs – cross-sectional and longitudinal, and identify sources of errors. The special considerations involved in formulating research designs in international marketing research are discussed. Several ethical issues that arise at this stage of the marketing research process are considered. The reader can develop a better appreciation of the concepts presented in this chapter by first considering the following examples, which illustrate cross-sectional and longitudinal research designs.

EXAMPLE

Cross-sectional research prevents airlines from 'Flying by the seat of their pants'[1]

An international survey of airline passengers, employing a cross-sectional design in which each respondent was interviewed only once, found that convenient schedules and seating comfort were passengers' most important considerations in selecting an airline. Lots of legroom, wide seats and general spaciousness were desirable characteristics for a trip that lasted between two and five hours. In keeping with the results of this survey, Lufthansa, the German international airline, emphasised convenient schedule to a large number of destinations, seating comfort, and 'unparalleled on-board service' in its advertising.

Airlines such as Lufthansa frequently make use of surveys based on cross-sectional designs

GLOBALCASH PROJECT

Preparing for monetary union

Pan-European banks preparing services and systems for the introduction of monetary union in Europe needed to know what corporate clients expected from their banks. There was much uncertainty within banks and with corporate clients of what should be done in preparation for monetary union. To cope with this uncertainty, a three-phase longitudinal design in which GlobalCash respondents throughout Europe were interviewed repeatedly was conducted. Phase 1, six months before the launch of EMU, involved 400 telephone interviews. Phase 2, conducted immediately after the launch of EMU, and phase 3, conducted six months after the launch, each involved 100 interviews with respondents who had participated in phase 1. Comparison of the findings through the three phases indicated that corporate clients had developed a strong understanding of EMU and had developed clear expectations of the services they expected from their banks. Each phase helped to guide promotional campaigns in banks and served as a guide to how successful previous campaigns had been. ■

As these examples indicate, two main types of research designs are employed in marketing research. An understanding of the fundamentals of research design and its components enables the researcher to formulate a design that is appropriate for the problem at hand.

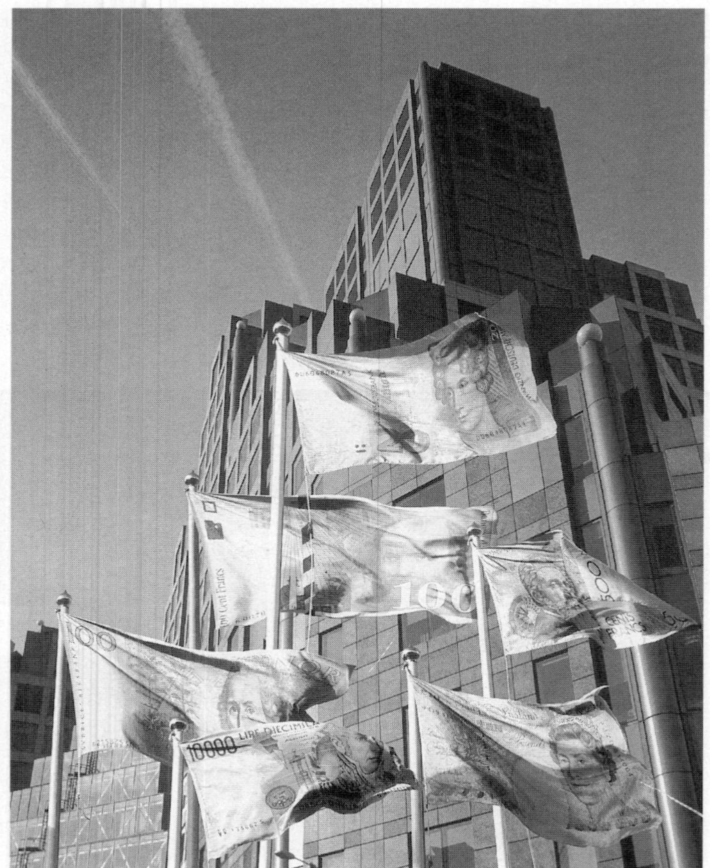

The GlobalCash study helped pan-European banks prepare services and systems for the introduction of monetary union in Europe
Tony Stone

RESEARCH DESIGN DEFINITION

Research design
A framework or blueprint for conducting the marketing research project. It specifies the details of the procedures necessary for obtaining the information needed to structure or solve marketing research problems.

A **research design** is a framework or blueprint for conducting a marketing research project. It details the procedures necessary for obtaining the information needed to structure or solve marketing research problems. Although a broad approach to the problem has already been developed, the research design specifies the details – the practical aspects – of implementing that approach. A research design lays the foundation for conducting the project. A good research design will ensure that the marketing research project is conducted effectively and efficiently. Typically, a research design involves the following components, or tasks:

1 Define the information needed (Chapter 2).
2 Design the exploratory, descriptive, or causal phases of the research (Chapters 3 through 9).
3 Specify the means of measurement and/or elicit data (Chapters 10 and 11).
4 Construct and pre-test a questionnaire (interviewing form) or an appropriate form for data collection (Chapter 12).
5 Specify the sampling process and sample size (Chapters 13 and 14).
6 Develop a plan of data analysis (Chapter 16).

Each component will be discussed in detail in the subsequent chapters. First, we must further develop our understanding of research design by examining the concept from the perspective of the markets and the respondent.

RESEARCH DESIGN FROM THE MARKETER'S PERSPECTIVE

Marketing decision-makers seek support from marketing researchers that is of practical relevance to the decisions they face. To give practical support, the information they receive should be:

- *Accurate*, i.e. a valid representation of the phenomena under investigation, that has come from a reliable or consistent form of measurement, and that is sufficiently sensitive to the important differences in individuals being measured or understood. Combining these three criteria refers to the degree to which information is based on an accurate representation.
- *Current*, i.e. the degree to which information reflects events in the relevant time period, past and/or present.
- *Sufficient*, i.e. the completeness or clarity of a 'picture' that reflects the characteristics of the marketing phenomena under study.
- *Available*, i.e. that access to the relevant information can be made when a decision is imminent.
- *Relevant*, i.e. that the support given 'makes sense' to decision-makers so that they can use the findings to build upon their existing foundation of knowledge.

Generating information that fulfils all the above characteristics is extremely difficult, if not impossible to achieve in marketing research. An exception could be in the realms of basic marketing phenomena where the relevance of the information could be of concern, i.e. is the information too basic to be of any use? Realistically, trade-offs must be made among the above characteristics. Within the first characteristic of accuracy there are further trade-offs which are primarily caused by what the marketing researcher is attempting to measure or understand:[2]

1. The subject of investigation is usually the human being.
2. The process of measuring humans may cause them to change.
3. It is difficult to assess the effect of extraneous variables in marketing experiments and thus their applications are limited.

Given the complexity of the subjects under study, the context or environment in which measurements are taken, and the skills required to perform and interpret measurements, it is difficult (if not impossible) to gain completely objective and accurate measurements. Of all the potential trade-offs, if one were to remove *relevancy* then the whole rationale of supporting the marketing decision-maker has been removed. This means this characteristic can never be compromised.

Relevancy embraces, *inter alia*, the ability to plan and forecast from research findings, to be able to distinguish real differences in consumer traits, and to know that characteristics are representative of groups of individuals. With relevant information such as this, the marketer can build up a stronger understanding or awareness of markets and the forces that shape them. In building up this understanding, the marketer cannot turn to a single technique or even body of techniques that may be deemed the 'ideal' in ensuring that information is relevant. In different types of decision-making scenario, different techniques will offer the best support for that decision-maker. Establishing the best form of support is the essence of research design.

A fundamental starting point in deciding an appropriate design is viewing the process from the point of view of the potential subject or respondent to a marketing research study.

RESEARCH DESIGN FROM RESPONDENTS' PERSPECTIVES

The potential respondents to any marketing research study play an enormous part in deciding which research design will actually work in practice. A subject of study may be complex and needs time for respondents to reflect upon and put words to the questions posed. Certain methods are more likely to build up a rapport and trust, in these circumstances, putting the respondent in the right frame of mind, will get them to respond in a full and honest manner. Figure 3.1 is a framework that serves to remind how respondents may be accessed, and what kinds of response may be generated.

In Figure 3.1 the top horizontal layer represents issues that respondents can express a view about quickly, that are simple for them to reflect upon, relating to common everyday occurrences that are at the forefront of their mind. In such circumstances, simple structured questioning (or self-reporting) in a standardised manner is possible. Further, the same procedure can be conducted in a consistent manner to a whole array of 'types' of respondent such as age groups, social class and intellectual levels. If questions were posed on which newspapers someone reads, it is a reasonable assumption that one is aware of the title(s), the title(s)

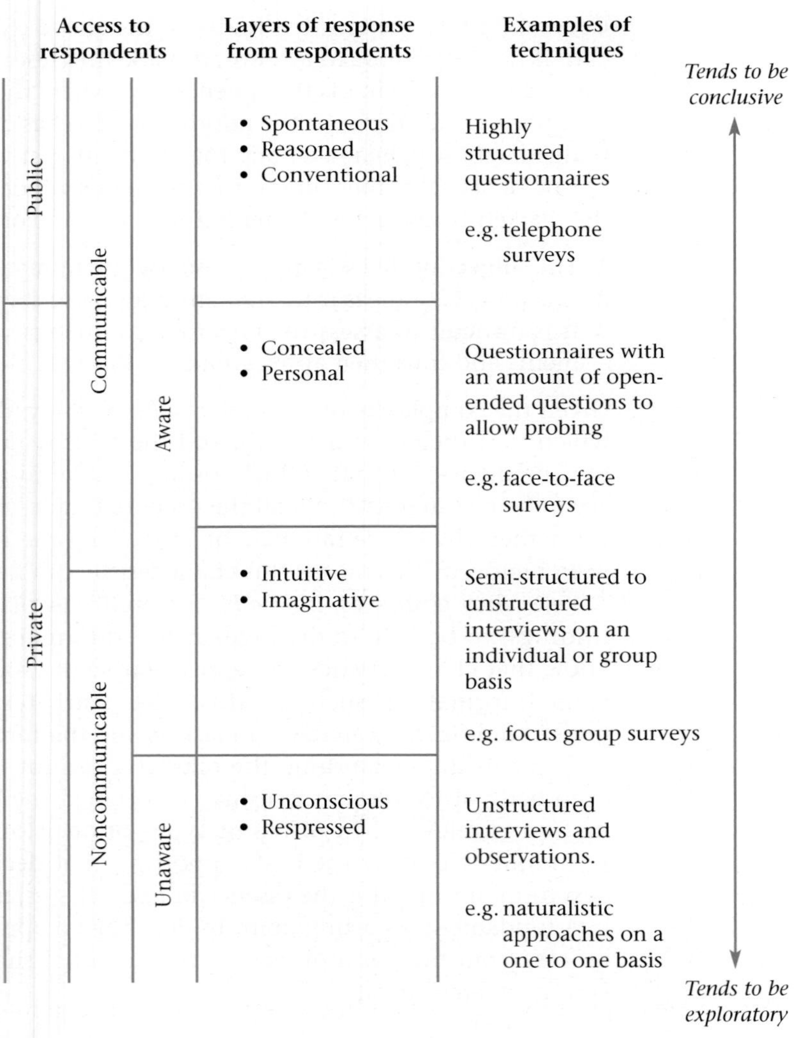

Figure 3.1 Responses to interviewing[3]

can be communicated and the topic is not a sensitive issue. In these circumstances, where answers to questions on reading habits are relatively easy to access and to respond to, highly structured questionnaires are appropriate. Clearly, in such situations quantitative techniques are applicable that allow very detailed descriptions or experiments to be made.

Progressing down, at the second level are issues that are more personal and more sensitive, such as the use of personal hygiene products. Again, structured questionnaires can measure the relevant issues but an amount of rapport may be needed to induce respondents to trust the interviewer and reveal their 'more personal' attitudes and behaviour.

At the third level are issues that require respondents to be creative. For example, if respondents were to be asked about their attitudes and behaviour towards eating yoghurt, this could be done in a very structured manner. Questions could be set to determine when it was eaten, favourite flavours and brands, where it was bought, how much was spent, etc. The same can be said of alcohol consumption, though this could well be a sensitive issue for many respondents. Now imagine a new product idea that mixes yoghurt and alcohol! What combination would work, and what types of consumer would be attracted to it? Would it be a dessert liqueur such as a Baileys Irish Cream or frozen yoghurt to compete with the Haagen Daas, luxury ice creams? Would champagne, advocaat, whisky or beer be the best alcoholic ingredient? Should any fruits be added? Individually? Forest fruits? Tropical fruits? How would it be packaged? What name would best suit it? What price level would it sell at? On what occasions would it be consumed?

Answering these questions demands a great amount of creativity and imagination. It demands that respondents reflect upon ideas, can play with ideas and words and dig deep to draw out ideas in a relaxed manner. Structured questionnaires cannot do this; such a scenario would work best with the use of focus groups.

At the fourth level may be issues that respondents may not be able to conceptualise, never mind be willing to express what they feel about a particular issue. An example of such an issue may be trying to understand the childhood influences of family and friends on an individual's perception and loyalty to brands of washing-up liquid. Respondents do not normally have to think through such issues or articulate them, until a marketing researcher comes along! In such circumstances, the characteristics of the individual determine what is the best way to probe and elicit appropriate responses. Nothing is standardised or consistent in these circumstances, the researcher having to shape the questions, probes and observations as they see fit in each interview.

Figure 3.1 illustrates exploratory and conclusive research being chosen based upon how respondents may react to the issues posed to them. Fuller descriptions of the approaches are presented in the next section.

RESEARCH DESIGN CLASSIFICATION

Conclusive research
Research designed to assist the decision-maker in determining, evaluating and selecting the best course of action to take in a given situation.

Exploratory research
One type of research design that has as its primary objective the provision of insights into and comprehension of the problem situation confronting the researcher.

Research designs may be broadly classified as exploratory or conclusive (see Figure 3.2). The differences between exploratory and **conclusive research** are summarised in Table 3.1. The primary objective of **exploratory research** is to provide insights into and an understanding of marketing phenomena. It is used in instances where the subject of the study cannot be measured in a quantitative manner. For example, if a researcher was trying to understand what 'atmosphere' meant in a restaurant, exploratory research may help to establish all the appropriate variables and how they connected together. What role did music play?

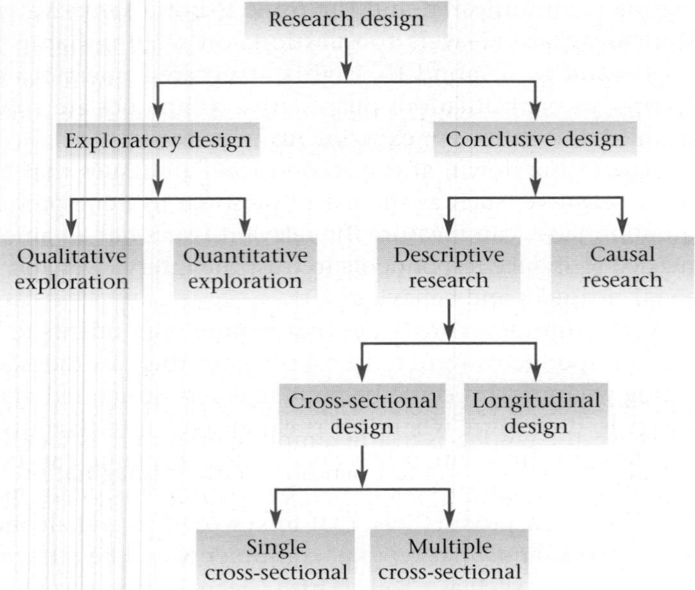

Figure 3.2 A classification of marketing research designs

Table 3.1 Differences between exploratory and conclusive research

	Exploratory	Conclusive
Objective	To provide insights and understanding of the nature of marketing phenomena To understand	To test specific hypotheses and examine relationships To measure
Characteristics	Information needed may be loosely defined Research process is flexible, unstructured and may evolve Samples are small Data analysis can be qualitative or quantitative	Information needed is clearly defined Research process is formal and structured Sample is large and aims to be representative Data analysis is quantitative
Findings/results	Can be used in their own right May feed into conclusive research May illuminate specific conclusive findings	Can be used in their own right May feed into exploratory research
Methods	Expert surveys Pilot surveys Secondary data Qualitative methods Unstructured observations Quantitative exploratory multivariate methods	Surveys Secondary data Databases Panels Structured observations Experiments

What type of music? How loud? What types of furniture? What colours and textures? What types of lighting? What architectural features? This list could go on of what 'atmosphere' may mean. It may not be quantifiable from the respondent's perspective, and from the perspective of the creative director in an advertising agency it would not convey meaning if in a quantitative format. Exploratory research may also be used in cases where you must define the problem more precisely, identify relevant courses of action, or gain additional insights before going on to confirm findings in a quantitative manner. The information needed will be loosely defined at this stage, by research questions rather than specific hypotheses or actual measurements. The research process that is adopted is characterised as being flexible, loosely structured and evolutionary in nature.

For example, it may consist of personal interviews with industry experts. The sample, selected to generate maximum insight, is small and non-representative. However, the emphasis in the sampling procedure is focused upon 'quality' individuals who are willing to open up, use their imagination, be creative and reveal perhaps sensitive thoughts and behaviour. 'Quality' also may emerge from their level of expertise; for example, there may only be a small population of chief executives in airline companies in Europe. If a small sample of, say, six chief executives from the largest and fastest developing airlines allowed access to a marketing researcher and revealed their attitudes and behaviour, insights may be gained that no quantitative study could achieve.

There are examples of quantitative findings being used for exploratory purposes. For example, within a survey that examines specific research questions and hypotheses lies the opportunity to examine additional connections between questions that had not been initially considered. Simple correlations through to multivariate techniques that explore potential connections between questions may be conducted; this process is known as data dredging. Exploratory research may be followed by further exploratory or conclusive research. Sometimes, exploratory research, particularly qualitative research, is all the research that is conducted.

The insights gained from exploratory research might be verified by conclusive research because the objective of conclusive research is to describe specific phenomena, to test specific hypotheses and examine specific relationships. This requires that the information needed is clearly specified.[4] Conclusive research is typically more formal and structured than exploratory research. It is based on large, representative samples, and the data obtained are subjected to quantitative analysis. The findings from this research are considered conclusive in nature. As shown in Figure 3.2, conclusive research designs may be either descriptive or causal, and descriptive research designs may be either cross-sectional or longitudinal. Each of these classifications is discussed further, beginning with exploratory research.

EXPLORATORY RESEARCH

As its name implies, the objective of exploratory research is to explore or search through a problem or situation to provide insights and understanding. Exploratory research could be used for any of the purposes listed in Table 3.2.

In general, exploratory research is meaningful in any situation where the researcher does not have enough understanding to proceed with the research project. Exploratory research is characterised by flexibility and versatility with respect to the methods because formal research protocols and procedures are not

Table 3.2 A summary of the uses of exploratory research designs

1	To obtain some background information where absolutely nothing is known about the problem area.
2	To define problems areas fully and to formulate hypotheses for further investigation and/or quantification.
3	Concept identification and exploration in the process of new product development.
4	During a preliminary screening process such as in new product development, in order to reduce a large number of possible projects to a smaller number of probable ones.
5	To identify relevant or salient behaviour patterns, beliefs, opinions, attitudes, motivations, etc. and to develop structures of these constructs.
6	To develop an understanding of the structure of beliefs and attitudes in order to aid the interpretation of data structures in multivariate data analyses.
7	To explore the reasons that lie behind the statistical differences between groups that may emerge from secondary data or surveys.
8	To explore sensitive or personally embarrassing issues from the respondents' and/or the interviewer's perspective.
9	To explore issues that respondents may hold deeply, that are difficult for themselves to rationalise and may find difficult to articulate.
10	To 'data dredge' or explore quantitative data to reveal hitherto unknown connections between different measured variables.

employed. It rarely involves structured questionnaires, large samples and probability sampling plans. Rather, researchers are alert to new ideas and insights as they proceed. Once a new idea or insight is discovered, they may redirect their exploration in that direction. That new direction is pursued until its possibilities are exhausted or another direction is found. For this reason, the focus of the investigation may shift constantly as new insights are discovered. Thus, the creativity and ingenuity of the researcher play a major role in exploratory research. Yet the abilities of the researcher are not the sole determinants of good exploratory research.

A further illustration of exploratory research is provided by the following example.

EXAMPLE

Fountain pens as signature of style[5]

How do you revive a semi-obsolete and dying product category? Montblanc found the answer through exploratory research. Montblanc Simplo GmbH conducted focus groups and in-depth interviews that provided the following insights:

1 Many consumers had a desire to view fountain pens as fashion accessories, much like jewellery, rather than inexpensive, utilitarian, and disposable.
2 The 'power of the pen' notion was still lingering in the minds of consumers.
3 The prestige-pricing phenomenon was applicable to fountain pens (many consumers associated higher price with higher prestige).

When these findings were confirmed by descriptive survey research, Montblanc positioned its fountain pens as a fashionable and prestigious item, a way of self-expression in a technological age. In the 1950s, the typed business letter represented power; however, with the arrival of the word processor everyone has the ability to produce perfectly typed documents. In the 1990s, a 'note, handwritten with a fountain pen and appended to the bottom of a letter . . . will indicate power'.

Valuable insights obtained through exploratory research using focus groups and depth interviews have enable Montblanc to position its fountain pens as 'signature of style'

Montblanc, whose fountain pen line varies from €200 for the Meisterstuck to €85,000 for the Royale, has also taken the lead in developing the lucrative 'limited edition' pen market. One example of a limited edition pen is Montblanc's Octavian pen. At €1500 each, the 4180 pens issued will be in demand by collectors. Aggressive marketing, aimed at satisfying underlying consumer needs discovered by exploratory research, has enabled Montblanc to position its fountain pens as a 'signature of style'.

Note that Montblanc did not rely exclusively on exploratory research. Once new positioning ideas were identified, they were further tested by descriptive research in the form of customer surveys.

DESCRIPTIVE RESEARCH

Descriptive research A type of conclusive research that has as its major objective the description of something, usually market characteristics or functions.

As the name implies, the major objective of **descriptive research** is to describe something, usually market characteristics or functions. Descriptive research as a conclusive research design is conducted for the reasons listed in Table 3.3.

Table 3.3 A summary of the uses of conclusive research designs

1	To describe the characteristics of relevant groups, such as consumers, salespeople, organisations, or market areas.
2	To estimate the percentage in a specified population exhibiting a certain form of behaviour.
3	To count the frequency of events, especially in the patterns of consumer behaviour.
4	To measure marketing phenomena to represent larger populations or target markets.
5	To be able to integrate findings from different sources in a consistent manner, especially in the use of marketing information systems and decision support systems.
6	To determine the perceptions of product or service characteristics.
7	To compare findings over time that allow changes in the phenomena to be measured.
8	To measure marketing phenomena in a consistent and universal manner.
9	To determine the degree to which marketing variables are associated.
10	To make specific predictions.

The Lufthansa and GlobalCash examples at the beginning of the chapter both employed descriptive research. These examples show that descriptive research assumes that the researcher has much prior knowledge about the problem situation.[6] A major difference between exploratory and descriptive research is that descriptive research is characterised by the prior formulation of specific research questions and hypotheses. Thus, the information needed is clearly defined. As a result, descriptive research is pre-planned and structured. It is typically based on large representative samples. A descriptive research design specifies the methods for selecting the sources of information and for collecting data from those sources.

Examples of descriptive studies in marketing research are as follows:

- Market studies describing the size of the market, buying power of the consumers, availability of distributors, and consumer profiles.
- Market share studies determining the proportion of total sales received by a company and its competitors.
- Sales analysis studies describing sales by geographic region, product line, type of the account and size of the account.
- Image studies determining consumer perceptions of the firm and its products.
- Product usage studies describing consumption patterns.
- Distribution studies determining traffic flow patterns and the number and location of distributors.
- Pricing studies describing the range and frequency of price changes and probable consumer response to proposed price changes.
- Advertising studies describing media consumption habits and audience profiles for specific television programmes and magazines.

These examples demonstrate the range and diversity of descriptive research studies.

Cross-sectional design
A type of research design involving the collection of information from any given sample of population elements only once.

Single cross-sectional design
A cross-sectional design in which one sample of respondents is drawn from the target population and information is obtained from this sample once.

Multiple cross-sectional design
A cross-sectional design in which there are two or more samples of respondents, and information from each sample is obtained only once.

Cross-sectional designs

The cross-sectional study is the most frequently used descriptive design in marketing research. **Cross-sectional designs** involve the collection of information from any given sample of population elements only once. They may be either single cross-sectional or multiple cross-sectional (Figure 3. 2). In **single cross-sectional designs**, only one sample of respondents is drawn from the target population, and information is obtained from this sample only once. These designs are also called sample survey research designs. In **multiple cross-sectional designs**, there are two or more samples of respondents, and information from each sample is obtained only once. Often, information from different samples is obtained at different times. The following examples illustrate single and multiple cross-sectional designs.

EXAMPLE

Designing coupons from cross-sections[7]

A cross-sectional study was conducted to determine the effectiveness of sales promotion coupons in stimulating sales as well as to assess coupon user and non-user profiles. The data were collected from 8000 households. The results showed that 31 per cent of all coupon-redeeming households accounted for 72 per cent of all redemptions. Demographically, heavy coupon redeemers were large households with children and annual incomes exceeding €30,000, with female heads of household aged 35 to 54 who worked part-time. Light users of coupons were smaller households with female heads who were younger and worked full-time. Such information was useful to consumer products firms like Procter & Gamble that rely heavily on coupon promotion, as it enabled them to target their promotions to heavy coupon redeemers.

EXAMPLE

Chase and Grabbits multiply like rabbits[8]

Eating behaviour trends were examined in a marketing research project commissioned by the Pillsbury Company. This project involved data from food diaries collected over three time waves. Each wave had a different sample of 1000 households for a total sample size of 3000 in the multiple cross-sectional design. Based on an analysis of eating patterns, the market was divided into five segments: Chase and Grabbits, Functional Feeders, Down Home Stokers, Careful Cooks and Happy Cookers. The changes in composition of these segments were examined over time. For example, the Chase and Grabbits experienced the biggest increase over the 15-year period (+136 per cent). Currently, this group represents 26 per cent of the total sample. Their desire for more convenience also increased over time. Says one Chase and Grabbit, 'Someday all you'll have to do is take a pill and it'll give you everything you need.' This information enabled the Pillsbury Company to target different products for different segments. For example, the Chase and Grabbit represented a prime segment for prepared foods and TV dinners.

The survey of coupon use, a single cross-sectional design, involved only one group of respondents who provided information only once. On the other hand, the Pillsbury study involved three different samples, each measured only once, with the measures obtained five years apart. Hence, the latter study illustrates a multiple cross-sectional design. A type of multiple cross-sectional design of special interest is cohort analysis.

Cohort analysis
A multiple cross-sectional design consisting of a series of surveys conducted at appropriate time intervals. The cohort refers to the group of respondents who experience the same event within the same interval.

Cohort analysis. **Cohort analysis** consists of a series of surveys conducted at appropriate time intervals, where the cohort serves as the basic unit of analysis. A cohort is a group of respondents who experience the same event within the same time interval.[9] For example, a birth (or age) cohort is a group of people who were born during the same time interval, such as 1951–60. The term cohort analysis refers to any study in which there are measures of some characteristics of one or more cohorts at two or more points in time.

It is unlikely that any of the individuals studied at time one will also be in the sample at time two. For example, the age cohort of people between 8 and 19 years was selected, and their soft drink consumption was examined every ten years for 30 years. In other words, every ten years a different sample of respondents was drawn from the population of those who were then between 8 and 19 years old. This sample was drawn independently of any previous sample drawn in this study from the population of 8 to 19 years. Obviously, people who were selected once were unlikely to be included again in the same age cohort (8 to 19 years), as these people would be much older at the time of subsequent sampling. This study showed that this cohort had increased consumption of soft drinks over time. Similar findings were obtained for other age cohorts (20–29, 30–39, 40–49, and 50+). Further, the consumption of each cohort did not decrease as the cohort aged. These results are presented in Table 3.4 in which the consumption of the various age cohorts over time can be determined by reading down the diagonal. These findings contradict the common belief that the consumption of soft drinks will decline with the greying of Western economies. This common but erroneous belief has been based on single cross-sectional studies. Note that if any column of Table 3.4 is viewed in isolation (as a single cross-sectional study) the consumption of soft drinks declines with age, thus fostering the erroneous belief.[10]

Cohort analysis is also used to predict changes in voter opinions during a political campaign. Well-known marketing researchers like MORI or Gallup, who specialise in political opinion research, periodically question cohorts of voters (people with similar voting patterns during a given interval) about their voting preferences to predict election results. Thus, cohort analysis is an important cross-sectional design. The other type of descriptive design is longitudinal design.

Table 3.4 Consumption of soft drinks by various age cohorts
(Percentage consuming on a typical day)

Age	*1950*	*1960*	*1969*	*1979*	
8–19	53	63	73	81	
20–29	45	61	76	76	C8
30–39	34	47	68	71	C7
40–49	23	41	59	68	C6
50+	18	29	50	52	C5
		C1	C2	C3	C4

C1: cohort born prior to 1900
C2: cohort born 1901–10
C3: cohort born 1911–20
C4: cohort born 1921–30
C5: cohort born 1931–40
C6: cohort born 1941–50
C7: cohort born 1950–59
C8: cohort born 1960–69

Longitudinal designs

Longitudinal design
A type of research design involving a fixed sample of population elements measured repeatedly. The sample remains the same over time, thus providing a series of pictures that, when viewed together, portray a vivid illustration of the situation and the changes that are taking place.

In **longitudinal designs**, a fixed sample (or samples) of population elements is measured repeatedly. A longitudinal design differs from a cross-sectional design in that the sample or samples remain the same over time. In other words, the same people are studied over time. In contrast to the typical cross-sectional design, which gives a snapshot of the variables of interest at a single point in time, a longitudinal study provides a series of 'pictures'. These 'pictures' give an in-depth view of the situation and the changes that take place over time. For example, the question, how did the German people rate the performance of President Helmut Kohl immediately after unification of West and East Germany? would be addressed using a cross-sectional design. A longitudinal design, however, would be used to address the question, how did the German people change their view of Kohl's performance during his presidency?

Panel
A sample of respondents who have agreed to provide information at specified intervals over an extended period.

Often, the term **panel** is used interchangeably with the term longitudinal design. A panel consists of a sample of respondents, generally households, which have agreed to provide information at specified intervals over an extended period. Panels are maintained by syndicated firms, and panel members are compensated for their participation with gifts, coupons, information, or cash.[11]

Data obtained from panels may provide information on market shares that are based on an extended period of time. It may also allow the researcher to examine changes in market share over time.[12] As the following section explains, these changes cannot be determined from cross-sectional data.

Relative advantages and disadvantages of longitudinal and cross-sectional designs

The relative advantages and disadvantages of longitudinal versus cross-sectional designs are summarised in Table 3.5. A major advantage of longitudinal design over the cross-sectional design is the ability to detect change as a result of repeated measurement of the same variables on the same sample.

Table 3.5 Relative advantages and disadvantages of longitudinal and cross-sectional designs

Evaluation criteria	*Cross-sectional design*	*Longitudinal design*
Detecting change	–	+
Large amount of data collection	–	+
Accuracy	–	+
Representative sampling	+	–
Response bias	+	–

Note: A + indicates a relative advantage over the other design, whereas a – indicates a relative disadvantage.

Table 3.6 Cross-sectional data may not show change

Brand purchased	*Time period*	
	Period 1 Survey	*Period 2 Survey*
Total surveyed	1000	1000
Brand A	200	200
Brand B	300	300
Brand C	500	500

Table 3.7 Longitudinal data may show substantial change

Brand purchased in Period 1	*Brand purchased in Period 2*			
	Brand A	*Brand B*	*Brand C*	*Total*
Total surveyed	200	300	500	1000
Brand A	100	50	50	200
Brand B	25	100	175	300
Brand C	75	150	275	500

Tables 3.6 and 3.7 demonstrate how cross-sectional data can mislead researchers about changes over time. The cross-sectional data reported in Table 3.6 reveal that the purchases of Brands A, B and C remain the same in periods 1 and 2. In each survey, 20 per cent of the respondents purchase Brand A, 30 per cent Brand B, and 50 per cent Brand C. The longitudinal data presented in Table 3.7 show that substantial change, in the form of brand switching, occurred in the study period. For example, only 50 per cent (100/200) of the respondents who purchased Brand A in period 1 also purchased it in period 2. The corresponding repeat purchase figures for Brands B and C are, respectively, 33.3 per cent

(100/300) and 55 per cent (275/500). Hence, during this interval Brand C experienced the greatest loyalty and Brand B the least. Table 3.7 provides valuable information on brand loyalty and brand switching (such a table is called a turnover table or a brand-switching matrix.)[13]

Longitudinal data enable researchers to examine changes in the behaviour of individual units and to link behavioural changes to marketing variables, such as changes in advertising, packaging, pricing and distribution. Since the same units are measured repeatedly, variations caused by changes in the sample are eliminated and even small changes are apparent.[14]

Another advantage of panels is that relatively large amounts of data can be collected. Because panel members are usually compensated for their participation, they are willing to participate in lengthy and demanding interviews. Yet another advantage is that panel data can be more accurate than cross-sectional data.[15] A typical cross-sectional survey requires the respondent to recall past purchases and behaviour; these data can be inaccurate because of memory lapses. Panel data, which rely on continuous recording of purchases in a diary, place less reliance on the respondent's memory. A comparison of panel and cross-sectional survey estimates of retail sales indicates that panel data give more accurate estimates.[16]

The main disadvantage of panels is that they may not be representative. Non-representativeness may arise because of:

1 *Refusal to cooperate*. Many individuals or households do not wish to be bothered with the panel operation and refuse to participate. Consumer panels requiring members to keep a record of purchases have a cooperation rate of 60 per cent or less.
2 *Mortality*. Panel members who agree to participate may subsequently drop out because they move away or lose interest. Mortality rates can be as high as 20 per cent per year.[17]
3 *Payment*. Payment may cause certain types of people to be attracted, making the group unrepresentative of the population.

Another disadvantage of panels is response bias. New panel members are often biased in their initial responses. They tend to increase the behaviour being measured, such as food purchasing. This bias decreases as the respondent overcomes the novelty of being on the panel, so it can be reduced by initially excluding the data of new members.[18] Seasoned panel members may also give biased responses because they believe they are experts or they want to look good or give the 'right' answer. Bias also results from boredom, fatigue and incomplete diary entries.

CAUSAL RESEARCH

Causal research
A type of conclusive research where the major objective is to obtain evidence regarding cause-and-effect (causal) relationships.

Causal research is used to obtain evidence of cause-and-effect (causal) relationships (see Table 3.2). Marketing managers continually make decisions based on assumed causal relationships. These assumptions may not be justifiable, and the validity of the causal relationships should be examined via formal research.[19] For example, the common assumption that a decrease in price will lead to increased sales and market share does not hold in certain competitive environments. Causal research is appropriate for the following purposes:

1 To understand which variables are the cause (independent variables) and which variables are the effect (dependent variables) of marketing phenomenon.
2 To determine the nature of the relationship between the causal variables and the effect to be predicted.
3 To test hypotheses.

Like descriptive research, causal research requires a planned and structured design. Although descriptive research can determine the degree of association between variables, it is not appropriate for examining causal relationships. Such an examination requires a causal design, in which the causal or independent variables are manipulated in a relatively controlled environment. A relatively controlled environment is one in which the other variables that may affect the dependent variable are controlled or checked as much as possible. The effect of this manipulation on one or more dependent variables is then measured to infer causality. The main method of causal research is experimentation.[20]

Due to the complexity and importance of this subject, Chapter 9 has been devoted to causal designs and experimental research.

EXAMPLE

Advertising your way to profits[21]

A causal study was undertaken to measure the effect of business-to-business advertising on the sales of a variety of products as well as to evaluate the effects of ad frequency schedules and varying media weight. The study involved a participating manufacturer, the publishers of the magazines used in the study, and a tightly controlled stratification of the magazine's circulation into three cells, which were to receive light, medium and heavy levels of advertising. Four products in the growth stage of the product lifecycle were chosen for advertisement. To obtain clear sales data on these products, distribution channel restrictions were necessary, so that sales could be linked to the balanced advertising cells. After the four products and the participating magazines had been selected, the advertising cells and levels for each product were defined. At the conclusion of the one-year study, findings supported the hypothesis that more advertising caused an increase in sales. The study also concluded that if a product is sold through dealers, both dealers and end-users should be targeted for ads. Further, increased advertising frequency can increase sales leads and result in higher profits. ■

In this experiment, the causal (independent) variable was advertising, which was manipulated to have three levels: light, medium, and heavy. The effect (dependent) variable was sales, and the influence of distribution on sales had to be controlled. Although the preceding example distinguished causal research from other types of research, causal research should not be viewed in isolation. Rather, the exploratory, descriptive and causal research designs often complement each other.

RELATIONSHIPS AMONG EXPLORATORY, DESCRIPTIVE AND CAUSAL RESEARCH

We have described exploratory, descriptive and causal research as major classifications of research designs, but the distinctions among these classifications are not absolute. A given marketing research project may involve more than one type of research design and thus serve several purposes.[22] Which combination of research designs to employ depends on the nature of the problem. We offer the following general guidelines for choosing research designs:

1 When little is known about the problem situation, it is desirable to begin with exploratory research. Exploratory research is appropriate for the following:
   (a) When the nature of the topic under study cannot be measured in a structured, quantifiable manner.
   (b) When the problem needs to be defined more precisely.
   (c) When alternative courses of action need to be identified.
   (d) When research questions or hypotheses need to be developed.
   (e) When key variables need to be isolated and classified as dependent or independent.
2 Exploratory research may be an initial step in a research design. It may be followed by descriptive or causal research. For example, hypotheses developed via exploratory research can be statistically tested using descriptive or causal research.
3 It is not necessary to begin every research design with exploratory research. It depends on the precision with which the problem has been defined and the researcher's degree of certainty about the approach to the problem. A research design could well begin with descriptive or causal research. To illustrate, a consumer satisfaction survey that is conducted annually need not begin with or include an exploratory phase.
4 Although exploratory research is generally the initial step, it need not be. Exploratory research may follow descriptive or causal research. For example, descriptive or causal research results in findings that are hard for managers to interpret. Exploratory research may provide more insights to help understand these findings.

The relationships between exploratory, descriptive and causal research are further illustrated by the following example of retail banking at Citibank.

EXAMPLE

Citibank banks on exploratory, descriptive and causal research[23]

Marketing research at Citibank is typical in that it is used to measure consumer awareness of products, to monitor their satisfaction and attitudes associated with the product, to track product usage, and to diagnose problems as they occur. To accomplish these tasks, Citibank makes extensive use of exploratory, descriptive and causal research. Often it is advantageous to offer special financial packages

Banks undertake exploratory, descriptive and causal research to understand the financial service needs of the consumers.

to specific groups of customers. In this case, a financial package is being designed for senior citizens. The following seven-step process was taken by marketing research to help in the design.

1 A task force was created to better define the market parameters to include all the needs of the many Citibank branches. A final decision was made to include customers of 55 years of age or older, retired, and in the upper half of the financial strata of that market.

2 Exploratory research in the form of secondary data analysis of the mature or older market was then performed, and a study of competitive products was conducted. Exploratory qualitative research involving focus groups was also carried out to determine the needs and desires of the market and the level of satisfaction with the current products. In the case of senior citizens, a great deal of diversity was found in the market. This was determined to be due to such factors as affluence, relative age, and the absence or presence of a spouse.

3 Exploratory research continued in the next stage of brainstorming. This involved the formation of many different financial packages targeted for the target market. In this case, ten ideas were generated.

4 The feasibility of the ten ideas generated in step 3 was then tested, based on whether these ideas were possible in relation to the business. The following list of questions was used as a series of hurdles that the ideas had to pass to continue on to the next step.
   (a) Can the idea be explained in a manner that the target market will easily understand?
   (b) Does the idea fit into the overall strategy of Citibank?
   (c) Is there available a description of a specific target market for the proposed product?
   (d) Does the research conducted so far indicate a potential match for target market needs, and is the idea perceived to have appeal to this market?
   (e) Is there a feasible outline of the tactics and strategies for implementing the programme?
   (f) Have the financial impact and cost of the programme been thoroughly evaluated and determined to be in line with company practices? In this study, only one idea generated from the brainstorming session made it past all the listed hurdles and on to step 5.

5 A creative work plan was then generated. This plan was to emphasise the competitive advantage of the proposed product as well as to delineate the specific features of the product better.

6 The previous exploratory research was now followed by descriptive research in the form of street interviews of people in the target market range. The survey showed that the list of special features was too long, and it was decided to drop the features more commonly offered by competitors.

7 Finally, the product was test marketed in six of the Citibank branches within the target market. Test marketing is a form of causal research.

Given successful test marketing results, the product was introduced nationally.

POTENTIAL SOURCES OF ERROR IN RESEARCH DESIGNS

Several potential sources of error can affect a research design. A good research design attempts to control the various sources of error. Although these errors are discussed in detail in subsequent chapters, it is pertinent at this stage to give brief descriptions.

Total error
The variation between the true mean value in the population of the variable of interest and the observed mean value obtained in the marketing research project.

Where the focus of a study is a quantitative measurement, the **total error** is the variation between the true mean value in the population of the variable of interest and the observed mean value obtained in the marketing research project. As shown in Figure 3.3, total error is composed of random sampling error and non-sampling error.

Random sampling error

Random sampling error
The error because the particular sample selected is an imperfect representation of the population of interest. It may be defined as the variation between the true mean value for the sample and the true mean value of the population.

Random sampling error occurs because the particular sample selected is an imperfect representation of the population of interest. Random sampling error is the variation between the true mean value for the population and the true mean value for the original sample. Random sampling error is discussed further in Chapters 13 and 14.

Non-sampling error

Non-sampling error
An error that can be attributed to sources other than sampling and that can be random or non-random.

Non-sampling errors can be attributed to sources other than sampling, and they may be random or non-random. They result from a variety of reasons, including errors in problem definition, approach, scales, questionnaire design, interviewing methods, and data preparation and analysis. Non-sampling errors consist of non-response errors and response errors.

Non-response error
A type of non-sampling error that occurs when some of the respondents included in the sample do not respond. This error may be defined as the variation between the true mean value of the variable in the original sample and the true mean value in the net sample.

A **non-response error** arises when some of the respondents included in the sample do not respond. The primary causes of non-response are refusals and not-at-homes (see Chapter 14). Non-response will cause the net or resulting sample to be different in size or composition from the original sample. Non-response error is defined as the variation between the true mean value of the variable in the original sample and the true mean value in the net sample.

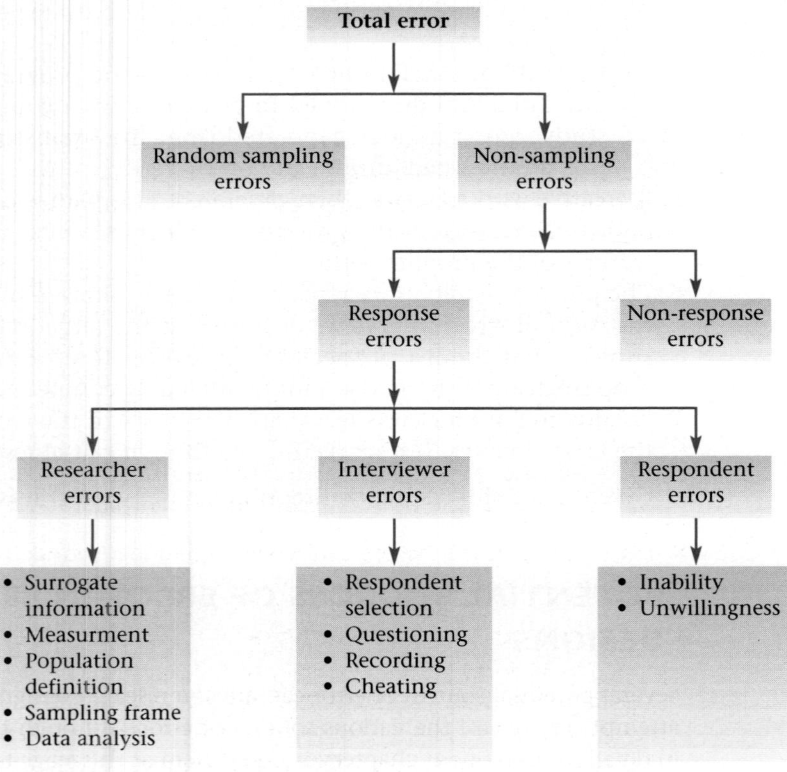

Figure 3.3 Potential sources of error in research designs

Response error
A type of non-sampling error arising from respondents who do respond but who give inaccurate answers or whose answers are mis-recorded or mis-analysed. It may be defined as a variation between the true mean value of the variable in the net sample and the observed mean value obtained in the market research project.

Response error arises when respondents give inaccurate answers or their answers are mis-recorded or mis-analysed. Response error is defined as the variation between the true mean value of the variable in the net sample and the observed mean value obtained in the marketing research project. Response errors can be made by researchers, interviewers or respondents.

Errors made by the researcher include surrogate information, measurement, population definition, sampling frame, and data analysis errors.

- *Surrogate information error* may be defined as the variation between the information needed for the marketing research problem and the information sought by the researcher. For example, instead of obtaining information on consumer choice of a new brand (needed for the marketing research problem), the researcher obtains information on consumer preferences because the choice process cannot be easily observed.
- *Measurement error* may be defined as the variation between the information sought and information generated by the measurement process employed by the researcher. While seeking to measure consumer preferences, the researcher employs a scale that measures perceptions rather than preferences.
- *Population definition error* may be defined as the variation between the actual population relevant to the problem at hand and the population as defined by the researcher. The problem of appropriately defining the population may be far from trivial, as illustrated by the case of affluent households.

EXAMPLE

How affluent is affluent?

The population of the affluent households was defined in four different ways in a study:

1 households with income of €50,000 or more;
2 the top 20 per cent of households, as measured by income;
3 households with net worth over €250,000; and
4 households with discretionary income to spend being 30 per cent higher than that of comparable households. ■

The number and characteristics of the affluent households varied depending on the definition, underscoring the need to avoid population definition error. Depending upon the way the population of affluent households was defined, the results of this study would have varied markedly.

- *Sampling frame error* may be defined as the variation between the population defined by the researcher and the population as implied by the sampling frame (list) used. For example, the telephone directory used to generate a list of telephone numbers does not accurately represent the population of potential consumers due to unlisted, disconnected and new numbers in service.
- *Data analysis error* encompasses errors that occur while raw data from questionnaires are transformed into research findings. For example, an inappropriate statistical procedure is used, resulting in incorrect interpretation and findings.

Response errors made by the interviewer include respondent selection, questioning, recording, and cheating errors.

- *Respondent selection error* occurs when interviewers select respondents other than those specified by the sampling design or in a manner inconsistent with the sampling design. For example, in a readership survey, a non-reader is selected for the interview but classified as a reader of the *European* in the 15- to 19-years-old category in order to meet a difficult quota requirement.

- *Questioning error* denotes errors made in asking questions of the respondents or in not probing, when more information is needed. For example, while asking questions an interviewer does not use the exact wording given in the questionnaire.
- *Recording error* arises due to errors in hearing, interpreting, and recording the answers given by the respondents. For example, a respondent indicates a neutral response (undecided) but the interviewer misinterprets that to mean a positive response (would buy the new brand).
- *Cheating error* arises when the interviewer fabricates answers to a part or whole of the interview. For example, an interviewer does not ask the sensitive questions related to respondent's debt but later fills in the answers based on personal assessment.

Response errors made by the respondent comprise inability and unwillingness errors.

- *Inability error* results from the respondent's inability to provide accurate answers. Respondents may provide inaccurate answers because of unfamiliarity, fatigue, boredom, faulty recall, question format, question content and other factors. For example, a respondent cannot recall the brand of toothpaste purchased four weeks ago.
- *Unwillingness error* arises from the respondent's unwillingness to provide accurate information. Respondents may intentionally misreport their answers because of a desire to provide socially acceptable answers, to avoid embarrassment, or to please the interviewer. For example, to impress the interviewer, a respondent intentionally says that they read *The Economist* magazine.

These sources of error are discussed in more detail in subsequent chapters; what is important here is that there are many sources of error. In formulating a research design, the researcher should attempt to minimise the total error, not just a particular source. This admonition is warranted by the general tendency among naive researchers to control sampling error with large samples. Increasing the sample size does decrease sampling error, but it may also increase non-sampling error, for example by increasing interviewer errors. Non-sampling error is likely to be more problematic than sampling error. Sampling error can be calculated, whereas many forms of non-sampling error defy estimation. Moreover, non-sampling error has been found to be the major contributor to total error, whereas random sampling error is relatively small in magnitude.[25] The point is that total error is important. A particular type of error is important only in that it contributes to total error.

Sometimes, researchers deliberately increase a particular type of error to decrease the total error by reducing other errors. For example, suppose that a mail survey is being conducted to determine consumer preferences for purchasing fashion clothing from department stores. A large sample size has been selected to reduce sampling error. A response rate of 30 per cent may be expected. Given the limited budget for the project, the selection of a large sample size does not allow for follow-up mailings. Past experience, however, indicates that the response rate could be increased to 45 per cent with one follow-up mailing and to 55 per cent with two follow-up mailings. Given the subject of the survey, non-respondents are likely to differ from respondents in many features. Hence, it may be desirable to reduce the sample size to make money available for follow-up mailings. While decreasing the sample size will increase random sampling error, the two follow-up mailings will more than offset this loss by decreasing non-response error.

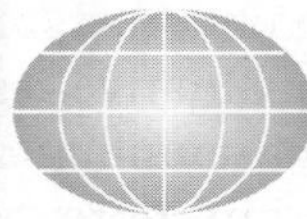

INTERNATIONAL MARKETING RESEARCH

While conducting international marketing research, it is important to realise that given environmental differences, the research design appropriate for one country may not be suitable in another. Consider the problem of determining household attitudes toward major appliances in Holland and Saudi Arabia. While conducting exploratory research in Holland, it is appropriate to conduct focus groups jointly with male and female heads of households. It would be inappropriate to conduct such focus groups in Saudi Arabia, however. Given the traditional culture, wives are unlikely to participate freely in the presence of their husbands. It would be more useful to conduct one-on-one in-depth interviews with both male and female heads of households being included in the sample. Procter & Gamble encountered a similar situation in Japan.

Proctor & Gamble wooing and exploring Japanese women[26]

The consumer market in Japan is one of the toughest, most competitive, fastest-moving markets in the world. Japan represents the cutting edge of world-wide product technology in many product categories. When Procter & Gamble started business in Japan, it conducted a detailed study of market characteristics and market profile. The target market for Proctor & Gamble was housewives who were largely responsible for the consumption of several products such as nappies, household cleaners, soaps and detergents. Exploratory research followed by descriptive research was undertaken for this purpose. Although focus groups are the most popular qualitative marketing research technique in Europe, exploratory research in Japan emphasised individual in-depth interviews. Given the Japanese cultural tendency not to openly disagree in group settings, one-on-one in-depth interviews were preferred. The descriptive surveys emphasised in-home personal interviews. Results showed that an average Japanese housewife was very uncompromising in her demands for high quality, value and service. She was a paragon of conservation and efficiency in the management of her household. About half the adult women in Japan were employed. They generally worked before marriage and after children were raised. Child rearing was the number one priority for Japanese mothers. When it came to foreign versus domestic brands, Japanese women preferred foreign name brand products that had style and status, such as fashionable clothing, French perfumes, wines, liquors and Gucci bags. They did not prefer functional products that were made in foreign countries, however, because they usually did not meet their exacting and demanding quality standards. Japanese women greatly preferred commercials that upheld traditional social and family values and roles rather than the typical Western examples. Although Proctor & Gamble initially made a few mistakes by misjudging Japanese nuance in instances such as the introduction of Camay toilet soap and Pampers nappies, this market profile study helped them to avoid costly mistakes later.

In many countries, particularly developing countries, consumer panels have not been developed, making it difficult to conduct descriptive longitudinal research. Likewise, in many countries the marketing support infrastructure – that is, retailing, wholesaling, advertising and promotional infrastructure – is lacking, making it infeasible to implement a causal design involving a field experiment. In formulating a research design, considerable effort is required to ensure the equivalence and comparability of secondary and primary data obtained from different countries. In the context of collecting primary data, qualitative research, survey methods, scaling techniques, questionnaire design and sampling considerations are particularly important. These topics are discussed in more detail in subsequent chapters.

ETHICS IN MARKETING RESEARCH

During the research design stage, not only are the concerns of the researcher and the client involved, but the rights of the respondents also must be respected. Although normally there is no direct contact between the respondents and the other stakeholders (client and researcher) during the research design phase, this is the stage when decisions, such as using hidden video or audio tape recorders, with ethical ramifications are made.

The basic question of the type of research design which should be adopted (i.e. descriptive or causal, cross-sectional or longitudinal) has ethical overtones. For example, when studying brand switching in toothpaste purchases, a longitudinal design is the only actual way to assess changes in an individual respondent's brand choice. A research firm that has not conducted many longitudinal studies may try to justify the use of a cross-sectional design. Is this ethical?

Researchers must ensure that the research design utilised will provide the information needed to address the marketing research problem that has been identified. The client should have the integrity not to misrepresent the project and should describe the constraints under which the researcher must operate and not make unreasonable demands. Longitudinal research takes time. Descriptive research might require interviewing customers. If time is an issue, or if customer contact has to be restricted, the client should make these constraints known at the start of the project.

Equally important, the responsibilities to the respondents must not be overlooked. The researcher should design the study so as not to violate the respondents' right to safety, right to privacy, or right to choose. Furthermore, the client must not abuse power to jeopardise the anonymity of the respondents.

INTERNET AND COMPUTER APPLICATIONS

The Internet can facilitate the implementation of different types of research designs.

Exploratory research

If a exploratory research design is to be utilised, forums, chat rooms or newsgroups can be used to discuss a particular topic to great depth. Files can be exchanged that can include moving images and sounds allowing questions and probes to be built around this material. Formal focus groups may be conducted with experts or individuals representing target groups, all on a global basis if needed.

Conclusive research

Many descriptive studies utilise secondary data in defining the nature of a problem, as a technique in its own right and as a means to develop sampling plans. The use of the Internet for these purposes is discussed in Chapter 4. In primary data collection, the Internet can be used for surveys (discussed in Chapter 8) and in panels (Chapters 4 and 8). The use of the Internet for causal research designs is discussed in Chapter 9.

In addition to Internet applications, computers can also help to control total error. By using computers, researchers can see how the various sources of error will affect the results and what levels of errors may be acceptable. It is relatively easy to estimate random sampling error when probability sampling schemes are used. Estimating the impact of various non-sampling errors, however, is much more problematic. Simulation can be conducted to determine how the distributions and levels of various non-sampling errors will affect final results.[27]

SUMMARY

A research design is a framework or blueprint for conducting the marketing research project. It specifies the details of how the project should be conducted. Research designs may be broadly classified as exploratory or conclusive. The primary purpose of exploratory research is to provide insights into the problem. Conclusive research is conducted to test specific hypotheses and examine specific relationships. The findings from conclusive research are used as input into managerial decision-making. Conclusive research may be either descriptive or causal.

The major objective of descriptive research is to describe market characteristics or functions. Descriptive research can be classified into cross-sectional and longitudinal research. Cross-sectional designs involve the collection of information from a sample of population elements at a single point in time. These designs can be further classified as single cross-sectional or multiple cross-sectional designs. In contrast, in longitudinal designs repeated measurements are taken on a fixed sample. Causal research is designed for the primary purpose of obtaining evidence about cause-and-effect (causal) relationships.

A research design consists of six components. Error can be associated with any of these components. The total error is composed of random sampling error and non-sampling error. Non-sampling error consists of non-response and response errors. Response error encompasses errors made by researchers, interviewers and respondents. In formulating a research design when conducting international marketing research, considerable effort is required to ensure the equivalence and comparability of secondary and primary data obtained from different countries. In terms of ethical issues, the researchers must ensure that the research design used will provide the information sought and that the information sought is the information needed by the client. The client should have the integrity not to misrepresent the project and should describe the situation within which the researcher must operate and must not make unreasonable demands. Every precaution should be taken to ensure the respondents' or subjects' right to safety, right to privacy, or right to choose.

QUESTIONS AND PROBLEMS

1 Define research design in your own words.

2 What expectations do marketing decision-makers have of research designs?

3 How does the subject of enquiry as seen by potential research respondents affect research design?

4 How does formulating a research design differ from developing an approach to a problem?

5 Differentiate between exploratory and conclusive research.

6 What are the major purposes for which exploratory research is conducted?

7 Describe how quantitative techniques may be used in exploratory research.

8 What are the major purposes for which descriptive research is conducted?

9 Discuss the advantages and disadvantages of panels.

10 Compare and contrast cross-sectional and longitudinal designs.

11 Describe cohort analysis. Why is it of special interest?

12 What is a causal research design? What is its purpose?

13 What is the relationship between exploratory, descriptive and causal research?

14 What potential sources of error can affect a research design?

15 Why is it important to minimise total error rather than any particular source of error?

NOTES

1 *ITAPA International Survey of Passenger Preferences* (Arlington, VA: International Airline Passengers Associations, 1987).

2 Boyd, H.W. Jr, Westfall, R. and Stasch, S.F., *Marketing Research, Text and Cases*, 7th edn (Irwin, Homewood, IL: Irwin, 1989), 49.

3 Adapted from Cooper, P. and Braithwaite, A. 'Qualitative technology – new perspectives on measurement and meaning through qualitative research', Market Research Society Conference, 2nd pre-conference workshop, 1979.

4 Kerlinger, F.N., *Foundations of Behavioural Research*, 3rd edn (New York: Holt, Rinehart and Winston, 1986), pp. 17–20.

5 Bird, L., 'Marketers Sell Pen as Signature of Style', *Wall Street Journal* (9 November 1993), B1, B7.

6 For an example of descriptive research, see Slater, S.E. and Narver, J.C., 'Does Competitive Environment Moderate the Market Orientation-Performance Relationship?', *Journal of Marketing* 58 (January 1994), 46–55.

7 'Coupon Use Low Among Young, Working Women', *Marketing News* (10 April 1987), 24.

8 'Eating Behaviour Trends Revealed in Pillsbury Study', *Quirk's Marketing Research Review* (June–July 1988), 14–15, 39, 44.

9 Glenn, N.D., *Cohort Analysis* (Beverly Hills: Sage Publications, 1981). For another application see Rentz, J.O. and Reynolds, F.D., 'Forecasting the Effects of an Ageing Population on Product Consumption: An Age-Period-Cohort Framework', *Journal of Marketing Research* (August 1991), 355–60.

10 Rentz, J.O., Reynolds, F.D. and Stout, R.G., 'Analyzing Changing Consumption Patterns with Cohort Analysis', *Journal of Marketing Research* 20 (February 1983), 12–20.

11 For example, see Elrod, T. and Keane, M.P., 'A Factor-Analytic Probit Model for Representing the Market Structure in Panel Data', *Journal of Marketing Research* 32 (February 1995), 1–16.

12 Markus, G.B., *Analysing Panel Data* (Beverly Hills: Sage Publications, 1979). For applications of panel data, see Chintagunta, P.K., Jain, D.C., and Vilcassim, N.J., 'Investigating Heterogeneity in Brand Preferences in Logit Models for Panel Data', *Journal of Marketing Research* (November 1991), 417–28; Kahn, B.E. and Raju, J.S., 'Effects of Price Promotions on Variety-Seeking and Reinforcement Behaviour', *Marketing Science* (Fall 1991), 316–37.

13 Table 3.7 can also be viewed as a transition matrix. It depicts the brand-buying changes from period to period. Knowing the proportion of consumers who switch allows for early prediction of the ultimate success of a new product or change in market strategy. See Sudman, S. and Ferber, R., *Consumer Panels* (Chicago: American Marketing Association, 1979), pp. 19–27.

14 Johnston, M.W., Parasuraman, A., Futrell, C.M., and Black, W.C., 'A Longitudinal Assessment of the Impact of Selected Organizational Influences on Salespeople's Organizational Commitment during Early Employment', *Journal of Marketing Research* (August 1990), 333–44.

15 Sudman, S. and Ferber, R., 'A Comparison of Alternative Procedures for Collecting Consumer Expenditure Data for Frequently Purchased Products', and Wright, R.A., Beisel, R.H., Oliver, J.D. and Gerzowski, M.C., 'The Use of a Multiple Entry Diary in a Panel Study on Health Care', both in Ferber, R. (ed.), *Readings in Survey Research* (Chicago: American Marketing Association, 1978), pp. 487–502 and 503–12; Wind, Y. and Lemer, D., 'On the Measurement of Purchase Data: Surveys Versus Purchase Diaries', *Journal of Marketing Research* 16 (February 1979), 39–47; and McKenzie, J., 'The Accuracy of Telephone Call Data by Diary Methods', *Journal of Marketing Research* 20 (November 1983), 417–27.

16 Sudman, S. and Ferber, R., *Consumer Panels* (Chicago: American Marketing Association, 1979), pp. 19–27. See also

Wernerfelt, B. 'Brand Loyalty and Market Equilibrium', *Marketing Science* (Summer 1991), 229–45.
17 Winer, R.S,. 'Attrition Bias in Econometric Models Estimated with Panel Data', *Journal of Marketing Research* 20 (May 1983), 177–86.
18 Motes, W.H., 'How to Solve Common Problems in Longitudinal Studies', *Marketing News* (6 January 1984), 3.
19 Cox, K.K. and Enis, B.M., *Experimentation for Marketing Decisions* (Scranton, PA: International Textbook, 1969), p. 5.
20 For an application of causal research see Unnava, R.H., Bumkrant, R.E. and Erevelles, S., 'Effects of Presentation Order and Communication Modality on Recall and Attitude', *Journal of Consumer Research* (21 December 1994), 481–90.
21 Naples, M.J. and Wulfsberg, R.M., 'The Bottom Line: Does Industrial Advertising Sell?', *Journal of Advertising Research*, (August–September 1987), RC4–RC16.
22 Cooper, P.J., Diamond, I. and High, S., 'Choosing and Using Contraceptives: Integrating Qualitative and Quantitative Research Methods in Family Planning', *Journal of the Market Research Society* 35 (October 1993), 325–40.
23 Brock, S., Lipson, S. and Levitt, R., 'Trends in Marketing Research and Development at Citicorp/Citibank', *Marketing Research: A Magazine of Management and Applications* 1(4) (December 1989), 3–8.
24 *Marketing News* (10 April 1987), 3.
25 Assael, H. and Keon, J., 'Non-sampling vs. Sampling Errors in Survey Research', *Journal of Marketing* 46 (Spring 1982), 114–23.
26 Artzt, E., 'Winning in Japan: Keys to Global Success', *Business Quarterly* (Winter 1989). Copyright 1989 by Business Quarterly. Reprinted with permission of Business Quarterly, published by the Westem Business School, The University of Westem Ontario, London, Canada.
27 Leung, J.W.K. and Lai, K.K., 'A Structured Methodology to Build Discrete-event Simulation Models', *Asia Pacific Journal of Operations Research* 14(1) (May 1997), 19–37; Malhotra, N.K., 'An Approach to the Measurement of Consumer Preferences Using Limited Information', *Journal of Marketing Research* 23 (February 1986), 33–40; Malhotra, N.K., 'Analyzing marketing research data with incomplete information on the dependent variable', *Journal of Marketing Research* 24 (February 1987), 74–84.

Chapter 4

Secondary data collection and analysis

Examination of secondary data is vital to the success of problem definition, sample planning and collection of primary data

OBJECTIVES

After reading this chapter, the student should be able to:

1 define the nature and scope of secondary data and distinguish secondary data from primary data;
2 analyse the advantages and disadvantages of secondary data and their uses in the various steps of the marketing research process;
3 evaluate secondary data using the criteria of: specifications, error, currency, objectives, nature and dependability;
4 describe, in detail, the different sources of secondary data including internal sources and external sources in the form of published materials, and syndicated services;
5 discuss in detail the syndicated sources of secondary data including household and consumer data obtained via surveys, mail diary panels, and electronic scanner services as well as institutional data related to retailers, wholesalers, and industrial or service firms;
6 explain the need to use multiple sources of secondary data and describe single-source data;
7 identify and evaluate the sources of secondary data useful in international marketing research;
8 understand the ethical issues involved in the use of secondary data.

OVERVIEW

Analysis of secondary data helps define the marketing research problem and develop an approach. In addition, before the research design for collecting primary data is formulated, the researcher should locate and analyse relevant secondary data. Secondary data can help in sample designs and in the details of primary research methods. In some projects, research may be largely confined to the analysis of secondary data because some routine problems may be addressed based only on secondary data. In addition, given the huge explosion of secondary data sources available, sufficient data may be accessed to solve a particular marketing research problem.

This chapter discusses the distinction between primary and secondary data. The advantages and disadvantages of secondary data are considered, and criteria for evaluating secondary data are presented, along with a classification of secondary data. Internal secondary data are described, and major sources of external secondary data – such as published materials, on-line and off-line databases, and syndicated services – are also discussed The sources of secondary data useful in international marketing research are discussed. Several ethical issues that arise in the use of secondary data are identified.

We begin by citing several examples to give you a flavour of secondary data. The first two examples describe studies that a variety of marketers may find of use in their own right and as a basis for tailored primary data collection. The third example shows how secondary data may be used in its own right as part of a geodemographic information system.

EXAMPLE

Generation Next: Keeping track of youth style[1]

The cosy certainties of the 1970s and the 1980s, when you could count on young people buying into everything from glam rock to new romanticism, have given way to a supermarket of style of 'pick and mix' from an infinitely diverse cultural shopping list. Today's youth are doing their own thing, they write their own rules: to listen to Bach one day and Jungle the next, to dress flower power at one party and Calvin Klein at another.

One attempt to keep track with the subtleties of youth lifestyles is through a panel named ROAR (Right of Admission Reserved) run by RSGB (Research Surveys of Great Britain). ROAR was commissioned by a consortium of media companies including Channel 4, The Guardian, Emap, KissFM, ad agency BMP and Carlton Screen Advertising. It is an in-depth study of the lifestyles of over 1000 15- to 24-year-olds that began in 1995 'to provide marketers with the best of both qualitative and quantitative worlds'.

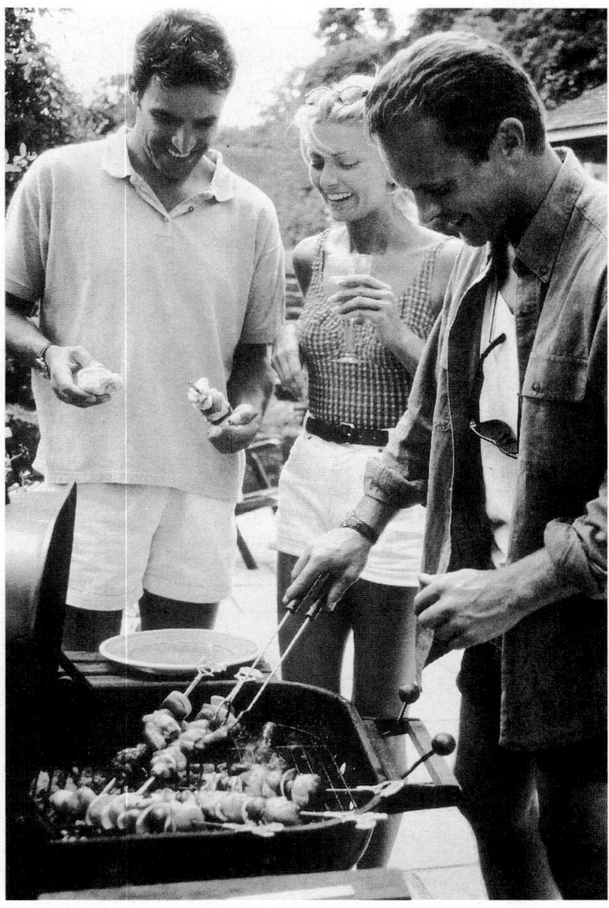

The ROAR panel is an in-depth study of the lifestyles of over 1000 15- to 24-year-olds. It is positioned as a giant club for the 90s, whose members are feted as the 'spokespeople for their generation'.
Tony Stone

ROAR's panel is positioned as a giant club for the 1990s, whose members are feted as the 'spokespeople for their generation' and kept involved through newsletters and competitions as well as their input into research studies. The study releases findings four times a year; clients can also request bespoke data. All marketers have to deal in percentages and figures. The scale of ROAR provides these statistics, but the qualitative focus groups also mean that the ambiguities can be fleshed out. ■

EXAMPLE

Reaching the pink pound[2]

Describe your dream consumer. If it is something like 'trend setting, affluent with no dependants and likely to spend significant proportions of disposable income on travel, fashion and entertainment', then the chances are you have a strong potential market within the gay community. What's more, those characteristics, identified in the recent report 'In the Pink?' from marketing consultants Grey Matter, are backed up by the cash to make them count. Various estimates put the value of the gay market between £6 bn and £8 bn. In a 1995 readership survey conducted by *Gay Times*, it was found that the average gay household brought in £36,000, which was considerably more than the typical straight family unit. The survey also found that 27 per cent had a college/university education compared with 9 per cent of the general population, 90 per cent had no dependants, employment levels and pension ownership was higher than the national average, 90 per cent eat out regularly and 79 per cent take two or more holidays a year.

Gay consumers have diverse characteristics. Being gay may influence their purchasing situations, but it does not mean that gay consumers are the same. Although gays cannot be regarded as a community of consumers, they can represent their community interest through their spending power. In other words, they may not all buy the same products but they can and will boycott a company they regard as exploitative, hypocritical or insensitive. ■

EXAMPLE

Making data go further

In the Netherlands, the use of Geodemographic Information Systems (GIS) is very sophisticated due to the range of data available from official sources such as utilities and the post office. Centre Parcs, the chain of holiday villages owned by Scottish and Newcastle, used a GIS to target potential visitors to its new Dutch centre.

Nicole Kessels, Centre Parcs' direct marketing manager (Netherlands) says: 'a segmentation system linked to our own database gives us a valuable insight into who our customers are, how they behave and where we can find potential new customers'. ■

PRIMARY VERSUS SECONDARY DATA

Primary data
Data originated by the researcher specifically to address the research problem.

Primary data are originated by a researcher for the specific purpose of addressing the problem at hand. The collection of primary data involves all six steps of the marketing research process (Chapter 1). Obtaining primary data can be expensive and time consuming.

Table 4.1 A comparison of primary and secondary data

Collection	*Primary data*	*Secondary data*
Purpose	For the problem at hand	For other problems
Process	Individually tailored	Rapid and relatively simple
Cost	High	Relatively low
Time	Long	Short

Secondary data
Data collected for some purpose other than the problem at hand.

Secondary data are data that have already been collected for purposes other than the problem at hand. The data may be seen as 'second hand', considering that the data have been generated in older projects for use on a new project. These data can generally be located quickly and inexpensively. The differences between primary and secondary data are summarised in Table 4.1. As compared with primary data, secondary data are collected rapidly and easily, at a relatively low cost, and in a short time. These differences between primary and secondary data lead to some distinct advantages and uses of secondary data.

ADVANTAGES AND USES OF SECONDARY DATA

As can be seen from the foregoing discussion, secondary data offer several advantages over primary data. Secondary data are easily accessible, relatively inexpensive and quickly obtained. Some secondary data, such as those provided by the National Censuses, are available on topics where it would not be feasible for a firm to collect primary data. Although it is rare for secondary data to provide all the answers to a non-routine research problem, such data can be useful in a variety of ways. Secondary data can help you:

1 Diagnose the research problem
2 Develop an approach to the problem
3 Develop a sampling plan
4 Formulate an appropriate research design (for example, by identifying the key variables to measure or understand)
5 Answer certain research questions and test some hypotheses
6 Interpret primary data with more insight
7 Validate qualitative research findings.

Given these advantages and uses of secondary data, we state the following general rule:

> *Examination of available secondary data is a prerequisite to the collection of primary data. Start with secondary data. Proceed to primary data only when the secondary data sources have been exhausted or yield marginal returns.*

There are rich dividends to be gained by following this rule. The following example illustrates the need to analyse internal secondary data, which gives focus to the collection and analysis of external secondary data and subsequent primary data collection.

EXAMPLE

External drive[3]

Databases have become something of an obsession with many marketers. They are collecting all kinds of information on their customers, sorting it and analysing it. The primary purpose of loyalty schemes might be to stop customers being nabbed by rivals, but their secondary aim is to monitor who they are and what they buy. With so many companies turning to database marketing, their reliance on outside sources of data should decrease considerably. After all, if all the information you require is at your fingertips, why look elsewhere for information?

In fact, the external data suppliers are booming as a result of the evolution of database marketing. However, why would companies that have spent so much time gathering their own data, add to the expense by buying more information from outside sources? Sean Flanagan, of Data by Design, says it is because marketers cannot get all the answers they need from in-house data.

'Companies that wish to enhance their marketing relationships with customers need to know not only when and what their customers buy from them and how much they spend, but why they bought and what stimulated them to do so'. ■

This example shows that analysis of secondary data held in databases can provide valuable insights, but in many instances, they do not reveal sufficient detail and so lay the foundation for conducting quantitative or qualitative research. The researcher should be cautious in using secondary data, however, because they have some limitations and disadvantages.

DISADVANTAGES OF SECONDARY DATA

Because secondary data have been collected for purposes other than the problem at hand, their usefulness to the current problem may be limited in several important ways, including relevance and accuracy. The objectives, nature and methods used to collect the secondary data may not be appropriate to the present situation. Also, secondary data may be lacking in accuracy or may not be completely current or dependable. Before using secondary data, it is important to evaluate them on these factors.[4] These factors are discussed in more detail in the following section.

CRITERIA FOR EVALUATING SECONDARY DATA

The quality of secondary data should be routinely evaluated, using the criteria of Table 4.2 discussed in the following sections.[5]

Specifications: research design used to collect the data

The specifications or the research design used to collect the data should be critically examined to identify possible sources of bias. Such methodological considerations include size and nature of the sample, response rate and quality, questionnaire design and administration, procedures used for fieldwork, and data analysis and reporting procedures. These checks provide information on the reliability and validity of the data and help determine whether they can be generalised to the problem at hand. The reliability and validity can be further ascertained by an examination of the error, currency, objectives, nature and dependability associated with the secondary data.

Table 4.2 Criteria for evaluating secondary data

Criteria	*Issues*	*Remarks*
Specifications and research design	■ Data collection method ■ Response rate ■ Population definition ■ Sampling method ■ Sample size ■ Questionnaire design ■ Fieldwork ■ Data analysis	Data should be reliable, valid and generalisable to the problem at hand.
Error and accuracy	Examine errors in ■ Approach ■ Research design ■ Sampling ■ Data collection ■ Data analysis ■ Reporting	Assess accuracy by comparing data from different sources.
Currency	Time lag between collection and publication. Frequency of updates	Census data are periodically updated by syndicated firms.
Objective	Why were the data collected?	The objective will determine the relevance of data.
Nature	■ Definition of key variables ■ Units of measurement ■ Categories used ■ Relationships examined	Reconfigure the data to increase their usefulness, if possible.
Dependability	Source: ■ Expertise ■ Credibility ■ Reputation ■ Trustworthiness	Preference should be afforded to an original rather than an acquired source.

Error: accuracy of the data

The researcher must determine whether the data are accurate enough for the purposes of the present study. Secondary data can have a number of sources of error or inaccuracy, including errors in the approach, research design, sampling, data collection, analysis, and reporting stages of the project. Moreover, it is difficult to evaluate the accuracy of secondary data because the researcher did not participate in the research. One approach is to find multiple sources of data if possible, and compare them using standard statistical procedures.

EXAMPLE

Number crunch[6]

In December 1997, the Audit Bureau of Circulations (ABC) met UK newspaper publishers and major media buyers from the Institute of Practitioners in Advertising. The meeting aimed to thrash out a formula that could restore ABC's credibility as a trading currency.

Most observers agreed that the ABC's troubles were a direct result of squabbling between media owners. As circulations have continued to slide, the press barons have fought to hold on to their market share through price cuts, promotions and enhanced editorial packages. This has introduced an unprecedented volatility into their sales figures. Not content with trumpeting their own gains, some companies have sought to show up the deficiencies in their rivals' sales figures.

Figures under fire

The argument is best understood through a straightforward example of what is at stake. Let us take the October 1997 ABC figure for *The Times*, which was 814,899. That figure was a monthly circulation average which, prior to the recent dispute, would have been the only official benchmark that agencies used as a negotiating point with press owners, (though they turn to data from the National Readership Survey and the Target Group Index to argue their case). At the heart of the dispute has been how that monthly figure is comprised. For example, were all the issues sold at the full price or were some given away cheaply as part of a subscription or promotional offer? Were any sold or given in bulk to an airliner or retailer, and if so how many? What about papers sold to Eire or Spain? Were they included in the total and if so how could that be justified as a piece of credible advertising data?

Another hot issue was the reliability of the monthly figure. Advertisers were dissatisfied with a number that they believe fails to reflect the reality of what they were buying. Director of press buying at The Media Centre, Tim Armes says, 'we'd like to know what each paper sells daily and we'd like to know week to week fluctuations. The papers all boast about Saturday but keep quiet about Tuesday and Thursday. If one day is dramatically higher than the average, you don't have to be a brain surgeon to realise the others are lower'. ■

As this example indicates, the accuracy of secondary data can vary, particularly if they relate to phenomena that are subject to change. Moreover, data obtained from different sources may not agree. In these cases, the researcher should verify the accuracy of secondary data by conducting pilot studies or by other appropriate methods. Often, by exercising creativity this can be done without much expense or effort.

Currency: when the data were collected

Secondary data may not be current and the time lag between data collection and publication may be long, as is the case with much census data. Moreover, the data may not be updated frequently enough for the purpose of the problem at hand. Marketing research requires current data; therefore, the value of secondary data is diminished, as they become dated. For instance, although the Census of Population data are comprehensive, they may not be applicable to major cities in which the population has changed rapidly during the last two years. Likewise, in the GlobalCash project, the lists of the largest companies in Europe had to be updated to reflect changes that take place in the two years between each study.

Objective: the purpose for which the data were collected

Data are invariably collected with some objective in mind, and a fundamental question to ask is why the data were collected in the first place. The objective for collecting data will ultimately determine the purpose for which that information is relevant and useful. Data collected with a specific objective in mind may not be appropriate in another situation. As explained in more detail later in the chapter, scanner volume tracking data are collected with the objective of examining aggregate movement of brands, including shifts in market shares. Such data on sales of orange juice, for example, would be of limited value in a study aimed at understanding how households select specific brands.

Nature: the content of the data

The nature, or content, of the data should be examined with special attention to the definition of key variables, the units of measurement, categories used and the relationships examined. If the key variables have not been defined or are defined in a manner inconsistent with the researcher's definition, then the usefulness of the data is limited. Consider, for example, secondary data on consumer preferences for TV programmes. To use this information, it is important to know how preference for programmes was defined. Was it defined in terms of the programme watched most often, the one considered most needed, most enjoyable, most informative, or the program of greatest service to the community?

Likewise, secondary data may be measured in units that may not be appropriate for the current problem. For example, income may be measured by individual, family, household or spending unit and could be gross or net after taxes and deductions. Income may be classified into categories that are different from research needs. If the researcher is interested in high-income consumers with gross annual household incomes of over €120,000, secondary data with income categories of less than €20,000, €20,001–€50,000, €50,001–€75,000 and more than €75,000 will not be of use. Determining the measurement of variables such as income may be a complex task, requiring the wording of the definition of income to be precise. Finally, the relationships examined should be taken into account in evaluating the nature of data. If, for example, actual behaviour is of interest, then data inferring behaviour from self-reported attitudinal information may have limited usefulness. Sometimes it is possible to reconfigure the available data – for example, to convert the units of measurement – so that the resulting data are more useful to the problem at hand.

Dependability: how dependable are the data?

An overall indication of the dependability of data may be obtained by examining the expertise, credibility, reputation and trustworthiness of the source. This information can be obtained by checking with others who have used the information provided by the source. Data published to promote sales, to advance specific interests, or to carry on propaganda should be viewed with suspicion. The same may be said of data published anonymously or in a form that attempts to hide the details of the data collection research design and process. It is also pertinent to examine whether the secondary data came from an original source, one that generated the data, or an acquired source, one that procured the data from an original source. Generally, secondary data should be secured from an original rather than an acquired source. There are at least two reasons for this rule. First, an original source is the one that specifies the details of the data collection research design, and second, an original source is likely to be more accurate and complete than a secondary source.

CLASSIFICATION OF SECONDARY DATA

Internal data
Data available within the organisation for whom the research is being conducted.

Figure 4.1 presents a classification of secondary data. Secondary data may be classified as either internal or external. **Internal data** are those generated within the organisation for which the research is being conducted. This information may be available in a ready-to-use format, such as information routinely supplied by the management decision support system. On the other hand, these data may exist within the organisation but may require considerable processing before they are useful to the researcher. For example, a variety of information

database program. This information can then be analysed in terms of a customer's activity over the life of the business relationship. A profile of heavy versus low users, signs of change in the usage relationships, or significant 'customer life cycle' events such as anniversaries can be identified and acted upon. These databases provide the essential tool needed to nurture, expand, and protect the customer relationship.[9] Given the huge growth in this form of data capture, a major part of Chapter 5 is devoted to this very important secondary data source.

PUBLISHED EXTERNAL SECONDARY SOURCES

Sources of published external secondary data include local authorities, regional and national governments, the EC, non-profit organisations (e.g. Chambers of Commerce), trade associations and professional organisations, commercial publishers, investment brokerage firms, and professional marketing research firms.[10] In fact, such a quantity of data are available that the researcher can be overwhelmed. Therefore, it is important to classify published sources (see Figure 4.2). Published external sources may be broadly classified as general business data or government data. General business sources comprise guides, directories, indexes and statistical data. Government sources may be broadly categorised as census data and other publications. These data types are discussed further with specific sources used as examples.

General business data

Businesses publish a lot of information in the form of books, periodicals, journals, newspapers, magazines, reports and trade literature. This information can be located by using guides, directories and indexes. Sources are also available to identify statistical data.

Guides. Guides are an excellent source of standard or recurring information. A guide may help identify other important sources of directories, trade associations and trade publications. Guides are one of the first sources a researcher should consult. The following example illustrates the use of the Electronic Buyer's Guide.

EXAMPLE

Keeping up to data[11]

The market for business information is growing and the shift towards electronic sources continues. According to market information specialist KeyNote, the business information market will grow by 44.5 per cent by 2000 and the electronic information sector will expand by 50.2 per cent. The choice of new media for directory publishers includes off-line methods, such as CD-ROM, and on-line, such as the Internet. In addition, while on-line systems account for most information sales, the use of CDs is growing faster.

Access to up-to-date information is a big attraction. There is a perception that on-screen information is more up-to-date than a book. However, many CD-ROM directories are not updated any more frequently than their paper equivalents. So, while information on the Internet can be kept up-to-date, CD-ROMS come into their own when storing large amounts of information.

Miller Freeman launched the Electronic Buyer's Guide in 1996 and by October 1997 it was on the Internet. There is some information available free of charge; if more information is wanted then there are charges. Alternatively, anyone who buys the guide on CD-ROM is given a password that gives them free access to the Internet directory. ■

Directories. Directories are helpful for identifying individuals or organisations that collect specific data. An example of a directory that you can examine on the Internet is Pronet's 'Global Interactive Business Directory'. This is a multi-lingual on-line link to the products, services and capabilities of over 150,000 companies organised by country and business directory. Another example is Europages, a reference business directory in Europe that classifies 500,000 companies in 30 European countries. Again, this can be accessed through the Internet and is available in English, French, German, Italian and Spanish versions.

Indexes. It is possible to locate information on a particular topic in several different publications by using an index and abstracts. Indexes and abstracts, therefore, can increase the efficiency of the search process. Several indexes and abstracts are available for both academic and business sources. Examples of newspaper indexes include the *Financial Times Index*, *Le Monde Index*, and the *British Newspaper Index*. These indexes allow researchers to identify sources of particular topics, industries and individuals.

An example of a marketing index is the *Marketing Surveys Index* published by Euromonitor. This is a most comprehensive and up-to-date directory of business research on European and world markets. The Index contains details of published research reports, a brief summary of its contents, a keyword index to the markets and products covered, and bibliographic details of the report.

A particularly useful abstract for marketing researchers is the *Market Research Abstracts* published by the Market Research Society in Britain. Major European and American Journals that relate to marketing research are reviewed and an abstract of each article is presented. The abstract is published twice a year. It is divided into sections that cover: survey techniques; statistics, models and forecasting; attitude and behaviour research; psychographics, personality and social psychology; advertising and media research; applications of research; industrial market research; market research and general applications; and new product development. Such an abstract allows the researcher to quickly identify and evaluate the worth of journal papers that are relevant to their particular study.

Non-government statistical data. Published statistical data are of great interest to researchers. Graphic and statistical analyses can be performed on these data to draw important insights. Examples of non-governmental statistical data include trade associations such as the European Fishing Tackle Trade Association

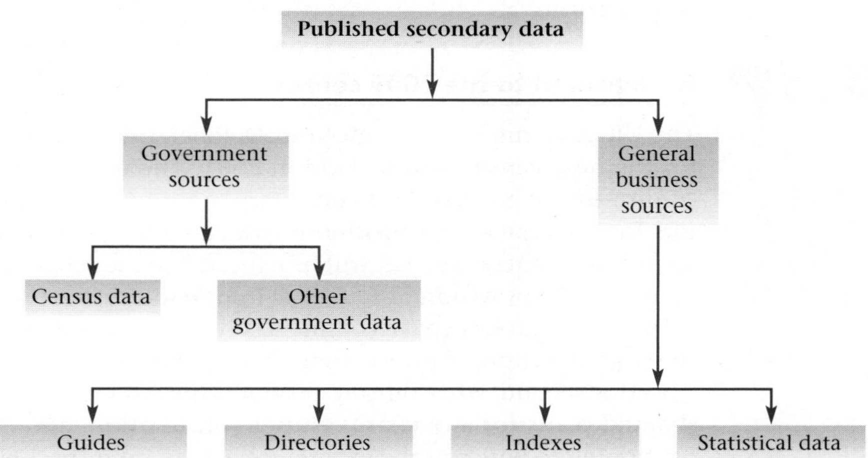

Figure 4.2
A classification of published secondary sources

(EFTTA). EFTTA collects and formats fishing tackle import and export statistics from the EC and other countries, where they are available. Another example is Euromonitor which publishes monthly market research journals covering subjects under the headings of Market Research Europe, Market Research GB, Market Research International and Retail Monitor International.

The United Nations provides an example of an organisation with a Statistics Division that provides a wide range of statistical outputs on a global basis. The Statistics Division produces printed publications of statistics and statistical methods in the fields of international merchandise trade, national accounts, demography and population, social indicators, gender, industry, energy, environment, human settlements and disability. The Division also produces general statistical compendiums including the *Statistical Yearbook* and *World Statistics Pocketbook*. Many of the Division's databases in these fields are available as electronic publications in the form of CD-ROM, diskette and magnetic tape and on the Internet.

Government sources

European governments and the EU also produce large amounts of secondary data. Each European country has its own statistical office which produces lists of the publications available (and the costs involved). Examples of national statistical offices include the Centraal Bureau voor de Statistiek Netherlands, Danmarks Statistik, the Federal Statistical Office of Germany, the French Institut National de la Statistique et des Études Economiques, and the British Office for National Statistics. All of these offices have Internet links that allow you to quickly examine the array of publications that they produce. Their publications may be divided into census data and other publications.

Census data. Most European countries produce either catalogues or newsletters that describe the array of census publications available and the plans for any forthcoming census. In Britain for example, *Census News* is a newsletter that contains the latest information about the 2001 census and previous censuses and is available four to six times a year. Census Marketing in Britain can supply unpublished data from the 1961, 1971, 1981 and 1991 censuses in the form of Small Area Statistics (SAS). SAS are available for standard census areas within England and Wales, such as Counties, Local Government Districts, London Boroughs, Wards, Civil Parishes and Enumeration Districts. Maps can also be purchased to complement the data. The following example illustrates an update on the 2001 British census.

EXAMPLE

Background to the 2001 census

The UK government announced in October 1992 that planning would proceed for the next censuses to be held in 2001. The decision follows a review which confirmed there would be a continuing need in both the public and private sectors for the type of information provided by the census and that there were no alternative sources. The UK will be expected to meet European legislative requirements for the provision of statistical information from the censuses in 2001.

Two major projects have commenced to consider the production of output and the dissemination of information. The first is concerned with policy and strategy, the second with output production and delivery. An essential part of shaping plans for any census is user consultation, and the Census Offices are continuing to build on the experience gained from the 1991 census by involving users in an active role for planning the 2001 operation. All census users are continuing to play an active and major role in the consultation process.

The 2001 census programme sets strategic assumptions from which the consideration of dissemination can begin. They currently are:

- Standard statistics for small and local populations should be available, with comparability between areas and over time.
- Customised output should be available at an early stage.
- Output should be in a form suitable for updating from other sources between censuses.
- The Census Offices should produce more customised products while preventing disclosure of information about identifiable individuals. ■

Census data can be kept in electronic formats allowing it to be analysed and presented in a variety of formats at a detailed geographical level. Given the long periods between national censuses and the amount of change that can occur in this period, other data sources are used to maintain an up-to-date picture of specific regions.

EXAMPLE

Netherlands demographic and boundary data

The Data Consultancy offers municipality and postcode data for the Netherlands. Visualising the relationship between Dutch 'depots' and clients, undertaking market penetration and demographic analyses for the Netherlands are now all possible. The range includes four-digit postcode centroids for geocoding, municipality and census tract boundaries with associated population for demographic analysis and one-to-four-digit postcode boundaries. Base mapping is available separately in the Automobile Association Automaps Europe dataset, which provides full coverage of the whole of Europe and is regularly updated by the AA. ■

Each European country has its own statistical office which produces lists of their available publications. The Institut National de la Statisique et des Études Economiques is the French national statistics office

Tony Stone

As well as general population censuses, national statistical offices produce an array of industrial censuses. These may include Industrial Production, Housing, Construction, Agriculture, Restaurants and Hotels, and Financial Services.

Other government publications. In addition to the census, national statistical offices collect and publish a great deal of statistical data. Examining the Department of Statistics and Research in Cyprus as an example, major industrial categories such as Agriculture, Construction, Retailing and Tourism are classified, with a whole array of available statistics. More generally, Demographic, Health, Household Income and Expenditure and Labour statistical reports are also available.

Examples of reports from the British Office for National Statistics include *Family Spending* and *Economic Trends*. *Family Spending* provides a snapshot of household spending in the UK, explaining in detail how consumers spend their money. Expenditure patterns are broken down by age, economic status, income and geography. *Economic Trends* provides monthly macroeconomic statistics of economic trends which include key data such as national accounts, gross domestic product, disposable income, balance of payments, trade in goods, prices, labour market information, industrial output, consumers sales credit and interest rates, as well as extensive commentary to put all this information into context.

In the EC, statistics are collected and published by the Statistical Office of the European Community (SOEC) in a series called Eurostat.[12] Tables normally contain figures for individual member states of the EU plus totals for all countries. Eurostat divides its publications into themes which are:

- *Theme 1* – General statistics
- *Theme 2* – Economy and finance
- *Theme 3* – Population and social conditions
- *Theme 4* – Energy and industry
- *Theme 5* – Agriculture, forestry and fisheries
- *Theme 6* – External trade
- *Theme 7* – Distributive trades, services and transport
- *Theme 8* – Environment
- *Theme 9* – Research and development

It also produces general titles which include: *Eurostat Yearbook* (annual); *Basic Statistics* (annual); *Europe in Figures* (annual); *Key Figures* (monthly) and *Eurostatistics* (monthly).

COMPUTERISED DATABASES

Most published information is also available in the form of computerised databases. Computerised databases contain information that has been made available in computer readable form for electronic distribution. In the 1980s and 1990s, the number of databases, as well as the vendors providing these services, has grown enormously. Computerised databases offer a number of advantages over printed data including:[13]

1 The data are current and up-to-date, as publishers and data compilers are now using computers as the primary production technology.
2 The search process is more comprehensive, quicker and simpler. On-line vendors provide ready access to hundreds of databases. Moreover, this information can be accessed instantaneously, and the search process is simplified as the vendors provide uniform search protocols and commands for accessing the database.

3 The cost of accessing these is relatively low, because of the accuracy of searching for the right data, and the speed of location and transfer of data.
4 It is convenient to access these data using a personal computer fitted with an appropriate communication device, such as a modem or a communication network.

While computerised database information can be helpful, it is vast and can be confusing. Thus a classification of computerised databases is helpful.

Classification of computerised databases

Computerised databases may be classified as on-line, Internet, or off-line as shown in Figure 4.3. On-line databases consist of a central data bank that is accessed with a computer (or dumb terminal) via a telecommunications network. Internet databases can be accessed, searched and analysed on the Internet. It is also possible to download data from the Internet and store it in the computer or an auxiliary storage device.[14] Off-line databases make the information available on diskettes and CD-ROM disks. Thus, off-line databases can be accessed at the user's location without the use of an external telecommunications network.[15]

On-line databases
Databases, stored in computers, that require a telecommunications network to access.

Internet databases
Internet databases can be accessed, searched and analysed on the Internet. It is also possible to download data from the Internet and store it on the computer or an auxiliary device.

Off-line databases
Databases that are available on diskette or CD-ROM.

On-line, Internet and **off-line databases** may be further classified as bibliographic, numeric, full text, directory or special-purpose databases. **Bibliographic databases** are composed of citations to articles in journals, magazines, newspapers, marketing research studies, technical reports, government documents and the like.[16] They often provide summaries or abstracts of the material cited. The earlier example of *Market Research Abstracts* is an example of a bibliographic database. Another example is the *Aslib Index to Theses*; this bibliographic database lists UK theses at masters and doctoral level and research degrees, including abstracts.

Bibliographic databases
Databases composed of citations to articles in journals, magazines, newspapers, marketing research studies, technical reports, government documents, and the like. They often provide summaries or abstracts of the material cited.

Numeric databases contain numerical and statistical information. For example, some numeric databases provide time series data about the economy and specific industries. The earlier examples of census-based numeric databases using data over a series of censuses provide an example of a numeric database.

Numeric databases
Databases containing numerical and statistical information that may be important sources of secondary data.

Full-text databases contain the complete text of the sources of the database. Examples include: *Searchbank: European ASAP* and *FT Discovery*. *Searchbank* has over 100 full-text journals on subjects including business, economic, current affairs and new technologies. It includes a spectrum of journals from professional trade publications through to refereed academic journals. *FT Discovery* presents the *Global News* link that gives full access to the Financial Times, World Reporter, Europe Intelligence Wire and Asia Intelligence Wire. It is possible to search on specific countries, sectors and publications.

Full-text databases
Databases that contain the complete text of secondary source documents comprising the database.

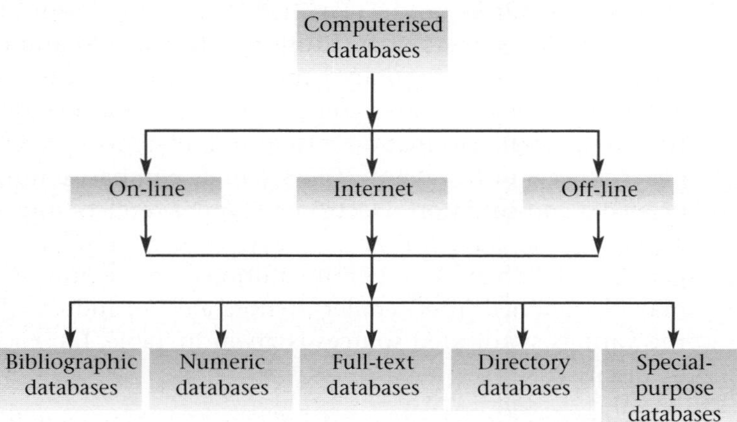

Figure 4.3
A classification of computerised databases

Directory databases Databases that provide information on individuals, organisations and services.

Directory databases provide information on individuals, organisations and services. *Europe Online 'The European Gateway to the Internet'* is an example of a directory that has channels based upon EU community activities, country channels and thematic channels such as Arts and Culture, Business and Finance, and Sport. Another example worth examining is the *ESOMAR* directory which provides details of member organisations throughout the world as well as many other publications of value to marketing researchers based in Europe.

Special-purpose databases Databases that contain information of a specific nature, e.g. data on a specialised industry.

Finally, there are **special-purpose databases**. For example, the Profit Impact of Market Strategies (PIMS) database is an ongoing database of research and analysis on business strategy compiled by the Strategic Planning Institute in Cambridge, Massachusetts. This database comprises more than 250 companies, which provide data on over 2000 businesses. Virtually all libraries of major universities maintain special-purpose databases of research activities that reflect the distinct specialisms of that university. Beyond the internally generated, special-purpose databases, university libraries and reference libraries maintain computerised databases with instructions relating to what may be accessed and how they may be accessed. Another library source worth examining for computerised sources is the European Commissions 'Libraries' site on the Internet. The site which is partially multilingual, is distributed by the EUROPA server. It provides access to three Web pages free of charge: one presents the services that the Commission's Main Library provides, the second gives access to the ECLAS catalogue common to all the institution's libraries, and the third opens the door to EUROLIB, the association of the Union's institutional and related libraries.

SYNDICATED SOURCES OF SECONDARY DATA

Syndicated service (sources) Information services offered by marketing research organisations that provide information from a common database to different firms that subscribe to their services.

In addition to published data or data available in the form of computerised databases, syndicated sources constitute the other major source of external secondary data. **Syndicated sources**, also referred to as syndicated services, are companies that collect and sell common pools of data designed to serve information needs shared by a number of clients (see Chapter 1). These data are not collected for the purpose of marketing research problems, but the data and reports supplied to client companies can be personalised to fit specific needs. For example, reports could be organised based on the clients' sales territories or product lines. Using syndicated services is frequently less expensive than collecting primary data. Figure 4.4 presents a classification of syndicated sources. Syndicated sources can be classified based on the unit of measurement (households and consumers or institutions). Household and consumer data may be obtained from surveys, diary panels or electronic scanner services. Information obtained through surveys consists of values and lifestyles, advertising evaluation, or general information related to preferences, purchase, consumption and other aspects of behaviour. Diary panels emphasise information on purchases or media consumption. Electronic scanner services might provide scanner data only, scanner data linked to diary panels, or scanner data linked to diary panels and (cable) TV. When institutions are the unit of measurement, the data may be obtained from retailers, wholesalers or industrial firms. An overview of the various syndicated sources is given in Table 4.3. Each of these sources will be discussed.

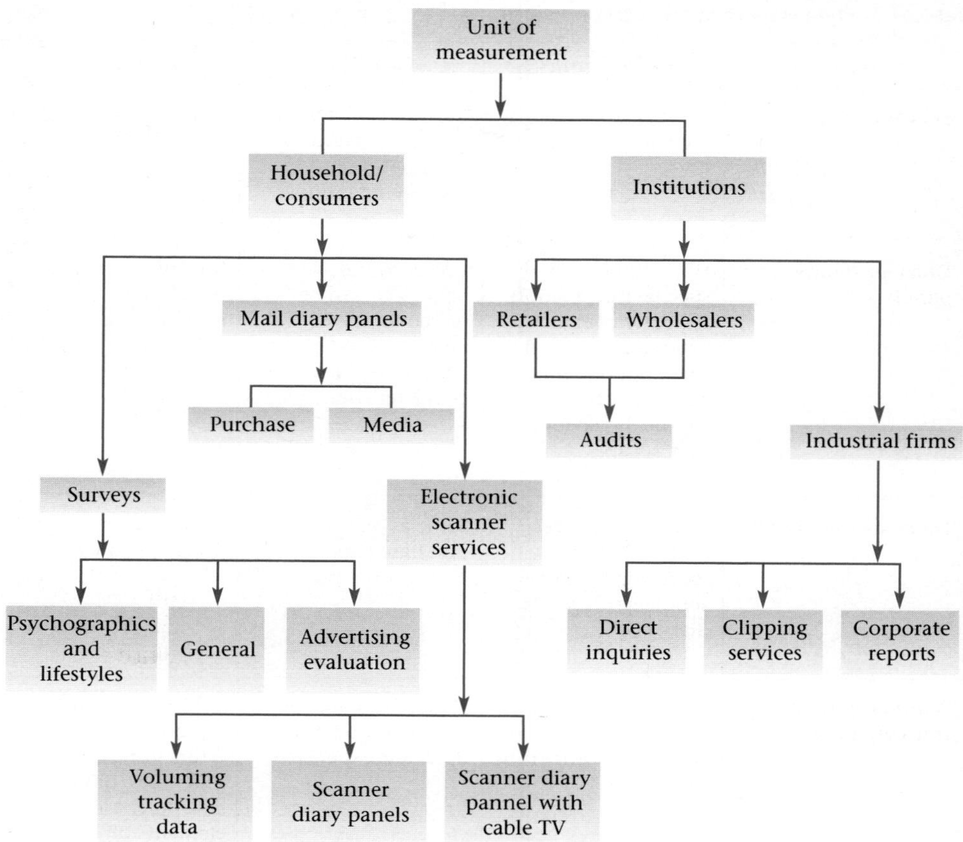

Figure 4.4
A classification of syndicated services

Surveys
Interviews with a large number of people using a questionnaire.

Omnibus survey
A distinctive form of survey that serves the needs of a syndicated group. The omnibus survey targets particular types of respondents such as geographic location, e.g. Luxembourg residents, or consumers of particular types of products, e.g. business air travellers. With that target group of respondents, a core set of questions can be asked with other questions added as syndicate members wish.

Psychographics
Quantified profiles of individuals based upon lifestyle characteristics.

Lifestyles
Distinctive patterns of living described by the activities people engage in, the interests they have, and the opinions they hold of themselves and the world around them.

SYNDICATED DATA FROM HOUSEHOLDS

Surveys and 'omnibus' surveys. Various syndicated services regularly conduct surveys and 'omnibus' surveys. In general, these surveys involve interviews with a large number of respondents using a pre-designed questionnaire. The distinction of the omnibus survey is that it targets particular types of respondents such as geographic location, e.g. Luxembourg residents, or consumers of particular types of products, e.g. business air travellers. With that target group of respondents, a core set of questions can be asked with other questions added as syndicate members wish. Other syndicate members can 'jump on the omnibus' and buy the answers to all the questionnaire responses or to specific questions of their choice. Surveys and omnibus surveys may be broadly classified based on their content as psychographics and lifestyles, advertising evaluation, or general surveys.

Psychographics and lifestyles. Psychographics refer to the psychological profiles of individuals and to psychologically based measures of lifestyle. Lifestyles refer to the distinctive modes of living of a society or some of its segments. Together, these measures are generally referred to as activities, interest and opinions.

Advertising evaluation. The purpose of advertising evaluation surveys is to assess the effectiveness of advertising using print and broadcast media. Television commercials are evaluated using either the recruited audience method or the in-home viewing method. In the former method, respondents are recruited and brought to a central viewing facility, such as a theatre or mobile viewing

Table 4.3 Overview of syndicated services

Type	*Characteristics*	*Advantages*	*Disadvantages*	*Uses*
Surveys	Surveys conducted at regular intervals	Most flexible way of obtaining data; information on underlying motives	Interviewer errors; respondent errors	Market segmentation, advertising theme selection and advertising effectiveness
Diary purchase panels	Households provide specific information regularly over an extended period of time; respondents asked to record specific behaviour as it occurs	Recorded purchase behaviour can be linked to the demographic/ psychographic characteristics	Lack of representativeness; response bias; maturation	Forecasting sales, market share and trends; establishing consumer profiles, brand loyalty and switching; evaluating test markets, advertising and distribution
Diary media panels	Electronic devices automatically recording behaviour, supplemented by a diary	Same as diary purchase panel	Same as diary purchase panel	Establishing advertising rates; selecting media programme or air time, establishing viewer profiles
Scanner volume tracking data	Household purchases are recorded through electronic scanners in supermarkets	Data reflect actual purchases; timely data, less expensive	Data may not be representative; errors in recording purchases; difficult to link purchases to elements of marketing mix other than price	Price tracking, modelling effectiveness of in-store modelling
Scanner diary panels with cable TV	Scanner panels of households that subscribe to cable TV	Data reflect actual purchases; sample control; ability to link panel data to household characteristics	Data may not be representative; quality of data limited	Promotional mix analyses, copy testing, new product testing, positioning.
Audit services	Verification of product movement by examining physical records or performing inventory analysis	Relatively precise information at the retail and wholesale levels	Coverage may be incomplete; matching of data on competitive activity may be difficult	Measurement of consumer sales and market share, competitive activity, analysing distribution patterns; tracking of new products
Industrial product syndicated services	Data banks on industrial establishments created through direct inquiries of companies, clipping services and corporate reports	Important source of information in industrial firms, particularly useful in initial phases of the projects	Data are lacking in terms of content, quantity and quality	Determining market potential by geographic area, defining sales territories, allocating advertising budget

laboratory. The respondents view the commercials and provide data regarding knowledge, attitudes, and preferences related to the product being advertised and the commercial itself.

In the in-home viewing method, consumers evaluate commercials at home in their normal viewing environment. New commercials can be pre-tested at the network level or in local markets. A survey of viewers is then conducted to assess the effectiveness of the commercials.

General surveys. Surveys are also conducted for a variety of other purposes, including examination of purchase and consumption behaviour. Because a variety of data can be obtained, survey data have numerous uses. They can be used for market segmentation, as with psychographic and lifestyle data, and for establishing consumer profiles. Surveys are also useful for determining product image, measurement and positioning, and conducting price perception analysis. Other notable uses include advertising theme selection and evaluation of advertising effectiveness.

Diary panels. Often, survey data can be complemented with data obtained from diary panels. Panels were discussed in Chapter 3 in the context of longitudinal research designs. Diary panels are samples of respondents who provide specified information at regular intervals over an extended period of time. These respondents may be organisations, households or individuals, although household diary panels are most common. The distinguishing feature of diary panels is that the respondents record specific behaviours as they occur, in a diary. Typically, the diary is returned to the research organisation every one to four weeks. Panel members are compensated for their participation with gifts, coupons, information or cash. Based on the content of information recorded, diary panels can be classified as diary purchase panels or diary media panels.

Diary purchase panels
A data gathering technique in which respondents record their purchases in a diary.

Diary media panels
A data gathering technique composed of samples of respondents whose television viewing behaviour is automatically recorded by electronic devices, supplementing the purchase information recorded in a diary.

Diary media panels. In diary media panels, electronic devices automatically record viewing behaviour, thus supplementing a diary. **Diary purchase panels** provide information useful for forecasting sales, estimating market shares, assessing brand loyalty and brand-switching behaviour, establishing profiles of specific user groups, measuring promotional effectiveness, and conducting controlled store tests. **Diary media panels** yield information helpful for establishing advertising rates by radio and TV networks, selecting appropriate programming, and profiling viewer or listener subgroups. Advertisers, media planners and buyers find panel information particularly useful.

Compared with sample surveys, diary panels offer certain distinct advantages.[17] Panels can provide longitudinal data (data can be obtained from the same respondents repeatedly). People who are willing to serve on panels may provide more and higher-quality data than sample respondents. In purchase diary panels, information is recorded at the time of purchase, eliminating recall errors.[18] Information recorded by electronic devices is accurate because it eliminates human errors.

The disadvantages of diary panels include lack of representativeness, maturation and response biases. They may under-represent certain groups such as minorities and those with low education levels. This problem is further compounded by refusal to respond and attrition of panel members. Over time, maturation sets in, and the panel members must be replaced (see Chapter 8). Response biases may occur, since simply being on the panel may alter behaviour. Because purchase or media data are entered by hand, recording errors are also possible (see Chapter 3).

Electronic scanner services

The following example illustrates the nature and scope of electronic scanner services as undertaken by A.C. Nielsen, who conduct consumer panel services in 18 countries around the world.

EXAMPLE

A.C. Nielsen – The business economist at work[19]

Most of A.C. Nielsen's revenue comes from selling information on *fast-moving consumer goods* (FMCG). This information is compiled from either scanner data obtained from thousands of supermarkets, pharmacists and department stores, or from a 40,000 household panel who electronically record every aspect of every goods purchase they made using that item's bar code.

They go beyond their standard forms of analysing and presenting existing data to more creative interpretations that attempt to tell the marketer something he or she does not know. Often, creativity is valued more than sophisticated econometric techniques – two examples of this are:

Inventory and sales data are available on food store retail sales, so an inventory–sales ratio can be calculated. This ratio had been increasing for several years up to 1992 when it began to shrink. Yet it is generally accepted that the size of the average new store is increasing, implying the need for additional inventories relative to sales. Coincidentally, more sophisticated inventory management techniques have become especially prevalent in food stores in recent years. Apparently, the ratio is being driven more by improved inventory management than the opening of new, larger stores. A discrete cause and effect cannot be proven, but a linkage between the ratio and better inventory control mechanisms is highly probable.

Analysis of consumer spending patterns in Asia is very difficult to do given the paucity of data available and the lack of data comparability across countries or spending components. By calculating consumer spending on food as a share of total consumer spending, and then ordering the results by per capita GDP, a relationship becomes obvious. Poorer countries spend proportionately more of their resources on food, around 50 per cent. For middle income countries, this ratio slides from around 40 to 20 per cent, and then holds steady near 20 per cent for the developed economies. The implication is that, as a country obtains a middle income status, because of this declining ratio, food sales will not grow as fast as other categories of consumer spending. ■

Although information provided by surveys and diary panels is useful, electronic scanner services are becoming increasingly popular. The role of scanned data as a foundation to developing sophisticated consumer databases is developed in Chapter 5. In this chapter we examine scanned data as a distinct source of syndicated data. **Scanner data** reflect some of the latest technological developments in the marketing research industry. **Scanner data** are collected by passing merchandise over a laser scanner that optically reads the bar-coded description (Universal Product Code, or UPC) printed on the merchandise. This code is then linked to the current price held in the computer memory and used to prepare a sales slip. Information printed on the sales slip includes descriptions as well as prices of all items purchased. Checkout scanners, now used in many retail stores, are revolutionising packaged goods marketing research.

Scanner data
Data obtained by passing merchandise over a laser scanner that reads the UPC code from the packages.

Volume tracking data
Scanner data that provide information on purchases by brand, size, price, and flavour or formulation.

Scanner diary panels
Scanner data where panel members are identified by an ID card, allowing information about each panel member's purchases to be stored with respect to the individual shopper.

Scanner diary panels with cable TV
The combination of a scanner diary panel with manipulations of the advertising that is being broadcast by cable television companies.

Three types of scanner data are available: **volume tracking data**, **scanner diary panels**, and **scanner diary panels with cable TV**. Volume tracking data provide information on purchases by brand, size, price and flavour or formulation, based on sales data collected from the checkout scanner tapes. This information is collected nationally from a sample of supermarkets with electronic scanners. In scanner diary panels, each household member is given an ID card that looks like a credit card. Panel members present the ID card at the checkout counter each time they shop. The checker keys in the ID numbers and each item of that customer's order. The information is stored by day of week and time of day.[20]

An even more advanced use of scanning, scanner diary panels with cable TV, combines diary panels with new technologies growing out of the cable TV industry. Households on these panels subscribe to one of the cable or TV systems in their market. By means of a cable TV 'split', the researcher targets different commercials into the homes of the panel members. For example, half the households may see test commercial A during the 6:00pm newscast while the other half see test commercial B. These panels allow researchers to conduct fairly controlled experiments in a relatively natural environment.[21]

Uses of scanner data. Scanner data are useful for a variety of purposes.[22] National volume tracking data can be used for tracking sales, prices and distribution; for modelling, and for analysing early warning signals. Scanner diary panels with cable TV can be used for testing new products, repositioning products, analysing promotional mix, and making advertising decisions, including budget, copy and media, and pricing. These panels provide marketing researchers with a unique controlled environment for the manipulation of marketing variables.

Advantages and disadvantages of scanner data. Scanner data have an obvious advantage over surveys and diary panels; they reflect purchasing behaviour that is not subject to interviewing, recording, memory, or expert biases. The record of purchases obtained by scanners is complete and unbiased by price sensitivity, because the panellist is not required to be overly conscious of price levels and changes. Another advantage is that in-store variables such as pricing, promotions and displays are part of the dataset. The data are also likely to be current and can be obtained quickly. Finally, scanner panels with cable TV provide a highly controlled testing environment.

A major weakness of scanner data is lack of representativeness. National volume tracking data may not be generalisable to the total population, because only large supermarkets have scanners. In addition, certain types of outlets such as food warehouses, pharmacists and mass merchandisers are excluded. Likewise, scanners have limited geographical dispersion and coverage.

The quality of scanner data may be limited by several factors. Not all products may be scanned. For example, to avoid lifting a heavy item, a clerk may use the register to ring it up. If an item does not scan on the first try, the clerk may key in the price and ignore the bar code. Sometimes a consumer purchases many flavours of the same item, but the clerk scans only one package and then rings in the number of purchases. Thus, the transaction is inaccurately recorded. With respect to scanner panels, the available technology permits the monitoring of only one TV set per household. Hence, there is a built-in bias if the household has more than one TV set. In addition, the system provides information on TV sets in use rather than actual viewing behaviour. Although scanner data provide behavioural and sales information, they do not provide information on underlying attitudes and preferences and the reasons for specific choices.

SYNDICATED DATA FROM INSTITUTIONS

Retailer and wholesaler audits

Audit
A data collection process derived from physical records or performing inventory analysis. Data are collected personally by the researcher, or by representatives of the researcher, and the data are based on counts usually of physical objects rather than people.

As Figure 4.4 shows, syndicated data are available for retailers and wholesalers as well as industrial firms. The most popular means of obtaining data from retailers and wholesalers is an audit. An **audit** is a formal examination and verification of product movement carried out by examining physical records or analysing inventory. Retailers and wholesalers who participate in the audit receive basic reports and cash payments from the audit service. Audit data focus on the products or services sold through the outlets or the characteristics of the outlets themselves.

Retail auditing for retailing information

Introduced in the USA in 1933, A.C. Nielsen pioneered food and drug indices to measure and understand the performance and dynamics of product sales. The Retail Measurement Service of A.C. Nielsen uses store audit data on product movement, market share, distribution, price and other market-sensitive information in over 80 countries across six continents. Using in-store scanning of product codes and store visits by auditors, sample and census information is gathered across food, household, health and beauty, durables, confectionery and beverage industries.

Retail audit data can be useful to consumer product firms. For example, if Colgate-Palmolive is contemplating the introduction of a new toothpaste brand, a retail audit can help determine the size of the total market and distribution of sales by type of outlet and by different regions.[23]

Wholesale audit services, the counterpart of retail audits, monitor warehouse withdrawals. Participating operators, who include supermarket chains, wholesalers and frozen-food warehouses, typically account for over 80 per cent of the volume in the area.

The uses of retail and wholesale audit data include:

1 determining the size of the total market and the distribution of sales by type of outlet, region, or city;
2 assessing brand shares and competitive activity;
3 identifying shelf space allocation and inventory problems;
4 analysing distribution problems;
5 developing sales potentials and forecasts;
6 developing and monitoring promotional allocations based on sales volume.

Audits provide relatively accurate information on the movement of many different products at the wholesale and retail levels. Furthermore, this information can be broken down by a number of important variables, such as brand, type of outlet, and size of market. Audits have limited coverage, however; not all markets or operators are included. In addition, audit information may not be timely or current, particularly compared with scanner data. Typically, there is a two-month gap between the completion of the audit cycle and the publication of reports. Another disadvantage is that, unlike scanner data, audit data cannot be linked to consumer characteristics. In fact, there may even be a problem in relating audit data to advertising expenditures and other marketing efforts. Some of these limitations are overcome in computerised audit panels.

Industry services. These provide syndicated data about industrial firms, businesses and other institutions. These data are collected by making direct inquiries, from clipping services and corporate reports. The range and sources of syndicated data available to industrial goods firms are more limited than those available to consumer goods firms. An example of this service is Dunn and Bradstreet's Market Identifiers.

Industry services information is useful for sales management decisions, including identifying prospects, defining territories, setting quotas, and measuring market potential by geographic areas. It can also aid in advertising decisions such as targeting prospects, allocating advertising budgets, selecting media, and measuring advertising effectiveness. This kind of information is useful for segmenting the market and for designing custom products and services for important segments.

Industry services represent an important source of secondary information on industrial firms. The information they provide can be valuable in the initial phases of a marketing project. They are limited in the nature, content, quantity and quality of information, however.

COMBINING INFORMATION FROM DIFFERENT SOURCES: SINGLE-SOURCE DATA

Single-source data
An effort to combine data from different sources by gathering integrated information on household and marketing variables applicable to the same set of respondents.

It is desirable to combine secondary information obtained from different sources. Combining data allows the researcher to compensate for the weakness of one method with the strengths of another. One outcome of the effort to combine data from different sources is **single-source data**. Single-source research follows a person's TV, reading and shopping habits. After recruiting a test panel of households, the research firm installs meters into each home's TV sets and periodically surveys family members on what they read. Their grocery purchases are tracked by UPC scanners. For background, most systems also track retail data, such as sales, advertising and promotion. Thus, single-source data provide integrated information on household variables, including media consumption and purchases and marketing variables, such as product sales, price, advertising, promotion and in-store marketing effort.[24]

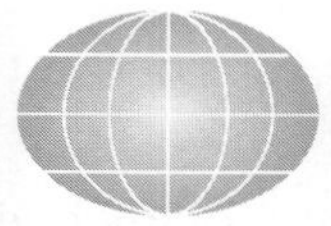

INTERNATIONAL MARKETING RESEARCH

A wide variety of secondary data are available for international marketing research. As with domestic research, the problem is not one of lack of data but one of the plethora of information available. Evaluation of secondary data is even more critical for international than for domestic projects. Different sources report different values for a given statistic, such as the gross domestic product (GDP), because of differences in the way the unit is defined. Measurement units may not be equivalent across countries. In France, for example, workers are paid a thirteenth monthly salary each year as an automatic bonus, resulting in a measurement construct that is different than other countries.[25] The accuracy of secondary data may also vary from country to country. Data from highly industrialised countries in Europe are likely to be more accurate than those from developing nations. Business and income statistics are affected by the taxation structure and the extent of tax evasion. Population censuses may vary in frequency and year in which the data are collected. In Britain, for example, the census is conducted every ten years, whereas in the People's Republic of China there was a 29-year gap between the censuses of 1953 and 1982. This situation, however, is changing quickly. Several syndicated firms are developing huge sources of international secondary data as illustrated in the following example.

EXAMPLE

Los Medios y Mercados de Latinoamerica (LMML)

Started in 1994 by Audits & Surveys worldwide, *Los Medios y Mercados de Latinoamerica* (The Markets and Media of Latin America) is the largest multinational survey of media and consumer habits that is conducted in Latin America to provide managers with important information for their marketing strategies. The study, which is repeated every year, aims at tracking the development of media and consumer habits in Latin America.

A recent multinational survey was conducted in 18 Latin America countries including Argentina, Brazil, Columbia, Mexico and Venezuela. It sampled 6634 respondents between the ages of 12 and 64. Its probability sample, representing urban as well as rural Latin America, can be projected to 280 million people or 79 million households.

The methodology for this survey involved two steps. First the personal interview technique was used to measure the variety of media including newspapers, multinational and local magazines, television and radio. Then a 25-page self-administered booklet was passed to the respondent to measure their product consumption and usage in over 100 categories and 800 brands. Demographic data gathered about the respondents included country/region, age, sex, employment status, occupation, education, household size, annual household income, car ownership, household goods owned and services taken.

Companies can easily use these data as the survey results are provided in a set of 14 printed volumes, and also in computer database formats including an SPSS format. ■

ETHICS IN MARKETING RESEARCH

Possible ethical dilemmas exist when using internal or external secondary data. Some ethical issues that are pertinent include:

- The unnecessary collection of primary data when the problem can be addressed based on secondary data alone.
- The use of only secondary data when primary data are needed.
- The use of secondary data that are not applicable.
- The use of secondary data that have been gathered through morally questionable means.
- Compromising the anonymity of customer details held on databases.

As was discussed in Chapter 2, the unnecessary collection of expensive primary data when the research problem can be addressed using only secondary data is unethical. In this case, the researcher is using a more expensive method that is less appropriate. Similarly, the exclusive reliance on secondary data when the research problem requires primary data collection could raise ethical concerns. This is particularly true if the researcher is charging a fixed fee for the project and the research design was not specified in advance. Here again, the researcher's profit goes up, but at the expense of the client.

The researcher is ethically obliged to ensure the relevance and usefulness of secondary data to the problem at hand. The secondary data should be evaluated by the criteria discussed earlier in this chapter. Only data judged to be appropriate should be used. It is also important for the data to be collected using procedures that are morally appropriate. Data can be judged unethical if they are gathered in a way that harms the respondents. Take, for example, information on credit card holders' buying patterns with accompanying demographics available from a syndicated service. These data were collected without the consent of the cardholders and may be considered an invasion of respondents' privacy. Although neither the client (a major bank) nor the researcher was involved in the unethical treatment of the respondents, should they use such research? This ethical dilemma becomes more complicated given the competition in the banking industry. A client with a moral objection to using such data realises that these data are available also to competitors and that by not using them, the client firm can be at a competitive disadvantage. Clearly, researchers and syndicate firms should not engage in any questionable or unethical practices, such as abuse of respondents' privacy, while generating secondary data. Privacy has, indeed, become a burning issue, as the following example indicates.

EXAMPLE

Is Boots taking advantage?[27]

You're in your local Boots paying for your toiletries. As the assistant swipes your Advantage card, she politely asks whether you're still suffering from that nasty little rash that started a couple of months ago. It's not that she remembers you, but that the card holds your medical history along with your shopping patterns. Boots has announced that it has examined including medical histories and even social security data on the card which might, for example, automatically say whether holders were entitled to free prescriptions.

If Boots were to pursue the idea, not only would it be making medical history along with commercial data, but it would also be sailing close to the wind on data protection law. Such a move has alarmed a number of agencies charged with looking out for the consumer, not least the Data Protection Registrar. ■

INTERNET AND COMPUTER APPLICATIONS

The World Wide Web as an on-line source of secondary data

The World Wide Web is a vital source of secondary data for the marketing researcher. The speed of the Internet can aid rapid problem diagnosis and data collection at various stages of the research process. Given the global nature of the technology, the Internet is a vital tool for the international marketing researcher. Searching the www is facilitated by using generalist search engines such as Yahoo! or AltaVista, which require a few key words to get hundreds of sites related to one subject. One can go directly to the Web sites of traditional suppliers of secondary data from government or business sources. Many of those sites also have inside search engines that sort data from the supplier's internal database. Information on the Web is of great value as generally it is current, though care must be taken to note when Web pages have been updated. It should be noted that not all secondary data on the Web is free. The Web may reveal the existence of data on a particular subject or industry but remember the costs involved in conducting quality research. Hence the Web may be used to give an awareness and a 'taste' of secondary data but it does not necessarily mean 'free' data.

Internal secondary data

Large organisations have intranets, which greatly facilitate the search for access to secondary data. The Coca-Cola Company for example, has developed powerful intranet applications that enable Coca-Cola managers worldwide to search for past and present research studies and a wide variety of marketing-related information on the basis of key words. Once located, the information can be accessed on-line. Even sensitive and restricted information can be accessed by obtaining permission electronically.

External secondary data

Information can be obtained by visiting various business-related sites that provide sales leads and mailing lists, business profiles and credit ratings. Various newspapers, magazines and journals can be accessed on the Web with excellent indexing facilities to locate particular subjects, companies and individuals. Government data for the European Community, individual countries through to regional and city councils can be accessed via the www though the quality and quantity of data available through government sources can vary enormously.

Syndicated sources of information

For syndicated sources of information one can visit the home pages of the various marketing research companies and providers of syndicated information. The A.C. Nielsen home page at www.acnielsen.com is a good example. This site provides links to various manufacturers and to various countries such as Britain, Canada and Spain. Another good source of syndicated data is Mintel, which can be reached at www.mintel.co.uk. Further, one could go to the Dunn and Bradstreet home page at www.dbisna.com/dbis/dnbhome.htm and directly access the services and syndicated information.

International secondary data

The Internet has emerged as the most extensive source of secondary information. The utility of the Internet for the marketing researcher is further enhanced due to the easy accessibility and retrieval of information and the ability to cross-validate information from a variety of sources.

SUMMARY

In contrast to primary data, which originate with the researcher for the specific purpose of the problem at hand, secondary data are data originally collected for other purposes. Secondary data can be obtained quickly and are relatively inexpensive. It has limitations, and should be carefully evaluated to determine their appropriateness for the problem at hand. The evaluation criteria consist of specifications, error, currency, objectivity, nature and dependability.

A wealth of information exists in the organisation for which the research is being conducted. This information constitutes internal secondary data. External data are generated by sources outside the organisation. These data exist in the form of published (printed) material, on-line and off-line databases, or information made available by syndicated services. Published external sources may be broadly classified as general business data or government data. General business sources comprise guides, directories, indexes and statistical data. Government sources may be broadly categorised as census data and other data. Computerised databases may be on-line or off-line. Both on-line and off-line databases may be further classified as bibliographic, numeric, full-text, directory or specialised databases.

Syndicated sources are companies that collect and sell common pools of data designed to serve a number of clients. Syndicated sources can be classified based on the unit of measurement (households and consumers or institutions). Household and consumer data may be obtained via surveys, diary purchase or media panels, or electronic scanner services. When institutions are the unit of measurement, the data may be obtained from retailers, wholesalers, or industrial units. It is desirable to combine information obtained from different secondary sources.

Several specialised sources of secondary data are useful for conducting international marketing research. The evaluation of secondary data becomes even more critical, however, because the usefulness and accuracy of these data can vary widely. Ethical dilemmas that can arise include the unnecessary collection of primary data, the use of only secondary data when primary data are needed, the use of secondary data that are not applicable, and the use of secondary data that have been gathered through morally questionable means.

QUESTIONS AND PROBLEMS

1 What are the differences between primary and secondary data?

2 What are the relative advantages and disadvantages of secondary data?

3 At what stages of the marketing research process can secondary data be used?

4 Why is it important to locate and analyse secondary data before progressing to primary data?

5 How may secondary data be used to validate qualitative research findings?

6 What is the difference between internal and external secondary data?

7 How can intranet technology help in the location and dissemination of secondary data?

8 By what criteria may secondary data be evaluated?

9 What criteria would you look for when examining the design and specifications of secondary data? Why is it important to examine these criteria?

10 To what extent should you use a secondary data source if you cannot see any explicit objectives attached to that research?

11 If you had two sources of secondary data for a project, the first being dependable but out of date, the second not dependable but up to date, which would you prefer?

12 Describe with examples, the main types of government and business secondary data sources.

13 List and describe the main types of syndicated sources of secondary data.

14 Explain what a diary panel is. What are the advantages and disadvantages of traditional and scanner diary panels?

15 What is an audit? Describe the uses, advantages and disadvantages of audits.

NOTES

1 Redhead, D., 'Generation Next', *Marketing*, (16 January 1997), 25.

2 Fry, A., 'Reaching the Pink Pound', (4 September 1997), 31.

3 Fletcher, K., 'External drive', *Marketing* (30 October 1997), 39.

4 Jacob, H., *Using Published Data: Errors and Remedies* (Beverly Hills: Sage Publications, 1984).

5 Stewart, D.W., *Secondary Research: Information Sources and Methods* (Beverly Hills: Sage Publications, 1984), 23–33.

6 Fry, A., 'Number Crunch', *Marketing* (4 December 1997), 29.

7 Bird, J., 'Switching on to Intranets', *Management Today* (December 1996), 78.

8 Miller, R., 'Where Next for Research?', *Marketing* (22 May 1997), 30.

9 Wang, P. and Spiegel, T., 'Database Marketing and Its Measurement of Success: Designing a Managerial Instrument to Calculate the Value of a Repeat Customer Base', *Journal of Direct Marketing* 8 (Spring 1994), 73–81.

10 Fries, J.R., 'Library Support for Industrial Marketing Research', *Industrial Marketing Management* 11 (February 1982), 47–51.

11 Miller, R., 'Keeping up to Data', *Marketing* (30 January 1997), 35.

12 Ramsay, A., *EIA Quick Guides, No. 4*. Manchester, (England: European Information Association).

13 Post, C., 'Marketing Data Marts Help Companies Stay Ahead of the Curve and in Front of the Competition', *Direct Marketing*, 59 (April 1997), 37–40.

14 Notess, G.R., 'Searching the Hidden Internet', *Database* 20 (June/July 1997), 37–40.

15 Quint, B., 'Assume the Position, Take the Consequences', *Information Today* 13 (June 1996), 11–13.

16 Notess, G.R., 'The Internet as an On-line Service: Bibliographic Databases on the Net', *Database* 19 (August/September 1996), 92–5.

17 Parfitt, J.H. and Collins, B.J.K., 'Use of Consumer Panels for Brand Share Predictions', *Journal of the Market Research Society* 38(4) (October 1996), 341–67; Ramaswamy, V. and Desarbo, W.S., 'SCULPTURE: A New Methodology for Deriving and Analyzing Hierarchical Product-market Structures from Panel Data', *Journal of Marketing Research* 27 (November 1990), 418–27.

18 Sudman, S., 'On the Accuracy of Recording of Consumer Panels I', *Journal of Marketing Research* (August 1964), 69–83; Sudman, S. and Bradburn, M. 'Response Effects in Surveys', *Journal of Marketing Research* (May 1964), 14–20; Sudman, S. and Ferber, R., *Consumer Panels* (Chicago: American Marketing Association 1978); and Sudman, S., *On the Accuracy of Recording of Consumer Panels II*, Learning Manual (New York: Neal-Schumen Publishers, 1981).

19 Handler, D., 'The Business Economist at Work: Linking Economics to Market Research: A.C. Nielsen', *Business Economics* 31 (October 96), 51.

20 Andrew, R.L. and Srinivasan, T.C., 'Studying Consideration Effects in Empirical Choice Models Using Scanner Panel Data', *Journal of Marketing Research* 32 (February 1995), 30–41; and Bucklin, R.E., Gupta, S. and Han, S., 'A Brand's Eye View of Response Segmentation in Consumer Brand Choice Behaviour', *Journal of Marketing Research* 32 (February 1995), 66–74.

21 It is possible to combine store-level scanner data with scanner panel data to do an integrated analysis. See for example, Russell, G.J. and Kamakura, W.A., 'Understanding Brand Competition Using Micro and Macro Scanner Data', *Journal of Marketing Research*, 31 (May 1994), 289–303.

22 Examples of scanner data applications include Fader, P.S. and McAlister, L., 'An Elimination by Aspects Model of Consumer Response to Promotion Calibrated on UPC Scanner Data', *Journal of Marketing Research* 27 (August 1990), 322–32; Waarts, E., Carree, M. and Wierenga, B., 'Full-Information Maximum Likelihood Estimation of Brand Positioning Maps Using Supermarket Scanning Data', *Journal of Marketing Research* 28 (November 1991), 483–90.

23 Based on information obtained from the suppliers.

24 For an application of single-source data, see Deighton, J., Henderson, C.M. and Neslin, S.A., 'The Effects of Advertising on Brand Switching and Repeat Purchasing', *Journal of Marketing Research* 31 (February 1994), 28–43.

25 Douglas, S.P. and Craig, C.S., *International Marketing Research* (Upper Saddle River, NJ: Prentice Hall, 1983).

26 Rydholm, J., 'A United Effort', *Quirk's Marketing Research Review* (October 1996).

27 Lee, J., 'Is Boots Taking Advantage?', *Marketing* (14 August 1997), 11.

Chapter 5

The use of databases and geodemographic information systems in secondary data collection and analyses

The ability to be able to collect, store and utilise as much data as quickly as possible on your customer base is crucial. Companies have to recognise that this trend represents a radical redesign of the whole area of selling and marketing into a customer-facing system where decisions come from customers into the company instead of the other way around. And IT is the enabling tool that allows companies to adopt this system successfully. The crux of an IT system is a database that allows fast access to information.[1]

OBJECTIVES

After reading this chapter, the student should be able to:

1 understand how databases are transforming the way that marketers develop marketing strategies;
2 describe how the 'loyalty card' has transformed the means of capturing consumer behaviour;
3 describe what a geodemographic information system is and explain how it may be used to integrate and display different types of data;
4 see how the link-up of different databases and survey data can form datawarehouses;
5 understand how databases are developing into powerful means to understand consumer behaviour through 'electronic observation';
6 understand how databases support traditional forms of marketing research;
7 understand the international data capture issues that can be enhanced with the use of databases and geodemographic information systems;
8 understand the ethical problems of having individual consumer data held on databases.

OVERVIEW

Marketing research as a function does not support marketing decision-making in isolation. As discussed in Chapter 1, it may be seen as being part of a broader marketing information system that supports strategic decision-making. Many information technology advances have been made in recent years which have fundamentally changed the way that marketing decisions are supported. For example, significant developments in database technology have meant that scanning systems in retail stores, loyalty card data, store panel data and survey data can be fused together to present very clear and up-to-date 'pictures' of consumers. As well as giving direct support to the marketer, these systems give more focus to marketing research activity and direct support to many stages of research.

This chapter describes how databases and geodemographic information systems (GIS) have developed to make major impacts upon how decision-makers are supported. The data collected and analysed through these mediums can be seen as secondary data sources. However, as with all good secondary data sources, they have a major impact upon the conduct and direction of primary data collection, analyses and interpretation.

We introduce our discussion with examples of the uses of databases. The database is not solely a marketing research tool. Databases can be used to generate direct sales and target promotion activities, which conflict with the philosophy of anonymity in marketing research. The examples illustrate something of the conflict between developing a richer understanding of consumers and the promotional activities associated with databases.

EXAMPLE

Getting to know you[2]

Huge banks of information, bringing together billions of EPOS bleeps, with millions of loyalty cards, have provided some surprising product associations. But is it really necessary to use all the data from every store, or would market research be able to do the job more easily and cheaply?

Edwina Dunn, Chief Executive of Marketing Database Consultant DunnHumby Associates presents the case for the huge data capture task. 'Some of the techniques mean you can link transactions to individual customers, and that is the breakthrough. When you start to look at customers and what they actually buy, your whole understanding of the market changes. Instead of saying "I wonder why we are selling fewer tins of beans?" you can actually say "I wonder why Mrs James is now reducing her weekly purchase of baked beans from two cans to one?" The power of that focus means that you can do a lot of things to study and stimulate that change.' ■

EXAMPLE

Locating the best international sites for Blockbuster Video[3]

Finding the best overseas locations for its retail outlets is a major priority for Blockbuster Video, the successful American video chain. The company has been expanding rapidly into Europe and recognised that the nature of each local market varied widely between countries. It needed a detailed understanding of each market before making investments in new sites.

Using Experian's marketing information system, MOSAIC Systems, Blockbuster was able to analyse the make-up of widely differing local communities and to identify the locations with the greatest profit potential. The system also has enabled Blockbuster to target promotional activities at its best prospective customers using the most effective media.

According to Ted Kerr, Blockbuster's managing director of developing territories: 'Experian has provided us with an excellent tool for evaluating potential store locations. It has enabled us to invest in markets such as Spain, Germany, Austria, Denmark and the Netherlands with much greater confidence.' ■

A map of MOSAIC groups in Stockholm
Experian

EXAMPLE

External drive[4]

One of the most important uses for external data is the kind of revealing analysis that can be achieved by combining and comparing it to an internal database. Dawn Orr, sales director for consumer data consultancy NDL, agrees that an in-house database full of transactional data is just the beginning. 'Then you look for how much they bought, and how often. This is known as recency/frequency/monetary, or RFM data. Then you build up from there.'

'Customers might buy the same product, pay the same way and appear to be alike. But if you look at the frequency of their purchases, one might be much more valuable to you than the other. RFM data can build a good picture of customers, but if companies don't look further outside their own databases, then that's about all they can do. You want to know about the longevity of expenditure of that customer, so you need to know about their lifestyle.' ■

THE USE OF THE DATABASE

In Chapter 1, when defining the nature and scope of marketing research, the definition presented from the European Society of Opinion and Marketing Research (ESOMAR) distinguished marketing research from other forms of data gathering, through the issue of the anonymity of respondents. It was stressed that in marketing research the identity of the provider of information is not disclosed. A distinction was made between marketing research and database marketing where the names and addresses of the people contacted are to be used for individual selling (sugging), promotional fund-raising or other non-research purposes (frugging).

The message from this distinction is clear. If marketing researchers were to collect data, promising anonymity and then breaking that promise, untold damage could be done to the profession. Potential respondents may be reluctant to talk to marketing researchers with disastrous effects upon response rates. Further, potential respondents may distort the 'truth', not revealing what they really feel or how they actually behave, fearing what may be done with this knowledge.

The distinction between anonymous questioning that makes 'pure' marketing research and database marketing is not so clear as it may first seem. The following two factors have made a significant impact upon the distinction between marketing research and database marketing.

1 *Analysis of existing customers*. It has long been contended that an essential part of a marketing information system is 'internal secondary data'. In other words, operational data that reveals, for example, who your customers are, where they are located, what they buy, how much they buy, how they have responded to promotional offers and how profitable they are. This operational data can be used as essential decision-making support. In many circumstances, this data was held within accounting departments or in operations, managing stock and distribution. In certain instances actual customer details were known; in other circumstances only broad details were known.

   With developments in database technology and cultural changes within organisations, marketing decision-makers are increasingly having access to this data. With the data, they can perform analyses to evaluate past marketing decisions. They can also set an array of targets, for example defining a target group of customers and measuring the amount of sales achieved in that target group. From the analyses, clear gaps may appear in their knowledge of consumers that will guide primary data collection on a quantitative or qualitative basis.

   Depending upon the characteristics of a marketplace, the identity of the customer may or may not be of importance to a decision-maker. With few customers and a need to nurture and develop marketing relationships, the identity of the customer is vital. With millions of customers of a fast-moving consumer good, the identity may not be so vital.

   Whether the customers' identity is apparent or not, the analyses of customer behaviour is a vital foundation to marketing decision-making and the planning of subsequent marketing research.

2 *Expectations of respondents*. As more organisations throughout developed Western economies adopt a marketing orientation, more measurements are being made of consumers. This does not solely apply to profit-making enterprises but also political organisations, hospitals, religious organisations and other 'non-profit' enterprises that may have had a paternalistic view of their 'customers' in the past. Marketing research respondents are becoming more sophisticated as consumers, and more particular about who they speak to and what they talk about. The outcome of more sophisticated consumers facing more measurements is that, generally, response rates are falling for all forms of marketing research.

   To cope with falling response rates, marketing researchers must design their measurement activities based upon a clear awareness of the expectations of their target respondents. Part of those expectations may be a desire for anonymity, but equally for certain individuals there may be a greater desire for a tangible reward. Consumers recognise that their views and behaviour have a value to marketers and in many instances want a tangible reward for imparting that knowledge.

   The most obvious example of a reward being given to consumers is through the use of the 'loyalty' or 'reward' card in supermarkets. The loyalty card on one level is a sales promotion device, used to promote certain items in a store and giving a reward for overall spending. At another level, it is a data capture device, electronically observing consumer behaviour. Many consumers recognise this and are willing to trade knowledge of their behaviour for the tangible rewards of the loyalty card scheme.

Changes in marketing decision-makers, consumers and the technology to capture behaviour and quickly perform sophisticated analyses have contributed to the problem of making a clear distinction between marketing research and database marketing. Database marketing activities are growing at a faster rate than 'traditional' marketing research. Many of the leading marketing research companies in Europe and the USA have long recognised the potential in databases from a research and profit perspective and are comfortable in combining the approaches. Such marketing research agencies perform database analyses with the same purpose as outlined in the definition of marketing research and with the same level of professional standards, especially when related to database analyses of identified customers. The research uses of the database that we outline in this chapter will illustrate why so many research companies and marketing decision-makers find the database indispensable.

SCANNING DEVICES

Scanner data
Data obtained by passing merchandise over a laser scanner that reads the UPC code from the packages.

One of the most fundamental technological breakthroughs that has allowed the monitoring of product sales is the bar code. With **scanning devices** to read bar codes, has come the ability to quickly count and analyse sales. If a new product is launched, scanning data can monitor sales on a daily basis, breaking down the sales by advertising region and the type of outlet. Marketing research companies that audit the sales of products and outlets have quickly grasped the technology as illustrated in the following example.

EXAMPLE

Checking out the goods[5]

Scanning has opened new horizons in the speed, scope and accuracy of market research. This is both in generic research – like that of researchers Nielsen, with its Homescan system, and AGB Market Information with Superpanel – and in-house research by retailing groups to spot early trends in product sales, test the effectiveness of merchandising techniques and promotions and to determine the locations of new stores. ■

This example shows that the scanning device can be used to rapidly answer questions on the effectiveness of promotions activities, price discounts or developing relationships with particular retailers. The scanning device is an electronic means of observation. Consumers do not answer any questions, do not identify themselves, they merely enjoy the benefits of supermarket queues moving far more quickly compared to the days of checkout clerks manually entering the prices for individual goods in their baskets.

What product bar codes and scanning devices do not do is classify consumers. Classification is fundamental to marketing research techniques and ultimately marketing segmentation techniques. Is the new brand of yoghurt more popular with younger age groups compared to older groups? Have more Calvin Klein shirts been sold to male or female buyers? The next technological development has allowed these questions to be answered, maintaining the technique of electronic observation.

CUSTOMER LOYALTY SCHEMES

For many marketers, a major part of their effort is placed upon retaining loyal customers. This focus matches the whole *raison d'être* of marketing, i.e. to satisfy customers so that they come back to buy more. To create loyal customers, great efforts are being made to build up a relationship with individual customers. This may seem an obvious strategy in industrial markets where a marketer may have a few major customers that they know well and may meet on a regular basis. It may also seem obvious in community stores where a shopkeeper may know and greet their customers personally and may have done so for many years. For FMCG marketers, with thousand or even millions of customers, huge product lines and numbers of daily transactions, building up loyalty may not be such an obvious strategy. In the business of banking and financial services, the ability to track 'loyalty' and the success of customer retention is transforming bank–customer relationships.

GLOBALCASH PROJECT

Loyal customers in the bank

In pan-European banks are many divisions that cover the spectrum from small domestic accounts through to large corporate accounts. In opening any account, banks ask many questions to allow their operations and transactions to work smoothly, to assess the creditworthiness of customers and to assess whether there are other services that they could offer to the customer.

Over time, a bank can build up a series of transaction records against a customer record. From this record, for example, banks can see who are their most profitable customers, who buys a range of connected services, who has been the most loyal over the years, to name but a few analyses.

They may find that certain customers have been banking with them for years, loyally saving a tiny sum paid over the counter each week. Such customers may cost a bank more to service than they can make on interest in the sum invested. A bank may look to means of making the transaction costs cheaper, offer other services that may increase profits or even charge customers a fee to pay in savings over the counter! ■

The essence of the GlobalCash example is that the operational data used to open and service accounts link customer identification against product usage. Any promotional offers, competitive activity, new products offerings, telephone banking services, or discounts, to name but a few marketing activities, can be analysed and related to classifications of customer. For other types of business, the key to this power of analysis lies in customer identification. The loyalty card is one means to do this but not the only one as the following example illustrates.

EXAMPLE

Doing a Dyson

The vacuum cleaner manufacturer Dyson has built a commanding market leadership position in many European countries. Like most vacuum cleaner manufacturers, Dyson sell their products through electrical retailers, department stores and catalogues. In order to find out who actually buys their products they enclose a guarantee card with each product. When completed and returned, the guarantee card reveals many characteristics of the customer, allowing them to link actual products purchases to customer types. A database of customers and their characteristics can be built and maintained. This practice is common for many electrical goods manufacturers allowing them to 'leap over' retailers to reach and identify final customers.

Where Dyson go one step further is in their commitment to the quality and innovation in their products. If a vacuum cleaner breaks down it is not returned to the retailer. The customer calls a courier who ships the broken cleaner to the Dyson factory. The cleaner is stripped down, repaired and repackaged to be couriered back to the customer the following day. A database is built up of this activity detailing customers, products and the nature of the problem encountered. This database is vital to product modification and new product development and, given the common 'key' of customer identification, builds onto the main customer database. ■

Loyalty card
At face value, the loyalty card is a sales promotion device used by supermarkets, pharmacists, department stores, petrol stations and even whole shopping centres and towns to encourage repeat purchases. For the marketing researcher, it is a device that can link customer characteristics to actual product purchases.

The **loyalty card** is the device that supermarkets, pharmacists, department stores, petrol stations and even whole shopping centres and towns have developed in order to link customer characteristics to actual product purchases. As discussed earlier, this is not the only purpose of the card; for many marketers it is just a sales promotion device.

The loyalty card may be offered to customers as they make a purchase in a store. They normally complete an application form which may include a name and address, demographic details, household details, media usage, and even some lifestyle characteristics. Once the customer uses their loyalty card, the products they have purchased are scanned and a link can be made through the 'swiped' card to their characteristics. In return, the customer earns 'points' for their total spend and may earn additional points for buying particular products. The points gained may be redeemed for cash, additional purchases or even goods and services in other retailers or restaurants.

From the marketing decision-makers' perspective, many benefits accrue from a loyalty card and product scanning system. The following list summarises the benefits to the marketer:

1 *Profile of customers can be built up*. The types of individual that are being attracted to a store can be monitored. The returns and contributions made by particular types of customer can be measured. Profiles of the 'ideal' customer type can be built up, and plans developed to attract that type of customer.
2 *Products used and not used*. The types of product that are being bought or not bought can be monitored. From the customer profile, other types of product can be added to the range offered. Cross-selling of related products can be undertaken. Linked to the customer profile, actual customer behaviour can be understood more fully.
3 *Communications that have worked and not worked*. Merchandising displays, money-off coupons, three for the price of two, a clip-out coupon from a local newspaper as examples, can be linked to individuals and products. The effectiveness of particular types of communication for particular types of consumer can be developed. Reassurance that the customer has made the right decision can be given where the size of purchase warrants it.
4 *Distribution methods can be tailored*. Certain customer types may prefer the convenience of a small store that they visit more than once a week for small purchases of 'staple' goods. Other customer types may shop once a month for the total household. Retailers can have different shop formats for different customers, may develop home delivery programmes or even develop Internet shopping systems.

The above four factors interact to allow marketing decision-makers to redefine their market(s) and the offerings they make to those markets. The iteration of target market definition and marketing mix tailored to those markets is at the heart of strategic marketing.

From the marketing researchers' perspective, many benefits also accrue from a loyalty card and product scanning system. The following list summarises the benefits to the marketer researcher:

1 *One big laboratory*. Experimental methods will be described in Chapter 9 but, in essence, the monitoring of customers, markets and interrelated marketing mix activities allows many causal inferences to be established. For example, what is the effect, and upon whom, of raising the price of Haagen Dazs ice cream by 10 per cent? What is the effect of inserting a cut-out coupon to give a discount on after-sun lotion, placed in *Cosmopolitan* magazine?
2 *Refining the marketing process*. With time series of responses to planned marketing activities, statistical models of consumer response can be built with associated probabilities of a particular outcome. Likewise, models of the consumer over their lifetime can be built. Again, statistical models can be built with associated probabilities of particular types of product being bought at different stages of a consumer's life.
3 *Develop clear understanding of 'gaps' in knowledge of consumers*. The scanner and loyalty card electronically observes behaviour but does not encapsulate attitudinal data. The nature and levels of satisfaction, what is perceived as good quality service, what brand image is associated with a particular brand of vodka, are examples of attitudinal data. The use of the database helps to identify target populations to measure and the attitudinal data that needs to be collected. In all there can be a much greater clarity in the nature of primary marketing research that tackles attitudinal issues.
4 *Link of behavioural and attitudinal data*. If attitudinal data is elicited from consumers, the data gathered can be analysed in its own right. It is possible, however, to link the gathered data back to the behavioural data in the database. The term of 'fusing' the data from different sources is used. The key to the fusing lies in identifying individual respondents so that one large dataset is built up. The notion of fusing together databases and survey data from different sources is at the heart of the building a strong understanding of consumers.

The above benefits show why many marketers and marketing researchers welcome the power that the database brings to them. There are drawbacks, however, that focus on the nature of the 'loyalty card'. As described earlier, loyalty card schemes can be seen as a sales promotion technique in much the same manner as giving trading stamps, a dividend or coupons to be redeemed after a period of saving. Compared to other sales promotion techniques, the loyalty card incurs huge operating costs. The following example gives an indication of what those costs may be and some indication that as a sales promotion technique they may not be so cost-effective. The real benefit lies in the data gathering and analysis process.

EXAMPLE

Data goes to market[6]

No one believes any longer that loyalty schemes alone will pay for themselves. In addition to giving away margin they incur huge operating costs. For example, Tesco and Sainsbury's had to build dedicated call centres which receive up to 70,000 calls a day from reward card holders. The total investment is certain to outweigh the additional spend from loyal customers, proof of which is still patchy.

However, the points-mean-prizes element of loyalty schemes is merely the bait to encourage customers to provide personal information. Every time the loyalty card is swiped at the point of sale, the retailers' systems are triggered to record the name of the shopper, the time they came to shop, the store they visited and the entire contents of their trolley. Armed with this kind of data, retailers are suddenly switching from their usual obsession with product performance and cost per square foot, to customer needs. The goal is not simply to make direct marketing propositions to customers but to use the data to improve the business through merchandising, space planning and customer service. ■

The term 'loyalty' has also come under much scrutiny. Many shoppers gather loyalty cards from a variety of stores and 'cherry pick' the best offers from each store. The contention is that the card does not create loyalty, it has to be excellent product and service delivery that satisfies consumers that creates loyalty, not the card. The following example contains a full, verbatim letter to *The Times* that neatly encapsulates a culture of using an array of loyalty cards, trading them off against each other to get the best deal and even exasperation at having a wallet or purse stuffed with bits of plastic! The example continues with a message to reinforce the view that the benefits of the card given to customers in return for allowing themselves to be electronically observed.

EXAMPLE

Am I more loyal?

'Sir, I have accumulated nine "loyalty" cards from various stores and supermarkets. Does this make me more loyal, or less?' Dr John Burscough[7]

The term 'loyalty' is often misused, argues Mathew Hooper, Managing Director of Interfocus.[8] 'It is created by a multitude of factors, of which rewards are just one. Reward schemes, can provide a better profile of customers, but they won't increase sales. Reward schemes do not make money, they cost money. The rewards are the price that you pay for gathering customer intelligence.

'A reward scheme only generates extra business if you use that intelligence to improve the fundamentals of product, price and service. Tesco's success is because of improvements it has made using data gathered with the loyalty card, not the card itself.' ■

The following example highlights the pioneers of database marketing as financial services firms and airlines. These companies have the ability to build up detailed customer records. The example illustrates something of the potential development of the technique, primarily for promotional purposes. In companies that do not have the ability to collect data on their consumers, the use of free-sample offers or competitions allows them to collect the type of data gathered in application forms for banks or loyalty cards in supermarkets. Another interesting aspect of the example is the use of geographic data; this will be explored in further depth in the next section. For many companies, the database is seen as a means to conduct direct marketing, the marketing research benefits taking a lesser priority. When companies realise the power of description and analysis of their markets the emphasis changes.

EXAMPLE

A computer on a white horse[9]

In a recent survey of 100 large British businesses by the Manchester Business School, more than half the respondents said that database marketing would be their main promotional tool within five years. Already, consumer goods firms are ploughing money into computer databases. Kraft, the food division of America's Philip Morris, has tapped in the addresses of 30 m customers who have replied to free-sample offers or other promotions. Unilever is centralising the customer data amassed by its British subsidiaries. However, the pioneers of database marketing are financial services firms and airlines, who tend to know a lot more about their customers.

American Express, for example, uses its customer database to tailor offers (such as a special sale at Harrods department store, or cheap airline tickets) to small groups of cardholders according to their spending patterns. In Belgium, it is testing a system that combines offers based on tallying cardholders' past spending with postal-code data: if a new restaurant opens, for instance, cardholders who live within walking distance and are known to eat out a lot might receive a special discount. ■

Customer database
A database that details characteristics of customers that can include names and addresses, geographic, demographic and buying behaviour data.

The realisation of the power of description and analysis that lies within the **customer database** is at the heart of the following example at the Automobile Association. Of note is the addition of competitive information. This was discussed in Chapter 4 when the use of the company intranet was illustrated. Two important issues emerge from the AA example. First, users are encouraged to be creative in exploring the database. The essence of marketing decision-making is creative, looking for new ideas and connections. The database allows that and can create more focused managers when looking for additional marketing research support. Second, users can monitor the outcome and progress of their decision-making. This facilitates an amount of learning, the development of models and ultimately decision support systems.

EXAMPLE

Database use at the AA[10]

At the Automobile Association (AA), a vast database is being compiled including everything from profiles of members to the latest prices being offered by competitors in the vehicle repair and recovery business. The 40 staff who currently have access to the database are being encouraged to use it creatively, says Nigel Clark, the AA's Finance Director. 'They get immediate access to a full analysis of how many members we have in each category, how many have left, and how growth compares to budget.'

It demystifies bureaucracy because staff do not have to go looking for paper reports to find answers to their questions. They might decide to target lapsed members with special offers, or introduce incentives for existing members to sign up their friends. Staff can then monitor the success of such strategies at any time by checking progress on the system. ■

The next examples in this section further illustrate the power of the database in consumer and market analyses. The speculation as to why four major companies would share and develop a consumer database focuses upon the power of retailers. As described earlier, the link of scanner data plus loyalty cards gives retailers great marketing and marketing research advantages. This has contributed to a shift of power from the major 'blue-chip' suppliers to retailers. In a situation where companies are not competing, sharing consumer data helps to build up a greater and more complete 'picture' of consumers. The following example heralds a future of alliances between companies to **share databases** Links between retailers and banks to share quite distinct but comprehensive behavioural databases are becoming more common. Even the acquisition of companies for the asset of a consumer database that could enhance a buying company's database will become more commonplace.

Shared database
A large database made up of customer databases from a number of non-competing companies.

EXAMPLE

Unite and conquer[11]

What's the real story behind the marketing link-up of Unilever, Bass, Cadbury-Schweppes and Kimberly-Clark, and will it lead to the formation of other 'consortia of giants'?

The most successful FMCG companies are renowned for being fiercely competitive and highly secretive. So news that four of them had formed an alliance to share potentially sensitive market information came as something of a shock when it was announced. Press reports have suggested that the real objective of the *Consumer Needs Consortium,* as it is known, is to stand united against the onslaught of retailer power. One of the biggest benefits of the consortium is that it offers all four member companies access to a substantial database of common consumers. For example, the mother who buys Kimberly-Clark's Huggies is also likely to use one of Lever Brothers detergent brands and probably indulges in the occasional bar of Cadbury's chocolate. And because the companies are largely non-competing there is little for them to worry about in terms of direct competition between their brand portfolios. ■

Building a database on the scale that is envisaged by these four companies is expensive. While the companies will be able to share some of their existing data on consumers, they will no doubt face certain restrictions under the Data Protection Act. This will force them to gather new information, perhaps from buying in new lists or response mailings, both of which are costly exercises but become cheaper once shared among four different companies.

EXAMPLE

Shuffling the decks[12]

The future may well be just two or three consortium schemes within a five- to seven-year time frame

Loyalty card schemes have become popular because they give companies an insight into their customers' behaviour. But at some stage this transactional view is recognised as limited; what is really needed is a universal view. While it is hard to imagine Tesco and Sainsbury's sharing information about their shoppers, it is not too difficult to see a supermarket, bank, petrol and clothing retailer getting together. The cost to retailers of handling and managing the data from millions of transactions may ultimately price the 'stand alone' loyalty card out of the market. ■

There are few questions about the huge costs involved in developing and administering loyalty card schemes. For many retailers however, the investment allows many marketing and marketing research benefits to be realised. It is only when viewed in the light of offering strategic decision-making power and a complement to an integrated marketing information system that such an investment makes sense. Used as a tactical promotional technique, the technique may be short-lived. There may be many arguments to justify databases as a promotion technique, comparing promotion costs to other promotion types such as advertising, especially given the ability to measure communication effects. However, like trading stamps, free glasses with petrol promotions and other promotion fads, these arguments may hold little validity when promotions move on to other innovations. When evaluating the costs in term of the value of the data captured, it can be seen that the technique is not a fad. The final examples in this section raise the question of the future of the technique as a sales promotion tool. For the power that is realised in consumer and market analyses, it is difficult to see alternative means of capturing comparable data. Whether consumers will continue to use the cards for their purchases is another question. The power of the systems and the types of decision support that they offer makes it difficult to see marketers looking elsewhere for support.

EXAMPLE

Playing the loyalty card[13]

One question is vexing the promotions industry: are the new rash of supermarket cards true loyalty schemes or mere sales promotion gimmicks, the attraction of which will be short-lived? With the launch of its Club Card, Tesco has outmanoeuvred its rivals. While other grocery multiples have been testing the water, opting for more selective launches, Tesco has taken to the concept wholeheartedly. Just what it is getting back for its money is more difficult to answer. The party line is that Tesco wanted to reward regular customers and its shoppers are delighted when their custom produces savings. ■

EXAMPLE

'Rush-hour' shoppers face higher prices[14]

Supermarkets and high street stores are secretly devising 'dual pricing' policies which could result in busy professionals who shop at peak times being charged more than daytime shoppers. The policy, which is being helped by the spread of sophisticated loyalty card schemes, is already being tested by several big chains including Safeway, Asda and B & Q, and is expected to become widespread in the next five years.

By charging more at weekends and in the evenings, for example, retailers hope to encourage 'time rich, cash poor' customers such as pensioners and single mothers to do their shopping in quiet weekday periods. This would leave stores less congested at peak times, making way for 'cash rich, time poor' shoppers who would be charged more, but benefit from shorter queues and better service. ■

Two-tier pricing has been used for years by telephone companies to encourage off-peak calls, and airlines and railways to ease congestion. Since 1995, retailers have gained enough information about customers' income, lifestyles and shopping habits to apply the same principles to selling groceries and other products. Most of the information has come from customer loyalty cards.

GEODEMOGRAPHIC INFORMATION SYSTEMS

Geodemographic information systems (GIS)
At a base level, a GIS matches geographic information with demographic information. This match allows subsequent data analyses to be presented on maps.

Computer mapping
Maps that solve marketing problems are called thematic maps. They combine geography with demographic information and a company's sales data or other proprietary information and are generated by a computer.

One of the main elements of database power illustrated in the preceding section is the linking of different data sources from both scanner data and customer databases. The ability to create those links and to graphically display analyses has been achieved with the development of **geodemographic information systems** (GIS). At a base level, a GIS matches geographic information with demographic information, allowing analyses to be presented on **maps**. This base can be built upon with data from customer databases, databases from other sources and surveys. The combined data again can be presented on maps and in conventional statistical tables.

The geographic dimension is vital as a base to the system. Growing up and living in different geographical locations has an effect upon what we buy and the nature of our lifestyle. Look around Europe! It is easy to see differences in consumers and their spending habits, between countries, regions within countries, between cities and towns, areas within a town, between different sides of a street. These differences emerge from a variety of factors. The following list summarises the main factors, using extreme examples in places. With closer analysis, more subtle differences can be seen which will be illustrated later in this chapter.

1 *Physical geography and climate.* Consumers living in hot Mediterranean climates in villages close to the sea will have many different needs and wants compared to consumers in Scandinavian inner cities.
2 *Economic history, working opportunities.* Consumers that make up the population that is primarily semi-skilled, working in a declining manufacturing sector can be compared to a location that attracts recent graduates and young families to work in a burgeoning financial services centre.
3 *Political and legal differences.* Locations with a history of political and legal domination can affect the types of property and subsequently the types of people that live there. The differences may be national, e.g. with policies that encourage state ownership of property, or regional, e.g. with structural plans to build new estates to buy on green-field sites on the outskirts of cities.
4 *Demographic make-up.* Consumers living in predominantly retirement areas, such as seaside towns, will have many different requirements to regions that are heavily populated with single young people.
5 *Infrastructure links.* Infrastructure can include the means to travel around an area as well as the facilities such as leisure, shopping and cultural being available. Areas with different levels and quality of infrastructure attract different types of consumer. Consumers based on families with three cars who may comfortably drive to and park at many facilities, have different needs and wants compared to an individual living alone who owns a bicycle rather than a car.
6 *Property types.* In different locations particular styles of property may dominate. The style may be for flats rather than houses, multi-storey rather than low-rise, detached rather than terraced, bungalow rather than house. The type, size, quality and costs of property types within an area attract different types of consumer.

Thus, differences can be seen between geographic locations that affect the lifestyle of residents, the array of products and services they buy, their ability to buy different types of products and services and their hopes, fears and aspirations. The founding premise of a geodemographic information system is that the type of property a consumer lives in says much about their lifestyle and consumption patterns. Property type also encapsulates the other five factors that discriminate between consumers living in different geographic regions. For example, consumers living in small one-bedroom flats over shops in a city centre will tend to have far different lifestyles and consumption patterns compared to consumers living in large detached rural properties. Consumers in different property types have different propensities or probabilities of buying particular goods and services and undertaking activities that make up their lifestyle. They also have different propensities to use and be exposed to different types of media.

From a marketing decision-making perspective, geography also plays a vital role. Knowing where one's consumers are located affects the means and costs of distribution. For example, should a retail outlet be built? Where should it be located to gain the most returns? What features and facilities should the outlet have? The location of consumers also affects the means to communicate with them. Are consumers dispersed over a wide area or tightly clustered together? Do they read the same type of newspaper or magazine? Do they watch the same television programmes or films at the cinema?

A map therefore forms the foundation of a geodemographic information system. A map that can identify all properties in a country, all roads, shopping centres and major facilities in towns and cities. On top of a base map can be laid a range of statistical measures. They typically originate from a number of sources and have the common feature of being able to relate to a specific postcode or zip code. An example of such a system is one produced by Experian. They have developed systems for: Australia, Belgium, Germany, Great Britain, Hong Kong, Ireland, Japan, New Zealand, Norway, South Africa, Spain, Sweden and the USA. Obviously the sources and detail of data available in each of the above countries differs, as does the legislation that determines what can be stored and analysed on databases. Typically for each country statistics can be gathered and used to develop individual systems from: the census, postal address files, electoral registers, consumer credit data, directories of company directors, mail order purchase records, car registrations and data on access to retail outlets.

From the data collected, the purpose is to classify consumers on a geodemographic basis. Experian define a **geodemographic classification** as:

Geodemographic classification
Geodemographic classification groups consumers together based on the types of neighbourhood in which they live. If a set of neighbourhoods are similar across a wide range of demographic measures, they will also offer similar potential across most products, brands, services and media.

> Geodemographic classification groups consumers together based on the types of neighbourhood in which they live. If a set of neighbourhoods are similar across a wide range of demographic measures, they will also offer similar potential across most products, brands, services and media.

From the data Experian have available in any specific country, they will perform cluster analyses (the technique detailed in Chapter 22) in order to produce a classification of household types. Experian select the factors they use to classify household types based upon the following rules:

1 *Balance*. They seek an appropriate balance between data from different sources, e.g. in age and household characteristics, housing data, socio-economic characteristics, financial data. No single type or source of data is allowed to dominate their analyses.
2 *Correlations avoided*. Variables that are highly correlated are avoided. From within sets of highly correlated variables, only the most predictive of behaviour are selected.
3 *Correlations encouraged*. Variables chosen should correlate with purchasing or media usage behaviour.
4 *Sample size*. Variables used should have a sufficient sample size to be valid at the level of geography at which they are used.
5 *Concentration*. Variables should not be concentrated in a small number of geographic areas, e.g. if a mail-order database were available that concentrated on a particular region or a small number of cities, it would not be used in analyses. From the classification built, propensities to behave in particular ways are calculated, if the classification is built upon small geographic 'pockets', generalisations to other locations may be difficult.
6 *Regular updates*. Variables are preferred that are regularly updated. This helps to reflect changes in consumers in terms of where they live and how they behave.

With the variables chosen for a particular country, cluster analyses are used to create the most powerful discrimination of consumer behaviour, lifestyles and attitudes. The analyses ensure that each of the descriptions used is reasonably homogeneous in terms of demographic measurements and consumer behaviour. As well as being able to discriminate and describe distinctive groups of consumers, the analyses have to produce 'pictures' of consumers that are meaningful to marketing decision-makers. For Sweden, the resulting analyses have produced a classification of 10 main consumer types. Table 5.1 lists these types and the percentages of each type in the population. Each individual type can be further classified, Sweden having a total of

30 groups. For example, *Elite families* at 7 per cent of the population can be further broken down into *Careerists in terraced houses* at 2.1 per cent of the population, *Elite professionals* at 2.2 per cent and *White collar metropolitan* at 2.6 per cent. Tables 5.2 and 5.3 show the main classifications for the Netherlands and the UK respectively. The Netherlands has a total of 41 sub-groups from its main classification of 10 groups, with the UK having 52 sub-groups from 12 main groups.

Table 5.1 Experian classification of the Swedish population

Classification descriptor	*% in Swedish population*
Elite families	7.0
Middle income industrial	8.9
Low-middle income in flats	13.2
Well educated in metropolitan areas	13.7
Younger low income	5.5
Pensioners	8.7
Families with high incomes	3.8
High income in villas	4.9
Middle-aged families	10.7
Countryside	23.6

Table 5.2 Experian classification of the Netherlands population

Classification descriptor	*% in Netherlands population*
Clever capitalists	12.6
Corporate careerists	9.1
Average families	13.9
Smart singles	8.2
Problem families	14.0
Low-rise pensioners	8.0
Christian grey families	9.8
Roman families	16.3
Conservative young families	5.8
Farmer families	2.3

Table 5.3 Experian classification of the UK population

Classification descriptor	*% in UK population*
High-income families	9.9
Suburban semis	11.0
Blue-collar owners	13.0
Low-rise council	14.4
Council flats	6.8
Victorian low status	9.4
Town houses and flats	9.4
Stylish singles	5.2
Independent elders	7.4
Mortgaged families	6.2
Country dwellers	7.0
Institutional areas	0.3

In the UK example in Table 5.3, *Stylish singles* may be further illustrated. Experian contend that 5.2 per cent of the UK population match the description in the following example. As in the Swedish example in Table 5.1, each main group can be split into further sub-groups and the example also shows the sub-category of *Chattering classes* which makes up 1.9 per cent of the total population.

The Swedish Mosaic Group 'Well educated metropolitans'
Experian

EXAMPLE

Stylish singles and the chattering classes

Stylish singles

These are individuals for whom self-expression is more important than conformity to any external set of social standards, typically very well educated and very involved in their work. They are highly interested in the behaviour of different social groups and enjoy living in a diverse, cosmopolitan and sometimes multicultural environment. This group is often too busy experimenting and experiencing life to want to get married early and postpone as long as possible the responsibility of looking after homes, gardens and children. These people prefer the vitality of the large city to the tranquillity of outer suburbs and spend money freely on fashion, foreign travel, the arts, entertainment and eating out.

Chattering classes

This group is conspicuous for its outstandingly high proportion of graduates, most of whom work in highly paid service jobs associated with the media, the arts, politics or education. These are areas of highly articulate but sceptical influencers and opinion formers who direct the cultural and political agenda of the nation.

Such people are international in their orientation, often uninterested in technology for its own sake, more comfortable with ideas and opinions than with the operational detail of day-to-day management. Such people enjoy exposure to other cultures – foreign business travel, multi-cultural environments, ethnic restaurants. They are avid readers of newspapers and magazines. Residents in these areas are particularly interested in specialist foods and wines. They hold equity in expensive houses rather than in stocks and shares. ■

To further illustrate the characteristics of the *Chattering classes*, Figures 5.1 and 5.2 show the incidence of particular demographic characteristics. The bars show index scores for individual characteristics. If a score of 100 is shown, this means that the chattering classes have the same proportion of that characteristic compared to the rest of Britain. As an example, in Figure 5.1, an index score of 230 for 'flats' shows that the chattering classes have a greater propensity to live in flats compared to all other groups in Britain. There are proportionately 2.3 times

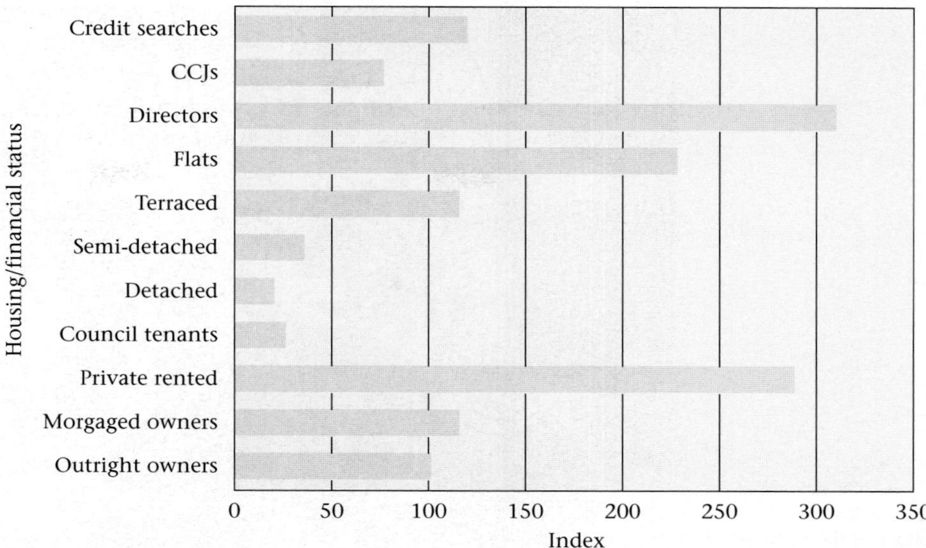

Figure 5.1
Housing and financial status of the *Chattering classes*

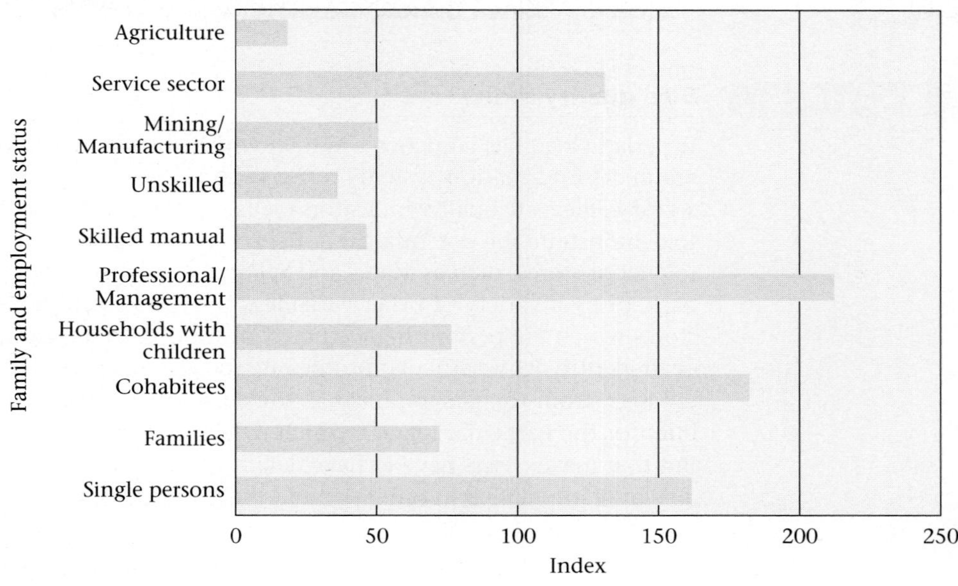

Figure 5.2
Family and work status of the *Chattering classes*

more *Chattering classes* that live in flats compared to the UK average. Similarly, one can see a very low propensity for individuals in this group to live in detached property with an index score of 20. Looking at Table 5.2, an index score of 180 shows a great propensity for *Chattering classes* to cohabit and a low propensity to work in unskilled and agricultural jobs.

With a geodemographic information system, it is possible to pinpoint where the *Chattering classes* are located throughout the country, whether they are clustered in particular regions or cities, or whether they are dispersed. As can be seen from the *Stylish singles* and *Chattering classes* example and Figures 5.1 and 5.2, a 'picture' of target consumers can be built up to facilitate segmentation and target marketing. From such classifications and the data that can be added from other databases, models of consumer behaviour can be developed. The following example illustrates how Experian have developed a model to calculate the potential for retail outlets.

A map of the propensity to buy 'Bensin' in Gothenburg
Experian

EXAMPLE

Site quality indicators[15]

Experian Goad has launched a system which shows the sort of power that geodemographical information systems can give to client companies, especially in the retail sector. Called site quality indicators (SQIs), it uses the accuracy of retail location maps to demonstrate the potential an outlet could have. This can be analysed by proximity to anchor stores, such as Marks and Spencer, how many minutes it is away from a car park, or by a variety of other variables. The model can be used to identify existing stores which are performing well or badly and then locations with a similar profile, or to identify why particular profiles are the way they are. The system pulls in a lot of datasets, from the geographical to the customer specific. From this, models can be built for the particular retailer, which reflect the baselines within their own business. But that means users have to have data on their customers already, and they must be able to manipulate it in order to build their own SQIs. ■

The above example also illustrates that the main power of the system comes from being able to add a customer database to the Experian database; this makes the 'picture' of consumers even clearer. Customers can be mapped out to see how far they live from a retail outlet or to see if they pass a competitor's store to reach a retail outlet. The profile of customers that a company has can be compared to national, regional or city profiles. Data that is captured on customer databases can be mapped out. For example, the ABN AMRO bank can map out which customers have responded to an offer to take out a personal loan at a discounted rate, as well as building up a profile of those that respond. The following example illustrates how Experian's data is merged with customer databases.

EXAMPLE

Micromarketer goes Dutch

The Dutch Air Miles franchise LMN, whose shareholders include Shell and ABN AMRO bank, use Experian's Micromarketer product to segment existing customers. It has built a database of 2.3 million customers and segments them geodemographically in order to facilitate targeted mailings. LMN's customer data is supplemented by Experian's data before segmentation. Gerard Zandbergen, Mosaic Micromarketer manager of Experian Netherlands says 'Data comes from several sources. One is the postal service. We also use market research bureaus and lists of private car owners.' Customers are segmented and the data fed into the GIS to provide a geographical element. Offers for visits to local theme parks and vouchers for local stores therefore go to people in specific regions. ■

In addition to customer behaviour being added to the geodemographic system, survey data can also be added. The key that would link the survey to the customer database may be either a named customer or a postcode. An example of the use of survey data may be in car retailing. A car retailer can map out who bought a new car from them. They may be able to profile and map out the types of individual that bought different types of car. The retailer may then profile and map out the buyers who return for servicing or to buy petrol or accessories. The manufacturer of the car sold and the retailer may conduct a satisfaction survey related to characteristics of the car and the service they received. The results of the survey can be analysed by the different Experian types and characteristics, and levels of customer satisfaction can be mapped out. Additional purchases or cars related to satisfaction or customer loyalty can be captured. It can be seen from the above that the means to build profiles of target markets, to measure the success of marketing decisions and the means to model consumer behaviour, can be built.

Graphical representations can be made of customer behaviour, their attitudes and their levels of satisfaction. Using this data, the car retailer additionally has the potential to measure the propensity of potential customers in new locations to buy particular, cars, petrol, accessories and so on.

LINKING DIFFERENT TYPES OF DATA

The previous example illustrated that different types of data can be merged and mapped out to represent customer characteristics. One rationale for linking data would be to perform segmentation analyses. Examining the means by which target markets can be segmented, it is clear to see that the five methods as illustrated in Figure 5.3 can be individually utilised or combined to build clearer 'pictures' or profiles of target consumers.

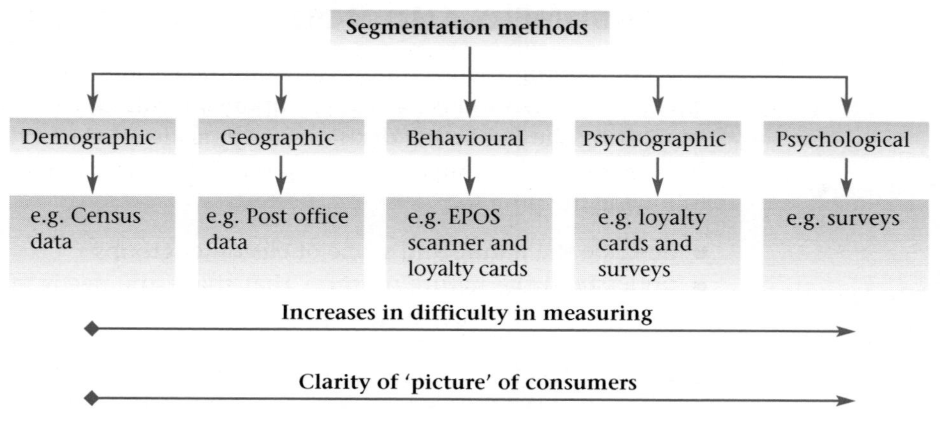

Figure 5.3
Methods of segmenting markets

Figure 5.3 gives examples of where data may be obtained from, to help build up profiles of customers and markets. In the example of 'psychographics' or lifestyle measurements, data may be generated from EPOS systems or surveys. In the case of the EPOS collection, the purchasing of particular types of products can indicate characteristics of a lifestyle. In a more direct manner, questions in a survey can help to build a profile of lifestyle behaviour. In its own right, 'lifestyle' can be a valid means to segment a market, perhaps positioning products and services to consumers who aspire to a particular lifestyle. However, being able to combine demographic measurements, broader behavioural characteristics and a knowledge of where these consumers live helps to build a 'picture' of consumers that facilitates strong marketing decision-making support.

Figure 5.3 indicates that as one moves from the demographic through to psychological characteristics the measurement process becomes more difficult. Putting aside the differences in techniques to capture 'demography', 'behaviour' or 'psychology', *what* is being captured becomes more difficult as one moves towards psychological variables. If one considers psychological variables that are vital to marketing which could be captured, examples such as satisfaction, loyalty, trust, and quality are not as easy to capture as questions such as gender, age or where one lives. Chapter 10 will explore the concept of measurement in more depth, but at this stage consider what 'satisfaction' actually means, and then the problems of measuring that concept in an accurate manner.

Conversely, as the measurements become more difficult to conduct, they add more to the 'picture' of consumer and market profiles. To say that a market is primarily female, aged between 25 to 40 and lives in a detached property with a mortgage, starts to build a 'picture' of target consumers. To add details of their media behaviour, the array of products and services they buy, characteristics of their lifestyle and their expectations helps to build up a rich and, for decision makers, very useful 'picture' of target consumers.

Examining the variety of data sources that can be used in the interrelated variables that build market profiles, it is clear to see a role for traditional survey work, scanned data, customer data, externally generated secondary data, and the use of loyalty cards. There is a clear interdependence among the different data sources with the increased sophistication of decision support systems that allow the 'fusing' of the data to be conducted.[16]

STAGES OF DEVELOPMENT IN USING DATABASES AND SURVEY DATA TO BUILD PROFILES OF CONSUMERS AND MODEL MARKETING DECISIONS

The last section discussed how different data could be combined to build strong 'pictures' of consumers. Reflecting upon the role of the marketing researcher in supporting the marketing decision-maker as detailed in Chapter 1, it is clear that the combination of survey data and databases plays a major role in fulfilling the following, helping to:

- describe the nature and scope of customer groups
- understand the nature of forces that shape the needs of customer groups and the marketer's ability to satisfy those groups
- test individual and interactive controllable marketing variables
- monitor and reflect upon past successes and failures in marketing decisions.

Building up a 'pictute' of target consumers. A geodemographic profile of the MOSAIC Swedish Sub Group "Home Sweet Home"
Experian

The actual implementation of the decision support systems that allow the combination of data sources to be used in supporting decision-makers can take a great deal of time, expense and organisational learning. It is not the intention here to go through the planning, training and organisational issues in making the systems work, but to broadly summarise the stages that an organisation may go through in combining survey and database data. Figure 5.4 summarises the stages of integration; the following descriptions develop the summarised stages in more detail.

1 *Analyse existing consumer database*. This data could include the daily operational transactions or enquiries made to a company. As an internal secondary data source it is the cheapest and most readily available data – providing the organisation culture allows access and analysis to marketing researchers.
2 *Use supplied geodemographic profiles*. There is a growing number of geodemographic systems vendors who have been in operation for up to 20 years. In this time they have been able to refine the data they collect and the analyses they produce to build consumer profiles. Companies can buy a base system 'off the shelf' and add in a variety of different databases.

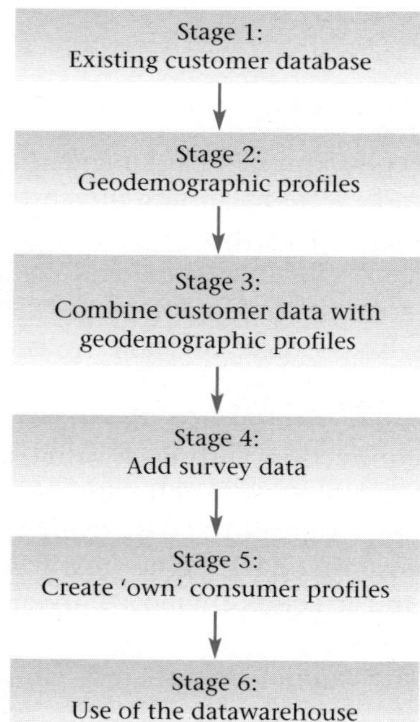

Figure 5.4
Stages of development in using databases and survey data to build profiles of consumers and model marketing decisions

3 *Combine existing consumer data with geodemographic profiles*. Using the mapping functions of the geodemographic system, existing customer data can be analysed using the profiles supplied with the system. Maps can be used to illustrate the catchment and types of customer and then evaluate potential in new locations.
4 *Use other surveys (either own or from external sources) that build on geodemographic sources and customer database*. Surveys conducted by a company where either a customer identification or postcode are recorded can be added. Survey data can be analysed using the geographic profiles and analyses represented using maps.
5 *Use combined data sources to create own profiles of customers*. Companies gain experience from using the geodemographic profiles and adding their own data. Over a period of time they may see that the generalised definitions of consumers from the geodemographic system do not accurately represent their existing and target customers. With the benefit and use of their own data, they may take the raw data from the geodemographics vendor and produce their own classifications.
6 *Use of the datawarehouse*. Essentially, this is using many database sources to build one huge database that may be accessed, allowing data to be fused and analysed. This would be done to suit particular reporting requirements or specific queries from either marketing research or marketing managers. With the growth and significance of this development in decision support, the next section describes the datawarehouse in more detail.

THE DATAWAREHOUSE

Datawarehouse
The datawarehouse may be seen as a 'super database', but more specifically it may be defined as a process of gathering disparate data from database and survey sources, and converting it into a consistent format that can aid business decision-making.

One of the most prolific users and innovators in **datawarehouses** is the banking industry. The following example illustrates the problems and opportunities for the banking industry from having many different departments with quite distinctive databases.

EXAMPLE

You say 'warehouse', I say 'database' ...[17]

Three major changes are sweeping through bank marketing: Banks are becoming even more customer driven, they are becoming increasingly information rich, and they are now dependent on constantly evolving computer technologies.

Being more customer driven results in a breaking down of the previously hermetically sealed functional areas of banking. Synergistic marketing and sales is now the name of the game. But as these invisible walls come tumbling down, banks are confronting the unintended result of departments with unique informational needs and personal computers: databases of highly valuable information that have no connection with each other. It is as if the tide has gone out, leaving tidal pools teeming with rich data separate from one another along a beach. In this case, the whole of the data really is greater than the sum of its parts. These pools of customer data are not just valuable in and of themselves. The greatest value is in the across-the-board juxtaposition of all the data pools with one another. That's where the confusing conceptual model of a datawarehouse comes in. 'Datawarehousing' then, is simply about the creation of a super database. ■

The datawarehouse may be seen as a 'super database', but more specifically it may be defined thus:[18]

A datawarehouse is as much a process of gathering disparate data, converting it into a consistent format that can aid business decision-making, as it is a configuration of software and hardware. Data warehouses empower users by providing them with access to a whole array of information in an organisation, making it available for use in other applications.

From this definition, the datawarehouse can be described as having the following three qualities:

1 It is a collection of integrated databases designed to support managerial decision-making and problem solving.
2 It essentially becomes a giant database that can include survey data held in a database format.
3 It physically separates an organisation's **operational data** systems from its decision support systems.

Operational data
Data generated about an organisation's customers, generated through day-to-day transactions.

At its most fundamental level, the datawarehouse has three components.

1 *Acquisition*. This includes all the programs, applications and various interfaces that extract data from earlier, existing databases. It continues with preparing this data and exporting it to the datawarehouse.
2 *Storage*. This is synonymous with any database. It simply involves a storage area to hold a vast amount of data from a variety of sources. The storage area is organised to make it easy to find and use the data. It will be updated from a variety of sources which could be through scanner and loyalty card data on customers, or through the use of intranet data as described in Chapter 4 when examining the compilation of competitor data.
3 *Access*. This encompasses both set reporting of pre-determined events and the means to perform individual analyses, querying 'what-if' scenarios. The process of exploring the databases matches the **data mining** techniques that will be illustrated in Chapter 6. As marketing researchers and decision-makers learn about markets and their effects upon those markets, the development of models is facilitated

Data mining
A range of data analysis techniques used to explore large datasets and carry out transformations of the data. Data mining may reveal hidden relationships or patterns in the data and acts as an aid to interpretation.

There has been a phenomenal growth in the use of databases to support marketing decision-making. In larger organisations with many divisions or where mergers and acquisitions have taken place, the datawarehouse has facilitated the 'fusing' of data from many sources. Such developments are seen as a threat by many in the marketing research industry. However, many marketing research companies and marketing research departments within companies are embracing database techniques, utilising the synergistic benefits of matching database analyses with traditional survey data. It is worth repeating the quote presented in Chapter 4 from Greg Ward, Development Director for Taylor Nelson, the largest marketing research company in the UK.

> The marketing research industry needs to acknowledge that databases are serious products and that both types of information have benefits. If you take the best of both – what we call information based marketing – you get something that is significantly more powerful. The 'them and us' situation does nobody any favours and the idea that the two disciplines bear no resemblance to each other is wrong.

As marketing decision-makers become more willing and able to interrogate databases and to creatively generate their own decision support, this does not mean the end of 'traditional' marketing research. As illustrated earlier when examining types of data that are used to build consumer and market profiles, psychological data plays a vital role that is fulfilled by qualitative and quantitative marketing research. The marketing researcher needs to develop a greater awareness of both how data captured through traditional methods can be integrated with data held on databases *and* how the combined data creatively supports decision-makers.

Databases and the development of datawarehouses are allowing a wider and shared use of data. The graphical formats of presenting data, especially using maps, break down many barriers in decision-makers who resist formal statistical analyses. They encourage managers to tailor output to their meet their individual needs. The creativity that is the hallmark of marketing decision-making is supported by the creative collection and connections between data. Where there are gaps in decision-makers' knowledge, they can be more focused and precise in determining what marketing research support they need. Many marketing researchers are rising to meet this challenge.

The final example in this section illustrates how innovative data capture and the formation of databases can be. Capturing data that represents media search behaviour through the Internet, like the bar code scanner or loyalty card, is a form of electronic observation. Applied in isolation the application illustrated can generate 'junk mail' as stated in the example. With the creative connection to other data sources, the marketing researcher moves to supporting a stronger total awareness of consumers and how best to satisfy them.

EXAMPLE

A nice little earner for the market researchers[19]

Visitors to company Web sites will soon be able to 'mine' data on the site for the information they want – but their activities are likely to be tracked and analysed for market research. As visitors wander through the Web site their preferences will be logged, recorded and even passed on, so they could be receiving junk email from other retailers almost instantly. Next time the person logs onto the site, they will be presented with the information, advertisements and other material that the computer remembers the user demanding last time.

IBM's Media Miner is being used by a newspaper in Germany to give used car buyers access to their classified database. Buyers can search for key words such as model, age, price range and so on, but can also search through the photographs by specifying a colour. Systems such as Media Miner will make it easier for people to find what they want on commercial Web sites, but they may be giving away a considerable amount of information about themselves while they do it. ■

INTERNATIONAL MARKETING RESEARCH

Linking databases through geodemographic information systems and datawarehouses is transforming international marketing research. Within individual companies, customers may be analysed from operational data within a country, showing different patterns of behaviour between different regions or cities and relating that behaviour to their marketing activities. When a company operates across borders, country differences become just another geographical variable.

Deciding to operate or develop in a particular country, companies may buy a geodemographic information system (should one be developed for that country). A GIS may be used as a foundation to add to their operational data. From this point they may go through the stages of database development as laid out in Figure 5.4.

The following example illustrates how a company looking at a particular country may use a GIS to great effect.

EXAMPLE

Making data go further

Expanding overseas may sound like a good idea, but ask any marketer who has attempted it and they will tell you how difficult it can be. Knowing the 'lie of the land' does not mean just a quick reconnaissance of the target market, it means detailed analysis. Geodemographical information systems (GIS) can offer a solution. Tesco, which is increasing its presence in Hungary and the Czech Republic by investing £700 m in three shopping malls in Prague and Budapest, is one of the many companies using GIS to plan overseas projects. The retailer recently said it plans to build six megastores per year in Eastern and Central Europe. Several established map and data providers are meeting the demand created by large users, such as Tesco. Experian, Claritas and Equifax provide GIS packages and data for European markets and for parts of Asia, Australasia and South Africa. ■

Performing analyses within countries is proving most fruitful, provided a base GIS has been established. Problems start where there is no base GIS. In many countries there are great problems in tracking down and combining data sources that can be relied upon. Further, even if reliable data can be located, legislation may make the use of certain data types illegal. In many developing countries, the data needed to build a GIS is sparse. With the data that is available, much experimentation is needed to enable valid classifications that reflect consumer types, which are useful to marketers and marketing researchers.

A further problem exists when making comparisons across countries using separate GIS systems for individual countries. As illustrated earlier when comparing Swedish, Dutch and UK classifications, there are different property types in each country, making cross-country comparisons difficult. Many GIS vendors have experimented and developed classification systems that allow comparisons between European countries. Building such classifications are difficult because of the inherent property differences between countries and differences in the data available for analysis.

The fusing together of different data sources – including customer data, geodemographic data and survey data – illustrates that the issues involved in understanding international markets are no different from those encountered with domestic markets.

ETHICS IN MARKETING RESEARCH

Marketing researchers are confronted by problems posed by the wording of ESOMAR and individual country marketing research associations' codes of conduct.[20] The codes specify that the compilation of lists, registers or databanks of names and addresses for any non-research purpose shall in no way be associated directly or indirectly with marketing research. However, the examples detailed in this chapter show that supporting marketing decision-makers through marketing research and databases can be seen as part of a total information industry. Evidence of the many leading marketing research agencies involved in data collection and analyses through databases illustrates that databases need not be 'cheap and nasty'. With due care it is possible to combine marketing research ethics and database marketing which has been achieved to a great extent in Canada. There are a growing number of companies that have used marketing research for many years that now combine the traditional role of marketing research manager with a wider role including database management. An essential part of this combined role lies in the management of customer databases, adding survey details with respondents' individual details being added.

Given the phenomenal growth of databases in marketing and the support they offer to marketing decision-makers, they are here to stay. With well-planned 'traditional' marketing research integrated into database analyses, the strategic power of consumer and market analyses is phenomenal. If marketers abuse their knowledge of consumers, they stand to do great harm to their brands and corporate image. For example, in bank databases there are many opportunities for the cross-selling of products. Rather than welcoming the approach from another division of a bank, trying to sell insurance to an investment client, there can be a reaction against the approach, affecting the original business. As discussed at the start of the chapter, consumers are more aware of how valuable knowledge of their behaviour is and how it is used by marketers. They are willing to trade this knowledge for the kind of rewards that are gained from the use of their loyalty cards. Marketers are aware of the dangers of abusing the knowledge that their customers impart to them. However, there are issues of civil liberties that cannot be ignored. These are touched upon in the following example.

EXAMPLE

Loyalty for sale[21]

Provided that shoppers like the benefits and do not object to a system which records every bar of chocolate and bottle of gin purchased, no great harm will be done. However there is a danger that, despite the safeguards of the Data Protection Act, this mass of information on consumers' habits could leak across the networks into unscrupulous hands. Issues of civil liberty would be raised if, for example, insurance companies could use the data to identify people whose purchases indicated an unhealthy lifestyle; or if the police could draw up a list of suspects by monitoring the purchase of specific items or unusual consumption patterns. ■

One of the benefits of the use of geodemographic systems is that in many cases the individual does not have to be identified, the postcode is a sufficient key to make a link between databases. This maintains the marketing research industry maxim of respondent confidentiality. The following example shows that the marketing research industry in the UK has recognised that the growth of databases has a major impact upon their work. Rather than dismissing the database 'industry', they are tackling the means to embrace the opportunities. Guidelines help marketing researchers to maintain the long recognised professional standards in the marketing research industry.

EXAMPLE

Research's spotlight puts its focus nearer the individual[22]

The research industry is now more involved with geodemographics (and now lifestyles) than ever. Most of the large syndicated surveys or panels are now able to cross-tabulate by neighbourhood classifications, in some cases by a number of them, as well as most of the media research surveys.

This is not new, the Target Group Index (TGI) has been available for analysis by geodemographics since 1980. What is more revolutionary is the linkage of marketing research with lifestyle data, the most public example being Claritas's Lifestyle Census by Taylor Nelson AGB.

Such linkages have been facilitated by the Market Research Society's Professional Standards Committee having published, in February 1995, *Guidelines for Handling Databases*, which addressed the issue of market research organisations wishing to link survey data to either client's customer databases or lifestyle databases. ■

INTERNET AND COMPUTER APPLICATIONS

The subject of collecting and analysing secondary data by the scanning of purchases, linking consumers to scanned data through store cards, geodemographic information systems, databases and datawarehouses is founded upon computer applications. Viewing and exploring these applications is the best means to illustrate the potential that lies in this technology. The enclosed multimedia guide to MOSAIC CD should be referred to at this point.

The multimedia guide to MOSAIC provides an insight into the values and lifestyles of British consumers. In the NEIGHBOURHOOD section, films, photographs, charts, text and sound commentary provide a clear visualisation of the 52 MOSAIC types and the 12 MOSAIC groups as described in this chapter. You can browse at random between the visualisation media; you can 'walk' through the 52 types in a rank order of their potential to consume particular products and types of media.

You can take a tour through a typical High Street that serves each of the 12 MOSAIC groups, look at poster sites that appeal to each of the consumer target groups, listen to street interviews espousing their social values.

In the TARGET GROUP section, you can identify over 100 products, services and media for the types of neighbourhood which offer the greatest market opportunity. For each of these products you can map the forms and individual postcodes within them where marketing effort is likely to yield the highest returns.

In the APPLICATIONS section you can hear experts, each a recognised authority in his or her field, explain the way MOSAIC is currently being used in applications as diverse as retail location decisions to actuarial analysis. You can view the software applications that marketers use to implement these targeting strategies from their own PCs, obtain the authoritative account of how MOSAIC is built and learn how to establish an accurate profile of target customers, whether from customer databases or from research surveys.

No technical manuals or training are required to use the CD. Help prompts can be accessed throughout the system and an 'i' button provides relevant information at any point.[23]

Start by working through the background material on 'How MOSAIC was built', follow this by examining 'MOSAIC profiling' and then the 'Background to Experian' the company that developed MOSAIC. From that base, explore and visualise how you may develop a rich picture of consumers that provides excellent support to marketing decision-making.

SUMMARY

Databases including customer operational data, geodemographic data and survey data are radically changing how marketing decision-making is being supported. There is much debate as to whether the use of databases is compatible with 'traditional' marketing research. With the junk mail connotations of databases and compromises of respondent anonymity, many marketing researchers may seek to keep the database at arm's length. However, handled with the professional acumen that marketing researchers have displayed for many years, the database presents great opportunities for the marketing researcher. In Europe, many of the leading marketing research agencies and research functions within companies have embraced the database.

There is also great debate as to whether the database is just a fad or whether it is going to fundamentally change how marketing researchers and marketers develop an understanding of consumers and markets. The following two examples illustrate the two sides of the debate.

EXAMPLE

Flight of fancy[24]

Database marketing may seem to involve a lot of effort for what some believe to be a fad or passing trend. A recent posting to an on-line mailing list contained a note that illustrated one subscriber's concern that database marketing is becoming a fad: 'I see database marketing becoming yet another fad only surviving through the proselytizations of soapbox opportunists eager to get in on the action of training and seminar circuits. What long-term value does it give us to know what colour underpants our customers wear or when their pet canary has a birthday? I guess my point is that we can't get carried away with gathering information just for the sake of gathering information.' The time, money and effort spent has to generate meaningful information that can be used to accomplish goals. ■

EXAMPLE

T-Groups[25]

Market research offers depth while databases offer breadth. If you combine the two you end up with something that is substantially bigger than the sum of its parts.

Imagine a cube which represents everything you need to know about the UK's 23 million homes, with everything they do, and think, down one side and then time represented by the depth. Databases collect from a strip across the top of the cube, while market research samples from a thin strip into its depth. If you slice both ways you get a T and where they cross is the T-Group. If you can identify and understand that group, you can fill in the rest of the cube. ■

The above example illustrates the synergistic effect of combining database with marketing research data and how interdependent the two 'industries' have become. For the marketer, databases help to build profiles of consumers, linked to the products, communications and distribution methods those consumers favour. For the marketing researcher, databases can present the opportunity to experiment in 'one big laboratory', build models of consumer behaviour, develop an understanding of the gaps in knowledge of consumers and make links between behavioural and attitudinal data.

Much of the data that offers these benefits has been gained using data that captures customer buying behaviour. The use of the 'loyalty card' is one example of the means to capture customer behaviour. Different types of data that include scanner data, loyalty card data and survey data may be combined using geodemographic information systems (GIS). Using base geographic and demographic data, existing customers may be mapped out and analysed, potential customers can be evaluated using the GIS.

Pulling together disparate database sources is done through the use of datawarehouses. The datawarehouse integrates databases and survey data, allowing creative connections between data to be explored. The development of datawarehouse expertise especially helps to cope with the problems of disparate databases from different countries.

The ethics of using databases provokes much debate in the marketing research industry. As many research practitioners grow more accustomed to using databases, marketing research guidelines and codes of practice are being developed to reflect the good practice that exists in many companies.

QUESTIONS AND PROBLEMS

1 Discuss the characteristics that have lessened the distinction between marketing research and database marketing.

2 How have 'reward' schemes affected consumers' expectations of tangible rewards for supplying information about themselves?

3 What kinds of data can be gathered through electronic scanner services?

4 Call in at a supermarket or store that operates a reward or loyalty card scheme that requires you to apply for membership. Pick up an application form and examine the nature of questions you are expected to answer. What marketing research use can be made of the data collected from this application form?

5 Describe the benefits to the marketing decision-maker of being able to capture data that identifies characteristics of consumers and their shopping behaviour in a store.

6 Describe the benefits to the marketing researcher of being able to capture data that identifies characteristics of consumers and their shopping behaviour in a store.

7 Why may the characteristics of consumers differ, based upon where they live?

8 What is a geodemographic classification of consumers?

9 How can the graphical representation of consumer characteristics using maps help marketing decision-making?

10 What benefits may be gained from fusing together customer characteristics held as internal secondary data, with a proprietary geodemographic information system, held as external secondary data?

11 How does the compilation of different types of data help to build a strong 'picture' of consumer characteristics?

12 Describe the stages of development in using databases and survey data to build profiles of consumers and model marketing decisions.

13 What is a datawarehouse?

14 Describe the main components of a datawarehouse.

15 What ethical problems exist with the use of databases that many traditional marketing researchers may find difficult to cope with?

NOTES

1 Smith, S. 'Losing Out in the Data Race', *Marketing* (27 February 1997), 30.

2 'Getting to Know You', *Grocer* (2 August 1997), 33.

3 Experian's World Wide Web Home Page.

4 Fletcher, K., 'External drive', *Marketing* (30 October 1997), 39–40.

5 Cobb, R., 'Checking out the Goods: Scanning Systems are Serving an Increasing Range of Roles other than just Product Sales', *Marketing* (1 November 1990), 36.

6 Field, C., 'Data goes to the market', *Computer Weekly* (16 January 1997), 44.

7 *The Times* (9 January 1998), 21.

8 Sumner-Smith, D., 'Knowing me, knowing you', *Marketing* (23 October 1997), 38.

9 'A computer on a white horse', *The Economist* 335 (1 April 1995), 51.

10 Bird, J., 'Logical Guides to Marketing', *Management Today* (February 1995), 58.

11 Richards, A., 'Unite and Conquer', *Marketing* (18 September 1997), 24–25.

12 'Shuffling the decks', *Marketing Week* (6 November 1997), 49–51.

13 Miles, L., 'Playing the loyalty card', *Marketing* (27 July, 1995), 111.

14 Rufford, N. and Nuki, P., 'Rush-hour Shoppers Face Higher Prices', *The Sunday Times* (7 December 1997), 5.

15 Reed, D., 'Simply Read', *Marketing Week* (2 October 1997).

16 A recent example of fusing research data with databases is presented in Leventhal, B., 'An Approach to Fusing Market Research with Database Marketing', *Journal of the Market Research Society* 39(4) (October 1997), 545–61.

17 Man, D., 'You say "warehouse", I say "database" . . .', *Bank Marketing* 29(4) (April 1997), 37.

18 Man, D., 'The Faqs on Datawarehousing', *Bank Marketing* 29(4) (April 1997), 38.

19 'A nice little earner for the market researchers', *The Times* (26 February 1997).

20 Hodgson, P., 'Databases: the Time for Decisions is Nigh', *Research* (October 1993), 19.

21 'Loyalty for sale', *Financial Times* (18 September 1998).

22 Sleight, P., 'Research's Spotlight Puts its Focus Nearer the Individual', *ResearchPlus* (May 1997) 4.

23 The Multimedia Guide to MOSAIC, The 1st Electronic Atlas of British Behaviour, 1997.

24 'Flight of fancy', *Direct Marketing* 60(1) (May 1997), 48.

25 Miller, R., 'Where Next for Research?' *Marketing* (22 May 1997), 31.

Chapter 6

Qualitative research: focus group interviews

Qualitative research helps the marketer to understand the richness, depth and complexity of consumers

OBJECTIVES

After reading this chapter, the student should be able to:

1 explain the difference between qualitative and quantitative research in terms of the objectives, sampling, data collection and analysis; and outcomes;
2 distinguish between various forms of qualitative research including direct procedures such as focus groups and in-depth interviews and indirect methods such as observation and projective techniques;
3 describe focus groups in detail, with emphasis on planning and conducting focus groups;
4 evaluate the advantages, disadvantages, and applications of focus groups;
5 describe alternative ways of conducting qualitative research in groups;
6 discuss the considerations involved in conducting qualitative research in an international setting, especially in contrasting European and US traditions of running focus groups;
7 understand the ethical issues involved in conducting qualitative research.

OVERVIEW

Qualitative research forms a major role in supporting marketing decision-making, primarily as an exploratory design. Researchers may undertake qualitative research to help define a research problem, to develop an approach or as a design in its own right. In developing an approach, qualitative research is often used for generating hypotheses and identifying variables that should be included in quantitative approaches. It may be used after or in conjunction with quantitative approaches where illumination of statistical findings are needed. In some cases qualitative approaches may be adopted in isolation, after secondary data sources have been thoroughly evaluated.

In this chapter, we discuss the differences between qualitative and quantitative research and the role of each in the marketing research project. We present a classification of qualitative research and cover focus groups in detail. The considerations involved in conducting qualitative research when researching international markets are discussed. Several ethical issues that arise in qualitative research are identified. The following examples give a flavour of qualitative research and its applications in marketing research.

EXAMPLE

A research commitment more than skin deep[1]

L'Oreal is the largest supplier of toiletries and cosmetics in the world, the group tucks under its umbrella some of the best known brands and companies in the beauty business: cosmetics houses Lancôme, Vichy, Helena Rubenstein; fragrance houses Guy Laroche, Cacharel, Ralph Lauren. The group's 1994 financial statement reported net profits soaring 13 per cent to 2.94 billion French francs.

Given the French penchant for qualitative research, and given the nature of the cosmetics industry, Anne Murray, Head of Research, was asked which type of research she favoured.

> We're not particularly pro quantitative or qualitative. Nevertheless, I do think qualitative in our area is very important. There are many sensitive issues to cover – environmental concerns, animal testing, intimate personal products. And increasingly, we have given to us very technical propositions from the labs, and what is a technical breakthrough to a man in a white coat, is not necessarily so to a consumer. So the research department has to be that interface between the technical side and the consumer. ■

EXAMPLE

There's trouble in classes for kids who wear glasses[2]

Dolland & Aitchison, the optician, which prides itself on its professionalism, decided to look at a small but significant sector of its market – children. Avoiding the tendency of many clients to talk only to parents, the company was determined that children should have their say too.

They commissioned Clarke Research, which does much work with children and families, to conduct qualitative research with children, aged from 5 to 12 years, and their parents. Research was carried out in 12 focus groups, each children's group having four friendship pairs, and including boys and girls spread by age and geographically. Each children's group was followed by a group of their parents (the children were taken to a local McDonalds while this went on).

Using projective techniques, Clarke Research asked children to describe the experience of wearing specs. This included asking them to draw pictures, to use words and cartoons to describe feelings and attitudes, and to make up mood boards. Some of what was learnt had been anticipated. Children described the experience of losing their specs, forgetting them, finding them uncomfortable, and getting them dirty. What had not been expected was that all the children spoken to had received some degree of harassment, teasing or outright bullying from non-spec wearing children. ■

These examples illustrate the rich insights into the underlying behaviour of consumers that can be obtained by using qualitative procedures.

PRIMARY DATA: QUALITATIVE VERSUS QUANTITATIVE RESEARCH

Qualitative research
An unstructured, primarily exploratory methodology based on small samples, intended to provide insight and understanding.

Quantitative research
A research methodology that seeks to quantify the data and, typically, applies some form of statistical analysis.

As explained in Chapter 4, primary data are originated by the researcher for the specific purpose of addressing the problem at hand. Primary data may be **qualitative** or **quantitative** in nature, as shown in Figure 6.1. The distinction between qualitative and quantitative research closely parallels the distinction between exploratory and conclusive research discussed in Chapter 3, but they are not identical. There are circumstances where qualitative research can be used to

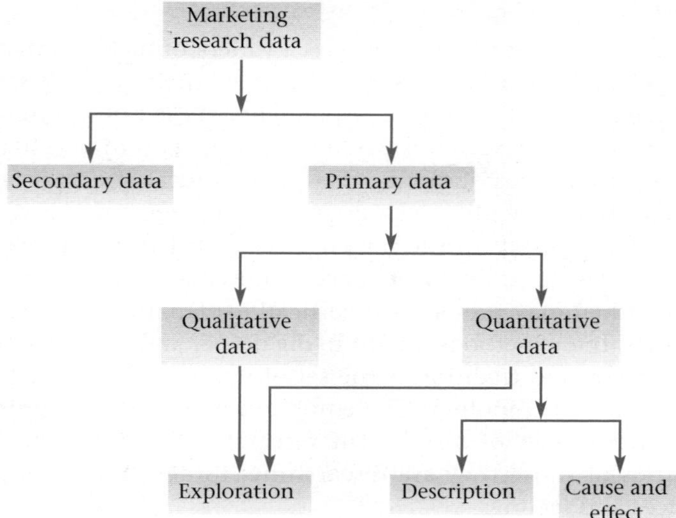

Figure 6.1
A classification of marketing research data

present detailed descriptions that cannot be measured in a quantifiable manner, for example, describing characteristics and styles of music that may be used in an advertising campaign. Conversely, there may be circumstances where quantitative measurements of specific hypotheses or questions related to a description or experiment have been tackled. There may be sufficient data to allow 'data mining' or an exploration of relationships between individual measurements to take place. The following example illustrates how exploratory quantitative research is growing, linked to the increasing amount of data available from both inside and outside organisations.

EXAMPLE

How the data mountain became a mountain of information[3]

Data visualisation is a data mining technique. As an example, a large tracking database covering the entire grocery purchasing of over 7000 households on a daily basis for a year was searched for common links. Links were presented visually in what can be best described as a sort of 'spirograph' picture. As the data levels are drilled through, the links become more and more specific.

We may start with a blank sheet of paper and identify a strong link between a Sainsbury main shopper and a Tesco shopper. We can quickly move on to discover that these shoppers are strongly linked with grocery purchasing within Tesco and from there highlight cereals, then ready to eat cereals, then key branded staple lines (Cornflakes, Weetabix, Rice Crispies) as being primary drivers for these shoppers.

Used in this way, data visualisation may not answer all our questions but, maybe more importantly, it ensures the right questions will be asked. What is it about Tesco's branded cereals offering that attracts Sainsbury shoppers? What else were they buying on these trips? How can these shoppers be targeted to bring them back to Sainsburys? ■

In general, qualitative research tends to be exploratory and quantitative research tends to be descriptive. The differences between the two research designs are summarised in Figure 6.1.

Qualitative research definition

Qualitative research encompasses a variety of methods that are flexible to enable respondents to reflect upon, and express their views. It seeks to encapsulate the experiences and feelings of respondents in their own terms.

Qualitative research is based on at least two intellectual traditions.[4] The first and perhaps most important is the set of ideas and associated methods from the broad area of depth psychology.[5] This movement was concerned with the less conscious aspects of the human psyche. It led to a development of methods to gain access to individuals' subconscious and/or unconscious levels. So, while an individual may present a superficial explanation of events to themselves or to others, these methods sought to dig deeper and penetrate the superficial.

The second tradition is the set of ideas and associated methods from sociology and anthropology. The emphases here are upon holistic understanding of the world-view of people. The researcher is expected to 'enter' the hearts and minds of those they are researching, to develop an empathy of their experiences and feelings.

Both traditions have a concern with developing means of communication between the researcher and those being researched. There may be intense interaction between the two parties in order to learn about the experiences of others. The following example illustrates differences between American and European marketing researchers in how they utilise the above traditions and practice qualitative research. Further differences will be tackled when focus groups are examined in more detail.

EXAMPLE

When East meets West, quite what does 'qualitative' mean?[6]

International marketers have always been aware that qualitative research as it developed in the US and Europe are quite different practices, stemming from different premises and yielding different results. American-style qualitative research started from the same evaluative premise as quantitative research but on a smaller scale. This made it cheaper, quicker and useful for checking out the less critical decisions. European-style qualitative research started from the opposite premise as quantitative research: it was developmental, exploratory and creative rather than evaluative. It was used as a tool of understanding, to get underneath consumer motivation.

The American style uses a detailed discussion guide which follows a logical sequence and is usually strictly adhered to. The interviewing technique involves closed questions and straight answers. This type of research is used primarily to inform about behaviour and to confirm hypotheses already derived from other sources. For this reason, clients who have attended groups often feel they do not need any further analysis; the group interaction supplies the answers. Transcripts are rarely necessary and reports are often summarised or even done away with altogether.

The European style is used primarily to gain new insight; it also works from a discussion guide, but in a less structured way. The interviewing technique is opportunistic and probing. Projective techniques are introduced to help researchers understand underlying motivations and attitudes. Because the purpose is understanding, which requires a creative synthesis of (sometimes unconscious) consumer needs and brand benefits, analysis is time consuming and usually involves full transcripts. ■

RATIONALE FOR USING QUALITATIVE RESEARCH

It is not always possible, or desirable, to use fully structured or formal methods to obtain information from respondents. Thus, there are several reasons to use qualitative research.

1. *Sensitive information*. Respondents may be unwilling to answer certain or give truthful answers to questions that invade their privacy, embarrass them, or have a negative impact on their ego or status. Questions that relate to sanitary products and contraception are examples of personally sensitive issues. In industrial marketing research, questions that relate to corporate performance and plans are examples of commercially sensitive issues.
2. *Subconscious feelings*. Respondents may be unable to provide accurate answers to questions that tap their subconscious. The values, emotional drives, and motivations residing at the subconscious level are disguised from the outer world by rationalisation and other ego defences. For example, a person may have purchased an expensive sports car to overcome feelings of inferiority. But, if asked, 'Why did you purchase this sports car?' he may say 'I got a great deal,' 'My old car was falling apart,' or 'I need to impress my customers and clients.'
3. *Complex phenomena*. The nature of what respondents are expected to describe may be difficult to capture with structured questions. For example, respondents may know what brands of wine they enjoy, what types of music they prefer or what images they regard as being prestigious. They may not be able to clearly explain why they have these feelings or where these feelings are coming from.
4. *The holistic dimension*. The object of taking a holistic outlook in qualitative research is to gain a comprehensive and complete picture of the whole context in which the phenomena of interest occur. It is an attempt to describe and understand as much as possible about the whole situation of interest. Each scene exists within a multi-layered and interrelated context and it may require multiple methods to ensure the researcher covers all angles. This orientation helps the researcher discover the interrelationships among the various components of the phenomena under study. The emphasis is upon developing an understanding the relationship of contexts with different forms of behaviour. Setting behaviour into context involves placing observations, experiences and interpretations into a larger perspective.[7] An example of this may be of measuring satisfaction with a meal in a restaurant. A questionnaire can break down components of the experience in the restaurant and quantify the extent of satisfaction with these. But what effect did the 'atmosphere' have upon the experience? What role did the type of music, the colour and style of furniture, aromas coming the kitchen, other people in the restaurant, the mood when entering the restaurant, feelings of relaxation or tension as the meal went on – all contribute to the feeling of atmosphere. Building up an understanding of the interrelationship of the context of consumption allows the qualitative researcher to build up this holistic view.

The following example of the Pepsi Next Generation illustrates marketing activities supported by qualitative marketing research, the type of information that needs eliciting from a target group and the qualitative technique used.

EXAMPLE

First get the language right, then tell them a story[8]

Teenagers immediately recognise a communication in their language and are very quick to judge whether advertisers have got it right. They see ads and either like them, reject them, ignore them or, in many cases, discuss them. Teenagers are so fluent in 'marketing speak' because marketing and advertising are perceived by them to be the kind of work which can be creative, interesting and acceptable. They discuss with one another the advertising which they perceive to be targeting them.

In the spring and summer of 1997, Pelgram Walters International conducted a study called Global Village. The Global Village hypothesis contended that teenagers around the world have a common language, which speaks to them in the filmed advertising medium. Part of the study consisted of focus group discussions of 12- to 18-year-olds.

Pepsi's Generation Next advertisement was criticised by more media literate teenage markets (Britain, Germany and the US) for stereotyping teens and misunderstanding who they are. The ad was a montage of very hip skateboarding teens, male teens wearing make up, perhaps implying that Pepsi is for the next generation which looks thus. The main complaint was 'we don't look like that', the teens saying that they were not all the same as one another. By aligning the brand image with these extreme images, the commercial was less appealing to mainstream teen consumers. ■

A CLASSIFICATION OF QUALITATIVE RESEARCH PROCEDURES

Direct approach
One type of qualitative research in which the purposes of the project are disclosed to the respondent or are obvious given the nature of the interview.

Indirect approach
A type of qualitative research in which the purposes of the project are disguised from the respondents.

A classification of qualitative research procedures is presented in Figure 6.2. These procedures are classified as either direct or indirect, based on whether the true purpose of the project is known to the respondents. A **direct approach** is not disguised. The purpose of the project is disclosed to the respondents or is otherwise obvious to them from the questions asked. Focus groups and in-depth interviews are the major direct techniques. In contrast, research that takes an **indirect approach** disguises the true purpose of the project. Observation and projective techniques, are the major indirect techniques. Each of these techniques is discussed in detail in this chapter and Chapter 7, beginning with focus groups.

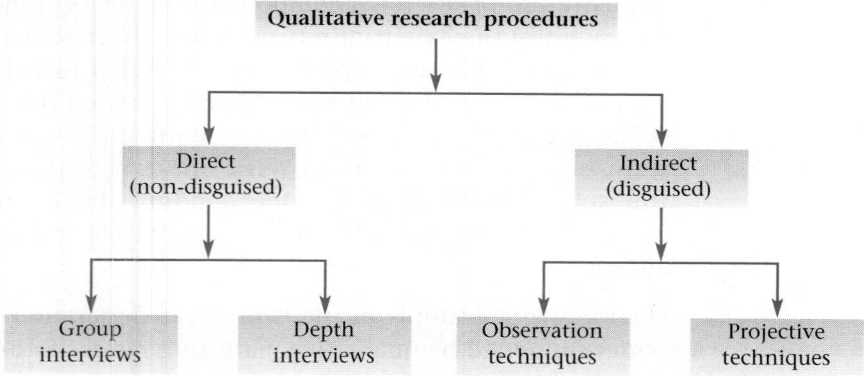

Figure 6.2
A classification of qualitative research procedures

FOCUS GROUP INTERVIEWS

Focus group
An interview conducted by a trained moderator among a small group of respondents in an unstructured and natural manner.

Moderator
An individual who conducts a focus group interview, by setting the purpose of the interview, questioning, probing and handling the process of discussion.

A **focus group** is an interview conducted by a trained moderator in a non-structured and natural manner with a small group of respondents. A **moderator** leads and develops the discussion. The main purpose of focus groups is to gain insights by creating a forum where respondents feel sufficiently relaxed to reflect and portray their feelings and behaviour – using their language and logic. The value of the technique lies in the unexpected findings often obtained from a free-flowing group discussion. Focus groups are the most important qualitative marketing research procedure, being used extensively in new product development, advertising development and image studies. They are so popular that many marketing research practitioners consider this technique synonymous with qualitative research.[9] Given their importance and popularity, we describe the salient characteristics of focus groups in detail.

What effect does 'atmosphere' have upon the experience of eating at a restaurant?
Tony Stone

Characteristics

The major characteristics of a focus group are summarised in Table 6.2. The key benefit of the focus group is the amount of creative discussion and other activities that may be generated. Group members have the time to reflect upon the stimulus that is presented to them. The stimulus may come from other group members or from the moderator. Using their intuition and imagination, group members can explain how they feel or behave, in words they are comfortable with, and using logic that is meaningful to them. The key drawback lies in how intimidating the group scenario may be to certain individuals. Many individuals may be self-conscious in expressing their ideas, feeling they may be ridiculed by others or they may be shy and unable to freely express themselves in a group. A focus group generally includes six to 12 members. Groups of fewer than six are unlikely to generate the momentum and group dynamics necessary for a successful session. Likewise, groups of more than 12 may be too crowded and may not be conducive to a cohesive and natural discussion.[10] Large groups have a tendency to splinter into sub-groups as group members 'fight' to get their views across.

Table 6.2 Characteristics of focus groups

Key benefit	Group members 'feed' off each other and creatively reveal ideas that the researcher may not have thought of or dared to tackle
Key drawback	Group members may feel intimidated or shy and may not reveal anything
Group size	6 to 12
Group composition	Homogeneous, respondents pre-screened
Physical setting	Relaxed, informal atmosphere
Time duration	1 to 6 hours
Recording	Use of audiocassettes, videotapes and notes from observations
Moderator	Observational, interpersonal and communication skills

A focus group generally should be homogeneous in terms of demographic and socio-economic characteristics. Commonality among group members avoids interactions and conflicts among group members on side issues.[11] Thus, for many topics, a women's group should not combine married homemakers with small children, young unmarried working women, and elderly divorced or widowed women because their lifestyles are substantially different. Moreover, the participants should be carefully screened to meet certain criteria. The participants must have had adequate experience with the object or issue being discussed. People who have already participated in numerous focus groups should not be included. These so-called professional respondents are atypical, and their participation leads to serious validity problems.[12]

The physical setting for the focus group is also important. A relaxed, informal atmosphere helps group members to forget they are being questioned and observed. What is meant by a relaxed, informal atmosphere may change depending upon the type of respondent and the subject being tackled. Examples of what 'relaxed and informal' means can include the home of a friend within a particular community, a works canteen, a village hall, a room in a leisure centre, a meeting room in a hotel or a purpose-built discussion group room. The poor acoustics and hard seats of a works canteen may not seem relaxed and informal. To group participants, however, it may be the place where they are happy to talk and willing to open up to a moderator. Light refreshments should be served before the session and made available throughout; these become part of a context of relaxation. The following example shows a development of conducting focus groups in places meaningful to the context of consuming a product.

EXAMPLE

New life in group discussions[13]

The issue of real context as opposed to simulation has always been thorny, but increasingly we are conducting groups wherever the product is seen, bought or used rather than in recruiter living rooms or in viewing facilities. This does not mean that all research needs to be conducted *in situ*. But designs do need to be designed which allow the findings from the real and the research environments to inform the overall recommendations. ■

Although a focus group may last from one to six hours, a duration of one and a half to two hours is typical. This period is needed to establish rapport with the participants and to explore, in depth, their beliefs, feelings, ideas, attitudes and insights regarding the topics of concern. Focus group interviews are invariably recorded, often on videotape, for subsequent replay, transcription and analysis. Videotaping has the advantage of recording facial expressions and body movements, but it can increase the costs significantly. Frequently, clients observe the session from an adjacent room using a one-way mirror. Video transmission technology enables the clients to observe focus group sessions live from a remote location.

The moderator plays a vital role in the success of a focus group. The moderator must establish rapport with the participants, keep the discussion moving forward, and **probe** the respondents to elicit insights. In addition, the moderator may have a central role in the analysis and interpretation of the data. Therefore, the moderator should possess skill, experience, knowledge of the discussion topic, and an understanding of the nature of group dynamics. The key characteristics of the moderator are summarised in the following list.

Probing
A motivational technique used when asking questions to induce the respondents to enlarge on, clarify, or explain their answers.

Qualities needed in the focus group moderator[14]

1 *Kindness with firmness*. The moderator must quickly develop an empathy with group members. From this the moderator should show kindness to make respondents feel welcome, combined with a firmness to stop particular individuals taking over the discussion.
2 *Permissiveness*. The moderator must be permissive, allowing the flow of discussion to develop as the group sees fit. However, he or she must be alert to signs that the group's cordiality or purpose is disintegrating.
3 *Involvement*. The moderator must encourage and stimulate intense personal involvement. In certain circumstances, this may mean becoming involved in the actual discussion itself. This can happen if a tendency for 'group speak' emerges. 'Group speak' happens when little debate or creativity in ideas develops, as particular individuals may not wish to be seen as going against a perceived group norm.
4 *Incomplete understanding*. The moderator must encourage respondents to be more specific about generalised comments by exhibiting a feigned naivety or incomplete understanding.

The moderator must encourage and stimulate intense personal involvement of the focus group members

5 *Encouragement*. The moderator must encourage unresponsive members to participate.
6 *Flexibility*. The moderator must be able to improvise and alter the planned outline amid the distractions of the group process.
7 *Sensitivity*. The moderator must be sensitive enough to guide the group discussion at an intellectual as well as emotional level. He or she must also be attuned to mood changes and issues that fire up enthusiastic responses or conversely cause the discussion to dry up.
8 *Observation*. As the group progresses, notes must be made of ideas or questions to come back to, interpretations of particular silences or bouts of laughter, and how group members are interacting with each other. These observations help the group discussion to progress well and the interpretation of the discussion to have greater meaning.

Planning and conducting focus groups

The procedure for planning and conducting focus groups is described in Figure 6.3.

Planning begins with an examination of the marketing research problem(s) and objectives. In most instances, the problem has been defined by this stage, but it is vital to ensure that the whole process is founded upon a clear awareness of the gaps in knowledge of marketing decision-makers. Given the problem definition, the objectives of using focus groups should be clarified. There should be a clear understanding of what information can be elicited using the technique.

Topic guide
A list of topics, questions and probes that are used by a moderator to help them manage a focus group discussion.

The next step is to develop a list of issues, or **topic guide**, that are to be tackled in the focus groups. This list may be a series of specific questions but is more likely to be a set of broad issues that can be developed into questions or probes as the focus group actually takes place. The specific question may be of help to the moderator who feels that a consistent set of points need to be presented to different groups in order to allow clear comparisons to be made. Specific questions also act as a 'prop' when the discussion is failing; indeed some group

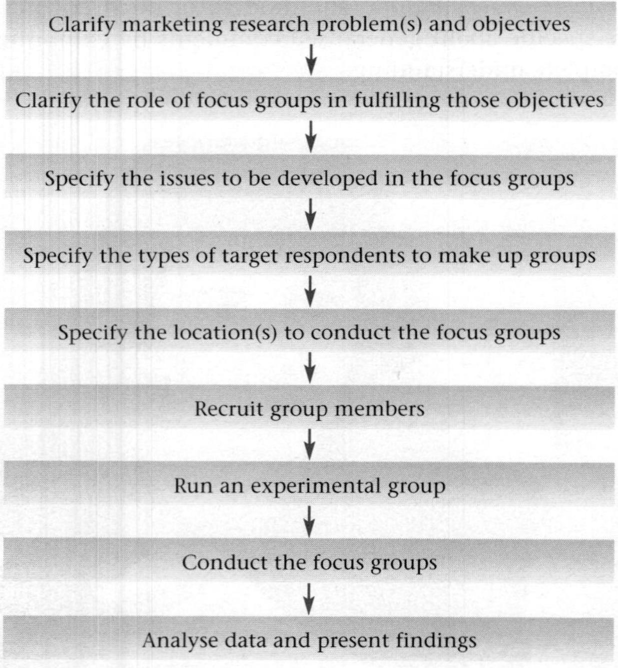

Figure 6.3
Procedure for planning and conducting focus groups

participants may expect their role to be to react to specific questions. If the moderator opens the discussion with a general question to make respondents comfortable with the subject and the purpose of the research, then specific questions, issues and probes can develop as the moderator tunes into the dynamics of the group. There may be additional, new issues that develop and, indeed, issues that group members do not see as being appropriate, and these can be discussed. The emphasis should be upon an *evolution and learning process* rather than administering a consistent set of questions.

The types of group members to take part in the discussions are then specified. From this specification, a questionnaire to screen potential participants is prepared. Typical information obtained from the questionnaire includes product familiarity and knowledge, usage behaviour, attitudes toward and participation in focus groups, and standard demographic characteristics. With the types of participants specified, consideration must be made of what would make them relaxed and comfortable. The following two examples illustrate traditions in the USA, Europe and in the UK, where focus groups are conducted. Note the UK tradition of recruiting and running focus groups within a community and even using the lounge of someone's house to run the group. The big advantage of this approach is that group participants are usually comfortable to attend and participate in an environment that is not alien to them.

EXAMPLE

See the USA, through the looking glass[15]

In the US, observing focus groups is a *policy*. Typically there will be five to eight observers, sometimes more, with agency and marketing company matching level for level to maintain a balance of power. American researchers and clients defend the value of observers. People with different perspectives can listen in a way that a moderator cannot, since the moderator is often 'dipping in for the moment' on one specific issue while the clients 'have the brand in their bones'. Probably the most deeply felt reason for being there is just being there; there is no substitute for the touchy-feely benefit of experiencing the consumer first-hand. More than ever, marketing people are isolated in their small worlds (probably in atypical New York or Chicago), making assumptions about their users. Seeing them is a reality check. Hearing tonality, watching body language, observing the consumer interact with the product, enriches the learning process. Sometimes brand people will get rejuvenated and creatives will get inspired. ■

PROBLEMS ASSOCIATED WITH THE US APPROACH[16]

- *Cost.* The travelling expenses on a recent four-group project in Dallas and Atlanta, over $15,000 for the nine observers from company and agency, more than doubled the cost of the research.
- *Incomplete data.* Clients may not have seen all the groups, leaving gaps in the total picture. Observers admit that they key in on the most lively and self-serving points; that they are identify positively and negatively with certain responses and filter accordingly; that they are attentive to ideas that affirm their positions and dismissive of contrary viewpoints.
- *Instant analysis.* Rather than waiting for a moderator's report or even the conclusions of the group, observers often jump to conclusions on little evidence or, worse still, stop listening once they have an 'impression' of the results.

- *Moderator reflection*. Often the moderator gets trapped into debriefing immediately after the group and taking positions that are hard to retreat from but which might be very different after a thoughtful review.
- *Effect on respondents*. There is little research on the effect of the two-way mirrors on respondents. The setting is not exactly conducive to natural expression and respondents may alter their responses for effect, stay silent or be self-conscious.

In the following example, the reactions of a decision-maker in observing comments made about their product are shown. In this example, the decision-maker conveys the value of the observation but recognises how raw the data are.

EXAMPLE

Through the looking glass[17]

Viewing laboratory
A room where a focus group may be conducted and simultaneously observed, usually by using a two-way mirror.

Which is the better marketing research environment: a member of the public's front room or a **viewing lab**? Traditionally, in the UK, the former was the unchallenged leader when it came to new product development and advertising campaign research. However, during the 1990s, the UK has taken a leap into viewing-lab territory.

Lucy Bannister, a director of qualitative research firm Davies Riley Smith Maclay, sees the UK catching up with the rest of the world. 'Clients in the UK have always thought of in-home research first because that is the way things developed historically. But I cannot think of any other country where this is the case, especially in Europe or in the US. Viewing labs have always been the norm outside the UK and marketers abroad think it is bizarre that we have this strange bias.' ■

A client's view of observing the focus group through the two-way mirror

'It's a strange experience, sitting on the other side of a two-way mirror watching your product being analysed in a focus group. It's like being locked out of your house and peering through the windows as burglars rifle through your drawers and take the piss out of your record collection.'

'You want to bang on the glass and plead with them to stop, but then they say something nice about your product and you want to grab the person next to you and shout "I thought of that!"'

'You tell yourself not to take the criticism too personally, to be professional, but it's hard when you've had sleepless nights agonising over minute details only to see them ignored or ripped apart in the space of half an hour.'

'It's great to get raw feedback like this, but remember just how raw it is. One group can say completely different things to another and some may just like the sport of making the suits behind the mirror suffer.' ■

Having decided on the location of the focus groups, the actual recruitment of group members progresses. This is one of the most difficult tasks as potential group members may be sceptical of what may happen at the group, sometimes fearing that they are exposing themselves to a hard sell campaign of time-share holidays or home improvements! If individuals have attended a focus group beforehand, the process of recruitment is easier, but getting the right type of respondent together at the right place and time can prove difficult. With the screening questionnaire, recruitment may take place on a face-to-face basis through street interviews or through database details by telephone. One of the traditions in the UK is to give the specification of group members to an individual in whose home the interviews are to take place. The advantage of this approach is their ability to persuade respondents that the process is a bona fide research process, it is rewarding and they make sure that individuals actually attend. The big disadvantage is ensuring that those recruited match the screening questionnaire requirements.

Group participants have to be rewarded for their attendance. Usually they enjoy the experience immensely once they are there but that does not ensure that they attend in the first place. Attendance can be rewarded with cash, a donation to charity or a gift. The following example illustrates the difficulties involved in recruitment and a marketing researcher's creative solution to the problem.

EXAMPLE

So how do you upstage a Ferrari owner?[18]

Researching an upmarket socially active audience is difficult at the best of times. The target is opinionated, demanding, often resistant to research and almost impossible to reach. So, when we got the brief to conduct focus groups among Ferrari, Porsche, top Mercedes and other exotic sports car-owners, we were tempted to panic. We knew we could find them, but how could we persuade them to participate?

We realised the one thing that would link our target, who were also defined as keen drivers, not just poseurs, was their love of cars and desire to know the latest news about new models (and to try them out if possible).

That's why we decided to offer the carrot of a drive around a race and proving track and the opportunity to meet the design and management team at our famous sports car maker. If anything might motivate people, who clearly already had sufficient money to indulge a very expensive taste, it should be this package. It worked like a dream, and we had a great success getting the right people to come and, more importantly, to participate. ■

Even when individuals have said that they will participate in the group, a telephone follow-up is necessary to remind and motivate group members.

Experimental group
An initial focus group run to test the setting of the interview, the opening question, topic guide and the mix of respondents that make up a group

The first group to be run should be seen as an **experimental group**. All aspects of running the group should be evaluated. Were the group members relaxed and comfortable? How did they react to the tape recorder, video or two-way mirror? What types of member interacted well? How did the initial question work in opening up and developing the discussion? How did the topic guide work, were there issues missing or issues that individuals would not tackle? How comfortable was the moderator handling the topics, did they have to interject to liven the discussion? With a reflection of these issues, any necessary alterations can be made to the way that the remaining focus groups are administered. There may be very useful information that emerges from the experimental group that can be included in the main analysis. However, if the group does not work well the information gleaned may be of little use but the lessons learnt are invaluable in running the remaining groups.

Finally, the focus groups can be actually run. The question arises here of how many groups should be run. Beyond the first experimental group, the number of groups needed can vary. If there is a great variety of types of individual that make up a target market, then many homogeneous groups may be needed to reflect the variety of types. If the target market is geographically widespread, then many groups may be needed to represent this diversity. The extent to which comparisons are sought in analyses will determine how many groups are needed. The complexity of the issues to be discussed will also determine the number of discussions needed. The following example summarises these issues.

EXAMPLE

Prospecting for that research gold[19]

The number of interviews or discussion groups required will depend on the nature or depth of the study. David Woodcock, Market Research Manager of Eurostar's European Passenger Services notes: 'In drawing samples the right way, you can get a good understanding with a small number of groups of what factors are driving people. A single group is unlikely to give representative results, although it could be used in the development of ideas, using respondents as a brain-storming group.' ■

The following example of Disneyland Paris illustrates the comparisons made in focus group analyses. The important markets they concentrated upon were France, Germany and the UK and so focus groups would be needed to represent each country. Further analyses of two distinct target groups were also needed. Thus, a minimum of six groups plus an experimental group would be needed, which would be doubled if it were felt to be important to run exclusively male and female groups.

EXAMPLE

An MR boost helps Disneyland Paris take off into profit[20]

Back in the summer of 1994 it's fair to say the team at Disneyland Paris were having a tough time of it: they were off the launch pad, but not yet up to full speed. Two years after opening, attendance figures, although impressive, had not lived up to expectations and there was even press speculation about the future of the park.

It was at this time that the Disney team asked The Added Value Company's Paris office to carry out research to understand the potential role of a new attraction. Even by Disney standards, Space Mountain looked as though it would be an amazing experience. It started with a catapult launch in a rocket ship up the outside of a mountain, with the daring space travellers experiencing zero gravity at the top. You were then plunged inside the darkness of the mountain, to travel through space at breathtaking speed, through meteorite storms and past flying asteroids.

Qualitative research groups were used, based on the need to get in-depth and rich consumer reactions to the new concept and to highlight which features were the most motivating. Groups were split between people who had already been to the theme park and those who had not visited, with two targets by lifestyle: parents of children aged 5–15 and young adults aged 25–35. Research was carried out in France, Germany and the UK, with an internal 'data merger' meeting used to share findings from the three countries and develop pan-European findings and conclusions. ■

In summary, the number of focus groups that should be conducted on a single subject depends on the:

1 complexity of issues;
2 number of consumer types targeted;
3 number of new ideas generated by each successive group;
4 time and budget available.

Mood board
A mood board is a collage created in a focus group setting. Focus group respondents are asked to snip words and pictures from magazines that they see representing the values a particular brand is perceived to have. In some circumstances, collages can also be made up from audio and video tapes.

Resources permitting, one should conduct additional discussion groups until the moderator can anticipate what will be said. As well as talking about issues, the moderator may choose times to add further stimulus to develop the discussion. One of the most frequently used forms of stimuli is the **mood board**. The following example describes the use of the mood board. Another example follows beyond the mood board to illustrate other types of stimuli used in focus group discussions.

EXAMPLE

The mood board[21]

The 'mood board' is really the creation of a collage. Focus group respondents are asked to snip words and pictures from magazines that they see representing the values a brand is perceived to have. The mood board has two main functions:

- *Reference point*. The moderator can use the mood board to reflect upon the discussion, in which case issues can emerge that were not so apparent in the heat of a discussion.
- *Enabling device*. It gets respondents to loosen up and talk more freely. The focus group is not to get respondents to talk rationally but to display what 'feels right' to them. The collage can help to express feelings they may not be able to put into words, or enable those words to have more clarity. This can happen by questioning what is in as well as not in a collage. ■

EXAMPLE

Art of the matter[22]

Paul Walton, Chairman of New Product Development Consultancy The Value Engineers, explains: 'In the early stages of a new product or brand reassessment project, words might be appropriate. Beyond the words come picture collages and as you learn more and you start to give the brand a clearer identity, you introduce mock-ups of packaging and other props to "three-dimensionalise" the world.'

Alex Authers, Research Director at Branding Consultancy New Solutions, argues the case for stimuli beyond the mood board: 'We've moved on from static visuals, to using videos. It's often useful to show a series of fast-edited clips set to some sort of soundtrack. People are now much more video literate. So, instead of having a mood board, we have a mood video. Video collages are particularly good for exploring the emotional resonances of brands.'

Other props used in qualitative research include swatches of material and even fragrances. Authers says smells and colours can 'help to create a mood and evoke a positioning'. ■

The analysis of data gleaned from focus groups is detailed in Chapter 7. However, at this point there are two essential points to note:

1. *Evolving analysis*. As focus groups may change and develop as new lessons are learnt, analysis is being conducted. In other words, the moderator makes observations and notes as discussions progress. The observations and notes are part of the total analysis in that they decide which issues to probe, which issues to drop and the form of summarising issues that may be presented to groups at certain stages of the discussion.
2. *Not just the narrative*. If the discussion is recorded then transcripts can be produced which can be analysed with proprietary software. These transcripts form a major part of the analysis procedure but the accumulation and reflection upon observations and notes forms a key part of the analysis.

Other variations of focus groups

Focus groups can use several variations of the standard procedure. These include:

- *Two-way focus group*. This allows one target group to listen to and learn from a related group. In one application, physicians viewed a focus group of arthritis patients discussing the treatment they desired. A focus group of these physicians was then held to determine their reactions.[23]
- *Dual-moderator group*. This is a focus group interview conducted by two moderators. One moderator is responsible for the smooth flow of the session, and the other ensures that specific issues are discussed.

- *Duelling-moderator group*. Here also there are two moderators, but they deliberately take opposite positions on the issues to be discussed. This allows the researcher to explore both sides of controversial issues.
- *Respondent-moderator group*. In this type of focus group, the moderator asks selected participants to play the role of moderator temporarily to improve group dynamics.
- *Client-participant group*. Client personnel are identified and made part of the discussion group. Their primary role is to offer clarifications that will make the group process more effective.
- *Mini group*. These groups consist of a moderator and only four or five respondents. They are used when the issues of interest require more extensive probing than is possible in the standard group of six to 12.

Advantages and disadvantages of focus groups

Focus groups offer several advantages over other data collection techniques. These may be summarised by the 10 Ss:[24]

1. *Synergy*. Putting a group of people together will produce a wider range of information, insight and ideas than will individual responses secured privately.
2. *Snowballing*. A bandwagon effect often operates in a group interview in that one person's comment triggers a chain reaction from the other participants.
3. *Stimulation*. Usually after a brief introductory period, the respondents want to express their ideas and expose their feelings as the general level of excitement over the topic increases in the group.
4. *Security*. Because the participants' feelings may be similar to those of other group members, they feel comfortable and are therefore willing to 'open up' and reveal thoughts where they may have been reluctant to if they were on their own.
5. *Spontaneity*. Because participants are not required to answer specific questions, their responses can be spontaneous and unconventional and should therefore provide an accurate idea of their views.
6. *Serendipity*. Ideas are more likely to arise unexpectedly in a group than in an individual interview. There may be issues that the moderator had not thought of. The dynamics of the group can allow these issues to develop and be discussed.
7. *Specialisation*. Because a number of participants are involved simultaneously, the use of a highly trained, but expensive, interviewer is justified.
8. *Scientific scrutiny*. The group interview allows close scrutiny of the data collection process in that observers can witness the session and it can be recorded for later analysis. Many individuals can be involved in the validation and interpretation of the collected data.
9. *Structure*. The group interview allows for flexibility in the topics covered and the depth with which they are treated. The structure can match the logical structure of issues from the respondents' perspective.
10. *Speed*. Because a number of individuals are being interviewed at the same time, data collection and analysis proceed relatively quickly.

The disadvantages of focus groups may be summarised by the five Ms:

1. *Misjudgement*. Focus group results can be more easily misjudged than the results of other data collection techniques. Focus groups are particularly susceptible to client and researcher biases.

2 *Moderation*. Focus groups are difficult to moderate. Moderators with all the desirable skills are rare. The quality of the results depends heavily on the skills of the moderator.
3 *Messiness*. The unstructured nature of the responses makes coding, analysis and interpretation difficult. Focus group data tend to be messy and need strong theoretical support to ensure that decision-makers can rely upon the analyses and interpretations.
4 *Misrepresentation*. Focus group results concentrate on distinct target groups. Trying to generalise to much wider groups can present great difficulties.
5 *Meeting*. There are problems in getting focus group participants together at the same time. This problem is even more acute with business research using managers. Given the amount of travel and tight schedules that many managers have, getting them together at the same time is very difficult. Add to this the issue of sensitive information, i.e. many managers are reluctant to reveal their company's behaviour and plans in front of other managers, and one can see that the focus group has limited use in business research.

OTHER TYPES OF QUALITATIVE GROUP DISCUSSIONS

Brainstorming[25]

Traditional brainstorming has been used for several decades. Whether formal or informal, the process is the same: think of as many ideas as you can and say them out loud; leave the evaluation until later; build on and combine others' ideas; be as imaginative as possible, the wilder the ideas the better. The group moderator seeks to nurture an atmosphere of creativity, tapping into the intuition of respondents, generating novel ideas and connections between ideas.

When it works well, ideas flow freely from an interplay that may never have occurred if the group had not brainstormed together.

Two problems plague traditional brainstorming: production blocking and evaluation apprehension.

- *Production blocking* occurs when a group member has an idea, but someone else is talking. When its their turn, they have forgotten the idea, think their idea is redundant or not that good. If the group is large or dominated by talkative people, they lose interest and do not say what they think.
- *Evaluation apprehension* occurs when respondents become anxious about what others think of their thoughts. Ideas may be censored, as there is a fear of being labelled as odd. When respondents feel this apprehension, they do not produce as many new and potentially useful ideas, they keep them to themselves and therefore defeat the purpose of brainstorming.

GLOBALCASH PROJECT

Industrial group discussions

As noted earlier, the focus group has limited use in industrial or business research. Getting managers together at the same time and place is a big operational problem. Getting managers to be open about their companies in a group scenario is also very difficult to achieve. In the GlobalCash project, group discussions were seen as important in order to explore and develop issues that could not be measured in a questionnaire. What was measured in the questionnaire, produced many statistics that needed further elaboration that could be tackled in a group discussion.

▶

To overcome the above issues, part of the incentive to complete the questionnaire was an invitation to take part in a 'closed forum for questionnaire respondents'. This meant that a date was set to present findings from the survey exclusively to questionnaire respondents. The date and meeting place of The Management Centre in Brussels were established well in advance to allow managers the chance to put the date in their diaries. The day started with an initial session of presenting statistical findings to the whole group of managers who had responded to the questionnaire. As questions were fielded in this forum, particular topics of interest were identified and focus groups named as 'workshops' were built around these topics. By mid-morning, groups of around 10–12 managers were together tackling a theme of importance to them. They were moderated by an academic researcher from one of the 20 business schools taking part in the GlobalCash project. With a loose set of topics to develop into questions and probes, the format for a focus group was achieved. In the afternoon, the same format continued with a presentation of questionnaire findings and further group discussions. By splitting the day in this manner, managers could attend and contribute to two subject areas of interest to them. Finally, individual managers could be identified who could be interviewed in depth on their own at a later date. The one-to-one in-depth interviews in the GlobalCash project will be illustrated in the next chapter. ■

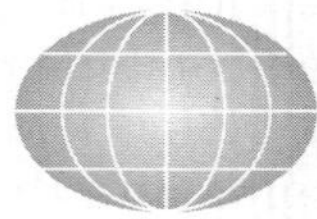

INTERNATIONAL MARKETING RESEARCH

If marketing decision-makers are not familiar with the foreign markets that they target, qualitative research can be crucial in international marketing research. In the initial stages of cross-national research, qualitative research can provide insights into the problem and help in developing an approach by generating relevant research questions and hypotheses, models and characteristics that influence the research design. Thus, qualitative research may reveal the differences between foreign and domestic markets. Focus groups can be used in many settings, in both industrialised and developing countries. The moderator should not only be trained in focus group design but should also be familiar with the language, culture and patterns of social interaction prevailing in that country. The focus group findings should be derived not only from the verbal contents but also from non-verbal cues such as voice intonations, inflections, expressions and gestures.[26] As indicated earlier in this chapter, there are different traditions in Europe and the USA in running focus groups. The qualitative marketing researcher should be aware of the two traditions as the expectations of group participants in different international environments may determine that one approach will be more successful than another.

International focus group traditions[27]

The term 'focus group discussion' is commonly used across all continents, yet it subsumes approaches that are different. There are two main schools of thought:

1 *Cognitive.* America researchers generally follow this tradition, which largely follows a format and interviewing style as used in quantitative studies. 'American-style groups' is shorthand in the UK for large groups (10 respondents on average), a structured procedure and a strong element of external validation. Within the cognitive approach, the analysis or articulation has

been worked on before, and so the interviews are largely meant to confirm or expand on known issues.

2 *Conative*. European researchers generally follow this tradition. This style assumes a different starting point, one that emphasises exploration, with analysis taking place during and after the group. There is less structure to the questions, with group members being encouraged to take their own paths of discussion, make their own connections and for the whole process to evolve.

Table 6.3 summarises the differences between the US (cognitive) and European (conative) approaches to conducting focus groups. Note the longer duration of the European approach to allow the exploration to develop. To maintain the interest and motivation of participants for this time period, the interview experience must be stimulating and enjoyable.

Table 6.3 The two schools of thought about 'focus group discussions'

Characteristics	*Cognitive*	*Conative*
Purpose	Demonstration	Exploration
Sample size	10–12	6–8
Duration	1.5 hours	1 to 6 hours
Interviewing	Logical sequence	Opportunistic
Questions	Closed	Open
Techniques	Straight question, questionnaires, hand shows, counting	Probing, facilitation, projectives, describing
Response required	Give answers	Debate issues
Interviewer	Moderator	Researcher
Observer's role	To get proof	To understand
Transcripts	Rarely necessary	Usually full
Analysis	On the spot	Time consuming
Focus of time	Pre-planning	Post-fieldwork
Accusations of other style	'Over-controlling'	'Formless'
Suited for	Information	Understanding
Output	To be confirmed in quantitative studies	Can be used in its own right to support decision-makers

ETHICS IN MARKETING RESEARCH

The researcher and the client must respect respondents when conducting qualitative research. This should include protecting the anonymity of respondents, not misleading or deceiving them, conducting research in a way not to embarrass or harm the respondents, and using the research results in an ethical manner.[28]

Many client managers believe that because they are footing the bill, they should be able to sit in on and observe a focus group or in-depth interview. However, the respondents' participation may be biased if they are aware of the client's presence. Therefore, some qualitative researchers allow their clients to observe a group discussion by introducing them as colleagues helping with the project. This deception raises ethical concerns related to the preservation of the respondents' anonymity. Some researchers may believe that this deception is small and acceptable because the respondent will not find out. It has been shown, however, that when introduced in this way, many participants accurately conclude that the observer is in fact the client. The mistrust generated by this interaction hurts the integrity of marketing research. This is illustrated in the following example, that lays out two primary reasons why qualitative researchers should understand the potential harm can be done with their techniques.

EXAMPLE

The need to pay greater attention to issues of the balance of power, to ensure public cooperation[29]

There are two primary reasons why researchers must be aware of the potential harm to respondents and the need to foster a continual willingness to cooperate in research:

1 Qualitative research is doubly dependent on public cooperation. Not only do we rely on respondents' cooperation in taking part, but the non-directive and open-ended nature of qualitative question techniques means that we also rely on their being positively engaged by the process, willing and eager to apply their minds, happy to reveal their thoughts.
2 The nature of qualitative interviews and groups means that moderators will always try to encourage respondents to reveal more. This brings with it a responsibility to ensure that safeguards are in place, to deter coercion and avoid the potential danger of abuse of power and control over respondents in qualitative research. ■

Ethical questions also arise when videotaping sessions with the respondents. Some of the pertinent questions are how much to tell participants and when should the clients be allowed access. When videotaping groups, regardless of whether or not they were aware of the camera during the meeting, at the end of the meeting, participants should be asked to sign a written declaration conveying their permission to use the recording. This declaration should disclose the full purpose of the video, including who will be able to view it. If any respondent refuses, the tape should either be destroyed or edited to omit that respondent's identity and comments completely. The researcher should be sensitive to the comfort level of the respondents and respect for the participants should warrant restraint. When a respondent feels uncomfortable and does not wish to go on, the researcher should not aggressively probe or confront any further. It has also been suggested that respondents should be allowed to reflect on all they have said at the end of the interview and should be given the opportunity to ask questions. This may help return the respondents to their pre-interview emotional state.

INTERNET AND COMPUTER APPLICATIONS

The Group System Support approach (GSS)[30] is a group interview that is run by an experienced facilitator and, additionally, a 'chauffeur' who assists with the technical tools that are an integral part of the approach. The GSS interview or meeting involves a small group of participants using sophisticated software on workstations that are connected by a local area network. The participants' workstations display requests for input and, as the participants' input answers, individual responses are also displayed. Participants' responses are sent over the local area network and assimilated at the chauffeur's workstation that acts as the focal point for the meeting. The chauffeur's screen is visible to the participants through a data show and overhead projection system.

Participants are asked to type answers to a question, straight into the computer in front of them. The facilitator, who guides the group through a series of questions and tasks, sets the pace, leads the discussion, poses questions and helps to interpret the answers. Participants may be asked to input as many ideas or answers they like or each person may be asked to contribute an equal number of answers. The facilitator must maintain focus and keep the discussion on track and a build a spirit of cooperation.

The feedback from participants are displayed anonymously on the public viewing screen, being processed simultaneously allowing everyone to contribute at the same time. The process allows the strengths of individual members to shine as well as allowing a group synergy. At distinct stages during a GSS, the facilitator can add notes to provoke further stimulus and discussion. The talk can be free flowing, or by the use of a timeserver can be tightly controlled. The facilitator can give their full attention to group dynamics without the need to control the speakers or to make notes. The GSS can be used in the 'reflective' format of the focus group discussion or the more 'frenetic' brainstorming session.

The important benefits of the GSS approach include:[31]

- All respondents feel they have the ability to contribute, their confidence is quickly built up.
- Domineering respondents do not take over the discussion.
- A great breadth of information may be collected.
- Tight control may be afforded over the direction of the discussion.

SUMMARY

Qualitative and quantitative research should be viewed as complementary. Qualitative research methods may be direct or indirect. In direct methods, respondents are able to discern the true purpose of the research, whereas indirect methods disguise the purpose of the research to some extent. The major direct methods are focus groups and depth interviews. The major indirect methods are observation and projection techniques. Focus group interviews are the most widely used qualitative research technique.

Focus groups are conducted by a moderator in a relaxed and informal manner with a small group of respondents. The moderator leads and develops the discussion. In a focus groups respondents can portray their feelings and behaviour – using their language and logic. The value of the technique lies in the unexpected findings that emerge when respondents are allowed to say what they really feel. Development in the use of the Internet and intranets means that group discussions can take place away from the traditional 'viewing' or meeting room. The maxim of respondents being relaxed and comfortable with the context and means of communicating still applies.

Qualitative research can reveal the salient differences between domestic and foreign markets. Whether focus groups or in-depth interviews should be conducted and how the findings should be interpreted depends heavily on the cultural differences. When conducting qualitative research, the researcher and the client must respect the respondents. This should include protecting the anonymity of respondents, honouring all statements and promises used to ensure participation, and conducting research in a way not to embarrass or harm the respondents.

QUESTIONS AND PROBLEMS

1 What are the primary differences between qualitative and quantitative research techniques?

2 What are the primary differences between a qualitative research design and qualitative research techniques?

3 Evaluate the rationale for using qualitative research techniques.

4 Evaluate the differences between a European and an American approach to qualitative research.

5 Differentiate between direct and indirect qualitative research. Give an example of each.

6 What does a 'comfortable setting' mean in the context of running a focus group?

7 To what extent can a moderator achieve an 'objective detachment' from a focus group discussion?

8 Why is the focus group moderator so important in obtaining quality results?

9 What are the relative advantages and disadvantages of being able to covertly observe a focus group discussion?

10 Why should one safeguard against professional respondents?

11 How many focus groups should be undertaken in any research project?

12 Describe the purpose and benefits of using stimulus material in a focus group.

13 What is the difference between a dual moderator and a duelling moderator group?

14 Evaluate the difficulties of conducting focus groups with industrial respondents.

15 What is 'lost' from quality of a focus group by the administration of a Group System Support approach?

NOTES

1 McElhatton, N., 'A research commitment more than skin deep', *Research* (May 1994), 10.

2 Clarke, B. and Saunders, M., 'There's Trouble in Classes for Kids who Wear Glasses', *ResearchPlus* (November 1997), 7.

3 Driver, L., 'How the Data Mountain Became a Mine of Information', *ResearchPlus* (November 1996), 6.

4 Sykes, W., 'Validity and Reliability in Qualitative Market Research: a review of the literature', *Journal of the Market Research Society*, 32(3), 289.

5 De Groot, G., 'Qualitative Research: Deep Dangerous or just Plain Dotty?' *European Research*, 14(3), 136–41.

6 Broadbent, K., 'When East meets West, Quite What Does "Qualitative' Mean?" *ResearchPlus* (March 1997), 14.

7 Gilmore, A. and Carson, D., '"Integrative" qualitative methods in a service context', *Marketing Intelligence and Planning*, 14(6), (June 1996), 21.

8 Flaster, C.,'First Get the Language Right, then Tell Them a Story', *ResearchPlus* (November 1997), 11.

9 Moran, W.T., 'The Science of Qualitative Research', *Journal of Advertising Research* 26 (June–July 1986), RC-16.

10 The group size of six to 12 is based on rules of thumb. For more discussion, see Fern, E.E. 'The Use of Focus Groups for Idea Generation: The Effects of Group Size, Acquaintanceship, and Moderator on Response Quantity and Quality', *Journal of Marketing Research* 19 (February 1982), 1–13.

11 Nelson, J.E. and Frontczak, N., 'How Acquaintanceship and Analyst Can Influence Focus Group Results', *Journal of Advertising* 17 (1988), 41–48.

12 Kahn, H., 'Professional Respondents Say They're Better for Research Than "Virgins", but They're Not', *Marketing News* (14 May 1982), section 1, p. 22.

13 Gordon, W., 'New Life for Group Discussions', *ResearchPlus* (July 1993), 1.

14 Adapted from Chase, D.A., 'The Intensive Group Interviewing in Marketing', *MRA Viewpoints* (1973).

15 Sonet, T., 'See the USA, Through the Looking Glass', *ResearchPlus* (June 1994), 6.

16 *Ibid.*

17 Dwek, R., 'Through the Looking Glass', *Marketing* (11 September 1997), 37.

18 Ellis, R., 'So How Do You Upstage a Ferrari Owner?', *ResearchPlus* (November 1994), 10.

19 Murphy, D., 'Fishing by the Net', *Marketing* (22 August 1996), 25.

20 Tayler, D., 'An MR Boost Helps Disneyland Paris Take Off into Profit', *ResearchPlus* (June 1997), 6.

21 Croft, M., 'Art of the Matter', *Marketing Week* (9 October 1997), 71.

22 *Ibid.*

23 Silverstein, M., 'Two-Way Focus Groups Can Provide Startling Information', *Marketing News* (4 January 1988), 31.

24 Hess, J.M. and King, R.L. (eds), *'Group Interviewing', New Science of Planning* (Chicago: American Marketing Association, 1968), p. 4.

25 Gallupe, R.B. and Cooper, W.H., 'Brainstorming Electronically', *Sloan Management Review*, 35(1) (Fall 1993), 27.

26 For perceptions of focus groups in the United States, Germany, and Japan, see McDonald, W.J., 'Provider Perceptions of Focus Groups Research Use: A Multi-country Perspective', *Journal of the Academy of Marketing Science*, 22 (Summer 1994), 265–73.

27 Goodyear, M., 'Divided by a Common Language: Diversity and Deception in the World of Global Marketing', *Journal of the Market Research Society* 38(2) (April 1996), 105.

28 *MRS Code of Conduct* (The Market Research Society).

29 Murphy, D., 'Fishing by the Net', *Marketing* (22 August 1996), 25.

30 Sweeney, J.C., Soutar, G.N., Hausknecht, D.R., Dallin, R.F. and Johnson, L.W., 'Collection of information from Groups: a Comparison of Two Methods', *Journal of the Market Research Society* 39(2), (April 1997), 397.

31 *Ibid.*

Chapter 7

Qualitative data collection and analysis

Qualitative analysis involves the process of making sense of data that is not expressed in numbers[1]

OBJECTIVES

After reading this chapter, the student should be able to:

1 describe depth interview techniques in detail, citing their advantages, disadvantages, and applications;
2 explain projective techniques in detail and compare association, completion, construction, and expressive techniques;
3 describe the process of analysing qualitative research findings;
4 discuss the considerations involved in analysing qualitative data collected from international markets;
5 understand the ethical issues involved in collecting qualitative data;
6 distinguish between different types of qualitative data analysis software packages;
7 understand the practical limitations and benefits of using software to analyse qualitative data.

OVERVIEW

Having established the purpose of qualitative research and described the major qualitative technique in marketing research – focus groups – this chapter moves on to describe other qualitative techniques and means to analyse qualitative data.

We cover the major technique of depth interviews in detail. We also consider the indirect procedures of observation and projective techniques with emphasis on association, completion, construction, and expressive techniques. When qualitative data is being collected, analysis progresses which develops fully when the interviews or observations are completed. The stages involved in analysing qualitative data are outlined and described. To be able to cope with the great amount of data generated from qualitative techniques, a great variety of software packages are available. The main types of package are described, emphasising what they do and what are their limitations and benefits. The considerations involved in analysing qualitative data when researching international markets are discussed. Several ethical issues that arise in qualitative research are identified. The following examples give a flavour of qualitative research techniques beyond focus groups and their applications in marketing research and marketing decision-making.

EXAMPLE

Fragrant ways to put the mind in the mood[2]

The aromachologist Joseph Precker is convinced that odour plays a far more important role in human affairs than we in the Westernised world have credited. 'The acceptance of the smell of a mate is a better prediction of compatibility and continuing relationship than many of the informal or formal "tests" of premarital and marital compatibility.'

The sense of smell is also one of the keys to product evaluation. The further one moves from functional products, the more important becomes the fragrance's role in fitting in with and complementing, even advancing, the image of the brand. Individual depth interviews and qualitative group discussions are vital if one is to evaluate the synergistic elements of brand name, pack, bottle design, concept and fragrance. This research evolves as the creative development of the various elements proceeds. The fragrance is refined, modified and then fine-tuned; up to 150 versions of a leading women's fine fragrance may be created. ■

EXAMPLE

Want to know why we buy what we do? Join the queue[3]

Observation of shoppers in-store allows manufacturers and retailers to identify and measure consumer behaviour at the point of sale. How long do shoppers spend at any given fixture? Where do they normally stop at the fixture? How do they react to promotional displays and gondola ends? Which brands do they handle and which brands do they select? (And which brands are consumed? . . . the single pack hurriedly and discreetly removed from a multipack to quieten the toddler screaming in the trolley).

Observation of consumers can be conducted in several ways, either by trained observers discreetly positioned by the fixture observing shoppers, or shadowing a pre-recruited shopper throughout the complete shopping cycle from home to store and back home again. The use of hidden cameras operated by remote control is becoming increasingly popular, although in most cases the camera study is not complete until an approach is made to the shopper to find out more about behavioural and classification details. ■

EXAMPLE

Keeping up with the kids[4]

Children have frequent preference and attitudinal shifts and marketers must be able to recognise and respond to these shifts by developing new products, refining marketing messages of existing brands and securing licensing rights to characters that are the current craze. This flexibility requires accurate and timely research data.

Part of the art in obtaining valid data from children is holding their interest. Different techniques are needed to those used to quiz adults, particularly with qualitative research and younger children.

'We can learn a lot by trying to look at children in context', says Angela Humphries, Director of Verve, the Children and Youth Unit of The Research Business. 'So, we go into their homes, go to McDonalds or go shopping with them to try to understand them in a more anthropological way. We want to get away from market research being in a vacuum.'

Research into younger children tends to be observational in nature. Disney's video arm, Buena Vista Home Entertainment, has traditionally watched the responses of children to products shown in viewing theatres. ■

DEPTH INTERVIEWS

Depth interview
An unstructured, direct, personal interview in which a single respondent probed by a highly skilled interviewer to uncover underlying motivations, beliefs, attitudes and feelings on a topic.

Depth interviews are another major method of obtaining qualitative data. We describe the general procedure for conducting depth interviews and then illustrate some specific techniques. The advantages, disadvantages and applications of depth interviews are also discussed.

Characteristics

Like focus groups, depth interviews are an unstructured and direct way of obtaining information but, unlike focus groups, depth interviews are conducted on a one-on-one basis. A depth interview is an unstructured, direct, personal interview in which a single respondent is probed by a highly skilled interviewer to uncover underlying motivations, beliefs, attitudes, and feelings on a topic.[5]

A depth interview may take from 30 minutes to over an hour. To illustrate the technique in the context of the GlobalCash project, the interviewer begins by asking a Finance Director a general question such as, 'Have pan-European banks helped you to prepare for the introduction of EMU?' The interviewer then encourages the subject to talk freely about his or her attitudes towards different banks' offerings. After asking the initial question, the interviewer uses an unstructured format with a topic guide to help them with important subject areas to cover. The subsequent direction of the interview is determined by the respondent's initial reply, the interviewer's probes for elaboration, and the respondent's answers. Suppose that the respondent replies to the initial question by saying, 'Bank X, our lead pan-European bank, has not been really helpful in developing our plans.' The interviewer might then pose a question such as 'Why do you think they have not been helpful?' If the answer is not very revealing ('They are lost, like all the other banks'), the interviewer may ask a probing question, such as 'In what ways are you looking for help from your lead bank?' Although the interviewer attempts to follow a rough outline of questions, the specific wording of the questions and the order in which they are asked is influenced by the subject's replies. Probing is of critical importance in obtaining meaningful responses and uncovering hidden issues. Probing is done by asking such questions as 'Why do you say that?' 'That's interesting, can you tell me more?' or 'Would you like to add anything else?' [6]

The interviewer must be alert to the issues that they wish to go through but also the issues that the respondent is willing to talk about. The questions and probes they put to respondents follow the interest and logic of the respondent, making them feel motivated to respond in a manner that suits them. As with a focus group discussion, the respondent should feel comfortable and relaxed. Answering in a manner that suits the respondent helps to make the interview more comfortable and relaxed. For a great amount of business research, the depth interview is the best way to gain access and to talk to managers. Much of the interviewing takes place in their office at a time that is convenient to them. Researchers can also observe characteristics of the manager in his or her office environment that can be of help in their analyses. Examples of this could be: levels of formality in the workplace, reports and books that the manager has around them for reference, the manager's use of IT equipment, or the tidiness of the workplace. These observations would be entirely based upon the purpose of the study, but the context of the office can be of help to the manager and the researcher. The following example illustrates the case for in-depth interviews for business marketing research.

EXAMPLE

In-depth research? A bit controversial![7]

The following arguments form the case for interviewing respondents individually instead of in groups for business to business markets:

- The best respondents tend also to be the busiest and most successful people. They can make time for an interview, but are rarely able to spare the much greater time needed for them to come to a discussion group at some location away from their office. So groups exclude the best respondents.
- Whereas mothers evaluating nappy ads or beer drinkers the latest lager have only their personal preferences to consider, it is very different for an executive evaluating copiers, airline ads or computer software. This is because their reactions are complicated by the type of job they do and who they work for. The discussion group methodology is dependent on the group's composition being fairly homogeneous; the job backgrounds of business people make them too varied to be entirely comfortable in a group.
- A lot of information comes from seeing the respondent at his or her desk, which is missed in a discussion group. Work schedules pinned to the wall, the working atmosphere, the freebies from suppliers on the desk, the way coffee is served, help fill out the picture.
- Groups do not allow the researcher enough thinking time. Two groups, each taking an hour and a half over successive evenings, do not even begin to compare with two or three full days of non-stop interviewing. Individual interviews give much more scope for experimentation. If one way does not work, it's only one respondent, not a whole group that is affected. ■

In the example of business marketing research, the context of the depth interview helped the frame of mind of the respondent and the researcher in their total understanding of the respondent. Another major application of depth interviews where the context of the interview plays a major part is in the interviewing of children. The following example illustrates the importance of context in interviewing children.

EXAMPLE

When not to rely on the young imagination[8]

Researchers into children and teenagers spend considerable time and energy pondering the best approach. Debates proliferate on methodological approaches and interviewing techniques: depth versus group, mini groups versus standard groups, friendship pairs versus stranger groups, this projective versus that and so on. These debates make researchers focus on the implications of how research is conducted and which approach provides the best results. However, one vitally important element is often overlooked, and that is the issue of context. In other words, we need to ensure that the situation in which we interview children is relevant to the research needs.

Like adults, children have multi-faceted personalities. The same teenager can be sullen at home, obstructive in the classroom, but the life and soul of the peer group. The essential difference between children and adults, however, is the extent to which different aspects of the persona can be accessed on one occasion and in one situation, the research setting.

Adults have insight into the different roles and behaviour, which they adopt in different contexts, can project other aspects of themselves and, in turn, bring these into the research situation. Children and young teenagers, on the other hand, react to the moment and thus project only one aspect of themselves. They lack the maturity, experience and self-knowledge to draw on other parts of themselves and therefore find it almost impossible to know, let alone admit or explore, how they might behave in another circumstance. ■

The above example also shows that question formulation, the very heart of marketing research, is debatably more important in interviewing children than when dealing with adults. A straightforward 'What do you think about x?' may throw children into confusion. A formulation such as 'If you were to call your friend about this, what would you tell them?' would be more likely to produce illuminating responses.

Friendship pair
A technique used to interview children as two friends or classmates together.

It also mentions another effective technique, the use of **friendship pairs** – interviewing two friends or classmates together. This helps to cut out lying because children are not alone with strangers and because if one tells a lie, the other tells on them. The ingrained honesty of children arguably makes them easier to research than adults, who of course are far more accomplished exponents of deception.

The interviewer's role is critical to the success of the depth interview. The interviewer should:

1 Do their utmost to develop an empathy with the respondent.
2 Make sure the respondent is relaxed and comfortable.
3 Be personable to encourage and motivate respondents.
4 Note issues that interest the respondent and develop questions around these issues.
5 Not be happy to accept brief 'yes' or 'no' answers.
6 Note where respondents have not explained issues clearly enough that need probing.

Advantages and disadvantages of depth interviews

Depth interviews have the following advantages: they can:

1 Uncover greater depth of insights than focus groups. This can happen through concentrating and developing an issue with the individual. In the group scenario, interesting and knowledgeable individuals cannot be solely concentrated upon.
2 Attribute the responses directly to the respondent, unlike focus groups where it is often difficult to determine which respondent made a particular response.
3 Result in a free exchange of information that may not be possible in focus groups because there is no social pressure to conform to group response. This makes them ideally suited to sensitive issues, especially commercially sensitive issues.
4 Be easier to arrange than the focus group as there are no so many individuals to coordinate and the interviewer can travel to the respondent

Depth interviews suffer from many of the disadvantages when compared to focus groups, and often to a greater extent:

1 Skilled interviewers capable of conducting depth interviews are expensive and difficult to find. The lack of structure makes the results susceptible to the interviewer's influence, and the quality and completeness of the results depend heavily on the interviewer's skills.
2 The data obtained are difficult to analyse and interpret, and the services of skilled psychologists are typically required for this purpose. As well as the transcripts of the interview, additional observations add to the analyses.
3 The length of the interview combined with high costs means that the number of depth interviews in a project tend to be few.

Despite these disadvantages, depth interviews do have many applications. Primarily they are used in business marketing research, and research on children as illustrated earlier. The following summarises the applications.[9]

Applications of depth interviews

1 Interviews with professional people (e.g. finance directors using banking services).
2 Interviews with children (e.g. attitudes towards a theme park).
3 Detailed probing of the respondent (e.g. new product development for cars).
4 Discussion of confidential, sensitive, or embarrassing topics (e.g. personal hygiene issues).
5 Situations where strong social norms exist and where the respondent may be easily swayed by group response (e.g. attitudes of university students toward sports).
6 Detailed understanding of complicated behaviour (e.g. the purchase of fashion goods).
7 Interviews with competitors, who are unlikely to reveal the information in a group setting (e.g. travel agents' perceptions of airline travel packages).
8 Situations where the product consumption experience is sensory in nature, affecting mood states and emotions (e.g. perfumes, bath soap).

The following example illustrates a case in which depth interviews were particularly helpful.

GLOBALCASH PROJECT

Why are you going to make more use of electronic banking?

The issues tackled in the GlobalCash project were guided largely by major pan-European banks from Britain, Finland, France, Germany, Norway, Spain and the USA who form a steering committee for the project. Each bank has different information requirements to support their marketing strategies, which means there is a big demand for a wide array of questions to be asked. This can be achieved to a great extent but it does not allow great depth to be achieved in many question areas. For example, the questionnaire asks companies what plans they have to make changes over the next two years. An example of a response to this question is 'make greater use of electronic banking'. Statistical analyses can reveal the proportion who are to make greater use of electronic banking, the types of industry they operate within, the types of existing system they have and the banks they work with.

Depth interviews are of great importance to probe the reasons behind this planned behaviour. Examples of questions and probes include: what reasons underlie the need to make greater use? Is the greater use driven by the services offered by banks or the IT systems being established within a company? Will there be greater integration between systems? Will hardware or software be purchased?

The whole GlobalCash questionnaire has many areas that can be probed, once patterns of response become apparent. Therefore, when around 50% of the responses to the questionnaire have been received, an interim report was presented to the steering committee of banks. The issues that they deem the most important to probe formed the topic guide for depth interviews.

With the completed questionnaires, profiles of the respondents can be analysed and those with behaviour relevant to the issues can be contacted. For example, 'sophisticated' users of cash management services can be profiled and for certain issues they may be contacted to conduct a depth interview. Around 60 depth interviews were conducted for the GlobalCash project, with a minimum of two interviews in any one country. Each interview had the same interviewer who ensured some consistency in the approach. He was supported by another interviewer in each country, who helped with translation where necessary but also helped with the cultural traditions of conducting the interviews and in interpreting the findings. ■

The GlobalCash example illustrates the value of depth interviews in uncovering responses that may be tackled in a superficial manner in a survey, allowing illustration of the meanings that underlie the statistical analyses.

PROJECTIVE TECHNIQUES

Projective technique
An unstructured and indirect form of questioning that encourages respondents to project their underlying motivations, beliefs, attitudes, or feelings regarding the issues of concern.

Both focus groups and depth interviews are direct approaches in which the true purpose of the research is disclosed to the respondents or is otherwise obvious to them. **Projective techniques** are different from these techniques in that they attempt to disguise the purpose of the research. A projective technique is an unstructured, indirect form of questioning that encourages respondents to project their underlying motivations, beliefs, attitudes, or feelings regarding the issues of concern.[10] In projective techniques, respondents are asked to interpret the behaviour of others rather than to describe their own behaviour. In interpreting the behaviour of others, respondents indirectly project their own motivations, beliefs, attitudes, or feelings into the situation. Thus, the respondent's attitudes are uncovered by analysing their responses to scenarios that are deliberately unstructured, vague and ambiguous. The more ambiguous the situation, the more respondents project their emotions, needs, motives, attitudes and values, as demonstrated by work in clinical psychology on which projective techniques are based.[11] As in psychology, these techniques are classified as association, completion, construction and expressive. Each of these classifications is discussed.[12]

Association techniques

Association techniques
A type of projective technique in which respondents are presented with a stimulus and are asked to respond with the first thing that comes to mind.

Word association
A projective technique in which respondents are presented with a list of words, one at a time. After each word, they are asked to give the first word that comes to mind.

In **association techniques**, an individual is presented with a stimulus and asked to respond with the first thing that comes to mind. Word association is the best known of these techniques. In **word association**, respondents are presented with a list of words, one at a time, and are asked to respond to each with the first word that comes to mind. The words of interest, called test words, are interspersed throughout the list, which also contains some neutral, or filler, words to disguise the purpose of the study. For example, in the GlobalCash study, individual banks may be examined with test words such as: location, speed, error, quality and price. The subject's response to each word is recorded verbatim and responses are timed so that respondents who hesitate or reason out (defined as taking longer than three seconds to reply) can be identified. The interviewer, not the respondent, records the responses. This controls for the time required for the respondent to write the response.

The underlying assumption of this technique is that association allows respondents to reveal their inner feelings about the topic of interest. Responses are analysed by calculating:

1 The frequency with which any word is given as a response.
2 The amount of time that elapses before a response is given.
3 The number of respondents who do not respond at all to a test word within a reasonable period.

Those who do not respond at all are judged to have an emotional involvement so high that it blocks a response. It is often possible to classify the associations as favourable, unfavourable, or neutral. An individual's pattern of responses and the details of the response are used to determine the person's underlying attitudes or feelings on the topic of interest, as shown in the following example.

EXAMPLE

Dealing with dirt

Word association was used to study women's attitudes toward detergents. Below is a list of stimulus words used and the responses of two women of similar age and household status. The sets of responses are quite different, suggesting that the women differ in personality and in their attitudes toward housekeeping. Ms M's associations suggest that she is resigned to dirt. She sees dirt as inevitable and does not do much about it. She does not do hard cleaning, nor does she get pleasure from her family. Ms C sees dirt too, but is energetic, factual-minded, and less emotional. She is actively ready to combat dirt, and she uses soap and water as her weapons.[13]

Stimulus	*Ms M*	*Ms C*
Washday	Everyday	Ironing
Fresh	And sweet	Clean
Pure	Air	Soiled
Scrub	Does not; husband does	Clean
Filth	This neighbourhood	Dirt
Bubbles	Bath	Soap and water
Family	Squabbles	Children
Towels	Dirty	Wash

These findings suggest that the market for detergents could be segmented based on attitudes. Firms (such as Procter & Gamble) that market several different brands of washing powders and detergents could benefit from positioning different brands for different attitudinal segments. ■

Procter & Gamble has positioned different detergent brands for different attitudinal segments, as revealed by the word association

There are several variations to the standard word association procedure illustrated here. Respondents may be asked to give the first two, three or four words that come to mind rather than only the first word. This technique can also be used in controlled tests, as contrasted with free association. In controlled tests, respondents might be asked, 'What banks come to mind first when I mention low error transactions'? More detailed information can be obtained from completion techniques, which are a natural extension of association techniques.

Completion technique
A projective technique that requires respondents to complete an incomplete stimulus situation.

Completion techniques

In completion techniques, respondents are asked to complete an incomplete stimulus situation. Common completion techniques in marketing research are sentence completion and story completion.

Sentence completion
A projective technique in which respondents are presented with a number of incomplete sentences and are asked to complete them.

Sentence completion. Sentence completion is similar to word association. Respondents are given incomplete sentences and are asked to complete them. Generally, they are asked to use the first word or phrase that comes to mind, as illustrated in the GlobalCash project.

GLOBALCASH PROJECT

Sentence completion

In the context of plans for European economic and monetary union, the following incomplete sentences may be used.

A manager who plans to convert to the Euro on 1 January 2000 is

....

A manager who selects a new pan-European bank based on price is

....

ABN AMRO is most preferred by

....

When I think of allocating business between banks, I

....

This example illustrates one advantage of sentence completion over word association: respondents can be provided with a more directed stimulus. Sentence completion may provide more information about the subjects' feelings than word association. Sentence completion is not as disguised as word association, however, and many respondents may be able to guess the purpose of the study. A variation of sentence completion is paragraph completion, in which the respondent completes a paragraph beginning with the stimulus phrase. A further expanded version of sentence completion and paragraph completion is story completion. ■

Story completion
A projective technique in which respondents are provided with part of a story and are required to give the conclusion in their own words.

Story completion. In story completion, respondents are given part of a story, enough to direct attention to a particular topic but not to hint at the ending. They are required to give the conclusion in their own words, as in the following example.

GLOBALCASH PROJECT

Story completion

A treasury manager had been conducting business with a leading domestic bank for over 10 years. Her company was planning to make more use of the Internet/email for financial communication. The manager that was her main contact at the bank knew little of the applications and benefits of Internet/email for her business. So, she spent three months in talks with a variety of software suppliers, primarily trying to get over the problem of integrating new software with the systems she already has. After going through a major selection process and being at the point where she is about to commit her company, another department of her bank contacts her with a Internet/email solution that solves her integration problems at a much cheaper price compared to her selection process.

What is the manager's response? Why?

The respondent's completion of this story will reveal characteristics of the relationship she 'enjoys' with the bank. How after such a lengthy relationship, the bank may take business for granted. What role is expected of the bank manager. What must happen in a relationship to get it to the point when switching to another bank is inevitable, whatever the costs. ■

Construction techniques

Construction technique
A projective technique in which respondents are required to construct a response in the form of a story, dialogue, or description.

Construction techniques are closely related to completion techniques. Construction techniques require the respondents to construct a response in the form of a story, dialogue, or description. In a construction technique, the researcher provides less initial structure to the respondents than in a completion technique. The two main construction techniques are picture response techniques and cartoon tests.

Picture response technique
A projective technique in which respondents are shown a picture and are asked to tell a story describing it.

Picture response techniques. The roots of **picture response techniques** can be traced to the thematic apperception test (TAT), which consists of a series of pictures of ordinary as well as unusual events. In some of these pictures, the persons or objects are clearly depicted, while in others they are relatively vague. The respondent is asked to tell stories about these pictures. The respondent's interpretation of the pictures gives indications of that individual's personality. For example, an individual may be characterised as impulsive, creative, unimaginative, and so on. The term thematic apperception test is used because themes are elicited based on the subject's perceptual interpretation (apperception) of pictures.

In marketing research uses of picture response techniques, respondents are shown a picture and asked to tell a story describing it. The responses are used to evaluate attitudes toward the topic and describe the respondents, as illustrated by the following.

EXAMPLE

Gimme a double shake and a lard on white

The light and healthy craze seems to be dying down for one segment of the population. In response to direct questioning, consumers are hesitant to say that they want food that is bad for them. This finding, however, emerged in a picture response test in which the respondents were asked to describe a picture depicting people consuming high-fat food rich in calories. A significant number of the respondents defended the behaviour of the people in the picture. They explained that the increased stress in everyday life has caused people to turn from tasteless rice cakes to comfort foods, loaded with the ingredients that make life worth living.

Many marketers have capitalised upon this finding by introducing products that contain large amounts of salt, fat and calories. Haagen-Dazs has introduced a line of deluxe ice creams called Extraas. The flavours include the new Triple Brownie Overload packed with fresh cream, sugar, chocolate liquor, butter, pecans and egg yolks. The Extraas line helped to increase Haagen-Dazs's market share. ■

Picture response techniques reveal that increased stress in everyday life has caused some people to turn to comfort foods, loaded with high fat and rich in calories

Cartoon tests
Cartoon characters are shown in a specific situation related to the problem. Respondents are asked to indicate the dialogue that one cartoon character might make in response to the comment(s) of another character.

Cartoon tests. In **cartoon tests**, cartoon characters are shown in a specific situation related to the problem. Respondents are asked to indicate what one cartoon character might say in response to the comments of another character. The responses indicate the respondents' feelings, beliefs, and attitudes toward the situation. Cartoon tests are simpler to administer and analyse than picture response techniques.

Expressive techniques

Expressive techniques
Projective techniques in which respondents are presented with a verbal or visual situation and are asked to relate the feelings and attitudes of other people to the situation.

In **expressive techniques**, respondents are presented with a verbal or visual situation and asked to relate the feelings and attitudes of other people to the situation. The respondents express not their own feelings or attitudes, but those of others. The two main expressive techniques are role playing and third-person technique.

Role playing
Respondents are asked to assume the behaviour of someone else.

In **role playing**, respondents are asked to play the role or to assume the behaviour of someone else. The researcher assumes that the respondents will project their own feelings into the role.[14] A major use of role playing is in uncovering the nature of a brand personality. The following example shows why the brand personality is of importance to the marketer and how an understanding of personality may be used in advertising.

EXAMPLE

It's a bit of an animal[15]

Brand personality

A brand has a man-made personality and it can survive only if those responsible for it think long term, safeguard its consistency, and ensure its adherence to and compatibility with the needs and attitudes of those for whom it caters. The brand's personality is sacrosanct. Its owners need to guard against squatters, parallel traders, plagiarists and the threat of the brand becoming generic. Above all, they must guard against inconsistency.[16]

Levi Strauss have done a superb job of managing their personality from a brand of workingmen's clothing to high priced, semi-fashion clothing for a huge world-wide audience of young (and not so young!) people. Buyers of Levi's had increasing amounts of money to spend and were bent on showing their growing independence by wearing informal clothes. Levi's product range was successfully broadened through the addition of shoes, shirts, skirts and jackets. Then, one day Levi's started to offer suits. People did not buy them. Suits were in conflict with the informal gear that Levi's stood for.

In another example, Peperami, the oddball snack product, strongly flavoured, meat based, in a world where sweet confectionery snacks are the norm. Advertising for the product could not be developed without first obtaining real insights into how consumers related to Peperami.

Research soon revealed that there was a widespread view of the brand's personality. Children and adults alike referred to it as bizarre, mischievous, anarchic, impulsive, rebellious and manic. More than 50 rough advertising concepts were then tested to establish how the brand personality could be expressed, from mere eccentricity to naked aggression. What emerged was a swaggering character with a mischievous desire to shock. All the ingredients were there for the advertising solution, the manic, animated Peperami, and the pay-off line, 'It's a bit of an animal'. ■

Brand personality can be uncovered using role-playing. In a group interview scenario, participants may be asked to play out the personality of a brand. In the Levi's example, the setting could be a cocktail bar after work on a Friday evening, with individuals acting out a Levi's brand, a Hugo Boss, a Ralph Lauren or a Benneton brand. What the individuals as brand do, what they say, how they interact with each other in the cocktail scenario, allows an expression of personality that straight questioning may not reveal. Video recording of the event, played back to the group acts as a means to discuss and elicit further meaning of a brand's personality, highlighting any positive and negative associations of the brand.

Third-person technique
A projective technique in which respondents are presented with a verbal or visual situation and are asked to relate the beliefs and attitudes of a third person situation.

Third-person technique. In the **third-person technique**, respondents are presented with a verbal or visual situation and are asked to relate the beliefs and attitudes of a third person rather than directly expressing personal beliefs and attitudes. This third person may be a friend, a neighbour, a colleague, or a 'typical' person. Again, the researcher assumes that the respondents will reveal personal beliefs and attitudes while describing the reactions of a third party. Asking an individual to respond in the third person reduces the social pressure to give an acceptable answer.

We conclude our discussion of projective techniques by describing their advantages, disadvantages and applications.

Advantages and disadvantages of projective techniques

Projective techniques have a major advantage over the unstructured direct techniques (focus groups and depth interviews): they may elicit responses that subjects would be unwilling or unable to give if they knew the purpose of the study. At times, in direct questioning, the respondent may intentionally or unintentionally misunderstand, misinterpret, or mislead the researcher. In these cases, projective techniques can increase the validity of responses by disguising the purpose. This is particularly true when the issues to be addressed are personal, sensitive, or subject to strong social norms. Projective techniques are also helpful when underlying motivations, beliefs, and attitudes are operating at a subconscious level.[17]

Projective techniques suffer from many of the disadvantages of unstructured direct techniques, but to a greater extent. These techniques generally require personal interviews with highly trained interviewers. Skilled interpreters are also required to analyse the responses. Hence, they tend to be expensive. Furthermore, there is a serious risk of interpretation bias. With the exception of word association, all are open-ended techniques, making the analysis and interpretation difficult.

Some projective techniques such as role playing require respondents to engage in what may seem to be unusual behaviour. Certain respondents may not have the self-confidence or the ability to fully express themselves with these techniques. In role playing, for example, the skills of acting may make one respondent more articulate at expressing their feelings compared to others. The same may be said of techniques where pictures and cartoons are put together and interpreted, in that distinctive skills may make certain respondents more adept and comfortable in expressing themselves. To counter this, one could argue that there is a great amount of skill required expressing oneself in an open ended depth interview. One could point to fiction writers or poets who are able to encapsulate particular feelings most clearly and succinctly, which again is a great skill.

With such skill requirements, the disadvantage of the technique lies in the nature of respondents who agree to participate, and how characteristic they are of distinct target markets.

Applications of projective techniques

Projective techniques are used less frequently than unstructured direct methods (focus groups and depth interviews). A possible exception may be word association, which is commonly used to test brand names and occasionally to measure attitudes about particular products, brands, packages or advertisements. As the examples have shown, projective techniques can be used in a variety of situations. The usefulness of these techniques is enhanced when the following guidelines are observed.

1. Projective techniques should be used because the required information cannot be accurately obtained by direct methods.
2. Projective techniques should be used in an exploratory manner to elicit issues that respondents find difficult to conceive and express.
3. Given their complexity, projective techniques should not be used naively.

Given these guidelines, projective techniques along with other qualitative techniques can yield valuable information.[18]

Qualitative observation or ethnographic techniques

The other major indirect qualitative method is observation. Quantitative observation as a technique is tackled at length in Chapter 8, but given that a major component of observation is qualitative and indirect, it is worth addressing at this point. Essentially, observation, or **ethnographic techniques**, can be used to capture characteristics of consumers that come 'naturally', that they may not be aware of, or they cannot express.

Ethnographic technique
A research approach based upon the observation of the customs, habits and differences between people in everyday situations.

Just as David Attenborough, in his Wildlife programmes, studies the behaviour of gorillas from a safe distance, camouflaged from view and in tones of hushed awe alternated with amused laughter, so can consumer behaviour be studied.[19] Consumers respond to the world they live in by adaptive behaviour of which they are mostly unaware. They do things in certain ways for reasons they cannot begin to articulate. They respond unconsciously to cues in the environment, to the behaviour of others around them, to their physical and psychological feelings, just like any other species. It generally happens in a fraction of a second.

The following example illustrates the use of observation at the point of purchase.

EXAMPLE

In the bag[20]

Increasingly, consumer decisions are being made at the point of purchase and to get at that moment of decision, the National Opinion Poll Research Group is using surveillance cameras in supermarkets, garage forecourts, newsagents, DIY and electrical stores.

Robert Lawson, NOP Associate Director, explains that shoppers are watched as they deliberate over prices, labels, promotions, struggle with trolleys, skip past certain aisles and queue at tills. Kids become bored and disruptive when parents are shopping for a fridge and as they drift away, they pull their parents too. The answer is to provide a distraction. Following work with NOP, electrical retailer Currys is placing different product categories next to each other, such as listening posts for music or videos that intrigue children and keep them quiet. The whole layout and atmosphere of stores can be changed to get the shopper to relax and spend more. The positioning of colourful fruit and vegetables at the front of the shop and the delicatessen counter placed along the back wall where its premium products have to be passed to reach everything else, all help shoppers load up their trolleys. Future improvements based on observation will see food displayed as meal groupings – all the ingredients for a barbecue or Indian meal, for example. ■

Beyond the point of purchase, the researcher may have the opportunity to observe the actual consumption of the product. In some product and service categories, the purchase and consumption take place simultaneously. For example, if the researcher wants to understand beer drinking behaviour and brand dynamics the best thing to do is to get as close as is possible to real behaviour as it happens. This means excursions into the world of the consumer, observing, listening, talking and being aware of the broader cultural context in which brand behaviour is taking place. In public houses, cafes and restaurants, the researcher can observe beer being ordered, served, consumed on its own, with snacks and meals, consumed in a group setting, with the mood and atmosphere changing, with different types of consumer drinking different brands. The consumers behave naturally, do not have to think through and explain their behaviour, they just do it!

This represents a major benefit of observation, i.e. that consumers can behave in a natural manner and do not have to think through or explain their behaviour or the motives for that behaviour. The major drawback lies in interpreting that behaviour. At a practical level, it is almost impossible to separate the gathering of data from the interpretation of that data. One technique used to overcome this problem involves the use of observation mixed with interviewing. The following example illustrates the use of depth interviewing and observation working together.

EXAMPLE

Asking the obvious[21]

The advertising agency, J. Walter Thompson, has a consumer research technique called InSitu, whereby unsuspecting shoppers are filmed in store and then questioned about their shopping decisions. When shoppers are quizzed about their purchases, they tend to forget what they were thinking at the time. However, once they are faced with a video of themselves, they quickly remember.

The technique has shown that shoppers do not acclimatise until they are about two-thirds of the way into a store, making promotions by the door relatively ineffectual. At the entrance they may be seen as 'pedestrians'; the key is to find points in the store where shoppers stand around and take in their environment.

JWT's interaction specialist Siamack Salari cites the example of pubs. 'No decisions are actually made at the bar, everyone decides what they want two metres away from it. So any promotions that cannot be seen from there are wasted.' ■

The next example also uses observations with interviews though the emphasis is upon interviewing first and using observations to enhance the interpretation of responses. The essential point to note is that of context in which the interview takes place. First, it allows access to individuals who may be difficult to talk to in normal circumstances. Second, the issues to be addressed are at the forefront of their mind, as they experience the services they are being questioned about. Third, how they behave in that context acts as powerful means to generate questions and interpret responses.

EXAMPLE

Boundary commission[22]

While as a general rule it is clearly not cost-effective to send researchers across the globe from one central source, there are circumstances in which an entirely centrally operated programme can get access to a group of international travellers without leaving the country. They do however, have to spend the day at the airport.

Janine Braier is Managing Director of Define Research & Marketing International, which operates a portfolio of products, called *Methods on the Move*. *Methods* take the qualitative research to the respondent, whether they are on a train, in a shop or idling away a couple of hours in an airport departure lounge. Encounters can take the form of in-depth one-to-one interviews or rolling group surveys in which quota-controlled respondents dip in for anything from ten minutes to two hours.

Braier says, 'obviously the more highly specified the target market, the more difficult it is to do research without lists of named customers. However, people are often willing to talk, as they may have nothing better to do. We can offer a very fast turnaround and we can ask questions to find out what is going on in people's heads as they stand in the actual environment. We notice emotion and body language; things people would not remember afterwards or else would rationalise after the event.' ■

In the above examples, there are circumstances where observation is completed in a covert manner, the consumers being completely unaware that they are being observed. In other circumstances, the researcher reveals his or her role at some point in the observation process. For the researcher there are questions as to which approach is the most revealing of how the consumer behaves but also which is the most ethical stance to adopt. Again, these issues will be tackled in more depth in Chapter 8. At this point, however, it is clear that observation can be a qualitative technique with a hidden research purpose. The next chapter will show that observation can be a quantitative technique with a clear research purpose revealed.

To summarise comparisons between qualitative techniques, Table 7.1 gives a relative comparison of focus groups, depth interviews, projective techniques and observation.

Table 7.1 A comparison of focus groups, depth interviews, projective techniques and qualitative observation

Criteria	*Focus groups*	*Depth interviews*	*Projective techniques*	*Observation*
Degree of structure	Relatively high	Relatively medium	Relatively low	Relatively low
Probing of individual respondents	Low	High	Medium	None when used in a covert manner and in isolation
Moderator bias	Relatively medium	Relatively high	Low to high	None when used in a covert manner and in isolation
Uncovering subconscious information	Low	Medium to high	High	High
Discovering innovative information	High	Medium	Low	Medium
Obtaining sensitive information	Low	Medium	High	High
Involving unusual behaviour or questioning	No	To a limited extent	Yes	Perhaps on the part of the researcher

The nature of qualitative research is such that within the broad categories above, there are numerous variations of the techniques with distinct strengths and weaknesses in eliciting and representing consumer feelings. Really, it is not possible to say that one technique is better or worse than the other. Faced with a given problem, it would seem to be the case of deciding which technique is the most appropriate to represent consumers.[23] What may affect this choice is the confidence that marketing decision-makers may have in particular techniques. Thus for example, any number of arguments may be made for the use of a projective technique as being the best way to indirectly tackle a sensitive issue. If the marketer who has to use the research findings does not believe it to be a trustworthy technique, then other, perhaps inappropriate, techniques may have to be used.

In all of the above techniques, a major question arises about the potential bias that may come from a moderator or researcher. A further question that develops from bias is one of analysis and interpretation of the data collected. These questions are vital in understanding how useful qualitative research is to marketing decision-makers and are tackled in the next section.

ANALYSING QUALITATIVE DATA

The techniques described in Chapter 6 and this chapter, show data being collected that does not result from pre-determined, structured measurements. Qualitative techniques allow a great variety of response styles and formats; they also allow questions and probes to evolve over the time of the research process. The evolution of questions, probes and even deciding who should be targeted for questions or observations means that some analysis takes place as data is being gathered. As the qualitative marketing researcher collects data in its many disparate forms, analysis continues. The key factors in developing analysis and interpretations of qualitative research lie in a combination of:

- theoretical understanding of the researcher(s) collecting and analysing the data;
- marketing understanding, i.e. appreciation of how decision-makers will use qualitative research findings.

The following example illustrates an advertising practitioner's reflections upon how qualitative researchers have improved their data collection and analysis procedures to offer strong support to decision-makers.

Cinderella's getting ready for the ball[24]

I think a lot of researchers have worked hard at understanding advertising and the advertising process and are now regarded as quite critical contributors. What has allowed them to become 'wise' advisors rather than providers of fuel for literal and obedient fools? I think the following:

1 *There has been more crossover between planners and qualitative researchers.* Qualitative researchers understand their role in the process of developing ads and building brands. They want to know what the creative brief is and what responses/feelings an ad is meant to elicit. For example, when developing a current and famous premium package lager, we purposely discussed what levels of initial bewilderment or mild alienation were acceptable. The campaign had to challenge consumers – hopefully the brightest ones would let their mates in on the secret jokes down the pub!
2 *Good researchers work to more 'holistic' views of how ads work and thus avoid mechanistic and simplistic diagnoses.* We may therefore use projective techniques to help consumers express feelings. Whatever it is, good researchers try and look at ads in totality not as a disaggregate series of frames.
3 *Good qualitative researchers, planners and clients are much more conscious about stimuli in ad research.* People put more effort into defining stimuli – e.g. using

film clips to get across production values or special effects, mood boards to give texture alongside traditional animatics, narratives or key frames. We have showed *Terminator* 2 to help consumers imagine products 'metamorphosing' from one thing to another and music snippets to conjure up different feelings of sensuality and sexuality.

4 *Interpretation has improved.* Good qualitative researchers know that consumers in group discussions are likely to be evaluative/judgemental, cynical and literal. It is the researcher's job to get them to 'imagine' beyond that and to interpret responses using one's cumulative knowledge of advertising chemistry. At one extreme, it's all about nurturing embryonic ideas, at the other about asking oneself whether this really has the legs?

Having a theoretical and marketing awareness is an outcome that good qualitative researchers aim for. To get to that point there are distinct stages of analysis that the qualitative marketing researcher should go through. These stages are outlined in Figure 7.1.

Data assembly

Data is assembled from a variety of sources. These would include:

- Memories of moderators or observers involved in the data collection process.
- Notes taken as interviewing or observations take place, or after the event.
- Audio tape recordings and transcripts of those recordings.
- Video tape recordings.
- Records made by respondents such as mood boards or collages.

Memory alone is fallible, unreliable and potentially biased. However, it should not be dismissed as a 'data source' in that it contributes much to the interpretation of other data sources. For example, the hesitation in replying to a question that a focus group respondent may display, upon reflection may be seen as someone evading the issue. After all the groups have been completed and the same question posed to others, the interpretation may change to the individual being embarrassed about an issue, primarily through becoming aware of his or her own ignorance. The moderator's memory helps them to recall how they were feeling at the point of setting the question, and recall the situation in other groups that gives meaning to: *a pause that shows up as a quiet spot in a audio or video recording.*

Data assembly
The gathering of data from a variety of disparate sources.

Data assembly also includes deciding lines of enquiry which should be developed and those that should be dropped. Given that qualitative research is primarily exploratory in nature, questions and probes are not fixed. As a interview or observation takes place, the researcher learns more about an issue and can develop a new question or probe and decide that a question, initially thought to be vital, is no longer relevant. There may be issues that can be compared over a series of interviews or observations, but the whole data collection and data assembly can evolve.

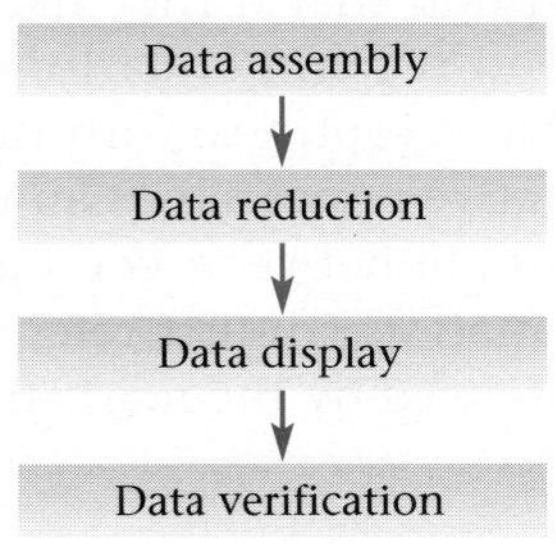

Figure 7.1
Stages of qualitative data analysis

Data reduction
The organising and structuring of qualitative data.

Data reduction involves handling the data. This process involves organising and structuring the data. It means having to throw some data away! Imagine a series of 10 focus group interviews and the amount of data that can be collected. There are the memories and notes of the moderator and any other observers who took part, there are the transcripts of what was actually said, and there may be contributions from respondents in the form of mood boards. The researcher has to decide what is relevant in all these data. Reducing the data involves a process of **coding**, which means breaking down the data into discrete chunks and attaching a reference to those chunks of data. With a reference, the chunks of data can be arranged and rearranged to search for patterns of similarity between interviews and observations or distinct differences between particular types of individual. (Coding data will be covered in more depth when the use of qualitative data analysis software is tackled.)

Coding data
Breaking down qualitative data into discrete chunks and attaching a reference to those chunks of data.

Data display
Involves summarising and presenting the structure that is seen in collected qualitative data.

Data display involves summarising and presenting the structure that is seen in the collected data. The display allows a 'public' view of how the researcher has made connections between the different 'data chunks'. Even if others may not have made the same connections and interpret the data in exactly the same manner, the logic of connections should be clear. The display may be in a graphical format, with boxes summarising issues that have emerged and connecting arrows showing the interconnection between issues. Verbatim quotes can be used to illustrate the issues or the interconnections. Pictures, drawings, music or advertisements can also be used to illustrate issues or interconnections. The overall structure allows the marketer to see the general meaning in the collected data. The illustration of issues or interconnections brings that meaning to life.

Data verification
Involves seeking alternative explanations of the interpretations of qualitative data, through other data sources.

Data verification involves seeking alternative explanations through other data sources. Researchers need to demonstrate that they have presented a valid meaning of the data that they have collected. They need to show that the structure or meaning they see is not just a reflection of their own views. This is where theoretical frameworks help to guide what may be reasonably expected as a meaning (bearing in mind that a true exploratory research technique may generate 'new' theory, or explanations that have not been published as theory to date). Other means to verify the data can be through seeking 'similar' research findings and explanations taken from different contexts, different time frames and different researchers. Though the findings from these different scenarios will not be the same, there can be themes that give qualitative researchers the confidence that they are representing a valid view of their respondents.

Practitioners' views on qualitative analysis

Most marketing decision-makers generally assume that researchers do what is necessary to analyse qualitative research, and assume that it is competently done.[25] Most make the tacit assumption that if they like the debrief (an oral presentation of the conclusions and recommendations) the analysis must have been all right. There are notable exceptions, with the following example illustrating that if the user of qualitative research has an understanding of the analysis process, they can discriminate between good and poor qualitative researchers. Good and poor in an analysis context refer to an understanding of relevant theory and the problems faced by the marketing decision-maker.

EXAMPLE

Money can't buy me qualitative research[26]

'I have sat in horror as debriefs have reflected little understanding (or even attempt at understanding) of how advertising can work. There are a great deal of obvious and unhelpful interpretations of what they should mean in terms of executional development presented as "the truth"' – *Rita Clifton, Director of Planning at Saatchi & Saatchi Advertising.*

'You might say, "she likes the personal stuff when it goes her way but not when it doesn't suit her". In fact, one of the researchers I have worked with extensively over the years has led to a "thumbs down" on about half the creative work we've researched. However, the difference is that the work was brilliantly analysed, in terms of effect versus consumer opinions, thoughtfully interpreted, with positive options suggested about what one would do to change the effect.' ■

It has been argued that marketing decision-makers *rarely ask* what qualitative researchers do with the data that they have collected, not having the level of discernment displayed by Rita Clifton above.[27] The main reasons for this include:

1 Decision-makers not knowing what ought to be done, and therefore having no criteria about what to look for, or what to expect.
2 It can be embarrassing to ask, as if impugning the researcher's professional standards.
3 It is hard to inspect a researcher's analysis; this is essentially a private display. Much of it is assumed to be done in the head and in this respect differs from moderation, debriefing, reporting or even to some extent recruitment.
4 Don't want to know! It might turn out to be a can of worms and in any case what would they do if they knew?

Some marketing decision-makers consider analysis to be not particularly important, arguing that:

1 Lengthy analysis might produce boring descriptions instead of insightful conclusions.
2 Qualitative research is about imagination, flair and personality, not about painstaking annotation.
3 Too much analysis can produce overkill; it can be mechanistic and boring – 'you cannot see the wood for the trees'.
4 Some well-known researchers are believed to get by without doing much in the way of analysis.

When pushed on how confident marketing decision-makers are with the conclusions and interpretations made of qualitative data, questions of validity come to the fore. Is the interpretation a valid one? Can it be dependable enough to build decisions upon? Building a valid view, which one can have confidence in, requires a view of coping with the data by 'pulling it apart – then pulling it together again'. Both these elements are important, and arguably, one cannot make a proper job of 'pulling it together' without first 'pulling it apart' thoroughly enough.[28]

Qualitative marketing researchers, in general, recognise what is involved in 'pulling together' qualitative data, by pulling it apart. An argument against the thoroughness of such a process lies in the time that it takes, traded off against the additional meaning that may be gleaned from the data. Researchers should form their analyses within a framework that suits an appropriate theoretical and/or marketing purpose of their work. Given the amount of seemingly disparate data that can be collected, a major development in coping with theoretical and marketing frameworks is the use of qualitative data analysis software. The Internet and Computer Applications section describes what this software does, highlighting the benefits and limitations of analysing qualitative data in this way.

INTERNATIONAL MARKETING RESEARCH

If one were to view the analysis of qualitative data as the feeding of data into an analysis package, and waiting for processed data to emerge, then international analysis would focus purely upon issues of language and translation. Such a perspective of qualitative data analysis is very narrow, ignoring the context and process of collecting the data in the interpretation of meaning that emerges from interviews and observations. The following example comes from a qualitative research practitioner, Mary Goodyear, who has a vast experience of running focus groups throughout the world, especially in developing nations. Her message is that essentially the technique in what it may elicit from the individual, wherever it is conducted throughout the world. Examining the society in which it is conducted, one sees a different approach needed to make the interview work. This also has a major impact upon analysing and interpreting the data collected.

EXAMPLE

The world over, a group is a group is a group[29]

A group is a group is a group. In terms of how to analyse the vagaries and priorities of the *individual*, human beings seem more or less the same wherever they live, whatever they eat and however they worship. But, it is important to recognise that international research is different. It differs in terms of analysing the social and cultural dynamics of the society – how the foreign society is structured, how power is gained and expressed, the roles allotted to men and women, and the interactions between different sectors of society. ■

The message from the above example is clear: qualitative researchers have to be aware of the cultural and societal norms that affect how they may interpret responses to questions and observations. Mary Goodyear's experiences form the next example, which shows that creative and insightful interpretation of qualitative data goes beyond 'understanding' an international environment. Qualitative researchers needs an acute self-awareness of how they 'see' – affecting the way they pose questions and interpret answers.

Recent studies suggest that in developing countries, consumers' relationship with brand values is different[30]

The process of analysis is just as fascinating as the travellers' tales of experience of fieldwork. Assessing a culture, a nation or a region raises some big issues, and questions most of one's own culturally determined assumptions. One of the big issues that have interested me in recent years has been to explore the definition and significance of brands. In our highly consumerised nation, we believe we know what we mean by a brand and what part it plays in our lives. But is there any reason to believe that it is defined and valued in the same way in societies where most goods are commodities and where the media's role is less dominant? I believe we should not confuse the appeal of television to its viewers in these countries with an *authority* over them. Word of mouth and the consensus of society is still the major decision-maker in their lives. ■

Consumers in any country use their social and cultural frames of reference to interpret questions posed to them by qualitative researchers and to present a response. Likewise, qualitative researchers use their social and cultural frames to present questions and interpret answers. If the researcher and the respondent share the same or similar social and cultural frames of reference, the analysis and interpretation of the data can be relatively straightforward. If the qualitative researcher goes into an international market, there is the potential for big differences in social and cultural frames between the researcher and researched. The qualitative researcher needs to develop an understanding of the social and cultural frames of the types of respondent in an international market. At the same time, they must have a strong awareness of their own social and cultural frames. Only when they have examined both perspectives can they start to interpret consumer responses in the manner that Mary Goodyear illustrates.

The process is summarised by leading qualitative researchers Virginia Valentine and Malcolm Evans as:[31]

> Consumers give a 'coded' version of the social and cultural relationship with products and brands that drive their 'feelings'. Because language (and language systems) are the medium of culture, the rules of language become the rules of the code. Qualitative research then becomes a matter of working with the code through understanding the rules of language.

Thus, simple literal translations of transcripts of interviews from international markets entered into a qualitative data analysis package are doomed to failure. Understanding the rules of language and understanding oneself are vital for the qualitative researcher to interpret interviews and observations. As the rules of language, with the social and cultural forces that shape those rules, become more alien to the researcher in international markets, the task of analysis and meaningful interpretation become more difficult.

ETHICS IN MARKETING RESEARCH

The essence of qualitative research is that consumers are examined in great depth. They may be questioned and probed in depth about subjects they hardly reflect upon on a day-to-day basis, never mind talk to strangers about. Great care must be taken not to upset or disturb respondents through such intensive questioning. In survey work, reassuring respondents that their responses will be confidential can work if there is a demonstrable link between their responses to questions and a means of aggregating all of the findings – making the individual response 'hidden'. In qualitative research, the process is far more intimate and the link between the response and the respondent is far more difficult to break. This is illustrated in the following example.

EXAMPLE

Just how 'anonymous' is a quali respondent?[32]

From both a practical and methodological perspective, 'confidentiality' in qualitative research is a different concept from confidentiality as applied to survey work. In survey work the emphasis is upon anonymity, i.e. the identity of individual respondents should not be revealed. This creates two problems for qualitative research.

1 Anonymity cannot be promised in qualitative research, especially in the light of current practices where it is increasingly common for clients and others to come to groups, or hear audiotapes, see videotapes and other primary data.

This issue further demands consideration of the question: where does the identity reside? In a name, a face, the voice, a turn of phrase maybe? It is of course also pertinent to ask: do respondents actually care if their identity is revealed?

2 In quantitative research, respondent identity is methodologically unimportant. The very essence of sampling theory is that a sufficiently large and randomly chosen sample will represent the views, behaviour or attitudes of any known population as a whole. As such, the identity of any one individual is irrelevant to quantitative findings. In sharp contrast, in qualitative research the relationship between the specific individuals and their views is at the heart of analysis and interpretation. You cannot reach qualitative findings without having 'revealed' the individual as part of the research process. Therefore, confidentiality through anonymity is a methodologically untenable concept wherever anyone other than the moderator is privy to any part of the research process. Yet at the same time, more clients attend groups and more groups take place in viewing facilities.

At the end of the second point above comes the reason why the marketing research industry is so concerned about how qualitative research respondents are handled. More consumers are being questioned in both domestic and business scenarios. If they are to 'open up' and reveal deeply held feelings, perhaps in front of a group of strangers, or if they are to take part in projective techniques that they may see as being unorthodox, they have to be reassured of how the data captured will be used. As well as the ethical questions of potentially damaging respondents come the problems of respondents either not willing to take part or if they do, to be very guarded with their responses. ■

The very important ethical issues of observing respondents will be tackled with quantitative observation in Chapter 8.

INTERNET AND COMPUTER APPLICATIONS

A major problem for the qualitative researcher is the sheer volume of data that they may collect. In an attempt to 'step into the shoes' of target consumers, a whole array of questions, probes, observations and answers have to be analysed. As with quantitative data analyses, it is possible to complete analyses without the aid of a computer. Using the computer should provide speed, memory, ease of data access and a much more efficient and ultimately effective process.

For the survey researcher, coding is one of a number of tasks in the preparation of data for entry and analysis by computer. Generally, it is a rule-based procedure, where a code, usually numeric, is assigned to each possible response to each question. For qualitative researchers, coding is not a separate task that precedes data analysis; *coding is the process by which data are analysed.*[33] Qualitative data analysis programs are designed to facilitate studying the content of textual documents using search, retrieval and collation routines of coded 'chunks' of data. The tasks involved in coding are similar for virtually all types of qualitative research – namely, breaking down or fracturing the data into segments, chunks or bits that share meaning. From coded data, the routines performed by the software aid the process of reviewing, categorising, comparing and discerning relationships within text.

The data analysis programs can be divided into the categories listed in Table 7.2.

Table 7.2 Classification of qualitative data analysis software

Qualitative data analysis software	*Characteristics*
Content analysis programs	Inventories of pre-specified words
Text analysis programs	Text description, showing patterns, developing hypotheses
Database managers	User familiarity, flexibility, longitudinal studies

Content analysis programs
A program designed to take an inventory of all pre-specified words contained in text. They are used primarily in exploratory phases of research.

Content analysis programs take an inventory of all pre-specified words contained in text. They are used primarily in exploratory phases of research. The programs can generate a frequency distribution of all words included in a text, for example, the number of times that the word 'relationship' is used in depth interviews with cash managers talking about the banks they work with in GlobalCash. Text frequency distributions are used to review and compare texts (which can be individual transcripts) of exploratory, open-ended interviews. Used in this way, a text frequency distribution can indicate new theoretical concepts and ideas as well as questions to be addressed in subsequent data collection. Text frequency distributions can also be used to support initial comparisons of two or more transcripts to determine which topics or themes they share, and those unique to each.

Text analysis programs
A program used primarily for text description and interpretation and, in the case of some programs, theory building.

Text analysis programs have been developed explicitly for the purposes of text description and interpretation and, in the case of some programs, theory building. These programs help to identify and code elements of theoretical interest. They aid in establishing connections and discovering relationships among different topics or themes that may exist in transcripts.

Text analysis programs have four basic functions:

1 *Attaching codes to segments of text.* Text analysis programs facilitate coding, marking and identifying the boundaries of segments of text. For example, the phrase 'our relationship has gone sour', taken verbatim from a transcript, can have a code attached to it. The researcher chooses the phrase, recognising that it is relevant to the overall research purpose. The software marks out the phrase in the transcript.
2 *Searching for and assembling coded segments of text.* This facilitates the quick and thorough retrieval of segments of interest. Thus, searching through for the word *'relationship'* can reveal codes where the term emerged in the interview and what was said about the relationship – sour or not.
3 *Searching for code sequences.* This facilitates the investigation of patterns and relationships. Looking for relationships with other coded segments of text may reveal a connection with 'service quality' codes. The researcher may deduce that as cash managers talk about 'relationships', they do so in a context of 'service quality'.
4 *Counting instances* in which particular codes, code sequences and corresponding counter-evidence exist. Thus, if a connection between codes exists, how often does it exist? Was it in just one interview or is there a pattern that emerges across interviews?

Text analysis programs play a major role in hypothesis development by determining the extent to which patterns and relationships occur in text. Progressive exploration, development and testing of emerging theory can be facilitated by searching for evidence and counter evidence.

Database managers. Given the widespread appeal of database packages, the diverse applications they can be used for, and their ability to handle complex datasets, database programs can play a major role in qualitative data analysis. Many of the functions performed by text retrieval and text analysis programs overlap with the functions performed by database managers. Database managers can be considered a third program category because of their powerful text management, storing, searching, retrieving, sorting, accumulating and summarising capabilities. They are most appropriate for large-scale, longitudinal studies in which information is updated, and added to periodically.

Practical issues to address in using qualitative data analysis packages

The practical issues of entering and preparing text for analysis must be addressed in considering the use of computers for qualitative data analysis. There are three basic approaches for entering text into computer readable files, i.e. assembling the data:

1 Typing data directly (including voice recognition programs).
2 Optically scanning the data.
3 Importing existing electronic files.

The format of assembling the data is important, as different software packages can manage the data in different formats. The qualitative researcher should be aware of these formats and what conversion processes may be needed to be able to use a particular package. The preparation necessary to run qualitative data analysis programs varies substantially from program to program. Therefore, an important consideration for the researcher thinking of using such programs is the fit of specific program functions to the analyses they are likely to conduct.

Once the text is prepared in a format appropriate for the software, the qualitative research package does not automate the analysis process, nor is that its purpose. Rather than automation, the purpose of software is to aid the researcher to analyse data in a systematic and thorough manner. The researcher seeks patterns, meanings and interconnections in their qualitative data. This can be conducted manually but by using software they can manipulate the data for more efficiently to help them see patterns, meaning and interconnections. The packages cannot interpret the meaning and connection of coded 'chunks' of data. The programs do facilitate, and in some cases, automate, the identification and coding of text. There is therefore a false assumption that identification and coding are simple and unproblematic, and critical evaluation and scrutiny of coded segments and code counts are not needed. By facilitating quick analyses, which focus on quantitative category relationships, the software may discourage more time-consuming, in-depth interpretations. Thus while the programs are intended as a means to allow the researcher to stay close to the data, their misuse can have the unintended result of distancing the researcher from the data.

Concerns with the use of computers[35]

As discussed earlier, many decision-makers that use qualitative marketing research do not question how analysis is completed, or indeed why it should be completed. The following arguments illustrate the nature of their concerns, putting aside the time it takes to complete analysis – even with the timesaving gained through analysis software.

1 *Machines take over.* The creative process expected of the qualitative researcher cannot be replaced by the computer.
2 *Mechanistic data analysis.* The sensitivity towards relationships and connections is lost.

3 *Loss of the overview*. The analyst concentrates on the detail of individual chunks of data and assigning codes to the data. This focus may detract from the overall context that may be missing from 'coded chunks'.
4 *Obsession with volume*. Given the ability to manipulate large amounts of data, there may be a push to increase number of interviews. This may be counter-productive in that the emphasis should be on the interrelated *qualities* of:
   (a) individual respondents
   (b) the interview process
5 *Exclusion of non-text data*. As noted earlier, qualitative 'text' includes notes, observations, pictures and music that make up the total 'picture' or representation of individuals. Most programs can only cope with the narrative of questions and answers recorded in transcripts.

The main conclusion from these limitations is that the qualitative analysis software does not obviate the need to creatively collect and interpret qualitative data. To 'creatively collect' qualitative data is a reminder that the analysis process occurs throughout the data collection process, and new respondents, questions and probes are developed as the research unfolds. The researcher is looking for ways to describe consumer behaviour and feelings, and to make connections between the issues that make up behaviour and feelings. Exploring the nature of behaviour, feelings and their interconnections requires the qualitative researcher to explore the data they collect from many perspectives. The big advantage of qualitative data analysis packages lies in the discipline of systematically choosing relevant and irrelevant data, and putting boundaries and descriptors to relevant data. This process of coding data into discrete 'chunks' allows them to fully explore the data they have collected.

An analogy can be made with someone who reads a large pile of questionnaires. Reading through them could give them a 'flavour' of the responses, and the ability to draw some conclusions and interpretations – but these would be very limited. With survey data entered in an analysis package, many analyses and connections can be made, with the results of sparking new ideas for other analyses and connections – all of which can be quickly and accurately performed. The same can be said of qualitative data analysis software. In short, the software can facilitate quick and accurate exploration, which can support creative and incisive analysis and interpretation. It facilitates, but does not replace that creativity.

SUMMARY

The direct qualitative technique of depth interviewing allows researchers to focus upon individuals with the qualities they deem to be important to their research objectives. With a 'quality individual' the researcher can question and probe to great depth and elicit a quality understanding of that individual's behaviour or feelings. The technique is well suited to tackling commercially and personally sensitive issues. It is also well suited to interviewing children.

The indirect projective techniques aim to project the respondent's motivations, beliefs, attitudes and feelings onto ambiguous situations. Projective techniques may be classified as association (word association), completion (sentence completion, story completion), construction (picture response, cartoon tests), and expressive (role-playing, third-person) techniques. Projective techniques are particularly useful when respondents are unwilling or unable to provide the required information by direct methods.

The other major indirect technique involves observation. Qualitative observation is used to great effect in its own right in applications such as understanding how consumers react at point-of-purchase displays. It is also used in conjunction with focus group and depth interviews, helping the researcher to understand the context of an interview and how consumers behave within that context.

Qualitative data analysis must be set in the context of a theoretical understanding of the issue being researched, and an understanding of the marketing decision-makers' use of the findings. To cope with the great amount of textual data that can be generated by qualitative research, many data analysis software packages have been developed. The main types of package can be classified into content analysis, textual analysis and database manager packages.

The main concern with the use of qualitative data analysis packages lies in the potential for them to be mechanistic and encouraging more interviews to be completed – sacrificing the quality of data capture. Used correctly they can facilitate a speedy and accurate exploration of qualitative data allowing creative and incisive analysis and interpretation.

Qualitative data may be collected from international markets. Though in essence the techniques of qualitative data collection are the same, social and cultural differences in the international market results in differences of approach. As qualitative data analysis starts as data collection unfolds, qualitative researchers must be aware of the social and cultural impact of their questions on target respondents. Such an awareness affects how they collect data, by posing questions, probing and interpreting responses. This should be done with the qualitative researchers' self-awareness of their own social and cultural values.

The essence of qualitative research is that consumers are questioned in depth, probed and observed to develop consumer understanding. There are ethical issues about what happens to the individual in this process and what happens with the resultant data. As well as the questions of individual anonymity lies issues of the 'damage' that may be done to respondents which may have severe implications for future recruitment and involvement in qualitative interviews and observations.

The quality of questioning, probing and observing and the quality of respondents are vital ingredients in the success of qualitative research. With a strong theoretical and marketing awareness, the qualitative researcher can produce insightful and useful interpretations of consumers. The interpretative process is what makes qualitative research such a useful tool for exploring markets, understanding consumers and solving problems. The very nature of qualitative research is that it is the *quality* of the ideas that count, not just their frequency in the data. All qualitative researchers can cite occasions when an off-the-cuff remark (perhaps made when an interview is over) from one respondent illuminated the research problem and provided a framework for understanding all that was going on. That remark was invaluable for the insight it gave and yet it was said once by one person.[36]

QUESTIONS AND PROBLEMS

1 What is a depth interview? Under what circumstances is it preferable to focus groups?

2 What are the major advantages of depth interviews?

3 What are the requirements of the researcher undertaking depth interviews? Why are these requirements particularly important when conducting interviews with managers?

4 What are projective techniques? Under what circumstances would projective techniques be used?

5 Under what circumstances may observation techniques be classified as a qualitative technique?

6 Describe the word association technique. Give an example of a situation in which this technique is especially useful.

7 When should projective techniques be employed?

8 What may be classified as 'data' when assembling data as part of the data analysis process?

9 Describe the combination of the key factors that are vital in developing analyses and interpretations of qualitative research.

10 What are the advantages and disadvantages of handing over audio tapes of qualitative interviews to a typist who has taken no part in the interviews?

11 How important is it for qualitative researchers to reflect upon their own social and cultural background in interpreting qualitative research findings?

12 Why is respondent anonymity particularly acute in qualitative research?

13 Evaluate the main concerns that exist with the use of computers in qualitative data analysis.

14 Describe the basic functions of text analysis programs.

15 What does the word 'coding' mean in the context of qualitative data analysis? What problems do you see associated with the process of coding?

NOTES

1 Tesch. R., *Qualitative Research – Analysis Types and Software Tools* (Farmer: New York, 1990).
2 Winter, F., 'Fragrant Ways to Put the Mind in the Mood', *ResearchPlus* (May 1997), 4.
3 Qureshi, B. and Smith, J., 'Want to Know Why We Buy What We Do? Join the Queue', *ResearchPlus* (November 1995), 8.
4 Gray, R., 'Keeping Up with the Kids', *Marketing* (24 April 1997), 26.
5 Knox, M.Z., 'In-Depth Interviews Can Reveal "What's in a Name"', *Marketing News*, 3 (January 1986), 4.
6 Payne, M.S., 'Individual In-Depth Interviews Can Provide More Details than Groups', *Marketing Today* (Atlanta: Elrick and Lavidge, 1982); and Payne, M.S., 'Resurgence of In-Depth Interviewing Leads to Better Qualitative Research', *Marketing Today* vol. 1 (Elrick and Lavidge, 1984).
7 Bloom, N., 'In-Depth Research? A Bit Controversial!' *ResearchPlus* (June 1993), 12.
8 Parke, A., 'When Not to Rely on the Young Imagination', *ResearchPlus* (March 1997), 14.
9 Sokolow, H., 'In-Depth Interviews Increasing in Importance', *Marketing News* (13 September 1985), 26.
10 Kassarjian, H.H., 'Projective Methods', in R. Ferber (ed.), *Handbook of Marketing Research* (New York: McGraw-Hill, 1974), 3.85–3.100.
11 Hollander, S.L., 'Projective Techniques Uncover Real Consumer Attitudes', *Marketing News* (4 January 1988), 34.
12 Lindzey, G., 'On the Classification of Projective Techniques', *Psychological Bulletin* (1959), 158–68.
13 'Interpretation Is the Essence of Projective Research Techniques', *Marketing News* (28 September 1984), 20.
14 For issues involved in role playing, see Suprenant, C., Churchill, G.A. and Kinnear, T.C. (eds), 'Can Role Playing Be Substituted for Actual Consumption?', *Advances in Consumer Research* (Provo, UT: Association for Consumer Research, 1984), 122–26.
15 *Campaign* (28 October 1994), S13.
16 Van Mesdag, M., 'Brand Strategy Needs Turning Back to Front', *Marketing Intelligence and Planning* 15(2–3) (Feb–March 1997), 157.
17 Schnee, R.K., 'Quality Research: Going Beyond the Obvious', *Journal of Advertising Research* 28 (February–March 1988), RC–9–RC-12; and Kerlinger, F.N., *Foundations of Behavioural Research* 3 (New York: Holt, Rinehart and Winston, 1986), 471.
18 For more on projective techniques, see Valentine, V. and Evans, M., 'The Dark Side of the Onion: Rethinking the Meaning of "Rational" and "Emotional" Responses', *Journal of the Market Research Society* 35 (April 1993), 125–44.
19 Gordon, W., 'Get Out and Meet the People if You Want their Money', *Marketing* (28 November 1996), 20.

20 Litherland, S., 'In the Bag', *Marketing* (14 September 1995), 43.

21 Snowden, R., 'Why JWT is Now Asking the Obvious', *Marketing* (14 September 1995), 16.

22 MacKenzie, S., 'Boundary Commission', *Marketing Week* (29 January 1998), 16.

23 Colwell, J., 'Qualitative Market Research: a Conceptual Analysis and Review of Practitioner Criteria', *Journal of the Market Research Society*, 32(1) (1990), 33.

24 Payne, G., 'Cinderella's Getting Ready for the Ball' *Research Plus,* (February 1993), 7.

25 Robson, S. and Hedges, A., 'Analysis and Interpretation of Qualitative Findings', *Journal of the Market Research Society*, 35(1) (1993), 30.

26 Clifton, R., 'Money Can't Buy Me . . . Qualitative Research', *ResearchPlus* (July 1993), 3.

27 Robson, S. and Hedges, A., *op.cit.*

28 *Ibid.*

29 Goodyear, M., 'The World Over, a Group is a Group is a Group', *ResearchPlus* (November 1992), 5.

30 Ibid.

31 Valentine, V. and Evans, M., 'The Dark Side of the Onion: Rethinking the Meanings of "rational" and "emotional" responses', *Journal of the Market Research Society* 35(2) (April 1993), 127.

32 Imms, M., 'Just How "Anonymous" is a Quali Respondent?' *Research* (April 1997), 20.

33 Catterall, M. and Maclaran, P., 'Using Computer Programs to Code Qualitative Data', *Marketing Intelligence and Planning* 14(4) (April 1996), 29.

34 Wolfe, R.A., Gephart, R.P. and Johnson, T.E., 'Computer-facilitated Qualitative Data Analysis: Potential Contributions to Management Research', *Journal of Management* 19(3) (Fall 1993), 637.

35 Dembrowski, S. and Hanmer-Lloyd, S., 'Computer Applications – a New Road to Qualitative Data Analysis?' *European Journal of Marketing* 29(11) (November 1995), 50.

36 Robson, S. and Hedges, A., *op. cit.*

Chapter 8

Survey and quantitative observation methods

No particular survey method is the best in all cases. Depending on the problem, none, one, two or many methods may be appropriate.

OBJECTIVES

After reading this chapter, the student should be able to:

1 discuss and classify survey methods available to marketing researchers, and describe various survey methods;
2 identify the criteria for evaluating survey methods, compare the different methods and evaluate which is the best for a particular research project;
3 explain and classify the different quantitative observation methods;
4 identify the criteria for evaluating observation methods, compare the different methods, and evaluate which, if any, is suited for a particular research project;
5 describe the relative advantages and disadvantages of observational methods and compare them to survey methods;
6 discuss the considerations involved in implementing surveys and observation methods in an international setting;
7 understand the ethical issues involved in conducting survey and observational research.

OVERVIEW

In this chapter, we focus on the major methods employed in descriptive research designs: surveys and quantitative observation. As explained in Chapter 3, descriptive research has as its prime objective the description of something, usually consumer or market characteristics. Survey and quantitative observation methods are vital techniques in descriptive research designs. Survey methods may be classified by mode of administration as: traditional telephone interviews, computer-assisted telephone interviews, personal in-home or office interviews, street interviews, computer-assisted personal interviews, postal surveys, electronic surveys and mail panels. We describe each of these methods and present a comparative evaluation of all the survey methods. Then we consider the major observational methods: personal observation including mystery shopping research, electronic observation, audit, content analysis, and trace analysis. The relative advantages and disadvantages of observation over survey methods and the considerations involved in conducting survey and observation research when researching international markets are also discussed. Several ethical issues that arise in survey research and observation methods are identified. To begin our discussion, here are some examples of these methods.

EXAMPLE

Lucas and New Holland[1]

When a farmer has a problem with their New Holland tractor or combine harvester, they contact the New Holland dealer. The dealer diagnoses the problem and, if the cause is the fuel injection pump, they contact the pump manufacturer – the Lucas distributor. In early 1995 New Holland expressed concerns about the service side of this relationship.

Three markets were deemed to be affected by this problem: Britain, France and Italy. The key objectives of the research programme were to examine the level of satisfaction among all players in the end user/New Holland dealer/Lucas distributor chain with the fuel injection equipment repairs carried out on their new Holland tractor(s) or combine(s). In terms of both support networks, the research aimed to explore the relationship between Lucas distributors and New Holland dealers and, in particular, to identify key areas for improvement.

Structured interviews were conducted over the telephone by members of BJM Research Consultancy's phone centre in London. In the case of Italy and France, British-based Italian and French Nationals formed the interviewing team. ■

EXAMPLE

Covert Research – where's the mystery?[2]

Mystery shopping, or mystery customer research, is a well-established research technique, involving observers contacting or visiting providers of goods and services as if they were really customers. It has been extensively applied by retailers, travel agents, restaurant chains, car dealers and financial services companies among others, to measure the attributes of the service provided by the company's staff and to make comparisons with competitors.

London Underground Ltd has been running an extensive programme of mystery shopping for several years, with investigators making frequent visits to tube stations to report on quality of service ranging from courtesy of staff to cleanliness of stations. Research Manager, Justin Gutmann, is using the programme to develop targeting systems for the business and has also been building the results into his 'Value of Improvements' model by station, by line and the network as a whole. ■

EXAMPLE

The ins and outs of gay discrimination[3]

Any survey which tries to find a random sample of gay men and lesbians through a doorstep screening exercise ('Excuse me, can you tell me whether anyone in this household is gay or lesbian?') would be almost certain to fail. In 1990–92, Social and Community Planning Research carried out the fieldwork for the National Survey of Sexual Attitudes and Lifestyles. This was a large random sample survey (almost 19,000 respondents), who had been asked a range of questions about sexual attitudes and behaviour including detailed questions about sexual experience with members of the same sex. Everything had been done to minimise under-reporting of sensitive areas, including homosexuality. Questions about sexual behaviour were asked in the context of a questionnaire that dealt with a series of related topics and the most sensitive questions were in a self-completion booklet. ■

EXAMPLE

More muscle from microchips[4]

Multimedia CAPI (Computer Assisted Personal Interviewing) builds on the technology used in conventional CAPI research but uses multimedia notebook computers, not only to collect data, but also to present TV ads and other material to respondents in their homes. The market research company BMRB has around 100 of its 500 strong fieldforce using the notebook computers which are capable of running footage at 25 frames per second (the same rate as video). The power of the notebook PCs gives BMRB considerable scope. Clips from TV ads can be shown on the screen and followed up with on-screen questionnaires, to which the respondent answers by clicking on the relevant box or, where an opinion is being sought, by speaking into the notebook's microphone. The spoken answers are saved and can be downloaded onto an audio tape, so that other researchers can listen to them at a later date.

> 'Previously, we would have summarised the answers in a report, but it's got so much more impact with the original intonation. You can see the force with which it was said. Hearing customers talk about a brand like this is very, very powerful', says BMRB director Graham Wilkinson.

The system is not limited to showing TV ad clips. Respondents can be shown different packaging treatments, or a piece of the client company's marketing communications, alongside competitors' material. Notebook computers can also help interviewers overcome language barriers. The questionnaire can be translated beforehand into any language and played back to the respondents.

Wilkinson and his team are investigating potential applications for the technology, such as sponsorship or readership research, product testing, advertisement pre-testing and researching sensitive issues. ■

SURVEY METHODS

Survey method
A structured questionnaire given to a sample of a population and designed to elicit specific information from respondents.

Structured data collection
Use of a formal questionnaire that presents questions in a prearranged order.

The **survey method** of obtaining information is based upon structured questioning of respondents. Respondents may be asked a variety of questions regarding their behaviour, intentions, attitudes, awareness, motivations, and demographic and lifestyle characteristics. These questions may be asked verbally, in writing, or via a computer, and the responses may be obtained in any of these forms. Typically, the questioning is structured. 'Structured' here refers to the degree of standardisation imposed on the data collection process. In **structured data collection**, a formal questionnaire is prepared and the questions are asked in a prearranged order; thus, the process is also direct. Whether research is classified as direct or indirect is based on whether the true purpose is known to the respondents. As explained in Chapter 6, a direct approach is non-disguised in that the purpose of the project is disclosed to the respondents or is otherwise obvious to them from the questions asked.

The structured direct survey, the most popular data collection method, involves administering a questionnaire. In a typical questionnaire, most questions are fixed-response alternative questions that require the respondent to select from a predetermined set of responses. Consider, for example, the following question designed to measure a dimension of attitude toward marketing research assessment:

	Strongly agree	*Agree*	*Neutral*	*Disagree*	*Strongly disagree*
I prefer written examinations compared to continual assessment	☐	☐	☐	☐	☐

The survey method has several advantages. First, the questionnaire is simple to administer. Second, the data obtained are reliable because the responses are limited to the alternatives stated. The use of fixed-response questions reduces the variability in the results that may be caused by differences in interviewers. Finally, coding, analysis and interpretation of data are relatively simple.[5]

Disadvantages are that respondents may be unable or unwilling to provide the desired information. For example, consider questions about motivational factors. Respondents may not be consciously aware of their motives for choosing specific brands or shopping at particular stores. Therefore, they may be unable to provide accurate answers to questions about their motives. Respondents may be unwilling to respond if the information requested is sensitive or personal. In addition, structured questions and **fixed-response alternatives** may result in loss of validity for certain types of data such as beliefs and feelings. Finally, wording questions properly is not easy (see Chapter 12 on questionnaire design). In other words, the survey imposes the language and logic of the researcher onto questionnaire respondents. Given this core characteristic of survey methods, great care must be taken to ensure that the language and logic used in questionnaires is meaningful and valid to potential respondents. Despite the above disadvantages, the survey approach is by far the most common method of primary data collection in marketing research.

Fixed-response alternative questions
Questions that require respondents to choose from a set of predetermined answers.

SURVEY METHODS CLASSIFIED BY MODE OF ADMINISTRATION

Survey questionnaires may be administered in three major modes: (1) telephone interviews, (2) personal interviews, and (3) mail interviews (see Figure 8.1). Telephone interviews may be further classified as traditional telephone interviews or computer-assisted telephone interviews. Personal interviews may be conducted in the home or office, as street interviews, or as computer-assisted personal interviews. The third major method, mail interviews, takes the form of ordinary mail surveys, electronic mail or surveys conducted using mail panels. We now describe each method.

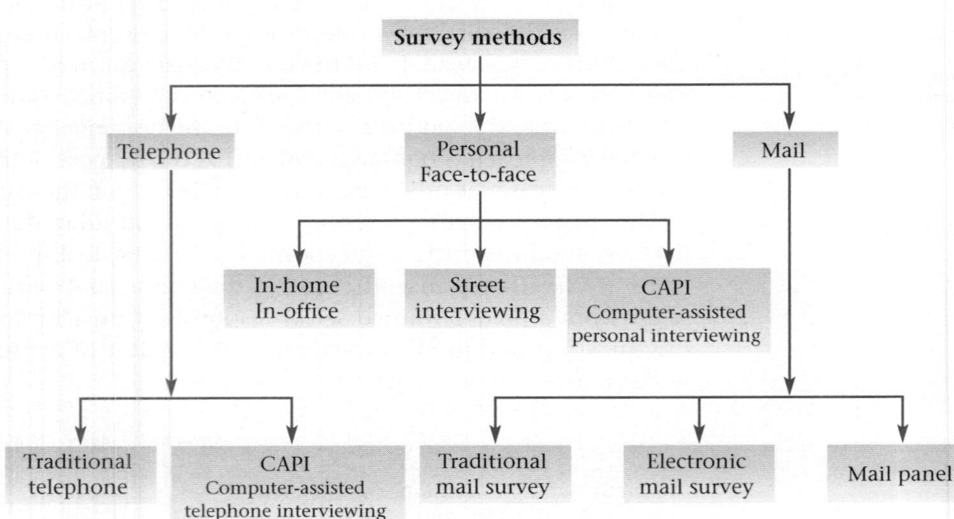

Figure 8.1
A classification of survey methods

TELEPHONE METHODS

As stated earlier, telephone interviews may be categorised as traditional or computer-assisted.

Traditional telephone interviews

Traditional telephone interviews involve phoning a sample of respondents and asking them a series of questions. The interviewer uses a paper questionnaire and records the responses with a pencil. From a central location, a wide geographical area can be covered including international markets. Given that respondents to telephone interviews have no visual prompts, have to write down answers to any open-ended questions and may have to flick through the questionnaire to find appropriate questions for a particular respondent (filtering), interviews tend to be short in duration and have questions with few options as answers. Today, this approach is rarely used in commercial marketing research, the common approach being a computer-assisted telephone interview.

Computer-Assisted telephone interviews (CATI)

Computer-assisted telephone interviewing (CATI) uses a computerised questionnaire administered to respondents over the telephone. A computerised questionnaire may be generated using a mainframe computer, a minicomputer or a personal computer. The interviewer sits in front of a terminal and wears a small headset. The terminal replaces a paper and pencil questionnaire, and the headset substitutes for a telephone. Upon command, the computer dials the telephone number to be called. When contact is made, the interviewer reads questions posed on the screen and records the respondent's answers directly into the computer memory bank, ready for immediate analysis. The following example illustrates how rapidly the technique has developed over the last 20 years. The main benefit of the technique illustrated here is the speed of collecting data and analyses. Speed is of the essence in areas where respondent attitudes can change quickly, an example being voting intentions for political parties, hence the widespread use of CATI for political opinion polls.

EXAMPLE

The fans of the phone pump the numbers up[6]

Little more than 20 years ago, the telephone simply was not adequate as a major research tool: there just weren't enough names in the phone book to guarantee workable results. Now it couldn't be more different: year on year, telephone proliferates. The areas of market research for which it is deemed unsuitable grows smaller.

The commercial world conducts business over the phone (no accident that telephone research thrives in business-to-business research); we are phone fluent now, at ease communicating down a phone line. By contrast, it is also an age of no-go areas, security fences and entryphones, a fragmented culture where people are loath to open doors of their homes to a stranger. Small wonder that traditional face-to-face interviewing is losing out.

Technology's most precious gift to the telephone, with features like auto dialling, is speed of delivery. The pace of collection and the immediacy of the data is more than a selling point. 'It's going to happen now, tonight and that's it,' enthuses Virginia Monk, who manages Network Research's telephone department. 'That's what I love about it: it's so instantaneous, so quick. I love the speed of it, to have the data come in, to play with it.'

Clients at Network are allowed in to witness the research at first hand. Potential problems are dealt with almost straightaway. Quotas and standards are checked there and then, call rates and refusal rates are constantly monitored. In comparison, traditional street and home interviewing seems fretful and wearing: it might be hours before a problem becomes known; in a telephone centre they can spot it the minute it pokes its head above ground.■

The computer systematically guides the interviewer. Only one question at a time appears on the screen. The computer checks the responses for appropriateness and consistency. It uses the responses as they are obtained to personalise the questionnaire. The data collection flows naturally and smoothly. Interviewing time is reduced, data quality is enhanced, and the laborious steps in the data collection process, coding questionnaires and entering data into the computer are eliminated. Because the responses are entered directly into the computer, interim and update reports on data collection or results can be provided almost instantaneously. The following example shows how technological developments allow flexibility in interviewing different types of respondent throughout Europe.

EXAMPLE

A pan-European view of the executive at lunch[7]

The general perception of CATI is, in the main, one of large sample size, reasonably short, simple, pre-coded questionnaires, conducted during a short fieldwork period. As computers that are much more powerful and updated software become available, we are finding that we can approach CATI surveys in a new way. Its abilities to deal with large sample sizes, complicated quota structures and complex, long, modular questionnaires enables us to deal with surveys which once would have caused untold sleepless nights.

As the interview covered exposure to newspapers, magazines, television (terrestrial, satellite and cable) and radio, at any time on any day, the questionnaire needed a comprehensive, pre-coded list of in excess of one hundred possibilities. On the first fieldwork day it became apparent that in mainland Europe, the borders are already down. Many Belgian, Dutch, French and German businessmen regularly listen to and watch each other's channels. Because the full European media list was available to each national version, we were able to update this listing as required. The CATI system also had to select three publications – our client's and two others – to be rated on 14 rotated statements – according to frequency of readership and whether they were international or not.

The survey not only collected comprehensive and accurate data, it was greatly enjoyed by respondents and interviewers alike, even though the interview length ranged from 20 minutes to a full hour, depending upon the executive's habits. The respondents could see the point and therefore the interviewers could probe and delve whilst enjoying the responses. 'High Fliers', after all, are not often quizzed about their breakfast, lunch and evening activities – and coding departments see what they get up to even less! ■

The biggest drawback of CATI lies in respondents' willingness to be interviewed by telephone. At times the technique may be confused in the minds of respondents with cold-call selling techniques. To overcome this problem requires interviewers who are trained to reassure respondents and to make the interviewing experience worthwhile. The following example illustrates the problem of response rates faced by telephone interviewers, showing what the potential causes of non-response may be.

EXAMPLE

Falling response rates from businesses[8]

Most phone calls are screened – how else could managers avoid calls from companies and individuals we don't, just now, want to talk to? Many businesses have set up formal procedures to minimise unnecessary calls to management. This is a hurdle well-trained interviewers are taught to circumvent. Interviewers run the gauntlet of three or four screenings and still secure an interview without in any way upsetting the interviewee.

In the past couple of years, however, the '(s)he's busy', '(s)he wouldn't be interested', '(s)he doesn't deal in that area', or '(s)he's in a meeting', has been joined by 'we don't allow market research interviews – it's company policy'. Even this will not deter telephone interviewers from seeking interviews but it is a continuing and worrying trend. ■

So why do companies which commission research themselves, restrict their own employees from participating? The reasons given are:

- The confidentiality of information divulged to interviewers.
- The length of interviews.
- The frequent apparent or real irrelevance of questions.
- The number of requests.
- *Taking part is seen as providing no direct benefit to the company.*

The last point is set in italic as a reminder to all researchers to place themselves in the shoes of potential respondents. The marketing researcher, and the decision-maker he or she supports, may have distinct information requirements, but why should respondents supply this information? What benefits do they gain from giving this information? This issue will be dealt with in Chapter 12 but here we have a reminder from a practitioner of the impact of ignoring the benefits that respondents gain from participating in a survey.

PERSONAL METHODS

Personal interviewing methods may be categorised as in-home, in-office, street, or computer-assisted.

Personal in-home and in-office interviews

In personal in-home interviews, respondents are interviewed face-to-face in their homes or in their workplace. The interviewer's task is to contact the respondents, ask the questions, and record the responses. In recent years, the use of personal in-home interviews has declined due to its high cost. Nevertheless, they are still used, particularly by syndicated firms, as illustrated in the following example. The use of omnibus surveys for marketing decision-makers is shown with examples of the types of marketing research projects.

EXAMPLE

Omnibus – the flexible research tool for many jobs[9]

The tracking aspect of an omnibus is important for a number of clients, not least because it enables:

- A continuous assessment of awareness and effectiveness of marketing/advertising activity.
- A monitor of opinion/behaviour in constantly changing competitive markets, which in addition may be highly fragmented.

- The accumulation of ongoing data to provide robust bases and thus build, for example, profiles of customers that would otherwise be inaccessible for small brands.
- Access to competitors' performance, without introducing overt bias among respondents' answers.
- Detection of early signs of change in a defined marketplace.
- Opportunities for syndication (with additional benefits, such as shared costs).

Omnimas offers omnibus facilities, each week interviewing 2000 adults face-to-face in their homes. A number of continuous tracking projects are conducted that range through:

- Advertising awareness tracking (which, depending on the client and subject matter, are conducted on a weekly, monthly or less frequent basis), monitoring whether the advertisement has been seen or heard and how it is communicated or interpreted.
- Regular (weekly) behavioural monitors (the Eating Out Of Home Monitor examines consumers' eating habits outside their own homes in restaurants and similar outlets).
- Ongoing tracking of people's awareness, usage and participation in loyalty schemes across a number of retail sectors.
- Using ongoing information about consumers' intentions to buy video titles to predict volume sales (data is supplied for Buena Vista Entertainment, the Disney Video Company). ■

In-office research is used extensively in business-to-business research to research subjects that cannot be effectively completed by telephone or mail. Managers being interviewed have the comfort and security of their office and can control the timing and pace of the interview. For the researcher, the big benefit of meeting managers in their office is the ability to build up a rapport, probe and gain the full attention of the manager.

Street interviews

In street interviews, respondents are intercepted while they are shopping in town centres or shopping centres. They may be questioned there and then in the street or taken to a specific test facility. The big advantage of the street interview is that it is more efficient for the respondent to come to the interviewer than for the interviewer to go to the respondent.[10] In the testing of new product formulations, test facilities are ideal to allow respondents the time and context to sample and evaluate products. The technique can also be used to test advertisements and other forms of marketing communications.

Computer-assisted personal interviews (CAPI)

In computer-assisted personal interviewing, the third form of personal interviewing, the respondent sits in front of a computer terminal and answers a questionnaire on the screen by using the keyboard or a mouse. There are several user-friendly electronic packages that design relatively simple questions for the respondent to understand. Help screens and courteous error messages are also provided. The colourful screens and on- and off-screen stimuli add to the respondent's interest and involvement in the task. This method has been classified as a personal interview technique because an interviewer is usually present to serve as a host or hostess and to guide the respondent as needed.

CAPI has been used to collect data at test facilities from street interviews, product clinics, conferences and trade shows. It may also be used for in-home or in-office interviews. You may wonder, however, how CAPI compares with the traditional method of conducting personal interviews, using paper-and-pencil questionnaires. The following example illustrates the benefits of CAPI compared to traditional interviewing.

EXAMPLE

How the omnibus hit the fast track – and now, hold very tight . . .[11]

The introduction of the CAPI overnight transformed the capabilities of the personal omnibus survey. The speed of delivering results improved dramatically, from three to four weeks, which was the norm for a paper survey, down to seven to eight days for a CAPI omnibus. There were also considerable improvements in data quality obtained by eliminating routing errors, providing the ability to build edits into questionnaire scripts and introducing more sophisticated field management systems.

The major impact of CAPI lay in the facility to produce and store complex and highly filtered questionnaire scripts, which transformed the scope of the omnibus as a data collection vehicle. For example, it became possible and cost efficient to hold complex batteries of questions, applying only to a small minority group, which are triggered when a target informant is identified. ■

A major development for marketers, especially in financial services has been the use of customer satisfaction surveys to guide strategic and operational decisions. The following example illustrates the use of CAPI where sections of a questionnaire may be tailored to examine characteristics of specific competitors. With traditional interview methods, the interviewer may have to carry a huge questionnaire to cope with over 400 banks in Germany, for example! With CAPI, when a particular bank is chosen, particular questions may be filtered out, specific questions may be asked, in all making the interview process far more efficient.

EXAMPLE

Check out the symptoms, but then provide the diagnosis[12]

An effective programme of satisfaction benchmarking for high street banks should ideally incorporate the following elements:

- A nationally representative sample of customers of all high street banks and major building societies.
- Sufficiently large sample sizes to allow the performance of named banks and building societies to be compared.
- Personal in-home interviewing, the only effective method of data collection for such research where customer lists are not available.
- Preferably, the interview should use CAPI: in addition to the usual benefits, it makes the interviewer's task far easier by controlling the supplier selection process automatically. ■

MAIL METHODS

Mail interviews, the third major form of survey administration, can be conducted via ordinary mail, electronic mail or the mail panel.

Mail interviews

In the traditional mail interview, questionnaires are mailed to pre-selected potential respondents. A typical mail interview package consists of the outgoing envelope, cover letter, questionnaire, return envelope, and possibly an incentive.[13] The respondents complete and return the questionnaires. There is no verbal interaction between the researcher and the respondent in the interview process.[14] There may be contact with potential respondents, to establish who is the correct person to send the questionnaire to, and motivating respondents to complete the survey.

Before data collection can begin, however, the respondents need to be at least broadly identified. Therefore, an initial task is to obtain a valid mailing list. Mailing lists can be compiled from telephone directories, customer databases, or association membership databases, or can be purchased from publication subscription lists or commercial mailing list companies.[15] Regardless of its source, a mailing list should be current and closely related to the population of interest. (Chapter 13 will detail the full sampling implications of this approach.) The researcher must also make decisions about the various elements of the mail interview package (see Table 8.1). Mail surveys are used for a variety of purposes including measurement of consumption of household purchases, as illustrated by the following example.

EXAMPLE

Foreign policy[16]

The British Market Research Bureau BMRB has been operating its widely used TGI (Target Group Index) research in the UK since 1969. In 1995 they were approached by a Russian company interested in compiling the same type of data under licence. BRMB's involvement was heaviest in the start-up period, but the company still follows the Russian research closely. The survey, which is used to correlate consumption and lifestyle with specific media, has also been launched in the Czech Republic, Slovakia, Poland, Hungary, Israel and China.

As a continuous single-source self-completion questionnaire running to about 100 pages, TGI requires more commitment from respondents than other research vehicles. 'Response rates have been remarkably good,' says TGI international Director Paul Dickinson. 'In the UK and in the USA, people have got a little tired of being asked questions, and often assume that you are trying to sell them something.' That kind of 'respondent fatigue' does not exist in these new markets, he explains. In fact, researchers involved in these markets report that projects can require more time than they would in the West simply because individual interviews take longer. ■

The remarkable feature of the Target Group Index survey was the size of the questionnaire – over 100 pages. With the right motivation, respondents can complete lengthy questionnaires in their own time, they can reflect upon particular issues and are under no pressure to quickly complete the survey. A 100-page interview would be most impractical for a face-to-face or telephone interview. The GlobalCash project had a long and complex questionnaire which was administered through the mail.

A postal survey throughout Europe

The GlobalCash questionnaire was sent by mail out to Treasury and Cash Managers in Europe's largest corporations. It covered many complex and technical issues, which had to be carefully translated into 10 European languages. In Switzerland for example, French, German, Italian or English versions were available, dependent upon which company and region was targeted. Before questionnaires were sent out, telephone calls were made to every company in the sampling frame. This call ensured that targeted respondents were correctly identified, all other postal details were correct and the purpose and benefits to the respondent were clear. A second telephone call was made, two weeks after the questionnaire was sent out, to further encourage a positive response. Given the wide geographic spread, the long and technical nature of the subject and little pressure to quickly generate analyses for the whole of Europe, the mail survey was the ideal survey technique. ■

Table 8.1 Some decisions related to the mail survey package

Outgoing envelope	Method of addressing	Envelope size, colour	Postage	
Covering letter	Personalisation	Sponsorship	Type of appeal	Signature
Questionnaire	Size, length and content	Colour and layout	Format and reproduction	Respondent anonymity
Instructions	As part of covering letter	A separate sheet	Alongside individual questions	
Return envelope	Whether to include one	Type of envelope	Postage	
Incentives	Feedback of findings	Monetary v. non-monetary	Prepaid v. promised amount	

Electronic mail

With the growth of use of email and Internet as means of communications, electronic mail has also become a feasible means to conduct surveys. Most survey analysis packages that include the function of questionnaire design have the ability to formulate the questionnaire into email and Internet formats. Big sampling problems exist with electronic mail which will be tackled in Chapter 13. For certain types of respondent and survey, for example evaluating the nature of an Internet home shopping service, some of the sampling problems may be tackled. The speed of administering the survey, collecting and analysing the data, linked with very low costs make this option very attractive and a rapidly growing option to conduct surveys. With increasing proportions of the population having access to email and the Internet, especially in businesses, the future looks extremely bright for this survey method. The following example summarises the advantages and disadvantages of this medium.

EXAMPLE

Advantages and disadvantages of surveys on the Web[17]

Advantages:

- *Speed.* Compared to a postal survey, especially on an international basis, the time taken can be reduced to a matter of days rather than weeks. Even if one includes the time taken to contact respondents by email, establish their willingness to take part in a survey, for them to reply, for the survey to be sent, for it to be completed and then emailed back (the procedure adopted to reduce the perception of 'junk' email), it can be completed far more quickly than a postal procedure.
- *Cost.* Once the electronic questionnaire is set up, it is almost as easy to mail it to 10 people as 10,000. This is without the printing, stationery and postage costs.
- *Quality of response.* Measured by the number and clarity of responses to open-ended questions.
- *Contacting certain target groups.* Mostly those who are regular users of the Internet, and certain business target markets.

Disadvantages:

- *Sampling frames.* Where are the lists of email numbers? Unlike telephone numbers, there is no published list of email addresses. This is being slowly rectified by the addition of email addresses to established directories used as sampling frames.
- *Access to the Web.* At present the penetration of households and businesses is low, though it is growing rapidly, and in businesses it is rapidly being adopted as the medium of communication. ■

Mail panels

Mail panels
A large and nationally representative sample of households that have agreed to participate in periodical mail questionnaires, product tests and telephone surveys.

Mail panels were introduced in Chapters 3 and 4. A **mail panel** consists of a large, nationally representative sample of households that have agreed to participate in periodic mail questionnaires, product tests and telephone surveys. The households are compensated with various incentives. Mail panels can be used to obtain information from the same respondents repeatedly. Thus, they can be used to implement a longitudinal design.

Not all survey methods are appropriate in a given situation. Therefore, the researcher should conduct a comparative evaluation to determine which methods are appropriate.

A COMPARATIVE EVALUATION OF SURVEY METHODS

Table 8.2 compares the different survey methods through a range of criteria. For any particular research project, the relative importance attached to these criteria will vary. The criteria consist of: flexibility of data collection, diversity of questions, use of physical stimuli, sample control, control of the data collection environment, control of field force, quantity of data, response rate, perceived anonymity, social desirability, obtaining sensitive information, potential for interviewer bias, potential to probe respondents, potential to build rapport, speed and cost.

Table 8.2 A comparative evaluation of survey methods

	Telephone interviews	*CATI*	*In-home In-office interviews*	*Street interviews*	*CAPI*	*Electronic mail surveys*	*Traditional mail surveys*	*Mail panels*
Flexibility of data collection	Moderate	Moderate to high	High	High	Moderate to high	Low	Low	Low
Diversity of questions	Low	Low	High	High	High	Moderate	Moderate	Moderate
Use of physical stimuli	Low	Low	High	High	High	Moderate to high	Moderate	Moderate
Sample control	Moderate	Moderate	Moderate to high	High	High	Low	Low	Moderate to high
Control of data collection environment	Moderate	Moderate	Moderate to high	High	High	Low	Low	Low
Control of field force	Moderate	Moderate	Low	Moderate	Moderate	High	High	High
Quantity of data	Low	Low	High	Moderate	Moderate	Moderate	Moderate	High
Response rate	Moderate	Moderate	High	High	High	High	Low	Low
Perceived respondent anonymity	Moderate	Moderate	Low	Low	Low	High	High	High
Social desirability	Low	Low	High	Moderate	Moderate	High	Moderate	Moderate
Obtaining sensitive information	High	High	Low	Low	Low to moderate	Moderate	High	High
Potential for interviewer bias	Moderate	Moderate	High	High	High	Low	Low	Low
Potential to probe respondents	Low	Low	High	High	High	Low	Low	Low
Potential to build rapport	Moderate	Moderate	High	Moderate to high	High	Low	Low	Moderate
Speed	High	High	Moderate	Moderate to high	Moderate to high	Moderate to high	Low	Low
Cost	Moderate	Moderate	High	Moderate to high	Moderate to high	Low	Low	Low to moderate

Flexibility of data collection

The personal interview, whether conducted as an in-home, in-office or a street interview, allows the highest flexibility of data collection. Because the respondent and the interviewer meet face to face, the interviewer can administer complex questionnaires, explain and clarify difficult questions, and even use unstructured techniques.

By contrast, the traditional telephone interview allows only moderate flexibility because it is more difficult to use unstructured techniques, ask complex questions, or obtain in-depth answers to open-ended questions over the telephone. CATI and CAPI allow somewhat greater flexibility because the researcher can use various question formats, can personalise the questionnaire, and can handle complex skip or filter patterns (directions for skipping questions in the questionnaire based on the subject's responses). Because the electronic and mail questionnaire allows for no interaction between the interviewer and the respondent, mail surveys and mail panels have low flexibility.

Diversity of questions

A variety of questions can be asked in a personal interview because the interviewer is present to clarify ambiguities. Thus in-home and in-office interviews, street interviews and CAPI allow for diversity. In electronic surveys, mail surveys and mail panels, less diversity is possible. In traditional telephone interviews and CATI, the respondent cannot see the questions while answering, and this limits the diversity of questions. For example, in a telephone interview or CATI, one could not ask respondents to rank 15 television programmes in terms of preference.

Use of physical stimuli

Often it is helpful or necessary to use physical stimuli such as products, product prototypes, commercials, or promotional displays during an interview. For the most basic example, a taste test involves tasting the product. In other cases, photographs, maps, or other audio-visual cues are helpful. In these cases, personal interviews conducted at central locations (guided through street interviews and CAPI) are more preferable to in-home interviews. In the central location, many intricate visual stimuli can be set up prior to the actual interview. In the electronic survey, visual and audio stimuli can be included, offering better potential for the use of physical stimuli than traditional mail. Mail surveys and mail panels are moderate on this dimension, because sometimes it is possible to mail the facilitating aids or even product samples. The use of physical stimuli is limited in traditional telephone interviews and CATI.

Sample control

Sample control
The ability of the survey mode to reach the units specified in the sample effectively and efficiently.

Sample control is the ability of the survey mode to reach the units specified in the sample effectively and efficiently.[18] At least in principle, in-home and in-office personal interviews offer the best sample control. It is possible to control which sampling units are interviewed, who is interviewed, the degree of participation of other members of the household, and many other aspects of data collection. In practice, to achieve a high degree of control, the researcher has to overcome several problems. It is difficult to find respondents at home during the day because many people work outside the home. Also, for safety reasons, interviewers are reluctant to venture into certain neighbourhoods and people have become cautious of responding to strangers at their door. Street interviews allow only a moderate degree of sample control. Although the interviewer has control over which respondents to intercept, the choice is limited to individuals who are walking down a street or through a shopping centre, and frequent shoppers have a greater probability of being included. Also, potential respondents can intentionally avoid or initiate contact with the interviewer. Compared with street interviews, CAPI offers slightly better control, as sampling quotas can be set and respondents randomised automatically.

Moderate to high sampling control can be achieved with traditional telephone interviews and CATI. Telephones offer access to geographically dispersed respondents and hard-to-reach areas. These procedures depend upon a **sampling frame**, a list of population units with their telephone numbers.[19] The sampling frames normally used are telephone directories, but telephone directories are limited in that:

Sampling frame
A representation of the elements of the target population that consists of a list or set of directions for identifying the target population.

1 Not everyone has a phone, while some individuals have a number of phone numbers partly due to the growing use of mobile phones.
2 Some individuals have unlisted phones or are ex-directory.
3 Directories do not reflect new phones in service or recently disconnected phones.

Electronic and traditional mail surveys require a list of addresses of individuals or households eligible for inclusion in the sample. Mail surveys can reach geographically dispersed respondents and hard-to-reach areas. However, mailing lists are sometimes unavailable, outdated or incomplete, especially for electronic addresses. Another factor outside the researcher's control is whether the questionnaire is answered and who answers it. Some subjects refuse to respond because of lack of interest or motivation; others cannot respond because they are illiterate.[20] Given these reasons, the degree of sample control in electronic and mail surveys is low.[21]

Mail panels, on the other hand, provide moderate to high control over the sample. They can provide samples matched to national census statistics on key demographic variables. It is also possible to identify specific user groups within a panel and to direct the survey to households with specific characteristics. Specific members of households in the panel can be questioned. Finally, low-incidence groups, groups that occur infrequently in the population, can be reached with panels, but there is a question of the extent to which a panel can be considered representative of the entire population.

Control of the data collection environment

The context in which a questionnaire is completed can affect the way that a respondent answers questions. An example of this would be the amount of distraction from other people around, noise and temperature. The degree of control a researcher has over the context or environment in which the respondent answers the questionnaire differentiates the various survey modes. Personal interviews conducted at central locations (from street interviews and CAPI) offer the greatest degree of environmental control. For example, the researcher can set up a special facility for demonstrating a product upon which a survey is based. In-home and in-office personal interviews offer moderate to good control because the interviewer is present. Traditional telephone interviews and CATI offer moderate control. The interviewer cannot see the environment in which the interview is being conducted, but he or she can sense the background conditions and encourage the respondent to be attentive and involved. In mail panels and especially electronic surveys and mail surveys, the researcher has little or no control over the environment.

Control of field force

Field force
Both the actual interviewers and the supervisors involved in data collection.

The field force consists of interviewers and supervisors involved in data collection. Because they require no such personnel, electronic surveys, mail surveys and mail panels eliminate field force problems. Traditional telephone interviews, CATI, street interviews and CAPI all offer moderate degrees of control because the interviews are conducted at a central location, making supervision relatively simple. In-home and in-office personal interviews are problematic in this respect. Because many interviewers work in many different locations, continual supervision is impractical.[22]

Quantity of data

In-home and in-office personal interviews allow the researcher to collect large amounts of data. The social relationship between the interviewer and the respondent, as well as the home environment, motivates the respondent to spend more time in the interview. Less effort is required of the respondent in a personal interview than in a telephone or mail interview. The interviewer records answers to open-ended questions and provides visual aids to help with lengthy and complex scales. Some personal interviews last for as long as 75 minutes. In contrast to in-home and in-office interviews, street interviews and CAPI provide only moderate amounts of data. Because these interviews are conducted in shopping centres and other central locations, a respondent's time is more limited. Typically, the interview time is 20 minutes or less. Electronic and traditional mail surveys also yield moderate amounts of data. Long questionnaires can be used because short questionnaires do not necessarily generate higher response rates than long ones. Mail panels, on the other hand, can generate large amounts of data because of the special relationship between the panel members and the sponsoring organisation.

Traditional telephone interviews and CATI result in the most limited quantities of data. They tend to be shorter than other surveys because respondents can easily terminate the telephone conversation at their own discretion. These interviews commonly last about 15 minutes, although longer interviews may be conducted when the subject matter is of interest to the respondents.[23]

Response rate

Response rate
The percentage of the total attempted interviews that are completed.

Survey **response rate** is broadly defined as the percentage of the total attempted interviews that are completed. Personal, in-home and in-office, street and CAPI yield the highest response rates. Problems caused by 'not-at-homes' can often be resolved by calling back at different times. Telephone interviews, traditional and CATI also suffer from not-at-homes or no-answers. Higher response rates are obtained by call-backs. Many telephone surveys attempt to call back at least three times.

Non-response bias
When actual respondents differ from those who refuse to participate.

Electronic surveys can generate high response rates, though with the limitation of its inability to reach certain types of respondent. Mail surveys have the poorest response rate. In a mail survey of randomly selected respondents, without any pre- or postmailing contact, response rates can be less than 15%. Such low response rate can lead to serious bias (**non-response bias**). This is because whether a person responds to a mail survey is related to how well the benefits of taking part in the survey are meaningful to the respondent and are clearly communicated to them. The magnitude of non-response bias increases as the response rate decreases. Response rates in mail panels are much higher than traditional mail methods because of assured respondent cooperation.

A comprehensive review of the literature covering 497 response rates in 93 journal articles found weighted average response rates of 81.7%, 72.3%, and 47.3% for, respectively, personal, telephone, and mail surveys.[24] The same review also found that response rates increase with

- Either prepaid or promised monetary incentives.
- An increase in the amount of monetary incentive.
- Non-monetary premiums and rewards (pens, pencils, books).
- Preliminary notification.
- Foot-in-the door techniques. These are multiple request strategies. The first request is relatively small, and all or most people agree to comply. The small request is followed by a larger request, called the **critical request**, which is actually the target behaviour.
- Personalisation (sending letters addressed to specific individuals).
- Follow-up letters.

Critical request
The target behaviour being researched.

A further discussion of improving response rates is found in Chapter 14.

Perceived anonymity

Percieved anonymity
The respondents' perceptions that their identities will not be discerned by the interviewer or researcher.

Perceived anonymity refers to the respondents' perceptions that their identities will not be discerned by the interviewer or the researcher. Perceived anonymity of the respondent is high in electronic surveys, mail surveys and mail panels and low in personal interviews (in-home, street, and CAPI). Traditional telephone interviews and CATI fall in the middle.

Social desirability/Sensitive information

Social desirability
The tendency of respondents to give answers that may not be accurate but that may be desirable from a social standpoint.

Social desirability is the tendency of respondents to give answers that are socially acceptable, whether or not they are true. As electronic surveys, mail surveys and mail panels do not involve any social interaction between the interviewer and the respondent, they are least susceptible to social desirability. Evidence suggests that such methods are good for obtaining sensitive information such as that related to financial or personal behaviour. Traditional telephone interviews and CATI are moderately good at avoiding socially desirable responses. Personal interviews – whether in-home, in-office, street, or computer-assisted – are limited in this respect, although the problem is somewhat mitigated in the case of CAPI.[25]

Potential for interviewer bias

An interviewer can bias the results of a survey by the manner in which he or she:

1 selects respondents (e.g. interviewing somebody else when required to interview a male 'head of household');
2 asks research questions (omitting questions);
3 poses questions in another way when respondents do not understand the question as presented on the questionnaire;
4 probes (e.g. by offering examples to encourage respondents);
5 records answers (recording an answer incorrectly or incompletely).

The extent of the interviewer's role determines the potential for bias.[26] In-home, in-office and street personal interviews are highly susceptible to interviewer bias. Traditional telephone interviews and CATI are less susceptible, although the potential is still there. For example, with inflection and tone of voice, interviewers can convey their own attitudes and thereby suggest answers.

CAPI have a low potential for bias, and electronic surveys, mail surveys and mail panels are free of it.

Potential to probe respondents

Though the interviewer has the potential to create bias in the responses elicited from respondents, it is balanced somewhat by the amount of probing that can be done. For example, a survey may ask respondents which brands of beer they have seen advertised on the television over the past month. A list of brands could be presented to respondents and they could simply look at the list and call out the names. What may be important in the survey is what brands they could remember. There may be a first response, of those that could be remembered unaided. A simple probe such as 'any others?' or 'any involving sports personalities?' could be recorded as a second response.

Much deeper prompts and probes can be conducted, within limits. The intention is not to turn the interview into a qualitative interview but, for example, some of the reasons that a respondent has chosen a brand may be revealed. In-home, in-office and street personal interviews have great potential for probing respondents. Traditional telephone interviews and CATI can also probe but not to the same extent as being face to face. CAPI has limited potential to probe though particular routines can be built into a survey to ask for further details. Electronic surveys, mail surveys and mail panels have very limited means to probe respondents.

Potential to build rapport with respondents

Another counter to the bias in the responses elicited from respondents by personal interviews is the amount of rapport that can be built up with respondents. Rapport may be vital to communicate why the survey is being conducted with a corresponding rationale for the respondent to spend time answering the questions. Beyond motivating respondents to take part in a survey, is the need for the respondent to answer truthfully, to reflect upon the questions properly and not to rush through the questionnaire. Building up a good rapport with respondents can be vital to gain a full and honest response to a survey.

In-home, in-office and street personal interviews have great potential to build up rapport with respondents. Traditional telephone interviews and CATI can also develop rapport but not to the same extent as being face to face. CAPI has limited potential to build up rapport through particular graphics and messages that can be built into a survey. When recruiting respondents to mail panels an amount of rapport can be built up. Electronic surveys and mail surveys have very limited means to build up a rapport with respondents.

Speed

Traditional telephone interviews and CATI are the fastest ways of obtaining information. When a central telephone facility is used, several hundred telephone interviews can be done per day. Data for even large national surveys can be collected in a manner of days or even within a day. Next in speed are street and CAPI interviews that reach potential respondents in central locations. In-home personal interviews are slower because there is dead time between interviews while the interviewer travels to the next respondent. To expedite data collection, interviews can be conducted in different markets or regions simultaneously. Mail surveys are typically the slowest. It usually takes several weeks to receive completed questionnaires; follow-up mailings take even longer. Mail panels and electronic surveys are faster than mail surveys because little follow-up is required.

Cost

Personal interviews tend to be the most expensive mode of data collection per completed response, whereas mail surveys tend to be the least expensive. In general, mail surveys, mail panel, traditional telephone, CATI, CAPI, street, and personal in-home interviews require progressively larger field staff and greater supervision and control. Hence, the cost increases in this order. Relative costs, however depend on the subject of inquiry and the procedures adopted.[27]

SELECTION OF SURVEY METHOD(S)

As is evident from Table 8.2 and the preceding discussion, no survey method is superior in all situations. Depending on such factors as information requirements, budgetary constraints (time and money), and respondent characteristics, none, one, two or even all methods may be appropriate. Remember that the various data collection modes are not mutually exclusive. Rather, they can be employed in a complementary fashion to build on each other's strengths and compensate for each other's weaknesses. The researcher can employ these methods in combination and develop creative methods. To illustrate, in a classic project, interviewers distributed the product, self-administered questionnaires, and return envelopes to respondents. Traditional telephone interviews were used for follow-up. Combining the data collection modes resulted in telephone cooperation from 97 per cent of the respondents. Furthermore, 82 per cent of the questionnaires were returned by mail.[28]

OBSERVATION METHODS

Quantitative observation
The recording and counting of behavioural patterns of people, objects and events in a systematic manner to obtain information about the phenomenon of interest.

Mystery shopping
A technique involving observers visiting providers of goods and services as if they were really customers, and recording characteristics of the service delivery.

Structured observation
Observation where the researcher clearly defines the behaviours to be observed and the methods by which they will be measured.

Quantitative observation methods are the second type of methodology used in descriptive research. Observation involves recording the behavioural patterns of people, objects and events in a systematic manner to obtain information about the phenomenon of interest. The observer does not question or communicate with the people being observed unless he or she takes the role of a **mystery shopper**. Information may be recorded as the events occur or from records of past events. Observational methods may be structured or unstructured, direct or indirect. Furthermore, observation may be conducted in a natural or a contrived environment.[29]

Structured versus unstructured observation

For **structured observation**, the researcher specifies in detail what is to be observed and how the measurements are to be recorded, such as when an auditor performs a stock or inventory analysis in a store. This reduces the potential for observer bias and enhances the reliability of the data. Structured observation is appropriate when the marketing research problem has been clearly defined and the information needed has been specified. In these circumstances, the details of the phenomenon to be observed can be clearly identified. Structured observation is suitable for use in conclusive research.

Unstructured observation Observation that involves a researcher monitoring all relevant phenomena, without specifying the details in advance.

In **unstructured observation** the observer monitors all aspects of the phenomenon that seem relevant to the problem at hand, such as when observing children playing with new toys. This form of observation is appropriate when the problem has yet to be formulated precisely and when flexibility is needed in observation to identify essential components of the problem and to develop hypotheses. In unstructured observation, potential for observer bias is high. For this reason, the observation findings should be treated as hypotheses to be tested rather than as conclusive findings. Thus, unstructured observation is most appropriate for exploratory research.

Disguised versus undisguised observation

In disguised observation, the respondents are unaware that they are being observed. Disguise enables respondents to behave naturally because people tend to behave differently when they know they are being observed. Disguise may be accomplished by using two-way mirrors, hidden cameras or inconspicuous electronic devices. Observers may be disguised as shoppers, sales assistants, or other appropriate roles. One of the most widespread techniques of observation is through the use of mystery shoppers. The following example illustrates what a mystery shopper may observe in a bank service delivery.

EXAMPLE

The mystery squad's tougher challenge[30]

Typically a mystery shopper would go into a bank, note practical things such as the number of counter positions open, number of people queuing, availability of specific leaflets, and then ask a number of specific questions. The mystery shopper takes the role of the ordinary 'man in the street', behaves just as a normal customer would, asks the same sort of questions a customer would, leaves and fills in a questionnaire detailing the various components of the visit. ■

Mystery shopping differs from conventional survey research in that it aims to collect facts rather than perceptions. Conventional customer service research is all about customer perceptions. Mystery shopping, on the other hand, aims to be as objective as possible and to record as accurately as possible what actually happened in encounters such as:

Personal visits

- How long were you in the queue?
- How many tills were open?
- Did the counter clerk apologise if you were kept waiting?
- What form of greeting or farewell were given?

Telephone calls

- How many rings before the phone was answered?
- Did the person who answered the phone go on to answer all your questions?
- Were you asked a password?
- How many times during the conversation was your name used?

In undisguised observation, the respondents are aware that they are under observation. For example, they may be aware of the presence of the observer. Researchers disagree on how much effect the presence of an observer has on behaviour. One viewpoint is that the observer effect is minor and short-lived.[31] The other position is that the observer can seriously bias the behaviour patterns.[32]

Natural versus contrived observation

Natural observation
Observing behaviour as it takes place in the environment.

Contrived observation
Observing behaviour in an artificial environment.

Natural observation involves observing behaviour as it takes places in the environment. For example, one could observe the behaviour of respondents eating fast food in Burger King. In **contrived observation**, respondents' behaviour is observed in an artificial environment, such as a test kitchen.

The advantage of natural observation is that the observed phenomenon will more accurately reflect the true phenomenon. The disadvantages are the cost of waiting for the phenomenon to occur and the difficulty of measuring the phenomenon in a natural setting.

OBSERVATION METHODS CLASSIFIED BY MODE OF ADMINISTRATION

As shown in Figure 8.3, observation methods may be classified by mode of administration as personal observation, electronic observation, audit, content analysis and trace analysis.

Personal observation

Personal observation
An observational research strategy in which human observers record the phenomenon being observed as it occurs.

In **personal observation**, a researcher observes actual behaviour as it occurs. The observer does not attempt to control or manipulate the phenomenon being observed but merely records what takes place. For example, a researcher might record the time, day and number of shoppers that enter a stop and observe where those shoppers 'flow' once they are in the shop. This information could aid in designing a store's layout and determining the location of individual departments, shelf locations, and merchandise displays.

Electronic observation

Electronic observation
An observational research strategy in which electronic devices, rather than human observers, record the phenomena being observed.

In **electronic observation**, electronic devices rather than human observers record the phenomenon being observed. The devices may or may not require the respondents' direct participation. They are used for continuously recording ongoing behaviour for later analysis.

Of the electronic devices that do not require respondents' direct participation, the A.C. Nielsen audimeter is best known. The audimeter is attached to a television set to record continually the channel to which a set is tuned. Recently, people meters have been introduced. People meters attempt to measure not only the channels to which a set is tuned but also who is watching.[33] Other common examples include turnstiles that record the number of people entering or leaving a building and traffic counters placed across streets to count the number of vehicles passing certain locations.

The most significant electronic observation form as detailed in Chapter 5 is through the use of the bar code on products. As goods are sold, optical scanners can determine which products have been sold. With a link to a 'loyalty card', electronic observation links the whole array of purchases made by a consumer to the actual identity of that consumer.

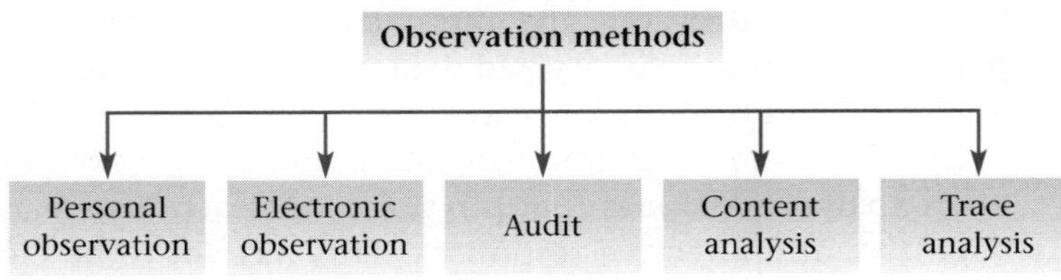

Figure 8.3
A classification of observation methods

The following example illustrates another example of electronic observation, used to monitor television viewing and related behaviour.

EXAMPLE

VCRs used to view home video market[34]

Video Cassette Recorders (VCRs) are used an average of seven hours a week, according to a study by AGB Television Research. This result was obtained from the first VCR study using AGB's FingerPrinting technology. AGB attaches a small device to a VCR that automatically measures recording, playback, and playing of pre-recorded tapes. This information is useful to firms like Blockbuster Video, which markets videos for home entertainment, education, and a variety of other purposes. ■

This study did not require direct involvement of the participants. In contrast, many electronic observation devices do require such involvement. These electronic devices may be classified into five groups: (1) eye tracking monitors, (2) pupilometers, (3) psychogalvanometers, (4) voice pitch analysers, and (5) devices measuring response latency. Eye-tracking equipment – such as oculometers, eye cameras, or eye view minuters – records the gaze movements of the eye. These devices can be used to determine how a respondent reads an advertisement or views a TV commercial and for how long the respondent looks at various parts of the stimulus. Such information is directly relevant to assessing advertising effectiveness. The pupilometer measures changes in the diameter of the pupils of the respondent's eyes. The respondent is asked to look at a screen on which an advertisement or other stimulus is projected. Image brightness and distance from the respondent's eyes are held constant. Changes in pupil size are interpreted as changes in cognitive (thinking) activity resulting from exposure to the stimulus. The underlying assumption is that increased pupil size reflects interest and positive attitudes toward the stimulus.[35]

Psycho-galvanometer An instrument that measures a respondent's galvanic skin response.

Galvanic skin response Changes in the electrical resistance of the skin that relate to a respondent`s affective state.

The **psycho-galvanometer** measures **galvanic skin response** (GSR) or changes in the electrical resistance of the skin.[36] The respondent is fitted with small electrodes that monitor electrical resistance and is shown stimuli such as advertisements, packages and slogans. The theory behind this device is that physiological changes such as increased perspiration accompany emotional reactions. Excitement leads to increased perspiration, which increases the electrical resistance of the skin. From the strength of the response, the researcher infers the respondent's interest level and attitudes toward the stimuli.[37]

Voice pitch analysis Measurement of emotional reactions through changes in the respondent's voice.

Voice pitch analysis measures emotional reactions through changes in the respondent's voice. Changes in the relative vibration frequency of the human voice that accompany emotional reaction are measured with audio-adapted computer equipment.[38]

Response latency The amount of time it takes to respond to a question.

Response latency is the time a respondent takes before answering a question. It is used as a measure of the relative preference for various alternatives.[39] Response time is thought to be directly related to uncertainty. Therefore, the longer a respondent takes to choose between two alternatives, the closer the alternatives are in terms of preference. On the other hand, if the respondent makes a quick decision, one alternative is clearly preferred. With the increased popularity of computer-assisted data collection, response latency can be recorded accurately and without the respondent's awareness.

Use of eye-tracking monitors, pupilometers, psychogalvanometers and voice pitch analysers assumes that physiological reactions are associated with specific cognitive and affective responses. This has yet to be clearly demonstrated.[40]

Furthermore, calibration of these devices to measure physiological arousal is difficult, and they are expensive to use. Another limitation is that respondents are placed in an artificial environment and know that they are being observed.

Audit

Pantry audit
A type of audit where the research inventories the brands, quantities and package sizes of products in a consumer's home.

In an audit, the researcher collects data by examining physical records or performing inventory analysis. Audits have two distinguishing features. First, data are collected personally by the researcher. Second, the data are based upon counts, usually of physical objects. Retail and wholesale audits conducted by marketing research suppliers were discussed in the context of secondary data (see Chapter 4). Here we focus on the role of audits in collecting primary data. In this respect, an important audit conducted at the consumer level, generally in conjunction with one of the survey methods, is the **pantry audit**. In a pantry audit, the researcher takes an inventory of brands, quantities, and package sizes in a consumer's home, perhaps in the course of a personal interview. Pantry audits greatly reduce the problem of untruthfulness or other forms of response bias. Obtaining permission to examine consumers' pantries can be difficult, however, and the fieldwork is expensive. Furthermore, the brands in the pantry may not reflect the most preferred brands or the brands purchased most often. Moreover, similar data can be obtained from scanned data more efficiently. For these reasons, pantry audits are no longer commonly used, audits are more common at the retail and wholesale level.

Content analysis

Content analysis
The objective, systematic and quantitative description of the manifest content of a communication.

Content analysis is an appropriate method when the phenomenon to be observed is communication, rather than behaviour or physical objects. It is defined as the objective, systematic and quantitative description of the manifest content of a communication.[41] It includes observation as well as analysis. The unit of analysis may be words (different words or types of words in the message), characters (individuals or objects), themes (propositions), space and time measures (length or duration of the message), or topics (subject of the message). Analytical categories for classifying the units are developed, and the communication is broken down according to prescribed rules. Marketing research applications involve observing and analysing the content or message of advertisements, newspaper articles, television and radio programmes, and the like. For example, the frequency of appearance of ethnic minorities and women, has been studied using content analysis. In the GlobalCash project, content analysis may be used to analyse magazine advertisements of the sponsoring and competing banks to compare their projected images.

Trace analysis

Trace analysis
An approach in which data collection is based on physical traces, or evidence, of past behaviour.

An observation method that can be inexpensive if used creatively is **trace analysis**. In trace analysis, data collection is based on physical traces, or evidence, of past behaviour. These traces may be left by the respondents intentionally or unintentionally. Several innovative applications of trace analysis have been made in marketing research.[42]

- The selective erosion of tiles in a museum indexed by the replacement rate was used to determine the relative popularity of exhibits.
- The number of different fingerprints on a page was used to gauge the readership of various advertisements in a magazine.

- The position of the radio dials in cars brought in for service was used to estimate share of listening audience of various radio stations. Advertisers used the estimates to decide on which stations to advertise.
- The age and condition of cars in a parking lot were used to assess the affluence of customers.
- The magazines people donated to charity were used to determine people's favourite magazines.

A COMPARATIVE EVALUATION OF OBSERVATION METHODS

A comparative evaluation of the observation methods is given in Table 8.3. The different observation methods are evaluated in terms of the degree of structure, degree of disguise, ability to observe in a natural setting, observation bias, measurement and analysis bias, and additional general factors.

Table 8.3 A comparative evaluation of observation methods

Criteria	*Personal observation*	*Electronic observation*	*Audit*	*Content analysis*	*Trace analysis*
Degree of structure	Low	Low to high	High	High	Medium
Degree of disguise	Medium	Low to high	Low	High	High
Natural setting	High	Low to high	High	Medium	Low
Observation bias	High	Low	Low	Medium	Medium
Analysis bias	High	Low to medium	Low	Low	Medium
General remarks	Most flexible	Can be intrusive	Expensive	Limited to communications	Limited traces available

Structure relates to the specification of what is to be observed and how the measurements are to be recorded. As can be seen from Table 8.3, personal observation is low, trace analysis is medium, and audit and content analysis are high on the degree of structure. Electronic observation can vary widely from low to high, depending on the methods used. Methods such as optical scanners are very structured in that the characteristics to be measured – for example, characteristics of items purchased scanned in supermarket checkouts – are precisely defined. Thus, these methods are high in the degree of structure. In contrast, electronic methods such as use of hidden cameras to observe children at play with toys tend to be unstructured.

The degree of disguise is low in the case of audits as it is difficult to conceal the identity of auditors. Personal observation offers a medium degree of disguise because there are limitations on the extent to which the observer can be disguised as a shopper, sales clerk, employee, and so forth. Trace analysis and content analysis offer a high degree of disguise because the data are collected 'after the fact', that is, after the phenomenon to be observed has taken place. Some electronic observations such as hidden cameras offer excellent disguise, whereas others, such as the use of psychogalvanometers, are very difficult to disguise.

The ability to observe in a natural setting is low in trace analysis because the observation takes place after the behaviour has occurred. It is medium in the case of content analysis because the communication being analysed is only a limited representation of the natural phenomenon. Personal observation and audits are excellent on this score because human observers can observe people or objects in a variety of natural settings. Electronic observation methods vary from low (e.g. use of psychogalvanometers) to high (e.g. use of turnstiles).

Observation bias is low in the case of electronic observation because a human observer is not involved. It is also low for audits. Although the auditors are humans, the observation usually takes place on objects and the characteristics to be observed are well defined, leading to low observation bias. Observation bias is medium for trace analysis and content analysis. In both these methods, human observers are involved and the characteristics to be observed are not very well defined. The observers typically do not interact with human respondents during the observation process, however, thus lessening the degree of bias. It is high for personal observation due to the use of human observers who interact with the phenomenon being observed.

Data analysis bias is low for audits and content analysis because the variables are precisely defined, the data are quantitative, and statistical analysis is conducted. Trace analysis has a medium degree of bias as the definition of variables is not very precise. Electronic observation methods can have a low (e.g. scanner data) to medium (e.g. hidden camera) degree of analysis bias, depending on the method. Unlike personal observation, the bias in electronic observation is limited to the medium level due to improved measurement and classification because the phenomenon to be observed can be recorded continuously using electronic devices.

In addition, personal observation is the most flexible because human observers can observe a wide variety of phenomena in a wide variety of settings. Some electronic observation methods, such as the use of psychogalvanometers, can be very intrusive, leading to artificiality and bias. Audits using human auditors tend to be expensive. Content analysis is well suited for and limited to the observation of communications. As mentioned earlier, trace analysis is a method that is limited to where consumers actually leave 'traces'. This occurs infrequently and very creative approaches are needed to capture these traces. The application of these criteria will lead to the identification of an appropriate method, if observation is at all suitable in the given situation.

A COMPARISON OF SURVEY AND OBSERVATION METHODS

Other than the use of scanner data, few marketing research projects rely solely on observational methods to obtain primary data.[43] This implies that observational methods have some major disadvantages as compared with survey methods. Yet these methods offer some advantages that make their use in conjunction with survey methods quite fruitful.

Relative advantages of observation

The greatest advantage of observational methods is that they permit measurement of actual behaviour rather than reports of intended or preferred behaviour. There is no reporting bias, and potential bias caused by the interviewer and the interviewing process is eliminated or reduced. Certain types of data can be collected only by observation. These include behaviour patterns of which the respondent is unaware or is unable to communicate. For example, information on babies' toy preferences is best obtained by observing babies at play, because they are unable to express themselves adequately. Moreover, if the observed phenomenon occurs frequently or is of short duration, observational methods may cost less and be faster than survey methods.

Relative disadvantages of observation

The most serious disadvantage of observation is that the reasons for the observed behaviour may not be determined because little is known about the underlying motives, beliefs, attitudes and preferences. For example, people observed buying a brand of cereal may or may not like it themselves; they may be purchasing that brand for someone else in the household. Another limitation of observation is that selective perception (bias in the researcher's perception) can bias the data. In addition, observational data can be time-consuming and expensive, and it is difficult to observe certain forms of behaviour such as personal activities. Finally, in some cases, the use of observational methods may border on being unethical. The ethical issues involved in monitoring the behaviour of people without their consent are still being debated.

To sum up, observation has the potential to provide valuable information when properly used. From a practical standpoint, it is best to view observation as a complement to survey methods, rather than as being in competition with them.

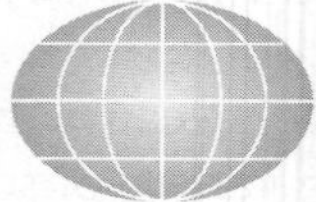

INTERNATIONAL MARKETING RESEARCH

The selection of appropriate interviewing methods is much more difficult because of the challenges of conducting research in foreign countries. Given the differences in the economic, structural, informational, technological and sociocultural environment, the feasibility and popularity of the different interviewing methods vary widely. In the United States and Canada, for example, the telephone has achieved almost total penetration of households. Consequently, telephone interviewing is a dominant mode of questionnaire administration. The same situation exists in some European countries, such as Sweden. In many other European countries, however, the telephone interview gets confused with telephone sales. This results in high refusal rates and scepticism of what the purpose of a survey is. In developing countries, the problem with the telephone is the number of households that have telephones.

Because of the low cost, mail interviews continue to be used in most developed countries where literacy is high and the postal system is well developed, for example in Canada, Denmark, Finland, Iceland, the Netherlands, Norway, Sweden and the United States. In many parts of Africa, Asia, and South America, however, the use of mail surveys and mail panels is low because of illiteracy and the large proportion of population living in rural areas.

The following example illustrates how CAPI technology has developed to allow consistent approaches to survey methods across Europe. It shows that by developing an appreciation of the cultural differences between countries, a methodology can be built that allows accurate and comparable surveys to be conducted.

EXAMPLE

CAPIBUS Europe[44]

The concept of the International Omnibus is not new; many research groups offer an international service. In reality, however, these have been little more than brokering services, bolting together whatever omnibus is available in each country, with little real standardisation.

Research Services Limited and the IPSOS group have tackled this problem by calling on the benefits of CAPI technology to introduce CAPIBUS Europe, a weekly omnibus survey covering the six major markets of Europe (Britain, France, Germany, Italy, Netherlands and Spain).

The use of computer technology means that questionnaires can be scripted in one location and transmitted electronically to other countries. While the need to ensure accurate translation remains, the problems involved in having different questionnaire formats, classification systems and data maps are minimised. At the end of a project, data is again transmitted electronically, to be aggregated by the lead agency in a standardised format for all markets. This can then be weighted to provide information on the European market as well as for each local market. ■

Selection of survey methods

No questionnaire administration method is superior in all situations. Table 8.4 presents a comparative evaluation of the major modes of collecting quantitative data in the context of international marketing research. In this table, the survey methods are discussed only under the broad headings of telephone, personal, mail and electronic interviews. The use of CATI, CAPI, electronic survey and mail panels depends heavily on the state of technological development in the country. Likewise, the use of street interviewing is contingent upon the dominance of shopping centres in the retailing environment. The major methods of interviewing should be carefully evaluated on the criteria given in Table 8.4, as shown.

Table 8.4 A comparative evaluation of survey methods for international marketing research

Criteria	*Telephone*	*Personal*	*Mail*	*Electronic*
High sample control	+	+	–	–
Difficulty in locating respondents at home	+	–	+	+
Inaccessibility of homes	+	–	+	+
Unavailability of a large pool of trained interviewers	+	–	+	+
Large population in rural areas	–	+	–	–
Unavailability of maps	+	–	+	+
Unavailability of current telephone directory	–	+	–	+
Unavailability of mailing lists	+	+	–	–
Low penetration of telephones	–	+	+	–
Lack of an efficient postal system	+	+	–	+
Low level of literacy	–	+	–	–
Face-to-face communication culture	–	+	–	–
Poor access to computers and Internet	+	+	+	–

Note: A + denotes an advantage, and a – denotes a disadvantage

The following example illustrates the combined efforts of British and French research companies working in the new market economy of Russia. It shows how important personal interviewing is at the present stage of market development. The ability to motivate and build up a rapport, showing that the interviewer is not from the tax authorities, helps to generate good response rates. It also shows some of the problems of conducting telephone surveys where the penetration of phones is low.

EXAMPLE

Foreign policy[45]

Taylor Nelson AGB, which recently merged with French Market Research company Sofres, has had a consumer research panel called Impulse running in Russia since August 1997. According to Managing Director Tim Kidd, Russians make good respondents, with a generally high level of education and a lively interest in market research itself. There are individuals in new markets – as in established ones – who do not get over those initial suspicions, but most will cooperate once they understand that the researcher is not an official, and will not shop them to the tax authorities.

Since the two 1000-strong samples used by Impulse are collected in Moscow and St Petersburg, telephone research is feasible, says Kidd. While many phones are shared, and network reliability is shaky, some 70 to 80 per cent of these populations do at least have access to a phone.

Should the lively interest in marketing research in Russia become abused by unprofessional or dubious researchers, the problems outlined in the next section could have a damaging effect on the widespread use of marketing research. ■

ETHICS IN MARKETING RESEARCH

The unethical use of survey research as a guise for targeting sales effort was discussed in Chapter 1. Respondents' anonymity, discussed in the context of qualitative research in Chapter 6, is salient in survey and observation research as well. Researchers are obligated to protect a respondent's identity and not disclose it to anyone outside the research organisation including the client. The client is not entitled to the names of respondents. The only instance where respondents' identity can be revealed to the client is when respondents are notified in advance and their consent is obtained prior to administering the survey. Even in such situations, the researcher should have the assurance that the respondents' trust will be kept by the client and their identities will not be used in a sales effort or misused in other ways.

Special care must be taken to ensure that any record which contains a reference to the identity of an informant is securely and confidentially stored during any period before such reference is separated from that record and/or destroyed.[46] Ethical lapses in this respect by unscrupulous researchers and marketers have resulted in a serious backlash for marketing research. The result has been a consistent fall in the levels of response rate, to all forms of survey method. This reinforces the message that considering the needs of survey respondents makes sound research sense as well as being ethically sound. Dubious practices may generate a response for a single survey but may create long-term damage to the marketing research industry.

Another issue facing the marketing research industry is image, as the public may not distinguish between telephone research and telemarketing. This identity crisis is exacerbated by the action of some firms to commit 'sugging and frugging', industry terms for selling or fund-raising under the guise of a survey (discussed in Chapter 1). This poor image has raised the cost of telephone research and made it difficult for researchers to obtain full and representative samples.

Although concerns for the respondents' psychological well-being are mild in survey data collection when compared with either qualitative or experimental research, researchers should not place respondents in stressful situations. Disclaimers such as 'there are no correct responses; we are only interested in your opinion' can relieve much of the stress innate to a survey.[47] In many face-to-face interview situations, respondents are given a 'thank you booklet' at the end of the interview. As well as saying a genuine thank you for taking part in a survey, the booklet briefly sets out the purpose and benefits of bona fide marketing research. The use of the 'thank you booklet' helps to educate the public to distinguish between genuine, professionally conducted marketing research and 'research' conducted as a front for generating sales leads.

Observation of people's behaviour without their consent is often done because informing the respondents may alter their behaviour.[48] But this can compromise the privacy of the respondents. One guideline is that people should not be observed for research in situations where they would not expect to be observed by the public. Therefore, public places like a shopping centre or a grocery aisle are fair game. These are places where people observe other people routinely. However, notices should be posted in these areas stating that they are under observation by marketing researchers. After the data have been collected, the researcher should solicit the necessary permission from the respondents.[49]

With the growth of mystery shopping, where the essence of the technique is that service deliverers cannot spot the observer, the debate over what is ethical practice has intensified. The following example taken from a seminar on mystery shopping illustrates some of the issues that the marketing research industry considers vital to debate for the future 'health' of the technique.

EXAMPLE

The ethical puzzle of mystery shopping[50]

'For us to believe we can do this without some form of public outrage would make us very naïve indeed.' This was the statement of Professor Roger Jowell to delegates attending the joint Social Research Association/Market Research Society Seminar on mystery shopping.

Mystery shopping has been going on for years in one form or another but was formally originated in the USA in the early 1970s. The definition of mystery consumer research used at the seminar states: 'The use of individuals *trained* to observe . . . by acting as a prospective customer.' Whether the individuals should be trained or not brought heated discussion, some suggesting that training would not encourage the shopper to act 'naturally' while others felt training was necessary in some form or another.

The contentious issue of competitive videoing was debated. One agency director said 'this is fly on the wall journalism' and clients should go to a production company rather than a marketing research agency. One agency had been asked by a client to mystery shop competitors only and, on turning to their code of conduct, found that there was nothing to stop them going ahead with this course of action.

Professor Jowell likened competitive shopping to industrial espionage, at which point Shirley Featherstone, Field Director of ACE Fieldwork, suggested that unlike industrial espionage, mystery shopping is information that is in the public domain.

Colin Brown, an independent consultant, explained that traditionally mystery shopping has been used:

- to campaign on public issues with which they have been able to make changes,
- as a monitor within companies to assess staff performance.

He then pointed to the latest tradition, that of enforcement, which results in people losing their jobs.■

The final point in the above example graphically illustrates how important ethical issues are in conducting marketing research. If potential respondents perceive marketing research as a means to generate sales and a 'snoop' on service delivery practices, then the goodwill needed to generate full and honest responses will wither.

INTERNET AND COMPUTER APPLICATIONS

The use of the Internet and computers has been discussed throughout this chapter. Internet surveys are gaining in popularity and have great potential. One reason is that the cost in most cases is less than personal, telephone or mail surveys. Also, the Internet survey is not as intrusive as the phone call in the middle of dinner. The on-line survey can be completed in one's own time and place. Quick response time is another advantage cited by those producing on-line surveys.

Another advantage of Internet marketing research is the ability to target specific populations or potential target markets. There is a growth of specialist directories that include email and internet addresses that serve the mean to target specific types of individual. The downside of the Internet is their representativeness of broader populations. Another limitation is the verification of who is actually responding to the survey. The absence of a human facilitator to motivate participants, security and privacy are also areas of concern.

SUMMARY

The two basic means of obtaining primary quantitative data in descriptive research are survey and observation. Survey involves the direct questioning of respondents, while observation entails recording respondent behaviour or the behaviour of service deliverers.

Surveys involve the administration of a questionnaire and may be classified, based on the method or mode of administration, as (1) traditional telephone interviews, (2) CATI, (3) in-home or in-office personal interviews, (4) street interviews, (5) CAPI, (6) traditional mail surveys, (7) electronic surveys, and (8) mail panels. Of these methods, CATI, CAPI and electronic surveys have grown enormously in their use in developed Western economies. Each method has some general advantages and disadvantages, however. Although these data collection methods are usually thought of as distinct and 'competitive', they should not be considered mutually exclusive in much the same manner as using quantitative and qualitative should not be considered mutually exclusive. It is possible to employ them productively in combination.

Quantitative observational methods may be classified as structured or unstructured, disguised or undisguised, and natural or contrived. The major methods are personal observation (including mystery shopping), electronic observation, audit, content analysis and trace analysis. As compared with surveys, the relative advantages of observational methods are that (1) they permit measurement of actual behaviour, (2) there is no reporting bias, and (3) there is less potential for interviewer bias. Also, certain types of data can best, or only, be obtained by observation. The relative disadvantages of observation are that: (1) very little can be inferred about motives, beliefs, attitudes and preferences; (2) there is a potential for observer bias; (3) most methods are time-consuming and expensive; (4) it is difficult to observe some forms of behaviour; and (5) questions of ethical methods of observation are far more contentious. Observation is rarely used as the sole method of obtaining primary data, but it can be usefully employed in conjunction with other marketing research techniques.

In collecting data from different countries, it is desirable to use survey methods with equivalent levels of reliability rather than to use the same method. Respondents' anonymity should be protected, and their names should not be turned over to the clients. People should not be observed without consent for research in situations where they would not expect to be observed by the public.

QUESTIONS AND PROBLEMS

1 With a context of the survey researcher imposing their language and logic upon potential respondents, what do you see as being the advantages and disadvantages of conducting surveys?

2 Discuss the dilemma faced by the survey designer who wishes to develop a survey that is not prone to interviewer bias but also sees that interviewer rapport with respondents is vital to the success of the survey.

3 Evaluate the reasons why response rates to industrial surveys are declining.

4 Why do interviewers need to probe respondents in surveys? What distinguishes survey probing from probing conducted in qualitative interviews?

5 What are the relevant factors for evaluating which survey method is best suited to a particular research project?

6 What are the distinct advantages of conducting a survey using CAPI technology compared to traditional paper questionnaires?

7 What are the key advantages of conducting interviews on the Web? Evaluate the potential that this technique holds for the future.

8 How would you classify Mystery Shopping as an observation technique? Why would you classify it in this way?

9 What may be electronically observed of supermarket consumers?

10 Explain using examples where content analysis may be used.

11 Describe the criteria by which you would evaluate the relative benefits of different observation techniques.

12 What is the difference between qualitative and quantitative observation?

13 Describe the relative advantages and disadvantages of observation?

14 Describe a marketing research problem in which both survey and observation methods could be used for obtaining the information needed.

15 What do you see as being the main ethical problems of mystery shopping?

NOTES

1 Olley, J., 'Lucas and New Holland', *Marketing Week* (14 October 1997), 11.

2 'Covert Research – Where's the Mystery', *Research* (August 1997), 34.

3 Thomson, K., 'The Ins and Outs of Gay Discrimination', *Research*, (July 1995), 12.

4 *Marketing* (9 October 1997), 33.

5 Surveys are commonly used in marketing research. See, for example, Weerahandi, S. and Moitra, S., 'Using Survey Data to Predict Adoption and Switching for Services', *Journal of Marketing Research* 32 (February 1995), 85–96; and Park, C.S and Srinivasan, V., 'A Survey-Based Method for Measuring and Understanding Brand Equity and Its Extendibility', *Journal of Marketing Research* 31 (May 1994), 271–88.

6 Savage, M., 'The Fans of the Phone Pump the Numbers Up', *Research* (September 1997), 30.

7 Kirby, R., 'A Pan-European View of the Executive at Lunch', *ResearchPlus* (October 1992), 7.

8 Burrows, S., Verbatim, *Research*, (September 1995), 20.

9 Luker, J. 'Omnibus – The Flexible Research Tool for Many Jobs', *ResearchPlus* (February 1996), 12.

10 Bush, A.J. and Hair Jr, J.E., 'An Assessment of the Mall-Intercept as a Data Collection Method', *Journal of Marketing Research* (May 1985), 158–67; and Rafael, J.E., 'Self Administered CRT Interview: Benefits Far Outweigh the Problems', *Marketing News* (9 November 1984), 16.

11 Denny, M., 'How the Omnibus Hit the Fast Track – and Now, Hold Very Tight', *ResearchPlus* (February 1996), 4.

12 Paton Walsh, E., 'Check Out the Symptoms, But Then Provide the Diagnosis, *ResearchPlus* (February 1997), 5.

13 Conant, J.S., Smart, D.T. and Walker, B.J., 'Mail Survey Facilitation Techniques: An Assessment and Proposal Regarding Reporting Practices', *Journal of Market Research Society* 32 (October 1990), 569–80; and James, J.M. and Bolstein, R., 'The Effect of Monetary Incentives and Follow-Up Mailings on the Response Rate and Response Quality in Mail Surveys', *Public Opinion Quarterly* 54 (Fall 1990), 346–61.

14 Mail surveys are common in institutional and industrial marketing research. See, for example, Ganesan, S. 'Determinants of Long-Term Orientation in Buyer Seller Relationships', *Journal of Marketing* 58 (April 1994), 1–19.

15 'Making a List, Selling It Twice', *Wall Street Journal* (20 May 1985), 64–65.

16 Gander, P., 'Foreign Policy', *Marketing Week* (30 April 1998), 45.

17 Comley, P., 'Will Working the Web Provide a Net Gain?', *Research* (December 1996), 16.

18 Childers, T.L. and Skinner, S.J., 'Theoretical and Empirical Issues in the Identification of Survey Respondents', *Journal of the Market Research Society* 27 (January 1985), 39–53.

19 Czaja, R., Blair, J. and Sebestik, J.P., 'Respondent Selection in a Telephone Survey: A Comparison of Three Techniques', *Journal of Marketing Research*, 19 (August 1982), 381–85; and O'Rourke, D. and Blair, J., 'Improving Random Respondent Selection in Telephone Interviews', *Journal of Marketing Research* 20 (November 1983), 428–32.

20 Conant, J.S., Smart, D.T. and Walker, B.J., 'Mail Survey Facilitation Techniques: An Assessment and Proposal Regarding Reporting Practices,' *Journal of Market Research Society*, 32 (October 1990), 569–80; and Martell, C. 'Illiteracy Hurts All, Author Says', *Wisconsin State Journal* (3 April 1985), 1–2.

21 Hubbard, R. and Little, E.L., 'Promised Contributions to Charity and Mail Survey Responses: Replications with Extension', *Public Opinion Quarterly* 52 (Summer 1988) 223–30; Erdos, P.L. and Ferber, R. (eds), 'Data Collection Methods: Mail Surveys', *Handbook of Marketing Research* (New York: McGraw-Hill, 1974), p. 102.

22 Guengel, P.C., Berchman, T.R. and Cannell, C.E., *General Interviewing Techniques: A Self Instructional Workbook for Telephone and Personal Interviewer Training* (Ann Arbor: Survey Research Center, University of Michigan, 1983).

23 Sudman, S., 'Sample Surveys', *Annual Review of Sociology* (1976), 107–20.

24 Yu, J. and Cooper, H., 'A Quantitative Review of Research Design Effects on Response Rates to Questionnaires', *Journal of Marketing Research* 20 (February 1983), 36–44. See also James, J.M. and Bolstein, R., 'The Effect of Monetary Incentives and Follow-Up Mailings on the Response Rate and Response Quality in Mail Surveys', *Public Opinion Quarterly* 54 (Fall 1990), 346–61.

25 Colombotos, J., 'Personal vs. Telephone Interviews Effect Responses', *Public Health Report* (September 1969), 773–820.

26 Cannell, C.E., Miller, P.U., Oksenberg, L. and Leinhardt, S. (eds), 'Research on Interviewing Techniques', *Sociological Methodology* (San Francisco: Jossey-Bass, 1981); Miller, P.U. and Cannell, C.E., 'A Study of Experimental Techniques for Telephone Interviewing', *Public Opinion Quarterly* 46 (Summer 1982), 250–69.

27 For assessing the effectiveness of surveys, see Martin, W.S., Stanford, R.E., Swan, J.E., Wren, B.M., Powers, T.L. and Duncan, W.J., *Journal of Business Research* 29 (January 1994), 39–45.

28 Payne, S.L., 'Combination of Survey Methods', *Journal of Marketing Research* (May 1964), 62.

29 Rust, L., 'How to Reach Children in Stores: Marketing Tactics Grounded in Observational Research', *Journal of Advertising Research* 33 (November–December 1993), 67–72.

30 McNeil, R., 'The Mystery Squad's Tougher Challenge', *ResearchPlus* (April 1994), 13.

31 Scott, C., Klein, D.M. and Bryant, J., 'Consumer Response to Humor in Advertising: A Series of Field Studies Using Behavioural Observation', *Journal of Consumer Research* 16 (March 1990), 498–501; and Kerlinger, F.N., *Foundations of Behavioural Research*, 3rd edn (New York: Holt, Rinehart and Winston, 1986), 538.

32 Webb, E.J., Campbell, D.T., Schwarts, K.D. and Sechrest, L., *Unobtrusive Measures: Non-reactive Research in the Social Sciences* (Chicago: Rand McNally, 1966), 113–14.

33 Gardner, F., 'Acid Test for the People Meter', *Marketing and Media Decisions* (19 April 1984), 74–75, 115.

34 'AGB's Finger Printing Measures VCR Use', *Marketing News* (9 May 1988), 13.

35 Russo, J.E. and Leclerc, F,. 'An Eye-Fixation Analysis of Choice Processes for Consumer Non-durables', *Journal of Consumer Research* 21 (September 1994), 274–90.
36 For an example of an application of GSR, see Abeele, P.V. and Maclachlan, D.L., 'Process Tracing of Emotional Responses to TV Ads: Revisiting the Warmth Monitor', *Journal of Consumer Research* 20 (March 1994), 586–600.
37 'Psychogalvanometer Testing "Most Predictive",' *Marketing News* (16 June 1981), 11.
38 Buckman, G.A., 'Uses of Voice-Pitch Analysis', *Journal of Advertising Research* 20 (April 1980), 69–73.
39 Aaker, D.A., Bagozzi, R.P., Carman, J.M. and MacLachlan, J.M., 'On Using Response Latency to Measure Preference', *Journal of Marketing Research* 17 (May 1980), 237–44.
40 Stewart, D.W., 'Physiological Measurement of Advertising Effects', *Psychology and Marketing* (Spring 1984), 43–48; and Stewart, D.W. and Furse, D.H., 'Applying Psychological Measures to Marketing and Advertising Research Problems', in Leigh, J.H. and Martin, C.R. (eds), *Current Issues in Advertising, 1982* (Ann Arbor: University of Michigan Press, 1982), 1–38.
41 Kolbe, R.H. and Burnett, M.S., 'Content-Analysis Research: An Examination of Applications with Directives for Improving Research Reliability and Objectivity', *Journal of Consumer Research* 18 (September 1991), 243–50; and Kassarjian, H.H., 'Social Values and the Sunday Comics: A Content Analysis', in Bagozzi, R.P. and Tybout, A.M. (eds), *Advances in Consumer Research,* vol. 10 (Ann Arbor, MI: Association for Consumer Research, 1983), pp. 434–38.
42 Bouchard, J.H. Jr, 'Unobtrusive Measures: An Inventory of Uses', *Sociological Methods and Research* (February 1976), 267–301; and Sechrest, L., *New Directions for Methodology of Behaviour Science: Unobtrusive Measurement Today* (San Francisco: Jossey-Bass, 1979).
43 Eay, M.L., *Unobtrusive Marketing Research Techniques* (Cambridge, MA: Marketing Science Institute, 1973), 13.
44 Denny, M., 'How the Omnibus Hit the Fast Track – and Now, Hold Very Tight', *ResearchPlus* (February 1996), 4.
45 Gander, P., 'Foreign Policy', *Marketing Week* (30 April 1998), 45.
46 Worcester, R.M. and Downham. J. (eds), 'ICC/ESOMAR International Code of Marketing and Social Research Practice', *Consumer Market Research Handbook* (Amsterdam: North-Holland, 1986) 813–26.
47 Tybout, A.M. and Zaltman, G., 'Ethics in Marketing Research: Their Practical Relevance', *Journal of Marketing Research* 11 (November 1974), 357–68.
48 Stafford, M.R. and Stafford, T.E., 'Participant Observation and the Pursuit of Truth: Methodological and Ethical Considerations', *Journal of the Market Research Society* 35 (January 1993), 63–76.
49 Smith, C.N. and Quelch, J.A., *Ethics in Marketing* (Homewood, IL: Richard D. Irwin, 1993).
50 Social Research Association & Market Research Society Joint Seminar, 11 September 1997.

Chapter 9

Causal research design: experimentation

Causality can never be proved; in other words, it can never be demonstrated decisively. Inferences of cause-and-effect relationships are the best that can be achieved

OBJECTIVES

After reading this chapter, the student should be able to:

1 explain the concept of causality as defined in marketing research and distinguish between the ordinary meaning and the scientific meaning of causality;
2 define and differentiate two types of validity: internal validity and external validity;
3 discuss the various extraneous variables that can affect the validity of results obtained through experimentation and explain how the researcher can control extraneous variables;
4 describe and evaluate experimental designs and the differences among pre-experimental, true experimental, quasi-experimental and statistical designs;
5 compare and contrast the use of laboratory versus field experimentation and experimental versus non-experimental designs in marketing research;
6 describe test marketing and its various forms: standard test market, controlled test market, and simulated test market;
7 understand the problems of internal and external validity of field experiments when conducted in international markets;
8 describe the ethical issues involved in conducting causal research and the role of debriefing in addressing some of these issues.

OVERVIEW

We introduced causal designs in Chapter 3, where we discussed their relationship to exploratory and descriptive designs and defined experimentation as the primary method employed in causal designs. This chapter explores the concept of causality further. We identify the necessary conditions for causality, examine the role of validity in experimentation, and consider the extraneous variables and procedures for controlling them. We present a classification of experimental designs and consider specific designs, along with the relative merits of laboratory and field experiments. An application in the area of test marketing is discussed in detail. The considerations involved in conducting experimental research when researching international markets are discussed. Several ethical issues which arise in experimentation are identified. We begin with some examples.

EXAMPLE

It's in the bag[1]

LeSportsac, filed a suit against Kmart Corporation after Kmart introduced a 'di Paris sac' line of bags which, *LeSportsac* claimed, looked like its bags. According to *LeSportsac*, Kmart led consumers to believe that they were purchasing *LeSportsac* bags when they were not. To prove its point, *LeSportsac* conducted causal research.

Two groups of women were selected in a field experiment. One group was shown two *LeSportsac* lightweight soft-sided bags from which all tags were removed and all words and designs were printed over within the distinctive *LeSportsac* ovals. The second group of women were shown two 'di Paris sac' bags with the brand name visible and bearing the tags and labels these bags carry in Kmart stores. Information was obtained from both groups of women to learn whether or not they perceived a single company or source or brand identification of masked bags, what identifications they made, if any, and the reasons they gave for doing so.

The sample consisted of 200 women in each group selected by age quotas in street interviews. The study indicated that many consumers could not distinguish the origin of the two makes of bags, supporting the position of *LeSportsac*. The field experiment helped *LeSportsac* convince the court of appeals to affirm the issuance of a preliminary injunction against Kmart. Kmart agreed to stop selling its 'di Paris sac'. ■

EXAMPLE

POP buys[2]

The Eckerd Drug Company conducted an experiment to examine the effectiveness of in-store radio advertisements to induce point-of purchase (POP) buys. Twenty statistically compatible stores were selected based on store size, geographical location, traffic flow count and age. Half of these were randomly selected as test stores, and the other half served as control stores. The test stores aired the radio advertisements, whereas the control stores' POP radio systems were removed. Tracking data in the form of unit sales and turnover were obtained for three periods of: seven days before the experiment, during the course of the four-week experiment, and seven days after the experiment. The products monitored varied from inexpensive items to small kitchen appliances. Results indicated that sales of the advertised products in the test stores at least doubled. Based on this evidence, Eckerd concluded that in-store radio advertising was highly effective in inducing POP buys, and they decided to continue it. ■

CONCEPT OF CAUSALITY

Causality
When the occurrence of X increases the probability of the occurrence of Y.

Experimentation is commonly used to infer causal relationships. The concept of **causality** requires some explanation. The scientific concept of causality is complex. 'Causality' means something very different to the average person on the street than to a scientist.[3] A statement such as 'X causes Y' will have the following meaning to an ordinary person and to a scientist.

The scientific meaning of causality is more appropriate to marketing research than is the everyday meaning.[4] Marketing effects are caused by multiple variables and the relationship between cause and effect tends to be probabilistic. Moreover, we can never prove causality (i.e. demonstrate it conclusively); we can only infer a cause-and-effect relationship. In other words, it is possible that the true causal relation, if one exists, will not have been identified. We further clarify the concept of causality by discussing the conditions for causality.

Ordinary meaning	*Scientific meaning*
X is the only cause of Y.	X is only one of a number of possible causes of Y.
X must always lead to Y.	The occurrence of X makes the occurrence of Y more probable (X is a probabilistic cause of Y).
It is possible to prove that X is a cause of Y.	We can never prove that X is a cause of Y. At best, we can infer that X is a cause of Y.

CONDITIONS FOR CAUSALITY

Before making causal inferences, or assuming causality, three conditions must be satisfied: (1) concomitant variation, (2) time order of occurrence of variables, and (3) elimination of other possible causal factors. These conditions are necessary but not sufficient to demonstrate causality. No one of these three conditions, nor all three conditions combined, can demonstrate decisively that a causal relationship exists.[5] These conditions are explained in more detail in the following sections.

Concomitant variation

Concomitant variation
A condition for inferring causality that requires that the extent to which a cause, X, and an effect, Y, occur together or vary together is predicted by the hypothesis under consideration.

Concomitant variation is the extent to which a cause, X, and an effect, Y, occur together or vary together in the way predicted by the hypothesis under consideration. Evidence pertaining to concomitant variation can be obtained in a qualitative or quantitative manner.

For example, in the qualitative case, the management of a bank may believe that the retention of customers is highly dependent on the quality of service in bank branches. This hypothesis could be examined by assessing concomitant variation. Here, the causal factor X is branch service and the effect factor Y is retention level. A concomitant variation supporting the hypothesis would imply that bank with satisfactory levels of service would also have a satisfactory retention of customers. Likewise, banks with unsatisfactory service would exhibit unsatisfactory retention of customers. If, on the other hand, the opposite pattern was found, we would conclude that the hypothesis was untenable.

For a quantitative example, consider a random survey of 1000 respondents regarding the purchase of shares from a bank branch. This survey yields the data in Table 9.1. The respondents have been classified into high- and low-education groups based on a median or even split. This table suggests that the purchase of shares is influenced by education level. Respondents with high education are likely to purchase more shares. Seventy-three per cent of the respondents with high education have a high purchase level, whereas only 64 per cent of those with low education have a high purchase level. Furthermore, this is based on a relatively large sample of 1000 people.

Table 9.1 Evidence of concomitant variation between purchase of shares and education

		Purchase of shares from a bank, Y		
		High	*Low*	
Education, X	*High*	363 (73%)	137 (27%)	500 (100%)
	Low	322 (64%)	178 (36%)	500 (100%)

Based on this evidence, can we conclude that high education causes high purchase of shares? Certainly not! All that can be said is that association makes the hypothesis more tenable; it does not prove it. What about the effect of other possible causal factors such as income? Shares can be expensive, so people with higher incomes may buy more of them. Table 9.2 shows the relationship between purchase of shares and education for different income segments. This is equivalent to holding the effect of income constant. Here again, the sample has been split at the median to produce high- and low-income groups of equal size. Table 9.2 shows that the difference in purchase of shares between high- and low-education respondents has been reduced considerably. This suggests that the association indicated by Table 9.1 may be spurious.

Table 9.2 Purchase of shares by income and education

		Low income purchase		
		High	*Low*	
Education	*High*	122 (61%)	78 (39%)	200 (100%)
	Low	171 (57%)	129 (43%)	300 (100%)

		High income purchase		
		High	*Low*	
Education	*High*	241 (80%)	59 (20%)	300 (100%)
	Low	151 (76%)	49 (24%)	200 (100%)

We could give you similar examples to show why the absence of initial evidence of concomitant variation does not imply that there is no causation. It is possible that considering a third variable will crystallise an association that was originally obscure. The time order of the occurrence of variables provides additional insights into causality.

Time order of occurrence of variables

The time order of occurrence condition states that the causing event must occur either before or simultaneously with the effect; it cannot occur afterwards. By definition, an effect cannot be produced by an event that occurs after the effect has taken place. It is possible, however, for each event in a relationship to be both a cause and an effect of the other event. In other words, a variable can be both a cause and an effect in the same causal relationship. To illustrate, customers who shop frequently in a particular supermarket are more likely to have a loyalty card for that supermarket. In addition, customers who have a loyalty card for a supermarket are likely to shop there frequently.

Consider banks and the retention of customers. If in-bank service is the cause of retention, then improvements in service must be made before, or at least simultaneously with, an increase in retention. These improvements might consist of training or hiring more counter staff. Then, in subsequent months, the retention of bank customers should increase. Alternatively, retention may increase simultaneously with the training or hiring of additional counter staff. On the other hand, suppose that a bank experienced an appreciable increase in the level of retaining customers and then decided to use some of that money generated to retrain its counter staff, leading to an improvement in service. In this case, bank service cannot be a cause of increased retention; rather, just the opposite hypothesis might be plausible.

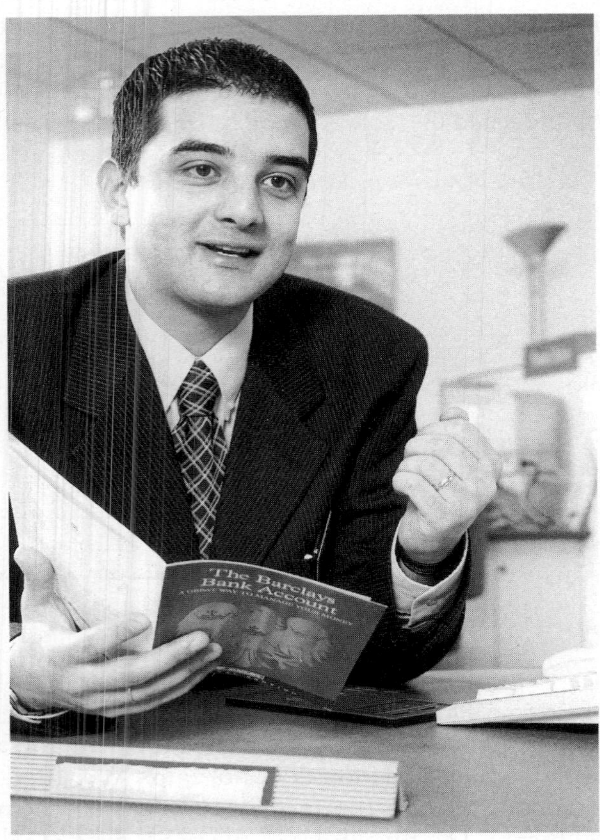

The management of a bank may believe that the retention of customers is highly dependent on the quality of service in bank branches

Absence of other possible causal factors

The absence of other possible causal factors means that the factor or variable being investigated should be the only possible causal explanation. Bank service may be a cause of retention if we can be sure that changes in all other factors affecting retention, pricing, advertising, promotional offers, product characteristics, competition and so forth, were held constant or were otherwise controlled.

In an after-the-fact examination of a situation, we can never confidently rule out all other causal factors. In contrast, with experimental designs it is possible to control some of the other causal factors. It is also possible to balance the effects of some of the uncontrolled variables so that only random variations resulting from these uncontrolled variables will be measured. These aspects are discussed in more detail later in this chapter. The difficulty of establishing a causal relationship is illustrated by the following example.

EXAMPLE

Which comes first?[6]

There are studies that contend that consumers increasingly make buying decisions in the store while they are shopping. Some studies indicate that as much as 80 per cent of buying decisions are made at point-of-purchase (POP). POP buying decisions have increased concurrently with increased advertising efforts in the stores. These include radio advertisements, ads on shopping trolleys and grocery bags, ceiling signs and shelf displays. It is difficult to ascertain from these data whether the increased POP decision-making is the result of increased advertising efforts in the store or whether the increase in store advertising results from attempts to capture changing consumer attitudes toward purchasing and to capture sales from the increase in POP decision-making. It is also possible that both variables may be both causes and effects in this relationship. ■

If, as the preceding example indicates, it is difficult to establish cause-and-effect relationships, what is the role of evidence obtained in experimentation?

Role of evidence

Evidence of concomitant variation, time order of occurrence of variables, and elimination of other possible causal factors, even if combined, still does not demonstrate conclusively that a causal relationship exists. If all the evidence is strong and consistent, however, it may be reasonable to conclude that there is a causal relationship. Accumulated evidence from several investigations increases our confidence that a causal relationship exists. Confidence is further enhanced if the evidence is interpreted in light of intimate conceptual knowledge of the problem situation. Controlled experiments can provide strong evidence on all the three conditions.

DEFINITIONS AND CONCEPTS

In this section, we define some basic concepts and illustrate them using examples, including the *LeSportsac* and Eckerd examples given at the beginning of this chapter.

Independent variables
Variables that are manipulated by the researcher and whose effects are measured and compared.

- **Independent variables**. Independent variables are variables or alternatives that are manipulated (i.e. the levels of these variables are changed by the researcher) and whose effects are measured and compared. These variables, also known as treatments, may include price levels, package designs, and advertising themes. In the two examples given at the beginning of this chapter, the treatments consisted of *LeSportsac* versus the 'di Paris sac' bags in the first example and in-store radio advertising (present versus absent) in the second.

Test units
Individuals, organisations, or other entities whose response to independent variables or treatments is being studied.

- **Test units**. Test units are individuals, organisations, or other entities whose response to the independent variables or treatments is being examined. Test units may include consumers, stores, or geographic areas. The test units were women in the *LeSportsac* case and stores in the Eckerd example.

Dependent variables
Variables that measure the effect of the independent variables on the test units.

- **Dependent variables**. Dependent variables are the variables that measure the effect of the independent variables on the test units. These variables may include sales, profits, and market shares. The dependent variable was brand or source identification in the *LeSportsac* example and sales in the Eckerd example.

Extraneous variables
Variables, other than the independent variables, which influence the response of the test units.

- **Extraneous variables**. Extraneous variables are all variables other than the independent variables that affect the response of the test units. These variables can confound the dependent variable measures in a way that weakens or invalidates the results of the experiment. Extraneous variables include bank size, bank location, and competitive effort. In the Eckerd example, store size, geographical location, traffic flow count, and age of the stores were extraneous variables that had to be controlled.

Experiment
The process of manipulating one or more dependent variables, while controlling for the extraneous variables.

- **Experiment**. An experiment is formed when the researcher manipulates one or more independent variables and measures their effect on one or more dependent variables, while controlling for the effect of extraneous variables.[7] Both the *LeSportsac* and Eckerd research projects qualify as experiments based on this definition.

Experimental design
The set of experimental procedures specifying (1) the test units and sampling procedures, (2) the independent variables, (3) the dependent variables, and (4) how to control the extraneous variables.

- **Experimental design**. An experimental design is a set of procedures specifying: (1) the test units and how these units are to be divided into homogeneous sub-samples, (2) what independent variables or treatments are to be manipulated, (3) what dependent variables are to be measured, and (4) how the extraneous variables are to be controlled.[8]

As a further illustration of these definitions, consider the following example.

EXAMPLE

Taking coupons at face value[9]

An experiment was conducted to test the effects of the face value of sales promotion coupons (i.e. the amount saved when a consumer next buys the product) on the likelihood of consumers redeeming those coupons, controlling for the frequency of brand usage. Personal interviews were conducted with 280 shoppers who were entering or leaving a supermarket. Subjects were randomly assigned to two treatment groups. One offered low-value coupons and the other high-value coupons for four products: Tide detergent, Kellogg's Cornflakes, Aim toothpaste, and Joy liquid detergent. During the interviews, the respondents answered questions about which brands they used and how likely they were to cash the coupons of the given face value the next time they shopped. An interesting finding was that higher face-value coupons produced higher likelihood of redemption among infrequent or non-buyers of the promoted brand but had little effect on regular buyers. ■

In the preceding experiment, the independent variable that was manipulated was the value of the coupon. The dependent variable was the likelihood of cashing the coupon. The extraneous variable that was controlled was brand usage. The test units were individual shoppers. The experimental design required the random assignment of test units (shoppers) to treatment groups (low or high value coupon).

DEFINITION OF SYMBOLS

To facilitate our discussion of extraneous variables and specific experimental designs, we define a set of symbols now commonly used in marketing research.[10]

X = the exposure of a group to an independent variable, treatment, or event, the effects of which are to be determined

O = the process of observation or measurement of the dependent variable on the test units or group of units

R = the random assignment of test units or groups to separate treatments

In addition, the following conventions are adopted:

- Movement from left to right indicates movement through time.
- Horizontal alignment of symbols implies that all those symbols refer to a specific treatment group.
- Vertical alignment of symbols implies that those symbols refer to activities or events that occur simultaneously.

For example, the symbolic arrangement

$$X \quad 0_1 \quad 0_2$$

means that a given group of test units was exposed to the treatment variable (X) and the response was measured at two different points in time 0_1 and 0_2.

Likewise, the symbolic arrangement

$$\begin{matrix} R & X_1 & 0_1 \\ R & X_2 & 0_2 \end{matrix}$$

means that two groups of test units were randomly assigned to two different treatment groups at the same time, and the dependent variable was measured in the two groups simultaneously.

VALIDITY IN EXPERIMENTATION

When conducting an experiment, a researcher has two goals: (1) to draw valid conclusions about the effects of independent variables on the study group and (2) to make valid generalisations to a larger population of interest. The first goal concerns internal validity, the second, external validity.[11]

Internal validity

Internal validity
A measure of accuracy of an experiment. It measures whether the manipulation of the independent variables, or treatments, actually caused the effects on the dependent variable(s).

Internal validity refers to whether the manipulation of the independent variables or treatments actually caused the observed effects on the dependent variables. Thus, internal validity refers to whether the observed effects on the test units could have been caused by variables other than the treatment. If the observed effects are influenced or confounded by extraneous variables, it is difficult to draw valid inferences about the causal relationship between the independent and dependent variables. Internal validity is the basic minimum that must be present in an experiment before any conclusion about treatment effects can be made. Without internal validity, the experimental results are confounded. Control of extraneous variables is a necessary condition for establishing internal validity.

External validity

External validity
A determination of whether the cause-and-effect relationships found in the experiment can be generalised.

External validity refers to whether the cause-and-effect relationships found in the experiment can be generalised. In other words, can the results be generalised beyond the experimental situation, and if so, to what populations, settings, times, independent variables and dependent variables can the results be projected?[12] Threats to external validity arise when the specific set of experimental conditions does not realistically take into account the interactions of other relevant variables in the real world.

It is desirable to have an experimental design that has both internal and external validity, but in applied marketing research we often have to trade one type of validity for another.[13] To control for extraneous variables, a researcher may conduct an experiment in an artificial environment. This enhances internal validity, but it may limit the generalisability of the results, thereby reducing external validity. For example, fast-food chains test customers' preferences for new formulations of menu items in test kitchens. Can the effects measured in this environment be generalised to fast-food outlets? (Further discussion on the influence of artificiality on external validity may be found in the section of this chapter on laboratory versus field experimentation.) Despite these deterrents to external validity, if an experiment lacks internal validity, it may not be meaningful to generalise the results. Factors that threaten internal validity may also threaten external validity, the most serious of these being extraneous variables.

EXTRANEOUS VARIABLES

The need to control extraneous variables to establish internal and external validity has already been discussed. In this section, we classify extraneous variables in the following categories: history, maturation, testing effects, instrumentation, statistical regression, selection bias and mortality.

History
Specific events that are external to the experiment but that occur at the same time as the experiment.

Contrary to what the name implies, **history** (H) does not refer to the occurrence of events before the experiment. Rather, history refers to specific events that are external to the experiment but that occur at the same time as the experiment. These events may affect the dependent variable. Consider the following experiment:

$$0_1 \quad X_1 \quad 0_2$$

where 0_1 and 0_2 are measures of personal loan applications in a specific region and X_1 represents a new promotional campaign. The difference $(0_2 - 0_1)$ is the treatment effect. Suppose that the experiment revealed that there was no difference between $0_2 - 0_1$. Can we then conclude that the promotional campaign was ineffective? Certainly not! The promotional campaign X_1 is not the only possible explanation of the difference between 0_2 and 0_1. The campaign might well have been effective. What if general economic conditions declined during the experiment and the local area was particularly hard hit by redundancies through several employers closing down their operations (history)? Conversely, even if there was some difference between 0_2 and 0_1, it may be incorrect to conclude that the campaign was effective if history was not controlled, because the experimental effects might have been confounded by history. The longer the time interval between observations, the greater the possibility that history will confound an experiment of this type.[14]

Maturation

Maturation
An extraneous variable attributable to changes in the test units themselves that occur with the passage of time.

Maturation (MA) is similar to history except that it refers to changes in the test units themselves. These changes are not caused by the impact of independent variables or treatments but occur with the passage of time. In an experiment involving people, maturation takes place as people become older, more experienced, tired, bored or uninterested. Tracking and market studies that span several months are vulnerable to maturation, since it is difficult to know how respondents are changing over time.

Maturation effects also extend to test units other than people. For example, consider the case in which the test units are banks. Banks change over time in terms of personnel, physical layout, decoration, and the range of products and services they have to offer.

Testing effects

Testing effects
Effects caused by the process of experimentation.

Testing effects are caused by the process of experimentation. Typically, these are the effects on the experiment of taking a measure on the dependent variable before and after the presentation of the treatment. There are two kinds of testing effects: (1) main testing effect (MT) and (2) interactive testing effect (IT).

Main testing effect
An effect of testing occurring when a prior observation affects a later observation.

The **main testing effect** (MT) occurs when a prior observation affects a later observation. Consider an experiment to measure the effect of advertising on attitudes towards a brand of beer. The respondents are given a pre-treatment questionnaire measuring background information and attitude toward the brand. They are then exposed to the test commercial embedded in a television programme. After viewing the commercial, the respondents again answer a questionnaire measuring, among other things, attitude toward the beer brand. Suppose that there is no difference between the pre- and post-treatment attitudes. Can we conclude that the commercial was ineffective? An alternative explanation might be that the respondents tried to maintain consistency between their pre- and post-treatment attitudes. As a result of the main testing effect, post-treatment attitudes were influenced more by pre-treatment attitudes than by the treatment itself. The main testing effect may also be reactive, causing the respondents to change their attitudes simply because these attitudes have been measured. The main testing effect compromises the internal validity of the experiment.

Interactive testing effect
An effect in which a prior measurement affects the test unit's response to the independent variable.

In the **interactive testing effect** (IT), a prior measurement affects the test unit's response to the independent variable. Continuing with our beer advertising experiment, when people are asked to indicate their attitudes toward a brand, they become aware of that brand: they are sensitised to that brand and become more likely to pay attention to the test commercial than people who were not included in the experiment. The measured effects are then not generalisable to the population; therefore, the interactive testing effects influence the experiment's external validity.

Instrumentation

Instrumentation
An extraneous variable involving changes in the measuring instrument, in the observers, or in the scores themselves.

Instrumentation (I) refers to changes in the measuring instrument, in the observers, or in the scores themselves. Sometimes measuring instruments are modified during the course of an experiment. In the beer advertising experiment, using a newly designed questionnaire to measure the post-treatment attitudes could lead to variations in the responses obtained. Consider an experiment in which sales at a shoe shop are measured before and after exposure to a promotional offer of a discounted music festival ticket (treatment). A non-experimental price change between 0_1 and 0_2 results in a change in instrumentation because sales will be measured using different unit prices. In this case, the treatment effect ($0_2 - 0_1$) could be attributed to a change in instrumentation.

As shown above, instrumentation effects are likely when interviewers make pre- and post-treatment measurements. The effectiveness of interviewers can be different at different times.

Statistical regression

Statistical regression
An extraneous variable that occurs when test units with extreme scores move closer to the average score during the course of the experiment.

Statistical regression effects (SR) occur when test units with extreme scores move closer to the average score during the course of the experiment. In the beer advertising experiment, suppose that some respondents had either very favourable or very unfavourable attitudes towards the brand. On post-treatment measurement, their attitudes might have moved toward the average. People's attitudes change continuously. People with extreme attitudes have more room for change, so variation is more likely. This has a confounding effect on the experimental results, because the observed effect (change in attitude) may be attributable to statistical regression rather than to the treatment (test commercial).

Selection bias

Selection bias
An extraneous variable attributable to the improper assignment of test units to treatment conditions.

Selection bias (SB) refers to the improper assignment of test units to treatment conditions. This bias occurs when selection or assignment of test units results in treatment groups that differ on the dependent variable before the exposure to the treatment condition. If test units self-select their own groups or are assigned to groups on the basis of the researchers' judgement, selection bias is possible. For example, consider an experiment in which two different displays (old *static display* and new *audio-visual display*) are assigned to different bank branches. The banks in the two groups may not be equivalent initially. They may vary with respect to an essential characteristic, such as branch size, which is likely to affect the sales of personal loans, regardless of which display was assigned to a bank.

Mortality

Mortality
An extraneous variable attributable to the loss of test units while the experiment is in progress.

Mortality (MO) refers to the loss of test units while the experiment is in progress. This happens for many reasons, such as test units refusing to continue in the experiment. Mortality confounds results because it is difficult to determine if the lost test units would respond in the same manner to the treatments as those that remain. Consider again the merchandising display experiment. Suppose that during the course of the experiment, branch managers in three banks in the new *audio-visual display* drop out because they feel the noise is not conducive to negotiations with certain types of client. The researcher could not determine whether the average sales of the personal loans for the new display would have been higher or lower if these three banks had continued in the experiment.

The various categories of extraneous variables are not mutually exclusive, they can occur jointly and also interact with each other. To illustrate, testing–maturation–mortality refers to a situation in which, because of pre-treatment measurement, the respondents' beliefs and attitudes change over time and there is a differential loss of respondents from the various treatment groups.

CONTROLLING EXTRANEOUS VARIABLES

Confounding variables
Variables used to illustrate that extraneous variables can confound the results by influencing the dependent variable, synonymous with extraneous variables.

Extraneous variables represent alternative explanations of experimental results. They pose a serious threat to the internal and external validity of an experiment. Unless they are controlled, they affect the dependent variable and thus confound the results. For this reason, they are also called **confounding variables**. There are four ways of controlling extraneous variables: randomisation, matching, statistical control and design control.

Randomisation

Randomisation
A method of controlling extraneous variables that involves randomly assigning test units to experimental groups by using random numbers. Treatment conditions are also randomly assigned to experimental groups.

Randomisation refers to the random assignment of test units to experimental groups by using random numbers. Treatment conditions are also randomly assigned to experimental groups. For example, respondents are randomly assigned to one of three experimental groups. One of the three versions of a test commercial, selected at random, is administered to each group. As a result of random assignment, extraneous factors can be represented equally in each treatment condition. Randomisation is the preferred procedure for ensuring the prior equality of experimental groups,[15] but it may not be effective when the sample size is small because it merely produces groups that are equal on average. It is possible, though, to check whether randomisation has been effective by measuring the possible extraneous variables and comparing them across the experimental groups.

Matching

Matching
A method of controlling extraneous variables that involves matching test units on a set of key background variables before assigning them to the treatment conditions.

Matching involves comparing test units on a set of key background variables before assigning them to the treatment conditions. In the display experiment, banks could be matched on the basis of turnover, size, proportion of domestic to corporate clients, or location. Then one bank from each matched pair would be assigned to each experimental group.

Matching has two drawbacks. First, test units can be matched on only a few characteristics, so the test units may be similar on the variables selected but unequal on others. Second, if the matched characteristics are irrelevant to the dependent variable, then the matching effort has been futile.[16]

Statistical control

Satistical control
A method of controlling extraneous variables by measuring the extraneous variables and adjusting for their effects through statistical methods.

Statistical control involves measuring the extraneous variables and adjusting for their effects through statistical analysis. This was illustrated in Table 9.2, which examined the relationship (association) between purchase of shares and education, controlling for the effect of income. More advanced statistical procedures, such as analysis of covariance (ANCOVA), are also available. In ANCOVA, the effects of the extraneous variable on the dependent variable are removed by an adjustment of the dependent variable's mean value within each treatment condition. ANCOVA is discussed in more detail in Chapter 18.

Design control

Design control
A method of controlling extraneous variables that involves using specific experimental designs.

Design control involves the use of experiments designed to control specific extraneous variables. The types of controls possible by suitably designing the experiment are illustrated with the following example.

EXAMPLE

Experimenting with new products[17]

Controlled-distribution electronic test markets are used increasingly to conduct experimental research on new products. This method makes it possible to control for several extraneous factors that affect new product performance and manipulate the variables of interest. It is possible to ensure that a new product (1) obtains the right level of supermarket acceptance and all commodity volume distribution, (2) is positioned in the correct aisle in each supermarket, (3) receives the right number of facings on the shelf, (4) has the correct everyday price, (5) never has out-of-stock problems, and (6) obtains the planned level of trade promotion, display, and price features on the desired time schedule. Thus, a high degree of internal validity can be obtained. ■

Although test marketing is considered in more detail later in this chapter, the preceding example shows that controlled-distribution electronic test markets can be effective in controlling specific extraneous variables. Extraneous variables can also be controlled by adopting specific experimental designs, as described in the next section.

A CLASSIFICATION OF EXPERIMENTAL DESIGNS

Pre-experimental designs
Designs that do not control for extraneous factors by randomisation.

True experimental designs
Experimental designs distinguished by the researcher randomly assigning test groups to experimental groups and also randomly assigning treatments to experimental groups.

Quasi-experimental designs
Designs that apply part of the procedures of true experimentation yet lack full experimental control.

Statistical designs
Designs that allow for the statistical control and analysis of external variables.

Experimental designs may be classified as **pre-experimental**, **true experimental**, **quasi-experimental**, and **statistical designs** (Figure 9.1). Pre-experimental designs do not employ randomisation procedures to control for extraneous factors.

Examples of these designs include the one-shot case study, the one-group pre-test–post-test design, and the static group. In true experimental designs, the researcher can randomly assign test units to experimental groups and treatments to experimental groups. Included in this category are the pre-test–post-test control group design, the post-test-only control group design, and the Solomon four-group design. Quasi-experimental designs result when the researcher is unable to achieve full manipulation of scheduling or allocation of treatments to test units but can still apply part of the apparatus of the experimentation. Two such designs are time series and multiple time series designs. A statistical design is a series of basic experiments that allows for statistical control and analysis of external variables. The basic designs used in statistical designs include pre-experimental, true experimental, and quasi-experimental. Statistical designs are classified based on their characteristics and use. The important statistical designs include randomised block design Latin square design and factorial designs.[18]

We begin our discussion with the first type, pre-experimental designs.

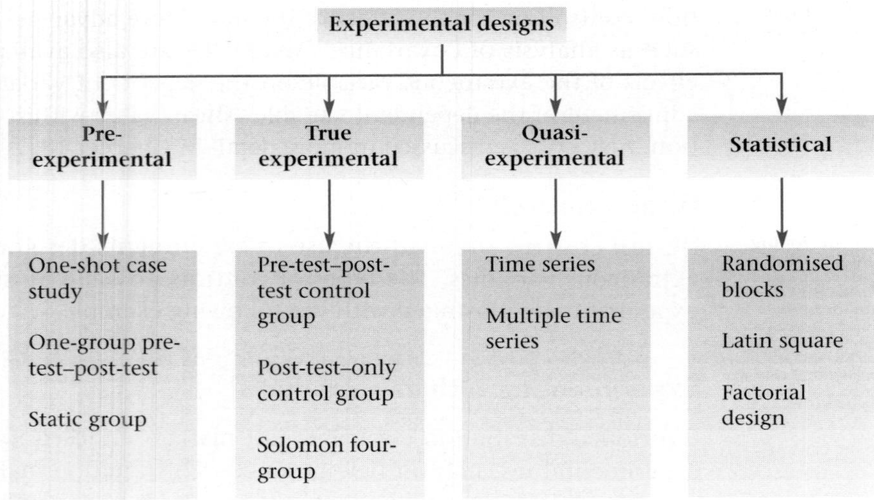

Figure 9.1
A classification of experimental designs

PRE-EXPERIMENTAL DESIGNS

These designs are characterised by an absence of randomisation. Three specific designs are described: the one-shot case study, the one-group pre-test–post-test design, and the static group.

One-shot case study

One-shot case study
A pre-experimental design in which a single group of test units is exposed to a treatment X, and then a single measurement on the dependent variable is taken.

Also known as the after-only design, the **one-shot case study** may be symbolically represented as

$$X \quad 0_1$$

A single group of test units is exposed to a treatment X, and then a single measurement on the dependent variable is taken (0_1). There is no random assignment of test units. Note that the symbol **R** is not used, because the test units are self-selected or selected arbitrarily by the researcher.

The danger of drawing valid conclusions from experiments of this type can be easily seen. It does not provide a basis of comparing the level of $\mathbf{0_1}$ to what would happen when **X** was absent. In addition, the level of $\mathbf{0_1}$ might be affected by many extraneous variables, including history, maturation, selection, and mortality. Lack of control for these extraneous variables undermines the internal validity. For these reasons, the one-shot case study is more appropriate for exploratory than for conclusive research.

One-group pre-test–post-test design
A pre-experimental design in which a group of test units is measured twice.

One-group pre-test–post-test design

The **one-group pre-test–post-test design** may be symbolised as

$$0_1 \quad X_1 \quad 0_2$$

In this design, a group of test units is measured twice. There is no control group. First a pre-treatment measure is taken ($\mathbf{0_1}$) then the group is exposed to the treatment (**X**). Finally, a post-treatment measure is taken ($\mathbf{0_2}$). The treatment effect is computed as ($\mathbf{0_2} - \mathbf{0_1}$) but the validity of this conclusion is questionable since extraneous variables are largely uncontrolled. History, maturation, testing (both main and interactive testing effects), instrumentation, selection, mortality and regression could possibly be present. The following example shows how this design is used.

EXAMPLE

Cinematic performance

It is possible to use the one-group pre-test–post-test design to measure the effectiveness of test commercials. Respondents are recruited to central cinema locations in different test cities. At the central location, respondents are first administered a personal interview to measure, among other things, attitudes toward the brand being portrayed in the commercial (0_1). Then they watch a TV programme containing the test commercial (X). After viewing the TV programme, the respondents are again administered a personal interview to measure attitudes towards the same brand (0_2). The effectiveness of the test commercial is measured as ($0_2 - 0_1$). ■

Static group design

Static group
A pre-experimental design in which there are two groups: the experimental group (EG), which is exposed to the treatment, and the control group (CG). Measurements on both groups are made only after the treatment, and test units are not assigned at random.

The **static group** is a two-group experimental design. One group, called the experimental group (EG), is exposed to the treatment, and the other, called the control group (CG), is not. Measurements on both groups are made only after the treatment, and test units are not assigned at random. This design may be symbolically described as

$$\begin{array}{lll} \text{EG:} & X & 0_1 \\ \text{CG:} & & 0_2 \end{array}$$

The treatment effect would be measured as ($\mathbf{0_1} - \mathbf{0_2}$). Notice that this difference could also be attributed to at least two extraneous variables (selection and mortality). Because test units are not randomly assigned, the two groups (EG and CG) may differ before the treatment, and selection bias may be present. There may also be mortality effects, as more test units may withdraw from the experimental group than from the control group. This would be particularly likely to happen if the treatment were unpleasant.

In practice, a control group is sometimes defined as the group that receives the current level of marketing activity, rather than a group that receives no treatment at all. The control group is defined this way because it is difficult to reduce current marketing activities such as advertising and personal selling to zero. We illustrate the static group and several other designs in the context of the GlobalCash project.

GLOBALCASH PROJECT

Static group

A static group comparison to measure the effectiveness of a product placement for a bank, within the context of a feature film would be conducted as follows. Two groups of respondents would be recruited on the basis of convenience. Only the experimental group would be exposed to the feature film containing the product placement. Then, attitudes toward the bank of both the experimental and control group respondents would be measured. The effectiveness of the product placement would be measured as $(0_1 - 0_2)$. ■

TRUE EXPERIMENTAL DESIGNS

The distinguishing feature of the true experimental designs, as compared with pre-experimental designs, is randomisation. In true experimental designs, the researcher randomly assigns test units to experimental groups and treatments to experimental groups. True experimental designs include the pre-test–post-test control group design, the post-test-only control group design, and the Solomon four-group design.

Pre-test–post-test control group design

Pre-test–post-test control group design
An experimental design in which the experimental group is exposed to the treatment but the control group is not. Pre-test and post-test measures are taken on both groups.

In the **pre-test–post-test control group design**, test units are randomly assigned to either the experimental or the control group and a pre-treatment measure is taken on each group. This design is symbolised as:

$$\begin{array}{lllll} \text{EG:} & R & 0_1 & X & 0_2 \\ \text{CG:} & R & 0_3 & & 0_4 \end{array}$$

The treatment effect (TE) is measured as

$$(0_2 - 0_1) - (0_4 - 0_3)$$

This design controls for most extraneous variables. Selection bias is eliminated by randomisation. The other extraneous effects are controlled as follows:

$$\begin{aligned} 0_2 - 0_1 &= TE + H + MA + MT + IT + I + SR + MO \\ 0_4 - 0_3 &= H + MA + MT + I + SR + MO \\ &= EV \text{ (extraneous variables)} \end{aligned}$$

where the symbols for the extraneous variables are as defined previously. The experimental result is obtained by

$$(0_2 - 0_1) - (0_4 - 0_3) = TE + IT$$

Interactive testing effect is not controlled, because of the effect of the pre-test measurement on the reaction of units in the experimental group to the treatment.

GLOBALCASH PROJECT

Pre-test–post-test control group

In the context of measuring the effectiveness of a product placement in a feature film for a bank, a pre-test–post-test control group design would be implemented as follows. A sample of respondents would be selected at random. Half of these would be randomly assigned to the experimental group, and the other half would form the control group. Respondents in both groups would be administered a questionnaire to obtain a pre-test measurement on attitudes toward the bank. Only the respondents in the experimental group would be exposed to the feature film containing the product placement. Then, a questionnaire would be administered to respondents in both groups to obtain post-test measures on attitudes toward the bank. ■

As this example shows, the pre-test–post-test control group design involves two groups and two measurements on each group. A simpler design is the post-test-only control group design.

Post-test-only control group design

Post-test-only control group design Experimental design in which the experimental group is exposed to the treatment but the control group is not and no pre-test measure is taken.

The **post-test-only control group design** does not involve any pre-measurement. It may be symbolised as

$$\begin{array}{llll} \text{EG:} & \text{R} & \text{X} & 0_1 \\ \text{CG:} & \text{R} & & 0_2 \end{array}$$

The treatment effect is obtained by

$$\text{TE} = 0_1 - 0_2$$

This design is fairly simple to implement. Because there is no pre-measurement, the testing effects are eliminated, but this design is sensitive to selection bias and mortality. It is assumed that the two groups are similar in terms of pre-treatment measures on the dependent variable because of the random assignment of test units to groups. Because there is no pre-treatment measurement, this assumption cannot be checked. This design is also sensitive to mortality. It is difficult to determine if those in the experimental group who discontinue the experiment are similar to their counterparts in the control group. Yet another limitation is that this design does not allow the researcher to examine changes in individual test units.

It is possible to control for selection bias and mortality through carefully designed experimental procedures. Examination of individual cases is often not of interest. On the other hand, this design possesses significant advantages in terms of time, cost and sample size requirements. It involves only two groups and only one measurement per group. Because of its simplicity, the post-test-only control group design is probably the most popular design in marketing research.[19] Note that, except for pre-measurement, the implementation of this design is very similar to that of the pre-test–post-test control group design.

Solomon four-group design An experimental design that explicitly controls for interactive testing effects, in addition to controlling for all the other extraneous variables.

In this example, the researcher is not concerned with examining the changes in the attitudes of individual respondents. When this information is desired, the **Solomon four-group design** should be considered. The Solomon four-group design overcomes the limitations of the pre-test–post-test control group and post-test-only control group designs in that it explicitly controls for interactive testing effect, in addition to controlling for all the other extraneous variables (EV). However, this design has practical limitations: it is expensive and time-consuming to implement. Hence, it is not considered further.[20]

In all true experimental designs, the researcher exercises a high degree of control. In particular, the researcher can control when the measurements are taken, on whom they are taken, and the scheduling of the treatments. Moreover, the researcher can randomly select the test units and randomly expose test units to the treatments. In some instances, the researcher cannot exercise this kind of control; then quasi-experimental designs should be considered.

QUASI-EXPERIMENTAL DESIGNS

A quasi-experimental design results when the researcher can control when measurements are taken and on whom they are taken but lacks control over the scheduling of the treatments and is also unable to expose test units to the treatments randomly. Quasi-experimental designs are useful because they can be used in cases when true experimentation cannot, and because they are quicker and less expensive. Because full experimental control is lacking, the researcher must consider the specific variables that are not controlled. Popular forms of quasi-experimental designs are time series and multiple time series designs.[21]

Time series design

Time series testing
A quasi-experimental design that involves periodic measurements on the dependent variable for a group of test units. Then the treatment is administered by the researcher or occurs naturally. After the treatment, periodic measurements are continued to determine the treatment effect.

The **time series design** involves a series of periodic measurements on the dependent variable for a group of test units. The treatment is then administered by the researcher or occurs naturally. After the treatment, periodic measurements are continued to determine the treatment effect. A time-series experiment may be symbolised as:

$$0_1\ 0_2\ 0_3\ 0_4\ 0_5\ 0_6\ 0_7\ 0_8\ 0_9\ 0_{10}$$

This is a quasi-experiment, because there is no randomisation of test units to treatments, and the timing of treatment presentation, as well as which test units are exposed to the treatment, may not be within the researcher's control.

Taking a series of measurements before and after the treatment provides at least partial control for several extraneous variables. Maturation is at least partially controlled, because it would not affect 0_5 and 0_6 alone but would also influence other observations. By similar reasoning, main testing effect and statistical regression are controlled as well. If the test units are selected randomly or by matching, selection bias can be reduced. Mortality may pose a problem, but it can be largely controlled by paying a premium or offering other incentives to respondents.

The major weakness of the time series design is the failure to control history. Another limitation is that the experiment may be affected by the interactive testing effect because multiple measurements are being made on the test units. Nevertheless, time series designs are useful, as illustrated by this example. The effectiveness of a test commercial (X) may be examined by broadcasting the commercial a predetermined number of times and examining the data from a pre-existing test panel. Although the marketer can control the scheduling of the test commercial, it is uncertain when or whether the panel members are exposed to it. The panel members' purchases before, during, and after the campaign are examined to determine whether the test commercial has a short-term effect, a long-term effect, or no effect.

Multiple time series design

Multiple time series design
A time series design that includes another group of test units to serve as a control group.

The **multiple time series design** is similar to the time series design except that another group of test units is added to serve as a control group. Symbolically, this design may be described as

$$\begin{array}{llllllllllll} \text{EG:} & O_1 & O_2 & O_3 & O_4 & O_5 & X & O_6 & O_7 & O_8 & O_9 & O_{10} \\ \text{CG:} & O_{11} & O_{12} & O_{13} & O_{14} & O_{15} & & O_{16} & O_{17} & O_{18} & O_{19} & O_{20} \end{array}$$

If the control group is carefully selected, this design can be an improvement over the simple time series experiment. The improvement lies in the ability to test the treatment effect twice: against the pre-treatment measurements in the experimental group and against the control group. To use the multiple time series design to assess the effectiveness of a commercial, the test panel example would be modified as follows. The test commercial would be shown in only a few of the test cities. Panel members in these cities would make up the experimental group. Panel members in cities where the commercial was not shown would constitute the control group. Another application of multiple time series design is illustrated in the following example.

EXAMPLE

Splitting commercials shows their strength[22]

A multiple time series design was used to examine the build-up effect of increased advertising. The data were obtained from Burke Marketing Services from a split-cable TV advertising field experiment. In the split-cable system, one group of households was assigned to the experimental panel and an equivalent group was assigned to the control panel. The two groups were matched on demographic variables. Data were collected for 76 weeks. Both panels received the same level of advertising for the first 52 weeks for the brand in question. For the next 24 weeks, the experimental panel was exposed to twice as much advertising as the control panel. The results indicated that the build-up effect of advertising was immediate with a duration of the order of the purchase cycle. Information of this type can be useful in selecting advertising timing patterns (allocating a set of advertising exposures over a specified period to obtain maximum impact). ■

In concluding our discussion of pre-experimental, true experimental and quasi-experimental designs, we summarise in Table 9.3 the potential sources of invalidity that may affect each of these designs. It should be remembered that potential sources of invalidity are not the same as actual errors.

STATISTICAL DESIGNS

Statistical designs consist of a series of basic experiments that allow for statistical control and analysis of external variables. In other words, several basic experiments are conducted simultaneously. Thus, statistical designs are influenced by the same sources of invalidity that affect the basic designs being used. Statistical designs offer the following advantages:

1 The effects of more than one independent variable can be measured.
2 Specific extraneous variables can be statistically controlled.
3 Economical designs can be formulated when each test unit is measured more than once.

Table 9.3 Potential sources of invalidity of experimental designs

	Source of invalidity							
	Internal							External
Design	*History*	*Maturation*	*Testing*	*Instrumentation*	*Regression*	*Selection*	*Mortality*	*Interaction of testing and X*
Pre-experimental designs								
One shot case study X O	–	–				–	–	
One group pre-test–post-test design O X O	–	–	–	–	?			–
Static group comparison X O O	+	?	+	+	+	–	–	
True experimental designs								
Pre-test–post-test control group R O X O R O O	+	+	+	+	+	+	+	–
Post-test only control group design R X O R O	+	+	+	+	+	+	+	+
Quasi-experimental designs								
Time series O O O X O O O	–	+	+	?	+	+	+	–
Multiple time series O O O X O O O O O O O O O	+	+	+	+	+	+	+	–

Note: A minus sign indicates a definite weakness, a plus sign indicates that the factor is controlled, a question mark denotes a possible source of concern, and a blank means that the factor is not relevant.

The most common statistical designs are the randomised block design, the Latin square design, and the factorial design.

Randomised block design

Randomised block design
A statistical design in which the test units are blocked on the basis of an external variable to ensure that the various experimental and control groups are matched closely on that variable.

A **randomised block design** is useful when there is only one major external variable – such as sales, store size, or income of the respondent – that might influence the dependent variable. The test units are blocked, or grouped, on the basis of the external variable. The researcher must be able to identify and measure the blocking variable. By blocking, the researcher ensures that the various experimental and control groups are matched closely on the external variable.

GLOBALCASH PROJECT

Randomised block design

Let us extend the effectiveness of a product placement in a feature film for a bank example. The purpose of this experiment would be to measure the impact of environmental concern in a film character related to the bank. Suppose that a pan-European bank like ABN-AMRO were to sponsor a film that included shots using their buildings, logos and examples of the way they run their business. They would naturally be concerned that the image portrayed in the film enhanced the corporate image that they wish to project.

To test this, three test film clips, A, B and C, show respectively, a character in the film with no environmental concern, some environmental concern, and high environmental concern. Which of these would be the most effective? Management feels that the respondents' evaluation of the product placement will be influenced by the extent of their usage of a bank. So bank usage is identified as the blocking variable and the randomly selected respondents are classified into four blocks (heavy, medium, light, or non-users of the bank). Respondents from each block are randomly assigned to the treatment groups (test film clips A, B, and C). The results reveal that the some environmental concern commercial (B) was most effective overall (see Table 9.4). ■

Table 9.4 An example of a randomised block design

		Treatment groups		
Block number	**Bank usage**	**Film A**	**Film B**	**Film C**
1	*High*			
2	*Medium*			
3	*Light*			
4	*None*			

As this example illustrates, in most marketing research situations, external variables such as sales, bank size, bank type, bank location, plus characteristics of the respondent can influence the dependent variable. Therefore, randomised block designs are generally more useful than completely random designs. Their main limitation is that the researcher can control for only one external variable. When more than one variable must be controlled, the researcher must use Latin square or factorial designs.

Latin square design

Latin square design
A statistical design that allows for the statistical control of two non-interacting external variables in addition to the manipulation of the independent variable.

A **Latin square design** allows the researcher to control statistically two non-interacting external variables as well as to manipulate the independent variable. Each external or blocking variable is divided into an equal number of blocks or levels. The independent variable is also divided into the same number of levels. A Latin square is conceptualised as a table (see Table 9.5), with the rows and the columns representing the blocks in the two external variables. The levels of the independent variable are then assigned to the cells in the table. The assignment rule is that each level of the independent variable should appear only once in each row and each column, as shown in Table 9.5.

GLOBALCASH PROJECT

Randomised block design

To illustrate the Latin square design, suppose that in the previous example, in addition to controlling for bank usage, the researcher also wanted to control for interest in increasing the electronic automation of cash transactions (defined as high, medium, or low). To implement a Latin square design, bank usage would also have to be blocked at three rather than four levels, (e.g., by combining the low and non-users into a single block). Assignments of the three test film clips could then be made as shown in Table 9.5. Note that each film clip – A, B, or C – appears once, and only once, in each row and each column.

Although Latin square designs are popular in marketing research, they are not without limitations. They require equal number of rows, columns, and treatment levels, which is sometimes problematic. Note that in the above example, the low and non-patrons had to be combined to satisfy this requirement. In addition, only two external variables can be controlled simultaneously. An additional variable can be controlled with an expansion of this design into a Greco-Latin square. Finally, Latin squares do not allow the researcher to examine interactions of the external variables with each other or with the independent variable. To examine interactions, factorial designs should be used. ■

Table 9.5 An example of a Latin square design

	Interest in increasing electronic automation		
Bank usage	**High**	**Medium**	**Low**
High	B	A	C
Medium	C	B	A
Light & None	A	C	B

Note: A, B, & C denote the three test commercials, which have respectively, no environmental concern, some concern, high concern.

Factorial design

Factorial design
A statistical experimental design used to measure the effects of two or more independent variables at various levels and to allow for interactions between variables.

A **factorial design** is used to measure the effects of two or more independent variables at various levels. Unlike the randomised block design and the Latin square, factorial designs allow for interactions between variables.[23] An interaction is said to take place when the simultaneous effect of two or more variables is different from the sum of their separate effects. For example, an individual's favourite drink might be coffee and her favourite temperature level might be cold, but this individual might not prefer cold coffee, leading to an interaction.

A factorial design may also be conceptualised as a table. In a two-factor design, each level of one variable represents a row and each level of another variable represents a column. Multidimensional tables can be used for three or more factors. Factorial designs involve a cell for every possible combination of treatment variables. Suppose that in the previous example, in addition to examining the effect of environmental concern, the researcher was also interested in simultaneously examining the effect of amount of information about the bank that came over in the film clip. Further, the amount of bank information was also varied at three levels (high, medium and low). As shown in Table 9.6, this would require 3 × 3 = 9 cells. The respondents would be randomly selected and randomly assigned to the nine cells. Respondents in each cell would receive a specific treatment combination. For example, respondents in the upper left corner cell would view a film clip that had no environmental concern and low bank information. The results revealed a significant interaction between the two factors or variables. Respondents with low amount of bank information preferred the high environmental concern film clip (C). Those with high amount of bank information, however, preferred the no environmental concern film clip (A). Notice that although Table 9.6 may appear somewhat similar to Table 9.4, the random assignment of respondents and data analysis are very different for the randomised block design and the factorial design.[24]

Table 9.6 An example of a factorial design

	Amount of environmental concern		
Amount of bank information	**No concern**	**Some concern**	**High concern**
Low			
Medium			
High			

Another example of a factorial design follows.

EXAMPLE

Price and information are for the dogs[25]

Burke Marketing Research conducted an experiment prior to the launch of a new dog food. They wished to determine the effect of price and competitive brand information on purchase intentions. A two-factor design was used. Price was manipulated to have four levels: one discount, two parity (or mid range prices), and one premium. Competitive brand information was varied at two levels: whether or not information on competitive brands was provided. Approximately 240 respondents were randomly assigned to one of eight (4 × 2) treatment conditions. Respondents were asked to indicate their purchase intentions for the new product on a five-point scale. The results indicated that neither price nor competitive brand information had a significant effect on purchase intentions. ■

The main disadvantage of a factorial design is that the number of treatment combinations increases multiplicatively with an increase in the number of variables or levels. In the Burke Marketing Research example, if the price had been manipulated at six levels and competitive brand information at three levels (no information, partial information and full information), the number of cells would have jumped from 8 to 18. All the treatment combinations are required if all the main effects and interactions are to be measured. If the researcher is interested in only a few of the interactions or main effects, fractional factorial designs may be used. As their name implies, these designs consist of only a fraction or portion of the corresponding full factorial design.

LABORATORY VERSUS FIELD EXPERIMENTS

Field environment
An experimental location set in actual market conditions.

Laboratory environment
An artificial setting for experimentation in which the researcher constructs the desired conditions.

Experiments may be conducted in laboratory or field environment. A laboratory environment is an artificial one that the researcher constructs with the desired conditions specific to the experiment. The term **field environment** is synonymous with actual market conditions. Our experiment to measure the effectiveness of a film clip could be conducted in a **laboratory environment** by showing the film in a test cinema. The same experiment could also be conducted in a field environment by running the full test film (rather than clips) in conventional cinemas. The differences between the two environments are summarised in Table 9.7.

Laboratory experiments have the following advantages over field experiments: the laboratory environment offers a high degree of control because it isolates the experiment in a carefully monitored environment. Therefore, the effects of history can be minimised. A laboratory experiment also tends to produce the same results if repeated with similar subjects, leading to high internal validity. Laboratory experiments tend to use a small number of test units, last for a shorter time, be more restricted geographically, and are easier to conduct than field experiments. Hence, they are generally less expensive as well.

Demand artefacts
Responses given because the respondents attempt to guess the purpose of the experiment and respond accordingly.

As compared with field experiments, laboratory experiments suffer from some main disadvantages. First, the artificiality of the environment may cause reactive error in that the respondents react to the situation itself rather than to the independent variable. Also, the environment may cause **demand artefacts**, a phenomenon in which the respondents attempt to guess the purpose of the experiment and respond accordingly. For example, while viewing the film clip, the respondents may recall pre-treatment questions about the brand and guess that the commercial is trying to change their attitudes toward the brand.[27] Finally, laboratory experiments are likely to have lower external validity than field experiments. Because a laboratory experiment is conducted in an artificial environment, the ability to generalise the results to the real world may be diminished.

Table 9.7 Laboratory versus field experiments

Factor	*Laboratory*	*Field*
Environment	Artificial	Realistic
Control	High	Low
Reactive error	High	Low
Demand artefacts	High	Low
Internal validity	High	Low
External validity	Low	High
Time	Short	Long
Number of units	Small	Large
Ease of implementation	High	Low
Cost	Low	High

It has been argued that artificiality or lack of realism in a laboratory experiment need not lead to lower external validity. One must be aware of the aspects of the laboratory experiment that differ from the situation to which generalisations are to be made. External validity will be reduced only if these aspects interface with the independent variables explicitly manipulated in the experiment, as is often the case in applied marketing research. Another consideration, however, is that laboratory experiments allow for more complex designs than field experiments. Hence, the researcher can control for more factors or variables in the laboratory setting, which increases external validity.[28]

The researcher must consider all these factors when deciding whether to conduct laboratory or field experiments.[29] Field experiments are less common in marketing research than laboratory experiments, although laboratory and field experiments play complementary roles.[30]

EXPERIMENTAL VERSUS NON-EXPERIMENTAL DESIGNS

In Chapter 3, we discussed three types of research designs: exploratory, descriptive and causal. Of these, only causal designs are truly appropriate for inferring cause-and-effect relationships. Although descriptive survey data are often used to provide evidence of 'causal' relationships, these studies do not meet all the conditions required for causality. For example, it is difficult in descriptive studies to establish the prior equivalence of the respondent groups with respect to both the independent and dependent variables. On the other hand, an experiment can establish this equivalence by random assignment of test units to groups. In descriptive research, it is also difficult to establish time order of occurrence of variables. In an experiment, however, the researcher controls the timing of the measurements and the introduction of the treatment. Finally, descriptive research offers little control over other possible causal factors.

We do not wish to undermine the importance of descriptive research designs in marketing research. As mentioned in Chapter 3, descriptive research constitutes the most popular research design in marketing research, and we do not want to imply that it should never be used to examine causal relationships. Indeed, some authors have suggested procedures for drawing causal inferences from descriptive (non-experimental) data.[31] Rather, our intent is to alert the reader to the limitations of descriptive research for examining causal relationships. Likewise, we also want to make the reader aware of the limitations of experimentation.[32]

LIMITATIONS OF EXPERIMENTATION

Experimentation is an important marketing research methodology given the ability to infer causal relationships. However, the methodology has limitations of time, cost and administration of an experiment.

Time

Experiments can be time consuming, particularly if the researcher is interested in measuring the long-term effects of the treatment, such as the effectiveness of an advertising campaign. Experiments should last long enough so that the post-treatment measurements include most or all the effects of the independent variables.

Cost

Experiments are often expensive. The requirements of experimental group control group, and multiple measurements significantly add to the cost of research.

Administration

Experiments can be difficult to administer. It may be impossible in measuring human activity, to control for the effects of the extraneous variables, particularly in a field environment. Field experiments often interfere with a company's ongoing operations, and obtaining cooperation from the retailers, wholesalers and others involved may be difficult. Finally, competitors may deliberately contaminate the results of a field experiment.

APPLICATION: TEST MARKETING

Test marketing
An application of a controlled experiment done in limited, but carefully selected, test markets. It involves a replication of the planned national marketing programme for a product in test markets.

Test markets
A carefully selected part of the marketplace particularly suitable for test marketing.

Test marketing, also called market testing, is an application of a controlled experiment conducted in limited but carefully selected parts of the marketplace called **test markets**. It involves a replication of a planned national marketing programme in test markets. Often, the marketing mix variables (independent variables) are varied in test marketing and the sales (dependent variable) are monitored so that an appropriate national marketing strategy can be identified. The two major objectives of test marketing are (1) to determine market acceptance of the product and (2) to test alternative levels of marketing mix variables. Test-marketing procedures may be classified as standard test markets, controlled and mini-market tests, and simulated test marketing.

Standard test market

Standard test market
A test market in which the product is sold through regular distribution channels. For example, no special considerations are given to products simply because they are being test-marketed.

In a **standard test market**, test markets are selected and the product is sold through regular distribution channels. Typically, the company's own sales force is responsible for distributing the product. Sales personnel stock the shelves, restock, and take inventory at regular intervals. One or more combinations of marketing mix variables (product, price, distribution and promotional levels) are employed.

Designing a standard test market involves deciding what criteria are to be used for selecting test markets, how many test markets to use, and the duration of the test. Test markets must be carefully selected. The criteria for selection of test markets are described in the following example. In general, the more test markets that can be used, the better. If resources are limited, at least two test markets should be used for each programme variation to be tested. Where external validity is important, however, at least four test markets should be used.

EXAMPLE

Criteria for the selection of test markets[33]

Test markets should have the following qualities:

1 Be large enough to produce meaningful projections. They should contain at least 2% of the potential target population.
2 Be representative demographically.
3 Be representative with respect to product consumption behaviour.
4 Be representative with respect to media usage.
5 Be representative with respect to competition.
6 Be relatively isolated in terms of media and physical distribution.
7 Have normal historical development in the product class.
8 Have marketing research and auditing services available.
9 Not be overtested.

The duration of the test depends on the repurchase cycle for the product, the probability of competitive response, cost considerations, the initial consumer response, and company philosophy. The test should last long enough for repurchase activity to be observed. This indicates the long-term impact of the product. If competitive reaction to the test is anticipated, the duration should be short. The cost of the test is also an important factor. The longer a test, the more it costs, and at some point, the value of additional information is outweighed by its costs. Recent evidence suggests that tests of new brands should run for at least ten months. An empirical analysis found that the final test market share was reached in ten months 85% of the time and in 12 months 95% of the time. Test marketing can be very beneficial to a product's successful introduction, as the following example demonstrates.

EXAMPLE

Bass joins exclusive Czech beer club[35]

Bass has acquired 34% of Staropramen, a Prague brewer. It launched the Czech beer in six-month test markets in Manchester and Liverpool in bottles, and on draft and in bottles in London. The introduction was backed with a comprehensive promotional package designed to encourage consumer trial and future purchase. This included sampling nights, point-of-sale material and glassware.

A standard test market, such as the Bass example, constitutes a one-shot case study. In addition to the problems associated with this design, test marketing faces two unique problems. First, competitors often take actions such as increasing their promotional efforts to contaminate the test marketing program. When Procter & Gamble test-marketed a hand-and-body lotion, the market leader, Cheeseborough Ponds, started a competitive buy-one-get-one-free promotion for its flagship brand, Vaseline Intensive Care lotion. This encouraged consumers to stock up on Vaseline Intensive Care lotion and as a result, the Procter & Gamble product did poorly in the test market. Procter & Gamble still launched the line nationally. Ponds again countered with the same promotional strategy. Vaseline Intensive Care settled with a market share of 22% while Procter & Gamble achieved but 4%.[36] ■

Another problem is that while a firm's test marketing is in progress, competitors have an opportunity to beat it to the national market. Sometimes it is not feasible to implement a standard test market using the company's personnel. Instead, the company must seek help from an outside supplier, in which case the controlled test market may be an attractive option.

Controlled test market

Controlled test market
A test-marketing programme conducted by an outside research company in field experimentation. The research company guarantees distribution of the product in retail outlets that represent a predetermined percentage of the market.

In a **controlled test market**, the entire test-marketing programme is conducted by an outside research company. The research company guarantees distribution of the product in retail outlets that represent a predetermined percentage of the market. It handles warehousing and field sales operations, such as stocking shelves, selling and stock control. The controlled test market includes both mini-market (or forced distribution) tests and the smaller controlled store panels. This service is provided by a number of research firms, including A.C. Nielsen.

Simulated test market

Simulated test market
A quasi-test market in which respondents are pre-selected; they are then interviewed and observed on their purchases and attitudes toward the product.

Also called a laboratory test or test market simulation, a **simulated test market** yields mathematical estimates of market share based on initial reaction of consumers to a new product. The procedure works as follows. Typically, respondents are intercepted in busy locations, such as shopping centres, and pre-screened for product usage. The selected individuals are exposed to the proposed new product concept and given an opportunity to buy the new product in a real-life or laboratory environment. Those who purchase the new product are interviewed about their evaluation of the product and repeat purchase intentions. The trial and repeat-purchase estimates so generated are combined with data on proposed promotion and distribution levels to project a share of the market.[37]

Simulated test markets can be conducted in 16 weeks or less. The information they generate is confidential and the competition cannot obtain it. They are also relatively inexpensive. Simulated test markets can cost around 10% of a standard test market. The following example illustrates the benefits of the simulated test market. It illustrates the demise of the traditional test market procedure. The final sentence should be read remembering the problems faced by Unilever on the launch of Persil Power. It demonstrates that the compromise of the simulated test market adheres to the philosophy of test marketing and can overcome many the pitfalls of test marketing.

EXAMPLE

Why new products are bypassing the market test[38]

Once upon a time any self-respecting packaged goods marketer launching a new product would first put it out to test in a television region. That traditional routine, from concept to prototype, from qualitative research to quantitative research to test marketing, has all but disappeared.

There are many reasons for test marketing's demise. Marketers have become obsessed with speed to market. They are afraid that test marketing will reveal their hand and allow competitors to rush in with copycats. TV sales houses are increasingly selling air time on a national or pan-regional basis, and charging a premium to advertisers wanting to buy in individual regions. And, crucially, the big grocery chains have turned against the practice. They have centralised their distribution, and they need a very good reason to incur the hassle of earmarking a product for delivery to stores in just one region.

Marketers claim that consumer research techniques are now so sophisticated that full-blown tests are no longer necessary. Besides, once they have invested in R&D plus new plant, and created an advertising campaign, they might just as well go nationally immediately. ■

There are a number of specific drawbacks to the new state of affairs. Product development is becoming so expensive that brand managers are increasingly opting for ersatz innovation in the form of low-risk, low-investment range and line extensions (except perhaps in soft drinks and confectionery, whose heavy sales through impulse outlets makes them less reliant on the grocery multiples). And those who can afford to lay out big money on NPD are always liable to make some equally big mistake. Would the Persil Power debacle have happened if Unilever had employed traditional test marketing?

DETERMINING A TEST MARKETING STRATEGY

The first decision to be made is whether or not to test market the proposed new product, or whatever element of the marketing programme that is under consideration. As shown in Figure 9.2, this decision must take into account the competitive environment; the socio-cultural environment, particularly consumer preferences and past behaviours; the need to keep the firm's marketing efforts secret; and the overall marketing strategy of the firm. If the marketing research already undertaken to develop the new product provides compelling positive evidence, or if factors such as pre-empting competitive moves dominate, the new product may well be introduced nationally without test marketing. If the decision is to conduct test marketing, however, simulated test marketing may be conducted first, followed by controlled test marketing, then standard test marketing, and, if the results are positive, national introduction. Of course, very positive results at any stage may directly lead to national introduction, circumventing subsequent testing.

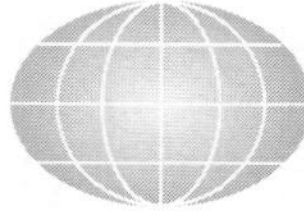

INTERNATIONAL MARKETING RESEARCH

If field experiments are difficult to conduct in developed Western economies, the challenge they pose is greatly increased in the international arena. In many countries, the marketing, economic, structural, information and technological environment is not developed to the extent that it is in Europe and the United States. For example, in many countries, TV stations are owned and operated by a government that may place severe restrictions on television advertising. This makes field experiments that manipulate advertising levels extremely difficult. Consider, for example, M & M/Mars, which has set up massive manufacturing facilities in Russia and advertises its sweets on television. Yet, the sales potential has not been realised. Is Mars advertising too much, too little, or just enough? Although the answer could be determined by conducting a field experiment that manipulated the level of advertising, such causal research is not feasible given the tight control of the Russian government on television stations.

Likewise, the lack of major supermarkets in the Baltic states makes it difficult for Procter & Gamble to conduct field experiments to determine the effect of in-store promotions on the sales of its detergents. In some countries in Asia, Africa and South America, a majority of the population lives in small towns and villages. Yet basic infrastructure such as roads, transportation and warehouse facilities are lacking, making it difficult to achieve desired levels of distribution. Even when experiments are designed, it is difficult to control for the time order of occurrence of variables and the absence of other possible causal factors, two of the necessary conditions for causality. Because the researcher has little control over the environment, control of extraneous variables is particularly problem-

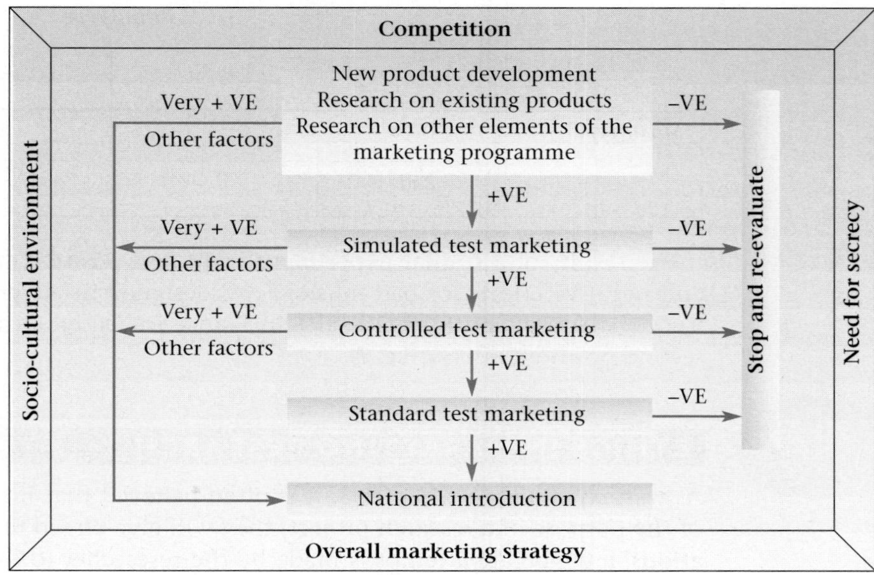

Figure 9.2
Selecting a test-marketing strategy

atic. Furthermore, it may not be possible to address this problem by adopting the most appropriate experimental design as environmental constraints may make that design infeasible.

Thus, the internal and external validity of field experiments conducted overseas is generally lower than in Europe and the United States. Although pointing to the difficulties of conducting field experiments in other countries, we do not wish to imply that such causal research cannot or should not be conducted. To the contrary, as the following example indicates, creatively designed field experiments can result in rich findings.

EXAMPLE

What you hear is what you get[39]

PepsiCo's strategy to fight arch-rival Coca-Cola in France was through increased spending on advertisements. Part of PepsiCo's campaign was to use singers and celebrities such as Rod Stewart, Tina Turner, Gloria Estefan, and M.C. Hammer in their commercials as well as publicity tours. Marketing research, however, revealed that overplaying American celebrities may be detrimental in the French market. Pepsi thought that this was probably a weakness Coke had because Europeans considered Coca-Cola's marketing effort was considered as 'too American' in Europe. Pepsi, therefore, decided to use taste as a competitive tool. The key was to highlight the product superiority, although not directly, as comparative advertising was prohibited in France. They came up with music as a means of communicating. How did this work?

Research showed that attitude toward the brand is influenced by attitude toward the ad, especially in low involvement products such as soft drinks. Sweet and melodious music played for Pepsi would transfer good feelings from the music to the brand Pepsi. Similarly, repugnant and undesirable music played for Coke would also transfer from the music to the brand Coke. This mechanism is called classical conditioning. To test these hypotheses, a two-factor experiment could be designed. The two factors would be type of music and the brand preferred, each varied at two levels as shown. A test commercial for each experimental condition would be run for a month, with each commercial being played in a different city. At the end of campaign, central location interviews would be used to examine the effect on brand.

		Brand type	
		Pepsi	*Coke*
Music type	*Good*		
	Bad		

The results of a similar experiment indicated positive effects for good music and negative effects for bad music. Pepsi designed its advertising based on these findings. Subsequently, retail sales in France increased although it still is in the second position, after Coke. ■

ETHICS IN MARKETING RESEARCH

As was explained in Chapter 8, it is often believed that if respondents are aware of the purpose of a research project, they will give biased responses. In these situations, a deliberate attempt is made by the researcher to disguise the purpose of the research. This is often necessary with experimentation, where disguise is needed to produce valid results. Take, for example, a project conducted to determine the effectiveness of television commercials for a breakfast cereal. The respondents are recruited and brought to a central facility. They are told that they will be watching a television programme on nutrition and then will be asked some questions. Interspersed in the programme is a test commercial for the breakfast cereal as well as commercials for some other products (filler commercials). After viewing the programme and the commercials, the respondents are given a questionnaire to complete. The questionnaire obtains evaluations on the programme content, the test commercial and some of the filler commercials. Note, the evaluations of the programme content and the filler commercials are not of interest but are obtained to reinforce the nature of the disguise. If the respondents knew that the true purpose was to determine the effectiveness of the test commercial, their responses might be biased. Disguising the purpose of the research however, should not lead to deception.

Although this seems like a paradox, one solution is to disclose the possible existence of deception before the start of the experiment and allow the participants the right to redress at the conclusion of the experiment. The following four items should be conveyed: (1) inform respondents that in an experiment of this nature, a disguise of the purpose is often required for valid results; (2) inform them of the general nature of the experiment and what they will be asked to do; (3) make sure they know that they can leave the experiment at any time; and (4) inform them that the study will be fully explained after the data have been gathered and at that time, they may request that their information be withdrawn.

Debriefing
After the experiment, informing test subjects what the experiment was about and how the experimental manipulations were performed.

The procedure outlined in item (4) is called **debriefing**. It could be argued that disclosure in this way would also bias results. There is evidence, however, indicating that data collected from subjects informed of the possibility of deception and those not informed is similar.[40] Debriefing can alleviate the stress caused by the experiment and make the experiment a learning experience for the respondents. However, if not handled carefully, debriefing itself can be unsettling to subjects. In the breakfast cereal example above, respondents may find it disheartening that they spent their time evaluating a cereal commercial. The researcher should anticipate and address this issue in the debriefing session.

One further ethical concern in experimentation involves using the appropriate experimental design to control errors caused by extraneous variables. It is the responsibility of the researcher to use the most applicable experimental design for the problem. As the following example illustrates, determining the most appropriate experimental design for the problem requires not only an initial evaluation but also continuous monitoring.

EXAMPLE

Correcting errors early: A stitch in time saves nine[41]

A marketing research firm specialising in advertising research examined the effectiveness of a television commercial for Nike athletic shoes. A one-group pre-test–post-test design was used. Attitudes held by the respondents toward Nike athletic shoes were obtained prior to being exposed to a sports programme on TV and several commercials, including the one for Nike. Attitudes were again measured after viewing the programme and the commercials. Initial evaluation based on a small sample found the one-group pre-test–post-test design adopted in this study to be susceptible to demand artefacts: respondents attempt to guess the purpose of the experiment and respond accordingly. Because time and financial constraints make redesigning the study difficult at best, the research continued with correction. Continuing a research project after knowing errors were made in the early stages is not ethical behaviour. Experimental design problems should be disclosed immediately to the client. Decisions whether to redesign or accept the flaws should be made jointly. ■

INTERNET AND COMPUTER APPLICATIONS

The Internet can be a useful vehicle for conducting causal research. Different experimental treatments can be displayed at different Web sites. Respondents can then be recruited to visit these sites and respond to a questionnaire that obtains information on the dependent and extraneous variables. Thus, the Internet can provide a mechanism for controlled experimentation, although in a laboratory type of environment.

An example of testing the effectiveness of advertisements can be used to illustrate the use of the Internet in causal research. Different advertisements can be posted on different Web sites. Matched or randomly selected respondents can be recruited to visit these sites, with one group visiting only one site. If any pre-treatment measures have to be obtained, respondents can answer a questionnaire posted on the site. Then they are exposed to a particular advertisement at that site. After viewing the advertisement, the respondents answer additional questions providing post-treatment measures. Control groups can also be implemented in a similar way. Thus, all types of experimental designs that we have considered can be implemented in this manner.

To complement the Internet, microcomputers and mainframe software can be used in the design and analysis of experiments. For example, the statistical analysis package Minitab can be used to design experiments. Although similar in use to SPSS, SAS or BMDP, Minitab includes functions and documentation specifically for industrial-quality control work in which factorial designs are encountered. For example, researchers investigating restaurant atmosphere, might want to examine some of the interactions of independent variables. The dependent variable in this experiment could be the respondent's rating of the restaurant as a setting for a romantic meal. Three factors would be included in this 2 × 2 × 2 study. Assuming two lighting levels (i.e. low or medium), two

Experimental research can help determine the optimal value of Internet coupons in the task of getting on-line customers to visit stores such as bookshops

sound types (piped music or live music), and two olfactory stimuli (i.e. spicy smells or sweet/confectionery smells), the best combinations of restaurant atmospherics can be examined.

SUMMARY

The scientific notion of causality implies that we can never prove that *X* causes *Y*. At best, we can only infer that *X* is one of the causes of *Y* in that it makes the occurrence of *Y* probable. Three conditions must be satisfied before causal inferences can be made: (1) concomitant variation, which implies that *X* and *Y* must vary together in a hypothesised way; (2) time order of occurrence of variables, which implies that *X* must precede *Y*; and (3) elimination of other possible causal factors, which implies that competing explanations must be ruled out. Experiments provide the most convincing evidence of all three conditions. An experiment is formed when one or more independent variables are manipulated or controlled by the researcher and their effect on one or more dependent variables is measured.

In designing an experiment, it is important to consider internal and external validity. Internal validity refers to whether the manipulation of the independent variables actually caused the effects on the dependent variables. External validity refers to the generalisability of experimental results. For the experiment to be valid, the researcher must control the threats imposed by extraneous variables, such as history, maturation, testing (main and interactive testing effects), instrumentation, statistical regression, selection bias and mortality. There are four ways of controlling extraneous variables: randomisation, matching, statistical control and design control.

Experimental designs may be classified as pre-experimental, true experimental, quasi-experimental and statistical designs. An experiment may be conducted in a laboratory environment or under actual market conditions in a real-life setting. Only causal designs encompassing experimentation are appropriate for inferring cause-and-effect relationships.

Although experiments have limitations in terms of time, cost, and administration, they are becoming increasingly popular in marketing. Test marketing is an important application of experimental design.

The internal and external validity of field experiments conducted in developing nations is generally lower than in the developed Western economies. The level of development in many countries is lower and the researcher lacks control over many of the marketing variables. The ethical issues involved in conducting causal research include disguising the purpose of the experiment. Debriefing can be used to address some of these issues.

QUESTIONS AND PROBLEMS

1 What are the requirements for inferring a causal relationship between two variables?

2 Differentiate between internal and external validity.

3 List any five extraneous variables and give an example to show how each can reduce internal validity.

4 Describe the various methods for controlling extraneous sources of variation.

5 What is the key characteristic that distinguishes true experimental designs from pre-experimental designs?

6 List the steps involved in implementing the post-test-only control group design. Describe the design symbolically.

7 What is a time series experiment? When is it used?

8 How is a multiple time series design different from a basic time series design?

9 What advantages do statistical designs have over basic designs?

10 What are the limitations of the Latin square design?

11 Compare the characteristics of laboratory and field experimentation.

12 Should descriptive research be used for investigating causal relationships? Why or why not?

13 What is test marketing? What are the three types of test marketing?

14 What is the main difference between a standard test market and a controlled test market?

15 Describe how simulated test marketing works.

NOTES

1 'Surveys Help Settle Trade Dress Infringement Case', *Quirk's Marketing Research Review* (October–November 1987), 16, 17, 33.

2 'POP Radio Test Airs the Ads In-Store', *Marketing News* (24 October 1986), 16.

3 Kenny, D.A., *Correlation and Causality* (New York: Wiley, 1979), chapter 1.

4 For several references on the use of experiments in marketing, see Gardner, D.M. and Belk, R.W., *A Basic Bibliography on Experimental Design in Marketing* (Chicago: American Marketing Association, 1980).

5 Selltiz, C., Jahoda, M., Deutsch, M. and Cook, S.W., *Research Methods in Social Relations* (New York: Holt, Rinehart and Winston, 1959), 83–88.

6 *Fortune* (23 November 1987),12.

7 Brown, S.R. and Melamed, L.E., *Experimental Design and Analysis* (Newbury Park, CA: Sage Publications, 1990).

8 See the study employing experimental designs: Hoch, S.J., Dreze, X. and Purk, M.E., 'EDLP, Hi-Lo, and Margin Arithmetic', *Journal of Marketing* 58 (October 1994), 16–27.

9 Shoemaker, R.W. and Tibrewala, V., 'Relating Coupon Redemption Rates to Past Purchasing of the Brand', *Journal of Advertising Research* 25 (October-November 1985), 40–47.

10 Banks, S., *Experimentation in Marketing* (New York: McGraw-Hill, 1965), 168–79.

11 In addition to internal and external validity, there also exist construct and statistical conclusion validity. Construct validity addresses the question of what construct, or characteristic, is in fact being measured and is discussed in Chapter 11 on measurement and scaling. Statistical conclusion validity addresses the extent and statistical significance of the covariation that exists in the data and is discussed in the chapters on data analysis. See Cook, T.D. and Campbell, D.T., *Quasi-Experimentation* (Chicago: Rand McNally, 1979), 52–53; and, Campbell, D.T. and Stanley, J.C., *Experimental and Quasi Experimental Designs for Research* (Chicago: Rand McNally, 1966).

12 Lynch, J.G. Jr, 'On the External Validity of Experiments in Consumer Research', *Journal of Consumer Research* 9 (December 1982), 225–44.

13 Lynch, J.G. Jr, 'The Role of External Validity in Theoretical Research', Calder, B.J., Phillips, L.W. and Tybout, A., 'Beyond External Validity', and McGrath, J.E and Brinberg, D., 'External Validity and the Research Process', *Journal of Consumer Research* (June 1983), 109–11, 112–14, and 115–24.

14 O'Herlihy, C., 'Why Ad Experiments Fail', *Journal of Advertising Research* (February 1980), 53–58.

15 Cook, T.D. and Campbell, D.T., *Quasi-Experimentation* (Chicago: Rand McNally, 1979), 52–53.

16 Brown, S.R. and Melamed, L.E., *Experimental Design and Analysis* (Newbury Park, CA: Sage Publications, 1990).

17 Tarshis, A.M., 'Natural Sell-in Avoids Pitfalls of Controlled Tests', *Marketing News* (24 October 1986), 14.

18 Other experimental designs are also available. See Winer, R.S., 'Analysis of Advertising Experiments', *Journal of Advertising Research* (June 1980) 25–31.

19 For some applications of this design, see Demirdjian, Z.S., 'Sales Effectiveness of Comparative Advertising', *Journal of Consumer Research* (December 1983) 362–65; and Duncan, C.P. and Nelson, J.E., 'Effects of Humour in a Radio Advertising Experiment', *Journal of Advertising* (1985) 33–40.

20 For an application of the Solomon four-group design, see Mizerski, R.W., Allison, N.K. and Calvert, S., 'A Controlled Field Study of Corrective Advertising Using Multiple Exposures and a Commercial Medium', *Journal of Marketing Research* 17 (August 1980) 341–48.

21 Banks, S. *Experimentation in Marketing* (New York: McGraw-Hill, 1965), 168–79.

22 Krishnamurthi, L., Narayan, J. and Raj, S.P. 'Intervention Analysis of a Field Experiment to Assess the Build-up Effect of Advertising', *Journal of Marketing Research* 23 (November 1986) 337–45.

23 For applications of factorial designs, see Leclerc, F. Schmitt, B.H. and Dube, L., 'Foreign Branding and Its Effects on Product Perceptions and Attitudes', *Journal of Marketing Research* 31 (May 1994), 263–70.
24 Bemmaor, A.C. and Mouchoux, D. 'Measuring the Short-Term Effect of In-Store Promotion and Retail Advertising on Brand Sales: A Factorial Experiment', *Journal of Marketing Research* 28 (May 1991), 202–14.
25 Miller, J.B., Bruvold, N.T. and Kernan, J.B., 'Does Competitive-Set Information Affect the Results of Concept Tests?', *Journal of Advertising Research* (April–May 1987) 16–23.
26 Barnes, J.H. Jr and Seymour, D.T., 'Experimenter Bias: Task, Tools, and Time', *Journal of the Academy of Marketing Science* (Winter 1980), 1–11.
27 Lim, J. and Summers, J.O., 'A Non-Experimental Investigation of Demand Artefacts in a Personal Selling Situation', *Journal of Marketing Research* (August 1984), 251–58.
28 Lynch, J.G. Jr, 'On the External Validity of Experiments in Consumer Research', *Journal of Consumer Research* 9, (December 1982), 225–44.
29 Farris, P.W. and Reibstein, D.J., 'Overcontrol in Advertising Experiments', *Journal of Advertising Research* (June-July 1984), 37–42.
30 Houston, M.J. and Rothschild, M.L., 'Policy-Related Experiments on Information Provision: A Normative Model and Explication', *Journal of Marketing Research* (November 1980) 432–49; and Sawyer, A.G., Worthing, P.M. and Sendak, P.E., 'The Role of Laboratory Experiments to Test Marketing Strategies', *Journal of Marketing* 43 (Summer 1979), 60–67.
31 Blalock, H.M. Jr, *Causal Inferences in Non-experimental Research* (Chapel Hill: University of North Carolina Press, 1964) and Cook, T.D. and. Campbell, D.T., *Quasi-Experimentation* (Chicago: Rand McNally, 1979), chapter 7.
32 In some situations, surveys and experiments can complement each other and may both be used. For example, the results obtained in laboratory experiments may be further examined in a field survey. See Johnston, W.J. and Kim, K. 'Performance, Attribution, and Expectancy Linkages in Personal Selling', *Journal of Marketing* 58 (October 1994) 68–81.
33 Reprinted with permission from *Marketing News* published by the American Marketing Association, Chicago, 1 March 1985, p. 15.
34 'Test Marketers on Target', *Sales and Marketing Management* (11 March 1985) 81–116, and 'The Time Test of Test Marketing Is Time', *Sales and Marketing Management* (14 March 1983) 74.
35 'Bass Joins Exclusive Czech Beer Club', *Grocer* 216 (7174) (22 October 1994), 34.
36 'How to Improve Your Chances for Test-Market Success', *Marketing News* (6 January 1984) 12.
37 For issues related to the validity of simulated test market, see Urban, G.L. and Katz, G.M., 'Pre-Test Market Models: Validation and Managerial Implications', *Journal of Marketing Research* 20 (August 1983) 221–34.
38 'Why New Products Are Bypassing the Market Test', *Management Today* (October 1995) 12.
39 Crumley, B., 'French Cola Wars', *Advertising Age* (17 December 1990) 22.
40 Holmes, D.S. and Bennett, D.H., 'Experiments to Answer Questions Raised by the Use of Deception in Psychological Research: I. Role Playing as an Alternative to Deception; II. Effectiveness of Debriefing after a Deception; III. Effect of Informed Consent on Deception', *Journal of Personality and Social Psychology* 29 (1974), 358–67.
41 Ferrell, O.C. and Skinner, S.J., 'Ethical Behavior and Bureaucratic Structure in Marketing Research Organisations', *Journal of Marketing Research* 25 (1988), 103–9.

Chapter 10

Measurement and scaling: fundamentals and comparative scaling

'When you can measure what you are speaking about and express it in numbers, you know something about it'
– Lord Kelvin

OBJECTIVES

After reading this chapter, the student should be able to:

1. introduce the concepts of measurement and scaling and show how scaling may be considered an extension of measurement;
2. discuss the primary scales of measurement and differentiate nominal, ordinal, interval and ratio scales;
3. classify and discuss scaling techniques as comparative and non-comparative and describe the comparative techniques of paired comparison, rank order, constant sum and Q-sort scaling;
4. explain the concept of verbal protocols and discuss how they could be employed to measure consumer response to advertising;
5. discuss the considerations involved in implementing the primary scales of measurement in an international setting;
6. understand the ethical issues involved in selecting scales of measurement.

OVERVIEW

Once the information to be obtained is specified and the type of research design has been determined (Chapters 3 through to 9), the researcher can move to the next phase of the research design. Should the research design be quantitative in nature, decisions need to be made on measurement and scaling procedures. This chapter describes the concepts of scaling and measurement and discusses four primary scales of measurement: nominal, ordinal, interval and ratio. We describe both comparative and non-comparative scaling techniques and explain comparative techniques in detail. Non-comparative techniques are covered in Chapter 11. The considerations involved in implementing the primary scales of measurement when researching international markets are discussed. The chapter concludes with a discussion of several ethical issues that arise in measurement and scaling are identified.

To begin, we give some examples of the uses of the primary scales of measurement.

EXAMPLE

Car war – Japan making a spearhead[1]

For the first time, European journalists had given their car-of-the-year award to a Japanese model, Nissan's new British-made Micra. This came as big blow to European car manufacturers who have been trying to keep the Japanese onslaught at bay. 'They will change the competitive balance', warns Bruce Blythe, Ford of Europe Inc.'s head of business strategy. How did the Japanese do it? Nissan conducted a survey of European consumers' preferences for cars using interval scales to capture the magnitude of the preference differences. The use of interval scales enabled Nissan to compare the differences between car features and determine which features were preferred. The findings revealed distinct consumer preferences. So the Japanese made inroads by transplants in production and building technical centres in Europe to customise to local styling tastes and preferences. By 1995 the Japanese were producing 775,000 cars a year in Europe, 75 per cent of them in Britain. The Japanese were taking away share from Renault in the French, Italian and Spanish markets. ■

GLOBALCASH PROJECT

Quality in pan-European banks

Pan-European banks that sponsored the GlobalCash project see their customers' priorities of service quality as being vital in shaping their service offerings. In the GlobalCash study, service quality components were listed and respondents requested to indicate their priorities. It required respondents to reflect upon their priorities and thus involved more time compared to if they had been asked to evaluate which components were 'important'. If respondents felt that all the service quality components were of equal importance, they could indicate this by giving them an equal number. This rarely happened. As corporate clients revealed their priorities through rank order scaling (which is ordinal in nature), banks could change their emphases in delivering service quality. ■

MEASUREMENT AND SCALING

Measurement
The assignment of numbers or other symbols to characteristics of objects according to certain pre-specified rules.

Measurement means assigning numbers or other symbols to characteristics of objects according to certain pre-specified rules.[2] We measure not the object but some characteristic of it. Thus, we do not measure consumers, only their perceptions, attitudes, preferences or other relevant characteristics. In marketing research, numbers are usually assigned for one of two reasons. First, numbers permit statistical analysis of the resulting data. Second, numbers facilitate a universal communication of measurement rules and results.

The most important aspect of measurement is the specification of rules for assigning numbers to the characteristics. The assignment process must be isomorphic: there must be one-to-one correspondence between the numbers and the characteristics being measured. For example, the same Euro (€) figures are assigned to households with identical annual incomes. Only then can the numbers be associated with specific characteristics of the measured object, and vice versa. In addition, the rules for assigning numbers should be standardised and applied uniformly. They must not change over objects or time.

Scaling
The generation of a continuum upon which measured objects are located.

Scaling may be considered an extension of measurement. Scaling involves creating a continuum upon which measured objects are located. To illustrate, consider a scale for locating consumers according to the characteristic 'attitude towards banks'. Each respondent is assigned a number indicating an unfavourable attitude (measured as 1), a neutral attitude (measured as 2), or a favourable attitude (measured as 3). Measurement is the actual assignment of 1, 2 or 3 to each respondent. Scaling is the process of placing the respondents on a continuum with respect to their attitude toward banks. In our example, scaling is the process by which respondents would be classified as having an unfavourable, neutral or positive attitude.

PRIMARY SCALES OF MEASUREMENT

There are four primary scales of measurement, nominal, ordinal, interval, and ratio.[3] These scales are illustrated in Figure 10.1, and their properties are summarised in Table 10.1 and discussed in the following sections.

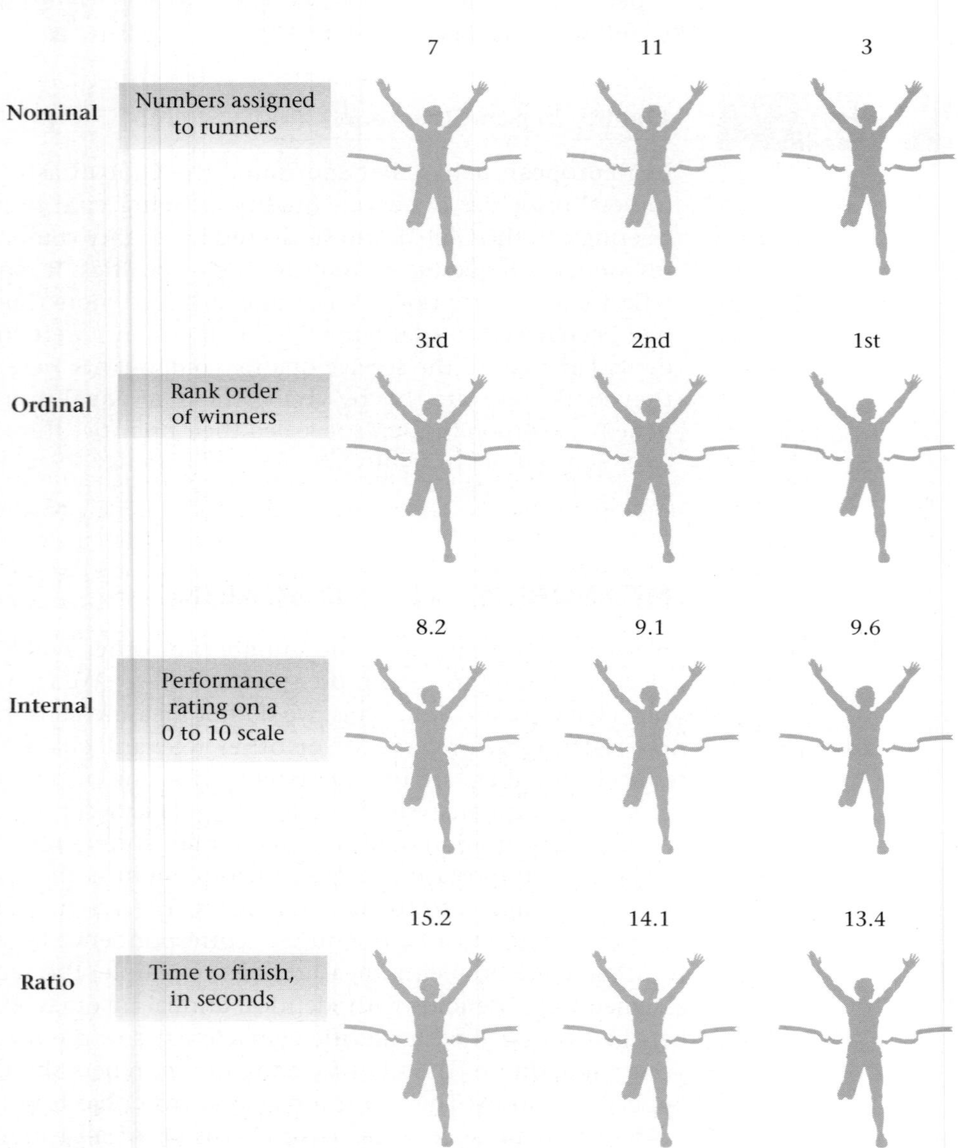

Figure 10.1 An illustration of primary scales of measurement

Table 10.1 Primary scales of measurement

Scale	*Basic characteristics*	*Common examples*	*Marketing examples*	*Permissible statistics*	
				Descriptive	*Inferential*
Nominal	Numbers identify and classify objects	Student registration numbers, numbers on football players' shirts	Gender classification, bank types	Percentages, mode	Chi-square, binomial test
Ordinal	Numbers indicate the relative positions of the objects but not the magnitude of differences between them	Rankings of the top 4 teams in the football World Cup	Ranking of service quality delivered by a number of banks. Rank order of favourite television programmes	Percentile, median	Rank-order correlation, Friedman ANOVA
Interval	Differences between objects can be compared; zero point is arbitrary	Temperature (Fahrenheit, Celsius)	Attitudes, opinions, index numbers	Range, mean, standard deviation	Product-moment correlations, *t*-tests, ANOVA, regression, factor analysis
Ratio	Zero point is fixed; ratios of scale values can be computed	Length, weight	Age, income, costs, sales, market shares	Geometric mean, harmonic mean	Coefficient of variation

Nominal scale

Nominal scale
A scale whose numbers serve only as labels or tags for identifying and classifying objects with a strict one-to-one correspondence between the numbers and the objects.

A **nominal scale** is a figurative labelling scheme in which the numbers serve only as labels or tags for identifying and classifying objects. For example, the numbers assigned to the respondents in a study constitute a nominal scale, thus a female respondent may be assigned a number 1 and a male respondent 2. When a nominal scale is used for the purpose of identification, there is a strict one-to-one correspondence between the numbers and the objects. Each number is assigned to only one object, and each object has only one number assigned to it.

Common examples include student registration numbers at their college or university and numbers assigned to football players or jockeys in a horse race. In marketing research, nominal scales are used for identifying respondents, brands, attributes, banks and other objects.

When used for classification purposes, the nominally scaled numbers serve as labels for classes or categories. For example, you might classify the control group as group 1 and the experimental group as group 2. The classes are mutually exclusive and collectively exhaustive. The objects in each class are viewed as equivalent with respect to the characteristic represented by the nominal number. All objects in the same class have the same number, and no two classes have the same number.

The numbers in a nominal scale do not reflect the amount of the characteristic possessed by the objects. For example, a high number on a football player's shirt does not imply that the footballer is a better player than one with a low number or vice versa. The same applies to numbers assigned to classes. The only permissible operation on the numbers in a nominal scale is counting. Only a limited number of statistics, all of which are based on frequency counts, are permissible. These include percentages, mode, chi-square and binomial tests (see Chapter 17). It is not meaningful to compute an average student registration number, the average sex of the respondents in a survey, or the number assigned to an average bank, as in the following example.

GLOBALCASH PROJECT

Nominal scale

In the GlobalCash project, the numbers 1 through to 100 were assigned to banks that were revealed as those most frequently used (from the 1996 GlobalCash study) (see extracts from the list in Table 10.2). Thus, bank 48 referred to Credit Lyonnais in France. It did not imply that Credit Lyonnais was in any way superior or inferior to Den Danske Bank, which was assigned the number 54. Any reassignment of the numbers, such as transposing the numbers assigned to Credit Lyonnais and Den Danske Bank, would have no effect on the numbering system, because the numerals did not reflect any characteristics of the banks. It is meaningful to make statements such as '25 per cent of French respondents named Credit Lyonnais as their lead bank'. Although the average of the assigned numbers is 50.5, it is not meaningful to state that the number of the average bank is 50.5. When all the questionnaires were returned from the GlobalCash survey, over 400 banks were named, each assigned an unique number. ■

Table 10.2 Illustration of primary scales of measurement

Nominal scale		*Ordinal scale*		*Interval scale*		*Ratio scale*
No.	*Bank*	*Preference rankings*		*Preference ratings*		
				1–7	*11–17*	
1	ABN AMRO	1	10	7	17	60%
11	Banco Bilbao Vizcaya			4	14	0%
23	Bank Brussels Lambert			5	15	0%
27	Bank of Ireland			7	17	0%
37	Budapest Bank			5	15	0%
44	Citibank	3	50	5	15	30%
48	Credit Lyonnais			6	16	0%
54	Den Danske Bank			6	16	0%
56	Deutsche Bank	2	25	7	17	10%
80	Okobank Finland			2	12	0%

Ordinal scale

Ordinal scale
A ranking scale in which numbers are assigned to objects to indicate the relative extent to which some characteristic is possessed. Thus, it is possible to determine whether an object has more or less of a characteristic than some other object.

An **ordinal scale** is a ranking scale in which numbers are assigned to objects to indicate the relative extent to which the objects possess some characteristic. An ordinal scale allows you to determine whether an object has more or less of a characteristic than some other object, but not how much more or less. Thus, an ordinal scale indicates relative position, not the magnitude of the differences between the objects. The object ranked first has more of the characteristic as compared with the object ranked second, but whether the object ranked second is a close second or a poor second is not known. Common examples of ordinal scales include quality rankings, rankings of teams in a tournament and occupational status. In marketing research, ordinal scales are used to measure relative attitudes, opinions, perceptions and preferences. Measurements of this type include 'greater than' or 'less than' judgements from the respondents.

In an ordinal scale, as in a nominal scale, equivalent objects receive the same rank. Any series of numbers can be assigned that preserves the ordered relationships between the objects. For example, ordinal scales can be transformed in any way as long as the basic ordering of the objects is maintained.[4] In other words, any monotonic positive (order preserving) transformation of the scale is permissible, since the differences in numbers are void of any meaning other than order (see the following example). For these reasons, in addition to the counting operation allowable for nominal scale data, ordinal scales permit the use of statistics based on centiles. It is meaningful to calculate percentile, quartile, median (Chapter 17), rank-order correlation (Chapter 19) or other summary statistics from ordinal data.

GLOBALCASH PROJECT

Ordinal scale

Table 10.2 gives a particular respondent's preference rankings. Respondents ranked three banks in order of who they preferred to do business with, showing their 'lead bank', 'second bank' and 'third bank', by assigning a rank 1 to the lead, rank 2 to the second bank, and so on. Note that ABN AMRO (ranked 1), is preferred to Deutsche Bank (ranked 2), but how much it is preferred we do not know. Also, it is not necessary that we assign numbers from 1 to 3 to obtain a preference ranking. The second ordinal scale, which assigns a number 10 to ABN AMRO, 25 to Deutsche, 50 to Citibank, is an equivalent scale, as it was obtained by a monotonic positive transformation of the first scale. The two scales result in the same ordering of the banks according to preference. ■

Interval scale

Interval scale
A scale in which the numbers are used to rank objects such that numerically equal distances on the scale represent equal distances in the characteristic being measured.

In an **interval scale**, numerically equal distances on the scale represent equal values in the characteristic being measured. An interval scale contains all the information of an ordinal scale, but it also allows you to compare the differences between objects. The difference between any two scale values is identical to the difference between any other two adjacent values of an interval scale. There is a constant or equal interval between scale values. The difference between 1 and 2 is the same as the difference between 2 and 3, which is the same as the difference between 5 and 6. A common example in everyday life is a temperature scale. In marketing research, attitudinal data obtained from rating scales are often treated as interval data.[5]

In an interval scale, the location of the zero point is not fixed. Both the zero point and the units of measurement are arbitrary. Hence, any positive linear transformation of the form $y = a + bx$ will preserve the properties of the scale. Here, x is the original scale value, y is the transformed scale value, b is a positive constant, and a is any constant. Therefore, two interval scales that rate objects A, B, C, and D as 1, 2, 3 and 4 or as 22, 24, 26 and 28 are equivalent. Note that the latter scale can be derived from the former by using $a = 20$ and $b = 2$ in the transforming equation.

Because the zero point is not fixed, it is not meaningful to take ratios of scale values. As can be seen, the ratio of D to B values changes from 2:1 to 7:6 when the scale is transformed. Yet, ratios of differences between scale values are permissible. In this process, the constants *a* and *b* in the transforming equation drop out in the computations. The ratio of the difference between *D* and *B* to the difference between *C* and *B* is 2:1 in both the scales.

Statistical techniques that may be used on interval scale data include all those that can be applied to nominal and ordinal data in addition to the arithmetic mean, standard deviation (Chapter 17), product moment correlations (Chapter 19), and other statistics commonly used in marketing research. Certain specialised statistics such as geometric mean, harmonic mean and coefficient of variation, however, are not meaningful on interval scale data. The GlobalCash example gives a further illustration of an interval scale.

GLOBALCASH PROJECT

Interval scale

In Table 10.2, a respondent's preferences for conducting any transactions with the ten named banks are expressed on a seven-point rating scale. What is being measured differs from the ordinal scale example. A company may appoint several banks to handle transactions, using the bank's expertise in particular industries or in particular regions. In the ordinal scale example, preference was expressed for which bank a company respondent liked to work with – out of the three the company had appointed. In this example, the company rates banks based on their experience with the bank – a bank that may not be of their choice to do business with, it is one of their client's banks. We can see that although Den Danske received a preference rating of 6 and Okobank a rating of 2, this does not mean that Den Danske is preferred three times as much as Okobank. When the ratings are transformed to an equivalent 11 to 17 scale (next column), the ratings for these stores become 16 and 12, and the ratio is no longer 3:1. In contrast, the ratios of preference differences are identical on the two scales. The ratio of the preference difference ABN AMRO and Okobank to the preference difference between Budapest Bank and Okobank is 5:3 on both the scales. ■

Ratio scale

Ratio scale
The highest scale, this scale allows the researcher to identify or classify objects, rank order the objects, and compare intervals or differences. It is also meaningful to compute ratios of scale values.

A **ratio scale** possesses all the properties of the nominal, ordinal and interval scales, and, in addition, an absolute zero point. Thus, in ratio scales we can identify or classify objects, rank the objects, and compare intervals or differences. It is also meaningful to compute ratios of scale values. Not only is the difference between 2 and 5 the same as the difference between 14 and 17, but also 14 is seven times as large as 2 in an absolute sense. Common examples of ratio scales include height, weight, age and money. In marketing, sales, costs, market share and number of customers are variables measured on a ratio scale.

Ratio scales allow only proportionate transformations of the form $y = bx$, where b is a positive constant. One cannot add an arbitrary constant, as in the case of an interval scale. An example of this transformation is provided by the conversion of yards to feet ($b = 3$). The comparisons between the objects are identical whether made in yards or feet.

All statistical techniques can be applied to ratio data. These include specialised statistics such as geometric mean, harmonic mean, and coefficient of variation. The ratio scale is further illustrated in the context of the GlobalCash example.

GLOBALCASH PROJECT

Ratio scale

In the ratio scale illustrated in Table 10.2, respondents were asked to indicate the percentage of business transactions that they conduct with each of the banks they named as lead, second and third banks. Note that since this respondent conducted 60 per cent of their business transactions with ABN AMRO and 10 per cent with Deutsche Bank, this person conducted six times as much business in ABN AMRO compared to Deutsche Bank. Also, the zero point is fixed, since 0 means that the respondent did not do any business with that bank (though their clients may have, hence their exposure to the bank). Note that the rank order of the amount of business conducted with the three banks does not match the rank order of preference of doing business with a particular bank – named as 'lead', 'second' and 'third'. Companies working in a particular region where a bank has expertise may be 'forced' to conduct business with that bank. However, they may prefer to do business with another bank but the percentage of business is low as they do not have a particular industry or regional expertise. ■

The four primary scales (discussed here) do not exhaust the measurement level categories. It is possible to construct a nominal scale that provides partial information on order (the partially ordered scale). Likewise, an ordinal scale can convey partial information on distance, as in the case of an ordered metric scale. A discussion of these scales is beyond the scope of this text.[6]

A COMPARISON OF SCALING TECHNIQUES

Comparative scales
One of two types of scaling techniques in which there is direct comparison of stimulus objects with one another.

The scaling techniques commonly employed in marketing research can be classified into comparative and non-comparative scales (see Figure 10.2). **Comparative scales** involve the direct comparison of stimulus objects. For example, respondents may be asked whether they prefer Coke or Pepsi. Comparative scale data must be interpreted in relative terms and have only ordinal or rank order properties. For this reason, comparative scaling is also referred to as non-metric scaling. As shown in Figure 10.2, comparative scales include paired comparisons, rank order, constant sum scales, Q-sort and other procedures. The major benefit of comparative scaling is that small differences between stimulus objects can be detected. As they compare the stimulus objects, respondents are forced to choose between them.

In addition, respondents approach the rating task from the same known reference points. Consequently, comparative scales are easily understood and can be applied easily. Other advantages of these scales are that they involve fewer theoretical assumptions, and they also tend to reduce halo or carryover effects from one judgement to another.[7] The major disadvantages of comparative scales include the ordinal nature of the data and the inability to generalise beyond the stimulus objects scaled. For instance, to compare Virgin Cola to Coke and Pepsi the researcher would have to do a new study. These disadvantages are substantially overcome by the non-comparative scaling techniques.

Non-comparitive scales
One of two types of scaling techniques in which each stimulus object is scaled independently of the other objects in the stimulus set.

In **non-comparative scales**, also referred to as monadic or metric scales, each object is scaled independently of the others in the stimulus set. The resulting data are generally assumed to be interval or ratio scaled.[8] For example, respondents may be asked to evaluate Coke on a 1 to 6 preference scale (1 = not all preferred, 6 = greatly preferred). Similar evaluations would be obtained for Pepsi

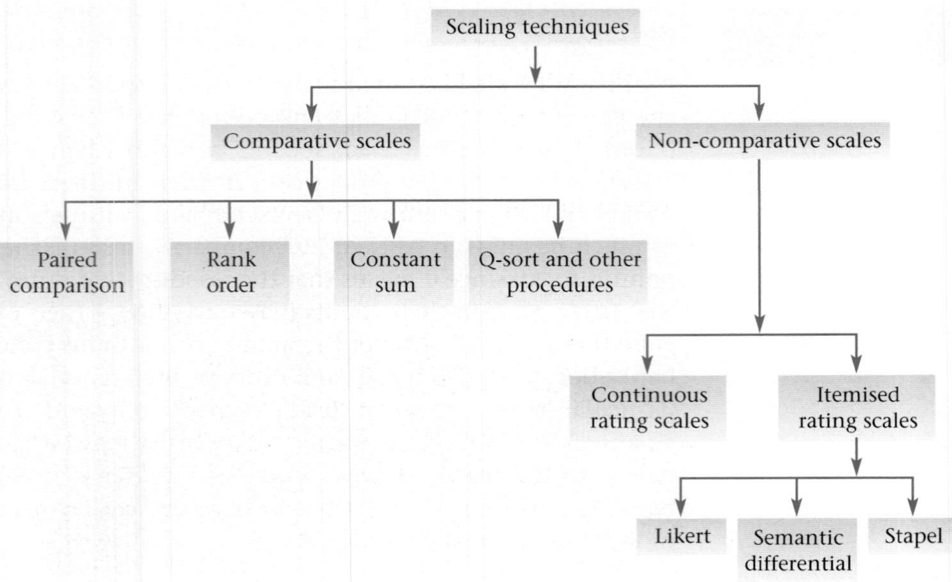

Figure 10.2
A classification of scaling techniques

and Virgin Cola. As can be seen in Figure 10.2, non-comparative scales can be continuous rating or itemised rating scales. The itemised rating scales can be further classified as Likert, semantic differential, or Stapel scales. Non-comparative scaling is the most widely used scaling technique in marketing research. Given its importance, Chapter 11 is devoted to non-comparative scaling. The rest of this chapter focuses on comparative scaling techniques.

COMPARATIVE SCALING TECHNIQUES

Paired comparison scaling

Paired comparison scaling
A comparative scaling technique in which a respondent is presented with two objects at a time and asked to select one object in the pair according to some criterion. The data obtained are ordinal in nature.

As its name implies, in **paired comparison scaling** a respondent is presented with two objects and asked to select one according to some criterion.[9] The data obtained are ordinal in nature. A respondent may state that he or she prefers Belgian chocolate to Swiss, likes Kellogg's cereals better than supermarket home brands, or likes Adidas more than Nike. Paired comparison scales are frequently used when the stimulus objects are physical products. Coca-Cola is reported

A paired comparison test.

to have conducted more than 190,000 paired comparisons before introducing New Coke.[10] Paired comparison scaling is the most widely used comparative scaling technique.

Figure 10.3 shows paired comparison data obtained to assess a respondent's bottled beer preferences. As can be seen, this respondent made ten comparisons to evaluate five brands. In general, with n brands, $[n(n - 1)/2]$ paired comparisons include all possible pairings of objects.[11]

The Munich Oktoberfest – perhaps not the best place to conduct paired comparisons of bottled beer preferences.
Tony Stone

Paired comparison data can be analysed in several ways.[12] The researcher can calculate the percentage of respondents who prefer one stimulus over another by summing the matrices of Figure 10.3 for all the respondents, dividing the sum by the number of respondents, and multiplying by 100. Simultaneous evaluation of all the stimulus objects is also possible. Under the assumption of transitivity, it is possible to convert paired comparison data to a rank order.

Transitivity of preference
An assumption made to convert paired comparison data to rank order data. It implies that if brand A is preferred to brand B and brand B is preferred to brand C, then brand A is preferred to brand C.

Transitivity of preference implies that if brand A is preferred to B, and brand B is preferred to C, then brand A is preferred to C. To arrive at a rank order, the researcher determines the number of times each brand is preferred by summing the column entries in Figure 10.3. Therefore, this respondent's order of preference, from most to the least preferred, is Carlsberg, Holsten, Stella Artois, Budvar and Grolsch. It is also possible to derive an interval scale from paired comparison data using the Thurstone case V procedure. Refer to the appropriate literature for a discussion of this procedure.[13]

Several modifications of the paired comparison technique have been suggested. One involves the inclusion of a neutral/no difference/no opinion response. Another extension is graded paired comparisons. In this method, respondents are asked which brand in the pair is preferred and how much it is preferred. The degree of preference may be expressed by how much more the respondent is willing to pay for the preferred brand. The resulting scale is a Euro metric scale. Another modification of paired comparison scaling is widely used in obtaining similarity judgements in multidimensional scaling (see Chapter 23).

Instructions
We are going to present you with ten pairs of bottled beer brands. For each pair, please indicate which of the two brands of beer in the pair you prefer.

Recording form

	Holsten	Stella Artois	Grolsch	Carlsberg	Budvar
Holsten		0	0	1	0
Stella Artois	1[a]		0	1	0
Grolsch	1	1		1	1
Carlsberg	0	0	0		0
Budvar	1	1	0	1	
Number of times preferred[b]	3	2	0	4	1

[a] 1 in a particular box means that the brand in that column was preferred over the brand in the corresponding row. A 0 means that the row brand was preferred over the column brand.

[b] The number of times a brand was preferred is obtained by summing the 1s in each column.

Figure 10.3
Obtaining bottled beer preferences using paired comparisons

Paired comparison scaling is useful when the number of brands is limited, since it requires direct comparison and overt choice. With a large number of brands, however, the number of comparisons becomes unwieldy. Other disadvantages are that violations of the assumption of transitivity may occur, and the order in which the objects are presented may bias the results.[14] Paired comparisons bear little resemblance to the marketplace situation, which involves selection from multiple alternatives. Also respondents may prefer one object over certain others, but they may not like it in an absolute sense. The following example provides further insights into paired comparison scaling.

EXAMPLE

Paired comparison scaling[15]

The most common method of taste testing is paired comparison. The consumer is asked to sample two different products and select the one with the most appealing taste. The test is done in private, either in homes or other predetermined sites. A minimum of 1000 responses is considered an adequate sample. A blind taste test for a soft drink, where imagery, self-perception and brand reputation are very important factors in the consumer's purchasing decision, may not be a good indicator of performance in the marketplace. The introduction of New Coke illustrates this point. New Coke was heavily favoured in blind paired comparison taste tests, but its introduction was less than successful, because image plays such a significant role in the purchase of Coke. ■

Rank order scaling

Rank order scaling
A comparative scaling technique in which respondents are presented with several objects simultaneously and asked to order or rank them according to some criterion.

After paired comparisons, the most popular comparative scaling technique is **rank order scaling**. In rank order scaling respondents are presented with several objects simultaneously and asked to order or rank them according to some criterion. For example, respondents may be asked to rank brands of cars according to overall preference. As shown in Figure 10.4, these rankings are typically obtained by asking the respondents to assign a rank of 1 to the most preferred brand, 2 to the second most preferred, and so on, until a rank of n is assigned to the least

Instructions

Rank the various brands of car in order of preference. Begin by picking out the one brand that you like most and assign it a number 1. Then find the second most preferred brand and assign it a number 2. Continue this procedure until you have ranked all the brands of car in order of preference. The least preferred brand should be assigned a rank of 10.

No two brands should receive the same rank number

The criterion of preference is entirely up to you. There is no right or wrong answer. Just try to be consistent.

	Brand	*Rank order*
1	Porsche	
2	Jaguar	
3	BMW	
4	Bristol	
5	Aston Martin	
6	Mercedes	
7	McLaren	
8	Ferrari	
9	Lamborghini	
10	Bentley	

Figure 10.4
Preference for car brands using rank order scaling

preferred brand. Like paired comparison, this approach is also comparative in nature, and it is possible that the respondent may dislike the brand ranked 1 in an absolute sense. Furthermore, rank order scaling also results in ordinal data. See Table 10.2, which uses rank order scaling to derive an ordinal scale.

Rank order scaling is commonly used to measure preferences for brands as well as attributes. Rank order data are frequently obtained from respondents in conjoint analysis (see Chapter 23), since rank order scaling forces the respondent to discriminate among the stimulus objects. Moreover, as compared with paired comparisons, this type of scaling process more closely resembles the shopping environment. It also takes less time and eliminates intransitive responses. If there are n stimulus objects, only $(n - 1)$ scaling decisions need be made in rank order scaling. However, in paired comparison scaling, $[n(n - 1)/2]$ decisions would be required. Another advantage is that most respondents easily understand the instructions for ranking. The major disadvantage is that this technique produces only ordinal data.

Finally, under the assumption of transitivity, rank order data can be converted to equivalent paired comparison data, and vice versa. This point was illustrated by Figure 10.3. Hence, it is possible to derive an interval scale from rankings using the Thurstone case V procedure. Other approaches for deriving interval scales from rankings have also been suggested.[16]

Constant sum scaling

Constant sum scaling
A comparative scaling technique in which respondents are required to allocate a constant sum of units such as points, dollars, chits, stickers, or chips among a set of stimulus objects with respect to some criterion.

In **constant sum scaling**, respondents allocate a constant sum of units, such as points or Euros, among a set of stimulus objects with respect to some criterion. As shown in Figure 10.5, respondents may be asked to allocate 100 points to attributes of a bottled beers in a way that reflects the importance they attach to each attribute. If an attribute is unimportant, the respondent assigns it zero points. If an attribute is twice as important as some other attribute, it receives twice as many points. The sum of all the points is 100. Hence, the name of the scale.

Instructions

Below are eight attributes of bottled beers. Please allocate 100 points among the attributes so that your allocation reflects the relative importance you attach to each attribute. The more points an attribute receives, the more important an attribute is. If an attribute is not at all important, assign it no points. If an attribute is twice as important as some other attribute, it should receive twice as many points.

Form

AVERAGE RESPONSES OF THREE SEGMENTS				
	Attribute	Segment I	Segment II	Segment III
1	Bitterness	8	2	17
2	Hop flavours	2	4	20
3	Fragrance	3	9	19
4	Country where brewed	9	17	4
5	Price	53	5	7
6	High alcohol level	7	60	9
7	Aftertaste	5	0	15
8	Package design	13	3	9
	Sum	100	100	100

Figure 10.5 Importance of bottled beer attributes using a constant sum scale

The attributes are scaled by counting the points assigned to each one by all the respondents and dividing by the number of respondents. These results are presented for three groups, or segments, of respondents in Figure 10.5. Segment I attaches overwhelming importance to price. Segment II considers a high alcoholic level to be of prime importance. Segment III values bitterness, hop flavours, fragrance and the aftertaste. Such information cannot be obtained from rank order data unless they are transformed into interval data. Note that the constant sum also has an absolute zero; 10 points are twice as many as 5 points, and the difference between 5 and 2 points is the same as the difference between 57 and 54 points. For this reason, constant sum scale data are sometimes treated as metric. Although this may be appropriate in the limited context of the stimuli scaled, these results are not generalisable to other stimuli not included in the study. Hence, strictly speaking, the constant sum should be considered an ordinal scale because of its comparative nature and the resulting lack of generalisability. It can be seen that the allocation of points in Figure 10.5 is influenced by the specific attributes included in the evaluation task.

The main advantage of the constant sum scale is that it allows for fine discrimination among stimulus objects without requiring too much time. It has two primary disadvantages, however. Respondents may allocate more or fewer units than those specified. For example, a respondent may allocate 108 or 94 points. The researcher must modify such data in some way or eliminate this respondent from analysis. Another potential problem is rounding error if too few units are used. On the other hand, the use of a large number of units may be too taxing on the respondent and cause confusion and fatigue.

Q-sort and other procedures

Q-sort scaling
A comparative scaling technique that uses a rank order procedure to sort objects based on similarity with respect to some criterion.

Q-sort scaling was developed to discriminate among a relatively large number of objects quickly. This technique uses a rank order procedure in which objects are sorted into piles based on similarity with respect to some criterion. For example, respondents are given 100 attitude statements on individual cards and asked to place them into 11 piles, ranging from 'most highly agreed with' to 'least highly agreed with'. The number of objects to be sorted should not be less than 60 nor more than 140; a reasonable range is 60 to 90 objects.[17] The number of objects to be placed in each pile is pre-specified, often to result in a roughly normal distribution of objects over the whole set.

Another comparative scaling technique is magnitude estimation.[18] In this technique, numbers are assigned to objects such that ratios between the assigned numbers reflect ratios on the specified criterion. For example, respondents may be asked to indicate whether they agree or disagree with each of a series of statements measuring attitude toward banks. Then they assign a number between 0 to 100 to each statement to indicate the intensity of their agreement or disagreement. Providing this type of numbers imposes a cognitive burden on the respondents. Finally, mention must be made of Guttman scaling, or scalogram analysis, a procedure for determining whether a set of objects can be ordered into an internally consistent, uni-dimensional scale.

VERBAL PROTOCOLS

Verbal protocol
A technique used to understand respondents' cognitive responses or thought processes by having them think aloud while completing a task or making a decision.

A particularly useful approach for measuring cognitive responses or thought processes consists of **verbal protocols**. Respondents are asked to 'think out loud' and verbalise anything going through their heads while making a decision or performing a task.[19] The researcher says, 'If you think anything, say it aloud, no matter how trivial the thought may be'. Even with such explicit instruction, the respondent may be silent. At these times, the researcher will say, 'Remember to say aloud everything you are thinking'. Everything that the respondent says is tape recorded. This record of the respondent's verbalised thought processes is referred to as a protocol.[20]

Protocols have been used to measure consumers' cognitive responses in actual shopping trips as well as in simulated shopping environments. An interviewer accompanies the respondent and holds a microphone into which the respondent talks. Protocols, thus collected, have been used to determine the attributes and cues used in making purchase decisions, product usage behaviour, and the impact of the shopping environment on consumer decisions. Protocol analysis has also been employed to measure consumer response to advertising. Immediately after seeing an ad, the respondent is asked to list all the thoughts that came to mind while watching the ad. The respondent is given a limited amount of time to list the thoughts so as to minimise the probability of collecting thoughts generated after, rather than during, the message. After the protocol has been collected, the individual's thoughts or cognitive responses are coded into three categories.[21]

Category	*Definition*	*Example*
Support argument	Support the claim made by the message	'Diet Coke tastes great'
Counter-argument	Refute the claim made by the message	'Diet Coke has an aftertaste'
Source derogation	Negative opinion about the source of the message	'Coca-Cola is not an honest company'

Protocols are, typically, incomplete. The respondent has many thoughts that she or he cannot or will not verbalise. The researcher must take the incomplete record and infer from it a measure of the underlying cognitive response.

INTERNATIONAL MARKETING RESEARCH

In the four primary scales, the level of measurement increases from nominal to ordinal to interval to ratio scale. This increase in measurement level is obtained at the cost of complexity. From the viewpoint of the respondents, nominal scales are the simplest to use whereas the ratio scales are the most complex. Respondents in many developed countries, due to higher education and consumer sophistication levels, are quite used to providing responses on interval and ratio scales. It has been argued[22] that opinion formation may not be well crystallised in some developing countries, however. Hence, these respondents experience difficulty in expressing the gradation required by interval and ratio scales. Preferences can, therefore, be best measured by using ordinal scales. In particular, the use of binary scales (e.g. preferred/not preferred), the simplest type of ordinal scale, has been recommended. For example, while measuring preferences for jeans in Europe, Levi Strauss and Company could ask consumers to rate their preferences for wearing jeans on specified occasions using a seven-point interval scale. Consumers in Papua New Guinea, however, could be shown a pair of jeans and simply asked whether or not they would prefer to wear them for a specific occasion (e.g. when shopping, working, relaxing on a holiday). Bear in mind however that this example is very generalised, given the vast array of differences in intellectual ability and motivation to participate in marketing research throughout Europe and indeed Papua New Guinea!

It should also be noted that comparative scales, except for paired comparisons, require comparisons of multiple stimulus objects and are, therefore, taxing on the respondents. In contrast, in non-comparative scales, each object is scaled independently of others in the stimulus set, that is, objects are scaled one at a time. Hence, non-comparative scales are simpler to administer and more appropriate in cultures where the respondents are less educated or are unfamiliar with marketing research.

ETHICS IN MARKETING RESEARCH

The researcher has the responsibility to use the appropriate type of scales to get the data needed to answer the research questions and test any hypotheses. Take, for example, a newspaper like *Der Spiegel* wanting information on the personality profiles of its readers and non-readers. Information on the personality characteristics might best be obtained by giving respondents (readers and non-readers) several Velcro nameplates, each listing one personality characteristic. Respondents are also given a felt board on which to arrange the nameplates. The researcher then instructs the respondents to rank order the personality characteristics, listing, in order, those they believe describe their personality best first, and those which do not describe themselves last. This results in ordinal data. Although it will provide rich insight into the personality characteristics by allowing respondents to compare personality characteristics, shuffle them, compare again and reshuffle, these data cannot easily be used in multivariate analysis. To examine differences in the personality characteristics of readers and non-readers and relate them to other consumer behaviour variables, interval scale data are needed. It is the obligation of the researcher to obtain the data that are most appropriate given the research questions that they have negotiated with the marketing decision-making they are supporting, providing the task is manageable by the target respondents. The following example illustrates this issue.

EXAMPLE

Sealing ethical dilemmas[23]

In a study designed to measure ethical judgements of marketing researchers, scale items from a previously developed and tested scale were used. After a pre-test was conducted on a convenience sample of 65 marketing professionals, it became apparent that some original scale items were worded in a way that did not reflect current usage. Therefore, these items were updated. For example, an item that was gender specific, such as 'He pointed out that ...', was altered to read 'The project manager pointed out that ... '. Respondents were requested to show their approval or disapproval of the stated action (item) of a marketing research director with regard to specific scenarios. Realising that a binary or dichotomous scale would be too restrictive, approval or disapproval was indicated by having respondents supply interval level data via five point scales with descriptive anchors of 1 = disapprove, 2 = disapprove somewhat, 3 = neither approve or disapprove, 4 = approve somewhat, and 5 = approve. In this way, scaling dilemmas were resolved.

After the data have been collected, they should be analysed correctly. If nominal scaled data are gathered then statistics permissible for nominal scaled data must be used. Likewise, when ordinal scale data are collected, statistical procedures developed for use with interval or ratio data should not be used. Conclusions based on the misuse of statistics are misleading. In the *Der Spiegel* example, ordinal data would be collected. If after collection the client wishes to know how the readers and the non-readers differed, the researcher should treat these data correctly and use non-metric techniques for analysis (discussed in Chapter 17). When the researcher lacks the expertise or the computer software to compute these statistics, ethical dilemmas arise. Researchers know that they should admit to their shortcomings and should see to it that correct statistics are computed. Either an outside statistician should be hired or the relevant software should be obtained. Admitting your shortcomings, however, is rarely easy.

INTERNET AND COMPUTER APPLICATIONS

All the primary scales of measurement that we have considered can be implemented on the Internet. The same is true for the commonly used comparative scales. Paired comparisons involving verbal, visual or auditory comparisons can be implemented with ease. However, taste, smell and touch comparisons are difficult to implement. It may also be difficult to implement specialised scales such as the Q-sort. The process of implementing comparative scales may be facilitated by searching the Internet for similar scales that have been implemented by other researchers.

SUMMARY

Measurement is the assignment of numbers or other symbols to characteristics of objects according to set rules. Scaling involves the generation of a continuum upon which measured objects are located. The four primary scales of measurement are nominal, ordinal, interval and ratio. Of these, the nominal scale is the most basic in that the numbers are used only for identifying or classifying objects. In the ordinal scale, the next higher-level scale, the numbers indicate the relative position of the objects but not the magnitude of difference between them. The interval scale permits a comparison of the differences between the objects. Because it has an arbitrary zero point, however, it is not meaningful to calculate ratios of scale values on an interval scale. The highest level of measurement is represented by the ratio scale in which the zero point is fixed. The researcher can compute ratios of scale values using this scale. The ratio scale incorporates all the properties of the lower-level scales.

Scaling techniques can be classified as comparative or non-comparative. Comparative scaling involves a direct comparison of stimulus objects. Comparative scales include paired comparisons, rank order, constant sum and the Q-sort. The data obtained by these procedures have only ordinal properties. Verbal protocols, where the respondent is instructed to think out loud, can be used for measuring cognitive responses.

Respondents in many developed countries, due to higher education and consumer sophistication levels, are quite used to providing responses on interval and ratio scales. In developing countries, however, preferences may be best measured by using ordinal scales. Ethical considerations require that appropriate type of scales be used to get the data needed to answer the research questions and test the hypotheses.

QUESTIONS AND PROBLEMS

1 What is measurement?

2 Highlight any marketing phenomena that you feel may be problematic in terms of assigning numbers to characteristics of that phenomena.

3 What are the primary scales of measurement?

4 Describe and illustrate with examples, the differences between a nominal and an ordinal scale.

5 What are the implications of having an arbitrary zero point in an interval scale?

6 What are the advantages of a ratio scale over an interval scale? Are these advantages significant?

7 What is a comparative rating scale ?

8 What is a paired comparison?

9 What are the advantages and disadvantages of paired comparison scaling?

10 Describe the constant sum scale. How is it different from the other comparative rating scales?

11 What types of respondent may have difficulty in coping with rank-order and constant sum scaling?

12 Describe the Q-sort methodology.

13 What is a verbal protocol? How are verbal protocols used?

14 Identify the type of scale (nominal, ordinal, interval or ratio) used in each of the following.

Give reasons for your choice.

(a) I like to listen to the radio when I am revising for exams

Disagree				*Agree*
1	2	3	4	5

(b) How old are you? ____________

(c) Rank the following activities in terms of your preference by assigning a rank from 1 to 5.

(1 = most preferred, 2 = second most preferred, etc.)
(i) Reading magazines
(ii) Watching television
(iii) Going to the cinema
(iv) Shopping for clothes
(v) Eating out

(d) What is your university/college registration number? __________

(e) In an average week day, how much time do you spend doing class assignments?
(i) Less than 15 minutes
(ii) 15 to 30 minutes
(iii) 31 to 60 minutes
(iv) 61 to 120 minutes
(v) More than 120 minutes

(f) How much money did you spend last week in the Student Union Bar? ______

15 Suppose each of the questions (a) through to (f) in Question 14 were administered to 100 respondents. Identify the kind of analysis that should be done for each question to summarise the results.

NOTES

1 *Business Week* (14 December 1992).

2 Doucette, W.R. and Wiederholt, J.B., 'Measuring Product Meaning for Prescribed Medication Using a Means-End Model', *Journal of Health Care Marketing* 12 (March 1992), 48–54; and Nunnally, J.C., *Psychometric Theory,* 2nd edn (New York: McGraw-Hill, 1978), 3.

3 Stevens, S., 'Mathematics, Measurement and Psychophysics', in Stevens, S. (ed.), *Handbook of Experimental Psychology* (New York: Wiley, 1951).

4 Barnard, N.R. and Ehrenberg, A.S.C., 'Robust Measures of Consumer Brand Beliefs', *Journal of Marketing Research* 27 (November 1990), 477–84; and Perreault, W.D. Jr, and Young, F.W., 'Alternating Least Squares Optimal Scaling: Analysis of Nonmetric Data in Marketing Research', *Journal of Marketing Research* 17 (February 1980), 1–13.

5 Albaum, G., Best, R. and Hawkins, D.I., 'Measurement Properties of Semantic Scale Data', *Journal of the Market Research Society* (January 1977), 21–28; and Taylor, M., 'Ordinal and Interval Scaling', *Journal of the Market Research Society* 25 (4), 297–303.

6 For a discussion of these scales, refer to Coombs, C.H., 'Theory and Methods of Social Measurement', in Festinger, L. and Katz, D. (eds), *Research Methods in the Behavioural Sciences* (New York: Holt, Rinehart and Winston, 1953).

7 Bastell, R.R. and Wind, Y., 'Product Development: Current Methods and Needed Developments', *Journal of the Market Research Society* 8 (1980), 122–26.

8 There is, however, some controversy regarding this issue. See Mullet, G.M., 'Itemised Rating Scales: Ordinal or Interval', *European Research* (April 1983), 49–52.

9 Corfman, K.P., 'Comparability and Comparison Levels Used in Choices among Consumer Products', *Journal of Marketing Research* 28 (August 1991), 368–74; Buchanan, B.S. and Morrison, D.G., 'Taste Tests', *Psychology and Marketing* (Spring 1984), 69–91.

10 'Coke's Flip-Flop Underscores Risks of Consumer Taste Tests', *Wall Street Journal* (18 July 1985), 25.

11 It is not necessary to evaluate all possible pairs of objects, however. Procedures such as cyclic designs can significantly reduce the number of pairs evaluated. A

treatment of such procedures may be found in Malhotra, N.K., Jain, A.K. and Pinson, C., 'The Robustness of MDS Configurations in the Case of Incomplete Data', *Journal of Marketing Research* 25 (February 1988), 95–102.

12 For an advanced application involving paired comparison data, see Dillon, W.R., Kumar, A. and de Borrero, M.S., 'Capturing Individual Differences in Paired Comparisons: An Extended BTL Model Incorporating Descriptor Variables', *Journal of Marketing Research* 30 (February 1993), 42–51.

13 Thurstone, L.L., *The Measurement of Values* (Chicago: University of Chicago Press, 1959). For an application of the case V procedure, see Malhotra, N.K., 'Marketing Linen Services to Hospitals: A Conceptual Framework and an Empirical Investigation Using Thurstone's Case V Analysis', *Journal of Health Care Marketing* 6 (March 1986), 43–50.

14 Daniles, E. and Lawford, J., 'The Effect of Order in the Presentation of Samples in Paired Comparison Tests', *Journal of the Market Research Society* 16 (April 1974), 127–33.

15 Davis, T., 'Taste Tests: Are the Blind Leading the Blind?', *Beverage World* (April 1987), 43–48, 85.

16 Hays, W.L., *Quantification in Psychology* (Belmont, CA: Brooks/Cole, 1967), 35–39.

17 Kerlinger, F., *Foundations of Behavioural Research*, 3rd edn (New York: Holt, Rinehart and Winston, 1973), 583–92.

18 Moskowitz, H.R., Jacobs, B. and Firtle, N., 'Discrimination Testing and Product Decisions', *Journal of Marketing Research* (February 1980), 84–90.

19 Hayes, J.R. 'Issues in Protocol Analysis', in Ungson, G.R. and Braunste, D.N. (eds), *Decision Making: An Interdisciplinary Inquiry* (Boston: Kent Publishing, 1982), 61–77.

20 For an application of verbal protocols, see Gardial, S.E., Clemons, D.S., Woodruff, R.B., Schumann, D.W. and Bums, M.J., 'Comparing Consumers' Recall of Prepurchase and Postpurchase Product Evaluation Experiences', *Journal of Consumer Research* 20 (March 1994), 548–60.

21 Mick, D.G., 'Levels of Subjective Comprehension in Advertising Processing and Their Relations to Ad Perceptions, Attitudes, and Memory', *Journal of Consumer Research* 18 (March 1992), 411–24; Wright, P.L., 'Cognitive Processes Mediating Acceptance of Advertising', *Journal of Marketing Research* 10 (February 1973), 53–62; and Wright, P.L.,'Cognitive Responses to Mass Media Advocacy and Cognitive Choice Processes', in Petty, R., Ostrum, T. and Brock, T., (eds), *Cognitive Responses to Persuasion* (New York: McGraw-Hill, 1978).

22 Malhotra, N.K., 'A Methodology for Measuring Consumer Preferences in Developing Countries', *International Marketing Review* 5 (Autumn 1988), 52–66.

23 Akaah, I.P., 'Differences in Research Ethics Judgements Between Male and Female Marketing Professionals', *Journal of Business Ethics* 8 (1989), 375–81.

Chapter 11

Measurement and scaling: non-comparative scaling techniques

Scales should be evaluated by examining reliability and validity

OBJECTIVES

After reading this chapter, the student should be able to:

1 describe the non-comparative scaling techniques, distinguish between continuous and itemised rating scales, and explain Likert, semantic differential, and Stapel scales;
2 discuss the decisions involved in constructing itemised rating scales with respect to the number of scale categories, balanced versus unbalanced scales, odd or even number of categories, forced versus non-forced choice, degree of verbal description, and the physical form of the scale;
3 discuss the criteria used for scale evaluation and explain how to assess reliability, validity and generalisability;
4 discuss the considerations involved in implementing non-comparative scales in an international setting;
5 understand the ethical issues involved in developing non-comparative scales;

OVERVIEW

As discussed in Chapter 10, scaling techniques are classified as comparative or non-comparative. The comparative techniques, consisting of paired comparison, rank order, constant sum and Q-sort scaling were discussed in the last chapter. The subject of this chapter is non-comparative techniques, which are composed of continuous and itemised rating scales. We discuss the popular itemised rating scales – the Likert, semantic differential, and Stapel scales – as well as the construction of multi-item rating scales. We show how scaling techniques should be evaluated in terms of reliability and validity and consider how the researcher selects a particular scaling technique. Mathematically derived scales are also presented. The considerations involved in implementing non-comparative scales when researching international markets are discussed. The chapter concludes with a discussion of several ethical issues that arise in rating scale construction. We begin with two examples of the use of common non-comparative scaling techniques.

EXAMPLE

Super Markets[1]

In a survey of services industries conducted by the Gallup Organisation, respondents were asked to rate services on a 10-point Likert scale, with 1 signifying low quality and 10 signifying very high quality. Over half the respondents gave supermarkets a rating of 8 or better. Restaurants and banks were also well regarded. Hotels, department stores, insurance companies, car repair companies and airlines ended up in the middle. Towards the bottom of the scale were local government, public transport and estate agents. From these findings, local governments, public transport authorities and estate agents have the biggest task in improving their services and communicating their improvements to their constituents and customers. ■

EXAMPLE

Fashion brand preferences among young consumers[2]

The awareness of branded fashion products of 7- to 10-year-old consumers, that included brands such as Nike, Reebok and Adidas was investigated. The impact of social influences such as advertising, endorsement by popular figures, peer groups and the family was also studied. The questionnaire used in the study consisted of a series of semantic differential scales and questions about who influenced decisions when choosing clothes. The objective of the questionnaire was to systematically elicit aspects of the perceptions and evaluations of brands at an individual level. The study established which attributes and dimensions were used by young consumers that differentiated them from teenagers and young adults. ■

NON-COMPARATIVE SCALING TECHNIQUES

Non-comparative scales One of two types of scaling techniques in which each stimulus object is scaled independently of the other objects in the stimulus set.

Respondents using a **non-comparative** scale employ whatever rating standard seems appropriate to them. They do not compare the object being rated either with another object or to some specified standard, such as 'your ideal brand'. They evaluate only one object at a time; thus, non-comparative scales are often referred to as monadic scales. Non-comparative techniques consist of continuous and itemised rating scales, which are described in Table 11.1 and discussed in the following sections.

Continuous rating scale

Continuous rating scale A measurement scale that has respondents rate the objects by placing a mark at the appropriate position on a line that runs from one extreme of the criterion variable to the other. The form may vary considerably. Also referred to as graphic rating scale.

In a **continuous rating scale**, also referred to as a graphic rating scale, respondents rate the objects by placing a mark at the appropriate position on a line that runs from one extreme of the criterion variable to the other. Thus, the respondents are not restricted to selecting from marks previously set by the researcher. The form of the continuous scale may vary considerably. For example, the line may be vertical or horizontal; scale points, in the form of numbers or brief descriptions, may be provided; and if provided, the scale points may be few or many. Three versions of a continuous rating scale are illustrated opposite.

Table 11.1 Basic non-comparative scales

Scale	*Basic characteristics*	*Examples*	*Advantages*	*Disadvantages*
Continuous rating scale	Place a mark on a continuous line	Reaction to TV commercials	Easy to construct	Scoring can be cumbersome unless computerised
Itemised rating scales				
Likert scale	Degree of agreement on a 1 (strongly disagree) to 5 (strongly agree) scale	Measurement of attitudes	Easy to construct, administer and understand	More time-consuming
Semantic differential	Seven-point scale with bipolar labels	Brand, product, and company images	Versatile	Controversy as to whether the data are interval
Stapel scale	Unipolar ten-point scale, –5 to +5, without a neutral point (zero).	Measurement of attitudes and images	Easy to construct, administered over phone	Confusing and difficult to apply

GLOBALCASH PROJECT

Continuous rating scales

How would you rate Dresdner Bank in handling pan-European cash management transactions?

Version 1

Probably the worst ~~~~~~~~~~~~~~~~~~~~~~~✓~~~~~~~~~Probably the best

Version 2

Probably the worst ~~~~~~~~~~~~~~~~~~~~~~~✓~~~~~~~~~Probably the best
0 10 20 30 40 50 60 70 80 90 100

Version 3

Very bad *Neither good or bad* *Very good*
Probably the worst ~~~~~~~~~~~~~~~~~~~~~~~✓~~~~~~~~~Probably the best
0 10 20 30 40 50 60 70 80 90 100

Once the respondent has provided the ratings, the researcher divides the line into as many categories as desired and assigns scores based on the categories into which the ratings fall.[3] In the GlobalCash project example, the respondent exhibits an favourable attitude toward Dresdner. These scores are typically treated as interval data. ■

Note: In the forthcoming examples using Dresdner Bank, the scores presented do not represent actual measurements taken in Global Cash.

The advantage of continuous scales is that they are easy to construct; however, scoring is cumbersome and unreliable.[4] Moreover, continuous scales provide little new information. Hence, their use in marketing research has been limited. Recently, however, with the increased popularity of computer-assisted personal interviewing and other technologies, their use has become more frequent.[5]

ITEMISED RATING SCALES

Itemised rating scale
A measurement scale having numbers or brief descriptions associated with each category. The categories are ordered in terms of scale position.

In an **itemised rating scale**, respondents are provided with a scale that has a number or brief description associated with each category. The categories are ordered in terms of scale position; and the respondents are required to select the specified category that best describes the object being rated. Itemised rating scales are widely used in marketing research and form the basic components of more complex scales, such as multi-item rating scales. We first describe the commonly used itemised rating scales – the Likert, semantic differential, and Stapel scales – and then examine the major issues surrounding the use of itemised rating scales.

Likert scale

Likert scale
A measurement scale with five response categories ranging from 'strongly disagree' to 'strongly agree' that requires respondents to indicate a degree of agreement or disagreement with each of a series of statements related to the stimulus objects.

Named after its developer, Rensis Likert, the **Likert scale** is a widely used rating scale that requires the respondents to indicate a degree of agreement or disagreement with each of a series of statements about the stimulus objects.[6] Typically, each scale item has five response categories, ranging from 'strongly disagree' to 'strongly agree'. We illustrate with a Likert scale for evaluating attitudes toward Dresdner in the context of the GlobalCash project.

To conduct the analysis, each statement is assigned a numerical score, ranging either from –2 to +2 or 1 to 5. The analysis can be conducted on an item-by-item basis (profile analysis), or a total (summated) score can be calculated for each respondent by summing across items. Suppose that the Likert scale in the GlobalCash example was used to measure attitudes toward the Bank of Ireland as well as Dresdner. Profile analysis would involve comparing the two banks in terms of the average respondent ratings for each item, such as level of electronic banking support, level of transaction detail, and service levels. The summated approach is most frequently used, and as a result, the Likert scale is also referred to as a summated scale.[7] When using this approach to determine the total score for each respondent on each bank, it is important to use a consistent scoring procedure so that a high (or low) score consistently reflects a favourable response. This requires that the categories assigned to the negative statements by the respondents be scored by reversing the scale. Note that for a negative statement, an agreement reflects an unfavourable response, whereas for a positive statement, agreement represents a favourable response. Accordingly, a 'strongly agree' response to a favourable statement and a 'strongly disagree' response to an unfavourable statement would both receive scores of five.[8] In the following GlobalCash example, if a higher score is to denote a more favourable attitude, the scoring of items 2, 4, 5 and 7 will be reversed. The respondent to this set of statements has an attitude score of 22. Each respondent's total score for each bank is calculated. A respondent will have the most favourable attitude toward the bank with the highest score. The procedure for developing summated Likert scales is described later in the section on multi-item scales.

Likert scale

Instructions

Listed below are different opinions about Dresdner Bank. Please indicate how strongly you agree or disagree with each by putting an ✗ next to your choice on the following scale:

1 = Strongly disagree, 2 = Disagree, 3 = Neither agree nor disagree, 4 = Agree, 5 = Strongly agree

	Strongly disagree	*Disagree*	*Neither agree nor disagree*	*Agree*	*Strongly agree*
1. Dresdner delivers high quality banking services	1	2✗	3	4	5
2. Dresdner has poor customer operational support	1	2✗	3	4	5
3. I prefer to conduct transactions with Dresdner	1	2	3✗	4	5
4. Dresdner does not have a good European branch network	1	2	3	4✗	5
5. The electronic banking security at Dresdner is terrible	1	2	3	4✗	5
6. Account managers at Dresdner display great knowledge of cash management	1✗	2	3	4	5
7. I do not like Dresdner advertisments	1	2	3	4✗	5
8. Dresdner has good published quality standards	1	2	3	4✗	5
9. Dresdner provides credit on excellent terms	1	2✗	3	4	5

The Likert scale has several advantages. It is easy to construct and administer, and respondents readily understand how to use the scale, making it suitable for mail, telephone or personal interviews. The major disadvantage of the Likert scale is that it takes longer to complete than other itemised rating scales because respondents have to read and fully reflect upon each statement.

Semantic differential
A seven-point rating scale with end points associated with bipolar labels.

Semantic differential scale

The **semantic differential** is a seven-point rating scale with end points associated with bipolar labels that have semantic meaning. In a typical application, respondents rate objects on a number of itemised, seven-point rating scales bounded at each end by one of two bipolar adjectives, such as 'cold' and 'warm'.[9] We illustrate this scale by presenting a respondent's evaluation of Dresdner on five attributes.

Semantic differential scale

Instructions

This part of the study measures what certain banks mean to you. You judge them on a series of descriptive scales bounded at each end by one of two bipolar adjectives. Please mark ✗ the blank that best indicates how accurately each adjective describes what the bank means to you.

Form

Dresdner Bank is:

Powerful :__:__:__:__: __:✗:__: Weak
Unreliable :__:__:__:__:__:✗:__: Reliable
Modern :__:__:__:__:__:__:✗: Old-fashioned
Hi-tech :__:__:__:__:__:✗:__: Low-tech
Careful :__:✗:__:__:__:__:__: Careless

The respondents mark the blank that best indicates how they would describe the object being rated.[10] Thus, in our example, Dresdener Bank is evaluated as somewhat weak, reliable, very old fashioned, low-tech and careful. The negative adjective or phrase sometimes appears at the left side of the scale and sometimes at the right. This controls the tendency of some respondents, particularly those with very positive or very negative attitudes, to mark the right- or left-hand sides without reading the labels.

Individual items on a semantic differential scale may be scored on either a –3 to +3 or a 1 to 7 scale. The resulting data are commonly analysed through profile analysis. In profile analysis, means or median values on each rating scale are calculated and compared by plotting or statistical analysis. This helps determine the overall differences and similarities among the objects. To assess differences across segments of respondents, the researcher can compare mean responses of different segments. Although the mean is most often used as a summary statistic, there is some controversy as to whether the data obtained should be treated as an interval scale.[11] On the other hand, in cases when the researcher requires an overall comparison of objects, such as to determine bank preference, the individual item scores are summed to arrive at a total score.

Its versatility makes the semantic differential a popular rating scale in marketing research. It has been widely used in comparing brand, product, and company images. It has also been used to develop advertising and promotion strategies and in new product development studies.[12] Several modifications of the basic scale have been proposed.[13]

Stapel scale

Stapel scale
A scale for measuring attitudes that consists of a single adjective in the middle of an even -numbered range of values.

The Stapel scale, named after its developer, Jan Stapel, is a unipolar rating scale with ten categories numbered from –5 to +5, without a neutral point (zero).[14] This scale is usually presented vertically. Respondents are asked to indicate by selecting an appropriate numerical response category how accurately or inaccurately each term describes the object. The higher the number, the more accurately the term describes the object, as shown in the GlobalCash project. In this example, Dresdner is perceived as not having high-quality products and having somewhat poor service.

GLOBALCASH PROJECT

Stapel scale

Instructions

Please evaluate how accurately each word or phrase describes each named European bank. Select a positive number for the phrases you think descibe the bank accurately. The more accurately you think the phrase describes the bank, the larger the plus number you should choose. You should select a minus number for the phrases you think do not describe the bank accurately. The less accurately you think the phrase describes the bank, the larger the negative number you should choose. You can select any number from +5 for phrases you think are very accurate, to –5 for phrases you think are very inaccurate.

Form

Dresdener Bank

+5	+5
+4	+4
+3	+3
+2	+2✗
+1	+1
High quality	*Poor service*
–1	–1
–2	–2
–3	–3
–4✗	–4
–5	–5

The data obtained by using a Stapel scale can be analysed in the same way as semantic differential data. The Stapel scale produces results similar to the semantic differential.[15] The Stapel scale's advantages are that it does not require a pre-test of the adjectives or phrases to ensure true bipolarity and that it can be administered over the telephone. Some researchers, however, believe the Stapel scale is confusing and difficult to apply. Of the three itemised rating scales considered, the Stapel scale is used least.[16] Nonetheless, this scale merits more attention than it has received.

NON-COMPARATIVE ITEMISED RATING SCALE DECISIONS

As is evident from the discussion so far, non-comparative itemised rating scales need not be used as originally proposed but can take many different forms. The researcher must make six major decisions when constructing any of these scales.

1 The number of scale categories to use
2 Balanced versus unbalanced scale
3 Odd or even number of categories
4 Forced versus non-forced choice
5 The nature and degree of the verbal description
6 The physical form of the scale.

Number of scale categories

Two conflicting considerations are involved in deciding the number of scale categories or response options. The greater the number of scale categories, the finer the discrimination among stimulus objects that is possible. On the other hand, most respondents cannot handle more than a few categories. Traditional guidelines suggest that the appropriate number of categories should be seven plus or minus two: between five and nine.[17] Yet there is no single optimal number of categories. Several factors should be taken into account in deciding on the number of categories.

If the respondents are interested in the scaling task and are knowledgeable about the objects, many categories may be employed. On the other hand, if the respondents are not very knowledgeable or involved with the task, fewer categories should be used. Likewise, the nature of the objects is also relevant. Some objects do not lend themselves to fine discrimination, so a small number of categories is sufficient. Another important factor is the mode of data collection. If telephone interviews are involved, many categories may confuse the respondents. Likewise, space limitations may restrict the number of categories in mail questionnaires.

How the data are to be analysed and used should also influence the number of categories. In situations where several scale items are added together to produce a single score for each respondent, five categories are sufficient. The same is true if the researcher wishes to make broad generalisations or group comparisons. If, however, individual responses are of interest or if the data will be analysed by sophisticated statistical techniques, seven or more categories may be required. The size of the correlation coefficient, a common measure of relationship between variables (Chapter 19), is influenced by the number of scale categories. The correlation coefficient decreases with a reduction in the number of categories. This, in turn, has an impact on all statistical analysis based on the correlation coefficient.[18]

Balanced versus unbalanced scale

Balanced scale
A scale with an equal number of favourable and unfavourable categories.

In a **balanced scale**, the number of favourable and unfavourable categories is equal; in an unbalanced scale, the categories are unequal in number.[19] Examples of balanced and unbalanced scales are given in Figure 11.1. In general, in order to obtain objective data, the scale should be balanced. If the distribution of responses is likely to be skewed, however, either positively or negatively, an unbalanced scale with more categories in the direction of skewness may be appropriate. If an unbalanced scale is used, the nature and degree of imbalance in the scale should be taken into account in data analysis.

Balanced scale

Clinique moisturiser for men is:

Extremely good	
Very good	✓
Good	
Bad	
Very Bad	
Extremely bad	

Unbalanced scale

Clinique moisturiser for men is:

Extremely good	
Very good	✓
Good	
Somewhat good	
Bad	
Very bad	

Figure 11.1
Balanced and unbalanced scales

Odd or even number of categories

With an odd number of categories, the middle scale position is generally designated as neutral or impartial.[20] The presence, position and labelling of a neutral category can have a significant influence on the response.[21] The Likert scale is a balanced rating scale with an odd number of categories and a neutral point.

The decision to use an odd or even number of categories depends on whether some of the respondents may be neutral on the response being measured. If a neutral or indifferent response is possible from at least some of the respondents, an odd number of categories should be used. If, on the other hand, the researcher wants to force a response or believes that no neutral or indifferent response exists, a rating scale with an even number of categories should be used. A related issue is whether the choice should be forced or non-forced.

Forced versus non-forced choice

Forced rating scale
A rating scale that forces respondents to express an opinion because a 'no opinion' or 'no knowledge' option is not provided.

On **forced rating scales** the respondents are forced to express an opinion because a 'no opinion' option is not provided. In such a case, respondents without an opinion may mark the middle scale position. If a sufficient proportion of the respondents do not have opinions on the topic, marking the middle position will distort measures of central tendency and variance. In situations where the respondents are expected to have no opinion, as opposed to simply being reluctant to disclose it, the accuracy of data may be improved by a non-forced scale that includes a 'no opinion' category.[22]

Nature and degree of verbal description

The nature and degree of verbal description associated with scale categories varies considerably and can have an effect on the responses.[23] Scale categories may have verbal, numerical or even pictorial descriptions. Furthermore, the researcher must decide whether to label every scale category, scale some categories, or only extreme scale categories. Surprisingly, providing a verbal description for each category may not improve the accuracy or reliability of the data. Yet, an argument can be made for labelling all or many scale categories to reduce scale ambiguity. The category descriptions should be located as close to the response categories as possible.[24]

The strength of the adjectives used to anchor the scale may influence the distribution of the responses. With strong anchors (1 = completely disagree, 7 = completely agree), respondents are less likely to use the extreme scale categories. This results in less variable and more peaked response distributions. Weak anchors (1 = generally disagree, 7 = generally agree), in contrast, produce uniform or flat distributions. Procedures have been developed to assign values to category descriptors to result in balanced or equal interval scales.[25]

Physical form of the scale

A number of options are available with respect to scale form or configuration. Scales can be presented vertically or horizontally. Categories can be expressed by boxes, discrete lines or units on a continuum and may or may not have numbers assigned to them. If numerical values are used, they may be positive, negative, or both. Several possible configurations are presented in Figure 11.2.

Two unique rating scale configurations used in marketing research are the thermometer scale and the smiling face scale. For the thermometer scale, the

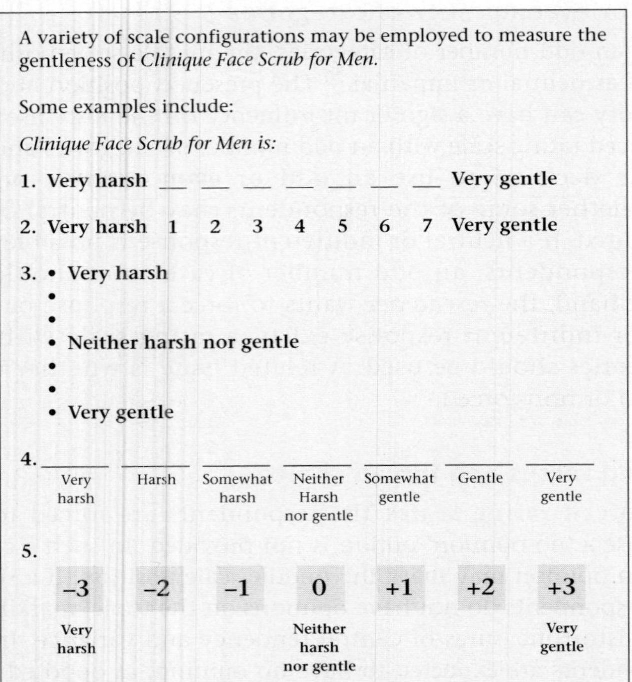

A variety of scale configurations may be employed to measure the gentleness of Clinique Face Scrub for Men.
Some examples include:
Clinique Face Scrub for Men is:
1. Very harsh ___ ___ ___ ___ ___ ___ ___ Very gentle
2. Very harsh 1 2 3 4 5 6 7 Very gentle
3. • Very harsh
•
•
• Neither harsh nor gentle
•
•
• Very gentle
4. Very harsh
Harsh
Somewhat harsh
Neither Harsh nor gentle
Somewhat gentle
Gentle
Very gentle
5. −3 −2 −1 0 +1 +2 +3
Very harsh
Neither harsh nor gentle
Very gentle

Figure 11.2 Rating scale configurations

higher the temperature the more favourable the evaluation. Likewise, happier faces indicate evaluations that are more favourable. These scales are especially useful for children.[26] Examples of these scales are shown in Figure 11.3. Table 11.2 summarises the six decisions in designing rating scales.

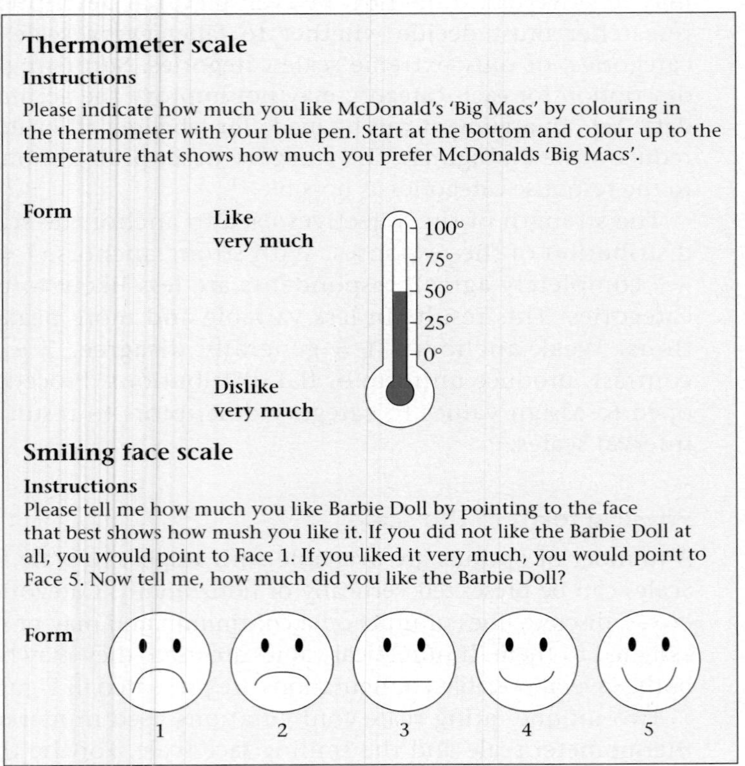

Thermometer scale
Instructions
Please indicate how much you like McDonald's 'Big Macs' by colouring in the thermometer with your blue pen. Start at the bottom and colour up to the temperature that shows how much you prefer McDonalds 'Big Macs'.
Form
Like very much
100°
75°
50°
25°
0°
Dislike very much
Smiling face scale
Instructions
Please tell me how much you like Barbie Doll by pointing to the face that best shows how mush you like it. If you did not like the Barbie Doll at all, you would point to Face 1. If you liked it very much, you would point to Face 5. Now tell me, how much did you like the Barbie Doll?
Form
1
2
3
4
5

Figure 11.3 Some unique rating scale configurations

Table 11.2 Summary of itemised rating scale decisions

1. **Number of categories**	Although there is no single, optimal number, traditional guidelines suggest that there should be between five and nine categories.
2. **Balanced versus unbalanced**	In general, the scale should be balanced to obtain objective data.
3. **Odd or even number of categories**	If a neutral or indifferent scale response is possible from at least some of the respondents, an odd number of categories should be used.
4. **Forced versus unforced**	In situations where the respondents are expected to have no opinion, the accuracy of the data may be improved by a non-forced scale.
5. **Verbal description**	An argument can be made for labelling all or many scale categories. The category descriptions should be located as close to the response categories as possible.
6. **Physical form**	A number of options should be tried and the best one selected.

MULTI-ITEM SCALES

The development of multi-item rating scales requires considerable technical expertise.[27] Figure 11.4 presents a sequence of operations needed to construct multi-item scales. The characteristic to be measured is frequently called a construct. Scale development begins with an underlying theory of the construct being measured. A theory is necessary not only for constructing the scale but also for interpreting the resulting scores. The next step is to generate an initial

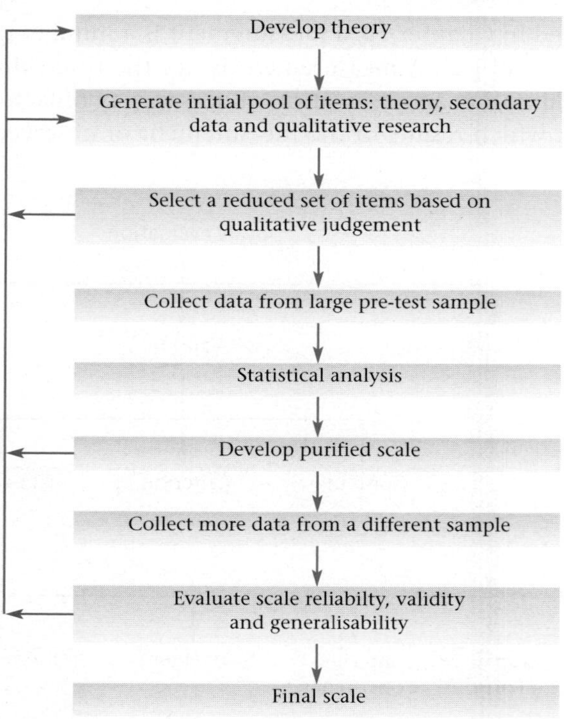

Figure 11.4
Devlopment of a multi-item scale

pool of scale items. Typically, this is based on theory, analysis of secondary data and qualitative research. From this pool, a reduced set of potential scale items is generated by the judgement of the researcher and other knowledgeable individuals. Some qualitative criterion is adopted to aid their judgement. The reduced set of items is still too large to constitute a scale. Thus, further reduction is achieved in a quantitative manner.

Data are collected on the reduced set of potential scale items from a large pre-test sample of respondents. The data are analysed using techniques such as correlations, factor analysis, cluster analysis, discriminant analysis and statistical tests discussed later in this book. As a result of these statistical analyses, several more items are eliminated, resulting in a purified scale. The purified scale is evaluated for reliability and validity by collecting more data from a different sample (see the following section). On the basis of these assessments, a final set of scale items is selected. As can be seen from Figure 11.4, the scale development process is an iterative one with several feedback loops.[28]

SCALE EVALUATION

A multi-item scale should be evaluated for accuracy and applicability.[29] As shown in Figure 11.5, this involves an assessment of reliability, validity and generalisability of the scale. Approaches to assessing reliability include test–retest reliability, alternative-forms reliability and internal consistency reliability. Validity can be assessed by examining content validity, criterion validity and construct validity.

Before we can examine reliability and validity we need an understanding of measurement accuracy; it is fundamental to scale evaluation.

Measurement accuracy

As mentioned in Chapter 10, a measurement is a number that reflects some characteristic of an object. A measurement is not the true value of the characteristic of interest but rather an observation of it. A variety of factors can cause **measurement error**, which results in the measurement or observed score being different

Measurement error
The variation in the information sought by the researcher and the information generated by the measurement process employed.

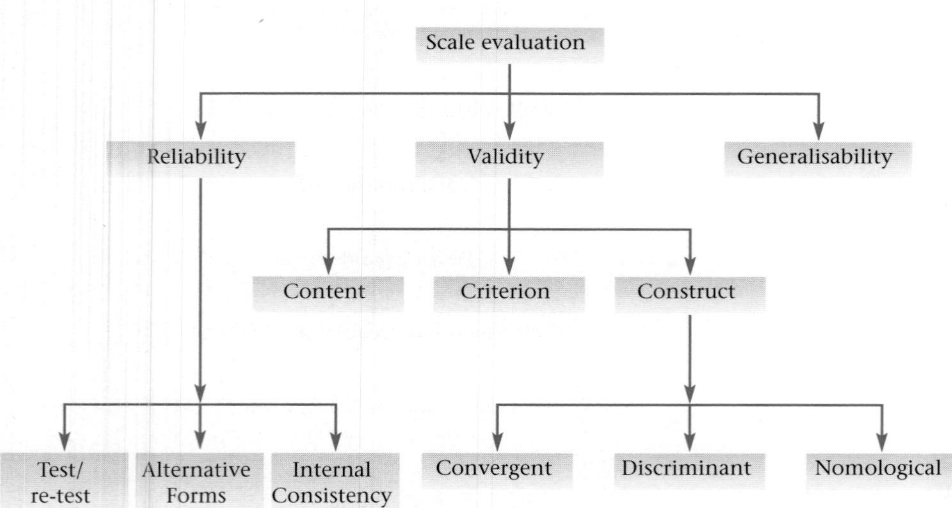

Figure 11.5
Scale evaluation

from the true score of the characteristic being measured (see Table 11.3). The **true score model** provides a framework for understanding the accuracy of measurement.[30] According to this model,

True score model
A mathematical model that provides a framework for understanding the accuracy of measurement.

$$X_O = X_T + X_S + X_R$$

where

X_O = the observed score or measurement
X_T = the true score of the characteristic
X_S = systematic error
X_R = random error

Note that the total measurement error includes the systematic error, X_S, and the random error, X_R. **Systematic error** affects the measurement in a constant way. It represents stable factors that affect the observed score in the same way each time the measurement is made, such as mechanical factors (see Table 11.3). **Random error**, on the other hand, is not constant. It represents transient factors that affect the observed score in different ways each time the measurement is made, such as transient personal or situational factors. The distinction between systematic and random error is crucial to our understanding of reliability and validity.

Systematic error
An error that affects the measurement in a constant way and represents stable factors that affect the observed score in the same way each time the measurement is made.

Random error
An error that arises from random changes or differences in respondents or measurement situations.

Reliability

Reliability refers to the extent to which a scale produces consistent results if repeated measurements are made.[31] Systematic sources of error do not have an adverse impact on reliability, because they affect the measurement in a constant way and do not lead to inconsistency. In contrast, random error produces inconsistency, leading to lower reliability. Reliability can be defined as the extent to which measures are free from random error, **XR**. If **XR = 0**, the measure is perfectly reliable.

Reliability
The extent to which a scale produces consistent results if repeated measurements are made on the characteristic.

Reliability is assessed by determining the proportion of systematic variation in a scale. This is done by determining the association between scores obtained from different administrations of the scale. If the association is high, the scale yields consistent results and is therefore reliable. Approaches for assessing reliability include the test–re-test, alternative-forms, and internal consistency methods.

Test–re-test reliability. In **test–re-test reliability**, respondents are administered identical sets of scale items at two different times, under as nearly equivalent

Test–re-test reliability
An approach for assessing reliability, in which respondents are administered identical sets of scale items at two different times, under as nearly equivalent conditions as possible.

Table 11.3 Potential sources of error in measurement

1	Other relatively stable characteristics of the individual that influence the test score, such as intelligence, social desirability, and education.
2	Short-term or transient personal factors, such as health, emotions, fatigue.
3	Situational factors, such as the presence of other people, noise, and distractions.
4	Sampling of items included in the scale: addition, deletion, or changes in the scale items.
5	Lack of clarity of the scale, including the instructions or the items themselves.
6	Mechanical factors, such as poor printing, overcrowding items in the questionnaire, and poor design.
7	Administration of the scale, such as differences among interviewers.
8	Analysis factors, such as differences in scoring and statistical analysis.

conditions as possible. The time interval between tests or administrations is typically two to four weeks. The degree of similarity between the two measurements is determined by computing a correlation coefficient (see Chapter 19). The higher the correlation coefficient, the greater the reliability.

Several problems are associated with the test–re-test approach to determining reliability. First, it is sensitive to the time interval between testing. Other things being equal, the longer the time interval, the lower the reliability. Second, the initial measurement may alter the characteristic being measured. For example, measuring respondents' attitude toward low-alcohol beer may cause them to become more health conscious and to develop a more positive attitude toward low-alcohol beer. Third, it may be impossible to make repeated measurements (for example, the research topic may be the respondent's initial reaction to a new product). Fourth, the first measurement may have a carryover effect to the second or subsequent measurements. Respondents may attempt to remember answers they gave the first time. Fifth, the characteristic being measured may change between measurements. For example, favourable information about an object between measurements may make a respondent's attitude more positive. Finally, the test–re-test reliability coefficient can be inflated by the correlation of each item with itself. These correlations tend to be higher than correlations between different scale items across administrations. Hence, it is possible to have high test–re-test correlations because of the high correlations between the same scale items measured at different times even though the correlations between different scale items are quite low. Because of these problems, a test–re-test approach is best applied in conjunction with other approaches, such as alternative-forms reliability.

Alternative-forms reliability
An approach for assessing reliability that requires two equivalent forms of the scale to be constructed and then the same respondents to be measured at two different times.

Alternative-forms reliability. In **alternative-forms reliability**, two equivalent forms of the scale are constructed. The same respondents are measured at two different times, usually two to four weeks apart. The scores from the administrations of the alternative scale forms are correlated to assess reliability.[32]

There are two major problems with this approach. First, it is time-consuming and expensive to construct an equivalent form of the scale. Second, it is difficult to construct two equivalent forms of a scale. The two forms should be equivalent with respect to content. In a strict sense, this requires that the alternative sets of scale items should have the same means, variances and intercorrelations. Even if these conditions are satisfied, the two forms may not be equivalent in content. Thus, a low correlation may reflect either an unreliable scale or non-equivalent forms.

Internal consistency reliability
An approach for assessing the internal consistency of the set of items by summing the individual consistencies for the items in the set to form a total score for the scale.

Internal consistency reliability. **Internal consistency** reliability is used to assess the reliability of a summated scale where several items are summed to form a total score. In a scale of this type, each item measures some aspect of the construct measured by the entire scale, and the items should be consistent in what they indicate about the characteristic. This measure of reliability focuses on the internal consistency of the set of items forming the scale.

Split-half reliability
A form of internal consistency reliability in which the items constituting the scale are divided into two halves and the resulting half scores are correlated.

The simplest measure of internal consistency is **split-half reliability**. The items on the scale are divided into two halves and the resulting half scores are correlated. High correlations between the halves indicate high internal consistency. The scale items can be split into halves based on odd- and even-numbered items or randomly. The problem is that the results will depend on how the scale items are split. A popular approach to overcoming this problem is to use the coefficient alpha.

Coefficient alpha
A measure of internal consistency reliability that is the average of all possible split-half coefficients resulting from different splittings of the scale items.

The **coefficient alpha**, or Cronbach's alpha, is the average of all possible split-half coefficients resulting from different ways of splitting the scale items.[33] This coefficient varies from 0 to 1, and a value of 0.6 or less generally indicates unsatisfactory internal consistency reliability. An important property of coefficient alpha is that its value tends to increase with an increase in the number of scale items. Therefore, coefficient alpha may be artificially, and inappropriately, inflated by including several redundant scale items.[34] Another coefficient that can be employed in conjunction with coefficient alpha is coefficient beta. Coefficient beta assists in determining whether the averaging process used in calculating coefficient alpha is masking any inconsistent items.

Some multi-item scales include several sets of items designed to measure different aspects of a multidimensional construct. For example, bank image is a multidimensional construct that includes country of origin, range of products, quality of products, service of bank personnel, credit terms, investment rates, convenience of location, and physical layout of branches. Hence, a scale designed to measure bank image would contain items measuring each of these dimensions. Because these dimensions are somewhat independent, a measure of internal consistency computed across dimensions would be inappropriate. If several items are used to measure each dimension, however, internal consistency reliability can be computed for each dimension.

Validity

Validity
The extent to which differences in observed scale scores reflect true differences among objects on the characteristic being measured, rather than systematic or random errors.

The **validity** of a scale may be defined as the extent to which differences in observed scale scores reflect true differences among objects on the characteristic being measured, rather than systematic or random error. Perfect validity requires that there be no measurement error ($X_O = X_T$, $X_R = 0$, $X_S = 0$). Researchers may assess content validity criterion validity or construct validity.[35]

Content validity
A type of validity, sometimes called face validity, that consists of a subjective but systematic evaluation of the representativeness of the content of a scale for the measuring task at hand.

Content validity. **Content validity**, sometimes called face validity, is a subjective but systematic evaluation of how well the content of a scale represents the measurement task at hand. The researcher or someone else examines whether the scale items adequately cover the entire domain of the construct being measured. Thus, a scale designed to measure bank image would be considered inadequate if it omitted any of the major dimensions (range of products, quality of products, service of bank personnel, etc.). Given its subjective nature, content validity alone is not a sufficient measure of the validity of a scale, yet it aids in a common-sense interpretation of the scale scores. A more formal evaluation can be obtained by examining criterion validity.

Criterion valisity
A type of validity that examines whether the measurement scale performs as expected in relation to other variables selected as meaningful criteria.

Criterion validity. **Criterion validity** reflects whether a scale performs as expected in relation to other variables selected (criterion variables) as meaningful criteria. Criterion variables may include demographic and psychographic characteristics, attitudinal and behavioural measures, or scores obtained from other scales. Based on the time period involved, criterion validity can take two forms, concurrent validity and predictive validity.

Concurrent validity is assessed when the data on the scale being evaluated and on the criterion variables are collected at the same time. The original instruments and the short versions would be administered simultaneously to a group of respondents and the results compared. To assess predictive validity, the researcher collects data on the scale at one point in time and data on the criterion variables at a future time. For example, attitudes toward breakfast cereals could be used to predict future purchases of cereals by members of a scanner panel. Attitudinal data are obtained from the panel members, and then their future purchases are tracked with scanner data. The predicted and actual purchases are compared to assess the predictive validity of the attitudinal scale.

Construct validity
A type of validity that addresses the question of what construct or characteristic the scale is measuring. An attempt is made to answer theoretical questions of why a scale works and what deductions can be made concerning the theory underlying the scale

Construct validity. **Construct validity** addresses the question of what construct or characteristic the scale is, in fact, measuring. When assessing construct validity, the researcher attempts to answer theoretical questions about why the scale works and what deductions can be made concerning the underlying theory. Thus, construct validity requires a sound theory of the nature of the construct being measured and how it relates to other constructs. Construct validity is the most sophisticated and difficult type of validity to establish. As Figure 11.5 shows, construct validity includes convergent, discriminant and nomological validity.

Convergent validity
A measure of construct validity that measures the extent to which the scale correlates positively with other measures of the same construct.

Discriminant validity
A type of construct validity that assesses the extent to which at measure does not correlate with other constructs from which it is supposed to differ.

Nomological validity
A type of validity that assesses the relationship between theoretical constructs. It seeks to confirm significant correlations between the constructs as predicted by a theory.

Convergent validity is the extent to which the scale correlates positively with other measures of the same construct. It is not necessary that all these measures be obtained by using conventional scaling techniques. **Discriminant validity** is the extent to which a measure does not correlate with other constructs from which it is supposed to differ. It involves demonstrating a lack of correlation among differing constructs. **Nomological validity** is the extent to which the scale correlates in theoretically predicted ways with measures of different but related constructs. A theoretical model is formulated that leads to further deductions, tests and inferences. Gradually, a nomological net is built in which several constructs are systematically interrelated. We illustrate construct validity in the context of a multi-item scale designed to measure self concept.

EXAMPLE

To thine own self be true[36]

The following findings would provide evidence of construct validity for a multi-item scale to measure self concept:

- High correlations with other scales designed to measure self-concepts and with reported classifications by friends (convergent validity)
- Low correlations with unrelated constructs of brand loyalty and variety seeking (discriminant validity)
- Brands that are congruent with the individual's self-concept are more preferred, as postulated by the theory (nomological validity)
- A high level of reliability ■

Notice that a high level of reliability was included as an evidence of construct validity in this example. This illustrates the relationship between reliability and validity.

Relationship between reliability and validity

The relationship between reliability and validity can be understood in terms of the true score model. If a measure is perfectly valid, it is also perfectly reliable. In this case, $X_O = X_T$, $X_R = 0$, and $X_S = 0$. Thus, perfect validity implies perfect reliability. If a measure is unreliable, it cannot be perfectly valid, since at a minimum $X_O = X_T + X_R$. Furthermore, systematic error may also be present, that is, $X_S \neq 0$. Thus, unreliability implies invalidity. If a measure is perfectly reliable, it may or may not be perfectly valid, because systematic error may still be present ($X_O = X_T + X_S$). Although lack of reliability constitutes negative evidence for validity, reliability does not in itself imply validity. Reliability is a necessary, but not sufficient, condition for validity.

Generalisability

Generalisability
The degree to which a study based on a sample applies to the population as a whole.

Generalisability refers to the extent to which one can generalise from the observations at hand to a universe of generalisations. The set of all conditions of measurement over which the investigator wishes to generalise is the universe of generalisation. These conditions may include items, interviewers, and situations of observation. A researcher may wish to generalise a scale developed for use in personal interviews to other modes of data collection, such as mail and telephone interviews. Likewise, one may wish to generalise from a sample of items to the universe of items, from a sample of times of measurement to the universe of times of measurement, from a sample of observers to a universe of observers, and so on.[37]

In generalisability studies, measurement procedures are designed to investigate each universe of interest by sampling conditions of measurement from each. For each universe of interest, an aspect of measurement called a facet is included in the study. Traditional reliability methods can be viewed as single-facet generalisability studies. A test–re-test correlation is concerned with whether scores obtained from a measurement scale are generalisable to the universe scores across all times of possible measurement. Even if the test–re-test correlation is high, nothing can be said about the generalisability of the scale to other universes. To generalise to other universes, generalisability theory procedures must be employed.

CHOOSING A SCALING TECHNIQUE

In addition to theoretical considerations and evaluation of reliability and validity, certain practical factors should be considered in selecting scaling techniques for a particular marketing research problem.[38] These include the level of information (nominal, ordinal, interval or ratio) desired, the capabilities of the respondents, the characteristics of the stimulus objects, the method of administration, the context, and cost.

As a general rule, using the scaling technique that will yield the highest level of information feasible in a given situation will permit using the greatest variety of statistical analyses. Also, regardless of the type of scale used, whenever feasible, several scale items should measure the characteristic of interest. This provides more accurate measurement than a single-item scale. In many situations, it is desirable to use more than one scaling technique or to obtain additional measures using mathematically derived scales.

MATHEMATICALLY DERIVED SCALES

All the scaling techniques discussed in this chapter require the respondents to evaluate directly various characteristics of the stimulus objects. In contrast, mathematical scaling techniques allow researchers to infer respondents' evaluations of characteristics of stimulus objects. These evaluations are inferred from the respondents' overall judgements of the objects. Two popular mathematically derived scaling techniques are multidimensional scaling and conjoint analysis, which are discussed in detail in Chapter 23.

INTERNATIONAL MARKETING RESEARCH

In designing the scale or response format, respondents' educational or literacy levels should be taken into account.[39] One approach is to develop scales that are pan-cultural, or free of cultural biases. Of the scaling techniques we have considered, the semantic differential scale may be said to be pan-cultural. It has been tested in a number of countries and has consistently produced similar results.

EXAMPLE

Copying the name Xerox[40]

Xerox was a name well received in the former Soviet Union since the late 1960s. In fact, the act of copying documents was called Xeroxing, a term coined after the name of the company. It was a brand name people equated with quality. With the disintegration of the Soviet Union into the Commonwealth of Independent States, however, Xerox's sales started to fall. The management initially considered this problem to be the intense competition with strong competitors such as Canon, Ricoh, Mitsubishi and Minolta. First attempts to make the product more competitive did not help. Subsequently, marketing research was undertaken to measure the image of Xerox and its competitors. Semantic differential scales were used as this type of scale is considered pan-cultural. The bipolar labels used were carefully tested to ensure that they had the intended semantic meaning in the Russian context.

The results of the study revealed that the real problem was a growing negative perception of Russian customers toward Xerox products. What could have gone wrong? The problem was not with Xerox, but with several independent producers of copying machines that had illegally infringed on Xerox trademark rights. With the disintegration of the Soviet Union, the protection of these trademarks was unclear and trademark infringement kept growing. As a result, customers developed a misconception that Xerox were selling low-quality products. Among other courses of action, Xerox ran a corporate campaign on the national Russian TV and radio networks as well as in local print media. The campaign emphasised Xerox's leadership position in the commonwealth countries where quality demands were very high. This was a definite step in removing some misconceptions of Russian consumers toward Xerox. Xerox also registered its trademark separately in each republic. ■

Semantic differential scales have been used to measure the image of Xerox and its competitors in Russia.

Although the semantic differential worked well in the Russian context, an alternative approach is to develop scales that use a self-defined cultural norm as a base referent. For example, respondents may be required to indicate their own anchor point and position relative to a culture-specific stimulus set. This approach is useful for measuring attitudes that are defined relative to cultural norms (e.g. attitude toward marital roles). In developing response formats, verbal rating scales appear to be the most suitable. Even less educated respondents can readily understand and respond to verbal scales. Special attention should be devoted to determining equivalent verbal descriptors in different languages and cultures. The end points of the scale are particularly prone to different interpretations. In some cultures, 1 may be interpreted as best, whereas in others it may be interpreted as worst, regardless of how it is scaled. It is important that the scale end points and the verbal descriptors be employed in a manner consistent with the culture.

Finally, in international marketing research, it is critical to establish the equivalence of scales and measures used to obtain data from different countries. This topic is complex and is discussed in some detail in Chapter 23.

ETHICS IN MARKETING RESEARCH

Ethical issues can arise in the construction of non-comparative scales. Consider, for example, the use of scale descriptors. The descriptors used to frame a scale can be manipulated to bias results in any direction. They can be manipulated to generate a positive view of the client's brand or a negative view of a competitor's brand. A researcher who wants to project the client's brand favourably can ask respondents to indicate their opinion of the brand on several attributes using seven-point scales framed by the descriptors 'extremely poor' to 'good'. Using a strongly negative descriptor with only a mildly positive one has an interesting effect. As long as the product is not the worst, respondents will be reluctant to rate the product extremely poorly. In fact, respondents who believe the product to be only mediocre will end up responding favourably. Try this yourself. How would you rate BMW cars on the following attributes?

Reliability:	Horrible	1	2	3	4	5	6	7	*Good*
Performance:	Very poor	1	2	3	4	5	6	7	*Good*
Quality:	One of the worst	1	2	3	4	5	6	7	*Good*
Prestige:	Very low	1	2	3	4	5	6	7	*Good*

Did you find yourself rating BMW cars positively? Using this same technique, a researcher can negatively bias evaluations of competitors' products by providing mildly negative descriptors against strong positive descriptors.

Thus we see how important it is to use balanced scales with comparable positive and negative descriptors. When this guide is not practised, responses are biased and should be interpreted accordingly. This concern also underscores the need to adequately establish the reliability, validity and generalisability of scales before using them in a research project. Scales that are invalid, unreliable or not generalisable to the target market provide the client with flawed results and misleading findings, thus raising serious ethical issues. The researcher has a responsibility to both the client and respondents to ensure the applicability and usefulness of the scale.

INTERNET AND COMPUTER APPLICATIONS

Continuous rating scales may be easily implemented on the Internet. The cursor can be moved on the screen in a continuous fashion to select the exact position on the scale that best describes the respondent's evaluation. Moreover, the scale values can be automatically scored by the computer, thus increasing the speed and accuracy of processing the data.

Similarly, it is also easy to implement all of the three itemised rating scales on the Internet. Moreover, using the Internet one can search for and locate cases and examples where scales have been used by other researchers. It is also possible that other researchers have reported reliability and validity assessments for multi-item scales. Before generating new scales, a researcher should first examine similar scales used by other researchers and consider using them if they meet the measurement objectives.

SUMMARY

In non-comparative scaling, each object is scaled independently of the other objects in the stimulus set. The resulting data are generally assumed to be interval or ratio scaled. Non-comparative rating scales can be either continuous or itemised. The itemised rating scales are further classified as Likert, semantic differential, or Stapel scales. When using non-comparative itemised rating scales, the researcher must decide on the number of scale categories, balanced versus unbalanced scales, odd or even number of categories, forced versus non-forced choices, nature and degree of verbal description, and the physical form or configuration.

Multi-item scales consist of a number of rating scale items. These scales should be evaluated in terms of reliability and validity. Reliability refers to the extent to which a scale produces consistent results if repeated measurements are made. Approaches to assessing reliability include test–re-test, alternative-forms and internal consistency. Validity, or accuracy of measurement, may be assessed by evaluating content validity, criterion validity and construct validity.

The choice of particular scaling techniques in a given situation should be based on theoretical and practical considerations. Generally, the scaling technique used should be the one that will yield the highest level of information feasible. Also, multiple measures should be obtained.

In international marketing research, special attention should be devoted to determining equivalent verbal descriptors in different languages and cultures. The misuse of scale descriptors also raises serious ethical concerns. The researcher has a responsibility to both the client and respondents to ensure the applicability and usefulness of the scales.

QUESTIONS AND PROBLEMS

1 What is a semantic differential scale? For what purpose is this scale used?

2 Describe the Likert scale.

3 What are the major decisions involved in constructing an itemised rating scale? How many scale categories should be used in an itemised rating scale? Why?

4 Should an odd or even number of categories be used in an itemised rating scale ?

5 What is the difference between forced and non-forced scales?

6 How does the nature and degree of verbal description affect the response to itemised rating scales?

7 What are multi-item scales?

8 What is reliability?

9 What are the differences between test–re-test and alternative-forms reliability?

10 Describe the notion of internal consistency reliability.

11 What is validity?

12 What is criterion validity? How is it assessed?

13 How would you assess the construct validity of a multi-item scale?

14 What is the relationship between reliability and validity?

15 How would you select a particular scaling technique?

NOTES

1 Edel, R., 'New Technologies Add Dimensions to Copy Testing', *Advertising Age* (24 November 1986).

2 Hogg, M.K., Bruce, M. and Hill, A.J., 'Fashion Brand Preferences Among Young Consumers', *International Journal of Retail and Distribution Management* 26 (8) (August 1998), 293.

3 Nanayana, C.L., 'Graphic Positioning Scale: An Economical Instrument for Surveys', *Journal of Marketing Research* 14 (February1977), 118–22.

4 Gregg, A.O., 'Some Problems Concerning the Use of Rating Scales for Visual Assessment', *Journal of the Market Research Society* 22 (January 1980) 29–43.

5 For arguments in favour of graphic rating scales, see Lampert, S.I., 'The Attitude Pollimeter: A New Attitude Scaling Device', *Journal of Marketing Research* (November 1979), 578–82; and Tillinghast, D.S., 'Direct Magnitude Scales in Public Opinion Surveys', *Public Opinion Quarterly* (Fall 1980), 377–84.

6 Likert, R., 'A Technique for the Measurement of Attitudes', *Archives of Psychology*, 140 (1932).

7 Weiss, A.M. and Anderson, E., 'Converting from Independent to Employee Salesforces: The Role of Perceived Switching Costs', *Journal of Marketing Research* 29 (February 1992), 101–15.

8 Sumrall, D.A., Eyuboglu, N. and Ahlawat, S.S., 'Developing a Scale to Measure Hospital Sales Orientation', *Journal of Health Care Marketing* (December 1991), 39–50.

9 Dickson, J. and Albaum, G., 'A Method for Developing Tailor-Made Semantic Differentials for Specific Marketing Content Areas', *Journal of Marketing Research* 14 (February 1977), 87–91.

10 Saffe, E.D. and Nebenzahl, I.D., 'Alternative Questionnaire Formats for Country Image Studies', *Journal of Marketing Research* 21 (November 1984), 463–71.

11 There is little difference in the results based on whether the data are ordinal or interval; however, see Gaiton, J., 'Measurement Scales and Statistics: Resurgence of an Old Misconception', *Psychological Bulletin* 87 (1980), 564–67.

12 Malhotra, S., Van Auken, S. and Lonial, S.C., 'Adjective Profiles in Television Copy Testing', *Journal of Advertising Research* (August 1981), 21–25.

13 Evans, R.H., 'The Upgraded Semantic Differential: A Further Test', *Journal of the Market Research Society* 22 (1980), 143–47; and Swan, S.E. and Futrell, C.M., 'Increasing the Efficiency of the Retailer's Image Study', *Journal of the Academy of Marketing Science* (Winter 1980), 51–57.

14 Stapel, J., 'About 35 Years of Market Research in the Netherlands', *Markonderzock Kwartaalschrift* 2 (1969), 3–7.

15 Hawkins, D.I., Albaum, G. and Best, R., 'Stapel Scale or Semantic Differential in Marketing Research?', *Journal of Marketing Research* 11 (August 1974), 318–22; and Menezes, D. and Elbert, N.E., 'Alternative Semantic Scaling Formats for Measuring Store Image: An Evaluation', *Journal of Marketing Research* 16 (February 1979), 80–87.

16 Upah, G.D. and Cosmas, S.C., 'The Use of Telephone Dials as Attitude Scales', *Journal of the Academy of Marketing Science* (Fall 1980), 416–26.

17 Cox III, E.P., 'The Optimal Number of Response Alternatives for a Scale: A Review', *Journal of Marketing Research* 17 (November 1980), 407–22, and Reynolds, F.D. and Neter, J., 'How Many Categories for Respondent Classification', *Journal of the Market Research Society* 24 (October 1982), 345–46; and Lawrence, R.J., 'Reply', *Journal of the Market Research Society* 24 (October 1982), 346–48.

18 Givon, M.M. and Shapira, Z., 'Response to Rating Scales: A Theoretical Model and Its Application to the Number of Categories Problem', *Journal of Marketing Research* (November 1984), 410–19; and Stem, Jr, D.E. and Noazin, S., 'The Effects of Number of Objects and Scale Positions on Graphic Position Scale Reliability', in Lusch, R.E. et al., *1985 AMA Educators' Proceedings* (Chicago: American Marketing Association, 1985), 370–72.

19 Schuman, H. and Presser, S., *Questions and Answers in Attitude Surveys* (New York: Academic Press, 1981), 179–201.

20 Spagna, G.J., 'Questionnaires: Which Approach Do You Use?', *Journal of Advertising Research* (February-March 1984), 67–70.

21 Holdaway, E.A., 'Different Response Categories and Questionnaire Response Patterns', *Journal of Experimental Education* (Winter 1971), 59.

22 Bishop, G.E., Oldendick, R.W. and Tuchfarber, A.J., 'Effects of Filter Questions in Public Opinion Surveys', *Public Opinion Quarterly* (Winter 1983), 528–46; Hawkins, D.I. and Coney, K.A., 'Uninformed Response Error in Survey Research', *Journal of Marketing Research* (August 1981), 370–74; and Schneider, K.C., 'Uninformed Response Rate in Survey Research', *Journal of Business Research* (April 1985), 153–62.

23 Friedman, H.H. and Leefer, J.R., 'Label versus Position in Rating Scales', *Journal of the Academy of Marketing Science* (Spring 1981), 88–92; and Haley, R.I. and Case, P.B., 'Testing Thirteen Attitude Scales for Agreement and Brand Discrimination', *Journal of Marketing* (Fall 1979), 20–32; and Wildt, A.R. and Mazis, M.B., 'Determinants of Scale Response: Label versus Position', *Journal of Marketing Research* (May 1978), 261–67.

24 Andrews, E.M., 'Construct Validity and Error Components of Survey Measures', *Public Opinion Quarterly* (Summer 1984), 432; Churchill, Jr, G.A. and Peter, J.P.,'Research Design Effects on the Reliability of Rating Scales', *Journal of Marketing Research* (November 1984), 365–66; and Stern, Jr, D.E., Lamb Jr, C.W. and MacLachlan, D.L., 'Remote versus Adjacent Scale Questionnaire Designs', *Journal of the Market Research Society* (January 1978), 3–13.

25 Schofield, A., 'Adverbial Qualifiers for Adjectival Scales', *Journal of the Market Research Society* (July 1975), 204–7; and Bartram, P. and Yelding, D., 'Reply', *Journal of the Market Research Society* (July 1975), 207–8.

26 Goldberg, M.E., Gorn, G.J. and Gibson, W., 'TV Messages for Snack and Breakfast Foods: Do They Influence Children's Preferences?', *Journal of Consumer Research* 5 (September 1978), 73–81.

27 For an example of a multi-item scale, see Kohli, A.K., Jaworski, B.J. and Kumar, A., 'MARKOR: A Measure of Market Orientation', *Journal of Marketing Research* 31 (November 1993), 467–77. An application may be found in Siguaw, J.A., Brown, G. and Widing II, R.E., 'The Influence of the Market Orientation of the Firm on Sales Force Behavior and Attitude', *Journal of Marketing Research* 31 (February 1994), 106–16.

28 For example, see Malhotra, N.K., 'A Scale to Measure Self Concepts, Person Concepts, and Product Concepts', *Journal of Marketing Research* 18 (November 1981), 456–64.

29 Greenleaf, E.A., 'Improving Rating Scale Measures by Detecting and Correcting Bias Components in Some Response Styles', *Journal of Marketing Research* 29 (May 1992), 176–88.

30 The true score model is not the only theory of measurement. See Lord, E.M. and Novick, M.A., *Statistical Theories of Mental Test-Scores* (Reading, MA: Addison-Wesley, 1968).

31 Perreault, Jr, W.D. and Leigh, L.E., 'Reliability of Nominal Data Based on Qualitative Judgements', *Journal of Marketing Research* 25 (May 1989), 135–48; and Peter, J.P., 'Reliability: A Review of Psychometric Basics and Recent Marketing Practices', *Journal of Marketing Research* 16 (February 1979), 6–17.

32 Segal, M.N., 'Alternate Form Conjoint Reliability', *Journal of Advertising Research* 4 (1984), 31–38.

33 Cronbach, L.J., 'Coefficient Alpha and the Internal Structure of Tests', *Psychometrika* 16 (1951), 297–334.

34 Peterson, R.A., 'A Meta-Analysis of Cronbach's Coefficient Alpha', *Journal of Consumer Research* 21 (September 1994), 381–91.

35 Singh, J. and Rhoads, G.K., 'Boundary Role Ambiguity in Marketing-Oriented Positions: A Multidimensional, Multifaceted Operationalization', *Journal of Marketing Research* 28 (August 1991), 328–38; and Peter, J.P., 'Construct Validity: A Review of Basic Issues and Marketing Practices', *Journal of Marketing Research* 18 (May 1981), 133–45.

36 For further details on validity, see Spiro, R.L. and Weitz, B.A., 'Adaptive Selling: Conceptualization, Measurement, and Nomological Validity', *Journal of Marketing Research* 27 (February 1990), 61–69; and Schmitt, N. and Stults, D.M., 'Methodology Review: Analysis of Multitrait-Multimethod Matrices', *Applied Psychological Measurement* 10 (1986), 1–22.

37 For a discussion of the generalisability theory and its applications in marketing research, see Rentz, J.O., 'Generalisability Theory: A Comprehensive Method for Assessing and Improving the Dependability of Marketing Measures', *Journal of Marketing Research* 24 (February 1987), 19–28; and Peter, J.P., 'Reliability, Generalisability, and Consumer Research', in Perreault, Jr, W.D. (ed.), *Advances in Consumer Research* vol. 4 (Atlanta: Association for Consumer Research, 1977), 394, 400; and Peter, J.P., 'Reliability: A Review of Psychometric Basis and Recent Marketing Practices', *Journal of Marketing Research* 16 (February 1979), 6–17.

38 Hawkins, D.I., Albaum, G. and Best, R., 'Stapel Scale or Semantic Differential in Marketing Research?', *Journal of Marketing Research* 11 (August 1974), 318–22; and Haley, R.I. and Case, P.B., 'Testing Thirteen Attitude Scales for Agreement and Brand Discrimination', *Journal of Marketing* (Fall 1979), 20–32; Lampert, S.I., 'The Attitude Pollimeter: A New Attitude Scaling Device', *Journal of Marketing Research* (November 1979), 578–82; and Menezes, D. and Elbert, N.E., 'Alternative Semantic Scaling Formats for Measuring Store Image: An Evaluation', *Journal of Marketing Research* 16 (February 1979), 80–87.

39 Martin, I.M. and Eroglu, S., 'Measuring a Multidimensional Construct: Country Image', *Journal of Business Research* 28 (November 1993), 191–210.

40 Mckay, B., 'Xerox Fights Trademark Battle', *Advertising Age International* (27 April 1992), 1–39.

Chapter 12

Questionnaire design

The questionnaire must motivate the respondent to cooperate, become involved, and provide complete, honest and accurate answers

OBJECTIVES

After reading this chapter, the student should be able to:

1 explain the purpose of a questionnaire and its objectives of asking questions that respondents can and will answer, encouraging respondents, and minimising response error;
2 understand the array of trade-offs that have to be made in the total process of questionnaire design;
3 describe the process of designing a questionnaire, the steps involved, and guidelines that must be followed at each step;
4 discuss the considerations involved in designing questionnaires for international marketing research;
5 understand the ethical issues involved in questionnaire design.

OVERVIEW

Questionnaire or form design is an important step in formulating a research design. Once the researcher has specified the nature of research design (Chapters 3 to 9) and determined the scaling procedures (Chapters 10 and 11), they can develop a questionnaire or an observational form. This chapter discusses the importance of questionnaires and how different events interrelate forcing questionnaire designers to make trade-offs a particular stages. Next, we describe the objectives of a questionnaire and the steps involved in designing questionnaires. We provide several guidelines for developing sound questionnaires. The considerations involved in designing questionnaires when conducting international marketing research are discussed. The chapter concludes with a discussion of several ethical issues that arise in questionnaire design.

We begin with an example to introduce questionnaire design which illustrates the nature of research task that can be tackled through the use of the questionnaire. The second example illustrates how target respondents affect the design and implementation of a questionnaire.

EXAMPLE

Winkling out the joys of financial research[1]

The Financial Research Survey (FRS) is, in principle, very simple: take a sample of people and ask them what financial products they use, which brand, how and where bought. Consider, though, the huge range of financial products available, the multitude of brands, and the diversity of channels of distribution. The result is a formidable questionnaire of 173 questions. Consider, too, that the inevitable result of a market with many brands is many brands with low penetration. To cater for this, the FRS sample is vast: roughly 30,000 per six-month reporting period. In theory then, each reporting period could deliver well over five million consumer responses. In reality, few consumers use every conceivable variety of financial product, so the actual number is somewhat less. To support this task, FRS provides a small team of client executives to present and support the data collected. ■

EXAMPLE

Finding the elusive young through cooperative parents[2]

ACCESS to Youth is a specialist survey that comprises around 1100 in-home interviews targeted at 7- to 19-year-olds. In surveying this age group it was noted that children become fatigued more quickly than adults, and this could affect data quality. In this project strict controls were placed on the interview length – it did not exceed 10 minutes. Wording was kept simple; complicated questions must be avoided. The research showed that the ease with which children were able to answer questions correlated with age. The older they were, the easier they found the question; and the more times they were asked the question the easier they found it. It was also found that children found it more difficult to understand the traditional four- or five-point agree/disagree scale and so a simplified three- point scale was used. Interviewers should be correctly briefed on how to conduct interviews with children. They needed to be patient and must treat the child as an equal – impatience or a condescending manner affect the child's ease and hence influence the answers they give. ■

QUESTIONNAIRES

As discussed in Chapter 8, survey and observation are the two basic methods for obtaining quantitative primary data in descriptive research. Both methods require some procedure for standardising the data collection process so that the data obtained are internally consistent and can be analysed in a uniform and coherent manner. If 40 different interviewers conduct personal interviews or make observations in different parts of the country, the data they collect will not be comparable unless they follow specific guidelines and ask questions and record answers in a standard way. A standardised questionnaire or form will ensure comparability of the data, increase speed and accuracy of recording, and facilitate data processing.

Questionnaire definition

Questionnaire
A structured technique for data collection consisting of a series of questions, written or verbal, that a respondent answers.

A **questionnaire**, whether it is called a schedule, interview form, or measuring instrument, is a formalised set of questions for obtaining information from respondents. Typically, a questionnaire is only one element of a data collection package that might also include (1) field work procedures, such as instructions for selecting, approaching and questioning respondents (see Chapter 15); (2) some reward, gift or payment offered to respondents; and (3) communication aids, such as maps, pictures, advertisements and products (as in personal interviews) and return envelopes (in mail surveys). Regardless of the form of administration, a questionnaire is characterised by some specific objectives.

Objectives of a questionnaire

Any questionnaire has three specific objectives. First, it must translate the information needed into a set of specific questions that the respondents can and will answer. Developing questions that respondents can and will answer and that will yield the desired information is difficult. Two apparently similar ways of posing a question may yield different information. Hence, this objective is a challenge.

Second, a questionnaire must uplift, motivate and encourage the respondent to become involved in the interview, to cooperate, and to complete the interview. Figure 12.1 uses a basic marketing model of exchange of values between two parties to illustrate this point. Before designing any questionnaire or indeed any research technique, the researcher must evaluate 'what is the respondent going to get out of this'. In other words, the marketing researcher must have an empathy with the respondent and appreciate what they go through when approached and questioned. Such an appreciation of what respondents go through affects the design of how they are approached, the stated purpose of the research, the rewards for taking part and the whole process of capturing the data.

Not all respondents are the same in what they seek from a questionnaire or interview process. In Figure 12.1, some respondents may want to see some personal benefit, perhaps a tangible reward, while others may be happy to see the social benefits. Taking care in appreciating what the respondent expects from the questioning process nurtures responses that have been well thought through, are honest and accurate.

Third, a questionnaire should minimise response error. The potential sources of error in research designs were discussed in Chapter 3, where response error was defined as the error that arises when respondents give inaccurate answers or when their answers are mis-recorded or mis-analysed. A questionnaire can be a major source of response error. Minimising this error is an important objective of questionnaire design.

What the respondent may want from the researcher:

- Tangible reward
- Confidentiality
- Interesting subject and experience
- Personal benefits from seeing the research completed
- Social benefits from seeing the research completed
- Being 'chosen' as a respondent with expertise on the subject
- Research organisation known for excellence in research
- Rapport and trust

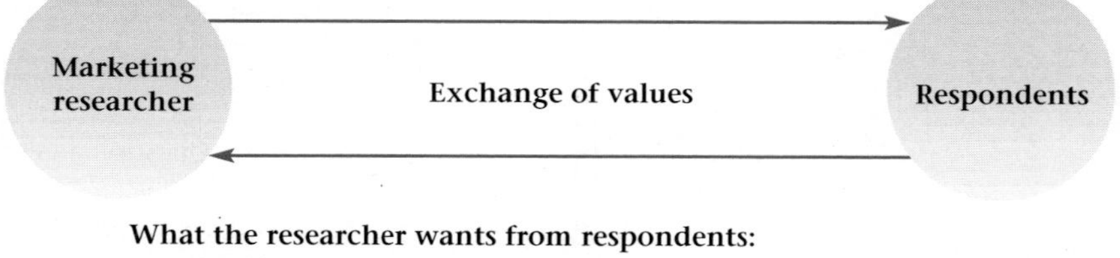

Marketing researcher — **Exchange of values** — **Respondents**

What the researcher wants from respondents:

- Honesty
- Takes in the reason for the study
- Follows the instructors in completing the study
- Thinks through the issues before forming an answer
- Says good things about the rationale for marketing research
- Says good things about the research process

Figure 12.1
Exchange of values between marketing researchers and respondents

QUESTIONNAIRE DESIGN PROCESS

The great weakness of questionnaire design is lack of theory. Because there are no scientific principles that guarantee an optimal or ideal questionnaire, questionnaire design is a skill acquired through experience. Similarly, the correct grammatical use of language does not guarantee the optimal questionnaire. There may be certain respondents who do not communicate in a 'correct' grammatical manner; such questionnaires may be confusing and meaningless. Therefore, this section presents guidelines and rules to help develop the craft of questionnaire design. Although these guidelines and rules can help you avoid major mistakes, the fine-tuning of a questionnaire comes from the creativity of a skilled researcher.

Developing the craft of questionnaire design requires the creative 'trade-off' of many factors. Figure 12.2 helps to illustrate some of the trade-offs that the questionnaire designer faces, that can make the design process so difficult. Chapter 2 discussed the problems of establishing the nature of marketing problems and corresponding marketing research problems. Different techniques and sources of information were outlined to help in the diagnosis process.

1 The 'source of idea' represents the culmination of marketing decision-maker and marketing researchers' diagnoses and the data they have available at the time of commissioning a marketing research project.
2 From the diagnoses, and the statement of marketing and research problems, emerge specific research questions. Based upon the diagnoses, 'question purposes' are established. Some research problems may be tackled through actual measurements in questionnaires. Other research problems may not be tackled by questionnaires. For example, in the GlobalCash project, banks wished to know which criteria companies use to choose a bank. Tackling this issue is a straightforward task of establishing criteria and applying scales of importance to these criteria. Banks further wished to know what forces were shaping these criteria and how these forces interacted. The latter issues are qualitative in nature and were captured in follow-up in-depth interviews. At this stage, priorities have to be set establishing what can be measured with a questionnaire, and out of the array of issues that could be measured, what are seen as the most, down to the least important.

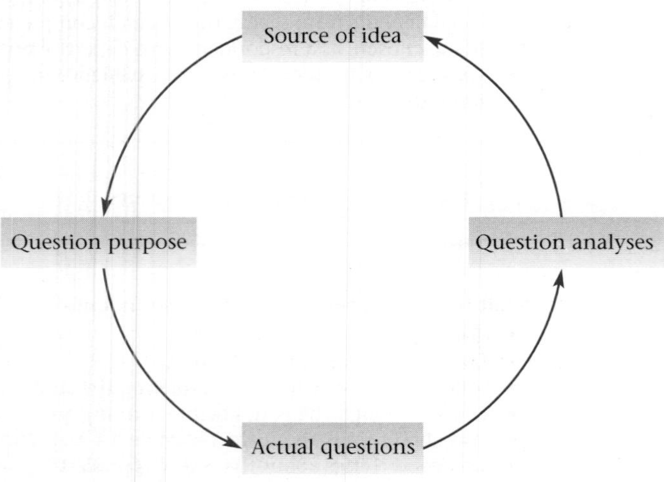

Figure 12.2
Trade-offs faced by the questionnaire designer

3 With clear question purposes, the process of establishing a form of setting 'actual questions' can begin. At this point, the researcher has to put themselves 'in the shoes' of the potential respondent. It is fine to say that certain questions need to be answered, but this has to be balanced with an appreciation of whether respondents are able or indeed willing to answer particular questions. For example in the GlobalCash project, banks wished to know which banks individual companies use in every European country. The purpose of such a question was to establish which banks were gaining market share and to see if companies were concentrating their business with fewer banks. This seems a straightforward question until one realises the enormity of the task. There are over 20 European countries and in some countries, the norm is to conduct business with a large number of banks. In Italy, for example, one company conducted business with 70 banks! Thus, the task of remembering all the banks and writing them down places an enormous burden on the respondent. Making the question closed by listing all the banks does not help either; in Germany for example there are over 400 banks that could be listed. The trade-off made, was to ask respondents who their 'lead bank' was, i.e. with whom they did most business. This ensured that the task was not too onerous for the respondent, enabling a more complete and accurate response. The trade-off was that it did not completely satisfy the set question purpose.

4 Knowing how the data collected is to be analysed does not happen when questionnaires have been returned from respondents. 'Question analyses' must be thought through from an early stage. The connections between questions and the appropriate statistical tests that fulfil the question purposes should be established as the questionnaire is designed. Again, trade-offs have to be considered. In Chapter 10, different scale types were linked to different statistical tests. As one progresses from nominal to ordinal to interval and then ratio scales, more powerful statistical analyses can be performed. However, as one progresses through these scale types, the task for respondents becomes more onerous. This trade-off can be illustrated again using questions from the GlobalCash project. Companies were asked who they thought were the top four cash management banks in their country (ordinal scale). Respondents were then asked why they thought the top two banks were perceived to be best and second-best. This could be completed in a number of ways. A list of characteristics could be given and respondents asked to tick those that they thought matched the bank. This would be easy for respondents to undertake and produce nominal data. The same set of characteristics could be listed with respondents asked to rank order them. This task requires more thought and effort, though now produces the more powerful ordinal data. The same list could have been presented and respondents asked to allocate 100 points using a constant sum scale. This would have been an even more onerous task but would have produced the more powerful interval scale. The questionnaire designer has to consider how onerous the task is for respondents, especially when set in the context of all the other questions the respondent is being asked, and trade this off against the meaning they get from the data.

5 The meaning that is taken from the data comes back to the 'source of idea' i.e. the marketing decision-maker and marketing researchers' diagnoses and the data they had available at the time of commissioning a marketing research project. By now they may have collected other data, interpreted existing data differently, or been exposed to new forces in the marketplace. They may even now see what questions they should have been asking!

The purpose of Figure 12.2 is to show that there can be no theory to encapsulate these trade-offs. Each research project will have different demands and emphases. With the experience of designing a number of questionnaires, the 'art' of questionnaire design is developed and the balance understood to meet different demands and emphases.

In order to develop a further understanding of questionnaire design, the process will be presented as a series of steps, as shown in Figure 12.3, and we present guidelines for each step. The process outlined in Figure 12.2 shows that in practice the steps are interrelated and the development of a questionnaire involves much iteration and interconnection between stages.[3]

SPECIFY THE INFORMATION NEEDED

The first step in questionnaire design is to specify the information needed. This is also the first step in the research design process. Note that as the research project progresses, the information needed becomes more and more clearly defined. It is helpful to review the components of the problem and the approach, particularly the research questions, hypotheses and characteristics that influence the research design. To further ensure that the information obtained fully addresses all the components of the problem, the researcher should prepare a set of dummy tables. A dummy table is a blank table used to catalogue data. It portrays how the analysis will be structured once the data have been collected.

It is also vital to have a clear idea of the target respondents. The characteristics of the respondent group have a great influence on questionnaire design.

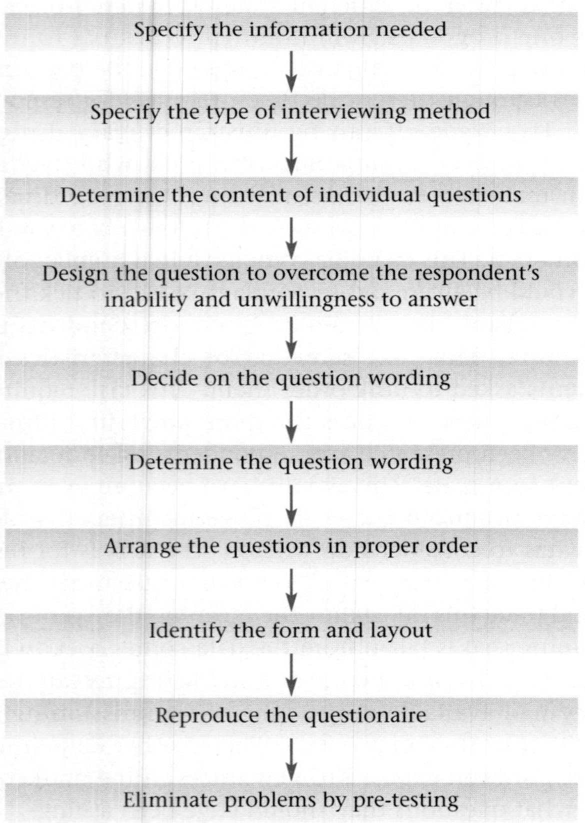

Figure 12.3
Questionnaire design process

Questions that are appropriate for finance directors and treasurers of large multinational companies may not be appropriate for retired persons. The more diversified the respondent group, the more difficult it is to design a single questionnaire appropriate for the entire group.

TYPE OF INTERVIEWING METHOD

An appreciation of how the type of interviewing method influences questionnaire design can be obtained by considering how the questionnaire is administered under each method (see Chapter 8). In personal interviews, respondents see the questionnaire and interact face to face with the interviewer. Thus, lengthy, complex and varied questions can be asked. In telephone interviews the respondents interact with the interviewer, but they do not see the questionnaire. This limits the type of questions that can be asked to short and simple ones. Mail and electronic questionnaires are self administered, so the questions must be simple and detailed instructions must be provided. In computer-assisted interviewing (CAPI and CATI), complex skip patterns and randomisation of questions to eliminate order bias can be easily accommodated. Questionnaires designed for personal and telephone interviews should be written in a conversational style.

INDIVIDUAL QUESTION CONTENT

Once the information needed is specified and the type of interviewing method decided, the next step is to determine individual question content: what to include in individual questions.[4]

Is the question necessary?

Every question in a questionnaire should contribute to the information needed or serve some specific purpose. If there is no satisfactory use for the data resulting from a question, that question should be eliminated.

In certain situations, however, questions may be asked that are not directly related to the needed information. It is useful to ask some neutral questions at the beginning of the questionnaire to establish involvement and rapport, particularly when the topic of the questionnaire is sensitive or controversial. Sometimes **filter questions** are asked to disguise the purpose or sponsorship of the project. For example, rather than limiting the questions to the brand of interest, questions about competing brands may also be included to disguise the sponsorship. Questions unrelated to the immediate problem may sometimes be included to generate client support for the project. At times, certain questions may be duplicated for the purpose of assessing reliability or validity.[5]

Filter question
An initial question in a questionnaire that screens potential respondents to ensure they meet the requirements of the sample.

Are several questions needed instead of one?

Once we have ascertained that a question is necessary, we must make sure that it is sufficient to get the desired information. Sometimes several questions are needed to obtain the required information in an unambiguous manner. Consider the question, 'Do you think Coca-Cola is a tasty and refreshing soft drink?' A yes answer will presumably be clear, but what if the answer is no? Does this mean that the respondent thinks that Coca-Cola is not tasty, that it is not refreshing, or that it is neither tasty nor refreshing? Such a question is called a **double-barrelled question** because two or more questions are

Double-barrelled question
A single question that attempts to cover two issues. Such questions can be confusing to respondents and result in ambiguous responses.

combined into one. To obtain the required information, two distinct questions should be asked: 'Do you think Coca-Cola is a tasty soft drink?' and 'Do you think Coca-Cola is a refreshing soft drink?'

Another example of multiple questions embedded in a single question is the 'why' question. In the context of the GlobalCash study, consider the question, 'Why do you bank at ABN AMRO?' The possible answers may include: 'for their cash flow forecasting software', 'it has a more conveniently located network of branches', and 'it was recommended by a respected colleague at a conference'. Each answer relates to a different question embedded in the why question. The first tells why the respondent banks with the pan-European bank, the second reveals what the respondent likes about ABN AMRO compared with other banks, and the third tells how the respondent learned about ABN AMRO. The three answers are not comparable and any one answer may not be sufficient. Complete information may be obtained by asking two separate questions: 'What do you like about ABN AMRO compared with other banks?' and 'How did you first develop a relationship with ABN AMRO?' Most 'why' questions about the use of a product or choice alternative involve two aspects: (1) attributes of the product and (2) influences leading to knowledge of it.[6]

OVERCOMING INABILITY TO ANSWER

Researchers should not assume that respondents can provide accurate or reasonable answers to all questions. The researcher should attempt to overcome the respondents' inability to answer. Certain factors limit the respondents' ability to provide the desired information. The respondents may not be informed, may not remember, or may be unable to articulate certain types of responses.

Is the respondent informed?

Respondents are often asked about topics on which they are not informed. A parent may not be informed about their child's daily purchasing or vice versa (especially when one considers that the sons and daughters can have an age range from 0 to around 80!).

In situations where not all respondents are likely to be informed about the topic of interest, filter questions that measure familiarity, product use, and past experience should be asked before questions about the topics themselves.[7] Filter questions enable the researcher to filter out respondents who are not adequately informed.

The GlobalCash questionnaire included questions related to different banks, ranging from small domestic banks to large American and pan-European banks. It was likely that many respondents would not be sufficiently informed about a wide array of banks, so information on the use of different banks was obtained as well as perceptions of which banks were felt to be the 'best'. This allowed for separate analysis of data on banks of which the respondents had no experience. A 'don't know' option appears to reduce uninformed responses without reducing the overall response rate or the response rate for questions about which the respondents have information. Hence, this option should be provided unless there are explicit reasons for not doing so.[8]

Can the respondent remember?

Many things that we might expect everyone to know are remembered by only a few. Test this on yourself. Can you remember the brand name of the socks you are wearing (presuming you are wearing them), what you had for lunch a week ago, or what you were doing a month ago today? Further, do you know how many litres of soft drinks you consumed during the last four weeks? Evidence indicates that consumers are particularly poor at remembering quantities of products consumed. In situations where factual data were available for comparison, it was found that consumer reports of product usage exceeded actual usage by 100 per cent or more.[9]

The inability to remember leads to errors of omission, telescoping and creation. Omission is the inability to recall an event that actually took place. **Telescoping** takes place when an individual telescopes or compresses time by remembering an event as occurring more recently than it actually occurred.[10] For example, a respondent reports three trips to the supermarket in the last two weeks when, in fact, one of these trips was made 18 days ago. Creation error takes place when a respondent 'remembers' an event that did not actually occur.

Telescoping
A psychological phenomenon that takes place when an individual telescopes or compresses time by remembering an event as occurring more recently than it actually occurred.

The ability to remember an event is influenced by (1) the event itself, (2) the time elapsed since the event, and (3) the presence or absence of events that would aid memory. We tend to remember events that are important or unusual or that occur frequently. People remember their wedding anniversary and birthday. Likewise, more recent events are remembered better. A grocery shopper is more likely to remember what he purchased on his last shopping trip as compared with what he bought three shopping trips ago. Think back to Chapter 5 and how the use of scanner data and the loyalty card overcomes this problem for the researcher. Not only can a huge list be of groceries be captured but also how much was paid for each item.

Research indicates that questions that do not provide the respondent with cues to the event, and that rely on unaided recall, can underestimate the actual occurrence of an event. For example, testing whether respondents were exposed to a beer commercials at the cinema could be measured in an unaided manner by questions like, 'What brands of beer do you remember being advertised last night at the cinema?' (having established that the respondent was at a cinema last night). Naming a brand shows that they saw the advert, took in the brand name and could recall it – three different stages. An aided recall approach attempts to stimulate the respondent's memory by providing cues related to the event of interest. Thus, the important features to measure may be that they saw the advert and took in the brand name – the fact that they cannot say the brand name may not affect their purchasing intentions. The aided recall approach would list a number of beer brands and then ask, 'Which of these brands were advertised last night at the cinema?' In presenting cues, the researcher must guard against biasing the responses by testing out several successive levels of stimulation. The influence of stimulation on responses can then be analysed to select an appropriate level of stimulation.

Can the respondent articulate?

Respondents may be unable to articulate certain types of responses. For example, if asked to describe the atmosphere of the bank branch they would prefer to patronise, most respondents may be unable to phrase their answers. On the other hand, if the respondents are provided with alternative descriptions of bank atmosphere, they will be able to indicate the one they like the best. If the respondents are unable to articulate their responses to a question, they are likely to ignore that question and refuse to respond to the rest of the questionnaire. Thus, respondents should be given aids such as pictures, maps and descriptions to help them articulate their responses.

OVERCOMING UNWILLINGNESS TO ANSWER

Even if respondents are able to answer a particular question, they may be unwilling to do so, either because too much effort is required, the situation or context may not seem appropriate for disclosure, no legitimate purpose or need for the information requested is apparent, or the information requested is sensitive.

Effort required of the respondents

Most respondents are unwilling to devote much effort to providing information. Suppose that the researcher is interested in determining from which shops a respondent bought goods on his or her most recent shopping trip. This information can be obtained in at least two ways. The researcher could ask the respondent to list all the items purchased on his or her most recent shopping trip, or the researcher could provide a list of shops and ask the respondent to indicate the applicable ones. The second option is preferable, because it requires less effort from respondents.

Context

Some questions may seem appropriate in certain contexts but not in others. For example, questions about personal hygiene habits may be appropriate when asked in a survey sponsored by a health organisation but not in one sponsored by a breakfast cereal manufacturer. Respondents are unwilling to respond to questions they consider to be inappropriate for the given context. Sometimes, the researcher can manipulate the context in which the questions are asked so that the questions seem appropriate.

Legitimate purpose

Respondents are also unwilling to divulge information that they do not see as serving a legitimate purpose. Why should a firm marketing breakfast cereals want to know their age, income and occupation? Explaining why the data are needed can make the request for the information seem legitimate and may increase the respondents' willingness to answer. A statement such as, 'To determine how the consumption of cereal and preferences for cereal brands vary among people of different ages, incomes and occupations, we need information on . . . ' can make the request for information seem legitimate.

Sensitive information

Respondents may be unwilling to disclose, at least accurately, sensitive information because this may cause embarrassment or threaten the respondent's prestige or self-image, or be seen as too personal and an invasion of privacy. If pressed for the answer, respondents may give biased responses, especially during personal interviews[11] (see Table 8.2). Sensitive topics include money, personal hygiene, family life, political and religious beliefs, involvement in accidents or crimes. In industrial surveys, sensitive questions may encompass much of what a company does, especially if it reveals strategic activities and plans. The techniques described in the following section can be adopted to increase the likelihood of obtaining information that respondents are unwilling to give.

Increasing the willingness of respondents

Respondents may be encouraged to provide information which they are unwilling to give by the following techniques.[12]

1 Place sensitive topics at the end of the questionnaire. By then, initial mistrust has been overcome, rapport has been created, legitimacy of the project has been established, and respondents are more willing to give information.
2 Preface the question with a statement that the behaviour of interest is common. For example, before requesting information on credit card debt, say 'Recent studies show that most European consumers are in debt'. This technique describes the use of counter-biasing statements.
3 Ask the question using the third-person technique (see Chapter 6): phrase the question as if it referred to other people.
4 Hide the question in a group of other questions that respondents are willing to answer. The entire list of questions can then be asked quickly.
5 Provide response categories rather than asking for specific figures.[13] Do not ask, 'What is your household's annual income?' Instead, ask the respondent to indicate an appropriate income category. In personal interviews, give the respondents cards that list the numbered choices. The respondents then indicate their responses by number.
6 Use randomised techniques. In these techniques, respondents are presented with two questions, one sensitive and the other a neutral question with a known probability of yes responses (e.g. 'Is your birthday in March?'). They are asked to select one question randomly by flipping a coin, for example. The respondent then answers the selected question yes or no, without telling the researcher which question is being answered.[14] Given the overall probability of a yes response, the probability of selecting the sensitive question, and the probability of a yes response to the neutral question, the researcher can determine the probability of yes response to the sensitive question using the law of probability. The researcher cannot, however, determine which respondents have answered yes to the sensitive question.[15]

CHOOSING QUESTION STRUCTURE

A question may be unstructured or structured. In the following sections, we define unstructured questions and discuss their relative advantages and disadvantages and then consider the major types of structured questions: multiple-choice, dichotomous and scales.[16]

Unstructured questions

Unstructured questions
Open-ended questions that respondents answer in their own words.

Unstructured questions are open-ended questions that respondents answer in their own words. They are also referred to as free-response or free-answer questions. The following are some examples:

- What is your occupation?
- What do you think of people who patronise secondhand clothes shops?
- Who is your favourite film personality?

Open-ended questions are good first questions on a topic. They enable the respondents to express general attitudes and opinions that can help the researcher interpret their responses to structured questions. Unstructured questions have a much less biasing influence on response than structured questions. Respondents are free to express any views. Their comments and explanations can provide the researcher with rich insights. Hence, unstructured questions are useful in exploratory research.

A principal disadvantage is that potential for interviewer bias is high. Whether the interviewers record the answers verbatim or write down only the main points, the data depend on the skills of the interviewers. Tape recorders should be used if verbatim reporting is important.

Another major disadvantage of unstructured questions is that the coding of responses is costly and time-consuming.[17] The coding procedures required to summarise responses in a format useful for data analysis and interpretation can be extensive. Implicitly, unstructured or open-ended questions give extra weight to respondents who are more articulate. Also, unstructured questions are not very suitable for self-administered questionnaires (mail and CAPI), because respondents tend to be briefer in writing than in speaking.

Pre-coding can overcome some of the disadvantages of unstructured questions. Expected responses are recorded in multiple-choice format, although the question is presented to the respondents as an open-ended question. Based on the respondent's reply, the interviewer selects the appropriate response category. Because the response alternatives are limited, this approach may be satisfactory when the respondent can easily formulate the response and when it is easy to develop pre-coded categories. In general, open-ended questions are useful in exploratory research and as opening questions. Otherwise, their disadvantages outweigh their advantages in a large survey.[18]

Structured questions

Structured questions Questions that pre-specify the set of response alternatives and the response format. A structured question could be multiple-choice, dichotomous, or a scale.

Structured questions specify the set of response alternatives and the response format. A structured question may be multiple-choice, dichotomous, or a scale.

Multiple choice questions. In multiple-choice questions, the researcher provides a choice of answers and respondents are asked to select one or more of the alternatives given. Consider the following question: Which of the following items have you purchased in the last two months? Please tick as many as apply.

Several of the issues discussed in Chapter 11 with respect to itemised rating scales also apply to multiple-choice answers. Two additional concerns in designing multiple-choice questions are the number of alternatives that should be included and order or position bias.

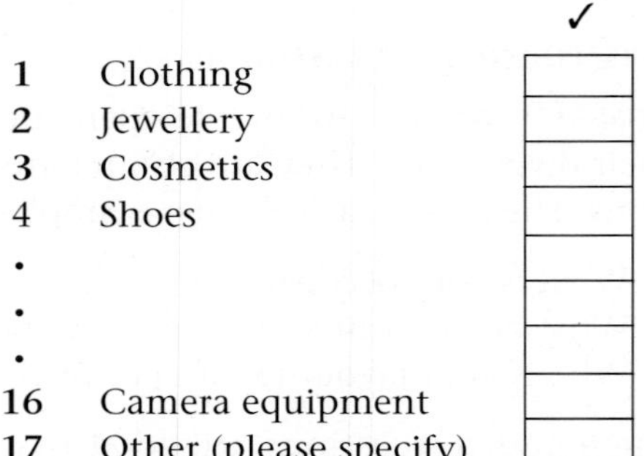

The response alternatives should include the set of all possible choices. The general guideline is to list all alternatives that may be of importance and to include an alternative labelled 'other (please specify)', as shown above. The response alternatives should be mutually exclusive. Respondents should also be able to identify one, and only one, alternative, unless the researcher specifically allows two or more choices (for example, 'Please indicate all the brands of soft drinks that you have consumed in the past week'). If the response alternatives are numerous, consider using more than one question to reduce the information processing demands on the respondents.

Order bias (position bias) A respondent's tendency to choose an alternative merely because it occupies a certain position or is listed in a certain order.

Order or position bias is the respondents' tendency to tick an alternative merely because it occupies a certain position or is listed in a certain order. Respondents tend to check the first or the last statement in a list, particularly the first.[19] For a list of numbers (quantities or prices), there is a bias toward the central value on the list. To control for order bias, several forms of the questionnaire should be prepared with the order in which the alternatives are listed varied from form to form. Each alternative should appear once in each of the extreme positions, once in the middle, and once somewhere in between.[20]

Multiple-choice questions overcome many of the disadvantages of open-ended questions because interviewer bias is reduced and these questions are administered quickly. Also, coding and processing of data are much less costly and time-consuming. In self-administered questionnaires, respondent cooperation is improved if the majority of the questions are structured.

Multiple-choice questions are not without disadvantages. Considerable effort is required to design effective multiple-choice questions. Qualitative techniques may be required to determine the appropriate response alternatives. It is difficult to obtain information on alternatives not listed. Even if an 'other (please specify)' category is included, respondents tend to choose among the listed alternatives. In addition, showing respondents the list of possible answers produces biased responses.[21] There is also the potential for order bias.

Dichotomous question A structured question with only two response alternatives, such as yes and no.

Dichotomous questions. A **dichotomous question** has only two response alternatives, such as yes or no, or agree or disagree. Often, the two alternatives of interest are supplemented by a neutral alternative, such as 'no opinion', 'don't know', 'both', or 'none', as in this example.[22]

Do you intend to buy a new laptop computer within the next six months?

	✓
Yes	☐
No	☐
Don't know	☐

Note that this question could also be framed as a multiple-choice question using response alternatives 'Definitely will buy', 'Probably will buy', 'Probably will not buy', and so forth. The decision to use a dichotomous question should be guided by whether the respondents approach the issue as a yes-or-no question. Although decisions are often characterised as series of binary or dichotomous choices, the underlying decision-making process may reflect uncertainty that can best be captured by multiple-choice responses. For example, two individuals may be equally likely to buy a new laptop computer within the next six months if the economic conditions remain favourable. One individual, who is being optimistic about the economy, will answer yes, however, while the other, feeling pessimistic, will answer no.

Another issue in the design of dichotomous questions is whether to include a neutral response alternative. If it is not included, respondents are forced to choose between yes and no even if they feel indifferent. On the other hand, if a neutral alternative is included, respondents can avoid taking a position on the issue, thereby biasing the results. We offer the following guidelines. If a substantial proportion of the respondents can be expected to be neutral, include a neutral alternative. If the proportion of neutral respondents is expected to be small, avoid the neutral alternative.[23]

The general advantages and disadvantages of dichotomous questions are very similar to those of multiple-choice questions. Dichotomous questions are the easiest type of questions to code and analyse, but they have one acute problem. The response can be influenced by the wording of the question. To illustrate, the statement 'Individuals are more to blame than social conditions for crime and lawlessness in this country', produced agreement from 59.6 per cent of the respondents. On a matched sample that responded to the opposite statement, 'Social conditions are more to blame than individuals for crime and lawlessness in this country', however, 43.2 per cent (as opposed to 40.4 per cent) agreed.[24] To overcome this problem, the question should be framed in one way on one-half of the questionnaires and in the opposite way on the other half. This is referred to as the split ballot technique.

Scales were discussed in detail in Chapters 10 and 11. To illustrate the difference between scales and other kinds of structural questions, consider the question about intentions to buy a new laptop computer. One way of framing this using a scale is as follows:

Do you intend to buy a new laptop computer within the next six months?

Definitely will not buy	Probably will not buy	Undecided	Probably will buy	Definitely will buy
1	2	3	4	5

This is only one of several scales that could be used to ask this question (see Chapters 10 and 11).

CHOOSING QUESTION WORDING

Question wording is the translation of the desired question content and structure into words that respondents can clearly and easily understand. Deciding on question wording is perhaps the most critical and difficult task in developing a questionnaire. If a question is worded poorly, respondents may refuse to answer it or answer it incorrectly. The first condition, known as item non-response, can increase the complexity of data analysis.[25] The second condition leads to response error, discussed earlier. Unless the respondents and the researcher assign exactly the same meaning to the question, the results will be seriously biased.[26]

To avoid these problems, we offer the following guidelines: (1) define the issue, (2) use ordinary words, (3) use unambiguous words, (4) avoid leading questions, (5) avoid implicit alternatives, (6) avoid implicit assumptions, (7) avoid generalisations and estimates, and (8) use positive and negative statements.

Define the issue

A question should clearly define the issue being addressed. Consider the following question:

Which brand of shampoo do you use?

A well defined question is needed to determine which brand of shampoo a person uses.

On the surface, this may seem to be a well-defined question, but we may reach a different conclusion when we examine it in terms of 'who', 'what', 'when', and 'where'. 'Who' in this question refers to the respondent. It is not clear, though, whether the researcher is referring to the brand the respondent uses personally or the brand used by the household. 'What' is the brand of shampoo. But what if more than one brand of shampoo is being used? Should the respondent mention the most preferred brand, the brand used most often, the brand used most recently, or the brand that comes to mind first? 'When' is not clear; does the researcher mean last time, last week, last month, last year, or ever? As for 'where', it is implied that the shampoo is used at home, but this is not stated clearly. A better wording for this question would be:

Which brand or brands of shampoo have you personally used at home during the last month? In case of more than one brand, please list all the brands that apply.

Use ordinary words

Ordinary words should be used in a questionnaire, and they should match the vocabulary level of the respondents.[27] In other words, even though we may speak the same language as our potential respondents, there may be particular colloquialisms and ways of using words and terms they use which we should acquaint ourselves with. When choosing words, bear the mind the intellectual level of the target group of respondents, and how comfortable they are with technical terms related to any products or services we are measuring. Most respondents do not understand technical marketing words. For example, instead of asking, 'Do you think the distribution of soft drinks is adequate?' ask, 'Do you think soft drinks are readily available when you want to buy them?' Never forget that you are imposing your language upon respondents in the form of a questionnaire. Your language communicates and puts respondents in a particular frame of mind as they answer the questions you pose. Unless that language is meaningful to respondents they will be in a frame of mind that you do not intend, and be answering different questions than the ones you set.

Use unambiguous words

The words used in a questionnaire should have a single meaning that is known to the respondents.[28] A number of words that appear unambiguous have different meanings to different people.[29] These include 'usually', 'normally', 'frequently', 'often', 'regularly', 'occasionally', and 'sometimes'. Consider the following question:

In a typical month, how often do you visit a bank?

	✓
Never	☐
Occasionally	☐
Sometimes	☐
Often	☐
Regularly	☐

The answers to this question are fraught with response bias, because the words used to describe category labels have different meanings for different respondents. Three respondents who visit a bank once a month may tick three different categories: occasionally, sometimes and often. A much better wording for this question would be the following:

In a typical month, how often do you visit a bank?

	✓
Less than once	☐
1 or 2 times	☐
3 or 4 times	☐
More than 4 times	☐

Note that this question provides a consistent frame of reference for all respondents. Response categories have been objectively defined, and respondents are no longer free to interpret them in their own way.

In deciding on the choice of words, researchers should consult a dictionary and thesaurus and ask the following questions of each word used:

1 Does it mean what we intend?
2 Does it have any other meanings?
3 If so, does the context make the intended meaning clear?
4 Does the word have more than one pronunciation?
5 Is there any word of similar pronunciation that might be confused with this word?
6 Is a simpler word or phrase suggested?

Avoid leading or biasing questions

Leading question
A question that gives the respondent a clue as to what the answer should be.

A **leading question** is one that clues the respondent to what the answer should be, as in the following:

Do you think that patriotic French people should buy imported cars when that would put French workers out of employment?

	✓
Yes	☐
No	☐
Don't know	☐

This question would lead respondents to a 'No' answer. After all, how could patriotic French people put French people out of work? Therefore, this question would not help determine the preferences of French people for imported versus domestic cars.

Bias may also arise when respondents are given clues about the sponsor of the project. Respondents tend to respond favourably toward the sponsor. The question, 'Is Colgate your favourite toothpaste?' is likely to bias the responses in favour of Colgate. A more unbiased way of obtaining this information would be to ask, 'What is your favourite toothpaste brand?' Likewise, the mention of a prestigious or non-prestigious name can bias the response; as in, 'Do you agree with the British Dental Association that Colgate is effective in preventing cavities?'[30]

Avoid implicit alternatives

Implicit alternative
An alternative that is not explicitly expressed.

An alternative that is not explicitly expressed in the options is an **implicit alternative**. Making an implied alternative explicit may increase the percentage of people selecting that alternative, as in the two following questions.

1 *Do you like to fly when travelling short distances?*
2 *Do you like to fly when travelling short distances, or would you rather drive?*

In the first question, the alternative of driving is only implicit, but in the second question, it is explicit. The first question is likely to yield a greater preference for flying than the second question.

Questions with implicit alternatives should be avoided unless there are specific reasons for including them.[31] When the alternatives are close in preference or large in number, the alternatives at the end of the list have a greater chance of being selected. To overcome this bias, the split ballot technique should be used to rotate the order in which the alternatives appear.

Avoid implicit assumptions

Questions should not be worded so that the answer is dependent on implicit assumptions about what will happen as a consequence. Implicit assumptions are assumptions that are not stated in the question, as in the following example.[32]

1 *Are you in favour of a balanced national budget?*
2 *Are you in favour of a balanced national budget if it would result in an increase in personal income tax?*

Implicit in question 1 are the consequences that will arise as a result of a balanced national budget. There might be a cut in defence expenditures, an increase in personal income tax, a cut in health spending, and so on. Question 2 is a better way to word this question. Question 1's failure to make its assumptions explicit would result in overestimating the respondents' support for a balanced national budget.

Avoid generalisations and estimates

Questions should be specific, not general. Moreover, questions should be worded so that the respondent does not have to make generalisations or compute estimates. Suppose that we were interested in households' annual per capita expenditure on groceries. If we asked respondents the question:

What is the annual per capita expenditure on groceries in your household?

they would first have to determine the annual expenditure on groceries by multiplying the monthly expenditure on groceries by 12 or the weekly expenditure by 52. Then they would have to divide the annual amount by the number of persons in the household. Most respondents would be unwilling or unable to perform these calculations. A better way of obtaining the required information would be to ask the respondents two simple questions:

What is the monthly (or weekly) expenditure on groceries in your household?

and

How many members are there in your household?

The researcher can then perform the necessary calculations.

Use positive and negative statements

Many questions, particularly those measuring attitudes and lifestyles, are worded as statements to which respondents indicate their degree of agreement or disagreement. Evidence indicates that the response obtained is influenced by the directionality of the statements: whether they are stated positively or negatively. In these cases, it is better to use dual statements, some of which are positive and others are negative. Two different questionnaires could be prepared. One questionnaire would contain half-negative and half-positive statements in an interspersed way. The direction of these statements would be reversed in the other questionnaire. An example of dual statements was provided in the summated Likert scale in Chapter 11 designed to measure attitudes toward Dresdener Bank.

DETERMINING THE ORDER OF QUESTIONS

The order of questions is of equal importance to the wording used in the questions. As noted in the last section, questions communicate and set respondents in a particular frame of mind. The frame of mind in which they are set affects how they perceive individual questions and respond to those questions. As well as understanding the characteristics of language in target respondents, questionnaire designers must be aware of the logical connections between questions – as perceived by target respondents. The following issues help to determine the order of questions.

Opening questions

The opening questions can be crucial in gaining the confidence and cooperation of respondents. They should be interesting, simple and non-threatening. Questions that ask respondents for their opinions can be good opening questions, because most people like to express their opinions. Sometimes such questions are asked although they are unrelated to the research problem and their responses are not analysed.[33] Though classification questions seem simple to start a questionnaire, issues like age, gender and income can be seen as sensitive. Opening a questionnaire with these questions tends to make respondents concerned about the purpose of these questions and indeed the whole survey.

Type of information

Classification information Socio-economic and demographic characteristics used to classify respondents.

Identification information A type of information obtained in a questionnaire that includes name, address and phone number.

The type of information obtained in a questionnaire may be classified as (1) basic information, (2) **classification information**, and (3) **identification information**. Basic information relates directly to the research problem. Classification information, consisting of socio-economic and demographic characteristics, is used to classify the respondents, understand the results and validate the sample (see Chapter 13). Identification information includes name, address and telephone number. Identification information may be obtained for a variety of purposes, including verifying that the respondents listed were actually interviewed and to send promised incentives or prizes. As a general guideline, basic information should be obtained first, followed by classification, and finally identification information. The basic information is of greatest importance to the research project and should be obtained first, before we risk alienating the respondents by asking a series of personal questions.

Difficult questions

Difficult questions or questions that are sensitive, embarrassing, complex or dull should be placed late in the sequence. After rapport has been established and the respondents become involved, they are less likely to object to these questions. Thus, in the GlobalCash project, information about the banks that companies use and how they rated those banks was asked at the end of the section on basic information. Likewise, income should be the last question in the classification section (if it is to be used at all).

Effect on subsequent questions

Questions asked early in a sequence can influence the responses to subsequent questions. As a rule of thumb, general questions should precede the specific questions. This prevents specific questions from biasing responses to the general questions. Consider the following sequence of questions:

Q1: What considerations are important to you in selecting a bank?
Q2: In selecting a bank, how important is convenience of location?

Note that the first question is general whereas the second is specific. If these questions were asked in the reverse order, respondents would be clued about convenience of location and would be more likely to give this response to the general question.

Funnel approach A strategy for ordering questions in a questionnaire in which the sequence starts with the general questions, which are followed by progressively specific questions, to prevent specific questions from biasing general questions.

Going from general to specific is called the **funnel approach**. The funnel approach is particularly useful when information has to be obtained about respondents' general choice behaviour and their evaluations of specific products.[34] Sometimes the inverted funnel approach may be useful. In this approach, questioning starts with specific questions and concludes with the general questions. The respondents are compelled to provide specific information before making general evaluations. This approach is useful when respondents have no strong feelings or have not formulated a point of view.

Logical order

Questions should be asked in a logical order. All questions that deal with a particular topic should be asked before beginning a new topic. When switching topics, brief transitional phrases should be used to help respondents switch their train of thought.

Branching question
A question used to guide an interviewer through a survey by directing the interviewer to different spots on the questionnaire depending on the answers given.

Branching questions should be designed carefully.[35] Branching questions direct respondents to different places in the questionnaire based on how they respond to the question at hand. These questions ensure that all possible contingencies are covered. They also help reduce interviewer and respondent error and encourage complete responses. Skip patterns based on the branching questions can become quite complex. A simple way to account for all contingencies is to prepare a flowchart of the logical possibilities and then develop branching questions and instructions based on it. A flowchart used to assess the use of electronic payments in clothes purchases via the Internet is shown in Figure 12.4.

Placement of branching questions is important and the following guidelines should be followed: (1) the question being branched (the one to which the respondent is being directed) should be placed as close as possible to the question causing the branching, and (2) the branching questions should be ordered so that the respondents cannot anticipate what additional information will be required. Otherwise, the respondents may discover that they can avoid detailed questions by giving certain answers to branching questions. For example, the respondents should first be asked if they have seen any of the listed commercials before they are asked to evaluate commercials. Otherwise, the respondents will quickly discover that stating that they have seen a commercial leads to detailed questions about that commercial and that they can avoid detailed questions by stating that they have not seen the commercial.

FORM AND LAYOUT

The format, spacing and positioning of questions can have a significant effect on the results,[36] particularly in self-administered questionnaires. It is a good practice to divide a questionnaire into several parts. Several parts may be needed for questions pertaining to the basic information.

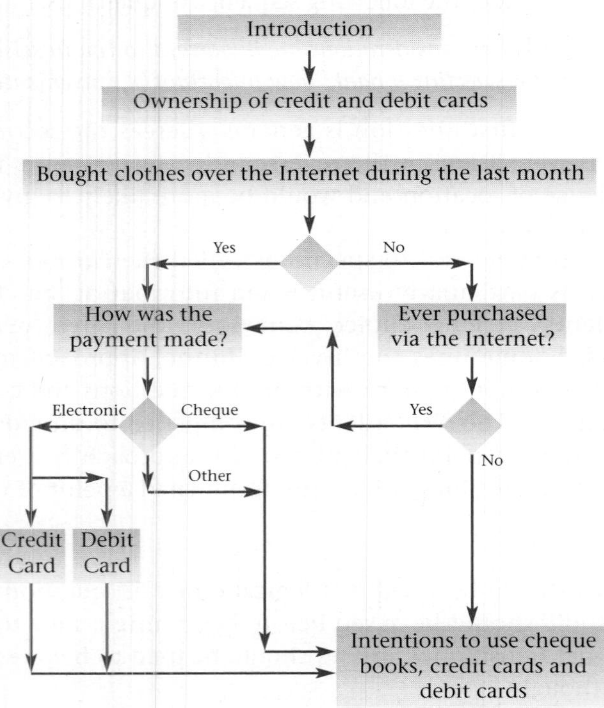

Figure 12.4 Flowchart for questionnaire design

Pre-coding
In questionnaire design, assigning a code to every conceivable response before data collection.

The questions in each part should be numbered, particularly when branching questions are used. Numbering of questions also makes the coding of responses easier. In addition, the questionnaires should preferably be pre-coded. In **pre-coding**, the codes to enter in the computer are printed on the questionnaire. Typically, the code identifies the line number and the column numbers in which a particular response will be entered. Coding of questionnaires is explained in more detail in Chapter 16 on data preparation.

The questionnaires themselves should be numbered serially. This facilitates the control of questionnaires in the field as well as the coding and analysis. Numbering makes it easy to account for the questionnaires and to determine if any have been lost. A possible exception to this rule is mail questionnaires. If these are numbered, respondents assume that a given number identifies a particular respondent. Some respondents may refuse to participate or answer differently under these conditions.

REPRODUCTION OF THE QUESTIONNAIRE

How a questionnaire is reproduced for administration can influence the results. For example, if the questionnaire is reproduced on poor-quality paper or is otherwise shabby in appearance, the respondents will think that the project is unimportant and the quality of response will be adversely affected. Therefore, the questionnaire should be reproduced on good-quality paper and have a professional appearance.

When a printed questionnaire runs to several pages, it should take the form of a booklet rather than a number of sheets of paper clipped or stapled together. Booklets are easier for the interviewer and the respondents to handle and do not easily come apart with use. They allow the use of a double-page format for questions and look more professional.

Each question should be reproduced on a single page (or double-page spread). A researcher should avoid splitting a question, including its response categories. Split questions can mislead the interviewer or the respondent into thinking that the question has ended at the end of a page. This will result in answers based on incomplete questions.

Vertical response columns should be used for individual questions. It is easier for interviewers and respondents to read down a single column rather than sideways across several columns. Sideways formatting and splitting, done frequently to conserve space, should be avoided.

The tendency to crowd questions together to make the questionnaire look shorter should be avoided. Overcrowded questions with little blank space between them can lead to errors in data collection and yield shorter and less informative replies. Moreover, they give the impression that the questionnaire is complex and can result in lower cooperation and completion rates. Although shorter questionnaires are more desirable than longer ones, the reduction in size should not be obtained at the expense of crowding.[37]

Directions or instructions for individual questions should be placed as close to the questions as possible. Instructions relating to how the question should be administered or answered by the respondent should be placed just before the question. Instructions concerning how the answer should be recorded or how the probing should be done should be placed after the question (for more information on probing and other interviewing procedures, see Chapter 15). It is a common practice to distinguish instructions from questions by using distinctive type (such as capital or boldfaced letters).

Although colour does not influence response rates to questionnaires, it can be employed advantageously in some respects. Colour coding is useful for branching questions. The next question to which the respondent is directed is printed in a colour that matches the space in which the answer to the branching question was recorded. Surveys directed at different respondent groups can be reproduced on paper of a different colour. In the GlobalCash survey, the questionnaire was printed with different coloured covers to identify which country the response came from.

The questionnaire should be reproduced in such a way that it is easy to read and answer. The type should be large and clear. Reading the questionnaire should not impose a strain.

PILOT-TESTING

Pilot-presting
Testing the questionnaire on a small sample of respondents for the purpose of improving the questionnaire by identifying and eliminating potential problems.

Pilot-testing refers to testing the questionnaire on a small sample of respondents to identify and eliminate potential problems.[38] Even the best questionnaire can be improved by pilot-testing. As a general rule, a questionnaire should not be used in the field survey without adequate pilot-testing.[39] A pilot-test should be extensive. All aspects of the questionnaire should be tested, including question content, wording, sequence, form and layout, question difficulty, and instructions. The respondents in the pilot-test should be similar to those who will be included in the actual survey in terms of background characteristics, familiarity with the topic, and attitudes and behaviours of interest.[40] In other words, respondents for the pilot-test and for the actual survey should be drawn from the same population.

Pilot-tests are best done by personal interviews, even if the actual survey is to be conducted by mail or telephone, because interviewers can observe respondents' reactions and attitudes. After the necessary changes have been made, another pilot-test could be conducted by mail or telephone if those methods are to be used in the actual survey. The latter pilot-tests should reveal problems peculiar to the interviewing method. To the extent possible, a pilot-test should involve administering the questionnaire in an environment and context similar to that of the actual survey.

A variety of interviewers should be used for pilot-tests. The project director, the researcher who developed the questionnaire, and other key members of the research team should conduct some pilot-test interviews. This will give them a good feel for potential problems and the nature of the expected data. Most of the pilot-test interviews, however, should be conducted by regular interviewers. It is good practice to employ both experienced and new interviewers. Experienced interviewers can easily perceive uneasiness, confusion and resistance in the respondents, and new interviewers can help the researcher identify interviewer-related problems. Ordinarily the pilot-test sample size is small, varying from 15 to 30 respondents for the initial testing, depending on the heterogeneity of the target population. The sample size can increase substantially if the pilot-testing involves several stages.

Protocol analysis and debriefing are two commonly used procedures in pilot-testing. In protocol analysis, the respondent is asked to 'think aloud' while answering the questionnaire, as explained in Chapter 10. Typically, the respondent's remarks are tape-recorded and analysed to determine the reactions invoked by different parts of the questionnaire. Debriefing occurs after the questionnaire has been completed. Respondents are told that the questionnaire they just completed was a pilot-test and the objectives of pilot-testing are described to them. They are then asked to describe the meaning of each question, to explain their answers, and to state any problems they encountered while answering the questionnaire.

Editing involves correcting the questionnaire for the problems identified during pilot-testing. After each significant revision of the questionnaire, another pilot-test should be conducted, using a different sample of respondents. Sound pilot-testing involves several stages. One pilot-test is a bare minimum. Pilot-testing should be continued until no further changes are needed.

Finally, the responses obtained from the pilot-test should be coded and analysed. The analysis of pilot-test responses can serve as a check on the adequacy of the problem definition and the data and analysis required to obtain the necessary information. The dummy tables prepared before developing the questionnaire will point to the need for the various sets of data. If the response to a question cannot be related to one of the pre-planned dummy tables, either those data are superfluous or some relevant analysis has not been foreseen. If part of a dummy table remains empty, a necessary question may have been omitted. Analysis of pilot-test data helps to ensure that all data collected will be utilised and that the questionnaire will obtain all the necessary data.[41]

Table 12.1 summarises the questionnaire design process in the form of a checklist.

Table 12.1 Questionnaire design checklist

Step 1: Specify The Information Needed

1. Ensure that the information obtained fully addresses all the components of the problem. Review components of the problem and the approach, particularly the research questions, hypotheses, and characteristics that influence the research design.
2. Prepare a set of dummy tables.
3. Have a clear idea of characteristics and motivations of the target population.

Step 2: Type of Interviewing Method

1. Review the type of interviewing method determined based on considerations discussed in Chapter 8.

Step 3: Individual Question Content

1. Is the question necessary?
2. Are several questions needed instead of one to obtain the required information in an unambiguous manner?
3. Do not use double-barrelled questions.

Step 4: Overcome Inability and Unwillingness to Answer

1. Is the respondent informed?
2. If the respondent is not likely to be informed, filter questions that measure familiarity, product use, and past experience should be asked before questions about the topics themselves.
3. Can the respondent remember?
4. Avoid errors of omission, telescoping and creation.
5. Questions that do not provide the respondent with cues can underestimate the actual occurrence of an event.
6. Can the respondent articulate?
7. Minimise the effort required of the respondent.
8. Is the context in which the questions are asked appropriate?
9. Make the request for information seem legitimate.
10. If the information is sensitive:
    a. Place sensitive topics at the end of the questionnaire.
    b. Preface the question with a statement that the behaviour of interest is common.
    c. Ask the question using the third-person technique.
    d. Hide the question in a group of other questions that respondents are willing to answer.
    e. Provide response categories rather than asking for specific figures.
    f. Use randomised techniques, if appropriate.

Step 5: Choose Question Structure

1. Open-ended questions are useful in exploratory research and as opening questions.
2. Use structured questions whenever possible.
3. In multiple-choice questions, the response alternatives should include the set of all possible choices and should be mutually exclusive.

▶

4. In a dichotomous question, if a substantial proportion of the respondents can be expected to be neutral, include a neutral alternative.
5. Consider the use of the split ballot technique to reduce order bias in dichotomous and multiple-choice questions.
6. If the response alternatives are numerous, consider using more than one question to reduce the information processing demands on the respondents.

Step 6: Choose Question Wording

1. Define the issue in terms of 'who', 'what', 'when', and 'where'.
2. Use ordinary words. Words should match the vocabulary level of the respondents.
3. Avoid ambiguous words: usually, normally, frequently, often, regularly, occasionally, sometimes, etc.
4. Avoid leading questions that cue the respondent to what the answer should be.
5. Avoid implicit alternatives that are not explicitly expressed in the options.
6. Avoid implicit assumptions.
7. Respondent should not have to make generalisations or compute estimates.
8. Use positive and negative statements.

Step 7: Determine the Order of Questions

1. The opening questions should be interesting, simple and non-threatening.
2. Qualifying questions should serve as the opening questions.
3. Basic information should be obtained first, followed by classification and finally identification information.
4. Difficult, sensitive or complex questions should be placed late in the sequence.
5. General questions should precede the specific questions.
6. Questions should be asked in a logical order.
7. Branching questions should be designed carefully to cover all possible contingencies.
8. The question being branched should be placed as close as possible to the question causing the branching, *and* the branching questions should be ordered so that the respondents cannot anticipate what additional information will be required.

Step 8: Form and Layout

1. Divide a questionnaire into several parts.
2. Questions in each part should be numbered.
3. The questionnaire should be pre-coded.
4. The questionnaires themselves should be numbered serially.

Step 9: Reproduce the Questionnaire

1. The questionnaire should have a professional appearance.
2. A booklet format should be used for long questionnaires.
3. Each question should be reproduced on a single page (or double-page spread).
4. Vertical response columns should be used.
5. Grids are useful when there are a number of related questions that use the same set of response categories.
6. The tendency to crowd questions to make the questionnaire look shorter should be avoided.
7. Directions or instructions for individual questions should be placed as close to the questions as possible.

Step 10: Pilot-test

1. Pilot-testing should always be done.
2. All aspects of the questionnaire should be tested, including question content, wording, sequence, form and layout, question difficulty, and instructions.
3. The respondents in the pilot-test should be similar to those who will be included in the actual survey.
4. Begin the pilot-test by using personal interviews.
5. The pilot-test should also be conducted by mail or telephone if those methods are to be used in the actual survey.
6. A variety of interviewers should be used for pilot-tests.
7. The pilot-test sample size should be small, varying from 15 to 30 respondents for the initial testing.
8. Use protocol analysis and debriefing to identify problems.
9. After each significant revision of the questionnaire, another pilot-test should be conducted, using a different sample of respondents.
10. The responses obtained from the pilot-test should be coded and analysed.

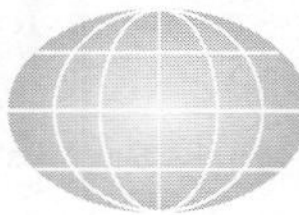

INTERNATIONAL MARKETING RESEARCH

The questionnaire or research instrument should be adapted to the specific cultural environment and should not be biased in terms of any one culture. This requires careful attention to each step of the questionnaire design process. The information needed should be clearly specified. It is important to take into account any differences in underlying consumer behaviour, decision-making processes, psychographics, lifestyles and demographic variables. In the context of demographic characteristics, information on marital status, education, household size, occupation, income and dwelling unit may have to be specified differently for different countries, as these variables may not be directly comparable across countries. For example, household definition and size varies greatly, given the extended family structure in some countries and the practice of two or even three families living under the same roof.

Although personal interviewing may dominate as a survey method in many Western countries, different survey methods may be favoured in different countries. Hence, the questionnaire may have to be suitable for administration by more than one method. For ease of comprehension and translation, it is desirable to have two or more simple questions rather than a single complex question. In overcoming the inability to answer, the variability in the extent to which respondents in different cultures are informed about the subject matter of the survey should be taken into account. Respondents in some parts of the world may not be as well informed on many issues as people in Europe.

The use of unstructured or open-ended questions may be desirable if the researcher lacks knowledge about the determinants of response in other countries. Because they do not impose any response alternatives, unstructured questions also reduce cultural bias, but they are more affected by differences in educational levels than structured questions. They should be used with caution in countries with high illiteracy rates.

The questionnaire may have to be translated for administration in different cultures. The researcher must ensure that the questionnaires in different languages are equivalent. The special procedures designed for this purpose are discussed in Chapter 25. The following example illustrates the problems of translation.

EXAMPLE

If you board the Asian 'bus, better mind your language[42]

On the surface it would appear that the omnibus service could be made very standardised in Asia, even more so than in Europe where one must deal with a different language in almost every country. One might conclude that a questionnaire in Chinese could be used with little or no modification in a number of countries such as China, Hong Kong, Taiwan and Malaysia, thus avoiding the problems of timing, cost and inaccuracies generally associated with translations. However, due to vast differences in the region in terms of language, culture and geography, the 'standard' omnibus survey becomes less standard than would first meet the eye. While the omnibus is a very cost-effective and efficient way of conducting research in Asia, great care must be taken in order to make best use of this service, particularly by companies thinking of entering these markets. Countries such as Japan, Korea and Thailand are typical of South East Asia in that they each possess a single culture and a single language. In both Singapore and Malaysia, for example, omnibus questionnaires are always printed in three languages: English, Mandarin and Malay. In Malaysia, in addition to Mandarin which is spoken by all 'Chinese-literate' consumers, there are three other commonly spoken dialects which have to be dealt with at the respondent level: Cantonese, Hokkien and Hakka. In Singapore the commonly spoken dialects are Cantonese, Hokkien and Teochew. ■

Pilot-testing the questionnaire is complicated in international research because linguistic equivalence must be pilot-tested. Two sets of pilot-tests are recommended. The translated questionnaire should be pilot-tested on monolingual subjects in their native language, and the original and translated versions should also be administered to bilingual subjects. The pilot-test data from administration of the questionnaire in different countries or cultures should be analysed and the pattern of responses compared to detect any cultural biases.

ETHICS IN MARKETING RESEARCH

The researcher must be mindful of the demands placed on the respondents when designing questionnaires. Because the administration of the questionnaire is a substantial intrusion by the researcher, several ethical concerns arise pertaining to the researcher–respondent relationship. Ethical issues impinging on the researcher–client relationship may also have to be addressed.

In consideration of the respondents, exceedingly long questionnaires should be avoided. As a general guideline, the following are generally considered 'overly long': a personal interview in-home over 60 minutes, a telephone interview over 30 minutes, a street interview over 30 minutes.[43] Overly long questionnaires are burdensome on the respondents and adversely affect the quality of responses. Similarly, questions that are confusing, exceed the respondents' ability, are difficult, or otherwise improperly worded, should be avoided.

Overly sensitive questions deserve special attention. A real ethical dilemma exists for researchers investigating social problems such as poverty, drug use and sexually transmitted diseases like AIDS, or conducting studies of highly personal products like feminine hygiene products or financial products.[44] Candid and truthful responses are needed to generate meaningful results. But how do we obtain such data without asking sensitive questions that invade respondents' privacy? When asking sensitive questions, researchers should attempt to minimise the discomfort of the respondents. It should be made clear at the beginning of the questionnaire that respondents are not obligated to answer any question that makes them uncomfortable.[45]

One researcher–client issue worth mentioning is piggybacking, which occurs when a questionnaire contains questions pertaining to more than one client. One client's questions take up a part of the questionnaire, while a second client's study takes up the rest. Although there is some risk that one study will contaminate the other or that the questionnaire may not be very coherent, piggybacking can substantially reduce the cost. Thus, it can be a good way for clients with limited research budgets to collect primary data they would not be able to afford otherwise. In these cases all clients must be aware of and consent to the arrangement. Unfortunately, piggybacking is sometimes used without disclosure to the clients for the sole purpose of increasing the researcher's profit. This is unethical.

Finally, the researcher has the ethical responsibility of designing the questionnaire so as to obtain the required information in an unbiased manner. Deliberately biasing the questionnaire in a desired direction – for example, by asking leading questions – cannot be condoned. In deciding the question structure, the most appropriate rather than the most convenient option should be adopted. Also, the questionnaire should be thoroughly pilot-tested before fieldwork begins, or an ethical breach has occurred.

INTERNET AND COMPUTER APPLICATIONS

The questionnaire design process outlined in this chapter also applies to Internet questionnaires. See the enclosed SNAP5 demo CD to examine examples of questionnaires designed for the Internet.

Internet questionnaires share many of the features of CAPI questionnaires. The questionnaire can be designed using a wide variety of stimuli such as graphics, pictures, advertisements, animations, sound clips and full-motion video. Moreover, the researcher can control the amount of time that the stimuli are available to the respondents, and the number of times a respondent can access each stimulus. This greatly increases the range and complexity of questionnaires that can be administered over the Internet. As in the case of CATI and CAPI, complicated skip patterns can be programmed into the questionnaire. The questions can be personalised and answers to previous questions can be inserted into subsequent questions. The various types of scales, such as ordinal ranking scales, Likert scales, semantic differential scales and Stapel scales can be utilised.

The Mercator Company that produce SNAP5 also produce a test bank of questionnaires that relate to specific industries, e.g. leisure and hospitality, and specific topics such as customer satisfaction measurement. These test banks are available on CD formats, allowing particular questions to be selected and adapted to meet the specific purposes of a new survey. Cutting and pasting questions from these test bank CDs allows questionnaires to be developed and adapted for use in CATI, CAPI, Internet or traditional paper formats.

SUMMARY

To collect quantitative primary data, a researcher must design a questionnaire. A questionnaire has three objectives. It must translate the information needed into a set of specific questions the respondents can and will answer. It must motivate respondents to complete the interview. It must also minimise response error.

Designing a questionnaire is an art rather than a science. This is primarily caused by the interrelationship of stages and the trade-offs that questionnaire designers make in balancing: the source of ideas, question purposes, actual questions and question analyses. The questionnaire design process begins by specifying (1) the information needed and (2) the type of interviewing method. The next step (3) is to decide on the content of individual questions.

The question should overcome the respondents' inability to answer (4). Respondents may be unable to answer if they are not informed, cannot remember, or cannot articulate the response. The unwillingness of the respondents to answer must also be overcome. Respondents may be unwilling to answer if the question requires too much effort, is asked in a situation or context deemed inappropriate, does not serve a legitimate purpose, or solicits sensitive information. Then comes the decision regarding the question structure (5). Questions can be unstructured (open-ended) or structured, to varying degrees. Structured questions include multiple-choice, dichotomous questions, and scales.

Determining the wording of each question (6) involves defining the issue, using ordinary words, using unambiguous words, and using dual statements. The researcher should avoid leading questions, implicit alternatives, implicit assumptions, and generalisations and estimates. Once the questions have been worded, the order in which they will appear in the questionnaire must be decided (7). Special consideration should be given to opening questions, type of information, difficult questions, and the effect on subsequent questions. The questions should be arranged in a logical order.

The stage is now set for determining the form and layout of the questions (8). Several factors are important in reproducing the questionnaire (9). These include appearance, use of booklets, fitting entire question on a page, response category format, avoiding overcrowding, placement of directions, colour coding, easy-to-read format, and cost. Last but not least is pilot-testing (10). Important issues are the extent of pilot-testing, nature of respondents, type of interviewing method, type of interviewers, sample size, protocol analysis and debriefing, and editing and analysis.

The questionnaire or research instrument should be adapted to the specific cultural environment and should not be biased in terms of any one culture. Also, the questionnaire may have to be suitable for administration by more than one method because different interviewing methods may be used in different countries. For ease of comprehension and translation, it is desirable to have simple, rather than complex, questions.

QUESTIONS AND PROBLEMS

1 What is the purpose of questionnaires?

2 What expectations does the marketing researcher have of potential questionnaire respondents – in terms of how they will react to the experience of completing a questionnaire?

3 What does the marketing researcher have to offer potential questionnaire respondents? Why should this question be considered?

4 How would you determine whether a specific question should be included in a questionnaire?

5 What are the reasons that respondents may be (a) unable to answer and (b) unwilling to answer the question asked?

6 Explain the errors of omission, telescoping and creation. What can be done to reduce such errors?

7 Explain the concepts of aided and unaided recall.

8 What can a researcher do to make the request for information seem legitimate?

9 What are the advantages and disadvantages of unstructured questions?

10 What are the issues involved in designing multiple-choice questions?

11 What are the guidelines available for deciding on question wording?

12 What is a leading question? Give an example.

13 What is the proper order for questions intended to obtain basic, classification and identification information?

14 What guidelines are available for deciding on the form and layout of a questionnaire?

15 Describe the issues involved in pilot-testing a questionnaire.

NOTES

1 Wales, G., 'Winkling out the Joys of Financial Research', *ResearchPlus* (March 1994), 3.

2 Abel, S., 'Finding the Elusive Young through Co-operative Parents', *ResearchPlus* (February 1996).

3 These guidelines are drawn from several books on questionnaire design: Backstrom, C.H. and Hursh-Csar, G., *Survey Research* (Cambridge, MA: Wiley, 1981); Berdie, D.R. and Anderson, J.F., *Questionnaires: Design and Use* (Metuchen, NJ: Scarecrow Press, 1974); Blankenship, A.B., *Professional Telephone Surveys* (New York: McGraw-Hill, 1977), 94–95; Dillman, D., *Mail and Telephone Surveys: The Total Design Method* (New York: Wiley, 1978); Erdos, P.L., *Professional Mail Surveys* (Malabar, FL: Robert E. Krieger, 1983); Korhauser, A. and Sheatsley, P.B., 'Questionnaire Construction and Interview Procedure', in Selltiz, C., Wrightsman, L.S. and Cook, S.W., *Research Methods in Social Relations*, 3rd edn (New York: Holt, Rinehart and Winston, 1976), 541–73; Labau, P., *Advanced Questionnaire Design* (Orlando, FL: Abt Books, 1981); Schuman, H. and Presser, S., *Questions and Answers in Attitude Surveys* (Orlando, FL: Academic Press, 1981); and Sudman, S. and Bradburn, N.M., *Asking Questions* (San Francisco: Jossey-Bass, 1983). For earlier references on questionnaire design, see Daniel, W.G., *Questionnaire Design: A Selected Bibliography for the Survey Researcher* (Monticello, IL: Vance Bibliographics, 1979).

4 Kleinsorge, I.K. and Koenig, H.E., 'The Silent Customers: Measuring Customer Satisfaction in Nursing Homes', *Journal of Health Care Marketing* (December 1991), 2–13.

5 Hague, P., 'Good and Bad in Questionnaire Design', *Industrial Marketing Digest*, vol. 12, Third Quarter 1987, 161–70.

6 Boyd, Jr, H.W., Westfall, R. and Stasch, S.E., *Marketing Research: Text and Cases*, 7th edn (Homewood, IL: Richard D. Irwin, 1989), 277.

7 Bishop, G.E., Oldendick, R.W. and Tuchfarber, A.J., 'Effects of Filter Questions in Public Opinion Surveys', *Public Opinion Quarterly* 46 (Spring 1982), 66–85.

8 Hawkins, D.I. and Coney, K.A., 'Uninformed Response Error in Survey Research', *Journal of Marketing Research* (August 1981), 373.

9 Haller, T., *Danger: Marketing Researcher at Work* (Westport, CT: Quotum Books, 1983), p. 149.

10 Cook, W.A., 'Telescoping and Memory's Other Tricks', *Journal of Advertising Research* (February–March 1987), 5–8; and Sudman, S., Finn, A. and Lannom, L., 'The Use of Bounded Recall Procedures in Single Interviews', *Public Opinion Quarterly* (Summer 1984), 520–24.

11 Malrin, J.H. and Moskowitz, J.M., 'Anonymous versus Identifiable Self-Reports', *Public Opinion Quarterly* (Winter 1983), 557–66.

12 Marquis, K.H., Marquis, M.S. and Polich, M.J., 'Response Bias and Reliability in Sensitive Topic Surveys', *Journal of the American Statistical Association* (June 1986), 381–89; Mangione, T.W., Hingson, R. and Barrett, J., 'Collecting Sensitive Data: A Comparison of Three Survey Strategies', *Sociological Methods and Research* 10 (February 1982), 337–46; and Marquis, K.H. et al., *Response Errors in Sensitive Topic Survey: Estimates, Effects, and Correction Options* (Santa Monica, CA: Rand Corporation, 1981).

13 Peterson, R.A.,'Asking the Age Question: A Research Note', *Public Opinion Quarterly* (Spring 1984), 379–83; and Sheth, J.N., LeClaire, Jr. A. and Wachspress, D., 'Impact of Asking Race Information in Mail Surveys', *Journal of Marketing* (Winter 1980), 67–70.

14 See Burton, B.K. and Near, J.P., 'Estimating the Incidence of Wrongdoing and Whistle-blowing: Results of a Study Using Randomized Response Technique', *Journal of Business Ethics* 14 (January 1995), 17–30.

15 Geurtz, M.D., 'Using a Randomized Response Research Design to Eliminate Non-Response and Response Biases in Business Research', *Journal of the Academy of Marketing Science* (Spring 1980), 83–91; Stem, Jr, D.E., Chao, W.T. and Steinhorst, R.K., 'A Randomisation Dance for Mail Survey Applications of the Randomized Response Model', in Bagozzi, R.P. et al., *Marketing in the 80's* (Chicago: American Marketing Association 1980), pp. 320–23; Stem, Jr., D.E. and Steinhorst, R.K., 'Telephone Interview and Mail Questionnaire Applications of the Randomized Response Model', *Journal of the American Statistical Association* (September 1984), 555–64; and Tracy P.E. and Fox, J.A., 'The Validity of Randomized Response for Sensitive Measurements', *American Sociological Review* 46 (April 1981), 187–200.

16 Seiberling, S., Taylor, S. and Ursic, M., 'Open-Ended Question vs. Rating Scale', in Rogers III, J.C. (ed.), *Developments in Marketing Science: Proceedings of the Seventh Annual Conference of the Academy of Marketing Science*, vol. 6 (Ann Arbor, MI: Books on Demand, 1983), pp. 440–45; and Spagna, G.J., 'Questionnaires: Which Approach Do You Use?', *Journal of Advertising Research* 24 (February–March 1984), 67–70.

17 Jones, S., 'Listening to Complexity', *Journal of the Market Research Society* (January 1981), 26–39; and McDonald, C., 'Coding Open-Ended Answers with the Help of a Computer', *Journal of the Market Research Society* (January 1982), 9–27.

18 Payne, S.L., 'Are Open-Ended Questions Worth the Effort?', *Journal of Marketing Research* 2 (November 1965), 417–18.

19 Krosnick, J.A. and Alwin, D.E., 'An Evaluation of a Cognitive Theory of Response-Order Effects in Survey Measurement', *Public Opinion Quarterly*, (Summer 1987), 201–19; and Payne, S.L., *The Art of Asking Questions* (Princeton, NJ: Princeton University Press, 1951), 141.

20 Blunch, N.J., 'Position Bias in Multiple-Choice Questions', *Journal of Marketing Research* 21 (May 1984), 216–20, has argued that position bias in multiple-choice questions cannot be eliminated by rotating the order of the alternatives. This viewpoint is contrary to the common practice.

21 Bishop, G.E., 'Experiments with the Middle Response Alternative in Survey Questions', *Public Opinion Quarterly* (Summer 1987), 220–32; and Schuman, H. and Presser, S., *Questions and Answers in Attitude Surveys* (Orlando, FL: Academic Press, 1981).

22 Bishop, G.E., Oldendick, R.W. and Tuchfarber, A.J., 'What Must My Interest in Politics Be If I Told You I Don't Know', *Public Opinion Quarterly* (Summer 1984), 510–19; and Mizerski, R.W., Freiden, J.B. and Green, Jr, R.C., 'The Effect of the "Don't Know" Option on TV Ad Claim

Recognition Tests', in *Advances in Consumer Research* 10 (Association for Consumer Research, 1983), 283–87.
23 Kalton, G. and Schuman, H., 'The Effect of the Question on Survey Responses: A Review', *Journal of the Royal Statistical Society* Series A, 145, Part 1 (1982), 44–45.
24 Schuman, H. and Presser, S., 'Question Wording as an Independent Variable in Survey Analysis', *Sociological Methods and Research* (November 1977), 155.
25 Omura, G.S., 'Correlates of Item Non-response', *Journal of the Market Research Society* (October 1983), 321–30; and Presser, S., 'Is Inaccuracy on Factual Survey Items Item-Specific or Respondent-Specific?', *Public Opinion Quarterly* (Spring 1984), 344–55.
26 Morgan, F.W., 'Judicial Standards for Survey Research: An Update and Guidelines', *Journal of Marketing* 54 (January 1990), 59–70; and Peterson, R.A. and Kerin, R.A., 'The Quality of Self-Report Data: Review and Synthesis,' in Enis, B. and Roering, K., (eds), *Annual Review of Marketing 1981* (Chicago: American Marketing Association, 1981), pp. 5–20.
27 O'Brien, J., 'How Do Market Researchers Ask Questions?', *Journal of the Market Research Society* 26 (April 1984), 93–107; Duncan, O.D. and Schuman, H., 'Effects of Question Wording and Context', *Journal of the American Statistical Association* (June 1980), 269–75; Smith, T.W., 'Qualifications to Generalised Absolutes', *Public Opinion Quarterly* (Summer 1981), 224–30; and Webb, N. 'Levels of Adult Numeracy', *Journal of the Market Research Society* (April 1984), 129–39; and Shepherd, P., 'Literacy and Numeracy and Their Implication for Survey Research', *Journal of the Market Research Society* (April 1984), 147–58.
28 Smith, T.W., 'That Which We Call Welfare by Any Other Name Would Smell Sweeter. An Analysis of the Impact of Question Wording on Response Patterns', *Public Opinion Quarterly* (Spring 1987), 75–83.
29 Billins, P., 'Research on Research'; and Robinson, P., 'Language in Data Collection', both in *Journal of the Market Research Society* (Spring 1982), 69–85.
30 Schuman, H. and Presser, S., 'Question Wording as an Independent Variable in Survey Analysis', *Sociological Methods and Research* (November 1977), 155.
31 Bishop, G.E., Oldendick, R.W. and Tuchfarber, A.J., 'Effects of Presenting One Versus Two Sides of an Issue in Survey Questions', *Public Opinion Quarterly* 46 (Spring 1982), 66–85; and Neumann, E.N. and Worcester, B., 'International Opinion Research', *European Research* (July 1984), 124–31.
32 Andrews, E.M., 'Construct Validity and Error Components of Survey Measures', *Public Opinion Quarterly* (Summer 1984), 409–42; and Jaffe, E.D. and Nebenzahl, I.D., 'Alternative Questionnaire Formats for Country Image Studies', *Journal of Marketing Research* (November 1984), 463–71.
33 Krosnick, J.A. and Alwin, D.E., 'An Evaluation of a Cognitive Theory of Response-Order Effects in Survey Measurement', *Public Opinion Quarterly* (Summer 1987), 201–19; Crespi, I. and Morris, D., 'Question Order Effect', *Public Opinion Quarterly* (Fall 1984), 578–91; and Schuman, H., Kalton, G. and Ludwig, J., 'Context and Contiguity in Survey Questionnaires', *Public Opinion Quarterly* (Spring 1983), 112–15.
34 Rating a brand on specific attributes early in a survey may affect responses to a later overall brand evaluation. For example, see Bickart, B.A., 'Carryover and Backfire Effects in Marketing Research', *Journal of Marketing Research* 30 (February 1993), 52–62.
35 Messmer, D.J. and Seymour, D.J., 'The Effects of Branching on Item Non-response', *Public Opinion Quarterly* 46 (Summer 1982), 270–77.
36 Mayer, C.S. and Piper, C., 'A Note on the Importance of Layout in Self-Administered Questionnaires', *Journal of Marketing Research* 19 (August 1982), 390–91.
37 Dickinson, S.R. and Kirzner, E., 'Questionnaire Item Omission as a Function of Within-Group Question Position', *Journal of Business Research* (February 1985), 71–75; and Herzog, A.R. and Bachman, J.G., 'Effects of Questionnaire Length on Response Quality', *Public Opinion Quarterly* 45 (Winter 1981), 549–59.
38 Hunt, S.D., Sparkman, Jr, R.D. and Wilcox, J., 'The Pre-test in Survey Research: Issues and Preliminary Findings', *Journal of Marketing Research* (May 1982), 269–73.
39 Zelnio, R.N. and Gagnon, J.P., 'The Construction and Testing of an Image Questionnaire', *Journal of the Academy of Marketing Science* (Summer 1981), 288–99.
40 Diamantopoulos, A., Schlegelmilch, B.B. and Reynolds, N., 'Pre-testing in Questionnaire Design: The Impact of Respondent Characteristics on Error Detection', *Journal of the Market Research Society* 36 (October 1994), 295–314.
41 Reynolds, N., Diamantopoulos, A. and Schlegelmilch, B.B., 'Pre-testing in Questionnaire Design: A Review of the Literature and Suggestions for Further Research', *Journal of the Market Research Society* 35 (April 1993), 171–82.
42 Hutton, G., 'If You Board the Asian 'Bus, Better Mind your Language', *ResearchPlus* (February 1996), 7.
43 *Rules of Conduct and Good Practice of the Professional Marketing Research Society of Canada* (1984).
44 Laczniak, G.R. and Murphy, P.E., *Ethical Marketing Decisions: the Higher Road* (Needhan Heights, MA: Allyn and Bacon, 1993).
45 Tybout, A.M. and Zaltman, G., 'Ethics in Marketing Research: Their Practical Relevance', *Journal of Marketing Research* 11 (1974), 357–68.

Chapter 13

Sampling: design and procedures

When determining the characteristics of a population, it is often advantageous to examine a part of the population (a sample) rather than the whole (a census)

OBJECTIVES

After reading this chapter, the student should be able to:

1 differentiate a sample from a census and identify the conditions that favour the use of a sample versus a census;
2 discuss the sampling design process: definition of the target population, determination of the sampling frame, selection of sampling technique(s), determination of sample size, execution of the sampling process and validating the sample;
3 classify sampling techniques as non-probability and probability sampling techniques;
4 describe the non-probability sampling techniques of convenience, judgmental, quota and snowball sampling;
5 describe the probability sampling techniques of simple random, systematic, stratified and cluster sampling;
6 identify the conditions that favour the use of non-probability sampling versus probability sampling;
7 understand the sampling design process and the use of sampling techniques in international marketing research;
8 identify the ethical issues related to the sampling design process and the use of appropriate sampling techniques.

OVERVIEW

Sampling is one component of a research design. The formulation of the research design is the third step of the marketing research process. At this stage, the information needed to address the marketing research problem has been identified and the nature of the research design (exploratory, descriptive or causal) has been determined. If a quantitative methodology is being adopted, scaling and measurement procedures will have been specified, and a questionnaire designed. The next step is to design suitable sampling procedures. Sampling design involves several basic questions: (1) Should a sample be taken? (2) If so, what process should be followed? (3) What kind of sample should be taken? (4) How large should it be? and (5) What can be done to control and adjust for non-response errors?

This chapter introduces the fundamental concepts of sampling and the qualitative considerations necessary to answer these questions. We address the question of whether or not to sample and describe the steps involved in sampling. Next, we present non-probability and probability sampling techniques. We discuss the use of sampling techniques in international marketing research and identify the relevant ethical issues. Statistical determination of sample size, and the causes for, control of, and adjustments for non-response error are discussed in Chapter 14.

We begin with the following example, which illustrates the usefulness of sampling.

EXAMPLE

Can football give brands 110% recall?[1]

The European Football Championship held in England in 1996, proved that football is the world's number one sport. More than 1.3 million tickets were sold and 250,000 overseas visitors followed their teams to England. The 31 matches were watched in more than 190 countries around the world by a global cumulative television audience of 6.7 billion; 445 million tuned in to watch the final itself.

Commercial support for the event came from a group of eleven official sponsors who were: Carlsberg, Canon, Coca-Cola, Fuji Film, General Motors, JVC, McDonalds, MasterCard, Phillips, Snickers and Umbro. Such a weight of marketing activity represented a major investment for the sponsors and it was vital that they were able to evaluate its effectiveness. Many individual sponsors conducted their own studies but a study was conducted for the sponsor group to evaluate the impact of EURO 96 as a sponsorship opportunity.

The survey to evaluate sponsorship effectiveness was a two-wave study, the first taking place eight months prior to the tournament, the second immediately after the final. The research was carried out in four markets, the national football teams of each one having successfully qualified for the finals, thus ensuring a consistent level of interest in the tournament across the sample:

UK: Host nation
France: Host to the 98 World Cup
Germany: Tournament favourites
Russia: East European nation

In each market a sample of 500 individuals aged 12 to 65 was interviewed at each wave, quota controls being imposed on sex, age and socio-economic group to match the incidence of each within the general population. ■

This example illustrates the various aspects of sampling design, clearly founded in a marketing and research problem. The target population is defined, the sampling technique is established with criteria for quotas and the sample size for each country and survey wave is set.

SAMPLE OR CENSUS

Population
The aggregate of all the elements, sharing some common set of characteristics, that comprise the universe for the purpose of the marketing research problem.

The objective of most marketing research projects is to obtain information about the characteristics or parameters of a **population**. A population is the aggregate of all the elements that share some common set of characteristics and that comprise the universe for the purpose of the marketing research problem. The population parameters are typically numbers, such as the proportion of consumers who are loyal to a particular brand of toothpaste. Information about

Census
A complete enumeration of the elements of a population or study objects.

Sample
A subgroup of the elements of the population selected for participation in the study.

population parameters may be obtained by taking a **census** or a **sample**. A census involves a complete enumeration of the elements of a population. The population parameters can be calculated directly in a straightforward way after the census is enumerated. A sample, on the other hand, is a subgroup of the population selected for participation in the study. Sample characteristics, called statistics, are then used to make inferences about the population parameters. The inferences that link sample characteristics and population parameters are estimation procedures and tests of hypotheses. These inference procedures are considered in Chapters 17 to 23.

Table 13.1 summarises the conditions favouring the use of a sample versus a census. Budget and time limits are obvious constraints favouring the use of a sample. A census is both costly and time-consuming to conduct. A census is unrealistic if the population is large, as it is for most consumer products. In the case of many industrial products, however, the population is small, making a census feasible as well as desirable. For example, in investigating the use of certain machine tools by Italian car manufacturers, a census would be preferred to a sample. Another reason for preferring a census in this case is that variance in the characteristic of interest is large. For example, machine tool usage of Fiat may vary greatly from the usage of Ferrari. Small population sizes as well as high variance in the characteristic to be measured favour a census.

If the cost of sampling errors is high (e.g. if the sample omitted a major manufacturer like Ford, the results could be misleading), a census, which eliminates such errors, is desirable. High cost of non-sampling errors, on the other hand, would favour sampling.

Table 13.1 Sample versus census

	Conditions favouring the use of	
	Sample	**Census**
1. Budget	*Small*	*Large*
2. Time available	*Short*	*Long*
3. Population size	*Large*	*Small*
4. Variance in the characteristic	*Small*	*Large*
5. Cost of sampling errors	*Low*	*High*
6. Cost of non-sampling errors	*High*	*Low*
7. Nature of measurement	*Destructive*	*Non-destructive*
8. Attention to individual cases	*Yes*	*No*

A census can greatly increase non-sampling error to the point that these errors exceed the sampling errors of a sample. Non-sampling errors are found to be the major contributor to total error, whereas random sampling errors have been relatively small in magnitude.[2] Hence, in most cases, accuracy considerations would favour a sample over a census.

A sample may be preferred if the measurement process results in the destruction or contamination of the elements sampled. For example, product usage tests result in the consumption of the product. Therefore, taking a census in a study that requires households to use a new brand of photographic film would not be feasible. Sampling may also be necessary to focus attention on individual cases, as in the case of depth interviews. Finally, other pragmatic considerations, such as the need to keep the study secret, may favour a sample over a census.

THE SAMPLING DESIGN PROCESS

The sampling design process includes six steps, which are shown sequentially in Figure 13.1. These steps are closely interrelated and relevant to all aspects of the marketing research project, from problem definition to the presentation of the results. Therefore, sample design decisions should be integrated with all other decisions in a research project.[3]

Define the target population

Target population
The collection of elements or objects that possess the information sought by the researcher and about which inferences are to be made.

Sampling design begins by specifying the **target population**. The target population is the collection of elements or objects that possess the information sought by the researcher and about which inferences are to be made. The target population must be defined precisely. Imprecise definition of the target population will result in research that is ineffective at best and misleading at worst. Defining the target population involves translating the problem definition into a precise statement of who should and should not be included in the sample.

Element
An object that possesses the information sought by the researcher and about which inferences are to be made.

Sampling unit
The basic unit containing the elements of the population to be sampled.

The target population should be defined in terms of elements, sampling units, extent and time. An **element** is the object about which or from which the information is desired. In survey research, the element is usually the respondent. A **sampling unit** is an element, or a unit containing the element, that is available for selection at some stage of the sampling process. Suppose that Clinique wanted to assess consumer response to a new line of lipsticks and wanted to sample females over 25 years of age. It may be possible to sample females over 25 directly, in which case a sampling unit would be the same as an element. Alternatively, the sampling unit might be households. In the latter case, households would be sampled and all females over 25 in each selected household would be interviewed. Here, the sampling unit and the population element are different. Extent refers to the geographical boundaries, and the time factor is the period under consideration. We use the GlobalCash project to illustrate.

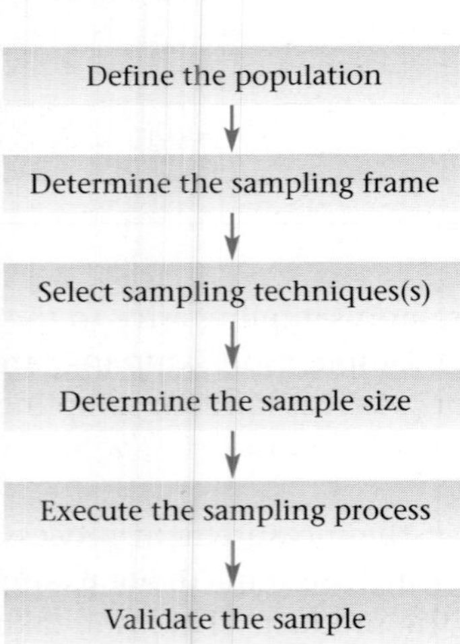

Figure 13.1
The sampling design process

GLOBALCASH PROJECT

Target population

The target population for the GlobalCash project was defined as follows:

Elements: managers responsible for cash management decisions
Sampling units: the largest companies and non-banking financial institutions in a country
Extent: 19 European countries plus the centres of taxation concessions in Ireland and Belgium
Time: 2000

Defining the target population may not be as easy as it was in this example. Consider a marketing research project assessing consumer response to a new brand of men's moisturiser. Who should be included in the target population? All men? Men who have used a moisturiser during the last month? Men of 17 years of age or older? Should females be included, because some women buy moisturiser for men that they know? These and similar questions must be resolved before the target population can be appropriately defined.[4]

Determine the sampling frame

Sampling frame
A representation of the elements of the target population that consists of a list or set of directions for identifying the target population.

A **sampling frame** is a representation of the elements of the target population. It consists of a list or set of directions for identifying the target population. Examples of a sampling frame include the telephone book, an association directory listing the firms in an industry, a mailing list on a database purchased from a commercial organisation, a city directory, or a map.[5] If a list cannot be compiled, then at least some directions for identifying the target population should be specified such as random-digit dialling procedures in telephone surveys.

Often it is possible to compile or obtain a list of population elements, but the list may omit some elements of the population or may include other elements that do not belong. Therefore, the use of a list will lead to sampling frame error, which was discussed in Chapter 3.[6]

In some instances, the discrepancy between the population and the sampling frame is small enough to ignore. In most cases, however, the researcher should recognise and attempt to treat the sampling frame error. The main approach is to redefine the population in terms of the sampling frame. If the telephone book is used as a sampling frame, the population of households could be redefined as those with a correct listing in the telephone book in a given area. Although this approach is simplistic, it does prevent the researcher from being misled about the actual population being investigated.[7] The major drawback of redefining the population based upon available sampling frames is that the nature of the research problem may be compromised. Who is being measured and ultimately to whom the research findings may be generalised may not match the target group of individuals identified in a research problem definition. Evaluating the accuracy of sampling frames matches the issues of evaluating secondary data (see Chapter 3).

Select a sampling technique

Selecting a sampling technique involves several decisions of a broader nature. The researcher must decide whether to use a Bayesian or traditional sampling approach, to sample with or without replacement, and to use non-probability or probability sampling.

Bayesian approach
A selection method where the elements are selected sequentially. The Bayesian approach explicitly incorporates prior information about population parameters as well as the costs and probabilities associated with making wrong decisions.

In the **Bayesian approach**, the elements are selected sequentially. After each element is added to the sample, the data are collected, sample statistics computed, and sampling costs determined. The Bayesian approach explicitly incorporates prior information about population parameters as well as the costs and probabilities associated with making wrong decisions. This approach is theoretically appealing. Yet it is not used widely in marketing research because much of the required information on costs and probabilities is not available. In the traditional sampling approach, the entire sample is selected before data collection begins. Because the traditional approach is the most common approach used, it is assumed in the following sections.

Sampling with replacement
A sampling technique in which an element can be included in the sample more than once.

Sampling without replacement
A sampling technique in which an element cannot be included in the sample more than once.

In **sampling with replacement**, an element is selected from the sampling frame and appropriate data are obtained. Then the element is placed back in the sampling frame. As a result, it is possible for an element to be included in the sample more than once. In **sampling without replacement**, once an element is selected for inclusion in the sample, it is removed from the sampling frame and therefore cannot be selected again. The calculation of statistics is done somewhat differently for the two approaches, but statistical inference is not very different if the sampling frame is large relative to the ultimate sample size. Thus, the distinction is important only when the sampling frame is small compared with the sample size.

The most important decision about the choice of sampling technique is whether to use probability or non-probability sampling. Given its importance, the issues involved in this decision are discussed in great detail in this chapter.

If the sampling unit is different from the element, it is necessary to specify precisely how the elements within the sampling unit should be selected. With in-home personal interviews and telephone interviews, merely specifying the address or the telephone number may not be sufficient. For example, should the person answering the doorbell or the telephone be interviewed, or someone else in the household? Often, more than one person in a household may qualify. For example, both the male and female head of household may be eligible to participate in a study examining family leisure-time activities. When a probability sampling technique is being employed, a random selection must be made from all the eligible persons in each household. A simple procedure for random selection is the next birthday method. The interviewer asks which of the eligible persons in the household has the next birthday and includes that person in the sample.

Determine the sample size

Sample size
The number of units to be included in a study.

Sample size refers to the number of elements to be included in the study. Determining the sample size is complex and involves several qualitative and quantitative considerations. The qualitative factors are discussed in this section, and the quantitative factors are considered in Chapter 14. Important qualitative factors to be considered in determining the sample size include (1) the importance of the decision, (2) the nature of the research, (3) the number of variables, (4) the nature of the analysis, (5) sample sizes used in similar studies, (6) incidence rates, (7) completion rates, and (8) resource constraints.

In general, for more important decisions, more information is necessary, and that information should be obtained very precisely. This calls for larger samples, but as the sample size increases, each unit of information is obtained at greater cost. The degree of precision may be measured in terms of the standard deviation of the mean. The standard deviation of the mean is inversely proportional to the square root of the sample size. The larger the sample, the smaller the gain in precision by increasing the sample size by one unit.

The nature of the research also has an impact on the sample size. For exploratory research designs, such as those using qualitative research, the sample size is typically small. For conclusive research, such as descriptive surveys, larger samples are required. Likewise, if data are being collected on a large number of variables, larger samples are required. The cumulative effects of sampling error across variables are reduced in a large sample.

If sophisticated analysis of the data using multivariate techniques is required, the sample size should be large. The same applies if the data are to be analysed in great detail. Thus, a larger sample would be required if the data are being analysed at the subgroup or segment level than if the analysis is limited to the aggregate or total sample.

Sample size is influenced by the average size of samples in similar studies. Table 13.2 gives an idea of sample sizes used in different marketing research studies. These sample sizes have been determined based on experience and can serve as rough guidelines, particularly when non-probability sampling techniques are used.

Finally, the sample size decision should be guided by a consideration of the resource constraints. In any marketing research project, money and time are limited. Other constraints include the availability of qualified personnel for data collection. The sample size required should be adjusted for the incidence of eligible respondents and the completion rate, as explained in the next chapter.

Table 13.2 Sample sizes used in marketing research studies

Type of study	*Minimum size*	*Typical range*
Problem identification research (e.g. market potential)	500	1000–2500
Problem-solving research (e.g. pricing)	200	300–500
Product tests	200	300–500
Test marketing studies	200	300–500
TV, radio, or print advertising (per commercial/ad tested)	150	200–300
Test-market audits	10 stores	10–20 stores
Focus groups	2 groups	4–12 groups

Execute the sampling process

Execution of the sampling process requires a detailed specification of how the sampling design decisions with respect to the population, sampling frame, sampling unit, sampling technique and sample size are to be implemented. If households are the sampling unit, an operational definition of a household is needed. Procedures should be specified for empty housing units and for call-backs in case no one is at home.

Sample validation

Once data is collected from a sample or indeed as it is being collected, comparisons between the structure of the sample and the target population should be made. Sample validation aims to account for sampling frame error by screening the respondents in the data collection phase. Respondents could be screened with respect to demographic characteristics, familiarity, product usage and other characteristics to ensure that they satisfy the criteria for the target population. Screening can eliminate inappropriate elements contained in the sampling frame, but it cannot account for elements that have been omitted. The success of the process depends upon the accuracy of base statistics that describe a population.

We illustrate the process of sample design decisions with an example of a continuous tracking survey.

EXAMPLE

Taking the peoples' temperature – right across Europe[8]

Since the earliest days of the European Economic Community, the Commission's information, communication, culture and audio-visual directorate, Directorate General X, has conducted regular polls across Europe. In 1996 the need for speed and flexibility in EU surveys led to the introduction of the Continuous Tracking Survey or CTS. The origin of the CTS was a policy initiative on information and communication, established in 1993 as a result of the decline in support for the EU in the period leading up to the Single Market and the ratification of the Maastricht Treaty.

The sample design for this study involved:

1 *Target population*: adults aged 18 years and over (element) in a household with a working telephone number (sampling unit) in individual EU countries (extent) during the survey period (time).
2 *Sampling frame*: computer program for generating random digit dialling (except in Germany where the code of practice forbids this approach).
3 *Sampling unit*: working telephone numbers.
4 *Sampling technique*: random sampling.
5 *Sample size*: 800 in each of 16 sampling areas making a total of 12,800 interviews in each four-week wave of interviewing – a total of 140,000 interviews each year.
6 *Execution*: CATI, random digit dialling followed by the random selection of individuals in households. 19 variants of the questionnaire to include people living in countries where more than one national language is common.
7 *Validation*: Sample characteristics compared to census statistics in each country.

A CLASSIFICATION OF SAMPLING TECHNIQUES

Non-probability sampling
Sampling techniques that do not use chance selection procedures but rather rely on the personal judgement of the researcher.

Sampling techniques may be broadly classified as non-probability and probability (see Figure 13.2). **Non-probability sampling** relies on the personal judgement of the researcher rather than on chance to select sample elements. The researcher can arbitrarily or consciously decide what elements to include in the sample. Non-probability samples may yield good estimates of the population characteristics, but they do not allow for objective evaluation of the precision of the sample results. Because there is no way of determining the probability of selecting any particular element for inclusion in the sample, the estimates obtained are not statistically projectable to the population. Commonly used non-probability sampling techniques include convenience sampling, judgemental sampling, quota sampling and snowball sampling (see the next section).

Probability sampling
A sampling procedure in which each element of the population has a fixed probabilistic chance of being selected for the sample.

In **probability sampling**, sampling units are selected by chance. It is possible to pre-specify every potential sample of a given size that could be drawn from the population, as well as the probability of selecting each sample. Every potential sample need not have the same probability of selection, but it is possible to specify the probability of selecting any particular sample of a given size. This requires not only a precise definition of the target population but also a general specification of the sampling frame. Because sample elements are selected by chance, it is possible to determine the precision of the sample estimates of the characteristics of interest. Confidence intervals, which contain the true popula-

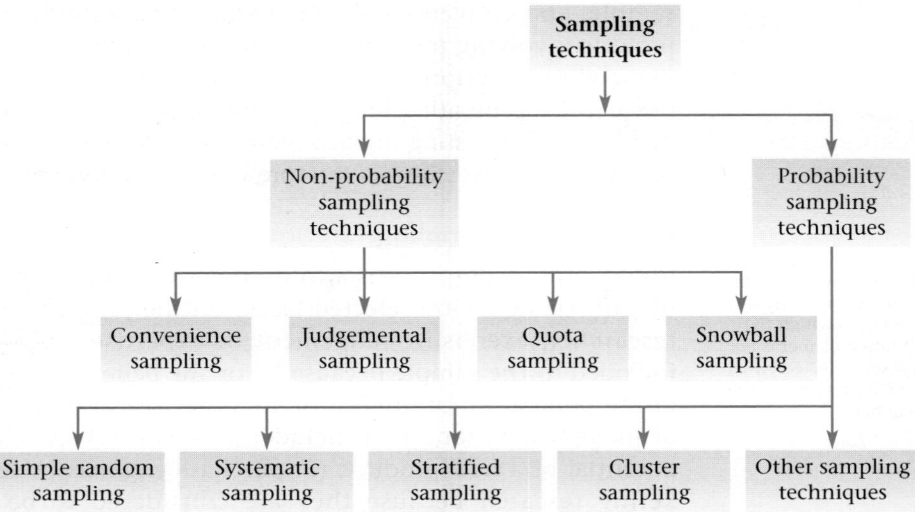

Figure 13.2
A classification of sampling techniques

tion value with a given level of certainty, can be calculated. This permits the researcher to make inferences or projections about the target population from which the sample was drawn. Classification of probability sampling techniques are based on

- Element versus cluster sampling
- Equal unit probability versus unequal probabilities
- Unstratified versus stratified selection
- Random versus systematic selection
- Single-stage versus multistage techniques

All possible combinations of these five aspects result in 32 different probability sampling techniques. Of these techniques, we consider simple random sampling, systematic sampling, stratified sampling, and cluster sampling in depth and briefly touch on some others. First, however, we discuss non-probability sampling techniques.

NON-PROBABILITY SAMPLING TECHNIQUES

Convenience sampling

Convenience sampling
A non-probability sampling technique that attempts to obtain a sample of convenient elements. The selection of sampling units is left primarily to the interviewer.

Convenience sampling attempts to obtain a sample of convenient elements. The selection of sampling units is left primarily to the interviewer. Often, respondents are selected because they happen to be in the right place at the right time. Examples of convenience sampling include: (1) use of students, church groups and members of social organisations, (2) street interviews without qualifying the respondents, (3) some forms of email and Internet survey, (4) tear-out questionnaires included in a newspaper or magazine, and (5) journalists interviewing 'people on the street'.[9] Convenience sampling is the least expensive and least time-consuming of all sampling techniques. The sampling units are accessible, easy to measure, and cooperative. Despite these advantages, this form of sampling has serious limitations. Many potential sources of selection bias are present, including respondent self-selection. Convenience samples are not representative of any definable population. Hence, it is not theoretically meaningful to generalise to any population from a convenience sample, and convenience samples are not appropriate for marketing research projects involving population inferences. Convenience samples are not recommended for descriptive or causal research, but they can be used in exploratory research for generating ideas, insights or hypotheses. Convenience samples can be used for pre-testing questionnaires, or pilot studies. Even in these cases, caution should be exercised in interpreting the results.

Judgemental sampling

Judgemental sampling
A form of convenience sampling in which the population elements are purposely selected based on the judgement of the researcher.

Judgemental sampling is a form of convenience sampling in which the population elements are selected based on the judgement of the researcher. The researcher, exercising judgement or expertise, chooses the elements to be included in the sample because he or she believes that they are representative of the population of interest or are otherwise appropriate. Common examples of judgemental sampling include: (1) test markets selected to determine the potential of a new product, (2) purchase engineers selected in industrial marketing research because they are considered to be representative of the company, (3) product testing with individuals who may be particularly fussy or who hold extremely high expectations, (4) expert witnesses used in court, and (5) supermarkets selected to test a new merchandising display system. The use of this technique is illustrated in the context of the GlobalCash project.

GLOBALCASH PROJECT

Sampling technique

In the GlobalCash study, at least two cash managers in every country surveyed were selected for an additional interview, based on judgement. Many of the companies and indeed cash manager respondents were known to members of the research team. If the individual manager was not known, characteristics of the respondent organisations were known. The purpose of the interviews was to explore the reasons behind why cash managers carry out specific activities or plan certain events. To be able to fulfil this purpose in an in-depth interview situation meant that managers were needed who:

- were willing to give up at least two hours to discuss issues,
- were able to articulate the reasons for their behaviour,
- were 'sophisticated' in their approach to cash management,
- had a wide array of experience of pan-European banks.

Perhaps the most subjective element of this list is the issue of 'sophistication'. This does not necessarily mean the most technically complex or the use of state-of-the-art technology, but the use of creative solutions to cash management problems. In this example, judgement was used to select specific managers who met the above criteria. Judgemental sampling is inexpensive, convenient and quick, yet it does not allow direct generalisations to a specific population, usually because the population is not defined explicitly. Judgemental sampling is subjective and its value depends entirely on the researcher's judgement, expertise and creativity. It may be useful if broad population inferences are not required. As in the GlobalCash example, judgement samples are frequently used in commercial marketing research projects. ■

Quota sampling

Quota sampling
A non-probability sampling technique that is a two-stage restricted judgemental sampling. The first stage consists of developing control categories or quotas of population elements. In the second stage, sample elements are selected based on convenience or judgement.

Quota sampling may be viewed as two-stage restri that is used extensively in street interviewing.

The first stage consists of developing control characteristics, ulation elements such as age or gender. To develop these quotas, sampling lists relevant control characteristics and determines the distribution characteristics in the target population, such as Males 49 per cent, Femal per cent. Often, the quotas are assigned so that the proportion of the sample elements possessing the control characteristics is the same as the proportion of population elements with these characteristics. In other words, the quotas ensure that the composition of the sample is the same as the composition of the population with respect to the characteristics of interest.

In the second stage, sample elements are selected based on convenience or judgement. Once the quotas have been assigned, there is considerable freedom in selecting the elements to be included in the sample. The only requirement is that the elements selected fit the control characteristics. This technique is illustrated with the following example.

EXAMPLE

How is epilepsy perceived?

A study was undertaken by the Scottish Epilepsy Association to determine the perceptions of the condition of epilepsy by the adult population in the city of Glasgow. A quota sample of 500 adults was selected. The control characteristics were sex, age and propensity to donate to a charity. Based on the composition of the adult population of the city, the quotas assigned were as follows:

		Male		*Female*		*Totals*
		48%		*52%*		
Propensity to donate		*Have a flag*	*No flag*	*Have a flag*	*No flag*	
Age		*50%*	*50%*	*50%*	*50%*	
18 to 30	25%	30	30	33	32	**125**
31 to 45	40%	48	48	52	52	**200**
46 to 60	15%	18	18	19	20	**75**
Over 60	20%	24	24	26	26	**100**
Totals		**120**	**120**	**130**	**130**	
Totals		**240**		**260**		**500**

Note that the percentages of gender and age within the target population can be taken from local census statistics. The percentages of 'propensity to donate' could not be gleaned from secondary data sources and so were split on a 50/50 basis. The interviews were conducted on a Saturday when it was customary to see charity 'flag sellers' operating. One of the hypotheses to be tested in the study was the extent to which those who donated to charities on flag days were more are of the condition of epilepsy and how to treat epileptic sufferers. Thus the ruction to interviewers was to split interviews between those who wore the that they had bought from a street collector and those who had not bought It was recognised that this was a crude measure of propensity to donate to but was the only tangible clue that could be consistently observed. ■

...his example, quotas were assigned such that the composition of the sample was the same as that of the population. In certain situations, however, it is desirable either to under- or over-sample elements with certain characteristics. To illustrate, it may be desirable to over-sample heavy users of a product so that their behaviour can be examined in detail. Although this type of sample is not representative, it may nevertheless be very relevant.

Even if the sample composition mirrors that of the population with respect to the control characteristics, there is no assurance that the sample is representative. If a characteristic that is relevant to the problem is overlooked, the quota sample will not be representative. Relevant control characteristics are often omitted because there are practical difficulties associated with including many control characteristics. Because the elements within each quota are selected based on convenience or judgement, many sources of selection bias are potentially present. The interviewers may go to selected areas where eligible respondents are more likely to be found. Likewise, they may avoid people who look unfriendly or are not well dressed or those who live in undesirable locations. Quota sampling does not permit assessment of sampling error.[10]

Quota sampling attempts to obtain representative samples at a relatively low cost. Its advantages are the lower costs and greater convenience to the interviewers in selecting elements for each quota. Recently, tighter controls have been imposed on interviewers and interviewing procedures that tend to reduce selection bias, and guidelines have been suggested for improving the quality of street interview quota samples.[11] Under certain conditions, quota sampling obtains results close to those for conventional probability sampling.[12]

Snowball sampling

Snowball sampling
A non-probability sampling technique in which an initial group of respondents is selected randomly. Subsequent respondents are selected based on the referrals or information provided by the initial respondents. By obtaining referrals from referrals, this process may be carried out in waves.

In snowball sampling, an initial group of respondents is selected, usua... random. After being interviewed, these respondents are asked to identify ... who belong to the target population of interest. Subsequent respond... selected based on the referrals. By obtaining referrals from referrals, th... may be carried out in waves, thus leading to a snowballing effect. Ev... probability sampling is used to select the initial respondents, the fi... a non-probability sample. The referrals will have demographic ... graphic characteristics more similar to the persons referring the... occur by chance.[13]

A major objective of snowball sampling is to estimate chara... rare in the population. Examples include users of particular ge... services, such as food stamps, whose names cannot be r... groups, such as widowed males under 35; and membe... population. Snowball sampling is used in industrial b... tify buyer–seller pairs. The major advantage of s... substantially increases the likelihood of locating ... population. It also results in relatively low... Snowball sampling is illustrated by the follow...

EXAMPLE

Sampling horse owners

Dalgety animal feeds wished to questi... nd feeding of their horses. They could not lo... d all horse owners with the exception of ma... shed to contact owners who had one or tw... was not well understood and held great ma... oach involved locating interviewers at horse feed outlets. The interviewers ascertained basic characteristics of horse owners but more importantly they invited them along to focus groups. When the focus groups were conducted, issues of horse care and feeding were developed in greater detail to allow the construction of a meaningful postal questionnaire. As a rapport and trust was built up with those that attended the focus groups, names as referrals were given that allowed a sampling frame for the first wave of respondents to the subsequent postal survey. The process of referrals continued allowing a total of four waves and a response of 800 questionnaires. ■

In this example, note the non-random selection of the initial group of respondents through focus group invitations. This procedure was more efficient than random selection, which given the absence of an appropriate sampling frame would be very cumbersome. In other cases where an appropriate sampling frame exists, random selection of respondents through probability sampling techniques is more appropriate.

PROBABILITY SAMPLING TECHNIQUES

Probability sampling techniques vary in terms of sampling efficiency. Sampling efficiency is a concept that reflects a trade-off between sampling cost and precision. Precision refers to the level of uncertainty about the characteristic being measured. Precision is inversely related to sampling errors but positively related to cost. The greater the precision, the greater the cost, and most studies require a trade-off. The researcher should strive for the most efficient sampling design, subject to the budget allocated. The efficiency of a probability sampling technique may be assessed by comparing it with that of simple random sampling.

Simple random sampling

Simple random sampling
A probability sampling technique in which each element has a known and equal probability of selection. Every element is selected independently of every other element, and the sample is drawn by a random procedure from a sampling frame.

In **simple random sampling** (SRS), each element in the population has a known and equal probability of selection. Furthermore, each possible sample of a given size (n) has a known and equal probability of being the sample actually selected. This implies that every element is selected independently of every other element. The sample is drawn by a random procedure from a sampling frame. This method is equivalent to a lottery system in which names are placed in a container, the container is shaken and the names of the winners are then drawn out in an unbiased manner.

To draw a simple random sample, the researcher first compiles a sampling frame in which each element is assigned a unique identification number. Then random numbers are generated to determine which elements to include in the sample. The random numbers may be generated with a computer routine or a table (see Table 1 shown in the Appendix of Statistical Tables). Suppose that a sample of size ten is to be selected from a sampling frame containing 800 elements. This could be done by starting with row 1 and column 1 of Table 1, considering the three right most digits, and going down the column until ten numbers between 1 and 800 have been selected. Numbers outside this range are ignored. The elements corresponding to the random numbers generated constitute the sample. Thus, in our example, elements 480, 368, 130, 167, 570, 562, 301, 579, 475 and 553 would be selected. Note that the last three digits of row 6 (921) and row 11 (918) were ignored, because they were out of range.

SRS has many desirable features. It is easily understood, the sample results may be projected to the target population, and most approaches to statistical inference assume that the data have been collected by simple random sampling. SRS suffers from at least four significant limitations, however. First, it is often difficult to construct a sampling frame that will permit a simple random sample to be drawn. Second, SRS can result in samples that are very large or spread over large geographic areas, thus increasing the time and cost of data collection. Third, SRS often results in lower precision with larger standard errors than other probability sampling techniques. Fourth, SRS may or may not result in a representative sample. Although samples drawn will represent the population well on average, a given simple random sample may grossly misrepresent the target population. This is more likely if the size of the sample is small. For these reasons, SRS is not widely used in marketing research. Procedures such as systematic sampling are more popular.

Systematic sampling

Systematic sampling
A probability sampling technique in which the sample is chosen by selecting a random starting point and then picking every *i*th element in succession from the sampling frame.

In **systematic sampling**, the sample is chosen by selecting a random starting point and then picking every *i*th element in succession from the sampling frame. The sampling interval, i, is determined by dividing the population size N by the sample size n and rounding to the nearest integer. For example, there are 100,000 elements in the population and a sample of 1000 is desired. In this case, the sampling interval, i, is 100. A random number between 1 and 100 is selected. If, for example, this number is 23, the sample consists of elements 23, 123, 223, 323, 423, 523, and so on.[15]

Systematic sampling is similar to SRS in that each population element has a known and equal probability of selection. It is different from SRS, however, in that only the permissible samples of size n that can be drawn have a known and equal probability of selection. The remaining samples of size n have a zero probability of being selected.

For systematic sampling, the researcher assumes that the population elements are ordered in some respect. In some cases, the ordering (for example, alphabetic listing in a telephone book) is unrelated to the characteristic of interest. In other instances, the ordering is directly related to the characteristic under investigation. For example, credit card customers may be listed in order of outstanding balance, or firms in a given industry may be ordered according to annual sales. If the population elements are arranged in a manner unrelated to the characteristic of interest, systematic sampling will yield results quite similar to SRS.

On the other hand, when the ordering of the elements is related to the characteristic of interest, systematic sampling increases the representativeness of the sample. If firms in an industry are arranged in increasing order of annual sales, a systematic sample will include some small and some large firms. A simple random sample may be unrepresentative because it may contain, for example, only small firms or a disproportionate number of small firms. If the ordering of the elements produces a cyclical pattern, systematic sampling may decrease the representativeness of the sample. To illustrate, consider the use of systematic sampling to generate a sample of monthly department store sales from a sampling frame containing monthly sales for the last 60 years. If a sampling interval of 12 is chosen, the resulting sample would not reflect the month-to-month variation in sales.[16]

Systematic sampling is less costly and easier than SRS because random selection is done only once. Moreover, the random numbers do not have to be matched with individual elements as in SRS. Because some lists contain millions of elements, considerable time can be saved, which reduces the costs of sampling. If information related to the characteristic of interest is available for the population, systematic sampling can be used to obtain a more representative and reliable (lower sampling error) sample than SRS. Another relative advantage is that systematic sampling can even be used without knowledge of the composition (elements) of the sampling frame. For example, every *i*th person leaving a shop or passing a point in the street can be intercepted. For these reasons, systematic sampling is often employed in consumer mail, telephone and street interviews, as illustrated by the following example.

EXAMPLE

Tennis's systematic sampling returns a smash[17]

Tennis magazine conducted a postal survey of its subscribers to gain a better understanding of its market. Systematic sampling was employed to select a sample of 1472 subscribers from the publication's domestic circulation list. If we assume that the subscriber list had 1,472,000 names, the sampling interval would be 1000 (1,472,000/1472). A number from 1 to 1000 was drawn at random. Beginning with that number, every 1000th was selected.

An 'alert' postcard was mailed one week before the survey. A second, follow-up, questionnaire was sent to the whole sample ten days after the initial questionnaire. There were 76 post office returns, so the net effective mailing was 1396. Six weeks after the first mailing, 778 completed questionnaires were returned, yielding a response rate of 56 per cent. ■

Stratified sampling

Stratified sampling
A probability sampling technique that uses a two-step process to partition the population into subsequent sub-populations, or strata. Elements are selected from each stratum by a random procedure.

Stratified sampling is a two-step process in which the population is partitioned into sub-populations, or strata. The strata should be mutually exclusive and collectively exhaustive in that every population element should be assigned to one and only one stratum and no population elements should be omitted. Next, elements are selected from each stratum by a random procedure, usually SRS. Technically, only SRS should be employed in selecting the elements from each stratum. In practice, sometimes systematic sampling and other probability sampling procedures are employed. Stratified sampling differs from quota sampling in that the sample elements are selected probabilistically rather than based on convenience or judgement. A major objective of stratified sampling is to increase precision without increasing cost.[18]

The variables used to partition the population into strata are referred to as stratification variables. The criteria for the selection of these variables consist of homogeneity, heterogeneity, relatedness and cost. The elements within a stratum should be as homogeneous as possible, but the elements in different strata should be as heterogeneous as possible. The stratification variables should also be closely related to the characteristic of interest. The more closely these criteria are met, the greater the effectiveness in controlling extraneous sampling variation. Finally, the variables should decrease the cost of the stratification process by being easy to measure and apply. Variables commonly used for stratification include demographic characteristics (as illustrated in the example for quota sampling), type of customer (credit card versus non-credit card), size of firm, or type of industry. It is possible to use more than one variable for stratification, although more than two are seldom used because of pragmatic and cost considerations. Although the number of strata to use is a matter of judgement, experience suggests the use of no more than six. Beyond six strata, any gain in precision is more than offset by the increased cost of stratification and sampling.

Another important decision involves the use of proportionate or disproportionate sampling. In proportionate stratified sampling, the size of the sample drawn from each stratum is proportionate to the relative size of that stratum in the total population. In disproportionate stratified sampling, the size of the sample from each stratum is proportionate to the relative size of that stratum and to the standard deviation of the distribution of the characteristic of interest among all the elements in that stratum. The logic behind disproportionate sampling is simple. First, strata with larger relative sizes are more influential in determining the population mean, and these strata should also exert a greater influence in deriving the sample estimates. Consequently, more elements should be drawn from strata of larger relative size. Second, to increase precision, more elements should be drawn from strata with larger standard deviations and fewer elements should be drawn from strata with smaller standard deviations. (If all the elements in a stratum are identical, a sample size of one will result in perfect information.) Note that the two methods are identical if the characteristic of interest has the same standard deviation within each stratum.

Disproportionate sampling requires that some estimate of the relative variation, or standard deviation of the distribution of the characteristic of interest, within strata be known. As this information is not always available, the researcher may have to rely on intuition and logic to determine sample sizes for each stratum. For example, large retail stores might be expected to have greater variation in the sales of some products as compared with small stores. Hence, the size of large stores in a sample may be disproportionately large. When the researcher is primarily interested in examining differences between strata, a common sampling strategy is to select the same sample size from each stratum.

Stratified sampling can ensure that all the important sub-populations are represented in the sample. This is particularly important if the distribution of the characteristic of interest in the population is skewed. For example, very few households have annual incomes that allow them to own a second home overseas. If a simple random sample is taken, households that have a second home overseas may not be adequately represented. Stratified sampling would guarantee that the sample contains a certain number of these households. Stratified sampling combines the simplicity of SRS with potential gains in precision. Therefore, it is a popular sampling technique.

Cluster sampling

Cluster sampling
A two-step probability sampling technique where the target population is first divided into mutually exclusive and collectively exhaustive sub-populations called clusters and then, a random sample of clusters is selected based on a probability sampling technique such as simple random sampling. For each selected cluster, either all the elements are included in the sample or a sample of elements is drawn probabilistically.

In **cluster sampling**, the target population is first divided into mutually exclusive and collectively exhaustive sub-populations, or clusters. Then, a random sample of clusters is selected, based on a probability sampling technique such as SRS. For each selected cluster, either all the elements are included in the sample or a sample of elements is drawn probabilistically. If all the elements in each selected cluster are included in the sample, the procedure is called one-stage cluster sampling. If a sample of elements is drawn probabilistically from each selected cluster, the procedure is two-stage cluster sampling. As shown in Figure 13.3, two-stage cluster sampling can be either simple two-stage cluster sampling involving SRS or probability proportionate to size (PPS) sampling. Furthermore, a cluster sample can have multiple (more than two) stages, as in multistage cluster sampling.

The key distinction between cluster sampling and stratified sampling is that in cluster sampling only a sample of sub-populations (clusters) is chosen, whereas in stratified sampling all the sub-populations (strata) are selected for further sampling. The objectives of the two methods are also different. The objective of cluster sampling is to increase sampling efficiency by decreasing costs, but the objective of stratified sampling is to increase precision. With respect to homogeneity and heterogeneity, the criteria for forming clusters are just the opposite

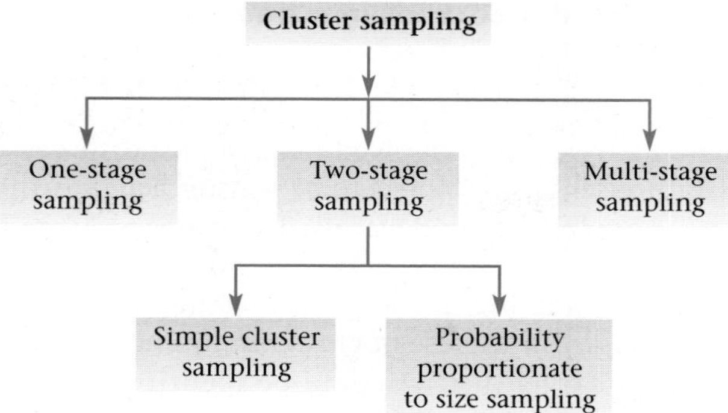

Figure 13.3
Types of cluster sampling

of that for strata. Elements within a cluster should be as heterogeneous as possible, but clusters themselves should be as homogeneous as possible. Ideally, each cluster should be a small-scale representation of the population. In cluster sampling, a sampling frame is needed only for those clusters selected for the sample.

Area sampling
A common form of cluster sampling in which the clusters consist of geographic areas such as counties, housing tracts, blocks, or other area descriptions.

A common form of cluster sampling is **area sampling**, in which the clusters consist of geographic areas, such as counties, housing districts, or blocks. If only one level of sampling takes place in selecting the basic elements (for example, if the researcher samples blocks and then all the households within the selected blocks are included in the sample), the design is called single-stage area sampling. If two (or more) levels of sampling take place before the basic elements are selected (if the researcher samples blocks and then samples households within selected blocks), the design is called two-stage (or multistage) area sampling. The distinguishing feature of one-stage area sampling is that all the households in the selected blocks (or geographic areas) are included in the sample.

There are two types of two-stage designs, as shown in Figure 13.3. One type involves SRS at the first stage (e.g. sampling blocks) as well as the second stage (e.g. sampling households within blocks). This design is called simple two-stage cluster sampling. In this design the fraction of elements (e.g. households) selected at the second stage is the same for each sample cluster (e.g. selected blocks).

This design is appropriate when the clusters are equal in size, that is, when the clusters contain approximately the same number of sampling units. If they differ greatly in size, however, simple two-stage cluster sampling can lead to biased estimates. Sometimes the clusters can be made of equal size by combining clusters. When this option is not feasible, probability proportionate to size (PPS) sampling can be used.

Probability proportionate to size
A selection method where the probability of selecting a sampling unit in a selected cluster varies inversely with the size of the cluster. Therefore, the size of all the resulting clusters is approximately equal.

In **probability proportionate to size** (PPS) sampling, the clusters are sampled with probability proportional to size. The size of a cluster is defined in terms of the number of sampling units within that cluster. Thus, in the first stage, large clusters are more likely to be included than small clusters. In the second stage, the probability of selecting a sampling unit in a selected cluster varies inversely with the size of the cluster. Thus, the probability that any particular sampling unit will be included in the sample is equal for all units, because the unequal first stage probabilities are balanced by the unequal second stage probabilities. The numbers of sampling units included from the selected clusters are approximately equal.

Cluster sampling has two major advantages: feasibility and low cost. These advantages are illustrated in the following example where alternative means of drawing a sample were severely restricted without incurring great costs.

EXAMPLE

Sport and leisure demands in schools

The Sports Council has supported marketing research in the South West of England that has facilitated new facilities and sports development in a range of cities. The methodology involved using a postal survey which was sent to individuals in households. The electoral register acted as the sampling frame and a systematic sampling method was used. A major problem lay in sampling younger members of the community who were not named on the electoral register and had no known sampling frame that marketing researchers could access.

The solution lay in the use of cluster sampling techniques. All schools and colleges within a target district could be identified. A random sample of all the classes within the schools and colleges was taken (between the ages of 12 and 18). With the selected classes, permission was gained to administer the questionnaire to the whole class. This resulted in a very cost-effective means of data collection. As all the class completed the task together, a consistent means to motivate respondents and instructions could be given. ■

In many situations the only sampling frames readily available for the target population are clusters, not population elements. In the above example, the schools and their classes are known but not the pupils. It is often impossible to compile a list of all consumers in a population, given the resources and constraints. Lists of geographical areas, telephone exchanges and other clusters of consumers, however, can be constructed relatively easily. Cluster sampling is the most cost-effective probability sampling technique. This advantage must be weighed against several limitations. Cluster sampling results in relatively imprecise samples, and it is difficult to form heterogeneous clusters, because, for example, households in a block tend to be similar rather than dissimilar.[19] It can be difficult to compute and interpret statistics based on clusters. The strengths and weaknesses of cluster sampling and the other basic sampling techniques are summarised in Table 13.3. Figure 13.4 describes the procedures for drawing probability samples.

Other probability sampling techniques

In addition to the four basic probability sampling techniques, there are a variety of other sampling techniques. Most of these may be viewed as extensions of the basic techniques and were developed to address complex sampling problems. Two techniques with some relevance to marketing research are sequential sampling and double sampling.

Sequential sampling A probability sampling technique in which the population elements are sampled sequentially, data collection and analysis are done at each stage, and a decision is made as to whether additional population elements should be sampled.

In **sequential sampling**, the population elements are sampled sequentially, data collection and analysis are done at each stage, and a decision is made as to whether additional population elements should be sampled. The sample size is not known in advance, but a decision rule is stated before sampling begins. At each stage, this rule indicates whether sampling should be continued or whether enough information has been obtained. Sequential sampling has been used to determine preferences for two competing alternatives. In one study, respondents were asked which of two alternatives they preferred, and sampling was terminated when sufficient evidence was accumulated to validate a preference. It has also been used to establish the price differential between a standard model and a deluxe model of a consumer durable.[20]

Double sampling A sampling technique in which certain population elements are sampled twice.

In **double sampling**, also called two-phase sampling, certain population elements are sampled twice. In the first phase, a sample is selected and some information is collected from all the elements in the sample. In the second

Table 13.3 Strengths and weaknessesof basic sampling techniques

Technique	*Strengths*	*Weaknesses*
Non-probability sampling		
Convenience sampling	Least expensive, least time consuming, most convenient.	Selection bias, sample not representative, not recommended for descriptive or causal research
Judgemental sampling	Low cost, convenient, not time consuming	Does not allow generalisation, subjective
Quota sampling	Sample can be controlled for certain characteristics	Selection bias, no assurance of representativeness
Snowball sampling	Can estimate rare characteristics	Time consuming
Probability sampling		
Simple random sampling (SRS)	Easily understood, results projectable	Difficult to construct sampling frame, expensive, lower precision, no assurance of representativeness
Systematic sampling	Can increase representativeness, easier to implement than SRS, sampling frame not always necessary	Can decrease representativeness
Stratified sampling	Includes all important sub-populations, precision	Difficult to select relevant stratification variables, not feasible to stratify on many variables, expensive
Cluster sampling	Easy to implement, cost-effective	Imprecise, difficult to compute and interpret results

phase, a sub-sample is drawn from the original sample and additional information is obtained from the elements in the sub-sample. The process may be extended to three or more phases, and the different phases may take place simultaneously or at different times. Double sampling can be useful when no sampling frame is readily available for selecting final sampling units but when the elements of the frame are known to be contained within a broader sampling frame. For example, a researcher wants to select households in a given city that consume apple juice. The households of interest are contained within the set of all households, but the researcher does not know which ones they are. In applying double sampling, the researcher would obtain a sampling frame of all households in the first phase. This would be constructed from the city directory or purchased. Then a sample of households would be drawn, using systematic random sampling to determine the amount of apple juice consumed. In the second phase, households that consume apple juice would be selected and stratified according to the amount of apple juice consumed. Then a stratified random sample would be drawn and detailed questions regarding apple juice consumption asked.[21]

Simple random sampling

1. Select a suitable sampling frame.
2. Each element is assigned a number from 1 to N (population size).
3. Generate n (sample size) different random numbers between 1 and N using a software package or a table of simple random numbers (Table 1 in the Appendix of statistical Tables). To use Table 1, select the appropriate number of digits (e.g. if $N = 900$, select three digits). Arbitrarily select a beginning number. The proceed up or down until n different numbers between 1 and N have been selected. Discard 0, duplicate numbers, and numbers greater than N.
4. The numbers generated denote the elements that should be included in the sample.

Systematic sampling

1. Select a suitable sampling frame.
2. Each element is assigned a number from 1 to N (population size).
3. Determine the sampling interval, i, $i = N/n$. If i is a fraction, round to the nearest integer.
4. Select a random number, r, between 1 and i, as explained in simple random sampling.
5. The elements with the following numbers will comprise the systematic random sample:

   $r, r + i, r + 2i, r + 3i, r + 4i \ldots r + (n-1)i$.

Stratified sampling

1. Select a suitable sampling frame.
2. Select the stratification variable(s) and the number of strata, H.
3. Divide the entire population into H strata. Based on the classification variable, each element of the population is assigned to one of the H strata.
4. In each stratum, number the elements from 1 to N_h (the population size of stratum h).
5. Determine the sample size of each stratum, n_h, based on proportionate or disproportionate stratified sampling, where

$$\sum_{h=1}^{H} n_h = n$$

6. In each stratum, select a simple random sample of size n_h.

Cluster sampling

We describe the procedure for selecting a two-stage PPS sample, because this represents the most commonly used general case.

1. Assign a number from 1 to N to each element in the population.
2. Divide the population into C clusters of which c will be included in the sample.
3. Calculate the sampling interval, i, $i = N/c$. If i is a fraction, round to the nearest integer
4. Select a random number, r, between 1 and i, as explained in simple random sampling.
5. Identify elements with the following numbers: $r, r + i, r + 2i, r + 3i \ldots, r + (c-1)i$.
6. Select the clusters that contain the identified elements.
7. Select sampling units within each selected cluster based on SRS or systematic sampling. The number of sampling units selected from each sample cluster is approximately the same and equal to n/c.
8. If the population of the cluster exceeds the sampling interval i, that cluster is selected with certainty. That cluster is removed from further consideration. Calculate the new proportion size, N^*, the number of clusters to be selected c^* ($= c - 1$), and the new sampling interval i^*. Repeat this process until each of the remaining clusters has a population less than the relevant sampling interval. If b clusters have been selected with certainty, select the remaining $c - b$ clusters according to steps 1 to 7. The fraction of units to be sampled from each cluster selected with certainty is the overall sampling fraction $= n/N$. Thus, for clusters selected with certainty, we would select $n_s = n/N(N_1 + N_2 + \ldots + Nb)$ units. The units selected from clusters selected under PPS sampling will therefore be $n^* = n - n_s$.

CHOOSING NON-PROBABILITY VERSUS PROBABILITY SAMPLING

The choice between non-probability and probability samples should be based on considerations such as the nature of the research, relative magnitude of non-sampling versus sampling errors, and variability in the population, as well as statistical and operational considerations (see Table 13.4). For example, in exploratory research, the findings may be treated as preliminary and the use of probability sampling may not be warranted. On the other hand, in conclusive research where the researcher wishes to use the results to estimate overall market shares or the size of the total market, probability sampling is favoured. Probability samples allow statistical projection of the results to a target population.

For some research problems, highly accurate estimates of population characteristics are required. In these situations, the elimination of selection bias and the ability to calculate sampling error make probability sampling desirable. Probability sampling will not always result in more accurate results, however. If non-sampling errors are likely to be an important factor, then non-probability sampling may be preferable because the use of judgement may allow greater control over the sampling process.

Another consideration is the homogeneity of the population with respect to the variables of interest. A heterogeneous population would favour probability sampling because it would be more important to secure a representative sample. Probability sampling is preferable from a statistical viewpoint, as it is the basis of most common statistical techniques.

Table 13.4 Choosing non-probability vs probability sampling

Factors	*Conditions favouring the use of*	
	Non-probability sampling	*Probability sampling*
Nature of research	Exploratory	Conclusive
Relative magnitude of sampling and non-sampling errors	Non-sampling errors are larger	Sampling errors are larger
Variability in the population	Homogeneous (low)	Heterogeneous (high)
Statistical considerations	Unfavourable	Favourable
Operational considerations	Favourable	Unfavourable

Probability sampling is sophisticated and requires statistically trained researchers. It generally costs more and takes longer than non-probability sampling, especially in the establishment of accurate sampling frames. In many marketing research projects, it is difficult to justify the additional time and expense. Therefore, in practice, the objectives of the study dictate which sampling method will be used.

USES OF NON-PROBABILITY AND PROBABILITY SAMPLING

Non-probability sampling is used in concept tests, package tests, name tests and copy tests where projections to the populations are usually not needed. In such studies, interest centres on the proportion of the sample that gives various responses or expresses various attitudes. Samples for these studies can be drawn using methods such as street interviewing and quota sampling. On the other hand, probability sampling is used when there is a need for highly accurate estimates of market share or sales volume for the entire market. National market tracking studies, which provide information on product category and brand usage rates as well as psychographic and demographic profiles of users, use probability sampling. Studies that use probability sampling generally employ telephone interviews. Stratified and systematic sampling are combined with some form of random-digit dialling to select the respondents.

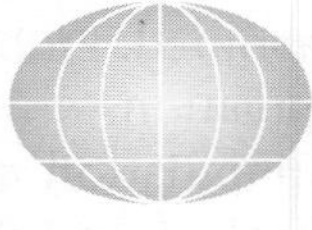

INTERNATIONAL MARKETING RESEARCH

Implementing the sampling design process in international marketing research is seldom easy. Several factors should be considered in defining the target population. The relevant element (respondent) may differ from country to country. In Europe, children play an important role in the purchase of children's cereals. In countries with authoritarian child-rearing practices, however, the mother or father may be the relevant element. Accessibility also varies across countries. In Mexico, houses cannot be entered by strangers because of boundary walls and servants. Additionally, dwelling units may be unnumbered and streets unidentified, making it difficult to locate designated households.[22]

Developing an appropriate sampling frame is a difficult task. In many countries, particularly in developing countries, reliable information about the target population may not be available from secondary sources. Government data may be unavailable or highly biased. Population lists may not be available commercially. The time and money required to compile these lists may be prohibitive. For example, in Saudi Arabia, there is no officially recognised census of population, no elections and hence no voter registration records, and no accurate maps of population centres. In this situation, the interviewers could be instructed to begin at specified starting points and to sample every *n*th dwelling until the specified number of units has been sampled.

Given the lack of suitable sampling frames, the inaccessibility of certain respondents, such as women in some cultures, and the dominance of personal interviewing, probability sampling techniques are uncommon in international marketing research. Imagine the problems involved in tracking down an accurate sampling frame in the following example.

EXAMPLE

Post-Deng China with a new 'middle class' of 35 million households[23]

China has been transformed from a centralised state system offering only two imported items (cigarettes and soft drinks) into a socialist market economy where consumers can buy Rolex watches, Burberry raincoats, Cadbury's chocolate, Kentucky Fried Chicken, Colgate toothpaste and Nike sports shoes and other international brands. With a population of 1.2 billion it is not surprising that companies are keen to enter China, where even niche markets can be huge.

While 'middle class' is a Western concept and as such does not exist in China, there are 'Xiao Kang' or Little Rich households. Xiao Kang is a state of society in Confucius ideology where people live and work happily, which in today's context means that the people eat well, dress smartly, live in nicely furnished homes fully equipped with consumer durables. There are estimated to be in the region of 35 million Xiao Kang families in China, a large and lucrative segment of population that totals 1.2 billion. ■

Quota sampling has been used widely in the developed and developing countries in both consumer and industrial surveys. Quota sampling has a long history of working well in Britain, France and Germany, a sampling method that is seen as 'unthinkable' for many USA marketing researchers.[24] Snowball sampling is also appealing when the characteristic of interest is rare in the target population or when respondents are hard to reach. For example, it has been suggested that in Saudi Arabia graduate students be employed to hand-deliver questionnaires to relatives and friends.[25] These initial respondents can be asked for referrals to other potential respondents and so on. This approach would result in a large sample size and a high response rate.

Sampling techniques and procedures vary in accuracy, reliability and cost from country to country. If the same sampling procedures are used in each country, the results may not be comparable.[26] To achieve comparability in sample composition and representativeness, it may be desirable to use different sampling techniques in different countries.

ETHICS IN MARKETING RESEARCH

The researcher has several ethical responsibilities to both the client and the respondents pertaining to sampling. With regard to the client, the researcher must develop a sampling design that best fits the project in an effort to minimise the sampling and non-sampling errors (see Chapter 3). When probability sampling can be used it should be.

When non-probability or convenience sampling is used, effort should be made to obtain a representative sample. It is unethical and misleading to treat non-probability samples as probability samples and to project the results to a target population. Appropriate definition of the population and the sampling frame, and application of the correct sampling techniques are essential if the research is to be conducted and the findings used ethically.

Researchers must be extremely sensitive to preserving the anonymity of the respondents when conducting business-to-business research with small populations, particularly when reporting the findings to the client. When the population size is small, it is easier to discern the identities of the respondents than when the samples are drawn from a large population. Special care must be taken when sample details are too revealing and when using verbatim quotations in reports to the client. This problem is acute in areas such as employee research. Here a breach of a respondent's anonymity can cost the respondent a pay rise, a promotion, or, at worst, employment. In such situations, special effort should be made to protect the identities of the respondents.

INTERNET AND COMPUTER APPLICATIONS

Sampling potential respondents who are surfing the Internet is meaningful if the sample generated is representative of the target population. More and more industries are meeting this criterion. In software, computers, networking, technical publishing, semiconductors, and graduate education, it is rapidly becoming feasible to use the Internet for sampling respondents for quantitative research, such as surveys. For internal customer surveys, where the client's employees share a corporate email system, an intranet survey is practical, even if workers have no access to the external Internet.

To avoid sampling errors, the researcher must be able to control the pool from which the respondents are selected. Also, it must be ensured that the respondents do not respond more than once. These requirements are met by email surveys, in which the researcher selects specific respondents. Furthermore, the surveys can be encoded to match the returned surveys with their corresponding outbound emailings. This can also be accomplished with Web surveys by emailing invitations to selected respondents and asking them to visit the Web site on which the survey is posted. In this case, the survey is posted in a hidden location on the Web, which is protected by a password. Hence, non-invited Web surfers are unable to access it.

Non-probability as well as probability sampling techniques can be implemented on the Internet. Moreover, the respondents can be pre-recruited or tapped on-line. Tapping visitors to a Web site is an example of convenience sampling. Based on the researcher's judgement, certain qualifying criteria can be introduced to pre-screen the respondents. Even quotas can be imposed. However, the extent to which quotas will be met is limited by the number as well as the characteristics of visitors to the site.

Likewise, simple random sampling is commonly used. To prevent gathering information from the same professional respondents (professional in this context meaning respondents who take part in many surveys for their own enjoyment) some companies use a 'click-stream intercept', which randomly samples on-line users and gives them the opportunity to participate or decline.

Microcomputers and mainframes can make the sampling design process more effective and efficient. Computers can be used in the specification of the sampling frame. Geodemographic information systems such as Experian handle lists of population elements as well as geographical maps. Database packages can also be used to store and manipulate sampling frames, especially when the sampling frame is built up from multiple sources and duplicates need to be identified and eliminated. Once the sampling frame has been determined, simulations can be used to generate random numbers and select the sample directly from the database.

SUMMARY

Information about the characteristics of a population may be obtained by conducting either a sample or a census. Budget and time limits, large population size, and small variance in the characteristic of interest favour the use of a sample. Sampling is also preferred when the cost of sampling error is low, the cost of non-sampling error is high, the nature of measurement is destructive, and attention must be focused on individual cases. The opposite set of conditions favours the use of a census.

Sampling design begins by defining the target population in terms of elements, sampling units, extent and time. Then the sampling frame should be determined. A sampling frame is a representation of the elements of the target population. It consists of a list of directions for identifying the target population. At this stage, it is important to recognise any sampling frame errors that may exist. The next step involves selecting a sampling technique and determining the sample size. In addition to quantitative analysis, several qualitative considerations should be taken into account in determining the sample size. Execution of the sampling process requires detailed specifications for each step in the sampling process. Finally, the selected sample should be validated by comparing characteristics of the sample with known characteristics of the target population.

Sampling techniques may be classified as non-probability and probability techniques. Non-probability sampling techniques rely on the researcher's judgement. Consequently, they do not permit an objective evaluation of the precision of the sample results, and the estimates obtained are not statistically projectable to the population. The commonly used non-probability sampling techniques include convenience sampling, judgemental sampling, quota sampling and snowball sampling.

In probability sampling techniques, sampling units are selected by chance. Each sampling unit has a non-zero chance of being selected, and the researcher can prespecify every potential sample of a given size that could be drawn from the population as well as the probability of selecting each sample. It is also possible to determine the precision of the sample estimates and inferences and make projections to the target population. Probability sampling techniques include simple random sampling, systematic sampling, stratified sampling, cluster sampling, sequential sampling and double sampling. The choice between probability and non-probability sampling should be based on the nature of the research, degree of error tolerance, relative magnitude of sampling and non-sampling errors, variability in the population, and statistical and operational considerations.

When conducting international marketing research, it is desirable to achieve comparability in sample composition and representativeness even though this may require the use of different sampling techniques in different countries. It is unethical and misleading to treat non-probability samples as probability samples and to project the results to a target population.

QUESTIONS AND PROBLEMS

1 Under what conditions would a sample be preferable to a census? A census preferable to a sample?

2 Describe the sampling design process.

3 How should the target population be defined? How does this definition link with the definition of a marketing research problem?

4 What is a sampling unit? How is it different from the population element?

5 To what extent may the availability of sampling frames determine the definition of a population?

6 What qualitative factors should be considered in determining the sample size?

7 How do probability sampling techniques differ from non-probability sampling techniques? What factors should be considered in choosing between probability and non-probability sampling?

8 What is the least expensive and least time-consuming of all sampling techniques? What are the major limitations of this technique?

9 What is the major difference between judgmental and convenience sampling? Give examples of where each of these techniques may be successfully applied.

10 Describe snowball sampling. How may the technique be supported by qualitative research techniques?

11 What are the distinguishing features of simple random sampling?

12 Describe the procedure for selecting a systematic random sample.

13 Describe stratified sampling. What are the criteria for the selection of stratification variables?

14 What are the differences between proportionate and disproportionate stratified sampling?

15 Describe the cluster sampling procedure. What is the key distinction between cluster sampling and stratified sampling?

NOTES

1 Easton, S. and Mackie, P., 'Can Football Give Brands 110% Recall?', *ResearchPlus* (June 1997), 10.

2 Assael, H. and Keon, J., 'Non-sampling vs. Sampling Errors in Sampling Research', *Journal of Marketing* (Spring 1982), 114–23.

3 This discussion is based on: Bartos, R., 'Alfred Politz: Sampling Innovator', *Journal of Advertising Research* 26 (February–March 1986), 26–29; Frankel, M.R., 'Sampling Theory', in Rossi, P.H., Wright, J.D. and Anderson, A.B. (eds), *Handbook of Survey Research* (Orlando, FL: Academic Press, 1983), 21–67; Jaeger, R.M., *Sampling in Education and the Social Sciences* (New York: Longman, 1984) 28–29; and Kalron, G., *Introduction to Survey Sampling* (Beverly Hills: Sage Publications, 1982).

4 Sudman, S., 'Applied Sampling', in Rossi, P.H., Wright, J.D. and Anderson, A.B., (eds), *Handbook of Survey Research* (Orlando, FL: Academic Press, 1983), 145–94.

5 Blair, E., 'Sampling Issues in Trade Area Maps Drawn from Shopper Surveys', *Journal of Marketing*, 47 (Winter 1983), 98–106.

6 For a comparison of directory-based sampling with random-digit dialling, see Czaja, R., Blair, J. and Sebestik, J.P., 'Respondent Selection in a Telephone Survey: A Comparison of Three Techniques', *Journal of Marketing Research* (August 1982); Ellison, P., 'Phone Directory Samples Just as Balanced as Samples from Computer Random Digit Dialling', *Marketing News* (11 January 1980), 8; and Moberg, P.E., 'Biases in Unlisted Phone Numbers', *Journal of Advertising Research* (August–September 1982), 51–55.

7 For the effect of sample frame error on research results, see Fish, K.E., Barnes, J.H. and Banahan III, B.F., 'Convenience or Calamity', *Journal of Health Care Marketing* 14 (Spring 1994), 45–49.

8 Phillips, A. 'Taking the Peoples' Temperature – Right across Europe', *ResearchPlus* (November 1996), 6.

9 For an application of convenience sampling, see Mittal, B., 'An Integrated Framework for Relating Diverse Consumer Characteristics to Supermarket Coupon Redemption', *Journal of Marketing Research* 31 (November 1994), 533–45.

10 Jaeger, R.M., *Sampling in Education and the Social Sciences* (New York: Longman, 1984).

11 Sudman, S., 'Improving the Quality of Shopping Center Sampling', *Journal of Marketing Research* 17 (November 1980), 423–31.

12 Kalton, G., *Introduction to Survey Sampling* (Beverly Hills: Sage Publications, 1982).

13 For an application of snowball sampling, see Frankwick, G.L., Ward, J.C., Hutt, M.D. and Reingen, P.H., 'Evolving Patterns of Organisational Beliefs in the Formation of Strategy', *Journal of Marketing* 58 (April 1994), 96–110.

14 If certain procedures for listing members of the rare population are followed strictly, the snowball sample can be treated as a probability sample. See Kalton, G. and Anderson, D.W., 'Sampling Rare Populations', *Journal of the Royal Statistical Association* (1986), 65–82; Biemacki, P. and Waldorf, D., 'Snowball Sampling: Problems and Techniques of Chain Referred Sampling', *Sociological Methods and Research* 10 (November 1981), 141–63; and Rothbart, G.S., Fine, M. and Sudman, S.,'On Finding and Interviewing the Needles in the Haystack: The Use of Multiplicity Sampling', *Public Opinion Quarterly* 46 (Fall 1982), 408–21.

15 When the sampling interval, *i*, is not a whole number, the easiest solution is to use as the interval the nearest whole number below or above *i*. If rounding has too great an effect on the sample size, add or delete the extra cases.

16 For an application of systematic random sampling, see Chakraborty, G., Ettenson, R. and Gaeth, G., 'How Consumers Choose Health Insurance', *Journal of Health Care Marketing* 14 (Spring 1994), 21–33.

17 'Readership Survey Serves Tennis Magazine's Marketing Needs', *Quirk's Marketing Research Review* (May 1988), 75–76.

18 For an application of stratified random sampling, see Weerahandi, S. and Moitra, S., 'Using Survey Data to Predict Adoption and Switching for Services', *Journal of Marketing Research* 32 (February 1995), 85–96.

19 Geographic clustering of rare populations, however, can be an advantage. See Sudman, S., 'Efficient Screening Methods for the Sampling of Geographically Clustered Special Populations', *Journal of Marketing Research* 22 (February 1985), 20–29.

20 Anderson, E.J., Gorton, K. and Tudor, R., 'The Application of Sequential Analysis in Market Research', *Journal of Marketing Research* 17 (February 1980), 97–105.

21 For more discussion of double sampling, see Frankel, M.R. and Frankel, L.R., 'Probability Sampling', in Ferber, R. (ed.), *Handbook of Marketing Research* (New York: McGraw-Hill, 1974), 2-230–2-246.

22 For the use of different non-probability and probability sampling techniques in cross-cultural research, see Saeed, S. and Jeong, I., 'Cross-Cultural Research in Advertising: An Assessment of Methodologies', *Journal of the Academy of Marketing Science* 22 (Summer 1994), 205–15.

23 Hutton, G., 'The Land Where the Little Rich Have Big Three Aspirations', *ResearchPlus* (March 1997), 12.

24 Taylor, H. 'Horses for Courses: How Survey Firms in Different Countries Measure Public Opinion with Very Different Methods', *Journal of the Market Research Society* 37 (3) (July 1995), 218.

25 Tuncalp, S., 'The Marketing Research Scene in Saudi Arabia', *European Journal of Marketing* 22 (5) (1988) 15–22.

26 Webster, L., 'Comparability in Multi-Country Surveys', *Journal of Advertising Research* 6 (December 1966), 14–18.

Chapter 14

Sampling: final and initial sample size determination

Statistical approaches to determining sample size are based on estimating the unknown population values of parameters by means of sample statistics

OBJECTIVES

After reading this chapter, the student should be able to:

1 define key concepts and symbols pertinent to sampling;
2 understand the concepts of the sampling distribution, statistical inference, and standard error;
3 discuss the statistical approach to determining sample size based on simple random sampling and the construction of confidence intervals;
4 derive the formulas to determine statistically the sample size for estimating means and proportions;
5 discuss the non-response issues in sampling and the procedures for improving response rates and adjusting for non-response;
6 understand the difficulty of statistically determining the sample size in international marketing research;
7 identify the ethical issues related to sample size determination, particularly the estimation of population variance.

OVERVIEW

In Chapter 13, we considered the role of sampling in research design formulation, described the sampling process, and presented the various non-probability and probability sampling techniques.

This chapter focuses on the determination of sample size in simple random sampling. We define various concepts and symbols and discuss the properties of the sampling distribution. Additionally, we describe statistical approaches to sample size determination based on confidence intervals. We present the formulas for calculating the sample size with these approaches and illustrate their use. We briefly discuss the extension to determining sample size in other probability sampling designs. The sample size determined statistically is the final or net sample size; that is, it represents the completed number of interviews or observations. To obtain this final sample size, however, a much larger number of potential respondents have to be contacted initially. We describe the adjustments that need to be made to the statistically determined sample size to account for incidence and completion rates and calculate the initial sample size. We also cover the non-response issues in sampling, with a focus on improving response rates and adjusting for non-response. We discuss the difficulty of statistically determining the sample size in international marketing research and identify the relevant ethical issues.

Statistical determination of sample size requires knowledge of the normal distribution and the use of normal probability tables. The normal distribution is bell-shaped and symmetrical. Its mean, median and mode are identical (see Chapter 17). Information on the normal distribution and the use of normal probability tables is presented in Appendix 14A. The following example illustrates the statistical aspects of sampling.

EXAMPLE

Has there been a shift in opinion?

The sample size in surveys used to opinion polls published in most newspapers are influenced by statistical considerations. The allowance for sampling error may be limited to around three percentage points.

The table that follows can be used to determine the allowances that should be made for sampling error. The computed confidence intervals take into account the effect of the sample design on sampling error. These intervals indicate the range (plus or minus the figure shown) within which the results of repeated samplings in the same time period could be expected to vary, 95 per cent of the time, assuming that the sample procedure, survey execution and questionnaire used were the same.

Recommended allowance for sampling error of a percentage

In percentage points (at 0.95 confidence level for a sample size of 456)	
Percentage near 10	3
Percentage near 20	4
Percentage near 30	4
Percentage near 40	5
Percentage near 50	5
Percentage near 60	5
Percentage near 70	4
Percentage near 80	4
Percentage near 90	3

The table should be used as follows: If a reported percentage is 43, look at the row labelled 'percentages near 40'. The number in this row is 5, the 43 per cent obtained in the sample is subject to a sampling error of ±5 percentage points. Another way of saying this is that very probably (95 times out of 100) the average of repeated samplings would be somewhere between 38 and 48 per cent, with the most likely figure being 43 per cent.

The fortunes of political parties measured through opinion polls are regularly reported in newspapers throughout Europe. The next time that you read a report of a political opinion poll, examine the sample size used, the confidence level assumed and the stated margin of error. When comparing the results of a poll with a previous poll, consider whether a particular political party or politician has *really* grown or slumped in popularity, or the reported changes can be accounted for within the set margin of error as summarised in this example. ■

DEFINITIONS AND SYMBOLS

Confidence intervals and other statistical concepts that play a central role in sample size determination are defined in the following list.

- *Parameter.* A parameter is a summary description of a fixed characteristic or measure of the target population. A parameter denotes the true value that would be obtained if a census rather than a sample was undertaken.
- *Statistic.* A statistic is a summary description of a characteristic or measure of the sample. The sample statistic is used as an estimate of the population parameter.
- *Finite population correction.* The finite population correction (fpc) is a correction for overestimation of the variance of a population parameter – for example, a mean or proportion – when the sample size is 10 per cent or more of the population size.
- *Precision level.* When estimating a population parameter by using a sample statistic, the precision level is the desired size of the estimating interval. This is the maximum permissible difference between the sample statistic and the population parameter.
- *Confidence interval.* The confidence interval is the range into which the true population parameter will fall, assuming a given level of confidence.
- *Confidence level.* The confidence level is the probability that a confidence interval will include the population parameter.

The symbols used in statistical notation for describing population and sample characteristics are summarised in Table 14.1.

Table 14.1 Symbols for population and sample variables

Variable	*Population*	*Sample*
Mean	μ	$\bar{X}$
Proportion	π	p
Variance	σ^2	s^2
Standard deviation	σ	s
Size	N	n
Standard error of the mean	$\sigma_{\bar{x}}$	$S_{\bar{x}}$
Standard error of the proportion	σ_p	S_p
Standardised variate (z)	$\frac{X - \mu}{\sigma}$	$\frac{X - \bar{X}}{S}$
Coefficient of variation (C)	$\frac{\sigma}{\mu}$	$\frac{S}{\bar{X}}$

THE SAMPLING DISTRIBUTION

Sampling distribution The distribution of the values of a sample statistic computed for each possible sample that could be drawn from the target population under a specified sampling plan.

The **sampling distribution** is the distribution of the values of a sample statistic computed for each possible sample that could be drawn from the target population under a specified sampling plan.[1] Suppose that a simple random sample of five hospitals is to be drawn from a population of 20 hospitals. There are $(20 \times 19 \times 18 \times 17 \times 16)/(1 \times 2 \times 3 \times 4 \times 5)$, or 15,504 different samples of size 5 that can be drawn. The relative frequency distribution of the values of the mean of these 15,504 different samples would specify the sampling distribution of the mean.

An important task in marketing research is to calculate statistics, such as the sample mean and sample proportion, and use them to estimate the corresponding true population values. This process of generalising the sample results to the population results is referred to as statistical inference. In practice, a single sample of predetermined size is selected, and the sample statistics (such as mean and proportion) are computed. Theoretically, to estimate the population parameter from the sample statistic, every possible sample that could have been drawn should be examined. If all possible samples were actually to be drawn, the distribution of the statistic would be the sampling distribution. Although in practice only one sample is actually drawn, the concept of a sampling distribution is still relevant. It enables us to use probability theory to make inferences about the population values.

The important properties of the sampling distribution of the mean, and the corresponding properties for the proportion, for large samples (30 or more) are as follows:

1 The sampling distribution of the mean is a normal distribution (see Appendix 14A). Strictly speaking, the sampling distribution of a proportion is a binomial. For large samples (n = 30 or more), however, it can be approximated by the normal distribution.

2 The mean of the sampling distribution of the mean $\left(\bar{X} = \left(\sum_{i=1}^{n} X_i\right)/n\right]$ or of the proportion
(p) equals the corresponding population parameter value, μ or π, respectively.

3 The standard deviation is called the standard error of the mean or the proportion to indicate that it refers to a sampling distribution of the mean or the proportion and not to a sample or a population. The formulas are:

Mean	Proportion
$\sigma_{\bar{x}} = \frac{\sigma}{\sqrt{n}}$	$\sigma_p = \sqrt{\frac{\pi(1-\pi)}{n}}$

4 Often the population standard deviation, σ, is not known. In these cases, it can be estimated from the sample by using the following formula:

$$s = \sqrt{\frac{\sum_{i=1}^{n} (X_i - \bar{X})^2}{n-1}}$$

$$s = \sqrt{\frac{\sum_{i=1}^{n} X_i^2 - \frac{\left(\sum_{i=1}^{n} X_i\right)^2}{n}}{n-1}}$$

In cases where σ is estimated by s, the standard error of the mean becomes

$$\text{est. } \sigma\bar{X} = \frac{s}{\sqrt{n}}$$

where 'est.' denotes that s has been used as an estimate of σ.

Assuming no measurement error, the reliability of an estimate of a population parameter can be assessed in terms of its standard error.

5 Likewise, the standard error of the proportion can be estimated by using the sample proportion p as an estimator of the population proportion, π as

$$\text{est. } S_p = \sqrt{\frac{p\,(1-p)}{n}}$$

6 The area under the sampling distribution between any two points can be calculated in terms of z values. The z value for a point is the number of standard errors a point is away from the mean. The z values may be computed as follows:

$$z = \frac{\bar{X} - \mu}{\sigma_{\bar{X}}}$$

For example, the areas under one side of the curve between the mean and points that have z values of 1.0, 2.0, and 3.0 are, respectively,0.3413, 0.4772, and 0.4986. (See Table 2 in the Appendix of Statistical Tables.) In the case of proportion, the computation of z values is similar.

7 When the sample size is 10 per cent or more of the population size, the standard error formulas will overestimate the standard deviation of the population mean or proportion. Hence, these should be adjusted by a finite population correction factor defined by

$$\sqrt{\frac{N-n}{N-1}}$$

In this case,

$$\sigma_{\bar{X}} = \frac{\sigma}{\sqrt{n}}\sqrt{\frac{N-n}{N-1}}$$

STATISTICAL APPROACHES TO DETERMINING SAMPLE SIZE

Several qualitative factors should also be taken into consideration when determining the sample size (see Chapter 13). These include the importance of the decision, the nature of the research, the number of variables, the nature of the analysis, sample sizes used in similar studies, incidence rates (the occurrence of behaviour or characteristics in a population), completion rates, and resource constraints. The statistically determined sample size is the net or final sample size: the sample remaining after eliminating potential respondents who do not qualify or who do not complete the interview. Depending on incidence and completion rates, the size of the initial sample may have to be much larger. In commercial marketing research, limits on time, money and expert resources can exert an overriding influence on sample size determination. In the GlobalCash project, the sample size was determined based on these considerations.

The statistical approach to determining sample size that we consider is based on traditional **statistical inference**.[2] In this approach the precision level is specified in advance. This approach is based on the construction of confidence intervals around sample means or proportions.

Statistical inference
The process of generalising the sample results to the population results.

THE CONFIDENCE INTERVAL APPROACH

The confidence interval approach to sample size determination is based on the construction of confidence intervals around the sample means or proportions

Standard error
The standard deviation of the sampling distribution of the mean or proportion.

using the **standard error** formula. As an example, suppose that a researcher has taken a simple random sample of 300 households to estimate the monthly amount invested in savings schemes and found that the mean household monthly investment for the sample is €182. Past studies indicate that the population standard deviation σ can be assumed to be €55.

We want to find an interval within which a fixed proportion of the sample means would fall. Suppose that we want to determine an interval around the population mean that will include 95 per cent of the sample means, based on samples of 300 households. The 95 per cent could be divided into two equal parts, half below and half above the mean, as shown in Figure 14.1. Calculation of the confidence interval involves determining a distance below ($\bar{X}_L$) and above ($\bar{X}_U$) the population mean ($\bar{X}$), which contains a specified area of the normal curve.

z value
The number of standard errors a point is away from the mean.

The *z* **values** corresponding to $\bar{X}_L$ and $\bar{X}_U$ may be calculated as

$$z_L = \frac{\bar{X}_L - \mu}{\sigma_{\bar{X}}}$$

$$z_u = \frac{\bar{X}_u - \mu}{\sigma_{\bar{X}}}$$

where $z_L = -z$ and $z_U = +z$. Therefore, the lower value of $\bar{X}$ is

$$\bar{X}_L = \mu - z\sigma_{\bar{X}}$$

and the upper value of $\bar{X}$ is

$$\bar{X}_U = \mu + z\sigma_{\bar{X}}$$

Note that μ is estimated by $\bar{X}$. The confidence interval is given by

$$\bar{X} \pm z\sigma_{\bar{X}}$$

We can now set a 95% confidence interval around the sample mean of €182. As a first step, we compute the standard error of the mean:

$$\sigma_{\bar{X}} = \frac{\sigma}{\sqrt{n}} = \frac{55}{\sqrt{300}} = 3.18$$

From Table 2 in the Appendix of Statistical Tables, it can be seen that the central 95 per cent of the normal distribution lies within ±1.96 *z* values. The 95 per cent confidence interval is given by

$$\begin{aligned} &\bar{X} \pm 1.96\,\sigma_{\bar{X}} \\ &= 182.00 \pm 1.96\,(3.18) \\ &= 182.00 \pm 6.23 \end{aligned}$$

Thus, the 95% confidence interval ranges from €175.77 to €188.23. The probability of finding the true population mean to be within €175.77 and €188.23 is 95 per cent.

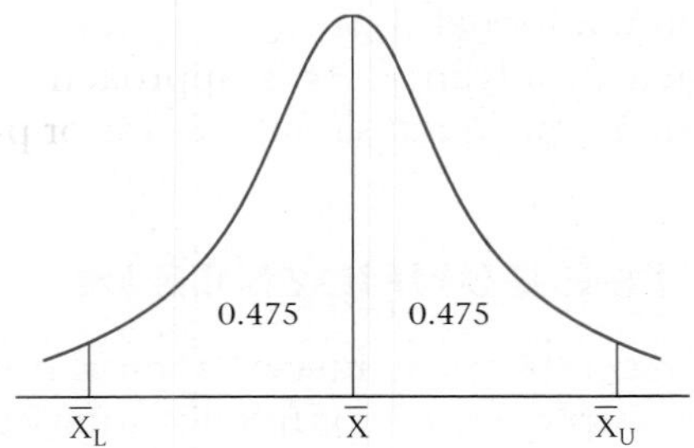

Figure 14.1
95 per cent confidence interval

Sample size determination: means

The approach used here to construct a confidence interval can be adapted to determine the sample size that will result in a desired confidence interval.[3] Suppose that the researcher wants to estimate the monthly household savings investment more precisely so that the estimate will be within ± €5.00 of the true population value. What should be the size of the sample? The following steps, summarised in Table 14.2, will lead to an answer.

1 Specify the level of precision. This is the maximum permissible difference (D) between the sample mean and the population mean. In our example, $D = \pm$ €5.00.

2 Specify the level of confidence. Suppose that a 95 per cent confidence level is desired.

3 Determine the z value associated with the confidence level using Table 2 in the Appendix of Statistical Tables. For a 95 per cent confidence level, the probability that the population mean will fall outside one end of the interval is 0.025 (0.05/2). The associated z value is 1.96.

4 Determine the standard deviation of the population. The standard deviation of the population may be known from secondary sources. If not, it might be estimated by conducting a pilot study. Alternatively, it might be estimated on the basis of the researcher's judgement. For example, the range of a normally distributed variable is approximately equal to plus or minus three standard deviations, and one can thus estimate the standard deviation by dividing the range by six. The researcher can often estimate the range based on knowledge of the phenomenon.

Table 14.2 Sample size determination for means and proportions

Steps	Means	Proportions
1 Specify the level of precision.	$D = \pm$€5.00	$D = p - \pi = \pm.05$
2 Specify the confidence level (CL).	CL = 95%	CL = 95%
3 Determine the z value associated with the CL.	z value is 1.96	z value is 1.96
4 Determine the standard deviation of the population.	Estimate σ: $\sigma = 55$	Estaimate π: $\pi = 0.64$
5 Determine the sample size using the formula for the standard error.	$n = \frac{\sigma^2 z^2}{D^2}$ $n = \frac{55^2(1.96)^2}{5^2}$ $= 465$	$n = \frac{\pi(1-\pi)z^2}{D^2}$ $n = \frac{0.64(1-0.64)(1.96)^2}{(0.05)^2}$ $= 355$
6 If the sample size represents 10% of the population, apply the finite population correction (fpc).	$n_c = \frac{nN}{N+n-1}$	$n_c = \frac{nN}{N+n-1}$
7 If necessary, re-estimate the confidence interval by employing s to estimate σ.	$= \bar{X} \pm zs_{\bar{x}}$	$p \pm zs_p$
8 If precision is specified in relative rather than absolute terms, determine the sample size by substituting for D.	$D = R\mu$ $n = \frac{C^2 z^2}{R^2}$	$D = R\pi$ $n = \frac{z^2(1-\pi)}{R^2\pi}$

5 Determine the sample size using the formula for the standard error of the mean.

$$z = \frac{\bar{X} - \mu}{\sigma_{\bar{X}}}$$

$$= \frac{D}{\sigma_{\bar{X}}}$$

or

$$\sigma_{\bar{x}} = \frac{D}{z}$$

or

$$\frac{\sigma}{\sqrt{n}} = \frac{D}{z}$$

or

$$n = \frac{\sigma^2 \quad z^2}{D^2}$$

In our example,

$$n = \frac{55^2 \, (1.96)^2}{5^2}$$

$$= 464.83$$

$$= 465 \text{ (rounded to the next highest integer)}$$

It can be seen from the formula for sample size that sample size increases with an increase in the population variability, degree of confidence, and the precision level required of the estimate.

6 If the resulting sample size represents 10 per cent or more of the population, the finite population correction (fpc) should be applied. The required sample size should then be calculated from the formula

$$n_c = \frac{nN}{N + n - 1}$$

where

n = sample size without fpc
n_c = sample size with fpc

7 If the population standard deviation, σ, is unknown and an estimate is used, it should be re-estimated once the sample has been drawn. The sample standard deviation, s, is used as an estimate of σ. A revised confidence interval should then be calculated to determine the precision level actually obtained.

Suppose that the value of 55.00 used for was an estimate because the true value was unknown. A sample of n = 465 is drawn, and these observations generate a mean $\bar{X}$ of 180.00 and a sample standard deviation s of 50.00. The revised confidence interval is then

$$\bar{X} \pm zs_{\bar{x}} = 180.00 \pm 1.96 \frac{50.0}{\sqrt{465}}$$

$$= 180.00 \pm 4.55$$

$$\text{or } 175.45 \leq \mu \leq 184.55$$

Note that the confidence interval obtained is narrower than planned, because the population standard deviation was overestimated, as judged by the sample standard deviation.

8 In some cases, precision is specified in relative rather than absolute terms. In other words, it may be specified that the estimate be within plus or minus R percentage points of the mean. Symbolically,

$$D = R\mu$$

In these cases, the sample size may be determined by

$$n = \frac{\sigma^2 \quad z^2}{D^2}$$

$$= \frac{C^2 \quad z^2}{R^2}$$

where the coefficient of variation $C = \sigma/\mu$ would have to be estimated.

The population size, N, does not directly affect the size of the sample, except when the finite population correction factor has to be applied. Although this may be counterintuitive, upon reflection it makes sense. For example, if all the population elements are identical on the characteristics of interest, then a sample size of one will be sufficient to estimate the mean perfectly. This is true whether there are 50, 500, 5,000, or 50,000 elements in the population. What directly affects the sample size is the variability of the characteristic in the population. This variability enters into the sample size calculation by way of population variance σ^2 or sample variance s^2.

Sample size determination: proportions

If the statistic of interest is a proportion rather than a mean, the approach to sample size determination is similar. Suppose that the researcher is interested in estimating the proportion of households possessing a debit card. The following steps should be followed.[4]

1 Specify the level of precision. Suppose that the desired precision is such that the allowable interval is set as $D = p - \pi = \pm\ 0.05$.
2 Specify the level of confidence. Suppose that a 95% confidence level is desired.
3 Determine the z value associated with the confidence level. As explained in the case of estimating the mean, this will be $z = 1.96$.
4 Estimate the population proportion π. As explained earlier, the population proportion may be estimated from secondary sources, from a pilot study, or based on the judgement of the researcher. Suppose that based on secondary data the researcher estimates that 64% of the households in the target population possess a debit card. Hence, $\pi = 0.64$.
5 Determine the sample size using the formula for the standard error of the proportion.

$$\sigma_p = \frac{p - \pi}{z}$$

$$= \frac{D}{z}$$

$$= \sqrt{\frac{\pi\,(1 - \pi)}{n}}$$

or

$$n = \frac{\pi\,(1 - \pi)\, z^2}{D^2}$$

In our example,

$$n = \frac{0.64\ (1 - 0.64)(1.96)^2}{(0.05)^2}$$

$$= 354.04$$

$$= 355 \text{ (rounded to the next highest integer)}$$

6 If the resulting sample size represents 10 per cent or more of the population, the finite population correction (fpc) should be applied. The required sample size should then be calculated from the formula

$$n_c = \frac{nN}{N + n - 1}$$

where

n = sample size without fpc
n_c = sample size with fpc

7 If the estimate of π turns out to be poor, the confidence interval will be more or less precise than desired. Suppose that after the sample has been taken, the proportion p is calculated to have a value of 0.55. The confidence interval is then re-estimated by employing s_p to estimate the unknown σ_p as

$$p \pm zs_p$$

where

$$S_p = \sqrt{\frac{p(1 - p)}{n}}$$

In our example

$$S_p = \sqrt{\frac{0.55\ (1 - 0.55)}{355}}$$

$$= 0.0264$$

The confidence interval, then, is

$$0.55 \pm 1.96(0.0264) = 0.55 \pm 0.052$$

which is wider than that specified. This is because the sample standard deviation based on $p = 0.55$ was larger than the estimate of the population standard deviation based on $\pi = 0.64$.

If a wider interval than specified is unacceptable, the sample size can be determined to reflect the maximum possible variation in the population. This occurs when the product is the greatest, which happens when π is set at 0.5. This result can also be seen intuitively. Since one half of the population has one value of the characteristic and the other half the other value, more evidence would be required to obtain a valid inference than if the situation was more clear cut and the majority had one particular value. In our example, this leads to a sample size of

$$n = \frac{0.5\ (0.5)\ (1.96)^2}{(0.05)^2}$$

$$= 384.16$$

$$= 385 \text{ rounded to the next higher integer.}$$

8 Sometimes, precision is specified in relative rather than absolute terms. In other words, it may be specified that the estimate be within plus or minus R percentage points of the population proportion. Symbolically,

$$D = R\pi$$

In such a case, the sample size may be determined by

$$n = \frac{z^2 (1 - \pi)}{R^2 \pi}$$

MULTIPLE CHARACTERISTICS AND PARAMETERS

In the preceding examples, we focused on the estimation of a single parameter. In commercial marketing research, several characteristics, not just one, are of interest in any project. The researcher is required to estimate several parameters, not just one. The calculation of sample size in these cases should be based on a consideration of all the parameters that must be estimated.

For example, suppose that in addition to the mean household spend at a supermarket, it was decided to estimate the mean household spend on clothes and on gifts. The sample sizes needed to estimate each of the three mean monthly expenses are given in Table 14.3 and are 465 for supermarket shopping, 246 for clothes, and 217 for gifts. If all the three variables were equally important, the most conservative approach would be to select the largest value of $n = 465$ to determine the sample size. This will lead to each variable being estimated at least as precisely as specified. If the researcher was most concerned with the mean household monthly expense on clothes, however, a sample size of $n = 246$ could be selected.

Table 14.3 Sample size for estimating multiple parameters

	Variable Monthly household spend on		
	Supermarket	**Clothes**	**Gifts**
Confidence level	95%	95%	95%
z value	1.96	1.96	1.96
Precision level (D)	€5	€5	€4
Standard deviation of the population (σ)	€55	€40	€30
Required sample size (n)	465	246	217

So far, the discussion of sample size determination has been based on the methods of traditional statistical inference and has assumed simple random sampling. Next, we discuss the determination of sample size when other sampling techniques are used.

OTHER PROBABILITY SAMPLING TECHNIQUES

The determination of sample size for other probability sampling techniques is based on the same underlying principles. The researcher must specify the level of precision and the degree of confidence and estimate the sampling distribution of the test statistic.

In simple random sampling, cost does not enter directly into the calculation of sample size. In the case of stratified or cluster sampling, however, cost has an important influence. The cost per observation varies by strata or cluster, and the researcher needs some initial estimates of these costs.[5] In addition, the researcher must take into account within-strata variability or within- and between-cluster variability. Once the overall sample size is determined, the sample is apportioned among strata or clusters. This increases the complexity of the sample size formulas. The interested reader is referred to standard works on sampling theory for more information.[6] In general, to provide the same reliability as simple random sampling, sample sizes are the same for systematic sampling, smaller for stratified sampling, and larger for cluster sampling.

ADJUSTING THE STATISTICALLY DETERMINED SAMPLE SIZE

The sample size determined statistically represents the final or net sample size that must be achieved to ensure that the parameters are estimated with the desired degree of precision and the given level of confidence. In surveys, this represents the number of interviews that must be completed. To achieve this final sample size, a much greater number of potential respondents have to be contacted. In other words, the initial sample size has to be much larger because typically the **incidence rates** and **completion rates** are less than 100 per cent.[7]

Incidence rate
The rate of occurrence of persons eligible to participate in the study expressed as a percentage.

Completion rate
The percentage of qualified respondents who complete the interview. It enables researchers to take into account anticipated refusals by people who qualify.

Incidence rate refers to the rate of occurrence or the percentage of persons eligible to participate in the study. Incidence rate determines how many contacts need to be screened for a given sample size requirement.[8] For example, suppose that a study of book purchasing calls for a sample of female heads of households aged 25 to 55. Of the women between the ages of 20 and 60 who might reasonably be approached to see if they qualify, approximately 75 per cent are heads of households, aged 25 to 55. This means that, on average, 1.33 women would be approached to obtain one qualified respondent. Additional criteria for qualifying respondents (for example, product usage behaviour) will further increase the number of contacts. Suppose that an added eligibility requirement is that the women should have bought a book during the last two months. It is estimated that 60% of the women contacted would meet this criteria. Then the incidence rate is $0.75 \times 0.6 = 0.45$. Thus the final sample size will have to be increased by a factor of (1/0.45) or 2.22.

Similarly, the determination of sample size must take into account anticipated refusals by people who qualify. The completion rate denotes the percentage of qualified respondents who complete the interview. If, for example, the researcher expects an interview completion rate of 80% of eligible respondents, the number of contacts should be increased by a factor of 1.25. The incidence rate and the completion rate together imply that the number of potential respondents contacted – that is, the initial sample size-should be 2.22×1.25 or 2.77 times the sample size required. In general, if there are c qualifying factors with an incidence of $Q_1 \times Q_2 \times Q_3 \times .....Q_c$, each expressed as a proportion, the following are true:

$$\text{Incidence rate} = Q1 \times Q2 \times Q3 \text{ K } Qc,$$

$$\text{Initial sample size} = \frac{\text{final sample size}}{\text{incidence rate} \times \text{completion rate}}$$

NON-RESPONSE ISSUES IN SAMPLING

The two major non-response issues in sampling are improving response rates and adjusting for non-response. Non-response error arises when some of the potential respondents included in the sample do not respond (see Chapter 3). This is one of the most significant problems in survey research. Non-respondents may differ from respondents in terms of demographic, psychographic, personality, attitudinal, motivational and behavioural variables.[9] For a given study, if the non-respondents differ from the respondents on the characteristics of interest, the sample estimates will be seriously biased. Higher response rates, in general, imply lower rates of non-response bias, yet response rate may not be an adequate indicator of non-response bias. Response rates themselves do not indicate whether the respondents are representative of the original sample.[10] Increasing the response rate may not reduce non-response bias if the additional respondents are not different from those who have already responded but do differ from those who still do not respond. As low response rates increase the probability of non-response bias, an attempt should be made to improve the response rate.[11] As detailed in Chapter 12, the marketing researcher should build up an awareness of what motivates their target respondents to participate in a research study. The following section details the techniques involved in improving response rates and adjusting for non-response.

Improving the response rates

The primary causes of low response rates are refusals and not-at-homes, as shown in Figure 14.2.

Refusals. Refusals, which result from the unwillingness or inability of people included in the sample to participate, result in lower response rates and increased potential for non-response bias. Given the potential differences between responders and non-responders, researchers should attempt to lower refusal rates. This can be done by prior notification, motivating the respondents, incentives, good questionnaire design and administration, and follow-up.

Prior notification. In prior notification, potential respondents are sent a letter notifying them of the imminent mail, telephone or personal survey. Prior notification increases response rates as the respondent's attention is drawn to the purpose of a study and the potential benefits, without the apparent 'chore' of the

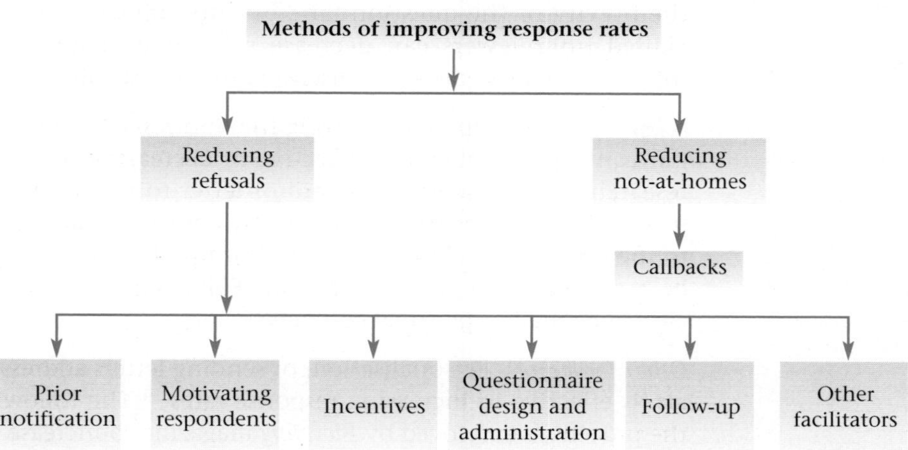

Figure 14.2
Improving response rates

questionnaire. With the potential respondent's attention focused upon the purpose and benefits, the chances increase for a greater reception when approached to actually complete a survey.[12]

Motivating the respondents. Potential respondents can be motivated to participate in the survey by increasing their interest and involvement. Two of the ways this can be done are the foot-in-the-door and door-in-the-face strategies. Both strategies attempt to obtain participation through the use of sequential requests. As explained briefly in Chapter 8, in the foot in-the-door strategy, the interviewer starts with a relatively small request, such as 'Will you please take five minutes to answer five questions', to which a large majority of people will comply. The small request is followed by a larger request, the critical request, that solicits participation in the survey or experiment. The rationale is that compliance with an initial request should increase the chances of compliance with the subsequent request. The door-in-the-face is the reverse strategy. The initial request is relatively large and a majority of people refuse to comply. The large request is followed by a smaller request, the critical request, soliciting participation in the survey. The underlying reasoning is that the concession offered by the subsequent critical request should increase the chances of compliance. Foot-in-the-door is more effective than door-in-the-face.[13]

Incentives. Response rates can be increased by offering monetary as well as non-monetary incentives to potential respondents. Monetary incentives can be pre-paid or promised. The pre-paid incentive is included with the survey or questionnaire. The promised incentive is sent to only those respondents who complete the survey. The most commonly used non-monetary incentives are premiums and rewards, such as pens, pencils, books, and offers of survey results. Pre-paid incentives have been shown to increase response rates to a greater extent than promised incentives. The amount of incentive can vary from trivial amounts to tens of euros. The amount of incentive has a positive relationship with response rate but the cost of large monetary incentives may outweigh the value of additional information obtained.

Questionnaire design and administration. A well-designed questionnaire can decrease the overall refusal rate as well as refusals to specific questions (see Chapter 12). Likewise, the skill used to administer the questionnaire in telephone and personal interviews can increase the response rate. Trained interviewers are skilled in refusal conversion or persuasion. They do not accept a no response without an additional plea. The additional plea might emphasise the brevity of the questionnaire or importance of the respondent's opinion. Skilled interviewers can decrease refusals by about 7 per cent on average. Interviewing procedures are discussed in more detail in Chapter 15.

Follow-up. Follow-up, or contacting the non-respondents periodically after the initial contact, is particularly effective in decreasing refusals in mail surveys. The researcher might send a postcard or letter to remind non-respondents to complete and return the questionnaire. Two or three mailings are needed in addition to the original one. With proper follow-up, the response rate in mail surveys can be increased to 80 per cent or more. Follow-ups can also be done by telephone, electronic mail or personal contacts.

Other facilitators. Personalisation, or sending letters addressed to specific individuals, is effective in increasing response rates.[14] The following example illustrates the procedure employed by *Bicycling* magazine to increase its response rate.[15]

EXAMPLE

Bicycling magazine's procedure for increasing response to mail surveys

Bicycling magazine conducts a semi-annual survey of individual bicycle dealers. The following procedure is used to increase the response to the survey:

1 An 'alert' letter is sent to advise the respondent that a questionnaire is coming.
2 A questionnaire package is mailed five days after the 'alert' letter. The package contains a cover letter, a five-page questionnaire, a new $1 bill, and a stamped return envelope.
3 A second package containing a reminder letter, a questionnaire, and a stamped return envelope is mailed five days after the first package.
4 A follow-up postcard is mailed a week after the second package.
5 A second follow-up postcard is mailed a week after the first.

In a recent survey, 1000 questionnaires were mailed to bicycle dealers, and 68 per cent of these were returned. This represents a good response rate in a mail survey. ■

With care and attention in motivating respondents, *Bicycling* was able to achieve good response rates.

Not-at-homes. The second major cause of low response rates is not-at-homes. In telephone and in-home personal interviews, low response rates can result if the potential respondents are not at home when contact is attempted. A study analysing 182 commercial telephone surveys involving a total sample of over one million consumers revealed that a large percentage of potential respondents was never contacted. The median non-contact rate was 40 per cent. In nearly 40 per cent of the surveys, only a single attempt was made to contact potential respondents. The results of 259,088 first-call attempts using a sophisticated random-digit dialling system shows that less than 10 per cent of the calls resulted in completed interviews, and 14.3 per cent of those contacted refused to participate.[16]

The likelihood that potential respondents will not be at home varies with several factors. People with small children are more likely to be at home. Consumers are more likely to be at home on weekends than on weekdays and in the evening as opposed to during the afternoon. Pre-notification and appointments increase the likelihood that the respondent will be at home when contact is attempted.

The percentage of not-at-homes can be substantially reduced by employing a series of call-backs, or periodic follow-up attempts to contact non-respondents. The decision about the number of call-backs should weigh the benefits of reducing non-response bias against the additional costs. As call-backs are completed, the call-back respondents should be compared with those who have already responded to determine the usefulness of making further call-backs. In most consumer surveys, three to four call-backs may be desirable. Although the first call yields the most responses, the second and third calls have higher response per call. It is important that call-backs be made and controlled according to a prescribed plan.

Adjusting for non-response

High response rates decrease the probability that non-response bias is substantial. Non-response rates should always be reported, and whenever possible, the effects of non-response should be estimated. This can be done by linking the non-response rate to estimated differences between respondents and non-respondents. Information on differences between the two groups may be obtained from the sample itself. For example, differences found through call-backs could be extrapolated, or a concentrated follow-up could be conducted on a sub-sample of the non-respondents. Alternatively, it may be possible to estimate these differences from other sources.[17] To illustrate, in a survey of owners of vacuum cleaners, demographic and other information may be obtained for respondents and non-respondents from their guarantee cards. For a mail panel, a wide variety of information is available for both groups from syndicate organisations. If the sample is supposed to be representative of the general population, then comparisons can be made with census figures. Even if it is not feasible to estimate the effects of non-response, some adjustments can still be made during data analysis and interpretation.[18] The strategies available to adjust for non-response error include sub-sampling of non-respondents, replacement, substitution, subjective estimates, trend analysis, simple weighting, and imputation.

Sub-sampling of non-respondents. Sub-sampling of non-respondents, particularly in the case of mail surveys, can be effective in adjusting for non-response bias. In this technique, the researcher contacts a sub-sample of the non-respondents, usually by means of telephone or personal interviews. This often results in a high response rate within that sub-sample. The values obtained for the sub-sample are then projected to all the non-respondents, and the survey results are adjusted to account for non-response. This method can estimate the effect of non-response on the characteristic of interest.

Replacement. In replacement, the non-respondents in the current survey are replaced with non-respondents from an earlier, similar survey. The researcher attempts to contact these non-respondents from the earlier survey and administer the current survey questionnaire to them, possibly by offering a suitable incentive. It is important that the nature of non-response in the current survey be similar to that of the earlier survey. The two surveys should use similar kinds of respondents, and the time interval between them should be short. As an example, as the GlobalCash survey is repeated two years later, the non-respondents in the present survey may be replaced by the non-respondents in the original survey.

Substitution
A procedure that substitutes for non-respondents other elements from the sampling frame who are expected to respond.

Substitution. In **substitution**, the researcher substitutes for non-respondents other elements from the sampling frame who are expected to respond. The sampling frame is divided into subgroups that are internally homogeneous in terms of respondent characteristics but heterogeneous in terms of response rates. These subgroups are then used to identify substitutes who are similar to particular non-respondents but dissimilar to respondents already in the sample. Note that this approach would not reduce non-response bias if the substitutes are similar to respondents already in the sample.

Subjective estimates. When it is no longer feasible to increase the response rate by sub-sampling, replacement or substitution, it may be possible to arrive at subjective estimates of the nature and effect of non-response bias. This involves evaluating the likely effects of non-response based on experience and available information. For example, married adults with young children are more likely to be at home than single or divorced adults or than married adults with no children. This information provides a basis for evaluating the effects of non-response due to not-at-homes in personal or telephone surveys.

Trend analysis
A method of adjusting for non-response in which the researcher tries to discern a trend between early and late respondents. This trend is projected to non-respondents to estimate their characteristic of interest.

Trend analysis. Trend analysis is an attempt to discern a trend between early and late respondents. This trend is projected to non-respondents to estimate where they stand on the characteristic of interest. For example, Table 14.4 presents the results of several waves of a mail survey. The characteristic of interest is money spent on shopping in supermarkets during the last two months. The known value of the characteristic for the total sample is given at the bottom of the table. The value for each successive wave of respondents becomes closer to the value for non-respondents. For example, those responding to the second mailing spent 79 per cent of the amount spent by those who responded to the first mailing. Those responding to the third mailing spent 85 per cent of the amount spent by those who responded to the second mailing. Continuing this trend, one might estimate that those who did not respond spent 91 per cent [85 + (85 – 79)] of the amount spent by those who responded to the third mailing. This results in an estimate of €252 (277 × 0.91) spent by non-respondents and an estimate of €88 for the average amount spent in shopping at supermarkets during the last two months for the overall sample. Note that the actual amount spent by the respondents was €230 rather than the €252 and that the actual sample average was €275 rather than the €288 estimated by trend analysis. Although the trend estimates are wrong, the error is smaller than the error that would have resulted from ignoring the non-respondents. Had the non-respondents been ignored, the average amount spent would have been estimated at €335 for the sample.

Weighting
A statistical procedure that attempts to account for non-response by assigning differential weights to the data depending on the response rates.

Weighting. Weighting attempts to account for non-response by assigning differential weights to the data depending on the response rates.[19] For example, in a survey on personal computers, the sample was stratified according to income.

Table 14.4 Use of trend analysis in adjusting for non-response

	Percentage response	*Average Euro expenditure*	*Percentage of previous wave's response*
First mailing	12	412	–
Second mailing	18	325	79
Third mailing	13	277	85
Non-response	(57)	(230)	91
Total	100	275	

The response rates were 85 per cent, 70 per cent, and 40 per cent, respectively, for the high-, medium-, and low-income groups. In analysing the data, these subgroups are assigned weights inversely proportional to their response rates. That is, the weights assigned would be 100/85, 100/70, and 100/40, respectively, for the high-, medium-, and low-income groups. Although weighting can correct for the differential effects of non-response, it destroys the self-weighting nature of the sampling design and can introduce complications. Weighting is further discussed in Chapter 16 on data preparation.

Imputation
A method to adjust for non-response by assigning the characteristic of interest to the non-respondents based on the similarity of the variables available for both non-respondents and respondents.

Imputation. **Imputation** involves imputing, or assigning, the characteristic of interest to the non-respondents based on the similarity of the variables available for both non-respondents and respondents.[20] For example, a respondent who does not report brand usage may be imputing the usage of a respondent with similar demographic characteristics. Often there is a high correlation between the characteristic of interest and some other variables. In such cases, this correlation can be used to predict the value of the characteristic for the non-respondents (see Chapter 13).

INTERNATIONAL MARKETING RESEARCH

When conducting marketing research in foreign countries, statistical estimation of sample size may be difficult because estimates of the population variance may be unavailable. Hence, the sample size is often determined by qualitative considerations, as discussed in Chapter 13: (1) the importance of the decision, (2) the nature of the research, (3) the number of variables, (4) the nature of the analysis, (5) sample sizes used in similar studies, (6) incidence rates, (7) completion rates, and (8) resource constraints. If statistical estimation of sample size is at all attempted, it should be realised that the estimates of the population variance may vary from country to country. For example, in measuring consumer preferences, a greater degree of heterogeneity may be encountered in countries where consumer preferences are not that well developed. Thus, it may be a mistake to assume that the population variance is the same or to use the same sample size in different countries.

EXAMPLE

The Chinese take to the sky[21]

The airline industry seems to have a strong and promising market potential in China. The airline market in China is growing rapidly. With billions of Euros spent, China is trying to satisfy surging demand and to catch up with the rest of the world. The domestic airline traffic is growing at a rate of up to 30 per cent a year. Strong economic growth, surging foreign trade, and a revival in tourism as the memory of the massacre in Tiananmen Square recedes, have helped to fuel the boom. China is making rapid progress in increasing its fleet and training pilots. For millions of Chinese, air travel is a relatively new experience and many more millions have never flown. Hence, Chinese preferences for air travel are likely to exhibit much more variability compared with Europeans. In a survey to compare attitudes toward air travel in China and European countries, the sample size of the Chinese survey would have to be larger than the European survey in order for the two survey estimates to have comparable precision. ■

For millions of Chinese, travel is a relatively new experience and Chinese preferences for air travel are likely to exhibit much more variability as compared with the preferences of Western travellers.

ETHICS IN MARKETING RESEARCH

As discussed in this chapter, statistical methods can be used to determine the sample size and, therefore, have an impact on the cost of the project. While this is usually an objective way of determining the sample size, it is, nonetheless, susceptible to fraud. The sample size is heavily dependent on the standard deviation of the variable and there is no way of knowing the standard deviation until the data have been collected. To resolve this paradox, the computation of the sample size must be performed using an estimate of the standard deviation. This estimate is derived based on secondary data, judgement or a small pilot study. By inflating the standard deviation, it is possible to increase the sample size and thus the project revenue. Using the sample size formula it can be seen that increasing the standard deviation by 20 per cent, for example, will increase the sample size by 44 per cent. But this is clearly unethical.

Ethical dilemmas can arise even when the standard deviation is estimated honestly. It is possible, indeed common, that the standard deviation in the actual study is different from that estimated initially. When the standard deviation is larger than initially estimated, the confidence interval will also be larger than desired. When such a situation arises, the researcher has the responsibility to disclose this to the client and jointly decide on a course of action. The ethical ramifications of mis-communicating the confidence intervals of survey estimates based on statistical samples are underscored in political polling.

EXAMPLE

Surveys serve up elections

The dissemination of some survey results has been strongly criticised as manipulative and unethical. In particular, the ethics of releasing political poll results before and during the election have been questioned. Opponents of such surveys claim that voters are misled by these results. First, before the election, voters are influenced by whom the polls predict will win. If they see that the candidate they favour is trailing, they may decide not to vote; they assume that there is no way their candidate can win. The attempt to predict the election results while the election is in progress has come under even harsher criticism. Opponents of this practice feel that this predisposes voters to vote for the projected winner or that it may even discourage voters from voting, even though the polls have not closed, because the media projects that there is already a winner. Furthermore, not only are the effects of these projections questionable, but frequently the accuracy of the projections is questionable as well. Although voters may be told a candidate has a certain percentage of the votes within ± per cent, the confidence interval may be much larger, depending on the sample size.

Researchers also have the ethical responsibility to investigate the possibility of non-response bias. The methodology adopted and the extent of non-response bias found should be clearly communicated. ■

INTERNET AND COMPUTER APPLICATIONS

The main use of the Internet in sample size calculations is to track down potential sampling frames that could be used to define and classify a population. With different sampling frames collected and 'cleaned' in a database package, the ultimate population size can be determined. If there is a finite size to a population, all means of tracking down elements of that population. The Internet can play a vital role in that task.

Using database packages and recording the identity of survey respondents, the researcher can keep track of non-respondents. The database can help to determine if there is a particular geographical location or type of non-respondent to a survey. The rapid identification of non-respondents enables researchers to develop tactics to encourage a response.

Microcomputers and mainframes can determine the sample size for various sampling techniques. For simple applications, appropriate sample size formulas can be entered using spreadsheet programs. The researcher specifies the desired precision level, confidence level and population variance and the program determines the appropriate sample size for the study. By incorporating the cost of each sampling unit, the sample size can be adjusted based upon budget considerations.

SUMMARY

The statistical approaches to determining sample size are based on confidence intervals. These approaches may involve the estimation of the mean or proportion. When estimating the mean, determination of sample size using the confidence interval approach requires the specification of precision level, confidence level and population standard deviation. In the case of proportion, the precision level confidence level and an estimate of the population proportion must be specified. The sample size determined statistically represents the final or net sample size that must be achieved. To achieve this final sample size, a much greater number of potential respondents have to be contacted to account for reduction in response due to incidence rates and completion rates.

Non-response error arises when some of the potential respondents included in the sample do not respond. The primary causes of low response rates are refusals and not-at-homes. Refusal rates may be reduced by prior notification, motivating the respondents, incentives, proper questionnaire design and administration, and follow-up. The percentage of not-at-homes can be substantially reduced by call-backs. Adjustments for non-response can be made by sub-sampling non-respondents, replacement, substitution, subjective estimates, trend analysis, simple weighting and imputation.

The statistical estimation of sample size is even more complicated in international marketing research because the population variance may differ from one country to the next. The preliminary estimation of population variance for the purpose of determining the sample size also has ethical ramifications.

QUESTIONS AND PROBLEMS

1 Define:
   (a) the sampling distribution,
   (b) finite population correction,
   (c) confidence intervals.

2 What is the standard error of the mean?

3 What is the procedure for constructing a confidence interval around a mean?

4 Describe the difference between absolute precision and relative precision when estimating a population mean.

5 How do the degree of confidence and the degree of precision differ?

6 Describe the procedure for determining the sample size necessary to estimate a population mean, given the degree of precision and confidence and a known population variance. After the sample is selected, how is the confidence interval generated?

7 Describe the procedure for determining the sample size necessary to estimate a population mean, given the degree of precision and confidence but the population variance is unknown. After the sample is selected, how is the confidence interval generated?

8 How is the sample size affected when the absolute precision with which a population mean is estimated is doubled?

9 How is the sample size affected when the degree of confidence with which a population mean is estimated is increased from 95 to 99 per cent?

10 Define what is meant by absolute precision and relative precision when estimating a population proportion.

11 Describe the procedure for determining the sample size necessary to estimate a population proportion given the degree of precision and confidence. After the sample is selected, how is the confidence interval generated?

12 How can the researcher ensure that the generated confidence interval will be no larger than the desired interval when estimating a population proportion?

13 When several parameters are being estimated, what is the procedure for determining the sample size?

14 Define incidence rate and completion rate. How do these rates affect the determination of the final sample size?

15 What strategies are available for adjusting for non-response?

NOTES

1 A discussion of the sampling distribution may be found in any basic statistics textbook. For example, see Berenson, M.L. and Levine, D.M., *Basic Business Statistics: Concepts and Applications,* 5th edn (Englewood Cliffs, NJ: Prentice Hall, 1992).

2 Other statistical approaches are also available. A discussion of these is beyond the scope of this book, however. The interested reader is referred to Nowell, C. and Stanley, L.R., 'Length-Biased Sampling in Mall Intercept Surveys', *Journal of Marketing Research* 28 (November 1991), 475–79; Gillett, R., 'Confidence Interval Construction by Stein's Method: A Practical and Economical Approach to Sample Size Determination', *Journal of Marketing Research* 26 (May 1989), 237; Frankel, M., 'Sampling Theory', in Rossi, P.H., Wright, J.D. and Anderson, A.B. (eds), *Handbook of Survey Research* (New York: Academic Press, 1983), 21–67; Kish, L., *Survey Sampling* (New York: Wiley, 1965), 102; and Sudman, S., *Applied Sampling* (New York: Academic Press, 1976), 85–105.

3 Kraemer, H.C. and Thiemann, S., *How Many Subjects?* (Newbury Park, CA: Sage Publications, 1988).

4 Frankel, M. 'Sampling Theory', in Rossi, P.H., Wright, J.D. and Anderson, A.B., (eds), *Handbook of Survey Research* (New York: Academic Press, 1983), 21–67.

5 For a discussion of estimating sample costs, see Kish, L., *Survey Sampling* (New York: Wiley, 1965); and Sudman, S., *Applied Sampling* (New York: Academic Press, 1976).

6 See, for example, Sudman, S., 'Applied Sampling', in Rossi, P.H., Wright, J.D. and Anderson, A.B. (eds), *Handbook of Survey Research* (Orlando, FL: Academic Press, 1983), 145–94.

7 Adjusting for incidence and completion rates is discussed in Pol, L.G. and Pak, S., 'The Use of Two Stage Survey Design in Collecting Data from Those Who Have Attended Periodic or Special Events', *Journal of the Market Research Society* 36 (October 1994), 315–26.

8 Lee, K.G., 'Incidence Is a Key Element', *Marketing News* (13 September 1985), 50.

9 Martin, C., 'The Impact of Topic Interest on Mail Survey Response Behaviour', *Journal of the Market Research Society* 36 (October 1994), 327–38.

10 McDaniel, S.W., Madden, C.S. and Verille, P., 'Do Topic Differences Affect Survey Non-response?', *Journal of the Market Research Society* (January 1987) 55–66; and Leslie, L., 'Are High Response Rates Essential to Valid Surveys?', *Social Science Research* (September 1971), 332–34.

11 For minimising the incidence of non-response and adjusting for its effects, see Brown, M., 'What Price Response?', *Journal of the Market Research Society* 36 (July 1994), 227–44.

12 Armstrong, J.S. and Lusk, E.J., 'Return Postage in Mail Surveys: A Meta-Analysis', *Public Opinion Quarterly* (Summer 1987), 233–48; and Yu, J. and Cooper, H., 'A Quantitative Review of Research Design Effects on Response Rates to Questionnaires', *Journal of Marketing Research* 20 (February 1983), 36–44.

13 Fern, E.E., Monroe, K.B. and Avila, R.A., 'Effectiveness of Multiple Request Strategies: A Synthesis of Research Results', *Journal of Marketing Research* 23 (May 1986), 144–53.

14 Greer, T.V. and Lohtia, R., 'Effects of Source and Paper Color on Response Rates in Mail Surveys', *Industrial Marketing Management* 23 (February 1994), 47–54.

15 *Bicycling Magazine's 1987 Semi-annual Study of US Retail Bicycle Stores* (September 1987).

16 Kerin, R.A. and Peterson, R.A., 'Scheduling Telephone Interviews', *Journal of Advertising Research* (May 1983), 44.

17 Dillman, D.A., *Mail and Telephone Surveys: The Total Design Method* (New York: Wiley, 1978), 53.

18 Pearl, D.K. and Fairley, D., 'Testing for the Potential for Non-response Bias in Sample Surveys', *Public Opinion Quarterly* 49 (Winter 1985), 553–60.

19 Ward, J.C., Russick, B. and Rudelius, W., 'A Test of Reducing Call-backs and Not-at-Home Bias in Personal Interviews by Weighting At-Home Respondents', *Journal of Marketing Research* 2 (February 1985), 66–73.

20 Chapman, D.W., 'Survey of Non-response Imputation Procedures', *Proceedings of the Social Statistics Section*, American Statistical Association, Part I (Washington, DC: American Statistical Association, 1976), 245–51.

21 *The Economist*, 'Another Chinese Take-Off' (19 December 1992).

APPENDIX 14A: THE NORMAL DISTRIBUTION

In this appendix, we provide a brief overview of the **normal distribution** and the use of the normal distribution table. The normal distribution is used in calculating the sample size, and it serves as the basis for classical statistical inference. Many continuous phenomena follow the normal distribution or can be approximated by it. The normal distribution can, likewise, be used to approximate many discrete probability distributions.[1]

The normal distribution has some important theoretical properties. It is bell-shaped and symmetrical in appearance. Its measures of central tendency (mean, median, and mode) are all identical. Its associated random variable has an infinite range ($-\infty < X < +\infty$).

The normal distribution is defined by the population mean μ and population standard deviation σ. Since an infinite number of combination of μ and σ exist, an infinite number of normal distributions exist and an infinite number of tables would be required. By standardising the data, however, we need only one table, such as Table 2 in the Appendix of Statistical Tables. Any normal random variable X can be converted to a standardised normal random variable z by the formula

$$z = \frac{X - \mu}{\sigma}$$

Note that the random variable z is always normally distributed with a mean of 0 and a standard deviation of 1. The normal probability tables are generally used for two purposes: (1) finding probabilities corresponding to known values of X or z, and (2) finding values of X or z corresponding to known probabilities. Each of these uses is discussed.

Finding probabilities corresponding to known values

Suppose that Figure 14A.1 represents the distribution of the number of engineering contracts received per year by an engineering firm. Because the data span the entire history of the firm, Figure 14A.1 represents the population. Therefore, the probabilities or proportion of area under the curve must add up to 1.0. The Marketing Director wishes to determine the probability that the number of contracts received next year will be between 50 and 55. The answer can be determined by using Table 2 of the Appendix of Statistical Tables.

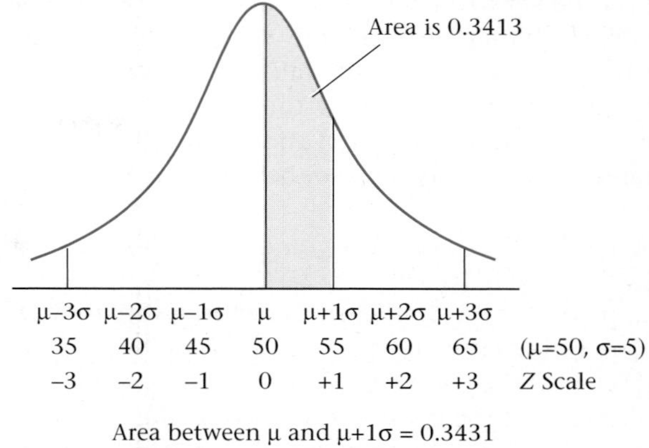

Figure 14 A.1 Finding probability corresponding to a known value

Table 2 gives the probability or area under the standardised normal curve from the mean (zero) to the standardised value of interest, z. Only positive entries of z are listed in the table. For a symmetrical distribution with zero mean, the area from the mean to $+z$ (i.e. z standard deviations above the mean) is identical to the area from the mean to $-z$ (z standard deviations below the mean).

Note that the difference between 50 and 55 corresponds to a z value of 1.00. Note that to use Table 2, all z values must be recorded to two decimal places. To read the probability or area under the curve from the mean to $z = +1.00$, scan down the z column of Table 2 until the z value of interest (in tenths) is located. In this case, stop in the row $z = 1.00$. Then, read across this row until you intersect the column containing the hundredths place of the z value. Thus, in Table 2, the tabulated probability for $z = 1.00$ corresponds to the intersection of the row $z = 1.0$ with the column $z = 0.00$. This probability is 0.3413. As shown in Figure 14A.1, the probability is 0.3413 that the number of contracts received by the firm next year will be between 50 and 55. It can also be concluded that the probability is 0.6826 (2 × 0.3413) that the number of contracts received next year will be between 45 and 55.

This result could be generalised to show that for any normal distribution, the probability is 0.6826

[1] This material is drawn from Berenson, M. L. and Levine, D. M., *Basic Business Statistics: Concepts and Applications*, 6th edn (Upper Saddle River, NJ: Prentice Hall, 1996). Adapted by permission of Prentice Hall, Inc. Upper Saddle River, NJ.

that a randomly selected item will fall within ±1 standard deviations above or below the mean. Also, it can be verified from Table 2 that there is a 0.9544 probability that any randomly selected normally distributed observation will fall within ±2 standard deviations above or below the mean and a 0.9973 probability that the observation will fall within ±3 standard deviations above or below the mean.

Finding values corresponding to known properties values

Suppose that the Marketing Director wishes to determine how many contracts must come in so that 5 per cent of the contracts for the year have come in. If 5 per cent of the contracts have come in, 95% of the contracts have yet to come. As shown in Figure 14A.2, this 95% can be broken down into two parts: contracts above the mean (i.e. 50%) and contracts between the mean and the desired *z* value (i.e. 45%). The desired *z* value can be determined from Table 2, since the area under the normal curve from the standardised mean, 0, to this *z* must be 0.4500. From Table 2, we search for the area or probability 0.4500. The closest value is 0.4495 or 0.4505. For 0.4495, we see that the *z* value corresponding to the particular *z* row (1.6) and *z* column (0.04) is 1.64. The *z* value, however, must be recorded as negative (i.e. $z = -1.64$), since it is below the standardised mean of 0. Similarly, the *z* value corresponding to the area of 0.4505 is −1.65. Since 0.4500 is midway between 0.4495 and 0.4505, the appropriate *z* value could be midway between the two *z* values and estimated as −1.645. The corresponding *X* value can then be calculated from the standardisation formula, as follows:

$$X = \mu + z\sigma$$
$$= 50 + (-1.645)5$$
$$= 41.775$$

Suppose that the Marketing Director wanted to determine the interval in which 95% of the contracts for next year are expected to lie. As can be seen from Figure 14A.3, the corresponding *z* values are ±1.96. This corresponds to *X* values of 50 ± (1.96)5, or 40.2 and 59.8. This range represents the 95% confidence interval.

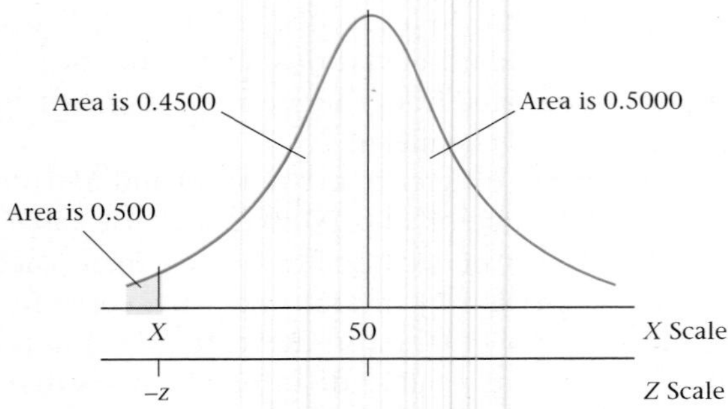

Figure 14A.2 Finding values corresponding to known probabilities

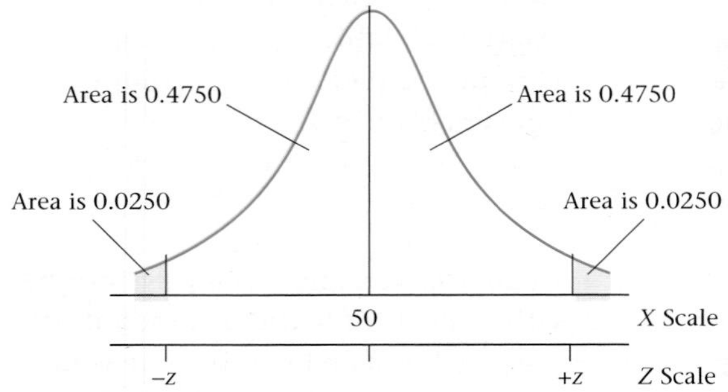

Figure 14A.3 Finding values corresponding to known probabilities: confidence interval

PROFESSIONAL PERSPECTIVES for Part II

Trevor Fenwick
Trevor is the Managing Director of Euromonitor, having over 20 years' experience in market research analysis and the business publishing fields. Euromonitor was established in 1972 and specialises in researching global consumer markets; it now publishes over 200 new surveys every year, from market reports to statistical reference books, CD-ROMS, directories and journals. He is a Director and Past Chairman of the Directory and Database Publishers Association, a Board member of the Confederation of Information and Communications Industries and the European Association of Directory and Database Publishers.

How on-line retrieval is devaluing research

TREVOR FENWICK

Only a few short years ago, researchers looking for information on a new or unfamiliar market had their work cut out. If they were lucky, hours of sleuthing might reveal the existence of the data they wanted in a research report. If they were *really* lucky they might find that the report publisher's office was still open, that the report was 'on the shelf' and could be couriered to the researcher there and then.

Such a scenario, as any researcher working in the early 1980s will tell you, can only be described as improbable. The reality would be more likely that the publisher's office was closed for the evening, or the report was being reprinted or was out of stock.

The growth in the availability of published market research on-line has changed all that. Now, researchers can turn on their PCs, go on-line and, by using relatively simple search commands, establish whether the information exists and joy of joys, take delivery of it there and then. This you would think, would be good for all – the user, who now has instant access to the data; the information publisher, who is selling more; and the on-line host. Unfortunately, this win-win-win scenario has not turned out to be the case.

At Euromonitor we are now finding that the unique ability of on-line searching to select, or 'cherry pick', small slices of data, coupled with the hosts' inability (or refusal), to price that data at a level which compensates the publisher for the loss of a hard copy report sale, results in the increasing loss of substantial revenues.

The only counter-argument of the hosts is that their user clients are primarily advertising, marketing and financial service companies who would not have bought complete hard copy reports in any case.

If this is true, which it is not, we publishers would not be unhappy. The unfortunate reality is that our industry clients are switching from copy on-line and then not even taking whole reports but selecting small sections of information.

Market research reports are expensive to reproduce; analysts have to be paid, survey data bought, manufacturers interviewed and overheads covered. Euromonitor pricing reflects our belief that the whole is greater than the sum of the parts. The hosts wrongly believe that the value is spread evenly throughout and is divisible by the number of lines.

The on-line provision of market research data is a relatively new phenomenon both for the research publishers and the on-line industry. Hosts have based their pricing policies on those successfully used for the huge scientific and technical full-text databases which are ideally suited to on-line searching and on which the on-line industry has established itself. Some do not exist at all in hard copy. In these cases there can be no substitution from, or erosion of, hard copy sales. Others are retrospective text databases. Here publishers have already achieved their revenues from the sales of the original print publication.

Publishers of the second type of database do not mind too much about low pricing. Indeed it is vital to achieve maximum usage volumes. These databases are typically very large and large databases mean lots of searching (good for the producer and the host) and comprehensive coverage of the subject (good for the user).

The fact that this approach cannot be applied to research reports will come as no surprise to those of us in the research industry. We are used to producing high added-value, specialist information, often for very small target client markets, and know that it is impossible to double the size of our market by halving the costs of our services.

The growth of hosts in this specialist field can hardly be seen as a success when all they have achieved is to take a product for which there was already an established market and to offer it to that same market at a much reduced price. On such sand-like foundations will great industries not be built.

Electronic distribution of research data has not increased the supply of or demand for that data. It has just made what is available more easily available and, because of the fundamental misunderstanding of the size and nature of the market for research information, has reduced, not increased, the potential revenue to the research industry.

The irony of this situation is that most, if not all, report publishers are fully committed to the electronic distribution of data. It matters not to us how we deliver our product. It does matter that the resulting revenues are sufficient to cover our costs and let us invest in new research. It is clearly a benefit to users who appreciate the convenience, speed of access and delivery. All that has to be resolved is the simple matter of realistic pricing of the data accessed. Unless the hosts address this issue they may find themselves presiding over an elegant but ultimately empty bookcase.

Originally published in *Research*, March 1994, p. 13

Today the nation; tomorrow the globe

RICHARD WEBBER

It is now some 15 years since geodemographics first established itself in Britain as a target marketing tool. Today there are maybe 500 organisations regularly using geodemographic segmentation systems to improve various aspects of their marketing efficiency. One thing is for sure: until now the way geodemographics has been sold and accessed has made it very difficult to broaden its use. Today its users are principally statistical analysts working within specialist units inside large consumer goods and services organisations.

Richard Webber

Richard is the Managing Director of the Marketing Division of Experian, the UK's leading supplier of geomarketing systems and segmentation software. He is arguably Europe's leading authority on geodemographic segmentation.

Since 1974, when he built his first demographic system in the UK, Richard has specialised in the development and application of geodemographic sytems and segmentation software. Today, Experian's geodemographic classification and segmentation software – Mosiac – can be applied in 15 international markets and covers 700 million consumers worldwide.

The advent of new multimedia visualisation tools is now beginning to make geodemographics accessible to a wider audience which, in my opinion, is likely to expand in two directions: first, from large organisations into smaller companies and consultancies, many populated by refugees from large companies and familiar with these systems from them; second, into employees in large organisations who have direct contact with customers and are responsible for the implementation of segmentation strategies across the counter or the phone line.

New delivery media such as CD and the Internet will provide this wider access, often using metered access which, for smaller users, will replace annual directory or software licence charges. We have already seen examples of this trend in list rental where the electoral roll, segmented by MOSAIC, can now be accessed from a CD on a metered basis.

If suppliers are to deliver services to smaller users profitably, much more business applications know-how will have to be embedded in the product itself, as computer-based training (CBT). This may be expensive to develop but will reduce the heavy costs of the field salesforce, account management and user training. Given the complexity of geodemographic applications, many users may find CBT superior to face-to-face. It will, I believe, soon extend to education in the business applications these systems are designed to address.

A key consequence of the downsizing of applications systems will be the emergence of intermediaries as solutions providers. Until today, only a specialist list broker could supply geodemographically targeted names and addresses for list rental. With the universe of UK names on a CD, the small business arm of a UK bank or even an office supply retailer can realistically establish itself as a source of targeted names and addresses for its clients' mailings.

Most large organisations are recognising the need to provide front-line staff with better information on the customers they deal with. Branch managers of pubs or restaurant chains are increasingly encouraged to manage their own local communications activities as well as to adapt their product to the local populations.

The type of targeting once applied centrally, via mass mailing, now has to be applied in remote locations, by telemarketing staff and counter clerks. Because face-to-face (or ear-to-ear) communications score so much higher per contact than direct mail, the financial return from segmentation is correspondingly higher. Realising these returns will depend upon the extent to which geodemographic segmentation can be accessed and properly understood across the enterprise.

A further change that we can confidently anticipate is the greater use of psychographic information: until now, geodemographic users have concentrated on who to communicate with. Increasingly, we will see the systems used to modify the message, proposition or incentive to different customer segments.

Lastly, I believe that, as the world becomes a single market and consumers a global village, manufacturers and service providers will increasingly look to common global segmentation systems which can be applied consistently across their different markets. Countries may differ in language or domestic architecture, but it is increasingly apparent that all advanced societies exhibit a common set of types of neighbourhoods, each sharing common attitudes, values and material aspirations.

Meeting the needs of the multinational target marketer is just one reason why we can expect to see a rapid consolidation of the geodemographic industry in the next few years.

Originally published in *ResearchPlus*, May 1997, p. 9.

Virginia Monk
Virginia is a Board Director at Network Research & Marketing. Her specialised technique is telephone research, although she has a broad research experience including face-to-face and postal techniques. For the most part, her experience is as a researcher, although, in the past she has had overall responsibility for telephone centres in both the implementation of C.A.T.I. and the training and development of centre staff. Virginia is committee member of the Market Research Society's Telephone Interest Group.

Ringing home

VIRGINIA MONK

Telephone research in the early years was something of an *enfant terrible* in the industry. It was fast, somewhat brash and always something of an alternative, rather than a technique of choice for many types of study. If it were a car, it would have been something like a Caterham Seven – very basic, raw but went like a bullet. Designed for the enthusiast, it was not something that you would choose to go to Sainsburys in. These days, telephone research is a mainstream saloon. That said, unlike in the US, where telephone has enjoyed the status of technique of choice for years, for many in the UK, telephone research still occupies minority status.

Personal interviewing still dominates fieldwork by volume. Why it does is open to debate. Telephone can hold its own in terms of complexity of the interview, response rate, data quality, sample spread, speed and cost. The occasions when stimulus material is a vital part of an interview are insufficient to justify the continuing strength of face-to-face interviewing. And the number of personnel and systems dedicated to quality control in a telephone centre is far greater than that in place in a face-to-face environment.

Telephone research began to take off in this country with the advent of large and predominantly CATI-based centres. Originally, these were major pieces of capital investment for what now look to be very bare bone set-ups. Many CATI stations were dumb, single-purpose machines sitting in utility-style booths. Most phones were direct lines with no switch and call supervision was very limited. Although costs per seat are a little lower now, the actual specification is far higher. Modern centres might not *look* very different, but the scale of change has been dramatic. They have very powerful PCs, fast servers, headsets and telephone switches with features that could only have been dreamt of just ten years ago.

Researchers, clients, centre managers and supervisors can monitor interviews remotely. Verbatim comments can be automatically recorded, computers can randomly digit dial, questionnaires can switch to different languages, codeframes can be built 'on the fly' and so on. The list is almost endless.

Centralised telephone research was only part of an ongoing change in the wider world. Over a single generation, the travelling salesman has all but disappeared from the high street. Computer-based stock systems now determine and predict demand. Direct sales of financial services and travel have emerged as major forces in business. It's all about technology and centralisation, and therefore manageable efficiency. These days, business is based upon direct access at the point of sale and the telemarketing industry is all about this.

Unfairly treated as a *bête noir* by much of the research industry, telemarketing is a major force, now not just larger than the telephone side of research, but many, many times larger than the entirety of market research. There are now more people working in call centres in the UK than doctors, accountants, solicitors and dentists, *put together*. Such scale demands that it be treated with some respect.

It too has exploited technology, direct communication and centralisation. Even the most modern telephone research facility struggles to come anywhere near the amount of kit available to a call centre. There can be little doubt either that call centre personnel are better trained, better paid and have better career paths than the relatively lowly telephone interviewer. First Direct, for example, trains its call centre personnel for at least seven weeks. ADS, a telemarketing agency, promises at least two weeks' continuous training before making a live call.

Compare this to the one-day IQCS standard and it is easy to see the difference and the potential threat of telemarketing to telephone research as a professional business service. (It should be said of course that training for telephone research is no less detailed than for face-to-face: the centralised nature of the former means that ongoing training is possible.) Perhaps rather conveniently, it takes more than a call centre to produce a decent piece of market research – it is after all only a place of production of the raw data.

In the field of customer service monitoring, however, telemarketing operations may well pose something of a threat. In a customer satisfaction survey, the client is usually announced to the respondent. Thus, the interviewer is a direct ambassador of the brand. Greater care will need to be taken in the conduct of such calls and this will put pressure on the current casual employment practices used in the research industry.

Legislation on part-time working and employment rights has frequently been cited as a major peril lurking around the corner. No longer. The issue is becoming so complex that it is very difficult to see how the '*as required*' basis of employment for interviewers can continue to be common practice for much longer. The legal consequences for availability of interviewers for ad hoc research are obvious. Permanently employed interviewers are likely to mark not just an improvement in quality, but perhaps a shift in the right direction in terms of professionalism, coming up to the standards commonly employed by telemarketing, once branded as cowboys.

There are further restrictions coming around the corner in terms of unsolicited calls, which are certainly going to make it harder to conduct certain studies. Final details are not yet available, but certainly it is no longer going to be a simple matter of putting together a set of telephone numbers and dialling them.

A research firm in Germany has received a court ban on making any unsolicited telephone calls. While this was a case with special characteristics, it has sent tremors across the industry and highlights the potential threat to the business as a whole.

The decline in response rates is well documented. In the USA, for example, an estimated 32% of households have caller ID to screen calls and recently published figures estimate refusal rates for telephone research at 46%. This is in no way a problem specific to telephone research, however. Incentives may become more commonplace and the use of panels may increase still further. Essentially, the more complicated it becomes to reach a qualifying, amenable respondent, so telephone will probably prosper. It is in the field of face-to-face interviewing that response rates will become more problematic, as a result of the cost involved in non-productive time spent between interviews.

The brave new world has long been heralded as the interviewerless environment and, at last, this is taking shape in the form of the Internet. But without a panel, or a decent directory of email addresses, Web-based research will always struggle to achieve the kind of speed and sample management available to telephone.

However, the opportunity of mixed mode interviewing comprising part telephone recruitment/part Internet completion does at least mean that visuals can now be added to its suite of capabilities. Telephone researchers and telephone operations personnel are well placed to take advantage of Internet-based research since they already possess many of the skills required of a CATI study and Internet research is not dissimilar in structure. As telephone research has learned, the Internet will not make its mark if it sets out its stall based upon low cost per interview.

So, telephone research has not stood still over the past 15 years or so. It has adopted many new tools and has surfed the current trends in customer satisfaction measurement and multi-country research. There may be a few challenges to come, but telephone specialists are a hardy bunch. The early pioneers are now battle-hardened veterans. They will survive. Cue Gloria Gaynor soundtrack . . .

Originally published in *Research*, Sept 1998, pp. 56–57.

CATI sans frontières

Tim Macer

Tim is a consultant and course provider to 8 of the top 10 market research firms in Britain, and leading research agencies in Canada, Denmark, Germany, Italy, the Netherlands, Norway, Switzerland and the United States. He works on both the implementation of technology and the development of skills and expertise. As a software reviewer, he contributes regularly to the industry-respected magazine Research *on all aspects of IT in marketing research.*

TIM MACER

Pollux interviews, the French CATI/CAPI system, has been relaunched in a new Windows incarnation with the name Converso. The reason is probably more an attempt to reposition this networked PC interviewing system as a telemarketing and MR application than it is to shake off a name that was less than ideal in the UK marketplace. DOS-based Pollux certainly pushed the envelope of what was possible under DOS, but it did not sit well on the Windows desktop alongside other applications such as the unstoppable Microsoft Office. Now, without its dated interface, it is possible to see that as CATI systems go, this is rather a good one.

Unusually for CATI, screens can hold more than one question, and answers can be selected from check-boxes, drop-down lists, buttons or by typing in. For the interviewer, there are strong searching features to ease the task of finding the right answer when there are too many to display on one screen. Most CATI systems buckle under the strain of handling open-ended questions where the answers are used to supplement lists and drive choices later on in the interview. Even if you manage to do it, the data are often a mess. Using a 'semi-open' type of question, coupled with what is called a 'transfer question', Converso makes what is to other systems difficult or impossible, simple and straightforward.

Qualitative interviewers will be interested in the navigation buttons that can be added to the top of the screen that allow you to jump to different sections of the questionnaire at will. These allow you to complete the interview in any order you choose or quickly abandon one line of questioning in favour of another. Coupled with seemingly limitless handling of open-ended responses, this should be a serious contender for introducing CAPI to quallies, especially since you can design the interview yourself too.

Script design is easy. Questions and screens are created simultaneously in a virtually syntaxless environment, using options from the toolbar and selecting objects from a floating palette to drag and drop into shape. A knowledge of some syntax is only required for routing and operations involving logic (include/exclude masking of question, for instance). For the language die-hards, a mark-up language is provided to get questions entered in bulk.

One potential hazard is that, with so much flexibility in the layout of the screen, compared with the rigidity of other systems, the time taken to design the script could expand in a Parkinsonian manner, since it encourages no end of tinkering to produce the perfect layout. Used wisely, it could mean greater clarity for the interviewer and super-looking self-administered interviews.

Supervisor functions are well supported, and can be configured to meet individual requirements. By using an ODBC-compliant database to hold the interviews, the data are very accessible and customised reports can easily be created.

As Denis Harang, Managing Director of Conversoft in France points out: 'For anyone able to work with the (Microsoft) Office software, it will be very easy to learn Converso, as it is exactly the same way of working. But on the other hand the software is very powerful – this is a professional system. And it is also very open'.

I applaud the developers on their approach to making Converso an open system. They have gone out of their way to allow sophisticated users to develop their own applications alongside Converso, sharing files and exchanging data with the system, even while interviews are taking place. Neither is there any expectation to analyse your data using their own built-in tab module, as the exporting facilities are excellent.

Converso also offers full multimedia support. Images and video can also be shown on screen in CAPI, and sound clips played over the phone in CATI. But it stops short of providing any support for the Web, which is a pity. Another slight blemish is that some of the options still appear in French, and some of the naming conventions used would mean a lot more to the Francophone.

A more serious problem is Converso's knack of deleting data if an interview has to go back to a previous question in an interview. This was an issue raised by several users I spoke to, as in most cases, when you move forwards again, the answers previously collected are lost. It stands out as an unfriendly feature in an otherwise most user-friendly package.

The majority of Converso users are in France. But in Liverpool, Dialogue Market Research report success in their use of Converso's forerunner, Pollux. Lynne Gill, Managing Director, marvels at the flexibility of the product: 'We use it for everything: CATI, face-to-face and data entry, even depth interviews by telephone. One of our strong points is the richness and the depth of the verbatim data we can get. Our clients often praise us for this.' The limitless open-ended fields and good support provided for verbatims allow them to exploit this to the maximum. The ability to play advertising jingles and capture voice in the new version has made Dialogue keen to upgrade to Converso.

'When we were looking for a system, we chose Pollux because of its compatibility with other packages, especially Word, Access, Excel and SPSS,' Lyne Gill explained. 'I've looked at other packages with claims of compatibility and found them all very disappointing.'

Researcher Claire Emmerson saw a lot of advantages in the Windows version: 'It's going to be easier to use. I think the graphical interface will make it easier to make more complex things.'

Dave Darby, Dialogue's Operations manager, is an experienced user of Pollux, and was looking forward to using Converso. 'The key thing is that you don't need to be a programmer to set up scripts – but some technical ability is definitely a help.' He often works from a questionnaire in Word, importing all the text into Pollux. 'It takes just a couple of hours. Basically, all you have to do is add the routing.'

It would be a pity if, like all their finest cheeses and wines, we allowed the French to keep all the best programs to themselves. This gourmet software has ripened beautifully and deserves a wider tasting.

Pros

- Very easy to write scripts
- Open system
- Good integration with MS Office
- Sophisticated handling of verbatims

Cons

- Data loss when going back in interviews
- Not fully translated from French
- No support for Web-based interviewing

Originally published in *Research*, January 1999.

Peter Wills

Peter is the founder and Managing Director of Mercator. The company is based in Bristol, UK and is one of the world's leading suppliers of software for survey processing, as well as providing extensive bureau services for its clients. Peter oversees all sales and marketing operations for both the HQ operation and the US office based in Boston, Massachusetts.

On-line market research surveys on the Internet

PETER WILLS

Market researchers have been slow to take up the Internet as an alternative medium for data collection. This may well be due to reservations about any new and possibly unproven technology. However, mastering on-line research techniques, with the help of user-friendly software packages that now exist, is no more difficult than mastering any new PC application, and the advantages of conducting research via the Internet are numerous.

The growth of the Internet is prodigious. The number of individuals who are on-line is increasing rapidly each day. The Web population is no longer dominated by academics and 'techies' and the Internet is proving to be one of the most remarkable technologies of the 20th century.

The following facts provide a level of support for this observation:

- Traffic on the Internet is doubling every 100 day (source: US Commerce Department).
- Over 100 million people were on-line by April 1998, and it is estimated that this number will increase to 327 million by the year 2000 (source: The Computer Industry Almanac)
- The Internet reached 50 million people in just 4 years. By comparison, it took television 13 years to achieve the same level of penetration, and it took radio over 30 years to reach that level.
- 10 million people in the US used on-line facilities to purchase something by the end of 1997, an increase from 4.7 million six months before (source: **www.ecommerce.gov**).
- The total number of Web sites has increased five-fold in just two years. The number was a staggering one million in 1997, but by April 1999 it had increased to over five million. It is estimated that there are already over 320 million pages on the World Wide Web/ (source: Nua Internet surveys – **www.nua.ie**).
- The cost of computing continues to fall, with a basic PC, as predicted, costing under US $599 (£375) (source: Forrester Research).
- By 2006, it is estimated that Americans will spend $666 billion on computers, a huge increase over the $2.1 billion spent in 1992.

Faced with these facts, the market research industry has a window of opportunity to get on-line and offer some leadership in the technology that is expanding at an alarming rate. The possibilities include:

1. Desk research
2. Conducting quantitative surveys on the Internet
3. Qualitative surveys on the Internet.

DESK RESEARCH

Market researchers have always been taught to use desk research as the first step before generating primary data by means of questionnaires and fieldwork. In former times, desk research was tedious, time-consuming and generally expensive. It often involved lengthy trips to the library to access files and printed materials, and often the information would not be up-to-date. Accessing on-line databases was always possible but required considerable IT expertise and was often expensive. Today, desk research is comprehensive, quick, up-to-date and concise. Many researchers have direct on-line access via the Internet to both the World Wide Web and commercial on-line host services. These services are often supported by subscriptions to vast libraries of data supplied on CD-ROM and easily accessible from a PC.

Information on the World Wide Web is generally free of charge, but it is not always up-to-date or in-depth. However, it is an ideal first step in forming an initial overview and helping to target sources for further investigation. Suppliers of on-line databases will use the Web as a 'taster' to provide sufficient information to get the research started, and then offer on-line database information on a chargeable basis, for the most current data available.

The following list provides some useful starting points for Website information gathering:

www.bbc.co.uk – BBC on-line
www.cnn.com – up-to-date news from CNN
www.coi.gov.uk – Central Office of Information
www.dialog.com The Dialog Corporation
www.dnb.com – Dunn & Bradstreet
www.economist.com – *The Economist*
www.wsj.com – *Wall Street Journal*
www.Embpage.org – embassy data on individual countries
www.infoplease.com – US database of encyclopaedia, almanacs & dictionaries
www.iris-net.org/ factbook – basic national data collated by IRIS – International Research Institutes
www.keynote.com.uk – research reports to order plus some free summaries
www.mediainfo.com/emedia/ – Editor and Publisher Interactive Media Links
www.mediauk.com/director/index.html – the UK's radio, television, magazines and newspapers
www. oecd.org – Organisation for Economic Co-operation and Development
www.odci.gov – Central Intelligence Agency
www.ons.gov.uk – Office for National Statistics
www.open.gov.uk – CCTA Government Information Service
www.quirks.com – Quirk's *Marketing Research* magazine
www.researchinfo.com – Market research information site
www.statistics.gov.uk/statbase/mainmenu.asp – UK National Statistics Online
www.statmarket.com – WebSideStory's HitBOX Tracker of raw data computed from hundreds of daily Internet users

In addition the following are some of the most well-known search engines. These search for any Web sites and Web pages that contain your selected word(s) or phrase(s):

www.aol.com
www.altavista.com
www.excite.co.uk
www.go.com
www.goto.com
www.hotbot.com
www.lycos.com
www.snap.com
www.yahoo.co.uk

The new management tool that's no mystery

David Backinsell

David has more than 20 years' experience in sales and marketing, particularly in customer service delivery, service performance measurement and customer relationship management. Over the past decade he has worked at the forefront of developments in a growing branch of marketing – Customer Relationship Management. David is a director of NOP Mystery Shopping and of Berry Consulting – CRM consultants. He has lectured and written extensively on effective service delivery, performance measurement systems, and using customer knowledge management to enhance customer lifetime value.

DAVID BACKINSELL

In 1991, and as an early advocate of mystery shopping, I was discussing the merits of measuring service performance with a couple of senior market researchers. I recall such phrases as 'a passing fad' being used to describe the then-infant methodology. The researchers failed themselves and the research sector on two counts: by confusing performance measurement with market research; and by ignoring a significant opportunity for the research industry to contribute to the range of performance measures now being used.

Today more than half the UK agencies listed in the current MRS members directory claim a mystery shopping capability. And the largest mystery shopping agency is among the Top 10 UK research agencies by revenue. So perhaps the most significant trend in mystery shopping is that it has gained acceptance as a mainstream management tool. It is used to measure – from the customer perspective – the service performance of an organisation, thereby enabling sources of both employee and customer satisfaction and dissatisfaction to be better understood – and better managed.

Despite a difficult birth, mystery shopping has survived adolescence and is maturing. It has done so largely on the back of what is plain common sense – that understanding and meeting customer's expectations must be good for business. Yet today it is the changing nature of managers' needs for information that drives the trends in mystery shopping practice and application.

To appreciate the trends in mystery shopping, the underlying trends in management thinking and practice need to be examined. Mystery shopping must be located within current management thinking, if it is to be seen appropriately – as a tool that is used for managing, among other things, employee and customer satisfaction.

Effective management requires an information system that enables users to see their business as a series of links in an economic chain. This chain must be understood as a whole in order to manage costs, and thereby manage yields (results). At the centre of managing yields is one question: which single activity (of the business) is at the centre of costs and of results? In every commercial activity (and in most non-commercial activities too), the answer is 'serving the customer'.

It is helpful to view the economic chain as a simple input–process–output model, in which human and other resource 'inputs' flow through the 'process' of product or service delivery, thereby creating 'results'. Using this model, we can identify the two key trends in management thinking which are affecting the development of mystery shopping. These are:

- locating customer service within the process element of the value chain;
- the resulting need to relate measures of process performance to measures of inputs (such as employee satisfaction) and outputs (such as customer satisfaction).

Let's look more closely at the first of these, the process 'trend'. Managers now see service delivery as the process that has the most directly measurable effect on profitable growth. The process has many discrete, albeit interlinked, elements, each of which is a 'moment of truth' for the customer. That is to say, each element carries within it the seeds of customer satisfaction – or dissatisfaction (a central reason for mystery shoppers using the 'sample size of one' – you only get one chance to make a good first impression!). And this demands that managers have an in-depth understanding of the different moments of truth that make up the customer's current (service) experience – which impacts on their overall current satisfaction. That mystery shopping is now used by organisations of all sizes (including those with but a single retail outlet) confirms this as a function of effective management, not of business size.

The second trend is that of relating process to inputs and outputs. The trend is based simply on managers needing to integrate different sets of information in order to build a comprehensive picture of business performance. (The growing application of concepts such as the Balanced Score Card reflect this need to integrate information from a variety of sources.) Thus there are managers evaluating the performance of individual retail outlets based on a combination of mystery shopping scores (the customer perspective), outlet revenues and profitability (the financial perspective), staff turnover, stock shrinkage, prospect conversion (the employee perspective), and so on.

So why don't businesses use customer satisfaction research instead of mystery shopping? Well, customer satisfaction is an output – of the input and process stages of our model. In order to understand what lies behind outputs, it is necessary to look at inputs and processes. And managers have demonstrated that, by improving customer service delivery, organisations can make significant and sustainable gains in the market – they can manage yields. The factors that contribute to service quality – communication, competence, courtesy, responsiveness, etc. – are almost all a function of staff attitudes and behaviour towards the customer. Employees with the right attitude, the right incentives, the right training, the right amount of 'empowerment', and who listen to customers, are the key to designing and providing services that create such outputs.

It is this understanding – of the need for excellence and differentiation at the customer interface – that has led to an increasing use of mystery shopping to generate certain types of information – information that cannot be generated by other means (such as conventional customer satisfaction research). In other words, mystery shopping is now one of the range of management (measurement) tools that are required in order to achieve and maintain standards of service delivery.

Based on these underlying trends in management thinking and practice, there are some further trends which point the way to how mystery shopping is developing.

Historically, almost all business performance measurement has used objective data. Today there is an acceptance of the need for subjective information, not only to flesh out objective data but also, more specifically, because customer service is relative – to respond to the expectations of individual customers. Increasingly, mystery shopping assessments are gathering subjective, as well as objective, data.

At the same time, it is also now accepted that different customers, when in different purchase environments, expect different levels of service. The underlying trend here is the growing need to identify and respond to these different service expectations.

Multiplying the number of different service expectations by the number of different elements within a service process could lead to unmanageable complexity. Thus another emerging trend is a 'two tier' approach to mystery shopping. Core service process elements are measured using only objective data. Process weaknesses thus identified are explored in greater detail through the use of more comprehensive sets of metrics, the results of which are enhanced and refined using subjective data.

Increasingly organisations are using mystery shopping assessments to 'audit' tactical activities, such as in-store promotions. The trend seen here is for assessors to be profiled for core brand allegiance rather than as mainstream customers profiled against geodemographic factors. In such cases, assessment findings are used to guide brand-reinforcing strategies rather than the development of the underlying service delivery process.

As the use of customer-centric performance measures becomes more commonplace (including central and local government), mystery shopping assessments have become more detailed, and require greater assessment skills. Today, leading mystery shopping agencies use IQCS-qualified assessors who have received generic training (e.g. in techniques of observation, memory retention and memory recall), in addition to project-specific training and briefing.

The key to service process 'quality' is designing systems that allow the right job to be done first time. This means identifying: what are the important features of the service delivery process (the roles of people, technology, facilities, etc.); what capacity the process provides; the extent to which it helps ensure quality standards; how it helps differentiate the service from competitors; how it meets customers' expectations; and if it provides barriers to entry (structural competitive advantage). It is managers' needs to identify these features, factors and influences that drive developments in mystery shopping.

Out of the mouths of babes

Marsha Hemingway
After working for Blue Chip companies such as Procter and Gamble, Marsha worked as a freelance moderator specialising in children's research. Now seen as a leading specialist in this area, she has also developed specialisms in new product development for the food and drink industry. In 1995, Good Sense Research was set to combine consumer science skills and develop sensory techniques for product development. Marsha is the Managing Director of Good Sense Research, she also works as an independent moderator on stand-alone qualitative research projects.

MARSHA HEMINGWAY

In the 1990s, children from a very young age tend to know what they like, but have difficulty in explaining why. As they move through the maturation process, their communication skills gradually improve to help them express their reasons, but the initial impact of 'I like it' or 'I don't like it' does not deviate.

It is important for products to have street cred and be visually attractive in children's terms, because children can generate sales through pester power. Products must also deliver, i.e. they must taste good/feel comfy/help you 'run faster'.

The researcher is challenged to discover methodologies to generate measurable responses in all product fields connected to children. The child researcher must help the child to explain the reasons behind their definitive choices by providing them with scenario, tools or games. The use of projective techniques and avoidance of direct questioning is paramount.

Young children aged three, four or five are easily tired and switch off if they do not understand. Six- and seven-year-olds are inventive and will simply make it up if they feel pressured to answer. Eight- and nine-year-olds may demand more and more information from you before answering and 10–11-year-olds may lie just for the hell of it. Although this is a sweeping generalisation, it serves the purpose of outlining the fundamental problems in interviewing children. Not only are there a number of age-specific issues, but the gender difference immediately doubles this figure.

In devising appropriate methodologies, the researcher must be cognisant of the stages of development and commensurate verbal skills, motor abilities and concentration spans.

Each project must be carefully assessed to determine the variables and each one set up with a series of different 'measurements'. We recommend each issue in question is presented to the child using up to three varying projective techniques. This acts as a double check to ensure that the child understands the issue as we set it and that we understand their responses as they were intended.

Apparently simple expressions can be wrongly interpreted with devastating effects. For example, the phrase, 'Are you in the pink?' meaning 'feeling good' was misunderstood, as was the phrase 'Are you green?' meaning 'feeling jealous'. However, the phrase 'Are you a little lemon?' meaning to be 'off colour', to kids meant 'gay'!

Drawing pictures, telling stories into cassette recorders and role play are all well-known techniques for qualitative research. Increasingly, we need to find appropriate scales for quantitative research. Various exercises utilising post boxes, smiley faces and frustration scales have been successfully developed to help children make their choices more obvious.

In toy research, a basic problem is to understand how 'good' the winning is (in some games it is not all that clear!). At Waddington Games, we play tested board games by running teams side by side with frequent whistle blowing to make children 'change sides'. The uproar when they were winning and did not want to change sides was an excellent indicator of how well the game was going.

When play-testing Scalextric, the critical element was to balance the frustration experienced when the cars flew off the track with the frustration experienced when the cars were 'fixed' to the track and therefore never crashed (deemed to be 'boring'). So we invented a scale for frustration linked to 'head banging'!

The Get Set! range of craft kits was launched after extensive research among children. Initial exploratory research indicated that craft kits currently on the market were too 'adult', with complex instructions in a small typeface and featuring finished products on the lid that children could not possibly achieve. To this audience the craft kit was synonymous with failure – failure to achieve, failure to satisfy and disappointment for both the child and a feeling of having let down the purchaser, i.e. mum.

After considerable home trial and observed play sessions, the strategy for the Get Set range was established – to offer at least three levels of achievement for each product:

1 a simple basic result easily achieved by a young or less able older child;
2 a sophisticated end result to motivate or aim for;
3 an intermediate level.

The box should look attractive when opened – not simple a few items loosely packed. The 'ingredients' should be items not generally available in the home, so that mums felt the purchase was worthwhile. The overall pack designs needed to be modern and clearly demonstrate the contents. Several pack designs were rejected by children who described them as 'one by people who grew up in the sixties' and 'how they [adults] remember their own childhood – not like today'.

The results were quantified in Saturday Workshop sessions. This scenario provides researchers with the opportunity to pre-recruit large numbers of children in hour-long sessions with trained observers and video cameras. The use of scales pre-tested to generate response to the stimuli leads to detailed quantitative analysis and fast turnaround of results.

The debate of who the decision-maker is continues and varies with product field. In working on children's shoes, we have generated a mathematical model to provide weightings for synergy in mum/child responses – amazingly different between mums of boys and mums of girls. This technique has also worked with clothing for children.

In food testing, 'yuks', 'ughs' and 'yums' are easy to extract, but the product development managers require finer detail and more specific flavour responses. We found ways to adapt our standard sensory analysis so that children are first 'coached' in flavour/texture descriptors using various product trials and scale illustrations. Currently, we are working on direct data entry using various child-orientated computer-generated rankings.

The research structures chosen for child research are consistent with the standard practice for all market researchers, but within this framework specific techniques are required that allow for the varying abilities of children to communicate. Pre-planning is critical to isolate the variables and providing task completion exercises in a controlled environment provides accurate and useful data. The skill of the researcher is then challenged to adapt the wealth of information provided into a results package that is meaningful to the client; after all, what can you do with the information that the 'spacehopper is a socially acceptable masturbatory technique'?

The key to product testing is to match the child's imagination and creativity while always ensuring that techniques are scientifically based, reproducible and consistently applied.

Originally published in *Research*, February 1999, pp. 50–51.

Part III

DATA COLLECTION, PREPARATION AND ANALYSIS

This part presents a practical and managerially oriented discussion of fieldwork, the fourth step in the marketing research process. We offer several guidelines for interviewer training, supervision, and conducting interviews. When the field work is complete, the researcher moves on to data preparation and analysis, the fifth step of the marketing research process. In this step we emphasise the importance and discuss the process of preparing quantitative data to make them suitable for analysis. Then we describe the various quantitative data analysis techniques. We cover not only the basic techniques of frequency distribution, cross-tabulation and hypothesis testing, but also the commonly used multivariate techniques of analysis of variance and regression. Finally, we describe the more advanced techniques: discriminant, factor, and cluster analysis, as well as multidimensional scaling and conjoint analysis. In the discussion of each statistical techniques, the emphasis is on explaining the procedure, interpreting the results, and managerial implications, rather than on statistical elegance.

Chapter 15

Fieldwork

The key to fieldwork is investing in the selection, training, supervision, and evaluation of fieldworkers

OBJECTIVES

After reading this chapter, the student should be able to:

1 describe the fieldwork process and explain the selecting, training and supervising of fieldworkers, validating fieldwork and evaluating fieldworkers;
2 discuss the training of fieldworkers in making the initial contact, asking the questions, probing, recording the answers and terminating the interview;
3 discuss supervising fieldworkers in terms of quality control and editing, sampling control, control of cheating and central office control;
4 describe evaluating fieldworkers in areas of cost and time, response rates, quality of interviewing and the quality of data;
5 explain the issues related to fieldwork when conducting international marketing research;
6 discuss ethical aspects of fieldwork.

OVERVIEW

Fieldwork is a vital process, helping to generate sound marketing research data. During this phase, fieldworkers make contact with potential respondents, administer the questionnaires or observation forms, record the data, and turn in the completed forms for processing. A personal interviewer administering questionnaires door to door, an interviewer intercepting shoppers in the street, a telephone interviewer calling from a central location, a worker mailing questionnaires from an office, an observer counting customers in a particular section of a store, and others involved in data collection and supervision of the process are all fieldworkers.

The marketing researcher faces two major problems when managing fieldwork operations. First of all, fieldwork should be carried out in a consistent manner so that regardless of who administers a questionnaire, the same process is adhered to. This is vital to allow comparisons between all completed questionnaires. Second, fieldworkers to some extent have to approach and motivate potential respondents in a manner that sets the correct purpose for a study and motivates the respondent to spend time answering the questions properly. This cannot be done in a 'robotic' manner, it requires good communication skills and an amount of empathy with respondents, but could be interpreted as a means to bias responses. These two problems may be seen as conflicting, but for the marketing researcher, fieldwork management means resolving these conflicts for each individual data gathering process. This makes fieldwork an essential task in the generation of sound research data.

This chapter describes the nature of fieldwork and the general fieldwork/data collection process. This process involves selecting, training and supervising fieldworkers, validating fieldwork, and evaluating fieldworkers. We briefly discuss fieldwork in the context of international marketing research and identify the relevant ethical issues. To begin, we illustrate the role of fieldwork within the marketing research process with an example detailing fieldwork activities across four European countries.

EXAMPLE

Americanism unites Europeans[1]

An image study conducted by Research International, a British market research company, showed that despite unification of the European market, European consumers still tend to favour American products. The survey was conducted in Britain, Germany, Italy and the Netherlands. In each country, local interviewers and supervisors were used because it was felt they would be able to identify better with the respondents. The fieldworkers, however, were trained extensively and supervised closely to ensure quality results and to minimise the variability in country-to-country results due to differences in interviewing procedures.

A total of 6724 personal interviews were conducted. Some of the findings were that Europeans gave US products high marks for being innovative and some countries also regarded them as fashionable and of high quality. Interestingly, France, usually considered anti-American, also emerged as pro-American. Among the 1034 French consumers surveyed, 40 per cent considered US products fashionable and 38 per cent believed that they were innovative, whereas 15 per cent said US products were of high quality. In addition, when asked what nationality they preferred for a new company in their area, a US company was the first choice. These findings were comparable and consistent across the four countries. A key to the discovery of these findings was the use of local fieldworkers and extensive training and supervision which resulted in high-quality data. ■

This example illustrates the importance of fieldwork in the context of the process turning research questions into marketing information that can be relied upon.

THE NATURE OF FIELDWORK

Marketing research data are rarely collected by the persons who design the research. Researchers have two major options for collecting their data: they can develop their own organisations or they can contract with a fieldwork agency. In either case, data collection involves the use of some kind of field force. The field force may operate either in the field (personal in-home or in-office, street interview, computer-assisted personal interviewing, and observation) or from an office (telephone and mail and electronic mail surveys). The fieldworkers who collect the data typically may have little formal marketing research or marketing training. Their training primarily focuses upon the essential tasks of selecting the correct respondents, motivating them to take part in the research, eliciting the correct answers from them, accurately recording the answers and conveying those answers for analyses. An appreciation of why these tasks fit into the overall context of conducting marketing research is important but it is not necessary for the fieldworker to be trained in the whole array of marketing research skills.

FIELDWORK AND DATA COLLECTION PROCESS

All fieldwork involves selecting, training and supervising persons who collect data.[2] The validation of fieldwork and the evaluation of fieldworkers are also parts of the process. Figure 15.1 represents a general framework for the fieldwork and data collection process. Even though we describe a general process, it should be recognised that the nature of fieldwork varies with the mode of data collection and that the relative emphasis on the different steps will be different for telephone, personal and mail interviews.

SELECTING FIELDWORKERS

The first step in the fieldwork process is the selection of fieldworkers. The researcher should (1) develop job specifications for the project, taking into account the mode of data collection; (2) decide what characteristics the fieldworkers should have; and (3) recruit appropriate individuals.[3] Interviewers' background characteristics, opinions, perceptions, expectations and attitudes can affect the responses they elicit.[4]

For example, the social acceptability of a fieldworker to the respondent may affect the quality of data obtained, especially in personal interviewing. Researchers generally agree that the more characteristics the interviewer and the respondent have in common, the greater the probability of a successful interview, as illustrated in the following example.

EXAMPLE

Searching for common ground[5]

In a survey dealing with emotional well-being and mental health, older interviewers got better cooperation from older respondents than younger interviewers, and this performance appeared to be independent of years of experience. When the interviewer and the respondent were of the same race the cooperation rate was higher than when there was a mismatch on race. ■

Thus, to the extent possible, interviewers should be selected to match respondents' characteristics. The job requirements will also vary with the nature of the problem and the type of data collection method. But there are some general qualifications of fieldworkers:

- *Healthy*. Fieldwork can be strenuous, and workers must have the stamina required to do the job.
- *Outgoing*. Interviewers should be able to establish rapport with respondents. They should be able to relate quickly to strangers.

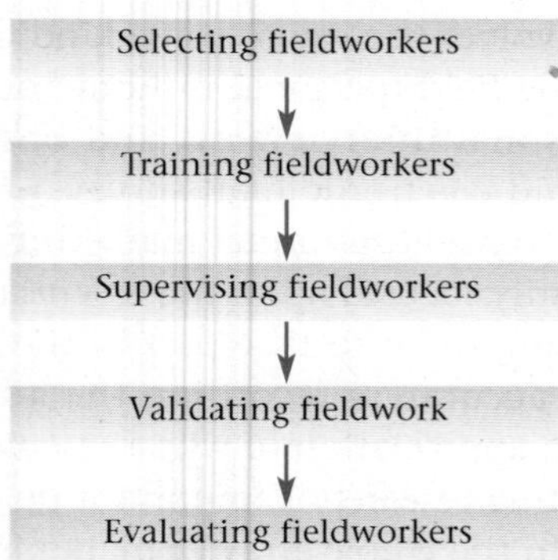

Figure 15.1 Fieldwork/data collection process

- *Communicative*. Effective speaking, observation and listening skills are a great asset.
- *'Pleasant' appearance*. If a fieldworker's physical appearance is unusual (from the respondents' perspective), the data collected may be biased.
- *Educated*. Interviewers must have good reading and writing skills.
- *Experienced*. Experienced interviewers are likely to do a better job in following instructions, obtaining respondent cooperation, and conducting the interview, as illustrated in the following example.

EXAMPLE

Your experience counts[6]

Research has found the following effects of interviewer experience on the interviewing process.

- Inexperienced interviewers are more likely to commit coding errors, to misrecord responses, and to fail to probe.
- Inexperienced interviewers have a particularly difficult time filling quotas of respondents.
- Inexperienced interviewers have larger refusal rates. They also accept more 'don't know' responses and refusals to answer individual questions. ■

TRAINING FIELDWORKERS

Training fieldworkers is critical to the quality of data collected. Training may be conducted in person at a central location or, if the interviewers are geographically dispersed, by mail. Training ensures that all interviewers administer the questionnaire in the same manner so that the data can be collected uniformly. Training should cover making the initial contact, asking the questions, probing, recording the answers and terminating the interview.[7]

Making the initial contact

The initial contact can result in cooperation or the loss of potential respondents.[8] It also sets the potential respondent in a 'frame of mind' to answer subsequent questions. Thus interviewers should be trained to make opening remarks that will convince potential respondents that their participation is important. They should also motivate potential respondents to reflect properly upon the questions posed to them and to answer honestly.

Asking the questions

Even a slight change in the wording, sequence, or manner in which a question is asked can distort its meaning and bias the response.[9] Asking questions is an art. Training in asking questions can yield high dividends in eliminating potential sources of bias. Changing the phrasing or order of questions during the interview can make significant differences in the response obtained. The following are guidelines for asking questions in a consistent manner:[10]

1. Be thoroughly familiar with the purpose of the questionnaire.
2. Be thoroughly familiar with the structure of the questionnaire.
3. Ask the questions in the order in which they appear in the questionnaire.
4. Use the exact wording given in the questionnaire.
5. Read each question slowly.

6 Repeat questions that are not understood.
7 Ask every applicable question.
8 Follow instructions, working through any filter questions, and probe carefully.

Probing

Probing
A motivational technique used when asking survey questions to induce the respondents to enlarge on, clarify, or explain their answers and to help the respondents focus on the specific content of the interview.

Probing is intended to motivate respondents to enlarge on, clarify or explain their answers. Probing also helps respondents focus on the specific content of the interview and provide only relevant information. Probing should not introduce any bias. An example of the effect of interviewer bias comes from a survey in which one of the authors helped in data analysis (but not in the management of the whole research process!). The survey related to bread and cake buying habits with one particular question focusing upon 'large cakes' that respondents had bought over the previous 12 months. In analysing the data a percentage had replied '*Christmas cake*'. When analysed further, all the respondents who said '*Christmas cake*' had been interviewed by the same interviewer. The conclusion from this analysis was that the interviewer in question had used their own probe to make the interview process work. None of the other interviewers had used this probe which meant there was an inconsistent approach in eliciting answers from respondents. The paradox faced by the survey designers in this example was that the 'rogue' interviewer *may* have used a probe that elicited a true representation of large cake purchasing, the other interviewers consistently failing to draw out a 'true' response.

To help in the process of probing, the following list details are some commonly used techniques.[11]

1 *Repeating the question.* Repeating the question in the same words can be effective in eliciting a response.
2 *Repeating the respondent's reply.* Respondents can be stimulated to provide further comments by repeating verbatim their replies. This can be done as the interviewer records the replies.
3 *Using a pause or silent probe.* A silent probe, or an expectant pause or look, can cue the respondent to provide a more complete response. The silence should not become embarrassing, however.
4 *Boosting or reassuring the respondent.* If the respondent hesitates, the interviewer should reassure the respondent with comments such as, 'There are no right or wrong answers. We are just trying to get your opinions'. If the respondent needs an explanation of a word or phrase, the interviewer should not offer an interpretation, unless written instructions to do so have been provided. Rather, the responsibility for the interpretation should be returned to the respondent. This can be done with a comment such as, 'Just whatever it means to you'.
5 *Eliciting clarification.* The respondent's motivation to cooperate with the interviewer and provide complete answers can be aroused with a question: 'I don't quite understand what you mean by that. Could you please tell me a little more?'
6 *Using objective or neutral questions or comments.* The following example provides several examples of the common questions or comments used as probes.[12] Corresponding abbreviations are also provided. The interviewer should record the abbreviations on the questionnaire in parentheses next to the question asked.

EXAMPLE

Commonly used probes and abbreviations

Standard interviewer's probe	Abbreviation
Any other reason?	(AO?)
Any others?	(Other?)
Anything else?	(AE or Else?)
Could you tell me more about your thinking on that?	(Tell more)
How do you mean?	(How mean?)
Repeat question	(RQ)
What do you mean?	(What mean?)
Which would be closer to the way you feel?	(Which closer?)
Why do you feel this way?	(Why?)
Would you tell me what you have in mind?	(What in mind?)

The above list seems straightforward but there are hidden dangers. For example probing '*why*' respondents behave in a particular manner or feel about a particular issue takes the interview into the realms of the qualitative interview. Compare the context of the street interview with a short structured questionnaire to the context of the qualitative interview with a questioning approach structured to the respondent and where a greater amount of rapport may be developed. The latter scenario is much more conducive to eliciting '*why*' respondents behave or feel as they do. The simple question '*why*' is an example of a seemingly simple question that can create many problems of consistency in fieldwork. In the greater majority of circumstances, '*why*' should be treated as a qualitative issue.

Recording the answers

Although recording respondent answers seems simple, several mistakes are common.[13] All interviewers should use the same format and conventions to record the interviews and edit completed interviews. Although the rules for recording answers to structured questions vary with each specific questionnaire, the general rule is to check the box that reflects the respondent's answer. The general rule for recording answers to unstructured questions is to record the responses verbatim. The following guidelines help to record answers to unstructured questions.

1 Record responses during the interview.
2 Use the respondent's own words.
3 Do not summarise or paraphrase the respondent's answers.
4 Include everything that pertains to the question objectives.
5 Include all probes and comments.
6 Repeat the response as it is written down.

Terminating the interview

The interview should not be closed before all the information is obtained. Any spontaneous comments the respondent offers after all the formal questions have been asked should be recorded. The interviewer should answer the respondent's questions about the project. The respondent should be left with a positive feeling about the interview. It is important to thank the respondent and express appreciation.

The Association of Market Survey Organisations (AMSO) publishes a 'Thank You' pamphlet that can be handed out to respondents who have taken part in an interview. As well as thanking respondents for their cooperation, it serves the purpose of educating respondents about the nature and purpose of marketing research, distinguishing marketing research from 'sugging' and 'frugging' as explained in Chapter 1.

The pamphlet explains why the respondent was chosen, the manner in which the interview was conducted and the purpose of marketing research interviewing. The following example presents extracts from the AMSO pamphlet.

EXAMPLE

Your time has been of great value. Thank you!

Thank you, for taking the time to give this interview; we hope you enjoyed it. Your interviewer is professionally trained by the company for which he/she works, a company which belongs to the Association of Market Survey Organisations. The Association exists to ensure that its members maintain the highest professional standards of market research. Your interviewer carries an identity card which guarantees they are a genuine market researcher.
AND ...
The way in which you were interviewed. In order to make sure that a representative sample was interviewed you may have been asked certain questions about your age, occupation, income and other decriptive details. These questions will be used in the research analysis to check the sample against other statistical information.

The questionnaire which the interviewer used will have been carefully constructed and tested by experienced researchers. The interviewer will have been instructed to read out the questions exactly as they are printed, and is not allowed to change the wording or give a personal opinion. These precautions are taken to ensure that your answers are not influenced in any way by the interviewer. ■

To encapsulate the process of interviewer training, the following list summarises the nature and scope of areas in which a marketing research interviewer should be trained.

1 The marketing research process: how a study is developed, implemented and reported.
2 The importance of the interviewer to this process; the need for honesty, objectivity, organisational skills and professionalism.
3 Confidentiality of the respondent and the client.
4 Familiarity with marketing research terminology.
5 The importance of following the exact wording and recording responses verbatim.
6 The purpose and use of probing and clarifying techniques.
7 The reason for and use of classification and respondent information questions.
8 A review of samples of instructions and questionnaires.
9 The importance of the respondent's positive feelings about survey research.

Conversely, marketing researchers should be trained in the 'experience' of gathering data in the field with a practical knowledge of what works in terms of:

- motivating potential respondents to take part in a survey,
- questions that will elicit the required data,
- probes that can be consistently applied,
- an interview process that does not confuse or cause boredom in the respondent.

SUPERVISING FIELDWORKERS

Supervising fieldworkers means making sure that they are following the procedures and techniques in which they were trained. Supervision involves quality control and editing, sampling control, control of cheating, and central office control.[14]

Quality control and editing

Quality control of fieldworkers requires checking to see if the field procedures are being properly implemented.[15] If any problems are detected, the supervisor should discuss them with the fieldworkers and provide additional training if necessary. To understand the interviewers' problems related to a specific study, the supervisors should also do some interviewing. Supervisors should collect questionnaires and other forms and edit them daily. They should examine the questionnaires to make sure all appropriate questions have been completed, that unsatisfactory or incomplete answers have not been accepted, and that the writing is legible.

Supervisors should also keep a record of hours worked and expenses. This will allow a determination of the cost per completed interview, whether the job is moving on schedule, and if any interviewers are having problems.

Sampling control

Sampling control
An aspect of supervising that ensures that the interviewers strictly follow the sampling plan rather than select sampling units based on convenience or accessibility.

An important aspect of supervision is **sampling control**, which attempts to ensure that the interviewers are strictly following the sampling plan rather than selecting sampling units based on convenience or accessibility.[16] Interviewers tend to avoid homes, offices, people (sampling units) that they perceive as difficult or undesirable. If the sampling unit is not at home for example, interviewers may be tempted to substitute the next available unit rather than call back. Interviewers sometimes stretch the requirements of quota samples. For example, a 58-year-old person may be placed in the 46-to-55 category and interviewed to fulfil quota requirements.

To control these problems, supervisors should keep daily records of the number of calls made, the number of not-at-homes, the number of refusals, the number of completed interviews for each interviewer, and the total for all interviewers under their control.

CATI Systems enable on-line supervisors to monitor the screen as well as the conversation

Central office control

Supervisors provide quality and cost-control information to the central office so that a total progress report can be maintained. In addition to the controls initiated in the field, other controls may be added at the central office to identify potential problems. Central office control includes tabulation of quota variables, important demographic characteristics, and answers to key variables.

VALIDATING FIELDWORK

An interviewer may falsify part of an answer to make it acceptable or may fake answers. The most blatant form of cheating occurs when the interviewer falsifies the entire questionnaire, merely filling in fake answers without contacting the respondent. Cheating can be minimised through proper training, supervision and validation of fieldwork.[17] One means to achieve this is by asking respondents to give their names and telephone numbers at the end of an interview. This is used to allow supervisors to randomly select respondents, to telephone them to ensure that the interview was conducted which is a key part of the validation of fieldwork. Validating fieldwork means verifying that the fieldworkers are submitting authentic interviews. To validate the study, the supervisors call 10 to 25 per cent of the respondents to inquire whether the fieldworkers actually conducted the interviews. The supervisors ask about the length and quality of the interview, reaction to the interviewer, and basic demographic data. The demographic information is cross-checked against the information reported by the interviewers on the questionnaires. The major drawback of this approach is that respondents may not trust interviewers with a name and telephone number, perhaps believing that it is to be used to generate a sale, i.e. it can be confused with a 'sugging' or 'frugging' approach.

EVALUATING FIELDWORKERS

It is important to evaluate fieldworkers to provide them with feedback on their performance as well as to identify the better fieldworkers and build a better, high-quality field force. The evaluation criteria should be clearly communicated to the fieldworkers during their training. The evaluation of fieldworkers should be based on the criteria of cost and time, response rates, quality of interviewing, and quality of data.[18]

Cost and time

Interviewers can be compared in terms of the total cost (salary and expenses) per completed interview. If the costs differ by city size, comparisons should be made only among fieldworkers working in comparable cities. Fieldworkers should also be evaluated on how they spend their time. Time should be broken down into categories such as actual interviewing, travel and administration.

Response rates

It is important to monitor response rates on a timely basis so that corrective action can be taken if these rates are too low.[19] Supervisors can help interviewers with an inordinate number of refusals by listening to the introductions they use and providing immediate feedback. When all the interviews are over, different fieldworkers' percentage of refusals can be compared to identify the more able interviewers.

Quality of interviewing

To evaluate interviewers on the quality of interviewing, the supervisor must directly observe the interviewing process. The supervisor can do this in person or the held worker can record the interview on tape. The quality of interviewing should be evaluated in terms of (1) the appropriateness of the introduction, (2) the precision with which the fieldworker asks questions, (3) the ability to probe in an unbiased manner, (4) the ability to ask sensitive questions, (5) interpersonal skills displayed during the interview, and (6) the manner in which the interview is terminated.

Quality of data

The completed questionnaires of each interviewer should be evaluated for the quality of data. Some indicators of quality data are that (1) the recorded data are legible; (2) all instructions, including skip patterns, are followed; (3) the answers to unstructured questions are recorded verbatim; (4) the answers to unstructured questions are meaningful and complete enough to be coded; and (5) item non-response occurs infrequently.

INTERNATIONAL MARKETING RESEARCH

The selection, training, supervision and evaluation of fieldworkers is critical in international marketing research. Local fieldwork agencies are unavailable in many countries. Therefore, it may be necessary to recruit and train local fieldworkers or import trained foreign workers. The use of local fieldworkers is desirable, because they are familiar with the local language and culture. They can create an appropriate climate for the interview and sensitivity to the concerns of the respondents. Extensive training may be required and close supervision may be necessary. As observed in many countries, interviewers tend to help the respondent with the answers and select household or sampling units based on personal considerations rather than the sampling plan. Validation of fieldwork is critical. Proper application of fieldwork procedures can greatly reduce these difficulties and result in consistent and useful findings.

ETHICS IN MARKETING RESEARCH

Marketing researchers and fieldworkers should make respondents feel comfortable participating in research activities. This is vital in order to elicit the correct responses for a specific project but also more broadly for the health of the marketing research industry. A respondent who feels that their trust has been abused, who found an interview to be cumbersome and boring or who fails to see the purpose of a particular study, is less likely to participate in further marketing research efforts. Collectively, the marketing research industry has the responsibility to look after their most precious assets – willing and honest respondents.

Many marketing researchers do not meet respondents face to face, or if they have done it may have occurred many years ago. Not being in the field, marketing researchers can lose an awareness of what it is like to actually collect data in the field. Without this awareness, research designs that on paper seem feasible, in the field are difficult to administer in a consistent manner. If there are problems in collecting data in the field it may not always be attributable to the training and quality of fieldworkers, the blame may lie with the research designer. The marketing researcher therefore, has an ethical responsibility to the fieldworker and the respondent. Their responsibility lies in an awareness of the process that the fieldworker and respondent go through in the field for each individual piece of research they design. Poor research design can leave fieldworkers facing very disgruntled respondents and can cause great damage.

Good marketing researchers have an awareness of their responsibilities to fieldworkers and respondents. The marketing researcher may take great care in understanding the difficulties of collecting data in the field. They may go to great pains to ensure that the data gathering process works well for the fieldworker and respondent alike. The fieldworker may have been told about the purpose of the study, the purpose of particular questions, the means to select and approach respondents and the means to correctly elicit responses from respondents. However, fieldworkers may behave in an unethical manner. They may cut corners in terms of selecting the correct respondents, posing questions and probes and in recording responses. In such circumstances the fieldworker can cause much damage to an individual study and to the long-term relationship with potential respondents. Thus it becomes a vital part of fieldworker training to demonstrate the ethical responsibilities they have in collecting data.

The use of codes of conduct and guidelines can help fieldworkers to be aware of their responsibilities. However, good marketing researchers who foster an ethical approach to the use of their fieldworkers create the atmosphere whereby such codes and guidelines work in practice.

INTERNET AND COMPUTER APPLICATIONS

Regardless of which method is used for interviewing (telephone, personal, mail or electronic), the Internet can play a valuable role in all the phases of fieldwork: selection, training, supervision, validation and evaluation of field workers. As far as selection is concerned, interviewers can be located, interviewed and hired by using the Internet. This process can be initiated, for example, by posting job vacancies notices for interviewers at the company Web site, bulletin boards and other suitable locations. While this would confine the search to only Internet-savvy interviewers, this may well be a qualification to look for in the current marketing research environment.

Similarly, the Internet with its multimedia capabilities can be a good supplementary tool for training the fieldworkers in all aspects of interviewing. Training in this manner can complement personal training programmes and add value to the process. Supervision is enhanced by facilitating communication between the supervisors and the interviewers via email and secured chatrooms. Central office control can be strengthened by posting progress reports, quality and cost control information on a secured location at a Web site, so that it is easily available to all the relevant parties.

Validation of fieldwork, especially for personal and telephone interviews, can be easily accomplished for those respondents who have an email address or access to the Internet. These respondents can be sent a short verification survey by email or asked to visit a Web site where the survey is posted. Finally, the evaluation criteria can be communicated to the field workers during the training stage by using the Internet, and performance feedback can also be provided to them by using this medium.

Microcomputers and mainframes can be used in fieldwork for respondent selection, interviewer planning, supervision and control. Computers can also be used to manage mailing lists. For example, mailing lists can be sorted according to postal codes, geographical regions (which may include drive times from the centre of a city or from a shopping centre) or other pre-specified respondent

Call disposition
Call disposition records the outcome of an interview call.

characteristics. Computers can generate accurate and timely reports for supervision and control purposes. These include quota reports, **call disposition** reports, incidence reports, top-line reports of respondent data, and interviewer productivity reports. Automatic reporting enhances supervision and control and increases the overall quality of data collection. Because less time is spent compiling reports, more time can be spent on data interpretation and on supervision.

SUMMARY

Researchers have two major options in the generation of sound research data: developing their own organisations or contracting with fieldwork agencies. In either case, data collection involves the use of a field force. Fieldworkers should be healthy, outgoing, communicative, pleasant, educated and experienced. They should be trained in important aspects of fieldwork, including making the initial contact, asking the questions, probing, recording the answers, and terminating the interview. Supervising fieldworkers involves quality control and editing, sampling control, control of cheating, and central office control. Validating fieldwork can be accomplished by calling 10 to 25 per cent of those who have been identified as interviewees and inquiring whether the interviews took place. Fieldworkers should be evaluated on the basis of cost and time, response rates, quality of interviewing, and quality of data collection.

Fieldwork should be carried out in a consistent manner so that regardless of who administers a questionnaire, the same process is adhered to. This is vital to allow comparisons between collected data. Fieldworkers to some extent have to approach and motivate potential respondents in a manner that sets the correct purpose for a study and motivates the respondent to spend time answering the questions properly. This cannot be done in a 'robotic' manner; it requires good communication skills and an amount of empathy with respondents. This makes the issue of managing fieldwork an essential task in the generation of sound research data.

Selecting, training, supervising and evaluating fieldworkers is even more critical in international marketing research because local fieldwork agencies are not available in many countries. Ethical issues include making the respondents feel comfortable in the data collection process so that their experience is positive.

QUESTIONS AND PROBLEMS

1. Why do marketing researchers need to use fieldworkers?
2. Describe the fieldwork/data collection process.
3. What qualifications should fieldworkers possess?
4. What are the guidelines for asking questions?
5. Describe and illustrate the differences between probing in a survey and in a depth interview.
6. Evaluate what may be done to help interviewers probe correctly and consistently?
7. Outline the advantages and disadvantages of the interviewer developing a rapport with respondents.
8. How should the answers to unstructured questions be recorded?
9. How should the fieldworker terminate the interview?
10. What aspects are involved in the supervision of fieldworkers?

11 How can respondent selection problems be controlled?

12 What is validation of fieldwork? How is this done?

13 Describe the criteria that should be used for evaluating fieldworkers.

14 Describe the major sources of error related to fieldwork.

15 Comment on the following field situations, making recommendations for corrective action.
   (a) One of the interviewers has an excessive rate of refusals in in-home personal interviewing.
   (b) In a CATI situation, many phone numbers are giving a busy signal during the first dialling attempt.
   (c) An interviewer reports that at the end of the interviews, many respondents asked if they had answered the questions correctly.
   (d) While validating the fieldwork, a respondent reports that she cannot remember being interviewed over the telephone, but the interviewer insists that the interview was conducted.

NOTES

1 Wentz, L., 'Poll: Europe Favors US Products', *Advertising Age* (23 September 1991).

2 Fowler Jr, E. and Mangione, T.W., 'The Role of Interviewer Training and Supervision in Reducing Effects on Survey Data', in *Proceedings of the American Statistical Association Meetings, Survey Research Methods Section* (Washington, DC: American Statistical Association, 1983), 124–28; and Andrews, L., 'Interviewers: Recruiting, Selecting, Training, and Supervising', in Farber, R., (ed.), *Handbook of Marketing Research* (New York: McGraw-Hill, 1974), 124–32.

3 Groves, R.M. and Magilavy, L.J., 'Measuring and Explaining Interviewer Effects in Centralized Telephone Surveys', *Public Opinion Quarterly* 50 (Summer 1986), 251–66.

4 Coulter, P.B., 'Race of Interviewer Effects on Telephone Interviews', *Public Opinion Quarterly* 46 (Summer 1982), 278–84; and Singer, E., Frankel, M.R. and Glassman, M.B., 'The Effect of Interviewer Characteristics and Expectations on Response', *Public Opinion Quarterly* 41 (Spring 1983), 68–83.

5 Barker, R.E., 'A Demographic Profile of Marketing Research Interviewers', *Journal of the Market Research Society* 29 (July 1987), 279–92.

6 Collins, M. and Butcher, B. 'Interviewer and Clustering Effects in an Attitude Survey', *Journal of the Market Research Society* 25 (January 1983), 39–58; and Johnson, R.E.Q., 'Pitfalls in Research: The Interview as an Illustrative Model', *Psychological Reports* 38 (1976), 3–17.

7 Guenzel, P.J., Berkmans, T.R. and Cannell, C.F., *General Interviewing Techniques* (Ann Arbor, MI: Institute for Social Research, 1983).

8 Miller, P.V. and Cannell, C.E., 'A Study of Experimental Techniques for Telephone Interviewing', *Public Opinion Quarterly* (Summer 1982), 250–67.

9 Bradburn, N.M. and Sudman, S., *Improving Interview Method and Questionnaire Design* (San Francisco: Jossey-Bass, 1979), 26.

10 This section follows closely the material in *Interviewer's Manual*, rev. edn (Ann Arbor: Survey Research Centre, Institute for Social Research, University of Michigan, 1976); and Guenzel, P.J., Berkmans, T.R. and Cannell, C.E., *General Interviewing Techniques* (Ann Arbor, MI: Institute for Social Research, 1983).

11 For an extensive treatment of probing, see *Interviewer's Manual*, rev. ed (Ann Arbor: Survey Research Centre, Institute for Social Research, University of Michigan, 1976), 15–19.

12 *Interviewer's Manual*, rev. edn (Ann Arbor: Survey Research Centre, Institute for Social Research, University of Michigan, 1976), 16. Reprinted by permission of the Institute for Social Research.

13 Morton-Williams, J. and Sykes, W., 'The Use of Interaction Coding and Follow-Up Interviews to Investigate Comprehension of Survey Questions', *Journal of the Market Research Society* 26 (April 1984), 109–27.

14 Fowler Jr, E.J. and Mangione, T.W., 'The Role of Interviewer Training and Supervision in Reducing Effects on Survey Data', in *Proceedings of the American Statistical Association Meetings, Survey Research Methods Section* (Washington, DC: American Statistical Association. 1983), 124–28.

15 Collins, M. and Butcher, B., 'Interviewer and Clustering Effects in an Attitude Survey', *Journal of the Market Research Society* 25 (January 1983), 39–58.

16 Czaja, R., Blair, J. and Sebestik, J.P., 'Respondent Selection in Telephone Survey: A Comparison of Three Techniques', *Journal of Marketing Research* (August 1982), 381–85.

17 Tull, D.S. and Richards, L.E., 'What Can Be Done about Interviewer Bias', in Sheth, J. (ed.), *Research in Marketing* (Greenwich, CT: JAI Press, 1980), pp. 143–62.

18 Two useful general sources are: Anderson, R., Kasper, J. and Frankel, M.R., *Total Survey Error* (San Francisco: Jossey-Bass, 1979); and Rothman, J. 'Acceptance Checks for Ensuring Quality in Research', *Journal of the Market Research Society* 22 (July 1980), 192–204.

19 'On the Definition of Response Rates', *CASRO Special Report* (Port Jefferson, NY: Council of American Survey Research Organisations, 1982).

Chapter 16

Data preparation

Care exercised at the data preparation stage can substantially enhance the quality of the statistical results

OBJECTIVES

After reading this chapter, the student should be able to:

1 discuss the nature and scope of data preparation and the data preparation process;
2 explain questionnaire checking and editing and the treatment of unsatisfactory responses by returning to the field, assigning missing values and discarding unsatisfactory responses;
3 describe the guidelines for coding questionnaires including the coding of structured and unstructured questions;
4 discuss the data cleaning process and the methods used to treat missing responses: substitution of a neutral value, imputed response, casewise deletion and pairwise deletion;
5 state the reasons for and methods of statistically adjusting data: weighting, variable re-specification and scale transformation;
6 describe the procedure for selecting a data analysis strategy and the factors influencing the process;
7 classify statistical techniques and give a detailed classification of univariate techniques as well as a classification of multivariate techniques;
8 understand the intra-cultural, pan-cultural, and cross-cultural approaches to data analysis in international marketing research;
9 identify the ethical issues related to data processing, particularly discarding of unsatisfactory responses, violation of the assumptions underlying the data analysis techniques, and evaluation and interpretation of results.

OVERVIEW

After the research problem has been defined and a suitable approach developed, an appropriate research design formulated and the field work conducted, the researcher can move to data preparation and analysis. This does not mean, however, that decisions related to data preparation and analysis occur after data has been collected. Before the raw data contained in the questionnaires can be subjected to statistical analysis, they must be converted into a form suitable for analysis. The suitable form and the means of analysis should be considered as a research design is developed. This ensures that the output of the analyses will satisfy the research objectives set for a particular project.

The care exercised in the data preparation phase has a direct effect upon the quality of statistical results and ultimately the support offered to marketing decision-makers. Paying inadequate attention to data preparation can seriously compromise statistical results, leading to biased findings and incorrect interpretation.

This chapter describes the data collection process, which begins with checking the questionnaires for completeness. Then, we discuss the editing of data and provide guidelines for handling illegible, incomplete, inconsistent, ambiguous or otherwise unsatisfactory responses. We also describe coding, transcribing and data cleaning, emphasising the treatment of missing responses and statistical adjustment of data. We discuss the selection of a data analysis strategy and classify statistical techniques. The intra-cultural, pan-cultural and cross-cultural approaches to data analysis in international marketing research are explained. Finally, the ethical issues related to data processing are identified with emphasis on discarding of unsatisfactory responses, violation of the assumptions underlying the data analysis techniques, and evaluation and interpretation of results.

We begin with an illustration of the data preparation process in the GlobalCash project.

GLOBALCASH PROJECT

Data preparation

In the GlobalCash project, the data were obtained by postal questionnaires. The questionnaires were edited by a supervisor as they were being returned from individual European countries by the respective business schools. The questionnaires were checked for incomplete, inconsistent and ambiguous responses. Questionnaires with problematic responses were queried with the respective business schools (who kept copies of the original questionnaires). In some circumstances, the business schools were asked to re-contact the respondents to clarify certain issues. Twenty questionnaires were discarded because the proportion of unsatisfactory responses was large. This resulted in a final sample size of 1075.

A codebook was developed for coding the questionnaires. Coding was extremely difficult given the large number of banks and banking software companies that operate throughout Europe, the number of different names these banks may be known by and the need for translation in certain open-ended questions. The data were transcribed directly into a survey analysis package via keypunching. The SNAP software used for data entry and analysis has a built-in error-check that identifies out-of-range responses. About 10 per cent of the data were verified for other keypunching errors. The data were cleaned by identifying logically inconsistent responses. Most of the rating information was obtained using five-point scales, so responses of 0, 6 and 7 were considered out of range and a code of 9 was assigned to missing responses. If an out-of-range response was keyed in, the SNAP software package did not allow any continuation of data entry; an audible warning was made. In statistically adjusting the data, dummy variables were created for the categorical variables. New variables that were composites of original variables were also created. Finally, a data analysis strategy was developed. ■

The GlobalCash example describes the various phases of the data preparation process. Note that the process is initiated while the fieldwork is still in progress. A systematic description of the data preparation process follows.

Table 16.3 Codes applicable to Question 57 in the GlobalCash survey

Country	Code	Country	Code	Country	Code
Australia	1	France	9	Norway	17
Austria	2	Germany	10	Portugal	18
Belgium	3	Greece	11	Spain	19
Canada	4	Ireland	12	Sweden	20
Channel Islands	5	Italy	13	Switzerland	21
Czech Republic	6	Japan	14	UK	22
Denmark	7	Luxembourg	15	USA	23
Finland	8	Netherlands	16	West Indies	24

Table 16.4 Example of a multiple choice question from the GlobalCash survey

Question 51 – During the next two years, which of the following changes does your company plan to make? (please tick appropriate boxes)

1	✓	Treasury function to be more centralised
2		Make more use of treasury vehicles
3		Move more towards an in-house bank
4		Out-source certain treasury functions – to banks
5	✓	Put domestic banking out to tender
6	✓	Make greater use of electronic banking
7		Treasury function to be more automated
8		Integrate more services under the treasury function
9	✓	Reduce number of people in the treasury function

In essence, each of the options presented in Question 51 is an individual 'yes' or 'no' question. In the example shown, the respondent has replied 'yes' to the first, fifth, sixth and ninth variables. This question would be coded as shown in Table 16.5. The 'ticks' above have been coded as a '1' to represent 'yes' and '0' as 'no'. The pattern in Table 16.4 is represented by record 1. Table 16.5 shows that a single question can have many variables. Besides the multiple choice question type, questions that bring together a number of rating and

Table 16.5 GlobalCash, Question 51 spreadsheet presentation

Individual fields in columns									
Variables	V642	V643	V644	V645	V646	V647	V648	V649	V650
Records in rows	Question 51								
1	1	0	0	0	1	1	0	0	1
2	1	1	0	0	0	1	1	0	0
3	0	0	1	1	1	0	0	0	0
4	1	1	0	0	1	0	1	1	1
…*n*	0	1	1	0	0	1	1	0	0

ranking scales contain a number of variables in each question. In the GlobalCash survey some questions listed 250 banks on a multiple choice basis which meant that single questions contained 250 variables or 250 individual 'yes' 'no' questions.

A summary of the whole questionnaire, showing the position of the fields and the key to all the codes used is called a codebook. Table 16.6 shows an extract from the GlobalCash codebook.

Codebook

Codebook
A book containing coding instructions and the necessary information about variables in the dataset.

A **codebook** contains instructions and the necessary information about variables in the dataset. A codebook guides the 'coders' in their work and helps the researcher identify and locate the variables properly. Even if the questionnaire has been pre-coded, it is helpful to prepare a formal codebook. As illustrated in Table 16.6, a codebook generally contains the following information: (1) variable number, (2) column number, (3) question name, (4) question number, (5) coding instructions.

Table 16.6 Extract from the GlobalCash survey codebook

Variable number	*Column number*	*Question name*	*Question number*	*Coding instructions*
v642 to v650	1245 to 1249	Plans over next 2 years	Q. 51	'1' for any box ticked '0' for a non-response
v651	1250	Treasury type	Q. 52	Subsidiary = '1' Country treasury = '2' Regional treasury = '3' European treasury = '4' Group treasury = '5' Missing value = '9'
v652	1251	Industry	Q. 53	Enter number as seen alongside ticked box. Missing value = '99'
v653	1252	World-wide sales	Q. 54a	Enter actual value in $US millions
v654	1253	Home sales	Q. 54b	Enter actual value in $US millions
v655	1254	Countries operate in	Q. 55	1 = '1' 2 to 5 = '2' 6 to 10 = '3' 11 to 15 = '4' over 15 = '5' Missing value = '9'
v656	1255	Position	Q. 56	Treasurer = '1' Finance director = '2' Accountant = '3' Chief executive = '4' Cash manager = '5' Other = '6' Missing value = '9'
v657	1256	Parent country	Q. 57	Australia = '1' Austria = '2' FULL LIST IN TABLE 16.3

Coding questions

The coding of structured questions, be they single or multiple choice, is relatively simple because the response options are predetermined. The researcher assigns a code for each response to each question and specifies the appropriate field or column in which it will appear; this is termed 'pre-coding'.[2] The coding of unstructured or open-ended questions is more complex; this is termed 'post-coding'.[3] Respondents' verbatim responses are recorded on the questionnaire. One option the researcher has is to go through all the completed questionnaires, list the verbatim responses and then develop and assign codes to these responses. Another option that is allowed on some data entry packages such as SNAP is to enter the verbatim responses directly onto the computer, allowing a print-off of the collective responses and codes to be assigned before all of the questionnaires have been entered. The coding process here is similar to the process of assigning codes in the analysis of qualitative data as described in Chapter 7. The verbatim responses to 1000 questionnaire responses may generate 1000 different answers. The words may be different but the essence of the response may mean that 20 issues have been addressed. The researcher decides what those 20 issues are, names the issues and assigns codes from 1 to 20, and then goes through all the 1000 questionnaires to enter the code alongside the verbatim response.

The following guidelines are suggested for coding unstructured questions and questionnaires in general.[4] Category codes should be mutually exclusive and collectively exhaustive. Categories are mutually exclusive if each response fits into one and only one category code. Categories should not overlap. Categories are collectively exhaustive if every response fits into one of the assigned category codes. This can be achieved by adding an additional category code of 'other' or 'none of the above'. An absolute maximum of 10% of responses should fall into the 'other' category; the researcher should strive to assign all responses into meaningful categories.

Category codes should be assigned for critical issues even if no one has mentioned them. It may be important to know that no one has mentioned a particular response. For example, a bank may be concerned about their new Web page design. In a question 'How did you learn about Credit Card X', the Web should be included as a distinct category, even if no respondents gave this as an answer.

Data should retain as much detail as possible. For example, if data on the exact number of trips made on commercial airlines by business travellers have been obtained, they should be coded as such rather than grouped into two category codes of 'infrequent flyers' and 'frequent flyers'. Obtaining information on the exact number of trips allows the researcher to later define categories of business travellers in several different ways. If the categories were pre-defined, the subsequent analyses of data would be limited to those categories.[5]

TRANSCRIBING

Transcribing data involves transferring the coded data from the questionnaires or coding sheets onto disks or magnetic tapes or more commonly, directly into computers by keypunching. If the data have been collected via CATI or CAPI, this step is unnecessary because the data are entered directly into the computer as they are collected. Besides keypunching, the data can be transferred by using mark sense forms, optical scanning, or computerised sensory analysis (see Figure 16.4). Mark sense forms require responses to be recorded in a pre-designated area coded for that response, and the data can then be read by a machine. Optical scanning involves direct machine reading of the codes and simultaneous transcription. A familiar example of optical scanning is the transcription of universal product code (UPC) data, scanned at supermarket checkout counters. Technological advances have resulted in computerised sensory analysis systems, which automate the data collection process. The questions appear on a computerised gridpad, and responses are recorded directly into the computer using a sensing device.

Except for CATI and CAPI, an original record exists which can be compared to what was either automatically read or keypunched. Errors can occur in an automatic read or keypunching process, and it is necessary to verify the dataset, or at least a portion of it, for keypunching errors.

A second operator re-punches the data from the coded questionnaires. The transcribed data from the two operators are compared record by record. Any discrepancy between the two sets of transcribed data is investigated to identify and correct for keypunching errors. Verification of the entire data set will double the time and cost of data transcription. Given the time and cost constraints, and that experienced keypunch operators are quite accurate, it is sufficient to verify only 10 to 25 per cent of the data. With automatically read data, the completed data set that has been read can be compared with original records. Again, a percentage may be selected and checks made to see what may have caused differences between the original record and the read data (e.g. respondents entering two ticks when only one was requested).

When CATI, CAPI or the Internet are employed, data are verified as they are collected. In the case of inadmissible responses, the computer will prompt the interviewer or respondent. In the case of admissible responses, the interviewer or the respondent can see the recorded response on the screen and verify it before proceeding.

The selection of a data transcription method is guided by the type of interviewing method used and the availability of equipment. If CATI, CAPI or the Internet are used, the data are entered directly into the computer. Keypunching via a computer terminal is most frequently used for ordinary telephone, in-home, street interviewing and traditional mail interviews. The use of computerised sensory analysis systems in personal interviews is increasing with the growing use of handheld computers, however. Optical scanning can be used in structured and repetitive surveys, and mark sense forms are used in special cases.

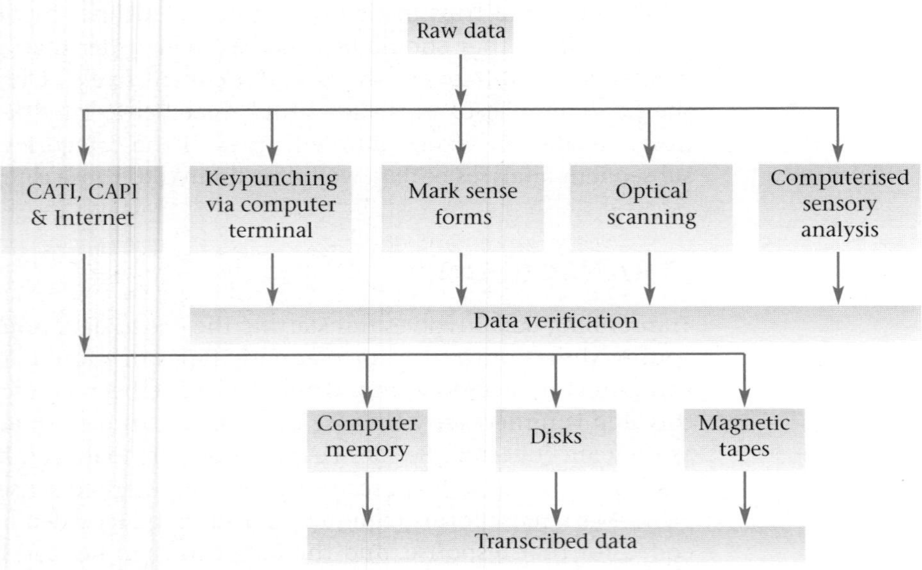

Figure 16.4
Data transcription

DATA CLEANING

Data cleaning
Thorough and extensive checks for consistency and treatment of missing responses.

Data cleaning includes consistency checks and treatment of missing responses. Even though preliminary consistency checks have been made during editing, the checks at this stage are more thorough and extensive, because they are made by computer.

Consistency checks

Consistency checks
A part of the data cleaning process that identifies data that are out of range, logically inconsistent, or have extreme values. Data with values not defined by the coding scheme are inadmissible.

Consistency checks identify data that are out of range, logically inconsistent, or have extreme values. Out-of-range data values are inadmissible and must be corrected. For example, respondents have been asked to express their degree of agreement with a series of lifestyle statements on a 1 to 5 scale. Assuming that 9 has been designated for missing values, data values of 0, 6, 7 and 8 are out of range. Computer packages can be programmed to identify out-of-range values for each variable and will not progress to another variable within a record until a value in the set range is entered. Other packages can be programmed to print out the respondent code, variable code, variable name, record number, column number and out-of-range value. This makes it easy to check each variable systematically for out-of-range values. The correct responses can be determined by going back to the edited and coded questionnaire.

Responses can be logically inconsistent in various ways. For example, a respondent may indicate that he charges long-distance calls to a calling card from a credit card company, although he does not have such a credit card. Or a respondent reports both unfamiliarity with and frequent usage of the same product. The necessary information (respondent code, variable code, variable name, record number, column number, and inconsistent values) can be printed to locate these responses and to take corrective action.

Finally, extreme values should be closely examined. Not all extreme values result from errors, but they may point to problems with the data. For example, in the GlobalCash survey, companies were asked how many banks they use for domestic business. Certain Italian companies recorded 70 or more banks when the mean for all respondents was around six. In these circumstances the extreme values can be identified and the actual figure validated in many cases by re-contacting the respondent or examining secondary data sources.

Consistency checks are extremely valuable in identifying data that are out of range, are logically inconsistent, or have extreme values

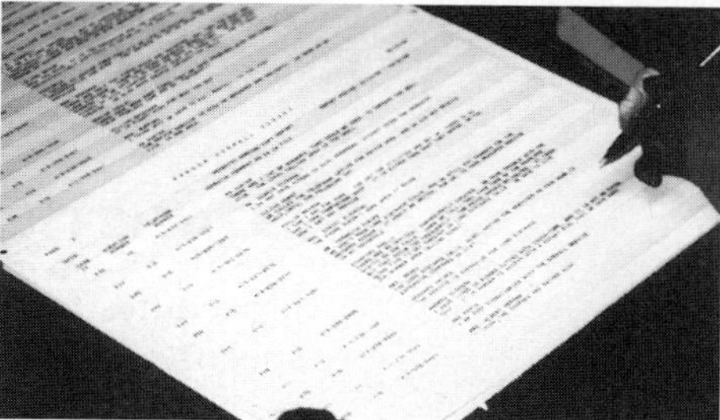

Treatment of missing responses

Missing responses
Values of a variable that are unknown because these respondents provided ambiguous answers to the question.

Missing responses represent values of a variable that are unknown either because respondents provided ambiguous answers or because their answers were not properly recorded. Treatment of missing responses poses problems, particularly if the proportion of missing responses is more than 10 per cent. The following options are available for the treatment of missing responses.[6]

Substitute a neutral value. A neutral value, typically the mean response to the variable, is substituted for the missing responses. Thus, the mean of the variable remains unchanged, and other statistics such as correlations are not affected much. Although this approach has some merit, the logic of substituting a mean value (say 4) for respondents who, if they had answered, might have used either high ratings (6 or 7) or low ratings (1 or 2) is questionable.[7]

Substitute an imputed response. The respondents' pattern of responses to other questions is used to impute or calculate a suitable response to the missing questions. The researcher attempts to infer from the available data the responses the individuals would have given if they had answered the questions. This can be done statistically by determining the relationship of the variable in question to other variables based on the available data. For example, product usage could be related to household size for respondents who have provided data on both variables. Given that respondent's household size, the missing product usage response for a respondent could then be calculated. This approach, however, requires considerable effort and can introduce serious bias. Sophisticated statistical procedures have been developed to calculate imputed values for missing responses.[8]

Casewise deletion
A method for handling missing values in which all cases or respondents with any missing values are not automatically discarded; rather, for each calculation, only the cases or respondents with complete responses are considered.

Casewise deletion. In casewise deletion, cases or respondents with any missing responses are discarded from the analysis. Because many respondents may have some missing responses, this approach could result in a small sample. Throwing away large amounts of data is undesirable because it is costly and time-consuming to collect data. Furthermore, respondents with missing responses could differ from respondents with complete responses in systematic ways. If so, casewise deletion could seriously bias the results.

Pairwise deletion. In pairwise deletion, instead of discarding all cases with any missing values, the researcher uses only the cases or respondents with complete responses for each calculation. As a result, different calculations in an analysis may be based on different sample sizes. This procedure may be appropriate when (1) the sample size is large, (2) there are few missing responses, and (3) the variables are not highly related. Yet this procedure can produce unappealing or even infeasible results.

The different procedures for the treatment of missing responses may yield different results, particularly when the responses are not missing at random and the variables are related. Hence, missing responses should be kept to a minimum. The researcher should carefully consider the implications of the various procedures before selecting a particular method for the treatment of non-response.

STATISTICALLY ADJUSTING THE DATA

Procedures for statistically adjusting the data consist of weighting, variable respecification and scale transformations. These adjustments are not always necessary but can enhance the quality of data analysis.

Weighting

Weighting
A statistical adjustment to the data in which each case or respondent in the database is assigned a weight to reflects its importance relative to other cases or respondents.

In weighting, each case or respondent in the database is assigned a weight to reflect its importance relative to other cases or respondents. The value 1.0 represents the unweighted case. The effect of weighting is to increase or decrease the number of cases in the sample that possess certain characteristics. (See Chapter 14, which discussed the use of weighting to adjust for non-response bias.)

Weighting is most widely used to make the sample data more representative of a target population on specific characteristics. For example, it may be used to give greater importance to cases or respondents with higher-quality data. Yet another use of weighting is to adjust the sample so that greater importance is attached to respondents with certain characteristics. If a study is conducted to determine what modifications should be made to an existing product, the researcher might want to attach greater weight to the opinions of heavy users of the product. This could be accomplished by assigning weights of 3.0 to heavy users, 2.0 to medium users, and 1.0 to light users and non-users. Because it destroys the self-weighting nature of the sample design, weighting should be applied with caution. If used, the weighting procedure should be documented and made a part of the project report.[9]

EXAMPLE

Determining the weight of community centre users

A mail survey was conducted in the Scottish city of Edinburgh to determine the patronage of a community centre. The resulting sample composition differed in age structure from the area population distribution as compiled from recent census data. Therefore, the sample was weighted to make it representative in terms of age structure. The weights applied were determined by dividing the population percentage by the corresponding sample percentage. The distribution of age structure for the sample and population, as well as the weights applied, are given in the following table.

Age group percentage	*Sample percentage*	*Population*	*Weight*
13 to 18	4.32	6.13	1.42
19 to 24	5.89	7.45	1.26
25 to 34	12.23	13.98	1.14
35 to 44	17.54	17.68	1.01
45 to 54	14.66	15.59	1.06
55 to 64	13.88	13.65	0.98
65 to 74	15.67	13.65	0.87
74 plus	15.81	11.87	0.75
Totals	100	100	

Age groups under-represented in the sample received higher weights whereas over-represented age groups received lower weights. Thus, the data for a respondent aged 13 to 18 would be overweighted by multiplying with 1.42 whereas the data for a respondent aged 75 or over would be underweighted by multiplying by 0.75. ■

Variable re-specification

Variable re-specification
The transformation of data to create new variables or the modification of existing variables so that they are more consistent with the objectives of the study.

Variable re-specification involves the transformation of data to create new variables or to modify existing variables. The purpose of re-specification is to create variables that are consistent with the objectives of the study. For example, suppose that the original variable was product usage, with ten response categories.

These might be collapsed into four categories: heavy, medium, light and non-user. Or, the researcher may create new variables that are composites of several other variables. In the GlobalCash study for example, a composite variable was created based upon how many European countries a company operates and the categories of the size of global sales. Likewise, one may take the ratio of variables. If the amount of purchases at a clothes (X_1) and the amount of purchases where a credit card was used (X_2) have been measured, the proportion of purchases charged to a credit card can be a new variable, created by taking the ratio of the two (X_2/X_1). Other re-specifications of variables include square root and log transformations, which are often applied to improve the fit of the model being estimated.

Dummy variables
A re-specification procedure using variables that take on only two values, usually 0 or 1.

An important re-specification procedure involves the use of **dummy variables** for re-specifying categorical variables. Dummy variables are also called binary, dichotomous, instrumental or qualitative variables. They are variables that may take on only two values, such as 0 or 1. The general rule is that to re-specify a categorical variable with K categories, $K - 1$ dummy variables are needed. The reason for having $K - 1$, rather than K, dummy variables is that only $K - 1$ categories are independent. Given the sample data, information about the Kth category can be derived from information about the other $K - 1$ categories. Consider sex, a variable having two categories. Only one dummy variable is needed. Information on the number or percentage of males in the sample can be readily derived from the number or percentage of females. The following example further illustrates the concept of dummy variables.

Dummy variable coding is frequently used to classify consumers of frozen foods.

EXAMPLE

'Frozen' consumers treated as dummies

In a survey of consumer preferences for frozen foods, the respondents were classified as heavy users, medium users, light users and non-users, and they were originally assigned codes of 4, 3, 2 and 1, respectively. This coding was not meaningful for several statistical analyses. To conduct these analyses, product usage was represented by three dummy variables, X_1, X_2 and X_3, as shown.

Multivariate statistical techniques can be classified as dependence techniques or interdependence techniques (see Figure 16.7). **Dependence techniques** are appropriate when one or more variables can be identified as dependent variables and the remaining as independent variables. When there is only one dependent variable, cross-tabulation, analysis of variance and covariance, regression, two-group discriminant analysis and conjoint analysis can be used. If there is more than one dependent variable, however, the appropriate techniques are multivariate analysis of variance and covariance, canonical correlation and multiple discriminant analysis. In **interdependence techniques**, the variables are not classified as dependent or independent; rather, the whole set of interdependent relationships is examined. These techniques focus on either variable interdependence or inter-object similarity. The major technique for examining variable interdependence is factor analysis. Analysis of inter-object similarity can be conducted by cluster analysis and multidimensional scaling.[14]

Dependence techniques Multivariate techniques apppropriate when one or more of the variables can be identified as dependent variables and the remaining as independent variables.

Interdependence techniques Multivariate statistical techniques that attempt to group data based on underlying similarity and thus allow for interpretation of the data structures. No distinction is made as to which variables are dependent and which are independent

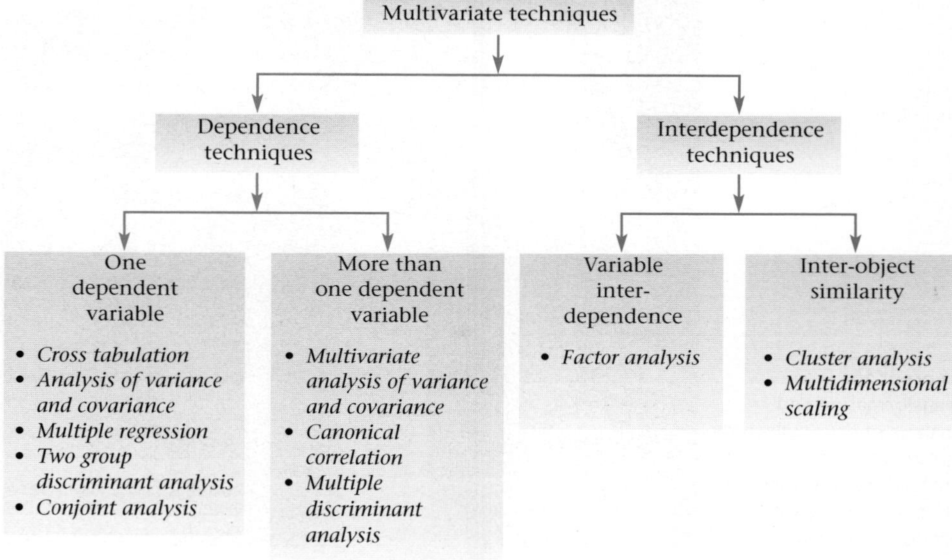

Figure 16.7
A classification of multivariate techniques

INTERNATIONAL MARKETING RESEARCH

Before analysing the data, the researcher should ensure that the units of measurement are comparable across countries or cultural units. For example, the data may have to be adjusted to establish currency equivalents or metric equivalents. Furthermore, standardisation or normalisation of the data may be necessary to make meaningful comparisons and achieve consistent results.

EXAMPLE

A world-wide scream for ice cream[15]

Over half the sales of Haagen-Dazs, the US ice cream manufacturer, came from international markets. How did this come about? Marketing research conducted in several European countries (e.g. Britain, France and Germany) and several Asian countries (e.g. Japan, Singapore and Taiwan) revealed that consumers were hungry for a high-quality ice cream with a high quality image and were willing to pay a premium price for it. These consistent findings emerged after the price of ice cream in each country was standardised to have a mean of zero and a standard deviation of unity. Standardisation was desirable because the prices were specified in different local currencies and a common basis was needed for comparison across countries. Also, in each country, the premium price had to be defined in relation to the prices of competing brands. Standardisation accomplished both these objectives.

Based on these findings, Haagen-Dazs first introduced the brand at a few high-end retailers; it then built company-owned stores in high-traffic areas; and finally it rolled into convenience stores and supermarkets. It maintained the premium quality brand name by starting first with few high-end retailers. It also supplied free freezers to retailers. Hungry for quality products, consumers in the new markets paid double or triple the price of home brands. In the United States, Haagen-Dazs remains popular, although faced with intense competition and a health-conscious market. This added to the impetus to enter international markets. ■

Appropriate transformation and analysis of data collected in several countries have enabled Haagen-Dazs to effectively market its products worldwide

Data analysis could be conducted at three levels: (1) individual, (2) within country or cultural unit, and (3) across countries or cultural units. Individual level analysis requires that the data from each respondent be analysed separately. For example, one might compute a correlation coefficient or run a regression analysis for each respondent. This means that enough data must be obtained from each individual to allow analysis at the individual level, which is often not feasible. Yet it has been argued that in international marketing or cross-cultural research, the researcher should possess a sound knowledge of the consumer in each culture. This can best be accomplished by individual level analysis.[16]

Intra-cultural analysis Within-country analysis of international data

Pan-cultural analysis Across-country analysis in which the data for all respondents from all the countries are pooled and analysed

In within-country or cultural unit analysis, the data are analysed separately for each country or cultural unit. This is also referred to as **intra-cultural analysis**. This level of analysis is quite similar to that conducted in domestic marketing research. The objective is to gain an understanding of the relationships and patterns existing in each country or cultural unit. In across-countries analysis, the data of all the countries are analysed simultaneously. Two approaches to this method are possible. The data for all respondents from all the countries can be pooled and analysed. This is referred to as **pan-cultural analysis**. Alternatively, the data can be aggregated for each country, and then these aggregate statistics can be analysed. For example, one could compute means of variables for each country, and then compute correlations on these means. This is referred to as **cross-cultural analysis**. The objective of this level of analysis is to assess the comparability of findings from one country to another. The similarities as well as the differences between countries should be investigated. When examining differences, not only differences in means but also differences in variance and distribution should be assessed. All the statistical techniques that have been discussed in this book can be applied to within-country or across-country analysis and, subject to the amount of data available, to individual-level analysis as well.[17]

Cross-cultural analysis
A type of across-countries analysis in which the data could be aggregated for each country and these aggregate statistics analysed

ETHICS IN MARKETING RESEARCH

New ethical issues can arise during the data preparation and analysis step of the marketing research process. While checking, editing, coding, transcribing and cleaning, researchers can get some idea about the quality of the data. Sometimes it is easy to identify respondents who did not take the questionnaire seriously or who otherwise provided data of questionable quality. Consider, for example, a respondent who ticks the 'neither agree nor disagree' response to all the 20 items measuring attitudes toward spectator sports. Decisions as to whether such respondents should be discarded or not included in analyses can raise ethical concerns. A good rule of thumb is to make such decisions during the data preparation phase before conducting any analysis.

In contrast, suppose that the researcher conducted the analysis without first attempting to identify unsatisfactory responses. The analysis, however, does not reveal the expected relationship; the analysis does not show that attitude toward spectator sports influences attendance of spectator sports. The researcher then decides to examine the quality of data obtained. In checking the questionnaires, a few respondents with unsatisfactory data are identified. These respondents are eliminated and the reduced data set analysed to obtain the expected results. Discarding respondents after analysing the data raises ethical concerns, particularly if the report does not state that the initial analysis was inconclusive. Moreover, the procedure used to identify unsatisfactory respondents and the number of respondents discarded should be clearly disclosed, as in the following example.

EXAMPLE

Elimination of decision makers unwilling to be ethical[18]

In a study of MBA's responses to marketing ethics dilemmas, respondents were required to respond to fourteen questions regarding ethically ambiguous scenarios by writing a simple sentence regarding what action they would take if they were the manager. The responses were then analysed to determine if the respondent's answer was indicative of ethical behaviour. However, in the data preparation phase, six respondents out of the 561 total respondents were eliminated from further analysis because their responses indicated that they did not follow the directions which told them to state clearly their choice of action. This is an example of ethical editing of the data. The criterion for unsatisfactory responses is clearly stated, the unsatisfactory respondents are identified before the analysis, and the number of respondents eliminated is disclosed. ■

While analysing the data, the researcher may also have to deal with ethical issues. The assumptions underlying the statistical techniques used to analyse the data must be satisfied to obtain meaningful results. For example, the error terms in bivariate regression must be normally distributed about zero, with a constant variance, and be uncorrelated (Chapter 19). The researcher has the responsibility to test these assumptions and take appropriate corrective actions if necessary. The appropriateness of the statistical techniques used for analysis should be discussed when presenting the results. When this is not done, ethical questions can be raised.

The last ethical concern relates to interpretation of the results, drawing conclusions and making recommendations. 'There are few fields of scientific activity that are as susceptible to fraud as some aspects of consumer research. In many cases, what is really being paid for by a client is an interpretation of detailed data; the temptations that beset the researcher in such a situation are very real.'[19] While interpretations, conclusions and recommendations necessarily involve the subjective judgement of the researcher, this judgement must be exercised honestly, free from personal biases or agendas of the researcher or the client.

INTERNET AND COMPUTER APPLICATIONS

The enclosed SNAP CD should be used at this point to illustrate many of the data collection, preparation and analyses tasks outlined in this chapter. SNAP has different means of entering survey data which includes optical scanning, Internet surveys, CATI, CAPI and a 'fast-entry' mode. There is even an option whereby the actual questionnaire appears on the screen, allowing boxes to be ticked, numbers to be entered and verbatim responses to be typed in. In the 'fast-entry' mode, the researcher should have a clear understanding of the issues of field positions and question coding. With other data entry modes, the field positions and coding are completed by default. This default means that the physical format of the questionnaire does not need to be cluttered with field and coding references.

With multiple choice questions, SNAP has an option where a tick is entered for each choice made. In spreadsheet programs, a multiple choice question takes up one column for each possible answer in a question. For example, if a list of 20 television programmes were presented in a question, and the respondent asked which of the programmes they had seen in the last week, the respondent could tick any number from 0 to 20. In a spreadsheet program, this answer would require 20 columns to be completed in a binary format, i.e. a '1' for all the programmes seen and a '0' for those not seen. In SNAP, a list of all 20 appears on screen and a tick is required for only those programmes seen. This may seem a small detail but in the GlobalCash project, Question One contained 12 multiple choice variables with 24 choices in each variable. This would have meant 288 columns in a spreadsheet and 288 data entries. In SNAP, this was reduced to the very few actual choices made which normally ranged between 1 to 10. Not only does this mean huge time savings, there are also much tighter error controls.

Another error control feature of the SNAP program is its ability to set defaults for each question that controls the range of values that may be entered. If a five-point Likert Scale is used and a '7' is entered, there is an audible warning and the data entry halts until the error is corrected. There is the option to set whatever percentage of verification is required, the program then randomly selecting questionnaires to be re-entered. The program also allows logical connections between questions to be set up, completing a comprehensive error avoidance and checking ability.

As well as entering numbers and ticks, verbatim responses can be entered as directly into the program. The verbatim data can be transferred to qualitative data analysis packages if needed, or can be postcoded and a new variable established.

Transformation of responses, filtering of particular answers for analysis and weighting options can all be performed with SNAP. SNAP performs basic descriptive statistical analyses and the range of statistical techniques detailed in Chapter 17. It also allows the variable labels and all the data to be transferred for use in other statistical packages. One of the main formats for this transfer is a universal SSS file format. It also has the means to transfer to an SPSS format, allowing the whole survey and data to be analysed using the mainframe and PC format of SPSS. Turn to the SNAP CD demo to see all these functions illustrated.

SUMMARY

Data preparation begins with a preliminary check of all questionnaires for completeness and interviewing quality. Then, more thorough editing takes place. Editing consists of screening questionnaires to identify illegible, incomplete, inconsistent or ambiguous responses. Such responses may be handled by returning questionnaires to the field, assigning missing values or discarding unsatisfactory respondents.

The next step is coding. A numeric or alphanumeric code is assigned to represent a specific response to a specific question along with the column position or field that code will occupy. It is often helpful to prepare a codebook containing the coding instructions and the necessary information about the variables in the dataset. The coded data are transcribed onto disks, magnetic tapes or entered directly into a data analysis package. Mark sense forms, optical scanning or computerised sensory analysis may also be used.

Cleaning the data requires consistency checks and treatment of missing responses. Options available for treating missing responses include substitution of a neutral value such as a mean, substitution of an imputed response, casewise deletion, and pairwise deletion. Statistical adjustments such as weighting, variable re-specification, and scale transformations often enhance the quality of data analysis. The selection of a data analysis strategy should be based on the earlier steps of the marketing research process, known characteristics of the data, properties of statistical techniques, and the background and philosophy of the researcher. Statistical techniques may be classified as univariate or multivariate.

Before analysing the data in international marketing research, the researcher should ensure that the units of measurement are comparable across countries or cultural units. The data analysis could be conducted at three levels: (1) individual, (2) within country or cultural unit (intra-cultural analysis, and (3) across countries or cultural units: pan-cultural or cross-cultural analysis). Several ethical issues are related to data processing, particularly the discarding of unsatisfactory responses, violation of the assumptions underlying the data analysis techniques, and evaluation and interpretation of results.

QUESTIONS AND PROBLEMS

1 Describe the data preparation process. Why is this process needed?

2 What activities are involved in the preliminary checking of questionnaires that have been returned from the field?

3 What is meant by editing a questionnaire?

4 How are unsatisfactory responses that are discovered in editing treated?

5 What is the difference between pre-coding and post-coding?

6 Describe the guidelines for the coding of unstructured questions.

7 What does transcribing the data involve?

8 What kinds of consistency checks are made in cleaning the data?

9 What options are available for the treatment of missing data?

10 What kinds of statistical adjustments are sometimes made to the data?

11 Describe the weighting process. What are the reasons for weighting?

12 What are dummy variables? Why are such variables created?

13 Explain why scale transformations are made.

14 Which scale transformation procedure is most commonly used? Briefly describe this procedure.

15 What considerations are involved in selecting a data analysis strategy?

NOTES

1 Dadzie, K.Q., 'Demarketing Strategy in Shortage Marketing Environment', *Journal of the Academy of Marketing Science* (Spring 1989), 157–65.

2 Alreck, P.L. and Settle, R.B., *The Survey Research Handbook* (Homewood, IL: Richard D. Irwin,1985), 254–86.

3 For a detailed discussion of coding, see Sidel, P.S., 'Coding', in Ferber, R., (ed.), *Handbook of Marketing Research* (New York: McGraw-Hill, 1974), 2-178–2.199.

4 Pope, J., *Practical Marketing Research* (New York: AMACOM, 1981), 89–90.

5 The American Lawyer, *The American Lawyer Subscriber Study*, 1987.

6 Malhotra, N.K., 'Analysing Marketing Research Data with Incomplete Information on the Dependent Variable', *Journal of Marketing Research* 24 (February 1987), 74–84.

7 A meaningful and practical value should be imputed. The value imputed should be a legitimate response code. For example, a mean of 3.86 may not be practical if only single-digit response codes have been developed. In such cases, the mean should be rounded to the nearest integer.

8 Malhotra, N.K., 'Analysing Marketing Research Data with Incomplete Information on the Dependent Variable', *Journal of Marketing Research* 24 (February 1987), 74–84.

9 Some weighting procedures require adjustments in subsequent data analysis techniques. See Sharot,T., 'Weighting Survey Results', *Journal of the Market Research Society* 28 (July 1986), 269–84; and Frankel, M.R., *Inference from Survey Samples* (Ann Arbor: Institute for Social Research, University of Michigan,1971).

10 Woodside, A.G., Nielsen, R.L., Walters, F. and Muller, G.D., 'Preference Segmentation of Health Care Services: The Old-Fashioneds, Value Conscious, Affluents, and Professional Want-It-Alls', *Journal of Health Care Marketing*, (June 1988), 14–24.

11 See Frank, R.E., 'Use of Transformations', *Journal of Marketing Research* (August 1966), 247–53, for specific transformations frequently used in marketing research.

12 For a similar data analysis strategy, see Malhotra, N.K., 'Modelling Store Choice Based on Censored Preference Data', *Journal of Retailing* (Summer 1986), 128–44; and Birks, D.F. and Birts, A.N., 'Service quality in domestic banks', in Birks, D.F., (ed.), *Global Cash Management in Europe* (Houndmills: Macmillan, 1998), 175–205.

13 Bivariate techniques have been included here with multivariate techniques. Although bivariate techniques are concerned with pairwise relationships, multivariate techniques examine more complex simultaneous relationships among phenomena. See Sheth, J.N., 'What Is Multivariate Analysis?', in Sheth, J.N. (ed.), *Multivariate Methods for Market and Survey Research* (Chicago: American Marketing Association, 1977).

14 Green, P.E., *Analysing Multivariate Data* (Hinsdale, IL: Dryden Press, 1978).

15 Maremont, M., 'They're All Screaming for Haagen-Dazs', *Business Week* (14 October 1991).

16 Tan, C.T., McCullough, J. and Teoh, J., 'An Individual Analysis Approach to Cross-Cultural Research', in Wallendorf, M. and Anderson, P. (eds), *Advances in Consumer Research*, vol. 14 (Provo, UT: Association for Consumer Research, 1987), 394–97.

17 See, for example, Spiller, L.D. and Campbell, A.J., 'The Use of International Direct Marketing by Small Businesses in Canada, Mexico, and the United States: A Comparative Analysis', *Journal of Direct Marketing* 8 (Winter 1994), 7–16; and Nyaw, M-K. and Ng, I.,'A Comparative Analysis of Ethical Beliefs: A Four Country Study', *Journal of Business Ethics* 13 (July 1994), 543–56.

18 Zinkhan, G.M., Bisesi, M. and Saxton, M.J., 'MBAs' Changing Attitudes toward Marketing Dilemmas: 1981–1987', *Journal of Business Ethics* 8 (1989), 963–74.

19 Day, R.L., 'A Comment on Ethics in Marketing Research', *Journal of Marketing Research* 12 (1974), 232–33.

Chapter 17

Frequency distribution, cross-tabulation and hypothesis testing

Frequency distribution, cross-tabulation and hypothesis testing provide valuable insights into the data and guide the rest of the data analysis as well as the interpretation of the results

OBJECTIVES

After reading this chapter, the student should be able to:

1 describe the significance of preliminary data analysis and the insights that can be obtained from such an analysis;
2 discuss data analysis associated with frequencies including measures of location, measures of variability and measures of shape;
3 explain data analysis associated with cross-tabulations and the associated statistics: chi-square, phi coefficient, contingency coefficient, Cramer's *V* and lambda coefficient;
4 describe data analysis associated with parametric hypothesis testing for one sample, two independent samples and paired samples;
5 understand data analysis associated with non-parametric hypothesis testing for one sample, two independent samples and paired samples.

OVERVIEW

Once the data have been prepared for analysis (Chapter 16), the researcher should conduct basic analyses. This chapter describes basic data analyses including frequency distribution, cross-tabulation and hypothesis testing. First, we describe the frequency distribution and explain how it provides both an indication of the number of out-of range, missing or extreme values as well as insights into the central tendency, variability and shape of the underlying distribution. Next, we introduce hypothesis testing by describing the general procedure. Hypothesis testing procedures are classified as tests of associations or tests of differences. We consider the use of cross-tabulation for understanding the associations between variables taken two or three at a time. Although the nature of the association can be observed from tables, statistics are available for examining the significance and strength of the association. Finally, we present tests for examining hypotheses related to differences based on one or two samples.

Many commercial marketing research projects do not go beyond basic data analysis. These findings are often displayed using tables and graphs, as discussed further in Chapter 24. Although the findings of basic analysis are valuable in their own right, they also provide guidance for conducting multivariate analysis. The insights gained from the basic analysis are also invaluable in interpreting the results obtained from more sophisticated statistical techniques. To provide the reader with a flavour of these techniques, we illustrate the use of cross-tabulation, chi-square analysis and hypothesis testing.

GLOBALCASH PROJECT

Basic data analyses

In the GlobalCash project, basic data analysis formed the foundation for conducting subsequent multivariate analysis. Data analysis began by obtaining a frequency distribution and descriptive statistics for each variable. In addition to identifying possible problems with the data, this information provided a good idea of the data and insights into how specific variables should be treated in subsequent analyses. For example, should some variables be treated as categorical, and if so, how many categories should there be? Several two- and three-variable cross-tabulations were also conducted to identify associations in the data. The effects of variables with two categories on the metric dependent variables of interest were examined by means of *t* tests and other hypotheses testing procedures. ■

The Belgium bank Generale have sponsored the GlobalCash project over many years.

GLOBALCASH PROJECT

Bank accounts outside one's home country

Measures of companies' plans over the next two years were conducted in the GlobalCash project. Results showed differences in the nature of these plans in different countries. The following table focuses upon the results from German respondents. The first question tackled was the intention to change the number of banks a company has business relationships with. The responses to this question was broken down into respondents who plan, or do not plan for their treasury function to be more automated. Cross-tabulation and chi-square analysis provided the following:

	Treasury function to be more automated? (%)	
Intend to change the number of banks you use?	**Yes**	**No**
No	59	74
Increase	6	7
Decrease	35	19
	$\chi^2 = 6.51$	p = < 0.05

These results indicate that in German companies, there is little difference in the plans to automate, when companies plan to increase the number of banks they work with. Where a decrease in the number of banks is planned, a much higher proportion plan have more automation in their treasury function. ■

EXAMPLE

Catalogues are risky business[1]

Twelve product categories were examined to compare shopping by catalogue with store shopping. The hypothesis that there is no significant difference in the overall amount of risk perceived when buying products by catalogue compared with buying the same products in a retail store was rejected. The hypothesis was tested by computing 12 (one for each product) paired-observations t tests. Mean scores for overall perceived risk for some of the products in both buying situations are presented in the following table, with higher scores indicating greater risk.

	Overall perceived risk	
Product	*Catalogue*	*Store*
Shoes	58.60	50.80*
Pocket calculator	49.62	42.00*
Hi-fi	48.89	41.98*
Portable television	48.53	40.91*
Digital camera	48.13	39.52*
Athletic socks	35.22	30.22*
Perfume	34.85	29.79*
CDs	32.65	28.74*

* Significant at 0.01 level

As can be seen, a significantly ($p < 0.01$) higher overall amount of perceived risk was attached to products purchased by catalogue as compared with those purchased from a retail store. ■

The first GlobalCash example illustrates the role of basic data analysis used in conjunction with multivariate procedures, whereas the other two examples show how such analysis can be useful in its own right. The cross-tabulation and chi-square analysis in the GlobalCash plans example and the paired t tests in the catalogue shopping example enabled us to draw specific conclusions from the data. Before these types of conclusions are drawn, it is useful to examine the frequency distributions of the relevant variables.

FREQUENCY DISTRIBUTION

Marketing researchers often need to answer questions about a single variable. For example:

- How many users of the brand may be characterised as brand loyal?
- What percentage of the market consists of heavy users, medium users, light users and non-users?
- How many customers are very familiar with a new product offering? How many are familiar, somewhat familiar, or unfamiliar with the brand? What is the mean familiarity rating? Is there much variance in the extent to which customers are familiar with the new product?
- What is the income distribution of brand users? Is this distribution skewed toward low income brackets?

Frequency distribution
A mathematical distribution whose objective is to obtain a count of the number of responses associated with different values of one variable and to express these counts in percentage terms.

The answers to these kinds of questions can be determined by examining **frequency distributions**. In a frequency distribution, one variable is considered at a time.

The objective is to obtain a count of the number of responses associated with different values of the variable. The relative occurrence, or frequency, of different values of the variable is expressed in percentages. A frequency distribution for a variable produces a table of frequency counts, percentages, and cumulative percentages for all the values associated with that variable.

Table 17.1 gives the frequency distribution of the replies to a question on selecting banks in the GlobalCash project. Respondents were asked to rank order the top five criteria they use in selecting a cash management bank. One of those criteria was a 'good electronic banking system' and the replies to that criterion are shown in Table 17.1. In the table, the first column contains the labels assigned to the different categories of the variable and the second column indicates the codes assigned to each value. Note that a code of 9 has been assigned to missing values. The third column gives the number of respondents ticking each value. For example, 203 respondents ticked value 1, indicating that they felt that a good electronic banking system was their most important criterion when selecting a cash management bank. The fourth column displays the percentage of respondents ticking each value.

Table 17.1 Rating of 'good electronic banking system' as a criterion in selecting a cash management bank

Value label	*Value*	*Frequency (N)*	*Percentage*	*Valid percentage*	*Cumulative percentage*
Most important criteria	1	203	18.8	18.9	18.9
2nd most important	2	166	15.4	15.5	34.4
3rd	3	138	12.8	12.8	47.2
4th	4	104	9.6	9.7	56.9
5th	5	77	7.1	7.2	64.1
Not rated	6	386	35.8	35.9	100.0
Missing	9	5	0.5	MISSING	
TOTAL		1079	100.0	100.0	

The fifth column shows percentages calculated by excluding the cases with missing values. If there are no missing values, columns 4 and 5 are identical. The last column represents cumulative percentages after adjusting for missing values. As can be seen, of the 1079 respondents who participated in the survey, 18.8% entered a figure '1' indicating the criteria was the 'most important'. If the five respondents with missing values are excluded, this changes to 18.9%. Examining the cumulative percentage column, it is clear that 47.2% of respondents would rate 'a good electronic banking system' as being in their top three criteria in selecting a cash management bank. In other words, 47.2% of the respondents with valid responses indicated a value of 3 or less.

A frequency distribution helps determine the extent of item non-response. It also indicates the extent of illegitimate responses. Values of 0, 7 and 8 would be illegitimate responses, or errors. The cases with these values could be identified and corrective action could be taken. The presence of outliers or cases with extreme values can also be detected. For example, in the case of a frequency distribution of household size, a few isolated families with household sizes of 9 or more might be considered outliers. A frequency distribution also indicates the shape of the empirical distribution of the variable. The frequency data may be used to construct a histogram, or a vertical bar chart in which the values of the variable are portrayed along the *x* axis and the absolute or relative frequencies of the values are placed along the *y* axis.

Figure 17.1 is a histogram of the frequency data in Table 17.1. From the histogram, one could examine whether the observed distribution is consistent with an expected or assumed distribution.

STATISTICS ASSOCIATED WITH FREQUENCY DISTRIBUTION

A frequency distribution is a convenient way of looking at different values of a variable. A frequency table is easy to read and provides basic information, but sometimes this information may be too detailed and the researcher must summarise it by the use of descriptive statistics.[2] The most commonly used statistics associated with frequencies are measures of location (mean, mode and median), measures of variability (range, interquartile range, standard deviation and coefficient of variation), and measures of shape (skewness and kurtosis).[3]

Measures of location

Measures of location
A statistic that describes a location within a data set. Measures of central tendency describe the centre of the distribution.

The **measures of location** that we discuss are measures of central tendency because they tend to describe the centre of the distribution. If the entire sample is changed by adding a fixed constant to each observation, then the mean, mode and median change by the same fixed amount.

Mean
The average; that value obtained by summing all elements in a set and dividing by the number of elements.

Mean. The **mean**, or average value, is the most commonly used measure of central tendency. It is used to estimate the mean when the data have been collected using an interval or ratio scale. The data should display some central tendency, with most of the responses distributed around the mean.

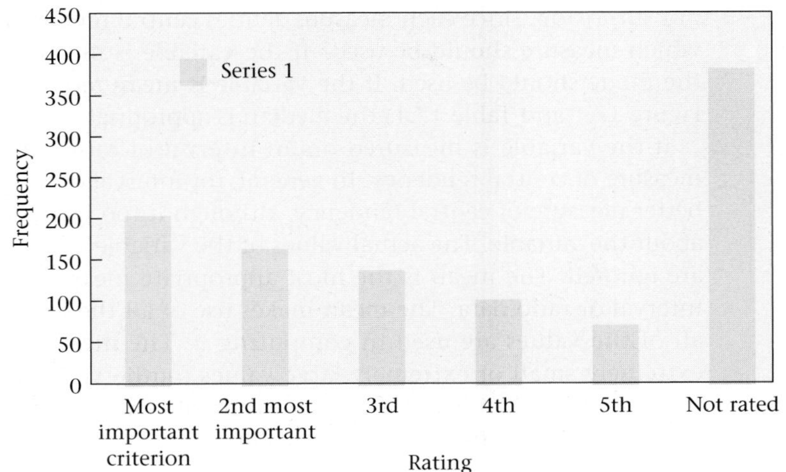

Figure 17.1
Frequency of 'good electronic banking system' as a criterion in selecting a cash management bank

The mean, $\bar{X}$, is given by

$$\bar{X} = \frac{\sum_{i=1}^{n} X_i}{n}$$

where

X_i = observed values of the variable X
n = number of observations (sample size)

The mean is an appropriate measure of central tendency when the variable is based upon interval or ration scaled data. Generally, the mean is a robust measure and does not change markedly as data values are added or deleted. For the frequencies given in Table 17.1, the mean value is calculated as follows:

$$\bar{X} = \frac{(203 \times 1) + (166 \times 2) + (138 \times 3) + (104 \times 4) + (77 \times 5) + (386 \times 6)}{1079}$$

$$= \frac{203 + 332 + 414 + 416 + 385 + 2316}{1079}$$

$$= \frac{4066}{1079}$$

$$= 3.768$$

Mode
A measure of central tendency given as the value that occurs with the most in a sample distribution.

Mode. The **mode** is the value that occurs most frequently. It represents the highest peak of the distribution. The mode is a good measure of location when the variable is inherently categorical or has otherwise been grouped into categories. The mode in Table 17.1 is 6.000.

Median
A measure of central tendency given as the value above which half of the values fall and below which half of the values fall.

Median. The **median** of a sample is the middle value when the data are arranged in ascending or descending order. If the number of data points is even, the median is usually estimated as the midpoint between the two middle values by adding the two middle values and dividing their sum by 2. The median is the 50th percentile. The median is an appropriate measure of central tendency for ordinal data. In Table 17.1, the middle value is 4.000, so the median is 4.000.

As can be seen from Table 17.1, the three measures of central tendency for this distribution are different (mean = 3.768, mode = 6.000, median = 4.000). This is not surprising, since each measure defines central tendency in a different way. So which measure should be used? If the variable is measured on a nominal scale, the mode should be used. If the variable is measured on an ordinal scale, (as in Figure 17.1 and Table 17.1) the median is appropriate.

If the variable is measured on an interval or ratio scale, the mode is a poor measure of central tendency. In general, for interval or ratio data, the median is a better measure of central tendency, although it too ignores available information about the variable. The actual values of the variable above and below the median are ignored. The mean is the most appropriate measure of central tendency for interval or ratio data. The mean makes use of all the information available since all of the values are used in computing it. The mean, however, is sensitive to extremely small or extremely large values (outliers). When there are outliers in the data, the mean is not a good measure of central tendency, and it is useful to consider both the mean and the median.

Measures of variability

Measures of variability
A statistic that indicates the distribution's dispersion.

The **measures of variability**, which are calculated on interval or ratio data, include the range, interquartile range, variance or standard deviation, and coefficient of variation.

Range
The difference between the smallest and largest values of a distribution.

Range. The **range** measures the spread of the data. It is simply the difference between the largest and smallest values in the sample

$$\text{range} = X_{largest} - X_{smallest}$$

As such, the range is directly affected by outliers. If all the values in the data are multiplied by a constant, the range is multiplied by the same constant. The range in Table 17.1 is 6 – 1 = 5.000.

Interquartile range
The range of a distribution encompassing the middle 50% of the observations.

Interquartile range. The **interquartile range** is the difference between the 75th and 25th percentile. For a set of data points arranged in order of magnitude, the *p*th percentile is the value that has *p*% of the data points below it and (100 – *p*) % above it. If all the data points are multiplied by a constant, the interquartile range is multiplied by the same constant. The interquartile range in Table 17.1 is 6 – 2 = 4.000.

Variance
The mean squared deviation of all the values of the mean.

Standard deviation
The square root of the variance.

Variance and standard deviation. The difference between the mean and an observed value is called the deviation from the mean. The **variance** is the mean squared deviation from the mean. The variance can never be negative. When the data points are clustered around the mean, the variance is small. When the data points are scattered, the variance is large. If all the data values are multiplied by a constant, the variance is multiplied by the square of the constant. The **standard deviation** is the square root of the variance. Thus, the standard deviation is expressed in the same units as the data, rather than in squared units. The standard deviation of a sample, s_x, is calculated as:

$$s_x = \sqrt{\sum_{i=1}^{n} \frac{(X_i - \bar{X})^2}{n-1}}$$

We divide by $n - 1$ instead of n because the sample is drawn from a population and we are trying to determine how much the responses vary from the mean of the entire population. The population mean is unknown, however; therefore, the sample mean is used instead. The use of the sample mean makes the sample seem less variable than it really is. By dividing by $n - 1$ instead of by n, we compensate for the smaller variability observed in the sample. For the data given in Table 17.1, the variance is calculated as follows:

$$s^2_x = \frac{\{203 \times (1\text{–}3.768)^2 + 166 \times (2\text{–}3.768)^2 + 138 \times (3\text{–}3.768)^2 + 104 \times (4\text{–}3.768)^2 + 77 \times (5\text{–}3.768)^2 + 386 \times (6\text{–}3.768)^2\}}{1073}$$

$$= \frac{1555.35 + 518.87 + 81.40 + 5.60 + 116.87 + 1922.98}{1073}$$

$$= \frac{4201.09}{1073}$$

$$= 3.91$$

The standard deviation, therefore, is calculated as

$$s_x = \sqrt{3.91}$$
$$= 1.98$$

Coefficient of variation
A useful expression in sampling theory for the standard deviation as a percentage of the mean.

Coefficient of variation. The coefficient of variation is the ratio of the standard deviation to the mean expressed as a percentage, and it is a unitless measure of relative variability. The coefficient of variation, CV, is expressed as

$$CV = \frac{s_x}{\bar{X}}$$

The coefficient of variation is meaningful only if the variable is measured on a ratio scale. It remains unchanged if all the data values are multiplied by a constant. Since the data in Table 17.1 are not measured on a ratio scale, it is not meaningful to calculate the coefficient of variation.

Measures of shape

In addition to measures of variability, measures of shape are also useful in understanding the nature of the distribution. The shape of a distribution is assessed by examining skewness and kurtosis.

Skewness. Distributions can be either symmetric or skewed. In a symmetric distribution, the values on either side of the centre of the distribution are the same, and the mean, mode and median are equal. The positive and corresponding negative deviations from the mean are also equal. In a skewed distribution, the

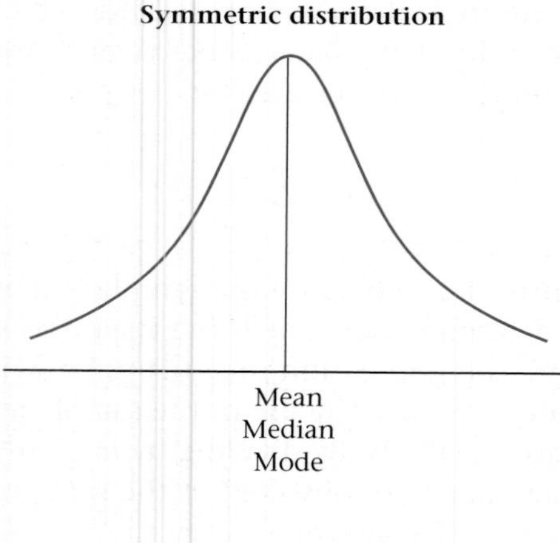

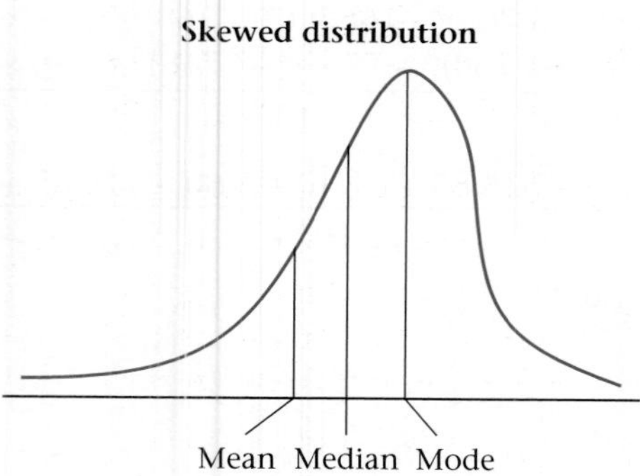

Figure 17.2 Skewness of a distribution

Skewness
A characteristic of a distribution that assesses its symmetry about the mean.

positive and negative deviations from the mean are unequal. **Skewness** is the tendency of the deviations from the mean to be larger in one direction than in the other. It can be thought of as the tendency for one tail of the distribution to be heavier than the other (see Figure 17.2). The skewness value for the data of Table 17.1 is –0.352, indicating a negative skew.

Kurtosis
A measure of the relative peakedness of the curve defined by the frequency distribution.

Kurtosis. **Kurtosis** is a measure of the relative peakedness or flatness of the curve defined by the frequency distribution. The kurtosis of a normal distribution is zero. If the kurtosis is positive, then the distribution is more peaked than a normal distribution. A negative value means that the distribution is flatter than a normal distribution. The value of this statistic for Table 17.1 is –0.0113, indicating that the distribution is flatter than a normal distribution.

INTRODUCTION TO HYPOTHESIS TESTING

This section provides an introduction to hypothesis testing. Basic analysis invariably involves some hypothesis testing. Examples of hypotheses generated in marketing research abound:

- A cinema is being patronised by more than 10 per cent of the households in a city.
- The heavy and light users of a brand differ in terms of psychographic characteristics.
- One hotel has a more 'luxurious' image than its close competitor.
- Familiarity with a restaurant results in greater preference for that restaurant.

Chapter 14 covered the concepts of the sampling distribution, standard error of the mean or the proportion, and the confidence interval.[4] All these concepts are relevant to hypothesis testing and should be reviewed. We now describe a general procedure for hypothesis testing that can be applied to test hypotheses about a wide range of parameters.

A GENERAL PROCEDURE FOR HYPOTHESIS TESTING

The following steps are involved in hypothesis testing (Figure 17.3).

1. Formulate the null hypothesis H_0 and the alternative hypothesis H_1.
2. Select an appropriate statistical technique and the corresponding test statistic.
3. Choose the level of significance, α.
4. Determine the sample size and collect the data. Calculate the value of the test statistic.
5. Determine the probability associated with the test statistic under the null hypothesis, using the sampling distribution of the test statistic. Alternatively, determine the critical values associated with the test statistic that divide the rejection and non-rejection region.
6. Compare the probability associated with the test statistic with the level of significance specified. Alternatively, determine whether the test statistic has fallen into the rejection or the non-rejection region.
7. Make the statistical decision to reject or not reject the null hypothesis.
8. Express the statistical decision in terms of the marketing research problem.

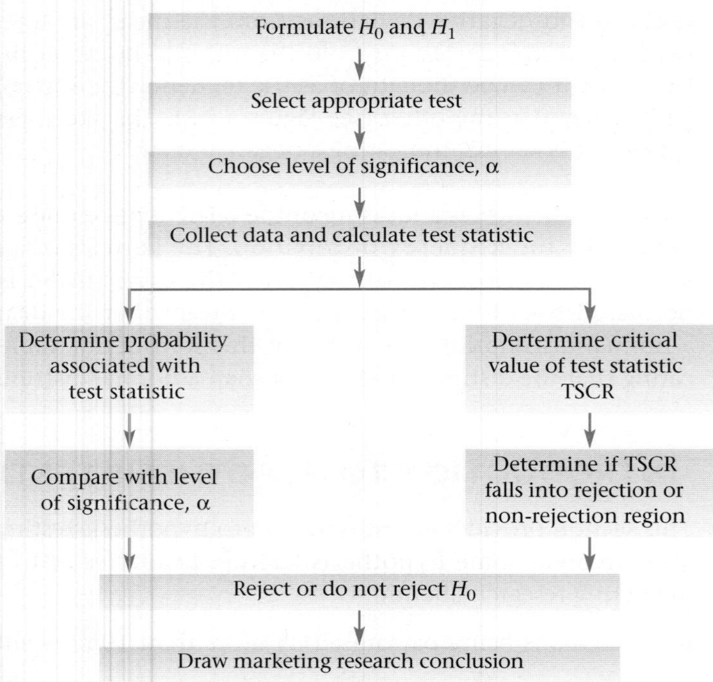

Figure 17.3
A general procedure for hypothesis testing

Step 1: Formulating the hypothesis

> **Null hypothesis**
> A statement in which no difference or effect is expected. If the null hypothesis is not rejected, no changes will be made.

> **Alternative hypothesis**
> A statement that some difference or effect is expected. Accepting the alternative hypothesis will lead to changes in opinions or actions.

The first step is to formulate the null and alternative hypothesis. A **null hypothesis** is a statement of the status quo, one of no difference or no effect. If the null hypothesis is not rejected, no changes will be made. An **alternative hypothesis** is one in which some difference or effect is expected. Accepting the alternative hypothesis will lead to changes in opinions or actions. Thus, the alternative hypothesis is the opposite of the null hypothesis.

The null hypothesis is always the hypothesis that is tested. The null hypothesis refers to a specified value of the population parameter (e.g. μ,σ,π), not a sample statistic (e.g. $\bar{X}$). A null hypothesis may be rejected, but it can never be accepted based on a single test. A statistical test can have one of two outcomes: that the null hypothesis is rejected and the alternative hypothesis accepted or that the null hypothesis is not rejected based on the evidence. It would be incorrect, however, to conclude that since the null hypothesis is not rejected, it can be accepted as valid. In classical hypothesis testing, there is no way to determine whether the null hypothesis is true.

In marketing research, the null hypothesis is formulated in such a way that its rejection leads to the acceptance of the desired conclusion. The alternative hypothesis represents the conclusion for which evidence is sought. For example, a garage is considering introducing a collection and delivery system when customers' cars need repairs. Given the investment in personnel to make this plan work well, it will only be introduced if it is preferred by more than 40 per cent of the customers. The appropriate way to formulate the hypotheses is

$$H_0\colon \pi \le 0.40$$

$$H_1\colon \pi > 0.40$$

If the null hypothesis H_0 is rejected, then the alternative hypothesis H_1 will be accepted and the new collection and delivery service introduced. On the other hand, if H_0 is not rejected, then the new collection and delivery service should not be introduced unless additional evidence is obtained.

One-tailed test
A test of the null hypothesis where the alternative hypothesis is expressed directionally.

Two-tailed test
A test of the null hypothesis where the alternative hypothesis is not expressed directionally.

The test of the null hypothesis is a **one-tailed test** because the alternative hypothesis is expressed directionally: the proportion of customers who express a preference is greater than 0.40. On the other hand, suppose that the researcher wanted to determine whether the new collection and delivery service is different (superior or inferior) from the existing form of getting a car to the garage for repairs, which is preferred by 40 per cent of the customers. Then a **two-tailed test** would be required, and the hypotheses would be expressed as

$$H_0: \pi = 0.40$$

$$H_1: \pi \neq 0.40$$

In commercial marketing research, the one-tailed test is used more often than a two-tailed test. Typically, there is some preferred direction for the conclusion for which evidence is sought. For example, the higher the profits, sales and product quality, the better. The one-tailed test is more powerful than the two-tailed test. The power of a statistical test is discussed further in step 3.

Step 2: Selecting an appropriate test

Test statistic
A measure of how close the sample has come to the null hypothesis. It often follows a well-known distribution, such as the normal, *t*, or chi-square distribution.

To test the null hypothesis, it is necessary to select an appropriate statistical technique. The researcher should take into consideration how the **test statistic** is computed and the sampling distribution that the sample statistic (e.g. the mean) follows. The test statistic measures how close the sample has come to the null hypothesis. The test statistic often follows a well-known distribution, such as the normal, *t*, or chi-square distribution. Guidelines for selecting an appropriate test or statistical technique are discussed later in this chapter. In our example, the *z* statistic, which follows the standard normal distribution, would be appropriate. This statistic would be computed as follows:

$$z = \frac{p - \pi}{\sigma_p}$$

where

$$\sigma_p = \sqrt{\frac{\pi\,(1 - \pi)}{n}}$$

Step 3: Choosing level of significance

Whenever we draw inferences about a population, there is a risk that an incorrect conclusion will be reached. Two types of error can occur.

Type I error
An error that occurs when the sample results lead to the rejection of a null hypothesis that is in fact true. Also known as alpha error.

Level of significance
The probability of making a type 1 error.

Type II error
An error that occurs when the sample results lead to acceptance of a null hypothesis that is in fact false. Also known as beta error.

Type I error. **Type I error** occurs when the sample results lead to the rejection of the null hypothesis when it is in fact true. In our example, a type I error would occur if we concluded, based on sample data, that the proportion of customers preferring the new collection and delivery service was greater than 0.40, when in fact it was less than or equal to 0.40. The probability of type I error (a) is also called the **level of significance**. The type I error is controlled by establishing the tolerable level of risk of rejecting a true null hypothesis. The selection of a particular risk level should depend on the cost of making a type I error.

Type II error. **Type II error** occurs when, based on the sample results, the null hypothesis is not rejected when it is in fact false. In our example, the type II error would occur if we concluded, based on sample data, that the proportion of

Step 8: Marketing research conclusion

The conclusion reached by hypothesis testing must be expressed in terms of the marketing research problem. In our example, we conclude that there is evidence that the proportion of customers preferring the new service plan is significantly greater than 0.40. Hence, the recommendation would be to introduce the new collection and delivery service.

As can be seen from Figure 17.6, hypotheses testing can be related to either an examination of associations or an examination of differences. In tests of associations the null hypothesis is that there is no association between the variables (H_0: . . . is NOT related to . . .). In tests of differences the null hypothesis is that there is no difference (H_0: . . . is NOT different than . . .). Tests of differences could relate to distributions, means, proportions, or medians or rankings. First, we discuss hypotheses related to associations in the context of cross-tabulations.

CROSS-TABULATIONS

Although answers to questions related to a single variable are interesting, they often raise additional questions about how to link that variable to other variables. To introduce the frequency distribution, we posed several representative marketing research questions. For each of these, a researcher might pose additional questions to relate these variables to other variables. For example:

- How many brand loyal users are males?
- Is product use (measured in terms of heavy users, medium users, light users and non-users) related to interest in outdoor leisure activities (high, medium and low)?
- Is familiarity with a new product related to age and income levels?
- Is product ownership related to income (high, medium and low)?

Cross-tabulation
A statistical technique that describes two or more variables simultaneously and results in tables that reflect the joint distribution of two or more variables that have a limited number of categories or distinct values.

The answers to such questions can be determined by examining **cross-tabulations**. A frequency distribution describes one variable at a time, but a cross-tabulation describes two or more variables simultaneously. Cross-tabulation results in tables that reflect the joint distribution of two or more variables with a limited number of categories or distinct values. The categories of one variable are cross-classified with the categories of one or more other variables. Thus, the frequency distribution of one variable is subdivided according to the values or categories of the other variables.

Using the GlobalCash project as an example, suppose that interest was expressed in determining whether the number of European countries that a com-

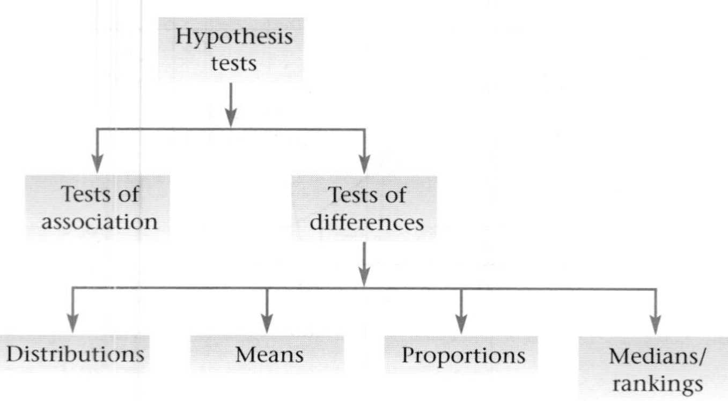

Figure 17.6
A broad classification of hypothesis testing procedures

pany operates in was associated with the plans to change the number of banks they do business with. The cross-tabulation is shown in Table 17.2. A cross-tabulation includes a cell for every combination of the categories of the two variables. The number in each cell shows how many respondents gave that combination of responses. In Table 17.2, 105 operated in only one European country and did not plan to change the number of banks they do business with.

Table 17.2 Number of countries in Europe that a company operates in and plans to change the number of banks that a company does business with

	In how many countries does your company operate?					
Do you intend to change the number of banks you use?	**1**	**2 to 5**	**6 to 10**	**11 to 15**	**over 15**	Row total
No	105	130	115	92	172	614
Increase	12	22	7	9	14	64
Decrease	34	57	64	44	95	294
Column total	151	209	186	145	281	972

The marginal totals in this table indicate that of the 972 respondents with valid responses on both the variables, 614 had no plans to change, 64 would increase and 294 would decrease the number of banks they do business with. Based on how many European countries a company operates in, 151 operate in one country, 209 in 2 to 5 countries, 186 in 6 to 10 countries, 145 in 11 to 15 countries and 281 in more than 15 countries. Note that this information could have been obtained from a separate frequency distribution for each variable. In general, the margins of a cross-tabulation show the same information as the frequency tables for each of the variables. Cross-tabulation tables are also called **contingency tables**. The data are considered to be qualitative or categorical data, because each variable is assumed to have only a nominal scale.[5]

Contingency table
A cross-tabulation table. It contains a cell for every combination of categories of the two variables.

Cross-tabulation is widely used in commercial marketing research because (1) cross-tabulation analysis and results can be easily interpreted and understood by managers who are not statistically oriented; (2) the clarity of interpretation provides a stronger link between research results and managerial action; (3) a series of cross-tabulations may provide greater insights into a complex phenomenon than a single multivariate analysis; (4) cross-tabulation may alleviate the problem of sparse cells, which could be serious in discrete multivariate analysis; and (5) cross-tabulation analysis is simple to conduct and appealing to less-sophisticated researchers.[6] We will discuss cross-tabulation for two and three variables.

Two variables

Cross-tabulation with two variables is also known as bivariate cross-tabulation. Consider again the cross-classification of the number of countries in Europe that a company operates in and plans to change the number of banks that a company does business with, given in Table 17.2. Is operating in a high number of European countries related to plans to reduce bank numbers? It appears to be from Table 17.2. We see that disproportionately more of the respondents who operate in over 15 European countries plan to decrease the number of banks that they do business with compared with those that operate in 15 or fewer countries. Computation of percentages can provide more insights.

Because two variables have been cross-classified, percentages could be computed either column-wise, based on column totals (Table 17.3), or row-wise, based on row totals (Table 17.4). Which table is more useful?

Table 17.3 Plans to change the number of banks that a company does business with by number of countries in Europe that a company operates in

	In how many countries does your company operate?				
Do you intend to change the number of banks you use?	**1**	**2 to 5**	**6 to 10**	**11 to 15**	**over 15**
No	70%	62%	62%	63%	61%
Increase	8%	11%	4%	6%	5%
Decrease	23%	27%	34%	30%	34%
Column total	100%	100%	100%	100%	100%

Table 17.4 Number of countries in Europe that a company operates in by plans to change the number of banks that a company does business with

	In how many countries does your company operate?					
Do you intend to change the number of banks you use?	**1**	**2 to 5**	**6 to 10**	**11 to 15**	**over 15**	Row total
No	17%	21%	19%	15%	28%	100%
Increase	19%	34%	11%	14%	22%	100%
Decrease	12%	19%	22%	15%	32%	100%

The answer depends on which variable will be considered as the independent variable and which as the dependent variable.[7] The general rule is to compute the percentages in the direction of the independent variable, across the dependent variable. In our analysis, number of countries may be considered as the independent variable and planned changes as the dependent variable, and the correct way of calculating percentages is shown in Table 17.3. Note that while 70 per cent of those operating in one country do not plan to make any changes, 61 per cent of those who operate in over 15 countries plan to change their number of banks. This seems plausible given the costs and complexity of operating many bank accounts in many countries. Companies faced with such an array of accounts may be seeking to make further cuts and savings, especially with the introduction of European Monetary Union.

Note that computing percentages in the direction of the dependent variable across the independent variable, as shown in Table 17.4, is not meaningful in this case. Table 17.4 implies that plans to change the number of bank relationships influences companies' decisions to operate in certain numbers of European countries. This latter finding seems implausible. It is possible, however, that the association between 'change plans' and 'numbers of countries' is mediated by a third variable, such as the country where an ultimate parent company in a group operates from, e.g. although Hitachi has operations in Britain, Germany and Italy, their ultimate parentage is Japanese. It is possible that companies whose group parentage is in areas of the globe whose economic conditions are more or less favourable than Europe, are affected in the extent of planned changes to their bank relationships. This kind of possibility points to the need to examine the effect of a third variable.

Three variables

Often the introduction of a third variable clarifies the initial association (or lack of it) observed between two variables. As shown in Figure 17.7, the introduction of a third variable can result in four possibilities:

1 It can refine the association observed between the two original variables.
2 It can indicate no association between the two variables, although an association was initially observed. In other words, the third variable indicates that the initial association between the two variables was spurious.
3 It can reveal some association between the two variables, although no association was initially observed. In this case, the third variable reveals a suppressed association between the first two variables.
4 It can indicate no change in the initial association.[8]

These cases are explained with examples based on a sample of 1000 respondents. Although these examples are contrived to illustrate specific cases, such cases are not uncommon in commercial marketing research.

Refine an initial relationship. An examination of the relationship between the purchase of 'designer' clothing and marital status resulted in the data reported in Table 17.5. The respondents were classified into either high or low categories based on their purchase of 'designer' clothing. Marital status was also measured in terms of two categories: currently married or unmarried. As can be seen from Table 17.5, 52 per cent of unmarried respondents fell in the high-purchase category as opposed to 31 per cent of the married respondents. Before concluding that unmarried respondents purchase more 'designer' clothing than those who are married, a third variable, the buyer's gender, was introduced into the analysis.

Table 17.5 Purchase of 'designer' clothing by relationship status

	Marital status	
Purchase of 'designer' clothing	**Married**	**Unmarried**
High	31%	52%
Low	69%	48%
Column	100%	100%
Number of respondents	700	300

The buyer's gender was selected as the third variable based on past research. The relationship between purchase of 'designer' clothing and marital status was re-examined in light of the third variable, as shown in Table 17.6. In the case of females, 60 per cent of the unmarried respondents fall in the high-purchase category compared with 25 per cent of those who are married. On the other hand, the percentages are much closer for males, with 40 per cent of the unmarried respondents and 35 per cent of the married respondents falling in the high-purchase category. Hence, the introduction of gender (third variable) has refined the relationship between marital status and purchase of 'designer' clothing (original variables). Unmarried respondents are more likely to fall into the high-purchase category than married ones, and this effect is much more pronounced for females than for males.

Table 17.6 Purchase of 'designer' clothing by marital status and gender

	Gender			
	Male *Marital status*		*Female* *Marital status*	
Purchase of 'designer' clothing	**Married**	**Unmarried**	**Married**	**Unmarried**
High	35%	40%	25%	60%
Low	65%	60%	75%	40%
Column	100%	100%	100%	100%
Number of respondents	400	120	300	180

Initial relationship was spurious. A researcher working for an advertising agency promoting a car brands costing more than €60,000 was attempting to explain the ownership of expensive cars (see Table 17.7). The table shows that 32 per cent of those with university degrees own an expensive (more than €60,000) car compared with 21 per cent of those without university degrees. The researcher was tempted to conclude that education influenced ownership of expensive cars. Realising that income may also be a factor, the researcher decided to re-examine the relationship between education and ownership of expensive cars in the light of income level. This resulted in Table 17.8. Note that the percentages of those with and without university degrees who own expensive cars are the same for each income group. When the data for the high-income and low-income groups are examined separately, the association between education

Table 17.7 Ownership of expensive cars by education level

	Education	
Own expensive car	**Degree**	**No degree**
Yes	32%	21%
No	68%	79%
Column	100%	100%
Number of respondents	250	750

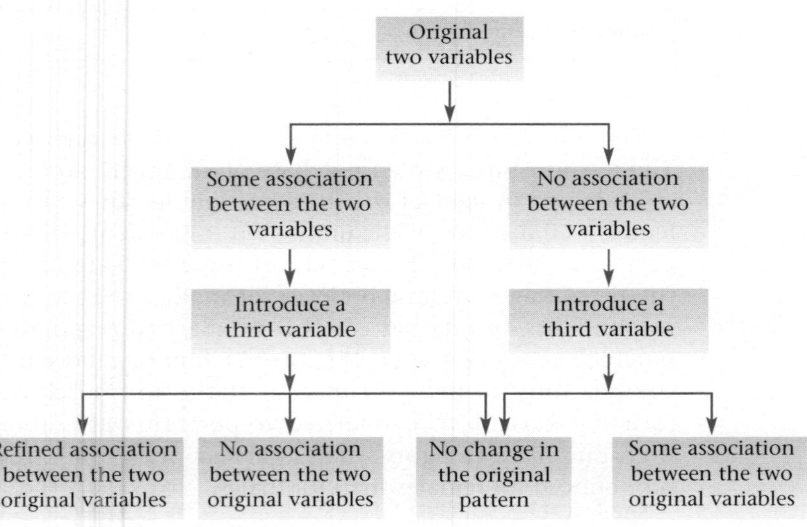

Figure 17.7
The introduction of a third variable in cross-tabulation

Table 17.8 Ownership of expensive cars by education and income levels

	Income			
	Low income Education		*High income Education*	
Own expensive car	**Degree**	**No degree**	**Degree**	**No degree**
Yes	20%	20%	40%	40%
No	80%	80%	60%	60%
Column totals	100%	100%	100%	100%
Number of respondents	100	700	150	50

and ownership of expensive cars disappears, indicating that the initial relationship observed between these two variables was spurious.

Reveal suppressed association. A researcher suspected desire to travel abroad may be influenced by age. A cross-tabulation of the two variables produced the results in Table 17.9, indicating no association. When gender was introduced as the third variable, Table 17.10 was obtained. Among men, 60 per cent of those under 45 indicated a desire to travel abroad compared with 40 per cent of those 45 or older. The pattern was reversed for women, where 35 per cent of those under 45 indicated a desire to travel abroad as opposed to 65 per cent of those 45 or older. Since the association between desire to travel abroad and age runs in the opposite direction for males and females, the relationship between these two variables is masked when the data are aggregated across gender as in Table 17.9. But when the effect of gender is controlled, as in Table 17.10, the suppressed association between preference and age is revealed for the separate categories of males and females.

Table 17.9 Desire to travel abroad by age

	Age	
Desire to travel abroad by age	**Under 45**	**45 or older**
Yes	50%	50%
No	50%	50%
Column totals	100%	100%
Number of respondents	500	500

Table 17.10 Desire to travel abroad by age and gender

	Gender			
	Male Age		*Female Age*	
Desire to travel abroad	**Under 45**	**45 or older**	**Under 45**	**45 or older**
Yes	60%	40%	35%	65%
No	40%	60%	65%	35%
Column totals	100%	100%	100%	100%
Number of respondents	300	300	250	200

No change in initial relationship. In some cases, the introduction of the third variable does not change the initial relationship observed, regardless of whether the original variables were associated. This suggests that the third variable does not influence the relationship between the first two. Consider the cross-tabulation of family size and the tendency to eat in fast-food restaurants frequently, as shown in Table 17.11. The respondents' families were classified into small- and large-size categories based on a median split of the distribution, with 500 respondents in each category. No association is observed. The respondents were further classified into high- or low-income groups based on a median split. When income was introduced as a third variable in the analysis, Table 17.12 was obtained. Again, no association was observed.

Table 17.11 Eating frequently in fast-food restaurants by family size

Eat frequently in fast-food restaurants	*Family size*	
	Small	*Large*
Yes	65%	65%
No	35%	35%
Column totals	100%	100%
Number of respondents	500	500

Table 17.12 Eating frequently in fast-food restaurants by family size and income

	Income			
	Low income Family size		*High income Family size*	
Eat frequently in fast-food restaurants	**Small**	**Large**	**Small**	**Large**
Yes	65%	65%	65%	65%
No	35%	35%	35%	35%
Column total	100%	100%	100%	100%
Number of respondents	250	250	250	250

General comments on cross-tabulation

Even though more than three variables can be cross-tabulated, the interpretation is quite complex. Also, because the number of cells increases multiplicatively, maintaining an adequate number of respondents or cases in each cell can be problematic. As a general rule, there should be at least five expected observations in each cell for the computed statistics to be reliable. Thus, cross-tabulation is an inefficient way of examining relationships when there are several variables. Note that cross-tabulation examines association between variables, not causation. To examine causation, the causal research design framework should be adopted (see Chapter 9).

STATISTICS ASSOCIATED WITH CROSS-TABULATION

We now discuss the statistics commonly used for assessing the statistical significance and strength of association of cross-tabulated variables. The statistical significance of the observed association is commonly measured by the chi-square statistic. The strength of association, or degree of association, is important from a practical or substantive perspective. Generally, the strength of association is of interest only if the association is statistically significant. The strength of the association can be measured by the phi correlation coefficient, the contingency coefficient, Cramer's *V*, and the lambda coefficient. These statistics are described in detail.

Chi square

Chi-square statistic
The statistic used to test the statistical significance of the observed association in a cross-tabulation. It assists us in determining whether a systematic association exists between the two variables.

The **chi-square statistic** (χ^2) is used to test the statistical significance of the observed association in a cross-tabulation. It assists us in determining whether a systematic association exists between the two variables. The null hypothesis, H_0, is that there is no association between the variables. The test is conducted by computing the cell frequencies that would be expected if no association were present between the variables, given the existing row and column totals. These expected cell frequencies, denoted f_e, are then compared with the actual observed frequencies, f_o, found in the cross-tabulation to calculate the chi-square statistic. The greater the discrepancies between the expected and actual frequencies, the larger the value of the statistic. Assume that a cross-tabulation has *r* rows and *c* columns and a random sample of *n* observations. Then the expected frequency for each cell can be calculated by using a simple formula:

$$f_e = \frac{n_r n_c}{n}$$

where

n_r = total number in the row
n_c = total number in the column
n = total sample size

For the data in Table 17.2, the expected frequencies for the cells going from left to right and from top to bottom, are

$$\frac{614 \times 151}{972} = 95.4 \qquad \frac{614 \times 219}{972} = 132 \qquad \frac{614 \times 186}{972} = 117.5$$

$$\frac{614 \times 145}{972} = 91.6 \qquad \frac{614 \times 281}{972} = 177.5 \qquad \frac{64 \times 151}{972} = 9.9$$

$$\frac{64 \times 209}{972} = 13.8 \qquad \frac{64 \times 186}{972} = 12.2 \qquad \frac{64 \times 145}{972} = 9.5$$

$$\frac{64 \times 281}{972} = 18.5 \qquad \frac{294 \times 151}{972} = 45.7 \qquad \frac{294 \times 209}{972} = 63.2$$

$$\frac{294 \times 186}{972} = 56.3 \qquad \frac{294 \times 145}{972} = 43.9 \qquad \frac{294 \times 281}{972} = 85$$

Then the value of χ^2 is calculated as follows:

$$\chi^2 = \sum_{\text{all cells}} \frac{(f_0 - f_e)^2}{f_e}$$

For the data in Table 17.2, the value of X^2 is calculated as

$$X^2 = \frac{(105-95.4)^2}{95.4} + \frac{(130-132)^2}{132} + \frac{(115-117.5)^2}{117.5} + \frac{(92-91.6)^2}{91.6} + \frac{(172-177.5)^2}{177.5} + \frac{(12-9.9)^2}{9.9} + \frac{(22-13.8)^2}{13.8} + \frac{(7-12.2)^2}{12.2} + \frac{(9-9.5)^2}{9.5} + \frac{(14-18.5)^2}{18.5} + \frac{(34-45.7)^2}{45.7} + \frac{(57-63.2)^2}{63.2} + \frac{(64-56.3)^2}{56.3} + \frac{(44-43.9)^2}{43.9} + \frac{(95-85)^2}{85} = 15.8$$

To determine whether a systematic association exists, the probability of obtaining a value of chi-square as large or larger than the one calculated from the cross-tabulation is estimated. An important characteristic of the chi-square statistic is the number of degrees of freedom (*df*) associated with it. In general, the number of degrees of freedom is equal to the number of observations less the number of constraints needed to calculate a statistical term. In the case of a chi-square statistic associated with a cross-tabulation, the number of degrees of freedom is equal to the product of number of rows (r) less one and the number of columns (c) less one. That is, $df = (r - 1) \times (c - 1)$.[9] The null hypothesis (H_0) of no association between the two variables will be rejected only when the calculated value of the test statistic is greater than the critical value of the chi-square distribution with the appropriate degrees of freedom, as shown in Figure 17.8.

Chi-square distribution
A skewed distribution whose shape depends solely on the number of degrees of freedom. As the number of degrees of freedom increases, the chi-square distribution becomes more symmetrical.

The **chi-square distribution** is a skewed distribution whose shape depends solely on the number of degrees of freedom.[10] As the number of degrees of freedom increases, the chi-square distribution becomes more symmetrical. Table 3 in the Statistical Appendix contains upper-tail areas of the chi-square distribution for different degrees of freedom. In this table, the value at the top of each column indicates the area in the upper portion (the right side, as shown in Figure 17.8) of the chi-square distribution. To illustrate, for 8 degrees of freedom, the value for an upper-tail area of 0.05 is 15.507. This indicates that for 2 degrees of freedom the probability of exceeding a chi-square value of 15.507 is 0.05. In other words, at the 0.05 level of significance with 8 degrees of freedom, the critical value of the chi-square statistic is 15.507.

For the cross-tabulation given in Table 17.2, there are $(3 - 1) \times (5 - 1) = 8$ degrees of freedom. The calculated chi-square statistic had a value of 15.8. Since this exceeds the critical value of 15.507, the null hypothesis of no association can be rejected, indicating that the association is statistically significant at the 0.05 level.

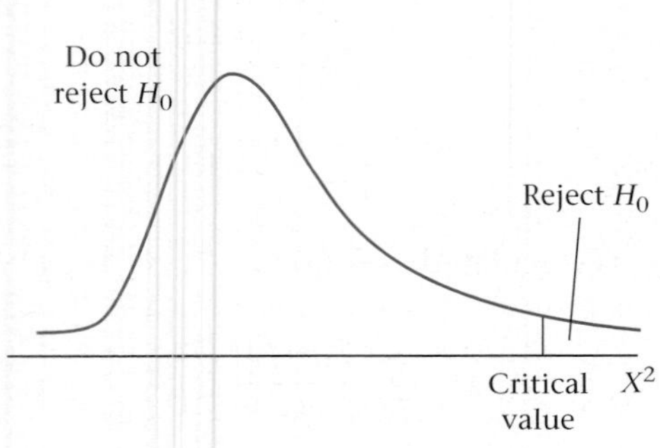

Figure 17.8 Chi-square test of association

The chi-square statistic can also be used in goodness-of-fit tests to determine whether certain models fit the observed data. These tests are conducted by calculating the significance of sample deviations from assumed theoretical (expected) distributions and can be performed on cross-tabulations as well as on frequencies (one-way tabulations). The calculation of the chi-square statistic and the determination of its significance is the same as illustrated above.

The chi-square statistic should be estimated only on counts of data. When the data are in percentage form, they should first be converted to absolute counts or numbers. In addition, an underlying assumption of the chi-square test is that the observations are drawn independently. As a general rule, chi-square analysis should not be conducted when the expected or theoretical frequencies in any of the cells is less than five. If the number of observations in any cell is less than ten, or if the table has two rows and two columns (a 2×2 table), a correction factor should be applied.[11] In the case of a 2×2 table, the chi-square is related to the phi coefficient.

Phi coefficient

Phi coefficient
A measure of the strength of association in the special case of a table with two rows and two columns (a 2×2 table).

The **phi coefficient** (ϕ) is used as a measure of the strength of association in the special case of a table with two rows and two columns (a 2×2 table). The phi coefficient is proportional to the square root of the chi-square statistic. For a sample of size n, this statistic is calculated as

$$\phi = \sqrt{\frac{\chi^2}{n}}$$

It takes the value of 0 when there is no association, which would be indicated by a chi-square value of 0 as well. When the variables are perfectly associated, phi assumes the value of 1 and all the observations fall just on the main or minor diagonal. (In some computer programs, phi assumes a value of –1 rather than + 1 when there is perfect negative association.) In the more general case involving a table of any size, the strength of association can be assessed by using the contingency coefficient.

Contingency coefficient

Contingency coefficient
A measure of the strength of association in a table of any size.

Although the phi coefficient is specific to a 2×2 table, the **contingency coefficient (C)** can be used to assess the strength of association in a table of any size. This index is also related to chi-square, as follows:

$$C = \sqrt{\frac{\chi^2}{\chi^2 + n}}$$

The contingency coefficient varies between 0 and 1. The 0 value occurs in the case of no association (i.e. the variables are statistically independent), but the maximum value of 1 is never achieved. Rather, the maximum value of the contingency coefficient depends on the size of the table (number of rows and number of columns). For this reason, it should be used only to compare tables of the same size. The value of the contingency coefficient for Table 17.2 is

$$C = \sqrt{\frac{\chi^2}{\chi^2 + n}}$$

$$= \frac{15.8}{987.8}$$

$$= 0.1264$$

This value of **C** indicates that the association is not very strong.

Another statistic that can be calculated for any table is Cramer's V.

Cramer's V

Cramer's V
A measure of the strength of association used in tables larger than 2×2.

Cramer's V is a modified version of the phi correlation coefficient, ϕ, and is used in tables larger than 2×2. When phi is calculated for a table larger than 2×2, it has no upper limit. Cramer's V is obtained by adjusting phi for either the number of rows or the number of columns in the table based on which of the two is smaller. The adjustment is such that V will range from 0 to 1. A large value of V merely indicates a high degree of association. It does not indicate how the variables are associated. For a table with r rows and c columns, the relationship between Cramer's V and the phi correlation coefficient is expressed as

$$V = \sqrt{\frac{\phi^2}{\min (r-1),(c-1)}}$$

or

$$V = \sqrt{\frac{\chi^2/n}{\min (r-1),(c-1)}}$$

The value of Cramer's V for Table 17.2 is

$$V = \sqrt{\frac{15.8 / 972}{8}}$$

$$= 0.045$$

Thus, the association is not strong.

Another statistic commonly estimated is the lambda coefficient.

Asymmetric lambda
A measure of the percentage improvement in predicting the value of the dependent variable given the value of the independent variable in contingency table analysis. Lambda also varies between 0 and 1.

Symmetric lambda
The symmetric lambda does not make an assumption about which variable is dependent. It measures the overall improvement when prediction is done in both directions.

Lambda coefficient

The lambda coefficient assumes that the variables are measured on a nominal scale. **Asymmetric lambda** measures the percentage improvement in predicting the value of the dependent variable, given the value of the independent variable. The lambda coefficient also varies between 0 and 1. A value of 0 means no improvement in prediction. A value of 1 indicates that the prediction can be made without error. This happens when each independent variable category is associated with a single category of the dependent variable.

Asymmetric lambda is computed for each of the variables (treating it as the dependent variable). The two asymmetric lambdas are likely to be different since the marginal distributions are not usually the same. A **symmetric lambda**, a kind of average of the two asymmetric values, is also computed. The symmetric lambda does not make an assumption about which variable is dependent. It measures the overall improvement when prediction is done in both directions.[12]

tau b
A test statistic that measures the association between two ordinal-level variables. It makes an adjustment for ties and is the most appropriate when the table of variables is square.

tau c
A test statistic that measures the association between two ordinal-level variables. It makes an adjustment for ties and is most appropriate when the table of variables is not square but a rectangle.

Gamma
A test statistic that measures the association between two ordinal-level variables. It does not make an adjustment for ties.

Other statistics

Other statistics like **tau *b***, **tau *c***, and **gamma** are available to measure association between two ordinal-level variables. All these statistics use information about the ordering of categories of variables by considering every possible pair of cases in the table. Each pair is examined to determine if its relative ordering on the first variable is the same as its relative ordering on the second variable (concordant), if the ordering is reversed (discordant), or if the pair is tied. The manner in which the ties are treated is the basic difference between these statistics. Both tau b and tau c adjust for ties. Tau b is the most appropriate with square tables in which the number of rows and the number of columns are equal. Its value varies between + 1 and –1. For a rectangular table in which the number of rows is different from the number of columns, tau *c* should be used. Gamma does not make an adjustment for either ties or table size. Gamma also varies between + 1 and –1 and generally has a higher numerical value than tau *b* or tau *c*. Other statistics for measuring the strength of association, namely product moment correlation, and non-metric correlation are discussed in Chapter 19.

CROSS-TABULATION IN PRACTICE

While conducting cross-tabulation analysis in practice, it is useful to proceed through the following steps.

1 Test the null hypothesis that there is no association between the variables using the chi-square statistic. If you fail to reject the null hypothesis, then there is no relationship.
2 If H_0 is rejected, then determine the strength of the association using an appropriate statistic (phi coefficient, contingency coefficient, Cramer's V, lambda coefficient, or other statistics), as discussed earlier.
3 If H_0 is rejected, interpret the pattern of the relationship by computing the percentages in the direction of the independent variable, across the dependent variable.

HYPOTHESIS TESTING RELATED TO DIFFERENCES

The previous section considered hypothesis testing related to associations. We now focus on hypothesis testing related to differences. A classification of hypothesis testing procedures for examining differences is presented in Figure 17.9. Note that this figure is consistent with the classification of univariate techniques presented in Figure 16.6. Hypothesis testing procedures can be broadly classified as parametric or non-parametric, based on the measurement scale of

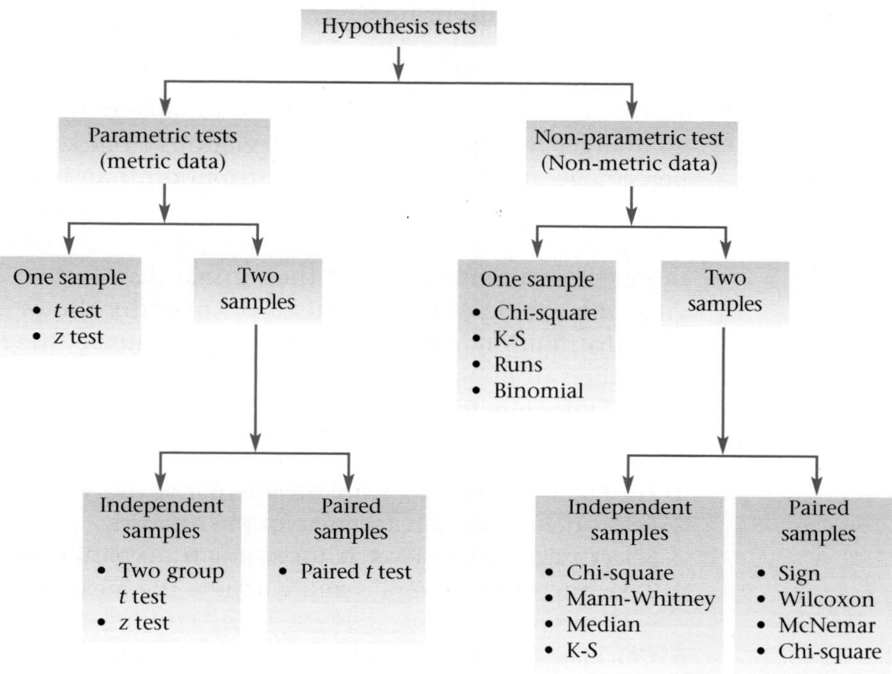

Figure 17.9
Hypothesis testing procedures

Parametric tests
Hypothesis testing procedures that assume that the variables of interest are measured on at least an interval scale.

Non-parametric tests
Hypothesis testing procedures that assume that the variables are measured on a nominal or ordinal scale.

the variables involved. **Parametric tests** assume that the variables of interest are measured on at least an interval scale. The most popular parametric test is the *t* test conducted for examining hypotheses about means. The *t* test could be conducted on the mean of one sample or two samples of observations. In the case of two samples, the samples could be independent or paired.

Non-parametric tests assume that the variables are measured on a nominal or ordinal scale. Non-parametric tests based on observations drawn from one sample include the Kolmogorov-Smirnov test, the chi-square test, the runs test and the binomial test. In case of two independent samples, the Mann-Whitney *U* test, the median test, and the Kolmogorov-Smirnov two sample tests are used for examining hypotheses about location. These tests are non-parametric counterparts of the two group *t* test. For paired samples, non-parametric tests include the Wilcoxon matched-pairs signed-ranks test and the sign test. These tests are the counterparts of the paired *t* test. Parametric as well as non-parametric tests are also available for evaluating hypotheses relating to more than two samples. These tests are considered in later chapters.

PARAMETRIC TESTS

t test
A univariate hypothesis test using the *t* distribution, which is used when the standard deviation is unknown and the sample size is small.

t statistic
A statistic that assumes that the variable has a symmetric bell-shaped distribution, that the mean is known (or assumed to be known), and that the population variance is estimated from the sample.

t distribution
A symmetrical bell-shaped distribution that is useful for sample testing ($n < 30$) testing.

Parametric tests provide inferences for making statements about the means of parent populations. A ***t* test** is commonly used for this purpose. This test is based on the Student's *t* statistic. The ***t* statistic** assumes that the variable is normally distributed and the mean is known (or assumed to be known) and the population variance is estimated from the sample. Assume that the random variable X is normally distributed, with mean μ and unknown population variance σ^2, which is estimated by the sample variance s^2. Recall that the standard deviation of the sample mean, $\bar{X}$, is estimated as $s_{\bar{X}} = s/\sqrt{n}$. Then, $t = (\bar{X} - \mu) / s_{\bar{X}}$ is t distributed with $n - 1$ degrees of freedom.

The ***t* distribution** is similar to the normal distribution in appearance. Both distributions are bell-shaped and symmetric. Compared with the normal distribution, however, the *t* distribution has more area in the tails and less in the centre. This is because population variance σ^2 is unknown and is estimated by the sample variance s^2. Given the uncertainty in the value of s^2, the observed values of t are more variable than those of z. Thus, we must go a larger number of standard deviations from zero to encompass a certain percentage of values from the *t* distribution than is the case with the normal distribution. Yet, as the number of degrees of freedom increases, the *t* distribution approaches the normal distribution. In fact, for large samples of 120 or more, the *t* distribution and the normal distribution are virtually indistinguishable. Table 4 in the Statistical Appendix shows selected percentiles of the *t* distribution. Although normality is assumed, the *t* test is quite robust to departures from normality.

The procedure for hypothesis testing, for the special case when the *t* statistic is used, is as follows.

1 Formulate the null (H_0) and the alternative (H_1) hypotheses.
2 Select the appropriate formula for the *t* statistic.
3 Select a significance level, α, for testing H_0. Typically, the 0.05 level is selected.[13]
4 Take one or two samples and compute the mean and standard deviation for each sample.
5 Calculate the *t* statistic assuming that H_0 is true.

6 Calculate the degrees of freedom and estimate the probability of getting a more extreme value of the statistic from Table 4. (Alternatively, calculate the critical value of the *t* statistic.)
7 If the probability computed in step 5 is smaller than the significance level selected in step 3, reject H_0. If the probability is larger, do not reject H_0. (Alternatively, if the value of the calculated *t* statistic in step 4 is larger than the critical value determined in step 5, reject H_0. If the calculated value is smaller than the critical value, do not reject H_0.) Failure to reject H_0 does not necessarily imply that H_0 is true. It only means that the true state is not significantly different than that assumed by H_0[14].
8 Express the conclusion reached by the *t* test in terms of the marketing research problem.

We illustrate the general procedure for conducting *t* tests in the following sections, beginning with the one-sample case.

One sample

In marketing research, the researcher is often interested in making statements about a single variable against a known or given standard. Examples of such statements include the market share for a new product will exceed 15 per cent, at least 65 per cent of customers will like a new package design, and 80 per cent of retailers will prefer a new pricing policy. These statements can be translated to null hypotheses that can be tested using a one-sample test, such as the *t* test or the *z* test. In the case of a *t* test for a single mean, the researcher is interested in testing whether the population mean conforms to a given hypothesis (H_0). Suppose that a new machine attachment would be introduced if it receives a mean of at least 7 on a ten-point scale (where 0 = Dreadful addition to machine and 10 = Exemplary addition to machine). A sample of 20 engineers is shown the attachment and asked to evaluate it. The results indicate a mean rating of 7.9 with a standard deviation of 1.6. A significance level of $\alpha = 0.05$ is selected. Should the part be introduced?

$$H_0 = \mu \leq 7.0$$

$$H_1 = \mu > 7.0$$

$$t = \frac{(\bar{X} - \mu)}{S_{\bar{X}}}$$

$$S_{\bar{X}} = \frac{s}{\sqrt{n}}$$

$$S_{\bar{X}} = \frac{1.6}{\sqrt{20}} = \frac{1.6}{4.472} = 0.358$$

$$t = \frac{(7.9 - 7.0)}{0.358} = \frac{0.9}{0.358} = 2.514$$

The degrees of freedom for the *t* statistic to test hypothesis about one mean are $n - 1$. In this case, $n - 1 = 20 - 1$, or 19. From Table 4 in the Statistical Appendix, the probability of getting a more extreme value than 2.514 is less than 0.05. (Alternatively, the critical *t* value for 19 degrees of freedom and a significance level of 0.05 is 1.7291, which is less than the calculated value.) Hence, the null hypothesis is rejected, favouring the introduction of the part.

z test
A univariate hypothesis test using the standard normal distribution.

Note that if the population standard deviation was assumed to be known as 1.5, rather than estimated from the sample, a **z test** would be appropriate. In this case, the value of the *z* statistic would be

$$z = \frac{\bar{X} - \mu}{\sigma_{\bar{X}}}$$

where

$$\sigma_{\bar{X}} = \frac{1.5}{20} = \frac{1.5}{4.472} = 0.335$$

and

$$z = \frac{7.9 - 7.0}{0.358} = \frac{0.9}{0.358} = 2.514$$

From Table 2 in the Statistical Appendix, the probability of getting a more extreme value of *z* than 2.514 is less than 0.05. (Alternatively, the critical *z* value for a one-tailed test and a significance level of 0.05 is 1.645, which is less than the calculated value.) Therefore, the null hypothesis is rejected, reaching the same conclusion arrived at earlier by the *t* test.

The procedure for testing a null hypothesis with respect to a proportion was illustrated earlier in this chapter when we introduced hypothesis testing.

Two independent samples

Independent samples
Two samples that are not experimentally related. The measurement of one sample has no effect on the values of the second sample.

Several hypotheses in marketing relate to parameters from two different populations: for example, the users and non-users of a brand differ in terms of their perceptions of the brand, the high-income consumers spend more on leisure activities than low-income consumers, or the proportion of brand loyal users in segment I is more than the proportion in segment 11. Samples drawn randomly from different populations are termed **independent samples**. As in the case for one sample, the hypotheses could relate to means or proportions.

Means. In the case of means for two independent samples, the hypotheses take the following form:

$$H_0: \mu_1 = \mu_2$$
$$H_1: \mu_1 \neq \mu_2$$

The two populations are sampled and the means and variances are computed based on samples of sizes *n*l and *n*2. If both populations are found to have the same variance, a pooled variance estimate is computed from the two sample variances as follows:

$$s^2 = \frac{\sum_{i=1}^{n_1} (X_{i_1} - \bar{X}_1)^2 + \sum_{i=1}^{n_2} (X_{i_2} - \bar{X}_2)^2}{n_1 + n_2 - 2}$$

The standard deviation of the test statistic can be estimated as

$$s_{\bar{X}_1 - \bar{X}_2} = \sqrt{s^2 \left(\frac{1}{n_1} + \frac{1}{n_2}\right)}$$

The appropriate value of *t* can be calculated as

$$t = \frac{(\bar{X}_1 - \bar{X}_2) - (\mu_1 - \mu_2)}{s_{\bar{X}_1 - \bar{X}_2}}$$

The degrees of freedom in this case are $(n_1 + n_2 - 2)$.

If the two populations have unequal variances, an exact t cannot be computed for the difference in sample means. Instead, an approximation to t is computed. The number of degrees of freedom in this case is usually not an integer, but a reasonably accurate probability can be obtained by rounding to the nearest integer.[15]

F **test**
A statistical test of the equality of the variances of two populations.

An ***F* test** of sample variance may be performed if it is not known whether the two populations have equal variance. In this case the hypotheses are

$$H_0: \sigma_1^2 = \mu_2^2$$
$$H_1: \mu_1^2 \neq \mu_2^2$$

F **statistic**
The ratio of two sample variances.

The ***F* statistic** is computed from the sample variances as follows:

$$F_{(n_1-1)'(n_2-1)} = \frac{s_1^{\,2}}{s_2^{\,2}}$$

where

n_1 = size of sample 1
n_2 = size of sample 2
$n_1 - 1$ = degrees of freedom for sample 1
$n_2 - 1$ = degrees of freedom for sample 2
$s_1^{\,2}$ = sample variance for for sample 1
$s_2^{\,2}$ = sample variance for for sample 2

F **distribution**
A frequency distribution that depends upon two sets of degrees of freedom: the degrees of freedom in the numerator and the degrees of freedom in the denominator.

As can be seen, the critical value of the ***F* distribution** depends on two sets of degrees of freedom: those in the numerator and those in the denominator. The critical values of F for various degrees of freedom for the numerator and denominator are given in Table 5 of the Statistical Appendix. If the probability of F is greater than the significance level α, H_0 is not rejected and t based on the pooled variance estimate can be used. On the other hand, if the probability of F is less than or equal to α, H_0 is rejected and t based on a separate variance estimate is used.

Using the GlobalCash example, suppose that the researcher wanted to determine whether respondents from Germany and the Netherlands who use Citibank for pan-European transactions prefer 'security' to other functions that need to be improved in their electronic banking functions.

A two independent samples t test was conducted, and the results are presented in Table 17.13. Note that the F test of sample variances has a probability that

Table 17.13 Two independent samples *t* test

Summary statistics			
	Number of cases	*Mean*	*Standard deviation*
German companies	135	3.9778	1.604
Dutch companies	132	4.3712	1.627

***F* test for equality of variances**	
***F** value*	*Two-tail probability*
1.03	0.871

***t* test**					
Pooled variance estimate			**Separate variance estimate**		
***t** value*	*Degrees of freedom*	*Two-tail probability*	***t** value*	*Degrees of freedom*	*Two-tail probability*
–1.99	265	0.048	–1.99	264.65	0.048

exceeds 0.05. Accordingly, H_0 cannot be rejected, and the t test based on the pooled variance estimate should be used. The t value is –1.99, and with 265 degrees of freedom, this gives a probability of 0.048, which is less than the significance level of 0.05. Therefore, the null hypothesis of equal means is rejected. Since the mean importance of 'user friendliness' for German companies is 3.9778 and for Dutch companies is 4.3712, Dutch companies (who use Citibank for pan-European transactions) attach significantly greater importance to 'user friendliness' when seeking improvements to electronic banking functions than German companies. We also show the t test using a separate variance estimate since most computer programs automatically conduct the t test both ways. As an application of the t test, consider the following example.

EXAMPLE

Shops seek to suit elderly to a 't'[16]

A study based on a sample of 789 respondents who were 65 or older attempted to determine the effect of lack of mobility on shop patronage. A major research question related to the differences in the physical requirements of dependent and self-reliant elderly persons. That is, did the two groups require different things to get to the shop or after they arrived at the shop? A more detailed analysis of the physical requirements conducted by two independent samples' t tests (shown in the table) indicated that dependent elderly persons are more likely to look for shops that offer home delivery and phone orders and for shops to which they have accessible transportation. They are also more likely to look for a variety of shops located close together. ■

Differences in physical requirements between dependent and self-reliant elderly

	MEAN*		
Physical requirement items	**Self-reliant**	**Dependent**	***t* test probability**
Delivery to home	1.787	2.000	0.023
Phone in order	2.030	2.335	0.003
Transportation to store	2.188	3.098	0.000
Convenient parking	4.001	4.095	0.305
Location close to home	3.177	3.325	0.137
Variety of shops close together	3.456	3.681	0.023

* Measured on a five-point scale from not important (1) to very important (5)

In this example, we tested the difference between means. A similar test is available for testing the difference between proportions for two independent samples.

Proportions. A case involving proportions for two independent samples is illustrated in Table 17.14, which gives the number of companies (employing more than 5000) that have their own 'in-house' banks in Germany and France.

Is the proportion the same in the German and French samples? The null and alternative hypotheses are:

$$H_0: \pi_1 = \pi_2$$
$$H_1: \pi_1 \neq \pi_2$$

Table 17.14 Comparing the proportions of German and French companies that have an 'in-house' bank

	Use an 'in-house' bank		
Sample	*Have an 'in-house' bank*	*Do not have an 'in-house' bank*	*Row totals*
Germany	160	40	200
France	120	80	200
Column totals	280	120	

A z test is used as in testing the proportion for one sample. In this case, however, the test statistic is given by

$$z = \frac{P_1 - P_2}{s_{\bar{P}_1 - \bar{P}_2}}$$

In the test statistic, the numerator is the difference between the proportions in the two samples, P_1 and P_2. The denominator is the standard error of the difference in the two proportions and is given by

$$s_{\bar{P}_1 - \bar{P}_2} = \sqrt{P(1 - P)\left[\frac{1}{n_1} + \frac{1}{n_2}\right]}$$

where

$$P = \frac{n_1 P_1 + n_2 P_2}{n_1 + n_2}$$

A significance level of $\alpha = 0.05$ is selected. Given the data in Table 17.14, the test statistic can be calculated as

$$P_1 - P_2 = 0.8 - 0.6 = 0.2$$

$$\text{P} = \frac{200 \times 0.8 + 200 \times 0.6}{200 + 200} = 0.7$$

$$s_{P_1 - P_2} = \sqrt{0.7 \times 0.3\left[\frac{1}{200} + \frac{1}{200}\right]} = 0.04583$$

$$z = \frac{0.2}{0.04583} = 4.36$$

Given a two-tail test, the area to the right of the critical value is $\alpha/2$, or 0.025. Hence, the critical value of the test statistic is 1.96. Since the calculated value exceeds the critical value the null hypothesis is rejected. Thus, the proportion of companies with 'in-house' banks (80 per cent for German companies and 60 per cent for French companies) is significantly different for the two samples.

Paired samples

In many marketing research applications, the observations for the two groups are not selected from independent samples. Rather, the observations relate to **paired samples** in that the two sets of observations relate to the same respondents. A sample of respondents may rate competing brands, may indicate the relative importance of two attributes of a product, or may evaluate a brand at two different times. The differences in these cases is examined by a **paired samples *t* test**. To compute t for paired samples, the paired difference variable, denoted by D, is

Paired samples
In hypothesis testing, the observations are paired so that the two sets of observations relate to the same respondents.

Paired samples *t* test
A test for differences in the means of paired samples.

formed and its mean and variance calculated. Then the t statistic is computed. The degrees of freedom are $n - 1$, where n is the number of pairs. The relevant formulas are

$$H_0: \mu_D = 0$$
$$H_1: \mu_D \neq 0$$
$$t_{n-1} = \frac{\bar{D} - \mu_D}{\frac{s_D}{\sqrt{n}}}$$

where

$$\bar{D} = \frac{\sum_{i=1}^{n} D_i}{n}$$

$$s_D = \sqrt{\frac{\sum_{i=1}^{n} (Di - \bar{D})^2}{n-1}}$$

The following example illustrates an application of a paired samples t test.

EXAMPLE

Seconds count[17]

A survey of 83 media directors of advertising agencies was conducted to determine the relative effectiveness of 15-second versus 30-second commercial advertisements. By use of a five-point rating scale (1 being excellent and 5 being poor), 15- and 30-second commercials were rated by each respondent for brand awareness, main idea recall, persuasion, and ability to tell an emotional story. The table indicates that 30-second commercials were rated more favourably on all the dimensions. Paired t tests indicated that these differences were significant, and the 15-second commercials were evaluated as less effective. ■

Mean rating of 15- and 30-second commercials on four communication variables							
Brand awareness		Main idea recall		Persuasion		Ability to tell an emotional story	
15	*30*	*15*	*30*	*15*	*30*	*15*	*30*
2.5	1.9	2.7	2.0	3.7	2.1	4.3	1.9

The difference in proportions for paired samples can be tested by using the McNemar test or the chi-square test, as explained in the following section on non-parametric tests.

NON-PARAMETRIC TESTS

Non-parametric tests are used when the variables are non-metric. Like parametric tests, non-parametric tests are available for testing variables from one sample, two independent samples, or two related samples.

One sample

Sometimes the researcher wants to test whether the observations for a particular variable could reasonably have come from a particular distribution, such as the normal, uniform, or Poisson distribution. Knowledge of the distribution is necessary for finding probabilities corresponding to known values of the variable or variable values corresponding to known probabilities (see Appendix 14A). The **Kolmogorov-Smirnov (KS) one-sample test** is one such goodness-of-fit test. The K-S compares the cumulative distribution function for a variable with a specified distribution. A_i denotes the cumulative relative frequency for each category of the theoretical (assumed) distribution, and O_i denotes the comparable value of the sample frequency. The K-S test is based on the maximum value of the absolute difference between A_i and O_i. The test statistic is

Kolmogorov-Smirnov one-sample test
A one-sample non-parametric goodness-of-fit test that compares the cumulative distribution function for a variable with a specified distribution.

$$K = \text{Max}| A_i - O_i |$$

The decision to reject the null hypothesis is based on the value of K. The larger K is, the more confidence we have that H_0 is false. Note that this is one-tailed test, since the value of K is always positive, and we reject H_0 for large values of K. For $\alpha = 0.05$, the critical value of K for large samples (over 35) is given by $1.36/n$.[18] Alternatively, K can be transformed into a normally distributed z statistic and its associated probability determined.

In the context of the GlobalCash project, suppose that one wanted to test whether the distribution of the importance attached 'security' in electronic banking functions was normal. A K-S one-sample test is conducted, yielding the data shown in Table 17.16.

Table 17.16 K-S one-sample test for normality

	Test distribution, Normal
Mean	4.19
Standard deviation	1.62
Cases	271

	Most extreme differences			
Absolute	**Positive**	**Negative**	**K-S z**	**Two-tailed p**
0.19754	0.13150	–0.19754	3.253	0.000

The largest absolute difference between the observed and normal distribution was $K = 0.1975$. The critical value for K is $1.36/271 = 0.005$. Since the calculated value of K is larger than the critical value, the null hypothesis is rejected. Alternatively, Table 17.16 indicates that the probability of observing a K value of 0.1975, as determined by the normalised z statistic, is less than 0.001. Since this is less than the significance level of 0.05, the null hypothesis is rejected, leading to the same conclusion. Hence, the distribution of the importance attached to 'security' deviates significantly from the normal distribution.

As mentioned earlier, the chi-square test can also be performed on a single variable from one sample. In this context, the chi-square serves as a goodness-of-fit test. It tests whether a significant difference exists between the observed number of cases in each category and the expected number. Other one-sample non-parametric tests include the **runs test** and the **binomial test**. The runs test is a test of randomness for the dichotomous variables. This test is conducted by determining whether the order or sequence in which observations are obtained is random. The binomial test is also a goodness-of-fit test for dichotomous variables. It tests the goodness of fit of the observed number of observations in each category to the number expected under a specified binomial distribution. For more information on these tests, refer to standard statistical literature.[19]

Runs test
A test of randomness for a dichotomous variable.

Binomial test
A goodness-of-fit statistical test for dichotomous variables. It tests the goodness of fit of the observed number of observations in each category to the number expected under a specified binomial distribution.

Two independent samples

Mann-Whitney *U* test
A statistical test for a variable measured on an ordinal scale comparing the difference in the location of two populations based on observations from two independent samples.

When the difference in the location of two populations is to be compared based on observations from two independent samples and the variable is measured on an ordinal scale, the **Mann-Whitney *U* test** can be used.[20] This test corresponds to the two independent sample *t* test, for interval scale variables, when the variances of the two populations are assumed equal.

In the Mann-Whitney *U* test, the two samples are combined and the cases are ranked in order of increasing size. The test statistic, *U*, is computed as the number of times a score from sample or group 1 precedes a score from group 2. If the samples are from the same population, the distribution of scores from the two groups in the rank list should be random. An extreme value of *U* would indicate a non-random pattern pointing to the inequality of the two groups. For samples of less than 30, the exact significance level for *U* is computed. For larger samples, *U* is transformed into a normally distributed *z* statistic. This *z* can be corrected for ties within ranks.

Since the distribution of importance attached to 'security' was determined to be non-normal, it is appropriate to examine again whether German companies attach different importance to Dutch companies in their views of electronic banking security. This time, though, the Mann-Whitney *U* test is used. The results are given in Table 17.17. Again, a significant difference is found between the two groups, corroborating the results of the two independent samples *t* test reported earlier. Since the ranks are assigned from the smallest observation to the largest, the higher mean rank (144.39) of German respondents indicates that they attach greater importance to electronic banking security than Dutch respondents (mean rank = 123.84).

Table 17.17 Mann-Whitney *U* Wilcoxon rank sum *W* test, importance of electronic banking security

Mean Rank	Cases		
123.84	135	Germany = 1.00	
144.39	132	Netherlands = 2.00	
	267	Total	
U	*W*	*z*	Corrected for ties, two-tailed p
7538.00	19060.00	−2.2219	0.0263

Note: *U* = Mann-Whitney test statistics, *W* = Wilcoxon *W* statistic, *z* = *U* transformed into a normally distributed *z* statistic

Two-sample median test
Non-parametric test statistic that determines whether two groups are drawn from populations with the same median. This test is not as powerful as the Mann-Whitney *U*.

Kolmogorov-Smirnov two-sample test
Non-parametric test statistic that determines whether two distributions are the same. It takes into account any differences in the two distributions, including median, dispersion and skewness.

Researchers often wish to test for a significant difference in proportions obtained from two independent samples. In this case, as an alternative to the parametric *z* test considered earlier, one could also use the cross-tabulation procedure to conduct a chi-square test.[21] In this case, we will have a 2 × 2 table. One variable will be used to denote the sample and will assume the value 1 for sample 1 and the value of 2 for sample 2. The other variable will be the binary variable of interest.

Two other independent-samples non-parametric tests are the median test and Kolmogorov-Smirnov test. The **two-sample median test** determines whether the two groups are drawn from populations with the same median. It is not as powerful as the Mann-Whitney *U* test because it merely uses the location of each observation relative to the median, and not the rank, of each observation. The **Kolmogorov-Smirnov two-sample test** examines whether the two distributions are the same. It takes into account any differences between the two distributions, including the median, dispersion, and skewness, as illustrated by the following example.

EXAMPLE

Directors change direction[22]

How do marketing research directors and users in Fortune 500 manufacturing firms perceive the role of marketing research in initiating changes in marketing strategy formulation? It was found that the marketing research directors were more strongly in favour of initiating changes in strategy and less in favour of holding back than were users of marketing research. Using the Kolmogorov-Smirnov test, these differences of role definition were statistically significant at the 0.05 level, as shown below. ■

The role of marketing research in strategy formulation

Stage/item			Responses (%)					Kolmogorov-Smirnov test
Strategy formulation	Sample	*n*	Absolutely must	Preferably should	May or may not	Preferably should not	Absolutely must not	Significance
'Initiate change in the marketing strategy of the firm whenever possible'	*D*	77	7	26	43	19	5	
	U	68	2	15	32	35	16	0.05

D = directors, *U* = users

In this example, the marketing research directors and users comprised two independent samples. The samples, however, are not always independent. In the case of paired samples, a different set of tests should be used.

Paired samples

Wilcoxon matched-pairs signed-ranks test
A non-parametric test that analyses the differences between the paired observations, taking into account the magnitude of the differences.

An important non-parametric test for examining differences in the location of two populations based on paired observations is the **Wilcoxon matched-pairs signed-ranks test**. This test analyses the differences between the paired observations, taking into account the magnitude of the differences. It computes the differences between the pairs of variables and ranks the absolute differences. The next step is to sum the positive and negative ranks. The test statistic, z, is computed from the positive and negative rank sums. Under the null hypothesis of no difference, z is a standard normal variate with mean 0 and variance 1 for large samples. This test corresponds to the paired t test considered earlier.[23]

The GlobalCash example is considered, where respondents rank the importance of electronic banking criteria such as 'security' and 'user friendliness'. As these are measured on ordinal rather than interval scales, we use the Wilcoxon test. The results are shown in Table 17.18 where a significant difference is found in the variables. There are 177 negative differences (importance attached to security is less than that attached to user friendliness). The mean rank of these negative differences is 99.89. On the other hand, there are only 14 positive differences (the importance attached to security exceeds that of user friendliness). The mean rank of these differences is 46.89. There are 80 ties, or observations with the same value for both variables. These numbers indicate that user friendliness is more important than security. Furthermore, the probability associated with the t statistic is less than 0.05, indicating that the difference is indeed significant.

Table 17.18 Wilcoxon matched pairs signed-ranks test

Security with User friendliness		
Mean rank	**Cases**	**Security-User friendliness**
99.88	177	–Ranks
46.89	14	+ Ranks
	80	Ties
	271	Total
z = –11.1262		2-tailed p = 0.000

Sign test
A non-parametric test for examining differences in the location of two populations, based on paired populations, that only compares the signs of the differences between pairs of variables without taking into account the magnitude of the differences.

Another paired sample non-parametric test is the **sign test**.[24] This test is not as powerful as the Wilcoxon matched-pairs signed-ranks test because it only compares the signs of the differences between pairs of variables without taking into account the magnitude of the differences. In the special case of a binary variable where the researcher wishes to test differences in proportions, the McNemar test can be used. Alternatively, the chi-square test can also be used for binary variables. The various parametric and non-parametric tests are summarised in Table 17.19.

Table 17.19 A summary of hypothesis testing

Sample	Application	Level of scaling	Test/comments
One sample			
One sample	Distributions	Non-metric	K-S and chi-square for goodness of fit Runs test for randomness Binomial test for goodness of fit for dichotomous variables
One sample	Means	Metric	t test, if variance is unknown
One sample	Proportions	Metric	z test, if variance is known
Two independent samples			
Two independent samples	Distributions	Non-metric	K-S two-sample test for examining the equivalence of two distributions
Two independent samples	Means	Metric	Two-group t test F test for equality of variances
Two independent samples	Proportions	Metric Non-metric	z test Chi-square test
Two independent samples	Rankings/ Medians	Non-metric	Mann-Whitney U test is more powerful than the median test
Paired samples			
Paired samples	Means	Metric	Paired t test
Paired samples	Proportions	Non-metric	McNemar test for binary variables Chi-square test
Paired samples	Rankings/ Medians	Non-metric	Wilcoxon matched pairs ranked-signs test is more powerful than the sign test

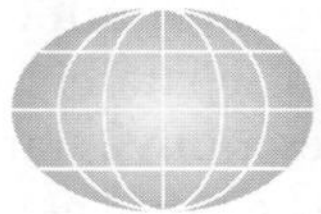

INTERNET AND COMPUTER APPLICATIONS

See the SNAP CD for examples of the computation of frequency distributions, cross-tabulations and testing hypotheses.

SPSS

The main program in SPSS is FREQUENCIES. It produces a table of frequency counts, percentages, and cumulative percentages for the vales of each variable. It gives all of the associated statistics except for the coefficient of variation. If the data are interval scaled and only the summary statistics are desired, the DESCRIPTIVES procedure can be used. All of the statistics computed by DESCRIPTIVES are available in FREQUENCIES. However, DESCRIPTIVES is more efficient because it does not sort values into a frequency table. An additional program, MEANS, computes means and standard deviations for a dependent variable over subgroups of cases defined by independent variables.

CROSSTABS displays cross-classification tables and provides cell counts, row and column percentages, the chi-square test for significance, and all the measures of the strength of the association that have been discussed. The major program for conducting *t* tests is T-TEST. This program can be used to conduct *t* tests on independent as well as paired samples. All the non-parametric tests that we have discussed can be conducted by using the NPAR TESTS program.

SAS

The main program is UNIVARIATE. In addition to providing a frequency table, this program provides all the associated statistics. Another procedure available is FREQ. For one-way frequency distribution, FREQ does not provide any associated statistics. If only summary statistics are desired, procedures such as MEANS, SUMMARY and TABULATE can be used.

FREQ displays cross-classification tables and provides cell counts, row and column percentages, the chi-square test for significance, and all the measures of the strength of the association that have been discussed. TABULATE can be used for obtaining cell counts and row and column percentages, although it does not provide any of the associated statistics. The program T-TEST can be used. The non-parametric tests may be conducted by using NPAR1WAY. This program will conduct the two independent samples test (Mann-Whitney, median and K-S) as well as the Wilcoxon test for paired samples.

BMDP

The main procedure in BMDP is 2D, which gives the frequency distribution and all the associated statistics except for the coefficient of variation. 1D provides the summary statistics for interval data but does not give the frequency distribution. 4D gives a frequency distribution for numeric and non-numeric data but does not compute the summary statistics.

4F displays cross-classification tables and provides cell counts, row and column percentages, the chi-square test for significance, and all the measures of the strength of the association that have been discussed. The parametric *t* tests in BMDP may be conducted by using the 3D program and the non-parametric tests by using 3S.

Minitab

The main function is Stats>Descriptive Statistics. The output values include the mean, median, mode, standard deviation, minimum, maximum and quartiles. A histogram in a bar chart or graph can be produced from the Graph>Histogram selection. Cross-tabulations, (cross tabs) and chi-square are under the Stats>Tables function. Each of these features must be selected separately under the Tables function. Parametric tests available in Minitab in descriptive stat function are *z* test means, *t* test for means, and two-sample *t* test. The non-parametric tests can be accessed under the Stat>Time Series function. The output includes the one-sample sign, one-sample Wilcoxon, Mann Whitney, Kruskal-Wallis, median test, Friedman, runs test, and pairwise differences.

Excel

In Excel the output produces the mean, standard error, median, mode, standard deviation, variance, kurtosis, skewness, range, minimum, maximum, sum, count, and confidence level. Frequencies can be selected under the histogram function. A histogram can be produced in bar format. The Data>Pivot Table performs crosstabs in Excel. To do additional analysis or customise data, select a different summary function such as max, min, average, or standard deviation. In addition, a custom calculation can be selected to calculate based on other cells in the data plane. ChiTest can be accessed under the Insert>Function>Statistical>ChiTest function. The available parametric tests include the *t* test: paired samples for means, *t* test: two independent samples assuming equal variances, *t* test: two independent samples assuming unequal variances, *z* test: two samples for means, and *F* test for variances of two samples.[25]

SUMMARY

Basic data analysis provides valuable insights and guides the rest of the data analysis as well as the interpretation of the results. A frequency distribution should be obtained for each variable in the data. This analysis produces a table of frequency counts, percentages and cumulative percentages for all the values associated with that variable. It indicates the extent of out-of range, missing or extreme values. The mean, mode and median of a frequency distribution are measures of central tendency. The variability of the distribution is described by the range, the variance or standard deviation, coefficient of variation, and interquartile range. Skewness and kurtosis provide an idea of the shape of the distribution.

Cross-tabulations are tables that reflect the joint distribution of two or more variables. In cross-tabulation, the percentages can be computed either by column, based on column totals, or by row, based on row totals. The general rule is to compute the percentages in the direction of the independent variable, across the dependent variable. Often the introduction of a third variable can provide additional insights. The chi-square statistic provides a test of the statistical significance of the observed association in a cross-tabulation. The phi coefficient, contingency coefficient, Cramer's *V*, and lambda coefficient provide measures of the strength of association between the variables.

Parametric and non-parametric tests are available for testing hypotheses related to differences. In the parametric case, the *t* test is used to examine hypotheses related to the population mean. Different forms of the *t* test are suitable for testing hypotheses based on one sample, two independent samples, or paired samples. In the non-parametric case, popular one-sample tests include the Kolmogorov-Smirnov, chi-square, runs and binomial tests. For two independent non-parametric samples, the Mann-Whitney *U* test, median test, and the Kolmogorov-Smirnov test can be used. For paired samples, the Wilcoxon matched-pairs signed-ranks test and the sign test are useful for examining hypotheses related to measures of location.

QUESTIONS AND PROBLEMS

1 Describe the procedure for computing frequencies.

2 What measures of location are commonly computed?

3 What measures of variability are commonly computed?

4 How is the relative flatness or peakedness of a distribution measured?

5 What is a skewed distribution? What does it mean?

6 What is the major difference between cross-tabulation and frequency distribution?

7 What is the general rule for computing percentages in cross-tabulation?

8 Define a spurious correlation.

9 What is meant by a suppressed association? How is it revealed?

10 Discuss the reasons for the frequent use of cross-tabulations. What are some of the limitations?

11 Present a classification of hypothesis testing procedures.

12 Describe the general procedure for conducting a *t* test.

13 What is the major difference between parametric and non-parametric tests?

14 Which non-parametric tests are the counterparts of the two independent samples *t* test for parametric data?

15 Which non-parametric tests are the counterparts of the paired samples *t* test for parametric data?

NOTES

1 Festervand, T.A., Snyder, D.R. and Tsalikis, J.D., 'Influence of Catalog vs. Store Shopping and Prior Satisfaction on Perceived Risk', *Journal of the Academy of Marketing Science* (Winter 1986), 28–36.

2 For an application of frequencies and descriptive statistics, see Bitner, M.J., Booms, B.H. and Mohr, L.A., 'Critical Service Encounters: The Employee's Viewpoint', *Journal of Marketing* 58 (October 1994), 95–106.

3 See any introductory statistics book for a more detailed description of these statistics; for example, see Berenson, M.L. and Levine, D.M., *Basic Business Statistics: Concepts and Applications*, 5th edn (Englewood Cliffs, NJ: Prentice Hall, 1992).

4 For our purposes, no distinction will be made between formal hypothesis testing and statistical inference by means of confidence intervals.

5 Excellent discussions of ways to analyse cross-tabulations can be found in Hellevik, O., *Introduction to Causal Analysis: Exploring Survey Data by Crosstabulation* (Beverly Hills: Sage Publications, 1984).

6 Feick, L.F., 'Analyzing Marketing Research Data with Association Models', *Journal of Marketing Research* 21 (November 1984), 376–86. For an application, see Becker, B.W. and Kaldenberg, D.O., 'Determination of Fees by Professionals: An Exploratory Investigation of Dentists', *Journal of Health Care Marketing* (September 1991), 28–35.

7 See the classic book by Zeisel, H., *Say It with Figures*, 5th edn (New York: Harper and Row, 1968).

8 See, for example, Hellevik, O., *Introduction to Causal Analysis: Exploring Survey Data by Crosstabulation* (Beverly Hills: Sage Publications, 1984); and Upton Graham, J.G., *The Analysis of Cross-Tabulated Data* (Chichester, England: Wiley, 1978).

9 Lancaster, H.O., *The Chi Squared Distribution* (New York: Wiley, 1969), or any basic statistics book.

10 Berenson, M.L. and Levine, D.M., *Basic Business Statistics: Concepts and Applications*, 5th edn (Englewood Cliffs, NJ: Prentice Hall), 1992.

11 Some statisticians, however, disagree. They feel that a correction should not be applied. See, for example, Overall, J.E., 'Power of Chi-Square Tests for 2 × 2 Contingency Tables with Small Expected Frequencies', *Psychological Bulletin* (January 1980), 132–35.

12 Significance tests and confidence intervals are also available for either lambda asymmetric or lambda symmetric. See Goodman, L.A. and Kruskal, W.H. 'Measures of Association for Cross Classification: Appropriate Sampling Theory', *Journal of the American Statistical Association* 88 (June 1963), 310–64.

13 Cowles, M. and Davis, C., 'On the Origins of the .05 Level of Statistical Significance', *American Psychologist* (May 1982), 553–58. See also Kotabe, M., Duhan, D.E., Smith, Jr, ▶

D.K. and Wilson, R.D., 'The Perceived Veracity of PIMS Strategy Principles in Japan: An Empirical Inquiry', *Journal of Marketing* 55 (January 1991), 26–41.

14 Technically, a null hypothesis cannot be accepted. It can be either rejected or not rejected. This distinction, however, is inconsequential in applied research.

15 The condition when the variances cannot be assumed to be equal is known as the Behrens-Fisher problem. There is some controversy over the best procedure in this case.

16 Lumpkin, J.R. and Hunt, J.B., 'Mobility as an Influence on Retail Patronage Behavior of the Elderly: Testing Conventional Wisdom', *Journal of the Academy of Marketing Science* (Winter 1989), 1–12.

17 Rosenblatt, J.A. and Mainprize, J., 'The History and Future of 15-Second Commercials: An Empirical Investigation of the Perception of Ad Agency Media Directors', in Lazer, W., Shaw, E. and Wee, C-H. (eds), *World Marketing Congress,* International Conference Series, Vol. 4 (Boca Raton, FL: Academy of Marketing Science, 1989), 169–77.

18 Harnett, D.L., *Statistical Methods* 3rd edn (Reading, MA: Addison-Wesley, 1982).

19 Conover, W.J., *Practical Nonparametric Statistics* 2nd edn (New York: Wiley, 1980).

20 There is some controversy over whether non-parametric statistical techniques should be used to make inferences about population parameters.

21 The *t* test in this case is equivalent to a chi-square test for independence in a 2 × 2 contingency table. The relationship is

$$X^2.95(1) = t^2.05(n_1 + n_2 - 2)$$

For large samples, the *t* distribution approaches the normal distribution and so the *t* test and the *z* test are equivalent.

22 Krum, J.R., Rau, P.A. and Keiser, S.K., 'The Marketing Research Process: Role Perceptions of Researchers And Users', *Journal of Advertising Research* (December–January 1988), 9–21.

23 For an example of Wilcoxon matched-pairs signed ranks test, see Kalwani, M.U. and Narayandas, N., 'Long-Term Manufacturer-Supplier Relationships: Do They Pay Off for Supplier Firms?', *Journal of Marketing* 59 (January 1995), 1–16.

24 Daniel, W.W. and Terrell, J.C., *Business Statistics*, 6th edn (Boston: Houghton Mifflin 1992); and Field, J.G., 'The World's Simplest Test of Significance', *Journal of the Market Research Society* (July 1971), 170–72.

25 Einspruch, E.L., *An Introductory Guide to SPSS for Windows* (Thousand Oaks, CA: Sage Publications, 1997); Spector, P.E., *SAS Programming for Researchers and Social Scientists* (Thousand Oaks, CA: Sage Publications, 1993); Norat, M.A., Software Reviews, *Economic Journal: The Journal of the Royal Economic Society* 107 (May 1997), 857–82; Wass, J., 'How Statistical Software Can Be Assessed', *Scientific Computing and Automation* (October 1966).

Chapter 18

Analysis of variance and covariance

Analysis of variance and analysis of covariance must have a dependent variable that has been measured using an interval or ratio scales: there must also be one or more independent variables that are all categorical or are combinations of categorical and interval or ratio variables

OBJECTIVES

After reading this chapter, the student should be able to:

1 discuss the scope of the analysis of variance (ANOVA) technique and its relationship to *t* test, and regression;
2 describe one-way analysis of variance including decomposition of the total variation, measurement of effects significance testing, and interpretation of results;
3 describe *n*-way analysis of variance and the testing of the significance of the overall effect, the interaction effect and the main effect of each factor;
4 describe analysis of covariance and show how it accounts for the influence of uncontrolled independent variables;
5 explain key factors pertaining to the interpretation of results with emphasis on interactions, relative importance of factors and multiple comparisons;
6 discuss specialised ANOVA techniques applicable to marketing such as repeated measures ANOVA, non-metric analysis of variance, and multivariate analysis of variance (MANOVA).

OVERVIEW

In Chapter 17, we examined tests of differences between two means or two medians. In this chapter, we discuss procedures for examining differences between more than two means or medians. These procedures are called analysis of variance and analysis of covariance. These procedures have traditionally been used for analysing experimental data, but they are also used for analysing survey or observational data.

We describe the analysis of variance and covariance procedures and discuss their relationship to other techniques. Then we describe one-way analysis of variance, the simplest of these procedures, followed by *n*-way analysis of variance and analysis of covariance. Special attention is given to issues in interpretation of results as they relate to interactions, relative importance of factors, and multiple comparisons. Some specialised topics such as repeated measures analysis of variance, non-metric analysis of variance, and multivariate analysis of variance are briefly discussed. We begin with an example illustrating the application of analysis of variance.

EXAMPLE

Antacids are treatment for ANOVA[1]

An investigation was conducted to determine the role of 'verbal content' and 'relative newness of a brand' in the effectiveness of a comparative advertising format, for over-the-counter antacids. The measure of attitude toward the sponsoring brand was the dependent variable. Three factors, advertising format, relative newness and verbal content, were the independent variables, each manipulated at two levels. *Advertising format* was either non-comparative (1st) or comparative (2nd). In the comparative format, well-known brands (Rolaids and Tums) were used for comparison. *Relative newness* was manipulated by changing the brand's sponsor. Alka-Seltzer (1st) was the sponsor in the well-established brand treatment, whereas Acid-Off (2nd) was the sponsor in the new brand condition. The name 'Acid-Off' was chosen based on a pre-test. Verbal content was manipulated to reflect factual (1st) or evaluative content (2nd) in an ad. The subjects were recruited at a shopping centre and randomly assigned to the treatment by an interviewer who was blind to the purpose of the study. A total of 207 responses was collected, 200 of which were usable. Twenty-five respondents were assigned to each of the eight (2 × 2 × 2) treatments.

A three-way analysis of variance was performed, with attitude as the dependent variable. The overall results were significant. The three-way interaction was also significant. The only two-way interaction that was significant was between ad format and relative newness. A major conclusion from these results was that a comparative format that emphasised factual information was best suited for launching a new brand. ■

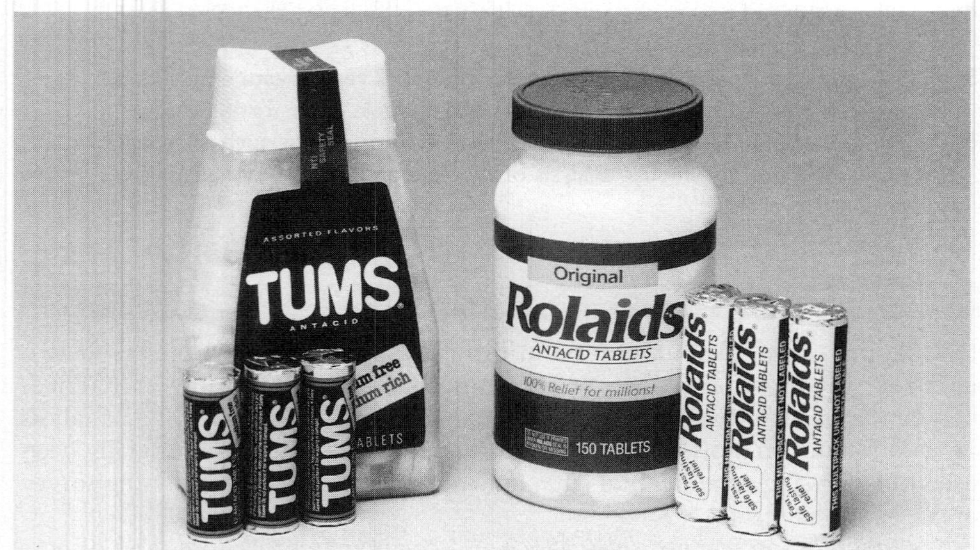

Analysis of variance revealed that comparative advertising, emphasising factual information, is best suited for launching a new brand of antacids

RELATIONSHIP AMONG TECHNIQUES

Analysis of variance (ANOVA)
A statistical technique for examining the differences among means for two or more populations.

Analysis of variance and analysis of covariance are used for examining the differences in the mean values of the dependent variable associated with the effect of the controlled independent variables, after taking into account the influence of the uncontrolled independent variables. Essentially, **analysis of variance (ANOVA)** is used as a test of means for two or more populations. The null hypothesis, typically, is that all means are equal. For example, suppose that the researcher was interested in examining whether heavy users, medium users, light users and non-users of yoghurt differed in their preference for Muller yoghurt, measured on a nine-point Likert scale. The null hypothesis that the four groups were not different in preference for Muller could be tested using analysis of variance.

Factor
Categorical independent variables. The independent variables must all be categorical (non-metric) to use ANOVA.

Treatment
In ANOVA, a particular combination of factor levels or categories.

One-way analysis of variance
An ANOVA technique in which there is only one factor.

n-way analysis of variance
An ANOVA model where two or more factors are involved.

Analysis of covariance (ANCOVA)
An advanced analysis of variance procedure in which the effects of one or more metric-scaled extraneous variables are removed from the dependent variable before conducting the ANOVA.

Covariate
A metric-independent variable used in ANCOVA.

In its simplest form, analysis of variance must have a dependent variable (preference for Muller yoghurt) that is metric (measured using an interval or ratio scale). There must also be one or more independent variables (product use: heavy, medium, light and non-users). The independent variables must be all categorical (non-metric). Categorical independent variables are also called **factors**. A particular combination of factor levels, or categories, is called a **treatment**. **One-way analysis of variance** (ANOVA) involves only one categorical variable, or a single factor. The differences in preference of heavy users, medium users, light users and non-users would be examined by one-way ANOVA. In one-way analysis of variance, a treatment is the same as a factor level (medium users constitute a treatment). If two or more factors are involved, the analysis is termed ***n*-way analysis of variance**. (If, in addition to product use, the researcher also wanted to examine the preference for Muller yoghurt of customers who are loyal and those who are not, an *n*-way analysis of variance would be conducted.)

If the set of independent variables consists of both categorical and metric variables, the technique is called **analysis of covariance** (ANCOVA). For example, analysis of covariance would be required if the researcher wanted to examine the preference of product use groups and loyalty groups, taking into account the respondents' attitudes toward nutrition and the importance they attached to dairy products. The latter two variables would be measured on nine-point Likert scales. In this case, the categorical independent variables (product use and brand loyalty) are still referred to as factors, whereas the metric-independent variables (attitude toward nutrition and importance attached to dairy products) are referred to as **covariates**.

The relationship of analysis of variance to *t* tests and other techniques, such as regression (see Chapter 19), is shown in Figure 18.1. These techniques all involve a metric-dependent variable. ANOVA and ANCOVA can include more than one independent variable (product use, brand loyalty, attitude, importance).

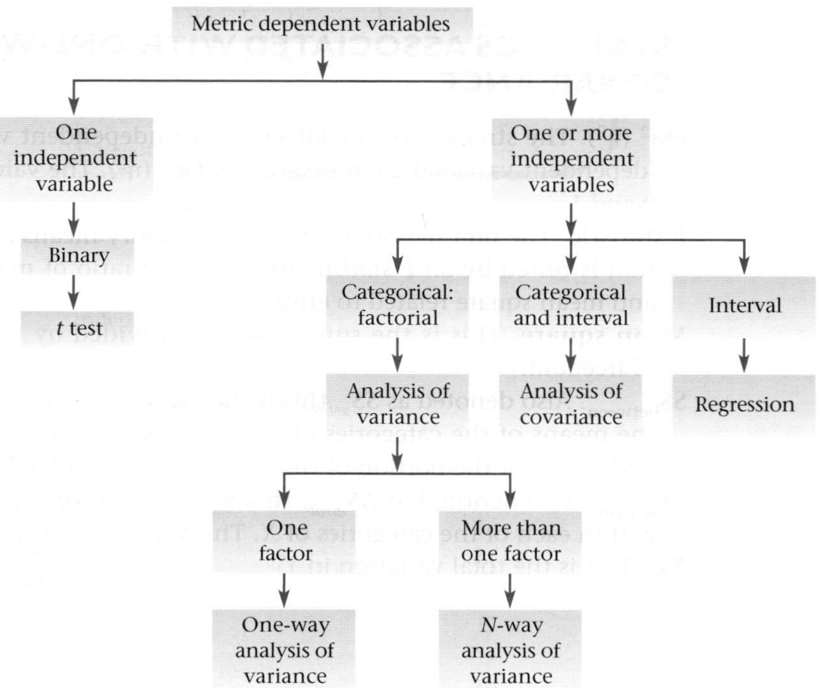

Figure 18.1
Relationship between t test, analysis of variance, analysis of covariance and regression

variation in the sample (dependent variable) and, based on the variability, determines whether there is reason to believe that the population means differ.

The total variation in Y, denoted by SS_y, can be decomposed into two components:

$$SS_y = SS_{between} + SS_{within}$$

where the subscripts *between* and *within* refer to the categories of X.[3] $SS_{between}$ is the variation in Y related to the variation in the means of the categories of X. It represents variation between the categories of X. In other words, $SS_{between}$ is the portion of the sum of squares in Y related to the independent variable or factor X. For this reason, $SS_{between}$ is also denoted as SS_x. SS_{within} is the variation in Y related to the variation within each category of X. SS_{within} is not accounted for by X. Therefore, it is referred to as SS_{error}. The total variation in Y may be decomposed as

$$SS_y = SS_x + SS_{error}$$

where

$$SS_y = \sum_{i=1}^{N} (Y_i - \bar{Y})^2$$

$$SS_x = \sum_{j=1}^{c} n(\bar{Y}_j - \bar{Y})^2$$

$$SS_{error} = \sum_{j}^{c} \sum_{i}^{n} (\bar{Y}_{ij} - \bar{Y}_j)^2$$

$\bar{Y}_i$ = individual observation
$\bar{Y}_j$ = mean for category j
$\bar{Y}$ = mean over the whole sample or grand mean
$\bar{Y}_{ij}$ = ith observation in the jth category

The logic of decomposing the total variation in Y, SS_y into $SS_{between}$ and SS_{within} to examine differences in group means can be intuitively understood. Recall from Chapter 17 that if the variation of the variable in the population was known or estimated, one could estimate how much the sample mean should vary because of random variation alone. In analysis of variance, there are several different groups (e.g. heavy, medium, and light users and non-users). If the null hypothesis is true and all the groups have the same mean in the population, one can estimate how much the sample means should vary because of sampling (random) variations alone. If the observed variation in the sample means is more than what would be expected by sampling variation, it is reasonable to conclude that this extra variability is related to differences in group means in the population.

In analysis of variance, we estimate two measures of variation: within groups (SS_{within}) and between groups ($SS_{between}$). Within-group variation is a measure of how much the observations, Y values, within a group vary. This is used to estimate the variance within a group in the population. It is assumed that all the groups have the same variation in the population. But because it is not known that all the groups have the same mean, we cannot calculate the variance of all the observations together. The variance for each of the groups must be calculated individually, and these are combined into an 'average' or 'overall' variance. Likewise, another estimate of the variance of the Y values may be obtained by examining the variation between the means. (This process is the reverse of determining the variation in the means, given the population variance σ.) If the population mean is the same in all the groups, then the variation in the sample means and the sizes of the sample groups can be used to estimate the variance of Y. The reasonableness of this estimate of the Y variance depends on whether the null hypothesis is true. If the null hypothesis is true and the population means are equal, the variance estimate based on between-group variation is correct. On the other hand, if the groups have different means in the population, the variance estimate based on between-group variation will be too large. Thus, by comparing the Y variance estimates based on between-group and within-group variation, we can test the null hypothesis.[4] Decomposition of the total variation in this manner also enables us to measure the effects of X on Y.

Measuring effects

The effects of X on Y are measured by SS_x. Since SS_x is related to the variation in the means of the categories of X, the relative magnitude of SS_x increases as the differences among the means of Y in the categories of X increase. The relative magnitude of SS_x also increases as the variations in Y within the categories of X decrease. The strength of the effects of X on Y are measured as follows:

$$\eta^2 = \frac{SS_x}{SS_y} = \frac{SS_y - SS_{error}}{SS_y}$$

The value of η^2 varies between 0 and 1. It assumes a value of 0 when all the category means are equal, indicating that X has no effect on Y. The value of η^2 will be 1 when there is no variability within each category of X but there is some variability between categories. Thus, η^2 is a measure of the variation in Y that is explained by the independent variable X. Not only can we measure the effects of X on Y, but we can also test for their significance.

Significance testing

In one-way analysis of variance, the interest lies in testing the null hypothesis that the category means are equal in the population.[5] In other words,

$$H_0\colon \mu_1 = \mu_2 = \mu_3 = \ldots = \mu_c$$

Under the null hypothesis, SS_x and SS_{error} come from the same source of variation. In such a case, the estimate of the population variance of Y can be based on either between category variation or within category variation. In other words, the estimate of the population variance of Y,

$$S_y^2 = \frac{SS_x}{c-1}$$

$$= \text{mean square due to } X$$

$$= MS_x$$

or

$$S_y^2 = \frac{SS_{error}}{N-c}$$

$$= \text{mean square due to error}$$

$$= MS_{error}$$

The null hypothesis may be tested by the F statistic based on the ratio between these two estimates:

$$F = \frac{SS_x/(c-1)}{SS_{error}/(N-c)} = \frac{MS_x}{MS_{error}}$$

This statistic follows the F distribution, with $(c - 1)$ and $(N - c)$ degrees of freedom (df). A table of the F distribution is given as Table 5 in the Statistical Appendix at the end of the book. As mentioned in Chapter 17, the F distribution is a probability distribution of the ratios of sample variances. It is characterised by degrees of freedom for the numerator and degrees of freedom for the denominator.[6]

Interpreting results

If the null hypothesis of equal category means is not rejected, then the independent variable does not have a significant effect on the dependent variable. On the other hand, if the null hypothesis is rejected, then the effect of the independent variable is significant. In other words, the mean value of the dependent variable will be different for different categories of the independent variable. A comparison of the category mean values will indicate the nature of the effect of the independent variable. Other salient issues in the interpretation of results, such as examination of differences among specific means, are discussed later. In the next section, we illustrate the application of the ANOVA technique.

ILLUSTRATIVE APPLICATIONS OF ONE-WAY ANALYSIS OF VARIANCE

We illustrate the concepts of ANOVA first with an example showing calculations done by hand and then by computer analysis. Suppose that a bank is attempting to determine the effect of direct mail offer of in-branch promotions of loans (X) on sales (Y). In-branch promotion is varied at three levels: high, medium and low. Fifteen branches are randomly selected, and five branches are randomly assigned to each treatment condition. The experiment lasts for four weeks. Sales of new loans are monitored, normalised to account for extraneous factors (branch size, traffic, etc.) and converted to a 0-to-10 scale. The data obtained (Y_{ij}) are reported in Table 18.2. The null hypothesis is that the category means are equal:

$$H_0: \mu_1 = \mu_2 = \mu_3$$

To test the null hypothesis, the various sums of squares are computed as follows:

$SS_y = (10 - 6)^2 + (9 - 6)^2 + (10 - 6)^2 + (8 - 6)^2 + (8 - 6)^2 + (6 - 6)^2 + (4 - 6)^2 + (7 - 6)^2 + (3 - 6)^2 + (5 - 6)^2 + (5 - 6)^2 + (6 - 6)^2 + (5 - 6)^2 + (2 - 6)^2 + (2 - 6)^2$
$= 16 + 9 + 16 + 4 + 4 + 0 + 4 + 1 + 9 + 1 + 1 + 0 + 1 + 16 + 16$
$= 98$
$SS_x = 5(9 - 6)^2 + 5(5 - 6)^2 + 5(4 - 6)^2$
$= 45 + 5 + 20$
$= 70$

$SS_{error} = (10 - 9)^2 + (9 - 9)^2 + (10 - 9)^2 + (8 - 9)^2 + (8 - 9)^2 + (6 - 5)^2 + (4 - 5)^2 + (7 - 5)^2 + (3 - 5)^2 + (5 - 5)^2 + (5 - 4)^2 + (6 - 4)^2 + (5 - 4)^2 + (2 - 4)^{-} + (2 - 4)^2$
$= 1 + 0 + 1 + 1 + 1 + 1 + 1 + 4 + 4 + 0 + 1 + 4 + 1 + 4 + 4$
$= 28$

It can be verified that

$$SS_y = SS_x + SS_{error}$$

Table 18.2 Effect of in-branch promotion on sales of new bank loans

	Normalised sales Level of in-branch promotion		
Branch No	*High*	*Medium*	*Low*
1	10	6	5
2	9	4	6
3	10	7	5
4	8	3	2
5	8	5	2
Category means: $\bar{Y}_j$	$\frac{45}{5} = 9$	$\frac{25}{5} = 5$	$\frac{20}{5} = 4$
Grand means: $\bar{Y}$	$= \frac{45 + 25 + 20}{15} = 6$		

as follows:

$$98 = 70 + 28$$

The strength of the effects of X on Y are measured as follows:

$$\eta^2 = \frac{SS_x}{SS_y}$$

$$= \frac{70}{98}$$

$$= 0.714$$

In other words, 71.4% of the variation in sales (Y) is accounted for by in-branch promotion (X), indicating a strong effect. The null hypothesis may now be tested.

$$F = \frac{SS_x/(c-1)}{SS_{error}/(N-c)} = \frac{MS_x}{MS_{error}}$$

$$F = \frac{70/(3-1)}{28/(15-3)}$$

$$F = 15.0$$

From Table 5 in the Statistical Appendix we see that for 2 and 12 degrees of freedom, the critical value of F is 6.93. Because the calculated value of F is greater than the critical value, we reject the null hypothesis. We conclude that the population means for the three levels of in-branch promotion are indeed different. The relative magnitudes of the means for the three categories indicate that a high level of in-branch promotion leads to significantly higher sales of bank loans.

We now illustrate the analysis of variance procedure using a computer program. In Chapter 17, in the context of the GlobalCash project, we examined whether respondents from Germany and the Netherlands who use Citibank for pan-European transactions prefer 'security' to other electronic banking functions. Let us examine the same question again, this time forming three size groups (large, medium and small) rather than two. The null hypothesis is

$$H_0: \mu_1 = \mu_2 = \mu_3$$

The results of conducting a one-way analysis of variance are presented in Table 18.3. The value of SS_x denoted by between-group sums of squares is 6.4123 with two df; that of SS_{error} (within-group sums of squares) is 695.6626 with 264 df. Therefore, $MS_X = 6.4123/2 = 3.2062$ and $MS_{error} = 695.6626/264 = 2.6351$. The value of $F = 3.2062/2.6351 = 1.2167$ with 2 and 264 degrees of freedom, resulting in a probability of 0.2979. Since the associated probability is larger than the significance level of 0.05, the null hypothesis of equal population means cannot be rejected. Alternatively, it can be seen from Table 5 in the Statistical Appendix that the critical value of F for 2 and 264 (∞) degrees of freedom is 4.61. Since the calculated value of F (1.2167) is less than the critical value, the null hypothesis cannot be rejected. As can be seen from Table 18.3, the sample mean – with values of 4.0217, 4.1209 and 4.3929 – are quite close to each other. In Chapter 17, when the respondents were divided into German and Dutch companies, a significant difference was observed in the importance attached to 'security' as a variable in the choice of electronic banking functions. When the sample is divided into three groups within these countries, no significant differences are observed.

The procedure for conducting one-way analysis of variance and the illustrative applications help us understand the assumptions involved.

Table 18.3 One-way ANOVA: effect of company size (in Germany and the Netherlands) on the importance of 'security' in electronic banking

Source	df	Sum of squares	Mean square	*F* ratio	*F* probability
Between groups	2	6.4123	3.2062	1.2167	0.2979
Within groups	264	695.6626	2.6351		
Total	266	702.0749			
Group	**Count**	**Mean**	**Standard deviation**	**Standard error**	
Group 1 – Large	92	4.0217	1.6440	0.1714	
Group 2 – Medium	91	4.1209	1.5765	0.1653	
Group 3 – Small	84	4.3929	1.6502	0.1801	
Total	267	4.1723	1.6246	0.0994	

ASSUMPTIONS IN ANALYSIS OF VARIANCE

The salient assumptions in analysis of variance can be summarised as follows.

1 Ordinarily, the categories of the independent variable are assumed to be fixed. Inferences are made only to the specific categories considered. This is referred to as the *fixed-effects model*. Other models are also available. In the *random-effects model*, the categories or treatments are considered to be random samples from a universe of treatments. Inferences are made to other categories not examined in the analysis. A *mixed-effects model* results if some treatments are considered fixed and others random.[7]

2 The error term is normally distributed, with a zero mean and a constant variance. The error is not related to any of the categories of X. Modest departures from these assumptions do not seriously affect the validity of the analysis. Furthermore, the data can be transformed to satisfy the assumption of normality or equal variances.

3 The error terms are uncorrelated. If the error terms are correlated (i.e. the observations are not independent), the F ratio can be seriously distorted.

In many data analysis situations, these assumptions are reasonably met. Analysis of variance is therefore a common procedure.

N-WAY ANALYSIS OF VARIANCE

In marketing research, one is often concerned with the effect of more than one factor simultaneously.[8] For example:

- How do consumers' intentions to buy a brand vary with different levels of price and different levels of distribution?
- How do advertising levels (high, medium and low) interact with price levels (high, medium and low) to influence a brand's sale?
- Do income levels (high, medium and low) and age (younger than 35, 35–55, older than 55) affect consumption of a brand?
- What is the effect of consumers' familiarity with a bank (high, medium and low) and bank image (positive, neutral and negative) on preference for taking a loan out with that bank?

Interaction
When assessing the relationship between two variables, an interaction occurs if the effect of X_1 depends on the level of X_2, and vice versa.

In determining such effects, n-way analysis of variance can be used. A major advantage of this technique is that it enables the researcher to examine **interactions** between the factors. Interactions occur when the effects of one factor on the dependent variable depend on the level (category) of the other factors. The procedure for conducting n-way analysis of variance is similar to that for one-way analysis of variance. The statistics associated with n-way analysis of variance are also defined similarly. Consider the simple case of two factors X_1 and X_2 having categories c_1 and c_2. The total variation in this case is partitioned as follows:

$$SS_{total} = SS \text{ due to } X_1 + SS \text{ due to } X_2 + SS \text{ due to interaction of } X_1 \text{ and } X_2 + SS_{within}$$

or

$$SS_y = SS_{x_1} + SS_{x_2} + SS_{x_1x_2} + SS_{error}$$

A larger effect of X_1 will be reflected in a greater mean difference in the levels of X_1 and a larger SS_{x_1}. The same is true for the effect of X_2. The larger the interaction between X_1 and X_2, the larger $SS_{x_1x_2}$ will be. On the other hand, if X_1 and X_2 are independent, the value of $SS_{x_1x_2}$ will be close to zero.[9]

Multiple η^2
The strength of the joint effect of two (or more) factors, or the overall effect.

The strength of the joint effect of two factors, called the overall effect, or **multiple η^2**, is measured as follows:

$$\text{multiple } \eta^2 = (SS_{x_1} + SS_{x_2} + SS_{x_1x_2})/SS_y$$

Significance of the overall effect
A test that some differences exist between some of the treatment groups.

The **significance of the overall effect** may be tested by an F test, as follows:

$$F = \frac{(SS_{x_1} + SS_{x_2} + SS_{x_1x_2})/\text{df}_n}{SS_{error}/\text{df}_d}$$

$$= \frac{SS_{x_1,x_2,x_1x_2}/\text{df}_n}{SS_{error}/\text{df}_d}$$

$$= \frac{MS_{x_1,x_2,\, x_1x_2}}{MS_{error}}$$

where

$$\begin{aligned} df_n &= \text{degrees of freedom for the numerator} \\ &= (c_1 - 1) + (c_2 - 1) + (c_1 - 1)(c_2 - 1) \\ &= c_1c_2 - 1 \end{aligned}$$

$$\begin{aligned} df_d &= \text{degrees of freedom for the denominator} \\ &= N - c_1c_2 \\ MS &= \text{mean square} \end{aligned}$$

Significance of the interaction effect
A test of the significance of the interaction between two or more independent variables.

If the overall effect is significant, the next step is to examine the **significance of the interaction effect**. Under the null hypothesis of no interaction, the appropriate F test is:

$$F = \frac{SS_{x_1x_2}/df_n}{SS_{error}/df_d} = \frac{MS_{x_1x_2}}{MS_{error}}$$

where

$$\begin{aligned} df_n &= (c_1 - 1)(c_2 - 1) \\ df_d &= N - c_1c_2 \end{aligned}$$

Significance of the main effect of each factor
A test of the significance of the main effect for each individual factor.

If the interaction effect is found to be significant, then the effect of X_1 depends on the level of X_2, and vice versa. Since the effect of one factor is not uniform but varies with the level of the other factor, it is not generally meaningful to test the **significance of the main effects**. It is meaningful to test the significance of each main effect of each factor, however, if the interaction effect is not significant.[10]

The significance of the main effect of each factor may be tested as follows for X_1:

$$F = \frac{SS_{x_1}/df_n}{SS_{error}/df_d} = \frac{MS_{x_1}}{MS_{error}}$$

where

$$\begin{aligned} df_n &= c_1 - 1 \\ df_d &= N - c_1c_2 \end{aligned}$$

The foregoing analysis assumes that the design was orthogonal, or balanced (the number of cases in each cell was the same). If the cell size varies, the analysis becomes more complex. The following application illustrates n-way analysis of variance.

An experiment was conducted to determine the effect of type of game and feedback on the amount of information sought while playing a promotional game.[11] Type of game was varied at two levels: whether the game required skill or was based on chance. The feedback factor was also varied at two levels: whether feedback on performance was provided or not. The subjects were 84 students who were randomly assigned to the different experimental conditions. The overall effect was significant (see Table 18.4).

As can be seen, the interaction effect was not significant. Hence, the main effects can be evaluated. The main effect of type of game was significant, whereas the main effect of feedback was not. Subjects sought more information when playing a game of skill than when playing a game of chance.

Table 18.4 Two-way analysis of variance

Source of variation	Sum of squares	df	Mean square	*F*	Sig. of *F*	ω^2
Type of game	390.01	1	390.01	6.62	0.012	0.06
Feedback	121.44	1	121.44	2.06	0.155	0.01
Two-way interaction	131.25	1	131.25	2.23	0.140	0.01
Residual	4714.29	80	58.93			

The following example illustrates the use of *n*-way analysis.

EXAMPLE

Country affects TV reception[12]

A study examined the impact of country affiliation on the credibility of product attribute claims for televisions. The dependent variables were the following product-attribute claims: good sound, reliability, crisp-clear picture and stylish design. The independent variables which were manipulated consisted of price, country affiliation and store distribution. A 2 × 2 × 2 between-subjects design was used. Two levels of price, 'low' and 'high', two levels of country affiliation, South Korea and Germany, and two levels of store distribution, Kaufhof and without Kaufhof, were specified.

Data were collected from two shopping centres in a large city. Thirty respondents were randomly assigned to each of the eight treatment cells for a total of 240 subjects. Table 1 presents the results for manipulations that had significant effects on each of the dependent variables.

Table 1 Analyses for significant manipulations

		Univariate		
Effect	*Dependent variable*	*F*	*df*	*p*
Country × price	**Good sound**	7.57	1232	0.006
Country × price	**Reliability**	6.57	1232	0.011
Country × distribution	**Crisp-clear picture**	6.17	1232	0.014
Country × distribution	**Reliability**	6.57	1232	0.011
Country × distribution	**Stylish design**	10.31	1232	0.002

The directions of country-by-distribution interaction effects for the three dependent variables are shown in Table 2. Although the credibility ratings for the crisp-clear picture, reliability and stylish design claims are improved by distributing the Korean-made TV set through Kaufhof rather than some other distributor, the same is not true of a German-made set. Similarly, the directions of country-by-price interaction effects for the two dependent variables are shown in Table 3. At the 'high' price level, the credibility ratings for the 'good sound' and 'reliability' claims are higher for the German-made TV set than for its Korean counterpart, but there is little difference related to country affiliation when the product is at the 'low' price.

This study demonstrates that credibility of attribute claims, for products traditionally exported to Germany by a company in a newly industrialised country,

Table 2 Country by distribution interaction means

Country × distribution	Crisp clear picture	Reliability	Stylish design
South Korea			
Kaufhof	3.67	3.42	3.82
Without Kaufhof	3.18	2.88	3.15
Germany			
Kaufhof	3.60	3.47	3.53
Without Kaufhof	3.77	3.65	3.75

Table 3 Country by price interaction means

Country × price	Good sound	Reliability
Low price		
Kaufhof	3.75	3.40
Without Kaufhof	3.53	3.45
High price		
Kaufhof	3.15	2.90
Without Kaufhof	3.73	3.67

can be significantly improved if the same company distributes the product through a prestigious German retailer and considers making manufacturing investments in Europe. Specifically, three product attribute claims (crisp-clear picture, reliability and stylish design) are perceived as more credible when the TVs are made in South Korea if they are also distributed through a prestigious German retailer. Also, the 'good sound' and 'reliability' claims for TVs are perceived to be more credible for a German-made set sold at a higher price, possibly offsetting the potential disadvantage of higher manufacturing costs in Europe. ■

ANALYSIS OF COVARIANCE

When examining the differences in the mean values of the dependent variable related to the effect of the controlled independent variables, it is often necessary to take into account the influence of uncontrolled independent variables. For example:

- In determining how consumers' intentions to buy a brand vary with different levels of price, attitude toward the brand may have to be taken into consideration.
- In determining how different groups exposed to different commercials evaluate a brand, it may be necessary to control for prior knowledge.
- In determining how different price levels will affect a household's breakfast cereal consumption, it may be essential to take household size into account.

In such cases, analysis of covariance should be used. Analysis of covariance includes at least one categorical independent variable and at least one interval or metric-independent variable. The categorical independent variable is called a *factor*, whereas the metric-independent variable is called a *covariate*. The most common use of the covariate is to remove extraneous variation from the dependent variable, because the effects of the factors are of major concern. The variation in the dependent variable due to the covariates is removed by an adjustment of the dependent variable's mean value within each treatment condition.

An analysis of variance is then performed on the adjusted scores.[13] The significance of the combined effect of the covariates, as well as the effect of each covariate, is tested by using the appropriate *F* tests. The coefficients for the covariates provide insights into the effect that the covariates exert on the dependent variable. Analysis of covariance is most useful when the covariate is linearly related to the dependent variable and is not related to the factors.[14]

Here we use the effect of 'security' as a variable in the choice of electronic banking functions, as discussed in Chapter 17 using a *t* test, to illustrate covariance. Suppose that the researcher feels that the number of banks they work with and the number of countries in which they operate world-wide, influence the dependent variable. Both these variables are measured on a ratio scale. As with a *t* test, respondents are divided into two groups based on a rough median split of the security variables, and an analysis of covariance is performed. The dependent variable consists of the importance attached to security. The factor of security can have two levels (high importance and low importance), and bank number and country number are the two covariates. The results are shown in Table 18.5. As can be seen, the effect of the two covariates combined, as well as the effect of each covariate, is significant. The main effect of security continues to be significant. The signs of the covariate coefficients indicate that the companies with greater numbers of banks with whom they work with as well as those operating in a few countries (this may be explained by particular countries of operation), attach greater importance to security in their choice of electronic banking functions.

Table 18.5 Analysis of covariance

Source of variation	Sum of squares	df	Mean square	*F*	Sig. of *F*
Covariates	47.387	2	23.693	9.678	0.000
No of banks	18.944	1	18.944	7.738	0.006
No of countries	20.222	1	20.222	8.260	0.004
Main effects	9.608	1	9.608	3.925	0.049
Security	9.608	1	9.608	3.925	0.049
Explained	56.995	3	18.998	7.761	0.000
Residual	638.945	261	2.448		
Total		695.940	264	2.636	
Covariate	Raw coefficient				
No of banks	0.019				
No of countries	–0.104				

ISSUES IN INTERPRETATION

Important issues involved in the interpretation of ANOVA results include interactions, relative importance of factors, and multiple comparisons.

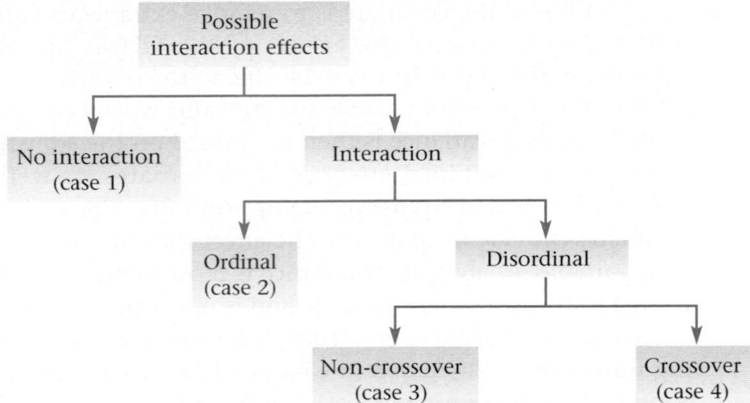

Figure 18.3
A classification of interaction effects

Interactions

Ordinal interaction
An interaction where the rank order of the effects attributable to one factor does not change across the levels of the second factor.

Disordinal interaction
The change in the rank order of the effects of one factor across the levels of another.

The different interactions that can arise when conducting ANOVA on two or more factors are shown in Figure 18.3. One outcome is that ANOVA may indicate that there are no interactions (the interaction effects are not found to be significant). The other possibility is that the interaction is significant. An interaction effect occurs when the effect of an independent variable on a dependent variable is different for different categories or levels of another independent variable. The interaction may be ordinal or disordinal. In **ordinal interaction**, the rank order of the effects related to one factor does not change across the levels of the second factor. **Disordinal interaction**, on the other hand, involves a change in the rank order of the effects of one factor across the levels of another. If the interaction is disordinal, it could be of a non-crossover or crossover type.[15]

These interaction cases are displayed in Figure 18.4, which assumes that there are two factors, X_1 with three levels (X_{11}, X_{12} and X_{13}) and X_2 with two levels (X_{21} and X_{22}). Case 1 depicts no interaction. The effects of X_1 on Y are parallel over the two levels of X_2. Although there is some departure from parallelism, this

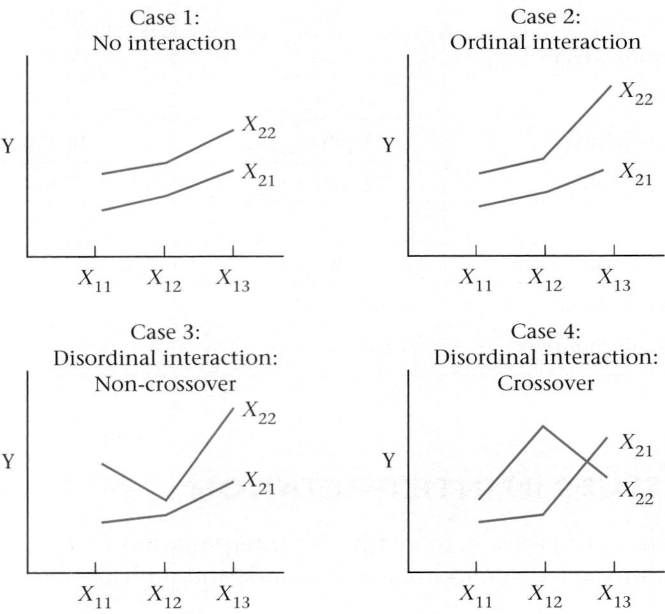

Figure 18.4
Patterns of interaction

is not beyond what might be expected from chance. Parallelism implies that the net effect of X_{22} over X_{21} is the same across the three levels of X_1. In the absence of interaction, the joint effect of X_1 and X_2 is simply the sum of their individual main effects.

Case 2 depicts an ordinal interaction. The line segments depicting the effects of X_1 and X_2 are not parallel. The difference between X_{22} and X_{21} increases as we move from X_{11} to X_{12} and from X_{12} to X_{13}, but the rank order of the effects of X_1 is the same over the two levels of X_2. This rank order, in ascending order, is X_{11}, X_{12}, X_{13}, and it remains the same for X_{21} and X_{22}.

Disordinal interaction of a non-crossover type is displayed by case 3. The lowest effect of X_1 at level X_{21} occurs at X_{11}, and the rank order of effects is X_{11}, X_{12}, and X_{13}. At level X_{22}, however, the lowest effect of X_1 occurs at X_{12}, and the rank order is changed to X_{12}, X_{11}, X_{13}. Because it involves a change in rank order, disordinal interaction is stronger than ordinal interaction.

In disordinal interactions of a crossover type, the line segments cross each other, as shown by case 4 in Figure 18.4. In this case, the relative effect of the levels of one factor changes with the levels of the other. Note that X_{22} has a greater effect than X_{21} when the levels of X_1 are X_{11} and X_{12}. When the level of X_1 is X_{13}, the situation is reversed, and X_{21} has a greater effect than X_{22}. (Note that in cases 1, 2 and 3, X_{22} had a greater impact than X_{21} across all three levels of X_1.) Hence, disordinal interactions of a crossover type represent the strongest interactions.[16]

Relative importance of factors

Omega squared (ω^2)
A measure indicating the proportion of the variation in the dependent variable explained by a particular independent variable or factor.

Experimental designs are usually balanced in that each cell contains the same number of respondents. This results in an orthogonal design in which the factors are uncorrelated. Hence, it is possible to determine unambiguously the relative importance of each factor in explaining the variation in the dependent variable.[17] The most commonly used measure in ANOVA is **omega squared**, ω^2. This measure indicates what proportion of the variation in the dependent variable is related to a particular independent variable or factor. The relative contribution of a factor X is calculated as follows:[18]

$$\omega_x^2 = \frac{SS_X - (\mathrm{df}_x \times MS_{error})}{SS_{total} + MS_{error}}$$

Normally, ω^2 is interpreted only for statistically significant effects.[19] In Table 18.4, ω^2 associated with type of game is calculated as follows:

$$\omega_x{}^2 = \frac{390.01 - (1 \times 58.93)}{5356.99 + 58.93}$$

$$= \frac{331.08}{5415.92}$$

$$= 0.06$$

In Table 18.4 note that:

$$SS_{total} = 390.01 + 121.44 + 131.25 + 4714.29$$

$$= 5356.99$$

As a guide to interpreting ω, a large experimental effect produces an ω^2 of 0.15 or greater, a medium effect produces an index of around 0.06, and a small effect produces an index of 0.01.[20] In Table 18.4, the effect produced by type of game is medium.

Multiple comparisons

The ANOVA F test examines only the overall difference in means. If the null hypothesis of equal means is rejected, we can only conclude that not all the group means are equal. Only some of the means may be statistically different, however, and we may wish to examine differences among specific means. This can be done by specifying appropriate **contrasts**, or comparisons used to determine which of the means are statistically different. Contrasts may be *a priori* or *a posteriori*. **A priori contrasts** are determined before conducting the analysis, based on the researcher's theoretical framework. Generally, *a priori* contrasts are used in lieu of the ANOVA F test. The contrasts selected are orthogonal (they are independent in a statistical sense).

A posteriori contrasts are made after the analysis. These are generally **multiple comparison tests**. They enable the researcher to construct generalised confidence intervals that can be used to make pairwise comparisons of all treatment means. These tests, listed in order of decreasing power, include least significant difference, Duncan's multiple range, Student-Newman-Keuls, Tukey's alternate procedure, honestly significant difference, modified least significant difference, and Scheffe's tests. Of these, least significant difference is the most powerful and Scheffe's the most conservative. For further discussion on a priori and a posteriori contrasts, refer to the literature.[21]

Our discussion so far has assumed that each subject is exposed to only one treatment or experimental condition. Sometimes subjects are exposed to more than one experimental condition, in which case repeated measures ANOVA should be used.

Contrasts
In ANOVA, a method of examining differences among two or more means of the treatment groups.

***A priori* contrasts**
Contrasts that are determined before conducting the analysis, based on the researcher's theoretical framework.

***A posteriori* contrasts**
Contrasts made after the analysis. These are generally multiple comparison tests.

Multiple comparison tests
A posteriori contrasts that enable the researcher to construct generalised confidence intervals that can be used to make pairwise comparisons of all treatment means.

REPEATED MEASURES ANOVA

In marketing research, there are often large differences in the background and individual characteristics of respondents. If this source of variability can be separated from treatment effects (effects of the independent variable) and experimental error, then the sensitivity of the experiment can be enhanced. One way of controlling the differences between subjects is by observing each subject under each experimental condition (see Table 18.6). In this sense, each subject serves as its own control. For example, in a survey attempting to determine

Table 18.6 Decomposition of the total variation: repeated measures ANOVA

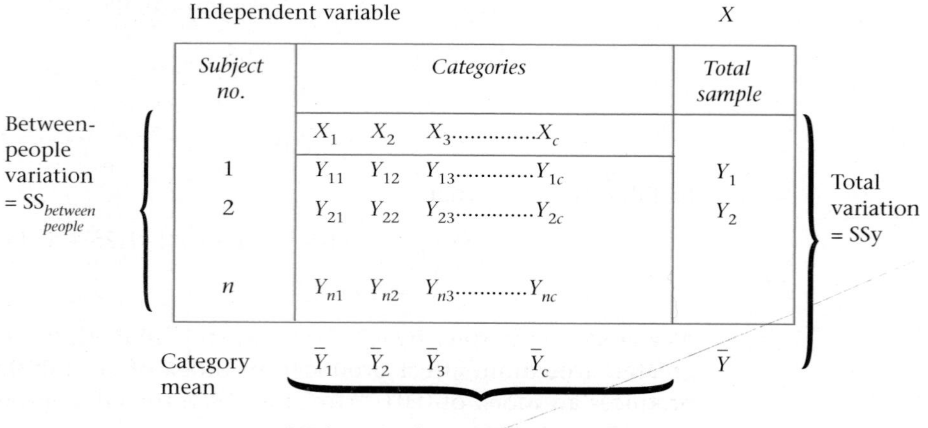

Independent variable X

Subject no.	*Categories*	*Total sample*
	X_1 X_2 X_3..............X_c	
1	Y_{11} Y_{12} Y_{13}.............Y_{1c}	Y_1
2	Y_{21} Y_{22} Y_{23}.............Y_{2c}	Y_2
n	Y_{n1} Y_{n2} Y_{n3}............Y_{nc}	
Category mean	$\bar{Y}_1$ $\bar{Y}_2$ $\bar{Y}_3$ $\bar{Y}_c$	$\bar{Y}$

differences in evaluations of various airlines, each respondent evaluates all the major competing airlines. In a study examining the differences among heavy users, medium users, light users and non-users of a brand, each respondent provides ratings on the relative importance of each attribute. Because repeated measurements are obtained from each respondent, this design is referred to as within-subjects design or **repeated measures analysis of variance**. This differs from the assumption we made in our earlier discussion that each respondent is exposed to only one treatment condition, also referred to as between-subjects design.[22] Repeated measures analysis of variance may be thought of as an extension of the paired-samples *t* test to the case of more than two related samples.

Repeated measures analysis of variance
An ANOVA technique used when respondents are exposed to more than one treatment condition and repeated measurements are obtained.

In the case of a single factor with repeated measures, the total variation, with $nc - 1$ degrees of freedom, may be split into between-people variation and within-people variation.

$$SS_{total} = SS_{between\ people} + SS_{within\ people}$$

The between-people variation, which is related to the differences between the means of people, has $n - 1$ degrees of freedom. The within-people variation has $n(c - 1)$ degrees of freedom. The within-people variation may, in turn, be divided into two different sources of variation. One source is related to the differences between treatment means, and the second consists of residual or error variation. The degrees of freedom corresponding to the treatment variation are $c - 1$ and that corresponding to residual variation are $(c - 1)(n - 1)$. Thus,

$$SS_{within\ people} = SS_x + SS_{error}$$

A test of the null hypothesis of equal means may now be constructed in the usual way:

$$F = \frac{SS_x / (c - 1)}{SS_{error}/(n - 1)(c - 1)}$$

$$= \frac{MS_x}{MS_{error}}$$

So far we have assumed that the dependent variable is measured on an interval or ratio scale. If the dependent variable is non-metric, however, a different procedure should be used.

Non-metric analysis of variance
An ANOVA technique for examining the difference in the central tendencies of more than two groups when the dependent variable is measured on an ordinal scale.

NON-METRIC ANALYSIS OF VARIANCE

Non-metric analysis of variance examines the difference in the central tendencies of more than two groups when the dependent variable is measured on an ordinal scale. One such procedure is the ***k*-sample median test**. As its name implies, this is an extension of the median test for two groups, which was considered in Chapter 17. The null hypothesis is that the medians of the *k* populations are equal. The test involves the computation of a common median over the *k* samples. Then, a $2 \times k$ table of cell counts based on cases above or below the common median is generated. A chi-square statistic is computed. The significance of the chi-square implies a rejection of the null hypothesis.

***k*-sample median test**
A non-parametric test used to examine differences among more than two groups when the dependent variable is measured on an ordinal scale.

A more powerful test is the **Kruskal-Wallis one-way analysis of variance**. This is an extension of the Mann-Whitney test (Chapter 17). This test also examines the difference in medians. The null hypothesis is the same as in the

Kruskal-Wallis one-way analysis of variance
A non-metric ANOVA test that uses the rank value of each case, not merely its location relative to the median.

k-sample median test, but the testing procedure is different. All cases from the *k* groups are ordered in a single ranking. If the *k* populations are the same, the groups should be similar in terms of ranks within each group. The rank sum is calculated for each group. From these, the Kruskal Wallis *H* statistic, which has a chi-square distribution, is computed.

The Kruskal-Wallis test is more powerful than the *k*-sample median test because it uses the rank value of each case, not merely its location relative to the median. If there are a large number of tied rankings in the data, however, the *k*-sample median test may be a better choice.

Non-metric analysis of variance is not popular in commercial marketing research. Another procedure that is also only rarely used is multivariate analysis of variance.

MULTIVARIATE ANALYSIS OF VARIANCE

Multivariate analysis of variance (MANOVA)
An ANOVA technique using two or more metric dependent variables.

Multivariate analysis of variance (MANOVA) is similar to analysis of variance (ANOVA) except that instead of one metric-dependent variable we have two or more. The objective is the same, since MANOVA is also concerned with examining differences between groups. Although ANOVA examines group differences on a single dependent variable, MANOVA examines group differences across multiple dependent variables simultaneously. In ANOVA, the null hypothesis is that the means of the dependent variable are equal across the groups. In MANOVA, the null hypothesis is that the vector of means on multiple dependent variables are equal across groups. Multivariate analysis of variance is appropriate when there are two or more dependent variables that are correlated. If there are multiple dependent variables that are uncorrelated or orthogonal, ANOVA on each of the dependent variables is more appropriate than MANOVA.[23]

As an example, suppose that four groups, each consisting of 100 randomly selected individuals, were exposed to four different commercials about the '3 Series' BMW. After seeing the commercial, each individual provided ratings on preference for the '3 Series', preference for BMW, and preference for the commercial itself. Because these three preference variables are correlated, multivariate analysis of variance should be conducted to determine which commercial is the most effective (produced the highest preference across the three preference variables). The following example illustrates the application of ANOVA and MANOVA in international marketing research.[24]

EXAMPLE

The commonality of unethical research practices world-wide

A study examined marketing professionals' perceptions of how common unethical practices in marketing research were across different countries, i.e. 'the commonality of unethical marketing research practices'. A sample of marketing professionals was drawn from Australia, Britain, Canada and the United States.

Respondents' evaluations were analysed using MANOVA and ANOVA techniques. The predictor variable was the 'country of respondent' and 15 evaluations of 'commonality' served as the criterion variables. The *F* values from the ANOVA analyses indicated that only two of the 15 commonality evaluations achieved significance ($p < 0.05$ or better). Further, the MANOVA *F* value was not statistically significant, implying the lack of overall differences in commonality evaluations across respondents of the four countries. It was concluded that marketing professionals in the four countries demonstrate similar perceptions of the commonality of unethical research practices. This finding is not surprising, given other research evidence that organisations in the four countries reflect similar corporate cultures. ■

INTERNET AND COMPUTER APPLICATIONS

The three computer packages, SPPP, SAS and BMDP, have programs for conducting analysis of variance and covariance available for the microcomputer and mainframe versions. In addition to the basic analysis that we have considered, these programs can also perform more complex analysis. Minitab and Excel also offer some programs. Given the importance of analysis of variance and covariance, several programs are available in each package.

SPSS

One-way ANOVA can be efficiently performed using the program ONEWAY. This program also allows the user to test a priori and a posteriori contrasts, which cannot be done in other SPSS programs. For performing *n*-way analysis of variance, the program ANOVA can be used. Although covariates can be specified, ANOVA does not perform a full analysis of covariance. For comprehensive analysis of variance or analysis of covariance, including repeated measures and multiple dependent measures, the MANOVA procedure is recommended. For non-metric analysis of variance, including the *k*-sample median test and Kruskal-Wallis one-way analysis of variance, the program NPAR TESTS should be used.

SAS

The main program for performing analysis of variance in the case of a balanced design is ANOVA. This program can handle data from a wide variety of experimental designs, including multivariate analysis of variance and repeated measures. Both a priori and a posteriori contrasts can be tested. For unbalanced designs, the more general GLM procedure can be used. This program performs analysis of variance, analysis of covariance, repeated measures analysis of variance, and multivariate analysis of variance. It also allows the testing of a priori and a posteriori contrasts. Whereas GLM can also be used for analysing balanced designs, it is not as efficient as ANOVA for such models. The VARCOMP procedure computes variance components. For non-metric analysis of variance, the NPAR1WAY procedure can be used. For constructing designs and randomised plans, the PLAN procedure can be used.

BMDP

For one-way analysis of variance, the program P1V can be used. It also performs analysis of covariance and can test user-specified contrasts of group means. The more general model, however, is P2V, which performs analysis of variance and covariance for a wide variety of fixed effect models. It can handle repeated measures and balanced as well as unbalanced designs. P4V, a more advanced program, can perform multivariate analysis of variance and covariance, including analysis of complex experimental designs. Another specialised program is P3V, which uses the maximum-likelihood approach for analysing fixed and random coefficients models. It allows for balanced as well as unbalanced designs. P8V is a general model that performs an analysis of variance for any complete design with equal cell sizes, including some complex designs. Non-parametric analysis of variance can be performed using P3S. Finally, P7D, in addition to providing histograms, can perform a one-way analysis of variance.

Minitab

Analysis of variance and covariance can be accessed from the Stats>ANOVA function. This function performs one way ANOVA, one-way unstacked ANOVA, two-way ANOVA, analysis of means, balanced ANOVA, analysis of covariance, general linear model, main effects plot, interactions plot, and residual plots. In order to compute the mean and standard deviation, the crosstab function must be used. To obtain *F* and *p* values, use the balanced ANOVA.

Excel

Both a one-way ANOVA and two-way ANOVA can be performed under the Tools>Data Analysis function. The two-way ANOVA has the features of a two factor with replication and a two factor without replication. The two factor with replication includes more than one sample for each group of data, while the two factor without replication does not include more than one sampling per group.

SUMMARY

In ANOVA and ANCOVA, the dependent variable is metric and the independent variable are all categorical and metric variables. One-way ANOVA involves a single independent categorical variable. Interest lies in testing the null hypothesis that the category means are equal in the population. The total variation in the dependent variable may be decomposed into two components: variation related to the independent variable and variation related to error. The variation is measured in terms of the sum of squares corrected for the mean (*SS*). The mean square is obtained by dividing the *SS* by the corresponding degrees of freedom (*df*). The null hypothesis of equal means is tested by an *F* statistic, which is the ratio of the mean square related to the independent variable to the mean square related to error.

N-way analysis of variance involves the simultaneous examination of two or more categorical independent variables. A major advantage is that the interactions between the independent variables can be examined. The significance of the overall effect, interaction terms, and the main effects of individual factors is examined by appropriate *F* tests. It is meaningful to the significance of main effects only if the corresponding interaction terms are not significant.

ANCOVA includes at least one categorical independent variable and at least one interval or metric-independent variable. The metric-independent variable, or covariate, is commonly used to remove extraneous variation from the dependent variable.

When analysis of variance is conducted on two or more factors, interactions can arise. An interaction occurs when the effect of an independent variable on a dependent variable is different for different categories or levels of another independent variable. If the interaction is significant, it may be ordinal or disordinal. Disordinal interaction may be of a non-crossover or crossover type. In balanced designs, the relative importance of factors in explaining the variation in the dependent variable is measured by omega squared (ω^2). Multiple comparisons in the form of a priori or a posteriori contrasts can be used for examining differences among specific means.

In repeated measures analysis of variance, observations on each subject are obtained under each treatment condition. This design is useful for controlling for the differences in subjects that exist prior to the experiment. Non-metric analysis of variance involves examining the differences in the central tendencies of two or more groups when the dependent variable is measured on an ordinal scale. Multivariate analysis of variance (MANOVA) involves two or more metric dependent variables.

QUESTIONS AND PROBLEMS

1 Discuss the similarities and differences between analysis of variance and analysis of covariance.

2 What is the relationship between analysis of variance and the *t* test?

3 What is total variation? How is it decomposed in a one-way analysis of variance?

4 What is the null hypothesis in one-way ANOVA? What basic statistic is used to test the null hypothesis in one-way ANOVA? How is this statistic computed?

5 How does *n*-way analysis of variance differ from the one-way procedure?

6 How is the total variation decomposed in *n*-way analysis of variance?

7 What is the most common use of the covariate in ANCOVA?

8 What is the difference between ordinal and disordinal interaction?

9 How is the relative importance of factors measured in a balanced design?

10 What is an a priori contrast?

11 What is the most powerful test for making a posteriori contrasts? Which test is the most conservative?

12 What is meant by repeated measures ANOVA? Describe the decomposition of variation in repeated measures ANOVA.

13 What are the differences between metric and non-metric analyses of variance?

14 Describe two tests used for examining differences in central tendencies in non-metric ANOVA.

15 What is multivariate analysis of variance? When is it appropriate?

NOTES

1 Iyer, E.S., 'The Influence of Verbal Content and Relative Newness on the Effectiveness of Comparative Advertising', *Journal of Advertising* 17 (1988), 15–21.

2 For applications of ANOVA, see Deshpande, R. and Stayman, D.M., 'A Tale of Two Cities: Distinctiveness Theory and Advertising Effectiveness', *Journal of Marketing Research* 31 (February 1994), 57–64.

3 See, for instance, Keppel, G., *Design and Analysis: A Researcher's Handbook*, 2nd edn (Englewood Cliffs, NJ: Prentice Hall, 1982).

4 Norusis, M., *The SPSS Guide to Data Analysis for SPSS/PC+* (Chicago: SPSS Inc., 1988).

5 Burdick, R.K., 'Statement of Hypotheses in the Analysis of Variance', *Journal of Marketing Research* (August 1983), 320–24.

6 The *F* test is a generalised form of the *t* test. If a random variable is *t* distributed with *N* degrees of freedom, then t^2 is *F* distributed with 1 and *N* degrees of freedom. Where there are two factor levels or treatments, ANOVA is equivalent to the two-sided *t* test.

7 Although computations for the fixed-effects and random-effects models are similar, interpretations of results differ. A comparison of these approaches is found in Neter, J., Wasserman, W. and Kutner, M., *Applied Linear Statistical Models*, 2nd edn (Homewood, IL: Richard D. Irwin, 1985).

8 We consider only the full factorial designs, which incorporate all possible combinations of factor levels. For example, see Dodds, W.B., Monroe, K.B. and Grewal, D., 'Effects of Price, Brand, and Store Information on Buyers' Product Evaluations', *Journal of Marketing Research* 28 (August 1991), 307–19.

9 Mayers, J.L., *Fundamentals of Experimental Design*, 3rd edn (Boston: Allyn and Bacon, 1979). See also Unnava, H.R., and Burnkrant, R.E., 'An Imagery-Processing View of the Role of Pictures in Print Advertisements', *Journal of Marketing Research* 28 (May 1991), 226–31.

10 Daniel, W.W. and Terrell, J.C., *Business Statistics*, 6th edn (Boston: Houghton Mifflin, 1992).

11 Hill, P.R. and Ward, J.C., 'Mood Manipulation in Marketing Research: An Examination of Potential Confounding Effects', *Journal of Marketing Research* 27 (February 1989), 97–104.

12 Chao, P. 'The Impact of Country Affiliation on the Credibility of Product Attribute Claims', *Journal of Advertising Research* (April–May 1989), 35–41.

13 Although this is the most common way in which analysis of covariance is performed, other situations are also possible. For example, covariate and factor effects may be of equal interest, or the set of covariates may be of major concern. For a recent application, see Lane Keller, K. and Aaker, D.A., 'The Effects of Sequential Introduction of Brand Extensions', *Journal of Marketing Research* 29 (February 1992), 35–50.

14 For a more detailed discussion, see Wildt, A.R. and Ahtola, O.T., *Analysis of Covariance* (Beverly Hills: Sage Publications, 1978).

15 Park, C.W., Milberg, S. and Lawson, R., 'Evaluation of Brand Extensions: The Role of Product Feature Similarity and Brand Concept Consistency', *Journal of Consumer Research* 18 (September 1991), 185–93; and Leigh, J.H. and Kinnear, T.C., 'On Interaction Classification', *Educational and Psychological Measurement* 40 (Winter 1980), 841–43.

16 For an examination of interactions using an ANOVA framework see Wansink, B., 'Advertising's Impact on Category Substitution', *Journal of Marketing Research* 31 (November 1994), 505–15; and Peracchio, L.A. and Meyers-Levy, J., 'How Ambiguous Cropped Objects in Ad Photos Can Affect Product Evaluations', *Journal of Consumer Research* 21 (June 1994), 190–204.

17 Sawyer, A. and Peter, J.P., 'The Significance of Statistical Significance Tests in Marketing Research,' *Journal of Marketing Research*, 20 (May 1983), 125; and Beltramini, R.F., 'A Meta-Analysis of Effect Sizes in Consumer Behavior Experiments', *Journal of Consumer Research* 12 (June 1985), 97–103.

18 This formula does not hold if repeated measurements are made on the dependent variable. See Dodd, D.H. and Schultz, Jr, R.E., 'Computational Procedures for Estimating Magnitude of Effect for Some Analysis of Variance Designs', *Psychological Bulletin* (June 1973), 391–95.

19 The ω^2 formula is attributed to Hays. See Hays, W.L., *Statistics for Psychologists* (New York: Holt, Rinehart and Winston, 1963). For an application, see Ratneshwar, S. and Chaiken, S., 'Comprehension's Role in Persuasion: The Case of Its Moderating Effect on the Persuasive Impact of Source Cues', *Journal of Consumer Research* 18 (June 1991), 52–62.

20 Cohen, J., *Statistical Power Analysis for the Behavioural Sciences* (New York: Academic Press, 1969).

21 Winer, B.S., *Statistical Principles in Experimental Design*, 2nd edn (New York: McGraw-Hill, 1971).

22 It is possible to combine between-subjects and within-subjects factors in a single design. See, for example, Broniarczyk, S.M. and Alba, J.W., 'The Importance of the Brand in Brand Extension', *Journal of Marketing Research* 31 (May 1994), 214–28; Krishna, A., 'The Effect of Deal Knowledge on Consumer Purchase Behavior', *Journal of Marketing Research* 31 (February 1994), 76–91.

23 Bray, J.H. and Maxwell, S.E., *Multivariate Analysis of Variance* (Beverly Hills: Sage Publications, 1985). For an application of MANOVA, see Olson, E.M., Walker, Jr., O.C. and Ruekert, R.W., 'Organizing for Effective New Product Development: The Moderating Role of Product Innovativeness', *Journal of Marketing* 59 (January 1995), 48–62.

24 Akaah, I.P., 'A Cross-National Analysis of the Perceived Commonality of Unethical Practices in Marketing Research', in Lazer, L., Shaw, E. and Wee, C-H. (eds), *World Marketing Congress*, International Conference Series, Vol. 4 (Boca Raton, FL: Academy of Marketing Science, 1989), 2–9.

Chapter 19

Correlation and regression

The product moment correlation is the most widely used statistic for summarising the strength of association between two metric variables. Regression analysis is a powerful and flexible procedure for analysing associative relationships between a metric dependent variable and one or more independent variables

OBJECTIVES

After reading this chapter, the student should be able to:

1 discuss the concepts of product moment correlation partial correlation and part correlation and show how they provide a foundation for regression analysis;
2 discuss non-metric correlation and measures such as Spearman's rho and Kendall's tau;
3 explain the nature and methods of bivariate regression analysis and describe the general model, estimation of parameters, standardised regression coefficient, significance testing, prediction accuracy, residual analysis and model cross-validation;
4 explain the nature and methods of multiple regression analysis and the meaning of partial regression coefficients;
5 describe specialised techniques used in multiple regression analysis, particularly stepwise regression, regression with dummy variables, and analysis of variance and covariance with regression.

OVERVIEW

Chapter 18 examined the relationship among the *t* test, analysis of variance and covariance, and regression. This chapter describes regression analysis, which is widely used for explaining variation in market share, sales, brand preference and other marketing results. This is done in terms of marketing management variables such as advertising, price, distribution and product quality. Before discussing regression however, we describe the concepts of product moment correlation and partial correlation coefficient, which lay the conceptual foundation for regression analysis.

In introducing regression analysis, we discuss the simple bivariate case first. We describe estimation, standardisation of the regression coefficients, and testing and examination of the strength and significance of association between variables, prediction accuracy, and the assumptions underlying the regression model. Next, we discuss the multiple regression model, emphasising the interpretation of parameters, strength of association, significance tests, and examination of residuals.

We then cover topics of special interest in regression analysis, such as stepwise regression, multicollinearity, relative importance of predictor variables, and cross-validation. We describe regression with dummy variables and the use of this procedure to conduct analysis of variance and covariance. We begin with some examples illustrating applications of regression analysis.

Multiple regression

In the GlobalCash project, multiple regression analysis was used to develop a model that explained bank preference in terms of respondents' evaluations of the banks in their own countries through four choice criteria. The dependent variable was the preference for individual domestic banks. The independent variables were the evaluations of each bank on balance reporting, domestic payments and collections, international payments and collections, and pooling and concentration (managing currencies from a variety of countries). The results indicated that all the factors of the choice criteria, except pooling and concentration, were significant in explaining bank preference. The coefficients of all the variables were positive, indicating that higher evaluations on each of the significant factors led to higher preference for that bank. The model had a good fit and good ability to predict bank preference. ■

EXAMPLE

Regression rings the right bell for Avon[1]

Avon Products were having significant problems with their sales staff. The company's business, dependent on sales representatives, was facing a shortage of sales representatives without much hope of getting new ones. Regression models were developed to reveal the possible variables that were fuelling this situation. The models revealed that the most significant variable was the level of the appointment fee that reps paid for materials. With data to back up its actions, the company lowered the fee. This resulted in an improvement in the recruitment and retention of sales reps. ■

These examples illustrate some of the uses of regression analysis in determining which independent variables explain a significant variation in the dependent variable of interest, the structure and form of the relationship, the strength of the relationship, and predicted values of the dependent variable. Fundamental to regression analysis is an understanding of the product moment correlation.

PRODUCT MOMENT CORRELATION

In marketing research, we are often interested in summarising the strength of association between two metric variables, as in the following situations:

- How strongly are sales related to advertising expenditures?
- Is there an association between market share and size of the sales force?
- Are consumers' perceptions of quality related to their perceptions of prices?

Product moment correlation (r)
A statistic summarising the strength of association between two metric variables.

In situations like these, the **product moment correlation**, r, is the most widely used statistic, summarising the strength of association between two metric (interval or ratio scaled) variables, say X and Y. It is an index used to determine whether a linear or straight line relationship exists between X and Y. It indicates the degree to which the variation in one variable, X, is related to the variation in another variable, Y. Because it was originally proposed by Karl Pearson, it is also known as the *Pearson correlation coefficient* and also referred to as simple correlation, bivariate correlation, or merely the correlation coefficient. From a sample of n observations, X and Y, the product moment correlation, r, can be calculated as

$$r = \frac{\sum_{i=1}^{n} (X_i - \bar{X})(Y_i - \bar{Y})}{\sqrt{\sum_{i=1}^{n} (X_i - \bar{X})^2 \sum_{i=1}^{n} (Y_i - \bar{Y})^2}}$$

Division of the numerator and denominatory by $n - 1$ gives

$$r = \frac{\dfrac{\sum_{i=1}^{n} (X_i - \bar{X})(Y_i - \bar{Y})}{n-1}}{\sqrt{\sum_{i=1}^{n} \dfrac{(X_i - \bar{X})^2}{n-1} \sum_{i-1}^{n} \dfrac{(Y_i - \bar{Y})^2}{n-1}}}$$

$$= \frac{COV_{xy}}{S_x S_y}$$

Covariance
A systematic relationship between two variables in which a change in one implies a corresponding change in the other ($COV_x y$).

In these equations, X and Y denote the sample means and S_x and S_y the standard deviations. COV_{xy}, the **covariance** between X and Y, measures the extent to which X and Y are related. The covariance may be either positive or negative. Division by $S_x S_y$ achieves standardisation so that r varies between –1.0 and +1.0. Note that the correlation coefficient is an absolute number and is not expressed in any unit of measurement. The correlation coefficient between two variables will be the same regardless of their underlying units of measurement.

As an example, suppose that a researcher wants to explain attitudes toward a respondent's city of residence in terms of duration of residence in the city. The attitude is measured on an 11-point scale (1 = do not like the city, 11 = very much like the city), and the duration of residence is measured in terms of the number of years the respondent has lived in the city. In a pre-test of 12 respondents, the data shown in Table 19.1 are obtained.

Table 19.1 Explaining attitude toward the city of residence

Respondent number	*Attitude toward the city*	*Duration of residence*	*Importance attached to weather*
1	6	10	3
2	9	12	11
3	8	12	4
4	3	4	1
5	10	12	11
6	4	6	1
7	5	8	7
8	2	2	4
9	11	18	8
10	9	9	10
11	10	17	8
12	2	2	5

The correlation coefficient may be calculated as follows:

$$\bar{X} = (10 + 12 + 12 + 4 + 12 + 6 + 8 + 2 + 18 + 9 + 17 + 2)/12$$
$$= 9.333$$
$$\bar{Y} = (6 + 9 + 8 + 3 + 10 + 4 + 5 + 2 + 11 + 9 + 10 + 2)/12$$
$$= 6.583$$

$$\sum_{i=1}^{n} (X_i - \bar{X})(Y_i - \bar{Y}) = (10 - 9.33)(6 - 6.58) + (12 - 9.33)(9 - 6.58) + (12 - 9.33)$$
$$(8 - 6.58) + (4 - 9.33)(3 - 6.58) + (12 - 9.33)(10 - 6.58) + (6 - 9.33)(4 - 6.58)$$
$$+ (8 - 9.33)(5 - 6.58) + (2 - 9.33)(2 - 6.58) + (18 - 9.33)(11 - 6.58) + (9 - 9.33)$$
$$(9 - 6.58) + (17 - 9.33)(10 - 6.58) + (2 - 9.33)(2 - 6.58)$$
$$= - 0.3886 + 6.4614 + 3.7914 + 19.0814 + 9.1314 + 8.5914 + 2.1014 + 33.5714$$
$$+ 38.3214 - 0.7986 + 26.2314 + 33.5714$$
$$= 179.6668$$

$$\sum_{i=1}^{n} (X_i - \bar{X})^2 = (10 - 9.33)^2 + (12 - 9.33)^2 + (12 - 9.33)^2 + (4 - 9.33)^2$$
$$+ (12 - 9.33)^2 + (6 - 9.33)^2 + (8 - 9.33)^2 + (2 - 9.33)^2 + (18 - 9.33)^2 + (9 - 9.33)^2$$
$$+ (17 - 9.33)^2 + (2 - 9.33)^2$$
$$= 0.4489 + 1.1289 + 7.1289 + 28.4089 + 7.1289 + 11.0889 + 1.7689$$
$$+ 53.7289 + 75.1689 + 0.1089 + 58.8289 + 53.7289$$
$$= 304.6668$$

$$\sum_{i=1}^{n} (Y_i - \bar{Y})^2 = (6 - 6.58)^2 + (9 - 6.58)^2 + (8 - 6.58)^2 + (3 - 6.58)^2 + (10 - 6.58)^2$$
$$+ (4 - 6.58)^2 + (5 - 6.58)^2 + (2 - 6.58)^2 + (11 - 6.58)^2 + (9 - 6.58)^2 + (10 - 6.58)^2$$
$$+ (2 - 6.58)^2$$
$$= 0.3364 + 5.8564 + 2.0164 + 12.8164 + 11.6964 + 6.6564 + 2.4964$$
$$+ 20.9764 + 19.5364 + 5.8564 + 11.6964 + 20.9764$$
$$= 120.9168$$

Thus,

$$r = \frac{179.6668}{\sqrt{(304.6668)(120.9168)}}$$
$$= 0.9361$$

In this example, $r = 0.9361$, a value close to 1.0. This means that respondents' duration of residence in the city is strongly associated with their attitude toward the city. Furthermore, the positive sign of r implies a positive relationship; the longer the duration of residence, the more favourable the attitude and vice versa.

Since r indicates the degree to which variation in one variable is related to variation in another, it can also be expressed in terms of the decomposition of the total variation (see Chapter 18). In other words,

$$r^2 = \frac{\text{explained variation}}{\text{total variation}}$$
$$= \frac{SS_x}{SS_y}$$
$$= \frac{\text{total variation} - \text{error variation}}{\text{total variation}}$$
$$= \frac{SS_y - SS_{error}}{SS_y}$$

Hence, r^2 measures the proportion of variation in one variable that is explained by the other. Both r and r^2 are symmetric measures of association. In other words, the correlation of X with Y is the same as the correlation of Y with X. It does not matter which variable is considered to be the dependent variable and which the independent. The product moment coefficient measures the strength of the linear relationship and is not designed to measure non-linear relationships. Thus $r = 0$ merely indicates that there is no linear relationship between X and Y. It does not mean that X and Y are unrelated. There could well be a non-linear relationship between them, which would not be captured by r (see Figure 19.1).

When computed for a population rather than a sample, the product moment correlation is denoted by the Greek letter rho, ρ. The coefficient r is an estimator of ρ. Note that the calculation of r assumes that X and Y are metric variables whose distributions have the same shape. If these assumptions are not met, r is deflated and underestimates ρ. In marketing research, data obtained by using rating scales with a small number of categories may not be strictly interval. This tends to deflate r, resulting in an underestimation of ρ.[2]

The statistical significance of the relationship between two variables measured by using r can be conveniently tested. The hypotheses are

$$H_0: \rho = 0$$
$$H_1: \rho \neq 0$$

The test statistic is[3]

$$t = r\left[\frac{n-2}{1-r^2}\right]^{1/2}$$

which has a t distribution with n–2 degrees of freedom.[4] For the correlation coefficient calculated based on the data given in Table 19.1,

$$\begin{aligned} t &= 0.9361\left[\frac{12-2}{1-(0.9361)^2}\right]^{1/2} \\ &= 8.414 \end{aligned}$$

and the degrees of freedom = 12 – 2 = 10. From the t distribution table (Table 4 in the Statistical Appendix), the critical value of t for a two-tailed test and $\alpha = 0.05$ is 2.228. Hence, the null hypothesis of no relationship between X and Y is rejected. This, along with the positive sign of r, indicates that attitude toward the city is positively related to the duration of residence in the city. Moreover, the high value of r indicates that this relationship is strong.

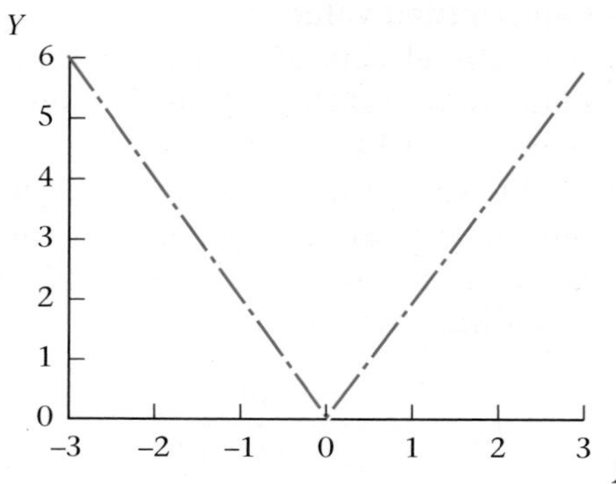

Figure 19.1
A non-linear relationship for which $r = 0$

In conducting multivariate data analysis, it is often useful to examine the simple correlation between each pair of variables. These results are presented in the form of a correlation matrix, which indicates the coefficient of correlation between each pair of variables. Usually, only the lower triangular portion of the matrix is considered. The diagonal elements all equal 1.00, since a variable correlates perfectly with itself. The upper triangular portion of the matrix is a mirror image of the lower triangular portion, since r is a symmetric measure of association. The form of a correlation matrix for five variables, V_1 through V_5 is as follows:

	V_1	V_2	V_3	V_4	V_5
V_1					
V_2	0.5				
V_3	0.3	0.4			
V_4	0.1	0.3	0.6		
V_5	0.2	0.5	0.3	0.7	

Although a matrix of simple correlations provides insights into pairwise associations, sometimes researchers want to examine the association between two variables after controlling for one or more other variables. In the latter case, partial correlation should be estimated.

PARTIAL CORRELATION

Whereas the product moment or simple correlation is a measure of association describing the linear association between two variables, a **partial correlation coefficient** measures the association between two variables after controlling for or adjusting for the effects of one or more additional variables. This statistic is used to answer the following questions:

Partial correlation coefficient
A measure of the association between two variables after controlling or adjusting for the effects of one or more additional variables.

- How strongly are sales related to advertising expenditures when the effect of price is controlled?
- Is there an association between market share and size of the sales force after adjusting for the effect of sales promotion?
- Are consumers' perceptions of quality related to their perceptions of prices when the effect of brand image is controlled?

As in these situations, suppose that a researcher wanted to calculate the association between X and Y after controlling for a third variable, Z. Conceptually, one would first remove the effect of Z from X. To do this, one would predict the values of X based on a knowledge of Z by using the product moment correlation between X and Z, r_{xz}. The predicted value of X is then subtracted from the actual value of X to construct an adjusted value of X. In a similar manner, the values of Y are adjusted to remove the effects of Z. The product moment correlation between the adjusted values of X and the adjusted values of Y is the partial correlation coefficient between X and Y, after controlling for the effect of Z, and is denoted by $r_{xy \cdot z}$. Statistically, since the simple correlation between two variables completely describes the linear relationship between them, the partial correlation coefficient can be calculated by a knowledge of the simple correlations alone, without using individual observations.

$$r_{xy.z} = \frac{r_{xy} - (r_{xz})(r_{yz})}{\sqrt{1 - r_{xz}^2}\sqrt{1 - r_{yz}^2}}$$

To continue our example, suppose that the researcher wanted to calculate the association between attitude toward the city, Y, and duration of residence, X_1, after controlling for a third variable, importance attached to weather, X_2. These data are presented in Table 19.1. The simple correlations between the variables are

$$r_{yx_1} = 0.9361 \qquad r_{yx_2} = 0.7334 \qquad r_{x_1x_2} = 0.5495$$

The required partial correlation may be calculated as follows:

$$r_{xy_1 \cdot x_2} = \frac{0.9361 - (0.5495)(0.7334)}{\sqrt{1 - (0.5495)^2}\sqrt{1 - (0.7334)^2}}$$

$$= 0.9386$$

As can be seen, controlling for the effect of importance attached to weather has little effect on the association between attitude toward the city and duration of residence.

Partial correlations have an order associated with them that indicates how many variables are being adjusted or controlled for. The simple correlation coefficient, r, has a zero order, because it does not control for any additional variables while measuring the association between two variables. The coefficient $r_{xy \cdot z}$ is a first-order partial correlation coefficient, because it controls for the effect of one additional variable, Z. A second-order partial correlation coefficient controls for the effects of two variables, a third-order for the effects of three variables, and so on. The higher order partial correlations are calculated similarly. The $(n + 1)$th order partial coefficient may be calculated by replacing the simple correlation coefficients on the right side of the preceding equation with the nth order partial coefficients.

Partial correlations can be helpful for detecting spurious relationships (see Chapter 17). The relationship between X and Y is spurious if it is solely because X is associated with Z, which is indeed the true predictor of Y. In this case, the correlation between X and Y disappears when the effect of Z is controlled. Consider a case in which consumption of a breakfast cereal brand (C) is positively associated with income (I), with $r_{ci} = 0.28$. Because this brand was popularly priced, income was not expected to be a significant factor. Therefore, the researcher suspected that this relationship was spurious. The sample results also indicated that income is positively associated with household size (H), $r_{hi} = 0.48$, and that household size is associated with breakfast cereal consumption, $r_{ch} = 0.56$. These figures seem to indicate that the real predictor of breakfast cereal consumption is not income but household size. To test this assertion, the first-order partial correlation between cereal consumption and income is calculated, controlling for the effect of household size. The reader can verify that this partial correlation, $r_{ci \cdot h}$, is 0.02, and the initial correlation between cereal consumption and income vanishes when the household size is controlled. Therefore, the correlation between income and cereal consumption is spurious. The special case when a partial correlation is larger than its respective zero-order correlation involves a suppressor effect (see Chapter 17).[4]

Part correlation coefficient
A measure of the correlation between Y and X when the linear effects of the other independent variables have been removed from X (but not from Y).

Another correlation coefficient of interest is the **part correlation coefficient**. This coefficient represents the correlation between Y and X when the linear effects of the other independent variables have been removed from X but not from Y. The part correlation coefficient, $r_{y(x.z)}$ is calculated as follows:

$$r_{y(x.z)} = \frac{r_{xy} - r_{yz}\, r_{xz}}{\sqrt{1 - r_{xz}^2}}$$

The part correlation between attitude toward the city and the duration of residence, when the linear effects of the importance attached to weather have been removed from the duration of residence, can be calculated as

$$r_{y(x_1 \cdot x_2)} = \frac{0.9361 - (0.5495)(0.7334)}{\sqrt{1 - (0.5495)^2}}$$

$$= 0.63806$$

The partial correlation coefficient is generally viewed as more important than the part correlation coefficient. The product moment correlation, partial correlation, and the part correlation coefficient all assume that the data are interval or ratio scaled. If the data do not meet these requirements, the researcher should consider the use of non-metric correlation.

EXAMPLE

Selling ads to home shoppers[5]

Advertisements play a very important role in forming attitudes and preferences for brands. In general, it has been found that for low-involvement products, attitude toward the advertisement mediates brand cognition (beliefs about the brand) and attitude toward the brand. What would happen to the effect of this mediating variable when products are purchased through a home shopping network? Home Shopping Budapest in Hungary conducted research to assess the impact of advertisements toward purchase. A survey was conducted where several measures were taken such as: attitude toward the product, attitude toward the brand, attitude toward the ad characteristics and brand cognitions. It was hypothesised that in a home shopping network, advertisements largely determined attitude toward the brand. To find the degree of association of attitude toward the ad with both attitude toward the brand and brand cognition, a partial correlation coefficient could be computed. The partial correlation would be calculated between attitude toward the brand and brand cognitions after controlling for the effects of attitude toward the ad on the two variables. If attitude toward the ad is significantly high, then the partial correlation coefficient should be significantly less than the product moment correlation between brand cognition and attitude toward the brand. Research was conducted which supported this hypothesis. Then, Saatchi and Saatchi designed the ads aired on Home Shopping Budapest to generate positive attitude toward the advertising. This turned out to be a major competitive weapon for the network. ■

NON-METRIC CORRELATION

At times the researcher may have to compute the correlation coefficient between two variables that are non-metric. It may be recalled that non-metric variables do not have interval or ratio scale properties and do not assume a normal distribution. If the non-metric variables are ordinal and numeric, Spearman's rho, ρ_s, and Kendall's tau, τ, are two measures of **non-metric correlation** which can be used to examine the correlation between them. Both these measures use rankings rather than the absolute values of the variables, and the basic concepts underlying them are quite similar. Both vary from –1.0 to +1.0.

Non-metric correlation
A correlation measure for two non-metric variables that relies on rankings to compute the correlation.

In the absence of ties, Spearman's ρ_s yields a closer approximation to the Pearson product moment correlation coefficient, *r*, than does Kendall's τ. In these cases, the absolute magnitude of τ tends to be smaller than Pearson's *r*. On the other hand, when the data contain a large number of tied ranks, Kendall's τ seems more appropriate. As a rule of thumb, Kendall's τ is to be preferred when a large number of cases fall into a relatively small number of categories (thereby leading to a large number of ties). Conversely, the use of Spearman's ρ_s is preferable when we have a relatively larger number of categories (thereby having fewer ties).[6]

The product moment as well as the partial and part correlation coefficients provide a conceptual foundation for bivariate as well as multiple regression analysis.

REGRESSION ANALYSIS

Regression analysis
A statistical procedure for analysing associative relationships between a metric-dependent variable and one or more independent variables.

Regression analysis is a powerful and flexible procedure for analysing associative relationships between a metric-dependent variable and one or more independent variables. It can be used in the following ways:

1 To determine whether the independent variables explain a significant variation in the dependent variable: whether a relationship exists.
2 To determine how much of the variation in the dependent variable can be explained by the independent variables: strength of the relationship.
3 To determine the structure or form of the relationship: the mathematical equation relating the independent and dependent variables.
4 To predict the values of the dependent variable.
5 To control for other independent variables when evaluating the contributions of a specific variable or set of variables.

Although the independent variables may explain the variation in the dependent variable, this does not necessarily imply causation. The use of the terms dependent or criterion variables and independent or predictor variables in regression analysis arises from the mathematical relationship between the variables. These terms do not imply that the criterion variable is dependent on the independent variables in a causal sense. Regression analysis is concerned with the nature and degree of association between variables and does not imply or assume any causality. Bivariate regression is discussed first, followed by multiple regression.

BIVARIATE REGRESSION

Bivariate regression
A procedure for deriving a mathematical relationship, in the form of an equation, between a single metric-dependent variable and a single metric-independent variable.

Bivariate regression is a procedure for deriving a mathematical relationship, in the form of an equation, between a single metric-dependent or criterion variable and a single metric-independent or predictor variable. The analysis is similar in many ways to determining the simple correlation between two variables. Since an equation has to be derived, however, one variable must be identified as the dependent variable and the other as the independent variable. The examples given earlier in the context of simple correlation can be translated into the regression context.

- Can variation in sales be explained in terms of variation in advertising expenditures? What is the structure and form of this relationship, and can it be modelled mathematically by an equation describing a straight line?
- Can the variation in market share be accounted for by the size of the sales force?
- Are consumers' perceptions of quality determined by their perceptions of price?

Before discussing the procedure for conducting bivariate regression, we define some important statistics.

STATISTICS ASSOCIATED WITH BIVARIATE REGRESSION ANALYSIS

The following statistics and statistical terms are associated with bivariate regression analysis.

Bivariate regression model. The basic regression equation is $Y_i = \beta_0 + \beta_1 X_i + e_i$, where Y = dependent or criterion variable, X = independent or predictor variable, β_0 = intercept of the line, β_1 = slope of the line, and e_i is the error term associated with the ith observation.

Coefficient of determination. The strength of association is measured by the coefficient of determination, r^2. It varies between 0 and 1 and signifies the proportion of the total variation in Y that is accounted for by the variation in X.

Estimated or predicted value. The estimated or predicted value of Y_i, is $\hat{Y}_i = a + bx$, where $\hat{Y}_i$ is the predicted value of Y_i, and a and b are estimators of β_0 and β_1, respectively.

Regression coefficient. The estimated parameter b is usually referred to as the non-standardised regression coefficient.

Scattergram. A scatter diagram, or scattergram, is a plot of the values of two variables for all the cases or observations.

Standard error of estimate. This statistic, the SEE, is the standard deviation of the actual Y values from the predicted $\hat{Y}$ values.

Standard error. The standard deviation of b, SE_b, is called the standard error.

Standardised regression coefficient. Also termed the beta coefficient or beta weight, this is the slope obtained by the regression of Y on X when the data are standardised.

Sum of squared errors. The distances of all the points from the regression line are squared and added together to arrive at the sum of squared errors, which is a measure of total error, $\sum e^2 j$

***t** statistic.* A t statistic with $n - 2$ degrees of freedom can be used to test the null hypothesis that no linear relationship exists between X and Y, or $H_0 : \beta_1 = 0$, where

$$t = \frac{b}{SE_b}$$

CONDUCTING BIVARIATE REGRESSION ANALYSIS

The steps involved in conducting bivariate regression analysis are described in Figure 19.2. Suppose that the researcher wants to explain attitudes toward the city of residence in terms of the duration of residence (see Table 19.1). In deriving such relationships, it is often useful to first examine a scatter diagram.

Scatter diagram

A scatter diagram, or scattergram, is a plot of the values of two variables for all the cases or observations. It is customary to plot the dependent variable on the vertical axis and the independent variable on the horizontal axis. A scatter diagram is useful for determining the form of the relationship between the variables. A plot can alert the researcher to patterns in the data or to possible problems. Any unusual combinations of the two variables can be easily identified. A plot of Y (attitude toward the city) against X (duration of residence) is given in Figure 19.3. The points seem to be arranged in a band running from the bottom left to the top right. One can see the pattern: as one variable increases, so

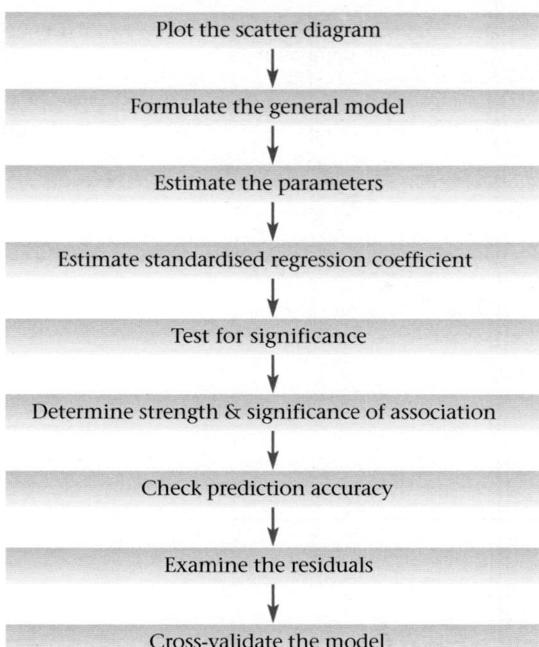

Figure 19.2
Conducting bivariate regression analysis

does the other. It appears from this scattergram that the relationship between X and Y is linear and could be well described by a straight line. How should the straight line be fitted to best describe the data?

Least squares procedure
A technique for fitting a straight line to a scattergram by minimising the vertical distances of all the points from the line.

The most commonly used technique for fitting a straight line to a scattergram is the **least squares procedure**. This technique determines the best-fitting line by minimising the vertical distances of all the points from the line. The best-fitting line is called the regression line. Any point that does not fall on the regression line is not fully accounted for. The vertical distance from the point to the line is the error, e_j (see Figure 19.4). The distances of all the points from the line are squared and added together to arrive at the sum of squared errors, which is a measure of total error, $\sum e_j^2$. In fitting the line, the least squares procedure minimises the sum of squared errors. If Y is plotted on the vertical axis and X on the horizontal axis, as in Figure 19.4, the best fitting line is called the regression of Y on X, since the vertical distances are minimised. The scatter diagram indicates whether the relationship between Y and X can be modelled as a straight line and, consequently, whether the bivariate regression model is appropriate.

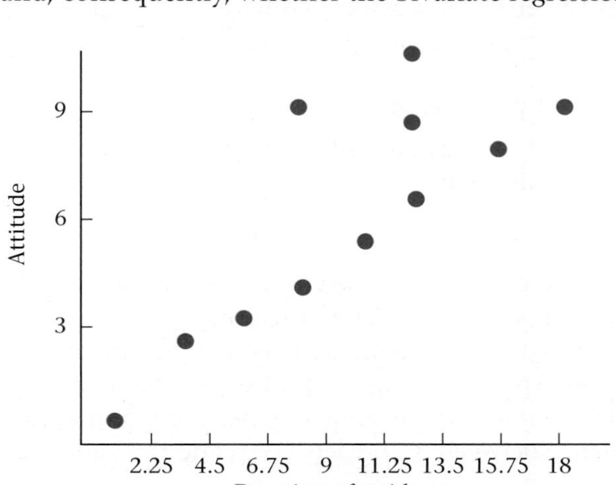

Figure 19.3
Plot of attitude with duration

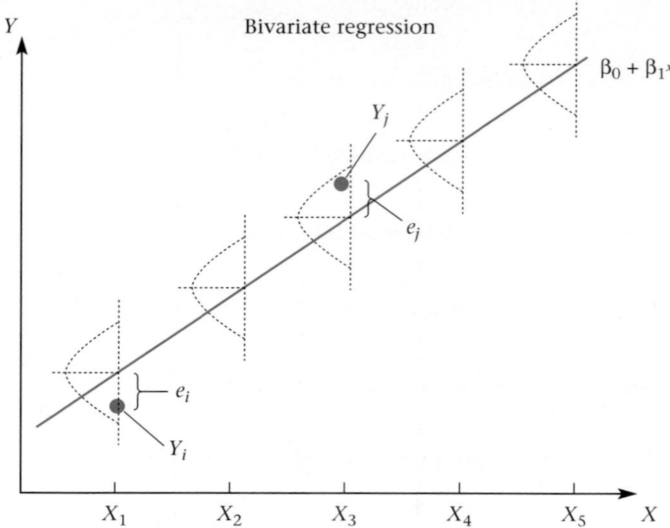

Figure 19.4
Bivariate regression

BIVARIATE REGRESSION MODEL

In the bivariate regression model, the general form of a straight line is

$$Y = \beta_0 + \beta_1 X$$

where

Y = dependent or criterion variable
X = independent or predictor variable
β_0 = intercept of the line
β_1 = slope of the line

This model implies a deterministic relationship in that Y is completely determined by X. The value of Y can be perfectly predicted if β_0 and β_1 are known. In marketing research, however, very few relationships are deterministic. Thus, the regression procedure adds an error term to account for the probabilistic or stochastic nature of the relationship. The basic regression equation becomes

$$Y_i = \beta_0 + \beta_1 X_i + e_i$$

where e_i is the error term associated with the ith observation.[7] Estimation of the regression parameters, β_0 and β_1, is relatively simple.

Estimation of parameters

In most cases, β_0 and β_1 are unknown and are estimated from the sample observations using the equation

$$\hat{Y}_i = a + bx_i$$

Estimated or predicted value
The value $Y_i = a + b_x$, where a and b are, respectively, estimators of β_0 and β_1, the corresponding population parameters.

where $\hat{Y}_i$ is the **estimated or predicted value** of Y_i, and a and b are estimators of β_0 and β_1 respectively. The constant b is usually referred to as the non-standardised regression coefficient. It is the slope of the regression line, and it indicates the expected change in Y when X is changed by one unit. The formulas for calculating a and b are simple.[8] The slope, b, may be computed in terms of the covariance between X and Y (COV_{xy}) and the variance of X as

$$b = \frac{COV_{xy}}{S^2_x}$$

$$= \frac{\sum_{i=1}^{n} (X_i - \bar{X})\ (Y_i - \bar{Y})}{\sum_{i=1}^{n} (X_i - \bar{X})^2}$$

$$= \frac{\sum_{i=1}^{n} X_i\ Y_i - n\ \bar{X}\ \bar{Y}}{\sum_{i=1}^{n} X_i^2 - n\ \bar{X}^2}$$

The intercept, a, may then be calculated using

$$a = \bar{Y} - b\bar{X}$$

For the data in Table 19.1, the estimation of parameters may be illustrated as follows:

$$\sum_{i=1}^{12} X_i\ Y_i = (10)(6) + (12)(9) + (12)(8) + (4)(3) + (12)(10) + (6)(4) + (8)(5) + (2)(2)$$
$$+ (18)(11) + (9)(9) + (17)(10) + (2)(2)$$
$$= 917$$

$$\sum_{i=1}^{12} X_i^2 = 10^2 + 12^2 + 12^2 + 4^2 + 12^2 + 6^2 + 8^2 + 2^2 + 18^2 + 9^2 + 17^2 + 2^2$$
$$= 1350$$

It may be recalled from earlier calculations of the simple correlation that

$$\bar{X} = 9.333$$
$$\bar{Y} = 6.583$$

Given $n = 12$, b can be calculated as

$$b = \frac{917 - (12)(9.333)(6.583)}{1350 - (12)(9.333)^2}$$
$$= 0.5897$$
$$a = \bar{Y} - b\ \bar{X}$$
$$= 6.583 - (0.5897)(9.333)$$
$$= 1.0793$$

Note that these coefficients have been estimated on the raw (untransformed) data. Should standardisation of the data be considered desirable, the calculation of the standardised coefficients is also straightforward.

Standardised regression coefficient

Standardisation is the process by which the raw data are transformed into new variables that have a mean of 0 and a variance of 1 (Chapter 16). When the data are standardised, the intercept assumes a value of 0. The term *beta coefficient* or *beta weight* is used to denote the standardised regression coefficient. In this case, the slope obtained by the regression of Y on X, B_{yx} is the same as the slope obtained by the regression of X on Y, B_{xy}. Moreover, each of these regression coefficients is equal to the simple correlation between X and Y

$$B_{yx} = B_{xy} = r_{xy}$$

There is a simple relationship between the standardised and non-standardised regression coefficients

$$B_{yx} = b_{yx} \left[\frac{S_x}{S_y} \right]$$

For the regression results given in Table 19.2, the value of the beta coefficient is estimated as 0.9361.

Once the parameters have been estimated, they can be tested for significance.

Table 19.2 Bivariate regression

Multiple R	0.93608
R^2	0.87624
Adjusted R^2	0.86387
Standard error	1.22329

Analysis of variance			
	df	**Sum of squares**	**Mean square**
Regression	1	105.95222	105.95222
Residual	10	14.96444	1.49644
F = 70.80266	Significance of F = 0.0000		

Variables in the equation					
Variable	***b***	**SE_b**	**Beta (β)**	***T***	**Sig. of *T***
DURATION	0.58972	0.07008	0.93608	8.414	0.0000
(Constant)	1.07932	0.74335		1.452	0.1772

Significance testing

The statistical significance of the linear relationship between X and Y may be tested by examining the hypotheses

$$H_0 : \beta_1 = 0$$
$$H_1 : \beta_1 \neq 0$$

The null hypothesis implies that there is no linear relationship between X and Y. The alternative hypothesis is that there is a relationship, positive or negative, between X and Y. Typically, a two-tailed test is done. A t statistic with $n - 2$ degrees of freedom can be used, where

$$t = \frac{b}{SE_b}$$

and SE_b denotes the standard deviation of b, called the *standard error*.[9] The t distribution was discussed in Chapter 17.

Using a software package, the regression of attitude on duration of residence, using the data shown in Table 19.1, yielded the results shown in Table 19.2. The intercept, a, equals 1.0793, and the slope, b, equals 0.5897. Therefore, the estimated equation is

$$\text{attitude } (\hat{Y}) = 1.0793 + 0.5891 \text{ (duration of residence)}$$

The standard error or standard deviation of b is estimated as 0.07008, and the value of the t statistic, $t = 0.5897/0.0700 = 8.414$, with $n - 2 = 10$ degrees of freedom. From Table 4 in the Statistical Appendix, we see that the critical value of t with 10 degrees of freedom and $\alpha = 0.05$ is 2.228 for a two-tailed test. Since the calculated value of t is larger than the critical value, the null hypothesis is rejected. Hence, there is a significant linear relationship between attitude toward the city and duration of residence in the city. The positive sign of the slope coefficient indicates that this relationship is positive. In other words, those who have lived in the city for a longer time have more positive attitudes toward the city.

Strength and significance of association

A related inference involves determining the strength and significance of the association between Y and X. The strength of association is measured by the coefficient of determination, r^2. In bivariate regression, r^2 is the square of the simple correlation coefficient obtained by correlating the two variables. The coefficient r^2 varies between 0 and 1. It signifies the proportion of the total variation in Y that is accounted for by the variation in X. The decomposition of the total variation in Y is similar to that for analysis of variance (Chapter 18). As shown in Figure 19.5, the total variation, SS_y may be decomposed into the variation accounted for by the regression line, SS_{reg}, and the error or residual variation, SS_{error} or SS_{res}, as follows:

$$SS_y = SS_{reg} + SS_{res}$$

$$SS_y = \sum_{i=1}^{n} (Y_i - \bar{Y})^2$$

$$SS_{reg} = \sum_{i=1}^{n} (\hat{Y}_i = \bar{Y})^2$$

$$SS_{res} = \sum_{i=1}^{n} (Y_i - \hat{Y}_i)^2$$

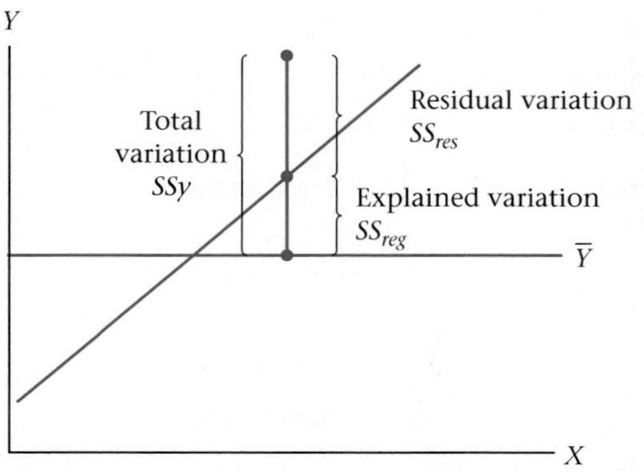

Figure 19.5 Decomposition of the total variation in bivariate regression

The strength of the association may then be calculated as follows

$$r^2 = \frac{SS_{reg}}{SS_y}$$

$$= \frac{SS_y - SS_{res}}{SS_y}$$

To illustrate the calculations of r^2, let us consider again the effect of attitude toward the city on the duration of residence. It may be recalled from earlier calculations of the simple correlation coefficient that

$$SS_{reg} = \sum_{i=1}^{n} (Y_i - \bar{Y})^2$$

$$= 120.9168$$

The predicted values $(\hat{Y})$ can be calculated using the regression equation

$$\text{attitude } (\hat{Y}) = 1.0793 + 0.5897 \text{ (duration of residence)}$$

For the first observation in Table 19.1, this value is

$$(\hat{Y}) = 1.0793 + 0.5897 \times 10 = 6.9763$$

For each successive observation, the predicted values are, in order, 8.1557, 8.1557, 3.4381, 8.1557, 4.6175, 5.7969, 2.2587, 11.6939, 6.3866, 11.1042, 2.2587. Therefore,

$$SS_{reg} = \sum_{i=1}^{n} (\hat{Y}_i - \bar{Y})^2$$

$$\begin{aligned}
= \; & (6.9763 - 6.5833)^2 + (8.1557 - 6.5833)^2 + (8.1557 - 6.5833)^2 + \\
& (3.4381 - 6.5833)^2 + (8.1557 - 6.5833)^2 + (4.6175 - 6.5833)^2 + \\
& (5.7969 - 6.5833)^2 + (2.2587 - 6.5833)^2 + (11.6939 - 6.5833)^2 + \\
& (6.3866 - 6.5833)^? + (11.1042 - 6.5833)^? + (2.2587 - 6.5833)^?
\end{aligned}$$

$$\begin{aligned}
= \; & 0.1544 + 2.4724 + 2.4724 + 9.8922 + 2.4724 + 3.8643 + 0.6184 + \\
& 18.7021 + 26.1182 + 0.0387 + 20.4385 + 18.7021
\end{aligned}$$

$$= 105.9524$$

$$SS_{res} = \sum_{i=1}^{n} (Y_i - \hat{Y}_i)^2$$

$$\begin{aligned}
& (6 - 6.9763)^2 + (9 - 8.1557)^2 + (8 - 8.1557)^2 + (3 - 3.4381)^2 + \\
& (10 - 8.1557)^2 + (4 - 4.6175)^2 + (5 - 5.7969)^2 + (2 - 2.2587)^2 + \\
& (11 - 11.6939)^2 + (9 - 6.3866)^2 + (10 - 11.1042)^2 + (2 - 2.2587)^2
\end{aligned}$$

$$= 14.9644$$

It can be seen that $SS_y = SS_{reg} + SS_{res}$. Furthermore,

$$r^2 = \frac{SS_{reg}}{SS_y}$$

$$= \frac{105.9524}{120.9168}$$

$$= 0.8762$$

Another equivalent test for examining the significance of the linear relationship between X and Y (significance of b) is the test for the significance of the coefficient of determination. The hypotheses in this case are

$$H_0: R^2pop = 0$$
$$H_1: R^2pop > 0$$

The appropriate test statistic is the F statistic

$$F = \frac{SS_{reg}}{SS_{res}/(n-2)}$$

which has an F distribution with 1 and $n - 2$ degrees of freedom. The F test is a generalised form of the t test (see Chapter 17). If a random variable is t distributed with n degrees of freedom, then t^2 is F distributed with 1 and n degrees of freedom. Hence, the F test for testing the significance of the coefficient of determination is equivalent to testing the following hypotheses:

$$H_0: \beta 1 = 0$$
$$H_1: \beta 1 \neq 0$$

or

$$H_0: \rho = 0$$
$$H_1: \rho \neq 0$$

From Table 19.2, it can be seen that

$$r^2 = \frac{105.9522}{105.9522 + 14.9644}$$
$$= 0.8762$$

which is the same as the value calculated earlier. The value of the F statistic is

$$F = \frac{105.9522}{14.9644/\ 10}$$
$$= 70.8027$$

with 1 and 10 degrees of freedom. The calculated F statistic exceeds the critical value of 4.96 determined from Table 5 in the Statistical Appendix. Therefore, the relationship is significant at $\alpha = 0.05$, corroborating the results of the t test. If the relationship between X and Y is significant, it is meaningful to predict the values of Y based on the values of X and to estimate prediction accuracy.

Prediction accuracy

To estimate the accuracy of predicted values, $\hat{Y}$, it is useful to calculate the standard error of estimate, SEE. This statistic is the standard deviation of the actual Y values from the predicted $\hat{Y}$ values.

$$\text{SEE} = \sqrt{\frac{\sum_{i=1}^{n}(Y_i - \hat{Y})^2}{n-2}}$$

$$\text{SEE} = \sqrt{\frac{SS_{res}}{n-2}}$$

or, more generally, if there are k independent variables

$$\text{SEE} = \sqrt{\frac{SS_{res}}{n-k-1}}$$

SEE may be interpreted as a kind of average residual or average error in predicting Y from the regression equation.[10]

Two cases of prediction may arise. The researcher may want to predict the mean value of Y for all the cases with a given value of X, say X_0, or predict the value of Y for a single case. In both situations, the predicted value is the same and is given by $\hat{Y}$, where

$$\hat{Y} = a + bX_0$$

But the standard error is different in the two situations, although in both situations it is a function of SEE. For large samples, the standard error for predicting mean value of Y is SEE/$\sqrt{n}$ and for predicting individual Y values it is SEE. Hence, the construction of confidence intervals (see Chapter 14) for the predicted value varies, depending upon whether the mean value or the value for a single observation is being predicted. For the data given in Table 19.2, the SEE is estimated as follows:

$$\text{SEE} = \sqrt{\frac{14.9644}{12-2}}$$

$$= 1.22329$$

The final two steps in conducting bivariate regression, namely examination of residuals and model cross-validation, are considered later, and we now turn to the assumptions underlying the regression model.

Assumptions

The regression model makes a number of assumptions in estimating the parameters and in significance testing, as shown in Figure 19.4:

1. The error term is normally distributed. For each fixed value of X, the distribution of Y is normal.[11]
2. The means of all these normal distributions of Y, given X, lie on a straight line with slope b.
3. The mean of the error term is 0.
4. The variance of the error term is constant. This variance does not depend on the values assumed by X.
5. The error terms are uncorrelated. In other words, the observations have been drawn independently.

Insights into the extent to which these assumptions have been met can be gained by an examination of residuals, which is covered in the next section on multiple regression.[12]

Multiple regression
A statistical technique that simultaneously develops a mathematical relationship between two or more independent variables and an interval-scaled dependent variable.

MULTIPLE REGRESSION

Multiple regression involves a single dependent variable and two or more independent variables. The questions raised in the context of bivariate regression can also be answered via multiple regression by considering additional independent variables:

- Can variation in sales be explained in terms of variation in advertising expenditures, prices and level of distribution?
- Can variation in market shares be accounted for by the size of the sales force, advertising expenditures and sales promotion budgets?
- Are consumers' perceptions of quality determined by their perceptions of prices, brand image and brand attributes?

Additional questions can also be answered by multiple regression:

- How much of the variation in sales can be explained by advertising expenditures, prices and level of distribution?
- What is the contribution of advertising expenditures in explaining the variation in sales when the levels of prices and distribution are controlled?
- What levels of sales may be expected given the levels of advertising expenditures, prices and level of distribution?

EXAMPLE

Global brands, local ads[13]

Europeans welcome brands from other countries, but when it comes to advertising, they seem to prefer brands from their own country. A survey conducted by Yankelovich and Partners and its affiliates found that most European consumers' favourite commercials were for local brands even though they were more than likely to buy foreign brands. Respondents in Britain, France and Germany named Coca-Cola as the most often purchased soft drink. The French, however, selected the famous award-winning spot for France's Perrier bottled water as their favourite commercial. Similarly, in Germany, the favourite advertising was for a German brand of non-alcoholic beer, Clausthaler. In Britain though, Coca-Cola was the favourite soft drink and also the favourite advertising. In the light of such findings, the important question was, does advertising help? Does it help increase the purchase probability of the brand or does it merely maintain the brand recognition rate high? One way of finding out was by running a regression where the dependent variable was the likelihood of brand purchase and the independent variables were brand attribute evaluations and advertising evaluations. Separate models with and without advertising could be run to assess any significant difference in the contribution. Individual *t* tests could also be examined to find out the significant contribution of both the brand attributes and advertising. The results could indicate the degree to which advertising plays an important part on brand purchase decisions. ■

Multiple regression model An equation used to explain the results of multiple regression analysis.

The general form of the **multiple regression model** is as follows:

$$y = \beta_0 + \beta_1 X_1 + \beta_2 X_2 + \beta_3 X_3 + \ldots + \beta_k X_k + e$$

which is estimated by the following equation:

$$\hat{Y} = a + b_1 X_1 + b_2 X_2 + b_3 X_3 + \ldots + b_k X_k$$

As before, the coefficient *a* represents the intercept, but the *b*'s are now the partial regression coefficients. The least squares criterion estimates the parameters in such a way as to minimise the total error, SS_{res}. This process also maximises the correlation between the actual values of Y and the predicted values of $\hat{Y}$. All the assumptions made in bivariate regression also apply in multiple regression. We define some associated statistics and then describe the procedure for multiple regression analysis.[14]

STATISTICS ASSOCIATED WITH MULTIPLE REGRESSION

Most of the statistics and statistical terms described under bivariate regression also apply to multiple regression. In addition, the following statistics are used:

Adjusted R^2. R^2, coefficient of multiple determination, is adjusted for the number of independent variables and the sample size to account for the diminishing returns. After the first few variables, the additional independent variables do not make much contribution.

Coefficient of multiple determination. The strength of association in multiple regression is measured by the square of the multiple correlation coefficient, R^2, which is also called the coefficient of multiple determination.

F test. The F test is used to test the null hypothesis that the coefficient of multiple determination in the population, R^2_{pop}, is zero. This is equivalent to testing the null hypothesis H_0: $\beta_1 = \beta_2 = \beta_3 = \ldots = \beta_k = 0$. The test statistic has an F distribution with k and $(n - k - 1)$ degrees of freedom.

Partial F test. The significance of a partial regression coefficient, β_i, of X_i may be tested using an incremental F statistic. The incremental F statistic is based on the increment in the explained sum of squares resulting from the addition of the independent variable X_i to the regression equation after all the other independent variables have been included.

Partial regression coefficient. The partial regression coefficient, b_1, denotes the change in the predicted value, $\hat{Y}$, per unit change in X_1 when the other independent variables, X_2 to X_k, are held constant.

CONDUCTING MULTIPLE REGRESSION ANALYSIS

The steps involved in conducting multiple regression analysis are similar to those for bivariate regression analysis. The discussion focuses on partial regression coefficients, strength of association, significance testing and examination of residuals.

Partial regression coefficients

To understand the meaning of a partial regression coefficient, let us consider a case in which there are two independent variables, so that

$$\hat{Y} = a + b_1X_1 + b_2X_2$$

First, note that the relative magnitude of the partial regression coefficient of an independent variable is, in general, different from that of its bivariate regression coefficient. In other words, the partial regression coefficient, b_1, will be different from the regression coefficient, b, obtained by regressing Y on only X_1. This happens because X_1 and X_2 are usually correlated. In bivariate regression, X_2 was not considered, and any variation in Y that was shared by X_1 and X_2 was attributed to X_1. In the case of multiple independent variables, however, this is no longer true.

The interpretation of the partial regression coefficient, b_1, is that it represents the expected change in Y when X_1 is changed by one unit but X_2 is held constant or otherwise controlled. Likewise, b_2 represents the expected change in Y

for a unit change in X_2, when X_1 is held constant. Thus, calling b_1 and b_2 partial regression coefficients is appropriate. It can also be seen that the combined effects of X_1 and X_2 on Y are additive. In other words, if X_1 and X_2 are each changed by one unit, the expected change in Y would be $(b_1 + b_2)$.

Conceptually, the relationship between the bivariate regression coefficient and the partial regression coefficient can be illustrated as follows. Suppose that one was to remove the effect of X_2 from X_1. This could be done by running a regression of X_1 on X_2. In other words, one would estimate the equation $\hat{X}_1 = a + bX_2$ and calculate the residual $X_r = (X_1 - \hat{X}_1)$. The partial regression coefficient, b_1, is then equal to the bivariate regression coefficient, b, obtained from the equation $\hat{Y} = a + bX_r$. In other words, the partial regression coefficient, b_1, is equal to the regression coefficient, b, between Y and the residuals of X_1 from which the effect of X_2 has been removed. The partial coefficient, b, can also be interpreted along similar lines.

Extension to the case of k variables is straightforward. The partial regression coefficient, b_1, represents the expected change in Y when X_1 is changed by one unit and X_2 through X_k are held constant. It can also be interpreted as the bivariate regression coefficient, b, for the regression of Y on the residuals of X_1, when the effect of X_2 through X_k has been removed from X_1.

The beta coefficients are the partial regression coefficients obtained when all the variables $(Y, X_1, X_2, \ldots X_k)$ have been standardised to a mean of 0 and a variance of 1 before estimating the regression equation. The relationship of the standardised to the non-standardised coefficients remains the same as before:

$$B_1 = b_1 \frac{S_{x1}}{S_y}$$

$$\vdots$$

$$B_k = b_k \frac{S_{xk}}{S_y}$$

The intercept and the partial regression coefficients are estimated by solving a system of simultaneous equations derived by differentiating and equating the partial derivatives to 0. Since these coefficients are automatically estimated by the various computer programs, we will not present the details. Yet it is worth noting that the equations cannot be solved if (1) the sample size, n, is smaller than or equal to the number of independent variables, k, or (2) one independent variable is perfectly correlated with another.

Suppose that in explaining the attitude toward the city, we now introduce a second variable, importance attached to the weather. The data for the 12 pre-test respondents on attitude toward the city, duration of residence, and importance attached to the weather are given in Table 19.1. The results of multiple regression analysis are depicted in Table 19.3. The partial regression coefficient for duration (X_1) is now 0.4811, different from what it was in the bivariate case. The corresponding beta coefficient is 0.7636.

The partial regression coefficient for importance attached to weather (X_2) is 0.2887, with a beta coefficient of 0.3138. The estimated regression equation is

$$(\hat{Y}) = 0.33732 + 0.48108X_1 + 0.28865X_2$$

or

$$\text{attitude} = 0.33732 + 0.48108 \text{ (duration)} + 0.28865 \text{ (importance)}$$

This equation can be used for a variety of purposes, including predicting attitudes toward the city, given a knowledge of the respondents' duration of residence in the city and the importance they attach to weather.

Table 19.3 Multiple regression

Multiple R	0.97210				
R^2	0.94498				
Adjusted R^2	0.93276				
Standard error	0.85974				
		Analysis of variance			
	df		**Sum of squares**		**Mean square**
Regression	2		114.26425		57.13213
Residual	9		6.65241		0.73916
F = 77.29364	Significance of F = 0.0000				
		Variables in the equation			
Variable	**b**	**SE_b**	**Beta (β)**	**T**	**Sig. of T**
Importance	0.28865	0.08608	0.31382	3.353	0.0085
DURATION	0.48108	0.05895	0.76363	8.160	0.0000
(Constant)	0.33732	0.56736		0.595	0.5668

Strength of association

The strength of the relationship stipulated by the regression equation can be determined by using appropriate measures of association. The total variation is decomposed as in the bivariate case

$$SS_y = SS_{reg} + SS_{res}$$

where

$$SS_y = \sum_{i=1}^{n} (Y_i - \bar{Y})^2$$

$$SS_{reg} = \sum_{i=1}^{n} (\hat{Y}_i - \bar{Y})^2$$

$$SS_{res} = \sum_{i=1}^{n} (Y_i - \hat{Y}_i)^2$$

The strength of association is measured by the square of the multiple correlation coefficient, R^2, which is also called the coefficient of multiple determination

$$R^2 = \frac{SS_{reg}}{SS_y}$$

The multiple correlation coefficient, R, can also be viewed as the simple correlation coefficient, r, between Y and $\hat{Y}$. Several points about the characteristics of R^2 are worth noting. The coefficient of multiple determination, R^2, cannot be less than the highest bivariate, r^2, of any individual independent variable with the dependent variable. R^2 will be larger when the correlations between the independent variables are low. If the independent variables are statistically independent (uncorrelated), then R^2 will be the sum of bivariate r^2 of each independent variable with the dependent variable. R^2 cannot decrease as more independent variables are added to the regression equation. Yet diminishing returns set in, so that after the first few variables, the additional independent variables do not make much of a contribution.[15] For this reason, R^2 is adjusted for the number of independent variables and the sample size by using the following formula:

$$\text{adjusted } R^2 = R^2 - \frac{k(1 - R^2)}{n - k - 1}$$

For the regression results given in Table 19.3, the value of R^2 is

$$R^2 = \frac{114.2643}{114.2643 + 6.6524}$$
$$= 0.9450$$

This is higher than the r^2 value of 0.8762 obtained in the bivariate case. The r^2 in the bivariate case is the square of the simple (product moment) correlation between attitude toward the city and duration of residence. The R^2 obtained in multiple regression is also higher than the square of the simple correlation between attitude and importance attached to weather (which can be estimated as 0.5379). The adjusted R^2 is estimated as

$$\text{adjusted } R^2 = 0.9450 - \frac{2(1.0 - 0.9450)}{12 - 2 - 1}$$
$$= 0.9328$$

Note that the value of adjusted R^2 is close to R^2 and both are higher than r^2 for the bivariate case. This suggests that the addition of the second independent variable, importance attached to weather, makes a contribution in explaining the variation in attitude toward the city.

Significance testing

Significance testing involves testing the significance of the overall regression equation as well as specific partial regression coefficients. The null hypothesis for the overall test is that the coefficient of multiple determination in the population, R^2_{pop}, is zero.

$$H_0: R^2_{pop} = 0$$

This is equivalent to the following null hypothesis:

$$H_0: \beta_1 = \beta_2 = \beta_3 = \ldots = \beta_k = 0$$

The overall test can be conducted by using an F statistic

$$F = \frac{SS_{reg}/k}{SS_{reg}/(n - k - 1)}$$
$$= \frac{R^2/k}{(1 - R^2)/(n - k - 1)}$$

which has an F distribution with k and $n - k - 1$ degrees of freedom.[16] For the multiple regression results given in Table 19.3,

$$F = \frac{114.2643/2}{6.6524/9} = 77.2938$$

which is significant at $\alpha = 0.05$.

If the overall null hypothesis is rejected, one or more population partial regression coefficients have a value different from 0. To determine which specific coefficients (β_i's) are nonzero, additional tests are necessary. Testing for the significance of the β_i's can be done in a manner similar to that in the bivariate case by using t tests. The significance of the partial coefficient for importance attached to weather may be tested by the following equation:

$$t = \frac{b}{SE_b}$$

$$= \frac{0.2887}{0.08608} = 3.353$$

which has a t distribution with $n - k - 1$ degrees of freedom. This coefficient is significant at $\alpha = 0.05$. The significance of the coefficient for duration of residence is tested in a similar way and found to be significant. Therefore, both the duration of residence and importance attached to weather are important in explaining attitude toward the city.

Some computer programs provide an equivalent F test, often called the partial F test, which involves a decomposition of the total regression sum of squares, SS_{reg}, into components related to each independent variable. In the standard approach, this is done by assuming that each independent variable has been added to the regression equation after all the other independent variables have been included. The increment in the explained sum of squares, resulting from the addition of an independent variable, X_i, is the component of the variation attributed to that variable and is denoted SS_{xi}.[17] The significance of the partial regression coefficient for this variable, β_i, is tested using an incremental F statistic

$$F = \frac{SS_{xi}/1}{SS_{res}/(n - k - 1)}$$

which has an F distribution with 1 and $(n - k - 1)$ degrees of freedom.

While high R^2 and significant partial regression coefficients are comforting, the efficacy of the regression model should be evaluated further by an examination of the residuals.

Examination of residuals

Residual
The difference between the observed value of Y_i and the value predicted by the regression equation $\hat{Y}_i$.

A **residual** is the difference between the observed value of Y_i and the value predicted by the regression equation $\hat{Y}_i$. Residuals are used in the calculation of several statistics associated with regression. In addition, scattergrams of the residuals – in which the residuals are plotted against the predicted values, $\hat{Y}_i$, time, or predictor variables – provide useful insights in examining the appropriateness of the underlying assumptions and regression model fitted.[18]

The assumption of a normally distributed error term can be examined by constructing a histogram of the residuals. A visual check reveals whether the distribution is normal. Additional evidence can be obtained by determining the percentages of residuals falling within ±1 SE or ±2 SE. These percentages can be compared with what would be expected under the normal distribution (68 per cent and 95 per cent, respectively). More formal assessment can be made by running the *K-S* one-sample test.

The assumption of constant variance of the error term can be examined by plotting the residuals against the predicted values of the dependent variable, $\hat{Y}_i$. If the pattern is not random, the variance of the error term is not constant. Figure 19.6 shows a pattern whose variance is dependent on the i values.

A plot of residuals against time, or the sequence of observations, will throw some light on the assumption that the error terms are uncorrelated. A random pattern should be seen if this assumption is true. A plot like the one in Figure 19.7

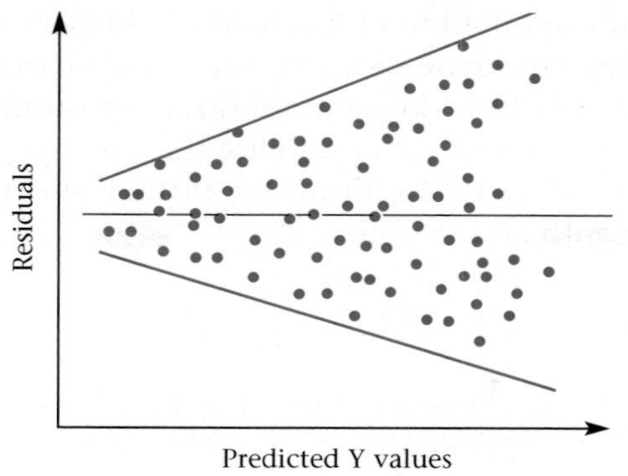

Figure 19.6
Residual plot indicating that variance is not constant

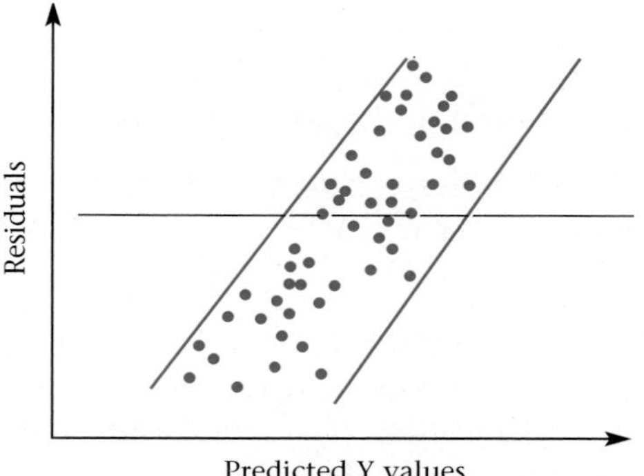

Figure 19.7
Plot indicating a linear relationship between residuals and time

indicates a linear relationship between residuals and time. A more formal procedure for examining the correlations between the error terms is the Durbin-Watson test.[19]

Plotting the residuals against the independent variables provides evidence of the appropriateness or inappropriateness of using a linear model. Again, the plot should result in a random pattern. The residuals should fall randomly, with relatively equal distribution dispersion about 0. They should not display any tendency to be either positive or negative.

To examine whether any additional variables should be included in the regression equation, one could run a regression of the residuals on the proposed variables. If any variable explains a significant proportion of the residual variation, it should be considered for inclusion. Inclusion of variables in the regression equation should be strongly guided by the researcher's theory. Thus, an examination of the residuals provides valuable insights into the appropriateness of the underlying assumptions and the model that is fitted. Figure 19.8 shows a plot that indicates that the underlying assumptions are met and that the linear model

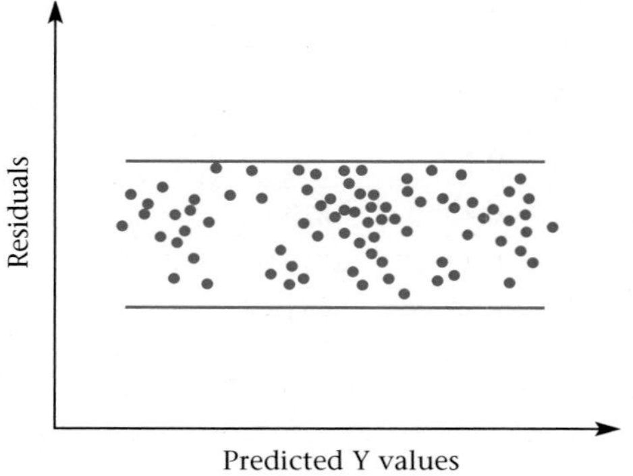

Figure 19.8
Plot of residuals indicating that a fitted model is appropriate

is appropriate. If an examination of the residuals indicates that the assumptions underlying linear regression are not met, the researcher can transform the variables in an attempt to satisfy the assumptions. Transformations, such as taking logs, square roots or reciprocals, can stabilise the variance, make the distribution normal or make the relationship linear. We further illustrate the application of multiple regression with an example.

EXAMPLE

At no 'Ad' ditional cost[20]

It is widely believed that consumer magazines' prices are subsidised by the advertising carried within the magazines. A study examined the contribution of advertising to the price per copy of magazines.

Multiple regression analysis was used to examine the relationships among price per copy and editorial pages, circulation, percentage of news-stand circulation, promotional expenditures, percentage of colour pages, and per copy advertising revenues. The form of the analysis was

$$\text{PPC} = b_0 + b_1(\text{ed. pages}) + b_2(\text{circ.}) + b_3(\text{\% news circ.}) + b_4(\text{PE}) + b_5(\text{\% colour}) + b_6(\text{ad revs.})$$

where

PPC = price per copy (in Euros)
ed. pages = editorial pages per average issue
circ. = the log of average paid circulation (in thousands)
% news circ. = percentage news-stand circulation
PE = promotional expenditures (in Euros)
% colour = percentage of pages printed in colour
ad revs. = per copy advertising revenues (in Euros)

Table 1 shows the zero-order Pearson product moment correlations among the variables. The correlations provide directional support for the predicted relationships and show that collinearity among the independent variables is sufficiently low so as not to affect the stability of the regression analysis. The highest correlation among the independent variables was between promotional expenditures and circulation ($r = 0.42$).

The results of the regression analysis using price per copy as the dependent variable are given in Table 2. Of the six independent variables, three were significant ($p < 0.05$): the number of editorial pages, average circulation, and percentage news-stand circulation. The three variables accounted for virtually all of the

Table 1 Zero order correlation matrix of variables in analyses

	Price per copy	*Price per edit. page*	*Circulation*	*Editorial pages*	*Promotion Expenditures*	*% colour pages*	*% news-stand circ.*
Price per edit. page	0.60[a]						
Circulation	–0.21[a]	–0.42[a]					
Editorial pages	0.52[a]	–0.30[a]	0.29[a]				
Promotion expenditures	–0.22[a]	–0.06	0.42[a]	–0.19			
% colour pages	0.01	–0.15	0.33[a]	0.19	–0.15		
% newstand circ.	0.46[a]	0.17	0.09	0.31[a]	0.26[a]	0.02	
Ad revenues per copy	0.29[a]	–0.04	–0.25[a]	0.30[a]	–0.14	0.15	0.08

[a] $p < 0.05$

explained variance ($R^2 = 0.51$; adjusted $R^2 = 0.48$). The direction of the coefficients was consistent with prior expectations: the number of editorial pages was positive, circulation was negative, and percentage news-stand circulation was positive. This was expected, given the structure of the magazine publishing industry, and confirmed the hypothesised relationship.

Promotional expenditures, use of colour, and per copy advertising revenues were found to have no relationship with price per copy, after the effects of circulation, percentage news-stand circulation and editorial pages were controlled in the regression analysis.

Because the effect of per copy advertising revenue was not significant, no support was found for the contention that advertising decreases the price per editorial page or the price per copy of consumer magazines. It was concluded that advertising in magazines is provided free to consumers but does not subsidise prices.■

Table 2 Regression analysis using price per copy as dependent variable

	b	SE	*F*
Dependent variable: Price per copy			
Independent variables:			
Editorial pages	0.0084	0.0017	23.04[a]
Circulation	–0.4180	0.1372	9.29[a]
Percentage news-stand circulation	0.0067	0.0016	18.46[a]
Promotional expenditures	0.13–04[b]	0.0000	0.59
Percentage colour pages	0.0227	0.0092	0.01
Per copy ad revenues	0.1070	0.0412	0.07
Overall $R^2 = 0.51$	df = 6,93	Overall F = 16.19[a]	

[a] $p < 0.05$
[b] Decimal moved in by four zeros

Multiple regression analysis shows that advertising in magazines is provided free to consumers but does not subsidise prices

3 It becomes difficult to assess the relative importance of the independent variables in explaining the variation in the dependent variable.
4 Predictor variables may be incorrectly included or removed in stepwise regression.

What constitutes serious multicollinearity is not always clear, although several rules of thumb and procedures have been suggested in the literature. Procedures of varying complexity have also been suggested to cope with multicollinearity.[25] A simple procedure consists of using only one of the variables in a highly correlated set of variables.

Alternatively, the set of independent variables can be transformed into a new set of predictors that are mutually independent by using techniques such as principal components analysis (see Chapter 21). More specialised techniques, such as ridge regression and latent root regression, can also be used.[26]

RELATIVE IMPORTANCE OF PREDICTORS

When multicollinearity is present, special care is required in assessing the relative importance of independent variables. In applied marketing research, it is valuable to determine the relative importance of the predictors. In other words, how important are the independent variables in accounting for the variation in the criterion or dependent variable?[27] Unfortunately, because the predictors are correlated, there is no unambiguous measure of relative importance of the predictors in regression analysis.[28] Several approaches, however, are commonly used to assess the relative importance of predictor variables.

1 *Statistical significance*. If the partial regression coefficient of a variable is not significant, as determined by an incremental F test, that variable is judged to be unimportant. An exception to this rule is made if there are strong theoretical reasons for believing that the variable is important.
2 *Square of the simple correlation coefficient*. This measure, R^2, represents the proportion of the variation in the dependent variable explained by the independent variable in a bivariate relationship.
3 *Square of the partial correlation coefficient*. This measure, $R^2yx_i.x_j.x_k$, is the coefficient of determination between the dependent variable and the independent variable, controlling for the effects of the other independent variables.
4 *Square of the part correlation coefficient*. This coefficient represents an increase in R^2 when a variable is entered into a regression equation that already contains the other independent variables.
5 *Measures based on standardised coefficients or beta weights*. The most commonly used measures are the absolute values of the beta weights, $|\beta_i|$, or the squared values, β_i^2. Because they are partial coefficients, beta weights take into account the effect of the other independent variables. These measures become increasingly unreliable as the correlations among the predictor variables increase (multicollinearity increases).
6 *Stepwise regression*. The order in which the predictors enter or are removed from the regression equation is used to infer their relative importance.

Given that the predictors are correlated, at least to some extent, in virtually all regression situations, none of these measures is satisfactory. It is also possible that the different measures may indicate a different order of importance of the predictors.[29] Yet if all the measures are examined collectively, useful insights may be obtained into the relative importance of the predictors.

CROSS-VALIDATION

Cross-validation
A test of validity that examines whether a model holds on comparable data not used in the original estimation.

Before assessing the relative importance of the predictors or drawing any other inferences, it is necessary to cross-validate the regression model. Regression and other multivariate procedures tend to capitalise on chance variations in the data. This could result in a regression model or equation that is unduly sensitive to the specific data used to estimate the model. One approach for evaluating the model for this and other problems associated with regression is cross-validation. **Cross-validation** examines whether the regression model continues to hold on comparable data not used in the estimation. The typical cross-validation procedure used in marketing research is

1 The regression model is estimated using the entire data set.
2 The available data are split into two parts, the *estimation sample* and the *validation sample*. The estimation sample generally contains 50 to 90 per cent of the total sample.
3 The regression model is estimated using the data from the estimation sample only. This model is compared with the model estimated on the entire sample to determine the agreement in terms of the signs and magnitudes of the partial regression coefficients.
4 The estimated model is applied to the data in the validation sample to predict the values of the dependent variable, $\hat{Y}_i$, for the observations in the validation sample.
5 The observed values, Y_i, and the predicted values, $\hat{Y}_i$, in the validation sample are correlated to determine the simple r^2. This measure, r^2, is compared with R^2 for the total sample and with R^2 for the estimation sample to assess the degree of shrinkage.

Double cross-validation
A special form of validation in which the sample is split into halves. One half serves as the estimation sample and the other as a validation sample. The roles of the estimation and validation halves are then reversed and the cross-validation process repeated.

A special form of validation is called double cross-validation. In **double cross-validation** the sample is split into halves. One half serves as the estimation sample, and the other is used as a validation sample in conducting cross-validation. The roles of the estimation and validation halves are then reversed, and the cross-validation is repeated.[30]

REGRESSION WITH DUMMY VARIABLES

Cross-validation is a general procedure that can be applied even in some special applications of regression, such as regression with dummy variables. Nominal or categorical variables may be used as predictors or independent variables by coding them as dummy variables. The concept of dummy variables was introduced in Chapter 16. In that chapter, we explained how a categorical variable with four categories (heavy users, medium users, light users, and non-users) can be coded in terms of three dummy variables, D_1, D_2 and D_3, as shown.

Product usage	*Original*	*Dummy variable code*		
category	*variable code*	D_1	D_2	D_3
Non-users	1	1	0	0
Light users	2	0	1	0
Medium users	3	0	0	1
Heavy users	4	0	0	0

Suppose that the researcher was interested in running a regression analysis of the effect of attitude toward the brand on product use. The dummy variables D_1, D_2, and D_3 would be used as predictors. Regression with dummy variables would be modelled as

$$\hat{Y}_i = a + b_1D_1 + b_2D_2 + b_3D_3$$

In this case, heavy users has been selected as a reference category and has not been directly included in the regression equation. Note that for heavy users, D_1, D_2 and D_3 assume a value of 0, and the regression equation becomes

$$\hat{Y}_i = a$$

For non-users, $D_1 = 1$, and $D_2 = D_3 = 0$, and the regression equation becomes

$$\hat{Y}_i = a+b_1$$

Thus, the coefficient b_1 is the difference in predicted Y_i for non-users, as compared with heavy users. The coefficients b_2 and b_3 have similar interpretations. Although heavy users was selected as a reference category, any of the other three categories could have been selected for this purpose.[31]

ANALYSIS OF VARIANCE AND COVARIANCE WITH REGRESSION

Regression with dummy variables provides a framework for understanding the analysis of variance and covariance. Although multiple regression with dummy variables provides a general procedure for the analysis of variance and covariance, we show only the equivalence of regression with dummy variables to one-way analysis of variance. In regression with dummy variables, the predicted $\hat{Y}$ for each category is the mean of Y for each category. To illustrate using the dummy variable coding of product use we just considered, the predicted $\hat{Y}$ and mean values for each category are as follows:

Product usage category	*Predicted value*	*Mean value*
	$\hat{Y}$	$\hat{Y}$
Non-users	$a + b_1$	$a + b_1$
Light users	$a + b_2$	$a + b_2$
Medium users	$a + b_3$	$a + b_3$
Heavy users	a	a

Given this equivalence, it is easy to see further relationships between dummy variable regression and one-way ANOVA.[32]

Thus, we see that regression in which the single independent variable with c categories has been recoded into $c - 1$ dummy variables is equivalent to one-way analysis of variance. Using similar correspondences, one can also illustrate how n-way analysis of variance and analysis of covariance can be performed using regression with dummy variables.

Dummy variable regression	**One-way ANOVA**
$SS_{res} = \sum_{i=1}^{n} (Y_i - \hat{Y}_i)^2$	$= SS_{within}$
$SS_{reg} = \sum_{i=1}^{n} (\hat{Y}_i - \bar{Y})^2$	$= SS_{between}$
R^2	$= \eta^2$
Overall F test	$= F$ test

INTERNET AND COMPUTER APPLICATIONS

The computer packages contain several programs to perform correlation analysis and regression analysis, calculating the associated statistics, performing tests for significance, and plotting the residuals.

SPSS

CORRELATIONS can be used for computing Pearson product moment correlations, PARTIAL CORR for partial correlations, and NONPAR CORR for Spearman's ρ_s and Kendall's τ. The main program is REGRESSION which calculates bivariate and multiple regression equations, associated statistics, and plots. It allows for easy examination of residuals. Stepwise regression can also be conducted. Regression statistics can be requested with PLOT, which produces simple scattergrams and some other types of plots.

SAS

The program CORR can be used for calculating Pearson, Spearman's, Kendall's and partial correlations. REG is a general purpose regression procedure that fits bivariate and multiple regression models using the least-squares procedure. All the associated statistics are computed, and residuals can be plotted. Stepwise methods can be implemented. RSREG is a more specialised procedure that fits a quadratic response surface model using least squares regression. It is useful for determining factor levels that optimise a response. The ORTHOREG procedure is recommended for regression when the data are ill conditioned. GLM uses the method of least squares to fit general linear models and can also be used for regression analysis. NLIN computes the parameters of a nonlinear model using least squares or weighted least-squares procedures.

BMDP

P8D computes Pearson product moment correlations. P1R estimates bivariate and multiple linear regressions. The associated statistics and plots of residuals can be obtained. P2R is a stepwise regression program providing various approaches. The order of entry or removal of variables can be pre-determined, partially specified, or determined only by the criteria for entry and removal of variables. P9R performs all possible subsets regression. It identifies 'best' subsets or predictors or can be used for multiple regression without selecting subsets. P4R computes regression analysis on a set of principal components obtained from the independent variables.

Minitab

Correlation can be computed using Stat>Basic statistics>Correlation function. It calculates Peason's product moment. The Spearman's procedure ranks the columns first and then performs the correlation on the ranked columns. To compute partial correlation use the menu commands Stat>Basic Statistics>Correlation and Stat>Regression>Regression. Regression analysis, under the Stats>Regression function, can perform simple, polynomial and multiple analysis. The output includes a linear regression equation, table of coefficients, R^2, R^2 adjusted, analysis of variance table, a table of fits and residuals that provide unusual observations. Other available features include stepwise, best subsets, fitted line plot and residual plots.

Excel

Correlations can be determined in Excel by using the Tools>Data analysis>Correlation function. Utilise the Correlation Worksheet function, when a correlation coefficient for two cell ranges is needed. There is no separate function for partial correlations. Regression can be accessed from the Tools>Data analysis menu. Depending on the features selected, the output can consist of a summary output table, including an ANOVA table, a standard error of Y estimate, coefficients, standard error of coefficients, R^2 values, and the number of observations. In addition, the function computes a residual output table, a residual plot, a line fit plot, normal probability plot, and a two-column probability data output table.

SUMMARY

The product moment correlation coefficient, r, measures the linear association between two metric (interval or ratio scaled) variables. Its square, r^2, measures the proportion of variation in one variable explained by the other. The partial correlation coefficient measures the association between two variables after controlling, or adjusting for, the effects of one or more additional variables. The order of a partial correlation indicates how many variables are being adjusted or controlled. Partial correlations can be very helpful for detecting spurious relationships.

Bivariate regression derives a mathematical equation between a single metric criterion variable and a single metric predictor variable. The equation is derived in the form of a straight line by using the least squares procedure. When the regression is run on standardised data, the intercept assumes a value of 0, and the regression coefficients are called beta weights. The strength of association is measured by the coefficient of determination, r^2, which is obtained by computing a ratio of SS_{reg} to SS_y. The standard error of estimate is used to assess the accuracy of prediction and may be interpreted as a kind of average error made in predicting Y from the regression equation.

Multiple regression involves a single dependent variable and two or more independent variables. The partial regression coefficient, b_1, represents the expected change in Y when X_1 is changed by one unit and X_2 to X_k are held constant. The strength of association is measured by the coefficient of multiple determination, R^2. The significance of the overall regression equation may be tested by the overall F test. Individual partial regression coefficients may be tested for significance using the incremental F test. Scattergrams of the residuals, in which the residuals are plotted against the predicted values, $\hat{Y}_i$, time, or predictor variables, are useful for examining the appropriateness of the underlying assumptions and the regression model fitted.

In stepwise regression, the predictor variables are entered or removed from the regression equation one at a time for the purpose of selecting a smaller subset of predictors that account for most of the variation in the criterion variable. Multicollinearity, or very high intercorrelations among the predictor variables, can result in several problems. Because the predictors are correlated, regression analysis provides no unambiguous measure of relative importance of the predictors. Cross-validation examines whether the regression model continues to hold true for comparable data not used in estimation. It is a useful procedure for evaluating the regression model.

Nominal or categorical variables may be used as predictors by coding them as dummy variables. Multiple regression with dummy variables provides a general procedure for the analysis of variance and covariance.

QUESTIONS AND PROBLEMS

1 What is the product moment correlation coefficient? Does a product moment correlation of 0 between two variables imply that the variables are not related to each other?

2 What are the main uses of regression analysis?

3 What is the least squares procedure?

4 Explain the meaning of standardised regression coefficients.

5 How is the strength of association measured in bivariate regression? In multiple regression?

6 What is meant by prediction accuracy?

7 What is the standard error of estimate?

8 What is multiple regression? How is it different from bivariate regression?

9 Explain the meaning of a partial regression coefficient. Why is it called that?

10 State the null hypothesis in testing the significance of the overall multiple regression equation. How is this null hypothesis tested?

11 What is gained by an examination of residuals?

12 Explain the stepwise regression approach. What is its purpose?

13 What is multicollinearity? What problems can arise because of multicollinearity?

14 Describe the cross-validation procedure.

15 Demonstrate the equivalence of regression with dummy variables to one-way ANOVA.

Chapter 20

Discriminant analysis

Discriminant analysis is used for discriminating among groups by analysing data with a categorical dependent variable and interval scaled independent variables

OBJECTIVES

After reading this chapter, the student should be able to:

1 describe the concept of discriminant analysis, its objectives and its applications in marketing research;
2 outline the procedures for conducting discriminant analysis including the formulation of the problem, estimation of the discriminant function coefficients, determination of significance, interpretation and validation;
3 discuss multiple discriminant analysis and the distinction between two-group and multiple discriminant analysis;
4 Explain stepwise discriminant analysis and describe the Mahalanobis procedure.

OVERVIEW

This chapter discusses the technique of discriminant analysis. We begin by examining the relationship of this procedure to regression analysis (Chapter 19) and analysis of variance (Chapter 18). We present a model and describe the general procedure for conducting discriminant analysis, with an emphasis on formulation, estimation, determination of significance, interpretation, and validation of the results. The procedure is illustrated with an example of two-group discriminant analysis, followed by an example of multiple (three-group) discriminant analysis. The stepwise discriminant analysis procedure is also covered.

We begin with examples illustrating the applications of two-group and multiple discriminant analysis.

GLOBALCASH PROJECT

Two-group discriminant analysis

In the GlobalCash project, two-group discriminant analysis was used. It helped to examine whether respondents who held accounts outside their home country, versus those who do not have accounts, attached different relative importance to nine factors of allocating business between banks. The dependent variable was whether the respondent's company held accounts outside their home country, and the independent variables were the importance attached to the nine factors of the choice criteria. The overall discriminant function was significant, indicating significant differences between the two groups. The results indicated that compared with respondents who do not have accounts, those companies holding accounts outside their home country attached a greater relative importance to a good relationship with a bank, electronic banking systems, service quality and level of commitment to their business. ■

EXAMPLE

Rebate redeemers[1]

A study of 294 consumers was undertaken to determine the correlates of 'rebate proneness', in other words, the characteristics of consumers who respond favourably to direct mail promotions that offer a rebate or discount. The predictor variables were four factors related to household shopping attitudes and behaviour and selected demographic characteristics (sex, age and income). The dependent variable was the extent to which respondents were predisposed to take up the offer of a rebate or discount, of which three levels were identified. Respondents who reported no purchases triggered by a rebate during the past 12 months were classified as *non-users*. Those who reported one or two such purchases as *light users*, and those with more than two purchases as *frequent users* of rebates. Multiple discriminant analysis was used to analyse the data.

Two primary findings emerged. First, consumers' perception of the effort/value relationship was the most effective variable in discriminating among frequent users, light users, and non-users of rebate offers. Clearly, rebate-sensitive consumers associate less effort with fulfiling the requirements of the rebate purchase, and are willing to accept a relatively smaller refund, than other customers. Second, consumers who were aware of the regular prices of products, so that they recognise bargains, are more likely than others to respond to rebate offers. ■

In the GlobalCash example, there were two groups of respondents (accounts outside home country and no accounts), whereas the rebate predisposition example examined three groups (non-users, light users, and frequent users of rebates). In both studies, significant inter-group differences were found using multiple predictor variables. An examination of differences across groups lies at the heart of the basic concept of discriminant analysis.

BASIC CONCEPT

Discriminant analysis
A technique for analysing marketing research data when the criterion or dependent variable is categorical and the predictor or independent variables are interval in nature.

Discriminant analysis is a technique for analysing data when the criterion or dependent variable is categorical and the predictor or independent variables are interval in nature.[2] For example, the dependent variable may be the choice of a brand of personal computer (A, B or C) and the independent variables may be ratings of attributes of PCs on a seven-point Likert scale. The objectives of discriminant analysis are as follows:

1 Development of discriminant functions, or linear combinations of the predictor or independent variables, that best discriminate between the categories of the criterion or dependent variable (groups).
2 Examination of whether significant differences exist among the groups, in terms of the predictor variables.
3 Determination of which predictor variables contribute to most of the intergroup differences.
4 Classification of cases to one of the groups based on the values of the predictor variables.
5 Evaluation of the accuracy of classification.

Two-group discriminant analysis
Discriminant analysis technique where the criterion variable has two categories.

Multiple discriminant analysis
Discriminant analysis technique where the criterion variable involves three or more categories.

Discriminant function
The linear combination of independent variables developed by discriminant analysis that will best discriminate between the categories of the dependent variable.

Discriminant analysis techniques are described by the number of categories possessed by the criterion variable. When the criterion variable has two categories, the technique is known as **two-group discriminant analysis**. When three or more categories are involved, the technique is referred to as **multiple discriminant analysis**. The main distinction is that in the two-group case, it is possible to derive only one **discriminant function**, but in multiple discriminant analysis, more than one function may be computed.[3]

Examples of discriminant analysis abound in marketing research. This technique can be used to answer questions such as the following:[4]

- In terms of demographic characteristics, how do customers who exhibit store loyalty differ from those who do not?
- Do heavy users, medium users and light users of soft drinks differ in terms of their consumption of frozen foods?
- What psychographic characteristics help differentiate between price-sensitive and non-price-sensitive buyers of groceries?
- Do market segments differ in their media consumption habits?
- What are the distinguishing characteristics of consumers who respond to direct mail solicitations?

RELATIONSHIP TO REGRESSION AND ANOVA

The relationships between discriminant analysis, analysis of variance (ANOVA), and regression analysis are shown in Table 20.1. We explain these relationships with an example in which the researcher is attempting to explain the amount of life insurance purchased in terms of age and income. All three procedures involve a single criterion or dependent variable and multiple predictor or independent variables. The nature of these variables differs, however. In analysis of variance and regression analysis, the dependent variable is metric or interval

Table 20.1 Similarities and differences among ANOVA, regression and discriminant analysis

	ANOVA	Regression	Discriminant analysis
Similarities			
Number of dependent variables	One	One	One
Number of independent variables	Multiple	Multiple	Multiple
Differences			
Nature of the dependent variable	Metric	Metric	Categorical
Nature of the independent variable	Categorical	Metric	Metric

scaled (amount of life insurance purchased in Euros), whereas in discriminant analysis, it is categorical (amount of life insurance purchased classified as high, medium, or low). The independent variables are categorical in the case of analysis of variance (age and income are each classified as high, medium or low) but metric in the case of regression and discriminant analysis (age in years and income in Euros, i.e. both measured on a ratio scale).

Two-group discriminant analysis, in which the dependent variable has only two categories, is closely related to multiple regression analysis. In this case, multiple regression, in which the dependent variable is coded as a 0 or 1 dummy variable, results in partial regression coefficients that are proportional to discriminant function coefficients (see the following section on the discriminant analysis model).

DISCRIMINANT ANALYSIS MODEL

Discriminant analysis model
The statistical model on which discriminant analysis is based.

The **discriminant analysis model** involves linear combinations of the following form:

$$D = b_0 + b_1X_1 + b_2X_2 + b_3X_3 + \ldots + b_kX_k$$

where

D = discriminant score
b = discriminant coefficients or weights
X = predictor or independent variable

The coefficients or weights (b) are estimated so that the groups differ as much as possible on the values of the discriminant function. This occurs when the ratio of between-group sum of squares to within-group sum of squares for the discriminant scores is at a maximum. Any other linear combination of the predictors will result in a smaller ratio. The technical details of estimation are described in Appendix 20A. Several statistics are associated with discriminant analysis.

STATISTICS ASSOCIATED WITH DISCRIMINANT ANALYSIS

The following are important statistics associated with discriminant analysis.

Canonical correlation. Canonical correlation measures the extent of association between the discriminant scores and the groups. It is a measure of association between the single discriminant function and the set of dummy variables that define the group membership.

Centroid. The centroid is the mean values for the discriminant scores for a particular group. There are as many centroids as there are groups, as there is one for each group. The means for a group on all the functions are the group centroids.

Classification matrix. Sometimes also called confusion or prediction matrix, the classification matrix contains the number of correctly classified and misclassified cases. The correctly classified cases appear on the diagonal, because the predicted and actual groups are the same. The off-diagonal elements represent cases that have been incorrectly classified. The sum of the diagonal elements divided by the total number of cases represents the hit ratio.

Discriminant function coefficients. The discriminant function coefficients (unstandardised) are the multipliers of variables, when the variables are in the original units of measurement.

Discriminant scores. The unstandardised coefficients are multiplied by the values of the variables. These products are summed and added to the constant term to obtain the discriminant scores.

Eigenvalue. For each discriminant function, the eigenvalue is the ratio of between-group to within-group sums of squares. Large eigenvalues imply superior functions.
F values and their significance. *F* values are calculated from a one-way ANOVA, with the grouping variable serving as the categorical independent variable. Each predictor, in turn, serves as the metric-dependent variable in the ANOVA.
Group means and group standard deviations. Group means and group standard deviations are computed for each predictor for each group.
Pooled within-group correlation matrix. The pooled within-group correlation matrix is computed by averaging the separate covariance matrices for all the groups.
Standardised discriminant function coefficients. The standardised discriminant function coefficients are the discriminant function coefficients and are used as the multipliers when the variables have been standardised to a mean of 0 and a variance of 1.
Structure correlations. Also referred to as discriminant loadings, the structure correlations represent the simple correlations between the predictors and the discriminant function.
Total correlation matrix. If the cases are treated as if they were from a single sample and the correlations are computed, a total correlation matrix is obtained.
Wilks' λ. Sometimes also called the *U* statistic, Wilks' λ for each predictor is the ratio of the within-group sum of squares to the total sum of squares. Its value varies between 0 and 1. Large values of λ (near 1) indicate that group means do not seem to be different. Small values of λ (near 0) indicate that the group means seem to be different.

The assumptions in discriminant analysis are that each of the groups is a sample from a multivariate normal population and that all the populations have the same covariance matrix. The role of these assumptions and the statistics just described can be better understood by examining the procedure for conducting discriminant analysis.

CONDUCTING DISCRIMINANT ANALYSIS

The steps involved in conducting discriminant analysis consist of formulation, estimation, determination of significance, interpretation and validation (see Figure 20.1). These steps are discussed and illustrated within the context of two-group discriminant analysis. Discriminant analysis with more than two groups is discussed later in this chapter.

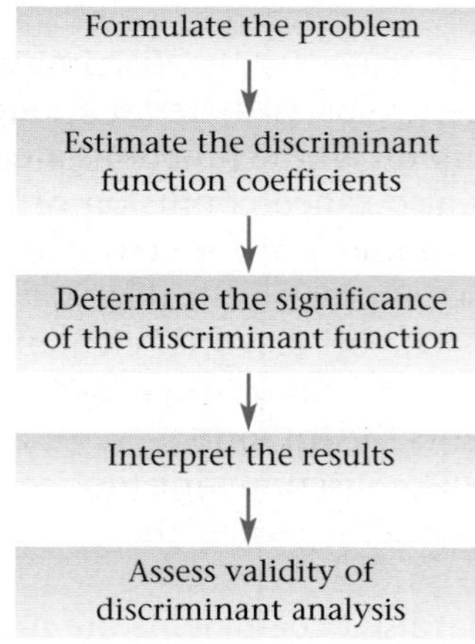

Figure 20.1 Conducting discriminant analysis

Formulation

The first step in discriminant analysis is to formulate the problem by identifying the objectives, the criterion variable, and the independent variables. The criterion variable must consist of two or more mutually exclusive and collectively exhaustive categories. When the dependent variable is interval or ratio scaled, it must first be converted into categories. For example, attitude toward the brand, measured on a six-point scale, could be categorised as unfavourable (1, 2, 3), or favourable (4, 5, 6). Alternatively, one could plot the distribution of the dependent variable and form groups of equal size by determining the appropriate cut-off points for each category. The predictor variables should be selected based on a theoretical model or previous research, or in the case of exploratory research, the experience of the researcher should guide their selection.

Analysis sample
Part of the total sample used to check the results of the estimation sample.

The next step is to divide the sample into two parts. One part of the sample, called the estimation or **analysis sample**, is used for estimation of the discriminant function. The other part, called the *holdout* or validation sample, is reserved for validating the discriminant function. When the sample is large enough, it can be split in half. One half serves as the analysis sample, and the other is used for validation. The role of the halves are then interchanged and the analysis is repeated. This is called double cross-validation and is similar to the procedure discussed in regression analysis (Chapter 19).

Validation sample
That part of the total sample used to check the results of the estimation sample.

Often, the distribution of the number of cases in the analysis and **validation samples** follows the distribution in the total sample. For instance, if the total sample contained 50 per cent loyal and 50 per cent non-loyal consumers, then the analysis and validation samples would each contain 50 per cent loyal and 50 per cent non-loyal consumers. On the other hand, if the sample contained 25 per cent loyal and 75 per cent non-loyal consumers, the analysis and validation samples would be selected to reflect the same distribution (25 per cent v. 75 per cent).

Finally, it has been suggested that the validation of the discriminant function should be conducted repeatedly. Each time, the sample should be split into different analysis and validation parts. The discriminant function should be estimated and the validation analysis carried out. Thus, the validation assessment is based on a number of trials. More rigorous methods have also been suggested.[5]

To illustrate two-group discriminant analysis better, let us look at an example. Suppose that we want to determine the salient characteristics of families that have visited a holiday resort during the last two years. Data were obtained from a

Two-group discriminant analysis can be used to determine the salient characteristics of families that have visited a holiday resort

pre-test sample of 42 households. Of these, 30 households, shown in Table 20.2, were included in the analysis sample and the remaining 12, shown in Table 20.3, were part of the validation sample. The households that visited a resort during the last two years were coded as 1; those that did not, as 2 (visit). Both the analysis and validation samples were balanced in terms of visit. As can be seen, the analysis sample contains 15 households in each category whereas the validation sample had six in each category. Data were also obtained on annual family income (income), attitude toward travel (travel, measured on a nine-point scale), importance attached to family holiday (holiday, measured on a nine-point scale), household size (hsize), and age of the head of the household (age).

Table 20.2 Information on resort visits: analysis sample

Number	*Resort visit*	*Annual family income (in 000s of Euros)*	*Attitude toward travel*	*Importance attached to family holiday*	*Household size*	*Age of head of household*	*Amount spent on family holiday*
1	1	50.2	5	8	3	43	M (2)
2	1	70.3	6	7	4	61	H (3)
3	1	62.9	7	5	6	52	H (3)
4	1	48.5	7	5	5	36	L (1)
5	1	52.7	6	6	4	55	H (3)
6	1	75.0	8	7	5	68	H (3)
7	1	46.2	5	3	3	62	M (2)
8	1	57.0	2	4	6	51	M (2)
9	1	64.1	7	5	4	57	H (3)
10	1	68.1	7	6	5	45	H(3)
11	1	73.4	6	7	5	44	H (3)
12	1	71.9	5	8	4	64	H (3)
13	1	56.2	1	8	6	54	M (2)
14	1	49.3	4	2	3	56	H (3)
15	1	62.0	5	6	2	58	H (3)
16	2	32.1	5	4	3	58	L (1)
17	2	36.2	4	3	2	55	L (1)
18	2	43.2	2	5	2	57	M(2)
19	2	50.4	5	2	4	37	M (2)
20	2	44.1	6	6	3	42	M (2)
21	2	38.3	6	6	2	45	L (1)
22	2	55.0	1	2	2	57	M (2)
23	2	46.1	3	5	3	51	L (1)
24	2	35.0	6	4	5	64	L (1)
25	2	37.3	2	7	4	54	L (1)
26	2	41.8	5	1	3	56	M (2)
27	2	57.0	8	3	2	36	M (2)
28	2	33.4	6	8	2	50	L (1)
29	2	37.5	3	2	3	48	L (1)
30	2	41.3	3	3	2	42	L (1)

Table 20.3 Information on resort visits: holdout sample

Number	*Resort visit*	*Annual family income (in 000s of Euros)*	*Attitude toward travel*	*Importance attached to family holiday*	*Household size*	*Age of head of household*	*Amount spent on family holiday*
1	1	50.8	4	7	3	45	M (2)
2	1	63.6	7	4	7	55	H (3)
3	1	54.0	6	7	4	58	M (2)
4	1	45.0	5	4	3	60	M (2)
5	1	68.0	6	6	6	46	H (3)
6	1	62.1	5	6	3	56	H (3)
7	2	35.0	4	3	4	54	L (1)
8	2	49.6	5	3	5	39	L (1)
9	2	39.4	6	5	3	44	H (3)
10	2	37.0	2	6	5	51	L (1)
11	2	54.5	7	3	3	37	M (2)
12	2	38.2	2	2	3	49	L (1)

Estimation

Once the analysis sample has been identified, as in Table 20.2, we can estimate the discriminant function coefficients. Two broad approaches are available. The **direct method** involves estimating the discriminant function so that all the predictors are included simultaneously. In this case, each independent variable is included, regardless of its discriminating power. This method is appropriate when, based on previous research or a theoretical model, the researcher wants the discrimination to be based on all the predictors. An alternative approach is the stepwise method. In **stepwise discriminant analysis**, the predictor variables are entered sequentially, based on their ability to discriminate among groups. This method, described in more detail later, is appropriate when the researcher wants to select a subset of the predictors for inclusion in the discriminant function.

Direct method
An approach to discriminant analysis that involves estimating the discriminant function so that all the predictors are included simultaneously.

Stepwise discriminant analysis
Discriminant analysis in which the predictors are entered sequentially based on their ability to discriminate between the groups.

The results of running two-group discriminant analysis on the data of Table 20.2 using a popular statistical analysis package are presented in Table 20.4. Some intuitive feel for the results may be obtained by examining the group means and standard deviations. It appears that the two groups are more widely separated in terms of income than other variables, and there appears to be more of a separation on the importance attached to the family holiday than on attitude toward travel. The difference between the two groups on age of the head of the household is small, and the standard deviation of this variable is large.

The pooled within-groups correlation matrix indicates low correlations between the predictors. Multicollinearity is unlikely to be a problem. The significance of the univariate F ratios indicates that when the predictors are considered individually, only income, importance of holiday and household size significantly differentiate between those who visited a resort and those who did not.

Because there are two groups, only one discriminant function is estimated. The eigenvalue associated with this function is 1.7862, and it accounts for 100 per cent of the explained variance. The canonical correlation associated with this function is 0.8007. The square of this correlation, $(0.8007)^2 = 0.64$, indicates that 64 per cent of the variance in the dependent variable (visit) is explained or accounted for by this model. The next step is determination of significance.

Table 20.4 Results of two-group discriminant analysis

Group means					
Visit	Income	Travel	Holiday	Hsize	Age
1	60.52000	5.40000	5.80000	4.33333	53.73333
2	41.91333	4.33333	4.06667	2.80000	50.13333
Total	51.21667	4.86667	4.93333	3.56667	51.93333
Group standard deviations					
1	9.83065	1.91982	1.82052	1.23443	8.77062
2	7.55115	1.95180	2.05171	0.94112	8.27101
Total	12.79523	1.97804	2.09981	1.33089	8.57395
Pooled within-groups correlation matrix					
Income	1.00000				
Travel	0.19745	1.00000			
Holiday	0.09148	0.08434	1.00000		
Hsize	0.08887	–0.01681	0.07046	1.00000	
Age	–0.01431	–0.19709	0.01742	–0.04301	1.00000

Wilks' λ (*U* statistic) and univariate *F* ratio with 1 and 28 degrees of freedom

Variable	Wilks' λ	*F*	Significance
Income	0.45310	33.80	0.0000
Travel	0.92479	2.277	0.1425
Holiday	0.82377	5.990	0.0209
Hsize	0.65672	14.64	0.0007
Age	0.95441	1.338	0.2572

Canonical discriminant functions

Function	Eigenvalue	Per cent of variance	Cumulative percentage	Canonical correlation	After function	Wilks' λ	Chi-square	df	Sig.
1*	1.7862	100.00	100.00	0.8007	0	0.3589	26.13	5	0.0001

* Marks the 1 canonical discriminant function remaining in the analysis

Standard canonical discriminant function coefficients

	Func 1
Income	0.74301
Travel	0.09611
Holiday	0.23329
Hsize	0.46911
Age	0.20922

Table 20.4 (continued)

Structure matrix: Pooled within-groups correlations between discriminating variables and canonical discriminant functions (variables ordered by size of correlation within function)

	Func 1
Income	0.82202
Hsize	0.54096
Holiday	0.34607
Travel	0.21337
Age	0.16354

Unstandardised canonical discriminant function coefficients

	Func 1
Income	0.8476710E-01
Travel	0.4964455E-01
Holiday	0.1202813
Hsize	0.4273893
Age	0.2454380E-01
(constant)	−7.975476

Canonical discriminant functions evaluated at group means (group centroids)

Group	**Func 1**
1	1.29118
2	−1.29118

Classification results for cases selected for use in analysis

			Predicted group membership	
	Actual group	**No. of cases**	**1**	**2**
Group	1	15	12	3
			80.0%	20.0%
Group	2	15	0	15
			0.0%	100%
Percentage of grouped cases correctly classified: 90%				

Classification results for cases not selected for use in analysis (holdout sample)

			Predicted group membership	
	Actual group	**No. of cases**	**1**	**2**
Group	1	6	4	2
			66.7%	33.3%
Group	2	6	0	6
			0.0%	100%
Percentage of grouped cases correctly classified: 83.33%				

Determination of significance

It would not be meaningful to interpret the analysis if the discriminant functions estimated were not statistically significant. The null hypothesis that, in the population, the means of all discriminant functions in all groups are equal can be statistically tested. In SPSS, this test is based on Wilks' λ. If several functions are tested simultaneously (as in the case of multiple discriminant analysis), the Wilks' λ statistic is the product of the univariate λ for each function. The significance level is estimated based on a chi-square transformation of the statistic. In testing for significance in the holiday resort example (see Table 20.4), it may be noted that the Wilks' λ associated with the function is 0.3589, which transforms to a chi-square of 26.13 with 5 degrees of freedom. This is significant beyond the 0.05 level.

Interpretation

The interpretation of the discriminant weights, or coefficients, is similar to that in multiple regression analysis. The value of the coefficient for a particular predictor depends on the other predictors included in the discriminant function. The signs of the coefficients are arbitrary, but they indicate which variable values result in large and small function values and associate them with particular groups.

Given the multicollinearity in the predictor variables, there is no unambiguous measure of the relative importance of the predictors in discriminating between the groups.[6] With this caveat in mind, we can obtain some idea of the relative importance of the variables by examining the absolute magnitude of the standardised discriminant function coefficients. Generally, predictors with relatively large standardised coefficients contribute more to the discriminating power of the function, as compared with predictors with smaller coefficients.

Some idea of the relative importance of the predictors can also be obtained by examining the structure correlations, also called canonical loadings or discriminant loadings. These simple correlations between each predictor and the discriminant function represent the variance that the predictor shares with the function. Like the standardised coefficients, these correlations must also be interpreted with caution.

An examination of the standardised discriminant function coefficients for the holiday resort example is instructive. Given the low inter-correlations between the predictors, one might cautiously use the magnitudes of the standardised coefficients to suggest that income is the most important predictor in discriminating between the groups, followed by household size and importance attached to the family holiday. The same observation is obtained from examination of the structure correlations. These simple correlations between the predictors and the discriminant function are listed in order of magnitude.

The unstandardised discriminant function coefficients are also given. These can be applied to the raw values of the variables in the holdout set for classification purposes. The group centroids, giving the value of the discriminant function evaluated at the group means, are also shown. Group 1, those who have visited a resort, has a positive value, whereas Group 2 has an equal negative value. The signs of the coefficients associated with all the predictors are positive, which suggests that higher family income, household size, importance attached to family holiday, attitude toward travel, and age are more likely to result in the family visiting the resort. It would be reasonable to develop a profile of the two groups in terms of the three predictors that seem to be the most important: income, household size, and importance of holiday. The values of these three variables for the two groups are given at the beginning of Table 20.4.

The determination of relative importance of the predictors is further illustrated by the following example.

EXAMPLE

Satisfied salespeople stay[7]

Discriminant analysis was used to determine what factors explained the differences between salespeople who left a large computer manufacturing company and those who stayed. The independent variables were company rating, job security, seven job satisfaction dimensions, four role-conflict dimensions, four role-ambiguity dimensions, and nine measures of sales performance. The dependent variable was the dichotomy between those who stayed and those who left. The canonical correlation, an index of discrimination ($R = 0.4572$), was significant (Wilks' $\lambda = 0.7909$, $F(26,113) = 1.7588$, $p = 0.0180$). This result indicated that the variables discriminated between those who left and those who stayed.

Discriminant analysis results

Variable	Coefficients	Standardised coefficients	Canonical loadings
1 Work[a]	0.0903	0.3910	0.5446
2 Promotion[a]	0.0288	0.1515	0.5044
3 Job security	0.1567	0.1384	0.4958
4 Customer relations[b]	0.0086	0.1751	0.4906
5 Company rating	0.4059	0.3240	0.4824
6 Working with others[b]	0.0018	0.0365	0.4651
7 Overall performance[b]	4.0148	–0.3252	0.4518
8 Time-territory management[b]	0.0126	0.2899	0.4496
9 Sales produced[b]	0.0059	0.1404	0.4484
10 Presentation skill[b]	0.0118	0.2526	0.4387
11 Technical information[b]	0.0003	0.0065	0.4173
12 Pay-benefits[a]	0.0600	0.1843	0.3788
13 Quota achieved[b]	0.0035	0.2915	0.3780
14 Management[a]	0.0014	0.0138	0.3571
15 Information collection[b]	–0.0146	4.3327	0.3326
16 Family[c]	–0.0684	–0.3408	–0.3221
17 Sales manager[a]	4.0121	–0.1102	0.2909
18 Coworker[a]	0.0225	0.0893	0.2671
19 Customer[c]	–0.0625	4.2797	–0.2602
20 Family[d]	0.0473	0.1970	0.2180
21 Job[d]	0.1378	0.5312	0.2119
22 Job[c]	0.0410	0.5475	–0.1029
23 Customer[d]	–0.0060	4.0255	0.1004
24 Sales manager[c]	–0.0365	–0.2406	–0.0499
25 Sales manager[d]	–0.0606	–0.3333	0.0467
26 Customer[a]	–0.0338	–0.1488	0.0192

Note: Rank order of importance is based on the magnitude of the canonical loadings:

[a] Satisfaction
[b] Performance
[c] Ambiguity
[d] Conflict

The results from simultaneously entering all variables in discriminant analysis are presented in the table. The rank order of importance, as determined by the relative magnitude of the canonical loadings, is presented in the first column. Satisfaction with the job and promotional opportunities were the two most important discriminators, followed by job security. Those who stayed in the company found the job to be more exciting, satisfying, challenging and interesting than those who left. ■

In this example, promotion was identified as the second most important variable based on the canonical loadings. However, it is not the second most important variable based on the absolute magnitude of the standardised discriminant function coefficients. This anomaly results from multicollinearity.

Characteristic profile
An aid to interpreting discriminant analysis results by describing each group in terms of the group means for the predictor variables.

Another aid to interpreting discriminant analysis results is to develop a **characteristic profile** for each group by describing each group in terms of the group means for the predictor variables. If the important predictors have been identified, then a comparison of the group means on these variables can assist in understanding the intergroup differences. Before any findings can be interpreted with confidence, however, it is necessary to validate the results.

Validation

Hit ratio
The percentage of cases correctly classified by the discriminant analysis.

As explained earlier, the data are randomly divided into two subsamples. One, the analysis sample, is used for estimating the discriminant function, and the validation sample is used for developing the classification matrix. The discriminant weights, estimated by using the analysis sample, are multiplied by the values of the predictor variables in the holdout sample to generate discriminant scores for the cases in the holdout sample. The cases are then assigned to groups based on their discriminant scores and an appropriate decision rule. For example, in two-group discriminant analysis, a case will be assigned to the group whose centroid is the closest. The **hit ratio**, or the percentage of cases correctly classified, can then be determined by summing the diagonal elements and dividing by the total number of cases.[8]

It is helpful to compare the percentage of cases correctly classified by discriminant analysis to the percentage that would be obtained by chance. When the groups are equal in size, the percentage of chance classification is 1 divided by the number of groups. How much improvement should be expected over chance? No general guidelines are available, although some authors have suggested that classification accuracy achieved by discriminant analysis should be at least 25 per cent greater than that obtained by chance.[9]

Most discriminant analysis programs also estimate a classification matrix based on the analysis sample. Because they capitalise on chance variation in the data, such results are invariably better than the classification obtained on the holdout sample.[10]

Table 20.4, of the holiday resort example, also shows the classification results based on the analysis sample. The hit ratio, or the percentage of cases correctly classified, is $(12 + 15)/30 = 0.90$, or 90 per cent. One might suspect that this hit ratio is artificially inflated, as the data used for estimation were also used for validation. Conducting classification analysis on an independent holdout set of data results in the classification matrix with a slightly lower hit ratio of $(4 + 6)/12 = 0.833$, or 83.3 per cent (see Table 20.4). Given two groups of equal size, by chance one would expect a hit ratio of $1/2 = 0.50$, or 50 per cent. Hence, the improvement over chance is more than 25 per cent, and the validity of the discriminant analysis is judged as satisfactory.

Another application of two-group discriminant analysis is provided by the following example.

EXAMPLE

Home bodies and couch potatoes[11]

Two-group discriminant analysis was used to assess the strength of each of five dimensions used in classifying individuals as TV users or non-users. The discriminant-analysis procedure was appropriate for this use because of the nature of the predefined categorical groups (users and non-users) and the interval scales used to generate individual factor scores.

Two equal groups of 185 elderly consumers, users and non-users (total $n = 370$), were created. The discriminant equation for the analysis was estimated by using a subsample of 142 respondents from the sample of 370. Of the remaining respondents, 198 were used as a validation subsample in a cross-validation of the equation. Thirty respondents were excluded from the analysis because of missing discriminant values.

The canonical correlation for the discriminant function was 0.4291, significant at the $p < 0.0001$ level. The eigenvalue was 0.2257. The table summarises the standardised canonical discriminant coefficients. A substantial portion of the variance is explained by the discriminant function. In addition, as the table shows, the home-orientation dimension made a fairly strong contribution to classifying individuals as users or non-users of television. Morale, security and health, and respect also contributed significantly. The social factor appeared to make little contribution.

The cross-validation procedure using the discriminant function from the analysis sample gave support to the contention that the dimensions aided researchers in discriminating between users and nonusers of television. As the table shows, the discriminant function was successful in classifying 75.76% of the cases. This suggests that consideration of the identified dimensions will help marketers understand the elderly market. ■

Summary of discriminant analysis

Standard canonical discriminant function coefficients	
Morale	0.27798
Security & health	0.39850
Home orientation	0.77496
Respect	0.32069
Social	–0.01996

Classification results for cases selected for use in the analysis

		Predicted group membership	
Actual group	**No. of cases**	**Non-users**	**Users**
TV non-users	77	56	21
		72.7%	27.3%
TV users	65	24	41
		36.9%	63.1%
Per cent of grouped cases correctly classified: 68.31%			

Classification results for cases selected for cross-validation

		Predicted group membership	
Actual group	**No. of cases**	**Non-users**	**Users**
TV non-users	108	85	21
		78.7%	21.3%
TV users	90	25	65
		27.8%	72.2%
Per cent of grouped cases correctly classified: 75.76%			

The extension from two-group discriminant analysis to multiple discriminant analysis involves similar steps and is illustrated with an application.

MULTIPLE DISCRIMINANT ANALYSIS

Formulation

The data presented in Tables 20.2 and 20.3 can also be used to illustrate three-group discriminant analysis. In the last column of these tables, the households are classified into three categories, based on the amount spent on family holiday (high, medium or low). Ten households fall in each category. The question of interest is whether the households that spend high, medium or low amounts on their holidays (amount) can be differentiated in terms of annual family income (income), attitude toward travel (travel), importance attached to family holiday (holiday), household size (hsize), and age of the head of household (age).[12]

Estimation

Table 20.5 presents the results of estimating three-group discriminant analysis. An examination of group means indicates that income appears to separate the groups more widely than any other variable. There is some separation on travel and holiday. Groups 1 and 2 are very close in terms of household size and age. Age has a large standard deviation relative to the separation between the groups. The pooled within-groups correlation matrix indicates some correlation of holiday and household size with income. Age has some negative correlation with travel. Yet these correlations are on the lower side indicating that although multicollinearity may be of some concern, it is not likely to be a serious problem. The significance attached to the univariate *F* ratios indicates that when the predictors are considered individually, only income and travel are significant in differentiating between the two groups.

Table 20.5 Results of three-group discriminant analysis

Group means					
Visit	**Income**	**Travel**	**Holiday**	**Hsize**	**Age**
1	38.57000	4.50000	4.70000	3.10000	50.30000
2	50.1100	4.00000	4.20000	3.40000	49.50000
3	64.97000	6.10000	5.90000	4.20000	56.00000
Total	51.21667	4.86667	4.93333	3.56667	51.93333
Group standard deviations					
1	5.29718	1.71594	1.88856	1.19722	8.09732
2	6.00231	2.35702	2.48551	1.50555	9.25263
3	8.61434	1.19722	1.66333	1.13529	7.60117
Total	12.79523	1.97804	2.09981	1.33089	8.57395
Pooled within-groups correlation matrix					
Income	1.00000				
Travel	0.05120	1.00000			
Holiday	0.30681	0.03588	1.00000		
Hsize	0.38050	0.00474	0.22080	1.00000	
Age	–0.20939	–0.34022	–0.01326	–0.02512	1.00000

Table 20.5 (continued)

Wilks' λ (*U* statistic) and univariate *F* ratio with 2 and 27 degrees of freedom

Variable	Wilks' λ	*F*	Significance
Income	0.26215	38.00	0.0000
Travel	0.78790	3.634	0.0400
Holiday	0.88060	1.830	0.1797
Hsize	0.87411	1.944	0.1626
Age	0.88214	1.804	0.1840

Canonical discriminant functions

Function	Eigenvalue	Percent of variance	Cumulative percentage	Canonical correlation	After function	Wilks' λ	Chi-square	df	Sig.
					0	0.1664	44.831	10	0.00
1*	3.8190	93.93	93.93	0.8902	1	0.8020	5.517	4	0.24
2*	0.2469	6.07	100.00	0.4450					

* Marks the two canonical discriminant function remaining in the analysis

Standard canonical discriminant function coefficients

	Func 1	Func 2
Income	1.04740	–0.42076
Travel	0.33991	0.76851
Holiday	–0.14198	0.53354
Hsize	–0.16317	0.12932
Age	0.49474	0.52447

Structure matrix: Pooled within-groups correlations between discriminating variables and canonical discriminant functions (variables ordered by size of correlation within function)

	Func 1	Func 2
Income	0.85556*	–0.27833
Hsize	0.19319*	0.07749
Holiday	0.21935	0.58829*
Travel	0.14899	0.45362*
Age	0.16576	0.34079*

Unstandardised canonical discriminant function coefficients

	Func 1	Func 2
Income	0.1542658	–0.6197148E-01
Travel	0.1867977	0.4223430
Holiday	–0.6952264E-01	0.2612652
Hsize	–0.1265334	0.1002796
Age	0.5928055E-01	0.6284206E-01
(constant)	–11.09442	–3.791600

Table 20.5 (continued)

Canonical discriminant functions evaluated at group means (group centroids)

Group	Func 1	Func 2
1	–2.04100	0.41847
2	–0.40479	–0.65867
3	2.44578	0.24020

Classification results for cases selected for use in analysis

			Predicted group membership		
	Actual group	**No. of cases**	**1**	**2**	**3**
Group	1	10	9	1	0
			90.0%	10.0%	.0%
Group	2	10	1	9	0
			10.0%	90.0%	.0%
Group	3	10	0	2	8
			.0%	20.0%	80.0%
Percentage of grouped cases correctly classified: 86.67%					

Classification results for cases not selected for use in analysis

			Predicted group membership		
	Actual group	**No. of cases**	**1**	**2**	**3**
Group	1	4	3	1	0
			75.0%	25.0%	.0%
Group	2	4	0	3	1
			.0%	75.0%	25.0%
Group	3	4	1	0	3
			25.0%	.0%	75.0%
Percentage of grouped cases correctly classified: 75.00%					

In multiple discriminant analysis, if there are G groups, $G - 1$ discriminant functions can be estimated if the number of predictors is larger than this quantity. In general, with G groups and k predictors, it is possible to estimate up to the smaller of $G - 1$, or k, discriminant functions. The first function has the highest ratio of between-groups to within-groups sum of squares. The second function, uncorrelated with the first, has the second highest ratio, and so on. Not all the functions may be statistically significant, however.

Because there are three groups, a maximum of two functions can be extracted. The eigenvalue associated with the first function is 3.8190, and this function accounts for 93.93 per cent of variance in the data. The eigenvalue is large, so the first function is likely to be superior. The second function has a small eigenvalue of 0.2469 and accounts for only 6.07 per cent of the variance.

the categorical variable and the predictor as the criterion variable. The predictor with the highest F ratio is the first to be selected for inclusion in the discriminant function, if it meets certain significance and tolerance criteria. A second predictor is added based on the highest adjusted or partial F ratio, taking into account the predictor already selected.

Each predictor selected is tested for retention based on its association with other predictors selected. The process of selection and retention is continued until all predictors meeting the significance criteria for inclusion and retention have been entered in the discriminant function. Several statistics are computed at each stage. In addition, at the conclusion, a summary of the predictors entered or removed is provided. The standard output associated with the direct method is also available from the stepwise procedure.

Mahalanobis procedure A stepwise procedure used in discriminant analysis to maximise a generalised measure of the distance between the two closest groups.

The selection of the stepwise procedure is based on the optimising criterion adopted. The **Mahalanobis procedure** is based on maximising a generalised measure of the distance between the two closest groups. This procedure allows marketing researchers to make maximal use of the available information.[15]

The Mahalanobis method was used to conduct a two-group stepwise discriminant analysis on the data pertaining to the visit variable in Tables 20.2 and 20.3. The first predictor variable to be selected was income, followed by household size and then holiday. The order in which the variables were selected also indicates their importance in discriminating between the groups. This was further corroborated by an examination of the standardised discriminant function coefficients and the structure correlation coefficients. Note that the findings of the stepwise analysis agree with the conclusions reported earlier by the direct method.

EXAMPLE

Satisfactory results of satisfaction programs in Europe[16]

These days, more and more computer companies are emphasising customer service programs rather than their erstwhile emphasis on computer features and capabilities. Hewlett-Packard learned this lesson in Europe. Research conducted in the European market revealed that there was a difference in emphasis on service requirements across age segments. Focus groups revealed that customers above 40 years of age had a hard time with the technical aspects of the computer and greatly required the customer service programs. On the other hand, young customers appreciated the technical aspects of the product that added to their satisfaction. To uncover the factors leading to differences in the two segments, further research in the form of a large single cross-sectional survey was done. A two-group discriminant analysis was conducted with satisfied and dissatisfied customers as the two groups and several independent variables such as technical information, ease of operation, variety and scope of customer service programs, etc. Results confirmed the fact that the variety and scope of customer satisfaction programs was indeed a strong differentiating factor. This was a crucial finding because Hewlett-Packard could better handle dissatisfied customers by focusing more on customer services than on technical details. Consequently, Hewlett-Packard successfully started three programs on customer satisfaction: customer feedback, customer satisfaction surveys, and total quality control. This effort resulted in increased customer satisfaction. ■

INTERNET AND COMPUTER APPLICATIONS

SPSS

In the mainframe version, the DISCRIMINANT procedure is used for conducting discriminant analysis. This is a general program that can be used for two-group or multiple discriminant analysis. Furthermore, the direct or the stepwise method can be adopted. A similar program, DSCRIMINANT, is available in the PC version.

SAS

The DISCRIM procedure can be used for performing two-group or multiple discriminant analysis. If the assumption of a multivariate normal distribution cannot be met, the NEIGHBOR procedure can be used. In this procedure, a non-parametric nearest neighbour rule is used for classifying the observations. CANDISC performs canonical discriminant analysis and is related to principal components analysis and canonical correlation. The STEPDISC procedure can be used for performing stepwise discriminant analysis. The mainframe and microcomputer versions are similar, except that the program NEIGHBOR is not available on the microcomputer version.

BMDP

The P7M program can be used to perform stepwise discriminant analysis. It does not print the standardised discriminant function coefficients. The P7M program is available in both mainframe and microcomputer versions.[17]

Minitab

Discriminant analysis can be conducted using the Stats>Multivariate> Discriminant Analysis function. It computes both linear and quadratic discriminant analysis in the classification of observations into two or more groups.

Excel

At the time of writing, discriminant analysis was not available.

SUMMARY

Discriminant analysis is useful for analysing data when the criterion or dependent variable is categorical and the predictor or independent variables are interval scaled. When the criterion variable has two categories, the technique is known as two-group discriminant analysis. Multiple discriminant analysis refers to the case when three or more categories are involved.

Conducting discriminant analysis is a five-step procedure. First, formulating the discriminant problem requires identification of the objectives and the criterion and predictor variables. The sample is divided into two parts. One part, the analysis sample, is used to estimate the discriminant function. The other part, the holdout sample, is reserved for validation. Estimation, the second step, involves developing a linear combination of the predictors, called discriminant functions, so that the groups differ as much as possible on the predictor values.

Determination of statistical significance is the third step. It involves testing the null hypothesis that, in the population, the means of all discriminant functions in all groups are equal. If the null hypothesis is rejected, it is meaningful to interpret the results.

The fourth step, the interpretation of discriminant weights or coefficients, is similar to that in multiple regression analysis. Given the multicollinearity in the predictor variables, there is no unambiguous measure of the relative importance of the predictors in discriminating between the groups. Some idea of the relative importance of the variables, however, may be obtained by examining the absolute magnitude of the standardised discriminant function coefficients and by examining the structure correlations or discriminant loadings. These simple correlations between each predictor and the discriminant function represent the variance that the predictor shares with the function. Another aid to interpreting discriminant analysis results is to develop a characteristic profile for each group, based on the group means for the predictor variables.

Validation, the fifth step, involves developing the classification matrix. The discriminant weights estimated by using the analysis sample are multiplied by the values of the predictor variables in the holdout sample to generate discriminant scores for the cases in the holdout sample. The cases are then assigned to groups based on their discriminant scores and an appropriate decision rule. The percentage of cases correctly classified is determined and compared with the rate that would be expected by chance classification.

Two broad approaches are available for estimating the coefficients. The direct method involves estimating the discriminant function so that all the predictors are included simultaneously. An alternative is the stepwise method in which the predictor variables are entered sequentially, based on their ability to discriminate among groups.

In multiple discriminant analysis, if there are G groups and k predictors, it is possible to estimate up to the smaller of $G - 1$, or k, discriminant functions. The first function has the highest ratio of between-group to within-group sums of squares; the second function, uncorrelated with the first, has the second highest ratio; and so on.

QUESTIONS AND PROBLEMS

1 What are the objectives of discriminant analysis?

2 Describe four examples of the application of discriminant analysis.

3 What is the main distinction between two-group and multiple discriminant analysis?

4 Describe the relationship of discriminant analysis to regression and ANOVA.

5 What are the steps involved in conducting discriminant analysis?

6 How should the total sample be split for estimation and validation purposes?

7 What is Wilks' λ? For what purpose is it used?

8 Define discriminant scores.

9 Explain what is meant by an eigenvalue.

10 What is a classification matrix?

11 Explain the concept of structure correlations.

12 How is the statistical significance of discriminant analysis determined?

13 Describe a common procedure for determining the validity of discriminant analysis.

14 When the groups are of equal size, how is the accuracy of chance classification determined?

15 How does the stepwise discriminant procedure differ from the direct method?

NOTES

1 Jolson, M.A., Wiener, J.L. and Rosecky, R.B., 'Correlates of Rebate Proneness', *Journal of Advertising Research* (February–March 1987), 33–43.

2 A detailed discussion of discriminant analysis may be found in Lachenbruch, P.A., *Discriminant Analysis* (New York: Hafner Press, 1975). For an application, see Allen, C.T., Machleit, K.A. and Schultz Kleine, S., 'A Comparison of Attitudes and Emotions as Predictors of Behaviour at Diverse Levels of Behavioural Experience', *Journal of Consumer Research* 18 (March 1992), 493–504.

3 Klecka, W.A., *Discriminant Analysis* (Beverly Hills: Sage, 1980). See also Sinclair, S.A. and Stalling, E.C., 'How to Identify Differences between Market Segments With Attribute Analysis', *Industrial Marketing Management* 19 (February 1990), 31–40.

4 For an application, see Sager, J.K. and Menon, A., 'The Role of Behavioural Intentions in Turnover of Salespeople', *Journal of Business Research* 29 (March 1994), 179–88, and Kijewski, V., Yoon E. and Young, G., 'How Exhibitors Select Trade Shows', *Industrial Marketing Management* 22 (November 1993), 287–98.

5 Crask, M.R. and Perreault, Jr., W.D., 'Validation of Discriminant Analysis in Marketing Research', *Journal of Marketing Research* 14 (February 1977), 60–68.

6 See Morrison, D.G., 'On the Interpretation of Discriminant Analysis', *Journal of Marketing Research* 6 (May 1969), 156–63. For use of other techniques in conjunction with discriminant analysis to aid interpretation, see Dant, R.P., Lumpkin. J.R. and Bush, R.P., 'Private Physicians or Walk-In Clinics: Do the Patients Differ?', *Journal of Health Care Marketing* (June 1990), 23–35.

7 Fern, E.E., Avila, R.A. and Grewal, D., 'Salesforce Turnover: Those Who Left and Those Who Stayed', *Industrial Marketing Management* (1989), 1–9. For another example in determining the relative importance of predictors, see Marks, R.B. and Totten, J.W., 'The Effects of Mortality Cues on Consumers' Ratings of Hospital Attributes', *Journal of Health Care Marketing* (September 1990), 4–12.

8 For the validation of discriminant analysis, see Bush, R.P., Ortinau, D.J. and Bush, A.J., 'Personal Value Structures and AIDS Prevention', *Journal of Health Care Marketing* 14 (Spring 1994), 12–20.

9 Hair, Jr., J.E., Anderson, R.E., Tatham, R.L. and Black, W.C., *Multivariate Data Analysis with Readings*, 4th edn (Englewood Cliffs, NJ: Prentice Hall, 1995), 178–255.

10 See Albaum, G. and Baker, K., 'The Sampling Problem in Validation of Multiple Discriminant Analysis', *Journal of the Market Research Society* 18 (July 1976).

11 Rahtz, D.R., Sirgy, M.J. and Kosenko, R., 'Using Demographics and Psychographic Dimensions to Discriminate between Mature Heavy and Light Television Users: An Exploratory Analysis', in Bahn, K.D., (ed.), *Developments in Marketing Science*, Vol. 11 (Blacksburg, VA: Academy of Marketing Science, 1988), 2–7.

12 For advanced discussion of multiple discriminant analysis, see Johnson, R.A. and Wichem, D.W., *Applied Multivariate Statistical Analysis* (Englewood Cliffs, NJ: Prentice Hall, 1982). For an application, see Dant, R.P. and Schul, P.L., 'Conflict Resolution Processes in Contractual Channels of Distribution', *Journal of Marketing* 56 (January 1992), 38–54.

13 For an application of multiple discriminant analysis, see O'Connor, S.J., Shewchuk, R.M. and Camey, L.W., 'The Great Gap', *Journal of Health Care Marketing* 14 (Summer 1994), 32–39.

14 Lim, J.S. and Zallocco, R., 'Determinant Attributes in Formulation of Attitudes Toward Four Health Care Systems', *Journal of Health Care Marketing* (June 1988), 25–30.

15 Hair, Jr, J.E., Anderson, R.E., Tatham, R.L. and Black, W.C., *Multivariate Data Analysis with Readings*, 4th edn (Englewood Cliffs, NJ: Prentice Hall, 1995), chapter 4.

16 Klopp, C. and Sterlicchi, J., 'Customer Satisfaction Just Catching on in Europe', *Marketing News* (28 May 1990).

17 Einspruch, E.L., *An Introductory Guide to SPSS for Windows* (Thousand Oaks, CA: Sage Publications, 1998); Spector, P.E., *SAS Programming for Researchers and Social Scientists* (Thousand Oaks, CA: Sage Publications, 1993); Norat, M.A., Software Reviews, *Economic Journal: The Journal of the Royal Economic Society* 107 (May 1997), 857–82; Seiter, C., 'The Statistical Difference', *Macworld* 10 (10) (October 1993), 116–21.

APPENDIX 20A: ESTIMATION OF DISCRIMINANT FUNCTION COEFFICIENTS

Suppose that there are G groups, $i = 1, 2, 3, \ldots, G$, each containing n_i observations on K independent variables, $X_1\ X_2, \ldots, X_k$. The following notations are used:

N = Total sample size

$$= \sum_{i=1}^{G} n_i$$

W_i = matrix of mean corrected sum of squares and cross-products for the ith group

W = matrix of pooled within-groups mean corrected sum of squares and cross-products

B = matrix of between-groups mean corrected sum of squares and cross-products

T = matrix of total mean corrected sum of squares and cross-products for all the N observations (= $W + B$)

$\bar{X}_i$ = vector of means of observations in the ith group

$\bar{X}$ = vector of grand means for all the N observations

λ = ratio of between groups to within group sums of squares

b = vector of discriminant coefficients or weights

Then,

$$T = \sum_{i=1}^{G} \sum_{j=1}^{n_i} (X_{ij} - \bar{X})\ (X_{ij} - \bar{X})'$$

$$W_i = \sum_{j=1}^{n_i} (X_{ij} - \bar{X}_i)\ (X_{ij} - \bar{X}_i)'$$

$$W = W_1 + W_2 + W_3 + \ldots + W_G$$
$$B = T - W$$

Define the linear composite $D = b'_1X$. Then, with reference to D, the between-groups and within-groups sums of squares are, b'_1Bb and b'_1Wb, respectively. To maximally discriminate the groups, the discriminant functions are estimated to maximise the between-group variability. The coefficients b are calculated to maximise λ, by solving

$$\text{Max } \lambda = \frac{b'Bb}{b'Wb}$$

Taking the partial derivative with respect to λ and setting it equal to zero, with some simplification, yields:

$$(B - \lambda W)b = 0$$

To solve for b, it is more convenient to premultiply by W^{-1} and solve the following characteristic equation:

$$(W^{-1}\ B - \lambda I)b = 0$$

The maximum value of λ is the largest eigenvalue of the matrix $W^{-1}\ B$, and b is the associated eigenvector. The elements of b are the discriminant coefficients, or weights, associated with the first discriminant function. In general, it is possible to estimate up to the smaller of $G - 1$ or k discriminant functions, each with its associated eigenvalue. The discriminant functions are estimated sequentially. In other words, the first discriminant function exhausts most of the between-group variability, the second function maximises the between-group variation that was not explained by the first one, and so on.

Chapter 21

Factor analysis

In factor analysis, there is no distinction between dependent and independent variables; rather, the whole set of interdependent variables is examined to identify underlying dimensions or factors

OBJECTIVES

After reading this chapter, the student should be able to:

1. describe the concept of factor analysis and explain how it is different from analysis of variance, multiple regression and discriminant analysis;
2. discuss the procedure for conducting factor analysis including problem formulation, construction of the correlation matrix, selection of an appropriate method, determination of the number of factors, rotation and interpretation of factors;
3. understand the distinction between principal component factor analysis and common factor analysis methods;
4. explain the selection of surrogate variables and their application with emphasis on their use in subsequent analysis;
5. describe the procedure for determining the fit of a factor analysis model using the observed and the reproduced correlations.

OVERVIEW

In analysis of variance (Chapter 18), regression (Chapter 19) and discriminant analysis (Chapter 20), one of the variables is clearly identified as the dependent variable. We now turn to a procedure, factor analysis, in which variables are not classified as independent or dependent. Instead, the whole set of interdependent relationships among variables is examined. This chapter discusses the basic concept of factor analysis and gives an exposition of the factor model. We describe the steps in factor analysis and illustrate them in the context of principal components analysis. Next, we present an application of common factor analysis. To begin, we provide some examples to illustrate the usefulness of factor analysis.

GLOBALCASH PROJECT

Factor analysis

In the GlobalCash project, the respondents' ratings of 11 service quality statements were factor analysed to determine the underlying service quality factors. Four factors emerged: close support, speed of activities, coping with errors and matching efficiency expectations. These factors, along with individual country characteristics, were used to profile market segments formed as a result of clustering. ■

EXAMPLE

Personal alarms[1]

In a study of personal alarms, women were asked to rate eight personal alarms using the following fifteen statements:

1 Feels comfortable in the hand
2 Could be easily kept in the pocket
3 Would fit easily into a handbag
4 Could be easily worn on the person
5 Could be carried to be very handy when needed
6 Could be set off almost as a reflex action
7 Would be difficult for an attacker to take it off me
8 Could keep a very firm grip on it if attacked
9 An attacker might be frightened that I might attack him with it
10 Would be difficult for an attacker to switch off
11 Solidly built
12 Would be difficult to break
13 Looks as if it would give off a very loud noise
14 An attacker might have second thoughts about attacking me if he saw me with it
15 I would be embarrassed to carry it around with me

The question was 'could these 15 variables be reduced to a smaller number of derived variables, known as factors, in such a way that too much information was not lost'? Factor analysis enabled these 15 variables to be reduced to four underlying dimensions or factors that women used to evaluate the alarms. Factor 1 seemed to measure a dimension of '*size*', on a continuum of small to large. Factor 2 tapped into aspects of the '*appearance*' of a personal alarm. Factor 3 revealed '*robustness*' characteristics with factor 4 related to '*hand feel*'. ■

BASIC CONCEPT

Factor analysis is a general name denoting a class of procedures primarily used for data reduction and summarisation. In marketing research, there may be a large number of variables, most of which are correlated and which must be reduced to a manageable level. Relationships among sets of many interrelated variables are examined and represented in terms of a few underlying factors. For example, bank image may be measured by asking respondents to evaluate banks on a series of items on a semantic differential scale. These item evaluations may then be analysed to determine the **factors** underlying bank image.

Factor analysis
A class of procedures primarily used for data reduction and summarisation.

Factor
An underlying dimension that explains the correlations among a set of variables.

In analysis of variance, multiple regression and discriminant analysis, one variable is considered the dependent or criterion variable, and the others

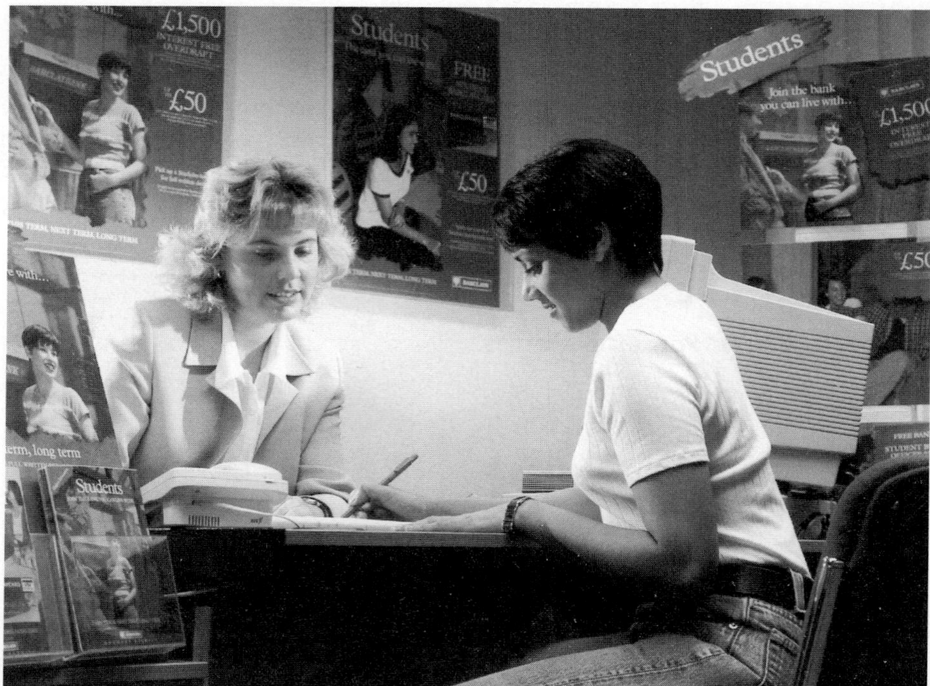

Understanding the factors that make up service quality is essential for good banking relationships

independent or predictor variables. But no such distinction is made in factor analysis. Rather, factor analysis is an **interdependence technique** in that an entire set of interdependent relationships is examined.[2]

Interdependence techniques
A multivariate statistical technique in which the whole set of interdependent relationships is examined.

Factor analysis is used in the following circumstances:

1 To identify underlying dimensions, or factors, that explain the correlations among a set of variables. For example, a set of lifestyle statements may be used to measure the psychographic profiles of consumers. These statements may then be factor analysed to identify the underlying psychographic factors.[3]
2 To identify a new, smaller, set of uncorrelated variables to replace the original set of correlated variables in subsequent multivariate analysis (regression or discriminant analysis). For example, the psychographic factors identified may be used as independent variables in explaining the differences between loyal and non-loyal consumers.
3 To identify a smaller set of salient variables from a larger set for use in subsequent multivariate analysis. For example, a few of the original lifestyle statements that correlate highly with the identified factors may be used as independent variables to explain the differences between the loyal and non-loyal users.

Factor analysis has numerous applications in marketing research. For example:

- Factor analysis can be used in market segmentation for identifying the underlying variables on which to group the customers. New car buyers might be grouped based on the relative emphasis they place on economy, convenience, performance, comfort and luxury. This might result in five segments: economy seekers, convenience seekers, performance seekers, comfort seekers and luxury seekers.
- In product research, factor analysis can be employed to determine the brand attributes that influence consumer choice. Toothpaste brands might be evaluated in terms of protection against cavities, whiteness of teeth, taste, fresh breath and price.
- In advertising studies, factor analysis can be used to understand the media consumption habits of the target market. The users of frozen foods may be heavy viewers of satellite TV, see a lot of videos, and listen to country music.

- In pricing studies, factor analysis can be used to identify the characteristics of price-sensitive consumers. For example, these consumers might be methodical, economy minded and home centred.

FACTOR ANALYSIS MODEL

Mathematically, factor analysis is somewhat similar to multiple regression analysis in that each variable is expressed as a linear combination of underlying factors. The amount of variance a variable shares with all other variables included in the analysis is referred to as communality. The covariation among the variables is described in terms of a small number of common factors plus a unique factor for each variable. These factors are not overtly observed. If the variables are standardised, the factor model may be represented as

$$X_i = A_{i1}F_1 + A_{i2}F_2 + A_{i3}F_3 + \dots + A_{im}F_m + V_iU_i$$

where

X_i = ith standardised variable
A_{ij} = standardised multiple regression coefficient of variable i on common factor j
F = common factor
V_i = standardised regression coefficient of variable i on unique factor i
U_i = the unique factor for variable i
m = number of common factors

The unique factors are correlated with each other and with the common factors.[4] The common factors themselves can be expressed as linear combinations of the observed variables

$$F_i = W_{i1}X_1 + W_{i2}X_2 + W_{i3}X_3 + \dots + W_{ik}X_k$$

where

F_i = estimate of ith factor
W_i = weight or factor score coefficient
k = number of variables

It is possible to select weights or factor score coefficients so that the first factor explains the largest portion of the total variance. Then a second set of weights can be selected so that the second factor accounts for most of the residual variance, subject to being uncorrelated with the first factor. This same principle could be applied to selecting additional weights for the additional factors. Thus, the factors can be estimated so that their factor scores, unlike the values of the original variables, are not correlated. Furthermore, the first factor accounts for the highest variance in the data, the second factor the second highest, and so on. A technical treatment of the factor analysis model is presented in Appendix 21A. Several statistics are associated with factor analysis.

STATISTICS ASSOCIATED WITH FACTOR ANALYSIS

The key statistics associated with factor analysis are as follows:

Bartlett's test of sphericity. Bartlett's test of sphericity is a test statistic used to examine the hypothesis that the variables are uncorrelated in the population.In other words, the population correlation matrix is an identify matrix; each variable correlates perfectly with itself ($r = 1$) but has no correlation with the other variables ($r = 0$).

Correlation matrix. A correlation matrix is a lower triangle matrix showing the simple correlations, r, between all possible pairs of variables included in the analysis. The diagonal elements, which are all 1, are usually omitted.

Communality. Communality is the amount of variance a variable shares with all the other variables being considered. This is also the proportion of variance explained by the common factors.

Eigenvalue. The eigenvalue represents the total variance explained by each factor.

Factor loadings. Factor loadings are simple correlations between the variables and the factors.

Factor loading plot. A factor loading plot is a plot of the original variables using the factor loadings as coordinates.

Factor matrix. A factor matrix contains the factor loadings of all the variables on all the factors extracted.

Factor scores. Factor scores are composite scores estimated for each respondent on the derived factors.

Kaiser-Meyer-Olkin (KMO) measure of sampling adequacy. The Kaiser-Meyer-Olkin (KMO) measure of sampling adequacy is an index used to examine the appropriateness of factor analysis. High values (between 0.5 and 1.0) indicate that factor analysis is appropriate. Values below 0.5 imply that factor analysis may not be appropriate.

Percentage of variance. The percentage of the total variance attributed to each factor.

Residuals. Residuals are the differences between the observed correlations, as given in the input correlation matrix, and the reproduced correlations, as estimated from the factor matrix.

Scree plot. A scree plot is a plot of the eigenvalues against the number of factors in order of extraction.

We describe the uses of these statistics in the next section, in the context of the procedure for conducting factor analysis.

CONDUCTING FACTOR ANALYSIS

The steps involved in conducting factor analysis are illustrated in Figure 21.1. The first step is to define the factor analysis problem and identify the variables to be factor analysed. Then a correlation matrix of these variables is constructed and a method of factor analysis is selected. The researcher decides on the number of factors to be extracted and the method of rotation. Next, the rotated factors should be interpreted. Depending on the objectives, the factor scores may be calculated, or surrogate variables selected, to represent the factors in subsequent multivariate analysis. Finally, the fit of the factor analysis model is determined. We discuss these steps in more detail in the following sections.[5]

Problem formulation

Problem formulation includes several tasks. First, the objectives of factor analysis should be identified. The variables to be included in the factor analysis should be specified based on past research, theory, and judgement of the researcher. It is important that the variables be appropriately measured on an interval or ratio scale. An appropriate sample size should be used. As a rough guideline, there should be at least four or five times as many observations (sample size) as there are variables.[6] In many marketing research situations, the sample size is small, and this ratio is considerably lower. In these cases, the results should be interpreted cautiously.

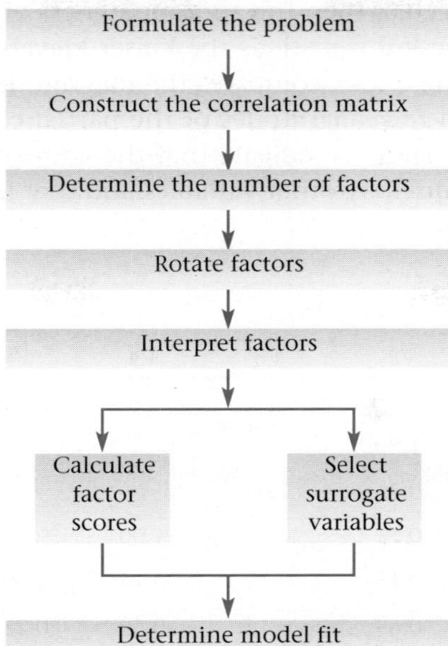

Figure 21.1
Conducting factor analysis

To illustrate factor analysis, suppose that the researcher wants to determine the underlying benefits consumers seek from the purchase of a toothpaste. A sample of 237 respondents was interviewed using street interviewing. The respondents were asked to indicate their degree of agreement with the following statements using a seven-point scale (1 = strongly disagree, 7 = strongly agree):

V_1 It is important to buy a toothpaste that prevents cavities.
V_2 1 like a toothpaste that gives shiny teeth.
V_3 A toothpaste should strengthen your gums.
V_4 I prefer a toothpaste that freshens breath.
V_5 Prevention of tooth decay should be an important benefit offered by a toothpaste.
V_6 The most important consideration in buying a toothpaste is attractive teeth.
V_7 A toothpaste should give you strong teeth.

A correlation matrix was constructed based on these ratings data. This construction process is discussed in the next section.

Construction of the correlation matrix

The analytical process is based on a matrix of correlations between the variables. Valuable insights can be gained from an examination of this matrix. For factor analysis to be appropriate, the variables must be correlated. In practice, this is usually the case. If the correlations between all the variables are small, factor analysis may not be appropriate. We would also expect that variables that are highly correlated with each other would also highly correlate with the same factor or factors.

Formal statistics are available for testing the appropriateness of the factor model. Bartlett's test of sphericity can be used to test the null hypothesis that the variables are uncorrelated in the population; in other words, the population correlation matrix is an identity matrix. In an identity matrix, all the diagonal terms are 1, and all off-diagonal terms are 0. The test statistic for sphericity is based on a chi-square transformation of the determinant of the correlation matrix. A large value of the test statistic will favour the rejection of the null hypothesis. If this hypothesis cannot be rejected, then the appropriateness of factor analysis should be questioned. Another useful statistic is the Kaiser-Meyer-Olkin (KMO) measure of sampling adequacy. This index compares the magnitudes of the observed correlation coefficients with the magnitudes of the partial correlation coefficients. Small values of the KMO statistic indicate that the correlations between pairs of variables cannot be explained by other variables and that factor analysis may not be appropriate.

Table 21.1 Correlation matrix

Variables	V1	V2	V3	V4	V5	V6	V7
V_1	1.00						
V_2	0.13	1.00					
V_3	0.67	0.21	1.00				
V_4	0.17	0.71	0.19	1.00			
V_5	0.70	0.15	0.49	0.13	1.00		
V_6	0.13	0.69	0.16	0.69	0.21	1.00	
V_7	0.56	0.22	0.73	0.27	0.72	0.31	1.00

The correlation matrix, constructed from the data obtained to understand toothpaste benefits, is shown in Table 21.1. There are relatively high correlations among V_1 (prevention of cavities), V_3 (strong gums), V_5 (prevention of tooth decay), and V_7 (strong teeth). We would expect these variable to correlate with the same set of factors. Likewise, there are relatively high correlations among V_2 (shiny teeth), V_4 (fresh breath) and V_6 (attractive teeth). These variables may also be expected to correlate with the same factors.[7]

The results of factor analysis are given in Table 21.2. The null hypothesis – that the population correlation matrix is an identity matrix – is rejected by Bartlett's test of sphericity. The value of the KMO statistic (0.61724) is also large (> 0.5). Thus factor analysis may be considered an appropriate technique for analysing the correlation matrix of Table 21.1.

Method of factor analysis

Once it has been determined that factor analysis is an appropriate technique for analysing the data, an appropriate method must be selected. The approach used to derive the weights or factor score coefficients differentiates the various methods of factor analysis. The two basic approaches are principal components analysis and common factor analysis. In principal components analysis, the total variance in the data is considered. The diagonal of the correlation matrix consists of unities, and full variance is brought into the factor matrix. **Principal components analysis** is recommended when the primary concern is to determine the minimum number of factors that will account for maximum variance in the data for use in subsequent multivariate analysis. The factors are called *principal components*.

Principal components analysis
An approach to factor analysis that considers the total variance in the data.

In **common factor** analysis, the factors are estimated based only on the common variance. Communalities are inserted in the diagonal of the correlation matrix. This method is appropriate when the primary concern is to identify the underlying dimensions and the common variance is of interest. This method is also known as *principal axis factoring*.

Common factor analysis
An approach to factor analysis that estimates the factors based only on the common variance.

Table 21.2 Results of principal components analysis

Bartlett test of sphericity = 1009.2719, significance = 0.00000
Kaiser-Meyer-Olkin measure of sampling adequacy = 0.61724

Initial statistics:

Variable	Communality	Factor	Eigenvalue	Per cent of variance	Cumulative percentage
V_1	1.00000	1	3.38111	48.3	48.3
V_2	1.00000	2	1.96150	28.0	76.3
V_3	1.00000	3	0.52851	7.6	83.9
V_4	1.00000	4	0.44928	6.4	90.3
V_5	1.00000	5	0.30112	4.3	94.6
V_6	1.00000	6	0.27965	4.0	98.6
V_7	1.00000	7	0.09883	1.4	100.0

Final statistics:

Variable	Communality	Factor	Eigenvalue	Per cent of variance	Cumulative percentage
V_1	0.73961	1	3.38111	48.3	48.3
V_2	0.80066	2	1.96150	28.0	76.3
V_3	0.70680				
V_4	0.80169				
V_5	0.72541				
V_6	0.78882				
V_7	0.77962				

Factor matrix:

	Factor 1	Factor 2
V_1	0.73011	–0.45448
V_2	0.58106	0.68046
V_3	0.75017	–0.37952
V_4	0.59422	0.66977
V_5	0.74088	–0.42013
V_6	0.60364	0.65149
V_7	0.82538	–0.31362

Rotated factor matrix

	Factor 1	Factor 2
V_1	0.85906	0.04039
V_2	0.09201	0.89005
V_3	0.83302	0.11348
V_4	0.10890	0.88872
V_5	0.84842	0.07478
V_6	0.12705	0.87902
V_7	0.85752	0.21043

Table 21.2 (continued)

Factor score coefficient matrix:

	Factor 1	Factor 2
V_1	0.30931	–0.06814
V_2	–0.05548	0.38315
V_3	0.29250	–0.03331
V_4	–0.04918	0.38087
V_5	0.30199	–0.05191
V_6	–0.04160	0.37478
V_7	0.29173	0.00697

Table 21.2 Reproduced correlation matrix

Variables	V_1	V_2	V_3	V_4	V_5	V_6	V_7
V_1	0.73961*	0.01501	–0.05020	0.04055	–0.03186	–0.01464	–0.18516
V_2	0.11499	0.80066*	0.03235	–0.09103	0.00538	–0.10407	–0.04620
V_3	0.72020	0.17765	0.70680*	–0.00157	–0.22524	–0.04559	–0.00821
V_4	0.12945	0.80103	0.19157	0.80169*	–0.02885	–0.10504	–0.01040
V_5	0.73186	0.14462	0.71524	0.15885	0.72541*	0.03648	–0.02327
V_6	0.14464	0.79407	0.20559	0.79504	0.17352	0.78882*	0.01608
V_7	0.74516	0.26620	0.73821	0.28040	0.74327	0.29392	0.77962*

The lower left triangle contains the reproduced correlation matrix; the diagonal, the communalities; and the upper right triangle, the residuals between the observed correlations and the reproduced correlations.

Other approaches for estimating the common factors are also available. These include the methods of unweighted least squares, generalised least squares, maximum likelihood, alpha method and image factoring. These methods are complex and are not recommended for inexperienced users.[8]

Table 21.2 shows the application of principal components analysis to the toothpaste example. Under initial statistics, it can be seen that the communality for each variable, *V*1 to *V*7, is 1.0 as unities were inserted in the diagonal of the correlation matrix. The eigenvalues for the factors are, as expected, in decreasing order of magnitude as we go from factor 1 to factor 7. The eigenvalue for a factor indicates the total variance attributed to that factor. The total variance accounted for by all the seven factors is 7.00, which is equal to the number of variables. Factor 1 accounts for a variance of 3.38111, which is (3.38111/7) or 48.3 per cent of the total variance. Likewise, the second factor accounts for (1.96150/7) or 28.0 per cent of the total variance, and the first two factors combined account for 76.3 per cent of the total variance. Several considerations are involved in determining the number of factors that should be used in the analysis.

Number of factors

It is possible to compute as many principal components as there are variables, but in doing so, no parsimony is gained. To summarise the information contained in the original variables, a smaller number of factors should be extracted.

The question is, how many? Several procedures have been suggested for determining the number of factors. These included *a priori* determination and approaches based on eigenvalues, scree plot, percentage of variance accounted for, split-half reliability, and significance tests.

***A priori* determination.** Sometimes, because of prior knowledge, the researcher knows how many factors to expect and thus can specify the number of factors to be extracted beforehand. The extraction of factor ceases when the desired number of factors have been extracted. Most computer programs allow the user to specify the number of factors, allowing for an easy implementation of this approach.

Determination based on eigenvalues. In this approach, only factors with eigenvalues greater than 1.0 are retained; the other factors are not included in the model. An eigenvalue represents the amount of variance associated with the factor. Hence, only factors with a variance greater than 1.0 are included. Factors with variance less than 1.0 are no better than a single variable because, due to standardisation, each variable has a variance of 1.0. If the number of variables is less than 20, this approach will result in a conservative number of factors.

Determination based on scree plot. A scree plot is a plot of the eigenvalues against the number of factors in order of extraction. The shape of the plot is used to determine the number of factors. Typically, the plot has a distinct break between the steep slope of factors, with large eigenvalues and a gradual trailing off associated with the rest of the factors. This gradual trailing off is referred to as the scree. Experimental evidence indicates that the point at which the scree begins denotes the true number of factors. Generally, the number of factors determined by a scree plot will be one or a few more than that determined by the eigenvalue criterion.

Determination based on percentage of variance. In this approach, the number of factors extracted is determined so that the cumulative percentage of variance extracted by the factors reaches a satisfactory level. What level of variance is satisfactory depends upon the problem. It is recommended that the factors extracted should account for at least 60 per cent of the variance, however.

Determination based on split half reliability. The sample is split in half, and factor analysis is performed on each half. Only factors with high correspondence of factor loadings across the two sub-samples are retained.

Determination based on significance tests. It is possible to determine the statistical significance of the separate eigenvalues and retain only those factors that are statistically significant. A drawback is that with large samples (size greater than 200), many factors are likely to be statistically significant, although from a practical viewpoint many of these account for only a small proportion of the total variance.

In Table 21.2, we see that the eigenvalue greater than 1.0 (default option) results in two factors being extracted. Our a priori knowledge tells us that toothpaste is bought for two major reasons. The scree plot associated with this analysis is given in Figure 21.2. From the scree plot, a distinct break occurs at three factors. Finally, from the cumulative percentage of variance accounted for, we see

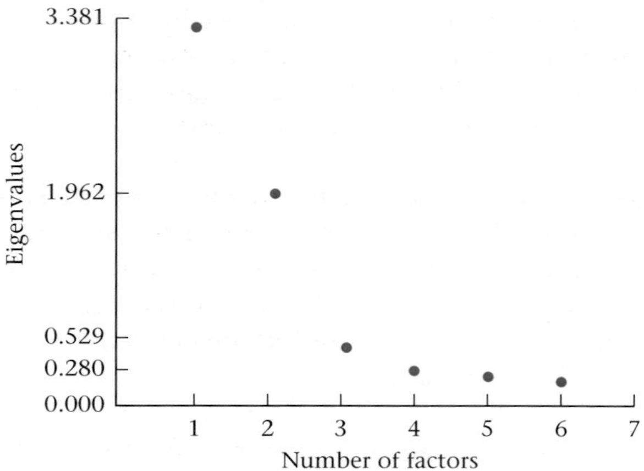

Figure 21.2
Scree plot

that the first two factors account for 76.3 per cent of the variance and that the gain achieved in going to three factors is marginal. Furthermore, split-half reliability also indicates that two factors are appropriate. Given the large sample size, statistical tests are not very useful. Thus, two factors appear to be reasonable in this situation.

The section labelled 'final statistics' in Table 21.2 gives relevant information after the desired number of factors have been extracted. It shows the communalities for the variables, along with the variance accounted for by each factor that is retained. The factor statistics are the same under the 'initial statistics' and 'final statistics' headings. This is always the case in principal components analysis, but the communalities for the variables are different because all the variances associated with the variables are not explained unless all the factors are retained. Interpretation of the solution is often enhanced by a rotation of the factors.

Rotation of factors

An important output from factor analysis is the factor matrix, also called the *factor pattern matrix*. The factor matrix contains the coefficients used to express the standardised variables in terms of the factors. These coefficients, the factor loadings, represent the correlations between the factors and the variables. A coefficient with a large absolute value indicates that the factor and the variable are closely related. The coefficients of the factor matrix can be used to interpret the factors.

Although the initial or unrotated factor matrix indicates the relationship between the factors and individual variables, it seldom results in factors that can be interpreted, because the factors are correlated with many variables. For example, in Table 21.2, factor 1 is highly correlated with all seven variables. How should this factor be interpreted? In such a complex matrix, it is difficult to interpret the factors. Therefore, through rotation, the factor matrix is transformed into a simpler one that is easier to interpret.

In rotating the factors, we would like each factor to have nonzero, or significant, loadings or coefficients for only some of the variables. Likewise, we would like each variable to have nonzero or significant loadings with only a few factors, and if possible, with only one. If several factors have high loadings with the same variable, it is difficult to interpret them. Rotation does not affect the communalities and the percentage of total variance explained. The percentage of variance accounted for by each factor does change, however. The variance explained by the individual factors is redistributed by rotation. Hence, different methods of rotation may result in the identification of different factors.

Orthogonal rotation
Rotation of factors in which the axes are maintained at right angles.

Varimax procedure
An orthogonal method of factor rotation that minimises the number of variables with high loadings on a factor, thereby enhancing the interpretability of the factors.

Oblique rotation
Rotation of factors when the axes are not maintained at right angles.

The rotation is called **orthogonal rotation** if the axes are maintained at right angles. The most commonly used method for rotation is the **varimax procedure**. This is an orthogonal method of rotation that minimises the number of variables with high loadings on a factor, thereby enhancing the interpret ability of the factors.[9] Orthogonal rotation results in factors that are uncorrelated. The rotation is called **oblique rotation** when the axes are not maintained at right angles, and the factors are correlated. Sometimes, allowing for correlations among factors can simplify the factor pattern matrix. Oblique rotation should be used when factors in the population are likely to be strongly correlated.

In Table 21.2, by comparing the varimax rotated factor matrix with the unrotated matrix (entitled factor matrix), we can see how rotation achieves simplicity and enhances interpretability. Although all seven variables correlated highly with factor 1 in the unrotated matrix, only variables V_1, V_3, V_5 and V_7 correlate highly with factor 1 after rotation. The remaining variables – V_2, V_4 and V_6 – correlate highly with factor 2. Furthermore, no variable correlates highly with both the factors. The rotated factor matrix forms the basis for interpretation of the factors.

Interpretation of factors

Interpretation is facilitated by identifying the variables that have large loadings on the same factor. That factor can then be interpreted in terms of the variables that load high on it. Another useful aid in interpretation is to plot the variables, using the factor loadings as coordinates. Variables at the end of an axis are those that have high loadings on only that factor and hence describe the factor. Variables near the origin have small loadings on both the factors. Variables that are not near any of the axes are related to both the factors. If a factor cannot be clearly defined in terms of the original variables, it should be labelled as an undefined or a general factor.

In the rotated factor matrix of Table 21.2, factor 1 has high coefficients for variables V_1 (prevention of cavities), V_3 (strong gums), V_5 (prevention of tooth decay) and V_7 (strong teeth). Therefore, this factor may be labelled a health benefit factor. Factor 2 is highly related with variables V_2 (shiny teeth), V_4 (fresh breath) and V6 (attractive teeth). Thus factor 2 may be labelled a social benefit factor. A plot of the factor loadings, given in Figure 21.3, confirms this interpretation. Variables V_1, V_3, V_5 and V_7 (denoted 1, 3, 5 and 7, respectively) are at the end of the horizontal axis (factor 1), whereas variables V_2, V_4 and V_6 (denoted 2, 4 and 6) are at the end of the vertical axis (factor 2). One could summarise the data by stating that consumers appear to seek two major kinds of benefits from a toothpaste: health benefits and social benefits.

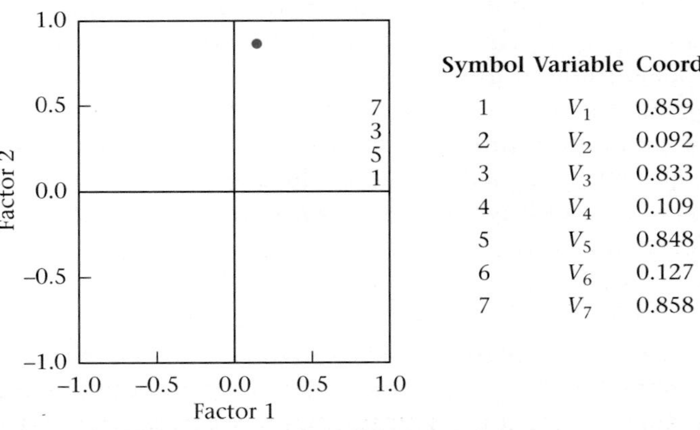

Symbol	Variable	Coordinates	
1	V_1	0.859	0.040
2	V_2	0.092	0.890
3	V_3	0.833	0.113
4	V_4	0.109	0.889
5	V_5	0.848	0.075
6	V_6	0.127	0.879
7	V_7	0.858	0.210

Figure 21.3
Factor loading plot

Factor scores

Factor scores
Composite scores estimated for each respondent on the derived factors.

Following interpretation, **factor scores** can be calculated, if necessary. Factor analysis has its own stand-alone value. If the goal of factor analysis is to reduce the original set of variables to a smaller set of composite variables (factors) for use in subsequent multivariate analysis, however, it is useful to compute factor scores for each respondent. A factor is simply a linear combination of the original variables. The **factor scores** for the ith factor may be estimated as follows:

$$F_i = W_{i1}X_1 + W_{i2}X_2 + W_{i3}X_3 + \ldots + W_{ik}X_k$$

where the symbols are as defined earlier in the chapter.

The weights or factor score coefficients used to combine the standardised variables are obtained from the factor score coefficient matrix. Most computer programs allow you to request factor scores. Only in the case of principal components analysis is it possible to compute exact factor scores. Moreover, in principal component analysis, these scores are uncorrelated. In common factor analysis, estimates of these scores are obtained, and there is no guarantee that the factors will be uncorrelated with each other. Factor scores can be used instead of the original variables in subsequent multivariate analysis. For example, using the factor score coefficient matrix in Table 21.2, one could compute two factor scores for each respondent. The standardised variable values would be multiplied by the corresponding factor score coefficients to obtain the factor scores.

Selection of Surrogate Variables

Surrogate variables
A subset of original variables selected for use in subsequent analysis.

Sometimes, instead of computing factor score, the researcher wishes to select surrogate variables. Selection of substitute or **surrogate variables** involves singling out some of the original variables for use in subsequent analysis. This allows the researcher to conduct subsequent analysis and to interpret the results in terms of original variables rather than factor scores. By examining the factor matrix, one could select for each factor the variables rather than factor scores. By examining the factor matrix, one could select for each factor the variable with the highest loading on that factor. That variable could then be used as a surrogate variable for the associated factor. This process works well if one factor loading for a variable is clearly higher than all other factor loadings. The choice is not as easy, however, if two or more variables have similarly high loadings. In such a case, the choice between these variables should be based on theoretical and measurement considerations. For example, theory may suggest that a variable with a slightly lower loading is more important than one with a slightly higher loading. Likewise, if a variable has a slightly lower loading but has been measured more precisely, it should be selected as the surrogate variable. In Table 21.2, the variables V_1, V_3, V_5 and V_7 all have high loadings on factor 1, and all are fairly close in magnitude. If prior knowledge suggests that prevention of tooth decay is a very important benefit, V_5 would be selected as the surrogate for factor 1. Also, the choice of a surrogate for factor 2 is not straightforward. Variables V_2, V_4 and V_6 all have comparable high loadings on this factor. If prior knowledge suggests that shiny teeth is the most important social benefit sought from a toothpaste, the researcher would select V_2.

Model fit

The final step in factor analysis involves the determination of model fit. A basic assumption underlying factor analysis is that the observed correlation between variables can be attributed to common factors. Hence, the correlations between the variables can be deduced or reproduced from the estimated correlations between the variables and the factors. The differences between the observed correlations (as given in the input correlation matrix) and the reproduced correlations (as estimated from the factor matrix) can be examined to determine model fit. These differences are called residuals. If there are many large residuals, the factor model does not provide a good fit to the data and the model should be reconsidered. In Table 21.2, we see that only four residuals are larger than 0.1, and six are larger than 0.05, indicating an acceptable model fit.

The following example further illustrates principal components factoring in the context of trade promotion.

EXAMPLE

Manufacturing promotion components[10]

The objective of this study was to develop a comprehensive inventory of manufacturer-controlled trade promotion variables and to demonstrate that an association exists between these variables and the retailer's promotion support decision. Retailer or trade support was defined operationally as the trade buyer's attitude toward the promotion.

Factor analysis was performed on the explanatory variables with the primary goal of data reduction. The principal components method, using varimax rotation, reduced the 30 explanatory variables to eight factors having eigenvalues greater than 1.0. For the purpose of interpretation, each factor was composed of variables that loaded 0.40 or higher on that factor. In two instances, where variables loaded 0.40 or above on two factors, each variable was assigned to the factor where it had the highest loading. Only one variable, ease of handling/stocking at retail, did not load at least 0.40 on any factor. In all, the eight factors explained 62% of the total variance. Interpretation of the factor-loading matrix was straightforward. Table 1 lists the factors in the order in which they were extracted.

Table 1 Factors influencing trade promotional support

Factor	Factor interpretation (% variance explained)	Loading	Variables included in the factor
*F*1	Item importance (16.3%)	0.77	Item is significant enough to warrant promotion
		0.75	Category responds well to promotion
		0.66	Closest trade competitor is likely to promote item
		0.64	Importance of promoted product category
		0.59	Item regular (non-deal) sales volume
		0.57	Deal meshes with trade promotional requirements
			Buyers estimate of sales increase on the basis of:
*F*2	Promotion elasticity (9.3%)	0.86	Price reduction and display
		0.82	Display only
		0.80	Price reduction only
		0.70	Price reduction, display and advertising
			Manufacturer's brand support in form of:
*F*3	Manufacturer brand support (8.2%)	0.85	Coupons
		0.81	Radio and television advertising
		0.80	Newspaper advertising
		0.75	Point of purchase promotion (e.g. display)

Table 1 (continued

Factor	Factor interpretation (% variance explained)	Loading	Variables included in the factor
*F*4	Manufacturer reputation (7.3%)	0.72	Manufacturer's overall reputation
		0.72	Manufacturer cooperates in meeting trade's promotional needs
		0.64	Manufacturer cooperates on emergency orders
		0.55	Quality of sales presentation
		0.51	Manufacturer's overall product quality
*F*5	Promotion wearout (6.4%)	0.93	Product category is over-promoted
		0.93	Item is over-promoted
*F*6	Sales velocity (5.4%)	–0.81	Brand market share rank[a]
		0.69	Item regular sales volume[a]
		0.46	Item regular sales volume
*F*7	Item profitability (4.5%)	0.79	Item regular gross margin
		0.72	Item regular gross margin[a]
		0.49	Reasonableness of deal performance requirements
*F*8	Incentive amount (4.2%)	0.83	Absolute amount of deal allowances
		0.81	Deal allowances as percentage of regular trade cost[a]
		0.49	Absolute amount of deal allowances[a]

[a]Denotes objectives (archival) measure

Stepwise discriminant analysis was conducted to determine which, if any, of the eight factors predicted trade support to a statistically significant degree. The factor scores for the eight factors were the explanatory variables. The dependent variable consisted of the retail buyer's overall rating of the deal (rating), which was collapsed into a three-group (low, medium and high) measure of trade support. The results of the discriminant analyses are shown in Table 2. All eight entered the discriminant functions. Goodness-of-fit measures indicated that, as a group, the eight factors discriminated between high, medium and low levels of trade support. Multivariate *F* ratios, indicating the degree of discrimination

Table 2 Discriminant analysis results: analysis on rating and performance ($n = 564$)

		Standardised discriminant coefficients Analysis of rating	
Factor		**Function 1**	**Function 2**
*F*1	Item importance	0.861	–0.253
*F*2	Promotion elasticity	0.081	0.398
*F*3	Manufacturer brand support	0.127	–0.036
*F*4	Manufacturer reputation	0.394	0.014
*F*5	Promotion wearout	–0.207	0.380
*F*6	Sales velocity	0.033	–0.665
*F*7	Item profitability	0.614	0.357
*F*8	Incentive amount	0.461	0.254
Wilks' λ (for each factor)		All significant at $p < 0.001$	
Multivariate *F* ratios		All significant at $p < 0.001$	
Percentage of cases correctly classified		65% correct ($t = 14.4$, $p < 0.001$)	

between each pair of groups, were significant at $p < 0.001$. Correct classification into high, medium and low categories was achieved for 65% of the cases. The order of entry into discriminant analysis was used to determine the relative importance of factors as trade support influencers, as shown in Table 3. ■

Table 3 Relative importance of trade support influencers (as indicated by order of entry into the discriminant analysis)

Analysis of rating	
Order of entry	**Factor name**
1	Item importance
2	Item profitability
3	Incentive amount
4	Manufacturer reputation
5	Promotion wearout
6	Sales velocity
7	Promotion elasticity
8	Manufacturer brand support

In the next section, we describe common factor analysis and provide applications of this method.

APPLICATIONS OF COMMON FACTOR ANALYSIS

The correlation matrix shown in Table 21.1 was analysed using the common factor analysis model. Instead of using unities in the diagonal, the communalities were inserted. The output, shown in Table 21.3, is similar to the output from principal components analysis presented in Table 21.2. The initial statistics table is the same as in Table 21.2 except that the communalities for the variables are no longer 1.0. Based on the eigenvalue criterion, again two factors are extracted. The final statistics, after extracting the factors, are different from the initial statistics. The first factor accounts for 43.6 per cent of the variance, whereas the second accounts for 23.4 per cent, in each case a little less than what was observed in principal components analysis.

Table 21.3 Results of common factor analysis

Bartlett test of sphericity = 1009.2719, significance = 0.00000
Kaiser-Meyer-Olkin measure of sampling adequacy = 0.61724

Initial statistics:

Variable	Communality	Factor	Eigenvalue	Per cent of variance	Cumulative percentage
V_1	0.68263	1	3.38111	48.3	48.3
V_2	0.60376	2	1.96150	28.0	76.3
V_3	0.71310	3	0.52851	7.6	83.9
V_4	0.60594	4	0.44928	6.4	90.3
V_5	0.72173	5	0.30112	4.3	94.6
V_6	0.58597	6	0.27965	4.0	98.6
V_7	0.76372	7	0.09883	1.4	100.0

Table 21.3 (continued)

Final statistics:

Variable	Communality	Factor	Eigenvalue	Per cent of variance	Cumulative percentage
V_1	0.63867	1	3.04960	43.6	43.6
V_2	0.70338	2	1.64092	23.4	67.0
V_3	0.60090				
V_4	0.70795				
V_5	0.62793				
V_6	0.67873				
V_7	0.73295				

Factor matrix:

	Factor 1	Factor 2
V_1	0.68096	–0.41829
V_2	0.56493	0.61987
V_3	0.69355	–0.34625
V_4	0.57868	0.61080
V_5	0.69067	–0.38846
V_6	0.58235	0.58275
V_7	0.79668	–0.31346

Rotated factor matrix

	Factor 1	Factor 2
V_1	0.79724	0.05541
V_2	0.09943	0.83276
V_3	0.76562	0.12135
V_4	0.11589	0.83338
V_5	0.78782	0.08533
V_6	0.13518	0.81268
V_7	0.83048	0.20797

Factor score coefficient matrix

	Factor 1	Factor 2
V_1	0.34295	–0.05898
V_2	–0.2312	0.36321
V_3	0.15844	–0.02150
V_4	–0.06357	0.36945
V_5	0.18444	–0.03433
V_6	–0.04586	0.32517
V_7	0.42645	0.00095

Table 21.3 (continued)

Reproduced correlation matrix:

Variables	V_1	V_2	V_3	V_4	V_5	V_6	V_7
V_1	0.63867*	0.00459	–0.05289	0.03143	0.06719	–0.02280	–0.11362
V_2	0.12541	0.70338*	0.03282	0.00447	0.00061	–0.00022	-0.03576
V_3	0.61711	0.17718	0.60090*	0.00015	–0.12352	–0.04212	0.06893
V_4	0.13857	0.70553	0.18985	0.70795*	–0.03241	–0.00294	0.00044
V_5	0.63281	0.14939	0.61352	0.16241	0.67293*	0.03416	0.04799
V_6	0.15280	0.69022	0.20212	0.69294	0.17584	0.67873*	0.02872
V_7	0.67362	0.25576	0.66107	0.26956	0.67201	0.28128	0.73295*

The lower left triangle contains the reproduced correlation matrix; the diagonal, the communalities; and the upper right triangle, the residuals between the observed correlations and the reproduced correlations.

The values in the unrotated factor pattern matrix of Table 21.3 are a little different than those in Table 21.2, although the pattern of the coefficient is similar. Sometimes however, the pattern of loadings for common factor analysis is different than that for principal components analysis, with some variables loading on different factors. The rotated factors matrix has the same pattern as that in Table 21.2, leading to a similar interpretation of the factors.

We end with another application of common factor analysis, in the context of consumer perception of rebates.

EXAMPLE

'Common' rebate perceptions[11]

Rebates are effective in obtaining new users, brand switching and repeat purchases among current users. A study was undertaken to determine the factors underlying consumer perception of rebates. A set of 24 items measuring consumer perceptions of rebates was constructed. Respondents were asked to express their degree of agreement with these items on five-point Likert scales. The data were collected by a one-stage area telephone survey conducted in the Memphis metropolitan area. A total of 303 usable questionnaires was obtained.

The 24 items measuring perceptions of rebates were analysed using common factor analysis. The initial factor solution did not reveal a simple structure of underlying rebate perceptions. Therefore, items that had low loadings were deleted from the scale, and the factor analysis was performed on the remaining items. This second solution yielded three interpretable factors. The factor loadings and the reliability coefficients are presented in the table below. The three factors contained four, four and three items, respectively. Factor 1 seemed to capture the consumers' perceptions of the efforts and difficulties associated with rebate redemption (efforts). Factor 2 was defined as a representation of consumers' faith in the rebate system (faith). Factor 3 represented consumers' perceptions of the manufacturers' motives for offering rebates (motives). The loadings of items on their respective factor ranged from 0.527 to 0.744. ■

Factor analysis of perceptions of rebates

	Factor loading		
Scale items[a]	**Factor 1**	**Factor 2**	**Factor 3**
Manufacturers make the rebate process too complicated	0.194	<u>0.671</u>	–0.127
Postal rebates are not worth the trouble involved	–0.031	<u>0.612</u>	0.352
It takes too long to receive the rebate cheque from the manufacturer	0.013	<u>0.718</u>	0.051
Manufacturers could do more to make rebates easier to use	0.205	<u>0.616</u>	0.173
Manufacturers offer rebates because consumers want them[b]	<u>0.660</u>	0.172	0.101
Today's manufacturers take real interest in consumer welfare[b]	<u>0.569</u>	0.203	0.334
Consumer benefit is usually the primary consideration in rebate offers[b]	<u>0.660</u>	0.002	0.318
In general, manufacturers are sincere in their rebate offers to consumers[b]	<u>0.716</u>	0.047	–0.033
Manufacturers offer rebates to get consumers to buy something they do not really need	0.099	0.156	<u>0.744</u>
Manufacturers use rebate offers to induce consumers to buy slow-moving items	0.090	0.027	<u>0.702</u>
Rebate offers require you to buy more of a product than you need	0.230	0.066	<u>0.527</u>
Eigenvalues	2.030	1.344	1.062
Percentage of explained variance	27.500	12.200	9.700

[a]The response categories for all items were strongly agree (1), agree (2) 1 neither agree nor disagree (3), disagree (4), strongly disagree (5) and don't know (6). 'Don't know' responses were excluded from data analysis.
[b]the scores of these items were reversed.

In this example, when the initial factor solution was not interpretable, items which had low loadings were deleted and the factor analysis was performed on the remaining items. If the number of variables is large (greater than 15), principal components analysis and common factor analysis result in similar solutions. Principal components analysis is less prone to misinterpretation, however, and is recommended for the non-expert.

INTERNET AND COMPUTER APPLICATIONS

SPSS[12]

The program FACTOR may be used for principal components analysis as well as for common factor analysis. Some other methods of factor analysis are also available and factor scores are available.

SAS

The program PRINCOMP performs principal components analysis and calculates principal components scores. To perform common factor analysis, the program FACTOR can be used. The FACTOR program also performs principal components analysis.

BMDP

Principal components analysis and common factor analysis can be performed with the 4M program.

Minitab

Factor analysis can be accessed using Multivariate>Factor analysis. Principal components or maximum likelihood can be used to determine the initial factor extraction. If maximum likelihood is used, specify the number of factors to extract. If a number is not specified with a principal component extraction, the program will set it equal to a number of variables in the data set.

Excel

At the time of writing, factor analysis was not available.

SUMMARY

Factor analysis is a class of procedures used for reducing and summarising data. Each variable is expressed as a linear combination of the underlying factors. Likewise, the factors themselves can be expressed as linear combinations of the observed variables. The factors are extracted in such a way that the first factor accounts for the highest variance in the data, the second the next highest, and so on. Additionally, it is possible to extract the factors so that the factors are uncorrelated, as in principal components analysis.

In formulating the factor analysis problem, the variables to be included in the analysis should be specified based on past research, theory, and the judgement of the researcher. These variables should be measured on an interval or ratio scale. Factor analysis is based on a matrix of correlation between the variables. The appropriateness of the correlation matrix for factor analysis can be statistically tested.

The two basic approaches to factor analysis are principal components analysis and common factor analysis. In principal components analysis, the total variance in the data is considered. Principal components analysis is recommended when the researcher's primary concern is to determine the minimum number of factors that will account for maximum variance in the data for use in subsequent multivariate analysis. In common factor analysis, the factors are estimated based only on the common variance. This method is appropriate when the primary concern is to identify the underlying dimensions and when the common variance is of interest. This method is also known as principal axis factoring.

The number of factors that should be extracted can be determined *a priori* or based on eigenvalues, scree plots, percentage of variance, split-half reliability or significance tests. Although the initial or unrotated factor matrix indicates the relationships between the factors and individual variables, it seldom results in factors that can be interpreted because the factors are correlated with many variables. Therefore, rotation is used to transform the factor matrix into a simpler one that is easier to interpret. The most commonly used method of rotation is the varimax procedure, which results in orthogonal factors. If the factors are highly correlated in the population, oblique rotation can be used. The rotated factor matrix forms the basis for interpreting the factors.

Factor scores can be computed for each respondent. Alternatively, surrogate variables may be selected by examining the factor matrix and selecting a variable with the highest or near highest loading for each factor. The differences between the observed correlations and the reproduced correlations, as estimated from the factor matrix, can be examined to determine model fit.

QUESTIONS AND PROBLEMS

1 How is factor analysis different from multiple regression and discriminant analysis?

2 What are the major uses of factor analysis?

3 Describe the factor analysis model.

4 What hypothesis is examined by Bartlett's test of sphericity? For what purpose is this test used?

5 What is meant by the term communality of a variable?

6 Briefly define the following: eigenvalue, factor loadings, factor matrix and factor scores.

7 For what purpose is the Kaiser-Meyer-Olkin measure of sampling adequacy used?

8 What is the major difference between principal components analysis and common factor analysis?

9 Explain how eigenvalues are used to determine the number of factors.

10 What is a scree plot? For what purpose is it used?

11 Why is it useful to rotate the factors? Which is the most common method of rotation?

12 What guidelines are available for interpreting the factors?

13 When is it useful to calculate factor scores?

14 What are surrogate variables? How are they determined?

15 How is the fit of the factor analysis model examined?

NOTES

1 Alt, M., *Exploring Hyperspace* (McGraw Hill, 1990), 74.

2 For a detailed discussion of factor analysis, see Dunteman, G.H., *Principal Components Analysis* (Newbury Park, CA: Sage Publications, 1989). For other applications, see Scheer, L.K. and Stern, L.W., 'The Effect of Influence Type and Performance Outcomes on Attitude toward the Influencer', *Journal of Marketing Research* 29 (February 1992), 128–42; and Wotnuba, T.R. and Tyagi, P.K., 'Met Expectations and Turnover in Direct Selling', *Journal of Marketing* 55 (July 1991), 24–35.

3 See, for example, Taylor, S., 'Waiting for Service: The Relationship between Delays and Evaluations of Service', *Journal of Marketing* 58 (April 1994), 56–69.

4 See Lastovicka, J.L. and Thamodaran, K., 'Common Factor Score Estimates in Multiple Regression Problems', *Journal of Marketing Research* 28 (February 1991), 105–12; and Dillon, W.R. and Goldstein, M., *Multivariate Analysis: Methods and Applications* (New York: Wiley, 1984), 23–99.

5 For an application of factor analysis, see Ganesan, S., 'Negotiation Strategies and the Nature of Channel Relationships', *Journal of Marketing Research* 30 (May 1993), 183–203.

6 Hair, Jr, J.E., Anderson, R.E., Tatham, R.L. and Black, W.C., *Multivariate Data Analysis with Readings*, 4th edn (Englewood Cliffs: Prentice Hall, 1995), 364–419.

7 Factor analysis is influenced by the relative size of the correlations rather than the absolute size.

8 See Chatterjee, S., Jamieson, L. and Wiseman, F., 'Identifying Most Influential Observations in Factor Analysis', *Marketing Science* (Spring 1991), 145–60; and Acito, F. and Anderson, R.D., 'A Monte Carlo Comparison of Factor Analytic Methods', *Journal of Marketing Research* 17 (May 1980), 228–36.

9 Other methods of orthogonal rotation are also available. The quartimax method minimises the number of factors needed to explain a variable. The equimax method is a combination of varimax and quartimax.

10 Curhan, R.C. and Kopp, R.J., 'Obtaining Retailer Support for Trade Deals: Key Success Factors', *Journal of Advertising Research* (December 1987–January 1988), 51–60.

11 Tat, P., Cunningham III, W.A. and Babakus, E., 'Consumer Perceptions of Rebates', *Journal of Advertising Research* (August–September 1988), 45–50.

12 Einspruch, E.L., *An Introductory Guide to SPSS for Windows* (Thousand Oaks, CA: Sage Publications, 1998); Spector, P.E., *SAS Programming for Researchers and Social Scientists*, (Thousand Oaks, CA: Sage Publications, 1993); Norat, M.A., Software Reviews, Economic Journal: *The Journal of the Royal Economic Society* 107 (May 1997), 857–82; Seiter, C., 'The Statistical Difference', *Macworld* 10 (10) (October 1993), 116–21.

APPENDIX 21A: FUNDAMENTAL EQUATIONS OF FACTOR ANALYSIS

In the factor analysis model, hypothetical components are derived that account for the linear relationship between observed variables.[1] The factor analysis model requires that the relationships between observed variables be linear and that the variables have non-zero correlations between them. The derived hypothetical components have the following properties:

1 They form a linearly independent set of variables. No hypothetical component is derivable from the other hypothetical components as a linear combination of them.
2 The hypothetical components' variables can be divided into two basic kinds of components: common factors and unique factors. These two components can be distinguished in terms of the patterns of weights in the linear equations that derive the observed variables from the hypothetical components' variables. A common factor has more than one variable with a nonzero weight or factor loading associated with the factor. A unique factor has only one variable with a nonzero weight associated with the factor. Hence, only one variable depends on a unique factor.
3 Common factors are always assumed to be uncorrelated with the unique factors. Unique factors are also usually assumed to be mutually uncorrelated, but common factors may or may not be correlated with each other.
4 Generally, it is assumed that there are fewer common factors than observed variables. The number of unique factors is usually assumed to be equal to the number of observed variables, however.

The following notations are used.

$\boldsymbol{X}$ = an n x 1 random vector of observed random variables $X_1, X_2, X_3, ..., X_n$

It is assumed that

$$E(\boldsymbol{X}) = 0$$

$E(\boldsymbol{XX'}) = \boldsymbol{Rxx}$, a correlation matrix with unities in the main diagonal

$\boldsymbol{F}$ = an m x 1 vector of m common factors $F_1, F_2, ..., F_m$

It is assumed that

$$E(\boldsymbol{F}) = 0$$

$E(\boldsymbol{FF'}) = \boldsymbol{R}_{ff}$, a correlation matrix

$\boldsymbol{U}$ = an n x 1 random vector of the n unique factors variables, $U_1, U_2, ..., U_n$

It is assumed that

$$E(\boldsymbol{U}) = 0$$
$$E(\boldsymbol{UU'}) = \boldsymbol{I}$$

The unique factors are normalised to have unit variances and are mutually uncorrelated.

$\boldsymbol{A}$ = an n x m matrix of coefficients called the factor pattern matrix

$\boldsymbol{V}$ = an n x n diagonal matrix of coefficients for the unique factors

The observed variables, which are the coordinates of $\boldsymbol{X}$, are weighted combinations of the common factors and the unique factors. The fundamental equation of factor analysis can then be written as

$$\boldsymbol{X} = \boldsymbol{AF} + \boldsymbol{VU}$$

The correlations between variables in terms of the factors may be derived as follows:

$$\begin{aligned} R_{xx} &= E(\boldsymbol{XX'}) \\ &= E\{(\boldsymbol{AF} + \boldsymbol{VU})(\boldsymbol{AF} + \boldsymbol{VU})'\} \\ &= E\{(\boldsymbol{AF} + \boldsymbol{VU})(\boldsymbol{F'A'} + \boldsymbol{U'V'})\} \\ &= E(\boldsymbol{AFF'A'} + \boldsymbol{AFU'V'} + \boldsymbol{VUF'A'} + \boldsymbol{VUU'V'}) \\ &= \boldsymbol{AR}_{ff}\boldsymbol{A'} + \boldsymbol{AR}_{fu}\boldsymbol{V'} + \boldsymbol{VR}_{uf}\boldsymbol{A'} + \boldsymbol{V}^2 \end{aligned}$$

Given that the common factors are uncorrelated with the unique factors, we have

$$\boldsymbol{R}_{fu} = \boldsymbol{R}_{uf}' = 0$$

Hence,

$$\boldsymbol{R}_{xx} = \boldsymbol{AR}_{ff}\boldsymbol{A'} + \boldsymbol{V}^2$$

Suppose that we subtract the matrix of unique factor variance, $\boldsymbol{V}^2$, from both sides. We then obtain

$$\boldsymbol{R}_{xx} - \boldsymbol{V}^2 = \boldsymbol{AR}_{ff}\boldsymbol{A'}$$

$\boldsymbol{R}_{xx}$ is dependent only on the common factor variables, and the correlations among the variables are related only to the common factors. Let $\boldsymbol{R}_c = \boldsymbol{R}_{xx} - \boldsymbol{V}^2$ be the reduced correlation matrix.

We have already defined the factor pattern matrix $\boldsymbol{A}$. The coefficients of the factor pattern matrix are weights assigned to the common factors when the observed variables are expressed as linear combinations of the common and unique factors. We now define the factor structure matrix. The coefficients of the factor structure matrix are the covariances between the observed variables and the factors. The

[1] The material in this appendix has been drawn from Stanley A. Muliak, *The Foundations of Factor Analysis* (New York: McGraw-Hill, 1972)

factor structure matrix is helpful in the interpretation of factors as it shows which variables are similar to a common factor variable. The factor structure matrix, A_s, is defined as

$$\begin{aligned} A_s &= E(XF') \\ &= E[(AF + VU)F'] \\ &= AR_{ff} + VR_{uf} \\ &= AR_{ff} \end{aligned}$$

Thus, the factor structure matrix is equivalent to the factor pattern matrix A multiplied by the matrix of covariances among the factors R_{ff}. Substituting A_s for AR_{ff}, the reduced correlation matrix becomes the product of factor structure and the factor pattern matrix.

$$\begin{aligned} R_c &= AR_{ff}A' \\ &= A_sA' \end{aligned}$$

Chapter 22

Cluster analysis

Like birds of a feather, consumers, banks, brands and other objects in the marketing environment that are similar in terms of key variables often flock (cluster) together, and such clusters are discovered using cluster analysis

OBJECTIVES

After reading this chapter, the student should be able to:

1 describe the basic concept and scope of cluster analysis and its importance in marketing research;
2 discuss the statistics associated with cluster analysis;
3 explain the procedure for conducting cluster analysis including formulating the problem, selecting a distance measure, selecting a clustering procedure, deciding on the number of clusters, interpreting clusters, and profiling clusters;
4 describe the purpose and methods for evaluating the quality of clustering results and assessing reliability and validity;
5 discuss the applications of non-hierarchical clustering and clustering of variables.

OVERVIEW

Like factor analysis (Chapter 21), cluster analysis examines an entire set of interdependent relationships. Cluster analysis makes no distinction between dependent and independent variables. Rather, interdependent relationships between the whole set of variables are examined. The primary objective of cluster analysis is to classify objects into relatively homogeneous groups based on the set of variables considered. Objects in a group are relatively similar in terms of these variables and different from objects in other groups. When used in this manner, cluster analysis is the obverse of factor analysis in that it reduces the number of objects, not the number of variables, by grouping them into a much smaller number of clusters.

This chapter describes the basic concept of cluster analysis. The steps involved in conducting cluster analysis are discussed and illustrated in the context of hierarchical clustering by using a popular computer program. Then an application of non-hierarchical clustering is presented, followed by a discussion of clustering of variables. We begin with two examples.

GLOBALCASH PROJECT

Cluster analysis of European companies plans over the next two years[1]

In the GlobalCash project, respondents were clustered on the basis of the changes that respondents said their companies would be making over the next two years. The results indicated that respondents could be clustered into 20 segments. Differences among the segments were statistically tested. Thus, each segment contained respondents who were relatively homogeneous with respect to their plans. The following descriptions encapsulate four of the distinct segments.

- *Restructure through new electronic systems* represented companies whose distinctive plans involved 'making greater use of electronic banking', 'automating the treasury function', 'installing a new treasury system' and 'restructuring cash management along pan-European lines'.
- *Quality focus* represented those companies whose only significant planned change was for 'bank service quality to become a major issue'.
- *All change* represented those companies that planned changes in most areas, perhaps the most volatile of all groups. Most of this group planned to use a pan-European bank and with that change would come a restructuring of cash management on pan-European lines and installation of a new treasury system.
- *Status quo* represented the companies with the lowest amounts of planned changes none of this group plan to have more automation in their treasury function, put their domestic banking out to tender, or use a netting system.

The headquarters of the Royal Bank of Canada – one of the major North American banks that sponsored the GlobalCash study.

EXAMPLE

Perceived product parity: once rarity, now reality[2]

How do consumers in different countries perceive brands in different product categories? Surprisingly, the answer is that the product perception parity rate is quite high. Perceived product parity means that consumers perceive all or most of the brands in a product category as similar to each other or at par.

A study by BBDO Worldwide showed that two thirds of consumers surveyed in 28 countries considered brands in 13 product categories to be at a parity. The product categories ranged from airlines to credit cards to coffee. Perceived parity averaged 63% for all categories in all countries. The Japanese have the highest perception of parity across all product categories at 99% and Colombians the lowest at 28%. Viewed by product category, credit cards have the highest parity perception at 76% and cigarettes the lowest at 52%.

BBDO clustered the countries based on product parity perceptions to arrive at clusters that exhibited similar levels and patterns of parity perceptions. The highest perception parity figure came from the Asia/Pacific region (83%), which included Australia, Japan, Malaysia and South Korea, and also France. It is no surprise that France was in this list because, for most products, French consumers use highly emotional, visual advertising that is feelings-oriented. The next cluster was US-influenced markets (65%), which included Argentina, Canada, Hong Kong, Kuwait, Mexico, Singapore and the United States. The third cluster, primarily European countries (60%) included Austria, Belgium, Denmark, Italy, the Netherlands, South Africa, Spain, the United Kingdom and Germany.

What all this means is that to differentiate the product or brand, advertising cannot just focus on product performance but must also relate the product to the person's life in an important way. Also, a much greater marketing effort will be required in the Asia/Pacific region and in France to differentiate the brand from competition and to establish a unique image. ■

Both examples illustrate the use of clustering to arrive at homogeneous segments for the purpose of formulating specific marketing strategies.

BASIC CONCEPT

Cluster analysis is a class of techniques used to classify objects or cases into relatively homogeneous groups called clusters. Objects in each cluster tend to be similar to each other and dissimilar to objects in the other clusters. Cluster analysis is also called classification analysis or numerical taxonomy.[3] We are concerned with clustering procedures that assign each object to one and only one cluster.[4] Figure 22.1 shows an ideal clustering situation in which the clusters are distinctly separated on two variables: quality consciousness (variable 1) and price sensitivity (variable 2). Note that each consumer falls into one cluster and there are no overlapping areas. Figure 22.2, on the other hand, presents a clustering situation more likely to be encountered in practice. In Figure 22.2, the boundaries for some of the clusters are not clear cut, and the classification of some consumers is not obvious, because many of them could be grouped into one cluster or another.

Both cluster analysis and discriminant analysis are concerned with classification. Discriminant analysis, however, requires prior knowledge of the cluster or group membership for each object or case included, to develop the classification rule. In contrast, in cluster analysis there is no a priori information about the

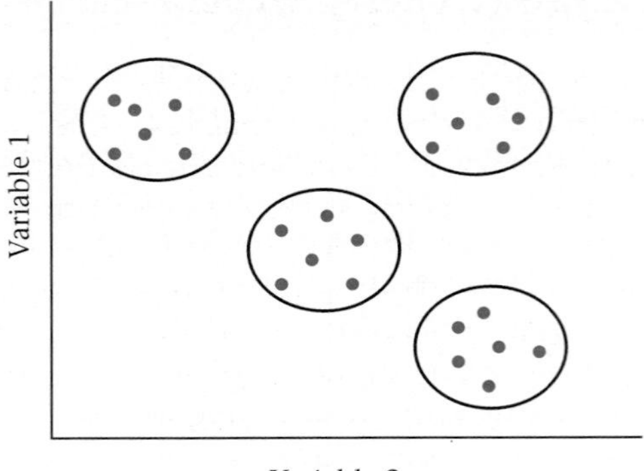

Figure 22.1
An ideal clustering solution

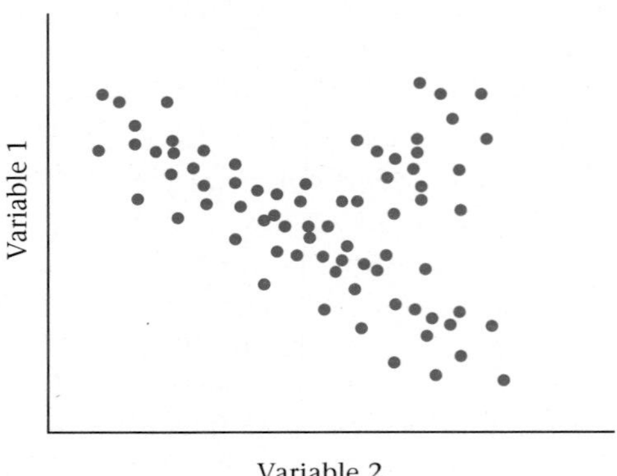

Figure 22.2
A practical clustering solution

group or cluster membership for any of the objects. Groups or clusters are suggested by the data, not defined *a priori*.[5] Cluster analysis has been used in marketing for a variety of purposes, including the following:[6]

- *Segmenting the market.* For example, consumers may be clustered on the basis of benefits sought from the purchase of a product. Each cluster would consist of consumers who are relatively homogeneous in terms of the benefits they seek.[7] This approach is called benefit segmentation.
- *Understanding buyer behaviours.* Cluster analysis can be used to identify homogeneous groups of buyers. Then the buying behaviour of each group may be examined separately, as happened in another area of the GlobalCash project. Respondents were clustered on the basis of choice criteria used in selecting a bank.
- *Identifying new product opportunities.* By clustering brands and products, competitive sets within the market can be determined. Brands in the same cluster compete more fiercely with each other than with brands in other clusters. A firm can examine its current offerings compared with those of its competitors to identify potential new product opportunities.
- *Selecting test markets.* By grouping cities into homogeneous clusters, it is possible to select comparable cities to test various marketing strategies.
- *Reducing data.* Cluster analysis can be used as a general data reduction tool to develop clusters or subgroups of data that are more manageable than individual observations. Subsequent multivariate analysis is conducted on the clusters rather than on the individual observations. For example, to describe differences in consumers' product usage behaviour, the consumers may first be clustered into groups. The differences among the groups may then be examined using multiple discriminant analysis.

STATISTICS ASSOCIATED WITH CLUSTER ANALYSIS

Before discussing the statistics associated with cluster analysis, it should be mentioned that most clustering methods are relatively simple procedures that are not supported by an extensive body of statistical reasoning. Rather, most clustering methods are heuristics, which are based on algorithms. Thus, cluster analysis contrasts sharply with analysis of variance, regression, discriminant analysis and factor analysis, which are based upon an extensive body of statistical reasoning. Although many clustering methods have important statistical properties, the fundamental simplicity of these methods needs to be recognized.[8] The following statistics and concepts are associated with cluster analysis.

Agglomeration schedule. An agglomeration schedule gives information on the objects or cases being combined at each stage of a hierarchical clustering process.
Cluster centroid. The cluster centroid is the mean values of the variables for all the cases or objects in a particular cluster.
Cluster centres. The cluster centres are the initial starting points in non-hierarchical clustering. Clusters are built around these centres or seeds.
Cluster membership. Cluster membership indicates the cluster to which each object or case belongs.
Dendrogram. A dendrogram, or tree graph, is a graphical device for displaying clustering results. Vertical lines represent clusters that are joined together. The position of the line on the scale indicates the distances at which clusters were joined. The dendrogram is read from left to right. Figure 22.8 is a dendrogram.
Distances between cluster centres. These distances indicate how separated the individual pairs of clusters are. Clusters that are widely separated are distinct and therefore desirable.
Icicle diagram. An icicle diagram is a graphical display of clustering results, so called because it resembles a row of icicles hanging from the eaves of a house. The columns correspond to the objects being clustered, and the rows correspond to the number of clusters. An icicle diagram is read from bottom to top. Figure 22.7 is an icicle diagram.
Similarity/distance coefficient matrix. A similarity/distance coefficient matrix is a lower-triangle matrix containing pairwise distances between objects or cases.

CONDUCTING CLUSTER ANALYSIS

The steps involved in conducting cluster analysis are listed in Figure 22.3. The first step is to formulate the clustering problem by defining the variables on which the clustering will be based. Then, an appropriate distance measure must be selected. The distance measure determines how similar or dissimilar the objects being clustered are. Several clustering procedures have been developed, and the researcher should select one that is appropriate for the problem at hand. Deciding on the number of clusters requires judgement on the part of the researcher. The derived clusters should be interpreted in terms of the variables used to cluster them and profiled in terms of additional salient variables. Finally, the researcher must assess the validity of the clustering process.

Formulating the problem

Perhaps the most important part of formulating the clustering problem is selecting the variables on which the clustering is based. Inclusion of even one or two irrelevant variables may distort an otherwise useful clustering solution. Basically,

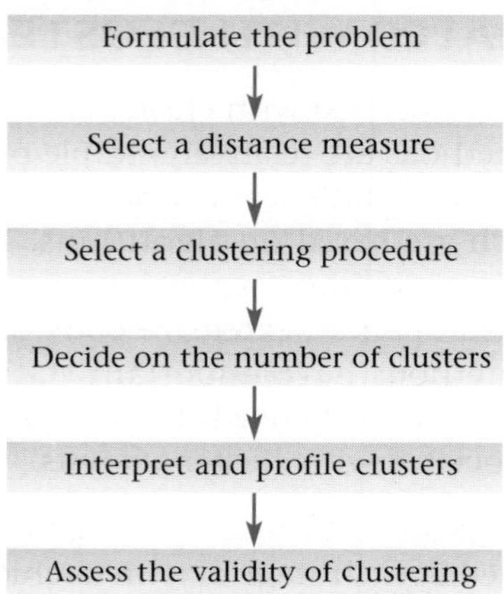

Figure 22.3
Conducting cluster analysis

the set of variables selected should describe the similarity between objects in terms that are relevant to the marketing research problem. The variables should be selected based on past research, theory or a consideration of the hypotheses being tested. In exploratory research, the researcher should exercise judgement and intuition.

To illustrate, we consider a clustering of consumers based on attitudes toward shopping. Based on past research, six attitudinal variables were identified. Consumers were asked to express their degree of agreement with the following statements on a seven-point scale (1 = disagree, 7 = agree):

V_1 Shopping is fun.
V_2 Shopping is bad for your budget.
V_3 I combine shopping with eating out.
V_4 I try to get the best buys while shopping.
V_5 I don't care about shopping.
V_6 You can save a lot of money by comparing prices.

Data obtained from a pre-test sample of 20 respondents are shown in Table 22.1. Note that, in practice, clustering is done on much larger samples of 100 or more. A small sample size has been used to illustrate the clustering process.

Selecting a distance or similarity measure

Because the objective of clustering is to group similar objects together, some measure is needed to assess how similar or different the objects are. The most common approach is to measure similarity in terms of distance between pairs of objects. Objects with smaller distances between them are more similar to each other than are those at larger distances. There are several ways to compute the distance between two objects.[9]

Euclidean distance
The square root of the sum of the squared differences in values for each variable.

The most commonly used measure of similarity is the **euclidean distance** or its square.[10] The euclidean distance is the square root of the sum of the squared differences in values for each variable. Other distance measures are also available. The *city-block* or *Manhattan distance* between two objects is the sum of the absolute differences in values for each variable. The *Chebychev distance* between two objects is the maximum absolute difference in values for any variable. For our example, we use the squared euclidean distance.

If the variables are measured in vastly different units, the clustering solution will be influenced by the units of measurement. In a supermarket shopping study, attitudinal variables may be measured on a nine-point Likert type scale;

Table 22.1 Attitudinal data for clustering

Case number	V_1	V_2	V_3	V_4	V_5	V_6
1	6	4	7	3	2	3
2	2	3	1	4	5	4
3	7	2	6	4	1	3
4	4	6	4	5	3	6
5	1	3	2	2	6	4
6	6	4	6	3	3	4
7	5	3	6	3	3	4
8	7	3	7	4	1	4
9	2	4	3	3	6	3
10	3	5	3	6	4	6
11	1	3	2	3	5	3
12	5	4	5	4	2	4
13	2	2	1	5	4	4
14	4	6	4	6	4	7
15	6	5	4	2	1	4
16	3	5	4	6	4	7
17	4	4	7	2	2	5
18	3	7	2	6	4	3
19	4	6	3	7	2	7
20	2	3	2	4	7	2

patronage, in terms of frequency of visits per month and the amount spent; and brand loyalty, in terms of percentage of grocery shopping expenditure allocated to the favourite supermarket. In these cases, before clustering respondents, we must standardise the data by re-scaling each variable to have a mean of zero and a standard deviation of unity. Although standardisation can remove the influence of the unit of measurement, it can also reduce the differences between groups on variables that may best discriminate groups or clusters. It is also desirable to eliminate outliers (cases with atypical values).[11]

Use of different distance measures may lead to different clustering results. Hence, it is advisable to use different measures and to compare the results. Having selected a distance or similarity measure, we can next select a clustering procedure.

Hierarchical clustering
A clustering procedure characterised by the development of a hierarchy or treelike structure.

Agglomerative clustering
A hierarchical clustering procedure where each object starts out in a separate cluster. Clusters are formed by grouping objects into bigger and bigger clusters.

Divisive clustering
A hierarchical clustering procedure where all objects start out in one giant cluster. Clusters are formed by dividing this cluster into smaller and smaller clusters.

Selecting a clustering procedure

Figure 22.4 is a classification of clustering procedures. Clustering procedures can be hierarchical or non-hierarchical. **Hierarchical clustering** is characterised by the development of a hierarchy or treelike structure. Hierarchical methods can be agglomerative or divisive. **Agglomerative clustering** starts with each object in a separate cluster. Clusters are formed by grouping objects into bigger and bigger clusters. This process is continued until all objects are members of a single cluster. **Divisive clustering** starts with all the objects grouped in a single cluster. Clusters are divided or split until each object is in a separate cluster.

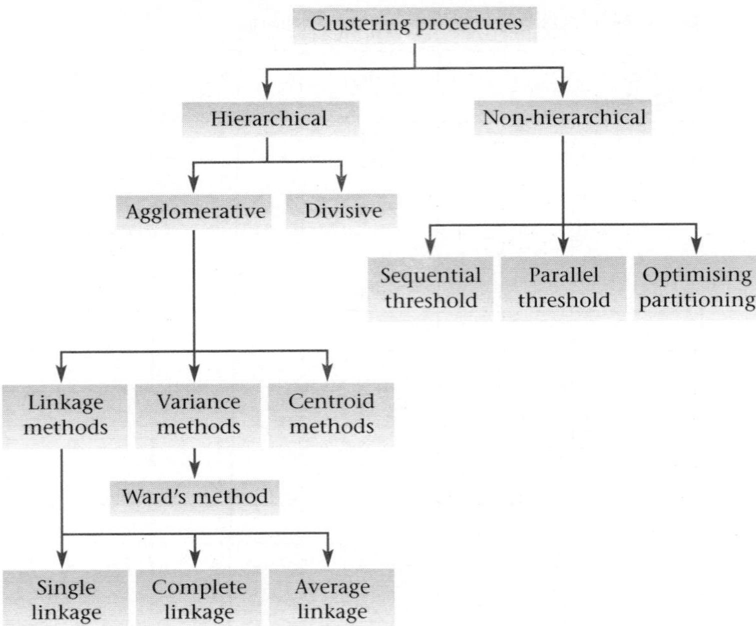

Figure 22.4
A classification of clustering procedures

Agglomerative methods are commonly used in marketing research. They consist of linkage methods, error sums of squares or variance methods, and centroid methods. **Linkage methods** include single linkage, complete linkage and average linkage. The **single linkage** method is based on minimum distance or the nearest neighbour rule. The first two objects clustered are those that have the smallest distance between them. The next shortest distance is identified, and either the third object is clustered with the first two or a new two-object cluster is formed. At every stage, the distance between two clusters is the distance between their two closest points (see Figure 22.5). Two clusters are merged at any stage by the single shortest link between them. This process is continued until all objects are in one cluster. The single linkage method does not work well when the clusters are poorly defined. The **complete linkage** method is similar to single linkage, except that it is based on the maximum distance or the farthest neighbour approach. In complete linkage, the distance between two clusters is calculated as the distance between their two farthest points. The average linkage method works similarly. In this method, however, the distance between two clusters is defined as the average of the distances between all pairs of objects, where one member of the pair is from each of the clusters (Figure 22.5). As can be seen, the average linkage method uses information on all pairs of distances, not merely the minimum or maximum distances. For this reason, it is usually preferred to the single and complete linkage methods.

Linkage methods
Agglomerative methods of hierarchical clustering that cluster objects based on a computation of the distance between them.

Single linkage
A linkage method based on minimum distance or the nearest neighbour rule.

Complete linkage
A linkage method that is based on maximum distance of the farthest neighbour approach.

The **variance methods** attempt to generate clusters to minimise the within-cluster variance. A commonly used variance method is **Ward's procedure**. For each cluster, the means for all the variables are computed. Then, for each object, the squared euclidean distance to the cluster means is calculated (Figure 22.6); and these distances are summed for all the objects. At each stage, the two clusters with the smallest increase in the overall sum of squares within cluster distances are combined. In the **centroid method**, the distance between two clusters is the distance between their centroids (means for all the variables), as shown in Figure 22.6. Every time objects are grouped, a new centroid is computed. Of the hierarchical methods, the average linkage method and Ward's procedure have been shown to perform better than the other procedures.[12]

Variance method
An agglomerative method of hierarchical clustering in which clusters are generated to minimise the within-cluster variance.

Ward's procedure
A variance method in which the squared euclidean distance to the cluster means is minimised.

Centroid method
A variance method of hierarchical clustering in which the distance between two clusters is the distance between their centroids (means for all the variables).

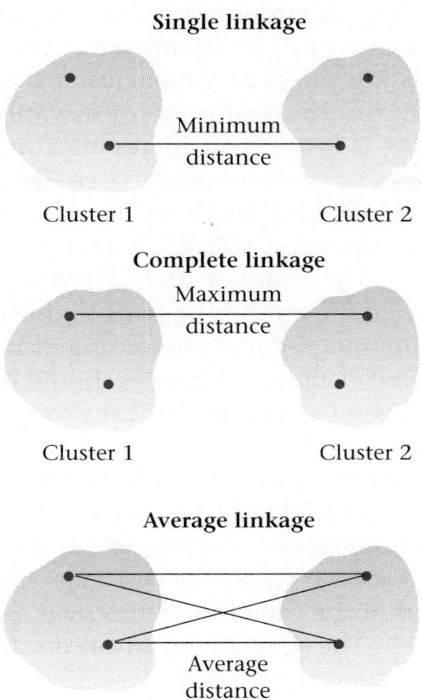

Figure 22.5 Linkage methods of clustering

Non-hierarchical clustering
A procedure that first assigns or determines a cluster centre and then groups all objects within a pre-specified threshold value from the centre.

Parallel threshold method
A non-hierarchical clustering method that specifies several cluster centres at once. All objects that are within a pre-specified threshold value from the centre are grouped together.

Optimising partitioning method
A non-hierarchical clustering method that allows for later reassignment of objects to clusters to optimise an overall criterion.

The second type of clustering procedures, the **non-hierarchical clustering** methods, are frequently referred to as *k*-means clustering. These methods include sequential threshold, parallel threshold, and optimising partitioning. In the sequential threshold method, a cluster centre is selected and all objects within a pre-specified threshold value from the centre are grouped together. A new cluster centre or seed is then selected, and the process is repeated for the unclustered points. Once an object is clustered with a seed, it is no longer considered for clustering with subsequent seeds. The **parallel threshold method** operates similarly except that several cluster centres are selected simultaneously and objects within the threshold level are grouped with the nearest centre. The **optimising partitioning method** differs from the two threshold procedures in that objects can later be reassigned to clusters to optimise an overall criterion, such as average within-cluster distance for a given number of clusters.

Two major disadvantages of the non-hierarchical procedures are that the number of clusters must be pre-specified and that the selection of cluster centres

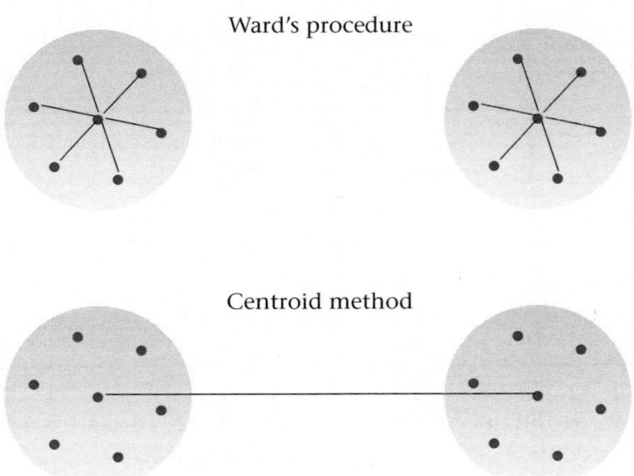

Figure 22.6 Other agglomerative clustering methods

is arbitrary. Furthermore, the clustering results may depend on how the centres are selected. Many non-hierarchical programs select the first k (k = number of clusters) cases without missing values as initial cluster centres. Thus, the clustering results may depend on the order of observations in the data. Yet non-hierarchical clustering is faster than hierarchical methods and has merit when the number of objects or observations is large. It has been suggested that the hierarchical and non-hierarchical methods be used in tandem. First, an initial clustering solution is obtained using a hierarchical procedure, such as average linkage or Ward's. The number of clusters and cluster centroids so obtained are used as inputs to the optimising partitioning method.[13]

The choice of a clustering method and choice of a distance measure are interrelated. For example, squared euclidean distances should be used with the Ward's and centroid methods. Several non-hierarchical procedures also use squared euclidean distances.

We will use Ward's procedure to illustrate hierarchical clustering. The output obtained by clustering the data of Table 22.1 is given in Table 22.2. Useful information is contained in the agglomeration schedule, which shows the number of cases or clusters being combined at each stage. The first line represents stage 1, with 19 clusters. Respondents 14 and 16 are combined at this stage, as shown in the columns labelled 'clusters combined'. The squared euclidean distance between these two respondents is given under the column labelled 'coefficient'. The column entitled 'stage cluster first appears' indicates the stage at which a cluster is first formed. To illustrate, an entry of 1 at stage 7 indicates that respondent 14 was first grouped at stage 1. The last column, 'next stage', indicates the stage at which another case (respondent) or cluster is combined with this one. Because the number in the first line of the last column is 7, we see that at stage 7, respondent 10 is combined with 14 and 16 to form a single cluster. Similarly, the second line represents stage 2 with 18 clusters. In stage 2, respondents 2 and 13 are grouped together.

Another important part of the output is contained in the icicle plot given in Figure 22.7. The columns correspond to the objects being clustered; in this case, they are the respondents labelled 1 to 20. The rows correspond to the number of

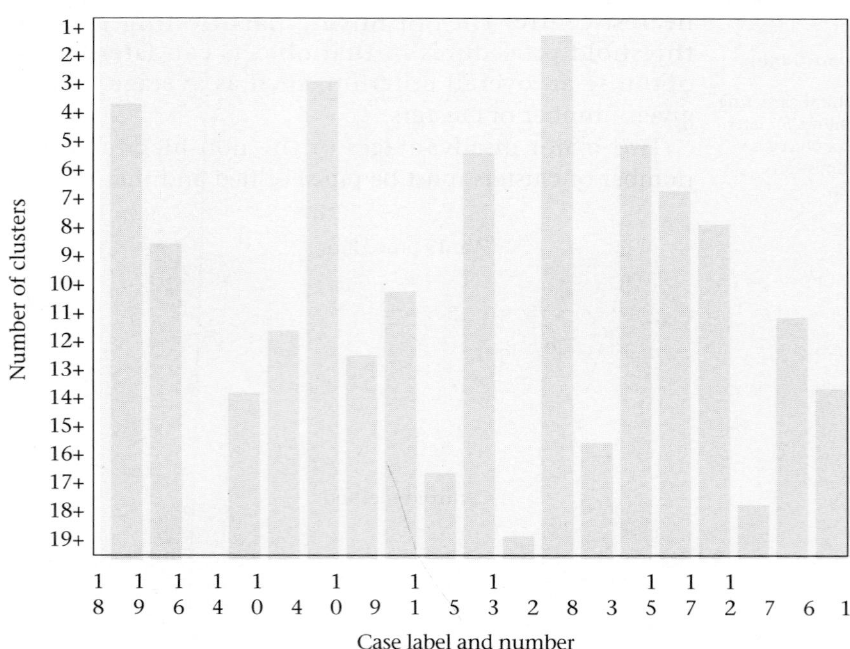

Figure 22.7
Vertical icicle plot using Ward's procedure

Table 22.2 Results of hierarchical clustering

Agglomeration schedule using Ward's procedure						
	Clusters combined			**Stage cluster first appears**		
Stage	**Cluster 1**	**Cluster 2**	**Coefficient**	**Cluster 1**	**Cluster 2**	**Next stage**
1	14	16	1.000000	0	0	7
2	2	13	2.500000	0	0	15
3	7	12	4.000000	0	0	10
4	5	11	5.500000	0	0	11
5	3	8	7.000000	0	0	16
6	1	6	8.500000	0	0	10
7	10	14	10.166667	0	1	9
8	9	20	12.666667	0	0	11
9	4	10	15.250000	0	7	12
10	1	7	18.250000	6	3	13
11	5	9	22.750000	4	8	15
12	4	19	27.500000	9	0	17
13	1	17	32.700001	10	0	14
14	1	15	40.500000	13	0	16
15	2	5	51.000000	2	11	18
16	1	3	63.125000	14	5	19
17	4	18	78.291664	12	0	18
18	2	4	171.291656	15	17	19
19	1	2	330.450012	16	18	0

Cluster membership of cases using Ward's procedure			
	Number of clusters		
Label Case	**4**	**3**	**2**
1	1	1	1
2	2	2	2
3	1	1	1
4	3	3	2
5	2	2	2
6	1	1	1
7	1	1	1
8	1	1	1
9	2	2	2
10	3	3	2
11	2	2	2
12	1	1	1
13	2	2	2
14	3	3	2
15	1	1	1
16	3	3	2
17	1	1	1
18	4	3	2
19	3	3	2
20	2	2	2

clusters. This figure is read from bottom to top. At first, all cases are considered as individual clusters. Since there are 20 respondents, there are 20 initial clusters. At the first step, the two closest objects are combined, resulting in 19 clusters. The last line of Figure 22.7 shows these 19 clusters. The two cases, respondents 14 and 16, that have been combined at this stage have no blank (white) space separating them. Row number 18 corresponds to the next stage, with 18 clusters. At this stage, respondents 2 and 13 are grouped together. Thus, at this stage there are 18 clusters; 16 of them consist of individual respondents, and two contain two respondents each. Each subsequent step leads to the formation of a new cluster in one of three ways: (1) two individual cases are grouped together, (2) a case is joined to an already existing cluster, or (3) two clusters are grouped together.

Another graphic device that is useful in displaying clustering results is the dendrogram (see Figure 22.8). The dendrogram is read from left to right. Vertical lines represent clusters that are joined together. The position of the line on the scale indicates the distances at which clusters were joined. Because many distances in the early stages are of similar magnitude, it is difficult to tell the sequence in which some of the early clusters are formed. It is clear, however, that in the last two stages, the distances at which the clusters are being combined are large. This information is useful in deciding on the number of clusters (see the next section).

It is also possible to obtain information on cluster membership of cases if the number of clusters is specified. Although this information can be discerned from the icicle plot, a tabular display is helpful. Table 22.2 contains the cluster membership for the cases, depending on whether the final solution contains two, three or four clusters. Information of this type can be obtained for any number of clusters and is useful for deciding on the number of clusters.

Deciding on the number of clusters

A major issue in cluster analysis is deciding on the number of clusters. Although there are no hard and fast rules, some guidelines are available.

1 Theoretical, conceptual or practical considerations may suggest a certain number of clusters. For example, if the purpose of clustering is to identify market segments, management may want a particular number of clusters.

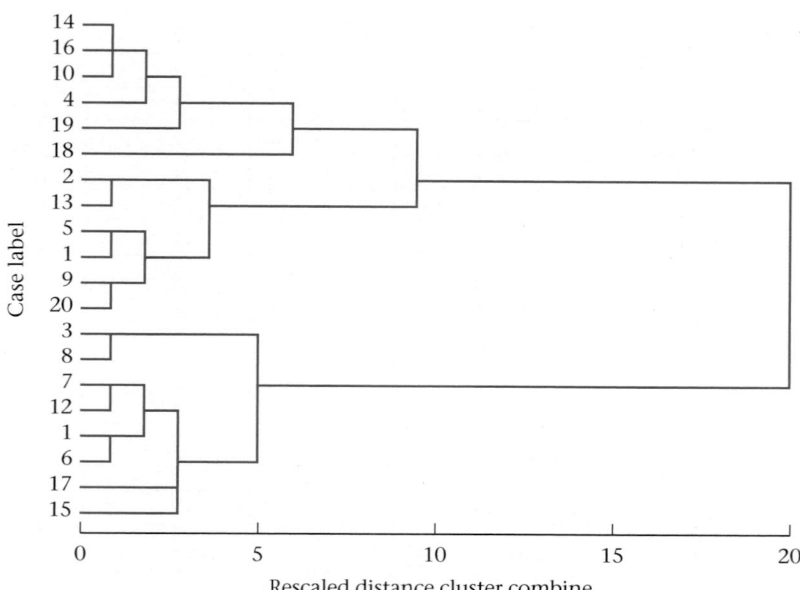

Figure 22.8 Dendrogram using Ward's procedure

2 In hierarchical clustering, the distances at which clusters are combined can be used as criteria. This information can be obtained from the agglomeration schedule or from the dendrogram. In our case, we see from the agglomeration schedule in Table 22.2 that the value in the 'coefficient' column suddenly more than doubles between stages 17 and 18. Likewise, at the last two stages of the dendrogram in Figure 22.8, the clusters are being combined at large distances. Therefore, it appears that a three-cluster solution is appropriate.
3 In non-hierarchical clustering, the ratio of total within-group variance to between-group variance can be plotted against the number of clusters. The point at which an elbow or a sharp bend occurs indicates an appropriate number of clusters. Increasing the number of clusters beyond this point is usually not worthwhile.
4 The relative sizes of the clusters should be meaningful. In Table 22.2, by making a simple frequency count of cluster membership, we see that a three-cluster solution results in clusters with eight, six and six elements. If we go to a four-cluster solution, however, the sizes of the clusters are eight, six, five and one. It is not meaningful to have a cluster with only one case, so a three-cluster solution is preferable in this situation.

Interpreting and profiling the clusters

Interpreting and profiling clusters involves examining the cluster centroids. The centroids represent the mean values of the objects contained in the cluster on each of the variables. The centroids enable us to describe each cluster by assigning it a name or label. If the clustering program does not print this information, it may be obtained through discriminant analysis. Table 22.3 gives the centroids or mean values for each cluster in our example. Cluster 1 has relatively high values on variables V_1 (Shopping is fun) and V_3 (I combine shopping with eating out). It also has a low value on V_5 (I don't care about shopping). Hence cluster 1 could be labelled 'fun-loving and concerned shoppers'. This cluster consists of cases 1, 3, 6, 7, 8, 12, 15 and 17. Cluster 2 is just the opposite, with low values on V_1 and V_3 and a high value on V_5 and this cluster could be labelled 'apathetic shoppers'. Members of cluster 2 are cases 2, 5, 9, 11, 13 and 20. Cluster 3 has high values on V_2 (Shopping upsets my budget), V_4 (I try to get the best buys while shopping) and V_6 (You can save a lot of money by comparing prices). Thus, this cluster could be labelled 'economical shoppers'. Cluster 3 is composed of cases 4, 10, 14, 16, 18 and 19. It is often helpful to profile the clusters in terms of variables that were not used for clustering, such as demographic, psychographic, product usage, media usage or other variables. For example, the clusters may have been derived based on benefits sought. Further profiling may be done in terms of demographic and psychographic variables to target marketing efforts for each cluster. The variables that significantly differentiate between clusters can be identified via discriminant analysis and one-way analysis of variance.

Table 22.3 Cluster centroids

	Means of variables					
Cluster number	V_1	V_2	V_3	V_4	V_5	V_6
1	5.750	3.625	6.000	3.125	1.750	3.875
2	1.667	3.000	1.833	3.500	5.500	3.333
3	3.500	5.833	3.333	6.000	3.500	6.000

Assessing reliability and validity

Given the several judgements entailed in cluster analysis, no clustering solution should be accepted without some assessment of its reliability and validity. Formal procedures for assessing the reliability and validity of clustering solutions are complex and not fully defensible.[14] Hence, we omit them here. The following procedures, however, provide adequate checks on the quality of clustering results.

1 Perform cluster analysis on the same data using different distance measures. Compare the results across measures to determine the stability of the solutions.
2 Use different methods of clustering and compare the results.
3 Split the data randomly into halves. Perform clustering separately on each half. Compare cluster centroids across the two sub-samples.
4 Delete variables randomly. Perform clustering based on the reduced set of variables. Compare the results with those obtained by clustering based on the entire set of variables.
5 In non-hierarchical clustering, the solution may depend on the order of cases in the data set. Make multiple runs using different order of cases until the solution stabilises.

We further illustrate hierarchical clustering with a study of differences in marketing strategy among British, Japanese and US firms.

EXAMPLE

It is a small world[15]

Data for a study of British, Japanese and US competitors were obtained from detailed personal interviews with chief executives and top marketing decision-makers for defined product groups in 90 companies. To control for market differences, the methodology was based upon matching 30 British companies with their major Japanese and American competitors in the British market. The study involved 30 triads of companies, each composed of a British, US and Japanese business that competed directly with one another.

Most of the data on the characteristics of the companies' performance, strategy, and organisation were collected on five-point semantic differential scales. The first stage of the analysis involved factor analysis of variables describing the firms' strategies and marketing activities. The factor scores were used to identify groups of similar companies using Ward's hierarchical clustering routine. A six-cluster solution was developed.

Strategic clusters

Cluster	I	II	III	IV	V	VI
Name	Innovators	Quality marketeers	Price promotors	Product marketeers	Mature marketeers	Aggressive pushers
Size	22	11	14	13	13	17
Successful (%)	55	100	36	38	77	41
Nationality (%)						
British	23	18	64	38	31	29
Japanese	59	46	22	31	15	18
American	18	36	14	31	54	53

Membership in the six clusters was then interpreted against the original performance, strategy and organisational variables. All the clusters contained some successful companies, although some contained significantly more than others. The clusters lent support to the hypothesis that successful companies were similar irrespective of nationality, since British, Japanese and US companies were found in all the clusters. There was, however, a preponderance of Japanese companies in the more successful clusters and a predominance of British companies in the two least successful clusters. Apparently, Japanese companies do not deploy strategies that are unique to them; rather, more of them pursue strategies that work effectively in the British market. ■

The findings indicate that there are generic strategies that describe successful companies irrespective of their industry. Three successful strategies can be identified. The first is the quality marketeers' strategy. These companies have strengths in marketing and research and development. They concentrate their technical developments on achieving high quality rather than pure innovation. These companies are characterised by entrepreneurial organisations, long-range planning, and well-communicated sense of mission. The second generic strategy is that of the innovators, who are weaker on advanced R & D but are entrepreneurial and driven by a quest for innovation. The last successful group is the mature marketeers, who are highly profit-oriented and have in-depth marketing skills. All three appear to consist of highly marketing-oriented business.

APPLICATIONS OF NON-HIERARCHICAL CLUSTERING

We illustrate the non-hierarchical procedure using the data in Table 22.1 and an optimising partitioning method. Based on the results of hierarchical clustering, a three-cluster solution was pre-specified. The results are presented in Table 22.4. The initial cluster centres are the values of the first three cases. The classification cluster centres are interim centres used for the assignment of cases. Each case is assigned to the nearest classification cluster centre. The classification centres are updated until the stopping criteria are reached. The final cluster centres represent the variable means for the cases in the final clusters.

Table 22.4 Results of non-hierarchical clustering

Initial cluster centres

Cluster	V_1	V_2	V_3	V_4	V_5	V_6
1	4.0000	6.0000	3.0000	7.0000	2.0000	7.0000
2	2.0000	3.0000	2.0000	4.0000	7.0000	2.0000
3	7.0000	2.0000	6.0000	4.0000	1.0000	3.0000

Classification cluster centres

Cluster	V_1	V_2	V_3	V_4	V_5	V_6
1	3.8135	5.8992	3.2522	6.4891	2.5149	6.6957
2	1.8507	3.0234	1.8327	3.7864	6.4436	2.5056
3	6.3558	2.8356	6.1576	3.6736	1.3047	3.2010

Table 24.4 (continued)

Case listing of cluster membership		
Case ID	Cluster	Distance
1	3	1.780
2	2	2.254
3	3	1.174
4	1	1.882
5	2	2.525
6	3	2.340
7	3	1.862
8	3	1.410
9	2	1.843
10	1	2.112
11	2	1.923
12	3	2.400
13	2	3.382
14	1	1.772
15	3	3.605
16	1	2.137
17	3	3.760
18	1	4.421
19	1	0.853
20	2	0.813

Final cluster centres						
Cluster	V_1	V_2	V_3	V_4	V_5	V_6
1	3.5000	5.8333	3.3333	6.0000	3.5000	6.0000
2	1.6667	3.0000	1.8333	3.5000	5.5000	3.3333
3	5.7500	3.6250	6.0000	3.1250	1.7500	3.8750

Distances between final cluster centres			
Cluster	1	2	3
1	0.0000		
2	5.5678	0.0000	
3	5.7353	6.9944	0.0000

Analysis of variance						
Variable	Cluster MS	df	Error MS	df	F	p
V_1	29.1083	2	0.6078	17.0	47.8879	0.000
V_2	13.5458	2	0.6299	17.0	21.5047	0.000
V_3	31.3917	2	0.8333	17.0	37.6700	0.000
V_4	15.7125	2	0.7279	17.0	21.5848	0.000
V_5	24.1500	2	0.7353	17.0	32.8440	0.000
V_6	12.1708	2	1.0711	17.0	11.3632	0.001

Table 2.4 (continued)

Number of cases in each cluster		
Cluster	**Unweighted cases**	**Weighted cases**
1	6.0	6.0
2	6.0	6.0
3	8.0	8.0
Missing	0.0	
Total	20.0	20.0

Table 22.4 also displays cluster membership and the distance between each case and its classification centre. Note that the cluster memberships given in Table 22.2 (hierarchical clustering) and Table 22.4 (non-hierarchical clustering) are identical. (Cluster 1 of Table 22.2 is labelled cluster 3 in Table 22.4, and cluster 3 of Table 22.2 is labelled cluster 1 in Table 22.4.) The distances between the final cluster centres indicate that the pairs of clusters are well separated. The univariate F test for each clustering variable is presented. These F tests are only descriptive. Because the cases or objects are systematically assigned to clusters to maximise differences on the clustering variables, the resulting probabilities should not be interpreted as testing the null hypothesis of no differences among clusters.

The following example of hospital choice further illustrates non-hierarchical clustering.

EXAMPLE

Segmentation with surgical precision[16]

Cluster analysis was used to classify respondents who preferred hospitals for in-patient care to identify hospital preference segments. The clustering was based on the reasons respondents gave for preferring a hospital. The demographic profiles of the grouped respondents were compared to learn whether the segments could be identified efficiently.

Using 'Quick Cluster', a minimum variance clustering method in the SPSS package, respondents were grouped based on their answers to hospital preference items. The squared euclidean distances between all clustering variables were minimised. Because different individuals perceive scales of importance differently, each individual's ratings were normalised before clustering. The results indicated that the respondents could be best classified into four clusters. The cross-validation procedure for cluster analysis was run twice, on halves of the total sample.

As expected, the four groups differed substantially by their distributions and average responses to the reasons for their hospital preferences. The names assigned to the four groups reflected the demographic characteristics and reasons for hospital preferences: '*old-fashioned*', '*affluent*', '*value conscious*', and '*professional want-it-alls*'. ■

CLUSTERING VARIABLES

Sometimes cluster analysis is also used for clustering variables to identify homogeneous groups. In this instance, the units used for analysis are the variables, and the distance measures are computed for all pairs of variables. For example, the correlation coefficient, either the absolute value or with the sign, can be used as a measure of similarity (the opposite of distance) between variables.

Hierarchical clustering of variables can aid in the identification of unique variables, or variables that make a unique contribution to the data. Clustering can also be used to reduce the number of variables. Associated with each cluster is a linear combination of the variables in the cluster, called the cluster component. A large set of variables can often be replaced by the set of cluster components with little loss of information. A given number of cluster components does not generally explain as much variance as the same number of principal components, however. Why, then, should the clustering of variables be used? Cluster components are usually easier to interpret than the principal components, even if the latter are rotated. We illustrate the clustering of variables with an example from advertising research. A study was conducted to identify feelings that are precipitated by advertising. A total of 655 feelings were reduced to a set of 180 that were judged by respondents to be most likely to be stimulated by advertising. This group was clustered on the basis of judgements of similarity between feelings resulting in 31 feeling clusters. These were divided into 16 positive and 15 negative clusters.[17]

INTERNET AND COMPUTER APPLICATIONS

SPSS[18]

The main program for hierarchical clustering of objects or cases is CLUSTER. Different distance measures can be computed, and all the hierarchical clustering procedures discussed here are available. For non-hierarchical clustering, the QUICK CLUSTER program can be used. This program is particularly helpful for clustering a large number of cases. All the default options will result in a *k*-means clustering. To cluster variables, the distance measures should be computed across variables using the PROXIMITIES program. This proximity matrix can be read into CLUSTER to obtain a grouping of the variables.

SAS

The CLUSTER program can be used for the hierarchical clustering of cases or objects. All the clustering procedures discussed here are available, as well as some additional ones. Non-hierarchical clustering of cases or objects can be accomplished using FASTCLUS. For clustering of variables, the VARCLUS program can be used. Dendrograms are not automatically computed but can be obtained using the TREE program.

BMDP

The main program for the clustering of cases using the hierarchical procedures is 2M. This program allows the use of several distance measures, but it permits the use of only single linkage, centroid, or *k* nearest neighbour clustering procedures. For non-hierarchical clustering, the KM program can be used for performing *k*-means clustering of cases. Clustering of variables can be done using the 1M program. It permits the use of single linkage, complete linkage and average linkage procedures. A special program, 3M, is available for constructing block clusters for categorical data. Subsets of cases are grouped into clusters that are alike for subsets of variables.

Minitab

Cluster analysis can be accessed in the Multivariate>Cluster observation function. Also available are Clustering of Variables and Cluster *K*-Means.

Excel

At the time of writing, cluster analysis was not available.

SUMMARY

Cluster analysis is used for classifying objects or cases, and sometimes variables, into relatively homogeneous groups. The groups or clusters are suggested by the data and are not defined *a priori*.

The variables on which the clustering is based should be selected based on past research, theory, the hypotheses being tested, or the judgement of the researcher. An appropriate measure of distance or similarity should be selected. The most commonly used measure is the euclidean distance or its square.

Clustering procedures may be hierarchical or non-hierarchical. Hierarchical clustering is characterised by the development of a hierarchy or treelike structure. Hierarchical methods can be agglomerative or divisive. Agglomerative methods consist of linkage methods, variance methods and centroid methods. Linkage methods are composed of single linkage, complete linkage and average linkage. A commonly used variance method is the Ward's procedure. The non-hierarchical methods are frequently referred to as *k*-means clustering. These methods can be classified as sequential threshold, parallel threshold, and optimising partitioning. Hierarchical and non-hierarchical methods can be used in tandem. The choice of a clustering procedure and the choice of a distance measure are interrelated.

The number of clusters may be based on theoretical, conceptual or practical considerations. In hierarchical clustering, the distances at which the clusters are being combined is an important criterion. The relative sizes of the clusters should be meaningful. The clusters should be interpreted in terms of cluster centroids. It is often helpful to profile the clusters in terms of variables that were not used for clustering. The reliability and validity of the clustering solutions may be assessed in different ways.

QUESTIONS AND PROBLEMS

1 Discuss the similarity and difference between cluster analysis and discriminant analysis.

2 What is a 'cluster'?

3 What are some of the uses of cluster analysis in marketing?

4 Briefly define the following terms: dendrogram, icicle plot, agglomeration schedule, and cluster membership.

5 What is the most commonly used measure of similarity in cluster analysis?

6 Present a classification of clustering procedures.

7 Upon what basis may a researcher decide which variables should be selected to formulate a clustering problem?

8 Why is the average linkage method usually preferred to single linkage and complete linkage?

9 What are the two major disadvantages of non-hierarchical clustering procedures?

10 What guidelines are available for deciding the number of clusters?

11 What is involved in the interpretation of clusters?

12 What role may qualitative methods play in the interpretation of clusters?

13 What are some of the additional variables used for profiling the clusters?

14 Describe some procedures available for assessing the quality of clustering solutions.

15 How is cluster analysis used to group variables?

NOTES

1 Birks, D.F. and Birts, A.N., 'Cash Management Market Segmentation', in Birks. D.F., (ed.), *Global Cash Management in Europe* (Houndsmill: Basingstoke, Macmillan, 1998), 83–109.

2 Giges, N., 'World's Product Parity Perception High', *Advertising Age* (20 June 1988).

3 For an recent application of cluster analysis, see Day, G.S. and Nedungali, P., 'Managerial Representation of Competitive Advantage', *Journal of Marketing* 58 (April 1994), 31–44.

4 Overlapping clustering methods that permit an object to be grouped into more than one cluster are also available. See Arabie, P., Carroll, J.D., DeSarbo, W. and Wind, J., 'Overlapping Clustering: A New Method for Product Positioning', *Journal of Marketing Research* 18 (August 1981), 310–17; and Arahie, P. and Carroll, J.D., 'MAPCLUS: A Hierarchical Programming Approach to Fitting the ADCLUS Model', *Psychometrika* (June 1980), 211–35.

5 Excellent discussions on the various aspects of cluster analysis may be found in Aldenderfer, M.S. and Blashfield, R.K., *Cluster Analysis* (Beverly Hills: Sage Publications, 1984); Everitt, B., *Cluster Analysis*, 2nd edn (New York: Halsted Press, 1980); and Romsburg, H.C., *Cluster Analysis for Researchers* (Belmont, CA: Lifetime Learning Publications, 1984).

6 These applications of cluster analysis in marketing have been identified by Punj, G. and Stewart, D., 'Cluster Analysis in Marketing Research: Review and Suggestions for Application', *Journal of Marketing Research* 20 (May 1983), 134–48.

7 For use of cluster analysis for segmentation, see 'Using Cluster Analysis for Segmentation', *Sawtooth News* 10 (Winter 1994–95), 6–7.

8 Aldenderfer, M.S. and Blashfield, R.K., *Cluster Analysis* (Beverly Hills: Sage Publications, 1984), 7–16.

9 For a detailed discussion on the different measures of similarity, and formulas for computing them, see Romsburg, H.C., *Cluster Analysis for Researchers* (Belmont, CA: Lifetime Learning Publications, 1984).

10 Hair, Jr., J.E. Anderson, R.E., Tatham, R.L. and Black, W.C., *Multivariate Data Analysis with Readings*, 4th edn (Englewood Cliffs, NJ: Prentice Hall, 1995), 420–83.

11 For further discussion of the issues involved in standardisation, see Romsburg, H.C., *Cluster Analysis for Researchers* (Belmont, CA: Lifelong Learning Publications, 1984), 77–91.

12 Milligan, G., 'An Examination of the Effect of Six Types of Error Perturbation on Fifteen Clustering Algorithms', *Psychometrika* 45 (September 1980), 325–42.

13 Punj, G. and Stewart, D., 'Cluster Analysis in Marketing Research: Reviews and Suggestions for Application', *Journal of Marketing Research* 20 (May 1983), 134–48.

14 For a formal discussion of reliability, validity, and significance testing in cluster analysis, see Funkhouser, G.R., 'A Note on the Reliability of Certain Clustering Algorithms', *Journal of Marketing Research* 30 (February 1983), 99–102; Klastorin, T.D., 'Assessing Cluster Analysis Results', *Journal of Marketing Research* 20 (February 1983), 92–98; and Arnold, S.J., 'A Test for Clusters', *Journal of Marketing Research* 16 (November 1979), 545–51.

15 Doyle, P., Saunders, J. and Wong, V., 'International Marketing Strategies and Organisations: A Study of U.S., Japanese, and British Competitors', in Bloom, P., Winer, R., Kassarjian, H.H., Scammon, D.L., Weitz, B., Spekman, R.E., Mahajan, V. and Levy, M., (eds), *Enhancing Knowledge Development in Marketing*, Series no. 55 (Chicago: American Marketing Association, 1989), 100–104.

16 Woodside, A.G., Nielsen, R.L., Walters, F. and Muller, G.D., 'Preference Segmentation of Health Care Services: The Old-Fashioneds, Value Conscious, Affluents, and Professional Want-It-Alls', *Journal of Health Care Marketing* (June 1988), 14–24.

17 Aaker, D.A., Stayman, D.M. and Vezina, R., 'Identifying Feelings Elicited by Advertising', *Psychology & Marketing* (Spring 1988), 1–16.

18 Einspruch, E.L., *An Introductory Guide to SPSS for Windows* (Thousand Oaks, CA: Sage Publications, 1998); Spector, P.E., *SAS Programming for Researchers and Social Scientists* (Thousand Oaks, CA: Sage Publications, 1993); Norat, M.A., Software Reviews, *Economic Journal: The Journal of the Royal Economic Society* 107 (May 1997), 857–82; Seiter, C., 'The Statistical Difference', *Macworld* 10 (10) (October 1993), 116–21.

Chapter 23

Multidimensional scaling and conjoint analysis

OBJECTIVES

After reading this chapter, the student should be able to:

1 discuss the basic concept and scope of multidimensional scaling (MDS) in marketing research and describe its various applications;
2 describe the steps involved in multidimensional scaling of perception data including formulating the problem, obtaining input data, selecting an MDS procedure, deciding on the number of dimensions, labelling the dimensions and interpreting the configuration, and assessing reliability and validity;
3 explain the multidimensional scaling of preference data and distinguish between internal and external analysis of preferences;
4 explain correspondence analysis and discuss its advantages and disadvantages;
5 understand the relationship between MDS, discriminant analysis, and factor analysis;
6 discuss the basic concepts of conjoint analysis, contrast it with MDS, and discuss its various applications;
7 describe the procedure for conducting conjoint analysis including formulating the problem, constructing the stimuli, deciding the form of input data, selecting a conjoint analysis procedure, interpreting the results, and assessing reliability and validity;
8 define the concept of hybrid conjoint analysis and explain how it simplifies the data collection task.

Multidimensional scaling represents the perceptions and preferences of respondents geometrically in a spatial map. Conjoint analysis determines the relative importance consumers attach to salient attributes and the utilities they attach to the levels of attributes

OVERVIEW

This final chapter on data analysis presents two related techniques for analysing consumer perceptions and preferences: multidimensional scaling (MDS) and conjoint analysis. We outline and illustrate the steps involved in conducting MDS and discuss the relationships among MDS, factor analysis, and discriminant analysis. Then we describe conjoint analysis and present a step-by-step procedure for conducting it. We also provide brief coverage of hybrid conjoint models.

We begin with examples illustrating MDS and conjoint analysis.

STATISTICS AND TERMS ASSOCIATED WITH MULTIDIMENSIONAL SCALING

The important statistics and terms associated with MDS include the following:

Similarity judgements. Similarity judgements are ratings on all possible pairs of brands or other stimuli in terms of their similarity using a Likert-type scale.
Preference rankings. Preference rankings are rank orderings of the brands or other stimuli from the most preferred to the least preferred. They are normally obtained from the respondents.
Stress. Stress is a lack-of-fit measure; higher values of stress indicate poorer fits.
R-square. *R*-square is a squared correlation index that indicates the proportion of variance of the optimally scaled data that can be accounted for by the MDS procedure.
Spatial map. Perceived relationships among brands or other stimuli are represented as geometric relationships among points in a multidimensional space called a spatial map.
Coordinates. Coordinates indicate the positioning of a brand or a stimulus in a spatial map.
Unfolding. The representation of both brands and respondents as points in the same space is referred to as unfolding.

CONDUCTING MULTIDIMENSIONAL SCALING

Figure 23.1 shows the steps in MDS. The researcher must formulate the MDS problem carefully because a variety of data may be used as input into MDS. The researcher must also determine an appropriate form in which data should be obtained and select an MDS procedure for analysing the data. An important aspect of the solution involves determining the number of dimensions for the spatial map. Also, the axes of the map should be labelled and the derived configuration interpreted. Finally, the researcher must assess the quality of the results obtained.[4] We describe each of these steps, beginning with problem formulation.

Formulating the problem

Formulating the problem requires that the researcher specify the purpose for which the MDS results would be used and select the brands or other stimuli to be included in the analysis. The number of brands or stimuli selected and the specific brands included determine the nature of the resulting dimensions and configurations. At a minimum, eight brands or stimuli should be included to

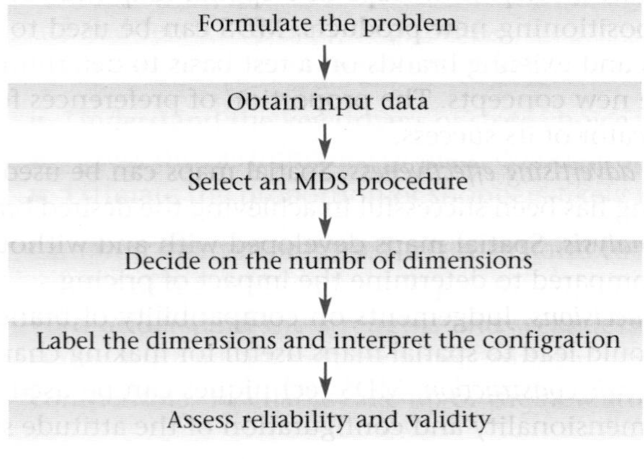

Figure 23.1 Conducting multidimensional scaling

obtain a well-defined spatial map. Including more than 25 brands is likely to be cumbersome and may result in respondent fatigue.

The decision regarding which specific brands or stimuli to include should be made carefully. Suppose that a researcher is interested in obtaining consumer perceptions of cars. If luxury cars are not included in the stimulus set, this dimension may not emerge in the results. The choice of the number and specific brands or stimuli to be included should be based on the statement of the marketing research problem, theory and the judgement of the researcher.

Multidimensional scaling will be illustrated in the context of obtaining a spatial map for ten brands of beer. These brands are Becks, Budvar, Budweiser, Carlsberg, Corona, Grolsch, Harp, Holsten, San Miquel and Stella Artois. Given the list of brands, the next question, then, is: how should we obtain data on these ten brands?

Obtaining input data

As shown in Figure 23.2, input data obtained from the respondents may be related to perceptions or preferences. Perception data, which may be direct or derived, is discussed first.

Perception data: direct approaches. In direct approaches to gathering perception data, respondents are asked to judge how similar or dissimilar various brands or stimuli are, using their own criteria. Respondents are often required to rate all possible pairs of brands or stimuli in terms of similarity on a Likert scale. These data are referred to as similarity judgements. For example, similarity judgements on all the possible pairs of bottled beer brands may be obtained in the following manner:

	Very dissimilar						**Very similar**
Becks versus Budweiser	1	2	3	4	5	6	7
Budweiser versus Carlsberg	1	2	3	4	5	6	7
Carlsberg versus Corona	1	2	3	4	5	6	7
....							
Becks versus Stella Artois	1	2	3	4	5	6	7

The number of pairs to be evaluated is $n(n - 1)/2$, where n is the number of stimuli. Other procedures are also available. Respondents could be asked to rank-order all the possible pairs from the most similar to the least similar. In another method, the respondent rank-orders the brands in terms of their similarity to an anchor brand. Each brand, in turn, serves as the anchor.

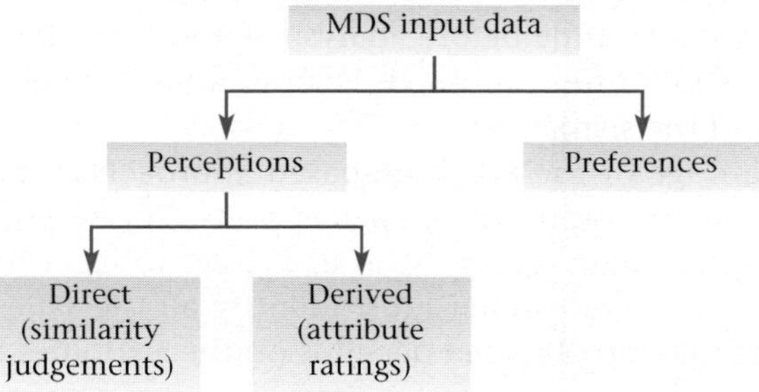

Figure 23.2 Input data for multidimensional scaling

In our example, the direct approach was adopted. Subjects were asked to provide similarity judgements for all 45 (10 × 9/2) pairs of bottled beer brands, using a seven-point scale. The data obtained from one respondent are given in Table 23.1.

Table 23.1 Similarity ratings of bottle beer brands

	Becks	*Budvar*	*Budweiser*	*Carlsberg*	*Corona*	*Grolsch*	*Harp*	*Holsten*	*San Miguel*	*Stella Artois*
Becks										
Budvar	5									
Budweiser	6	7								
Carlsberg	4	6	6							
Corona	2	3	4	5						
Grolsch	3	3	4	4	5					
Harp	2	2	2	3	5	5				
Holsten	2	2	2	2	6	5	6			
San Miguel	2	2	2	2	6	6	7	6		
Stella Artois	1	2	4	2	4	3	3	4	3	

Derived approaches
In MDS, attribute-based approaches to collecting perception data requiring respondents to rate the stimuli on the identified attributes using semantic differential or Likert scales.

Perception data: derived approaches. Derived approaches to collecting perception data are attribute-based approaches requiring the respondents to rate the brands or stimuli on the identified attributes using semantic differential or Likert scales.[5] For example, the different brands of bottled beer may be rated on attributes like these:

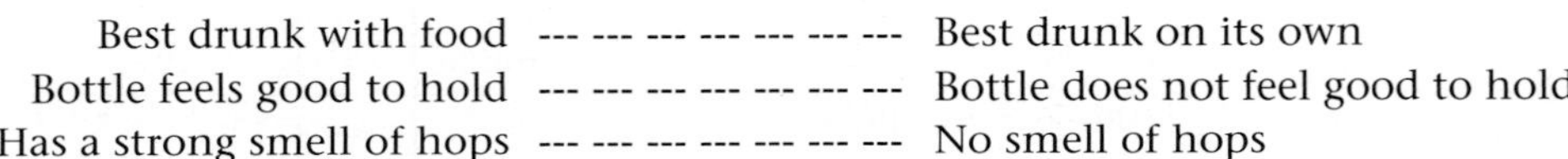

Best drunk with food --- --- --- --- --- --- --- Best drunk on its own
Bottle feels good to hold --- --- --- --- --- --- --- Bottle does not feel good to hold
Has a strong smell of hops --- --- --- --- --- --- --- No smell of hops

Sometimes an ideal brand is also included in the stimulus set. The respondents are asked to evaluate their hypothetical ideal brand on the same set of attributes. If attribute ratings are obtained, a similarity measure (such as Euclidean distance) is derived for each pair of brands.

Direct v. derived approaches. Direct approaches have the advantage that the researcher does not have to identify a set of salient attributes. Respondents make similarity judgements using their own criteria, as they would under normal circumstances. The disadvantages are that the criteria are influenced by the brands or stimuli being evaluated. If the various brands of cars being evaluated are in the same price range, then price will not emerge as an important factor. It may be difficult to determine before analysis if and how the individual respondent's judgements should be combined. Furthermore, it may be difficult to label the dimensions of the spatial map.

The advantage of the attribute-based approach is that it is easy to identify respondents with homogeneous perceptions. The respondents can be clustered based on the attribute ratings. It is also easier to label the dimensions. A disadvantage is that the researcher must identify all the salient attributes, a difficult task. The spatial map obtained depends on the attributes identified.

The direct approaches are more frequently used than the attribute-based approaches. It may, however, be best to use both these approaches in a complementary way. Direct similarity judgements may be used for obtaining the spatial map, and attribute ratings may be used as an aid to interpreting the dimensions of the perceptual map. Similar procedures are used for preference data.

Preference data. Preference data order the brands or stimuli in terms of respondents' preference for some property. A common way in which such data are obtained is preference rankings. Respondents are required to rank the brands from the most preferred to the least preferred. Alternatively, respondents may be required to make paired comparisons and indicate which brand in a pair they prefer. Another method is to obtain preference ratings for the various brands. (The rank-order, paired comparison, and rating scales were discussed in Chapters 10 and 11 on scaling techniques.) When spatial maps are based on preference data, distance implies differences in preference. The configuration derived from preference data may differ greatly from that obtained from similarity data. Two brands may be perceived as different in a similarity map yet similar in a preference map, and vice versa. For example, Becks and Harp may be perceived by a group of respondents as very different brands and thus appear far apart on a perception map. But these two brands may be about equally preferred and may appear close together on a preference map. We will continue using the perception data obtained in the bottled beer example to illustrate the MDS procedure and then consider the scaling of preference data.

Selecting an MDS procedure

Non-metric MDS
A type of multidimensional scaling which assumes that the input data are ordinal.

Metric MDS
A multidimensional scaling method that assumes that input data are metric.

Selecting a specific MDS procedure depends on whether perception or preference data are being scaled or whether the analysis requires both kinds of data. The nature of the input data is also a determining factor. **Non-metric MDS** procedures assume that the input data are ordinal, but they result in metric output. The distances in the resulting spatial map may be assumed to be interval scaled. These procedures find, in a given dimensionality, a spatial map whose rank orders of estimated distances between brands or stimuli best preserve or reproduce the input rank orders. In contrast, **metric MDS** methods assume that input data are metric. Since the output is also metric, a stronger relationship between the output and input data is maintained, and the metric (interval or ratio) qualities of the input data are preserved. The metric and non-metric methods produce similar results.[6]

Another factor influencing the selection of a procedure is whether the MDS analysis will be conducted at the individual respondent level or at an aggregate level. In individual-level analysis, the data are analysed separately for each respondent, resulting in a spatial map for each respondent. Although individual-level analysis is useful from a research perspective, it is not appealing from a managerial standpoint. Marketing strategies are typically formulated at the segment or aggregate level, rather than at the individual level. If aggregate-level analysis is conducted, some assumptions must be made in aggregating individual data. Typically, it is assumed that all respondents use the same dimensions to evaluate the brands or stimuli, but that different respondents weight these common dimensions differentially.

The data of Table 23.1 were treated as rank-ordered and scaled using a non-metric procedure. Because these data were provided by one respondent, an individual-level analysis was conducted. Spatial maps were obtained in one to four dimensions, and then a decision on an appropriate number of dimensions was made. This decision is central to all MDS analyses; therefore, it is explored in greater detail in the following section.

Deciding on the number of dimensions

The objective in MDS is to obtain a spatial map that best fits the input data in the smallest number of dimensions. Spatial maps are computed in such a way that the fit improves as the number of dimensions increases, however. Therefore, a compromise has to be made. The fit of an MDS solution is commonly assessed by the stress measure. Stress is a lack-of-fit measure; higher values of stress indicate poorer fits. The following guidelines are suggested for determining the number of dimensions.

1 *A priori knowledge*. Theory or past research may suggest a particular number of dimensions.
2 *Interpretability of the spatial map*. Generally, it is difficult to interpret configurations or maps derived in more than three dimensions.
3 *Elbow criterion*. A plot of stress versus dimensionality should be examined. The points in this plot usually form a convex pattern, as shown in Figure 23.3. The point at which an elbow or a sharp bend occurs indicates an appropriate number of dimensions. Increasing the number of dimensions beyond this point is usually not worth the improvement in fit. This criterion for determining the number of dimensions is called the **elbow criterion**
4 *Ease of use*. It is generally easier to work with two-dimensional maps or configurations than with those involving more dimensions.
5 *Statistical approaches*. For the sophisticated user, statistical approaches are also available for determining the dimensionality.[7]

Elbow criterion
A plot of stress versus dimensionality used in MDS. The point at which an elbow or a sharp bend occurs indicates an appropriate dimensionality.

Based on the plot of stress versus dimensionality (Figure 23.3), interpretability of the spatial map, and ease-of-use criteria, it was decided to retain a two-dimensional solution. This is shown in Figure 23.4.

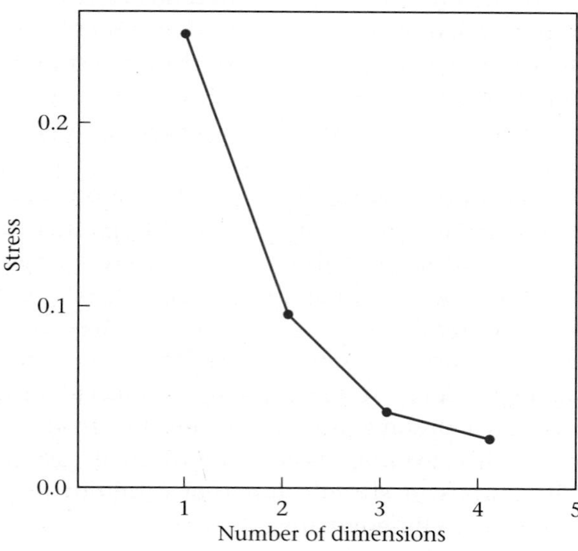

Figure 23.3
Plot of stress versus dimensionality

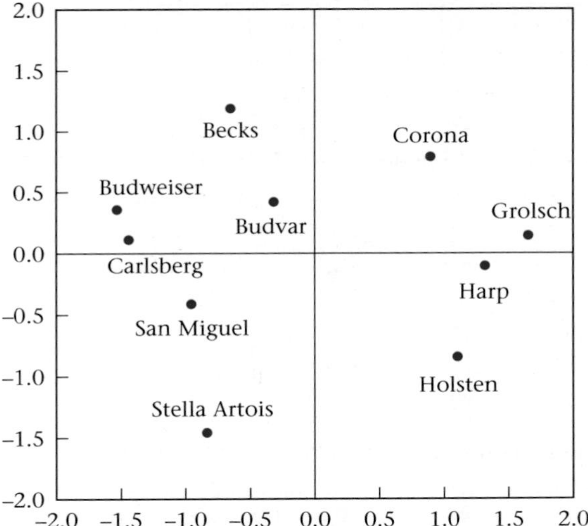

Figure 23.4
A spatial map of beer brands

Labelling the dimensions and interpreting the configuration

Once a spatial map is developed, the dimensions must be labelled and the configuration interpreted. Labelling the dimensions requires subjective judgement on the part of the researcher. The following guidelines can assist in this task:

1 Even if direct similarity judgements are obtained, ratings of the brands on researcher supplied attributes may still be collected. Using statistical methods such as regression these attribute vectors may be fitted in the spatial map (see Figure 23.5). The axes may then be labelled for the attributes with which they are most closely aligned.
2 After providing direct similarity or preference data, the respondents may be asked to indicate the criteria they used in making their evaluations. These criteria may then be subjectively related to the spatial map to label the dimensions.
3 If possible, the respondents can be shown their spatial maps and asked to label the dimensions by inspecting the configurations.
4 If objective characteristics of the brands are available (e.g. horsepower or kilometres per litre for cars), these could be used as an aid in interpreting the subjective dimensions of the spatial maps.

Often, the dimensions represent more than one attribute. The configuration or the spatial map may be interpreted by examining the coordinates and relative positions of the brands. For example, brands located near each other compete more fiercely than brands far apart. An isolated brand has a unique image. Brands that are farther along in the direction of a descriptor are stronger on that characteristic than others. Thus, the strengths and weaknesses of each product can be understood. Gaps in the spatial map may indicate potential opportunities for introducing new products.

In Figure 23.5, the vertical axis may be labelled as 'strength' representing the power of particular flavours and smells when the beer is first tasted. Brands with high positive values on this axis include Grolsch, Harp, Holsten and Corona. The horizontal axis may be labelled as 'aftertaste' representing the flavour of the beer that lingers on the palate after the beer has been drunk. Brands with large negative values on this dimension include Stella Artois, Holsten and San Miguel. Note that negative scores on the map do not necessarily represent negative

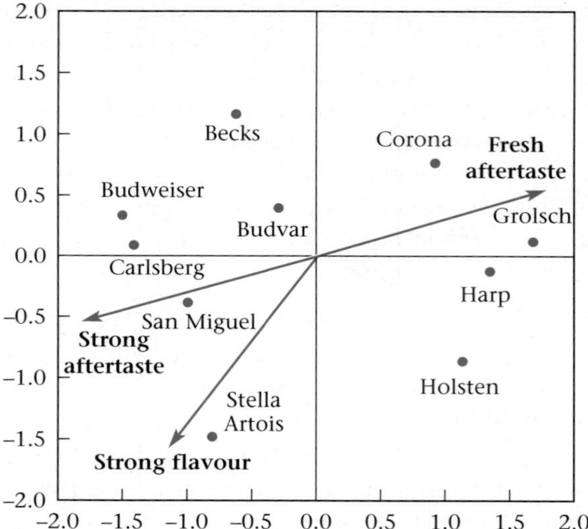

Figure 23.5
Using attribute vectors to label dimensions

characteristics for certain consumers. Thus, the strength of flavour from initial smell and taste through to a strong aftertaste in a brand such as Stella Artois may be seen as desirable characteristics for many beer drinkers.

The gaps in the spatial map indicate potential opportunities for new brands, for example, one that has a strong initial taste but does not have a strong lingering aftertaste.

Assessing reliability and validity

The input data, and consequently the MDS solutions, are invariably subject to substantial random variability. Hence, it is necessary that some assessment be made of the reliability and validity of MDS solutions. The following guidelines are suggested.

1 The index of fit, or *R*-square, should be examined. This is a squared correlation index that indicates the proportion of variance of the optimally scaled data that can be accounted for by the MDS procedure. Thus, it indicates how well the MDS model fits the input data. Although higher values of *R*-square are desirable, values of 0.60 or better are considered acceptable.

2 Stress values are also indicative of the quality of MDS solutions. Whereas *R*-square is a measure of goodness-of-fit, stress measures badness-of-fit, or the proportion of variance of the optimally scaled data that is not accounted for by the MDS model. Stress values vary with the type of MDS procedure and the data being analysed. For Kruskal's stress formula 1, the recommendations for evaluating stress values are as follows.[8]

Stress (%)	Goodness of fit
20	Poor
10	Fair
5	Good
2.5	Excellent
0	Perfect

3 If an aggregate-level analysis has been done, the original data should be split into two or more parts. MDS analysis should be conducted separately on each part and the results compared.
4 Stimuli can be selectively eliminated from the input data and the solutions determined for the remaining stimuli.
5 A random error term could be added to the input data. The resulting data are subjected to MDS analysis and the solutions compared.
6 The input data could be collected at two different points in time and the test-retest reliability determined.

Formal procedures are available for assessing the validity of MDS.[9] In the case of our illustrative example, the stress value of 0.095 indicates a fair fit. One brand, namely Stella Artois, is different from the others. Would the elimination of Stella Artois from the stimulus set appreciably alter the relative configuration of the other brands? The spatial map obtained by deleting Stella Artois is shown in Figure 23.6. There is some change in the relative positions of the brands, particularly Corona and Holsten. Yet the changes are modest, indicating fair stability.[10]

ASSUMPTIONS AND LIMITATIONS OF MDS

It is worthwhile to point out some assumptions and limitations of MDS. It is assumed that the similarity of stimulus A to B is the same as the similarity of stimulus B to A. There are some instances where this assumption may be violated. For example, New Zealand is perceived as more similar to Australia than Australia is to New Zealand.

MDS assumes that the distance (similarity) between two stimuli is some function of their partial similarities on each of several perceptual dimensions. Not much research has been done to test this assumption. When a spatial map is obtained, it is assumed that inter-point distances are ratio scaled and that the axes of the map are multidimensional interval scaled. A limitation of MDS is that dimension interpretation relating physical changes in brands or stimuli to changes in the perceptual map is difficult at best. These limitations also apply to the scaling of preference data.

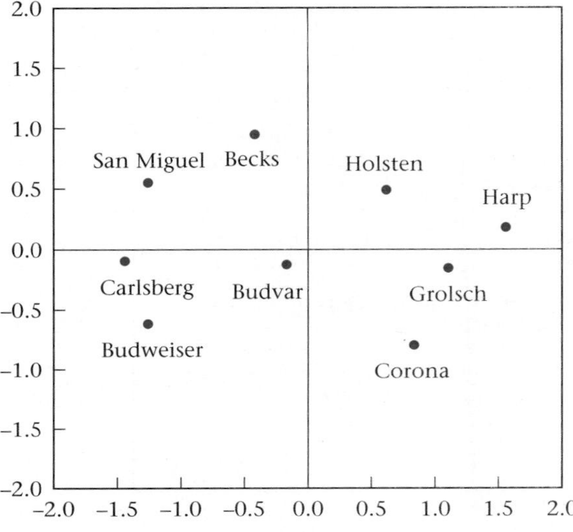

Figure 23.6
Assessment of stability by deleting one brand

SCALING PREFERENCE DATA

Internal analysis of preferences
A method of configuring a spatial map such that the spatial map represents both brands or stimuli and respondent points or vectors and is derived solely from the preference data.

External analysis of preferences
A method of configuring a spatial map such that the ideal points or vectors based on preference data are fitted in a spatial map derived from the perception data.

Analysis of preference data can be internal or external. In **internal analysis of preferences**, a spatial map representing both brands or stimuli and respondent points or vectors is derived upperly from the preference data. Thus, by collecting preference data, both brands and respondents can be represented in the same spatial map. In **external analysis of preferences**, the ideal points or vectors based on preference data are fitted in a spatial map derived from perception (e.g. similarities) data. To perform external analysis, both preference and perception data must be obtained. The representation of both brands and respondents as points in the same space, by using internal or external analysis, is referred to as *unfolding*.

External analysis is preferred in most situations.[11] In internal analysis, the differences in perceptions are confounded with differences in preferences. It is possible that the nature and relative importance of dimensions may vary between the perceptual space and the preference space. Two brands may be perceived to be similar (located closely to each other in the perceptual space), yet one brand may be distinctly preferred over the other (i.e. the brands may be located apart in the preference space). These situations cannot be accounted for in internal analysis. In addition, internal analysis procedures are beset with computational difficulties.[12]

We illustrate external analysis by scaling the preferences of our respondent into his spatial map. The respondent ranked the brands in the following order of preference (most preferred first): Stella Artois, Holsten, Harp, San Miguel, Carlsberg, Grolsch, Budvar, Budweiser, Corona and Becks. These preference rankings, along with the coordinates of the spatial map (Figure 23.5), were used as input into a preference scaling program to derive Figure 23.7. Notice the location of the ideal point. It is close to Stella Artois, Holsten, Harp and San Miguel, the four most preferred brands, and far from Corona and Becks, the two least preferred brands. If a new brand were to be located in this space, its distance from the ideal point, relative to the distances of other brands from the ideal point, would determine the degree of preference for this brand.

Although we have considered only quantitative data so far, qualitative data can also be mapped using procedures such as correspondence analysis.

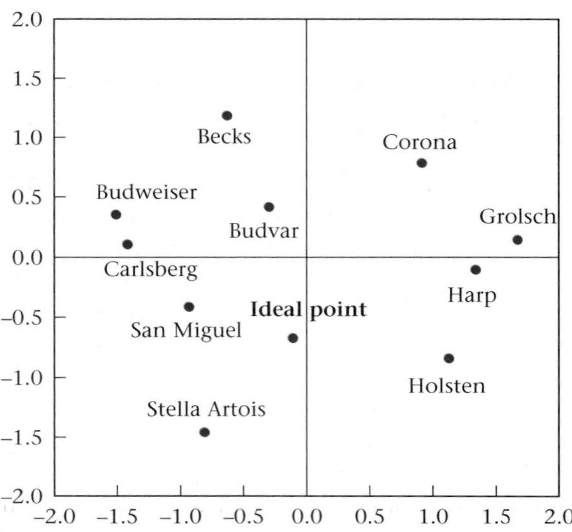

Figure 23.7
External analysis of preference data

CORRESPONDENCE ANALYSIS

Correspondence analysis
An MDS technique for scaling qualitative data that scales the rows and columns of the input contingency table in corresponding units so that each can be displayed in the same low-dimensional space.

Correspondence analysis is an MDS technique for scaling qualitative data in marketing research. The input data are in the form of a contingency table indicating a qualitative association between the rows and columns. Correspondence analysis scales the rows and columns in corresponding units so that each can be displayed graphically in the same low-dimensional space. These spatial maps provide insights into:

1 Similarities and differences within the rows with respect to a given column category
2 Similarities and differences within the column categories with respect to a given row category
3 Relationships among the rows and columns.[13]

The interpretation of results in correspondence analysis is similar to that in principal components analysis (Chapter 21), given the similarity of the algorithms. Correspondence analysis results in the grouping of categories (activities, brands or other stimuli) found within the contingency table, just as principal components analysis involves the grouping of the independent variables. The results are interpreted in terms of proximities among the rows and columns of the contingency table. Categories that are closer together than others are more similar in underlying structure.[14]

Compared with other multidimensional scaling techniques, the advantage of correspondence analysis is that it reduces the data collection demands imposed on the respondents, since only binary or categorical data are obtained. The respondents are merely asked to tick which attributes apply to each of several brands, or in the GlobalCash study, tick which events they plan to undertake over the next two years. The input data are the number of yes responses for each brand on each attribute. The brands and the attributes are then displayed in the same multidimensional space. The disadvantage is that between-set (i.e. between column and row) distances cannot be meaningfully interpreted. Correspondence analysis is an exploratory data analysis technique that is not suitable for hypothesis testing.[15]

MDS, including correspondence analysis, is not the only procedure available for obtaining perceptual maps. Two other techniques that we have discussed before, discriminant analysis (Chapter 18) and factor analysis (Chapter 21), can also be used for this purpose.

RELATIONSHIP AMONG MDS, FACTOR ANALYSIS AND DISCRIMINANT ANALYSIS

If the attribute-based approaches are used to obtain input data, spatial maps can also be obtained by using factor or discriminant analysis. In this approach, each respondent rates n brands on m attributes. By factor analysing the data, one could derive for each respondent n factor scores for each factor, one for each brand. By plotting brand scores on the factors, a spatial map could be obtained for each respondent. If an aggregate map is desired, the factor score for each brand for each factor can be averaged across respondents. The dimensions would be labelled by examining the factor loadings, which are estimates of the correlations between attribute ratings and underlying factors.[16]

The goal of discriminant analysis is to select the linear combinations of attributes that best discriminate between the brands or stimuli. To develop spatial maps by means of discriminant analysis, the dependent variable is the brand rated and the independent or predictor variables are the attribute ratings. A spatial map can be obtained by plotting the discriminant scores for the brands. The discriminant scores are the ratings on the perceptual dimensions, based on the attributes which best distinguish the brands. The dimensions can be labelled by examining the discriminant weights, or the weightings of attributes that make up a discriminant function or dimension.[17]

BASIC CONCEPTS IN CONJOINT ANALYSIS

Conjoint analysis
A technique that attempts to determine the relative importance consumers attach to salient attributes and the utilities they attach to the levels of attributes.

Conjoint analysis attempts to determine the relative importance consumers attach to salient attributes and the utilities they attach to the levels of attributes.[18] This information is derived from consumers' evaluations of brands or from brand profiles composed of these attributes and their levels. The respondents are presented with stimuli that consist of combinations of attribute levels. They are asked to evaluate these stimuli in terms of their desirability. Conjoint procedures attempt to assign values to the levels of each attribute so that the resulting values or utilities attached to the stimuli match, as closely as possible, the input evaluations provided by the respondents. The underlying assumption is that any set of stimuli – such as products, brands or banks – are evaluated as a bundle of attributes.[19]

Like multidimensional scaling, conjoint analysis relies on respondents' subjective evaluations. In MDS, however, the stimuli are products or brands. In conjoint analysis, the stimuli are combinations of attribute levels determined by the researcher. The goal in MDS is to develop a spatial map depicting the stimuli in a multidimensional perceptual or preference space. Conjoint analysis, on the other hand, seeks to develop the part-worth or utility functions describing the utility consumers attach to the levels of each attribute. The two techniques are complementary.[20]

Conjoint analysis has been used in marketing for a variety of purposes, including the following:

- *Determining the relative importance of attributes in the consumer choice process.* A standard output from conjoint analysis consists of derived relative importance weights. The relative importance weights indicate which attributes are important in influencing consumer choice.
- *Estimating market share of brands that differ in attribute levels.* The utilities derived from conjoint analysis can be used as input into a choice simulator to determine the share of choices, and hence the market share, of different brands.
- *Determining the composition of the most preferred brand.* Brand features can be varied in terms of attribute levels and the corresponding utilities determined. The brand features that yield the highest utility indicate the composition of the most preferred brand.
- *Segmenting the market based on similarity of preferences for attribute levels.* The part-worth functions derived for the attributes may be used as a basis for clustering respondents to arrive at homogeneous preference segments.[21]

Applications of conjoint analysis have been made in consumer goods, industrial goods and financial and other services. Moreover, these applications have spanned all areas of marketing. A recent survey of conjoint analysis reported applications in the areas of new product and concept identification, competitive analysis, pricing, market segmentation, advertising and distribution.[22]

STATISTICS AND TERMS ASSOCIATED WITH CONJOINT ANALYSIS

The important statistics and terms associated with conjoint analysis include the following:

Part-worth functions. The part-worth or *utility functions* describe the utility consumers attach to the levels of each attribute.
Relative importance weights. The relative importance weights are estimated and indicate which attributes are important in influencing consumer choice.
Attribute levels. The attribute levels denote the values assumed by the attributes.
Full profiles. Full profiles or complete profiles of brands are constructed in terms of all the attributes by using the attribute levels specified by the design.
Pairwise tables. In pairwise tables, the respondents evaluate two attributes at a time until all the required pairs of attributes have been evaluated.
Cyclical designs. Cyclical designs are designs employed to reduce the number of paired comparisons.
Fractional factorial designs. Fractional factorial designs are designs employed to reduce the number of stimulus profiles to be evaluated in the full-profile approach.
Orthogonal arrays. Orthogonal arrays are a special class of fractional designs that enable the efficient estimation of all main effects.
Internal validity. Internal validity involves correlations of the predicted evaluations for the holdout or validation stimuli with those obtained from the respondents.

CONDUCTING CONJOINT ANALYSIS

Figure 23.8 lists the steps in conjoint analysis. Formulating the problem involves identifying the salient attributes and their levels. These attributes and levels are used for constructing the stimuli to be used in a conjoint evaluation task. The respondents rate or rank the stimuli using a suitable scale, and the data obtained are analysed. The results are interpreted and their reliability and validity assessed. We now describe each of the steps of conjoint analysis in detail.

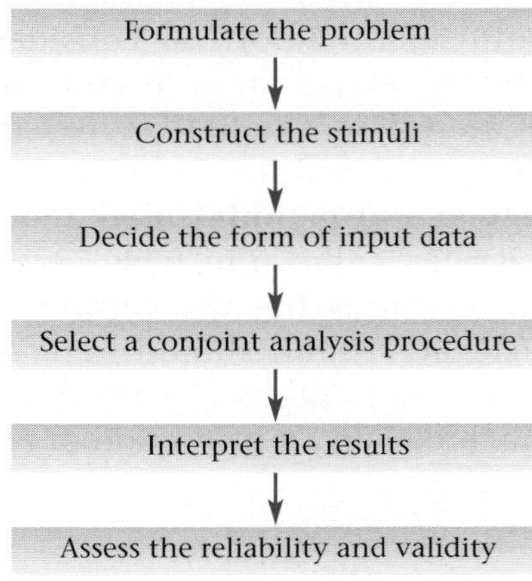

Figure 23.8 Conducting conjoint analysis

Formulating the problem

In formulating the conjoint analysis problem, the researcher must identify the attributes and attribute levels to be used in constructing the stimuli. Attribute levels denote the values assumed by the attributes. From a theoretical standpoint, the attributes selected should be salient in influencing consumer preference and choice. For example, in the choice of a car, price, fuel efficiency, interior space and so forth should be included. From a managerial perspective, the attributes and their levels should be actionable. To tell a manager that consumers prefer a sporty car to one that is conservative-looking is not helpful, unless sportiness and conservativeness are defined in terms of attributes over which a manager has control. The attributes can be identified through discussions with management and industry experts, analysis of secondary data, qualitative research and pilot surveys. A typical conjoint analysis study may involve six or seven attributes.

Once the salient attributes have been identified, their appropriate levels should be selected. The number of attribute levels determines the number of parameters that will be estimated and also influences the number of stimuli that will be evaluated by the respondents. To minimise the respondent evaluation task and yet estimate the parameters with reasonable accuracy, it is desirable to restrict the number of attribute levels. The utility or part-worth function for the levels of an attribute may be non-linear. For example, a consumer may prefer a medium-sized car to either a small or a large one. Likewise, the utility for price may be non-linear. The loss of utility in going from a low price to a medium price may be much smaller than the loss in utility in going from a medium price to a high price. In these cases, at least three levels should be used. Some attributes, though, may naturally occur in binary form (two levels): a car does or does not have a sunroof.

The attribute levels selected will affect the consumer evaluations. If the price of a car brand is varied at €14,000, €16,000 and €18,000, price will be relatively unimportant. On the other hand, if the price is varied at €20,000, €30,000 and €40,000, it will be an important factor. Hence, the researcher should take into account the attribute levels prevalent in the marketplace and the objectives of the study. Using attribute levels that are beyond the range reflected in the marketplace will decrease the believability of the evaluation task, but it will increase the accuracy with which the parameters are estimated. The general guideline is to select attribute levels so that the ranges are somewhat greater than those prevalent in the marketplace but not so large as to impact the believability of the evaluation task adversely.

We illustrate the conjoint methodology by considering the problem of how students evaluate boots, for example brands such as Dr Martens, Timberland, Bally and Caterpillar. Qualitative research identified three attributes as salient: the material used for the upper, the country or region in which they were designed and manufactured and the price. Each was defined in terms of three levels, as shown in Table 23.2. These attributes and their levels were used for constructing the conjoint analysis stimuli. It has been argued that pictorial stimuli should be used when consumers' marketplace choices are strongly guided by the product's styling, such that the choices are heavily based on an inspection of actual products or pictures of products.[23]

It has been argued that pictorial stimuli should be used when consumers' marketplace choices are strongly guided by the product's styling

Tony Stone

Table 23.2 Boot attributes and levels

	Level	
Attribute	**Number**	**Description**
Uppers	3	Leather
	2	Suede
	1	Imitation leather
Country	3	Italy
	2	America
	1	Far East
Price	3	€50
	2	€125
	1	€200

Constructing the stimuli

Two broad approaches are available for constructing conjoint analysis stimuli: the pairwise approach and the full-profile procedure. In the pairwise approach, also called *two-factor evaluations*, respondents evaluate two attributes at a time until all the possible pairs of attributes have been evaluated. This approach is illustrated in the context of the boots example in Figure 23.9. For each pair, respondents evaluate all the combinations of levels of both the attributes, which are presented in a matrix. In the full-profile approach, also called *multiple-factor evaluations*, full or complete profiles of brands are constructed for all the attributes. Typically, each profile is described on a separate index card. This approach is illustrated in the context of the boots example in Table 23.3.

It is not necessary to evaluate all the possible combinations, nor is it feasible in all cases. In the pairwise approach, it is possible to reduce the number of paired comparisons by using cyclical designs. Likewise, in the full-profile approach, the number of stimulus profiles can be greatly reduced by means of fractional factorial designs. A special class of fractional designs, orthogonal arrays, allow for the efficient estimation of all main effects.

You will be presented with information on Boots in terms of pairs of features described in the form of a matrix. For each matrix, please rank the nine feature combinations in terms of your preference. A rank of 1 should be assigned to the most preferred combination and 9 to least preferred.

Upper	Country: Italy	America	Far East
Leather			
Suede			
Imitation leather			

Price	Country: Italy	America	Far East
€50			
€125			
€200			

Upper	Price: €50	€125	€200
Leather			
Suede			
Imitation leather			

Figure 23.9 Pairwise approach to collecting conjoint data

Orthogonal arrays permit the measurement of all main effects of interest on an uncorrelated basis. These designs assume that all interactions are negligible. Orthogonal arrays are constructed from basic full factorial designs by substituting a new factor for selected interaction effects that are presumed to be negligible.[24] Generally, two sets of data are obtained. One, the estimation set, is used to calculate the part-worth functions for the attribute levels. The other, the holdout set, is used to assess reliability and validity.

The advantage of the pairwise approach is that it is easier for the respondents to provide these judgements. Its relative disadvantage, however, is that it requires more evaluations than the full-profile approach. Also, the evaluation task may be unrealistic when only two attributes are being evaluated simultaneously. Studies comparing the two approaches indicate that both methods yield comparable utilities, yet the full-profile approach is more commonly used.

Table 23.3 Full-profile approach to collecting conjoint data

Example of boot product profile	
Upper	Made of leather
Country	Designed and made in Italy
Price	Costing €200

The boots example follows the full-profile approach. Given three attributes, defined at three levels each, a total of $3 \times 3 \times 3 = 27$ profiles can be constructed. To reduce the respondent evaluation task, a fractional factorial design was employed and a set of nine profiles was constructed to constitute the estimation stimuli set (see Table 23.4). Another set of nine stimuli was constructed for validation purposes. Input data were obtained for both the estimation and validation stimuli. Before the data could be obtained, however, it was necessary to decide on the form of the input data.[25]

Deciding on the form of input data

As in the case of MDS, conjoint analysis input data can be either non-metric or metric. For non-metric data, respondents are typically required to provide rank-order evaluations. For the pairwise approach, respondents rank all the cells of each matrix in terms of their desirability. For the full-profile approach, they rank all the stimulus profiles. Rankings involve relative evaluations of the attribute levels. Proponents of ranking data believe that such data accurately reflect the behaviour of consumers in the marketplace.

Table 23.4 Boot profiles and their ratings

		Attribute levels[a]		
Profile number	*Upper*	*Country*	*Price*	*Preference rating*
1	1	1	1	9
2	1	2	2	7
3	1	3	3	5
4	2	1	2	6
5	2	2	3	5
6	2	3	1	6
7	3	1	3	5
8	3	2	1	7
9	3	3	2	6

[a]The attribute levels correspond to those in Table 23.2

In the metric form, respondents provide ratings, rather than rankings. In this case, the judgements are typically made independently. Advocates of rating data believe they are more convenient for the respondents and easier to analyse than rankings. In recent years, the use of ratings has become increasingly common.

In conjoint analysis, the dependent variable is usually preference or intention to buy. In other words, respondents provide ratings or rankings in terms of their preference or intentions to buy. The conjoint methodology, however, is flexible and can accommodate a range of other dependent variables, including actual purchase or choice.

In evaluating boot profiles, respondents were required to provide preference ratings for the boots described by the nine profiles in the estimation set. These ratings were obtained using a nine-point Likert scale (1 = not preferred, 9 = greatly preferred).

Ratings obtained from one respondent are shown in Table 23.4.

Selecting a conjoint analysis procedure

Conjoint analysis model
The mathematical model expressing the fundamental relationship between attributes and utility in conjoint analysis.

The basic **conjoint analysis model** may be represented by the following formula:[26]

$$U(X) = \sum_{i=1}^{m} \sum_{j=1}^{k_i} \alpha_{ij} x_{ij}$$

where

$U(X)$ = overall utility of an alternative

α_{ij} = the part-worth contribution or utility associated with the jth level $(1, j = 1, 2, \ldots, k_i)$ of the ith attribute $(i, i = 1, 2, \ldots, m)$

k_i = number of levels of attribute i

m = number of attributes

The importance of an attribute, I_i, is defined in terms of the range of the part-worths, α_{ij}, across the levels of that attribute:

$$I_i = \{\text{Max}(\alpha_{ij}) - \text{Min}(\alpha_{ij})\} \text{ for each } i$$

The attribute's importance is normalised to ascertain its importance relative to other attributes, W_i:

$$W_i = \frac{I_i}{\sum_{i=1}^{m} I_i}$$

so that

$$\sum_{i=1}^{m} W_i = 1$$

Several different procedures are available for estimating the basic model. The simplest is dummy variable regression (see Chapter 19). In this case, the predictor variables consist of dummy variables for the attribute levels. If an attribute has k_i levels, it is coded in terms of $k_i - 1$ dummy variables. If metric data are obtained, the ratings, assumed to be interval scaled, form the dependent variable. If the data are non-metric, the rankings may be converted to 0 or 1 by making paired comparisons between brands. In this case, the predictor variables represent the differences in the attribute levels of the brands being compared. Other procedures that are appropriate for non-metric data include LINMAP, MONANOVA and the LOGIT model.[27]

The researcher must also decide whether the data will be analysed at the individual respondent or the aggregate level. At the individual level, the data of each respondent are analysed separately. If an aggregate-level analysis is to be conducted, some procedure for grouping the respondents must be devised. One common approach is to estimate individual-level part-worth or utility functions first. Respondents are then clustered on the basis of the similarity of their part-worth functions. Aggregate analysis is then conducted for each cluster.[28] An appropriate model for estimating the parameters should be specified.[29]

The data reported in Table 23.4 were analysed using ordinary least squares (OLS) regression with dummy variables. The dependent variable was the preference ratings. The independent variables or predictors were six dummy variables, two for each variable. The transformed data are shown in Table 23.5. Since the data pertain to a single respondent, an individual-level analysis was conducted.

Table 23.5 Boot data coded for dummy variable regression

Preference ratings	*Attributes*					
	Upper		*Country*		*Price*	
Y	X_1	X_2	X_3	X_4	X_5	X_6
9	1	0	1	0	1	0
7	1	0	0	1	0	1
5	1	0	0	0	0	0
6	0	1	1	0	0	1
5	0	1	0	1	0	0
6	0	1	0	0	1	0
5	0	0	1	0	0	0
7	0	0	0	1	1	0
6	0	0	0	0	0	1

Table 23.6 Boot attributes and levels

	Level			
Attribute	*Number*	*Description*	*Utility*	*Importance*
Uppers	3	Leather	0.778	
	2	Suede	–0.556	
	1	Imitation leather	–0.222	0.268
Country	3	Italy	0.445	
	2	America	0.111	
	1	Far East	–0.556	0.214
Price	3	€50	1.111	
	2	€125	0.111	
	1	€200	–1.222	0.500

The part-worth or utility functions estimated for each attribute, as well the relative importance of the attributes, are given in Table 23.6.[30]

The model estimated may be represented as

$$U = b_0 + b_1X_1 + b_2X_2 + b_3X_3 + b_4X_4 + b_5X_5 + b_6X_6$$

where

X_1, X_2 = dummy variables representing upper
X_3, X_4 = dummy variables representing country
X_5, X_6 = dummy variables representing price

For upper, the attribute levels were coded as follows:

	X_1	X_2
Level 1	1	0
Level 2	0	1
Level 3	0	0

The levels of the other attributes were coded similarly. The parameters were estimated as follows:

$b_0 = 4.222$
$b_1 = 1.000$
$b_2 = 0.333$
$b_3 = 1.000$
$b_4 = 0.667$
$b_5 = 2.333$
$b_6 = 1.333$

Given the dummy variable coding, in which level 3 is the base level, the coefficients may be related to the part-worths. As explained in Chapter 19, each dummy variable coefficient represents the difference in the part-worth for that level minus the part-worth for the base level. For upper, we have the following:

$$\alpha_{11} - \alpha_{13} = b_1$$
$$\alpha_{12} - \alpha_{13} = b_2$$

To solve for the part-worths, an additional constraint is necessary. The part-worths are estimated on an interval scale, so the origin is arbitrary. Therefore, the additional constraint imposed is of the form

$$\alpha_{11} + \alpha_{12} + \alpha_{13} = 0$$

These equations for the first attribute, upper, are

$$\begin{aligned} \alpha_{11} - \alpha_{13} &= 1.000 \\ \alpha_{12} - \alpha_{13} &= -0.333 \\ \alpha_{11} + \alpha_{12} + \alpha_{13} &= 0 \end{aligned}$$

Solving these equations, we get

$$\begin{aligned} \alpha_{11} &= 0.778 \\ \alpha_{12} &= -0.556 \\ \alpha_{13} &= -0.222 \end{aligned}$$

The part-worths for other attributes reported in Table 23.6 can be estimated similarly. For country, we have

$$\begin{aligned} \alpha_{21} - \alpha_{23} &= b_3 \\ \alpha_{22} - \alpha_{23} &= b_4 \\ \alpha_{21} + \alpha_{22} + \alpha_{23} &= 0 \end{aligned}$$

For the third attribute, price, we have

$$\begin{aligned} \alpha_{31} - \alpha_{33} &= b_5 \\ \alpha_{32} - \alpha_{33} &= b_6 \\ \alpha_{31} + \alpha_{32} + \alpha_{33} &= 0 \end{aligned}$$

The relative importance weights were calculated based on ranges of part-worths, as follows:

$$\begin{aligned} \text{Sum of ranges of part-worths} &= [0.778 - (-0.556)] + [0.445 - (-0.556)] + [1.111 - (1.222)] \\ &= 4.668 \end{aligned}$$

$$\text{Relative importance of upper} = \frac{1.334}{4.668} = 0.286$$

$$\text{Relative importance of country} = \frac{1.001}{4.668} = 0.214$$

$$\text{Relative importance of price} = \frac{2.333}{4.668} = 0.500$$

The estimation of the part-worths and the relative importance weights provides the basis for interpreting the results.

Interpreting the results

For interpreting the results, it is helpful to plot the part-worth functions. The part-worth function values for each attribute given in Table 23.6 are graphed in Figure 23.10. As can be seen from Table 23.6 and Figure 23.10, this respondent has the greatest preference for a leather upper when evaluating boots. Second preference is for an imitation leather upper, and a suede upper is least preferred. An Italian boot is most preferred, followed by American and boots from the Far East. As may be expected, a price of €50.00 has the highest utility and a price of €200.00 the lowest. The utility values reported in Table 23.6 have only interval scale properties, and their origin is arbitrary. In terms of relative importance of the attributes, we see that price is number one. Second most important is upper, followed closely by country. Because price is by far the most important attribute for this respondent, this person could be labelled as price sensitive.

Assessing reliability and validity

Several procedures are available for assessing the reliability and validity of conjoint analysis results.[31]

1 The goodness of fit of the estimated model should be evaluated. For example, if dummy variable regression is used, the value of R^2 will indicate the extent to which the model fits the data. Models with poor fit are suspect.
2 Test-retest reliability can be assessed by obtaining a few replicated judgements later in data collection. In other words, at a later stage in the interview, the respondents are asked to evaluate certain selected stimuli again. The two values of these stimuli are then correlated to assess test-retest reliability.
3 The evaluations for the holdout or validation stimuli can be predicted by the estimated part-worth functions. The predicted evaluations can then be correlated with those obtained from the respondents to determine internal validity.
4 If an aggregate-level analysis has been conducted, the estimation sample can be split in several ways and conjoint analysis conducted on each sub-sample. The results can be compared across sub-samples to assess the stability of conjoint analysis solutions.

In running a regression analysis on the data of Table 23.5, an R^2 of 0.934 was obtained, indicating a good fit. The preference ratings for the nine validation profiles were predicted from the utilities reported in Table 23.6. These were

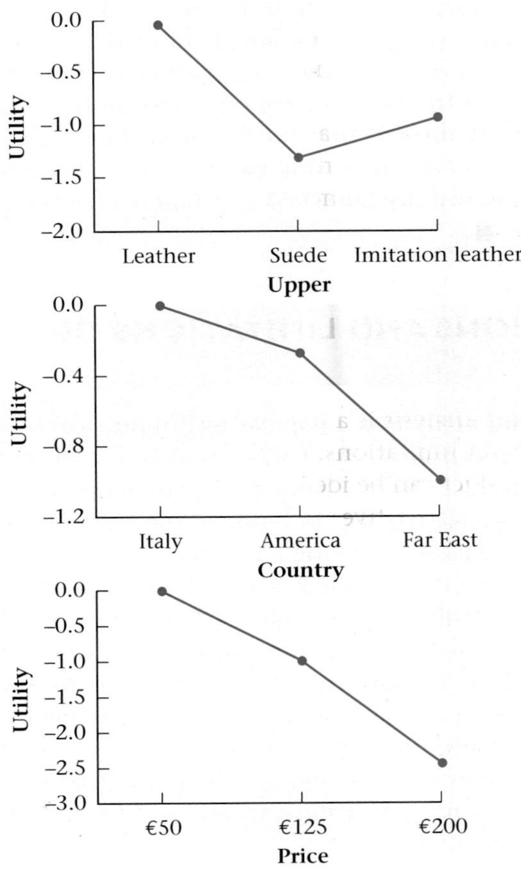

Figure 23.10
Part-worth functions

correlated with the input ratings for these profiles obtained from the respondent. The correlation coefficient was 0.95, indicating a good predictive ability. This correlation coefficient is significant at $\alpha = 0.05$.

The following example further illustrates an application of conjoint analysis.

EXAMPLE

Fab's fabulous foamy fight[32]

Competition in the clothes detergent market was brewing in Thailand. Superconcentrate detergent was fast becoming the prototype, with a market share of over 26% in the clothes detergent category. Market potential research in Thailand indicated that superconcentrates would continue to grow at around 40% a year. In addition, this category had already dominated other Asian markets such as Taiwan, Hong Kong and Singapore. Consequently, Colgate entered this new line of competition with *Fab Power Plus* with the objective of capturing 4% market share.

The main players in this market were Kao Corporation's *Attack* (14.6%), Lever Brother's *Breeze Ultra* (2.8%), Lion Corporation's *Pao M. Wash* (1.1%), and Lever's *Omo* (0.4%). Based on qualitative research and secondary data, Colgate assessed the critical factors for the success of superconcentrates. Some of these factors were environmental appeal, hand-wash and machine-wash convenience, superior cleaning abilities, optimum level of suds for hand-wash, and brand name. Research also revealed that no brand had both hand-wash and machine wash capabilities. *Pao Hand Force* was formulated as the hand-washing brand, and *Pao M. Wash* as the machine wash version. Lever's *Breezematic* was targeted for machine use.

Therefore, a formula that had both hand- and machine-wash capabilities was desirable. A conjoint study was designed, and these factors varied at either two or three levels. Preference ratings were gathered from respondents, and part-worth functions for the factors were estimated both at the individual and the group level. Results showed that the factor on hand-machine capability had a substantial contribution supporting earlier claims. Based on these findings, *Fab Power Plus* was successfully launched as a brand with both hand- and machine-wash capabilities. ■

ASSUMPTIONS AND LIMITATIONS OF CONJOINT ANALYSIS

Although conjoint analysis is a popular technique, like MDS, it carries a number of assumptions and limitations. Conjoint analysis assumes that the important attributes of a product can be identified. Furthermore, it assumes that consumers evaluate the choice alternatives in terms of these attributes and make trade-offs. In situations where image or brand name is important, however, consumers may not evaluate the brands or alternatives in terms of attributes. Even if consumers consider product attributes, the trade-off model may not be a good representation of the choice process. Another limitation is that data collection may be complex, particularly if a large number of attributes are involved and the model must be estimated at the individual level. This problem has been mitigated to some extent by procedures such as interactive or adaptive conjoint analysis and hybrid conjoint analysis. It should also be noted that the part-worth functions are not unique. For more technical issues, and for the limitations of conjoint analysis, refer to the literature.[33]

HYBRID CONJOINT ANALYSIS

Hybrid conjoint analysis A form of conjoint analysis that can simplify the data collection task and estimate selected interactions as well as all main effects.

Hybrid conjoint analysis is an attempt to simplify the burdensome data collection task required in traditional conjoint analysis. Each respondent evaluates a large number of profiles, yet usually only simple part-worth functions, without any interaction effects, are estimated. In the simple part-worths or main effects model, the value of a combination is simply the sum of the separate main effects (simple part-worths). In actual practice, two attributes may interact in the sense that the respondent may value the combination more than the average contribution of the separate parts. Hybrid models have been developed to serve two main purposes: (1) to simplify the data collection task by imposing less of a burden on each respondent and (2) to permit the estimation of selected interactions (at the subgroup level) as well as all main (or simple) effects at the individual level.

In the hybrid approach, the respondents evaluate a limited number, generally no more than nine, conjoint stimuli, such as full profiles. These profiles are drawn from a large master design and different respondents evaluate different sets of profiles so that over a group of respondents, all the profiles of interest are evaluated. In addition, respondents directly evaluate the relative importance of each attribute and desirability of the levels of each attribute. By combining the direct evaluations with those derived from the evaluations of the conjoint stimuli, it is possible to estimate a model at the aggregate level and still retain some individual differences.[34]

MDS and conjoint analysis are complementary techniques and may be used in combination, as the following example shows.

EXAMPLE

Weeding out the competition[35]

ICI Agricultural Products did not know whether it should lower the price of Fusilade, its herbicide. It knew that it had developed a potent herbicide, but it was not sure that the weed killer would survive in a price-conscious market. So a survey was designed to assess the relative importance of different attributes in selecting herbicides and measure and map perceptions of major herbicides on the same attributes. Personal interviews were conducted with 601 soybean and cotton farmers who had at least 200 acres dedicated to growing these crops and who had used herbicides during the past growing season. First, conjoint analysis was used to determine the relative importance of attributes farmers use when selecting herbicides. Then multidimensional scaling was used to map farmers' perceptions of herbicides. The study showed that price greatly influenced herbicide selections, and respondents were particularly sensitive when costs were more than €10 an hectare. But price was not the only determinant. Farmers also considered how much weed control the herbicide provided. They were willing to pay higher prices to keep weeds off their land. The study showed that herbicides that failed to control even one of the four most common weeds would have to be very inexpensive to attain a reasonable market share. Fusilade promised good weed control. Furthermore, multidimensional scaling indicated that one of Fusilade's competitors was considered to be expensive. Hence, ICI kept its original pricing plan and did not lower the price of Fusilade. ■

INTERNET AND COMPUTER APPLICATIONS

Several computer programs have been developed for conducting MDS analysis using microcomputers and mainframes. The ALSCAL program, available in the mainframe versions of SPSS and SAS, incorporates several different MDS models and can be used for conducting individual- or aggregate-level analysis. Other MDS programs are easily available and widely used. Most are available in both microcomputer and mainframe versions.

- MDSCAL 5M derives a spatial map of brands in a specified number of dimensions. Similarity data are used. A variety of input data formats and distance measures can be accommodated.
- KYST performs metric and non-metric scaling and unfolding using similarity data.
- INDSCAL, denoting individual differences scaling, is useful for conducting MDS at the aggregate level. Similarity data are used as input.
- MDPREF performs internal analysis of preference data. The program develops vector directions for preferences and the configuration of brands or stimuli in a common space.
- PREFMAP performs external analysis of preference data. This program uses a known spatial map of brands or stimuli to portray an individual's preference data. PREFMAP2 performs both internal and external analysis.
- PC-MDS contains a variety of multidimensional scaling algorithms, including factor analysis, discriminant analysis, and some other multivariate procedures.
- APM (adaptive perceptual mapping) is an adaptive scaling program, available for the microcomputer, that can handle up to 30 brands and 50 attributes. There is no limit on the number of respondents per study or the number of computers that can be used to collect the data.

If OLS regression is used as the estimation procedure in conjoint analysis, these programs are universally available. In particular, the microcomputer and mainframe versions of SPSS, SAS, BMDP, Minitab and Excel have several regression programs. (These were discussed in Chapter 19.) Several specialised programs are also available for conjoint analysis. MONANOVA (monotone analysis of variance) is a non-metric procedure that uses full-profile data. For pairwise data, the TRADEOFF procedure can be used. TRADEOFF is also a non-metric procedure that uses the rank ordering of preferences for attribute level pairs. Both MONANOVA and TRADEOFF are available for the mainframe and microcomputers. Other programs include LINMAP and ACA (adaptive conjoint analysis) and Sensus from Sawtooth Technologies. ACA focuses on the attributes and levels most relevant for each individual respondent. PC-MDS also contains a program for conjoint analysis.

SUMMARY

Multidimensional scaling is used for obtaining spatial representations of respondents' perceptions and preferences. Perceived or psychological relationships among stimuli are represented as geometric relationships among points in a multidimensional space. Formulating the MDS problem requires a specification of the brands or stimuli to be included. The number and nature of brands selected influences the resulting solution. Input data obtained from the respondents can be related to perceptions or preferences. Perception data can be direct or derived. The direct approaches are more common in marketing research.

The selection of an MDS procedure depends on the nature (metric or non-metric) of the input data and whether perceptions or preferences are being scaled. Another determining factor is whether the analysis will be conducted at the individual or aggregate level. The decision about the number of dimensions in which to obtain a solution should be based on theory, interpretability, elbow criterion, and ease-of-use considerations. Labelling of the dimensions is a difficult task that requires subjective judgement. Several guidelines are available for assessing the reliability and validity of MDS solutions. Preference data can be subjected to either internal or external analysis. If the input data are of a qualitative nature, they can be analysed via correspondence analysis. If the attribute-based approaches are used to obtain input data, spatial maps can also be obtained by means of factor or discriminant analysis.

Conjoint analysis is based on the notion that the relative importance that consumers attach to salient attributes, and the utilities they attach to the levels of attributes can be determined when consumers evaluate brand profiles that are constructed using these attributes and their levels. Formulating the problem requires an identification of the salient attributes and their levels. The pairwise and the full-profile approaches are commonly employed for constructing the stimuli. Statistical designs are available for reducing the number of stimuli in the evaluation task. The input data can be either non-metric (rankings) or metric (ratings). Typically, the dependent variable is preference or intention to buy.

Although other procedures are available for analysing conjoint analysis data, regression using dummy variables is becoming increasingly important. Interpreting the results requires an examination of the part-worth functions and relative importance weights. Several procedures are available for assessing the reliability and validity of conjoint analysis results.

QUESTIONS AND PROBLEMS

1 For what purposes are MDS procedures used?

2 Identify two marketing research problems where MDS could be applied. Explain how you would apply MDS in these situations.

3 What is meant by a spatial map?

4 Describe the steps involved in conducting MDS.

5 Describe the direct and derived approaches to obtaining MDS input data.

6 What factors influence the choice of an MDS procedure?

7 What guidelines are used for deciding on the number of dimensions in which to obtain an MDS solution?

8 Describe the ways in which the reliability and validity of MDS solutions can be assessed.

9 What is the difference between internal and external analysis of preference data?

10 What is involved in formulating a conjoint analysis problem?

11 Describe the full profile approach to constructing stimuli in conjoint analysis.

12 Describe the pairwise approach to constructing stimuli in conjoint analysis.

13 How can regression analysis be used for analysing conjoint data?

14 Graphically illustrate what is meant by part-worth functions.

15 What procedures are available for assessing the reliability and validity of conjoint analysis results?

NOTES

1 Green, P.E., Carmone, Jr, F.J. and Smith, S.M., *Multidimensional Scaling: Concepts and Applications* (Boston: Allyn and Bacon, 1989), 16–17.

2 Barrett, P., Burr, P. and Dolman, N., 'The Conjoint Path over the Cultural Divide', *Marketing Week* (14 October 1997).

3 For a review of MDS studies in marketing, see Cooper, L.G., 'A Review of Multidimensional Scaling in Marketing Research', *Applied Psychological Measurement* 7 (Fall 1983), 427–50.

4 An excellent discussion of the various aspects of MDS may be found in Davison, M.L., *Multidimensional Scaling* (New York: Wiley-Interscience,1983); Schiffman, S.S., Reynolds, M.L. and Young, E.W., *Introduction to Multidimensional Scaling: Theory, Methods, and Applications* (New York: Academic Press, 1981); and Kruskal, J.B. and Wish, M., *Multidimensional Scaling* (Beverly Hills, CA: Sage Publications, 1978).

5 Green, P.E., Carmone, Jr, F.J. and Smith, S.M., *Multidimensional Scaling: Concepts and Applications* (Boston: Allyn and Bacon, 1989); and Huber, J. and Holbrook, M.B., 'Using Attribute Ratings for Product Positioning: Some Distinctions among Compositional Approaches', *Journal of Marketing Research* 16 (November 1979), 507–16.

6 Malhotra, N.K., Jain, A.K. and Pinson, C., 'The Robustness of MDS Configurations in the Case of Incomplete Data', *Journal of Marketing Research* 25 (February 1988), 95–102; Green, P.E., 'On the Robustness of Multidimensional Scaling Techniques', *Journal of Marketing Research* 12 (1975), 73–81; and Weeks, D,G. and Bentler, P.M., 'A Comparison of Linear and Monotone Multidimensional Scaling Models', *Psychological Bulletin* 86 (1979), 349–54.

7 See Kruskal, J.B. and Wish, M., *Multidimensional Scaling* (Beverly Hill: Sage Publications, 1978), 89–92.

8 Kruskal's stress is probably the most commonly used measure for lack of fit. See Kruskal, J.B., 'Multidimensional Scaling by Optimising Goodness of Fit to a Nonmetric Hypothesis', *Psychometrika* 29 (March 1964), 1–27.

9 See Malhotra, N.K., 'Validity and Structural Reliability of Multidimensional Scaling', *Journal of Marketing Research* 24 (May 1987), 164–73.

10 For an examination of the reliability and validity of MDS solutions, see Steenkamp, J-B.E.M., Van Trijp, H.C.M., and Ten Berge, J.M.F., 'Perceptual Mapping Based on Idiosyncratic Sets of Attributes', *Journal of Marketing Research* 31 (February 1994), 15–27.

11 Hair, Jr, J.E., Anderson, R.E., Tatham, R.L. and Black, W.C., *Multivariate Data Analysis with Readings*, 4th edn (Englewood Cliffs: Prentice Hall, Inc., 1995), 484–555.

12 See, for example, DeSarbo, W.S. and Hoffman, D., 'Constructing MDS Joint Spaces From Binary Choice Data: A New Multidimensional Unfolding Threshold Model for Marketing Research', *Journal of Marketing Research* 24 (February 1987), 40–54.

13 For an application of correspondence analysis see Green, P.E. and Krieger, A.M., 'A Simple Approach to Target Market Advertising Strategy', *Journal of the Market Research Society* 35 (April 1993), 161–70.

14 Green, P.E., Carmone, Jr, F.J. and Smith, S.M., *Multidimensional Scaling: Concepts and Applications* (Boston: Allyn and Bacon, 1989), 16–17.

15 See Greenacre, M.J., 'The Carroll-Green-Schaffer Scaling in Correspondence Analysis: A Theoretical and Empirical Appraisal', *Journal of Marketing Research* 26 (August 1989), 358–65; Greenacre, M.J., *Theory and Applications of Correspondence Analyses* (New York: Academic Press, 1984); and Hoffman, D.L. and Franke, G.R., 'Correspondence Analysis: Graphical Representation of Categorical Data in Marketing Research', *Journal of Marketing Research* 23 (August 1986), 213–27.

16 For the use of factor analysis in constructing spatial maps, see Hasson, L., 'Monitoring Social Change', *Journal of the Market Research Society* 37 (January 1995), 69–80.

17 Hauser, J.R. and Koppelman, F.S., 'Alternative Perceptual Mapping Techniques: Relative Accuracy and Usefulness', *Journal of Marketing Research* 16 (November 1979), 495–506. Hauser and Koppelman conclude that factor analysis is superior to discriminant analysis.

18 For applications and issues in conjoint analysis, see Kohli, R. and Mahajan, V., 'A Reservation Price Model for Optimal Pricing of Multiattribute Products in Conjoint Analysis', *Journal of Marketing Research* 28 (August 1991), 347–54; Green, P.E., Krieger, A.M. and Agarwal, M.K., 'Adaptive Conjoint Analysis: Some Caveats and Suggestions', *Journal of Marketing Research* 28 (May 1991), 215–22; and Green, P.E. and Krieger, A.M., 'Segmenting Markets With Conjoint Analysis', *Journal of Marketing* 55 (October 1991), 20–31.

19 For a managerial overview of conjoint analysis, see Green, P.E. and Wind, Y., 'New Way to Measure Consumers' Judgements', *Harvard Business Review* (July–August 1975), 107–17.

20 For an overview of conjoint analysis in marketing, see Green, P.E. and Srinivasan, V., 'Conjoint Analysis in Marketing: New Developments with Implications for Research and Practic', *Journal of Marketing* 54 (October 1990), 3–19, and Green, P.E. and Srinivasan, V., 'Conjoint Analysis in Consumer Research: Issues and Outlook', *Journal of Consumer Research* 5 (September 1978), 102–23.

21 The various applications of conjoint analysis have been described in Cattin, P., and Wittink, D.R., 'Commercial Use of Conjoint Analysis: A Survey', *Journal of Marketing* 46 (Summer 1982), 44–53.

22 Wittink, D.R. and Cattin, P., 'Commercial Use of Conjoint Analysis: An Update', *Journal of Marketing* 53 (July 1989), 91–97. For using conjoint analysis to measure price sensitivity, see 'Multi-Stage Conjoint Methods to Measure Price Sensitivity', *Sawtooth News* 10 (Winter 1994–1995), 5–6.

23 Loosschilder, G.H., Rosbergen, E., Vriens, M. and Wittink, D.R., 'Pictorial Stimuli in Conjoint Analysis – to Support Product Styling Decisions', *Journal of the Market Research Society* 37 (January 1995), 17–34.

24 See Addleman, S., 'Orthogonal Main-Effect Plans for Asymmetrical Factorial Experiments', *Technometrics* 4 (February 1962), 21–36; Green, P.E., 'On the Design of Choice Experiments Involving Multifactor Alternatives', *Journal of Consumer Research* 1 (September 1974), 61–68; and Kuhfeld, W.F., Tobias, R.D. and Garratt, M., 'Efficient Experimental Designs with Marketing Applications', *Journal of Marketing Research* 31 (November 1994), 545–57.

25 More complex conjoint designs are also possible. See Oppewal, H., Louviere, J.J. and Timmermans, H.J.P., 'Modeling Hierarchical Conjoint Processes with Integrated Choice Experiments', *Journal of Marketing Research* 31 (February 1994), 15–27.

26 Jain, A.K., Acito, F., Malhotra, N.K. and Mahajan V., 'A Comparison of the Internal Validity of Alternative Parameter Estimation Methods in Decompositional Multiattribute Preference Models', *Journal of Marketing Research* (August 1979), 313–22.

27 Jain, A.K., Acito, F., Malhotra, N.K. and Mahajan, V., 'A Comparison of the Internal Validity of Alternative Parameter Estimation Methods in Decompositional Multiattribute Preference Models', *Journal of Marketing Research* (August 1979), 313–22; and Wittink, D.R. and Cattin, P., 'Alternative Estimation Methods for Conjoint Analysis: A Monte Carlo Study', *Journal of Marketing Research* 18 (February 1981), 101–6.

28 Moore, W.L., 'Levels of Aggregation in Conjoint Analysis: An Empirical Comparison', *Journal of Marketing Research* 17 (November 1980), 516–23.

29 Carmone, E.J. and Green, P.E., 'Model Mis-specification in Multiattribute Parameter Estimation', *Journal of Marketing Research* 18 (February 1981), 87–93.

30 For an application of conjoint analysis using OLS regression see Ostrom, A. and Iacobucci, D., 'Consumer Trade-Offs and the Evaluation of Services', *Journal of Marketing* 59 (January 1995), 17–28.

31 Malhotra, N.K., 'Structural Reliability and Stability of Nonmetric Conjoint Analysis', *Journal of Marketing Research* 19 (May 1982), 199–207; Leigh, T.W., MacKay, D.B. and Summers, J.O., 'Reliability and Validity of Conjoint Analysis and Self-Explicated Weights: A Comparison', *Journal of Marketing Research* 21 (November 1984), 456–62; and Segal, M.N., 'Reliability of Conjoint Analysis: Contrasting Data Collection Procedures', *Journal of Marketing Research* 19 (February 1982), 139–43.

32 Butler, D., 'Thai Superconcentrates Foam', *Advertising Age* (18 January 1993).

33 Green, P.E. and Srinivasan, V. 'Conjoint Analysis in Consumer Research: Issues and Outlook', *Journal of Consumer Research* (September 1978), 103–23.

34 For an exposition of hybrid models, see Green, P.E., 'Hybrid Models for Conjoint Analysis: An Expository Review', *Journal of Marketing Research* 21 (May 1984), 155–69.

35 Schneidman, D., 'Research Method Designed to Determine Price for New Products, Line Extensions', *Marketing News* (23 October 1987), 11.

PROFESSIONAL PERSPECTIVES for Part III

Bob McDonald
Bob is vice president Philadelphia client services. He joined Burke in 1973 and founded the company's Philadelphia-area client service office in 1976. He currently provides research design and analytic assistance to several client organizations and to Burke account representatives.

Cross-Tabulation

BOB McDONALD

Introduction

Although a variety of sophisticated statistical techniques are available, virtually all surveys and tests will initially, and often exclusively, rely on the 'counts' and percentages found in cross-tabulations. For example, when presented with test data of the nature of Table 1, management can readily interpret the results of this pairing of two television commercials in generating positive purchase intent:

	Commercial	
	"Warren's Tavern"	*"New Boston"*
Base—Viewers Per Ad	(200)%	(200)%
Positive Purchase Intent	46	67
Definitely Would Buy	18	31
Probably Would Buy	28	36

In the jargon of the trade, the headings are referred to as the 'banner':

Commercial	
"Warren's Tavern"	*"New Boston"*

The row captions are referred to as the 'stubs':

Positive Purchase Intent
Definitely Would Buy
Probably Would Buy

The terminology is simple, but the design and presentation of cross-tabular data, however, is not always as simplistic as the above example suggests. Consider the following points:

Banner design

- A total column may or may not be appropriate, based on the research design. Within an independent-cells test design in which the samples are not drawn proportionate to their presence in the population, an aggregated total (unless it is based on weighted columns) is clearly inappropriate.

- The banner should generally avoid the presentation of highly intercorrelated variables which, unsurprisingly, yield highly redundant results. For example, in a child's snack product test conducted among a sample of mothers of children and/or teenagers, looking at the cross-tabulations shows greater purchase interest among younger moms, among moms of fewer children, among employed moms, and among single moms. The point, of course, is that virtually the same subgroup is being 'read' four times, the proportional overlaps between the four classificatory segments being extensive. Although not technically 'wrong,' conclusions drawn from the correlated banner points could be misleading. A simple example shows:

	Number of children		
	1	*2*	*3*
	%	%	%
Positive purchase intent	90	80	60
base	120	100	80

It appears clear that positive purchase intent declines with the number of children in the household.

	Age of Mother	
	Under 25	*25 and Older*
Positive purchase intent	83%	74%
base	160	140

It is also clear that older mothers have a lower percentage of positive purchase intent.

	Age of Mother					
	Moms under 25 Number of Children:			*Moms 25 and Over Number of Children*		
	1	*2*	*3+*	*1*	*2*	*3+*
Positive purchase intent	90	80	60	90	80	60
base	85	55	20	35	45	60

Now, with the 'nested' tabulation, it is clear that the age of the mother isn't related to positive purchase intent, rather the distribution of mothers by number of children is very different for younger versus older moms.

Response categories

In many surveys the number of categories in which a measurement is taken is decided by the researcher without evidence of the consequence of using the selected categorization. For example, respondent age might be initially tabbed via three, four, five, or more subgroups. As a rule of thumb, use the largest number of categories you can (or get exact data if possible). Subsequent analysis always presents the opportunity for 'collapsing' to fewer groups. You can explore how the categories relate to other measures without concern that the categories you selected are artificially hiding relationships because they are too broad.

- Nature of the sample banner subgroups to be tested for statistically significant differences need be clearly recognized as either (1) completely independent groups (mutually exclusive), (2) completely matched (the same respondents), or (3) a partially overlapping mixture. Matched groups, of course, will often appear when, for example, two brands each with near 100 per cent awareness are rated. Where broader variation is seen in brand awareness levels, the overlapping mixture result occurs: Some respondents rate brand A/not B, some rate brand B/not A, and some rate both. The point, of course, is simply that maximal precision of interpretation will depend on the application of the most appropriate test (or tests) as directed by the nature of the subgroups.

- A distinction should be made between statistical versus managerial significance. Strict and complete reliance on the presence or absence of statistically significant differences is not always desirable.

Statistical variations that do not 'hang together' to cogently support the major results within the 'story' are also not high priority with management; they do not enhance their decisions nor forward their careers. Conversely, differences and patterns (typically termed 'directional') that do buttress the 'story' but 'miss' the 95 per cent confidence levels may potentially be of high priority, and when omitted because the 95 per cent bell was not rung represents a disservice to management.

Stub design

Because such a multitude of alternatives can not be assessed without excessive length, the following comments are offered to focus on only a few selected fundamental issues and basic decision themes in stub design.

- As elementary as it may seem, the order of presenting tables is not a given. The not uncommon practice of tables being ordered to match the sequence in which the questions appear within the interview frequently has little to endorse it other than its being easier than developing a custom flow that reveals the story the data tells.
- Each table needs to be considered as to the most meaningful base that is to be employed. Most often, this will reflect the respondents that asked the particular question and, therefore, can easily vary between tables due to interview skip patterns. (An overall brand satisfaction question tabbed on total, that is, makes little sense when only one-third of the survey respondents have ever tried the brand.) Likewise, some tables will clearly be more informative with the base 'floated' down to a particular subgroup from those asked.
- Ratios and percentage differences/changes need to be employed with caution and presented with appropriate caveats..
- Classic 'conversion ratios,' such as awareness-to-trial or trial-to-brand-used-most-often (BUMO), need to be carefully approached from two perspectives. First, if several brands are being profiled, the composition of awareness may differ substantively as to aware-tried versus aware-not tried ('Ford' versus 'Rolls Royce'). Because triers have experience-based perceptions and non-triers respond only from imagery, interbrand (and intergroup) differences may be misleading. Secondly, attention must be focused on the appropriate sample size on which a ratio is calculated. If, for example, comparisons are being made across brands (or across waves of a tracking survey) for trial-to-BUMO levels, and if a given brand has only a 10 per cent or 15 per cent trial penetration, the total survey sample of 300 interviews is irrelevant to the statistical evaluation; the 30 or 45 triers is the rather shaky foundation for the ratio.
- Two major problem sources for such data are typical:

1 As with ratios, small samples can become 'lost' in churning percentage change results. Consider an advertising agency wishing to stress the 'tripling' of a campaign's main message among ad recallers between the 'pre-' and 'post-' surveys. The key words, of course, are 'among ad recallers.' The fact that the latter have been measured at less than 15 per cent of target market

respondents in both survey waves has major relevance and makes citation of percentage changes in ad message playback an inane exercise.

2 Perhaps even a bit more slippery is the issue of the level of the first proportion; the lower it is, of course, the greater the potential there is for an 'out of the park homer.' Consider the following 'data':

	Pre-wave	*Post-wave*	*Percentage Change*
Base–total per wave	(200)%	(200)%	
Bought Inferno Salsa			
Past three months	2	6	+200

The above type of presentation is not unprecedented in survey reporting. The researcher needs to be highly attuned to the potential influence and effects of 'interested parties' having a hand in the creation of 'findings' such as this '200 percent increase in trial!'

Data Analysis: Multivariate Techniques

Sarah Evans
Senior Marketing Research Analyst, Burke, Inc. As a senior analyst, Sarah Evans consults on design, analysis, and results interpretation for Burke, Inc. Her diverse category experience includes consumer packaged goods, technology, telecommunications, business services, pharmaceuticals, automotive, travel, household durables, food service, financial services, and publishing.

SARAH EVANS

As a market researcher, much of what I love about this field is our ability to uncover peoples' perceptions and motivations and then help integrate these findings into marketing strategies. Often we need to examine our respondents' data with multivariate techniques to fully understand the complexity of the information we have. Our goal is to make the data 'speak' in a clearly understandable and believable voice.

The new researcher often gets caught up in applying the 'techniques' available and fails to keep in mind the study's objectives. This 'technique focus' has become even more prevalent in the past five years as menu-prompted statistical software packages make running these techniques even simpler. Here I share with you brief comments on my views of the use of several multivariate techniques (analysis of variance, multiple regression, discriminant analysis, factor analysis, cluster analysis, multidimensional scaling, and conjoint analysis) in hopes of easing the difficulties of analysis so that you have the best results possible to channel back to your marketing team.

Analysis of variance

ANalysis Of VAriance (ANOVA) is an extremely helpful tool in practical marketing research, as it is used most often to help reduce familywise error. Familywise error is the cumulative effect of type I error (saying that two numbers are different when in fact they are not different) across all paired comparisons. However, before you choose to use an ANOVA, you should make sure that your data are appropriate. ANOVA is an omnibus test, meaning that it looks for overall differences among all nominally scaled independent variables on a given interval or metric dependent variable. In addition to having a nominal independent variable like brands, products, or subgroups, and an interval or metric dependent variable like performance ratings, importance ratings, and awareness levels, you also need to meet a couple of other assumptions of ANOVA: 1) the sampled populations are normally distributed and 2) the population variances are equal.

another segment is looking for a point-and-click camera that yields clear pictures even if taken with an unsteady hand. These needs segments do not depend on the occasion of using the camera; consumers do not want an ensemble of three or four cameras to choose from depending on the occasion.

The second type we will call occasion-based segmentation, and these are performed in categories where needs and motivations do vary by occasion. For example, the selection of a restaurant will not always be based on the same needs. It will depend on time of day, who is in the party, day of the week, and cause for celebration, among other things. Occasion-based segmentations are commonly performed in food and drink categories as any one consumer may have several sets of needs depending on the circumstances of the occasion.

For both market- and occasion-based segmentations using cluster analysis, data should be at least interval level and you should have complete data on every respondent. Avoid, if possible, using substitution values for missing data, for instance replacing missing values with the mean of the remaining data. This may be unavoidable, but in the end you have to recognize that it will influence the outcome and you have essentially 'made-up data.'

Once you have the results, profile each of the segments by the variables included in the cluster analysis. First, understand which variables everyone is seeking and which variables no one is seeking; these variables are market-level characteristics, not segment-level characteristics. Separating them from the rest of the attributes will make identifying the segment-level needs easier. Second, sort the remaining attribute means from high to low within each segment. Jot down the key themes and give each segment a tentative name. Next, profile each of the clusters by variables outside of the cluster analysis including demographics, pyschographics, product usage, and behaviours. If the clusters aren't different on these variables that were not used in the clustering, it is likely that they will be of little use to management. If the clusters do display differences on these 'outside' variables, use this information combined with the variables from the cluster analysis to name the clusters and describe them, keeping in mind the overall goal of marketing products/services to each of these segments.

Multidimensional scaling

The simplest definition of multidimensional scaling (MDS) is that it draws a picture of relationships you have measured with numbers. Let's assume we want to try to understand how people perceive the following six quick-service restaurants: McDonald's, Burger King, Pizza Hut, Long John Silver's, Arby's, and KFC. The respondents rate the restaurants on a set of scales.

There are many ways to create the 'pictures' that help you understand how these restaurants are seen. With the rating scales, you could factor analyse the results in a restaurant by restaurant correlation matrix and plot the resulting factor loadings. You could treat the ratings for each restaurant as a 'group,' perform discriminant analysis, and plot the discriminant scores. The rating data can be used in an MDS program that essentially creates a picture in which the items that are closer together more often are closest on the picture and those distant from each other are further apart.

At this point you may say that this is too simple to be meaningful. On the contrary, its simplicity is part of its attraction. On the surface it is easy to understand and the pictures give a vivid portrayal of what respondents seem to be saying. Mathematically, it is more rigorous than it may first appear. Thus, if you get a multidimensional picture of your data and the analysis scheme tells you that it is a good fit, then you can have confidence that it is showing what is very likely a real structure for the way people see things.

Conjoint analysis

Unlike the preceding methods, conjoint analysis is not so much a multivariate technique as it is a family of research procedures for designing and analysing experiments. The purpose of the experiment is usually to determine the impact on choice or preference of each of the features of a product or service. What is common across conjoint studies is the assumption that a product or service is a bundle of features that are *con*sidered *joint*ly. For example, a candy bar is the combination of its ingredients, its size, its price, and its brand.

Conjoint has a wide variety of applications including the following examples:

- Identifying the product or service with the optimum combination of features
- Determining the relative contributions of each attribute and each attribute level to the overall evaluation of product/service
- Predicting market share among products/services with differing sets of features
- Measuring market opportunities for products not currently on the market
- Determining the profitability of possible products based on a comparison of feature costs to expected price and market share
- Understanding the potential for multiproduct or multibrand strategy, including an estimate of cannibalism
- Assessing the impact of deleting a product or brand from the market
- Determining how to change a current product to compete with new products entering the market
- Estimating the effect of eliminating some product features that are costly to provide but are of marginal value to customers
- Segmenting customers who place differing importance on features, possibly understanding the size of the segment who buys strictly on price or the size of the segment who buys strictly on brand

Irrespective of the approach you use to conjoint design and analysis, choosing the features and levels to include is of vital importance to the study's success. The tendency of new researchers is to want to include an overabundance of features thinking that the consumers are as involved in their category as they are. Humans tend to simplify decision processes, and as a result, including the five to eight most important features is generally sufficient to predict purchase interest. When selecting the final variables for inclusion in the conjoint, be sure to include only features that can add to or detract from overall choice, differentiate between products, be acted on, and be easily communicated.

Another issue for the new researcher is the tendency to overgeneralise the solution. If the change in levels of price tends to have a great impact on the preference for a product, one can not make the general statement that 'price is the most important characteristic.' What you have measured is that the change from one level of price to another among the prices you chose to test was more determinant of choice than a change from one level to another on other characteristics. You could have chosen price levels that were closer together and gotten a very different result.

Tim Macer

As a software reviewer, Tim contributes regularly to the industry respected magazine Research *on all aspects of IT in marketing research. Visit http:\\\www.macer.co.uk to examine current and back copies of his software reviews.*

Good news from the mining industry

TIM MACER

Data mining offers market researchers a wide range of sophisticated analysis and interpretative tools to remove the drudgery from seeking interesting findings in seemingly endless pages of cross-tab reports. Though not a new technique, it is still largely ignored by quantitative researchers. Similarly, most of the literature on data mining (and data warehousing) fails to mention market research at all.

There is much folklore surrounding data mining. As expert Bob Small pointed out in an article entitled 'Debunking Data Mining Myths',[1] much of what is attributed to data mining is incomplete, exaggerated or wrong'. One early myth he does not mention was the assertion that, with so much data available, most market research surveys would become redundant. Another is that data mining is somehow always connected with using a data warehouse and not with the kind of survey data we work with. Data warehousing involves a large-scale investment in creating a replicated and cleaned set of data from different sources within a company's systems which is then 'mined'. The analogy is of sifting through large amounts of data for the few nuggets of gold that you want.

Data mining is a battery of techniques for carrying out transformations on data as an aid to analysis and interpretation – and it only requires that you have a lot of data, not a datawarehouse. The Parallel Computer Centre at Queen's University Belfast lists the principal approaches in data mining as clustering, data summarisation, learning classification rules, finding dependency networks, analysing changes and detecting anomalies. As market researchers, we are more familiar with these as factor analysis, cluster analysis, tabulation, regression, correlation and correspondence analysis. Is this a case of old wine in new bottles? Have we been mining our data for years without realising it? The answer is probably not, because data mining actually takes analysis a stage further.

Doug Dow is Vice President in charge of data mining at SPSS. He has been applying data mining techniques to market research, and has encouraged several large clients in the USA to make the philosophical leap to this way of working. 'From traditional data analysis, you pull data out of its source, transform it slightly, and produce your tables. The first shift most researchers took was going for output you could cut and paste directly into your report. Data mining takes you a whole new step in that direction. You can apply the results of your analysis to creating a decision tree, write the rules for how people will behave and score this in your database, visually edit and clean your data. It challenges the traditional way of doing research – and it does create a nervousness with some researcher.'

Doug Dow's claim is that researchers could use SPSS data mining solutions to transform not only their data but the whole way they approach their data. The core SPSS product and their Chaid analysis product are widely used by researchers; others such as the AnswerTree decision-making and grouping tool are likely to make greater inroads into the market research community once users realise their power in sifting through a mountain of results to come out with the answers – whatever they might be. He speaks excitedly of the potential offered by the 'bi-directionality' of these tools, whereby you can aggregate data or follow it through to the individual. He talks of the ability to perform 'data brushing' to work on outliers and even modify their values. For instance, SPSS

[1] Small, R., *Information Week* (20 January 1997).

offer sophisticated tools for performing missing value analysis and ascribing answers to non-responses.

Doug Dow continues: 'Some may argue that the traditional cross-tabular tool is passé – and that newer technology is superseding it. But the staying power of the survey is the intentional data which you just can't get from any other source. Our clients in the US have been challenged to develop techniques to collect behavioural and intentional data and merge this with data from other sources in the organisation such as sales, marketing and customer service data.'

Martin Callingham, Group Market Research Director for Whitbread, finds data mining tools save him a lot of time and effort. He says, 'It requires an entire philosophical change because you are able to work at an individual not an aggregate level. What you are doing is trying to get at individual relationships in your data. I use the analogy of the sculptor who does not know the lie of the rock in advance, but as he chisels away, the form, the thing the sculptor is creating emerges from beneath all the layers. What is strange is that you don't seem to produce very much in the way of reams of output, because you only produce what you need.' Martin Callingharn uses the tools to steer him in the direction of what is interesting in the data. This is true data mining. He explains how he will often perform a one-dimensional cluster analysis on a key variable just as a simple way of breaking it out into groups, in the same way that traditionally you would divide it by percentage groupings or quartiles. He does a lot of work on derived variables. In the end, he is able to produce charts and some simple tables, so that superficially the end product of his analysis looks similar to that of a traditional researcher – but the way he got there is completely different.

He continues: 'For the most part, market researchers use computers in a cosmetic way to make their tabs look more pretty. With SPSS you can really do something different. I am not a statistician, I am just an ordinary researcher who has bothered to get his head stuck into these things. The hardest thing is to get your brain into a completely new way of working.'

But before you jump to the conclusion that data transformation, decision trees and data brushing are simply the latest and faddiest ways of fiddling the data, think back to your first reaction when the technique of weighting was explained to you. These tools also have a role to play in bringing the meaning out of data, and deserve our attention.

Originally published in *Research*, (June 1998).

Part IV

COMMUNICATION AND INTERNATIONAL DIMENSIONS OF MARKETING RESEARCH

Communicating research findings by preparing and presenting a formal report constitutes the sixth step in a marketing research project. With practical orientation, we provide guidelines for writing reports and preparing tables and graphs and also discuss oral presentation of the report. We finally focus on the international dimensions of marketing research. Although international marketing research has been discussed in previous chapters, this part presents additional details. We present a conceptual framework for international marketing research and illustrate, in detail, how the environment prevailing in the countries, cultural units or international markets being researched influences the way the marketing research process should be preformed.

Chapter 24

Report preparation and presentation

The quality of the report and presentation are often used as major indicators of the quality of the entire marketing research project

OBJECTIVES

After reading this chapter, the student should be able to:

1 discuss the basic requirements of report preparation including report format, report writing, graphs and tables;
2 discuss the nature and scope of the oral presentation;
3 describe the approach to the marketing research report from the client's perspective and the guidelines for reading the research report;
4 explain the reason for follow-up with the client and describe the assistance that should be given to the client and the evaluation of the research project;
5 understand the report preparation and presentation process in international marketing research;
6 identify the ethical issues related to the interpretation and reporting of the research process and findings to the client and the use of these results by the client.

OVERVIEW

Report preparation and presentation constitutes the sixth and final step in a marketing research project. It follows problem definition, developing an approach, research design formulation, fieldwork, and data preparation and analysis. This chapter describes the importance of this last step as well as a process for report preparation and presentation. We provide guidelines for report preparation, including report writing and preparing tables and graphs, and we discuss oral presentation of the report. Research follow-up, including assisting the client and evaluating the research process, is described. The special considerations for report preparation and presentation in international marketing research are discussed, and relevant ethical issues are identified. We begin with an example of the potential array of reports that can emerge from a marketing research project. This is followed with an example of the array of means to convey research findings. Both examples illustrate the different and important audiences that marketing research reports are presented to.

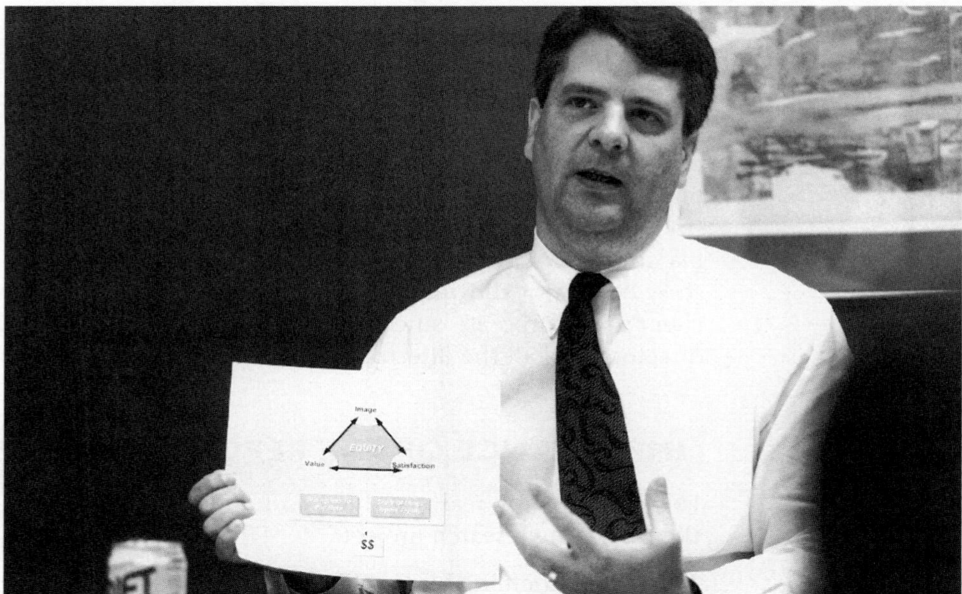

The importance of oral presentation cannot be over-emphasised since many executives form their lasting impressions about a project based on it

GLOBALCASH PROJECT

Report preparation and presentation

In the GlobalCash project, funding for the research came from 15 pan-European banks and trade associations throughout Europe such as the Dutch and the UK Association of Corporate Treasurers. With different sponsoring organisations, a number of formats of report presentation were made. As 19 European countries were surveyed, reports were prepared for each country. There were additional reports for the Nordic/Scandinavia region that combined the results from Denmark, Finland, Norway and Sweden plus an aggregated report for the whole of Europe. Given the importance of the introduction of European Monetary Union, interim reports (based upon 250 and then 500 responses) were presented as the total dataset was being compiled.

The aggregated European report compiled data from 1994, 1996 and 1998 in a written format. As well as the statistical findings, interpretation of the statistics were presented. For individual countries, statistics and interpretations were presented in electronic formats. As well as receiving the written and electronic findings, each of the sponsoring banks had an oral presentation. In some instances banks like Citibank and the Chase Manhattan Bank used video-conferencing to allow executives in the United States to participate in the oral presentation. Each oral presentation was tailored to the individual sponsoring bank. They wished to understand the impact of the findings upon their future strategy in the European cash market.

For the sponsoring trade associations, a written report for their country was presented. This report was shorter than the bank report in that individual bank ratings and performance were omitted. Again, an oral presentation was made to an association meeting which could number up to 300 delegates from a wide array of companies and banks within individual countries.

Finally a much shorter summary of the statistics was written and sent to all questionnaire respondents. ■

EXAMPLE

Taking it to the top[1]

A research agency, Elrick and Lavidge, conducted a research project to measure the relative effectiveness of television, print and radio as advertising media for a client firm. In addition, the effectiveness of ten TV commercials, radio commercials and print advertisements were assessed. Given the nature of the project, the oral presentation of the report was particularly important in communicating the findings. In addition to an overhead projector and slide projector, a VCR (for playing TV commercials), a tape recorder (for playing radio commercials), and a story board (for showing print ads) were used. The presentation was made to the client's top corporate officers – consisting of the chief executive, all the company directors, and all the director's assistants at one of their monthly meetings. ■

IMPORTANCE OF THE REPORT AND PRESENTATION

For the following reasons, the report and its presentation are important parts of the marketing research project:

1 They are the tangible products of the research effort. After the project is complete and management has made the decision, there is little documentary evidence of the project other than the written report. The report serves as a historical record of the project.
2 Management decisions are guided by the report and the presentation. If the first five steps in the project are carefully conducted but inadequate attention is paid to the sixth step, the value of the project to management will be greatly diminished.
3 The involvement of many marketing managers in the project is limited to the written report and the oral presentation. These managers evaluate the quality of the entire project on the quality of the report and presentation.
4 Management's decision to undertake marketing research in the future or to use the particular research supplier again will be influenced by the perceived usefulness of the report and the presentation.

PREPARATION AND PRESENTATION PROCESS

Figure 24.1 illustrates report preparation and presentation. The process begins by interpreting the results of data analysis in the light of the marketing research problem, approach, research design and fieldwork. Instead of merely summarising the statistical results, the researcher should present the findings in such a way that they can be used directly as input into decision-making. Wherever appropriate, conclusions should be drawn and recommendations made. Recommendations should be actionable. Before writing the report, the researcher should discuss the major findings, conclusions and recommendations with the key decision-makers. These discussions play a major role in ensuring that the report meets the client's needs and is ultimately accepted. These discussions should confirm specific dates for the delivery of the written report and other data.

The entire marketing research project should be summarised in a single written report or in several reports addressed to different readers. Generally, an oral presentation supplements the written documents. The client should be given an opportunity to read the report. After that, the researcher should take necessary

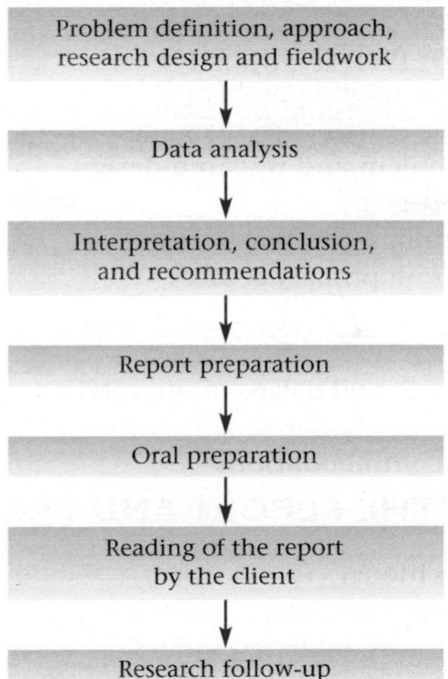

Figure 24.1 The report preparation and presentation process

follow-up actions. The researcher should assist the client in understanding the report, implementing the findings, undertaking further research and evaluating the research process in retrospect.

REPORT PREPARATION

Researchers differ in the way they prepare a research report. The personality, background, expertise and responsibility of the researcher, along with the marketing decision-maker to whom the report is addressed, interact to give each report a unique character. Yet there are guidelines for formatting and writing reports and designing tables and graphs.[2]

Report format

Report formats are likely to vary with the researcher or the marketing research firm conducting the project, the client for whom the project is being conducted, and the nature of the project itself. Hence, the following is intended as a guideline from which the researcher can develop a format for the research project at hand. Most research reports include the following elements:

I **Submission letter**
II **Title page**
III **Table of contents**
  (a) Main sections
  (b) List of tables
  (c) List of graphs
  (d) List of appendices
  (e) List of exhibits
IV **Executive summary**
  (a) Summary of prime objectives
  (b) Major findings
  (c) Conclusions & recommendations

V **Problem definition**
  (a) Background to the problem
  (b) Statement of the marketing problem
  (c) Statement of the research objectives – information needs
VI **Approach to the problem and research design**
  (a) Type of research design
  (b) Data collection from secondary sources
  (c) Data collection from primary sources
VII **Data analysis**
  (a) Methodology
  (b) Plan of data analysis and means to interpret results
VIII **Results**
IX **Conclusions and recommendations**
X **Limitations and caveats**
XI **Appendices**
  (a) Letter of authorisation
  (b) Questionnaire development and pre-testing
  (c) Questionnaires, forms, interview guides
  (d) Sampling techniques including error and confidence levels
  (e) Fieldwork
  (f) Lists including contact individuals and organisations

This format closely follows the earlier steps of the marketing research process. The results may be presented in several chapters of the report. For example, in a national survey, data analysis may be conducted for the overall sample and then the data for each geographic region may be analysed separately. If so, the results may be presented in five chapters instead of one.

Submission letter. A formal report generally contains a letter of submission that delivers the report to the client and summarises the researcher's overall experience with the project, without mentioning the findings. The letter should also identify the need for further action on the part of the client, such as implementation of the findings or further research that should be undertaken.

Title page. The title page should include the title of the report, information (name, address and telephone) about the researcher or organisation conducting the research, the name of the client for whom the report was prepared, and the date of release. The title should encapsulate the nature of the project.

Table of contents. The table of contents should list the topics covered and the appropriate page numbers. In most reports, only the major headings and subheadings are included. The table of contents is followed by a list of tables, list of graphs, list of appendices, and list of exhibits.

Executive summary. The executive summary is an extremely important part of the report, because this is often the only portion of the report that executives read. The summary should concisely describe the problem, approach, and research design that was adopted. A summary section should be devoted to the major results, conclusions and recommendations. The executive summary should be written after the rest of the report.

Problem definition. The problem definition section of the report gives the background to the problem. This part summarises elements of the marketing and research problem diagnosis. Key elements of any discussions with decision makers, industry experts and initial secondary data analyses are presented. Having set this context for the whole project a clear statement of the management decision problem(s) and the marketing research problem(s) should be presented.

Approach to the problem and research design. The approach to the problem section should discuss the broad approach that was adopted in addressing the problem. This section should summarise the theoretical foundations that guided the research, any analytical models formulated, research questions, hypotheses, and the factors that influenced the research design. The research design should specify the details of how the research was conducted, preferably with a graphical presentation of the stages undertaken, showing the relationships between stages. This should detail the methods undertaken in the data collection from secondary and primary sources. These topics should be presented in a non-technical, easy-to-understand manner. The technical details should be included in an appendix. This section of the report should justify the specific methods selected.

Data analysis. The section on data analysis should describe the plan of data analysis and justify the data analysis strategy and techniques used. The techniques used for analysis should be described in simple, non-technical terms, with examples to help the reader to interpret any statistics.

Results. The results section is normally the longest part of the report and may entail several chapters. It may be presented by (*a*) *forms of analysis*, for example, in a health care marketing survey of hospitals, the results were presented in four chapters. One chapter presented the overall results, another examined the differences between geographical regions, a third presented the differences between for-profit and non-profit hospitals, and a fourth presented the differences according to bed capacity. Often, results are presented not only at the aggregate level but also at the subgroup (market segment, geographical area, etc.) level. (*b*) *forms of data collection*, for example, a study may contain significant elements of secondary data collection and analyses, a series of focus group interviews and a survey. The results in such circumstances may be best presented by drawing conclusions from one method before moving onto another method. The conclusions derived from focus groups for example, may need to be established to show the link to a sample design and questions used in a survey. (*c*) *objectives*, there may be a series of research objectives whose fulfilment may incorporate a variety of data collection methods and levels of analysis. In these circumstances the results combine methods and levels of analyses to show connections and to develop and illustrate emerging issues.

The results should be organised in a coherent and logical way. Choosing whether to present by forms of analysis, forms of data collection or objectives, helps to build that coherence and logic. The presentation of the results should be geared directly to the components of the marketing research problem and the information needs that were identified. The nature of the information needs and characteristics of the recipients of the report ultimately determine the best way to present results.

Conclusions and recommendations. Presenting a mere summary of the statistical results is not enough. The researcher should interpret the results in light of the problem being addressed to arrive at major conclusions. Based on the results and conclusions, the researcher may make recommendations to the decision-makers. Sometimes, marketing researchers are not asked to make recommendations because they research only one area but do not understand the bigger picture at the client firm. The researcher may not have been fully involved in the diagnosis of the marketing and research problems and as such their interpretations may not fit into the context that the marketer understands.

In any research project there are many approaches that can be taken to analyse the data. This can result in a potential over-abundance of data (quantitative and/or qualitative) and distilling the 'meaning' from the data and presenting this in a clear report can result in much of the original meaning or richness being lost.[3] To maintain the meaning or richness, the researcher should strive to understand the nature of the decision making process that is being supported. Only then can sound interpretations of the collected data be made.

Limitations and caveats. All marketing research projects have limitations caused by time, budget, and other organisational constraints. Furthermore, the research design adopted may be limited in terms of the various types of errors, and some of these may be serious enough to warrant discussion. This section should be written with great care and a balanced perspective. On the one hand, the researcher must make sure that management does not overly rely on the results or use them for unintended purposes, such as projecting them to unintended populations. On the other hand, this section should not erode their confidence in the research or unduly minimise its importance.

Appendices

At the end of the report, documents can be compiled that may be used by different readers to help them to understand characteristics of the research project in more detail. These should include the letter of authorisation to conduct the research; this authorisation could include the agreed research proposal. Details that relate to individual techniques should be included relating to questionnaires, interview guides, sampling and fieldwork activities. The final part of the appendix should include lists of contacts, references used and further sources of reference.

REPORT WRITING

Readers. A report should be written for a specific reader or readers: the marketing managers who will use the results. The report should take into account the readers' technical sophistication and interest in the project as well as the circumstances under which they will read the report and how they will use it.[4]

Technical jargon should be avoided. As expressed by one expert, 'The readers of your reports are busy people; and very few of them can balance a research report, a cup of coffee, and a dictionary at one time.'[5] Instead of technical terms like maximum likelihood, heteroscedasticity, and non-parametric, use descriptive explanations. If some technical terms cannot be avoided, briefly define them in an appendix. When it comes to marketing research, decision-makers would rather live with a problem they cannot solve than accept a solution they cannot understand.

Often the researcher must cater to the needs of several audiences with different levels of technical sophistication and interest in the project. Such conflicting needs may be met by including different sections in the report for different readers or separate reports entirely.

Easy to follow. The report should be easy to follow.[6] It should be structured logically and written clearly. The material, particularly the body of the report, should be structured in a logical manner so that the reader can easily see the inherent connections and linkages. Headings should be used for different topics and subheadings for subtopics.

A logical organisation also leads to a coherent report. Clarity can be enhanced by using well-constructed sentences that are short and to the point. The words used should express precisely what the researcher wants to communicate. Difficult words, slang and clichés should be avoided. An excellent check on the clarity of a report is to have two or three people who are unfamiliar with the project read it and offer critical comments. Several revisions of the report may be needed before the final document emerges.

Presentable and professional appearance. The looks of a report are important. The report should be professionally reproduced with quality paper, typing and binding. The typography should be varied. Variation in type size and skilful use of white space can greatly contribute to the appearance and readability of the report.

Objective. Objectivity is a virtue that should guide report writing. Researchers can become so fascinated with their project that they overlook their scientific role. The report should accurately present the methodology, results and conclusions of the project, without slanting the findings to conform to the expectations of management. Decision-makers are unlikely to receive with enthusiasm a report that reflects unfavourably on their judgement or actions. Yet the researcher must have the courage to present and defend the results objectively.

Reinforce text with tables and graphs. It is important to reinforce key information in the text with tables, graphs, pictures, maps and other visual devices. Visual aids can greatly facilitate communication and add to the clarity and impact of the report. Guidelines for tabular and graphical presentation are discussed later.

Reinforce tables and graphs with text. Conversely it is important to illustrate tables and graphs with verbatim quotes from questionnaires and interviews. Quotes can bring to life the meaning in tables and graphs and used carefully can make the reading of the report far more interesting than a solid body of statistics.

Terse. A report should be terse and concise. Anything unnecessary should be omitted. If too much information is included, important points may be lost. Avoid lengthy discussions of common procedures. Yet brevity should not be achieved at the expense of completeness.

Guidelines for tables

Statistical tables are a vital part of the report and deserve special attention. We illustrate the guidelines for tables using data from the GlobalCash study. Table 24.1 presents the findings from two questions. The rows in Table 24.1 show how European companies plan to change their relationships with their existing banks once EMU is introduced. The columns in Table 24.1 summarise the number of relationships companies have with banks in their home countries. This number of relationships is termed the 'sourcing strategy', i.e. a *single* strategy means all transactions go through one bank, a *dual* strategy means that transactions go through two banks and a *multiple* strategy means that transactions go through more than two banks, in some instances up to 70 banks for some Italian companies!

The numbers in parentheses in the following paragraphs refer to the numbered sections of the table.

Title and number. Every table should have a number (1a) and title (1b). The title should be brief yet clearly descriptive of the information provided. Arabic numbers are used to identify tables so that they can be referenced in the text.[7]

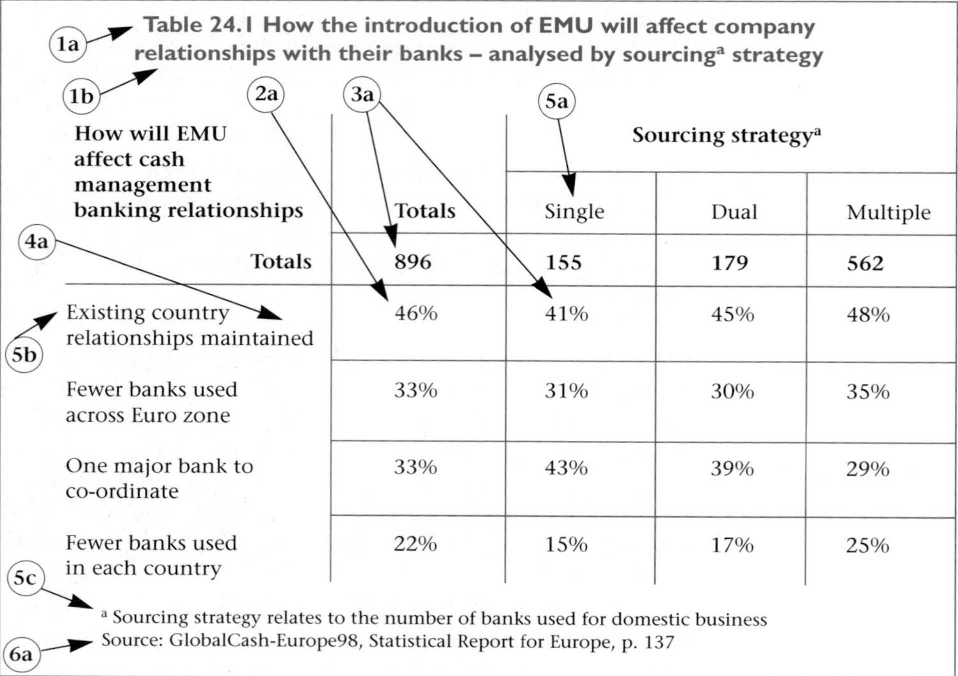

Table 24.1 How the introduction of EMU will affect company relationships with their banks – analysed by sourcing[a] strategy

How will EMU affect cash management banking relationships	Totals	Sourcing strategy[a]		
		Single	Dual	Multiple
Totals	**896**	**155**	**179**	**562**
Existing country relationships maintained	46%	41%	45%	48%
Fewer banks used across Euro zone	33%	31%	30%	35%
One major bank to co-ordinate	33%	43%	39%	29%
Fewer banks used in each country	22%	15%	17%	25%

[a] Sourcing strategy relates to the number of banks used for domestic business
Source: GlobalCash-Europe98, Statistical Report for Europe, p. 137

Arrangement of data items. The arrangement of data items in a table should emphasise the most significant aspect of the data. For example, when the data pertain to time, the items should be arranged by appropriate time period. When order of magnitude is most important, the data items should be arranged in that order (2a). If ease of locating items is critical, an alphabetical arrangement is most appropriate.

Basis of measurement. The basis or unit of measurement should be clearly stated (3a). In Table 24.1, the totals sample size is shown and the sub-sample sizes of the different sourcing strategies. The main body of data is shown in percentages. The % signs would normally be removed with a note to tell the reader that the main body is based upon: column percentages, or row percentages, or percentages related to the total sample size.

Leaders, rulings, spaces. The reader's eye should be guided to be able to read across the table clearly. This can be achieved with ruled lines (4a), alternate shaded rows, or white spaces with dotted lines leading from the row headings to the data.

Explanations and comments: headings, stubs, and footnotes. Explanations and comments clarifying the table can be provided in the form of captions, stubs and footnotes. Designations placed over the vertical columns are called headings (5a). Designations placed in the left-hand column are called stubs (5b). Information that cannot be incorporated in the table should be explained by footnotes (5c). Letters or symbols should be used for footnotes rather than numbers. The footnotes that are part of the original source should come after the main table, but before the source note.

Sources of the data. If the data contained in the table are secondary, the source of data should be cited (6a).

Guidelines for graphs

As a general rule, graphic aids should be employed whenever practical. Graphical display of information can effectively complement the text and tables to enhance clarity of communication and impact.[8] As the saying goes, a picture is worth a thousand words. The guidelines for preparing graphs are similar to those for tables. Therefore, this section focuses on the different types of graphical aids.[9] We illustrate several of these using the GlobalCash data from Table 24.1.

Geographic and other maps. Geographic and other maps, such as product positioning maps, can communicate relative location and other comparative information. Geographic maps form the bases of presentations in geodemographic analyses as discussed in Chapter 5. The maps used in geodemographic analyses can portray: customer locations and types, potential consumers, location of competitors, road networks to show consumer flows and other facilities that may attract consumers to certain locations.

Pie chart
A round chart divided into sections.

Round or pie charts. In a pie chart, the area of each section, as a percentage of the total area of the circle, reflects the percentage associated with the value of a specific variable. A pie chart is not useful for displaying relationships over time or relationships among several variables. As a general guideline, a pie chart should not require more than seven sections.[10] Figure 24.2 shows a pie chart for the sourcing strategies of European companies. Great care must be taken with 3D pie charts as the relative sizes of the pie segments become distorted.

Line chart
A chart that connects a series of data points using continuous lines.

Line charts. A line chart connects a series of data points using continuous lines. This is an attractive way of illustrating trends and changes over time. Several series can be compared on the same chart, and forecasts, interpolations and extrapolations can be shown. If several series are displayed simultaneously, each line should have a distinctive colour or form (see Figure 24.3).[11]

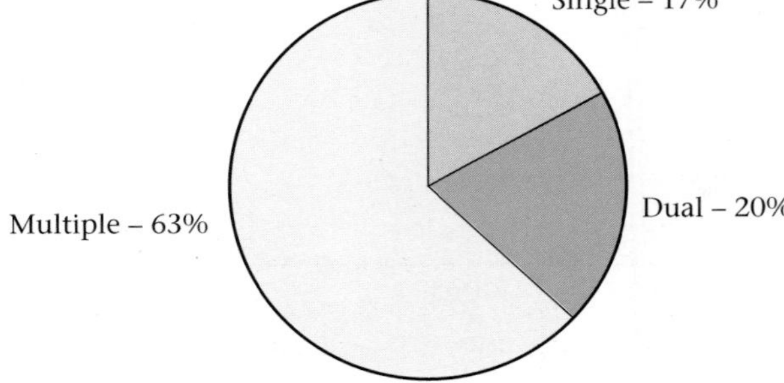

Figure 24.2
Pie chart that shows the percentage of European companies with different sourcing strategies for domestic banks

Bar chart
A chart that displays data in bars positioned horizontally or vertically.

Histogram
A vertical bar chart in which the height of the bars represents the relative or cumulative frequency of occurrence.

Histograms and bar charts. A **bar chart** displays data in various bars that may be positioned horizontally or vertically. Bar charts can be used to present absolute and relative magnitudes, differences and change. A **histogram** is a vertical bar chart in which the height of the bars represents the relative or cumulative frequency of occurrence of a specific variable (see Figure 24.4). Variations on the basic bar chart include the stacked bar chart (Figure 24.5) and the cluster bar chart (Figure 24.6). Stacked and cluster bar charts can work well with a few data items presented, to qualitatively represent differences between groups. As noted with pie charts, 3D charts should be used with great caution as they can distort the message and confuse an audience. Most graphics packages have a great array of 3D options; however, there are few circumstances where they can be used to present data in a clear and unbiased manner.

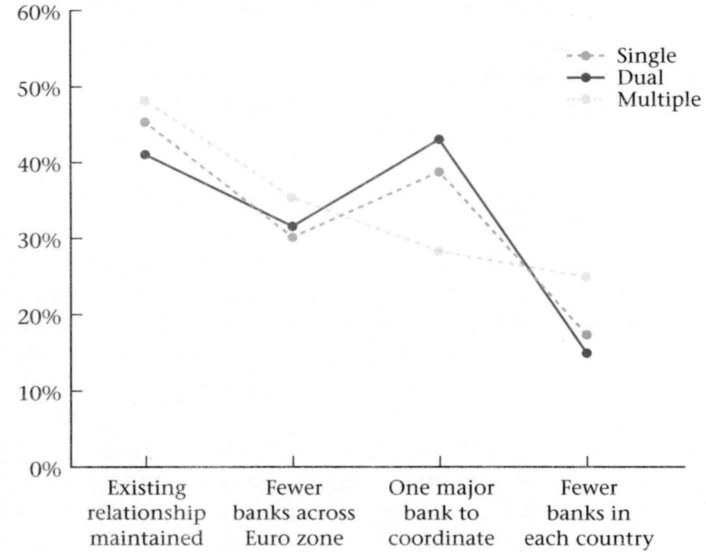

Figure 24.3
Line chart of how the introduction of EMU will affect cash management banking relationships

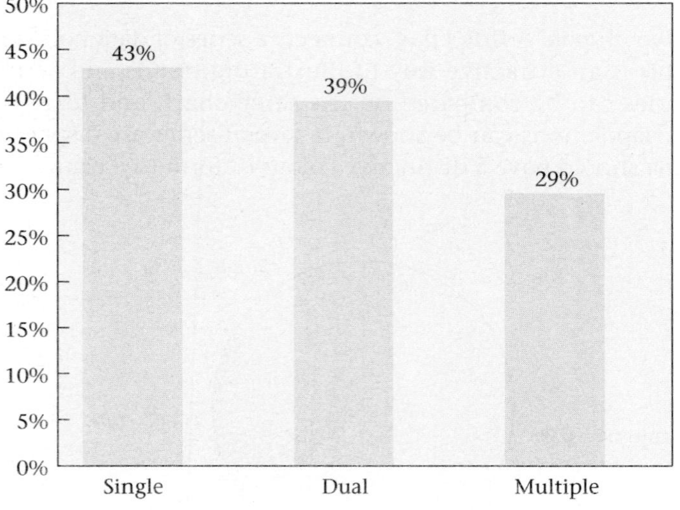

Figure 24.4
Bar chart that shows the percentage of company types that planned to use one major bank to coordinate cash transactions throughout Europe

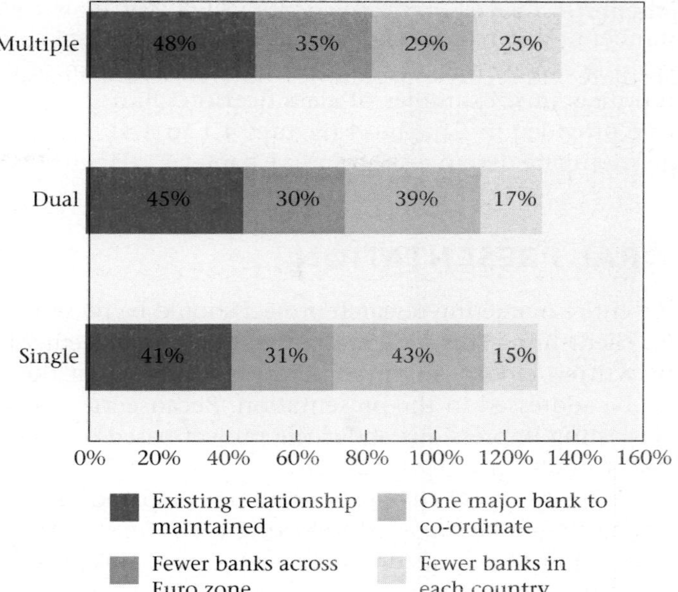

Figure 24.5
Stacked bar chart

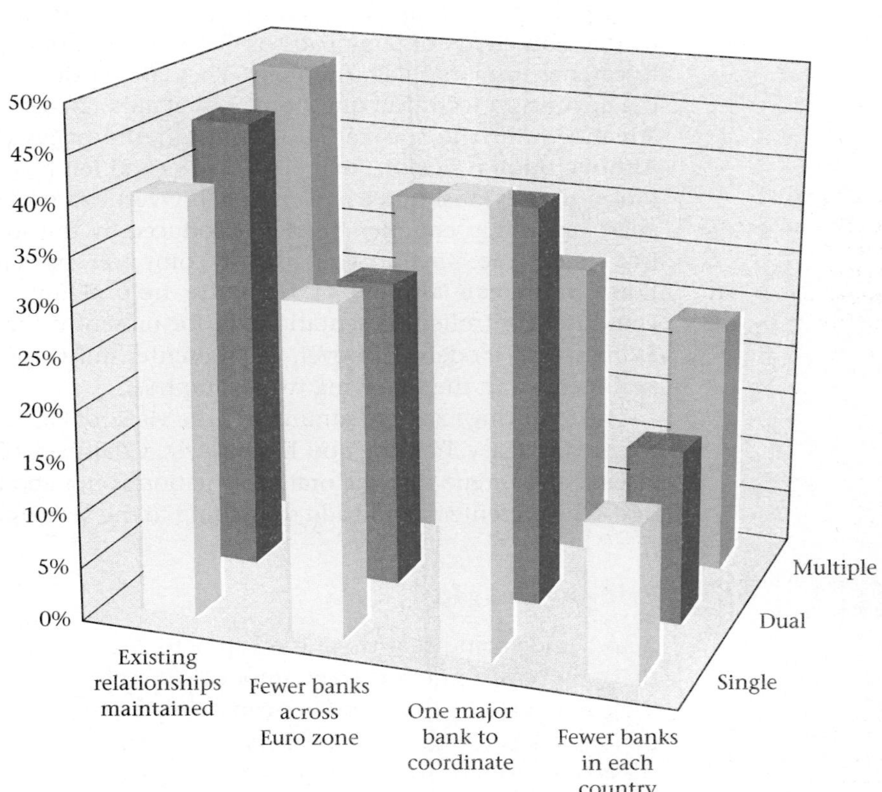

Figure 24.6
3D cluster bar

Schematic figures and flowcharts. Schematic figures and flowcharts take on a number of different forms. They can be used to display the steps or components of a process, as in Figure 24.1. Another useful form of these charts is classification diagrams. Examples of classification charts for classifying secondary data were provided in Chapter 4 (Figures 4.1 to 4.4). An example of a flowchart for questionnaire design was given in Chapter 12 (Figure 12.2).[12]

ORAL PRESENTATION

The entire marketing research project should be presented to the management of the client firm. This presentation will help management understand and accept the written report. Any preliminary questions that the management may have can be addressed in the presentation. Because many executives form their first and lasting impressions about the project based on the presentation, its importance cannot be overemphasised.[13]

The key to an effective presentation is preparation. A written script or detailed outline should be prepared following the format of the written report. The presentation must be geared to the audience. For this purpose, the researcher should determine the backgrounds, interests and involvement of those in the project, as well as the extent to which they are likely to be affected by it. The presentation should be rehearsed several times before it is made to the management.

Visual aids such as tables and graphs should be displayed with a variety of media. Flip charts of large pads of blank paper mounted on an easel enable the researcher to manipulate numbers. They are particularly useful in communicating answers to technical questions. Visual aids can also be drawn on the pages in advance, and the speaker flips through the pages during the presentation. Although not as flexible, magnetic boards and felt boards allow for rapid presentation of previously prepared material. Overhead projectors can present simple charts as well as complex overlays produced by the successive additions of new images to the screen. The use of computer packages such as Microsoft's Powerpoint can also be of immense help. They can be used for making computer-controlled presentations or for presenting technical information such as analytical models. However, the presenter must not lose sight of the message as illustrated in the following two examples.

The following example summarises the views of Cristina Stuart, managing director of SpeakEasy Training and Khalid Aziz, Chairman of the Aziz Corporation. In essence they argue that the oral presentation is not about the slick use of technology – the presenter should add something to the visual presentation.

EXAMPLE

Bridging the gap[14]

Actors understand that there is a gap between the speaker and the audience and that you have to do a certain amount of work to bridge that gap. Actors spend their lives at interviews and are constantly having to present themselves to new people. Like actors, some speakers use props to enhance their performance but these need to be handled with care. It is the person that must be persuasive, not the PC. People often hide behind their visuals but if that is all that you are presenting, you might as well have sent them in the post. Technology may be used where it is appropriate, but too often people overdo the visuals to the detriment of the message. Even at Microsoft, where with its PowerPoint software the medium is the message, the presenter presides over the technology, not the other way around. ■

EXAMPLE

Screen saviours[15]

Phillip Redding, deputy Managing Director of The Presentation Company emphasises that technology is only part of the presentation picture. For him, it is just as important to get the content and structure of the argument right, and to create designs that put them over in a powerful way. 'If the content and structure are not clear, the presentation is not going to stand a chance. People think that by adding 3D animation, the audience will be impressed. They will, but they still won't think the argument is very good.'

Video recorders (VCRs) and large-screen projectors are particularly effective in presenting focus groups and other aspects of field work that are dynamic in nature. It is important to maintain eye contact and to interact with the audience during the presentation. Sufficient opportunity should be provided for questions, both during and after the presentation. The presentation should be made interesting and convincing with the use of appropriate stories, examples, experiences, and quotations. Filler words like 'uh', 'y'know' and 'all right' should not be used.

Body language should be employed. Descriptive gestures are used to clarify or enhance verbal communication. Emphatic gestures are used to emphasise what is being said. Suggestive gestures are symbols of ideas and emotions. Prompting gestures are used to elicit a desired response from the audience. The speaker should vary the volume, pitch, voice quality, articulation and rate while speaking. The presentation should terminate with a strong closing. To stress its importance, the presentation should be sponsored by a top-level manager in the client's organisation. ■

After the presentation, key executives in the client firm should be given time to read the report in detail. Some guidelines are available for report reading.

READING THE RESEARCH REPORT

The following points should help in the writing of a report by putting the author in the shoes of the reader.[16]

Addresses the problem

The problem being addressed should be clearly identified and the relevant background information should be provided. The organisation sponsoring the research, as well as the one conducting the research, should be clearly identified. The report should not assume that the reader has prior knowledge of the problem situation, but should give all the relevant information. A report that does not provide such information has missed its mark, as well as its readers.

Research design

The research design should be clearly described in non-technical terms. If readers in the target audience of the report cannot understand the research design procedure, the fault lies with the researcher. The report should include a discussion of the information needs, data collection methods, scaling techniques, questionnaire design and pre-testing, sampling techniques and fieldwork. Justification should be provided for the specific methods used. Reports that do not contain, or otherwise make available, methodological details should be viewed with caution.

Execution of the research procedures

The reader should pay special attention to the manner in which the research procedures were executed. The people working on the project should be well qualified and properly trained. Proper supervision and control procedures should be followed. This is particularly important with respect to data collection, data preparation and statistical analysis.

Numbers and statistics

Numbers and statistics reported in tables and graphs should be examined carefully by the reader. Inappropriate numbers and statistics can be highly misleading. Consider, for example, percentages based on small samples or means reported for ordinal data. Unfortunately, the occurrence of these types of misleading statistics in reports is not uncommon.

Interpretations and conclusions

The findings should be reported in an objective and candid way. The interpretation of the basic results should be differentiated from the results per se. Any assumptions made in interpreting the results should be clearly identified. The limitations of the research should be discussed. Any conclusions or recommendations made without a specification of the underlying assumptions or limitations should be treated cautiously by the reader.

Generalisability

It is the responsibility of the researcher to provide evidence regarding the reliability, validity and generalisability of the findings. The report should clearly identify the target population to which the findings apply. Factors that limit the generalisability of the findings – such as the nature and representativeness of the sample, mode and time of data collections, and various sources of error – should be clearly identified. The reader should not attempt to generalise the findings of the report without explicit consideration of these factors.

Disclosure

Finally, the reader should carefully examine whether the spirit in which the report was written indicates an honest and complete disclosure of the research procedures and results. It is particularly important that procedures – for example, those used for the treatment of missing values or for weighting – that call for subjective judgement on the part of the researcher, be made known. If any negative or unexpected findings were obtained, they should be reported. The reader should feel free to ask for any relevant information that is not contained in the report.

A careful reading of the report using these guidelines will help the client to participate in research follow-up effectively.

RESEARCH FOLLOW-UP

The researcher's task does not end with the oral presentation. Two other tasks remain. The researcher should help the client understand and implement the findings and take follow-up action. Second, while it is still fresh in the researcher's mind, the entire marketing research project should be evaluated.

Assisting the client

After the client has read the report in detail, several questions may arise. Parts of the report, particularly those dealing with technical matters, may not be understood and the researcher should provide the help needed. Sometimes the researcher helps implement the findings. Often, the client retains the researcher to help with the selection of a new product or advertising agency, development of a pricing policy, market segmentation or other marketing actions. An important reason for client follow-up is to discuss further research projects. For example, the researcher and management may agree to repeat the study after two years. Finally, the researcher should help the client firm make the information generated in the marketing research project a part of the firm's marketing (management) information system (MIS) or decision support system (DSS), as discussed in Chapter 1. A key element in researchers being able to assist marketing decision-makers is the level of trust that exists between the two parties. The nature of personal interaction between managers and researchers is very important in creating trust in the researcher and consequently in the results of the research. The quality of personal interaction affects managers' perceptions of the overall quality of the report itself.[17] Trust between the decision-maker and the researcher has been found to influence the perceived quality of user–researcher interactions, the level of researcher involvement, the level of user commitment to the relationship and the level of market research utilisation.[18]

Evaluation of the research project

Although marketing research is scientific, it also involves creativity, intuition and expertise. Hence, every marketing research project provides an opportunity for learning, and the researcher should critically evaluate the entire project to obtain new insights and knowledge. The key question to ask is, 'Could this project have been conducted more effectively or efficiently?' This question, of course, raises several more specific questions. Could the problem have been defined differently so as to enhance the value of the project to the client or reduce the costs? Could a different approach have yielded better results? Was the research design that was used the best? How about the method of data collection? Should street interviews been used instead of telephone interviews? Was the sampling plan employed the most appropriate? Were the sources of possible design error correctly anticipated and kept under control, at least in a qualitative sense? If not, what changes could have been made? How could the selection, training and supervision of field workers be altered to improve data collection? Was the data analysis strategy effective in yielding information useful for decision-making? Were the conclusions and recommendations appropriate and useful to the client? Was the report adequately written and presented? Was the project completed within the time and budget allocated? If not, what went wrong? The insights gained from such an evaluation will benefit the researcher and the subsequent projects conducted.

INTERNATIONAL MARKETING RESEARCH

The guidelines presented earlier in this chapter apply to international marketing research as well, although report preparation may be complicated by the need to prepare reports for management in different countries and in different languages. In such a case, the researcher should prepare different versions of the report, each geared to specific readers. The different reports should be comparable, although the formats may differ. The guidelines for oral presentation are also similar to those given earlier, with the added proviso that the presenter should be sensitive to cultural norms. For example, making jokes, which is frequently done in many countries, is not appropriate in all cultures (which may also include particular organisational cultures). Most marketing decisions are made from facts and figures arising out of marketing research. But these figures have to pass the test and limits of logic, subjective experience and gut feelings of decision-makers. The subjective experience and gut feelings of managers could vary widely across countries necessitating that different recommendations be made for implementing the research findings in different countries. This is particularly important when making innovative or creative recommendations such as advertising campaigns.

ETHICS IN MARKETING RESEARCH

Many issues pertaining to research integrity arise during report preparation and presentation. A survey of 254 marketing researchers found that 33% believed that the most difficult ethical problems they face pertain to issues of research integrity. These issues included ignoring pertinent data, compromising the research design, deliberately misusing statistics, falsifying figures, altering research results and misinterpreting the results with the objective of supporting a personal or corporate point of view, and withholding information.[19] It is important that researchers deal with these issues in a satisfactory manner and prepare a report which accurately and fully discloses the details of all the procedures and findings.

Objectivity should be maintained throughout the research process. For example, when data are analysed and no meaningful results are found, researchers are tempted to see findings which are not supported by the analysis. One example is meaningfully interpreting a regression equation when all the independent variables turn out to be non-significant (Chapter 19). Ethical dilemmas can arise in these instances. The researchers are being paid for their expert interpretation of data, and can nothing meaningful be said? 'To arrive at some rational, logical, and convincing conclusion is so much more satisfying intellectually than to admit that the findings are inconsistent and inconclusive. No wonder we find ourselves mentally selecting and shaping what might otherwise be shapeless into a coherent, well-defined story.'[20] Such temptations must be resisted to avoid unethical conduct.

Like researchers, clients also have the responsibility for full and accurate disclosure of the research findings and are obligated to employ these findings honourably. For example, the public can be negatively affected by a client who distorts the research findings to develop a more favourable television advertising campaign. Ethical issues also arise when client firms, such as tobacco companies, use marketing research findings to formulate questionable marketing programmes.

INTERNET AND COMPUTER APPLICATIONS

Marketing research reports are being published or posted directly to the Web. Normally, these reports are not located in publicly accessible areas but in locations protected by passwords or corporate intranets. The various word-processing, spreadsheet and presentation packages have the capability to produce material in a format that can be posted directly to the Web, thus facilitating the process.

There are a number of advantages to publishing marketing research reports on the Web. These reports can incorporate all kinds of multimedia presentations including graphs, pictures, animation, audio and full-motion video. The dissemination is immediate and the reports can be accessed by authorised persons on-line on a worldwide basis. These reports can be electronically searched to identify materials of specific interest. For example, a manager in Kuala Lumpur can electronically locate the portions of a report that pertain to Malaysia or South East Asia. Storage or future retrieval is efficient and effortless. It is easy to integrate these reports to become part of a decision support system. The main disadvantage is that the readers may not have permanent access to the reports as Web sites may change periodically.

Originally, the main application of microcomputers was in word processing. However, with great developments in processor and software technology, a variety of word processors and other tools have evolved that allow for professional preparation and presentation of marketing research reports at reasonable costs. For example, not only do word processors include a dictionary, thesaurus and grammar checkers, they also have the ability to incorporate graphs, tables and images created with other software such as spreadsheets, graphics packages, and image processing tools. For further flexibility in text and image design, desktop publishing programs can be used.

Another important addition for reports and presentations is the inclusion of graphics. These can be in the form of clip art, scanned and manipulated images, and original graphics. Several companies offer a multitude of clip art images that are available for royalty-free distribution in reports. If however, the images that need to be included in a report are not available as clip art, images can be scanned using a flatbed or slide scanner and an image modification package.

A vast number of software programs are available for developing remarkable presentations with great ease. For example, Microsoft PowerPoint allows for the development of a slide show as a presentation. The development process is very simple, but the final product can be very intricate. In addition, some presentation programs also allow for the addition of sound and video clips for a more complete representation of data. With a little more effort, presentation software can be used to fully animate a presentation.

SUMMARY

Report preparation and presentation is the final step in the marketing research project. This process begins with interpretation of data analysis results and leads to conclusions and recommendations. Next, the formal report is written and an oral presentation made. After management has read the report, the researcher should conduct a follow-up, assisting management and undertaking a thorough evaluation of the marketing research project.

In international marketing research, report preparation may be complicated by the need to prepare reports for management in different countries and in different languages. Several ethical issues are pertinent, particularly those related to the interpretation and reporting of the research process and findings to the client and the use of these results by the client.

The final example presents a metaphor of the use of guitar in supporting presentations. It is a final reminder that the power of computing software can never replace the creative skills of conveying the story and impact of a piece of research upon a decision-making situation.

EXAMPLE

My paradigm is the guitar[21]

Developments in modern technology have had a profound impact on the art of business presentation, most notably through PC-driven presentations. There is no doubt that the standard of the visualisation of presentations has improved immeasurably, but has the presentation itself? Technically good presentations are becoming commonplace, perhaps even predictable. Predictability precedes boredom.

Presenters spend too much time at the PC creating a slide show and not enough on their performance. Presenters have forgotten to plan their personal involvement and the involvement of their audience.

> My paradigm is the guitar. The guitar represents a tool that supports presentation, rather like a PC, but that can never do the performance for you. From my own experience as a guitarist, presentations and gigs have many parallels. You have to prepare diligently, and have a good plan for the progress of the performance. You should know your material. You must be able to excite the audience and get them involved. You must be able to improvise and respond to requests. You should have a good guitar, but the good guitar on its own won't carry the day. You will. ■

QUESTIONS AND PROBLEMS

1. Describe the process of report preparation.
2. Why is the quality of report presentation vital to the success of a marketing research project?
3. Describe a commonly used format for writing marketing research reports.
4. Describe the following parts of a report: title page, table of contents, executive summary, problem definition, research design, data analysis, conclusions and recommendations.
5. Why is the 'limitations and caveats' section included in the report?
6. Discuss the importance of objectivity in writing a marketing research report.
7. Describe the guidelines for report writing.
8. How should the data items be arranged in a table?
9. What is a pie chart? For what type of information is it suitable? For what type of information is it not suitable?
10. Describe a line chart. What kind of information is commonly displayed using such charts?
11. What are the advantages and disadvantages of presenting data using 3D charts?
12. What is the purpose of an oral presentation? What guidelines should be followed in an oral presentation?
13. To what extent should marketing researchers interpret the information they present in a report?
14. Describe the evaluation of a marketing research project in retrospect.
15. Graphically represent the consumer decision-making process described in the following paragraph:

    The consumer first becomes aware of the need. Then the consumer simultaneously searches for information from several sources: retailers, advertising, word of mouth, and independent publications. After that a criterion is developed for evaluating the available brands in the marketplace. Based on this evaluation, the most preferred brand is selected.

NOTES

1 Information provided by Roger L. Bacik, Senior Vice-President, Elrick and Lavidge, Atlanta.

2 Sorrels, R.D., *Business Communication Fundamentals* (New York: Merrill Publishing, 1984).

3 Birks, D.F., 'Market Research', in Baker, M.J. *The Marketing Book,* 3rd edn (Butterworth Hiennemann, 1994), 262

4 Roman, K. and Raphaelson, J., *Writing That Works* (New York: HarperCollins, 1985).

5 Britt, S.H., 'The Writing of Readable Research Reports', *Journal of Marketing Research* (May 1971), 265.

6 Elliott, J., 'How Hard It Is to Write Easily', *Viewpoint: By, For, and About Ogilvy & Mather* 2 (1980), 18.

7 Ehrenberg, A.S.C., 'Rudiments of Numeracy', *Journal of the Royal Statistical Society*, Series A, 140 (1977), 277–97; and Ehrenberg, A.S.C., 'The Problem of Numeracy', *American Statistician* 35 (May 1981), 67–71.

8 Takeuchi, H., and Schmidt, A.H., 'New Promise of Computer Graphics', *Harvard Business Review* (January–February 1980), 122–31.

9 Lord, Jr., W.J. and Dawe, J., *Functional Business Communication*, 3rd edn (Englewood Cliffs, NJ: Prentice Hall, 1983).

10 Tufte, E.R., *The Visual Display of Quantitative Information* (Cheshire: CT Graphics Press, 1983).

11 Zelazny, G., *Say It with Charts* (Homewood, IL: Business One Irwin, 1991).

12 For an example of how graphs can enhance the presentation of research findings, see Figures 1 and 2 of Anderson, E.W., Fornell, C. and Lehmann, D.R., 'Customer Satisfaction, Market Share, and Profitability: Findings from Sweden', *Journal of Marketing* 58 (July 1994), 53–66.

13 Murphy, H.A. and Hildebrandt, H.W., *Effective Business Communications*, 5th edn (New York: McGraw-Hill, 1988).

14 Miller, R., 'In the Spotlight', *Marketing* (1997), 35.

15 Condon, R., 'Screen Saviours', *Marketing* (8 January 1998), 24.

16 Public Affairs Council, *Guidelines for the Public Use of Market and Opinion Research* (New York: Advertising Research Foundation, 1981).

17 Deshpande, R. and Zaltman, G., 'Factors Affecting the Use of Market Research Information: a Path Analysis', *Journal of Marketing Research* 19 (February 1982), 25.

18 Moorman, C., Deshpande, R. and Zaltman, G., 'Factors Affecting Trust in Market Research Relationships', *Journal of Marketing* 57 (January 1993), 81–101.

19 Hunt, S.D., Chonko, L.B. and Wilcox, J.B., 'Ethical Problems of Marketing Researchers', *Journal of Marketing Research* 21 (1984), 309–24.

20 Day, R.L., 'A Comment on 'Ethics in Marketing Research', *Journal of Marketing Research* 11 (1974), 232–33.

21 Willetts N.J., 'Going Live', *Marketing Week* (13 November 1997), 47–48.

Chapter 25

International marketing research

Marketing across national boundaries remains one of the most difficult activities for many manufacturers in many product and service areas. Likewise, the research problems involved in multi-country coordination can be formidable[1]

OBJECTIVES

After reading this chapter, the student should be able to:

1. develop a framework for conducting international marketing research;
2. explain in detail the marketing, governmental, legal, economic, structural, informational and technological, and socio-cultural environmental factors and how they have an impact on international marketing research;
3. describe characteristics of the use of secondary data, qualitative techniques, telephone, personal and mail survey methods in different countries;
4. discuss how to establish the equivalence of scales and measures including construct, operational, scalar and linguistic equivalence;
5. describe the processes of back translation and parallel translation in translating a questionnaire into a different language;
6. discuss the ethical considerations in international marketing research.

OVERVIEW

This chapter starts by evaluating the need for international marketing research. It then discusses the environment in which international marketing research is conducted, focusing on the marketing, government, legal, economic, structural, informational and technological, and socio-cultural environment.[2] Although discussions of how the six steps of the marketing research process should be implemented in an international setting took place in earlier chapters, here we present additional details on secondary data, qualitative techniques, survey methods, scaling techniques, and questionnaire translation. Relevant ethical issues in international marketing research are identified. We begin with some examples illustrating the role of marketing research in international marketing.

EXAMPLE

Boundary Commission[3]

The need for research across national borders grows each year. Improved communications and advancing technology may underpin the international corporate drive to expand into new markets. This can only be successful if companies are able to discover a sophisticated mixture of cultural, socio-economic and market information on precisely how another country may provide a new and appropriate market for their goods and services. Monika Bhaduri, Director of International Research at Taylor Nelson AGB, says: 'our main interface is with companies with research problems. They're looking to move into a new market with their vacuum cleaner or washing-up liquid. They may want to move into Europe or the US or, having been brought up corporately in the West, be looking to expand into new areas such as the Far East or Latin America.'

'Initially they need broad market understanding of factors like size, composition of population and ethnic or religious background. They then need to know what product acceptability they will have. This means finding out about the product category in that country: do men or women tend to buy it? What are the main brands now? How much do they cost? How and how often are they used and replaced? For example, is it important to know that in Spain and Portugal people tend to eat cereal with yoghurt rather than milk? Companies must also find out what the new market's legal and political restraints or requirements are on packaging.' ■

EXAMPLE

Researching a market of 2.4 billion feet[4]

There are more people with the surname Zhang than the entire population of the USA, and that's not to mention the Lis or the Wangs.

As recently as 20 years ago, China was a mysterious, secretive, inward-looking nation that few Westerners really knew anything about. Chinese ministries cranked out questionable statistics telling the Western world that tractor factory and steel production were on the rise regardless of the true situation. The few directories that existed tended to be poorly referenced and out of date as soon as they were published.

In the last 15 years, the situation has changed dramatically. With the arrival of mass communications and the information highway, market research as an industry has come of age in China. Whether you want to know the sort of toothpaste that Ms Zhang is likely to use or what kind of stockings she wears, somebody will be able to tell you. Fifteen years ago she would have been wearing a Mao suit – these days its more likely to be jeans and a T-shirt, Gucci shoes and Chanel. Incidentally, just for the record, there are more people with the surname Zhang than the entire population of the USA, and that's not to mention the Lis or the Wangs. So even if your target market was just people with the surname Zhang you could be talking to a sizeable market. For market researchers, China is the new frontier. ■

The first example illustrated the types of issues that international marketing research tackles, the second illustrates how research techniques are progressing in developing markets with vast marketing potential. The GlobalCash study, conducted across Europe, presented many challenges. The following example illustrates the dilemma faced over just one question in the questionnaire that was developed.

Open or closed questions?[5]

In the development of codes for a questionnaire, it is a simple task to assign numbers to closed questions such as 'do you use netting systems?', assigning '1' to a *yes* response and '2' to a *no*. In the GlobalCash study a coding problem arose in a questions that was open-ended in presentation but in reality was a closed list of banks and software companies. As an open-ended question, a single line was needed to establish a lead bank used in 21 European countries. If the question was presented in a closed format with boxes to tick, it would have had to cope with over 350 banks in Germany, 250 in Switzerland, 200 in France, 200 in Italy and 180 in Britain to start with. As well as being too cumbersome for the respondent, there might have been some confusion as to the correct name or initials of a bank which may be used within a particular country. Banks may also have merged and respondents may use the bank name pre-merger. Each business school had to 'translate' the shorthand versions of bank names used by respondents in their country. Thus there was much work that had to be done to code the open-ended question, but the alternative of creating a closed question would have been both cumbersome to the respondent and would miss the cultural nuances of how they name the banks they work with. ■

WHAT IS INTERNATIONAL MARKETING RESEARCH?

The term international marketing research can be used very broadly. It denotes research for true international products (international research), research carried out in a country other than the country of the research-commissioning organisation (foreign research), research conducted in all important countries where the company is represented (multinational research), and research conducted in and across different cultures (cross-cultural research). The latter category of cross-cultural research does not have to cross national boundaries. Many European countries have a vast array of ethnic groups, giving the marketing researcher many challenges in understanding consumers in these groups within their home country. The following example is a brief illustration of the array of problems faced by researchers working in a London local authority.

EXAMPLE

Qualitative research among ethnic minority communities in Britain[6]

Although the language barrier remains a problem among non-English speaking minorities in the UK, communicating or conducting research with them can still be done provided their traditional patterns of behaviour are observed. Two examples of the issues faced in studies of ethnic minorities in the London Borough of Newham include:

- Is there a difference between the Punjabi spoken by Pakistanis and Indians in Britain? This will depend on the exact area from which the people come: the written forms are entirely different, and the more formal spoken forms may differ too, but there can be no hard and fast rules. Punjabi is the language spoken in the Punjab region of India and Pakistan. Indian Punjabis usually speak Hindi (the national language of India) as well, while Pakistani Punjabis usually speak Urdu (the national language of Pakistan) as well.
- Should one use Bengali or Sylheti for written stimulus directed at the Bangladeshi population? Sylheti is not a written language, so if people from the Sylhet region are literate in their mother tongue, they will read Bengali. ■

The previous example supports the contention that, methodologically, there is no difference between domestic and international marketing research. In other words, marketing researchers have to adapt their techniques to their target respondents, and that the subtle cultural differences within a country offer the same challenges as the much more apparent differences over thousands of miles. The following example supports that contention but then shows why international marketing research should be examined as a distinct subject area.

EXAMPLE

The world over, a group is a group is a group[7]

It has become the convention to talk about international research as if it were a discrete sector of the industry. Methodologically, in qualitative research at least, it is not really very different from what is done at home. A group is a group is a group. However, it is important to realise that international research is different: firstly, in terms of analysing the social and cultural dynamics of the society, how the foreign society is structured, how power is gained and expressed, the roles allotted to men and women, the interactions between different sectors of society and so on. Secondly, in the practical problems involved in organising the research. ■

The first point established in the above example is that many of the cultural and societal assumptions that we take for granted have to be examined. Without such an examination we have the potential to be naïve in the questions we pose, who we pose those questions to and the manner in which we interpret the answers we generate. The second point reminds us of the features of the infrastructure that supports the research process, features that we may get used to, and take for granted. For example, without the benefits of accurate sampling frames, accurate and up-to-date secondary data and reliable and widespread use of telephones, our research plans may be weak. Our whole approach to organising and conducting research in international markets has to reflect these physical conditions.

In some circumstances, international marketing research can be very complex. We present a framework for understanding and dealing with these complexities.

A FRAMEWORK FOR INTERNATIONAL MARKETING RESEARCH

Conducting international marketing research can be much more complex than domestic marketing research. Although the basic six-step framework for domestic marketing research is applicable, the environment prevailing in the countries, cultural units or international markets that are being researched influences the way the six steps of the marketing research process should be performed. Figure 25.1 presents a framework for conducting international marketing research.

The environment

The differences in the environments of countries, cultural units or foreign markets should be considered when conducting international marketing research. These differences may arise in the marketing environment, government environment, legal environment, economic environment, structural environment, informational and technological environment and socio-cultural environment, as shown in Figure 25.1.

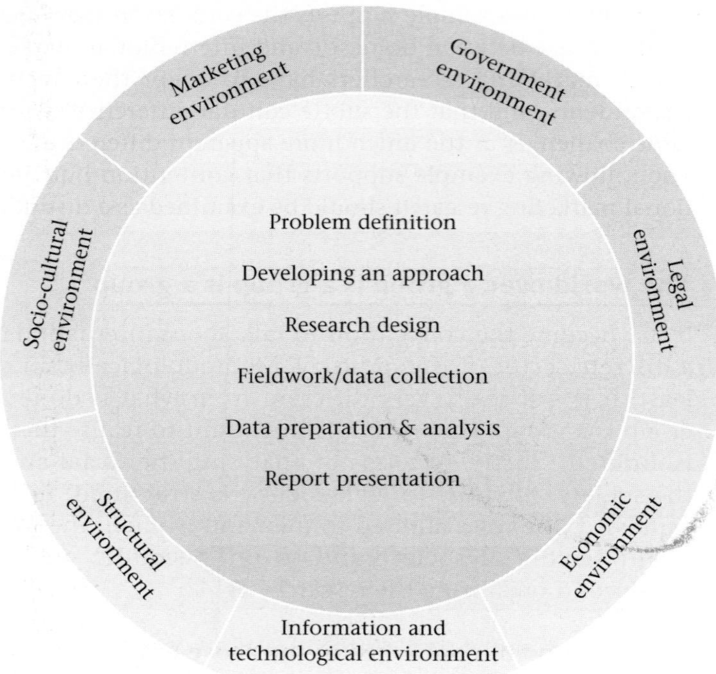

Figure 25.1
A framework for international marketing research

Marketing environment

The role of marketing in economic development varies in different countries. For example, many developing countries are frequently oriented toward production rather than marketing. Demand typically exceeds supply, and there is little concern about customer satisfaction, especially because the level of competition is low. In assessing the marketing environment, the researcher should consider the variety and assortment of products available, pricing policies, government control of media and the public's attitude toward advertising, the efficiency of the distribution system, the level of marketing effort undertaken, and the unsatisfied needs and behaviour of consumers. For example, surveys conducted in Europe usually involve questions on the variety and selection of merchandise. These questions would be inappropriate in many African countries, which are characterised by shortage economies. Likewise, questions about pricing may have to incorporate bargaining as an integral part of the exchange process. Questions about promotion should be modified as well. Television advertising, an extremely important promotion vehicle in Europe, is restricted or prohibited in many countries where TV stations are owned and operated by the government. Certain themes, words, and illustrations used in Europe are taboo in some countries. This is illustrated in the following example which describes characteristics of research in the Middle East.

EXAMPLE

Warming responses from the Levant to the Gulf[8]

The Middle East is one of the most fascinating and challenging areas for research. Market research is no longer a novelty for people in the Middle East and is relatively well developed in most countries. Local Arab females' mobility is generally restricted and all interviews have to be conducted at the recruiter's or respondent's home. However, this means that the chances of finding women at home and obtaining an interview from them are much higher than in Europe. Using visuals in research can be problematic if they are not carefully selected before they are sent and presented to local custom. It is particularly essential to control the amount of female skin visually exposed. One should never forget that sexual connotations, verbal as well as visual, are unacceptable in most Middle Eastern countries.

One of the main difficulties encountered in interviewing Arabs (and females in particular) is their natural tendency to want to please others, including researchers. Careful formulation of questions is essential to a fruitful interview or discussion, together with a non-complacent interviewer or moderator. Indeed, true feeling, opinions or preferences are often disguised, if felt to be socially unacceptable: ratings are generally higher, especially when related to product attributes or purchase propensity. ■

Government environment

An additional relevant factor is the government environment. The type of government has a bearing on the emphasis on public policy, regulatory agencies, government incentives and penalties, and investment in government enterprises. Some governments, particularly in developing countries, do not encourage foreign competition. High tariff barriers create disincentives to the efficient use of marketing research approaches. Also, the role of government in setting market controls, developing infrastructure, and acting as an entrepreneur should be carefully assessed. The role of government is also crucial in many advanced countries, where government has traditionally worked with industry toward a common national industrial policy. At the tactical level, the government determines tax structures, tariffs and product safety rules and regulations, often imposing special rules and regulations on foreign multinationals and their marketing practices. In many countries, the government may be an important member of the distribution channel. The government purchases essential products on a large scale and then sells them to consumers, perhaps on a rationed basis.

Legal environment

The legal environment encompasses common law, foreign law, international law, transaction law, antitrust, bribery and taxes. From the standpoint of international marketing research, particularly salient are laws related to the elements of the marketing mix. Product laws include those dealing with product quality, packaging, warranty and after-sales service, patents, trademarks and copyright. Laws on pricing deal with price fixing, price discrimination, variable pricing, price controls, and retail price maintenance. Distribution laws relate to exclusive territory arrangements, type of channels, and cancellation of distributor or wholesaler agreements. Likewise, laws govern the type of promotional methods that can be employed. Although all countries have laws regulating marketing activities, some countries have only a few laws that are loosely enforced and others have many complicated laws that are strictly enforced. In many countries the legal channels are clogged and the settlement of court cases is prolonged. In addition, home-country laws may also apply while conducting business or marketing research in foreign countries.

Economic environment

Economic environmental characteristics include economic size (gross domestic product, or GDP); level, source, and distribution of income; growth trends; and sectoral trends. A country's stage of economic development determines the size, the degree of modernisation, and the standardisation of its markets. Consumer, industrial and commercial markets become more standardised and consumers' work, leisure and lifestyles become more homogenised by economic development and advances in technology. The following example illustrates the problems inherent in understanding the characteristics of a country's stage of economic development and forecasting the potential that exists there.

EXAMPLE

The East gets out of the red and into the black[9]

Dr Rudolf Bretschneider, Managing Director of Austrian based FESSEL-GfK, is credited as the frontiersman in the GfK network to make the first bold steps into Eastern Europe: GfK credits itself with being the first Western agency to spot market research potential in the region. Bretschneider cautions against relying too greatly on official economic indicators which, given the substantial size of the black and grey markets, can never give more than an illusory and fragmentary picture. GfK discovered that they had overestimated their knowledge of the region. Their experience highlights the pace of change and the meteoric swings that are commonplace, requiring extra vigilance from all observers. ■

Structural environment

Structural factors relate to transportation, communication, utilities and infrastructure. For example, telephone usage in the Far East is much lower than in Europe, where many households do without telephones. Mail service is inefficient in many developing countries. Personal contact with respondents is difficult because city people work during the day and rural residents are inaccessible. Block statistics and maps are not available or can be obtained only with great difficulty. Many households are unidentified.

Based on geography alone, national samples in China and Indonesia are almost unthinkable. China is predominantly rural and Indonesia consists of several thousand islands. In Thailand, only 21 per cent of the population live in urban areas and two-thirds of the total urban population live in a single city, Bangkok. In these three countries, interviewing by telephone is, for the most part, not a consideration.[10]

Informational and technological environment

Elements of the informational and technological environment include information and communication systems, computerisation, use of electronic equipment, energy, production technology, science and invention. For example, in India, South Korea and many Latin American countries, advances in science and technology have not had a proportionate impact on the lifestyle of the majority of citizens. Computers and electronic information transfer have still to make an impact at grassroots level. Information handling and record keeping are performed in the traditional way. Again, this has an impact on the type of information that can be solicited from consumers, businesses and other enterprises.

Socio-cultural environment

Socio-cultural factors include values, literacy, language, religion, communication patterns, and family and social institutions. Relevant values and attitudes toward time, achievement, work, authority, wealth, scientific method, risk, innovation, change, and the Western world should be considered. The marketing research process should be modified so that it does not conflict with the cultural values.

In many developing countries, 60 per cent or more of the population is illiterate. In tradition-directed, less-developed societies, the ability of respondents to formulate opinions of their own seems to be all but absent; consequently, it is difficult to solicit information from these respondents. As a result, the sophisticated rating scales employed in Europe are not useful.. There may also be several distinct spoken languages and dialects in a given nation or region.

In India, for example, there are 19 major languages and more than 200 dialects. India is divided into linguistic states. The country can be described as a mini-Europe, each state like a separate country within Europe, with its own language and cultural peculiarities. A survey which even approaches national representation in scope will generally be printed in at least 12 languages.[11]

Finally, a country with a homogeneous family structure is likely to be more culturally homogeneous than a country with multiple family structures. For example, Japan is culturally more homogeneous than many European or African countries, which have many different kinds of family structures.

Each country's environment is unique, so international marketing research must take into consideration the environmental characteristics of the countries or foreign markets involved. Throughout the text we have discussed and illustrated how we can adapt the marketing research process to international situations. In the following sections, we provide additional details for implementing secondary data, qualitative techniques, survey methods, scaling techniques and questionnaire translation in international marketing research.[12]

SECONDARY DATA

Secondary data was covered in detail in Chapter 4. It is worth recalling where secondary data can support the research process, especially given some of the difficulties of conducting primary research in international markets. Secondary data can help to:

1 Diagnose the research problem
2 Develop an approach to the problem
3 Develop a sampling plan
4 Formulate an appropriate research design (for example, by identifying the key variables to measure or understand)
5 Answer certain research questions and test some hypotheses
6 Interpret primary data with more insight
7 Validate qualitative research findings

Obtaining secondary data on international markets to gain support for the above is much simpler with the advent of the Internet. The Internet may allow access into international markets which in the past may have required travel to the country and a great amount of time-consuming searching. Judicious use of the Internet does not mean that the international researcher will automatically gain support in the above areas. There may still be little or no secondary data that relates to the issues we wish to research in an international market. For what data we can obtain, the principles of evaluating secondary data, as set out in Table 4.2, still apply. Conducting an evaluation of the nature, specifications, accuracy, currency and dependability may be far more difficult in international markets. The process and specifications of research conducted in international markets may not be explicit; one may need a deep understanding of conducting primary research in a country to understand why data has been collected in a particular manner. Language is also a major issue, not only in reading and interpreting data, but in the definitions used in measurements. Finally, secondary research from a target country may have been heavily influenced by political forces. The researcher may need to be aware of such influences in order to interpret and make use of the findings.

The following example illustrates the limitations of existing data in Russia, even though there are very competent researchers in the country. Overcoming this problem has helped to produce data that can be relied upon and is more relevant to a number of marketers.

EXAMPLE

Rise, rise, you Russian middle classes ...[13]

All marketers need information to help understand their markets. One major problem is simply knowing who their consumers are. As one brand manager said: 'All my distribution is in Moscow and St Petersburg, but maybe only 30% of my final consumers are in these cities'. 1995 saw the introduction of the Target Group Index into Russia. Under licence from the British Market Research Bureau International, the Russian agency Comcon 2 has established the first single-source product and media survey covering all Russia. As in Britain, the objective is to gather information about the consumption and consumers of different goods and services, alongside their media preferences and attitudinal or lifestyle characteristics. Much previous research, while of high quality (the result of the high level of theoretical training of researchers within Russian universities), had been unsystematic and concentrated on the two major cities. ■

Another major development in the use of secondary data is in the development of geographic information systems. In the use of geodemographic classifications of consumers, systems already exist in Australia, Belgium, Britain, France, Germany, Hong Kong, Ireland, Italy, Japan, the Netherlands, New Zealand, Norway, South Africa, Spain, Sweden and the USA. The systems work well in defining consumers within each country and, as described in Chapter 5, can be used as a foundation to add transactional data generated within an organisation operating within each country. The international research problem emerges from the means of comparing classifications across the different countries. This problem emerges from the different data sources that are used to build the classifications in each country. There are different types of data that may be accessible, different standards and definitions used in data collection and different laws allowing the use, or not, of certain types of data.

Geodemographic databases can give an excellent introduction to a particular country and can form a foundation upon which other data sources can be built. At present, comparing consumer types across borders is problematic.

QUALITATIVE TECHNIQUES

Chapter 6 discussed the differences between European and USA researchers in their approach to focus groups. In essence, a USA approach is far more structured and tends to be a foundation for subsequent surveys, while the European approach tends to be more evolutionary and exploratory. The question of the perspective from which one plans and conducts qualitative research is not really important until other researchers or moderators from international markets become involved in the process. The approach adopted may not match the expectations of the decision-maker who will supported by the research. These circumstances are outlined and illustrated in the following example.

EXAMPLE

When East meets West, quite what does 'qualitative' mean?[14]

International marketers have always been aware that qualitative research as it developed in the US and in Europe were quite different practices, stemming from different premises and yielding different results. American-style qualitative research started from the same evaluative premise as quantitative research but on a smaller scale. European-style qualitative research started from the opposite premise: it was developmental, exploratory and creative rather than evaluative.

The rest of the world tended to adopt one or the other style of qualitative research depending upon the history and trading partners of the country. For example, India adopted the European model, whereas Japan largely followed the American model. The difficulty for the Asia Pacific region is that the influence of both schools are found there concurrently. The founders of commercial research in the region came from the UK, Australia, New Zealand and America, bringing with them varying approaches. From a marketer's point of view, the problem is that both styles of qualitative research are currently on offer under the same description. Marketers may not be sure what they are getting; even worse, some research agencies seem unclear about what they are offering, serving up a confused mixture of both styles of qualitative research, falling short of achieving the objectives of either approach. ■

Good qualitative research is an open process where researchers and decision-makers clearly understand the premises for exploring particular issues, probing certain individuals and the bases for interpreting data. In qualitative international marketing research, where there may be confusion about the premises for the whole approach, there is a much greater need for openness between all parties involved.

Conducting qualitative research in a number of countries may mean approaching a local research agency which is aware of local customs, language issues and administrative requirements. In examining more than one country, one must consider how consistent the approach is and how the findings from one country may be compared to another. For multi-country projects that are qualitative in nature, it may be impossible to find researchers with the cultural, linguistic and administrative experience that allows some consistency and means to compare findings. The following example illustrates how bilingual researchers working in teams tackle this problem.

EXAMPLE

In-depth research? A bit controversial[15]

Consumer markets like soft drinks or processed foods are important enough to be regularly researched across many countries. Wherever you go there are professional qualitative researchers who really understand them. The same cannot be said for most business-to-business markets. Just sending a topic guide and recruitment questionnaire to local agencies is not enough.

Some research agencies have responded by recruiting bilingual researchers, so that the same research team that does the 'home' interviews can with as much ease do interviews in target foreign countries. They feel that this is the only way to guarantee consistency in the way the research is carried out. More fundamentally, it is the only way to keep the approach flexible. Why is flexibility so important? True qualitative research entails wording questions to suit respondents: if necessary, to keep re-wording the question until the answer makes sense. It means the freedom to adapt the interview to suit the interviewer's developing understanding of the subject. ■

This example also illustrates the essence of qualitative research in terms of exploring through re-wording, of adapting an interview until sense is made. In international marketing research this calls for linguistic skills matching the native speaker in any target country.

SURVEY METHODS

The following sections discuss the major interviewing methods in light of the challenges of conducting research in foreign countries, especially Europe and developing countries.[16]

Telephone interviewing and CATI

In the USA and Canada, the telephone has achieved almost total penetration of households. In North America, telephone interviewing is the dominant mode of questionnaire administration. Throughout Europe there are also many countries, regions and cities that have almost total telephone penetration. Over recent years, telephone interviewing techniques in Europe have grown enormously. However, even with high penetration levels, many Europeans are reluctant to divulge personal details over the telephone. This means that the technique does not have the dominance seen in North America.

The successful use of the telephone in international research depends upon three factors. The first is the level of telephone penetration (see Chapter 8 for a discussion of the issues related to the selection of probability samples in telephone interviewing). The second is the completeness and accuracy of telephone directories (the growth of the use of mobile phones and 'ex-directory' numbers have compounded this factor). The third is the cultural acceptance of using the telephone to divulge personal details.

In Hong Kong for example, 96 per cent of households (other than those on outlying islands and on boats) can be contacted by telephone. With some persistence, evening telephone interviewing can successfully achieve interviews with 70 to 75 per cent of selected respondents. Residents are uninhibited about using telephones and relaxed about telephone interviews. Even in these circumstances, this is not the most important mode of data collection.[17]

In most developing countries, telephone penetration is low. There may be relatively high concentrations of telephone usage in particular cities and with particular types of consumer (especially in professional classes). Telephone interviews are most useful with respondents in these countries who are accustomed to business transactions by phone.

With the decline of costs for international telephone calls, multi-country studies can be conducted from a single location.[18] This greatly reduces the time and costs associated with the organisation and control of the research project in each country. Furthermore, international calls can obtain a high response rate, and the results have been found to be stable (i.e. the same results are obtained from the first 100 interviews as from the next 200 or 500). It is necessary to find interviewers fluent in the relevant languages, but in most major European cities this is not a problem.

In home and office personal interviews

In many European countries, home interviewing is the dominant means to conduct surveys. Given that in-home interviews require a large pool of qualified interviewers, are time-consuming and costly, this may seem odd. However, when one considers the quality of rapport that can be built up between the interviewer and respondent, the amount of probing and the quality of audiovisual stimuli that can be used, there are clear benefits that outweigh the costs. In many areas of industrial marketing research, the only means to contact certain managers may be through the personal interview, held in their office.

In international research this means understanding the cultural implications of entering someone's home or office. In the example 'Warming responses from the Levant to the Gulf' on page 684 it was noted that local Arab females' mobility is generally restricted and all interviews have to be conducted at the recruiter's or respondent's home. This meant that the chances of finding women at home and obtaining an interview from them were much higher than in Europe.

In the GlobalCash study, where in-office interviews were conducted throughout Europe, two interviewers were used. The first (who had a high level of technical knowledge of cash management) attended all the interviews to ensure that a consistent approach was used, especially when probing. The second was from a business school in the country being surveyed. The second interviewer guided the means to obtain the interviewer in the first instance, then ensured that the protocol was correct (given the type of respondent faced) and finally helped with any language difficulties. The following example further illustrates a cultural problem faced with in-office interviews.

EXAMPLE

Russian roulette: exciting once you learn the new rules[19]

Executives find it odd, and sometimes sinister, that people should just come to ask questions which often seem irrelevant. One respondent, a high official in a major city, kept interrupting the interview with offers to sell the product under discussion and asked our agency to supply some other products. He considered it fatuous that he should face a stream of questions without seeing any concrete result at the end. It is usually assumed that the researcher belongs to the company commissioning the research, even when the relationship is made clear. Guarantees that the respondents' identity will remain confidential can be treated with disbelief. ■

Street interviews

In many countries, with low telephone penetration and comparatively low literacy rates, the street interview offers an excellent means to survey. This is illustrated in the following example, showing Chinese respondents enjoying the marketing research task.

EXAMPLE

Foreign policy[20]

Interviewing is not usually an obstacle in mainland China, says TNAGB (Taylor Nelson Audits of Great Britain) Group Director for Greater China, Richard Necchi. The problem is ensuring that you have a representative sample to work from. Census data is simply not up to Western standards, he says, and researchers try to rely on Government statistics as little as possible. The huge migrant population of about 100 million also means that the actual population of certain cities is much greater than official figures suggest, and this problem is likely to grow. 'In China we have to do face to face every time, as there are so few telephones. But people love answering questions.' TNAGB compiles the TV ratings in China and has recently enlarged its sample to 12,200 households in 62 cities. ■

Provided that the environment of the street allows an interview to be conducted, the street interview is an excellent means to identify and interview individuals where there are poor or non-existent sampling frames. Given the congestion in many major international cities, the locations where interviews will be conducted have to be carefully selected. However, this does not differ from planning and conducting street interviews in 'home' markets. As with in-home and in-office interviews, the differences lie in the culture of approaching someone in the street and their willingness to divulge information to a stranger in the street.

Mail interviews

Because of their low cost, mail interviews continue to be used in most developed countries where literacy is high and the postal system is well developed. Mail surveys are, typically, more effective in industrial international marketing research, although it is difficult to identify the appropriate respondent within each firm and to personalise the address. This point was illustrated in the GlobalCash study where 6000 telephone calls were made throughout Europe to establish the identity of the target respondent and to check the postal details.

The growth of Internet usage has also meant a growth in the use of electronic mail surveys. Given the global nature of the Internet, for certain topics (such as home shopping using the Internet) this may be the cheapest and quickest means to conduct an international survey. However, given the sampling problems associated with Internet usage, great care must be taken in validating samples from such surveys. As the penetration of Internet usage increases globally, the technique has great potential for both survey work and qualitative techniques; it is ideally suited to reaching out across national boundaries.

The criteria for the selection of survey methods were discussed in Chapter 8. As discussed and illustrated in Chapter 8, an important consideration in selecting the methods of administering questionnaires is to ensure equivalence and comparability across countries. This is illustrated in the following example, where comparability between countries is of paramount importance. The example leads onto issues of equivalence in measurement and scaling.

EXAMPLE

Does luxury have a home country?[21]

In the late 1980s, RISC, an international consulting company, decided to launch a study on luxury goods. Consequently, they developed a number of questions about luxury brands which were added to the questionnaire administered to national representative samples of major European countries. In 1992 they decided to explore, in France, Germany and Italy, the particular issue of country images in relation to luxury. As a result, 2500 respondents in each country answered the question *'In your opinion, which country best understands the idea of luxury and reflects it through its products and brands?'*

Respondents could choose from a list of seven countries: Britain, France, Germany, Italy, Japan, Spain and the USA. They were then asked to select from the same list the country they spontaneously associated with ten general product related dimensions.

The fact that the same survey was conducted at the same time with exactly the same methodology in three countries was important because it allowed the magnitude of response biases due to *'patriotism'*, a factor often presented as an explanatory variable for country-of-origin effects. ■

MEASUREMENT AND SCALING

In international marketing research, it is critical to establish the equivalence of scales and measures used to obtain data from different countries.[22] As illustrated in Figure 25.2, this requires an examination of construct equivalence operational equivalence, scalar equivalence and linguistic equivalence.[23]

Construct equivalence
A type of equivalence that deals with the question of whether the marketing constructs have the same meaning and significance in different countries.

Conceptual equivalence
A construct equivalence issue that deals with whether the interpretation of brands, products, consumer behaviour and the marketing effort are the same in different countries.

Functional equivalence
A construct equivalence issue that deals specifically with whether a given concept or behaviour serves the same role or function in different countries.

Category equivalence
A construct equivalence issue that deals specifically with whether the categories in which brands, products and behaviour are grouped is the same in different countries.

Operational equivalence
A type of equivalence that measures how theoretical constructs are operationalised in different countries to measure marketing variables.

Construct equivalence deals with the question of whether the marketing constructs (for example, opinion leadership, variety seeking, and brand loyalty) have the same meaning and significance in different countries. In many countries, the number of brands available in a given product category is limited. In some countries, the dominant brands have become generic labels symbolising the entire product category. Consequently, a different perspective on brand loyalty may have to be adopted in these countries.

Construct equivalence comprises conceptual equivalence, functional equivalence and category equivalence. **Conceptual equivalence** deals with the interpretation of brands, products, consumer behaviour and marketing effort. For example, sales promotion techniques are an integral component of marketing effort throughout Europe. On the other hand, in countries with shortage economies, where the market is dominated by the sellers, consumers view sales with suspicion because they believe that the product being promoted is of poor quality. **Functional equivalence** examines whether a given concept or behaviour serves the same role or function in different countries. For example, in many developing countries, bicycles are predominantly a means of transportation rather than of recreation. Marketing research related to the use of bicycles in these countries must examine different motives, attitudes, behaviours, and even different competing products than such research would in Europe. **Category equivalence** refers to the category in which stimuli like products, brands and behaviours are grouped. In Europe, the category of the principal shopper may be defined as either the male or female head of household. This category may be inappropriate in countries where routine daily shopping is done by a domestic servant. Furthermore, the category 'household' itself varies across countries.

Operational equivalence concerns how theoretical constructs are operationalised to make measurements. In Europe, leisure may be operationalised as playing golf, tennis or other sports; watching television; or basking in the sun.

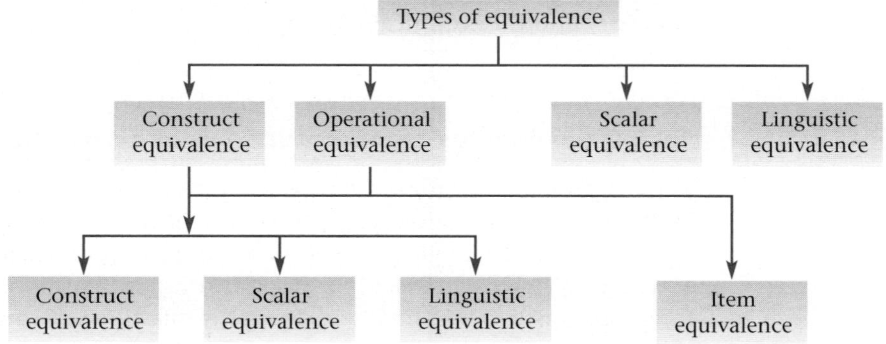

Figure 25.2 Scaling and measurement equivalence in international research

This operationalisation may not be relevant in countries where people do not play these sports or do not have round-the-clock TV transmission. Lying in the sun is generally not normal behaviour in countries with hot climates. **Item equivalence**, which is closely connected to operational equivalence, presupposes both construct and operational equivalence. To establish item equivalence, the construct should be measured by the same instrument in different countries.

Item equivalence
Proposes that the same instrument should be used in different countries.

Scalar equivalence, also called metric equivalence, is established if the other types of equivalence have been attained. This involves demonstrating that two individuals from different countries with the same value on some variable, such as brand loyalty, will score at the same level on the same test. Scalar equivalence has two aspects. The specific scale or scoring procedure used to establish the measure should be equivalent. The equivalence of response to a given measure in different countries should be considered. For example, do scores from the top box or from the top two boxes on a purchase-intent scale reflect similar likelihood of purchase in different countries? Finally, **linguistic equivalence** refers to both the spoken and the written language forms used in scales, questionnaires and interviewing. The scales and other verbal stimuli should be translated so that they are readily understood by respondents in different countries and have equivalent meaning.[24]

Scalar equivalence
The demonstration that two individuals from different countries with the same value on some variable will score at the same level on the same test; also called metric equivalence.

Linguistic equivalence
The equivalence of both spoken and written language forms used in scales and questionnaires.

QUESTIONNAIRE TRANSLATION

GLOBALCASH PROJECT

Translation into 10 languages[25]

Robert Kirby, who was the Telephone Research Director at Research Services Ltd and has many years' experience of pan-European telephone surveys, offers the following advice in coping with translation:

> Translations require the most rigorous checking. In my experience it is not advisable to use someone from a home country who can speak the language fluently, because frequently a current idiomatic knowledge is required. A translation agency with no expertise could have the idiom but not the interviewing skills.

His advice was valuable in the GlobalCash project. The GlobalCash questionnaire was translated from English into Czech, Finnish, French, German, Greek, Hungarian, Italian, Polish, Portuguese and Spanish. In the project there was the added dimension of confusing technical terms with terms such as 'netting' 'pooling' and 'concentration', which have a day-to-day usage that is entirely different to the financial usage. The translation for the GlobalCash project was undertaken by the business schools in the target countries that understood the idiom, the elicitation task required of finance directors in their country and the technical terms used. ■

EXAMPLE

Taking the peoples' temperature – right across Europe[26]

The continuous tracking survey of EU citizens' opinion of European issues use 19 variants of their questionnaire, to include people living in countries where more than one national language is common. All the questionnaires have to go through extensive checking, translation, back translation, harmonisation and piloting in the short time between finally agreeing the questionnaire and starting work. ■

As in the above examples, questions may have to be translated for administration in different cultures. Direct translation, in which a bilingual translator translates the questionnaire directly from a base language to the respondent's language, is frequently used. If the translator is not fluent in both languages and is not familiar with both cultures, however, direct translation of certain words and phrases may be erroneous. Procedures like back translation and parallel translation have been suggested to avoid these errors. In **back translation**, the questionnaire is translated from the base language by a bilingual speaker whose native language is the language into which the questionnaire is being translated. This version is then retranslated back into the original language by a bilingual whose native language is the initial or base language. Translation errors can then be identified. Several repeat translations and back translations may be necessary to develop equivalent questionnaires, and this process can be cumbersome and time-consuming.[27]

Back translation
A translation technique that translates a questionnaire from the base language by a translator whose native language is the one into which the questionnaire is being translated. This version is then retranslated back into the original language by someone whose native language is the base language. Translation errors can then be identified.

An alternative procedure is **parallel translation**. A committee of translators, each of whom is fluent in at least two of the languages in which the questionnaire will be administered, discusses alternative versions of the questionnaire and makes modifications until consensus is reached. In countries where several languages are spoken, the questionnaire should be translated into the language of each respondent subgroup. It is important that any non-verbal stimuli (pictures and advertisements) also be translated using similar procedures. The following example underscores the importance of translation that does not impose the structure of a 'home country' from which the research is commissioned, in this case Britain.

Parallel translation
A translation method in which a committee of translators, each of whom is fluent in at least two languages, discusses alternative versions of a questionnaire and makes modifications until consensus is reached.

EXAMPLE

The search for focus – brand values across Europe[28]

Land Rover wished to understand the values associated with their brand in Belgium, Britain, France, Germany, Italy, the Netherlands, Portugal and Spain. The project involved the use of CAPI and required the development of a questionnaire that could allow comparisons between the countries. The issue of questionnaire translation was a sensitive and pertinent one. What was crucial was that the translation was meaningful in all languages rather than forcing the English language requirements into the local language. The translation was a difficult process and required an understanding of both the research process and the cultural context of the individual markets. It was the case that certain concepts that are expressive in English could not easily be translated into other languages. For instance, the word 'aspirational' does not easily translate into French, Spanish or Italian with the same meaning as in English. Consequently, in order to ensure comparability the translation process involved a series or iterative steps changing the master questionnaire to fit what was achievable overall in each market. ■

ETHICS IN MARKETING RESEARCH

Ethical responsibilities for marketing research conducted abroad are very similar to those for research conducted domestically. In conducting marketing research across Europe (and indeed globally), ESOMAR produce a code of conduct that guides professional practice that protects the interests of all research stakeholders. In general, for each of the six stages of the marketing research design process, the same four stakeholders (client, researcher, respondent and public) should act honourably and respect their responsibilities to one another. For individual countries, a key development in honourable practice lies in the development of professional associations. Professional associations can guide researchers through the development of specific codes of practice that may reflect their culture and industrial heritage. For example, in the Czech Republic, Hungary, Poland and Russia, major market research suppliers are forming associations and introducing or discussing quality standard systems for fieldwork. Research was not unknown in the region prior to the collapse of communism and most countries have had a tradition of government-sponsored research spanning 40–50 years. Most major suppliers are investing in their future by training their staff in Western Europe and America.[29]

For all the similarities that may exist in conducting research in international markets, some ethical issues become more difficult to solve. Consider the dilemma presented by David Mendoza, Director of Gobi International, an Anglo-Russian industrial research company: 'Some people will, Soviet style, still refuse to answer any questions of any kind. Others, often the same type of former Soviet apparatchik, but totally disillusioned, will promise to tell you whatever you need in return for dollars. Frankly, this is highly unsatisfactory and something we try to avoid, although often there is no choice'.[30]

INTERNET AND COMPUTER APPLICATIONS

The Internet and computers can be extensively used in all phases of the international marketing research process. These uses parallel those discussed in earlier chapters and hence will not be repeated here. The fact that the Internet can be used to communicate with respondents and marketing decision-makers anywhere in the world has given a new dimension to international marketing research. For example, the on-line survey overcomes geographic boundaries and differences in postal systems to solicit responses from around the world. The on-line survey also takes advantage of one interviewer (the computer) that can present the same survey in several different translations.

The environmental characteristics of international markets detailed in this chapter present a formidable research task, especially when first learning about a country. The Internet is the ideal means to quickly access material that helps to shape an understanding of the environmental context of a particular country. This is particularly relevant in tracking down secondary data sources that may not be available in the home country of a researcher.

The Internet has also been extremely beneficial in conducting qualitative interviews. One of the most difficult administrative tasks in conducting focus groups is getting participants together at an agreed location. Because of the travel problems for certain respondents, many focus groups may have to be conducted to cover a wide geographic area. The Internet can help to overcome these problems, first of all by the convenience it offers the participants – not having to leave their homes – and second by the breaking down of geographic boundaries.

SUMMARY

With the globalisation of markets, international marketing research is burgeoning rapidly. As well as the technical requirements of conducting successful marketing research as outlined in this text, the researcher has to cope with new cultures and languages in targeted international markets. Given the array of ethnic groups within most European countries, the challenges of understanding new cultures and languages can exist within a 'home' country.

The environment prevailing in the international markets being researched influences all six steps of the marketing research process. Important aspects of this environment include the marketing, government, legal, economic, structural, informational and technological, and socio-cultural environment.

In collecting data from different countries, it is desirable to use techniques with equivalent levels of reliability rather than the same method. Repeating identical techniques across borders may result in subtle cultural and linguistic differences being ignored, which may have a great effect upon the nature and quality of data that is generated. It is critical to establish the equivalence of scales and measures in terms of construct equivalence, operational equivalence, scalar equivalence, and linguistic equivalence. Questionnaires used should be adapted to the specific cultural environment and should not be biased in favour of any one culture or language. Back translation and parallel translation are helpful in detecting translation errors.

The ethical concerns facing international marketing researchers are similar in many ways to the issues confronting domestic researchers. Working in countries where professional marketing research associations exist should allow access to codes of conduct that reflect the culture and industrial heritage of that country. However, the international researcher being exposed to an array of cultures and economic scenarios should always expect to find new situations and ethical dilemmas.

QUESTIONS AND PROBLEMS

1 Evaluate the meaning of 'international' from the perspective of the marketing researcher.

2 What characteristics distinguish international marketing research from domestic marketing research?

3 Describe the aspects of the environment of each country that should be taken into account in international marketing research.

4 Describe the importance of considering the marketing environment in conducting international marketing research.

5 What is meant by the structural environment? How do the variables comprising the structural environment influence international marketing research?

6 What is meant by the informational and technological environment? How do the variables comprising the informational and technological environment influence international marketing research?

7 What is meant by the socio-cultural environment? How do the variables comprising the socio-cultural environment influence international marketing research?

8 How should the researcher evaluate secondary data obtained from foreign countries?

9 Describe the factors that may influence the approach to qualitative techniques in different countries.

10 Select a country, using environmental characteristics to illustrate why CATI works particularly well as a survey technique.

11 Select a country, using environmental characteristics to illustrate why in-home interviewing does not work particularly well as a survey technique.

12 Select a country, using environmental characteristics to illustrate why Internet surveys work particularly well as a survey technique.

13 How should the equivalence of scales and measures be established when the data are to be obtained from different countries or cultural units?

14 What problems are involved in the direct translation of a questionnaire into another language?

15 Briefly describe the procedures that may be adopted to ensure translation is correctly conducted in the development of a questionnaire.

NOTES

1 Goodyear, M., Guest editorial – 'International Research and Marketing', *Journal of the Market Research Society* 38 (1) (January 1996), 1.

2 See Malhotra, N.K., 'Administration of Questionnaires for Collecting Quantitative Data in International Marketing Research', *Journal of Global Marketing* 4 (2) (1991), 63–92; and Malhotra, N.K., 'Designing an International Marketing Research Course: Framework and Content', *Journal of Teaching in International Business* 3 (1992), 1–27.

3 Mackenzie, S., 'Boundary Commission', *Marketing Week* (29 January 1998), 29.

4 Glasse, J., 'Researching a Market of 2.4 Billion Feet', *Research* (March 1995), 23.

5 Birks, D.F., 'Research Cash Management Practices', in Birks, D.F., *Global Cash Management in Europe*, (Basingstoke: Macmillan 1998, p. 39.

6 Sills, A. and Desai, P., 'Qualitative Research Amongst Ethnic Minorities in Britain', *Journal of the Market Research Society* 38 (3) (July 1996), 247.

7 Goodyear, M., 'The World Over, a Group is a Group is a Group', *ResearchPlus* (November 1992), 5.

8 Dunlop, C., 'Warming Responses from the Levant to the Gulf', *Research* (November 1995), 24.

9 Savage, M., 'The East Gets Out of the Red and Into the Black', *Research* (October 1997), 22.

10 Hutton, G., 'If You Board the Asian 'Bus, Better Mind Your Language', *ResearchPlus* (February 1996), 9.

11 *Ibid.*

12 See Dawar, N. and Parker, P., 'Marketing Universals: Consumers' Use of Brand Name, Price, Physical Appearance, and Retailer Reputation as Signals of Product Quality', *Journal of Marketing* 58 (April 1994), 81–95.

13 Wicken, G. and Koneva, E., 'Rise, Rise, You Russian Middle-classes', *ResearchPlus* (January 1996), 5.

14 Broadbent, K., 'When East Meets West, Quite What Does "Qualitative" Mean?', *ResearchPlus* (March 1997), 15.

15 Bloom, N., 'In-Depth Research? A Bit Controversial!', *ResearchPlus* (June 1993), 13.

16 The work on survey methods is drawn from Malhotra, N.K., 'Administration of Questionnaires for Collecting Quantitative Data in International Marketing Research', *Journal of Global Marketing* 4 (2) (1991), 63–92.

17 Davies, R.W.B., Minter, C.J.W., Moll, M. and Bottomley, D.T., 'Marketing Research in Hong Kong', *European Research* (May 1987), 114–20.

18 De Houd, M., 'Internationalised Computerized Telephone Research: Is it Fiction?', *Marketing Research Society Newsletter* 190 (January 1982), 14–15.

19 Mendonza, D., 'Russian Roulette: Exciting Once You Learn New Rules', *Research* (January 1995), 20.

20 Gander, P., 'Foreign Policy', *Marketing Week* (30 April 1998), 46.

21 Dubois, B. and Paternault, C., 'Does Luxury Have a Home Country? An Investigation of Country Images in Europe', *Marketing and Research Today* (May 1997), 80.

22 See also Min-Han, C., Lee, B.W. and Ro, K.K., 'The Choice of a Survey Mode in Country Image Studies', *Journal of Business Research* 29 (February 1994), 151–62.

23 See Bhalla, G. and Lin, L., 'Cross-Cultural Marketing Research: A Discussion of Equivalence Issues and Measurement Strategies', *Psychology and Marketing* 4 (4) (1987), 275–85. A similar discussion is also found in Douglas, S.P. and Craig, C.S., *International Marketing Research* (Englewood Cliffs, NJ: Prentice Hall, 1983).

24 Andrews, J.C., Durvasula, S. and Netemeyer, R.G., 'Testing the Cross-National Applicability of U.S. and Russian Advertising Belief and Attitude Measures', *Journal of Advertising* 23 (March 1994), 17–26.

25 Kirby, R., 'A Pan-European View of the Executive at Lunch', *ResearchPlus* (October 1992), 7.

26 Phillips, A., 'Taking the Peoples' Temperature – Right Across Europe', *ResearchPlus* (November 1996), 7.

27 For an application of back translation, see Wharton, R., Baird, I.S. and Lyles, M.A., 'Conceptual Frameworks Among Chinese Managers: Joint Venture Management and Philosophy', *Journal of Global Marketing* 5 (1-2) (1991), 163–81.

28 Bull, N. and Oxley, M., 'The Search for Focus – Brand Values across Europe', *Marketing and Research Today* (November 1996), 243.

29 Bartonova, M., 'The Markets Are Emerging – and Research is Hard on their Heels', *ResearchPlus* (January 1996), 4.

30 Mendoza, D., 'Russian Roulette: Exciting Once You Learn the New Rules', *Research* (January 1995), 21.

PROFESSIONAL PERSPECTIVES for Part IV

Michael R. Kuhn

Senior Vice President, Burke Customer Satisfaction Associates. Michael Kuhn is the region manager for Burke Marketing Research's western business group and manages all Burke client service activities in Arizona, Colorado, northern California, and the Pacific Northwest. He has been a practitioner of marketing research since coming to Burke as a project manager in 1971. Mr. Kuhn has worked for clients in a wide variety of consumer packaged goods companies, high-technology and industrial manufacturing concerns, and the travel and leisure industry. He also serves as director of Burke's customer satisfaction and external quality control programs for clients in the western United States.

Preparing and Presenting the Marketing Research Report

MICHAEL R. KUHN

In report writing and presentation, we take all the art and all the science of marketing research and not only attempt to interpret what they really mean but also to communicate them to others outside our field of expertise—others who may be relying on this information to make decisions involving many millions of dollars.

Chapter 24 of this text is an excellent framework within which the student or professional practitioner of marketing research can find direction and guidance for writing and organising effective reports and presentations. Often, there are pragmatic constraints that affect the final report. These constraints may be pressing, but it is possible to overcome them creatively and produce a report that is professional and meets the needs of the management. These constraints include time constraints, budget limitations, decentralised decision making, management indifference, and increasing scope and complexity of research projects. These constraints are discussed first. Then an example illustrates how these constraints can be accommodated without sacrificing the quality or usefulness of the report.

Time constraints

In today's information age, we as information providers are often pressured to hurry up the results of a study and to minimise formality. The time window for decision making is becoming narrower and narrower. Management wants specific answers from the marketing research project, and it wants them quickly. The world's competitive environment very often leads management to move more quickly than any of us would like, imposing the risk of making decisions from inadequately analysed and considered information.

Budget limitations

This particular problem takes its toll in two areas. First, world competition and the recent wave of leveraged buyouts have put extreme pressure on corporations to be cost-conscious, and consequently to reduce the size of all corporate staff organisations, including marketing research staffs. Yet there remains as much pressure as ever to deliver actionable and timely results. Second, budgets available for marketing research projects have also come under close corporate scrutiny. In spite of the fact that most firms' market information needs are growing, the researcher is being asked to do more with the same budget or even with less. To balance these pressures there is a tendency to shortcut either the scope, the depth, or both, of the final report and presentation.

Decentralised decision making

Many of our clients have undergone significant reorganizations during the past few years. The primary focus of the reorganization is to push decision making to the lowest possible line manager within an identifiable product, service, or business group. These line managers are interested primarily in the information that will answer their specific questions and help them move forward with a decision. Because they have responsibility for bottom line profit, these line managers often do not like the formal, corporate appearing research report, and they question whether the money spent to produce such a report is worthwhile.

Management indifference

The 'blood and toil' put into a formal research report sometimes goes unnoticed by management. To prevent this from happening, marketing researchers must make the information they deliver to managers easy to understand and digest, using a minimum of words and a maximum of charts, diagrams, and summary tables of relevant data. The goal is to make the report stand on its own and its worth self-evident.

Increasing scope and complexity of research projects

The old adage that says, 'The more I know, the more I know that I don't know' is true. In the field of marketing research, the trend is to ask all the questions and get all the answers that one can possibly squeeze into a research study. The smarter managers become, the more questions they ask. Management, in an effort to get more bang for the buck, frequently tries to load several projects onto one study of the same respondent group. This often means that the researcher is tempted to short-cut the formal reporting and presentation process.

Overcoming the constraints: an example

Although these constraints can be pressing, researchers should resist the tendency to compromise the report preparation and presentation process. Often the researcher can creatively overcome the constraints without sacrificing the professional quality of the report and deliver the information in a form that can be used directly as input into decision making. An example from our experience is cited to illustrate this point.

Burke was asked to design and implement a customer satisfaction and problem tracking monitor for a major gasoline company. The client company operated retail service stations in 40 major markets and wanted a survey conducted among its retail service station customers in every market on a quarterly basis. To further complicate matters, the service stations themselves fell into six different ownership and service delivery configurations. Some were dealer owned, whereas others were managed by the company. Some offered gasoline only, but others had minimarkets or auto service bays. We had to run surveys in a total of 3,950 service stations in 40 markets and report to three levels of non-research management within two weeks of the close of each quarterly period.

We were charged with designing a reporting scheme that would satisfactorily communicate the results of the quarterly surveys. It was important to illustrate the progress made by our client's retail gasoline stations in improving customer satisfaction. These reports were to be used by three levels of management: service station owners/managers, field marketing representatives, and corporate managers in charge of the retail marketing operations. None were professional marketing researchers.

Given the constraints, it was necessary to create documents that could be understood and used by a service station manager as well as by a corporate officer. Our answer to this dilemma is shown in Figures 1 and 2. Data was downloaded directly into a Burke-designed automated chart-making system. The figures are two examples of the charts we designed to show results from the quarterly customer surveys. A short written introduction was also provided, explaining how to read the chart and interpret the information for decision making and program development. Corporate charts included summaries of this same information by region and for the total United States. From these charts, managers could read the following key performance information:

1 Incidence of problem occurrences this period
2 Performance trend, each problem, this period to past four periods
3 Performance relative to same period one year ago
4 Performance relative to group norms

Concluding comments

Timing and cost considerations will continue to intensify, putting ever greater pressure on the marketing research professional to become more creative and efficient in delivering easy-to-understand and easy-to-digest research information. This information must be a tool that management can use with confidence to enhance the marketing and production decisions of the firm.

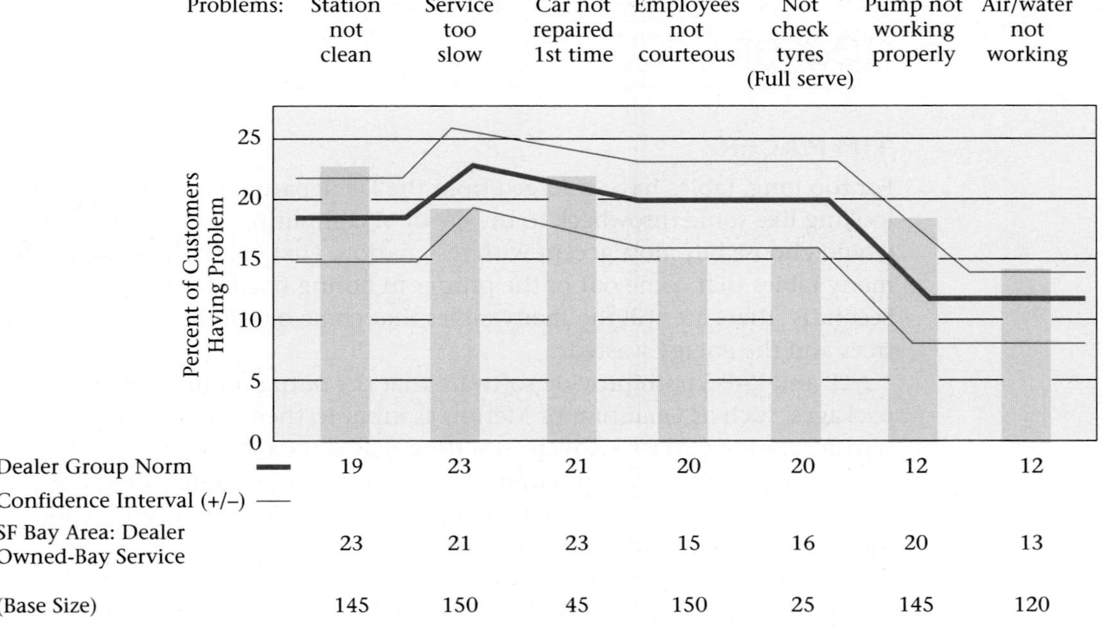

Figure 1 Problem Impact Analysis

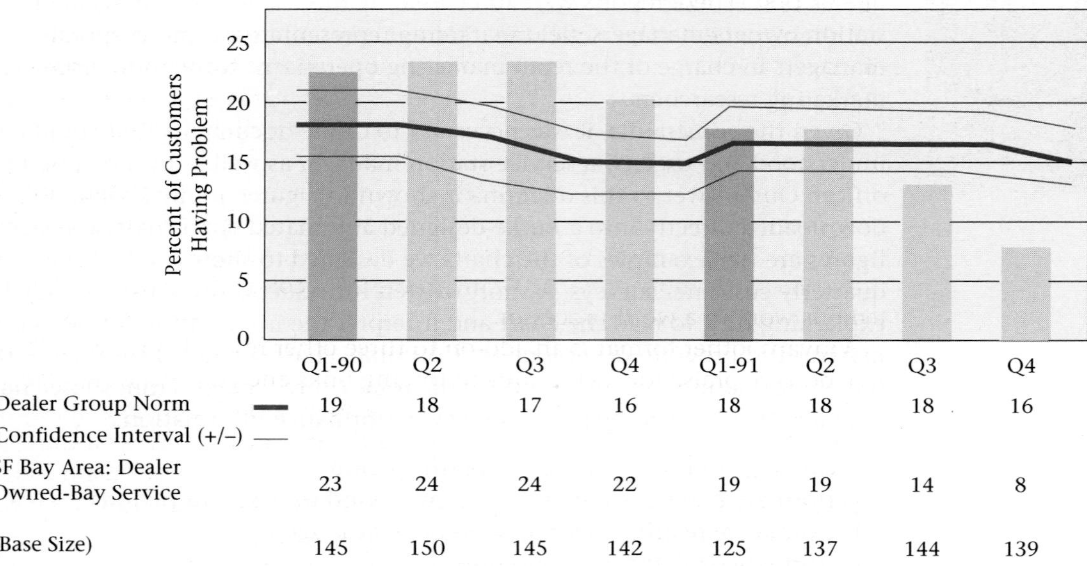

Figure 2 **Problem Trend Analysis**

Paperless presentation is a big step nearer . . .

TIM MACER

For too long, tables have emerged from the DP department to land on our desks looking like some throwback to the dawn of computing: something no-one would choose but most accept with resignation. First of all, there are still too many tables that come out of the printer in boring fixed-space typefaces. Secondly, there are still too many tables that come out of the printer. Pity the trees and the energy wasted.

ATP and IS-PC both provide software that the output of most major tabulation packages, such as Quantum or Merlin, as input to their own particular transformations. ATP's Winyaps is setting new standards in terms of stylish publication quality printed output, while IS-PC is about to release ITE 97, a full 32-bit version of their groundbreaking data delivery, archiving and report library tool that virtually eliminates the need to print tables at all.

Winyaps is a Windows version of ATP's YAPS package. Its mission is to transform ugly tables to beautiful ones. YAPS was created to post-process Quantum tables on UNIX systems. Winyaps handles all manner of tables within

Tim Macer

a simple point-and-click Windows interface, making this a product for the majority rather than the specialist minority. It contains a clever 'parsing' routine that deconstructs each table into its components of headings, captions and figures as it reads it in.

It then applies 'styles' to all the different components it has identified (over 20 of them), and each one is given a consistent treatment throughout the batch of tables. Graphics, icons or pictures can appear automatically, anywhere on the page, or in halftone in the background. The real beauty is that the transformation requires no human intervention.

Winyaps comes in two forms. Winyaps Professional lets you stylise tables mass produced by any of the old-style tabs packages. In my test, on a middling Pentium PC, Winyaps devoured over 200 fixed-spaced tables and turned them into something more presentable in around 20 seconds. This would be hours of tedious work in a word-processor.

Winyaps' other format is an add-on to three other research products. Here, ATP deserve praise for their efforts in forging links and providing seamless integration in an area still characterised by a singular lack of cooperation. At the moment, Winyaps can be called up from Quantime's Quantvert real-time analysis system, from Merlinco's Fastab – another on-line tab program – and from ITE. With the exception of Quantime, these providers are now offering Winyaps as an optional add-on module to their own products.

Leslie Sopp, head of Survey Centre at the Consumers Association said, 'We loved what we saw. We had been badgering Quantime for better output. When ATP produced Winyaps we welcomed it – it's great! It is much clearer, crisper and looks more professional.'

Justin Pieris, Survey Analysis Manager at CA, was equally enthusiastic 'We are big users of Quanvert. But the Quantime products just don't do the business when it comes to output. Winyaps maintains all the styles. You can produce tables that look just as they do in a magazine. It's marvellous and it's dead easy to use.' After a day spent defining all the styles for YAPS, all their tables come out to the standards of their house style – not the standards of a lineprinter circa 1979.

ITE takes a more revolutionary approach. It provides a complete solution to the need to produce and distribute large or bulky volumes of tables on paper by providing the means to disseminate them electronically, by disk, CD-ROM and now the Internet. ITE offers much better searching and browsing facilities, a neater tidier interface, better options for selecting and sorting information and better support for dropping selected data directly into spreadsheets, charts and wordprocessors. CA are also interested in the ITE and the connection with Winyaps means that the tables will have the same appearance no matter how they are produced. Justin Pieris commented: 'We are excited by ITE as a method of delivery to our internal clients.'

Mike Leigh, as DP director at Millward Brown International, has considerable experience of ITE and now, after beta testing it, of ITE97 too. He commented, 'You can now do more in the way of formatting and add graphics and logos. Navigation is easier, which I thought was good. You can also access many libraries at once. Overall, I'm quite impressed. The downside is that it is a 32-bit application, which will compromise supplying clients who are still restricted to 16 bits.'

Windows users must upgrade to Windows 95 or NT to use the 32-bit software, something which some sites are still reluctant to do. I asked Mike Leigh how he felt Millward Brown had benefited from using ITE. 'Eventually we are hoping that we will get away from sending out paper copies of reports and tables. It is a nicer way of distributing reports. It's pretty efficient in terms of disk space and it has a good library mechanism. It is essentially a simple product and it's easy to use.'

ITE is not limited to distributing tables and allows users to attach other items too. Millward Brown frequently attach all the other paperwork associated with a survey, such as graphs, written reports, even the original questionnaire. Information about sampling methodologies or weighting or all the other loose ends that can easily be mislaid can be attached to the ITE reports. As Mike Leigh pointed out: 'Our client service people find it very nice in that they have access to all their projects and their old data on screen ... they can review all aspects of the job from the one place.'

Perhaps the most encouraging development is the cooperation of three independent software houses – ATP, Merlinco and IS-PC – to share secrets about how their software works and produce proper integration for their clients to enjoy. With SPSS purchasing Quantime and In2itive, who have looked for common standards from day one, we can only hope that this spirit of cooperation will start to intoxicate all the major players.

Addendum

Two trends in data publishing have become hot topics since the above article was written: using the Internet to publish results and the provision of some elementary capabilities to manipulate published results.

ITE, featured in the above review, now incorporates a Web publisher to present ITE formatted results over the Internet, by anyone using a web browser to access the ITE web server. It also now offers a capability to perform significance testing, such as a *t*-test, on published data.

SPSS, an analytical and statistical tool widely used in academic as well as commercial circles, now offers a data publishing add-on, SPSS SmartViewer. Users can manipulate and re-arrange results online but cannot apply new statistics or perform calculations as there is no underlying data. Basically, tables are presented as a 'cube' which can then be sliced any way the user chooses. It is offered as a small utility to run on a PC, or over the Internet as SmartViewer Webserver.

The future looks certain to bring a further blurring of the boundaries between publishing and analysis. More importantly, given the astonishing growth of Internet technologies and the savings to be gained by using it as a published medium, Internet-based solutions are bound to take the lead in paperless presentation very soon, if they have not done so already.

Originally published in *Research*, (Dec 1997). Tim Macer produced an addendum in June 1999.

Appendix

Table I Simple random numbers

Line/ Col.	(1)	(2)	(3)	(4)	(5)	(6)	(7)	(8)	(9)	(10)	(11)	(12)	(13)	(14)
1	10480	15011	01536	02011	81647	91646	69179	14194	62590	36207	20969	99570	91291	90700
2	22368	46573	25595	85393	30995	89198	27982	53402	93965	34095	52666	19174	39615	99505
3	24130	48390	22527	97265	76393	64809	15179	24830	49340	32081	30680	19655	63348	58629
4	42167	93093	06243	61680	07856	16376	39440	53537	71341	57004	00849	74917	97758	16379
5	37570	39975	81837	16656	06121	91782	60468	81305	49684	60072	14110	06927	01263	54613
6	77921	06907	11008	42751	27756	53498	18602	70659	90655	15053	21916	81825	44394	42880
7	99562	72905	56420	69994	98872	31016	71194	18738	44013	48840	63213	21069	10634	12952
8	96301	91977	05463	07972	18876	20922	94595	56869	69014	60045	18425	84903	42508	32307
9	89579	14342	63661	10281	17453	18103	57740	84378	25331	12568	58678	44947	05585	56941
10	85475	36857	53342	53988	53060	59533	38867	62300	08158	17983	16439	11458	18593	64952
11	28918	69578	88231	33276	70997	79936	56865	05859	90106	31595	01547	85590	91610	78188
12	63553	40961	48235	03427	49626	69445	18663	72695	52180	20847	12234	90511	33703	90322
13	09429	93969	52636	92737	88974	33488	36320	17617	30015	08272	84115	27156	30613	74952
14	10365	61129	87529	85689	48237	52267	67689	93394	01511	26358	85104	20285	29975	89868
15	07119	97336	71048	08178	77233	13916	47564	81056	97735	85977	29372	74461	28551	90707
16	51085	12765	51821	51259	77452	16308	60756	92144	49442	53900	70960	63990	75601	40719
17	02368	21382	52404	60268	89368	19885	55322	44819	01188	65255	64835	44919	05944	55157
18	01011	54092	33362	94904	31273	04146	18594	29852	71685	85030	51132	01915	92747	64951
19	52162	53916	46369	58586	23216	14513	83149	98736	23495	64350	94738	17752	35156	35749
20	07056	97628	33787	09998	42698	06691	76988	13602	51851	46104	88916	19509	25625	58104
21	48663	91245	85828	14346	09172	30163	90229	04734	59193	22178	30421	61666	99904	32812
22	54164	58492	22421	74103	47070	25306	76468	26384	58151	06646	21524	15227	96909	44592
23	32639	32363	05597	24200	13363	38005	94342	28728	35806	06912	17012	64161	18296	22851
24	29334	27001	87637	87308	58731	00256	45834	15398	46557	41135	10307	07684	36188	18510
25	02488	33062	28834	07351	19731	92420	60952	61280	50001	67658	32586	86679	50720	94953
26	81525	72295	04839	96423	24878	82651	66566	14778	76797	14780	13300	87074	79666	95725
27	29676	20591	68086	26432	46901	20849	89768	81536	86645	12659	92259	57102	80428	25280
28	00742	57392	39064	66432	84673	40027	32832	61362	98947	96067	64760	64584	96096	98253
29	05366	04213	25669	26422	44407	44048	37937	63904	45766	66134	75470	66520	34693	90449
30	91921	26418	64117	94305	26766	25940	39972	22209	71500	64568	91402	42416	07844	69618
31	00582	04711	87917	77341	42206	35126	74087	99547	81817	42607	43808	76655	62028	76630
32	00725	69884	62797	56170	86324	88072	76222	36086	84637	93161	76038	65855	77919	88006
33	69011	65795	95876	55293	18988	27354	26575	08625	40801	59920	29841	80150	12777	48501
34	25976	57948	29888	88604	67917	48708	18912	82271	65424	69774	33611	54262	85963	03547
35	09763	83473	73577	12908	30883	18317	28290	35797	05998	41688	34952	37888	38917	88050
36	91567	42595	27959	30134	04024	86385	29880	99730	55536	84855	29088	09250	79656	73211
37	17955	56349	90999	49127	20044	59931	06115	20542	18059	02008	73708	83517	36103	42791
38	46503	18584	18845	49618	02304	51038	20655	58727	28168	15475	56942	53389	20562	87338
39	92157	89634	94824	78171	84610	82834	09922	25417	44137	48413	25555	21246	35509	20468
40	14577	62765	35605	81263	39667	47358	56873	56307	61607	49518	89656	20103	77490	18062
41	98427	07523	33362	64270	01638	92477	66969	98420	04880	45585	46565	04102	46880	45709
42	34914	63976	88720	82765	34476	17032	87589	40836	32427	70002	70663	88863	77775	69348
43	70060	28277	39475	46473	23219	53416	94970	25832	69975	94884	19661	72828	00102	66794
44	53976	54914	06990	67245	68350	82948	11398	42878	80287	88267	47363	46634	06541	97809
45	76072	29515	40980	07391	58745	25774	22987	80059	39911	96189	41151	14222	60697	59583

(continued)

Table I ***(Continued)***

Line/ Col.	(1)	(2)	(3)	(4)	(5)	(6)	(7)	(8)	(9)	(10)	(11)	(12)	(13)	(14)
46	90725	52210	83974	29992	65831	38857	50490	83765	55657	14361	31720	57375	56228	41546
47	64364	67412	33339	31926	14883	24413	59744	92351	97473	89286	35931	04110	23726	51900
48	08962	00358	31662	25388	61642	34072	81249	35648	56891	69352	48373	45578	78547	81788
49	95012	68379	93526	70765	10592	04542	76463	54328	02349	17247	28865	14777	62730	92277
50	15664	10493	20492	38301	91132	21999	59516	81652	27195	48223	46751	22923	32261	85653
51	16408	81899	04153	53381	79401	21438	83035	92350	36693	31238	59649	91754	72772	02338
52	18629	81953	05520	91962	04739	13092	97662	24822	94730	06496	35090	04822	86774	98289
53	73115	35101	47498	87637	99016	71060	88824	71013	18735	20286	23153	72924	35165	43040
54	57491	16703	23167	49323	45021	33132	12544	41035	80780	45393	44812	12515	98931	91202
55	30405	83946	23792	14422	15059	45799	22716	19792	09983	74353	68668	30429	70735	25499
56	16631	35006	85900	98275	32388	52390	16815	69293	82732	38480	73817	32523	41961	44437
57	96773	20206	42559	78985	05300	22164	24369	54224	35083	19687	11052	91491	60383	19746
58	38935	64202	14349	82674	66523	44133	00697	35552	35970	19124	63318	29686	03387	59846
59	31624	76384	17403	53363	44167	64486	64758	75366	76554	31601	12614	33072	60332	92325
60	78919	19474	23632	27889	47914	02584	37680	20801	72152	39339	34806	08930	85001	87820
61	03931	33309	57047	74211	63445	17361	62825	39908	05607	91284	68833	25570	38818	46920
62	74426	33278	43972	10119	89917	15665	52872	73823	73144	88662	88970	74492	51805	99378
63	09066	00903	20795	95452	92648	45454	69552	88815	16553	51125	79375	97596	16296	66092
64	42238	12426	87025	14267	20979	04508	64535	31355	86064	29472	47689	05974	52468	16834
65	16153	08002	26504	41744	81959	65642	74240	56302	00033	67107	77510	70625	28725	34191
66	21457	40742	29820	96783	29400	21840	15035	34537	33310	06116	95240	15957	16572	06004
67	21581	57802	02050	89728	17937	37621	47075	42080	97403	48626	68995	43805	33386	21597
68	55612	78095	83197	33732	05810	24813	86902	60397	16489	03264	88525	42786	05269	92532
69	44657	66999	99324	51281	84463	60563	79312	93454	68876	25471	93911	25650	12682	73572
70	91340	84979	46949	81973	37949	61023	43997	15263	80644	43942	89203	71795	99533	50501
71	91227	21199	31935	27022	84067	05462	35216	14486	29891	68607	41867	14951	91696	85065
72	50001	38140	66321	19924	72163	09538	12151	06878	91903	18749	34405	56087	82790	70925
73	65390	05224	72958	28609	81406	39147	25549	48542	42627	45233	57202	94617	23772	07896
74	27504	96131	83944	41575	10573	03619	64482	73923	36152	05184	94142	25299	94387	34925
75	37169	94851	39117	89632	00959	16487	65536	49071	39782	17095	02330	74301	00275	48280
76	11508	70225	51111	38351	19444	66499	71945	05422	13442	78675	84031	66938	93654	59894
77	37449	30362	06694	54690	04052	53115	62757	95348	78662	11163	81651	50245	34971	52974
78	46515	70331	85922	38329	57015	15765	97161	17869	45349	61796	66345	81073	49106	79860
79	30986	81223	42416	58353	21532	30502	32305	86482	05174	07901	54339	58861	74818	46942
80	63798	64995	46583	09785	44160	78128	83991	42865	92520	83531	80377	35909	81250	54238
81	82486	84846	99254	67632	43218	50076	21361	64816	51202	88124	41870	52689	51275	83556
82	21885	32906	92431	09060	64297	51674	64126	62570	26123	05155	59194	52799	28225	85762
83	60336	98782	07408	53458	13564	59089	26445	29789	85205	41001	12535	12133	14645	23541
84	43937	46891	24010	25560	86355	33941	25786	54990	71899	15475	95434	98227	21824	19535
85	97656	63175	89303	16275	07100	92063	21942	18611	47348	20203	18534	03862	78095	50136
86	03299	01221	05418	38982	55758	92237	26759	86367	21216	98442	08303	56613	91511	75928
87	79626	06486	03574	17668	07785	76020	79924	25651	83325	88428	85076	72811	22717	50585
88	85636	68335	47539	03129	65651	11977	02510	26113	99447	68645	34327	15152	55230	93448
89	18039	14367	61337	06177	12143	46609	32989	74014	64708	00533	35398	58408	13261	47908
90	08362	15656	60627	36478	65648	16764	53412	09013	07832	41574	17639	82163	60859	75567
91	79556	29068	04142	16268	15387	12856	66227	38358	22478	73373	88732	09443	82558	05250
92	92608	82674	27072	32534	17075	27698	98204	63863	11951	34648	88022	56148	34925	57031
93	23982	25835	40055	67006	12293	02753	14827	23235	35071	99704	37543	11601	35503	85171
94	09915	96306	05908	97901	28395	14186	00821	80703	70426	75647	76310	88717	37890	40129
95	59037	33300	26695	62247	69927	76123	50842	43834	86654	70959	79725	93872	28117	19233
96	42488	78077	69882	61657	34136	79180	97526	43092	04098	73571	80799	76536	71255	64239
97	46764	86273	63003	93017	31204	36692	40202	35275	57306	55543	53203	18098	47625	88684
98	03237	45430	55417	63282	90816	17349	88298	90183	36600	78406	06216	95787	42579	90730
99	86591	81482	52667	61582	14972	90053	89534	76036	49199	43716	97548	04379	46370	28672
100	38534	01715	94964	87288	65680	43772	39560	12918	80537	62738	19636	51132	25739	56947

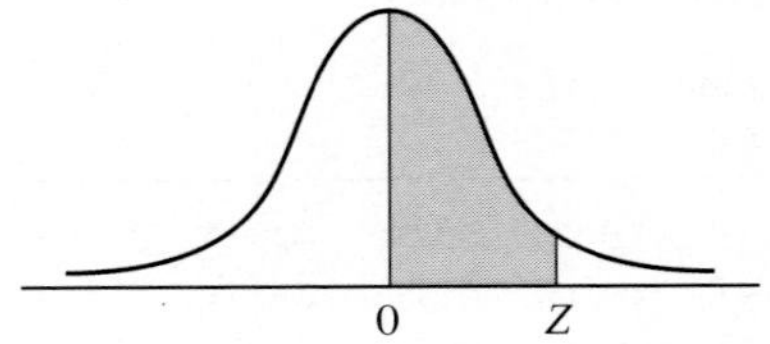

Table 2 Area under the normal curve

z	.00	.01	.02	.03	.04	.05	.06	.07	.08	.09
0.0	.0000	.0040	.0080	.0120	.0160	.0199	.0239	.0279	.0319	.0359
0.1	.0398	.0438	.0478	.0517	.0557	.0596	.0636	.0675	.0714	.0753
0.2	.0793	.0832	.0871	.0910	.0948	.0987	.1026	.1064	.1103	.1141
0.3	.1179	.1217	.1255	.1293	.1331	.1368	.1406	.1443	.1480	.1517
0.4	.1554	.1591	.1628	.1664	.1700	.1736	.1772	.1808	.1844	.1879
0.5	.1915	.1950	.1985	.2019	.2054	.2088	.2123	.2157	.2190	.2224
0.6	.2257	.2291	.2324	.2357	.2389	.2422	.2454	.2486	.2518	.2549
0.7	.2580	.2612	.2642	.2673	.2704	.2734	.2764	.2794	.2823	.2852
0.8	.2881	.2910	.2939	.2967	.2995	.3023	.3051	.3078	.3106	.3133
0.9	.3159	.3186	.3212	.3238	.3264	.3289	.3315	.3340	.3365	.3389
1.0	.3413	.3438	.3461	.3485	.3508	.3531	.3554	.3577	.3599	.3621
1.1	.3643	.3665	.3686	.3708	.3729	.3749	.3770	.3790	.3810	.3830
1.2	.3849	.3869	.3888	.3907	.3925	.3944	.3962	.3980	.3997	.4015
1.3	.4032	.4049	.4066	.4082	.4099	.4115	.4131	.4147	.4162	4177
1.4	.4192	.4207	.4222	.4236	.4251	.4265	4279	.4292	.4306	.4319
1.5	.4332	.4345	.4357	.4370	.4382	.4394	.4406	.4418	.4429	.4441
1.6	.4452	.4463	.4474	.4484	.4495	.4505	.4515	.4525	.4535	.4545
1.7	.4554	.4564	.4573	.4582	.4591	.4599	.4608	.4616	.4625	.4633
1.8	.4641	.4649	.4656	.4664	.4671	.4678	.4686	.4693	.4699	.4706
1.9	.4713	.4719	.4726	.4732	.4738	.4744	.4750	.4756	.4761	.4767
2.0	.4772	.4778	.4783	.4788	.4793	.4798	.4803	.4808	.4812	.4817
2.1	.4821	.4826	.4830	.4834	.4838	.4842	.4846	.4850	.4854	.4857
2.2	.4861	.4864	.4868	.4871	.4875	.4878	.4881	.4884	.4887	.4890
2.3	.4893	.4896	.4898	.4901	.4904	.4906	.4909	.4911	.4913	.4916
2.4	.4918	.4920	.4922	.4925	.4927	.4929	.4931	.4932	4934	.4936
2.5	.4938	.4940	.4941	.4943	.4945	.4946	.4948	.4949	.4951	.4952
2.6	.4953	.4955	.4956	.4957	.4959	.4960	.4961	.4962	.4963	.4964
2.7	.4965	.4966	.4967	.4968	.4969	.4970	.4971	.4972	.4973	.4974
2.8	.4974	.4975	.4976	.4977	.4977	.4978	.4979	.4979	.4980	.4981
2.9	.4981	.4982	.4982	.4983	.4984	.4984	.4985	.4985	.4986	.4986
3.0	.49865	.49869	.49874	.49878	.49882	.49886	.49889	.49893	.49897	.49900
3.1	.49903	.49906	.49910	.49913	.49916	.49918	.49921	.49924	.49926	.49929
3.2	.49931	.49934	.49936	.49938	.49940	.49942	.49944	.49946	.49948	.49950
3.3	.49952	.49953	.49955	.49957	.49958	.49960	.49961	.49962	.49964	49965
3.4	.49966	.49968	.49969	.49970	.49971	.49972	.49973	.49974	.49975	.49976
3.5	.49977	.49978	.49978	.49979	.49980	.49981	.49981	.49982	.49983	.49983
3.6	.49984	.49985	.49985	.49986	.49986	.49987	.49987	.49988	.49988	.49989
3.7	.49989	.49990	.49990	.49990	.49991	.49991	.49992	.49992	.49992	.49992
3.8	.49993	.49993	.49993	.49994	.49994	.49994	.49994	.49995	.49995	.49995
3.9	.49995	.49995	.49996	.49996	.49996	.49996	.49996	.49996	.49997	.49997

Entry represents area under the standard normal distribution from the mean to Z

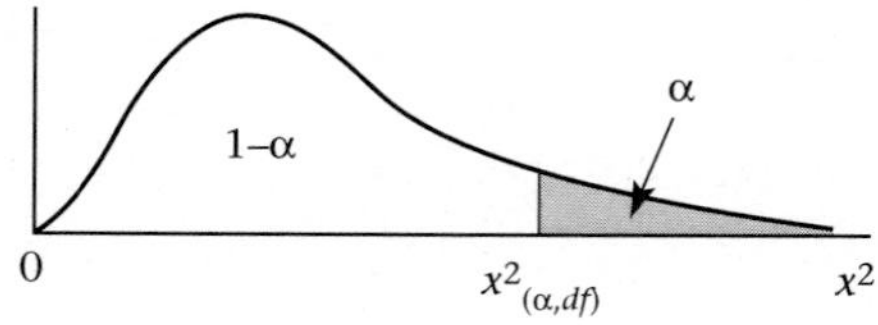

Table 3 Chi-square distribution

Degrees of Freedom	Upper Tail Areas (α)											
	.995	.99	.975	.95	.90	.75	.25	.10	.05	.025	.01	.005
1			0.001	0.004	0.016	0.102	1.323	2.706	3.841	5.024	6.635	7.879
2	0.010	0.020	0.051	0.103	0.211	0.575	2.773	4.605	5.991	7.378	9.210	10.597
3	0.072	0.115	0.216	0.352	0.584	1.213	4.108	6.251	7.815	9.348	11.345	12.838
4	0.207	0.297	0.484	0.711	1.064	1.923	5.385	7.779	9.488	11.143	13.277	14.860
5	0.412	0.554	0.831	1.145	1.610	2.675	6.626	9.236	11.071	12.833	15.086	16.750
6	0.676	0.872	1.237	1.635	2.204	3.455	7.841	10.645	12.592	14.449	16.812	18.548
7	0.989	1.239	1.690	2.167	2.833	4.255	9.037	12.017	14.067	16.013	18.475	20.278
8	1.344	1.646	2.180	2.733	3.490	5.071	10.219	13.362	15.507	17.535	20.090	21.955
9	1.735	2.088	2.700	3.325	4.168	5.899	11.389	14.684	16.919	19.023	21.666	23.589
10	2.156	2.558	3.247	3.940	4.865	6.737	12.549	15.987	18.307	20.483	23.209	25.188
11	2.603	3.053	3.816	4.575	5.578	7.584	13.701	17.275	19.675	21.920	24.725	26.757
12	3.074	3.571	4.404	5.226	6.304	8.438	14.845	18.549	21.026	23.337	26.217	28.299
13	3.565	4.107	5.009	5.892	7.042	9.299	15.984	19.812	22.362	24.736	27.688	29.819
14	4.075	4.660	5.629	6.571	7.790	10.165	17.117	21.064	23.685	26.119	29.141	31.319
15	4.601	5.229	6.262	7.261	8.547	11.037	18.245	22.307	24.996	27.488	30.578	32.801
16	5.142	5.812	6.908	7.962	9.312	11.912	19.369	23.542	26.296	28.845	32.000	34.267
17	5.697	6.408	7.564	8.672	10.085	12.792	20.489	24.769	27.587	30.191	33.409	35.718
18	6.265	7.015	8.231	9.390	10.865	13.675	21.605	25.989	28.869	31.526	34.805	37.156
19	6.844	7.633	8.907	10.117	11.651	14.562	22.718	27.204	30.144	32.852	36.191	38.582
20	7.434	8.260	9.591	10.851	12.443	15.452	23.828	28.412	31.410	34.170	37.566	39.997
21	8.034	8.897	10.283	11.591	13.240	16.344	24.935	29.615	32.671	35.479	38.932	41.401
22	8.643	9.542	10.982	12.338	14.042	17.240	26.039	30.813	33.924	36.781	40.289	42.796
23	9.260	10.196	11.689	13.091	14.848	18.137	27.141	32.007	35.172	38.076	41.638	44.181
24	9.886	10.856	12.401	13.848	15.659	19.037	28.241	33.196	36.415	39.364	42.980	45.559
25	10.520	11.524	13.120	14.611	16.473	19.939	29.339	34.382	37.652	40.646	44.314	46.928
26	11.160	12.198	13.844	15.379	17.292	20.843	30.435	35.563	38.885	41.923	45.642	48.290
27	11.808	12.879	14.573	16.151	18.114	21.749	31.528	36.741	40.113	43.194	46.963	49.645
28	12.461	13.565	15.308	16.928	18.939	22.657	32.620	37.916	41.337	44.461	48.278	50.993
29	13.121	14.257	16.047	17.708	19.768	23.567	33.711	39.087	42.557	45.722	49.588	52.336
30	13.787	14.954	16.791	18.493	20.599	24.478	34.800	40.256	43.773	46.979	50.892	53.672
31	14.458	15.655	17.539	19.281	21.434	25.390	35.887	41.422	44.985	48.232	52.191	55.003
32	15.134	16.362	18.291	20.072	22.271	26.304	36.973	42.585	46.194	49.480	53.486	56.328
33	15.815	17.074	19.047	20.867	23.110	27.219	38.058	43.745	47.400	50.725	54.776	57.648
34	16.501	17.789	19.806	21.664	23.952	28.136	39.141	44.903	48.602	51.966	56.061	58.964
35	17.192	18.509	20.569	22.465	24.797	29.054	40.223	46.059	49.802	53.203	57.342	60.275
36	17.887	19.233	21.336	23.269	25.643	29.973	41.304	47.212	50.998	54.437	58.619	61.581
37	18.586	19.960	22.106	24.075	26.492	30.893	42.383	48.363	52.192	55.668	59.892	62.883
38	19.289	20.691	22.878	24.884	27.343	31.815	43.462	49.513	53.384	56.896	61.162	64.181
39	19.996	21.426	23.654	25.695	28.196	32.737	44.539	50.660	54.572	58.120	62.428	65.476
40	20.707	22.164	24.433	26.509	29.051	33.660	45.616	51.805	55.758	59.342	63.691	66.766
41	21.421	22.906	25.215	27.326	29.907	34.585	46.692	52.949	56.942	60.561	64.950	68.053
42	22.138	23.650	25.999	28.144	30.765	35.510	47.766	54.090	58.124	61.777	66.206	69.336

(Continued)

Table 3 ***(Continued)***

Degrees of Freedom	Upper Tail Areas (α) .995	.99	.975	.95	.90	.75	.25	.10	.05	.025	.01	.005
43	22.859	24.398	26.785	28.965	31.625	36.436	48.840	55.230	59.304	62.990	67.459	70.616
44	23.584	25.148	27.575	29.787	32.487	37.363	49.913	56.369	60.481	64.201	68.710	71.893
45	24.311	25.901	28.366	30.612	33.350	38.291	50.985	57.505	61.656	65.410	69.957	73.166
46	25.041	26.657	29.160	31.439	34.215	39.220	52.056	58.641	62.830	66.617	71.201	74.437
47	25.775	27.416	29.956	32.268	35.081	40.149	53.127	59.774	64.001	67.821	72.443	75.704
48	26.511	28.177	30.755	33.098	35.949	41.079	54.196	60.907	65.171	69.023	73.683	76.969
49	27.249	28.941	31.555	33.930	36.818	42.010	55.265	62.038	66.339	70.222	74.919	78.231
50	27.991	29.707	32.357	34.764	37.689	42.942	56.334	63.167	67.505	71.420	76.154	79.490
51	28.735	30.475	33.162	35.600	38.560	43.874	57.401	64.295	68.669	72.616	77.386	80.747
52	29.481	31.246	33.968	36.437	39.433	44.808	58.468	65.422	69.832	73.810	78.616	82.001
53	30.230	32.018	34.776	37.276	40.308	45.741	59.534	66.548	70.993	75.002	79.843	83.253
54	30.981	32.793	35.586	38.116	41.183	46.676	60.600	67.673	72.153	76.192	81.069	84.502
55	31.735	33.570	36.398	38.958	42.060	47.610	61.665	68.796	73.311	77.380	82.292	85.749
56	32.490	34.350	37.212	39.801	42.937	48.546	62.729	69.919	74.468	78.567	83.513	86.994
57	33.248	35.131	38.027	40.646	43.816	49.482	63.793	71.040	75.624	79.752	84.733	88.236
58	34.008	35.913	38.844	41.492	44.696	50.419	64.857	72.160	76.778	80.936	85.950	89.477
59	34.770	36.698	39.662	42.339	45.577	51.356	65.919	73.279	77.931	82.117	87.166	90.715
60	35.534	37.485	40.482	43.188	46.459	52.294	66.981	74.397	79.082	83.298	88.379	91.952

For a particular number of degrees of freedom, entry represents the critical value of χ^2 corresponding to a specified upper tail area, α

For larger values of degrees of freedom (DF) the expression $z = \sqrt{2\chi^2} - \sqrt{2(DF) - 1}$ may be used and the resulting upper tail area can be obtained from the table of the standardised normal distribution.

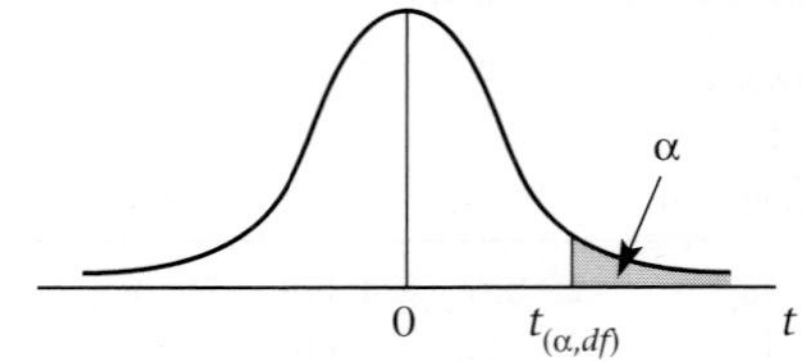

Table 4 t Distribution

Degress of Freedom	Upper Tail Areas .25	.10	.05	.025	.01	.005
1	1.0000	3.0777	6.3138	12.7062	31.8207	63.6574
2	0.8165	1.8856	2.9200	4.3027	6.9646	9.9248
3	0.7649	1.6377	2.3534	3.1824	4.5407	5.8409
4	0.7407	1.5332	2.1318	2.7764	3.7469	4.6041
5	0.7267	1.4759	2.0150	2.5706	3.3649	4.0322
6	0.7176	1.4398	1.9432	2.4469	3.1427	3.7074
7	0.7111	1.4149	1.8946	2.3646	2.9980	3.4995
8	0.7064	1.3968	1.8595	2.3060	2.8965	3.3554
9	0.7027	1.3830	1.8331	2.2622	2.8214	3.2498
10	0.6998	1.3722	1.8125	2.2281	2.7638	3.1693
11	0.6974	1.3634	1.7959	2.2010	2.7181	3.1058
12	0.6955	1.3562	1.7823	2.1788	2.6810	3.0545
13	0.6938	1.3502	1.7709	2.1604	2.6503	3.0123
14	0.6924	1.3450	1.7613	2,1448	2.6245	2.9768
15	0.6912	1.3406	1.7531	2.1315	2.6025	2.9467
16	0.6901	1.3368	1.7459	2.1199	2.5835	2.9208
17	0.6892	1.3334	1.7396	2.1098	2.5669	2.8982
18	0.6884	1.3304	1.7341	2.1009	2.5524	2.8784
19	0.6876	1.3277	1.7291	2.0930	2.5395	2.8609
20	0.6870	1.3253	1.7247	2.0860	2.5280	2.8453
21	0.6864	1.3232	1.7207	2.0796	2.5177	2.8314
22	0.6858	1.3212	1.7171	2.0739	2.5083	2.8188
23	0.6853	1.3195	1.7139	2.0687	2.4999	2.8073
24	0.6848	1.3178	1.7109	2.0639	2.4922	2.7969
25	0.6844	1.3163	1.7081	2.0595	2.4851	2.7874
26	0.6840	1.3150	1.7056	2.0555	2.4786	2.7787
27	0.6837	1.3137	1.7033	2.0518	2.4727	2.7707
28	0.6834	1.3125	1.7011	2.0484	2.4671	2.7633
29	0.6830	1.3114	1.6991	2.0452	2.4620	2.7564
30	0.6828	1.3104	1.6973	2.0423	2.4573	2.7500
31	0.6825	1.3095	1.6955	2.0395	2.4528	2.7440
32	0.6822	1.3086	1.6939	2.0369	2.4487	2.7385
33	0.6820	1.3077	1.6924	2.0345	2.4448	2.7333
34	0.6818	1.3070	1.6909	2.0322	2.4411	2.7284
35	0.6816	1.3062	1.6896	2.0301	2.4377	2.7238
36	0.6814	1.3055	1.6883	2.0281	2.4345	2.7195
37	0.6812	1.3049	1.6871	2.0262	2.4314	2.7154
38	0.6810	1.3042	1.6860	2.0244	2.4286	2.7116
39	0.6808	1.3036	1.6849	2.0227	2.4258	2.7079
40	0.6807	1.3031	1.6839	2.0211	2.4233	2.7045
41	0.6805	1.3025	1.6829	2.0195	2.4208	2.7012
42	0.6804	1.3020	1.6820	2.0181	2.4185	2.6981
43	0.6802	1.3016	1.681 1	2.0167	2.4163	2.6951

(Continued)

Table 4 *(Continued)*

Degrees of Freedom	Upper Tail Areas .25	.10	.05	.025	.01	.005
44	0.6801	1.3011	1.6802	2.0154	2.4141	2.6923
45	0.6800	1.3006	1.6794	2.0141	2.4121	2.6896
46	0.6799	1.3002	1.6787	2.0129	2.4102	2.6870
47	0.6797	1.2998	1.6779	2.0117	2.4083	2.6846
48	0.6796	1.2994	1.6772	2.0106	2.4066	2.6822
49	0.6795	1.2991	1.6766	2.0096	2.4049	2.6800
50	0.6794	1.2987	1.6759	2.0086	2.4033	2.6778
51	0.6793	1.2984	1.6753	2.0076	2.4017	2.6757
52	0.6792	1.2980	1.6747	2.0066	2.4002	2.6737
53	0.6791	1.2977	1.6741	2.0057	2.3988	2.6718
54	0.6791	1.2974	1.6736	2.0049	2.3974	2.6700
55	0.6790	1.2971	1.6730	2.0040	2.3961	2.6682
56	0.6789	1.2969	1.6725	2.0032	2.3948	2.6665
57	0.6788	1.2966	1.6720	2.0025	2.3936	2.6649
58	0.6787	1.2963	1.6716	2.0017	2.3924	2.6633
59	0.6787	1.2961	1.6711	2.0010	2.3912	2.6618
60	0.6786	1.2958	1.6706	2.0003	2.3901	2.6603
61	0.6785	1.2956	1.6702	1.9996	2.3890	2.6589
62	0.6785	1.2954	1.6698	1.9990	2.3880	2.6575
63	0.6784	1.2951	1.6694	1.9983	2.3870	2.6561
64	0.6783	1.2949	1.6690	1.9977	2.3860	2.6549
65	0.6783	1.2947	1.6686	1.9971	2.3851	2.6536
66	0.6782	1.2945	1.6683	1.9966	2.3842	2.6524
67	0.6782	1.2943	1.6679	1.9960	2.3833	2.6512
68	0.6781	1.2941	1.6676	1.9955	2.3824	2.6501
69	0.6781	1.2939	1.6672	1.9949	2.3816	2.6490
70	0.6780	1.2938	1.6669	1.9944	2.3808	2.6479
71	0.6780	1.2936	1.6666	1.9939	2.3800	2.6469
72	0.6779	1.2934	1.6663	1.9935	2.3793	2.6459
73	0.6779	1.2933	1.6660	1.9930	2.3785	2.6449
74	0.6778	1.2931	1.6657	1.9925	2.3778	2.6439
75	0.6778	1.2929	1.6654	1.9921	2.3771	2.6430
76	0.6777	1.2928	1.6652	1.9917	2.3764	2.6421
77	0.6777	1.2926	1.6649	1.9913	2.3758	2.6412
78	0.6776	1.2925	1.6646	1.9908	2.3751	2.6403
79	0.6776	1.2924	1.6644	1.9905	2.3745	2.6395
80	0.6776	1.2922	1.6641	1.9901	2.3739	2.6387
81	0.6775	1.2921	1.6639	1.9897	2.3733	2.6379
82	0.6775	1.2920	1.6636	1.9893	2.3727	2.6371
83	0.6775	1.2918	1.6634	1.9890	2.3721	2.6364
84	0.6774	1.2917	1.6632	1.9886	2.3716	2.6356
85	0.6774	1.2916	1.6630	1.9883	2.3710	2.6349
86	0.6774	1.2915	1.6628	1.9879	2.3705	2.6342
87	0.6773	1.2914	1.6626	1.9876	2.3700	2.6335
88	0.6773	1.2912	1.6624	1.9873	2.3695	2.6329
89	0.6773	1.2911	1.6622	1.9870	2.3690	2.6322
90	0.6772	1.2910	1.6620	1.9867	2.3685	2.6316
91	0.6772	1.2909	1.6618	1.9864	2.3680	2.6309
92	0.6772	1.2908	1.6616	1.9861	2.3676	2.6303
93	0.6771	1.2907	1.6614	1.9858	2.3671	2.6297
94	0.6771	1.2906	1.6612	1.9855	2.3667	2.6291
95	0.6771	1.2905	1.6611	1.9853	2.3662	2.6286

(Continued)

Table 4 *(Continued)*

Degrees of Freedom	Upper Tail Areas .25	.10	.05	.025	.01	.005
96	0.6771	1.2904	1.6609	1.9850	2.3658	2.6280
97	0.6770	1.2903	1.6607	1.9847	2.3654	2.6275
98	0.6770	1.2902	1.6606	1.9845	2.3650	2.6269
99	0.6770	1.2902	1.6604	1.9842	2.3646	2.6264
100	0.6770	1.2901	1.6602	1.9840	2.3642	2.6259
110	0.6767	1.2893	1.6588	1.9818	2.3607	2.6213
120	0.6765	1.2886	1.6577	1.9799	2.3578	2.6174
130	0.6764	1.2881	1.6567	1.9784	2.3554	2.6142
140	0.6762	1.2876	1.6558	1.9771	2.3533	2.6114
150	0.6761	1.2872	1.6551	1.9759	2.3515	2.6090
∞-	0.6745	1.2816	1.6449	1.9600	2.3263	2.5758

For a particular number of degrees of freedom, entry represents the critical value of t corresponding to a specified upper tail area α.

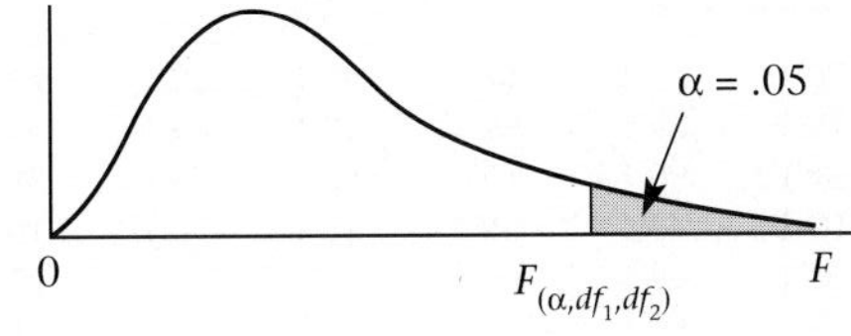

Table 5 ***F*** **Distribution**

Denominator df_2	Numerator df_1 1	2	3	4	5	6	7	8	9	10	12	15	20	24	30	40	60	120	∞
1	161.4	199.5	215.7	224.6	230.2	234.0	236.8	238.9	240.5	241.9	243.9	245.9	248.0	249.1	250.1	251.1	252.2	253.3	254.3
2	18.51	19.00	19.16	19.25	19.30	19.33	19.35	19.37	19.38	19.40	19.41	19.43	19.45	19.45	19.46	19.47	19.48	19.49	19.50
3	10.13	9.55	9.28	9.12	9.01	8.94	8.89	8.85	8.81	8.79	8.74	8.70	8.66	8.64	8.62	8.59	8.57	8.55	8.53
4	7.71	6.94	6.59	6.39	6.26	6.16	6.09	6.04	6.00	5.96	5.91	5.86	5.80	5.77	5.75	5.72	5.69	5.66	5.63
5	6.61	5.79	5.41	5.19	5.05	4.95	4.88	4.82	4.77	4.74	4.68	4.62	4.56	4.53	4.50	4.46	4.43	4.40	4.36
6	5.99	5.14	4.76	4.53	4.39	4.28	4.21	4.15	4.10	4.06	4.00	3.94	3.87	3.84	3.81	3.77	3.74	3.70	3.67
7	5.59	4.74	4.35	4.12	3.97	3.87	3.79	3.73	3.68	3.64	3.57	3.51	3.44	3.41	3.38	3.34	3.30	3.27	3.23
8	5.32	4.46	4.07	3.84	3.69	3.58	3.50	3.44	3.39	3.35	3.28	3.22	3.15	3.12	3.08	3.04	3.01	2.97	2.93
9	5.12	4.26	3.86	3.63	3.48	3.37	3.29	3.23	3.18	3.14	3.07	3.01	2.94	2.90	2.86	2.83	2.79	2.75	2.71
10	4.96	4.10	3.71	3.48	3.33	3.22	3.14	3.07	3.02	2.98	2.91	2.85	2.77	2.74	2.70	2.66	2.62	2.58	2.54
11	4.84	3.98	3.59	3.36	3.20	3.09	3.01	2.95	2.90	2.85	2.79	2.72	2.65	2.61	2.57	2.53	2.49	2.45	2.40
12	4.75	3.89	3.49	3.26	3.11	3.00	2.91	2.85	2.80	2.75	2.69	2.62	2.54	2.51	2.47	2.43	2.38	2.34	2.30
13	4.67	3.81	3.41	3.18	3.03	2.92	2.83	2.77	2.71	2.67	2.60	2.53	2.46	2.42	2.38	2.34	2.30	2.25	2.21
14	4.60	3.74	3.34	3.11	2.96	2.85	2.76	2.70	2.65	2.60	2.53	2.46	2.39	2.35	2.31	2.27	2.22	2.18	2.13
15	4.54	3.68	3.29	3.06	2.90	2.79	2.71	2.64	2.59	2.54	2.48	2.40	2.33	2.29	2.25	2.20	2.16	2.11	2.07
16	4.49	3.63	3.24	3.01	2.85	2.74	2.66	2.59	2.54	2.49	2.42	2.35	2.28	2.24	2.19	2.15	2.11	2.06	2.01
17	4.45	3.59	3.20	2.96	2.81	2.70	2.61	2.55	2.49	2.45	2.38	2.31	2.23	2.19	2.15	2.10	2.06	2.01	1.96
18	4.41	3.55	3.16	2.93	2.77	2.66	2.58	2.51	2.46	2.41	2.34	2.27	2.19	2.15	2.11	2.06	2.02	1.97	1.92
19	4.38	3.52	3.13	2.90	2.74	2.63	2.54	2.48	2.42	2.38	2.31	2.23	2.16	2.11	2.07	2.03	1.98	1.93	1.88
20	4.35	3.49	3.10	2.87	2.71	2.60	2.51	2.45	2.39	2.35	2.28	2.20	2.12	2.08	2.04	1.99	1.95	1.90	1.84
21	4.32	3.47	3.07	2,84	2.68	2.57	2.49	2.42	2.37	2.32	2.25	2.18	2.10	2.05	2.01	1.96	1.92	1.87	1.81
22	4.30	3.44	3.05	2.82	2.66	2.55	2.46	2.40	2.34	2.30	2.23	2.15	2.07	2.03	1.98	1.94	1.89	1.84	1.78
23	4.28	3.42	3.03	2.80	2.64	2.53	2.44	2.37	2.32	2.27	2.20	2.13	2.05	2.01	1.96	1.91	1.86	1.81	1.76
24	4.26	3.40	3.01	2.78	2.62	2.51	2.42	2.36	2.30	2.25	2.18	2.11	2.03	1.98	1.94	1.89	1.84	1.79	1.73
25	4.24	3.39	2.99	2.76	2.60	2.49	2.40	2.34	2.28	2.24	2.16	2.09	2.01	1.96	1.92	1.87	1.82	1.77	1.71
26	4.23	3.37	2.98	2.74	2.59	2.47	2.39	2.32	2.27	2.22	2.15	2.07	1.99	1.95	1.90	1.85	1.80	1.75	1.69
27	4.21	3.35	2.96	2.73	2.57	2.46	2.37	2.31	2.25	2.20	2.13	2.06	1.97	1.93	1.88	1.84	1.79	1.73	1.67
28	4.20	3.34	2.95	2.71	2.56	2.45	2.36	2.29	2.24	2.19	2.12	2.04	1.96	1.91	1.87	1.82	1.77	1.71	1.65
29	4.18	3.33	2.93	2.70	2.55	2.43	2.35	2.28	2.22	2.18	2.10	2.03	1.94	1.90	1.85	1.81	1.75	1.70	1.64
30	4.17	3.32	2.92	2.69	2.53	2.42	2.33	2.27	2.21	2.16	2.09	2.01	1.93	1.89	1.84	1.79	1.74	1.68	1.62
40	4.08	3.23	2.84	2.61	2.45	2.34	2.25	2.18	2.12	2.08	2.00	1.92	1.84	1.79	1.74	1.69	1.64	1.58	1.51
60	4.00	3.15	2.76	2.53	2.37	2.25	2.17	2.10	2.04	1.99	1.92	1.84	1.75	1.70	1.65	1.59	1.53	1.47	1.39
120	3.92	3.07	2.68	2.45	2.29	2.17	2.09	2.02	1.96	1.91	1.83	1.75	1,66	1.61	1.55	1.50	1.43	1.35	1.25
∞	3.84	3.00	2.60	2.37	2.21	2.10	2.01	1.94	1.88	1.83	1.75	1.67	1.57	1.52	1.46	1.39	1.32	1.22	1.00

(Continued)

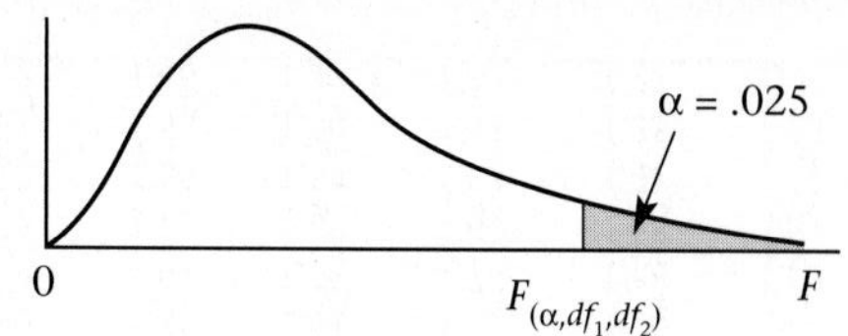

Table 5 *(Continued)*

Denominator df_2	Numerator df_1: 1	2	3	4	5	6	7	8	9	10	12	15	20	24	30	40	60	120	∞
1	647.8	799.5	864.2	899.6	921.8	937.1	948.2	956.7	963.3	968.6	976.7	984.9	993.1	997.2	1001	1006	1010	1014	1018
2	38.51	39.00	39.17	39.25	39.30	39.33	39.36	39.37	39.39	39.40	39.41	39.43	39.45	39.46	39.46	39.47	39.48	39.49	39.50
3	17.44	16.04	15.44	15.10	14.88	14.73	14.62	14.54	14.47	14.42	14.34	14.25	14.17	14.12	14.08	14.04	13.99	13.95	13.90
4	12.22	10.65	9.98	9.60	9.36	9.20	9.07	8.98	8.90	8.84	8.75	8.66	8.56	8.51	8.46	8.41	8.36	8.31	8.26
5	10.01	8.43	7.76	7.39	7.15	6.98	6.85	6.76	6.68	6.62	6.52	6.43	6.33	6.28	6.23	6.18	6.12	6.07	6.02
6	8.81	7.26	6.60	6.23	5.99	5.82	5.70	5.60	5.52	5.46	5.37	5.27	5.17	5.12	5.07	5.01	4.96	4.90	4.85
7	8.07	6.54	5.89	5.52	5.29	5.12	4.99	4.90	4.82	4.76	4.67	4.57	4.47	4.42	4.36	4.31	4.25	4.20	4.14
8	7.57	6.06	5.42	5.05	4.82	4.65	4.53	4.43	4.36	4.30	4.20	4.10	4.00	3.95	3.89	3.84	3.78	3.73	3.67
9	7.21	5.71	5.08	4.72	4.48	4.32	4.20	4.10	4.03	3.96	3.87	3.77	3.67	3.61	3.56	3.51	3.45	3.39	3.33
10	6.94	5.46	4.83	4.47	4.24	4.07	3.95	3.85	3.78	3.72	3.62	3.52	3.42	3.37	3.31	3.26	3.20	3.14	3.08
11	6.72	5.26	4.63	4.28	4.04	3.88	3.76	3.66	3.59	3.53	3.43	3.33	3.23	3.17	3.12	3.06	3.00	2.94	2.88
12	6.55	5.10	4.47	4.12	3.89	3.73	3.61	3.51	3.44	3.37	3.28	3.18	3.07	3.02	2.96	2.91	2.85	2.79	2.72
13	6.41	4.97	4.35	4.00	3.77	3.60	3.48	3.39	3.31	3.25	3.15	3.05	2.95	2.89	2.84	2.78	2.72	2.66	2.60
14	6.30	4.86	4.24	3.89	3.66	3.50	3.38	3.29	3.21	3.15	3.05	2.95	2.84	2.79	2.73	2.67	2.61	2.55	2.49
15	6.20	4.77	4.15	3.80	3.58	3.41	3.29	3.20	3.12	3.06	2.96	2.86	2.76	2.70	2.64	2.59	2.52	2.46	2.40
16	6.12	4.69	4.08	3.73	3.50	3.34	3.22	3.12	3.05	2.99	2.89	2.79	2.68	2.63	2.57	2.51	2.45	2.38	2.32
17	6.04	4.62	4.01	3.66	3.44	3.28	3.16	3.06	2.98	2.92	2.82	2.72	2.62	2.56	2.50	2.44	2.38	2.32	2.25
18	5.98	4.56	3.95	3.61	3.38	3.22	3.10	3.01	2.93	2.87	2.77	2.67	2.56	2.50	2.44	2.38	2.32	2.26	2.19
19	5.92	4.51	3.90	3.56	3.33	3.17	3.05	2.96	2.88	2.82	2.72	2.62	2.51	2.45	2.39	2.33	2.27	2.20	2.13
20	5.87	4.46	3.86	3.51	3.29	3.13	3.01	2.91	2.84	2.77	2.68	2.57	2.46	2.41	2.35	2.29	2.22	2.16	2.09
21	5.83	4.42	3.82	3.48	3.25	3.09	2.97	2.87	2.80	2.73	2.64	2.53	2.42	2.37	2.31	2.25	2.18	2.11	2.04
22	5.79	4.38	3.78	3.44	3.22	3.05	2.93	2.84	2.76	2.70	2.60	2.50	2.39	2.33	2.27	2.21	2.14	2.08	2.00
23	5.75	4.35	3.75	3.41	3.18	3.02	2.90	2.81	2.73	2.67	2.57	2.47	2.36	2.30	2.24	2.18	2.11	2.04	1.97
24	5.72	4.32	3.72	3.38	3.15	2.99	2.87	2.78	2.70	2.64	2.54	2.44	2.33	2.27	2.21	2.15	2.08	2.01	1.94
25	5.69	4.29	3.69	3.35	3.13	2.97	2.85	2.75	2.68	2.61	2.51	2.41	2.30	2.24	2.18	2.12	2.05	1.98	1.91
26	5.66	4.27	3.67	3.33	3.10	2.94	2.82	2.73	2.65	2.59	2.49	2.39	2.28	2.22	2.16	2.09	2.03	1.95	1.88
27	5.63	4.24	3.65	3.31	3.08	2.92	2.80	2.71	2.63	2.57	2.47	2.36	2.25	2.19	2.13	2.07	100	1.93	1.85
28	5.61	4.22	3.63	3.29	3.06	2.90	2.78	2.69	2.61	2.55	2.45	2.34	2.23	2.17	2.11	2.05	1.98	1.91	1.83
29	5.59	4.20	3.61	3.27	3.04	2.88	2.76	2.67	2.59	2.53	2.43	2.32	2.21	2.15	2.09	2.03	1.96	1.89	1.81
30	5.57	4.18	3.59	3.25	3.03	2.87	2.75	2.65	2.57	2.51	2.41	2.31	2.20	2.14	2.07	2.01	1.94	1.87	1.79
40	5.42	4.05	3.46	3.13	2.90	2.74	2.62	2.53	2.45	2.39	2.29	2.18	2.07	2.01	1.94	1.88	1.80	1.72	1.64
60	5.29	3.93	3.34	3.01	2.79	2.63	2.51	2.41	2.33	2.27	2.17	2.06	1.94	1.88	1.82	1.74	1.67	1.58	1.48
120	5.15	3.80	3.23	2.89	2.67	2.52	2.39	2.30	2.22	2.16	2.05	1.94	1.82	1.76	1.69	1.61	1.53	1.43	1.31
∞	5.02	3 69	3.12	2.79	2.57	2.41	2.29	2.19	2.11	2.05	1.94	1,83	1.71	1.64	1.57	1.48	1.39	1.27	1.00

(Continued)

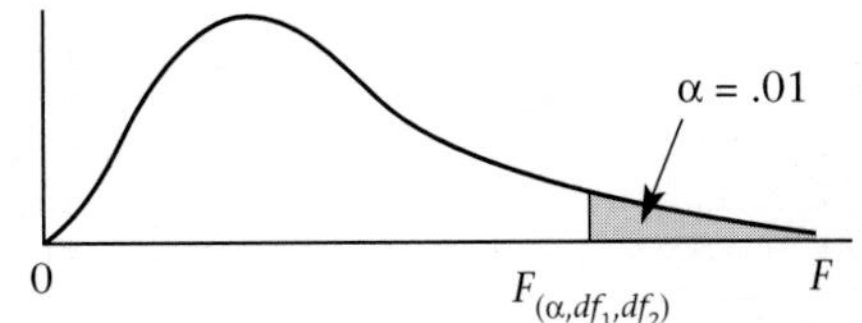

Table 5 ***(Continued)***

Denominator df_2	Numerator df_1: 1	2	3	4	5	6	7	8	9	10	12	15	20	24	30	40	60	120	∞
1	4052	4999.5	5403	5625	5764	5859	5928	5982	6022	6056	6106	6157	6209	6235	6261	6287	6313	6339	6366
2	98.50	99.00	99.17	99.25	99.30	99.33	99.36	99.37	99.39	99.40	99.42	99.43	99.45	99.46	99.47	99.47	99.48	99.49	99.50
3	34.12	30.82	29.46	28.71	28.24	27.91	27.67	27.49	27.35	27.23	27.05	26.87	26.69	26.60	26.50	26.41	26.32	26.22	26.13
4	21.20	18.00	16.69	15.98	15.52	15.21	14.98	14.80	14.66	14.55	14.37	14.20	14.02	13.93	13.84	13.75	13.65	13.56	13.46
5	16.26	13.27	12.06	11.39	10.97	10.67	10.46	10.29	10.16	10.05	9.89	9.72	9.55	9.47	9.38	9.29	9.20	9.11	9.02
6	13.75	10.92	9.78	9.15	8.75	8.47	8.26	8.10	7.98	7.87	7.72	7.56	7.40	7.31	7.23	7.14	7.06	6.97	6.88
7	12.25	9.55	8.45	7.85	7.46	7.19	6.99	6.84	6.72	6.62	6.47	6.31	6.16	6.07	5.99	5.91	5.82	5.74	5.65
8	11.26	8.65	7.59	7.01	6.63	6.37	6.18	6.03	5.91	5.81	5.67	5.52	5.36	5.28	5.20	5.12	5.03	4,95	4.86
9	10.56	8.02	6.99	6.42	6.06	5.80	5.61	5.47	5.35	5.26	5.11	4.96	4.81	4.73	4.65	4.57	4.48	4.40	4.31
10	10.04	7.56	6.55	5.99	5.64	5.39	5.20	5.06	4.94	455	4.71	4.56	4.41	4.33	4.25	4.17	4.08	4.00	3.91
11	9.65	7.21	6.22	5.67	5.32	5.07	4.89	4.74	4.63	4.54	4.40	4.25	4.10	4.02	3.94	3.86	3.78	3.69	3.60
12	9.33	6.93	5.95	5.41	5.06	4.82	4.64	4.50	4.39	4.30	4.16	4.01	3.86	3.78	3.70	3.62	3.54	3.45	3.36
13	9.07	6.70	5.74	5.21	4.86	4.62	4.44	4.30	4.19	4.10	3.96	3.82	3.66	3.59	3.51	3.43	3.34	3.25	3.17
14	8.86	6.51	5.56	5.04	4.69	4.46	4.28	4.14	4.03	3.94	3.80	3.66	3.51	3.43	3.35	3.27	3.18	3.09	3.00
15	8.68	6.36	5.42	4.89	4.56	4.32	4.14	4.00	3.89	3.80	3.67	3.52	3.37	3.29	3.21	3.13	3.05	2.96	2.87
16	8.53	6.23	5.29	4.77	4.44	4.20	4.03	3.89	3.78	3.69	3.55	3.41	3.26	3.18	3.10	3.02	2.93	2.84	2.75
17	8.40	6.11	5.18	4.67	4.34	4.10	3.93	3.79	3.68	3.59	3.46	3.31	3.16	3.08	3.00	2.92	2.83	2.75	2.65
18	8.29	6.01	5.09	4.58	4.25	4.01	3.84	3.71	3.60	3.51	3.37	3.23	3.08	3.00	2.92	2.84	2.75	2.66	2.57
19	8.18	5.93	5.01	4.50	4.17	3.94	3.77	3.63	3.52	3.43	3.30	3.15	3.00	2.92	2.84	2.76	2.67	2.58	2.49
20	8.10	5.85	4.94	4.43	4.10	3.87	3.70	3.56	3.46	3.37	3.23	3.09	2.94	2.86	2.78	2.69	2.61	2.52	2.42
21	8.02	5.78	4.87	4.37	4.04	3.81	3.64	3.51	3.40	3.31	3.17	3.03	2.88	2.80	2.72	2.64	2.55	2.46	2.36
22	7.95	5.72	4.82	4.31	3.99	3.76	3.59	3.45	3.35	3.26	3.12	2.98	2.83	2.75	2.67	2.58	2.50	2.40	2.31
23	7.88	5.66	4.76	4.26	3.94	3.71	3.54	3.41	3.30	3.21	3.07	2.93	2.78	2.70	2.62	2.54	2.45	2,35	2.26
24	7.82	5.61	4.72	4.22	3.90	3.67	3.50	3.36	3.26	3.17	3.03	2.89	2.74	2.66	2.58	2.49	2.40	2.31	2.21
25	7.77	5.57	4.68	4.18	3.85	3.63	3.46	3.32	3.22	3.13	2.99	2.85	2.70	2.62	2.54	2.45	2.36	2.27	2.17
26	7.72	5.53	4.64	4.14	3.82	3.59	3.42	3.29	3.18	3.09	2.96	2.81	2.66	2.58	2.50	2.42	2.33	2.23	2.13
27	7.68	5.49	4.60	4.11	3.78	3.56	3.39	3.26	3.15	3.06	2.93	2.78	2.63	2.55	2.47	2.38	2.29	2.20	2.10
28	7.64	5.45	4.57	4.07	3.75	3.53	3.36	3.23	3.12	3.03	2.90	2.75	2.60	2.52	2.44	2.35	2.26	2.17	2.06
29	7.60	5.42	4.54	4.04	3.73	3.50	3.33	3.20	3.09	3.00	2.87	2.73	2.57	2.49	2.41	2.33	2.23	2.14	2.03
30	7.56	5.39	4.51	4.02	3.70	3.47	3.30	3.17	3.07	2.98	2.84	2.70	2.55	2.47	2.39	2.30	2.21	2.11	2.01
40	7.31	5.18	4.31	3.83	3.51	3.29	3.12	2.99	2.89	2.80	2.66	2.52	2.37	2.29	2.20	2.11	2.02	1.92	1.80
60	7.08	4.98	4.13	3.65	3.34	3.12	2.95	2.82	2.72	2.63	2.50	2.35	2.20	2.12	2.03	1.94	1.84	1.73	1.60
120	6.85	4.79	3.95	3.48	3.17	2.96	2.79	2.66	2.56	2.47	2.34	2.19	2.03	1.95	1.86	1.76	1.66	1.53	1.38
∞	6.63	4.61	3.78	3.32	3.02	2.80	2.64	2.51	2.41	2.32	2.18	2.04	1.88	1.79	1.70	1.59	1.47	1.32	1.00

For a particular combination of numerator and denominator degrees of freedom, entry represents the critical values of F corresponding to a specified upper tail area α

Indexes

SUBJECT INDEX

NAMES INDEX

COMPANY INDEX

Credits

Chapter 1: Dyson, Paul Lange. Commerzbank, Commerzbank Frankfurt.

Chapter 2: Burke Professionals, NKM Photo. Chanel, Teri Stratford, Pearson Education.

Chapter 3: Lufthansa aircraft, Lufthansa German Airlines. Currency flags, Tony Stone Images. Mont Blanc pen, Nike Communications. Citibank, John Lei/Stock, Boston.

Chapter 4: Barbeque, Tony Stone Images. Businessman/Eiffel Tower, Tony Stone Images.

Chapter 5: Stockholm map, Experian. Well educated metropolitans, Experian. Goteborg map, Experian. Home Sweet Home, Experian.

Chapter 6: Couples in restaurant, Tony Stone Images. Moderator, NKM Photo.

Chapter 7: Washing powder, Teri Stratford, Pearson Education. Eating high fat food, Greg Davis/The Stock Market.

Chapter 9: Banker, Barclays Bank plc. Bookshop, Lee Snider/The Image Works.

Chapter 10: Paired test, Elrick & Lavidge. Oktoberfest, Tony Stone Images.

Chapter 11: Xerox sign, Jeff Greenberg/PhotoEdit.

Chapter 12: Washing hair, Bob Daemmrich/The Image Works.

Chapter 14: Cyclists, Jean Claude LeJeune/Stock, Boston. Airline, Chromo Sohm/Unicorn Stock Photos.

Chapter 15: Supervisor, NKM Photo.

Chapter 16: Checking, Pearson Education. Frozen food display, Barbara Rios/Photo Reserchers, Inc. Haagen-Dazs shop, James Leynse/Network Photographers Ltd.

Chapter 17: Bank, Royal Bank of Canada.

Chapter 18: Tums, Teri Stratford, Pearson Education.

Chapter 19: Magazines, Teri Stratford, Pearson Education.

Chapter 20: Family beach holiday, R. Ford Smith/The Stock Market.

Chapter 21: Student banking Barclays, Bank plc.

Chapter 22: Bank, Generale Bank.

Chapter 23: Couple, Tony Stone Images.

Chapter 24: Presentation, NKM Photo.

IMPORTANT: READ CAREFULLY

WARNING: BY OPENING THE PACKAGE YOU AGREE TO BE BOUND BY THE TERMS OF THE LICENCE AGREEMENT BELOW.

This is a legally binding agreement between You (the user or purchaser) and Pearson Education Limited. By retaining this licence, any software media or accompanying written materials or carrying out any of the permitted activities You agree to be bound by the terms of the licence agreement below.

If You do do not agree to these terms then promptly return the entire publication (this licence and all software, written materials, packaging and any other components received with it) with Your sales receipt to Your supplier for a full refund.

SINGLE USER LICENCE AGREEMENT

❒ YOU ARE PERMITTED TO:

- Use (load into temporary memory or permanent storage) a single copy of the software on only one computer at a time. If this computer is linked to a network then the software may only be installed in a manner such that it is not accessible to other machines on the network.
- Make one copy of the software solely for backup purposes or copy it to a single hard disk, provided you keep the original solely for back up purposes.
- Transfer the software from one computer to another provided that you only use it on one computer at a time.

❒ YOU MAY NOT:

Rent or lease the software or any part of this publication.

- Copy any part of the documentation, except where specifically indicated otherwise.
- Make copies of the software, other than for backup purposes.
- Reverse engineer, decompile or disassemble the software.
- Use the software on more than one computer at a time.
- Install the software on any networked computer in a way that could allow access to it from more than one machine on the network.
- Use the software in any way not specified above without the prior written consent of Pearson Education Limited.

ONE COPY ONLY

This licence is for a single user copy of the software

PEARSON EDUCATION LIMITED RESERVES THE RIGHT TO TERMINATE THIS LICENCE BY WRITTEN NOTICE AND TO TAKE ACTION TO RECOVER ANY DAMAGES SUFFERED BY PEARSON EDUCATION LIMITED IF YOU BREACH ANY PROVISION OF THIS AGREEMENT.

Pearson Education Limited owns the software You only own the disk on which the software is supplied.

LIMITED WARRANTY

Pearson Education Limited warrants that the diskette or CD rom on which the software is supplied are free from defects in materials and workmanship under normal use for ninety (90) days from the date You receive them. This warranty is limited to You and is not transferable. Pearson Education Limited does not warrant that the functions of the software meet Your requirements or that the media is compatible with any computer system on which it is used or that the operation of the software will be unlimited or error free.

You assume responsibility for selecting the software to achieve Your intended results and for the installation of, the use of and the results obtained from the software. The entire liability of Pearson Education Limited and its suppliers and your only remedy shall be replacement of the components that do not meet this warranty free of charge.

This limited warranty is void if any damage has resulted from accident, abuse, misapplication, service or modification by someone other than Pearson Education Limted. In no event shall Pearson Education Limtied or its suppliers be liable for any damages whatsoever arising out of installation of the software, even if advised of the possibility of such damages. Pearson Education Limited will not be liable for any loss or damage of any nature suffered by any party as a result of reliance upon or reproduction of or any errors in the content of this publication.

Pearson Education Limited does not limit its liability for death or personal injury caused by its negligence.

This licence agreement shall be governed by and interpreted and construed in accordance with English law.